INFLUENCES OUR APPROACH TO MODERN ECONOMIC ISSUES

AGGREGATE DEMAND

KEYNESIAN THEORY
John Maynard KEYNES 1883-1946

Alvin HANSEN 1887-1975

BUSINESS CYCLES
Wesley Clair MITCHELL 1874-1948

KEYNES

SWEDISH SCHOOL
Gunnar MYRDAL 1898- Nobel Prize 1974

FISHER

QUANTITY THEORY
Irving FISHER 1867-1947

A. C. PIGOU 1877-1959

ECONOMETRIC METHOD
Jan TINBERGEN 1903- Nobel Prize 1969

Ragnar A. K. FRISCH 1895-1973 Nobel Prize 1969

Lawrence R. KLEIN 1920- Nobel Prize 1980

RESOURCE ALLOCATION

EXTERNALITIES
A. C. PIGOU 1877-1959

Erik LINDAHL 1891-1960

IMPERFECT COMPETITION
E. H. CHAMBERLIN 1899-1967

Joan ROBINSON 1903-1983

INTERNATIONAL TRADE THEORY
Bertil OHLIN 1899-1979 Nobel Prize 1977

Jacob VINER 1892-1970

VINER

RESOURCE CONSERVATION
Harold HOTELLING 1895-1973

KNIGHT

CAPITAL THEORY AND GROWTH
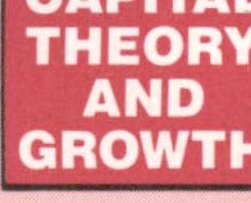

Joseph A. SCHUMPETER 1883-1950

Frank H. KNIGHT 1885-1972

Sir Roy HARROD 1900-1978

Sir John R. HICKS 1904- Nobel Prize 1972

HICKS

1. ROLE OF GOVERNMENT

Planning

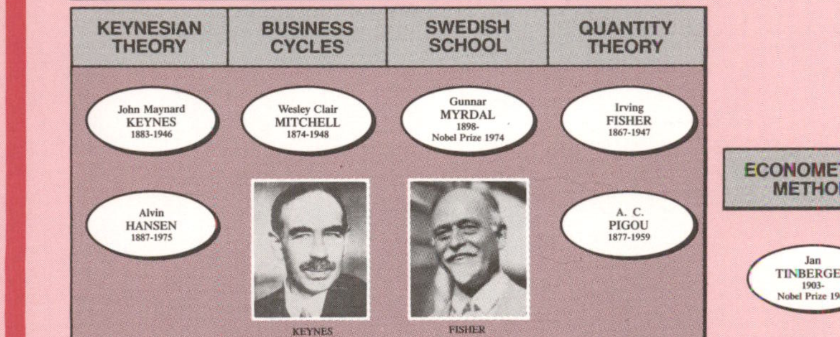
LEONTIEF

Wassily LEONTIEF 1906- Nobel Prize 1973

Gunnar MYRDAL 1898- Nobel Prize 1974

John Kenneth GALBRAITH 1908-

Libertarianism

Ludwig von MISES 1881-1973

F. A. HAYEK 1899- Nobel Prize 1974

Milton FRIEDMAN 1912- Nobel Prize 1976

2. MACROECONOMIC MEASUREMENT AND POLICY

Measurement

Simon KUZNETS 1901-1985 Nobel Prize 1971

Richard STONE 1913- Nobel Prize 1984

KUZNETS

Active Management

Paul A. SAMUELSON 1915- Nobel Prize 1970

James TOBIN 1918- Nobel Prize 1981

Sir John R. HICKS 1904- Nobel Prize 1972

James E. MEADE 1907- Nobel Prize 1977

Franco MODIGLINANI 1918- Nobel Prize 1985

TOBIN

Rules

Milton FRIEDMAN 1912- Nobel Prize 1976

FRIEDMAN

3. EFFICIENCY

Kenneth J. ARROW 1921- Nobel Prize 1972

Tjalling KOOPMANS 1910-1985 Nobel Prize 1975

Leonid KANTOROVICH 1912- Nobel Prize 1975

Paul A. SAMUELSON 1915- Nobel Prize 1970

Herbert A. SIMON 1916- Nobel Prize 1978

George STIGLER 1911- Nobel Prize 1982

Gerard DEBREU 1921- Nobel Prize 1983

SAMUELSON

4. EQUITY

Gunnar MYRDAL 1898- Nobel Prize 1974

Arthur M. OKUN 1928-1980

MYRDAL

5. GROWTH

Theodore W. SCHULTZ 1902- Nobel Prize 1979

Sir W. Arthur LEWIS 1915- Nobel Prize 1979

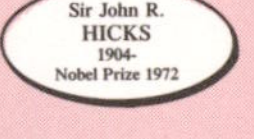

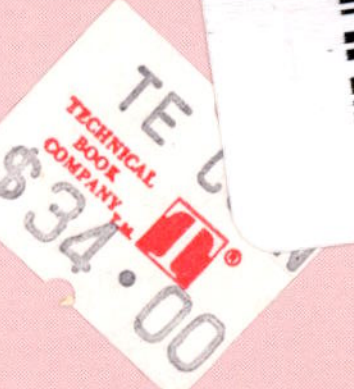

Note: Among contemporary economists, only Nobel Prize winners and retired economists are included.

Contributors:
Paul Wonnacott, University of Maryland
Ronald Wonnacott, University of Western Ontario
Dudley Dillard, University of Maryland
Robert F. Herbert, Auburn University
Hugh S. Norton, University of South Carolina

ECONOMICS

THIRD EDITION

ECONOMICS

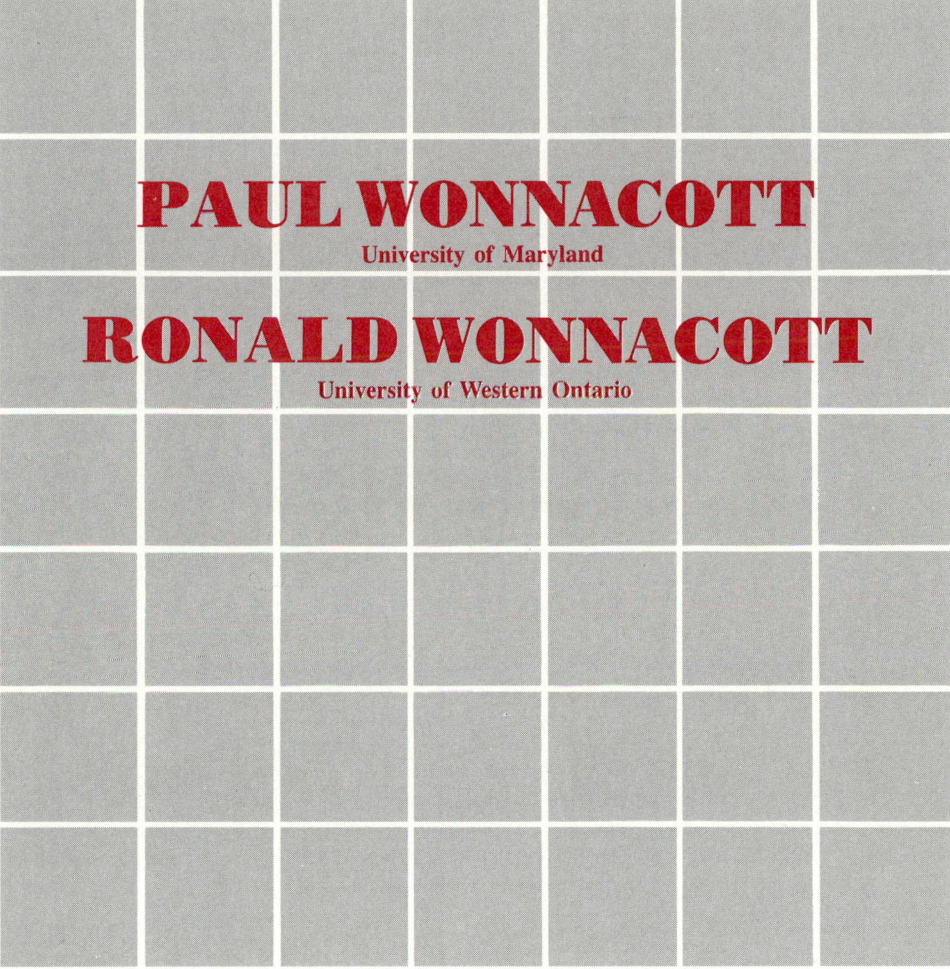

PAUL WONNACOTT
University of Maryland

RONALD WONNACOTT
University of Western Ontario

McGRAW-HILL BOOK COMPANY

New York St. Louis San Francisco Auckland Bogotá Hamburg Johannesburg London Madrid Mexico Montreal New Delhi Panama Paris São Paulo Singapore Sydney Tokyo Toronto

ECONOMICS

1 2 3 4 5 6 7 8 9 0 HALHAL 8 9 8 7 6 •

ISBN 0-07-071650-1

This book was set in Times Roman by York Graphic Services, Inc. (ECU)
The editors were Paul V. Short and Alison Meersschaert;
the designer was Nicholas Krenitsky;
the production supervisor was Joe Campanella.
New drawings were done by J & R Services, Inc.
Halliday Lithograph Corporation was printer and binder.
See Photo Credits on page 817.

Library of Congress Cataloging-in-Publication Data

Wonnacott, Paul.
Economics.

Includes bibliographical references and index.
1. Economics. I. Wonnacott, Ronald J. II. Title.
HB171.5.W76 1986 330 85-19783
ISBN 0-07-071650-1

ABOUT THE AUTHORS

Paul Wonnacott studied history as an undergraduate at the University of Western Ontario. He then switched to his second and greatest academic love—economics—receiving his Ph.D. from Princeton. He taught four years at Columbia University before taking up his present post at the University of Maryland. Most of his scholarly work has focused on international economics, including studies on U.S.-Canadian trade (with Ron Wonnacott) and on exchange rate flexibility. He has a keen interest in economic policy. While with the Council of Economic Advisers, he participated in work which led to the decision to adopt exchange rate flexibility in the early 1970s. His extracurricular activities include skiing and tennis.

Ronald J. Wonnacott received his Ph.D. in economics at Harvard in 1959, and has taught at that university, the University of Minnesota, and the University of Western Ontario. He has written widely on the subject of U.S.-Canadian trade relations, and on the economics of customs unions and free trade areas—much of this with his brother Paul. Their joint book, *Free Trade between the United States and Canada: The Potential Economic Effects* has contributed to the recent discussion of a possible free trade arrangement between the two countries. Ron Wonnacott has also co-authored books on statistics and econometrics with a third brother, Tom. He is a past president of the Canadian Economics Association and a Fellow of the Royal Society of Canada. He shares an enthusiasm for music, tennis, and skiing with Paul, and is a member of the Honourable Company of Edinburgh Golfers.

TO

Paul McCracken and

Grant Reuber

CONTENTS

PART THREE AGGREGATE DEMAND POLICIES

PART FOUR
GREAT MACROECONOMIC ISSUES OF OUR TIME

SUGGESTED OUTLINE FOR A ONE-SEMESTER COURSE

Note: Boxes and Appendixes may be omitted in a one-semester course.

PART ONE: BASIC ECONOMIC CONCEPTS

1. Economic Problems and Economic Goals
2. Scarcity and Choice (to p. 33)
3. Specialization, Exchange, and Money
4. Demand and Supply: The Market Mechanism
6. Business Organization and Finance (section on business accounting only, pp. 102–105)

PART TWO: HIGH EMPLOYMENT AND A STABLE PRICE LEVEL

7. Measuring National Product and National Income (to p. 130)
9. Explaining Unemployment and Inflation: Aggregate Supply and Aggregate Demand
10. Equilibrium with Unemployment: The Keynesian Approach

PART THREE: AGGREGATE DEMAND POLICIES

11. Fiscal Policy (to p. 215)
12. Money and the Banking System
13. The Federal Reserve and Monetary Policy (to p. 255)

PART FOUR: GREAT MACROECONOMIC ISSUES OF OUR TIME

[Omit this part.]

PART FIVE: MICROECONOMICS: IS OUR OUTPUT PRODUCED EFFICIENTLY?

20. Demand and Supply: The Concept of Elasticity
21. Demand
22. Costs and Perfectly Competitive Supply: The Short Run
23. Costs and Perfectly Competitive Supply: The Long Run
24. Perfect Competition and Economic Efficiency (to p. 495)
25. Monopoly (to p. 521)
26. Markets between Monopoly and Perfect Competition

PART SIX: ECONOMIC EFFICIENCY: ISSUES OF OUR TIME

27. How Much Should the Government Regulate Business? (except pp. 561–569)
28. Protecting the Environment in a Growing Economy: How Should Pollution Be Limited? (to p. 583)
30. Public Goods: What Should the Government Provide? (to p. 623)

PART SEVEN: MICROECONOMICS: HOW INCOME IS DISTRIBUTED

33. Wages in a Perfectly Competitive Economy
34. Wages in Imperfectly Competitive Labor Markets
35. Other Incomes (to p. 734)

PREFACE

An understanding of economics has never been more important than it is today. Because of new technology, we produce many goods that were unheard of a few decades ago. And we produce old products in new ways. Changes in government policies have opened new opportunities for some, and have constrained others. Changes in economic conditions have created new and difficult problems.

This third edition of *Economics* represents a major revision and update. We have made every effort to present current material on the major policy issues of our time, while continuing to build a solid foundation of basic economic ideas.

THE CHALLENGE OF ECONOMICS

Economics is like the music of Mozart. On one level, it holds great simplicity: Its basic ideas can be quickly grasped by those who first encounter it. On the other hand, below the surface there are fascinating subtleties that remain a challenge—even to those who spend a lifetime in its study. We therefore hold out this promise: In this introductory study, you will learn a great deal about how the economy works—the basic principles governing economic life that must be recognized by those in government and business who make policy decisions. At the same time, we can also promise that you won't be able to master it all. You should be left with an appreciation of the difficult and challenging problems of economics that remain unsolved.

Perhaps some day you will contribute to their solution.

HOW TO USE THIS BOOK

Our objective has been to make the basic propositions of economics as easy as possible to grasp. As each new topic is encountered, essential definitions are printed in red type, and key steps in the argument are emphasized with boldface type. These highlights should be studied carefully during the first reading, and during later review. (A glossary is provided at the end of the book, containing a list of definitions of terms used in this text plus other common economics terms that you may encounter in class or in readings.) The basic ideas of each chapter are summarized in the Key Points at the end of the chapter, and new concepts introduced in the chapter are also listed.

When you read a chapter for the first time, concentrate on the main text. Don't worry about the boxes, which are optional. They are set aside from the text to keep the main text as simple and straightforward as possible. The boxes fall into two broad categories: *First* are the boxes that provide levity or color—for example, Kurt Vonnegut's tale in Box 36-2 of the Handicapper-General whose aim is to ensure that people will not only start out equal but also finish that way. *Second* are the boxes that present detailed theoretical explanations that are not needed to grasp the main ideas in the text. If you want to glance at the boxes that are fun and easy to read, fine. But when you first read a chapter, don't worry about those that contain more difficult material. On the first reading, you may also skip starred (*) sections of the text, along with the footnotes and appendixes; these also tend to be more difficult. Particularly challenging are the footnotes marked (*). Come back to them later, after you have mastered the basic ideas.

Economics is not a spectator sport. You cannot learn just from observation; you must work at it. When you have finished reading a chapter, work on the problems listed at the end; they are designed to reinforce your understanding of important concepts. [The starred (*) problems are either based on material in a box, or are more difficult questions designed to provide a challenge to students who want to do more advanced work.] Because each chapter builds on preceding ones, and because the solution to some of the problems depends on those that come before, remember this important rule: Don't fall behind in a problem-solving course. To help you keep up, we recommend the *Study Guide* (third edition) which is designed specially to assist you in working through each chapter. It should be available in your bookstore.

TO THE INSTRUCTOR

As we have revised and updated this text, we have continued to keep in mind the two major questions posed in the first edition. Our uneasiness regarding the answers provided a major reason for writing this book.

For macroeconomics, the principal question was this: After studying introductory economics, are students able to understand public controversies over such topics as the level of government spending and taxation, monetary policy, and the desirability of price controls? Are we training our students to understand the front pages of the newspaper? For many years, the introductory course was aimed at teaching students how policy should be run; that is, at providing a cookbook of "right" answers. While many books express more doubts and qualifications than was the case a decade ago, we have altered the focus of the course even more by building up to the six controversial questions in Part 4: Is fiscal or monetary policy the key to aggregate demand? Should the authorities attempt to "fine-tune" aggregate demand? How can inflation exist at the same time as a high rate of unemployment? How does the economy adjust to inflation, and what complications does inflation present to the policymaker? Why have productivity and growth been disappointing since 1973? Should exchange rates be fixed or flexible?

While there are no simple, indisputably "correct" answers to these questions, we believe that the major issues can be presented clearly to beginning economics students, thereby providing them with an understanding of important, recurring public debates over macroeconomic policy.

For microeconomics, the question was this: Does the introductory study of microeconomics lack coherence? To the student, does microeconomics tend to become just one thing after another—a guided tour through the economist's workshop, introducing as many polished pieces of analytic machinery as possible for later use in more advanced courses? Most students do not continue to advanced economics courses. For them, there is little point in concentrating on analytic techiques for their own sake, when time could be spent studying interesting policy issues instead. Even for those who do continue in economics, we doubt that it is useful to focus so heavily on analytic techniques. True, such a focus gives students some headstart in their later courses; but it also increases the risk that they will be bored by repetition, and will miss some of the forest while concentrating on the trees. Therefore, we follow a simple rule of thumb: In introducing analytic concepts, we focus on those most useful in studying policy issues.

In the third edition, as in the first two, we have attempted to make microeconomics more interesting by organizing our discussion around two continuing themes: ***efficiency*** and ***equity.*** Efficiency is the focus of attention in Parts 5 and 6, and equity in Part 7.

Major Revisions

Like the world of high technology, the world of economics is changing rapidly. Huge pools of internationally mobile capital have led to fluctuations in currency values and third-world debt problems far beyond our experience of just a few years ago. The United States seems committed to spending and taxation policies which imply large budget deficits as far as the eye can see. Even after adjustment for inflation and the size of the economy, these deficits are unprecedented, except for wartime periods.

In these circumstances, professors may expect substantial updating of any economics text. We have responded by revising every chapter to some degree; in most cases, the revisions have been substantial. Here are some of the main changes.

In the *macroeconomic sections* of the book—Parts 2 through 4—two new chapters have been added. Chapter 8, "Fluctuations in Economic Activity: Unemployment and Inflation," reviews the major developments and problems in the U.S. economy. Two points are emphasized. (1) We have been successful in preventing a repeat of the Great Depression. Our greater understanding of macroeconomics has had a payoff in terms of better policies. (2) However, cycles have not been getting milder and milder; the recessions of 1973–1975 and 1981–1982 were more severe than those of the fifties and sixties. Macroeconomics is not a simple subject, with simple solutions to our problems. This theme provides the background for the later study of major unsettled questions in macroeconomics (Part 4).

Chapter 9, "Explaining Unemployment and Inflation: Aggregate Supply and Aggregate Demand," is designed to give students a broad overview before the detailed study of macroeconomics. In introducing the concepts of aggregate supply and aggregate demand, we have taken care to explain why we cannot simply assume that the aggregate curves slope the same way as the curves for an individual product. When drawing a demand or supply curve for an individual product—such as hamburgers or shoes—we consider the responses of buyers and sellers to changes in relative prices; they respond by switching to (or from) other products. For aggregate demand and aggregate supply, there is no such switching, because we are dealing with the overall price level, not changes in relative prices. Chapter 9 also provides an introduction to the differences between the Keynesian and classical schools. Although there are many points of agreement among macroeconomists, substantial areas of disagreement remain.

In the macroeconomic chapters, other changes include the following:

1. Much more attention is now paid to budget deficits and the growing national debt. There are major new sections on these topics in the chapter on fiscal policy (Chapter 11), and in the chapter on the relative importance of fiscal and monetary policies (Chapter 14). In this latter chapter, the new edition includes a discussion of the relationship between government deficits, interest rates, exchange rates, and trade deficits. At the same time, some dated topics have been dropped. For example, in a period when the government is having great difficulty in gaining control of the budget, it no longer seems necessary to have a section on fiscal drag.

2. The discussion of growth and productivity in Chapter 18 has been extensively rewritten and updated, with a major change in emphasis. No longer is the question simply one of why growth and productivity were disappointing in the 1970s. The new chapter also includes a discussion of growth and productivity in the early 1980s, and explores whether we are solving our productivity problems. We do not offer a categorical answer; sufficient information is not yet available. (There is an important relationship between productivity and the business cycle, and the strong cycle of the early 1980s has made it difficult to identify underlying trends in productivity.) This chapter includes a discussion of the supply-side strategy of the Reagan administration.

In the *microeconomic chapters,* major organizational changes have been made. The chapter on "Costs and Perfectly Competitive Supply" has been divided into two chapters; one describes the short run, and the other describes the long run . This division should provide students with more breathing space in the development of the basic microeconomic theory. Equally important has been the reorganization of the micro chapters into three broad groupings: the basic theory of product markets in a new Part 5, followed by a new Part 6 entitled "Economic Efficiency: Issues of Our Time," and finally, Part 7 on factor markets and the distribution of income.

The creation of new Part 6 offers several advantages. First, it highlights the policy issues in microeconomics, just as Part 4, "Great Macroeconomic Issues of Our Time," deals with the important macro policy questions. Second, it improves the flow of the book. The chapter on resources has been fully reworked so that it can be moved forward into this new Part 6, where it is linked to the chapter on pollution. Just as pollution imposes an external cost on those downstream or downwind, so too the extraction of a common property resource creates an external cost—in this case the cost to future generations who are left with less of the resource.

In response to changing conditions and suggestions of reviewers, the discussion of energy has been reduced in size, and is now included in the resource chapter (Chapter 29). While energy is still an important topic—OPEC is still used as an example of the opportunities and problems facing collusive oligopolists in Chapter 26—there is a shift in emphasis away from oil as a crisis commodity to oil as a vivid historical example of the complications that arise when the government controls a price. Finally, moving resources and energy forward into Part 6 improves the flow of Part 7 on income distribution. The chapter on the way in which markets distribute income is followed immediately by the controversies over how income *should* be distributed, and over the policies that the government can use to alter income patterns.

New material in microeconomics includes an expanded discussion of transactions and time costs in the chapter on demand (Chapter 21); a new section on contestable markets in the chapter on imperfect competition (Chapter 26); an updated description of the farm programs and their increasing costs in the 1980s; material on the rising rate of poverty; and sections on the breakup of AT&T and the new wave of giant mergers—including a description of greenmail, white knights, pac-man strategies, and other forms of shark repellant.

Looking Ahead

Because we have attempted to build the discussion in orderly steps, we recommend that teachers look ahead to later passages before introducing certain subjects. For example, before teaching the basics of microeconomics in Part 5, we suggest that teachers glance ahead to the most important initial building blocks—the highlighted ''Essential Ideas for Future Chapters'' in Chapters 20 to 23, and the first 10 pages of Chapter 24 where the concept of efficiency is explained in detail. Similarly, we recommend that instructors who wish to teach indifference curves not only read the first indifference curve appendix (in Chapter 21), but also look ahead to the second (in Chapter 24). In the second appendix, we consider a topic not found frequently in elementary texts; namely, how indifference curves can be used to illustrate the way in which a perfectly competitive economy results in an efficient allocation of resources. Students find this an interesting topic. And this use of indifference curves fits directly into our emphasis on efficiency throughout Parts 5 and 6 of this book.

Other Points of Interest

Finally, we draw your attention to a number of ways in which our treatment differs from that of many other economics texts.

- In emphasizing efficiency and the gains from specialization, we have given greater attention to economies of scale than is frequently the case. In Chapters 3 and 31, economies of scale are given billing almost equal to comparative advantage. In our opinion, economies of scale are an important source of gain from specialization, and they should not be avoided because of the difficult analytic problems to which they lead. Most of the analytic problems can be avoided in an introductory text.
- We consider the problem of financial instability in more detail than most other books. (For example, see the discussion of the instabilities of the monetary system during the Great Depression in Chapter 13, and the overview of financial instability in recent recessions in Box 13-2.) In our opinion, the Keynesian revolution resulted in too little attention to the financial side of the economy.
- We discuss the gold standard—and the problems which it raises—in more detail than most other books (pages 260 to 264). This topic is important for an understanding of history, particularly the problem of bank instability. Many students are fascinated by the gold standard. Like most economists, we believe that it would be a mistake to go back to the gold standard—particularly in its classical version, with the quantity of money determined by the quantity of gold. But we also believe it is important that students of economics know *why*.
- Because of our emphasis on major themes and problems, our discussion of international economics is organized differently from that in most books. The gains from trade and the effects of protection fit into the topic of efficiency, and therefore they are included in the microeconomic part of the book, in Chapters 31 and 32. But exchange rate arrangements are most closely related to such issues as inflation and unemployment, and they are therefore included with other macroeconomic topics, in Chapter 19. By keeping international topics next to the related domestic topics, we hope to counteract the neglect of international economics in many introductory courses.
- Students are introduced to the important idea of dynamic efficiency. Any detailed analysis of dynamic efficiency has traditionally been regarded as too difficult for an elementary course. Initially we sympathized with this view, until we discovered that most beginning students *can* handle a problem like the most efficient pattern of resource use over time (optional Box 29-3).
- We show how conflicts can exist not only between objectives such as equity and efficiency, but also between groups of people in the economy. For example, the theory of comparative advantage illustrates how foreign trade can increase a nation's real income. We go one step further, to emphasize how trade affects various

groups differently: Low-cost imports benefit consumers, but they hurt competing domestic producers. It is easy for students to identify such winners and losers. They thereby can appreciate the irony of complaints about agricultural price supports from business executives who benefit from tariffs that prop up the prices of the goods *they* produce. Moreover, this identification of different groups—and the differences in their political power—helps the student to answer one of the basic questions raised by the theory of public choice: Why is there a difference between what the government *should* do and what it *does* do?

- Other topics on which we have placed more-than-usual emphasis include externalities (Chapters 28 to 30) and the difficulty of policymaking when we face both a high rate of unemployment and high inflation (Chapter 16).

Alternative Course Designs

As already noted, some of the boxes in the text are used to introduce material that may be too difficult for some students, but highly enlightening for others. (See, for example, Box 24-2 on Pareto efficiency and Box 25-1 on the theory of the second best.) We hope that these boxes, along with similarly designed appendixes, will give you flexibility in designing your course.

In a further attempt to provide flexibility, we have brought all the macro chapters together into Parts 2 to 4, and all the micro chapters together into Parts 5 to 7. The majority of instructors who teach macro first can use the chapters in the order in which they appear in the book. Those who wish to teach micro first can cover Parts 1, 5, 6, 7, 2, 3, and 4, in that order. For instructors teaching a one-semester course, there are two paperback options: *An Introduction to Macroeconomics,* and *An Introduction to Microeconomics*. Those who wish to cover both macro and micro quickly in one semester should consult the Suggested Outline, preceding this Preface. To those who are teaching such a one-semester survey course, we would like to pass on a suggestion from veterans: Don't try to cover too much. A full year's work is simply too much for students to digest in one semester.

WE WISH TO THANK . . .

In developing this third edition, we have shamelessly accumulated intellectual debts to our colleagues and coworkers. We should like to thank our editor, Alison Meersschaert, for her insistence that every sentence be comprehensible to the undergraduate, and Michael Hartman, whose comprehensive review of the second edition provided a starting point for our revisions. We are particularly indebted to teachers of economics who have advised us or reviewed the text in its various drafts, and have provided a wealth of suggestions. These contributors—to this third edition as well as to earlier editions—are acknowledged on the following pages. To all, we express our sincere thanks.

Paul Wonnacott
Ronald Wonnacott

ACKNOWLEDGMENTS

Berhanu Abegaz
College of William and Mary

Carol Adams
University of California, Santa Cruz

Elisabeth Allison
Date Resources, Inc.

Clopper Almon
University of Maryland

Richard Anderson
Texas A&M University

Martin Bailey
University of Maryland

Anthony Barkume
California State University

Robert Barry
College of William and Mary

Peter Barth
University of Connecticut

Raymond C. Battalio
Texas A&M University

Marion Beaumont
California State University, Long Beach

Deepak Bhattasali
Boston University

Donna M. Bialik
Indiana University-Purdue University

John Bishop
University of Wisconsin

J. Lloyd Blackwell, III
University of North Dakota

Vin Blankenship
U.S. Department of Agriculture

Ake Blomqvist
University of Western Ontario

Gerald Breger
University of South Carolina

Charles Brown
University of Michigan

Michael Butler
University of North Alabama

James Ciccka
DePaul University

John Cooke
University of South Florida

David Conklin

Ed Corcoran
Community College of Philadelphia

William J. Corcoran
University of Nebraska at Omaha

Joseph Cox
University of Kansas

Dudley Dillard
University of Maryland

Richard B. DuBoff
Bryn Mawr College

Stanley Duobonis
Shippensburg State College

Thomas Fox
Pennsylvania State University

Mark Frankena
University of Western Ontario

K. K. Fung
Memphis State University

William J. Field
DePauw University

Richard Freeman
Harvard University

Eugene B. Gendel
Lafayette College

Marshall Goldman
Harvard University

Timothy Greening
Tulane University

James J. Grunloh
University of Wisconsin, Oshkosh

R. J. Gunderson
Northern Arizona State University

Curtis Harvey
University of Kentucky

Knick Harley
University of Western Ontario

Charles M. Hill
Prairie State College

P. J. Hill
University of Alaska

Catherine Hoffman
University of Idaho

Peter Howitt
University of Western Ontario

Phyllis Iseley
Norwich University

George Jakubson
Cornell University

John Kagel
Texas A&M University

Sol D. Kaufler
Los Angeles Pierce College

Tim Keely
Tacoma Community College

Kyoo Hong Kim
Bowling Green State University

Robert Kirk
Purdue University at Indianapolis

William Kleiner
Western Illinois University

Marvin Koster
American Enterprise Institute for Public Policy

Joseph Kreitzer
College of St. Thomas

Ulrich Lachler
University of Maryland

David Laidler
University of Western Ontario

Kathleen Langley
Boston University

Allen F. Larsen
St. Cloud State University

Douglas G. Madigan
Robert Morris College

James Mak
University of Hawaii at Manoa

John George Marcis
Kansas State University

Arthur Martel
Indiana University of Pennsylvania

Peter A. Martin
Purdue University

Forrest McCluer
Bates College

Francis J. McGrath
Iona College

Paul Meyer
University of Maryland

Patsy Miller

Tapan Monroe
University of the Pacific

Peter Morgan
University of Western Ontario

W. Douglas Morgan
University of California, Santa Barbara

Carolina A. Murphy
Fitchburg State College

Peter Murrell
University of Maryland

William Moscoff
San Gamon State University

Dennis Mueller
University of Maryland

Martin P. Oettinger
University of California, Davis

Lars Osberg
Dalhousie University

John Palmer
University of Western Ontario

Michael Parkin
University of Western Ontario

Jerry Pelovsky
College of the Sequoias

Martin Perline
Wichita State University

Hugh Peters
Sacramento City College

Barry Pfitzner
North Virginia Community College

Bette Polkinghorn
California State University

Jonas Prager
New York University

Marilyn Pugh
Prince George's Community College

Rex D. Rehnberg
Colorado State University

Chris Robinson
University of Western Ontario

Thomas Robinson
Clinton County Community College

Allen R. Sanderson
University of Chicago

Kenneth G. Scalet
York College of Pennsylvania

Robert Schwab
University of Maryland

Samuel Schrager
Villanova University

Dan Segebarth
Triton College

Michael Shields
South Illinois University

Mary Alice Shulman
Northwestern University

Martin Snowbarger
San Jose State University

Susan C. Stephenson
Drake University

LaVonna A. Straub
Western Illinois University

Charles Stuart
University of California, Santa Barbara

Mary R. Supel
College of St. Thomas

William Tabel
Thornton Community College

Frank D. Taylor
McLennan Community College

Norman Taylor
Franklin and Marshall College

Robert Thompson
Council of Economic Advisers

Roswell G. Townsend
Chatham College

Richard Tyson
University of Wisconsin, Stout

Holley Ulbrich
Clemson University

Joseph Walker
University of Montevallo

Victoria Zinde Walsh
University of Western Ontario

Paul Weinstein
University of Maryland

John Whalley
University of Western Ontario

William C. Wood
University of Virginia

Arthur Wright
University of Connecticut

Donald Yankovic
University of Toledo

Michael Zweig
SUNY at Stony Brook

PART ONE

BASIC ECONOMIC CONCEPTS

CHAPTER 1

ECONOMIC PROBLEMS AND ECONOMIC GOALS

Economy is the art of making the most out of life.

GEORGE BERNARD SHAW

Some years ago, a Japanese mass-circulation newspaper, the *Mainichi,* conducted a survey of 4,000 people, asking them what they thought of first when they heard the word *takai* (high). ''Mount Fuji,'' said 12%. The overwhelming majority—88%—said, ''Prices.'' In the United States, *The New York Times* and CBS conducted a poll shortly before the election of 1984, quizzing voters on the most important factor in determining their choice for president. While 18% said military affairs and foreign policy, 55% said the state of the economy. The importance of the economy in determining voting behavior has been borne out by history. In the United States, an elected president has been defeated at the polls only twice since 1912. In 1932, Herbert Hoover was defeated by Franklin D. Roosevelt. At that time, the economy was approaching the low point of the Great Depression, with more than one worker in five out of a job. Roosevelt promised hope. In 1980, Jimmy Carter was defeated by Ronald Reagan. In that year, the average level of prices paid by American families rose by 12.4%. Those two elections showed how much the American public cares about the problems of unemployment and inflation. With the rare exception of the individual who inherits great wealth, most of us spend a large part of our energy in the struggle to make a living.

Economics **is the study of how people make their living, how they acquire the food, shelter, clothing, and other material necessities and comforts of this world. It is a study of the problems they encounter and of the ways in which these problems can be reduced.**

In the words of Alfred Marshall, a great teacher and scholar of a century ago, ''economics is a study of mankind in the ordinary business of life.'' Under this broad definition, economics addresses many specific questions. To list but a few:

- What jobs will be available when we finish college? What will they pay?
- Why is it so difficult to get a job at some times and so easy at others?
- Does it pay to go to college?
- How are goods produced and exchanged? How do we choose which goods to produce?
- Why did our economy produce so much more in 1984 than in 1948?

Economics is a study of success, and it is a study of failure.

ECONOMIC PROGRESS

From the vantage point of our comfortable homes of the late twentieth century, it is easy for us to forget how many people, through history, have been losers in the struggle to make a living. Unvarnished economic history is the story of deprivation, of 80-hour weeks, of child labor—and of starvation. But also, it is the story of the slow climb of civilization toward the goal of relative affluence, where the general public as well as the fortunate few can have a degree of material well-being and leisure.

One of the most notable features of the U.S. economy has been its growth. Although there have been interruptions and setbacks, economic progress has been remarkable. Figure 1-1 shows one of the standard measures of success—the increase in total production per person. (The precise measure of production in this diagram is *gross national product,* or GNP for short. This concept will be explained in Chapter 7.) The average American now produces about twice as much as the average American of 1945, and four times as much as the average American at the turn of the century. Furthermore, the higher output is produced with less effort: The average workweek has declined about 25% during this century. Thus, economic progress in the United States has been reflected both in an increase in the goods and services that we produce and enjoy, and in a greater amount of leisure time.

A similar tale of success has occurred in many other countries, as illustrated in Figure 1-2. Between 1963 and 1983, output grew at an average annual rate of 3.9% in France, 3.1% in Germany, 3.5% in Italy, and 3.8% in Canada. Nor has growth been confined to the countries of Europe and North America. Particularly notable has been the growth of the Japanese economy. From the ashes of the Second World War, Japan has emerged as one of the leading success stories, with output per person that now exceeds that of Britain.[1] Other stories of success have come from the middle-income areas of East

[1]The success of the Japanese economy has made that country the subject of good-natured humor. In a speech at Miami University (Ohio), Paul McCracken of the University of Michigan, who served as chairman of the President's Council of Economic Advisers from 1969 to 1971, recalled that on his first trip to Japan in the fifties he had gone to offer the Japanese advice on growth policy. Added McCracken, "I've been trying to remember ever since what we told them."

There are substantial problems in comparing output per person in various countries. However, careful work indicates that Japan passed Britain about 1970. See Irving B. Kravis and others, *A System of International Comparisons of Gross Product and Purchasing Power,* United Nations International Comparison Project: Phase One (Baltimore: Johns Hopkins University Press, 1975), p. 231.

FIGURE 1-1
Production per person and hours worked
Source: Board of Governors of the Federal Reserve, *1984 Historical Chart Book.*

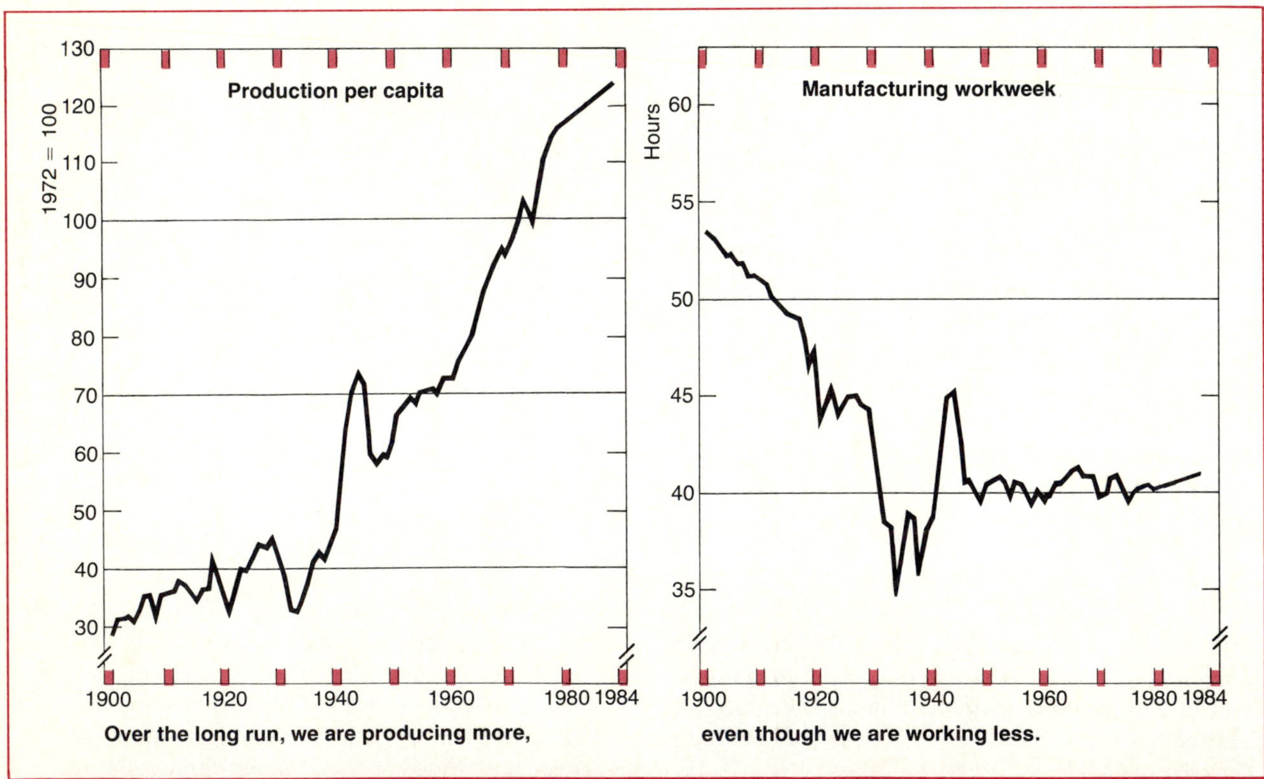

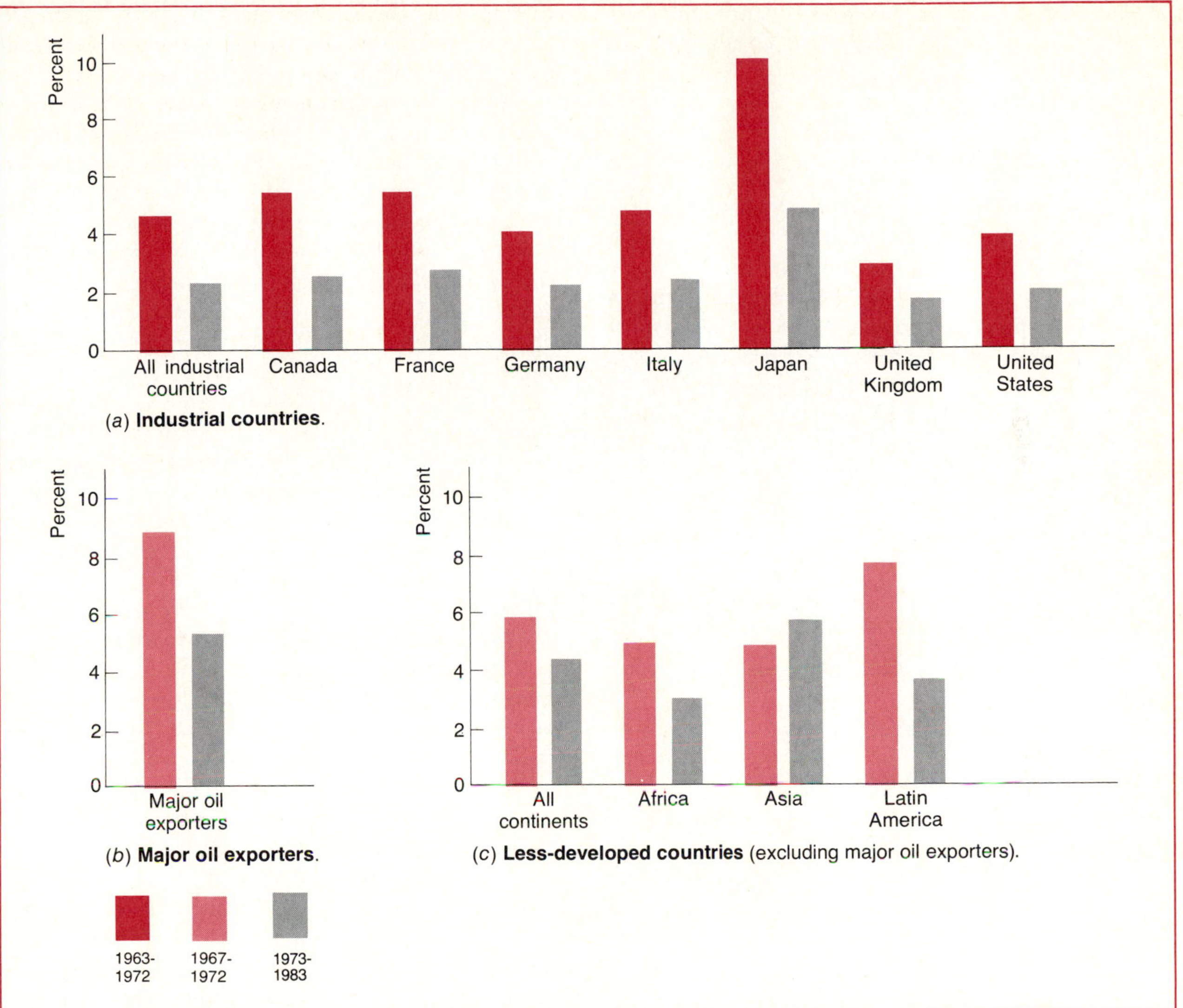

FIGURE 1-2

Annual rates of increase in output, 1963–1983

Growth has been rapid in many countries. Growth was particularly fast in Japan between 1963 and 1972, when output increased at an average annual rate of 10½%. Note that for most countries, growth has been much slower since 1973 than during the previous decade—with the less-developed economies of Asia being an exception. This slower growth may be traced in part to the disruptions caused by the rapid increase in the price of oil.

Sources: International Monetary Fund (IMF), *Annual Report, 1980,* pp. 8–12; IMF, *Annual Report, 1984,* pp. 7–10.

Asia—South Korea, Hong Kong, and Singapore—where output per person has grown at a very impressive rate of 6.7% per year.

ECONOMIC PROBLEMS

Although rapid growth has occurred in many countries, it has been neither universal nor automatic. In a number of countries, the standard of living remains abysmally low. The World Bank—an international institution whose major purpose is to lend to the developing countries—estimates that, between 1960 and 1982, output per person rose at an average annual rate of only 1.2% in the 25 poorest countries (excluding China). The record is even bleaker in the poorest of the poor, where the increase in population continuously threatens to outrun the increase in production. Output per person has actually declined in countries such as Chad, Nepal, and Uganda.[2]

In both rich countries and poor, substantial economic problems remain. Even in the relatively prosperous United States, we may wonder:

- Why are so many unable to find work, when so much needs to be done?
- Why do pockets of poverty remain in an affluent society?
- Why have prices spiraled upward?
- Why does the average black in America have a lower income than the average white?
- Are we really producing the right things? Should we produce more housing and fewer cars? Or more medical services and fewer sports spectaculars?
- Why is pollution such a problem? What should be done about it?

ECONOMIC POLICY

Why? and *What should be done*? are the two key questions in economics. The ultimate objective of economics is to *develop policies to deal with our problems*. However, before we can formulate policies, we must first make every effort to understand how the economy has worked in the past and how it works today. Otherwise, well-intentioned policies may go astray and lead to unforeseen and unfortunate consequences.

When economic policies are studied, the center of attention is usually the policies of the government—policies such as taxation, government spending programs, and the regulation of particular industries, such as electric power and the railroads. However, the policies of private businesses are also important. How should they organize production in order to make their goods at the lowest possible cost? What prices should a business charge? When should a supermarket increase the stocks of goods in its warehouse?

The Controversial Role of Government

For more than 200 years, economics has been dominated by a controversy over the proper role of government. In what circumstances should government take an active role? When is it best for government to leave decisions to the private participants in the economy? On this topic, the giants of economics have repeatedly met to do battle.

In 1776, Scottish scholar ***Adam Smith*** published his pathbreaking book, *An Inquiry into the Nature and Causes of the Wealth of Nations*.[3] Modern economics may be dated from that historic year, which was also notable for the Declaration of Independence. Smith's message was clear: Private markets should be liberated from the tyranny of government control. In pursuit of their private interests, individual producers would make the goods that consumers want. It is not, said Smith, "from the benevolence of the butcher, the brewer, or the baker that we expect our dinner, but from their regard to their own interest." There is an "invisible hand," he wrote, that causes the producer to promote the interests of society. Indeed, "by pursuing his own interest he frequently promotes that of the society more effectually than when he really intends to promote it." In general, said Smith, the government should be cautious in interfering with the operations of the private market. According to Smith, the best policy is generally one of ***laissez faire***—leave it alone. Government intervention usually makes things worse. For example, government imposi-

[2]World Bank, *World Development Report 1984*, pp. 218–219.

[3]Available in Modern Library edition (New York: Random House, 1937). Smith's book is commonly referred to as *The Wealth of Nations*.

tion of a tariff is generally harmful. (A *tariff,* or *duty,* is a tax on a foreign-produced good as it enters the country.) Even though a tariff generally helps domestic producers who are thereby given an advantage over foreign producers, the country as a whole loses. Specifically, a tariff increases the cost of goods available to consumers, and this cost to consumers outweighs the benefits to producers. Smith's work has been refined and modified during the past 200 years, but many of his laissez faire conclusions have stood up remarkably well. For example, there is still a very strong economic argument against high tariffs on imported goods. In recent decades, one of the principal areas of international cooperation has been the negotiation of lower tariffs.

During the Great Depression of the 1930s—a century and a half after the appearance of the *Wealth of Nations*—the laissez faire tradition in economics came under attack. In 1936, ***John Maynard Keynes*** published his *General Theory of Employment, Interest and Money* (also known, more simply, as the *General Theory*). In this book, Keynes (which rhymes with Danes) argued that the government has the duty to intervene in the economy to put the unemployed back to work. Of the several ways in which this could be done, one stood out in its simplicity. By building public works, such as roads, post offices, and dams, the government could provide jobs directly and thus provide a cure for the depression.

With his proposals for a more active role for government, Keynes drew the ire of many business executives. They feared that, as a result of his recommendations, the government would become larger and larger and private enterprise would gradually be pushed out of the picture. But Keynes did not foresee this result. He believed that, by providing jobs, the government could remove the explosive frustrations caused by the mass unemployment of the 1930s, and could make it possible for western political and economic institutions to survive. His objective was to modify our economic system and make it better. Unlike Karl Marx, he was not trying to destroy it. (For a brief introduction to the revolutionary ideas of Marx, see Box 1-1.)[4]

[4]Throughout this book, the boxes present illustrative and supplementary materials. They can be disregarded without losing the main thread of the discussion.

Thus, Smith and Keynes took apparently contradictory positions—Smith arguing for less government and Keynes for more.[5] It is possible, of course, that each was right. Perhaps the government should do more in some respects and less in others. Economic analysis does not lead inevitably to either an activist or a passive position on the part of the government. The economist's rallying cry should not be, "Do something." Rather, it should be, "Think first."

ECONOMIC GOALS

We have already noted that the ultimate goal of economics is to develop better policies to minimize our problems and to maximize the benefits from our daily toil. More specifically, there is widespread agreement that we should strive for the following goals:

1. ***A high level of employment.*** People willing to work should be able to find jobs reasonably quickly. Widespread unemployment is demoralizing, and it represents an economic waste. Society foregoes the goods and services that the unemployed could have produced.
2. ***Price stability.*** It is desirable to avoid rapid increases—or decreases—in the average level of prices.
3. ***Efficiency.*** When we work, we want to get as much as we reasonably can out of our productive efforts.
4. ***An equitable distribution of income.*** When many live in affluence, no group of citizens should suffer stark poverty.
5. ***Growth.*** Continuing growth, which would make possible an even higher standard of living in the future, is generally considered an important objective.

The list is far from complete. Not only do we want to produce more, but we want to do so without the degradation of our environment; the ***reduction of pollution*** is important. ***Economic freedom***—the right of people to

[5]Conflicting views over the proper role of government may be found in the works of two retired professors: the University of Chicago's Milton Friedman (for laissez faire) and Harvard's John Kenneth Galbraith (who argues for more government). See John Kenneth Galbraith, *The Affluent Society* (Boston: Houghton-Mifflin, 1958) and Milton Friedman and Rose Friedman, *Free to Choose* (New York: Harcourt Brace Jovanovich, 1980). We strongly recommend that if you read one of these books, you read them both. Each of the books puts forth a convincing case. Nevertheless, they are flatly contradictory.

choose their own occupations, to enter contracts, and to spend their incomes as they please—is a desirable goal. So, too, is ***economic security***—freedom from the fear that chronic illness or other catastrophe will place an individual or a family in a desperate financial situation.

The achievement of our economic goals provides the principal focus of this book. As a background for later chapters, let's look at the major goals in more detail.

1. A High Level of Employment

The importance of the objective of full employment was illustrated most clearly during the Great Depression of the 1930s, when the United States and many other countries conspicuously failed to achieve it. During the sharp contraction from 1929 to 1933, total output in the United States fell almost one-third, and spending for new buildings, machinery, and equipment declined by almost 80%. As the economy slid downward, more and more workers were thrown out of jobs. By 1933, one-quarter of the labor force was unemployed. (See Figure 1-3.) Long lines of the jobless gathered at factory gates in the hope of work; disappointment was their common fate. Nor was the problem quickly solved. The downward slide into the depths of the depression went on for a

BOX 1-1

KARL MARX

The main text refers to two towering economists—Adam Smith and John Maynard Keynes. In the formation of the intellectual heritage of most American economists, Smith and Keynes have played leading roles. But, if we consider the intellectual heritage of the world as a whole, Karl Marx is probably the most influential economist of all. In the Soviet Union, Marx is more than the source of economic "truth"; he is the messiah of the state religion.

Many business executives viewed Keynes as a revolutionary because he openly attacked accepted economic opinion and proposed fundamental changes in economic policy. But by revolutionary standards, Keynes pales beside Marx. The Marxist call to revolution was shrill and direct: "Workers of the world, unite! You have nothing to lose but your chains."

Why did they have nothing to lose? Because, said Marx, workers are responsible for the production of all goods. Labor is the sole source of value. But workers get only part of the fruits of their labor. A large—and in Marx's view, unearned—share goes to the exploiting class of capitalists. (Capitalists are the owners of factories, machinery, and other equipment.) Marx believed that, by taking up arms and overthrowing capitalism, workers could end exploitation and obtain their rightful rewards.

On our main topic—the role of government—Marx was strangely ambivalent. Who would own the factories and machines once the communist revolution had eliminated the capitalist class? Ownership by the state—by all the workers as a group—was the obvious solution, and in fact this has been the path taken by countries such as the Soviet Union. The revolution has led to state ownership of the means of production. Yet, Marx also believed that the revolution would eventually lead to the "withering away" of the state. There has been no perceptible sign of this withering away in Marxist societies.

period of 4 years, and the road back to a high level of employment was even longer. It was not until the beginning of the 1940s, when American industry began working around the clock to produce weapons, that many of the unemployed were able to find jobs. There was not a single year during the whole decade 1931–1940 that unemployment averaged less than 14% of the labor force.

A *depression* exists when there is a very high rate of unemployment over a long period of time.

Something had clearly gone wrong—disastrously wrong. Large-scale unemployment represents tremendous waste; time lost in involuntary idleness is gone forever. The costs of unemployment go beyond the loss of output: Unemployment also involves the dashing of hopes. Those unable to find work suffer frustration and a sense of worthlessness, and their skills are lost as they remain idle.

The term ***unemployed*** is reserved for those who are willing and able to work but are unable to find jobs. Thus, those of you who are full-time college students are not included among the unemployed. Your immediate task is to get an education, not a job. Similarly, the 70-

FIGURE 1-3

Output and unemployment in the United States, 1929–1984

During the Great Depression, output fell and the unemployment rate rose sharply to 25%. In recent decades, the unemployment rate has been much lower, although it did rise above 10% during the recession of 1981–1982.

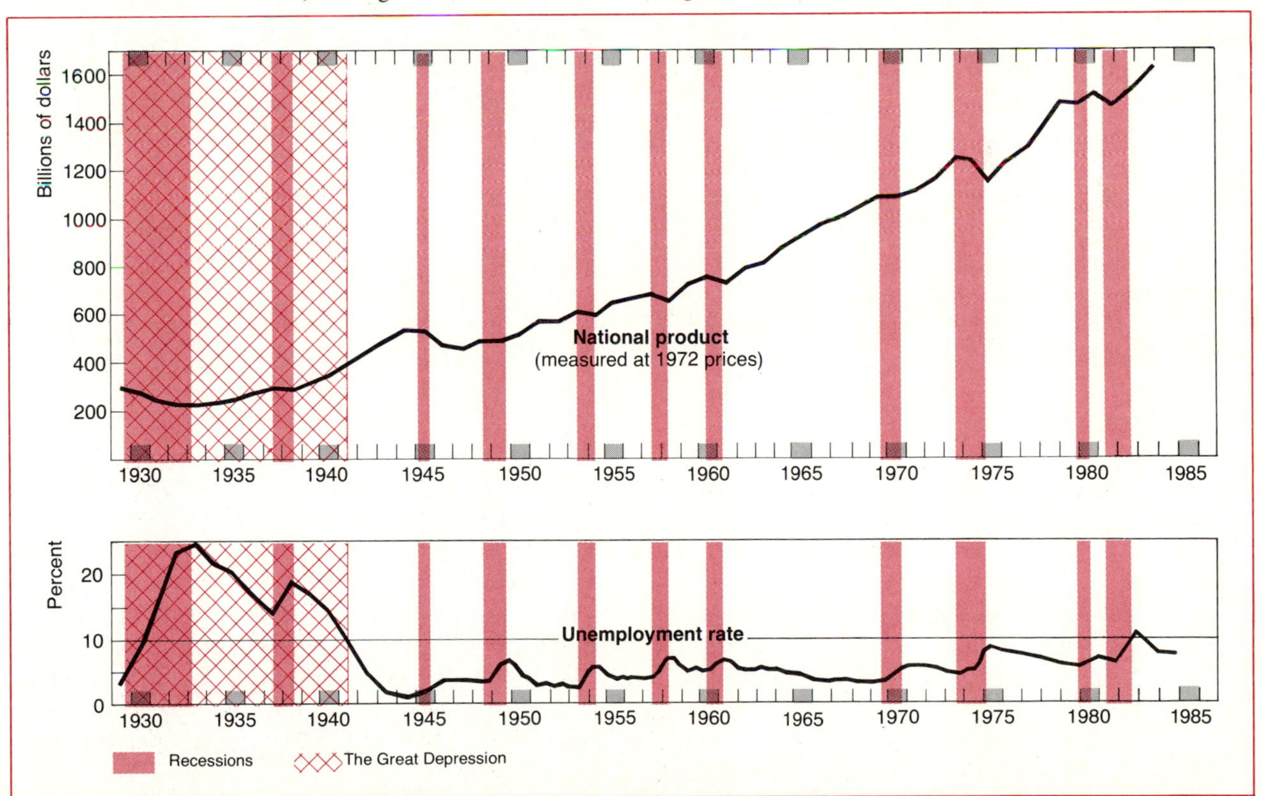

year-old retiree is not included in the statistics of the unemployed, nor are those in prisons or mental institutions, since they are not available for jobs.

A person is *unemployed* if he or she is available and looking for work but has not found it.

The unemployment rate is calculated as a percentage of the total labor force—the labor force being the sum of those who are actually employed, plus those who are unemployed. (Labor force and employment statistics are tied to the traditional definition of "jobs." Thus, for example, a mother who stays at home to raise her children is neither "in the labor force" nor "employed," although she certainly *works*.)

At the end of the Second World War, the Great Depression was still a fresh memory. The public, the politician, and the economist shared a common determination that a repeat of the 1930s could not be permitted. This determination was reflected in the ***Employment Act of 1946,*** which declared:

It is the continuing responsibility of the Federal Government to use all practical means . . . to promote maximum employment, production, and purchasing power.

Since the end of the Second World War, we have been successful in our determination to prevent a repetition of the unemployment of the 1930s, but the postwar period has not been an unbroken story of success. From time to time, there have been downturns in the economy—much more moderate, it is true, than the slide of 1929 to 1933, but downward movements nonetheless. These more moderate declines, or ***recessions,*** have been accompanied by an increase in the unemployment rate. In December 1982, during the worst recession of the past four decades, the unemployment rate rose to a peak of 10.6%. While we have been successful in preventing big depressions, the problem of periodic recessions has not been solved.

A *recession* is a decline in total output, income, employment, and trade, usually lasting 6 months to a year, and marked by widespread contractions in many sectors of the economy. (The decline is not confined to just one or two industries, such as steel or aircraft.)

2. Stability of the Average Price Level

Unemployment caused the downfall of Herbert Hoover in 1932. ***Inflation*** was a significant reason for the defeat of Jimmy Carter in 1980.

***Inflation* is an increase in the average level of prices. (Deflation is a fall in the average level of prices.)**

We can see in Figure 1-4 how the average of prices paid by consumers has risen through most of our recent history, with the period 1920–1933 being a notable exception. Prices rose most rapidly after World War I and for a brief period after World War II. Between 1973 and 1981, inflation was unusually severe for peacetime periods. (Detail on how to draw and interpret diagrams may be found in the appendix to this chapter and in the *Study Guide* which accompanies this text.)

While unemployment represents sheer waste—society loses the goods which might have been produced by those out of work—the problem with inflation is less obvious. When a price rises, there is both a winner and a loser. The loser is the buyer who has to pay more. However, there is a benefit to the seller, who gets more. On balance, it is not clear whether the society is better or worse off.

It is true, of course, that there is much resentment against inflation, but perhaps at least some of this resentment reflects a peculiarity of human nature. When people find the goods they *sell* rising in price, they see the increase as perfectly right, normal, and justified. On the other hand, when they find the goods they *buy* rising in price, they often view the increase as evidence of the seller's greed. When the price of wheat rises, farmers see themselves at last getting a reasonable return from their toil. When the price of oil increases, the oil companies argue that they are getting no more than the return neces-

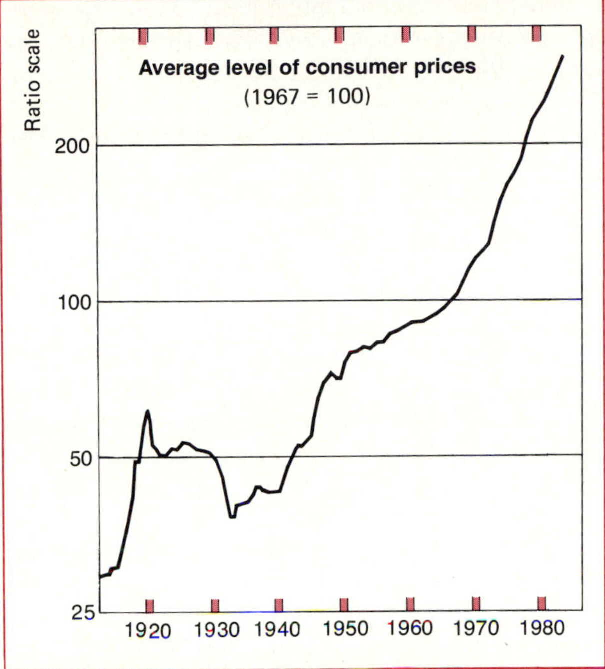

FIGURE 1-4
Consumer prices

Occasionally prices have fallen, for example, during the early 1930s. In recent decades, however, the trend of prices has been clearly upward. In 1974, and again in 1979 and 1980, the United States suffered from "double-digit" inflation—a rise in the average level of prices by more than 10% per year.

sary to finance the search for more oil. When the price of books rises, authors feel that they are getting no more than a "just" return for their creative efforts, and book publishers insist that they are being no more than adequately compensated for their risks. However, when the farmer, the oil company, the author, and the book publisher find that the prices of the goods they *buy* have increased, they believe they have been cheated by inflation. We may all be the victims of an illusion—the illusion that each of us can and should have a rise in the price of what we sell, but that the price of what we buy should remain stable. For the economy as a whole, this is not possible.

This two-sided nature of price increases—a gain to the seller but a loss to the buyer—means that it is difficult to evaluate the dangers of inflation. Indeed, there has been considerable controversy as to whether a low rate of inflation (say, 1% or 2% per annum) is dangerous, or whether, on the contrary, it may actually be beneficial to society. Some say that a small rate of inflation makes it easier for the economy to adjust to changes and to maintain a high level of employment.

However, when inflation gets beyond a moderate rate, there is widespread agreement that it becomes a menace. It becomes more than a mere transfer of money from the buyer to the seller; it interferes with the production and exchange of goods. This has most clearly been the situation during very rapid inflations, when economic activity was severely disrupted. ***Hyperinflation***—that is, a skyrocketing of prices at annual rates of 1,000% or more—occurs most commonly during or soon after a military conflict, when government spending shoots upward; for example, in the south during the Civil War, in Germany during the early 1920s, and in China during its Civil War in the late 1940s. A hyperinflation means that money rapidly loses its ability to buy goods. People are anxious to spend money as quickly as possible while they can still get something for it.

Clearly, hyperinflation of 1,000% or more per year is an extreme example. However, lower rates of inflation, amounting to 10% or less per year, can also have serious consequences:

1. Inflation hurts people living on fixed incomes and people who have saved fixed amounts of money for their retirement or for "a rainy day" (future illness or accident). The couple who put aside $1,000 in 1960 for their retirement have suffered a rude shock. In 1985, $1,000 bought no more than $300 bought in 1960.

2. Inflation can cause business mistakes. For good decisions, businesses need an accurate picture of what is going on. When prices are rising rapidly, the picture becomes obscured and out of focus. Decision-makers cannot see clearly. (For example, business accounting is done in dollar terms. When there is rapid inflation, some businesses may report profits when, on a more accurate calculation, they might actually be suffering losses. Consequently, inflation can temporarily hide problems.) Our economy is complex, and it depends on a continuous flow of accurate information. *Prices are an important link in the information chain.* For example, a high price should provide a signal to producers that consumers are especially anxious to get more of a particular product. But in a severe inflation, producers find it difficult to know whether this is the message, or whether the price of their product is rising simply because all prices are rising. In brief, *a severe inflation obscures the message carried by prices.*

Here, it is important to distinguish between a rise in the ***average level of prices*** (inflation) and a change in ***relative*** prices. Even if the average level of prices were perfectly stable (that is, no inflation existed), some *individual* prices would still change as conditions change in specific markets. For example, new inventions have cut the cost of producing computers, and computer companies have as a result been able to cut prices sharply. At the same time, U.S. energy prices (for oil, gasoline, electricity, etc.) have risen substantially during the past 15 years in response to the rise in the price of oil we import. The resulting fall in the price of computers relative to the price of oil has performed a useful function. It has encouraged businesses to use more of the relatively cheap computers in their operations and to conserve on the relatively expensive oil. (This is not, of course, to deny that the rise in the price of oil was painful, particularly to those living in the colder areas of the country.)

3. Efficiency

This illustration—of how businesses use more computers when they become cheaper—is one example of economic efficiency.

In an economy, both the unemployment rate and the inflation rate may be very low, but performance may still be poor. For example, fully employed workers may be engaged in a lot of wasted motion, and the goods being produced may not be those which are most needed. Obviously, this is not a satisfactory state of affairs.

***Efficiency* is the goal of getting the most out of our productive efforts. Inefficiency occurs when there is waste.**

Under this broad definition, two types of efficiency can be distinguished: ***technological efficiency*** and ***allocative efficiency.***

To illustrate *technological efficiency* (also known as *technical* efficiency), let us consider two bicycle manufacturers. One uses a large number of workers and many machines to produce 1,000 bicycles. The other uses fewer workers and fewer machines to produce the same number of bicycles. The second manufacturer is not a magician; he is simply a better manager. He is technologically efficient, whereas the first manufacturer is not. Technological inefficiency exists when the same output could be produced with fewer machines and fewer workers, working at a reasonable pace. (Technological efficiency does not require a sweatshop.) Technological inefficiency involves wasted motion and sloppy management; better management is the solution.

Allocative efficiency, on the other hand, involves the production of the *best combination of goods,* using the *lowest-cost combination of inputs.* How much food should we produce? How many houses? Suppose we produce only food and do so in a technologically efficient way, with no wasted motion. We will still not have achieved the goal of allocative efficiency because consumers want both food and housing.

Thus, allocative efficiency involves the choice of the right combination of outputs. It also involves using the best (lowest-cost) combination of inputs. Consider our earlier illustration. The cost of computers is coming down, while the cost of imported oil is rising. If businesses fail to adjust—and fail to conserve oil and to use computers more—there is allocative inefficiency.

Relative prices perform a key role in encouraging allocative efficiency. As we have noted, the decrease in the price of computers encourages businesses to use more computers and less of the other, relatively more expensive inputs.

4. An Equitable Distribution of Income

Ours is an affluent society, yet many people remain so poor they have difficulty in buying the basic necessities of life, such as food, clothing, and shelter. In the midst of plenty, some live in dire need. The moral question must then be faced: Should some people have so much while others have so little?

When the question is put this way, the compelling answer must surely be no. Our sense of justice is offended by extreme differences, and compassion requires that assistance be given to those crushed by illness and to those born and raised in cruel deprivation. In the view of the large majority, society has a responsibility to help those at the bottom of the economic ladder.

Our sense of equity, or justice, is offended by extreme differences. Thus, most people think of "equity" as a move toward "equality." But not all the way. The two words are far from synonymous. While there is widespread agreement that the least fortunate should be helped, there is no consensus that the objective of society should be an equal income for all. Some individuals are willing to work overtime; it is generally recognized as both just and desirable for them to have a higher income as a consequence. Otherwise, why should they work longer hours? Similarly, it is generally considered "right" for the hardworking to have a larger share of the pie. After all, they have contributed more to the production of the pie in the first place. On the other side, some people are loafers. If they were automatically given the same income as everyone else, our sense of equity would be offended. They don't deserve an equal share. And if everyone were guaranteed an equal income, how many would work?

There is no agreement on broad principles, such as how far we should go toward complete equality of incomes. The "best" division (or distribution) of income is ill-defined. Therefore, much of the discussion of income distribution has been focused on narrower questions, such as: What is happening to those at the bottom of the ladder? What is happening to the families who live in poverty?

Poverty is difficult to define in precise dollar terms. For one thing, not everyone's needs are the same. The sickly have the greatest need for medical care. Large families have the most compelling need for food and clothing. There is no simple, single measure of the "poverty line," below which families may be judged to be poor. Reasonable standards may, however, be established by taking into consideration such obvious complications as the number of individuals in a family. The poverty standards defined by the U.S. government are shown in Table 1-1.

TABLE 1-1
Poverty Standards, 1984

Size of family	Poverty standard
One person	$ 5,400
Two persons	6,980
Three persons	8,280
Four persons	10,610
Five persons	12,560
Six persons	14,210

According to U.S. government standards, families were poor in 1984 if their incomes fell below these figures. For example, a three-member family was poor if its income was less than $8,280.

There are two ways of raising people above the poverty line. The first is to increase the size of the national "pie." As the level of income rises throughout the economy, the incomes of those at the lower end will also generally rise. In the words of President John Kennedy, "A rising tide lifts all boats."

A second way to reduce poverty is to increase the share of the pie going to people with the lowest incomes. Thus, poverty may be combated by a ***redistribution of income.*** For example, the well-to-do may be taxed in order to finance government programs aimed at helping the poor. A number of government programs—particularly the "great society" programs of President Johnson—have attempted to raise the share of the nation's income going to the poorest families.

During the fifties and sixties, progress was made toward that goal. Between 1950 and 1969, the share of the poorest 20% of families rose from 4.5% to 5.6% of the national pie. Furthermore, a rising tide was lifting all boats. Because of the vigorous expansion of the economy, average family income rose about 40%—even after adjusting for inflation. The rising tide of income, together with the larger percentage going to the poor, combined to raise the incomes of the poorest fifth by more than 70% (again, after adjusting for inflation). Thus, the poorest of 1969 were much better off than the poorest of 1950. Nevertheless, they were still very poor by the overall standards of society.

Figure 1-5 shows the steady decline in the percentage of the population living in poverty during the 1960s, from 22.2% to 12.1%. After a brief reversal during the recession of 1970, the downward trend continued, reaching a low of 11.1% in 1973. Until 1979 there was little change, but since then the problem has gotten worse. We are still far short of the objective of eliminating poverty. Why is this task so difficult? One reason is unemployment. The unemployment rate has been much higher recently (averaging 7.4% in the decade from 1974 to 1983) than it was in 1973 (4.8%). As people lose their jobs, many of them fall into poverty. But unemployment has not been the only reason. Although the unemployment rate was no higher in 1981 than in 1976, the percentage of the population living in poverty was substantially higher (14.0% compared with 11.8%). Poverty has become a particularly perplexing problem.

5. Growth

In an economy with large-scale unemployment, output can be increased by putting the unemployed back to work. But once this is done, there is a limit to the amount that can be produced with the existing labor force and the existing factories and equipment. To increase output beyond this limit requires either an addition to the available resources (for example, an increase in the number of factories and machines) or an improvement in technology (that is, the invention of new, more productive machines or new ways of organizing production). When economists speak of growth, they typically mean an increase in output that results from technological improvement and additional factories, machines, or other resources.

The advantages of growth are obvious. If the economy grows, our incomes will be higher in the future. We and our children will have higher standards of material comfort. Moreover, some of the rising production can be used to benefit the poor without reducing the incomes of the rich. During the early 1960s, growth became a prominent national goal, both because of its economic advantages and in order to "keep ahead of the Russians."

FIGURE 1-5

The percentage of the population living in poverty

During the long expansion of the 1960s there was a substantial decline in the percentage of the population living in poverty. Since 1979, the percentage living in poverty has increased.

Source: Council of Economic Advisers, *Annual Report, 1985,* p. 264.

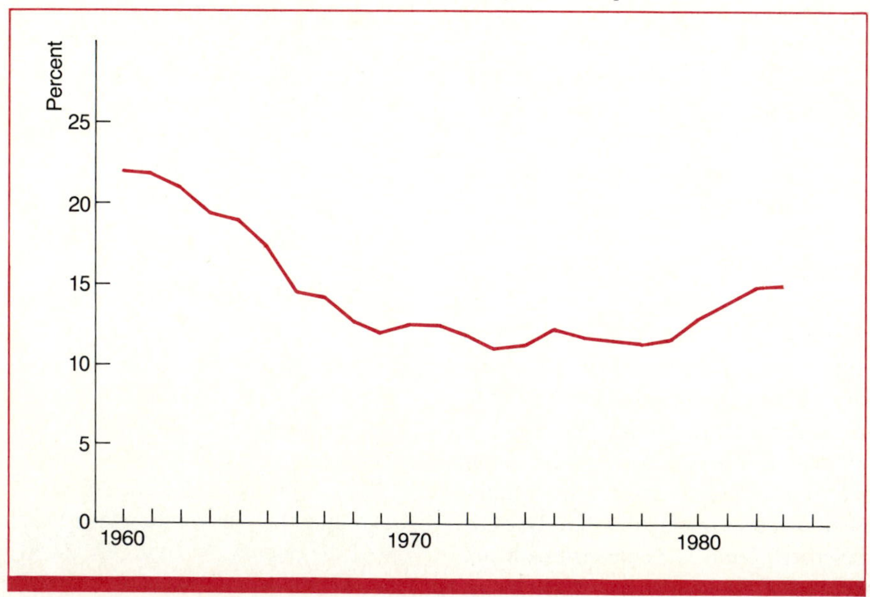

During the late 1960s and early 1970s, doubts began to develop about the importance of growth as an objective of economic policy. While its advantages are obvious, growth comes at a cost. If we are to grow more rapidly, more of our current efforts will have to be directed toward the production of machines and away from the production of consumption goods. In the future, of course, as the new machines begin operating, they will turn out more consumption goods—more clothing, furniture, or cars. Thus, current policies to stimulate growth will make possible higher consumption in the future. But, for the moment, consumption will be less. Thus, to evaluate a high-growth policy, we have to compare the advantage of higher *future* consumption with the sacrifice of lower *current* consumption.

Seen in this light, it is not clear that the faster the rate of growth, the better. Why, for example, should I live modestly, just so my children may at some future date live in luxury? Future generations should be considered, but so should the present one.

Even if we were concerned solely with the welfare of coming generations, it would not be so clear that the more growth, the better. Increasing levels of production use increasing quantities of raw materials. A moderate rate of growth may be in the best interests of future generations because it allows us to conserve raw materials.

Furthermore, very rapid rates of growth may harm the environment. If our primary objective is to produce more and more steel and automobiles, we may pay too little heed to the belching smoke of the steel mills or to the effect of the automobile on the quality of the air which we breathe. Thus, during the 1970s there was less emphasis on growth than there had been during the early 1960s, and more emphasis on other goals, such as preservation of the environment.

During the Reagan administration, the pendulum swung back toward growth as an objective. In part, this was a reaction to what some thought was excessive attention to the environment; in part, it reflected a similar view to that of the Kennedy administration, that vigorous growth was a way of dealing with many economic problems, including poverty. Kennedy's remark—"A rising tide lifts all boats"—again became popular in Washington. (In rebuttal, Herbert Stein observed: "Unfortunately, that is not true. A rising tide does not lift the boats that are under water. . . . Many kinds of poverty will not be significantly relieved by faster growth.")[6]

INTERRELATIONSHIPS AMONG ECONOMIC GOALS

The achievement of one goal may help in the achievement of others. As we have noted, growth may make it easier to solve the poverty problem. Additional income may be provided to the poor out of the growth in total income, without reducing the income of those at the top. Thus, social conflicts over the share of the pie may be reduced if the size of the pie is increasing.

Similarly, the poverty problem is easier to solve if the unemployment rate is kept low, so that large numbers of unemployed do not swell the ranks of the poor. When goals are ***complementary*** like this (that is, when achieving one helps to achieve the other), economic policymaking is relatively easy. By attacking on a broad front and striving for several goals, we can increase our chances of achieving each.

Unfortunately, however, economic goals are not always complementary. In many cases, they are in conflict. For example, when the unemployment problem is reduced, the inflation problem tends to get worse. There is a reason for this. Heavy purchasing by the public tends to reduce unemployment, but it also tends to increase inflation. It reduces unemployment because, as the public buys more cars, unemployed workers get jobs again in the auto factories; when families buy more homes, construction workers find it easier to locate jobs. At the same time, heavy purchasing tends to increase inflation because producers are more likely to raise their prices if buyers are clamoring for their products. Such conflicts among goals test the wisdom of policymakers. They feel torn in deciding which objective to pursue.

A PREVIEW

These, then, are the five major objectives of economic policy: *high employment, price stability, efficiency, an equitable distribution of income,* and *growth*. The first

[6]Herbert Stein, "Economic Policy, Conservatively Speaking," *Public Opinion*, Feb. 1981, p. 4. (Stein was Chairman of the Council of Economic Advisers from 1972 to 1974.)

two goals are related to the stability of the economy. If the economy is unstable, moving along like a roller coaster, its performance will be very unsatisfactory. As it heads downhill into recession, large numbers of people will be thrown out of work. Then, as it heads upward into a runaway boom, prices will soar as the public scrambles to buy the available goods. The first two goals may, therefore, be looked on as two aspects of a single objective: that of achieving an ***equilibrium*** with stable prices and a low unemployment rate. This will be the major topic in Parts 2, 3, and 4 (Chapters 7 through 19) of this book.

Equilibrium is the first of three main ''E's'' of economics. The second E—***efficiency***—will be studied in Parts 5 and 6 (Chapters 20 through 32). Are we getting the most out of our productive efforts? When does the free market—where buyers and sellers come together without government interference—encourage efficiency? Where the free market does not encourage efficiency, what (if anything) should be done?

Part 7 (Chapters 33 through 38) deals primarily with the third E—***equity***. If the government takes a laissez faire attitude, how much income will go to workers? To the owners of land? To others? How do labor unions affect the incomes of their members? How can the government improve the lot of the poor?

The final major objective—growth—cuts across a number of other major topics and thus appears periodically throughout the book. However, before we get into the meat of policy issues, we must first set the stage with some of the basic concepts and tools of economics. To that task we now turn in Chapters 2 through 6.

KEY POINTS

1. In the words of Alfred Marshall, ''economics is a study of mankind in the ordinary business of life.'' It is the study of how people make their living, how they acquire food, shelter, clothing, and other material necessities and comforts. It is a study of the problems they encounter, and of the ways in which these problems can be reduced.
2. During the twentieth century, substantial economic progress has been made in the United States and many other countries. We are producing much more, even though we spend less time at work than did our grandparents.
3. Nevertheless, substantial economic problems remain: problems such as poverty in the less-developed countries and at home, high rates of unemployment, and inflation.
4. One of the things we study in economics is how we can deal with our problems, either through private action or through government policies.
5. In the history of economic thought, the role of government has been controversial. Adam Smith in 1776 called for the liberation of markets from the tyranny of government control. By 1936, John Maynard Keynes was appealing to the government to accept its responsibilities and to undertake public works in order to get the economy out of the depression.
6. Important economic goals include:

    (*a*) An equilibrium with high employment and price stability.

    (*b*) Efficiency. *Allocative efficiency* involves the production of the right combination of goods, using the lowest-cost combination of inputs. *Technological efficiency* occurs when people produce goods with the smallest feasible quantity of inputs, while working at a reasonable pace.

    (*c*) Equity in the distribution of income.

    (*d*) A satisfactory rate of growth.

KEY CONCEPTS

economics
laissez faire
depression
recession
unemployment
inflation
hyperinflation
the average level of prices
relative prices
allocative efficiency
technological efficiency

poverty
equal distribution of income
equitable distribution of income
redistribution of income
growth
complementary goals
conflicting goals

PROBLEMS

1-1. According to Smith's "invisible hand," we are able to obtain meat, not because of the butcher's benevolence, but because of his self-interest. Why is it in the butcher's self-interest to provide us with meat? What does the butcher get in return?

1-2. Suppose another depression occurs like the depression of the 1930s. How would it affect you? (Thinking about this question provided a major motivation for a generation of economists. They were appalled at the prospect and determined to play a role in preventing a repeat of the Great Depression.)

1-3. The section on an equitable distribution of income reflects two views regarding the proper approach to poverty:

(*a*) The important thing is to meet the basic needs of the poor, that is, to provide at least a minimum income for the purchase of food, shelter, and other necessities.

(*b*) The important thing is to reduce inequality, that is, to reduce the gap between the rich and the poor.

These two views are not the same. For example, if there is rapid growth in the economy, objective (*a*) may be accomplished without any progress being made toward (*b*). Which is the more important objective? Why? Do you feel strongly about your choice? Why?

1-4. In Figure 1-1, observe that the downward trend in the length of the workweek ended about 1950. Before that date, part of the gains of the average worker came in the form of shorter hours. Since 1950, practically all the gains have consisted of higher wages and fringe benefits. Do you see any reason why the workweek leveled out in 1950?

1-5. Explain how an upswing in purchases by the public will affect (*a*) unemployment and (*b*) inflation. Does this result illustrate economic goals that are complementary or conflicting?

APPENDIX

DIAGRAMS USED IN ECONOMICS

Chapter 1 contains diagrams which illustrate important points, such as the increase in production per person since 1900 (Figure 1-1) and the fact that economic growth has slowed down since 1973 (Figure 1-2). In the study of economics, diagrams are frequently used—as you may see by flipping through this book. A picture is often worth a thousand words. Diagrams can fix important ideas in our minds. They present information in a vivid and eye-catching way. Unfortunately, they can also mislead. The first and lasting impression may be the wrong impression. This appendix explains some of the major types of diagrams used in economics. It also explains some of the ways in which diagrams may be used to impress or mislead, rather than inform.

Three major types of diagrams will be considered:

1. Diagrams that present and compare two facts.
2. Diagrams that show how something changes through time. For example, Figure 1-4 illustrates how the average level of prices has usually risen, but has sometimes fallen.
3. Diagrams that show how two variables are related; for example, how an increase in family income (variable 1) results in an increase in spending (variable 2).

1. A SIMPLE COMPARISON OF TWO FACTS

The simplest type of diagram brings together two facts for comparison. Often, the best method of presenting two facts—and the least likely to mislead—is to use a *bar chart* like the one in Figure 1-2. In the top left corner, the first bar shows that the average rate of growth of industrial countries between 1963 and 1972 was 4.6% per year, while the second bar shows that the rate was only 2.4% in the next decade. By comparing the heights of the two bars, we immediately see how growth rates have changed.

Things to Watch

Even such a simple diagram may carry a misleading message. There are several ''tricks'' which an unscrupulous writer can use to fool the reader.

Suppose, for example, that someone wants to present the performance of a country or a corporation in the most favorable light. Consider an example—a country whose steel production rose from 10 million tons in 1975 to 20 million tons in 1985.

Figure 1-6 is a bar chart illustrating this comparison in the simplest, most straightforward way. Glancing at the height of the two bars in this diagram, the reader gets the correct impression—steel production has doubled.

This is a very good performance but not a spectacular one. Suppose someone wants to ''gild the lily'' and make things look even better. Two easy ways of doing so—without actually lying—are illustrated in Figure 1-7.[7]

The left panel is designed to mislead because part of the diagram is omitted. The heights of the bars are measured from 5 million tons rather than zero. Thus the 1985 bar is three times as high as the 1975 bar, and the unwary

[7]For more detail on how readers may be misled, see the sprightly book by Darrell Huff, *How to Lie with Statistics* (New York: Norton, 1954).

FIGURE 1-6
A Simple Bar Chart
The simplest bar chart provides a comparison of two numbers, in this case the production of steel in 2 years. We see correctly that steel production has doubled.

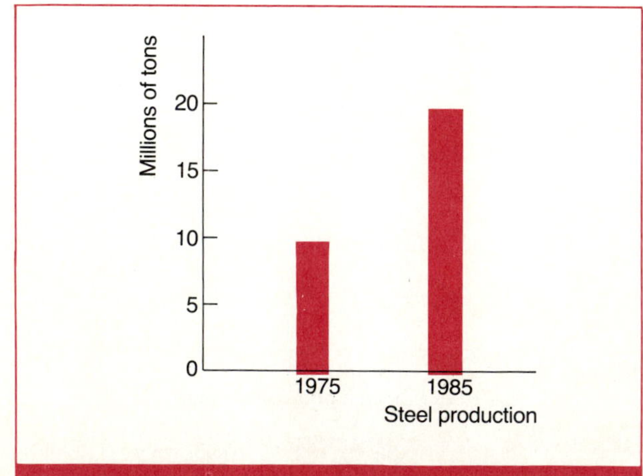

reader may be left with the wrong impression—that steel production is three times as high, whereas in fact it is only twice as high. This, then, is the first thing to watch out for: Do the numbers on the vertical axis start from zero? If not, the diagram may give the wrong impression.

The right panel shows another way in which the reader may be fooled. The bars of Figure 1-6 are replaced with something more interesting—pictures of steel mills. Because production has doubled, the steel mill on the right is twice as high as that on the left. But notice how this picture gives the wrong impression. The mill on the right is not only twice as high. It is also twice as wide, and we can visualize it as being twice as deep, too. Therefore, it isn't just twice as large as the mill on the left; it is many times as large. Thus, the casual reader may again be left with the wrong impression—that steel output has increased many fold, when in fact it has only doubled. This, then, is the second reason to be wary: Look carefully and skeptically at diagrams that use silhouettes or pictures. Do they leave you with an exaggerated impression of the changes that have actually occurred?

A third way to mislead is illustrated in Figure 1-8. In both panels, the facts are correct regarding the average price of common stock in the United States. (Each share of common stock represents part ownership of a company.) The left panel shows that, between 1929 and 1953, the average price of stocks did not change at all. The right panel shows facts which are equally true. Between 1932 and 1953—almost the same period of comparison—stock prices increased *six fold*. How can *both*

FIGURE 1-7

Variations on the simple bar chart

Readers may be misled by variations on the simple bar chart. Both of the above panels present the same information as in Figure 1-6. In the left panel, the vertical axis begins with 5 million tons, rather than zero. In the right panel, pictures are used, rather than bars. In each case, the reader may be left with the erroneous impression that steel production has more than doubled.

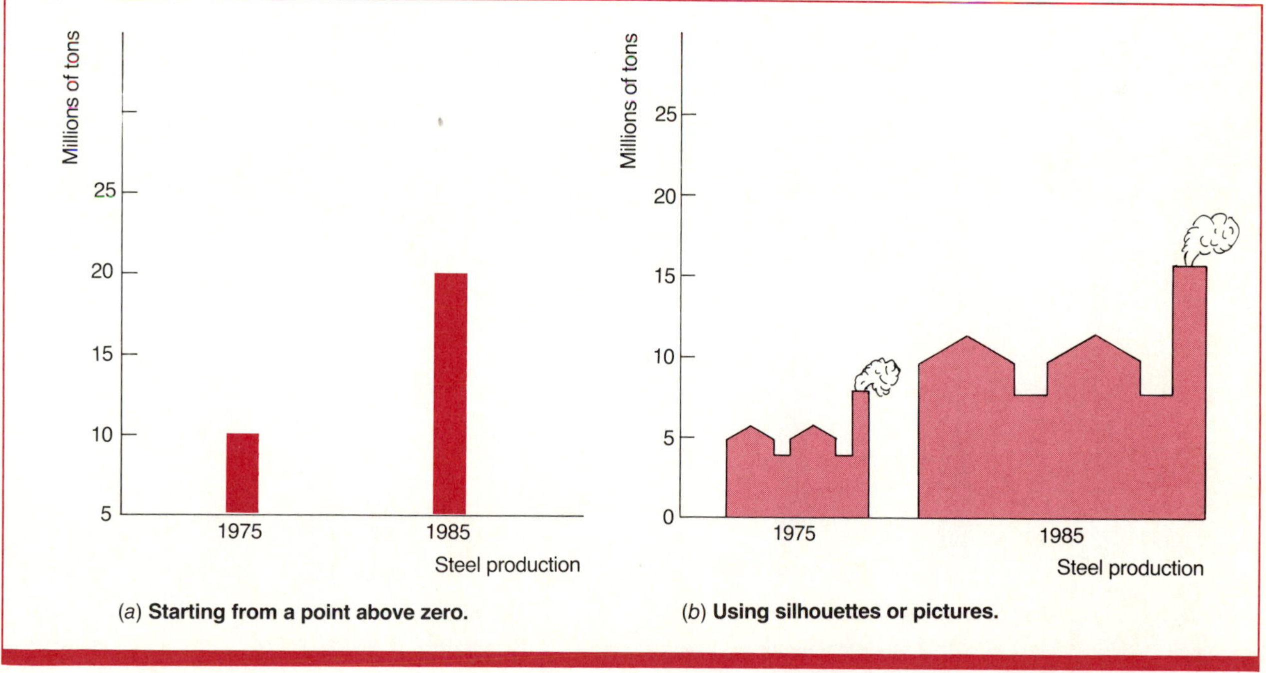

(*a*) **Starting from a point above zero.**

(*b*) **Using silhouettes or pictures.**

these panels be correct? The answer: Between 1929 and 1932, the most spectacular stock market collapse in American history occurred, with stocks losing five-sixths of their value.

Notice the contrast between the two panels. The left one implies that not much is be gained by entering the stock market. The right panel gives exactly the opposite impression: The stock market is the place to get rich. Thus, an author can give two completely different messages, depending on the choice of the initial ''base'' year (1929 or 1932). So beware. In any diagram showing how something has changed over time, ask yourself: Has the author slanted the results by selecting a base year designed to mislead?

2. TIME SERIES: HOW SOMETHING CHANGES THROUGH TIME

That last problem can be avoided by providing more information to the reader with a ***time series*** diagram, showing stock prices *every* year, not just a beginning and final year. Even better is to show stock prices every month. With a more detailed figure, the reader can see a much more complete story, including both the collapse of 1929–1932 and the way in which stock prices have risen since 1932.

A *time series* diagram shows how something (such as the price of stocks, the output of steel, or the unemployment rate) has changed through time.

However, even when we provide a detailed time series, a number of issues remain. Here are some of the most important.

Should We Measure from Zero?

In discussing a simple comparison between two facts, we seem to have settled the question of how we should measure up the vertical axis of a diagram. To start at any figure other than zero can be misleading—as in Figure

FIGURE 1-8

Comparisons depend on the times chosen

Comparisons may change even when seemingly minor changes are made in the dates. In 1953, stock prices were no higher on average than in 1929 (left panel). However, they were six times as high in 1953 as they had been in 1932.

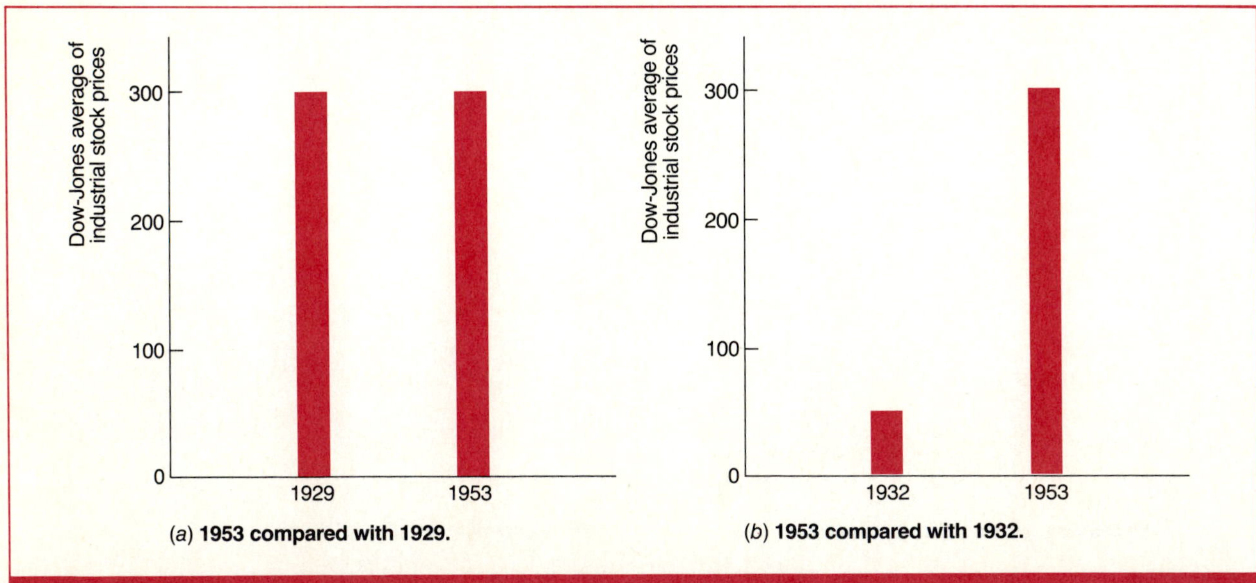

(*a*) **1953 compared with 1929.**

(*b*) **1953 compared with 1932.**

1-7*a*, when steel production was measured up from a starting point of 5 million tons.

However, once we provide the detailed information of a time series, we should reopen the question of how to measure along the vertical axis. The problem is that we now have two conflicting considerations. We would like to start from zero to avoid misleading the reader. On the other hand, starting from some other point may make the details of a diagram much easier to see.

This is illustrated in Figure 1-9, which shows the rate of unemployment in each year from 1974 to 1984. In the left panel, the unemployment rate is measured vertically, starting from zero. This gives us the best picture of how the overall unemployment rate compares in any 2 years we might like to choose (for example, 1974 and 1975). Contrast this with the right panel, where the measurement of unemployment starts above zero. Like Figure 1-7*a*, this panel can be misleading. For example, the first two bars might leave the impression that the unemployment rate tripled between 1974 and 1975, whereas in fact it increased by far less (from 5.6% to 8.3%).

However, the right panel has a major compensating advantage. It provides a much clearer picture of how the unemployment rate *changes* from year to year; the year-to-year differences are much more conspicuous. These year-to-year changes are very important, as they are one measure of fluctuations in the economy. Consequently, the right-hand diagram can be more informative.

If panel *b* is chosen, readers must be warned that we have not started from zero. One way is to leave a gap in the vertical bars to show that something has been left out. Alternatively, we can leave a gap in the vertical axis itself. (This alternative was used back in Figure 1-1, where there were no bars in which gaps could be left.)

How Should Growth Be Illustrated?

Some time series—such as a nation's population—have a strong tendency to grow through time. If we measure in the normal way along the vertical axis, the curve be-

FIGURE 1-9

A time series: The unemployment rate, 1974–1984

The reader is provided with much more information with a time series showing every year or every month rather than just 2 years. In this diagram, there is an advantage in starting the vertical measurement above zero. Observe that the detailed year-to-year changes stand out more clearly in the right panel than in the left. To warn the reader that something has been left out, a gap is left in the vertical bars.

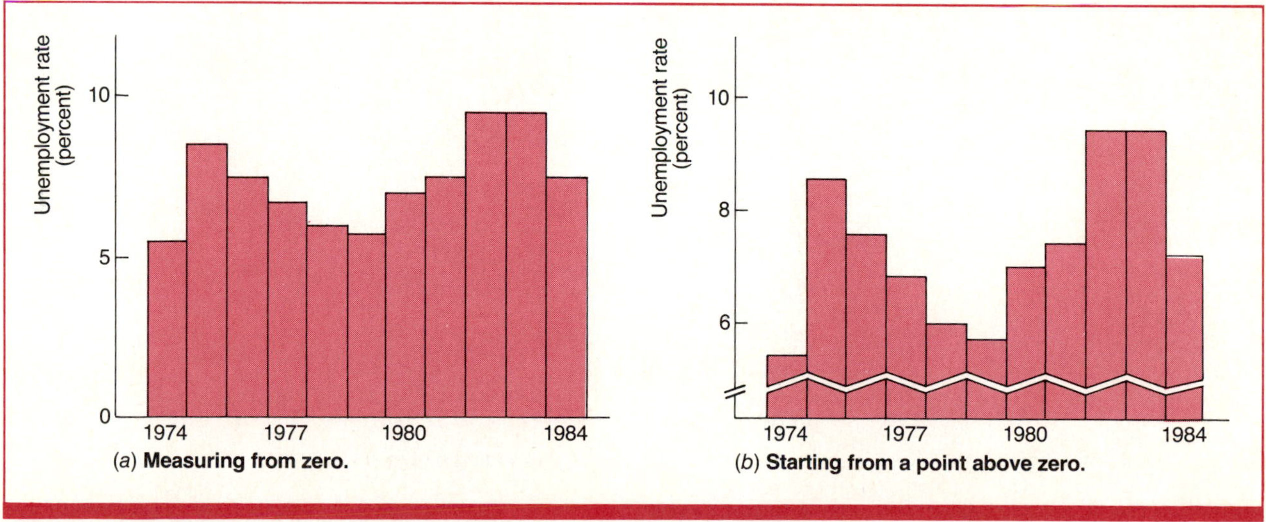

comes steeper and steeper through time, as shown in the left panel of Figure 1-10. There is nothing necessarily wrong with this presentation—the increase in the population between 1970 and 1980 (23 million) was in fact much greater than the increase between 1870 and 1880 (10 million).

However, there are two related problems with this figure. First, the numbers in the early years—before, say, 1820—are so small that details are hard to see. Second, we may be interested not just in the absolute numbers but in the *rate* at which population is growing. Thus, the 10 million increase in population in the 1870s represents a much greater rate of increase (2.3% per year) than the 23 million increase of the 1970s (1.1% per year).

To highlight the rate of growth, a ***ratio*** or ***logarithmic*** scale is used on the vertical axis in panel *b* of Figure 1-10. On such a scale, equal *percentage* changes show up as equal distances. For example, the vertical distance from 50 million to 100 million (an increase of 100%) is the same as the distance from 100 million to 200 million (also an increase of 100%). In such a diagram, if something grows at a *constant rate* (for example, by 2% per year), it shows up as a *straight line*. By looking for the steepest sections of the time series, we can identify the periods when population has grown at the most rapid rate. Similarly, back in Figure 1-4, which is also drawn on a ratio scale, the steepest parts of the curve show when the most rapid rates of inflation occurred.

A ratio scale is appropriate for a time series—like population—that grows. However, it is inappropriate for a series that does not have a strong tendency to grow. For example, there is no reason to expect more and more people to be living in poverty, and it would therefore be inappropriate to use a logarithmic scale in a figure showing the poverty rate.

FIGURE 1-10
Population of the United States, 1790–1980
By using a ratio scale, we can identify the periods when the rate of population growth was most rapid. It occurred when the slope of the curve in the right panel was steepest.

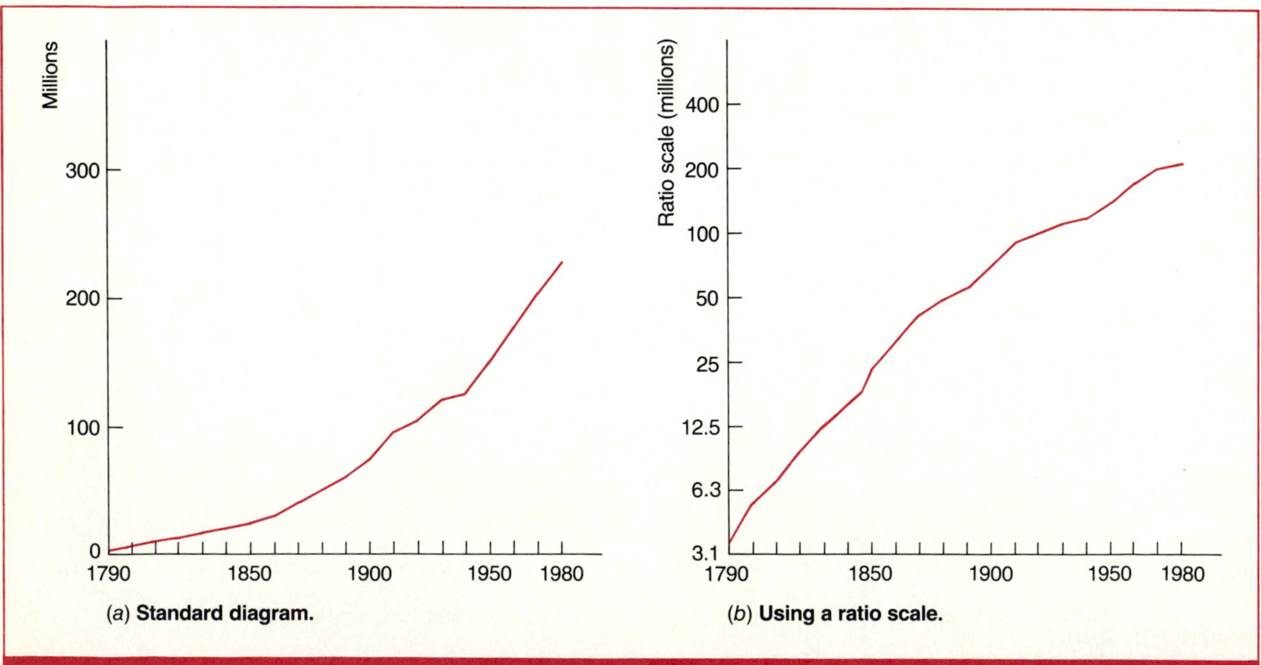

(*a*) **Standard diagram.**
(*b*) **Using a ratio scale.**

Finally, note that, when a logarithmic scale is used, the question of whether the vertical axis is measured from zero becomes irrelevant, since zero *cannot* appear on such a diagram. By looking at Figure 1-10*b*, we can see why. Each time we go up 1 centimeter (one notch on the vertical axis), the population doubles—from 50 to 100 million, and then to 200 million. We can make exactly the same statement the other way around: Each time we go down a centimeter, the population falls by half—from 50 million to 25 million, then 12.5 million, and so on. No matter how far we extend the diagram downward, each additional centimeter will reduce the population by one-half. Therefore, the population can *never* reach zero on such a diagram.

Real or Monetary Measures?

People often complain that the federal government is getting "too big." Suppose we wanted to look at the size of the government. How would we do so?

The most obvious way is to look at the amount the government spends. Measured in dollars, the growth of government spending has been truly stupendous over the past half century or so (Figure 1-11). But there are several shortcomings to this simple measure.

The first has to do with prices, which have risen substantially during the past half century. Inflation means that, even if the government had remained exactly the same size—building the same number of schools and roads, keeping the same number of soldiers in the army—it would have spent many more dollars; that is, its expenditures in dollar or ***nominal*** terms would have gone up rapidly. In order to eliminate the effects of inflation, government statisticians calculate what government expenditures *would have been if prices had not gone up,* that is, if prices had remained at the level existing in a single year. Such a measure of government expenditures—in ***constant-dollar*** or ***real*** terms—is shown in panel *a* of Figure 1-12. Observe how much more slowly government expenditures have grown when the effects of inflation are eliminated. (Further details on how real expenditures are calculated will be presented in a later chapter.)

Relative Measures

Even when measured in real terms, government expenditures have risen substantially. Does this, in itself, mean that the government is "too big?" The answer is, not necessarily. One reason is that, as the government has grown, so has the overall economy. Thus, we may ask the question: Has the government grown *relative to the economy*? (As in Figure 1-1, the size of the economy is measured by gross national product, or GNP.) In Figure 1-12, panel *b,* observe that government expenditures have not grown much relative to the economy (that is, as a percentage of GNP).

FIGURE 1-11

Federal government expenditures, measured in dollars

As measured by the number of dollars spent, the size of the federal government has expanded very rapidly.

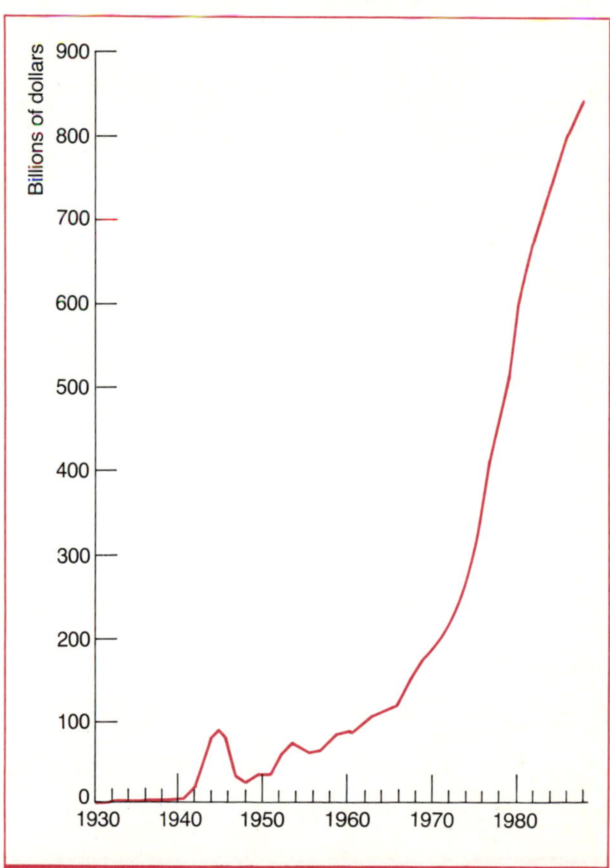

3. RELATIONSHIPS BETWEEN VARIABLES

Frequently, economists want to keep track of the relationship between two variables. Table 1-2 provides an illustration—the relationship between the incomes of households and their expenditures for the basic necessities (housing, food, and clothing). The top row (row *A*) indicates that the American family with an income of $10,000 spent $7,000 on the basic necessities. Similarly, row *B* shows that a family with an income of $20,000 spent $11,000 on these basics.

The data in Table 1-2 may be graphed as Figure 1-13, where income is measured along the horizontal axis and expenditures for basics up the vertical axis. (The lower left corner, labeled "0," represents the starting point from which both income and basic expenditures are measured. This point is called the ***origin***.) To plot the data in row *A* of the table, we measure $10,000 in income along the horizontal axis, and $7,000 in spending for basics up the vertical axis. This gives us point *A* in the diagram. Similarly, points *B*, *C*, and *D* represent corresponding rows *B*, *C*, and *D* in Table 1-2.

TABLE 1-2
Household Income and Expenditures for basics, 1985

	(1) Household income (after taxes)	(2) Expenditures for basics
A	$10,000	$ 7,000
B	20,000	11,000
C	30,000	14,500
D	40,000	17,500

FIGURE 1-12
Federal government expenditures: Alternative presentations
When the effects of inflation are removed in the left panel, the growth of government spending is much less spectacular than in Figure 1-11. As compared to the overall size of the economy (as measured by gross national product), the size of the federal government has grown relatively slowly, as can be seen in the right panel.

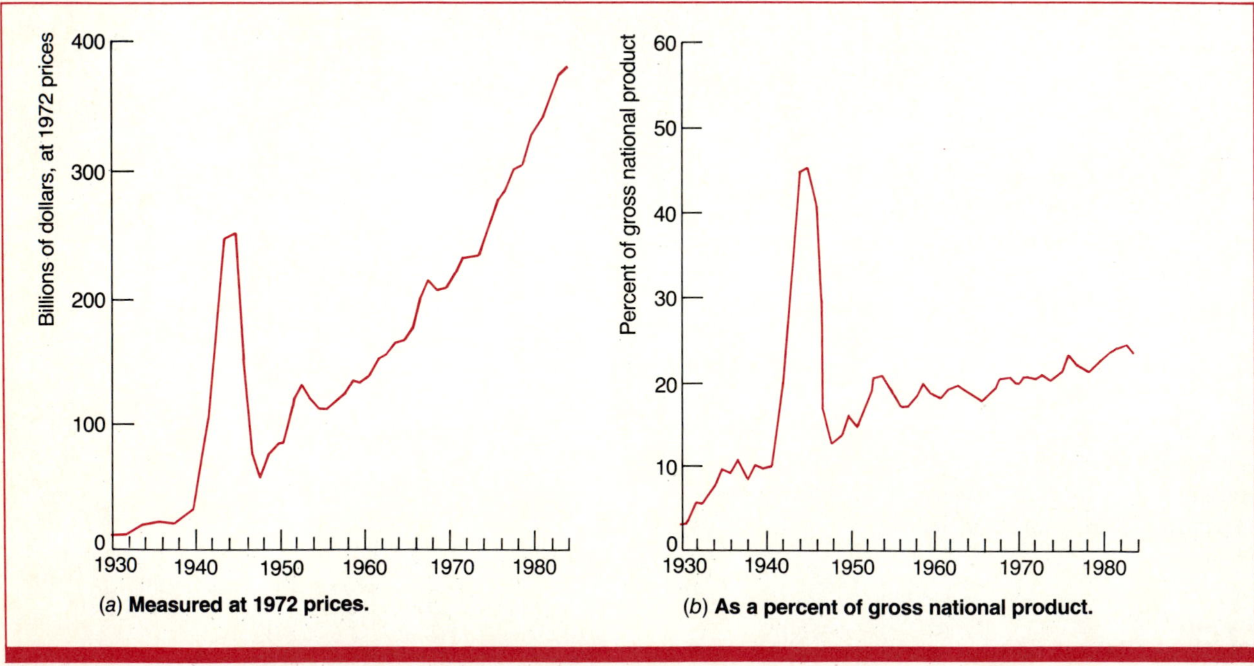

(*a*) **Measured at 1972 prices.**

(*b*) **As a percent of gross national product.**

One question which can be addressed with such a diagram is how expenditures on the basics change as income increases. For example, as income increases from $10,000 at point *A* to $20,000 at point *B*, basic expenditures rise from $7,000 to $11,000; that is, expenditures on the basics rise by $4,000 in response to the $10,000 increase in income.

This relation can be illustrated by drawing a line between points *A* and *B*, and looking at its ***slope***—slope being defined as the *vertical change* or *rise* (*HB*) *divided by the horizontal change* or *run* (*AH*). In this example, the slope is $4,000/$10,000 = 4/10. As incomes increase from point *A* to point *B*, families spend 40% of the increase on the basics.

Observe in this diagram that the slope becomes smaller and smaller as we go further and further to the right, that is, as we move to larger and larger incomes. Whereas the slope is 4/10 between *A* and *B*, it is only $3,000/$10,000, or 3/10, between *C* and *D*. This smaller slope makes sense. Families with high incomes already have good houses, food, and clothing. When their income goes up another $10,000, they don't spend much more on the basics; they have other things to do with their income.

Nevertheless, no matter how far to the right this diagram is extended, the line joining any two points will always slope *upward;* that is, the slope is always *positive*. The reason is that, as people's incomes rise, they always want somewhat better houses, food, and clothing.

However, in some relationships, there may be a *downward-sloping* curve. Figure 1-14 illustrates the situation facing a company producing a small business aircraft. The costs facing such a company are high—it has

FIGURE 1-13

How expenditures for basics are related to income

As family income increases (along the horizontal axis), the family's expenditures for the basics increase (as measured up the vertical axis). The *slope* of the line between any two points—such as *A* and *B*—show how strongly expenditures for basics respond (*HB*) to an increase in income (*AH*).

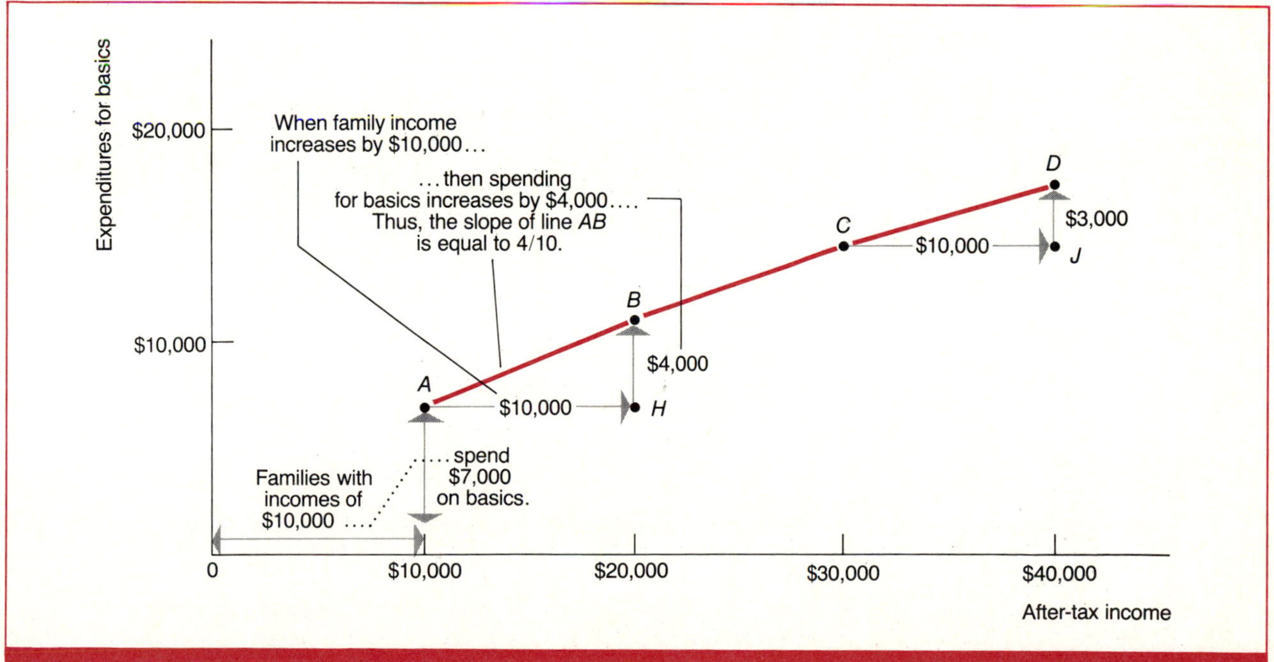

the expense of designing the aircraft and it requires an expensive plant for production. If the firm produces only a few units each year (say, 10 aircraft, measured along the horizontal axis), it will operate at point *A*. It will be unable to charge a price high enough to cover its costs, and it will therefore suffer a loss; that is, its profit (measured along the vertical axis) will be negative. As it sells more, its revenues will rise, and it will begin to make profits to the right of point *B*.

However, profits do not rise indefinitely. If the company were to produce a large number of planes—200, say—it would have to slash prices in order to sell them. This would reduce its profits. Thus, the profit curve at first slopes upward, reaches a peak at *C*, and then slopes downward.

Point *C* is very significant for the firm. At this point, the firm *maximizes its profits*. At this point, the curve ceases to slope upward and is just about to slope downward; that is, the slope is just about to switch from being positive to becoming negative. Thus, at the point of maximum profit, the slope of the curve is *zero*.

FIGURE 1-14

Output and profits

If the firm produces only a few planes, it cannot cover its costs. It suffers losses. (Profits are negative.) As production increases, its losses shrink as it approaches point *B*. Then, to the right of *B*, the firm begins to make profits. So long as output is less than 150 units, the profits curve has a *positive* slope; that is, it slopes upward. Profits reach a peak at point *C* and thereafter begin to decline. Thus, to the right of *C* the curve has a *negative* slope. At the point where the curve reaches its peak, it is horizontal. The slope is zero.

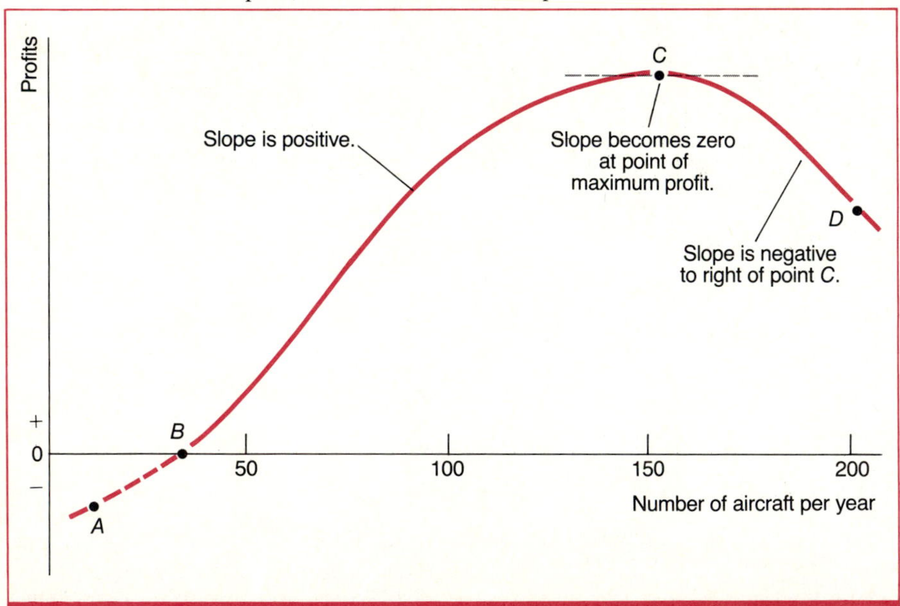

CHAPTER 2

SCARCITY AND CHOICE

Economics studies human behaviour as a relationship between ends and scarce means.

LIONEL ROBBINS

In Chapter 1 we surveyed a wide range of economic issues—economic progress, economic problems such as inflation and unemployment, and economic goals such as efficiency and equity. In this chapter, our objective is to become more specific by exploring the most important single concept in economics: ***scarcity.*** Consider, for a moment, the major economic developments in the United States during the twentieth century. The average worker now produces about four times as much as the worker at the turn of the century—and does so with less effort, in a shorter workweek. If the average worker can now produce so much, why don't we relax? If, with relatively little effort, we can have higher incomes than our grandparents, why do we worry about economic problems at all?

There are two fundamental reasons:

1. Our material ***wants*** are virtually unlimited or insatiable.
2. Economic ***resources*** are limited or scarce.

Because of these two basic facts, we cannot have everything we want. We therefore have to ***make choices.***

UNLIMITED WANTS

Consider, first, our wants. If the one-horse shay was good enough for great grandpa, why isn't it good enough for us?

Material wants arise for two reasons. First, each of us has basic biological needs: the need for food, shelter, and clothing. But there is also a second reason. Clearly, we are prepared to work more than is required to meet our minimum needs. We want more than the basic diet of vegetables and water needed to sustain life. We want more than a shack which will provide minimal protection from the weather. We want more than the minimum clothing needed to protect us from the cold. In other words, we want the goods and services which can make life more pleasant. Of course, the two basic reasons for material wants cannot be sharply separated. When we sit down to a gourmet meal at a restaurant, we satisfy our biological need for food. But we do something more. When we savor exotic foods in a comfortable and stylish atmosphere, we are getting both the basics and the "frills." These frills are sufficiently pleasant that we are willing to work to obtain them.

The range of consumer wants is exceedingly broad. We want ***goods,*** such as houses, cars, shoes, shirts, and tennis rackets. Similarly, we want ***services,*** such as medical care, haircuts, and laundry services. When we get what we want, it may whet our appetities for something more. If we own a Chevrolet, perhaps we will want an Oldsmobile next time. After we buy a house, we may wish to replace the carpets and drapes. Furthermore, as new products are introduced, we may want them too. We want video recorders, home computers, and a host of other products that earlier generations never even dreamed of. Even though it is conceivable that, some day, we will say, "Enough!" that day seems far away. Our material wants show no sign of being completely satisfied.

SCARCE RESOURCES

Not all wants can be satisfied because of the second fundamental fact. While our productive capacity is large, it is not without limit. There are only so many workers in the labor force, and we have only a certain number of machines and factories. In other words, our resources are limited.

Resources are the basic inputs used in the production of goods and services. Therefore, they are also frequently known as ***factors of production.*** They can be categorized under three main headings: land, capital, and labor.

Economists use the term ***land*** in a broad sense to include not only the arable land used by farmers and the city land used as building lots but also the other gifts of nature that come with the land. Thus, the minerals which are found under the soil and the water and sunlight which fall upon the soil are all part of the land resource.

Capital refers to buildings, equipment, and materials used in the productive process. An automobile assembly plant is "capital," and so are the machines in the plant and the steel with which automobiles will be built. In contrast to land, which has been *given* to us by nature, capital has been *produced* at some time in the past. This may have been the distant past; the factory may have been built 15 years ago. Or it may have been the recent past; the steel may have been manufactured last month. The process of producing and accumulating capital is known as ***investment.***

Unlike *consumer goods* (such as shoes, shirts, or food), *capital goods* or "investment goods" (such as tractors, factories, or machinery in the factories) are not designed to satisfy human wants directly. Rather, they are intended for use in the production of other goods. Capital produced now will satisfy wants only indirectly, and at a later time, when it is used in the production of consumer goods. The production of capital therefore means that someone has been *willing to wait*. When a machine is produced rather than a car, the choice has been made to forego the car now in order to produce the machine, making it possible to produce more cars or other goods in the future. Thus, capital formation involves a choice between consumption ***now*** and more consumption ***in the future.***

We should emphasize one point of terminology. Unless otherwise specified, economists use the term *capital* to mean ***real capital,*** not financial capital. In previous paragraphs, we've been referring to *real capital—the factories and machinery used to produce other goods.* ***Financial capital,*** on the other hand, consists of financial assets such as common stocks, bonds, or bank deposits. Such assets are important. The holder of a stock or bond, for example, has a form of wealth which is likely to produce income in the future in the form of dividends on the stock or interest on the bond. But, while an individual might consider 100 shares of General Motors stock as part of his or her "capital," they are *not* capital in the economic sense. They are not a resource with which goods and services can be produced.

Similarly, when economists talk of investment, they generally mean ***real investment***—the accumulation of machines and other real capital—and not financial investment (such as the purchase of a government bond).

Labor refers to the physical and mental talents of human beings as applied to the production of goods and services. The construction worker provides labor, and so does the college professor or the physician. (The professor produces educational services, and the doctor produces medical services.)[1]

One particular human resource deserves special emphasis: ***entrepreneurial ability.*** The *entrepreneur* is someone who:

1. *Organizes production,* bringing together the factors of production—land, labor, and capital—to make goods and services.
2. *Makes business decisions,* figuring out what goods to produce and how to produce them.
3. *Takes risk.* (There is no guarantee that business decisions will turn out to be correct.)
4. *Innovates,* introducing new products, new technology, and new ways of organizing business.

In order to be successful, an entrepreneur needs to be aware of changes in the economy. Is the market for adding machines declining while that of computers is expanding? If so, the successful entrepreneur will not build a new assembly line for adding machines, but will instead consider the production of computers. Some entrepreneurs can be spectacularly successful: for example,

[1]The preceding paragraphs have presented the traditional division of the factors of production into the categories of land, labor, and capital. While still popular, this traditional division is not universally used by present-day economists. In particular, some economists now talk of "human capital." This is the education and training which add to the productivity of labor. Human capital has two of the important characteristics of physical capital: (1) it requires a willingness to wait during the training period, when the trainee does not produce goods or services, and (2) it increases the productive capacity of the economy, since a trained worker can produce more than an untrained one.

Steve Jobs and Steve Wozniak, who set up Apple Computer while still in their twenties. Their mushrooming sales helped to make the microcomputer a common household appliance—and made them multimillionaires in the process (Box 2-1). Other entrepreneurs are engaged in much more prosaic, everyday tasks. The teenager who offers to cut a neighbor's lawn for $10 is an entrepreneur. So is the college student who has a business typing other students' papers. The key questions facing an entrepreneur are these: Are people willing to buy the product? Can the good or service be sold for enough to cover costs and have some profit left over?

Because entrepreneurs are the ones who undertake the production of new goods, they play a strategic role in determining the dynamism and growth of the economy. (The French word *entrepreneur* means, literally, "someone who undertakes" a task.)

TABLE 2-1
Production Possibilities

Options	Clothing (billions of yards)	Food (millions of tons)	Units of food that must be given up to produce one more unit of clothing (opportunity cost of clothing)
A	0	20	
			1
B	1	19	
			2
C	2	17	
			4
D	3	13	
			5
E	4	8	
			8
F	5	0	

SCARCITY AND CHOICE: THE PRODUCTION POSSIBILITIES CURVE

With unlimited wants and limited resources, we face the fundamental economic problem of ***scarcity.*** We cannot have everything we want; we must make *choices*.

The problem of scarcity—and the need to make choices—can be illustrated with a ***production possibilities curve*** (PPC). This curve shows what can be produced with our existing resources (land, labor, and capital) and with our existing technology. Although our resources are limited and our capacity to produce is likewise limited, we have an option as to what goods and services we produce. We may produce fewer cars and more aircraft, or less wheat and more corn.

In an economy with thousands of products, the choices before us are complex. In order to reduce the problem to its simplest form, consider a very basic economy, one with only two goods (cotton clothing and wheat). If we decide to produce more food (wheat), we will be able to produce less clothing.

The options open to us are shown in the production possibilities table (Table 2-1) and the corresponding production possibilities curve (Figure 2-1). Consider first an extreme example in which all our resources are directed toward the production of food. In this case, illustrated by option A, we would produce 20 million tons of food but

FIGURE 2-1
The production possibilities curve
The curve shows the combinations of two goods that can be produced with limited resources of land, labor, and capital.

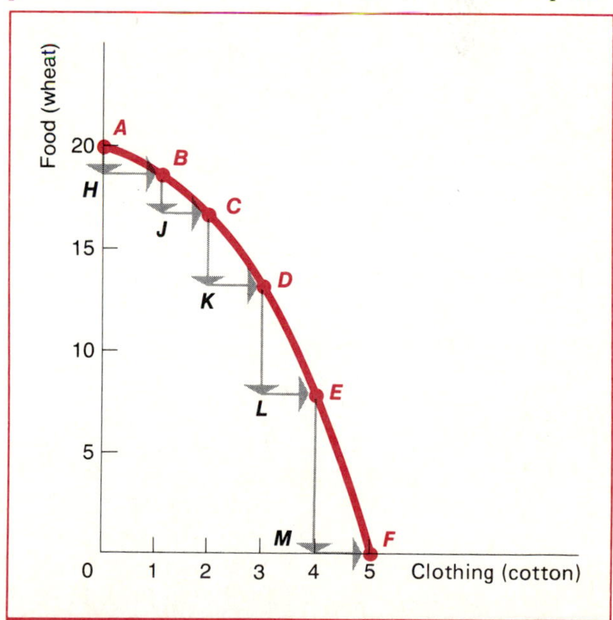

no clothing. This clearly does not represent a desirable composition of output. Although we would be well fed, we would be running around naked. However, no claim has been made that the points on the production possibilities curve are necessarily *desirable;* the only claim is that they are *possible*. And point A is possible.

At the other extreme, if we produced nothing but clothing, we would make 5 billion yards, as illustrated

BOX 2-1

A TALE OF TWO DREAMS

Even dreams are subject to demand curves.

JOHN HILTON
explaining the failure of the DeLorean automobile†

One task of the entrepreneur is to identify new opportunities and potential new products. In the business world, it is the entrepreneur who dreams dreams. But the entrepreneur must also be practical and hard-headed. Will the public share the dream? Will the new product sell?

Apple Computer

For Steve Jobs and Steve Wozniak, the answer was a resounding yes.

In the mid-1970s, the two college dropouts were employed in the electronics industry—Wozniak at Hewlett-Packard and Jobs as a designer of video games at Atari. In their spare time, they tinkered. In 1976, Wozniak built the first Apple, a small, easy-to-use computer. Jobs recognized its promise. They put together their available financial resources—$1,300—to start production in Jobs' garage.

For a fledgling electronics company, California's Silicon Valley was the place to be. An early task for the new entrepreneurs was to get funds for expansion by tapping into the local pool of venture capital. They were not immediately successful. One of their first prospects was put off by Jobs' cutoff jeans, sandals, and wispy beard. Then they made contact with A. C. Markkula, a former marketing manager at Intel (a maker of computer chips), who was delighted with the new machine. He put up $250,000, joined the company, and persuaded two venture capital firms to put up more money. Apple Computer was ready to go.

Wozniak quickly redesigned the original model. The trim, attractive Apple II was born. Sales surged: $800 thousand in 1977, $7.9 million in 1978, $100 million by 1980, $580 million by 1982, and $1.5 billion by 1984. The pace was frenetic. To Markkula, the problem was to "keep the race car on the track."

Apple's break-neck growth has created a major problem: how to keep the creative ferment and raw enthusiasm of a small company, while developing the structure and discipline needed in a large business. The team which developed Apple's Macintosh model—mostly young people in their twenties—wore T-shirts with their motto: "Working 90 hours a week, and loving every minute of it." The creativity of that group was remarkable, but the slightly madcap atmosphere exacted a toll. Many of Apple's young engineers burned out and left the company in their thirties. To create a more structured company, Apple in 1983 brought in a new president, John Sculley of Pepsi-Cola. Soon thereafter, Wozniak left, and Jobs was squeezed out of his managerial position.

DeLorean

The Apple dream has been generally happy, even if somewhat surreal. In contrast, the dream of John Zachary DeLorean has turned into a nightmare.

During his 17 years at General Motors, DeLorean rose close to the pinnacle of the automobile industry, managing the Pontiac and Chevrolet divisions and earning $650,000 a year. But he was restless and unhappy, chafing in the manager's role. In April, 1973, he left, to become a critic of General Motors and set up his own automobile firm to produce—in his words—an "ethical" car. His hint of social consciousness, his glittering lifestyle, and his willingness to take the big chance made him something of a folk hero.

Cars are very unlike computers. You can't start building them in your garage. An automobile assembly line takes vast amounts of capital, and most automobile companies are consequently very large. New entrants into the North American car market in the past half century have been conspicuously unsuccessful—Kaiser-Frazer, Tucker, and Bricklin. It took DeLorean 7 years to design his new car, acquire a factory, and begin production. In the process, he discovered that Puerto Rico and the British government were willing to pay handsomely to attract his factory, so eager were they to provide new jobs. In spite of a consulting firm's estimate that DeLorean's project had only one chance in ten of succeeding, the British government made the high bid, offering DeLorean more than $100 million to locate his plant in Northern Ireland.

Production of DeLorean's sleek stainless steel sports car began in 1981. The American introduction of the $26,000 vehicle was accompanied by extravagant hoopla, and sales were brisk at first. DeLorean ordered an increase in production to an annual rate of 20,000, even though his own market research estimated sales of no more than 12,000. By February of 1982, the company had an inventory of more than 4,000 unsold cars. Losses mounted. When DeLorean informed the British government that he would need $70 million more to keep his factory in operation, they coldly refused. In an angry debate in parliament, DeLorean's operation was denounced as a "rip-off." It was then that his problems really began. Within a few months, he was arrested on a drug charge. The prosecutors alleged that he had offered to put up almost $2 million to buy cocaine, in the hopes of making a quick profit with which to save his company. Although he was acquitted, he had lost his dream. His car company had collapsed.

†"The Decline and Fall of the DeLorean Dream," *Car and Driver*, July 1982, p. 70.

by point *F*. Again, this is a possible outcome, but not a desirable one. We would be well dressed as we faced starvation.

The Shape of the Production Possibilities Curve: Increasing Opportunity Costs

More interesting cases, and more reasonable ones, are those in which we produce some of each good. Consider how the economy might move from point *A* toward point *F*. At point *A* nothing is produced but food. It is grown on all types of arable land throughout the nation. In order to begin the production of clothing, we would plant cotton in the areas which are comparatively best suited for cotton production—those in Alabama and Mississippi. From these lands we would get a lot of cotton, while giving up just a small amount of food that might have been grown there. This is illustrated as we move from point *A* to point *B* on the production possibilities curve. Only one unit of food is given up in order to produce the first unit of clothing.

As we decide to produce more cotton, however, we must move to land which is somewhat less suited to the production of cotton. As a result, we do not get the second unit of clothing quite so easily. To produce it, we must give up more than one unit of food. This is illustrated in the move from point *B* to point *C*. As clothing production is increased by one more unit (from 1 to 2), food production falls by two units (from 19 to 17). The ***opportunity cost*** of the second unit of clothing—the food we have to give up to acquire it—is thus greater than the opportunity cost of the first unit.

The *opportunity cost* of a product is the alternative that must be given up to produce that product. (In this illustration, the opportunity cost of a unit of clothing is the wheat that must be given up when that unit of clothing is produced.)

Further increases in the production of clothing come at higher and higher opportunity costs. As we move to the third unit of clothing (from point *C* to *D*), we must start planting cotton in the farmlands of Iowa. A lot of food must be given up to produce that third unit of clothing. Finally, as we move from point *E* to point *F*, we are switching all our resources into the production of clothing. This comes at an extremely high opportunity cost in terms of lost output of food. Wheat production is stopped on the farms of North Dakota and Minnesota, which are no good at all for producing cotton. The wheat lands remain idle, and the farmers of North Dakota and Minnesota migrate further south, where they can make only minor contributions to cotton production. Thus, the last unit of clothing (the move from *E* to *F*) comes at a very high cost of eight units of food.

Thus, the *increasing opportunity cost of cotton is a reflection of the specialized characteristics of our resources*. Our resources are not completely adaptable to alternative uses. The lands of Minnesota and Mississippi are not equally well suited to the production of cotton and wheat. Thus, the opportunity cost of cotton rises as its production is increased.

As a result of increasing opportunity cost, the production possibilities curve *bows outward;* that is, it is *concave to the origin,* as shown in Figure 2-1. The arrows in this figure illustrate why. The horizontal increases in clothing production—from point *H* to *B*, from *J* to *C*, from *K* to *D*, and so on—are each one unit. The resulting reductions in food production—measured vertically from *A* to *H*, *B* to *J*, *C* to *K*, and so on—become larger and larger, making the slope of the curve increasingly steep as we move to the right.

While opportunity costs generally increase, as shown in Figure 2-1, it is not logically necessary that they must do so. In some cases, it is possible for opportunity costs to be constant. For example, beef cattle and dairy cattle can graze on similar land; it is possible that the resources used to raise beef are equally suited for dairy cattle. Thus, the opportunity cost of beef in terms of milk may be constant. If we drew a production possibilities curve with milk on one axis and beef on the other, we would get a straight line.

THE PRODUCTION POSSIBILITIES CURVE IS A "FRONTIER"

The production possibilities curve in Figure 2-1 illustrates what an economy is capable of producing. It shows the maximum possible combined output of the two goods. In practice, actual production can fall short of our capabilities. Obviously, if there is large-scale unemployment, we are wasting some of our labor resources. Such a situation is shown by point *U*, inside the production possibilities curve in Figure 2-2. Beginning at such a point, we could produce more food *and* more clothing (and move to point *D*) by putting the unemployed back to work. (With full employment, we alternatively could choose any other point on the production possibilities curve, such as *B*, *C*, or *E*.)

Thus, even though the production possibilities curve represents options open to the society, it does not include all conceivable options. The attainable options include not only the points on the curve but also all points in the shaded area inside the curve.

The production possibilities curve therefore traces out a *frontier*, or *boundary*, of the options open to us. We can pick a point on the frontier if we manage our affairs well and maintain a high level of employment. Or

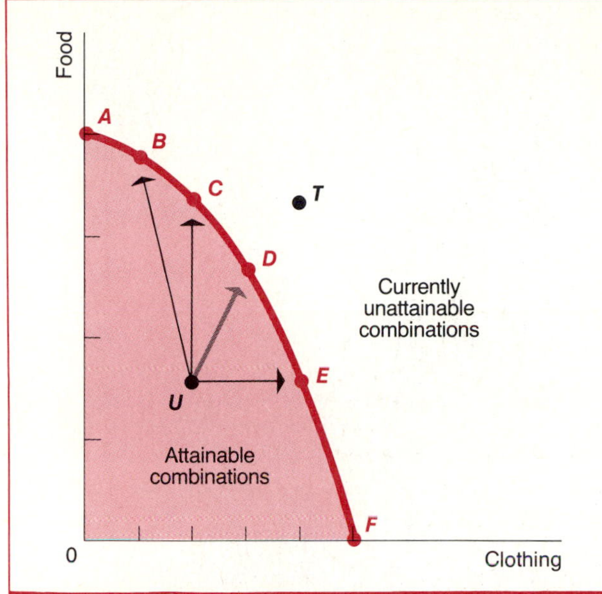

FIGURE 2-2

Unemployment and the production possibilities curve

Point *U* represents a position of large-scale unemployment. If people are put back to work, the economy can be moved to point *D*, with more food *and* more clothing.

With its limited resources, the society can choose any point along the production possibilities curve or any point within it. Points in the shaded area within the curve are undesirable; the society could do better by moving out to the curve. Points beyond the curve are unattainable with the resources currently available.

we can end up inside the curve if we mismanage the economy into a depression. But points (such as *T*) outside the curve are currently unattainable. We cannot reach them with our present quantities of land, labor, and capital and with our present technology.

In summary, the production possibilities curve illustrates three important concepts: scarcity, choice, and opportunity cost.

1. *Scarcity* is illustrated by the fact that combinations outside the curve cannot be attained. Even though we might want such combinations, we cannot have them with the resources available to us.

2. Because we cannot have combinations outside the curve, we must settle for a *choice* of one of the attainable combinations outlined by the PPC.

3. *Opportunity cost* is illustrated by the downward slope of the production possibilities curve.

GROWTH: THE OUTWARD SHIFT OF THE PRODUCTION POSSIBILITIES CURVE

As time passes, a point such as *T* (Figure 2-2) may come within our grasp as our productive capacity increases and the economy grows. There are three main sources of growth:

1. Technological improvement, representing new and better ways of producing goods

2. An increase in the quantity of capital

3. An increase in the labor force

Consider a change in technology. Suppose a new type of fertilizer were developed that substantially increased the output of our land, whether cotton or wheat were being grown. Then we would be able to produce more wheat and more cotton. The production possibilities curve would shift out to the new curve (PPC_2) shown in Figure 2-3.

***Growth* is defined as an outward movement of the production possibilities curve.**

While the new fertilizer illustrated in Figure 2-3 increases our ability to produce *both* wheat and cotton, other types of technological improvement may increase our ability to produce only *one* of them. For example, the development of a new disease-resistant strain of wheat will increase our ability to produce wheat but not cotton. In this case, illustrated in Figure 2-4, nothing will happen at point *F*, where the production possibilities curve meets the axis for cotton. If we direct all our resources to the production of cotton, we can still produce no more than shown by point *F*. However, if we direct all our resources to wheat, we can produce more; the other end of the PPC moves upward along the food axis, from *A* to *B*. Thus, the development of the new wheat causes the PPC to move upward, from PPC_1 to PPC_3.

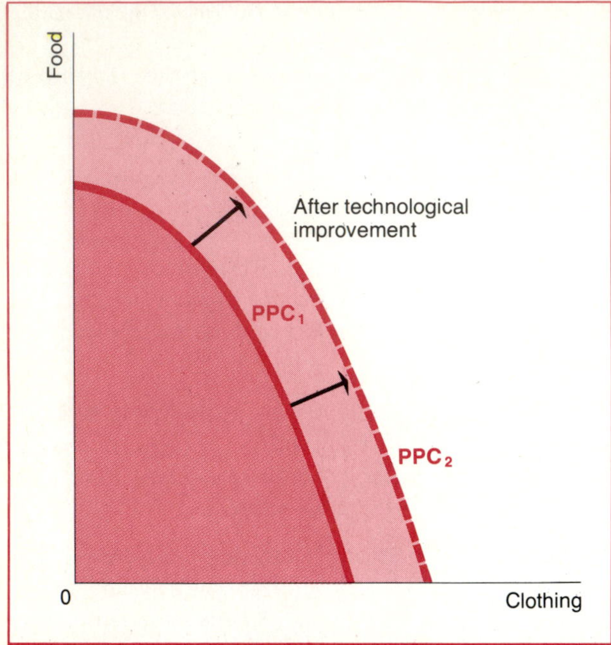

FIGURE 2-3
Technological improvement
As a result of the development of a new fertilizer, our productive capabilities increase. The production possibilities curve moves outward.

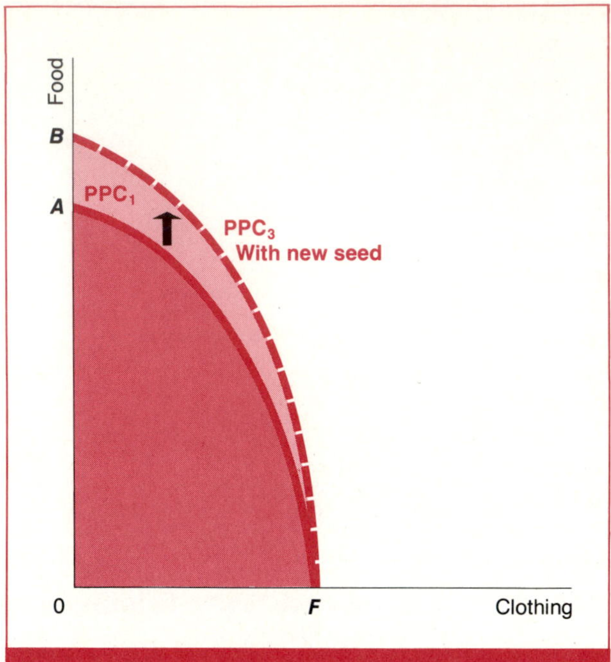

FIGURE 2-4
Technological improvement in a single good
When a new, improved strain of wheat is developed, the production possibilities curve moves out to PPC_3.

GROWTH: THE CHOICE BETWEEN CONSUMER GOODS AND CAPITAL GOODS

As an alternative to technological change, consider the second source of growth listed above: an increase in the quantity of capital. The capital we have today is limited. However, capital itself can be produced. The quantity of capital in the year 2000 will be determined in large part by how much capital we choose to produce this year and in coming years.

In order to study this choice, we must look at a different production possibilities curve—not one showing food and clothing, but rather, one showing the choice between the production of *capital goods* (such as machines and factories) and the production of *consumer goods* (such as food, clothing, and TV sets).

In Figure 2-5, two hypothetical economies are compared. Starting today, these two countries face the same initial production possibilities curve (PPC_{today}). The citizens of Extravagania (on the left) believe in living for the moment. They produce mostly consumption goods, and very few capital goods (at point *A*). As a result, their capital stock will be not much greater in 2000 than it is today, so their PPC will shift out very little. In contrast, the citizens of Thriftiana (on the right) keep down the production of consumer goods in order to build more capital goods (at point *B*). By the year 2000, their productive capacity will be greatly increased, as shown by the large outward movement of the PPC. Because they have given up so much consumption today, their income (and ability to consume) will be much greater in the future. Thus, any society faces a choice: How much consumption should it sacrifice now in order to be able to consume more in the future?

Economic Development: The Problem of Takeoff

For some countries, the question of growth may be approached in a relatively relaxed manner. For the United States, the issue is not a matter of life or death. Even if we consume most of our current output and grow only slowly, we will still be comfortable in the year 2000. The same is true for Japan and for the countries of Western Europe. (However, Japan conspicuously has not taken a relaxed approach to the growth question. Japan has been ''Thriftiana'' *par excellence,* investing a large share of national output in new plant and equipment and thus growing rapidly.)

Some other countries, however, face a much more critical situation. They are so poor that they can scarcely take a relaxed view either of the present or of the future. They face a cruel dilemma, illustrated in Figure 2-6. If they consume all their current output at point A, they will remain stuck on PPC_1. Their future will be just as bleak as the present.[2] On the other hand, if they want to grow, they will have to produce capital, and this means cutting back on their production of consumer goods. (If they choose the growth strategy and move initially to point B_1, then the production of consumer goods will decrease from A to B.) Since the already low level of consumption is depressed further, more people may starve.

In the long run, the growth strategy pays off. Because capital is produced at B_1, productive capacity

[2]In this simplified example, it is assumed that only capital changes and that technology and population remain constant. In fact, all three major determinants of growth (capital, labor, and technology) may change. If technology improves, growth may occur even in the absence of investment; the outlook may not be as bleak as suggested in the text. On the other hand, population pressures may make the outlook even worse. As population grows, output must grow if the already low standard of living is not to fall even lower. Thus, just to maintain the present standard, some capital formation may be required.

FIGURE 2-5
Capital formation now helps to determine future productive capacity

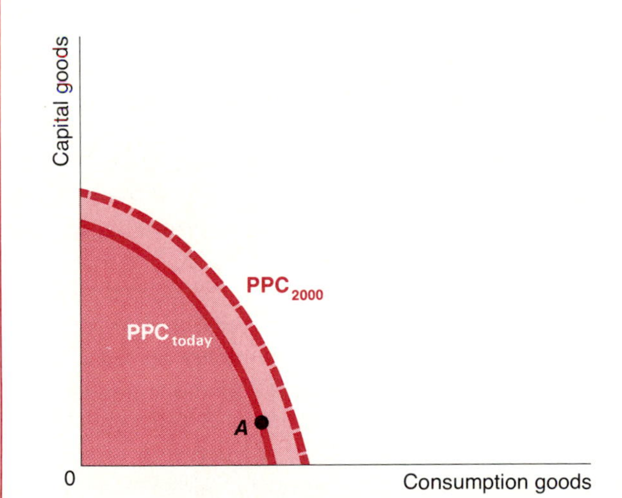

(*a*) **Extravagania.** Most productive capacity is directed toward the production of consumer goods (point ***A***). Little investment takes place. The result is slow growth.

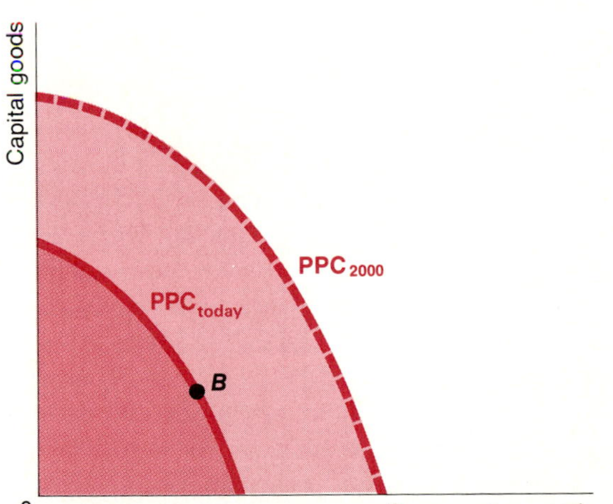

(*b*) **Thriftiana.** Much of current (today's) capacity is used to produce capital goods (point ***B***). The result is rapid growth, illustrated by a large outward movement of the production possibilities curve by the year 2000.

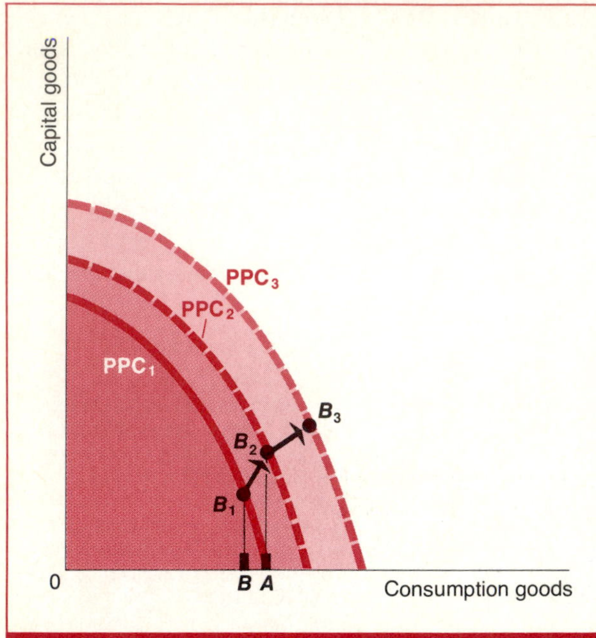

FIGURE 2-6

Takeoff into economic growth

If point B_1 is initially chosen (on PPC_1), growth will occur. The economy can move progressively to B_2, B_3, and beyond. However, the initial choice of B_1 rather than A will require people to forego some consumption goods, as measured by the distance AB. The problem, therefore, is: What short-term miseries will be caused by the choice of B_1 rather than A?

grows. The production possibilities curve shifts out to PPC_2. Now the nation can pick point B_2, where it not only produces capital goods but also consumes as much as it originally did at A. (B_2 is directly above point A.) The economy has achieved a ***takeoff***. Because it is now producing capital goods, its PPC is continuously moving out. Consequently, the nation can produce ever increasing amounts of both consumer and capital goods.

However, the long-run process does not solve the painful problem of the present: Should consumption be depressed, at the possible risk of starvation, in order to initiate the growth process? How can the economy take off without the danger of a crack-up halfway down the runway? (The danger may be political as well as economic. If a government chooses point B_1, the population may be unimpressed with "pie in the sky"—the promise of a brighter future. They may vote the government out, or rebel.)

One possible solution to this difficult dilemma lies with other countries. Richer countries can provide the resources for the early stages of growth, either by granting aid or through private investment. (For example, a Western European tractor manufacturer might build a plant in the developing country.) In this way, economic takeoff might occur without the sacrifices that capital formation normally requires.

AN INTRODUCTION TO ECONOMIC THEORY: THE NEED TO SIMPLIFY

The production possibilities curve is the first piece of theoretical equipment which the beginning economics student typically encounters. There will be many more. At this early stage, it is appropriate to address directly a problem which often bothers both beginning and advanced students of economics. The production possibilities curve, like many other theoretical concepts that will be introduced in later chapters, represents a gross simplification of the real world. When the PPC is drawn, it is assumed that only two types of goods can be produced—food and clothing, or consumer goods and capital goods. (Diagrams are limited to two alternatives because the printed page has only two dimensions.) Yet, obviously, there are thousands of goods produced in the modern economy. This raises a question: With our simple approach, can we say anything of relevance to the real world?

Since we have already used the production possibilities curve, it is not surprising that our answer to this question is yes. To see why, let us briefly consider the role of theory in economics. Economics is a study of such questions as how consumers behave; why cars are produced in Detroit and steel in Pittsburgh; why prices are sometimes stable and sometimes volatile. To study economics, we must consider *cause* and *effect*.

Theory Necessarily Involves Simplification

If we wished to describe the real world in detail, we could go on without end. A complete description would be useless as a guide to private behavior or public policy—it would be too complex. In a sense, theory is like a map. A road map is necessarily incomplete. In many ways, it is not very accurate and, indeed, downright wrong. Towns and villages are not round circles. Roads of various qualities do not really come in different colors. If a road map were more realistic, it would be less useful for its intended purpose. If it tried to show every house and every tree, it would be an incomprehensible jumble of detail. A road map is useful precisely because it is a simplification that shows in stark outline the various roads which may be traveled. Similarly, the objective of economic theory is to draw in stark outline the important relationships among producers and consumers.

When details are left out of a road map, it becomes more useful as a guide for the auto traveler. However, it becomes less useful for other purposes. A road map is a poor guide for airplane pilots. They need a map with the height of mountains marked clearly. A road map is a poor guide for sales managers, who need a map showing regional sales targets and staff assignments. The way in which a map is constructed depends upon its intended use. Various maps are "true," but they do not represent the "whole truth." An important question for a map user thus becomes: Do I have the best map for my purpose?

The same generalization holds for economic theory. If we wish to study long-run growth, we will use quite different theoretical tools from those we would use to study short-term fluctuations. If we want to study the consequences of price controls on the housing market, we will use different tools from those we would choose to investigate the economic consequences of a cut in the defense budget. Just as in the case of the map, the "best" theory cannot be identified unless we know the purposes for which it is to be used.

The production possibilities curve is a theoretical tool whose purpose is to illustrate the concept of scarcity. *If* we begin on the PPC, with our resources fully employed, we can come to a significant conclusion: To produce more of one good, we will have to cut back on the production of some other good or service. The "if" clause is important. It tells us that when we consider points along the PPC we are making an assumption—that resources are fully utilized. When the "if" clause is violated—that is, when the economy begins with large-scale unemployment—we reach quite a different conclusion. The economy *can* produce more consumer goods and more capital goods at the same time. Thus the "if" clause acts as a label on our theoretical road map. It tells us when the map can be used.

For the novice and old hand alike, it is essential to recognize and remember such "if" clauses. Failure to do so may lead us to use the wrong theory and make serious policy mistakes—just as the pilot who uses the wrong map may fly a plane into the nearest mountain top.

The Distinction between Positive and Normative Economics

The uses of theory are many, but they may be divided into two main families. ***Positive,*** or ***descriptive,*** economics aims at understanding how the economy works. It is directed toward explaining the world *as it is,* and how various forces can cause it to change. In contrast, ***normative*** economics deals with the way the world (or some small segment of it) *ought to be.*

A debate over a *positive* statement can often be settled by an appeal to the facts. For example, the following is a positive statement: "U.S. steel production last year was 100 million tons." By looking up the statistics, we can find out whether this was true. A more complicated positive statement is: "There are millions of barrels of oil in the rocks of Colorado." With a geological study, we can discover whether this is likely to be so. A third positive statement is: "If a ton of dynamite is exploded 100 feet below the surface, 1,000 barrels of oil will be released from the rocks." By experimentation, we can discover whether this is generally true.

A *normative* statement is more complex: for example, "We ought to extract oil in large quantities from the Colorado rocks." Facts are relevant here. If there is no oil in the rocks of Colorado (a positive conclusion), the normative statement that we ought to extract oil must be rejected for the very simple reason that it can't be done. However, facts alone will seldom settle a dispute over a normative statement, since it is based on something more—on a view regarding appropriate goals or ethical values. A normative statement involves a value judgment, a judgment about what *ought* to be. It is possible for well-informed individuals of exemplary character to disagree over normative statements, even when they agree completely regarding the facts. For example, they may agree that, in fact, a large quantity of oil is locked in the rocks of Colorado. Nevertheless, they may disagree whether it should be extracted. These differences may develop, perhaps, over the relative importance of the benefits of more heating oil as compared with the environmental cost that might accompany the extraction of oil.

Although some positive statements may be easily settled by looking at the facts, others may be much more difficult to judge. This is particularly true of statements making claims about causation. They may be quite controversial because the facts are not easily untangled. For example: "If there is no growth in the money stock next year, then inflation will fall to zero"; or, "If income tax rates are increased by 1%, government revenues will increase by $20 billion next year"; or, "Rent controls have little effect on the number of apartments offered for rent."

In evaluating such statements, economists and other social scientists have two major disadvantages as compared with natural scientists. First, experiments are difficult or impossible in many instances. Society is not the plaything of economists. They do not have the power to conduct an experiment in which one large city is subjected to rent control while a similar city is not, simply to estimate the effects of rent control. Nevertheless, economists do have factual evidence to study. By looking at situations where rent controls have actually been imposed by the government, they may be able to estimate the effects of those controls. Moreover, in special situations, economic experiments *are* possible, particularly when the government is eager to know the results. For example, experiments have been undertaken to find how major changes in the tax system may affect people's willingness to work. (The results will be reported in Chapter 37.)

The second disadvantage is that the social sciences deal with the behavior of people, and behavior can change. Suppose we estimate corporate profits next year to be $200 billion. We might carelessly conclude that, if the profits tax is raised by 10%, the government will receive an additional $20 billion in revenues. But this is not necessarily so. With a higher tax rate, businesses may behave differently in order to reduce the taxes they have to pay. Furthermore, even if we have evidence on how businesses have responded to a 10% tax increase in the past, we cannot be certain that they will respond the same way in the future. They may have become more imaginative in finding ways to avoid taxes. The possibility that people will learn and change has been one of the most interesting areas of research in economics in recent years.

In contrast, physical scientists study a relatively stable and unchanging universe. Gravity works the same today as it did in Newton's time.

KEY POINTS

1. *Scarcity* is a fundamental economic problem. Because wants are virtually unlimited and resources are scarce, we are faced with the need to make *choices*.

2. The choices open to society are illustrated by the *production possibilities curve*.

3. Not all resources are uniform. For example, the land of Mississippi is different from the land of Minnesota. As a consequence, opportunity cost generally increases as more of a good is produced. For example, as more cotton is produced, more and more wheat must be given up for each additional unit of cotton. As a result, the production possibilities curve normally bows outward.

4. The production posibilities curve is a frontier representing the choices open to society—*if* there is full utilization of the available resources of land, labor, and capital. If there is large-scale unemployment, production occurs at a point *within* this frontier.

5. The economy can grow and the production possibilities curve can move outward if (*a*) technology improves, (*b*) the capital stock grows, and/or (*c*) the labor force grows.

6. By giving up consumer goods at present, we can produce more capital goods and thus have a growing economy. The production of capital goods (investment) therefore represents a choice of more future production instead of present consumption.

7. For the poorest countries, a choice between present consumption and growth is particularly painful. If consumption is suppressed in order to grow more rapidly, people may starve. But growth is essential to raise a low standard of living.

8. Like other theoretical concepts, the production possibilities curve represents a simplification. Because the world is so complex, theory cannot reflect the whole truth. Nevertheless, a theory—like a road map—can be valuable if it is used correctly. In order to determine the appropriate uses of a theory, it is important to identify the assumptions on which the theory was developed.

KEY CONCEPTS

scarcity
resources
factors of production
land
labor
capital
investment
entrepreneur
production possibilities curve
increasing opportunity cost
growth
takeoff
positive economics
normative economics
theory

PROBLEMS

2-1. In Chapter 1, economics was defined broadly as the study of how people make their living, of the problems they encounter in doing so, and of the ways in which they can reduce these problems. Another common definition of economics is tied closely to the idea of scarcity: Economics is "the study of the allocation of scarce resources to satisfy alternative, competing human wants."

Clearly, scarcity is an important part of economics. We cannot have all the goods and services we want. However, one of the economic problems in Chapter 1 cannot be attributed to a scarcity of resources. Which one? Why is this problem not attributable to a scarcity of resources? Is this problem covered by the broader definition in Chapter 1?

2-2. "Wants aren't insatiable. The economic wants of David Rockefeller have been satisfied. There is no prospect that he will spend all his money before he dies. His consumption is not limited by his income." Do you agree? Does your answer raise problems for the main theme of this chapter, that not all wants can be satisfied with the goods and services produced from our limited resources? Why or why not?

2-3. "The more capital goods we produce, the more the U.S. economy will grow and the more we and our children will be able to consume in the future. Therefore, the government should encourage capital formation." Do you agree or disagree? Why?

2-4. Does the United States have a moral obligation to aid India with its economic development? Nigeria? Brazil? China?

2-5. Do your answers to Problems 2-3 and 2-4 fall under the heading of "positive" or "normative" economics? Why?

CHAPTER 3

SPECIALIZATION, EXCHANGE, AND MONEY

Money . . . is not . . . the wheels of trade: it is the oil which renders the motion of the wheels smooth and easy.

DAVID HUME

The past century has witnessed impressive economic progress, marked by a huge increase in the quantity of capital and a flood of new inventions. Tractors have been introduced into farming; airplanes speed the movement of people and goods; telephones and radio allow instant worldwide communication; computers help in the design of products. A long and impressive list could be quickly compiled. Today, the worker not only has more tools but also much better tools than the worker of the nineteenth century.

The new tools have led to a significant increase in the degree of ***specialization.*** The nineteenth-century carpenter produced a wide range of furniture and related wood products, from jewelry boxes to caskets. (Indeed, occupations were sometimes combined, with the same individual acting as both carpenter and undertaker.) On the early frontier, the settler was largely self-sufficient. Families grew their own food, built their own homes, and often made most of their own clothes. Not so today. Most farms are specialized, producing only one or a few products, such as wheat, corn, or beef. The worker in a modern factory tends a machine designed to produce a single piece of furniture or perhaps just a single leg of a piece of furniture. The results have not been an unmixed blessing. Modern workers are more prone to boredom, and they lack the sense of accomplishment enjoyed by the skilled workers of the past who could see their creations taking shape. However, the results have undoubtedly contributed to efficiency. By using specialized machinery, the modern worker has become very productive.

We can easily find examples where specialization contributes to efficiency. It is efficient for the United States to import coffee and to export wheat or business machines to pay for this coffee. True, coffee could be produced in the United States, but only with difficulty, and at a very high cost. Similarly, it is efficient to produce steel in Pittsburgh and corn in Kansas. Kansans presumably could produce their own steel, but the cost would be prohibitively high. Specialization likewise takes place within towns and cities. Barbers specialize in cutting hair, doctors in treating illnesses, and factory workers in producing such goods as bicycles, cars, and home appliances.

EXCHANGE: THE BARTER ECONOMY

Specialization requires *exchange*. Farmers who specialize in raising beef must exchange beef (beyond their families' direct requirements) for furniture, clothing, and other needs. There are two kinds of exchange: barter and exchange for money.

In a *barter* system, no money is used: One good or service is exchanged directly for another. The farmer specializing in the production of beef may find a hungry barber and thus get a haircut, or find a hungry tailor and thus exchange meat for a suit of clothes, or find a hungry doctor and thus obtain medical treatment. A simple barter transaction is illustrated in Figure 3-1. In a barter economy, there are dozens of such bilateral (two-way) transactions: between the farmer and the tailor, between

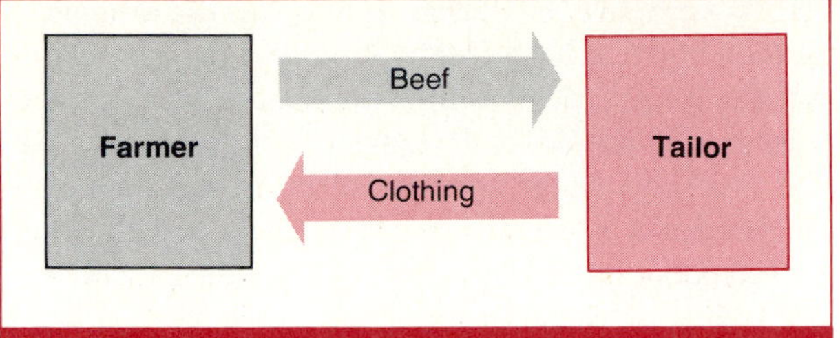

FIGURE 3-1
Barter
With barter, no money is used. The farmer exchanges beef directly for clothing. Transactions involve only two parties—in this case, the farmer and the tailor.

the farmer and the doctor, between the doctor and the tailor, and so on.

Clearly, barter is inefficient. Farmers spend half their time producing beef, and the other half searching for someone willing to make the right trade. Barter requires a ***coincidence of wants:*** Those engaged in barter must each have a product that the other wants. The farmer not only must find someone who wants beef, but that someone must also be able to provide something in exchange that the farmer wants. Furthermore, with barter, there is a problem of ***indivisibility.*** A suit of clothes—or an automobile, or a house—should be bought all at once and not in pieces. To illustrate, suppose a beef farmer who wants a suit of clothes has been lucky enough to find a tailor who wants meat and is willing to make a trade. The suit of clothes may be worth 100 pounds of beef, and the farmer may be quite willing to give up this amount. The problem is that the tailor may not be *that* hungry, perhaps wanting only 50 pounds. In a barter economy, what is the farmer to do? Get only the jacket from this tailor and set out to find another hungry tailor in order to obtain a pair of pants? If the farmer does so, what are the chances that the pants will match?

EXCHANGE WITH MONEY

With money, exchange is much easier. It is no longer necessary for wants to coincide. In order to get a suit of clothing, the farmer need not find a hungry tailor but only someone willing to pay money for the beef. The farmer can then take the money and buy the suit of clothes. Because money represents ***general purchasing power***—that is, it can be used to buy *any* of the goods and services offered for sale—money makes possible complex transactions among many parties. Figure 3-2 gives a simple illustration with three parties. Actual transactions in a monetary economy may be very complex, with dozens or hundreds of participants.

Money also solves the problem of indivisibility. The farmer can sell the whole carcass of beef for money and use the proceeds to buy a complete set of clothes. It doesn't matter how much beef the tailor wants.

In the simple barter economy, there is no clear distinction between seller and buyer, or between producer and consumer. When bartering beef for clothing, the farmer is at the same time both a seller (of beef) and a buyer (of clothing). In a monetary economy, in contrast, there is a clear distinction between seller and buyer. In the beef market, the farmer is the seller; the hungry tailor is the buyer. The farmer is the producer; the tailor is the consumer.

The distinction between the producer and the consumer in a money economy is illustrated in Figure 3-3. Producers—or ***businesses***—are put in the right-hand box, and consumers—or ***households***—in the left. Transactions between the two groups are illustrated in the loops. In the top loops, the transactions in consumer goods and services are shown. Beef, clothing, and a host of other products are sold in exchange for money.

In the lower loops, transactions in economic resources are shown. In a complex exchange economy, not only are consumer goods bought and sold for money; so are resources. In order to be able to buy food and other goods, households must have money income. They acquire money by providing the labor and other resources which are the inputs of the business sector. For example, workers provide their labor in exchange for wages and salaries, and owners of land provide their property in exchange for rents.

Figure 3-3 is simplified. For example, we have excluded the government, which is a major purchaser of goods and services. Remember the purpose of simplification discussed in Chapter 2: to show important relationships in sharp outline. Figure 3-3 shows the circular flow of payments, that is, how businesses use the receipts from sales to pay their wages, salaries, and other costs of production, while households use their income receipts from wages, salaries, etc., to buy consumer goods.

THE MONETARY SYSTEM

Because barter is so inefficient, people turn naturally to the use of money. In most societies, the government becomes deeply involved in the monetary system, issuing paper money and coins. But even if the government does nothing, a monetary system will evolve.

The very powerful tendencies for money to appear, and some of the important characteristics of a good monetary system, may be illustrated by a specific example of an economy that began without money: the prisoner-of-war camp of World War II.[1] Economic relations in such a camp were primitive; the range of goods was very limited. But some things were available: rations supplied by the German captors and the Red Cross parcels which arrived periodically. These parcels contained a variety of items such as canned beef, jam, margarine, and cigarettes. Nonsmokers who received cigarettes were obviously eager to trade them for other items. The basis was established for exchange.

[1]This illustration is based on R. A. Radford, "The Economic Organization of a P.O.W. Camp," *Economica,* November 1945, pp. 189–201.

FIGURE 3-2

Multilateral transactions in a money economy

In a money economy, multilateral transactions among many participants are possible. The farmer gets clothing from the tailor, even though the tailor doesn't want to buy the farmer's beef.

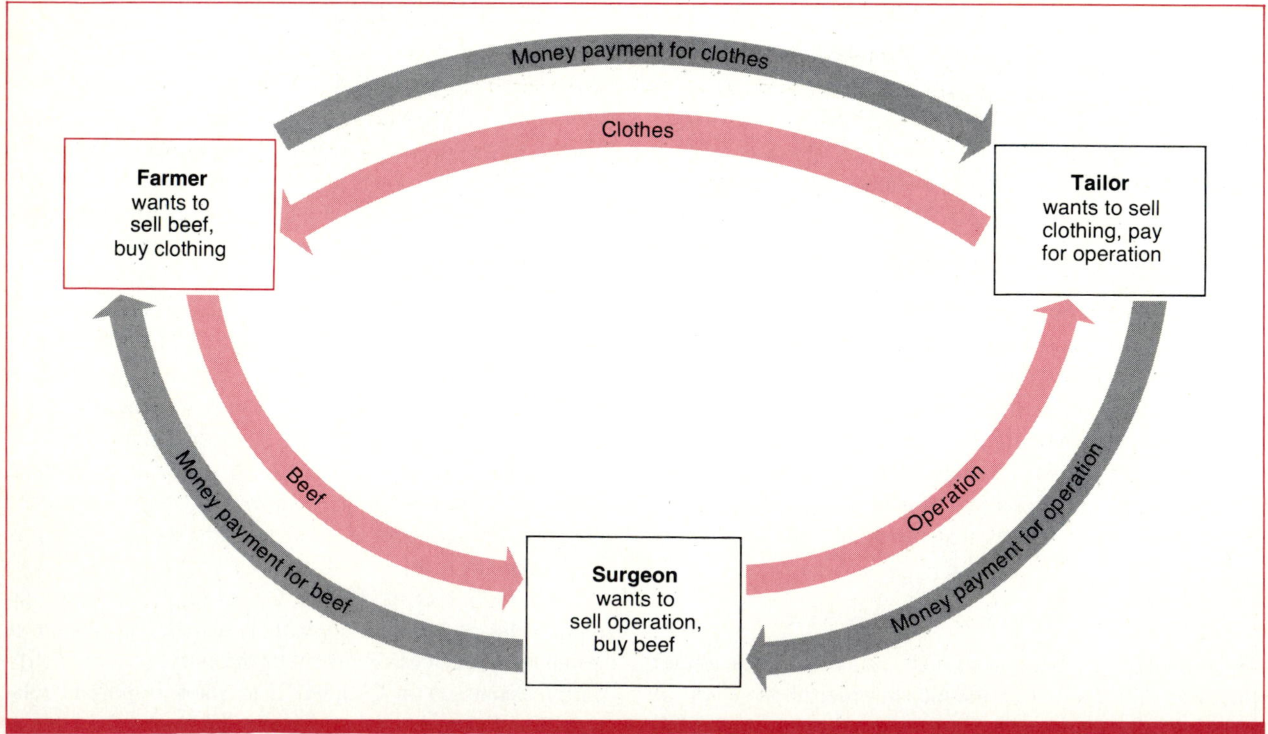

At first, trading was rough and ready, with no clear picture of the relative values of the various items. In one instance, a prisoner started around the camp with only a can of cheese and five cigarettes, and returned with a complete Red Cross parcel. He did so by buying goods where they were cheap and selling them where they were dear. However, as time went by, the prices of various goods tended to become stable, and all prices came to be quoted in terms of cigarettes. For example, a can of cheese was worth seven cigarettes. Cigarettes became not only the measuring rod for quoting prices, but also the common ***medium of exchange;*** that is, cigarettes were the item used to buy all other goods. Even non-smokers were willing to accept cigarettes in payment, although they had no desire to smoke. They knew that they would be able to use the cigarettes to buy chocolate, jam, or other items. In short, cigarettes became the money of the POW camp. This was a natural evolution; there was no government to decree that cigarettes were money, and no authority to enforce that choice. At other times and in other societies, other items have been used as money: items as diverse as beads, playing cards, porpoise teeth, rice, salt, wampum, stones, and even woodpecker scalps (Box 3-1).

FIGURE 3-3
The flow of goods, services, resources, and money payments in a simple economy
Monetary payments are shown in the outer loop. These pay for the flow of goods and services and resources shown in the inner loop.

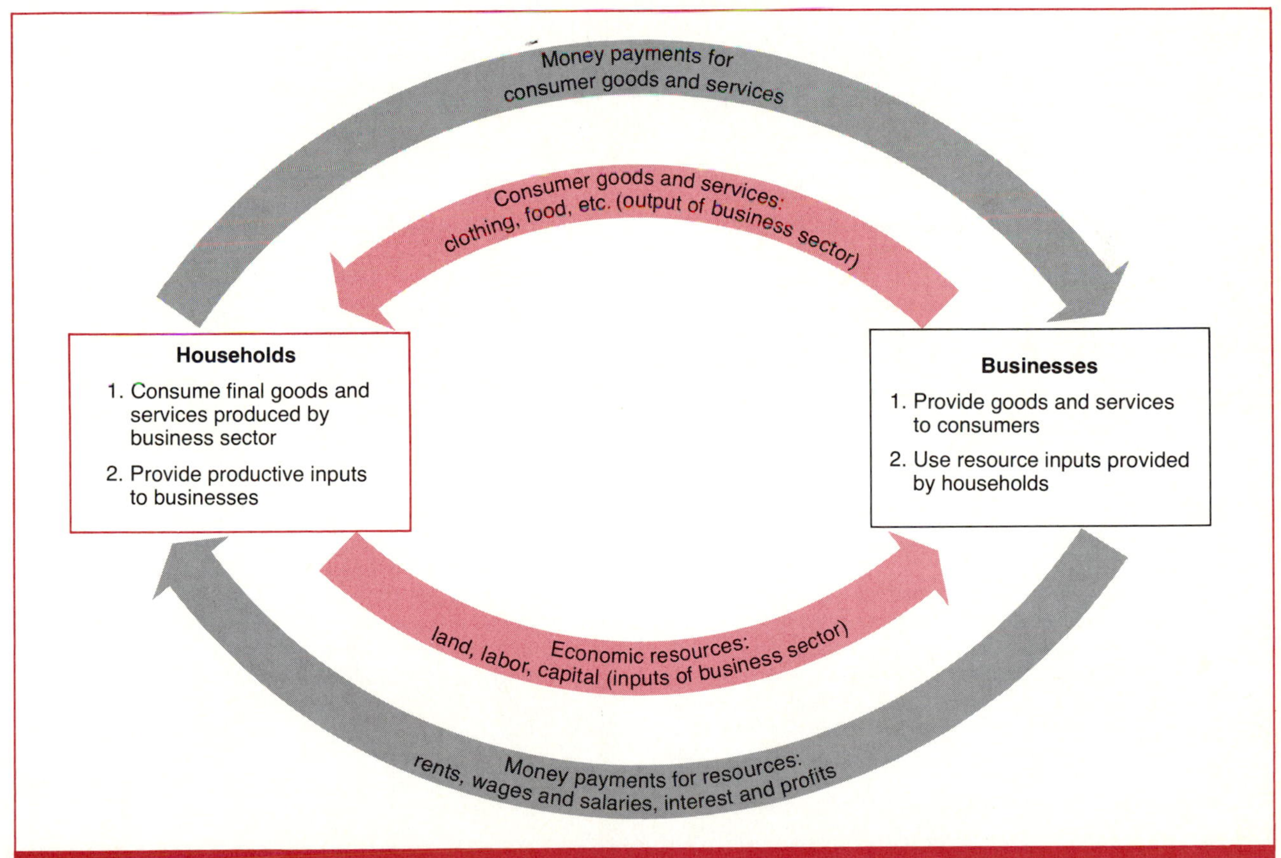

Monetary Problems in the POW Camp

Cigarette money made the primitive economy of the POW camp more efficient, but problems occurred, including problems quite similar to those of more advanced monetary systems. As part of the natural trend toward simplification, distinctions among different brands of cigarettes became blurred. Although all cigarettes were not equally desirable to smokers, all were equal as money. In paying for beef or other items, a cigarette was a cigarette. What was the consequence? Smokers held back the desirable brands for their personal use and spent the others. The less desirable cigarettes therefore were the ones used as money; the ''good'' cigarettes were smoked. This illustrates ***Gresham's law.*** This law, first enunciated by Elizabethan financier Sir Thomas Gresham (1519–1579), is popularly and loosely abbreviated: ''Bad money drives out good.'' In this case, ''bad'' cigarettes drove ''good'' cigarettes out of circulation as money. (The good cigarettes were smoked instead.)

Gresham's law: **If there are two types of money whose values in exchange are equal while their values in another use (like consumption) are different, the more valuable item will be retained for its other use while the less valuable item will continue to circulate as money. Thus, the ''bad'' (less valuable) money drives the ''good'' (more valuable) money out of circulation.**

The tendency for every cigarette to be treated as equal to every other cigarette caused another monetary problem. As a cigarette was a cigarette, prisoners often pulled out a few strands of tobacco before passing a cigarette along. This corresponds precisely to a problem when gold coins circulate: There is a temptation to ''clip'' coins by chipping off bits of gold. Furthermore, the cigarette currency became ''debased'': Some enterprising prisoners rolled cigarettes from pipe tobacco or broke down cigarettes and rerolled them, reducing the

BOX 3-1

EARLY MONEY ON THE ISLAND OF UAP†

On the south-sea island of Uap, the medium of exchange is called *fei.* This currency consists of large, solid, thick stone wheels ranging in diameter from 1 to 12 feet, and in the center a hole, so that the stones may be slung on poles and carried. They are not found on Uap itself, but are quarried in Babelthuap, some 400 miles away. Size is the most important factor, but also the *fei* must be of a certain fine, white, close-grained limestone. A traveler to Uap described the *fei* as follows:

> A feature of this stone currency, which is also an equally noteworthy tribute to Uap honesty, is that its owner does not need to actually possess it. After concluding a bargain which involves a *fei* too large to be conveniently moved, its new owner is quite content to accept the bare acknowledgment of ownership; and without so much as a mark to indicate the exchange, the coin remains undisturbed on the former owner's premises.
>
> There was in a village near by a family whose wealth was unquestioned—acknowledged by every one, and yet no one, not even the family itself, had ever laid eye on this wealth; it consisted of an enormous *fei* lying at the bottom of the sea! Many years ago an ancestor of this family, on an expedition after *fei,* secured this remarkable stone, which was placed on a raft to be towed homeward. A violent storm arose and the party, to save their lives, were obliged to cut the raft adrift, and the stone sank out of sight. When they reached home, they all testified that the *fei* was of magnificent proportions and extraordinary quality, and that it was lost through no fault of the owners. Thereupon it was universally considered that the mere accident of its loss overboard was too trifling to mention. The purchasing power of the stone remained, therefore, as valid as if it were leaning visibly against the side of the owner's house.

†Abridged, from Norman Angell, *The Story of Money* (New York: Garden City Publishing, 1929), pp. 88–89.

amount of tobacco in each. Similarly, governments have from time to time given in to the temptation to debase gold coins by melting them down and reissuing them with a smaller gold content. (Private entrepreneurs have had a strong incentive to do the same, but they have been discouraged throughout history by severe punishments against counterfeiting.)

However, it was not clipping or debasement which led to the greatest monetary problems in the POW camp. As long as there was a balanced inflow of both cigarettes and other goods, the exchange system of the camp worked reasonably well. But, from time to time, the weekly Red Cross issue of 25 or 50 cigarettes per prisoner was interrupted. As the existing stock of cigarettes was consumed by smokers, cigarettes became more and more scarce. Desperate smokers had to offer more and more to get cigarettes; their value skyrocketed. To put the same point another way: Other goods now exchanged for fewer and fewer cigarettes. A can of beef which previously sold for 20 cigarettes dropped in value to 15, 10, or even fewer cigarettes. Thus, there was a ***deflation***—a decline in the prices of other goods measured in terms of money.

As cigarettes became increasingly scarce and prices continued to fall, prisoners began to revert to barter in exchanging other goods. Smokers who had the few remaining cigarettes were reluctant to give them up to make purchases. Then, from time to time, thousands of cigarettes would arrive at the camp during a brief period. Prices soared. A can of beef that previously sold for 10 cigarettes now sold for 30 or 40. In other words, the value of cigarettes fell. Prisoners became reluctant to accept cigarettes in payment for other goods. (Remember: Nonsmokers accepted cigarette money only when they thought they would be able to buy other goods with it.) Once again, barter became common. Thus, *the monetary system worked smoothly only so long as a reasonable balance was kept between the quantity of money (cigarettes) and the quantity of other goods.*

Several characteristics of a good monetary system may be drawn out of this story of the "cigarette standard." A smoothly operating monetary system should be made up of money whose value is ***uniform.*** Nonuniform money will set Gresham's law into operation, with bad money driving good money out of circulation. In the United States, the Federal Reserve System has the responsibility to assure that money is uniform. It is the institution which issues paper currency. It matters not whether the $1 bill I have in my pocket is crisp and new or whether it is tattered and soiled. The Federal Reserve will replace it with a new bill of equal value when it becomes excessively worn. This means that it represents $1 in value to anyone. This uniformity in the value of each dollar bill obviously adds to the ease of exchange—and it means that Gresham's law does not operate in our modern economy. In accepting dollar bills, we need worry only about whether they are genuine; we need not quibble over their exact physical condition.

A second important characteristic of a good monetary system is that there be the ***proper quantity of money,*** neither too much nor too little. In the United States, the responsibility for controlling the quantity of money also lies with the Federal Reserve. This important topic will be studied in Part 3 of this book. (For other important characteristics of money, see Box 3-2.)

COMPARATIVE ADVANTAGE: A REASON TO SPECIALIZE

Money, the development of markets, and (perhaps equally important) the development of a sophisticated transportation and communications system all make possible a high degree of specialization of production. They make specialization possible and relatively smooth, but they don't provide a reason *why* specialization is advantageous in the first place. At the beginning of the chapter, an answer was suggested: Specialization can add to efficiency. It is now time to explain in more detail just *how*. A key concept in the explanation is the ***principle of comparative advantage.*** To understand this principle, it is useful to look first at the simpler concept of ***absolute advantage.***

A good is often made in the place which is best suited for its production: steel near the coal mines of Pennsylvania, corn in the fertile fields of Iowa, bananas in the tropical lands of Central America, coffee in the cool highlands of Colombia, and so on. In technical terms, there is some tendency for a good to be produced in the area that has an *absolute advantage* in its production.

A country (or region or individual) has an *absolute advantage* in the production of a good if it can produce that good with fewer resources (less land, labor, and capital) than can other countries (or regions or individuals).

Note that this principle applies to specialization among individuals within a city or town. Consider the case of the lawyer and the professional gardener. The lawyer is better at drawing up legal documents and the gardener generally is better at gardening, so it is in the interest of each to specialize in the occupation in which he or she has an absolute advantage.

However, the truth is often more complicated than this. By looking at the complications, we will be led to the idea of comparative advantage. Suppose a certain lawyer is better at gardening than the gardener; she's

BOX 3-2

WHY CIGARETTES?

In the POW camp, cigarettes emerged as the commonly accepted money. Why cigarettes? Why not canned carrots or beef?

There were three reasons. First, although not everyone wanted cigarettes for his personal use, the market value of cigarettes was high. Thus, cigarettes were chosen over canned carrots because canned carrots were practically worthless. If carrots had been the "money," exchange would have been cumbersome, with prisoners lugging around many cans in order to make exchanges. *A good money is one whose value is sufficiently high that the individual may conveniently carry a considerable purchasing power.* Thus, in the broader society, the money that evolved was precious metals—silver, and particularly gold. Lead did not (generally) become money because its value was relatively low and the use of lead would have been cumbersome. Of course, today our money is even more convenient than the precious metals: A \$20, \$50, or \$100 bill may be carried easily and inconspicuously.

Thus, cigarettes were preferred to canned carrots. But why did cigarettes become money, rather than canned beef? Canned meat, like cigarettes, had a high value. Here, we come to the second and third reasons why cigarettes became money. A package of cigarettes is *easily divisible* into subunits—the 20 individual cigarettes—each of which is relatively *durable.* A can of beef, on the other hand, cannot easily be subdivided. If it is opened and cut up, the individual chunks will be messy and will quickly spoil. Moreover, a 6-ounce piece of beef is not easily distinguished from a 7-ounce chunk. However, it is easy to tell if you have six cigarettes or seven.

Similarly, in the broader society, monies have developed which are easily divisible and durable. Precious metals, for example, are easily divisible into units of any size. The small units of gold or silver are durable—indeed, much more durable than the cigarettes of the POW camp. However, in another respect, gold and silver are less desirable than cigarettes. As in the case of beef, a 6-ounce piece of gold is not easily distinguished from a 7-ounce piece. Therefore, governments came into the picture, minting gold coins of specific value (such as \$20) which could immediately be identified.

But why did we have both gold *and* silver as money (for example, in the United States in the nineteenth century)? Gold is easily divisible—up to a point. Gold coins of \$50, \$20, or \$10 could easily be minted and were relatively convenient. However, suppose the government wanted to mint a gold coin worth 25 cents. It would be so tiny that it would be easily lost. While the high value of gold made it an obvious choice for coins of high value, it was very inconvenient for coins of low value. Here, silver was the obvious choice, since it was less valuable per ounce than gold.

In summary, the evolution of the "cigarette standard" illustrated a number of the characteristics which the item chosen for money should possess: It should be *sufficiently valuable* that a reasonably large purchasing power can be carried conveniently by an individual; it should be *easily divisible;* and it should be *durable.*

faster and more effective—in short, she has a "greener thumb." She has an absolute advantage in both the law and gardening. If absolute advantage were the key, she would practice law and do her own gardening as well. Does this necessarily happen? The answer: No. Unless this lawyer positively enjoys gardening as a recreation, she will leave the gardening to the professional. Why? Even though the lawyer, being an excellent gardener, can do as much gardening in 1 hour (let us say) as the gardener could in 2, she will be better off to stick to law and hire the gardener to work on the flowers and shrubbery. Why? In 1 hour's work, the lawyer can draw up a will, for which she charges $50. The gardener's time, in contrast, is worth only $5 per hour. By spending the hour on the law rather than gardening, the lawyer comes out ahead. She earns $50, and can hire the gardener for $10 to put in 2 hours to get the gardening done. The lawyer gains $40 by sticking to law for that 1 hour. (This is explained in more detail in Box 3-3.)

The gardener also gains through specialization. Although he has to work 10 hours in order to earn the $50 needed to hire the lawyer to draw up his will, it would take him much more time to draw up the will himself. He would have to spend many hours—as many as 100, perhaps—poring over law books just to learn the basic traps to avoid in drawing up a will. (Even after spending the 100 hours, he could not be sure that he might not have missed something very simple that the lawyer learned in her many years of study.) Thus, by spending 10 hours on gardening and using the income to buy the lawyer's time, the gardener gains: He gets a better will than he could have gotten by struggling with legal books for a full 100 hours.

Thus, absolute advantage is not necessary for specialization. The lawyer has an absolute advantage in both gardening and law; the gardener has an absolute disadvantage in both. But the lawyer has a *comparative advantage* in law; the gardener has a *comparative advantage* in gardening. When the gardener and the lawyer stick to their comparative advantage, *both gain from specialization*.

British economist ***David Ricardo*** enunciated the principle of comparative advantage in the early nineteenth century to illustrate how countries gain from international trade. But comparative advantage provides a general explanation of the advantages of specialization; it is just as relevant to domestic as to international trade. Nevertheless, it is customary to follow Ricardo and consider this principle as part of the study of international economics. We follow the custom and put off our more detailed analysis of comparative advantage to the chapter on international trade. For the moment, we note that the

BOX 3-3

ILLUSTRATION OF COMPARATIVE ADVANTAGE

A. *Assumptions:*
1. In 1 hour, the lawyer can plant 20 flowers.
2. In 1 hour, the gardener can plant 10 flowers. (Therefore, the lawyer has the *absolute advantage* in gardening.)
3. The lawyer's time, in the practice of law, is worth $50 per hour.
4. The gardener's time, in gardening, is worth $5 per hour.

B. *Question:* How should the lawyer have 20 flowers planted?

Option 1: Do the gardening herself, spending 1 hour.
Cost: She gives up the $50 she could have earned by practicing law for that hour.

Option 2: Stick to the law, and hire the gardener to plant the 20 flowers.
Cost: Two hours of gardener's time at $5 per hour, a total of $10.

C. *Decision:* Choose option 2.
Spend the available hour practicing law, earning $50.
Hire the gardener to do the planting for $10.
Net advantage over option 1: $40.

D. *Conclusion:* The lawyer has the *comparative advantage* in law.

concept of comparative advantage is related to opportunity cost.

If two individuals (or cities or nations) have different opportunity costs of producing a good or service, the individual (or city or nation) with the lower opportunity cost has the *comparative advantage* in that good or service.

The opportunity cost is the alternative foregone. To prepare a will, the lawyer's opportunity cost is the 20 flowers that she could have planted instead. (Details are in Box 3-3.) In contrast, the gardener would have faced a much higher opportunity cost to prepare a will. It would take him 100 hours, in which he alternatively could plant 1,000 flowers. Since the lawyer's opportunity cost of drawing up a will is lower than the gardener's (20 flowers vs. 1,000), the lawyer has the comparative advantage in law. She will specialize in this, leaving the flowers to the gardener. Furthermore, it follows directly that the gardener has the comparative advantage in gardening. To plant a flower, he gives up only one-thousandth of a will, compared to the one-twentieth foregone by the lawyer. Accordingly, the gardener will stick to his gardening and leave the drafting of the will to the lawyer.

Comparative advantage, then, provides one reason to specialize. It may be considered the first great propellant driving the wheels of commerce—while money acts as the grease, making the machine run with less friction. But there is also a second fundamental reason to specialize.

ECONOMIES OF SCALE: ANOTHER REASON TO SPECIALIZE

Consider two small cities which are identical in all respects. Suppose that the citizens of these cities want both bicycles and lawnmowers but that neither city has any advantage in the production of either good. Will each city then produce its own, without any trade existing between the two? Probably not. It is likely that one city will specialize in bicycles and the other in lawnmowers. Why?

The answer is ***economies of scale.*** To understand what this term means, first assume that there is no specialization. Each city directs half its productive resources into the manufacture of bicycles and half into the manufacture of lawnmowers, thus producing 1,000 bicycles and 1,000 lawnmowers. But if either city specializes by directing all its productive resources toward the manufacture of bicycles, it can acquire specialized machinery and produce 2,500 bicycles. Similarly, if the other city directs all its productive resources toward the manufacture of lawnmowers, it can produce 2,500. Note that each city, by doubling all inputs into the production of a single item, can more than double its output of that item from 1,000 to 2,500 units. Thus, economies of scale exist.

***Economies of scale* exist if an increase of *x*% in the quantity of every input causes the quantity of output to increase by more than *x*%. (For example, if all inputs are doubled, output more than doubles.)**

Even though neither city had any fundamental advantage in the production of either product, they can gain by specialization. Before specialization, their combined output was 2,000 bicycles and 2,000 lawnmowers. After specialization, they together make 2,500 bicycles and 2,500 lawnmowers.

While Ricardo's theory of comparative advantage dates back to the early nineteenth century, the explanation of economies of scale goes back even further, to Adam Smith's *Wealth of Nations* (1776). In Smith's first chapter, "Of the Division of Labour," there is a famous description of pin-making:

> A workman not educated to this business . . . could scarce, perhaps, . . . make one pin in a day, and certainly not twenty. But in the way in which this business is now carried on, not only the whole work is a peculiar trade, but it is divided into a number of branches. . . . One man draws out the wire, another straightens it, a third cuts it, a fourth points it, a fifth grinds it at the top for receiving the head. . . . Ten persons, therefore, could make among them upwards of forty-eight thousand pins in a day. Each person, therefore, . . . might be

considered as making four thousand and eight hundred pins in a day.[2]

What is the reason for the gain which comes from the division of pin-making into a number of separate steps? Certainly it is not that some individuals are particularly suited to drawing the wire, while others have a particular gift for straightening it. On the contrary, if two individuals are employed, it matters little which activity each is assigned. Adam Smith's "production line" is efficient because of economies of scale which depend on:

1. The introduction of specialized machinery
2. Specialization of the labor force on that machinery

Modern corporations also derive economies of scale from a third major source:

3. Specialized research and development, which make possible the development of new equipment and technology

In the modern world, economies of scale are very important as an explanation of specialization. They are a major reason why the manufacturers of automobiles and mainframe computers are few in number and large in size. It is partly because of economies of scale that the automobile industry is concentrated in the Detroit area, with Michigan shipping cars to other areas in exchange for a host of other products.

However, economies of scale explain much more than the trade among the regions, states, and cities *within* a country. They also are an important explanation of trade *between* countries. For example, economies of scale in the production of large passenger aircraft go on long after the U.S. market is met. Thus, there is a major advantage to Boeing in producing aircraft for the world market. There are gains to the aircraft buyers, too. For example, Norway can buy a Boeing 747 for a small fraction of the cost of manufacturing a comparable airplane.

In this chapter, the advantages of specialization and exchange have been studied. Exchange takes place in markets; how markets operate will be the subject of the next chapter.

KEY POINTS

1. Specialization contributes to efficiency.
2. Specialization requires exchange. The most primitive form of exchange is barter. This has the disadvantage that it depends on a coincidence of wants.
3. Much more complex exchange, with many participants, is feasible in an economy with money. Because exchange is so much easier and more efficient with money, money will evolve even in the absence of government action—as happened in the prisoner-of-war camp.
4. In the prisoner-of-war camp, some cigarettes were more desirable than others. The desirable cigarettes were smoked, leaving the less desirable cigarettes to circulate as money. This illustrated Gresham's law: "Bad money drives out good." In the modern U.S. economy, the Federal Reserve provides a *uniform* currency. Every dollar bill is worth the same as every other one; there is no "bad" money to drive "good" money out of circulation.
5. The Federal Reserve also has the responsibility to *control the quantity of money*. (How it does so will be explained in Chapter 13.)
6. There are two major reasons why there are gains from specialization and exchange: (*a*) comparative advantage and (*b*) economies of scale.
7. If two individuals (or regions or countries) have different opportunity costs of producing a good or service, the individual (or region or nation) with the lower opportunity cost has the *comparative advantage* in that good or service. An example is the lawyer who is better than the gardener at both the law and gardening. Even so, she does not do her gardening herself, because she gains by specializing in the law (her comparative advantage) and hiring the gardener to do the gardening (his comparative advantage).
8. Economies of scale exist if an increase of $x\%$ in the quantity of every input causes the quantity of output to increase by more than $x\%$.

[2]Adam Smith, *An Inquiry into the Nature and Causes of the Wealth of Nations* (Modern Library edition, New York: Random House, 1937), pp. 4–5.

KEY CONCEPTS

specialization
exchange
barter
coincidence of wants
indivisibility
general purchasing power
medium of exchange
Gresham's law
debasement of the currency
absolute advantage
comparative advantage
economies of scale

PROBLEMS

3-1. Most jobs are more specialized than they were 100 years ago. Why? What are the advantages of greater specialization? What are the disadvantages?

3-2. (*a*) Among the goods the United States exports are commercial aircraft, computers, and agricultural products such as soybeans and wheat. Why are these goods exported?

(*b*) Imports include automobiles, TV sets, oil, and agricultural products such as coffee and bananas. Why are these goods imported?

(*c*) The United States exports some agricultural products and imports others. Why? The United States exports many aircraft, but it also imports some. Why are we both exporters and importers of aircraft?

3-3. Suppose that one individual at your college is outstanding, being the best teacher and a superb administrator. If you were the college president, would you ask this individual to teach or to become the administrative vice-president? Why?

3-4. Draw a production possibilities curve (PPC) for the lawyer mentioned in Box 3-3, putting the number of wills drawn up in a week on one axis and flowers planted on the other. (Assume that the lawyer works 40 hours per week.) How does the shape of this PPC differ from that in Chapter 2?

***3-5.** Draw the production possibilities curve of one of the two identical cities described in the section on economies of scale. Which way does the curve bend? Does the opportunity cost of bicycles increase or decrease as more bicycles are produced?

---

*Problems marked with asterisks are more difficult than the others. They are designed to provide a challenge to students who want to do more advanced work.

CHAPTER 4

DEMAND AND SUPPLY:

THE MARKET MECHANISM

Do you know,
Considering the market, there are more
Poems produced than any other thing?
No wonder poets sometimes have to *seem*
So much more business-like than business men.
Their wares are so much harder to get rid of.

ROBERT FROST
New Hampshire

Although some countries are much richer than others, the resources of every country are limited. Choices must be made. Moreover, every economy involves some degree of specialization. In every economy, therefore, some mechanism is needed to answer the fundamental questions raised by specialization and by the need to make choices:

1. ***What*** goods and services will be produced? (How do we choose among the various options represented by the production possibilities curve?)
2. ***How*** will these goods and services be produced? For example, will cars be produced by relatively few workers using a great deal of machinery, or by many workers using relatively little capital equipment?
3. ***For whom*** will the goods and services be produced? Once goods are produced, who will consume them?

THE MARKET AND THE GOVERNMENT

There are two principal mechanisms by which these questions can be answered. First, answers can be provided by Adam Smith's ''invisible hand.'' If people are left alone to make their own transactions, the butcher and baker will provide the beef and bread for our dinner. In other words, answers may be provided by transactions among individuals and corporations in the ***market.***

In a *market,* an item is bought and sold. When transactions between buyers and sellers take place with little or no government interference, a *private* or *free* market exists.

The ***government*** provides the second method for determining what goods and services will be produced, how they will be produced, and for whom. The government affects the economy in four principal ways: by ***spending,*** by ***taxation,*** by ***regulation,*** and by ***public enterprises.***

1. *Spending.* When the government pays social security pensions to retirees, it influences *who* gets society's output; the recipient of a pension is able to buy more goods and services. When the government buys aircraft for the air force, those aircraft are produced; the government affects *what* is produced. When the government spends money for agricultural research, it influences *how* food will be produced.
2. *Taxes.* When the government collects taxes, it influences *who* gets society's output. A person who pays taxes has less left to buy goods and services. Taxes also affect *what* is produced. For example, a tax on gasoline encourages people to buy smaller cars. More small cars

are produced, and fewer large ones. Finally, the tax system may also influence *how* goods are produced. Incentives built into the tax law encourage businesses to use more machinery in producing goods. When they buy machinery, their taxes are reduced.

3. *Regulation*. Governmental regulations may also influence what, how, and for whom goods and services are produced. For example, the government prohibits production of some pesticides, and requires seat belts and other safety equipment in cars. It thereby affects *what* is produced. It requires producers of steel to limit their emissions of smoke into the atmosphere, thereby influencing *how* goods are produced. The government also regulates some prices—for example, the price of electricity. This keeps down the incomes of the electric companies' stockholders, executives, and workers. With less income, these people can buy less. Thus, the government influences *who* gets society's product.

4. *Public enterprises*. The government owns and operates some businesses, such as the Tennessee Valley Authority. It decides what these enterprises will produce and how they will produce it.

In addition to the market and the government, there are other institutions which help to answer the three basic questions: *What*? *How*? and *For whom*? For example, when a relief organization collects voluntary contributions of clothing or money for distribution to the poor or to the victims of a natural disaster, it is influencing *who* gets the output of society. Similarly, within the family, a mechanism other than the market or the government is used to determine how the budget for clothing, etc., is divided among the family members. Nevertheless, economists concentrate on the market and the government when they study the way in which society answers the three basic questions.

Conceivably, a nation might depend almost exclusively on private markets to make the three fundamental decisions. The government might be confined to a very limited role, providing defense, police, the courts, roads, and little else. At the other extreme, the goverment might try to decide almost everything, specifying what is to be produced and using a system of rationing and allocations to decide who gets the products. But the real world is one of compromise. In every actual economy, there is some *mixture* of markets and government decision-making.

However, reliance on the market varies substantially among countries. By international standards, the U.S. government plays a restricted role; most choices are made in the market. Particularly in the area of public enterprise, the U.S. government is a much smaller participant than the governments of other countries. This shows up clearly in Figure 4-1. In the United States, government enterprises undertake less than 5% of overall investment in structures and equipment. In most other countries, government enterprises undertake between 10% and 25% of such investment. In many foreign countries, the government owns the telephone system, the railroads, and the electric power plants. Some foreign governments also own factories that produce steel, automobiles, and other goods.

At the other end of the spectrum from the United States, the Soviet Union and other countries of Eastern Europe rely very heavily on government decision making. As ***Marxist*** nations, they reject the idea that the market should determine *for whom* goods will be produced. They do not permit individuals to own large amounts of capital. Individuals may of course own small capital goods, such as hoes or hammers, but the major forms of capital—factories and heavy machinery—are owned by the state. Therefore, individuals do not receive large dividend payments with which to buy a considerable fraction of the output of the economy. In contrast, most capital is privately owned in ***capitalist*** or ***free enterprise*** countries such as the United States.

In a Marxist nation, the government not only owns most of the capital, but it also is involved in detailed decisions as to which products will be produced with this capital. For example, the Soviet Union has a central planning agency which issues directives to the various sectors of the economy to produce specific quantities of goods. It would, however, be a mistake to conclude that government planning is a rigid and all-pervasive method of answering the three basic questions. Markets for goods exist in all Marxist countries, and some—particularly Hungary and Yugoslavia—allow many decisions to be made through the market. China is now engaged in a major experiment in which more reliance is being placed on the market.

A *capitalist* or *free enterprise economy* is one in which individuals are permitted to own large amounts of capital, and decisions are made primarily in markets, with relatively little government interference.

A *Marxist economy* is one in which the government owns most of the capital and makes many of the economic decisions. Political power is in the hands of a party pledging allegiance to the doctrines of Karl Marx.

Because the market is relatively important in the United States, it will be our initial concern. (Later chapters will deal with the economic role of the government in the United States and with the Marxist economic system.) This chapter explains how the market answers the three basic questions: What will be produced? How? For whom?

THE MARKET MECHANISM

In most markets, the buyer and the seller come face to face. When you buy a suit of clothes, you talk directly to the salesclerk; when you buy groceries, you physically enter the seller's place of business (the supermarket). However, physical proximity is not required to make a market. For example, in a typical stock market transac-

FIGURE 4-1

Investment in public enterprises, 1978–1981 (as a share of total fixed investment)

Public enterprises are much less important in the United States than in other countries. Although public enterprises undertake less than 5% of total investment in the United States, they undertake more than 10% in foreign countries—in some cases, much more. (For some countries in the figure, data do not cover the whole period but just 1 or 2 years within the period.)

Source: Robert H. Floyd, Clive S. Gray, and R. P. Short, *Public Enterprise in Mixed Economies* (Washington: International Monetary Fund, 1984), pp. 118–122.

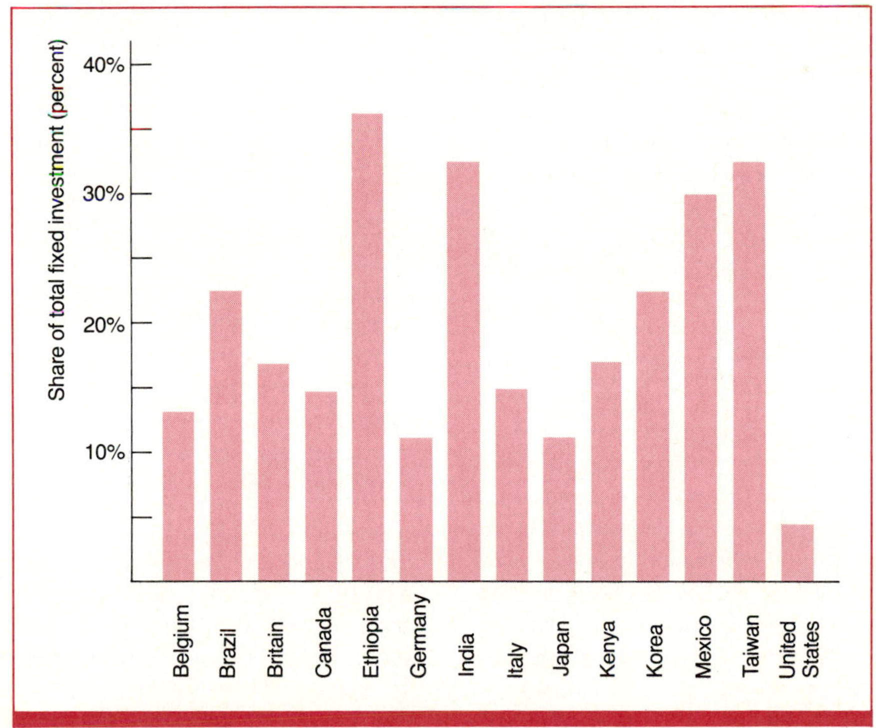

tion, someone in Georgia puts in a call to his broker to buy 100 shares of IBM common stock. About the same time, someone in Pennsylvania calls her broker to sell 100 shares. The transaction takes place on the floor of the New York Stock Exchange, where representatives of the two brokerage houses meet. The buyer and the seller of the stock do not leave their respective homes in Georgia and Pennsylvania.

Some markets are quite simple. For example, a barbershop is a "market" since haircuts are bought and sold there. The transaction is obvious and straightforward; the service of haircutting is produced on the spot. In other cases, markets are much more complex. Even the simplest everyday activity may be the culmination of a complicated series of market transactions.

As you sat at breakfast this morning drinking your cup of coffee, you were using products from distant areas. The coffee itself was probably produced in Brazil. The brew was made with water that perhaps had been delivered in pipes manufactured in Pennsylvania and purified with chemicals produced in Delaware. The sugar for the coffee may have been produced in Louisiana or the Carribean. Perhaps you used artificial cream made from soybeans grown in Missouri. Possibly, your coffee was poured into a cup made in New York State and stirred with a spoon manufactured in Taiwan from Japanese stainless steel which used Canadian nickel in its production. All this was for one cup of coffee.

In such a complex economy, something is needed to keep things straight, to bring order out of potential chaos. ***Prices*** bring order by performing two important, interrelated functions:

1. Prices provide ***information.***
2. Prices provide ***incentives.***

To illustrate, suppose we start from the example of chaos. Most of the coffee is in New York and most of the sugar in New Jersey. Coffee lovers in New Jersey would clamor for coffee, even at very high prices. The high price is a signal, providing *information* to coffee owners that there are eager buyers in New Jersey. It also provides them with an *incentive* to send coffee to New Jersey. In any market, the price provides the focus for interactions between buyers and sellers.

PERFECT AND IMPERFECT COMPETITION

Some markets are dominated by a few large firms; others have thousands of sellers. The "big three" automobile manufacturers (GM, Ford, and Chrysler) make most of the cars sold in the United States, with the rest provided by American Motors and a number of foreign firms. Such an industry, which is dominated by a few sellers, is an ***oligopoly.*** (The word *oligopoly* means "a few sellers," just as *oligarchy* means the "rule by a few.") Some markets are even more concentrated. For example, there is just one supplier of local telephone services to homes in your area; the telephone company has a ***monopoly.*** (However, there are a number of companies competing in the market for long-distance calls.) On the other hand, there are thousands of farmers producing wheat.

A *monopoly* exists when there is only *one seller.* An *oligopoly* exists when a *few sellers* dominate a market.

The number of participants in a market has a significant effect on the way in which the price is determined. In the wheat market, where there are thousands of buyers and thousands of sellers, no individual farmer produces more than a tiny fraction of the total supply. No single farmer can affect the price of wheat. For each one, the price is given; the individual farmer's decision is limited to the number of bushels of wheat to sell. Similarly, the millers realize that they are each buying only a small fraction of the wheat supplied. They realize that they cannot, as individuals, affect the price of wheat. Each miller's decision is limited to the number of bushels to be bought at the existing market price. In such a ***perfectly competitive*** market, *there is no pricing decision* for the individual seller and the individual buyer to make. Each buyer and seller is a ***price taker.***

***Perfect competition* exists when there are so many buyers and sellers that no single buyer or seller has any influence over the price. (Sometimes, this term is shortened simply to "competition.")**

In contrast, individual producers in an oligopolistic or a monopolistic market know that they have some control over price. For example, IBM sets the prices of its computers. That does not mean, of course, that it can set *any* price it wants and still be assured of making a profit. It can offer to sell at a high price, in which case it will sell only a few computers. Or it can charge a lower price, in which case it will sell more.

A *buyer* may also be large enough to influence price. General Motors is a large enough purchaser of steel to be able to bargain with the steel companies over the price of steel. When individual buyers or sellers can influence price, ***imperfect competition*** exists.

Imperfect competition **exists when any buyer or any seller is able to influence the price. Such a buyer or seller is said to have *market power.***

The term *competition* is used differently in economics and in business. Don't try to tell someone from Chrysler that the automobile market isn't competitive; Chrysler is very much aware of the competition from General Motors, Ford, and Japanese companies. Yet, according to the economist's definition, the automobile industry is far *less* competitive than the wheat industry.

An *industry* refers to all the producers of a good or service. For example, we may speak of the automobile industry, the wheat industry, or the accounting industry. Note that the term *industry* can refer to *any* good or service; it need not be manufactured.

A *firm* is a business organization that produces goods and/or services. A *plant* is an establishment at a single location used in the production of a good or service; for example: a factory, mine, farm, or store. Some firms, such as General Motors, have many plants. Others have only one; for example, the local independent drug store.

Because price is determined by impersonal forces in a perfectly competitive market, the competitive market is simplest and will therefore be considered first. The perfectly competitive market is also given priority because competitive markets generally operate more efficiently than imperfect markets, as we shall eventually show in Chapters 24 and 25.

THE PERFECTLY COMPETITIVE MARKET: DEMAND AND SUPPLY

We might as reasonably dispute whether it is the upper or the under blade of a pair of scissors that cuts a piece of paper, as whether the value is governed by utility [demand] or cost of production [supply.]

Alfred Marshall
Principles of Economics

In a perfectly competitive market, price is determined by ***demand*** and ***supply.***

Demand

Consider, as an example, the market for apples, in which there are many buyers and many sellers, with none having any control over the price. For the buyer, a high price acts as a deterrent. The higher the price, the fewer apples buyers purchase. Why is this so? As the price of apples rises, consumers switch to oranges or grapefruit or simply cut down on their total consumption of fruit. Similarly, the lower the price, the more apples are bought. A lower price brings new purchasers into the market, and each purchaser tends to buy more. The response of buyers to various possible prices is illustrated in the ***demand schedule*** in Table 4-1. This schedule is used to graph the ***demand curve*** in Figure 4-2. Points *A, B, C,* and *D* in Figure 4-2 represent the corresponding *A, B, C,* and *D* in Table 4-1.

A *demand schedule,* or *demand curve,* shows the quantities of a good or service that buyers would be willing and able to purchase at various market prices.

The demand schedule, or demand curve, applies to a *specific population* and to a *specific time period.* Clearly, the number of apples demanded during a month will exceed the number demanded during a week, and the number demanded by the people of Virginia will be less than the number demanded in the whole United

States. In a general discussion of theoretical issues, the population and time framework are not always stated explicitly, but it nevertheless should be understood that a demand curve applies to a specific time and population.

TABLE 4-1
The Demand Schedule for Apples

	(1) Price P (\$ per bushel)	(2) Quantity Q demanded (thousands of bushels per week)
A	\$10	50
B	8	100
C	6	200
D	4	400

FIGURE 4-2
The demand curve for apples
At each of the possible prices specified, there is a certain quantity of apples that people would be willing and able to buy. This information is provided in Table 4-1 and is reproduced in this diagram. On the vertical axis, the possible prices are shown. In each case, the quantity of apples that would be bought is measured along the horizontal axis. Since people are more willing to buy at a low price than at a high price, the demand curve slopes downward to the right.

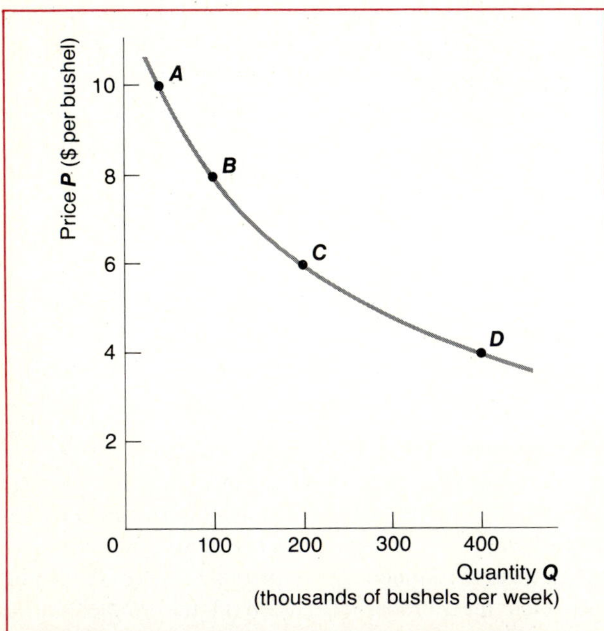

Supply

While the demand curve illustrates how buyers behave, the supply curve illustrates how sellers behave; it shows how much they would be willing to sell at various prices.

TABLE 4-2
The Supply Schedule for Apples

	(1) Price P (\$ per bushel)	(2) Quantity Q supplied (thousands of bushels per week)
F	\$10	260
G	8	240
H	6	200
J	4	150

FIGURE 4-3
The supply curve for apples
For each of the possible prices specified, the supply schedule (Table 4-2) indicates how many units the sellers would be willing to sell. This information is illustrated graphically in this figure, which shows how the supply curve slopes upward to the right. At a high price, suppliers will be encouraged to step up production and offer more apples for sale.

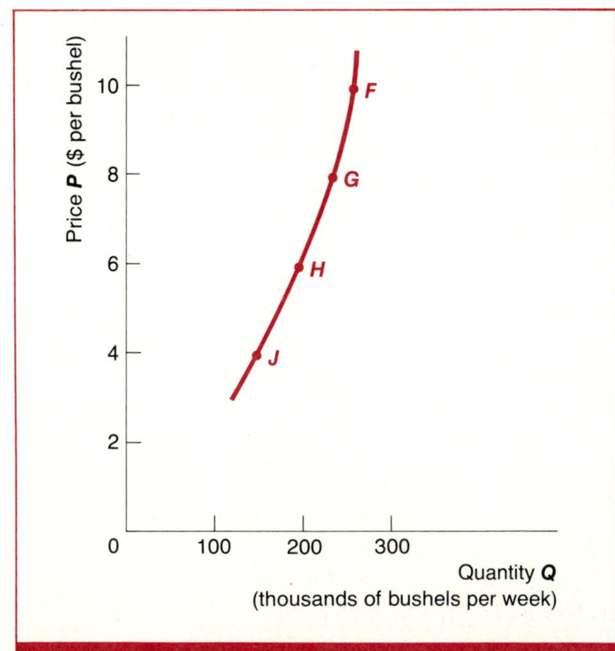

Needless to say, buyers and sellers look at high prices in a different light. Whereas a high price discourages buyers and causes them to switch to alternative products, a high price encourages suppliers to produce and sell more of the good. Thus, the higher the price, the higher the quantity supplied. This is shown in the ***supply schedule*** in Table 4-2 or, alternatively, in the ***supply curve*** in Figure 4-3. As in the case of the demand curve, the points on the supply curve (*F, G, H,* and *J*) are drawn from information given in the corresponding rows of Table 4-2.

A *supply schedule,* or *supply curve,* shows the quantities of a good or service that sellers would be willing and able to sell at various market prices.

The Equilibrium of Demand and Supply

The demand and supply curves may now be brought together in Figure 4-4. (See also Table 4-3.) To use the analogy of Alfred Marshall, this figure shows how the two blades of the scissors jointly determine price.

The ***market equilibrium*** occurs at point *E,* where the demand and supply curves intersect. At this equilibrium, the price is $6 per bushel and weekly sales are 200,000 bushels.

An *equilibrium* is a situation where there is no tendency to change.

To see why point *E* represents the equilibrium, consider what happens if the market price is initially at some

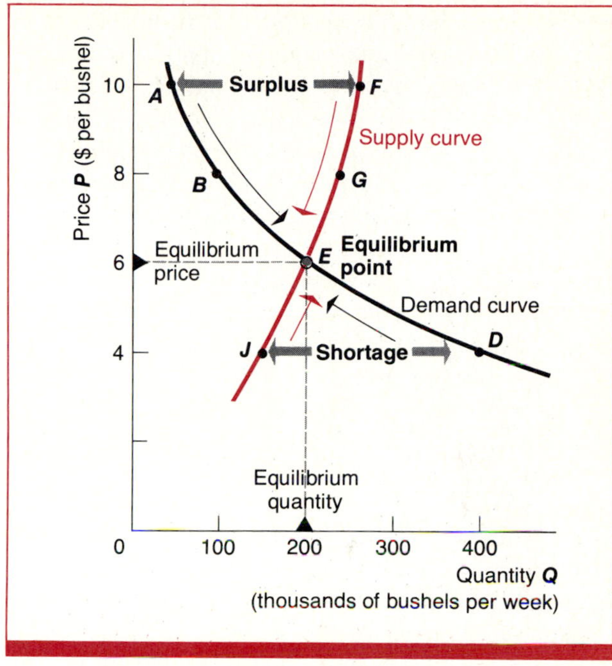

FIGURE 4-4
How demand and supply determine equilibrium price and quantity
Equilibrium exists at point *E,* where the quantity demanded equals the quantity supplied. At any higher price, the quantity supplied exceeds the quantity demanded. Because of the pressure of unsold stocks, competition among sellers causes the price to be bid down to the equilibrium of $6. Similarly, at a price less than the $6 equilibrium, forces are set in motion which raise the price. Because the quantity demanded exceeds the quantity supplied, eager buyers clamor for more apples and bid the price up to the equilibrium at $6.

TABLE 4-3
The Equilibrium of Demand and Supply

(1) Price *P* ($ per bushel)	(2) Quantity *Q* demanded (thousands of bushels per week)	(3) Quantity *Q* supplied (thousands of bushels per week)	(4) Surplus (+) or shortage (−) (4) = (3) − (2)	(5) Pressure on price
$10	50	260	Surplus +210	↓ Downward
8	100	240	Surplus +140	↓ Downward
6	**200**	**200**	**0**	**Equilibrium**
4	400	150	Shortage −250	↑ Upward

other level. Suppose, for example, that the initial price is \$10; that is, it is above the equilibrium price. What happens? Purchasers buy only 50,000 bushels (shown by point *A* in Figure 4-4), while sellers want to sell 260,000 bushels (point *F*). There is a large ***excess supply,*** or ***surplus,*** of 210,000 bushels. Some sellers are disappointed: They sell much less than they wish at the price of \$10. Unsold apples begin to pile up. In order to get them moving, sellers now begin to accept a lower price. The price starts to come down—to \$9, then \$8. Still there is a surplus, or an excess of the quantity supplied over the quantity demanded. (However, the surplus is now a smaller amount, *BG*). The price continues to fall. It does not stop falling until it reaches \$6, the equilibrium. At this price, buyers purchase 200,000 bushels, just the amount sellers want to sell. Both buyers and sellers are now satisfied with the quantity of their purchases or sales at the existing market price of \$6. Therefore, there is no further pressure on the price to change.

An *excess supply,* or *surplus,* exists when the quantity supplied exceeds the quantity demanded. (The price is above the equilibrium.)

Now consider what happens when the initial price is below the equilibrium, at, say, \$4. Eager buyers are willing to purchase 400,000 bushels (at point *D*), yet producers are willing to sell only 150,000 bushels (at point *J*). There is an ***excess demand,*** or ***shortage,*** of 250,000 bushels. As buyers clamor for the limited supplies, the price is bid upward. The price continues to rise until it reaches \$6, the equilibrium where there is no longer any shortage because the quantity demanded is equal to the quantity supplied. At point *E,* and only at point *E,* will the price be stable.

An *excess demand,* or *shortage,* exists when the quantity demanded exceeds the quantity supplied. (The price is below the equilibrium.)

SHIFTS IN THE DEMAND CURVE

The quantity of a product which buyers want to purchase depends on the price. As we have seen, the demand curve illustrates this relationship between price and quantity. But the quantity which people want to purchase also depends on other influences. For example, if incomes rise, people will want to buy more apples—and more of a whole host of other products, too.

The purpose of a demand curve is to show ***how the quantity demanded is affected by price, and by price alone.*** When we ask how much people want to buy at various prices, it is important that our answer not be disturbed by other influences. In other words, when we draw a demand curve for a good, we must *hold constant incomes and everything else that can affect the quantity demanded*—with the sole exception of the price of the good. We make the ***ceteris paribus*** assumption—that other things remain unchanged. (*Ceteris* is the same Latin word that appears in "*et cetera,*" which literally means "and other things." *Paribus* means "equal" or "unchanged.")

FIGURE 4-5

A change in the demand for apples

When incomes rise, there is an increase in the number of apples that people want to buy at any particular price. At a price of \$10, for example, the quantity of apples demanded increases from point A_1 to A_2. At other prices, the increase in incomes also causes an increase in the number of apples demanded. So the whole demand curve shifts to the right, from D_1 to D_2.

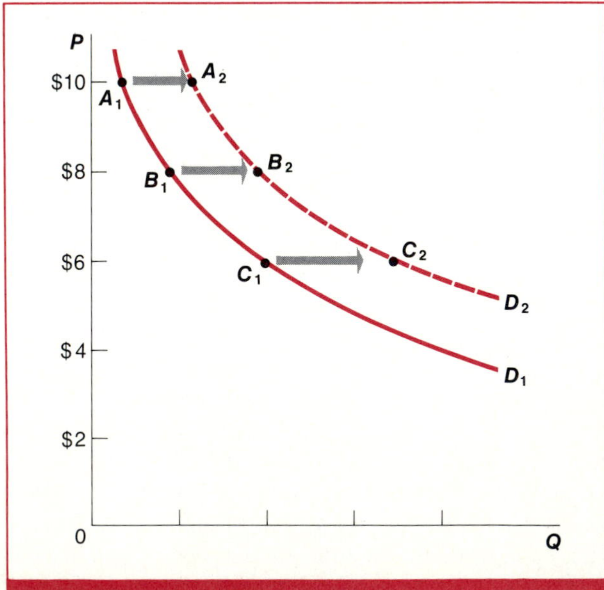

Of course, as time passes, other things do *not* remain constant. Through time, for example, incomes generally rise. When that happens, the quantity of apples demanded at any particular price increases. The whole demand curve shifts to the right, as illustrated in Figure 4-5. Since *economists use the term "demand" to mean the whole demand curve or demand schedule,* we may speak of this rightward shift in the curve more simply as an *increase in demand.*

Demand Shifters

A shift in the demand curve—that is, a change in demand—may be caused by a change in any one of a whole host of "other things." Some of the most important are:

1. *Income.* When incomes rise, people are able to buy more, and people do in fact buy more of the typical or ***normal good.*** For such a good, the number of units demanded at each price increases as incomes rise. Thus, the demand curve shifts to the right with rising incomes, as illustrated in Figure 4-5.

Not all goods are normal, however. As incomes rise, people may buy *less* of a good. For example, they may switch away from margarine and buy more butter, which they can afford now. If this happens—if the increase in income causes a leftward shift of the demand curve for margarine—the item is an ***inferior good.***

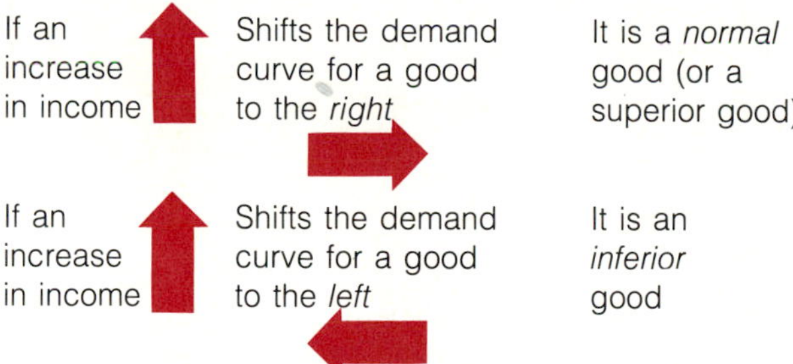

2. *Prices of related goods.* A rise in the price of one good can cause a shift in the demand curve for another good. For example, if the price of oranges were to double while the price of apples remained the same, buyers would be encouraged to buy apples instead of oranges. Thus, a rise in the price of oranges causes a rightward shift in the demand curve for apples. Goods such as apples and oranges—which satisfy similar needs or desires—are ***substitutes.*** Other examples are tea and coffee, butter and margarine, bus and train tickets, or heating oil and insulating materials.

For ***complements*** or ***complementary goods,*** exactly the opposite relationship holds. In contrast to substitutes—which are used *instead of* each other—complements are used *together,* as a package. For example, gasoline and automobiles are complementary goods. If the price of gasoline spirals upward, people become less eager to own automobiles. The demand curve for cars therefore shifts to the left. So it is with other complements, such as tennis rackets and tennis balls, or formal clothes and tickets to the senior prom.

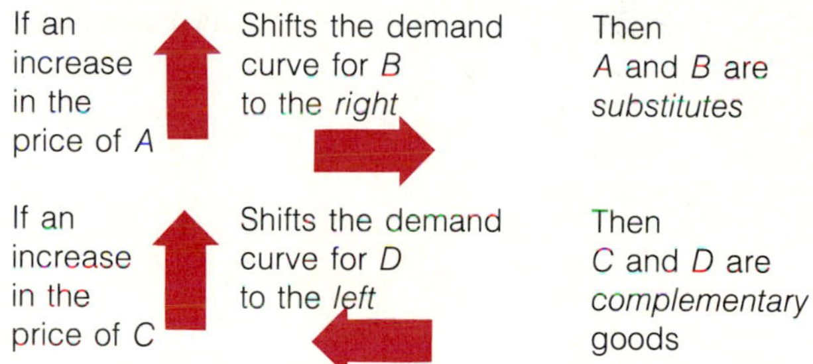

Finally, many goods are basically *unrelated,* in the sense that a rise in the price of one has no significant effect on the demand curve of the others. Thus, bus tickets and butter are unrelated, as are coffee and cameras.

3. *Tastes.* Tastes change over time. Because of increased interest in physical fitness, more people are jogging. This increases the demand for running shoes. Tastes are quite volatile for some products, particularly for fads like video games and Cabbage Patch dolls.

This list covers some of the most important demand shifters, but it is far from complete. To see how it might be extended, consider the following questions:

1. If the weather changes, how will the change affect the demand for skiing equipment? For snow tires?
2. If people expect cars to be priced $2,000 higher next year, what effect will this have on the demand for cars this year?
3. As more and more families get video cassette recorders, and thereby become able to skip through the

commercials with the fast scan button, how will this affect the demand by companies buying TV ads?[1] (A. C. Neilsen, a firm which rates TV shows as a service for advertisers, has found that, when people watch taped shows, half of them do in fact ''zap'' the commercials.)

WHAT IS PRODUCED: THE RESPONSE TO A CHANGE IN TASTES

At the beginning of this chapter, three basic questions were listed. To see how the market mechanism can help to answer the first of these questions—*What* will be produced?—consider what happens when there is a change in tastes. Suppose, for example, that people develop a desire to drink more tea and less coffee. This change in tastes is illustrated by a rightward shift in the demand curve for tea and a leftward shift in the demand curve for coffee.

As the demand for tea increases, the price is bid up by eager buyers. With a higher price, growers in Sri Lanka and elsewhere are encouraged to plant more tea. At the new equilibrium, shown as point E_2 in Figure 4-6, the price of tea is higher than it was originally (at E_1) and the consumers buy a larger quantity of tea. In the coffee market, the results are opposite. At the new equilibrium (F_2), the price is lower and a smaller quantity is bought.

Thus, competitive market forces cause producers to ''dance to the consumers' tune.'' In response to a change in consumer tastes, prices change. Tea producers are given an incentive to step up production, and coffee production is discouraged.

SHIFTS IN SUPPLY

While the market encourages producers to ''dance to the consumers' tune,'' the opposite is also true. As we shall

[1]Answer: It will reduce the demand. A New York advertising executive has estimated that this will result in a yearly loss of $200 million in ad revenues by 1987.

FIGURE 4-6
A change in tastes
A change in tastes causes the demand for tea to increase and the demand for coffee to decrease. As a result, more tea is bought at a higher price. Less coffee is bought, and the price of coffee falls.

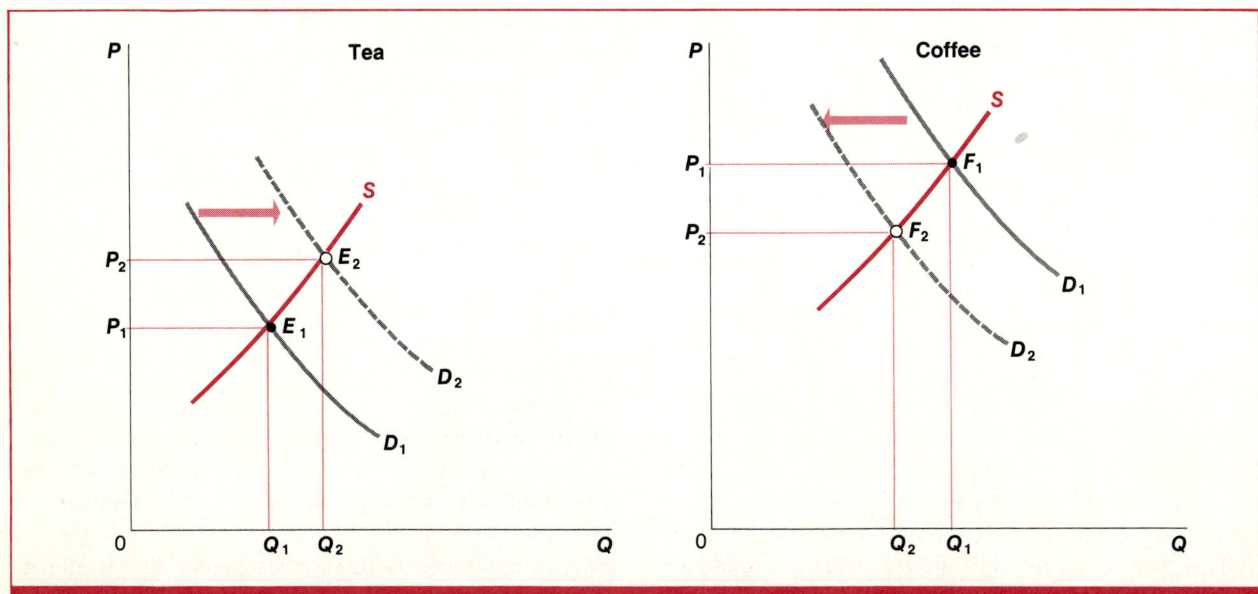

now show, consumers "dance to the producers' tune" as well. The market involves a complex interaction: Sellers respond to the desires of buyers, and buyers respond to the willingness of producers to sell.

Just as the demand curve reflects the desires of buyers, so too the supply curve illustrates the willingness of producers to sell. In an important respect, the two curves are similar. The objective of each is to show ***how the quantity is affected by the price of the good, and by this price alone.*** Thus, when we draw the supply curve, once again we make the *ceteris paribus* assumption. Everything (except the price of the good) that can affect the quantity supplied is held constant.

Supply Shifters

As in the case of demand, the "other things" that affect supply can change through time, causing the supply curve to shift. Some of these other things are:

1. *The cost of inputs*. For example, if the price of fertilizer goes up, farmers will be less willing to produce wheat at the previously prevailing price. The supply curve will shift to the left.

2. *Technology*. Suppose there is an improvement in technology that causes costs of production to fall. With lower costs, producers will be willing to supply more at any particular price. The supply curve will shift to the right.

(These first two points illustrate the dependence of the supply curve on the cost of production. The precise relationship between production costs and supply will be considered in detail in Chapters 22 and 23.)

3. *Weather*. This is particularly important for agricultural products. For example, a drought will cause a decrease in the supply of wheat (that is, a leftward shift in the supply curve), and a freeze in Florida will cause a decrease in the supply of oranges.

4. *The prices of related goods*. Just as items can be substitutes or complements in consumption, so too can they be substitutes or complements in production.

We saw earlier that substitutes in consumption are goods which can be consumed as *alternatives* to one another, satisfying the same wants (for example, apples and oranges). Similarly, ***substitutes in production*** are goods which can be produced as *alternatives* to one another using the same factors of production. Thus, corn and soybeans are substitutes in production: They can be grown on similar land. If the price of corn increases, farmers are encouraged to switch their lands out of the production of soybeans and into the production of corn. The amount of soybeans they are willing to supply at any given price decreases; the supply curve for soybeans shifts to the left.

We also saw earlier that complements in consumption are used *together* (for example, gasoline and automobiles). Similarly ***complements in production,*** or ***joint products,*** are produced together, as a package. Beef and hides provide an example. When more cattle are slaughtered for beef, more hides are produced in the process. An increase in the price of beef causes an increase in beef production, which in turn causes a rightward shift of the supply curve of hides.

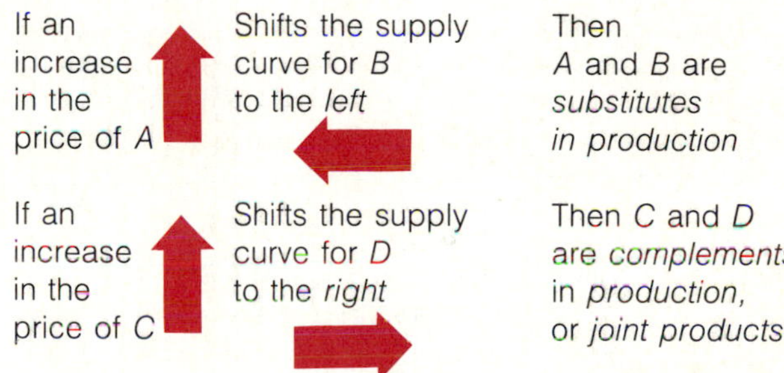

The Response to a Shift in the Supply Curve

To see how "consumers dance to the producers' tune," suppose that there is a frost in Brazil, which wipes out part of the coffee crop. As a result, the quantity of coffee available on the market is reduced; that is, the supply curve shifts to the left, as illustrated in Figure 4-7. With less coffee available, the price is bid upward. At the new equilibrium (G_2), the price is higher and the quantity sold is smaller.

How do consumers respond to the change in supply? Because of the higher price of coffee, consumers are discouraged from buying. Some consumers may feel indifferent about the choice between coffee and hot chocolate, and may switch to hot chocolate because it is now less expensive than coffee. Others may simply reduce their consumption of coffee, buying it only for very

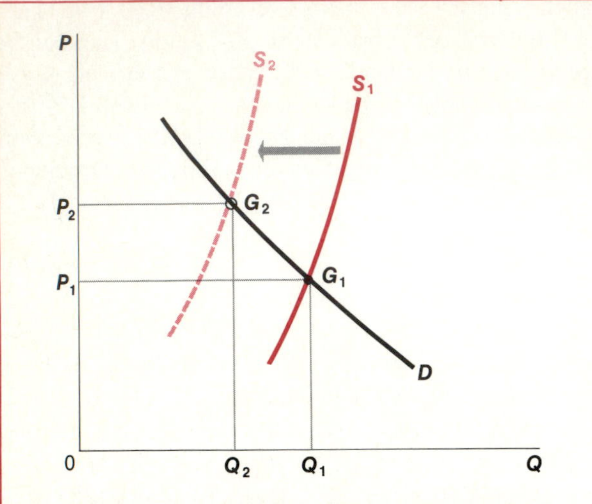

FIGURE 4-7
A shift in supply
A freeze in Brazil causes a leftward shift in the supply curve of coffee. The result is a movement of the equilibrium along the demand curve from G_1 to G_2. At the new equilibrium, there is a higher price and a smaller quantity is sold.

special occasions. Because of the limited quantity, it is not possible for all those who might like to drink coffee to get it. Anyone who is willing and able to pay the high price will get coffee; those who are unwilling or unable to pay the price will not get it. Thus, *the high price acts as a way of allocating the limited supply among buyers*. The coffee goes only to buyers who are sufficiently eager to be willing to pay the high price—and sufficiently affluent to be able to afford it.

SHIFTS IN A CURVE AND MOVEMENTS ALONG A CURVE

Because the term *supply* applies to a supply schedule or a supply curve, a change in supply means a *shift* in the entire curve. Such a shift took place in Figure 4-7 as a result of a freeze in Brazil.

In this figure, observe that the demand curve has not moved. However, as the supply curve shifts and the price consequently changes, there is a movement *along* the demand curve from G_1 to G_2. At the second point, less is bought than at the original point. The quantity of coffee demanded is less at G_2 than at G_1.

The distinction between *a shift in a curve* and a *movement along a curve* should be emphasized. What can we say about the move from G_1 to G_2?

1. It is correct to say that ''supply has decreased.'' Why? Because the entire supply curve has shifted to the left.
2. It is *not* correct to say that ''demand has decreased.'' Why? Because the demand curve has not moved.
3. It is, however, correct to say that ''the quantity demanded has decreased.'' Why? Because a smaller quantity is demanded at G_2 than at G_1.

A similar distinction should be made when the demand curve shifts. This is shown in Figure 4-8, based on

FIGURE 4-8
A shift in the demand for tea
This diagram, based on the left panel of Figure 4-6, shows that there is an increase in the quantity of tea supplied as the equilibrium moves from E_1 to E_2. However, supply does not change, since the supply curve does not move.

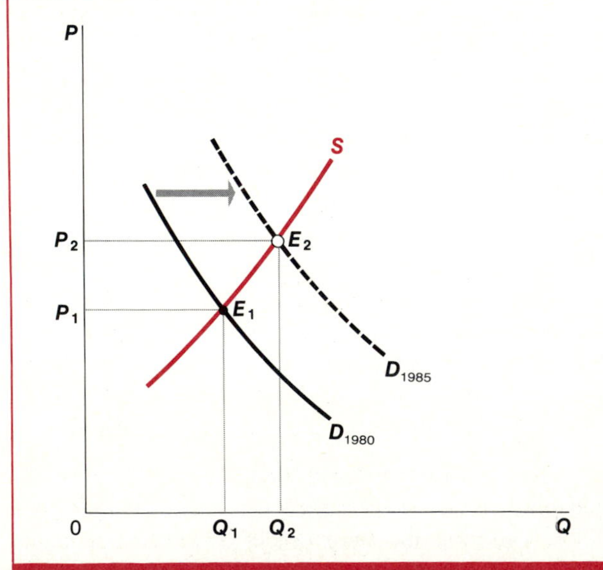

the left panel of Figure 4-6, where the demand for tea increases because of a change in tastes. The rightward movement of the demand curve causes the equilibrium to move *along* the *supply* curve, from E_1 to E_2. It is *not* correct to say that supply has increased, since the supply curve did not move. However, the *quantity supplied* did increase as the price rose. (Quantity Q_2 is greater than Q_1.)

The distinction between a *shift* in a curve and a movement *along* a curve is more than nit-picking. It is important for avoiding a classic error. History does not give us diagrams showing demand and supply curves, but it does give us quotations on prices and quantities. Suppose that, with a little research, we found that point E_1 in Figure 4-8 was observed in 1980 and point E_2 in 1985. If we are not careful, we might jump to the following *incorrect* conclusion:

The theory of the demand curve tells us that a rise in price should cause a decrease in the quantity demanded. Between 1980 and 1985, the price rose, but so did the quantity. Therefore, the facts contradict the theory of demand.

However, the facts do no such thing. The error in logic is this: Between 1980 and 1985, the demand curve *shifted*. As it shifted, equilibrium moved *along the supply curve*. Thus, the two points E_1 and E_2 trace out the supply curve, not the demand curve. Moreover, these two observations are exactly what we would expect as we move along a supply curve. When the price rises, so does the quantity.

(Unfortunately, the changes in equilibrium are seldom this simple. The reason is that, as time passes, both the demand and supply curves may shift. In this case, we do not know whether an increase in price will be accompanied by an increase or a decrease in the quantity sold.)

Finally, we reemphasize:

When supply shifts while demand remains stable, the points of equilibrium trace out the demand curve (Figure 4-7). When demand shifts while supply remains stable, the points of equilibrium trace out the supply curve (Figure 4-8).

THE INTERCONNECTED QUESTIONS OF WHAT, HOW, AND FOR WHOM

We have explored how two tunes are played. Demand is the tune played by consumers, and supply the tune played by producers. We have also seen how each group dances to the tune played by the other.

If we now want to go beyond the question of *what* will be produced to the other questions—*How*? *For whom*?—we must recognize that the world is even more complex. We don't merely have two tunes being played. We have a whole orchestra, with the tune played on any one instrument related to the tunes played on all the others.

The major segments of the economy are illustrated in Figure 4-9, which adds detail to Figure 3-3. The ***product markets*** for apples, coffee, bread, housing, etc., are represented by the upper box; we have concentrated on product markets thus far. The box at the bottom indicates that there are similar ***markets for factors of production,*** with their own demands and supplies. For example, to produce wheat, farmers need land—they create a demand for land. At the same time, those with land are willing to sell or rent it if the price is attractive—they create a supply of land.

In answering the question, *What* will be produced? we begin by looking at the top box, where the demand and supply for products come together. If there is a large demand for bread, we may expect a lot of it to be produced. But eventually we will also have to look at the lower box, where the demand and supply for the factors of production come together. Why are the factor markets relevant? Because the demand and supply in the upper box are influenced by what happens in the factor markets in the lower box.

As an example, consider what happened when oil was discovered in Alaska several decades ago. To build the pipeline needed to get the oil out, workers had to be hired. As a consequence, the demand for construction labor in Alaska increased sharply. The price of labor (that is, the wage rate) in Alaska shot up, and construction workers flocked in from the lower 48 states. The spiraling wage payments in Alaska (lower box) had repercussions on the demands for goods and services in Alaska (upper box). For example, the demand for Alaskan housing in the upper box increased as a result of the higher earnings of construction workers in the lower box.

How? and For Whom?

To answer the question "*What* will be produced?" we began by looking at the product markets in the upper box of Figure 4-9. To answer the questions *How*? and *For Whom*? we begin by looking at the lower box.

The factor prices established in the lower box help to determine *how* goods are produced. During the Black Death of 1348–1350 and subsequent plagues, an estimated quarter to a third of the Western European population died. As a consequence, labor supply was substan-

FIGURE 4-9

Markets answer the basic questions of what, how, and for whom

The product markets (top box) are most important in determining *what* is produced and the factor markets (lower box) in determining *how* goods are produced and *for whom*. However, there are many interrelationships among the two boxes. For example, incomes change in response to changing demand and supply conditions in the lower box, and these changing incomes in turn influence the demand for products in the upper box.

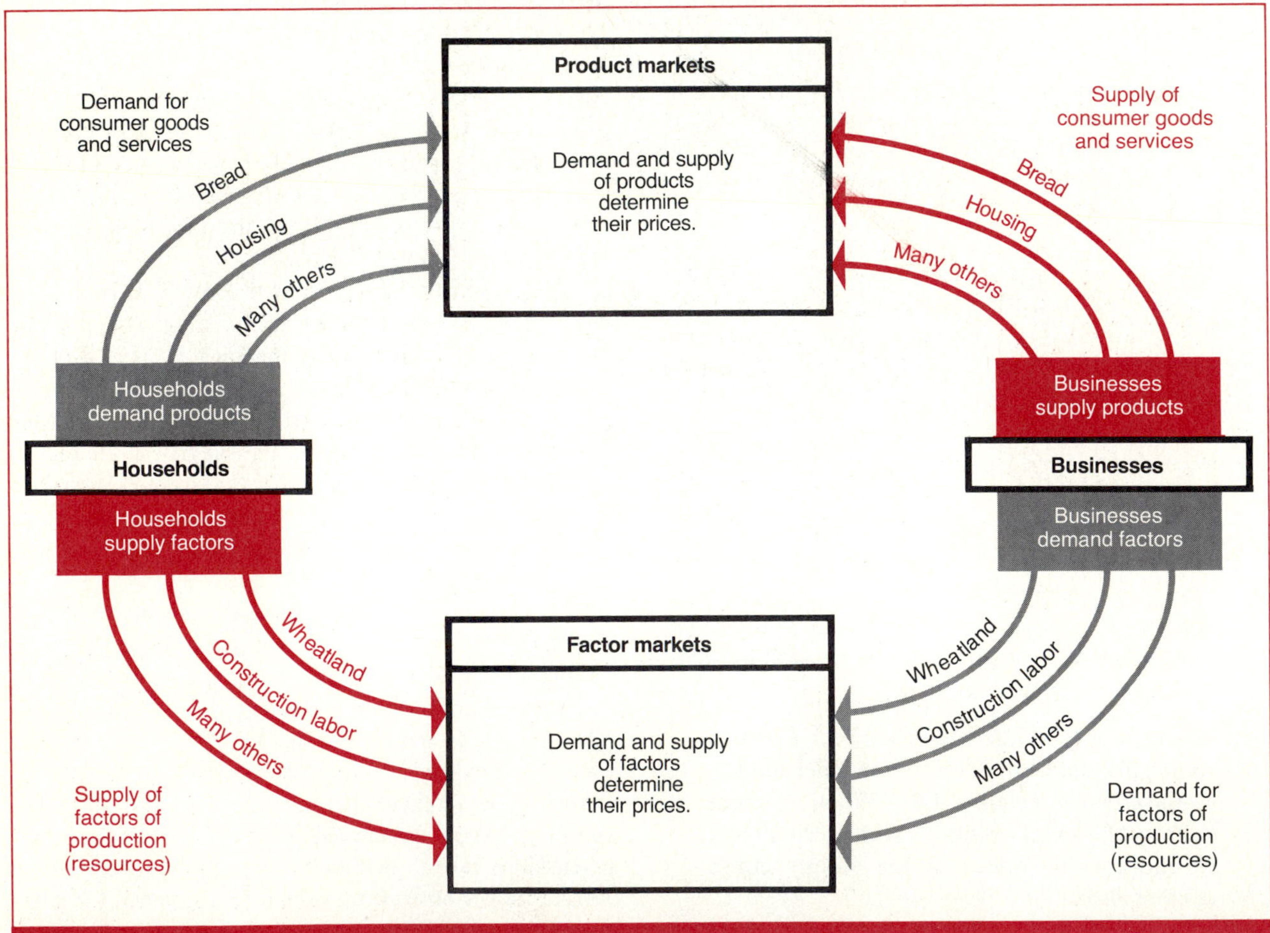

tially reduced and wages rose sharply, by 30% to 40%. Because of the scarcity of labor and its high price, wheat producers had an incentive to farm their lands with less labor. Wheat was produced with a different combination of labor and land. In those days, as today, the market mechanism was the way in which the society conserved its scarce supply of a factor (in this case, labor).

The answer to the question "*For whom* is the nation's output produced?" depends on incomes, which are determined by the interplay of supply and demand in factor markets (lower box in Figure 4-9). For example, the supply of doctors is small compared with the demand for doctors. The price of medical "labor" is therefore high; doctors generally have high incomes. On the other hand, unskilled labor is in large supply and is therefore cheap. Consequently, the unskilled worker receives a low income. (For further detail on the demand and supply for labor, see Appendix 4-A.)

Once again, we cannot look at only one box; we cannot look simply at the factor markets in the lower box. There are influences from the product markets (upper box) that must also be taken into account. For example, reconsider the Alaskan pipeline workers. The increase in demand for labor (in the lower box) drove their wage rate upward. However, that didn't mean that these workers lived like kings. Even though they had very high incomes, the Alaskan economy did not provide them with luxurious accommodations. Because of the tight supply conditions in the Alaskan housing market (upper box), rents for houses and hotel rooms soared. The incomes of construction workers went into paying these higher rents; their housing was not luxurious. At least in terms of living quarters, these workers did not get a much larger share of the nation's output after all.

THE MARKET MECHANISM: A PRELIMINARY EVALUATION

Some see private enterprise as a predatory target to be shot, others as a cow to be milked; but few are those who see it as a sturdy horse pulling the wagon.

Winston Churchill

There are thousands of markets in the United States and millions of interconnections among the markets. Changes in market conditions are reflected in changes in prices. As we have seen, prices provide information to market participants, they provide them with incentives to respond to changing conditions, and they bring order out of a potentially chaotic situation—even though there is no individual or government bureaucracy in control.

Strengths of the Market

In some ways, the market works very well. Specifically:

1. The market *gives producers an incentive to produce the goods that consumers want.* If people want more tea, the price of tea is bid up and producers are encouraged to produce more.

2. The market *provides an incentive to acquire useful skills.* For example, the high fees that doctors charge give students an incentive to undertake the long, difficult, and expensive training necessary to become a physician.

3. The market *encourages consumers to use scarce goods carefully.* For example, when the coffee crop is partially destroyed by bad weather, the price is driven up and people use coffee sparingly. Those who are relatively indifferent are encouraged to switch to tea. Even those who feel they must have coffee are motivated to conserve. With a high price of coffee, they are careful not to brew three cups when they intend to use only two.

4. Similarly, the price system *encourages producers to conserve scarce resources.* In the pasturelands of Texas, land is plentiful and cheap; it is used to raise cattle. In contrast, land is relatively scarce and expensive just outside New York or Tokyo. Because of its high price, it is used more intensively, for market gardening rather than livestock.

5. The market involves a *high degree of economic freedom.* Nobody forces people to do business with specific individuals or firms. People are not directed into specific lines of work by government officials; they are free to choose their own occupations. Moreover, if people save, they are free to use their savings to set themselves up in their own independent businesses.

6. Markets provide *information on local conditions.* For example, if an unusual amount of hay-producing land in a specific county is plowed up to grow corn, the price of hay in that county will tend to rise. The higher price of hay will signal farmers that they should put some of the land in this county back into hay. No government agency can hope to keep up-to-date and detailed information on the millions of localized markets like this one, each with its own conditions. (Note the amount of information that is relevant, even for this simple decision on whether hay or corn should be planted: the quality of the land, particularly its relative productivity in hay and corn; the number of cattle and horses that eat hay; the cost of fertilizer for hay and for corn; the cost of seed for each; and so on and on.)

In evaluating how well a market works, we should keep in mind the most important question of all: *compared to what*? Even a poor market may work better than the alternatives. Thus, one of the strongest arguments for the market parallels Winston Churchill's case for democracy: It doesn't work very well, but it does work better than the alternatives that have been tried from time to time.

The alternative of price controls: some problems Consider, for example, some of the problems which can arise if the government interferes with the market mechanism by fixing prices. Suppose, once again, that the coffee crop is partially destroyed by bad weather. If government controls prevent the price from rising, a shortage develops. Those who get to the store first are able to buy coffee at the low price. Because they have gotten the coffee cheaply, they may use it carelessly, brewing a large pot when they will only drink a few cups. Those who get to the store later find that coffee has been sold out; they have to do without completely.

Where government price controls result in shortages, people have an incentive to get to the store first, before their neighbors. In order to get scarce goods, they waste time standing in line. To use the quip applied to Britain in the early days after World War II, the society becomes a "queuetopia." The heavily regulated economies of Eastern Europe have had chronic shortages; buyers often have to line up to get scarce goods.

Moreover, as a result of price controls, goods may disappear from regular distribution channels and flow instead into illegal ***black markets.*** In this case, the scarce goods go to those willing to break the law.

A *black market* is one in which sales take place at a price above the legal maximum.

Price controls can create other problems. For example, in its desire to prevent labor unrest, the Polish government kept bread fixed at a low price—so low that it was less than the price of wheat which went into making the bread. Farmers found that it was cheaper to feed their livestock bread rather than grain. This represented a waste of the resources that had been used to make wheat into bread. Such a problem does not occur in a market economy: Nobody will produce bread from wheat if the bread sells for a lower price. (Problems also arise when the government controls rents. See Box 4-1.)

The Market Mechanism: Limitations and Problems

While the market has impressive strengths, it is also the target of substantial criticisms:

1. While the market provides a high degree of freedom for participants in the economy, *it may give the weak and the helpless little more than the freedom to starve*. In a market, producers do not respond solely to the needs or the eagerness of consumers to have products. Rather, they respond to the desires of consumers which are backed up with cash. Thus, under a system of *laissez faire,* the pets of the rich may have better meals and better health care than the children of the poor.

2. An unregulated system of private enterprise *may be quite unstable,* with periods of inflationary boom giving way to sharp recessions. Economic instability was a particularly severe problem in the early 1930s, when the economies of many countries collapsed into a deep depression.

3. In a system of laissez faire, *prices are not always the result of impersonal market forces*. As noted earlier, it is only in a perfectly competitive market that price is determined by the intersection of a demand and a supply curve. In many markets, one or more participants have the power to influence price. *The monopolist or oligopolist may restrict production* in order to keep the price high. (See Appendix 4-B.)

4. Activities by private consumers or producers may have undesirable *side effects*. Nobody owns the air or the rivers. Consequently, in the absence of government restraints, manufacturers use them freely as garbage dumps, harming those downwind or downstream. The market provides no incentive to limit such negative side effects.

5. Markets *simply won't work* in some areas. Where there is a military threat, individuals cannot provide their own defense. An individual who buys a rifle has no hope of standing against a foreign power. Organized military forces, financed by the government, are needed. The police and the judicial system are other services that can best be provided by the government. No matter how well the market works in general, people can't be permitted to "buy" a judge.

6. In a system of laissez faire, businesses may do an excellent job of satisfying consumer wants as expressed in the marketplace. But should the businesses be given high marks, if they have *created the wants in the first place by advertising*? In the words of retired Harvard Prof. John Kenneth Galbraith, "It involves an exercise of imagination to suppose that the taste so expressed originates with the consumer."[2] In this case, the producer is sovereign, not the consumer. According to Galbraith, the consumer is a puppet, manipulated by producers with the aid of Madison Avenue's bag of advertising tricks. Many of the wants which producers create and then satisfy are trivial: for example, the demands for automobile chrome and junk food.

(Without arguing the merits of each and every product, defenders of the market system make a countercase, based in part on the question: Compared with what? If market demands are dismissed, who then is to decide which products are "meritorious" and which are not? Government officials? Should not people be permitted the freedom to make their own mistakes? And why should we assume that created wants are without merit? After all, we are not born with a taste for art or good music. Our taste for good music is created when we listen to it. Galbraith certainly wouldn't suggest that symphony orchestras are without merit simply because they statisfy the desire for good music which they have created. But who then is to decide which "created" wants are socially desirable?)

If these criticisms of the market are taken far enough, they can be made into a case for replacing the market with an alternative system. Marxist economists lay particular emphasis on points 1 and 2 in their argument that the market should be replaced with central planning and government direction of the economy.

However, these criticisms are also often made by those who seek to reform, rather than replace, the market system. The recent economic history of Western Europe, North America, and many other parts of the globe has to a significant extent been written by such reformers. If the market does not provide a living for the weak and the helpless, its outcome should be modified by private and public assistance programs. If monopolists have excessive market power, they should be broken up or their market power should be restrained by the government. Where there are undesirable side effects, such as pollution, they should be limited by taxation or control programs. In defense, justice, the police, and other areas where the market won't work or works very poorly, the government should assume responsibility for the provision of services.

Although the market is a vital mechanism, it has sufficient weaknesses to provide the government with a major economic role. This role will be the subject of the next chapter.

[2]John Kenneth Galbraith, "Economics as a System of Belief," *American Economic Review,* May 1970, p. 474. See also Galbraith, *The New Industrial State* (Boston: Houghton Mifflin, 1967).

BOX 4-1

RENT CONTROL

Next to bombing, rent control seems in many cases to be the most efficient technique so far known for destroying cities, as the housing situation in New York City demonstrates.

ASSAR LINDBECK

New York City has had rent controls in one form or another since 1943, when they were introduced throughout the United States to protect industrial workers and the families of those serving overseas in the armed forces. (After the war, rent controls were abolished elsewhere in the nation.) Even if one wished to quibble with Lindbeck's devastating conclusion, the results cannot be considered encouraging.

The early effects of the imposition of rent controls are illustrated in the left panel of Figure 4-10. The maximum price which can legally be charged is set at P_1, below the free-market price of P_E. Consequently, the quantity of housing demanded exceeds the quantity supplied; there is a shortage of *AB* units. As a result, it is difficult to find an apartment. When a renter moves out, there is a scramble to get the vacant apartment, and "knowing the right person" becomes a valuable asset. This basic effect of rent control—that it becomes hard to find an apartment—is important.

However, even greater problems arise as time passes. Rent controls reduce the construction of new apartment buildings because they reduce the rental income which owners can hope to receive. Furthermore, if rent ceilings are fixed at low levels, owners may let their buildings go without proper maintenance and repair. When the buildings eventually deteriorate to the point where they cannot be rented, owners abandon them (Lindbeck's bombing effect).

This longer-run effect is shown in the right panel of Figure 4-10, where the demand curve and the short-run supply, S_S, are copied from the left panel. During the first year of rent control, the quantity of apartments supplied is reduced to *A*, on the short-run supply curve, S_S. With the rent ceiling continuing at P_1, the effects become more serious as time passes. Because few new buildings are constructed and owners skimp on maintenance and abandon their older buildings, the quantity of apartments declines. After a few years, the number of apartments falls to *F*, and then to *G*. Finally it approaches point *H* on the long-run supply curve. (The long-run supply curve, S_L, shows the ultimate effect, after apartment owners have adjusted completely to a new price.)

This illustrates the difficulties which can be created if rent controls are maintained over a long period. Over the short term, most tenants benefit from the controls. Observe that tenants pay a lower price, and they get almost the same amount of housing at *A* as at the free-market equilibrium *E*. (Nothing much happens to the quantity of apartments supplied in the first year of rent control.) Over the long run, however, it is very doubtful that renters benefit on average. While they still pay a lower price, they have less housing at *H* than at *E*. It is very hard for newcomers to find a place to live. (Desperate apartment-hunters have been known to watch the obituary columns, calling perfect strangers in the event of a death in the family to find if an apartment is becoming vacant.) Furthermore, something happens that does not show up on the diagram: The housing that still can be rented at point *H* may be shabby and run-down.

Another major effect of rent control is that owners are clearly worse off because their rental income has fallen. Since both sides lose, a substantial case can be made against long-term rent control.

The problems are, of course, reasonably obvious and were recognized in New York City. Several steps were taken to alleviate the situation. First, in order to provide an incentive for new construction, rent control was applied only to existing apartments, and not to newly constructed ones. (However, controls were subsequently extended to the new apartments, adversely affecting the rental income of owners. Because of this experience, it is now difficult to find any builder—in New York or elsewhere—who will believe the government when it promises that new buildings will be free from rent control.) Second, in order to give owners enough income to maintain existing apartment buildings, provisions were made to raise rents over time. Apartment dwellers are a politically powerful group, however, so a number of rather interesting formulae were devised to protect current tenants. Although the details of these formulae have varied from time to time, they contain one common element. The biggest upward adjustment in rent is permitted when an apartment becomes vacant.

This provision in turn creates another complication. The rent on a specific apartment depends less on its quality than on how recently it has changed occupants. Consequently, it has become more and more difficult to defend rent control as "fair." Furthermore, owners have an incentive to make life miserable for tenants, since the largest rent increases occur when they move out. Market incentives work. When the government provides a reward for making tenants miserable, then owners will make tenants miserable. It is not clear that the provision for rent increases actually contributes to its objective of better maintenance.

The New York experience conveys a strong message. A sensible long-run program of rent control is *very* difficult to design. It is easier to identify the problems than the solutions. There is an ominous long-term lesson for other parts of the country—such as Boston and a number of California cities—which have reintroduced rent controls during the past 15 years. Once introduced, rent controls are painful to remove. Just as the major gains to tenants come in the first few years of rent control, so the major penalties to tenants come in the first few years of decontrol. Rents may shoot upward, and there is little short-term increase in the number of apartments for rent. Any politician considering decontrol may have to face a group of enraged tenant voters.

A number of students of the housing market have suggested that the federal government prohibit rent controls, because they are so tempting for local politicians but have such strong negative long-run effects on the supply of housing.[†]

[†]For example, Anthony Downs, *Rental Housing in the 1980s* (Washington: Brookings, 1983), p. 9. Downs, a scholar at the Brookings Institution (a Washington think-tank), would couple a prohibition on rent controls with federal housing allowances for the poor.

FIGURE 4-10
Rent control

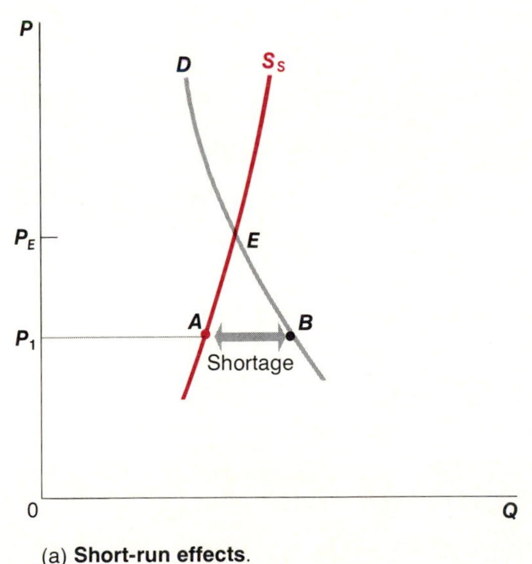

(a) **Short-run effects.**

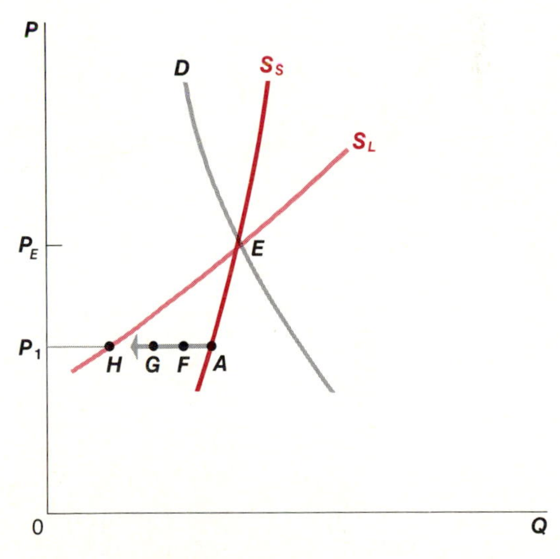

(b) **Long-run effects.**

KEY POINTS

1. Every economy has limited resources and involves specialization and exchange. In every economy, a mechanism is needed to answer three fundamental questions:

(*a*) *What* will be produced?

(*b*) *How* will it be produced?

(*c*) *For whom* will it be produced?

2. There are two principal mechanisms for answering these questions:

(*a*) The market, where individuals are free to make their own contracts and transactions.

(*b*) The government, which can use taxation, spending, regulation, and government-owned enterprises to influence *what, how,* and *for whom*.

In the real world, all countries rely on a *mixture* of markets and government actions. However, the mixture differs among countries. The United States places a relatively heavy reliance on the market. In the U.S.S.R. and other countries of Eastern Europe, the government has much more pervasive influence.

3. *Prices* play a key role in markets, providing information and incentives to buyers and sellers.

4. Markets vary substantially, with some being dominated by one or a few producers, while others have many producers and consumers. A market is *perfectly competitive* if there are many buyers and many sellers, with no single buyer or seller having any influence over the price.

5. In a perfectly competitive market, equilibrium price and quantity are established by the intersection of the demand and supply curves.

6. In drawing both the demand and supply curves, the *ceteris paribus* assumption is made—that "other things" do not change. Everything that can affect the quantity demanded or supplied—with the sole exception of price—is held constant when a demand or supply curve is constructed.

7. If any of these "other things"—such as consumer incomes or the prices of other goods—do change, the demand or supply curve will shift.

8. *What* the economy produces is determined primarily in the market for goods and services in the upper box of Figure 4-9. On the other hand, *how* and *for whom* are determined primarily in the factor markets (the lower box). However, there are numerous interactions among markets. The answer to each of the three questions depends on what happens in both the upper and lower boxes.

9. There is a substantial case to be made for the market system because it encourages firms to produce what people demand, and because it encourages the careful use of scarce goods and resources. Nevertheless, the market also has significant weaknesses, which provide the government with an important economic role.

KEY CONCEPTS

market
central planning
capitalist economy
free enterprise
mixed economy
monopoly
oligopoly
perfect competition
imperfect competition
market power
industry
firm
plant
demand
supply
equilibrium
surplus
shortage
ceteris paribus
demand shifter
inferior good
normal or superior good
substitutes
complementary goods
supply shifter
joint products
price control
black market

PROBLEMS

4-1. Figure 4-7 shows the effect of a Brazilian freeze on the coffee market. How might the resulting change in the price of coffee affect the tea market? Explain with a diagram showing the demand and supply for tea.

4-2. The relatively high incomes of doctors give students an incentive to study medicine. Other than the expected income and costs of training, what are the important things which affect career decisions?

4-3. It is often said that "the market has no ethics. It is impersonal." But individual participants in the market do have ethical values, and these values may be backed up with social pressures. Suppose that in a certain society it is considered not quite proper to be associated with a distillery. With the help of demand and supply diagrams, explain how this view will affect (*a*) the demand and/or supply of labor in the alcohol industry; (*b*) the willingness of people to invest their funds in the alcohol industry and the profitability of that industry.

4-4. Suppose that social sanctions are backed up by law, and that people caught selling marijuana are given stiff jail sentences. How will this affect the demand and supply of marijuana? The price of marijuana? The quantity sold? The incomes of those selling marijuana?

4-5. In Box 4-1, rent control is discussed. Extend the analysis by describing (*a*) the effects of rent control on the city's tax revenues; (*b*) what will happen if rent control is imposed for 20 years and then abruptly removed.

4-6. In 1984, several New York landlords were indicted for consipiracy, coercion, and extortion. Among other things, they were charged with encouraging thieves to move into their apartment buildings, and with having garbage dumped in the hallways.

(*a*) What conceivable motive could the landlords have for dumping garbage in their own buildings?

(*b*) What changes in law or in policy would you recommend to deal with this problem? How would your suggestion help? Are there any disadvantages to your recommendation? If you have no recommendation, describe possible policy changes and explain the advantages and disadvantages of each.

***4-7.** (This problem requires Box 4-1 as background.) "Rent control which applies only to structures in existence when the rent control law is passed will not affect new construction." Do you agree or not? Explain.

***4-8.** In distinguishing between substitutes and complements, the text listed a number of simple cases. Tea and coffee are substitutes, while cars and gasoline are complements.

However, it is worth looking more closely at one example that may not seem quite so simple: heating oil and insulation. How would you correct or rebut the following ***erroneous*** argument:

Heating oil and insulation are complements, not substitutes, because they are used together. In Alaska, they use a lot of heating oil and a lot of insulation. In California, they don't use much of either.

Try to answer this question without looking at the following hints. But consider them if you have difficulty.

(*a*) Think about the market for heating oil and insulation in a single city, say, St. Louis. When the price of heating oil goes up in St. Louis, do you think that this causes the demand curve for insulation to shift to the right or to the left? Does this make insulation a complement or substitute for heating oil, according to the definitions in the text?

(*b*) Are natural gas and oil substitutes or complements? Suppose the incorrect statement in quotation marks had mentioned heating oil and natural gas rather than heating oil and insulation.

(*c*) If we accept the erroneous quotation above, can't we argue in a similar manner that there are no such things as substitutes? For example, wouldn't we also accept the following incorrect conclusion: "In California, more apples and more oranges are sold than in Alaska. Therefore, apples and oranges are used together. They are complements, not substitutes." Do you see that this statement is incorrect because it departs from the standard assumption that "other things remain unchanged"? In identifying complements and substitutes, we must not switch from one location and population (Alaska) to another (California); we must look at a single set of people (those in St. Louis in the example above). Do you see why economists emphasize the assumption that "other things remain unchanged" (*ceteris paribus*)?

*Problems marked with asterisks are more difficult than the others. They are designed to provide a challenge for students who want to do more advanced work.

APPENDIX 4-A

THE DEMAND AND SUPPLY FOR LABOR:

THE MALTHUSIAN PROBLEM

If we wish to explain *specific* wage rates—for example, the high wage of construction workers in Alaska—we must look at that *specific* labor market. However, we may also be interested in the average wage earned by all labor in an economy. In that case, we must look at the market for all workers.

When we do so, we follow the normal practice and assume that "other things are unchanged." Specifically, we assume that the average price of goods and services remains unchanged. Thus, a change in the wage represents a change in the *real* wage, that is, a change in the quantity of goods and services that the wage will buy. When we show an increase in the wage, the increase permits the worker to buy more goods and services. It is not simply used up paying higher prices.

The aggregate labor market is quite different from a specific market (such as the market for construction workers). First, consider the supply. The supply curve for construction workers in Alaska slopes upward to the right: The higher the wage, the more workers are attracted from other industries and other states. In contrast, the supply of labor for the United States as a whole is approximately vertical, as shown in Figure 4-11. Even if the U.S. wage rate were to double, there would be little increase in the number of workers offering themselves for employment. The reason is that there are no "other industries" or "other states" from which workers can be attracted (although more workers might come in from other countries).

On the other hand, the demand curve for all U.S. labor does have the same general shape as the demand for labor in a specific industry; that is, it slopes downward to the right. The higher the wage rate, the fewer the jobs offered. At a high wage rate, businesses have an incentive to produce with less labor and more of other inputs, such as machinery. Furthermore, with the prices of goods remaining stable—in line with the *ceteris paribus* assumption—an increase in the wage rate reduces the profitability of producing goods, and therefore causes a reduction in output and in the number of jobs offered. With the demand and supply curves shown, the equilibrium is at point *E*.

Now, consider what happens through time. Population increases, and the supply curve for labor therefore shifts to the right. Forces are also at work causing the demand curve to shift. As time passes, the quantity of capital (machinery and equipment) increases, and this results in a rightward shift in the demand for labor.

FIGURE 4-11

The aggregate labor market

For the labor market as a whole, the supply curve is approximately vertical. A doubling of wage rates will not cause a large increase in the number of people who are willing to work.

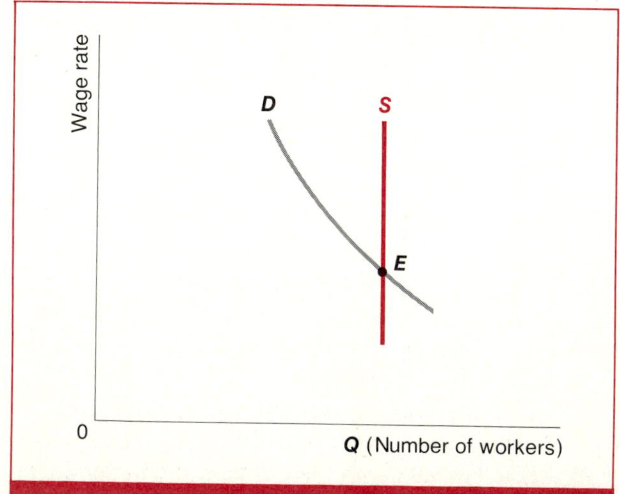

Why? As the quantity of machines and other capital increases, workers have more tools to work with. As a consequence, they can produce more goods; that is, their productivity rises. Therefore, employers are more anxious to hire workers and are able to pay them a higher wage.

With both the demand and supply curves for labor moving to the right, the net effect on wages depends on the relative strength of the two shifts. Consider the two cases illustrated in Figure 4-12. On the left is Japan, where recent population growth has been small; the supply of labor has therefore moved only slightly to the right. At the same time, the Japanese have directed a large proportion of their productive capacity into the production of new factories and equipment. As a result of the increase in the quantity of capital, the demand curve for labor has moved rapidly to the right. The net effect has been a rapid increase in the Japanese wage rate.

In the second panel, a quite different situation is illustrated, namely, a problem which concerns a number of the poorer countries in which population growth has been very rapid. Improvements in medical services have cut mortality rates while birth rates have remained high. As a result, the supply of labor has shifted rapidly to the right, to S_2. At the same time, a number of these countries have had trouble directing resources into the formation of capital. (Recall from Figure 2-6 that if they divert production away from satisfying their immediate consumption needs, the already low level of consumption may be depressed further.) As a consequence, there has been little increase in the capital stock, and the demand curve for labor has shifted outward much less rapidly than in Japan. As a result, wage rates in a number of the poorest countries have risen very little, if at all.

Thus, we come to a very important conclusion: *The key to an increase in the real wage is an increase in*

FIGURE 4-12
Shifts in the demand and supply of labor

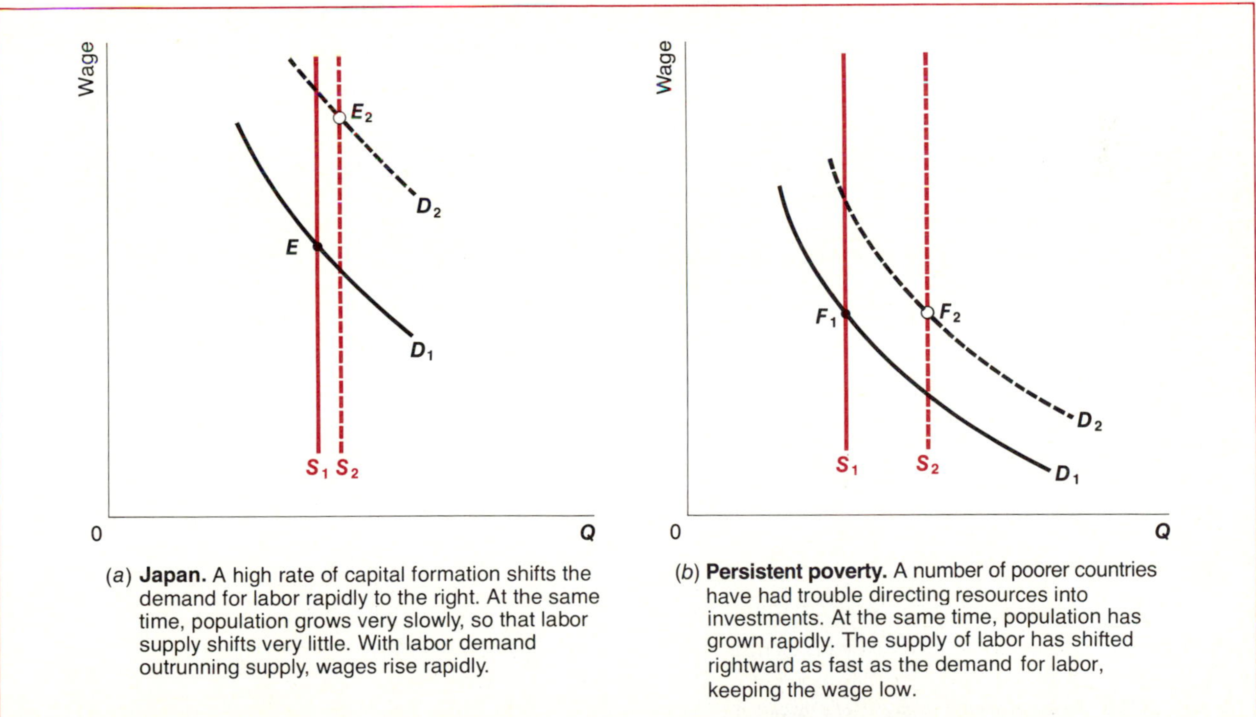

(*a*) **Japan.** A high rate of capital formation shifts the demand for labor rapidly to the right. At the same time, population grows very slowly, so that labor supply shifts very little. With labor demand outrunning supply, wages rise rapidly.

(*b*) **Persistent poverty.** A number of poorer countries have had trouble directing resources into investments. At the same time, population has grown rapidly. The supply of labor has shifted rightward as fast as the demand for labor, keeping the wage low.

productivity, which comes mainly from *improvements in technology* and from an *increase in the capital stock at the disposal of the average worker.*

THE MALTHUSIAN PROBLEM

There is a wide variation among the less-developed countries. In some, per capita output has risen rapidly in the past two decades; in others, it has remained relatively stagnant. The very poorest are haunted by the grim prospect described by the young English clergyman Thomas Malthus in his *Essay on the Principle of Population* (1798). Malthus emphasized that the scarcity of natural resources, particularly land, limits the production of food. Specifically, he argued that the output of food increases at best at an arithmetic rate (1, 2, 3, 4, 5, 6, and so on). However, the passion between the sexes means that population tends to increase at a geometric rate (1, 2, 4, 8, 16, 32, etc.):

> It may safely be pronounced that population, when unchecked, goes on doubling itself every twenty-five years, or increases in a geometrical ratio. The rate according to which the productions of the earth may be supposed to increase, will not be so easy to determine. Of this, however, we may be perfectly certain, that the ratio of their increase in a limited territory must be of a totally different nature from the ratio of the increase in population. A thousand millions are just as easily doubled every twenty-five years by the power of population as a thousand. But the food to support the increase from the greater number will by no means be obtained with the same facility. . . .
>
> It may be fairly pronounced, therefore, that considering the present average state of the earth, the means of subsistence, under circumstances the most favorable to human industry, could not possibly be made to increase faster than in an arithmetic ratio. . . . The ultimate check to population appears then to be a want of food, arising necessarily from the different ratios according to which population and food increase.[3]

Because of the tendency of population to outstrip food production, the income of the working class will be driven down to the subsistence level. During the nineteenth century, this proposition came to be known as the ***iron law of wages.***

After the wage reaches the subsistence level, poor nutrition and starvation will keep the population in check. There was a cruel implication to this theory. Public relief for the poor would do nothing in the long run to improve their condition. It would simply result in an upsurge in population; there would be more people to face starvation in the future.

The Malthusian problem is illustrated in Figure 4-13. Suppose that rapid growth has already driven the wage down to the subsistence level, as shown by the intersection of S_1 and D_1; the population is 2 million. Now, in the next 25-year period, population, if unchecked, would rise to 4 million (S_2). But food production can rise no more than enough to support 3 mil-

FIGURE 4-13
The Malthusian problem
The tendency for population to grow more rapidly than food production drives the wage down to the subsistence level at G_1. Thereafter, natural population growth would shift the supply of labor from S_1 to S_2, and reduce the wage rate *below* the subsistence level. However, people would starve, limiting the supply of workers to S_3, the number who can be paid the subsistence wage W_s.

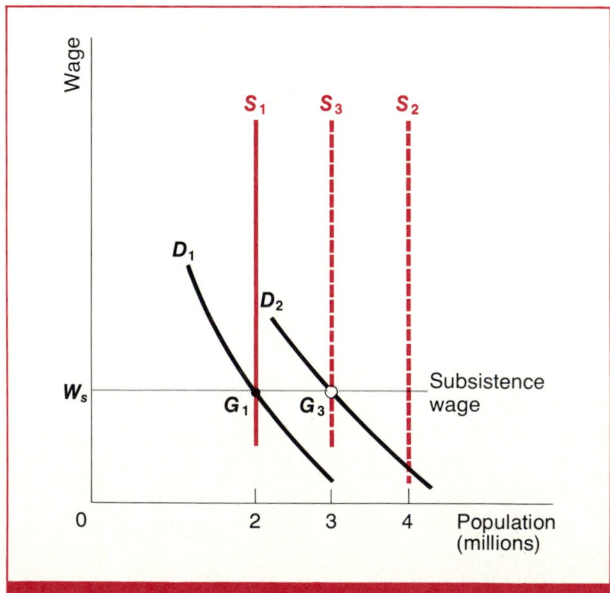

[3]Thomas Malthus, *An Essay on the Principle of Population* (London: Reeves and Turner, 1888 edition), pp. 5–6.

lion. Employers cannot pay 4 million a high enough wage to permit them all to survive; the demand for labor increases only to D_2. Starvation, war, or pestilence take their toll, keeping population down to the 3 million that can be supported by the available food (S_3).

As a general forecast, Malthus' theory proved inaccurate. The standard of living in most countries has risen markedly in the past 200 years. Birth control has been a greater restraint on population growth than Malthus anticipated. Food production has increased beyond Malthus' expectation because of the technological revolution that has included agriculture as well as manufacturing. Nevertheless, Malthus' theory—that there can be a race between population growth and the ability to produce—is worth remembering in a world which is becoming more crowded.

APPENDIX 4-B

PRICE IS DETERMINED BY DEMAND AND SUPPLY CURVES ONLY IN A PERFECTLY COMPETITIVE MARKET

It is only in a perfectly competitive market that the intersection of the demand and supply curves determines the price. To see why, consider the type of question the supply schedule answers. If the price of apples were, say, $10 per bushel, how many apples would suppliers be willing to sell? This is a question which is relevant in a perfectly competitive market. Individual orchard owners indeed ask themselves how many apples they want to sell at the going market price. Individually, they cannot affect that price, so each owner's decision is limited to the number of bushels to be sold.

However, that is not the sort of decision a monopolist or oligopolist (such as Chrysler) has to make. Such a firm does not take the market price as given. Instead, it quotes a price for its product. For example, at the beginning of the model year, Chrysler announces the prices of its cars. Because Chrysler, GM, and Ford set their own prices—rather than respond to a given market price—there is no supply curve for the auto industry.

On the other side of the market, a similar complication can arise. The demand curve is a meaningful concept only if there are many buyers, with none having any influence over price. In such a case, the demand-schedule question is relevant. If the price is, say, $10 per bushel, how many bushels will buyers be willing to purchase?

However, in a market with only one buyer (monopsony) or only a few buyers (oligopsony), the individual buyer *can* influence price. Therefore, the question a monopsonist will ask is not, "How many units will I buy at the given market price?" but rather, "What price shall I offer?" Thus, for example, the only manufacturer in a small town will have monopsony power in the labor market and will ask, "What wage rate shall I pay?" In such cases, where a single buyer sets market price rather than taking it as given, there is no demand curve.

The major market forms and the chapters in which they will be studied are outlined in Table 4-4.

TABLE 4-4
Types of Markets

Type	Characteristic	Is demand curve meaningful?	Is supply curve meaningful?	How is price determined?	Studied in Chapters
Perfect competition	Many buyers and sellers, with no single market participant affecting price	Yes	Yes	By intersection of demand supply curves	4, 24
Monopoly	One seller, many buyers	Yes	No	By seller, facing market demand	25
Monopsony	One buyer, many sellers	No	Yes	By buyer, facing market supply	34
More complex cases	Few buyers, few sellers	No	No	In complex manner	34

KEY POINTS

10. The wage rate depends on the demand and supply of labor.

11. Increases in the productivity of labor cause the demand for labor to increase. Increases in the quantity of capital are a principal cause of increases in the productivity of labor.

12. Population growth is the main cause for an increase in the supply of labor.

13. If the demand for labor shifts out faster than the supply of labor, wages will be pulled upward. If the supply shifts out faster than demand, wages will be depressed. If the tendency for population to increase keeps wages at a very low level and under downward pressure, the country faces the *Malthusian problem*.

14. Price is determined by the intersection of the demand and supply curves only in a perfectly competitive market.

KEY CONCEPTS

supply of labor in a specific market
supply of labor in the nation as a whole
productivity of labor
Malthusian problem
iron law of wages
monopsony

PROBLEM

4-9. (*a*) Suppose you are the manager of a local drug store. What does the supply curve of clerks look like?

(*b*) What does the supply curve of labor facing General Motors in Michigan look like?

(*c*) What does the supply curve for all labor in the United States look like?

(*d*) Explain why the curves in parts *a*, *b*, and *c* have different shapes.

CHAPTER 5

THE ECONOMIC ROLE OF GOVERNMENT

As new . . . problems arise beyond the power of men and women to meet as individuals, it becomes the duty of the Government itself to find new remedies.

FRANKLIN D. ROOSEVELT

Government is not the solution to our problem. Government is the problem.

RONALD REAGAN

The defects and limitations of the market system, outlined at the end of Chapter 4, provide reasons for government to participate in the economy. In the words of Abraham Lincoln, a legitimate objective of government is "to do for the people what needs to be done, but which they cannot, by individual effort, do at all, or do so well, for themselves."

In Chapter 4, we described briefly the four ways in which government affects the economy: by *spending,* by *taxation,* by *regulation,* and by running *public enterprises*. We saw that public enterprise is quite limited in the United States; it is much less important than in other countries. Accordingly, in this chapter, we will concentrate on the three other ways in which the government affects the economy—spending, taxation, and regulation.

In contrast with the private market, where people have an option of buying or not, government activities generally involve compulsion. Taxes *must* be paid; people are not allowed to opt out of the system when the time comes to pay income taxes. Similarly, government regulations involve compulsion; car manufacturers *must* install safety equipment. Compulsion sometimes exists even in a government spending program. Young people *must* go to school—although their parents do have the option of choosing a private school rather than one run by the government.

In later sections of this chapter, we will consider how the government can try to improve the outcome of the private market by the use of expenditures, taxation, and regulations. As a preliminary, it is necessary to look at some facts—how the government role has expanded and what the government is currently doing.

THE GROWTH OF GOVERNMENT EXPENDITURES

During the nineteenth and early twentieth centuries, U.S. government expenditures covered little more than the expenses of the Army and Navy, a few public works, and the salaries of a small number of government officials. Except for wartime periods when spending shot upward to pay for munitions, weapons, and personnel, government spending was small. As late as 1929, all levels of government—federal, state, and local—together spent less than $11 billion a year. Of this total, about three-quarters was spent at the state and local levels. Highway maintenance and education were typical government programs. This does not mean, however, that a rigid policy of *laissez faire* was followed. Even during the nineteenth century, governments at both the state and local levels participated in some important sectors of the economy. For example, governments helped railroads and canal systems to expand.

With the depression of the 1930s, a major increase in government activity began. Distress and unemployment were widespread, and it was increasingly hard to believe that the workings of the private market would lead to the best of all possible worlds. During the decade 1929–1939, federal government spending increased from $3 billion to $9 billion. Part of the increase was specifically aimed at providing jobs through new agencies, such as the Civilian Conservation Corps (CCC). Then, when the United States entered the Second World War in 1941, the government undertook huge spending to pay for military equipment and for the salaries of military personnel. By 1944, defense amounted to more than 40% of gross national product.

When the war ended in 1945, the nation demobilized and government spending fell by more than 50%. But the decline was only temporary. Over the past four decades, spending at all levels of government has increased rapidly, to total no less than $1,258 billion by 1984 (Figure 5-1).

Government Expenditures in Perspective

Clearly, government spending has become very large. It is hard for the average citizen, accustomed to dealing with a family budget measured in thousands of dollars, to comprehend government budgets measured in billions. A billion dollars may be more meaningful if it is reduced to a personal level: A billion dollars represents about $4.25 for every man, woman, and child in the United States. Thus, with total budgets exceeding $1,250 billion, our federal, state, and local governments spend about $5,300 per person.

The magnitude of a billion dollars may be illustrated in another way. When the government borrows $1 billion at an interest rate of 12% per annum, its interest payments amount to $325,000 *per day*.

The rapid increase in spending has in part been a reflection of the additional responsibilities undertaken by government. During the 1930s, innovations included the *social security* system, whose principal function is the payment of pensions to retired people. More recently, the government has introduced *medicare* to provide medical assistance to the elderly, and *medicaid* to provide such assistance to the needy. Expenditures for weapons and other military purposes have remained high for the past three decades because of the increasing complexity and cost of armaments and because of the cold war competition with the Soviet Union.

However, the expenditures shown in Figure 5-1 can give a misleading impression of the size of the government. While the government is spending more and more, so are private individuals and businesses. For both the

FIGURE 5-1

Government expenditures, 1929–1984

Since the mid-1950s, total government expenditures have risen from $100 billion to more than $1,250 billion.

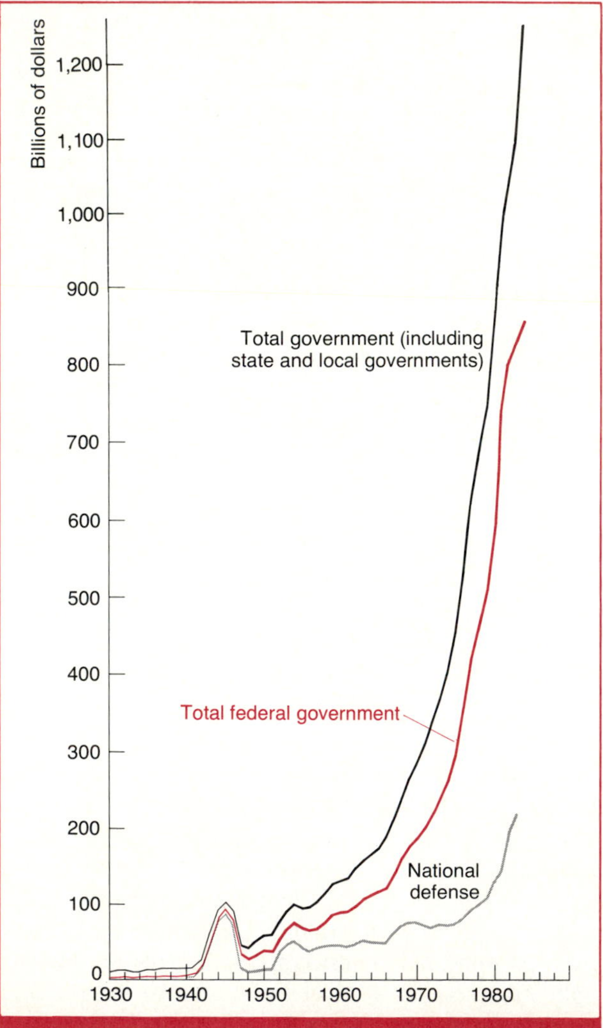

government and the private sectors, these rising expenditures reflect two major trends: More and more goods and services are being bought, and at higher and higher prices. We can see government expenditures in better perspective by examining them, not in dollar terms (as in Figure 5-1), but rather as a percentage of gross national product (GNP).

When we do this in the left panel of Figure 5-2, the increase in government expenditures becomes much less dramatic. Nevertheless, the trend has still been upward since 1930, with a big bulge during the Second World War.

Government Purchases versus Transfers

A further complication in measuring the size of the government arises because of the two major categories of government expenditures:

1. ***Purchases of goods and services***
2. ***Transfer payments***

Government purchases of goods include items such as paper, computers, and aircraft. The government purchases services when it hires schoolteachers, police officers, and employees for government departments. When the government purchases goods and services, *it makes a*

FIGURE 5-2

Two ways of looking at the relative size of government

The left panel shows total government expenditures, including both expenditures on goods and services, and the amounts redistributed in the form of transfers. Observe that total expenditures have become a larger and larger percent of national product. The right panel shows only the expenditures for goods and services. As a percent of national product, these expenditures have not changed much over the past three decades.

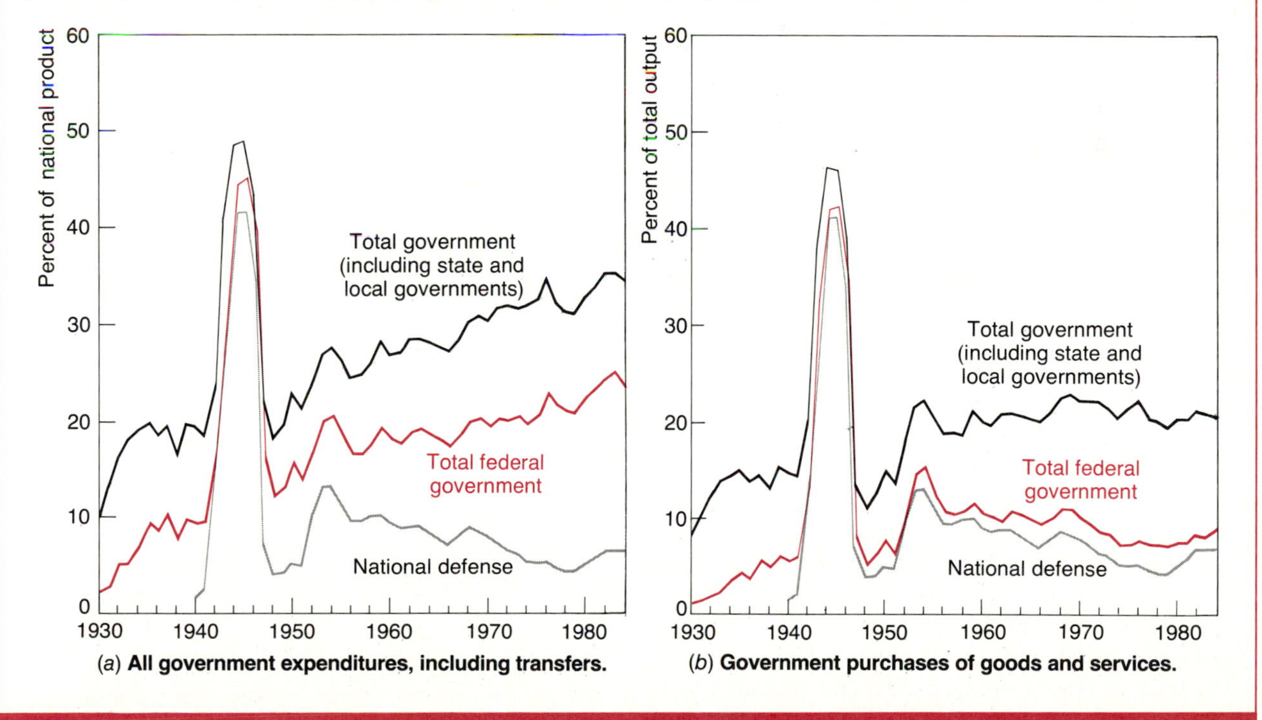

(*a*) **All government expenditures, including transfers.**

(*b*) **Government purchases of goods and services.**

direct claim on the productive capacity of the nation. For example, when the government orders a computer, the manufacturer uses glass, plastic, copper, silicon chips, machines, and labor to make the computer. Similarly, the purchase of services involves a claim on productive resources. The police officer hired by the government must spend time on the beat, and thus becomes unavailable for work in the private sector.

Government *transfer payments,* on the other hand, are payments *for which the recipient does not provide any good or service in return*. Transfer payments include social security and medicare benefits for the elderly and welfare payments such as medicaid. Of the transfer payments, the social security–medicare program provides *by far* the largest. Indeed, in 1984, social security and medicare accounted for 28% of total expenditures by the federal government.

A *transfer payment* is a payment by the government to an individual for which the individual does not provide a good or service in return. Social security benefits, unemployment compensation, and welfare payments are examples of transfers.

In contrast with government purchases, transfer payments represent no direct claim by the government on the productive capacity of the nation. For example, when the government pays social security pensions to retired people, there is no reallocation of the nation's product away from the private sector toward the government sector. Unlike the computer company that manufactures a computer and ships it to the government to get a payment from the government, the social security recipient provides neither a good nor a service in return for the benefit. This does not mean, of course, that the social security system is unimportant. When the government collects social security taxes from workers and employers and pays benefits to retirees, the pattern of consumer spending is affected. The old have more to spend, and workers have less. As a consequence, producers find themselves faced with greater demands for the things that retirees want and with smaller demands for the things workers want. Although the social security system affects the amount of the nation's product that various individuals can purchase, it does not redirect the economy toward production for the government.

The left panel of Figure 5-2 shows total government expenditures, *including transfers*. Another way of measuring the size of the government is to look only at government purchases of goods and services, that is, expenditures *excluding transfers,* as shown in the right panel. These are the expenditures that make a direct claim on the productive resources of the economy. Observe that as a percentage of national product, government purchases of goods and services are approximately what they were three decades ago. Purchases by state and local governments have gone up, but these increases have been approximately matched by the declining percentage for the federal government.

The two panels give two quite different impressions of the government's size. If we look only at purchases of goods and services in the right panel, the percentage of national product going to the government has been quite stable over the past three decades. If, on the other hand, we include transfers and look at total government expenditures in the left panel, the government's percentage is increasing. The government is not directly claiming a larger and larger share of the nation's product for itself. But it is claiming a larger and larger share, to be *redistributed* in the form of social security, welfare, and other transfer payments.

The main trends of the past three decades, as shown in Figure 5-2, may be summarized. *As a percentage of gross national product* (GNP):

1. The combined total of purchases of goods and services by all levels of government has been stable. An expansion at the state and local levels has been approximately offset by a decline at the federal level.
2. Government transfers have risen rapidly. This increase shows up in the contrast between the left panel of Figure 5-2, which includes transfers, and the right panel, which excludes them.[1]
3. Defense expenditures fell substantially between 1955 and 1979—specifically, from 9.6% of GNP to

[1]More precisely, there are two sets of expenditures that are included in the total government curve in panel *a* of Figure 5-2, but are excluded from the total government curve in panel *b:* (1) transfer payments to individuals, such as social security payments, and (2) interest on government debt.

4.6%. In recent years, defense expenditures have grown rapidly, rising to 6.0% of GNP by 1984. Under current plans, they are expected to rise to 6.7% of GNP by 1986 and 7.6% by 1990.

THE BUDGET OF THE FEDERAL GOVERNMENT

Table 5-1 provides details on federal government expenditures and on the taxes that financed these expenditures in fiscal year 1984.[2] Until the mid-1970s, defense expenditures were the largest single category of expenditure by the federal government. In 1976, the social security–medicare program took over first spot. In recent years, both defense and social security–medicare categories have grown rapidly, with defense expenditures coming on strongly since 1981 to put them in a virtual tie for first place with social security–medicare by 1984. But of the major categories, interest payments have grown by far the most rapidly, more than doubling between 1980 and 1984. There are two reasons for this rapid increase in interest payments: (1) interest rates have been higher in the early 1980s than they were during the 1970s; and (2) the government's debt, on which interest must be paid, grew more than 70%, from $915 billion in 1980 to $1,575 billion in 1984.

Federal Receipts

On the receipts side, the ***personal income tax*** is the largest source of federal government revenue. This tax is levied on taxable personal income, that is, on the incomes of individuals and families after the subtraction of

[2]The *fiscal year* is the year used in government or business accounts. For convenience, the fiscal year may begin in March, July, or October, rather than January. The federal government begins its fiscal year on Oct. 1. Thus, the 1984 fiscal year ran from Oct. 1, 1983 to Sept. 30, 1984.

TABLE 5-1
The Budget of the Federal Government, Fiscal 1984

	(1) Billions of dollars	(2) Percent of total	(3) Percent change since fiscal 1980
Budget outlays			
Social security and medicare	$235.8	27.7%	57.5%
National defense	227.4	26.7	69.7
Income security	112.7	13.2	30.3
Net interest	111.1	13.0	111.6
Health (excl. medicare)	30.4	3.6	31.0
Education, training, and social services	27.6	3.2	−13.2
Veterans benefits	25.6	3.0	20.8
Transportation	23.7	2.8	11.3
International affairs	15.9	1.9	25.2
Agriculture	13.6	1.6	54.5
Natural resources and environment	12.6	1.5	−8.7
Other	15.4	1.8	
	$851.8	100.0%	
Budget receipts			
Individual income taxes	$296.2	44.4%	21.4%
Social insurance taxes	241.7	36.2	53.2
Corporation income taxes	56.9	8.5	−11.9
Other	71.7	10.8	
Totals	$666.5	100.0%	

Budget deficit = outlays − receipts = $185.3 billion

various exemptions and deductions. For example, in 1984, each family was entitled to a deduction of $1,000 per family member, plus extra exemptions for the elderly and blind. Before calculating their taxable income, taxpayers are permitted to deduct state and local taxes, interest payments, charitable contributions, and some medical expenses.

For a married couple with two children, the income tax was levied at the rates shown in Table 5-2 in 1984. Because the tax system is complicated, a number of details are left out of this table. For example, those with incomes of less than $10,000 may pay less than shown.

The *average tax rate,* shown in the third column, is simply the total tax divided by income. Observe that, as income rises, the percentage of that income that has to be paid in tax also rises. Therefore, the income tax is ***progressive.***

If a tax takes a larger percentage of income as income rises, the tax is *progressive.*

If a tax takes a smaller percentage of income as income rises, the tax is *regressive.*

If a tax takes a constant percentage of income, the tax is *proportional.*

The ***marginal tax rate*** is shown in the last column; this is the tax rate on *additional* income. In the tax bracket with income between $15,900 and $20,000, for example, the marginal tax rate is 16%. Within this bracket, if income rises by $100 (for example, from $16,000 to $16,100), $16 more must be paid in taxes. It is the higher and higher marginal tax rates (column 4) which pull up the average tax rate (column 3).

While income taxes remain the largest single component of federal government revenues, social insurance taxes (to pay for social security and unemployment insurance) have risen rapidly, from 16% of total federal revenues in 1960 to 36% in 1984. Social security contributions, or taxes, are paid to finance old-age pensions, payments to the families of contributors who die or are disabled, and medicare. In 1985, the tax stood at 14.1% of wages and salaries up to a maximum income of $39,600; half the tax is collected from the employer and half from the employee. In order to finance the rapid increase in social security payouts, the social security tax has been increased repeatedly. It was 6% in 1960, 9.6% in 1970, and 12.25% in 1980. By 1990, it is scheduled to rise to 15.3%. The maximum income subject to tax will also rise, with the amount of increase depending on the increase in wages.

TABLE 5-2
Federal Income Tax for a Married Couple with Two Dependent Children and No Itemized Deductions, 1984

(1) Personal income	(2) Personal income tax	(3) Average tax rate (3) = (2) ÷ (1)	(4) Marginal tax rate (tax on additional income)
$ 7,400†	$ 0	0%	11%
9,500	231	2.4	12
11,600	483	4.2	14
15,900	1,085	6.8	16
20,000‡	1,741	8.7	18
28,600	3,456	12.1	25
39,200	6,274	16.0	33
64,000	15,168	23.7	42
113,400	36,630	32.3	49
166,400§	62,600	37.6	50

†There is a "zero tax bracket" of $3,400 per couple. In addition, there is an exemption of $1,000 per person. Therefore, a couple with two children do not begin to pay taxes until income passes $7,400 (that is, $3,400 plus the four exemptions of $1,000 each).
‡Above $20,000, some of the brackets are omitted for brevity.
§Above $166,400, the marginal rate remains constant at 50%.

The social security tax is ***regressive.*** Although it is collected at a flat percentage on incomes up to a limit of $36,900 in 1985, any additional income is exempt from the tax. Thus, the tax constitutes a higher percentage of the income of someone making $30,000 per year than of someone making $60,000. Nevertheless, if we look at the social security system *as a whole*—both taxes and benefits—we find that it favors lower-income people. They receive bigger benefits, compared to the taxes they paid, than do high-income people. While lower-income people pay a disproportionate share of the social security tax, they receive an even larger share of the benefits.

The tax on corporate income (profits) constitutes the third most important source of federal revenue. For profits above $100,000, the corporate income tax rate is 46%, with lower rates applying to the first $100,000. However, because of various credits and deductions, corporate tax payments are in fact much less than 46% of their profits. In recent decades, the corporate income tax has become less important as a source of revenue—falling from about 25% of total federal revenues in the 1950s to about 7.5% in 1983–1984.

Minor amounts of revenues are brought in by other taxes, such as *excise taxes*—on items such as cigarettes, alcoholic beverages, and gasoline—and *customs duties* imposed on goods imported into the United States.

Federal Government Deficits

When the government's revenues fall short of its expenditures, its budget is in ***deficit.*** In order to pay for the expenditures in excess of its revenues, the government borrows the difference.

If a government's revenues exceed its expenditures, it has a budget *surplus.*

If a government's expenditures exceed its revenues, it has a budget *deficit.*

If a government's revenues equal its expenditures, its budget is *balanced.* (The term "balanced budget" is often used loosely to mean that the budget is either in balance or in surplus; that is, revenues are at least as great as expenditures.)

In the past quarter century, the U.S. government has run a deficit every year except 1969. By the early 1980s, the deficits had grown to an unprecedented level for peacetime periods. For example, the federal deficit in fiscal 1984 amounted to $185 billion, or 5.2% of GNP (Figure 5-3). Furthermore, with the existing tax and spending programs, deficits of $200 billion or more were being forecast for future years. With the federal government borrowing more and more, its total debt doubled between 1980 ($915 billion) and 1985 ($1,840 billion). (Both numbers are for September 30, the end of the fiscal year.)

The large deficits were especially surprising because they occurred during the presidency of Ronald Reagan, who had vigorously attacked deficits before his election.

REAGANOMICS

The large deficits are one indication of how difficult it is to develop and execute an overall economic strategy—particularly when the objective is to make major changes in the role of the government.

When he came into office, President Reagan intended to change policy sharply. His economic program—which quickly was given the label "Reaganomics"—included the following objectives:

1. Increase *defense* expenditures.
2. Restrain and, where possible, reduce *domestic* spending by the federal government.
3. Restrain the growth of government *regulation.*
4. Cut *tax rates.* Specifically, the tax law enacted in 1981 provided for tax rates to be cut in stages over the period from 1981 to 1984.

These policies were based on a philosophy of what the government should and should not do. In the President's view, the major responsibilities of the government are to provide protection from external enemies and to provide the basis for an orderly society. Government had, however, gone far beyond its appropriate role and had become intrusively involved in telling business and the public what to do. One of his objectives, said Reagan, was to "get the government off the backs of the people." By loosening the heavy hand of the government, the administration hoped to invigorate the private enterprise economy, and to unloose a strong economic expansion.

Such a strong expansion would help to increase government revenues, since people must pay more in taxes when their incomes rise. Cuts in domestic programs would also help to lower government deficits. On the other hand, two factors would be at work to increase deficits: (1) higher defense spending and (2) lower tax rates.

The administration expected that a vigorous expansion and cuts in domestic programs would make it possible to bring deficits down. In the early budget projections made in 1981, the adminstration forecast a balanced budget by the end of President Reagan's first term in 1984.

However, in practice, deficits mounted. Why were the early, optimistic projections so wrong? Several causes might be cited:

1. Economic expansion was much less vigorous than the administration had hoped. It is true that the economy grew at a very healthy rate in 1983–1984, but this came only after the severe recession of 1981–1982. Because the economy grew less rapidly than expected for the 4 years as a whole, tax revenues were much less than expected. More than half the $185 billion deficit of 1984 could be accounted for by the lower-than-expected tax receipts, which in turn were attributable to slower-than-expected growth.

2. Domestic spending was more difficult to cut than expected. In particular, interest on the debt was much higher than the projections made in 1981. The higher interest payments were partly the result of federal government borrowing to finance the deficits of 1981–1983. In short, the deficits which the government had been running were adding to interest expenditures and making it even more difficult to avoid deficits in the future.[3]

[3]For a detailed explanation of why the Reagan administration failed to achieve its goal of balancing the budget during its first 4 years, see John C. Weicher, "Accounting for the Deficit," in Phillip Cagan, ed., *Contemporary Economic Problems, 1985* (Washington: American Enterprise Institute, 1985).

FIGURE 5-3

The federal budget: Expenditures, receipts, and deficits (as percentages of GNP)

Over the past decade, expenditures of the federal government have been substantially higher than its revenues, resulting in budget deficits. In 1984, the gap between expenditures and revenues amounted to 5.2% of gross national product. Figures for 1985 are estimates.

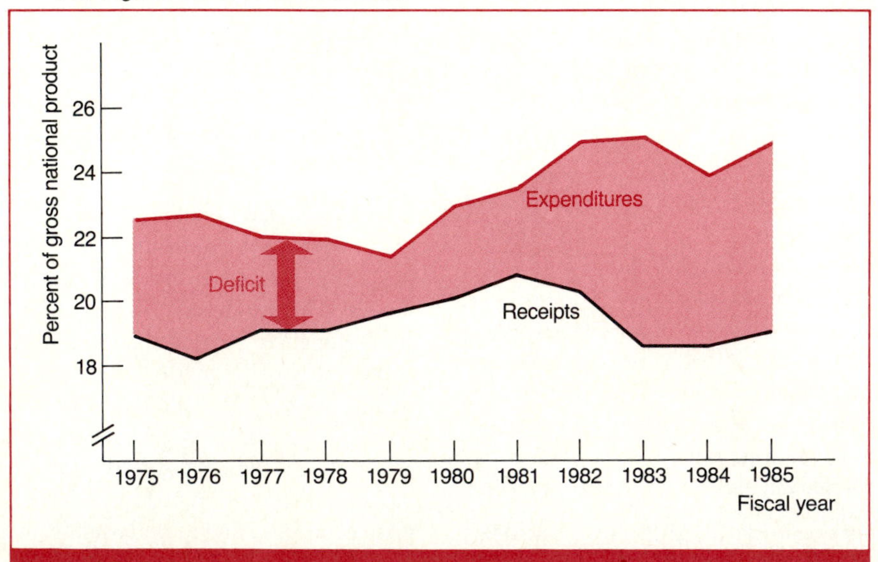

As the second Reagan administration began in 1985, the size of the deficit, and what should be done about it, dominated the debate over economic policy. The difficulty of cutting the budget was becoming increasingly clear. One fact in particular stood out. More than two thirds of total federal spending was made up of three large categories: (1) interest on the debt, which the government is contractually committed to pay; (2) national defense, which the administration had worked hard to build up; and (3) social security, which the President had pledged not to cut. Was it realistic to expect any sizable cuts in spending without including items 2 and 3? Was it realistic to expect any large reduction in the deficit without an increase in tax rates? Those were unwelcome—but unavoidable—questions for the Congress and the administration.

GOVERNMENT REGULATION

The government's budget, amounting to hundreds of billions of dollars, has a substantial effect on the types of goods produced and on who gets these goods. In addition, the government affects the economy through its regulatory agencies, such as the Environmental Protection Agency (EPA) that controls pollution. The cost of *administering* such agencies—which amounts to only 2% to 3% of the federal government's budget—is an inadequate measure of their importance. The cost to businesses of *complying* with these regulations is far higher. For example, it costs a steel mill much more to install pollution control devices than it costs the EPA to administer the regulations. The gains to the public—in the form of cleaner air—are likewise much greater than the small amounts which appear in the federal budget.

During the past century, a number of steps have been taken to limit the most flagrant abuses of private business. In 1890, the Sherman Act declared business mergers that create monopolies to be illegal. Then the Federal Trade Commission (FTC) was established in 1914 in the belief that monopolies should be prevented before the fact, rather than punished after they are created.

Regulation goes far beyond the control of monopoly. For example, the Food and Drug Administration (FDA) determines the effectiveness and safety of drugs before they are permitted on the market. The financial shenanigans of the 1920s—which contributed to the collapse into the Depression—led in 1933 to the establishment of the Securities and Exchange Commission (SEC) to regulate financial markets. The SEC requires corporations to disclose information about their finances. Banks are extensively regulated by the Federal Reserve System, the Federal Deposit Insurance Corporation, the Comptroller of the Currency, and state regulatory agencies. The Federal Power Commission (FPC) and the Federal Communications Commission (FCC) regulate power and broadcasting. The Federal Aviation Administration (FAA) sets and enforces safety standards for aircraft.

In the 1960s and 1970s, there was an upswing in regulatory activity, with the addition of such agencies as the Equal Employment Opportunity Commission (EEOC), the EPA, the Commodity Futures Trading Commission (CFTC), and the Occupational Safety and Health Administration (OSHA).

In many areas, regulation is relatively uncontroversial. For example, few people complain about the government agency (the FAA) that enforces safety standards on the airlines. Similarly, there is widespread support for government regulation aimed at keeping unsafe drugs off the market. The FDA drew particular praise because it had blocked the distribution of thalidomide, a drug to relieve nausea which caused birth defects when it was used in Europe.

However, doubts set in after the flurry of regulatory activity of the 1960s and 1970s. In particular, there were growing concerns that some government regulations were working at cross purposes. For example, the Justice Department and the FTC were charged with the responsibility of reducing monopoly abuse and increasing competition in the U.S. economy. But, at the same time, the Civil Aeronautics Board (CAB) was limiting competition among airlines. In order to fly a new route in competition with existing carriers, an airline needed approval of the CAB, and the CAB regularly turned down such requests. In addition, banking regulation set the interest rate which banks could offer to depositors and limited competition between banks and other financial institutions. During the Carter administration, major steps were taken to reduce regulation of banks and airlines. The deregulation of banks and airlines continued during the

Reagan administration. At the end of 1984, the CAB went out of business.

Under the Reagan administration, with its desire to reduce the regulatory hassles faced by business, enforcement of safety and environmental regulations became less vigorous. Particularly with respect to the environment, the policies of the administration stirred controversy. The EPA became a demoralized agency, touched by scandal. Critics of the administration pointed out that the EPA performed an essential function. Without it, there would be nothing in the competitive market system to give businesses any strong incentive to restrain pollution.

What is needed is a sense of balance. The private market mechanism has substantial defects. Corporations cannot on their own be counted on to pay sufficient attention to safety or to limiting pollution. But government agencies also have defects; they are not run by superhumans capable of solving all our problems. Furthermore, government regulation can be costly. While we use government agencies to deal with major failures of the market, we should be prepared to live with minor failures, where the cure may be worse than the defects themselves.

Regulation in the public interest is made particularly difficult because of the political clout of producers. When regulations are being developed, the affected industry makes its views known forcefully. But the views of consumers are diffuse and often remain underrepresented. In an extensive study of regulatory agencies, the Senate Government Operations Committee concluded that the public is outnumbered and outspent by industry in regulatory proceedings. The committee chairman observed that regulatory hearings "can be likened to the biblical battle of David and Goliath—except that David rarely wins." This conclusion should come as no surprise. For decades, an irreverent definition has circulated in Washington: A sick industry is one which cannot capture control of its regulatory agency.

The heavy influence of producers is not simply the result of a conspiracy of wealth. Rather, it is an intrinsic feature of a highly specialized economy. Each of us has a major, narrow, special interest as a producer, and each of us has a minor interest in a wide range of industries whose goods we consume. We are much more likely to react when our particular industry is affected by government policy; we are much less likely to express our diffuse interest as consumers. Narrow producer interests are expressed not only by business but also by labor. Unions concentrate their attention on events in their particular industry, even though the union members are also consumers, using a wide range of products. We repeat: The political clout of producers is primarily the result of modern technology and a high degree of specialization; it is not primarily a result of our particular system. It exists in a wide variety of political-economic systems, including those of Britain, France, Germany, Japan, and the Soviet Union.

STATE AND LOCAL GOVERNMENTS

Education is the biggest expenditure of state and local governments, accounting for 35.2% of the total in fiscal 1982–1983 (Table 5-3). Highways and welfare account for other large chunks of the budgets. (Some welfare programs, such as food stamps for the needy, are paid for entirely by the federal government. Other programs, among them Aid for Families with Dependent Children (AFDC), are partly financed by the federal government and partly by state and local governments.) Other important state and local expenditures are for police and fire protection, hospitals, and interest on the debt.

On the revenue side, states tax some of the same items as the federal government. Most states, and some local governments, have individual and corporation income taxes. Note, however, that income taxes provide a much smaller percentage of revenues for state and local governments than for the federal government. The two taxes that provide the largest revenues for states and localities are the *sales tax* (particularly important for state governments) and the *property tax* (the biggest source of tax revenues for local governments.)

Revenue Sharing

Another large source of revenues for state and local governments is not a tax at all, but rather grants from the federal government. Such grants amounted to 18.5% of total state and local revenues in fiscal 1982–1983 (Table 5-3).

Before 1972, virtually all federal government aid to

states and localities took the form of ***categorical grants***—that is, grants tied to specific programs, such as special education for the handicapped. Not only did the money come with strings attached, but it also required matching expenditures from state and local funds. In 1972, a new law was passed, providing for ***general revenue sharing***—that is, grants from the federal government with (practically) no strings attached.

Revenue sharing **involves grants from the federal government to state and/or local governments. Revenue sharing is** ***general*** **when it comes without restrictions on how it may be spent.**

Categorical grants **must be used for specific programs.**

Block grants **may be used in a broad area—such as education—and need not be spent on specific programs, such as reading programs for the handicapped.**

General revenue sharing has not been very large, amounting to only $5 billion in 1984. However, the idea of allowing the states and localities to decide how to spend funds was given a boost by President Reagan, who reduced the restrictions on categorical grants. Some categorical grants were combined into broader ***block grants,*** which gave states and localities more discretion over their use.

There were several reasons why revenue sharing was introduced. The federal government wanted to encourage specific progams and help states and localities bear the burden of such programs. This was the basic reason for establishing categorical grants in the first place. In 1972, the motivation for introducing general revenue sharing was the view that there was a mismatch between the revenues and responsibilities of the federal government, on the one hand, and the states and localities, on the other. Federal income tax revenues tend automatically to rise with a growing economy. But state and local tax revenues—based primarily on property and

TABLE 5-3
State and Local Government Expenditures and Revenues
(fiscal year 1982–1983)

	(1) Billions of dollars	(2) Percent of total	(3) Percent change since fiscal 1978–1979 (current dollars)
Expenditures			
Education	$164	35.2%	37.1%
Public welfare	60	12.9	44.4
Highways	37	7.9	28.9
All other	205	44.0	49.2
Total	$466	100%	42.4%
Revenues			
Sales and gross receipts tax	$100	20.6%	35.0%
Revenue from federal government	90	18.5	19.7
Property taxes	89	18.3	37.4
Individual income taxes	55	11.3	49.3
Corporation income taxes	14	2.9	18.2
All other	138	28.4	17.3
Total	$486	100%	41.8%

Surplus = revenues − expenditures
= $486 billion − $466 billion = $20 billion

sales taxes—may grow less rapidly. Yet many of the responsibilities of government lie at the state and local level. Advocates of general revenue sharing hoped to use the tax powers of the federal government to lessen the financial burdens on state and local governments.

However, this idea—that the federal government had excess taxing powers—seemed less and less valid as the federal government faced larger and larger deficits itself. At the same time, state and local governments were on average running surpluses, totalling $52 billion in 1984. Although most of these surpluses were used to build up pension funds for state and local workers—and were thus not "surplus" funds in an important sense—the states and localities as a group were in much better financial shape than the federal government. This has been one major reason for the leveling out in revenue sharing in recent years.

THE ECONOMIC ROLE OF THE GOVERNMENT: WHAT SHOULD THE GOVERNMENT DO?

With government budgets reaching hundreds of billions of dollars, and with an extensive list of government regulations, the U.S. economy is clearly a substantial distance away from a pure market system of laissez faire. What principles and objectives guide the government when it intervenes?

In part, government intervention is based on deep social attitudes that are often difficult to explain. Thirty years ago, Americans could look askance at government-financed, "socialized" medicine in Britain. Yet at the same time they could consider British education "undemocratic" because many well-to-do Britons sent their children to privately financed elementary and secondary schools. The British, on the other hand, were proud of their educational system and were puzzled by what they considered a quaint, emotional American objection to public financing of medical care. During the past three decades, the gap between the two societies has narrowed, with increasing governmental involvement in medicine in the United States and a decline in the importance of privately financed education in Britain.

The government intervenes in the economy for many reasons; it is hard to summarize them all. We will look at five of the main ones.

1. Providing What the Private Market Can't

Consider defense expenditures. For obvious political reasons, defense cannot be left to the private market. The prospect of private armies marching around the country is too painful to contemplate. But there also is an impelling economic reason why defense is a responsibility of the government.

The difference between defense and an average good is the following. If I buy food at the store, I get to eat it; if I buy a movie ticket, I get to see the film; if I buy a car, I get to drive it. In contrast, if I want a larger, better equipped army, my offer to purchase a rifle for the army will not add in any measurable way to my own security. My neighbor, and the average person in Alaska, Michigan, or Texas, will benefit as much from the extra rifle as I do. In other words, the benefit from defense expenditures *goes broadly to all citizens;* it *does not go specifically to the individual who pays*. If defense is to be provided, it must be financed by the government, which collects taxes to ensure that everyone contributes.

Such goods—where the benefit goes to the public regardless of who pays—are sometimes known as ***public goods.***

2. Externalities

An ***externality*** is a side effect—good or bad—of production or consumption. For example: When individuals are immunized against an infectious disease, they receive a substantial benefit; they are assured that they won't get the disease. But there is an ***external benefit*** as well, because others gain too: They are assured that the inoculated individuals will not catch the disease and pass it along to them. Similarly, there is an external benefit when people have their houses painted: The neighborhood becomes more attractive.

An ***external cost*** occurs when a factory pollutes the air. The cost is borne by those who breathe the polluted air.

An *externality* is a side effect of production or consumption. Persons or businesses other than the pro-

ducer or consumer are affected. An externality may be either positive (for example, vaccinations) or negative (for example, pollution).

Because of the effects on others, the government may wish to encourage activities which create external benefits and to discourage those with external costs. It can do so with the use of any of its three major tools: expenditures, regulations, or taxation. The government spends money for public health programs, for the immunization of the young. It has regulations on the types of automobiles which can be built, in order to reduce pollution. And taxes on gasoline or on polluting factories might likewise be used to discourage pollution.

The existence of an externality does not in itself make a compelling case for government action; the government should not be concerned with insignificant externalities or other trivial matters.[4] Thus, private incentives are generally enough to ensure that homes will be painted; the government does not usually intervene. However, there is growing concern over more serious externalities. While little was done about pollution two decades ago, major efforts are now directed toward cleaning up the air and water.

3. Merit Goods

Government intervention may also be based on the paternalistic view that people are not in all cases the best judges of what is good for them. According to this view, the government should encourage ***merit goods***—those that are deemed particularly desirable—and discourage the consumption of harmful products. People's inability to pick the "right" goods may be the result of shortsightedness, ignorance, addiction, or manipulation by producers. (Recall Chapter 4's brief discussion of Galbraith's views on created wants.)

In some cases, the government attempts merely to correct ignorance in areas where the public may have difficulty determining (or facing?) the facts. The requirement of a health warning on cigarette packages is an example. In other instances, the government goes further, to outright prohibition, as in the case of heroin and other hard drugs.

The view that "the government knows best" is generally greeted with skepticism. The government intervenes relatively sparingly to tell adults what they should or should not consume. (Children are, however, another matter; they are not allowed to reject the "merit" good, education.) However, substantial government direction does occur in welfare programs, presumably on the ground that those who get themselves into financial difficulties are least likely to make wise consumption decisions. Thus, part of the assistance to the poor consists of food stamps and housing programs rather than outright grants of money. In this way, the government attempts to direct consumption toward housing and milk for the children, rather than (perhaps) toward liquor for an alcoholic parent.

4. Helping the Poor

The market provides the goods and services desired by those with the money to buy, but it provides little for the poor. In order to help the impoverished and to move toward a more humane society, programs have been established to provide assistance for old people, the handicapped, and the needy.

There is much resentment of the "welfare mess," and not all of it comes from bigots who despise the poor. Because there were so many new programs introduced in a relatively brief period, particularly in the 1960s, it is perhaps inaccurate to speak of a welfare "system" at all. It's a patchwork. Recent presidents have struggled with this problem, and proposals for major change have included Nixon's family assistance program and Carter's welfare reform program—neither of which was enacted by Congress. One difficulty lies in how to reconcile conflicting objectives. How can help be given to the needy without weakening the incentive to work? How can as-

[4]The government does not, however, always exercise common sense. Many unnecessary or bizarre laws are on the books. For example, as part of a noise-abatement campaign, Lakefield, Ontario passed a law permitting birds to sing only 30 minutes during the day and 15 minutes at night. In Seattle, it is illegal to carry a concealed weapon more than 6 feet long. An ordinance in Danville, Pa. requires that "fire hydrants must be checked one hour before fires." These, and many other examples, may be found in Laurence J. Peter's book, *Why Things Go Wrong* (New York: Morrow, 1984). It is not only in government that things go wrong. Peter also quotes a number of errant newspaper headlines, for example: "Key Witness Takes Fifth in Liquor Probe."

sistance be guaranteed to abandoned mothers without giving irresponsible fathers an incentive to desert their families? How can the poverty-striken be given a place to live without creating ghettos of the poor? There are no easy answers to such questions.

5. The Government and Economic Stability

Finally, if we go back to the beginning of the upswing in government activity—to the depression of the thirties—we find that the primary motivation was not to affect the kinds of products made in the economy, nor specifically to aid the poor. Rather, the problem was the quantity of production. With unemployment rates running over 15% of the labor force year after year, the problem was to produce more—more of almost anything would help put people back to work. Since the dark days of the 1930s, a major responsibility of the government has been to promote a high level of employment and economic stability.

TAXATION

The art of taxation consists of plucking the goose so as to obtain the largest amount of feathers with the least possible amount of hissing.

Jean Baptiste Colbert,
Seventeenth-century French statesman

The major objective of taxation is to raise revenues—to obtain feathers without too much hissing. But other objectives are also important in the design of a tax system.

1. Neutrality

In many ways, the market system works admirably. Adam Smith's "invisible hand" provides the consuming public with a vast flow of goods and services. As a starting point, therefore, a tax system should be designed to be *neutral;* that is, it should disturb market forces as little as possible, unless there is a compelling reason to the contrary.

For the sake of illustration, consider a far-fetched example. Suppose that blue cars were taxed at 10% and green cars not at all. This tax would clearly not be neutral regarding blue and green cars. People would have an incentive to buy green cars; blue cars would practically disappear from the market. A tax which introduces such a distortion would make no sense.

While this illustration is silly, actual taxes do introduce distortions. For example, several centuries ago, houses in parts of Europe were taxed according to the number of windows. As a result, houses were built with fewer windows. To a lesser degree, the current property tax introduces a perverse incentive. If you have your house painted and your roof repaired, the government's evaluation of your house (the assessed value) may be raised and your taxes increased as a consequence. Therefore, property taxes encourage you to let your property deteriorate.

The problem is that every tax provides an incentive to do something to avoid it. So long as taxes must be collected, complete neutrality is impossible. The objective of the tax system must therefore be more modest: to aim toward neutrality. As a starting point in the design of a tax system, the disturbance to the market that comes from taxation should be minimized.

2. Nonneutrality: Meeting Social Objectives by Tax Incentives

There is, however, an important modification which must be made to the neutrality principle. In some cases, it may be desirable to disturb the private market.

For example, the government might tax polluting activities so that firms will do less polluting. The market is disturbed, but in a desirable way. Another example is the tax on cigarettes, which, in addition to its prime objective of raising revenue for the government, also discourages cigarette consumption. (Unfortunately, government policies are not always consistent. The government taxes cigarettes, forbids the advertising of cigarettes on TV, and requires health warnings on cigarette packages. But then the government turns around and subsidizes the production of tobacco.)

Taxation and regulation can be used to correct the failures of the private market. However, the two approaches are quite different in one respect. Regulation aims at *overriding* the market mechanism, forbiding or limiting specific behavior on the part of business. Taxation aims at *using* the market mechanism, but making it work better. When there are externalities, such as pollution, the signals of the market are incomplete; businesses or individuals who pollute the air do not have to pay the cost. Taxation of externalities can improve the outcome of the market by making the signals facing businesses and individuals more complete. Taxation might make polluters pay an amount to compensate for the external costs they are imposing on society, thereby giving them an incentive to reduce pollution.

3. Simplicity

To anyone who has spent the first two lovely weekends of April sweating over an income tax form, simplicity of the tax system is devoutly to be desired. Of course, we live in a complex world, and the tax code must to some degree reflect this complexity. But, as a result of decades of tinkering, the U.S. income tax has become ridiculously complicated. Indeed, it has become so complicated that the Internal Revenue Service (IRS) itself frequently gives incorrect answers to taxpayer inquiries. Mortimer Caplin, a former commissioner of the IRS, finds that the tax code has grown so "horrendously complex" that he has turned to an accounting firm to prepare his own return. So has Wilbur Mills, the ex-chairman of the House Ways and Means Committee—a committee that is largely responsible for writing the tax laws. (However, Donald Alexander, another former IRS chief, prepares his own tax return, since he thinks that those who write and enforce the law "should have to undergo the ordeal to see what it's like.")

A number of proposals have been made to simplify the tax system. Some people have flippantly suggested an ultrasimple, two-line tax form:

line 1: What did you make last year? $______.
line 2: Send it in.

More serious proposals abound—for example, those of (1) President Reagan in 1985, (2) the U.S. Treasury in 1984, (3) Democrats Bradley and Gephardt, and (4) Republicans Kemp and Kasten. While these four proposals differ substantially in detail, they have a number of common features. By eliminating some deductions and loopholes, they would all *broaden the tax base*—that is, they would increase the percentage of income on which tax is actually collected. With a broader base, a reduction in tax rates would be possible without reducing the government's revenues. Since the tax on upper brackets would not rise to such a high percentage, these are sometimes spoken of as proposals for a ***flatter tax.*** (A tax would be *completely* flat if there were only one tax rate—for example, 15%—applying to all income. See Box 5-1.)

4. Equity

Taxation represents coercion: Taxes are collected by force if necessary. Therefore, it is important that taxes both be fair and give the *appearance* of being fair. There are, however, two different principles for judging fairness.

The benefit principle This principle recognizes that the purpose of taxation is to pay for government services. Therefore, let those who gain the most from government services pay the most. If this principle is adopted, a question arises: Why not simply set prices for government services which people can voluntarily pay if they want the services? In other words, why not charge a price for a government service, just as General Motors charges for cars? This approach may work—for example, for a toll road from which drivers can be excluded if they do not pay. But it will not work for public goods that benefit people even if they do not pay—for example, defense, disease control programs, and air traffic control. Everyone will enjoy them, but no one will offer to pay for them. It is the function of the government to determine whether such programs are worthwhile. Once the decision is made to go ahead, people must be required to support the program through taxes.

If the ***benefit principle*** of taxation is followed, it is up to the government to estimate how much various individuals and groups benefit, and to set taxes accordingly. Individual citizens cannot be allowed to provide the estimates of how much they benefit personally; they have an incentive to understate their individual benefits in order to keep their taxes down.

Ability to pay If the government sets taxes according to the benefit principle, it does not redistribute income. People are simply taxed in proportion to their benefits from government programs. If the government wishes to redistribute income, it can set taxes according to the ***ability to pay.*** The basic measures of the ability to pay are income and wealth.

BOX 5-1

THE MORE OR LESS FLAT TAX

RUDOLPH G. PENNER†

The other day I heard a politician say that he strongly favored a "progressive, flat tax." I was not sure whether he was intent on murdering our language or our tax system. The latter may be a noble goal, but the truth is that the term "flat tax," which has recently become as popular as motherhood, is being used to describe a great variety of proposals put forth by individuals with very different goals.

Nevertheless, our tax system is badly in need of reform. Although the various proposals differ radically, they all share a few crucially important characteristics. All would reduce the large number of deductions, credits, and special exemptions that now riddle our income tax system and make it incomprehensible to most taxpayers. This would greatly expand the tax base and thereby allow a significant reduction in marginal rates without losing revenue for the government.

There was a time when public opinion polls showed that taxpayers felt that the property tax was our "most unfair" tax. Recently, it has lost its title to the income tax. That is disturbing because the personal income tax is the most important revenue source for the federal government, and it crucially depends on voluntary compliance.

Fairness is no longer considered to be a characteristic of the tax system. The best one can say about the system is that it is a hodgepodge. What's more, it is an incomprehensible hodgepodge.

Flat Tax Proposals

There are now at least ten proposals related to the flat tax. As already noted, they vary greatly, and some are anything but flat. Even the purest versions generally provide a generous basic exemption in order to ease the burden on low-income groups. Some variants, such as that of Senator Bill Bradley and Representative Richard A. Gephardt, would have more than one tax bracket and would more or less duplicate the effective progressivity of the current system. One of the most detailed pure proposals [with a single tax rate of 19%] was designed by Alvin Rabushka and Robert Hall of Stanford University.

The greatest appeal of the flat tax is its simplicity. The elimination of deductions, exemptions, and special credits greatly shortens the tax form; makes taxpayer compliance simpler; and makes it easier to administer. Hall and Rabushka claim that their tax form would fit on a postcard.

All of the variants of the flat tax system now being proposed possess some degree of progressivity. Where there is only one tax bracket, the progressivity comes from the basic allowances and exemptions. Under the Hall-Rabushka approach, for example, a couple with two children would face an average tax rate of 7.2% on $10,000 of income, 13.1% at $20,000, and 16.6% at $50,000. The rate gradually approaches 19% as income rises.

[The Bradley-Gephardt proposal] retains considerable progressivity and protects the bulk of the middle class by retaining homeowner deductions [for interest payments and property taxes]. I do not believe that one should completely rule out the possibility that the middle class would accept some tax increases in return for a much simpler system and one that treats equals more equally.

Our tax system has become a mess because politicians wanted to do all things for all people. There are few of us who do not benefit from one special provision or another. It may be time to make a deal. We might all agree to give up our special advantages in the interest of obtaining a more simple, efficient, and equitable system.

† Abridged, from Rudolph G. Penner, *The AEI Economist* (Washington: American Enterprise Institute), August 1982. Penner is now the director of the Congressional Budget Office.

If taxes are imposed according to the *benefit* principle, people pay taxes in proportion to the benefits they receive from government spending.

If taxes are imposed according to the *ability to pay* principle, higher taxes are paid by those with greater ability to pay, as measured by income and/or wealth.

If the government were to levy a progressive income tax and an inheritance tax, and at the same time provide assistance to those at the bottom of the economic ladder, it would substantially redistribute income from the rich to the poor. But the world is not so simple. The government levies many other taxes as well, and when they are all taken together, it is not so clear that the government is taking a substantially larger percentage of income from the rich than from the poor, as we shall see in the next section.

THE BURDEN OF TAXES: WHO ULTIMATELY PAYS?

It is difficult to determine who bears the burden of many of our taxes. For example, consider the relatively simple social security tax. Half this tax is deducted from the take-home pay of the worker. This half is regressive: An employee receiving $30,000 per year pays a larger percentage in social security taxes than does an employee receiving $60,000. But what about the other half of the tax which is levied on the employer? Does the tax come out of the corporation's profits? Or is it passed on to the consumer in the form of higher prices? Or, possibly, this half may also fall on the worker: If there were no social security tax, the employer might be willing to pay a higher wage. And, if the question of tax burden—of who ultimately pays—is complicated for the social security tax, it is even more complex for many other taxes. We simply do not have a very precise idea of who ultimately bears the burden of taxes.

The burden, or ***incidence,*** of all U.S. taxes—federal, state, and local—has been studied for many years by Joseph Pechman of the Brookings Institution, a Washington public policy research organization. He has made a number of estimates reflecting differences of opinion among economists as to who ultimately pays. His results are summarized in Figure 5-4. Even if the "most progressive" assumptions are made, the total tax system is only moderately progressive, rising from 20.6% of income for the lowest tenth of the population to 27.3% of income for the highest tenth. On the other hand, if the "least progressive assumptions" are made, the U.S. tax system is moderately regressive. The lowest tenth of the population pay 28.9% in taxes, while the top tenth pay only 24.9%. If one makes intermediate assumptions, the overall U.S. tax system is approximately proportional.

Whatever assumptions are made, progressivity is much less than one would expect on the basis of the income tax schedule shown earlier in Table 5-2. There are two major reasons: (1) Some taxes are proportional or even regressive, such as the employees' half of the social security tax and a number of taxes at the state and local levels; and (2) the existence of tax "loopholes," which are of particular benefit to the wealthy in allowing them to reduce their tax payments.

Tax Loopholes

"Loopholes" are provisions of the law which permit the reduction of taxes. Those who use the loopholes are acting perfectly *legally* to *avoid* taxes. (They therefore should be sharply distinguished from those who act *illegally* to *evade* taxes, perhaps by padding their deductions or understating their incomes.) The term *loophole* clearly implies that the provision is unfair, and as there can be strong disagreement over just what is fair, there is likewise disagreement over just what constitutes a loophole. However, here are some of the items which are often put on the list.

1. ***Investment tax credit.*** When a corporation or individual acquires business equipment, it is permitted to deduct 10% of the price of that equipment from its tax bill.
2. ***Tax-exempt securities.*** If you buy state or local government bonds, the interest you receive from them is exempt from federal income tax. Similarly, interest from federal government bonds is exempt from state and local taxes. Thus, individuals and corporations can reduce their income taxes by buying government bonds.

3. ***Capital gains.*** When an asset is sold for more than it cost, the seller has a capital gain. For example, if you buy General Motors stock for $2,000 and later sell it for $3,000, you have made a $1,000 capital gain. Long-term capital gains—that is, capital gains on assets held for 6 months or more—are taxed at 40% of the rate for ordinary income from wages or salaries.

4. ***Deduction of interest.*** In calculating taxable income, individuals are permitted to deduct the interest which they pay on loans. This provision is of particular benefit to those who are making large interest payments on home mortgages.

A *tax credit* is a subtraction from the tax payable. (For example, if a $1,000 machine is bought, the 10% investment tax credit means that $100 can be subtracted from the taxes which must be paid to the government.)

In contrast to a tax credit, a *deduction* is a subtraction from taxable income. Suppose an individual

FIGURE 5-4

Total federal, state, and local taxes, as a percent of income

The incidence of taxes depends in part on the assumptions as to ''who actually pays'' such taxes as the corporate income tax. On the most progressive assumptions, the overall tax system is moderately progressive. On the least progressive assumptions, it is moderately regressive. (The poor pay a higher percent in taxes, although the rich pay more in dollar terms.)

Source: Joseph A. Pechman, *Who Paid the Taxes, 1966–85?* (Washington: Brookings Institution, 1985), p. 4.

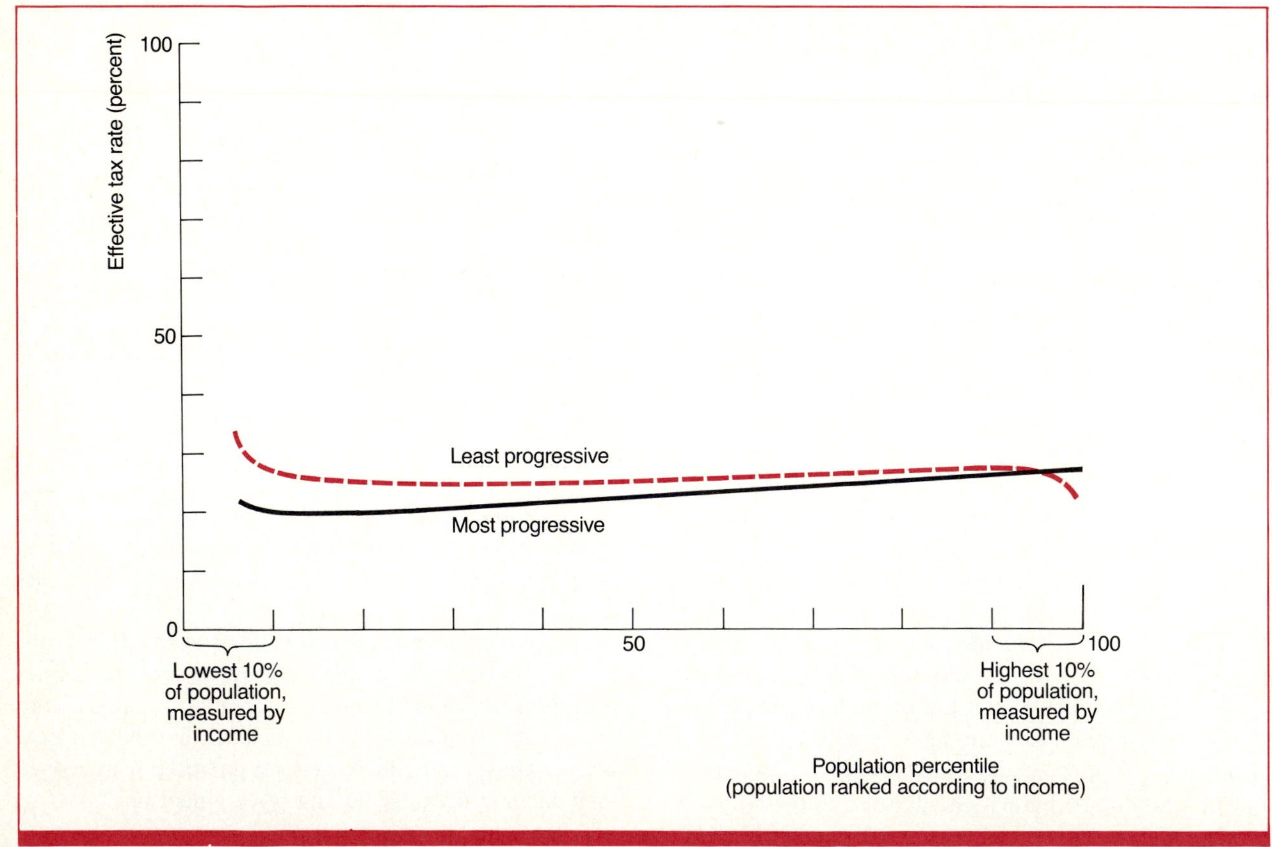

pays $1,000 in interest on a home mortgage. This $1,000 can be deducted from taxable income. For someone in the 33% tax bracket, this results in a $330 reduction in taxes. (Note that the tax saving depends on the tax bracket. Thus, a $1,000 deduction reduces taxes more for someone in the 33% tax bracket than for a person in a lower bracket. Note also that the $1,000 deduction is worth only $330 to this individual, while a $1,000 tax credit is worth the full $1,000 in tax savings.)

These—and other—loopholes have led to much controversy. Jimmy Carter was perhaps most critical when he labeled the tax system a "disgrace to the human race." There are, however, three major complications that have prevented President Carter—or anybody else—from succeeding in a comprehensive tax reform.

First is the disagreement over just what is fair. This disagreement inspired Senator Russell Long to poetry. The typical attitude, he observed, is, "Don't tax you; don't tax me; tax the fellow behind that tree."

The second complication is a political problem. Those who benefit from loopholes have an incentive to lobby to make sure they are not eliminated.

Finally, reform is complicated by the fact that fairness is only one of the major objectives in a tax system. Most of the loopholes were put in expressly to promote national goals which the proponents considered important. For example, the investment tax credit was introduced in the early 1960s at President Kennedy's request to stimulate investment.

In taxation, as in so many areas of economics, the policymaker is left with the problem of balancing conflicting national goals.

KEY POINTS

1. The defects and limitations of the market provide the government with an important economic role. The government affects the economy through expenditures, taxation, regulation, and publicly owned enterprises.
2. In dollar terms, government spending has skyrocketed since 1929. However, as a percentage of national product, the growth of government spending has been much slower. Indeed, if only purchases of goods and services are counted, the government's share of national product has been quite stable over the past three decades.
3. Of the federal expenditures, transfer payments have risen much more rapidly than expenditures for goods and services.
4. Personal income taxes, social security taxes, and corporate income taxes are the main sources of revenue for the federal government. At the state level, sales taxes are the most important source of tax revenues. For localities, property taxes are most important.
5. Federal government revenues have fallen far short of expenditures. As a result, the federal government has run large deficits, running as high as 6.5% of GNP in 1983.
6. Government regulatory agencies are active in many areas, regulating monopoly and protecting the public from misleading advertising, unsafe drugs, and pollution.
7. The primary reasons for government intervention in the economy are to:

    (*a*) Provide public goods that cannot be supplied by the market because individuals have no incentive to buy them. Individuals get the benefits regardless of who pays.

    (*b*) Deal with externalities, such as pollution.

    (*c*) Encourage the consumption of "merit" goods and discourage or prohibit harmful products.

    (*d*) Help the poor.

    (*e*) Help stabilize the economy.
8. A number of objectives are important in the design of a tax system:

    (*a*) In general, neutrality is a desirable objective.

    (*b*) In some cases, however, the government should alter market signals by taxation. For example, a tax can be used to discourage pollution.

    (*c*) Taxes should be reasonably simple and easily understood.

    (*d*) Taxes should be fair. There are two ways of judging fairness: the benefit principle and ability to pay.
9. The burden or "incidence" of taxes—that is, who ultimately pays the taxes—is hard to determine. But the rich don't bear as heavy a burden as the income tax rates suggest.

KEY CONCEPTS

regulation
transfer payment
income tax
marginal tax rate
average tax rate
progressive tax
regressive tax
proportional tax
deficit
surplus
balanced budget
revenue sharing
general revenue sharing
categorical grant
block grant
externality
tax neutrality
public good
merit good
broader tax base
flatter tax
benefit principle
ability-to-pay principle
incidence of taxes
tax loophole
investment tax credit
capital gain

PROBLEMS

5-1. "That government governs best which governs least." Do you agree? Why or why not? Does the government perform more functions than it should? If so, what activities would you like it to reduce or stop altogether? Are there any additional functions which the government should undertake? If so, what ones? How should they be paid for?

5-2. "State and local governments are closer to the people than is the federal government. Therefore, they should be given some of the functions of the federal government." Are there federal functions which might be turned over to the states and localities? Do you think they should be turned over? Why or why not? Are there federal functions which the states are incapable of handling?

5-3. The government engages in research. For example, the government has agricultural experimental stations, and during the Second World War the government developed the atomic bomb through the massive Manhattan Project. Why do you think the government engages in these two types of research, while leaving most other research to private business? Does the government have any major advantages in undertaking research? Any major disadvantages?

5-4. Consider two views of the tax system:

(*a*) "The government promotes social goals, such as the education and the arts, through direct payments. It also promotes education and the arts by encouraging private giving. This is done by making gifts deductible from taxable income. Tax deductions may be an even more effective way of supporting education, the arts, and other desirable causes than direct government grants. Therefore, such deductions do not constitute 'loopholes.' Rather, they represent an efficient way of achieving important social goals."

(*b*) "The income tax is a mess. Homeowners get a tax break, but renters do not. The rich are able to escape taxes by making gifts to universities, the arts, and to charities. The only way to get equity into the system is to eliminate all deductions, and make all income subject to tax."

Which of these arguments is stronger? Why?

CHAPTER 6

BUSINESS ORGANIZATION AND FINANCE

Business is a game—the greatest game in the world if you know how to play it.

THOMAS J. WATSON, SR., OF IBM

The government is an important participant in the U.S. economy, regulating business and providing such public goods as roads, health services, and defense. But the primary productive role is played by private business. Businesses use the resources of society—labor, land, and capital—to produce the goods and services that consumers, the government, and other businesses demand.

In future chapters, we will study the behavior of businesses. How much do they produce? At what prices do they sell? What combination of land, labor, and capital do they use in the productive process? How do they respond to changing market conditions? Questions such as these are central subjects of any introductory study of economics. This chapter provides background on the organization of businesses and the ways in which they obtain the money to finance expansion.

BUSINESS ORGANIZATIONS

There are three types of business organization: the ***single proprietorship,*** the ***partnership,*** and the ***corporation.*** The single proprietorship and the partnership are the most common forms of very small business, although even a one-person business may be a corporation. At the other end of the spectrum, large businesses are almost exclusively corporations, although there are some exceptions. For example, large law firms are partnerships.

Single Proprietorships and Partnerships: Their Advantages and Disadvantages

A single proprietorship is the easiest form of business to establish; there is little fuss or bother. If I decide to make pottery in my basement or design computer software in a spare bedroom, I may do so. I can begin tomorrow, without going through legal and organizational hassles. A single proprietorship has advantages for someone who wants to experiment with a new line of work—a fact that may explain why so many single proprietorships go out of business so quickly.

The single proprietorship is flexible and uncomplicated. The proprietor buys the materials needed, hires any help that is necessary and can be afforded, and undertakes to pay the bills. The profits of the business belong to the owner, to be shared by no one—except the government, which collects its share in the form of personal income taxes paid by the owner.

However, the single proprietorship has disadvantages. Most obviously, there are limits to how much one individual can manage. Consider a typical small enterprise, the gasoline station. In this sort of business, a single owner has problems. While help can be hired to operate the pumps, there are advantages in having someone around who is "in charge." Yet one individual would find it a crushing burden to try to be present during the long hours when a gas station is open. The obvious solution is to take on a partner, who will be jointly responsible.

Some partnerships are made up of just two people; others include dozens of partners. In a typical partnership, each partner agrees to provide some fraction of the work and some of the financing. In return, each partner receives an agreed share of the profits or suffers an agreed share of the loss. Again, the partnership is easily established; a simple oral agreement will do. However, this casual method is not recommended; it is a way to lose both business and friend. A formal partnership agreement, drawn up by a lawyer, can prevent much grief.

Both the single proprietorship and the partnership are simple and flexible, but they share the following major limitations:

1. If a proprietorship runs into difficulty, the owner can lose more than his or her initial investment. Personal assets may be lost in order to pay the *creditors*—that is, those to whom the business owes money. In short, a proprietor has ***unlimited liability*** for all the debts of the business.

In the standard type of partnership, partners similarly have unlimited liability; they can lose their personal assets as well as the money they originally put into the business. And, with a partnership, there is a particular form of risk: *Each partner is liable for the obligations undertaken by the other partner or partners,* and each partner runs the risk of being left "holding the bag" if the other partners are unable to meet their shares of the obligations of the partnership.

2. There is a problem with ***continuity.*** When a single proprietor dies, the business may too—although an heir may take over the shop or farm and continue to run it. Continuity is an even more awkward problem in a partnership. When a partner dies, the original partnership automatically ends and a new partnership must be formed. A new partnership agreement is likewise necessary whenever a new partner is admitted. This is not surprising; after all, each of the partners will be liable for the acts of the new partner.

3. There is the problem of ***financing growth.*** A partnership or proprietorship has a number of sources of financing: the personal wealth of the owner or owners; the profits made by the business which can be plowed back to purchase new equipment or buildings; the mortgaging of property; and borrowing from banks, suppliers, friends, and relatives. But proprietorships and partnerships may have difficulty borrowing the money needed for expansion. Because of the risk, banks are reluctant to lend large amounts to a struggling new enterprise.

Furthermore, it may also be difficult to bring in new owners to help with the financing. It is true that a carrot, in the form of a share of the profits, can be dangled in front of potential investors. But with the carrot comes a stick. In gaining a right to a share of the profits, a new partner also undertakes unlimited liability for the debts of the business. Consequently, outside investors will be reluctant to share in the partnership unless they have carefully investigated it and have developed an exceptionally high degree of confidence in the partners. This may make it very hard for a partnership to get the financing needed for expansion.

The Corporation

Corporation. An ingenious device for obtaining individual profit without individual responsibility.

Ambrose Bierce,
The Devil's Dictionary

The major advantage of the corporate form of organization is that it ***limits the liability*** of its owners: All they can lose is their initial investment. When new investors buy ***shares*** of the ***common stock*** of a business, they thereby acquire partial ownership of the business without facing the danger of unlimited liability. If the business goes bankrupt and is unable to pay its debts, the owners lose the purchase price of their shares but not their homes or other personal property.[1] By reducing the risks of investors, the corporate form of business makes it feasible to tap a wide pool of investment funds. Thus, the corporation is the form of business most suited to rapid growth with the use of outside funds.

Each *share of common stock* represents a fraction of the *ownership* (that is, a fraction of the *equity*) of a corporation.

Because of the limited liability, a corporation's creditors cannot lay claim to the personal property of the owners if the corporation fails—although they can claim

[1]Limited liability does not occur exclusively in corporations. There is a special type of partnership that represents a legal half-way point between the standard partnership, with its unlimited liability, and the corporation. These special partnerships have two classes of owners. The *general* partners have unlimited liability. The *limited* partners, as the name implies, have limited liability and are similar to the stockholders of a corporation. Such partnerships, with their two classes of owners, are quite common in real estate. They are used instead of corporations because of the tax advantages they offer.

the assets of the corporation itself. Corporations must inform those with whom they do business of this limited liability. In the United States, they do so by tacking to their corporate title the designation "Inc." or "Incorporated." The British have traditionally added "Ltd." or "Limited" to the title of their corporations, although the official designation was changed to "Public Limited Company," or "PLC," in 1980. The French and Spanish use a more colorful warning: Corporations' titles are followed by the letters S.A.—for *Société Anonyme* or *Sociedad Anonima* (anonymous society).

When the corporate form of business was first used in Britain some centuries ago, corporation charters were awarded only rarely, by special grants of the king and Parliament. These corporations were granted substantial privileges. Some were given special rights to conduct business in the British colonies—the East India Company, for example. During the nineteenth century, however, a major revolution occurred in business and legal thinking, and the modern corporation emerged. General incorporation laws were passed, granting to anyone the right to form a corporation. The formation of a corporation is generally a straightforward and uncomplicated legal procedure, although there are a few important exceptions—such as banking, where government regulation is important.

In addition to limited liability, the corporation offers the advantage of continuity. In law, the corporation is a fictitious "legal person." When one of the stockholders dies, the corporation survives; the shares of the deceased are inherited by his or her heirs, without the corporation's organization being disturbed. The heirs need not be concerned about accepting the shares, since they are not liable for the corporation's debts. Furthermore, the corporation survives if some of the stockholders want to get out of the business. These stockholders can sell their shares to anyone willing to buy; there is no need to reorganize the company.

Corporation Taxes

The profits of a proprietorship or a partnership are taxed as the personal income of the proprietor or partners. When a corporation is established, taxation becomes more complicated. From the viewpoint of the shareholder-owner, the corporate form of business organization may represent either a tax advantage or a tax disadvantage.

Consider an illustration. A corporation with 1 million shares outstanding makes pretax profits of $10 million, or $10 per share. The corporation is taxed as a separate entity; its total corporation profits tax might amount to, say, $3 million, or $3 per share. (The corporation income tax rate is 46% for all profits above $100,000 per year. But the effective tax rate is less than 46% because of the investment tax credit and other detailed provisions of the tax law.) This leaves $7 million in after-tax profits, or $7 per share. Of this $7, the corporation might retain $5 for expansion of the business and pay out the remaining $2 per share as dividends to the shareholders. In turn, the shareholders must include the dividends of $2 per share as part of their personal income and pay personal income tax—at rates up to a maximum of 50%, depending on their tax bracket. From the viewpoint of the shareholder-owner, the disadvantage of this arrangement is that *dividend income is taxed twice*. First, it is taxed when it is earned as part of the total profits of the corporation. Second, it is taxed again when it is paid out in dividends and becomes the personal income of the shareholder who receives it.

However, there also is a tax advantage. Consider the profits which are retained and not paid out in dividends. This income is taxed only once—and at a rate of only 30%. (Remember: It was part of the $10 million in profits on which $3 million of tax was paid.) For wealthy shareholders in a high tax bracket, the 30% tax paid on the retained corporate profit is less than they would have to pay in personal income taxes if the business were a proprietorship or a partnership. Furthermore, for a small corporation, the tax advantage is even greater, since low tax rates apply to the first $100,000 of corporate profits. (The tax rate is 15% for the first $25,000 of profits, 18% for the second $25,000, 30% for the third, and 40% for the fourth.) Particularly for a new, growing business, there thus may be a tax incentive to incorporate. By keeping dividends low and plowing most of the profits back into the business, total taxes can be kept low.

The double taxation of dividend income is a subject of sharp controversy. Not only does a question of fairness arise—since profits going into dividends are taxed twice while profits retained for expansion are taxed only once—but a tax incentive is also provided for big corporations to grow even bigger: When profits are retained for expansion, double taxation is avoided.

HOW A CORPORATION FINANCES EXPANSION

The corporation can obtain funds for expansion in the same way as a proprietorship or partnership, that is, by borrowing from banks or plowing profits back into the business. But a large corporation also has other options. It can issue common stock, bonds, or other securities.

Common Stock

When it sells additional shares of common stock, the corporation takes on new part-owners, since each share represents a fraction of the ownership of the corporation. As a part-owner, the purchaser of common stock not only receives a share of any dividends paid by the corporation but also gets the right to vote for the corporation's directors, who, in turn, choose the corporate officers and set the corporation's policies. (On the question of who actually controls a corporation, see Box 6-1.)

Bonds

Rather than take on new owners by issuing additional common stock, the corporation may raise funds by selling bonds. A bond represents a debt of the corporation; it is an I.O.U. that the corporation is obliged to repay, whether it is making profits or not. If the corporation doesn't pay, it can be sued by the bondholder.

A bond is a long-term form of debt which does not fall due for repayment until 10, 15, or more years from the time it was initially sold (issued) by the corporation. Bonds usually come in large denominations—for example, $100,000. The original buyer normally pays the corporation a sum equal to the face value of the bond; in effect, the original buyer is lending $100,000 to the corporation. In return for the $100,000, the corporation is committed to make two sets of payments to the bondholder:

1. Interest payments that must be made periodically—normally semiannually—during the life of the bond. If the interest rate is, say, 14% per annum on a bond with a $100,000 face value, the interest payment will be $7,000 (that is, 7%) every 6 months.

2. A payment of the $100,000 ***face value,*** or ***principal,*** when the date of maturity arrives; that is, the corporation must repay the amount of the loan at maturity.

Since a bond commits the corporation to make the payments of interest and principal, it provides the purchaser an assured, steady income—provided the corporation avoids bankruptcy. Common stock, on the other hand, involves a substantial risk. During periods of difficulty, the corporation may reduce or eliminate the dividend, and the market price of the stock may plummet. But, while bonds provide more safety than stocks, they offer less excitement. Unlike the owner of common stock, the bondholder cannot look forward to rising dividends if the company hits the jackpot. The bondholder will get no more than the interest and principal specified in the bond contract. Generally, bonds are safe, but they are also dull.

Bonds are not the only type of debt which a corporation can issue. It also may issue *notes,* which are similar to bonds, except that they have only a few years to maturity. *Commercial paper* is even shorter term, being normally issued for just a few months.

Some investors desire an income-earning security "between stocks and bonds," that is, one that will provide more safety than common stock while still offering a larger potential return than bonds if the company does well. These investors may choose *convertible bonds* or *preferred stock.*

Convertible Bonds

Convertible bonds are like ordinary bonds, with one additional feature. Before a given date, they may be exchanged for common stock in some fixed ratio—for example, 1 bond for 10 shares of common stock. If the outlook for the corporation becomes favorable, the holder of convertible bonds may exchange them for common stock and thus own shares of the growing corporation. If, on the other hand, the company fails to prosper, convertible bonds may be held to maturity, when the bondholder will receive repayment of the principal.

Because the holder has the option of converting, the interest rate on convertible bonds is normally less than the rate on regular bonds, often substantially less. Therefore, if you are thinking about buying convertible bonds, you have to weigh two conflicting considerations. The interest payments which you receive will be low, but you will have the option to convert into common stock, an option which may become valuable in the event the business is successful.

Preferred Stock

Preferred stock, like common stock, represents owner-

BOX 6-1

WHO CONTROLS THE CORPORATION?

Because stockholders elect the board of directors, who in turn choose management, it would seem at first glance that the corporation is run in the interest of its stockholders.

However, things are not necessarily that simple. If a company's stock is spread among a large number of shareholders, it may, in practice, be run by a group of insiders made up of the directors and senior management. The small stockholder's problem is akin to that of the consumer. In both cases, the stakes are not sufficiently great for the individual stockholders or consumers to make their views known forcefully. If you own only a few shares of stock, it is probably not even worth your time and your travel expenses to show up at the annual meeting. Furthermore, unless the corporation is doing very badly, you are likely to grant the management's request for your ***proxy;*** that is, you give them the authorization to vote on your behalf at the annual meeting. As a result, management is likely to be in control at the annual meeting.

This does not, however, mean that the management is absolutely immune from challenge: If the corporation's performance is weak, a dissident group of shareholders can get together. They may be successful in getting enough proxies to oust the old management. But this occurs only rarely. Throwing out management is a drastic step, which disrupts the everyday operation of the company. The standard advice given in the investment community is this: If you don't like the way the company is being run, don't fight management. Sell your stock. Vote with your feet.

The separation of ownership and control was pointed out in *The Modern Corporation and Private Property* by A. A. Berle and Gardner C. Means, published in 1932. They found that the stockholding of 44% of the 200 largest U.S. corporations was so dif-

fuse that no single family, corporation, or group of business associates owned as much as 10% of the stock. More recent work indicates that, by 1963, control was even more separated from ownership than it had been when Berle and Means wrote: What was true of 44% of the 200 largest corporations in the earlier period was by then true of 84.5%.

Where control is effectively in the hands of management rather than the owners, the question arises as to what difference this makes. There is an obvious community of interest between management and stockholders: Both groups want a corporation which is profitable. Management is obviously interested in the success of the corporation, since their jobs may be lost if the corporation goes under.

But, while similar, the interests of management and stockholders are not identical. Management may be more interested in the preservation of their jobs than in profits. Furthermore, management—like a government bureaucracy—may be interested in growth for its own sake, even if growth does not contribute to profits. Why is this so? The importance of your position is in part measured by the number of people who work for you.

ship and not debt. The corporation is legally obligated to make interest payments to bondholders, but it is not legally required to pay dividends to preferred or common stockholders.

Preferred stockholders, however, have a claim on profits which precedes—is "preferred" to—the claim of the common stockholder. The preferred stockholder has a right to receive specific dividends (for example, $2 per share) before the common stockholder can be paid any dividend at all. But, on the other hand, the preferred stockholder does not have the possibility of large gains open to the common stockholder. While the common stockholder may hope for rising dividends if the corporation prospers, the preferred shareholder will at most receive the specified dividend. (A rare form of stock, the *participating* preferred, provides an exception to this rule. It gives the holder the right to participate in the growth of the company's dividends.)

As a general rule, all types of securities—common stocks, preferred stocks, and bonds—may be resold by the original purchasers. Securities prices tend to reflect the judgment of buyers and sellers regarding the prospects of the corporation. Thus, for example, an announcement of a new product may make purchasers eager to buy the company's stock and make present stockholders reluctant to sell. As a result, the price of the stock will be bid up. Purchasers also look at the position and performance of the company as indicated by a study of its financial accounts.

BUSINESS ACCOUNTING: THE BALANCE SHEET AND THE INCOME STATEMENT

Business accounts are valuable not only as a source of information for potential buyers of the company's stock or bonds. They also are an important tool for helping management keep track of how well the company is doing and what it is worth. In addition, businesses are required to keep accounts for tax purposes.

There are two major types of business accounts:

1. The ***balance sheet,*** which gives a picture of the company's financial status at a *point* in time, for example, at the close of business on December 31 of last year.

2. The ***income statement***—also called the ***profit and loss statement***—which summarizes the company's transactions over a *period* of time, such as a year.

The income statement records the *flow* of payments into and out of a company *over a period* of time. It is like a record of the amount of water that has flowed into and out of Lake Michigan *during* a year. The balance sheet, on the other hand, measures the situation *at a specific point* in time. It is like a measure of the *stock* of water in Lake Michigan today at noon.

The Balance Sheet

The balance sheet shows (1) the ***assets*** which a company owns, (2) the ***liabilities*** which it owes, and (3) the value of the ***ownership*** of the stockholders. Assets must be exactly equal to the total of liabilities plus ownership. To use a simple illustration: If you have a car worth $7,000 (an asset), for which you still owe $4,000 to the bank (your debt or liability), then $3,000 is the value of your ownership in the car.

The same fundamental equation also holds for a corporation:

***Assets* = *liabilities* (what is owed) +**
***net worth* (the value of ownership)**

Assets are listed on the left side of the balance sheet, while liabilities and net worth are listed on the right. Because of the fundamental equation, the two sides must add to the same total: ***The balance sheet must balance.***

The *net worth* of a corporation—the amount the stockholders own—is equal to the assets minus the liabilities of the corporation.

As an example, consider Table 6-1, which shows the balance sheet of Wang Laboratories, a producer of word processors and small office computers.

The left-hand, asset side Wang has sizable assets in the form of cash (bank accounts), marketable short-term securities issued by other corporations or the government, and accounts receivable—for example, the value of computers which have already been delivered to customers but have not yet been paid for. Wang has sizable inventories of materials and parts and of completed office equipment. Wang also has major assets in the form of land, plant (buildings), and equipment.

The right-hand side, showing liabilities and net worth Wang has a number of short-term liabilities: amounts which Wang has not yet paid for the chips and other items it has bought from suppliers (accounts payable), wages and salaries not yet paid for work already performed (accrued liabilities), and other short-term debt. In addition, at mid-1984, Wang had an outstanding long-term debt of $359 million. (If debt matures within 1 year, it is short-term; in more than 1 year, long-term.)

In mid-1984, Wang's total assets were $2.25 billion and its liabilities were $1.00 billion. The net worth—the ownership of all stockholders—was therefore $1.25 billion. Of this, about half ($646 million) had been paid in by stockholders purchasing shares from the company. The other half ($603 million) represented retained earnings, that is, profits made over the years that had been plowed back into the business.[2]

In mid-1984, there were 138.7 million shares of Wang common stock outstanding. Each share represented an equity, or ***book value,*** of $9.01—that is, $1,249 million in net worth ÷ 138.7 million shares.

The *book value* of a stock is its net worth per share. It is calculated by dividing the total net worth of the company by the number of shares outstanding.

If you are thinking of buying common stock of a company, its book value is one of the things that should interest you. If it has a high book value, you will be buying ownership of a lot of assets. However, *don't get carried away by a high book value*. If the assets happen

[2]"Retained earnings" may sound like a pool of funds which the corporation has readily available. However, this is generally not the case. Most retained earnings are not held in the form of cash; most are used to buy equipment or other items.

Suppose that, in the first year of its operation, a corporation earns $1,000, and retains it all. (It pays no dividend.) The $1,000 may be used to buy a new machine. Then, as a result, the following changes occur in the balance sheet:

Change in:

Assets		Net worth	
Machinery	+$1,000	Retained earnings	+$1,000

The retained earnings have not been held in the form of idle cash; they have been put to work to buy machinery. The machinery shows up on the asset side. When the retained earnings are included in net worth, the balance sheet balances.

TABLE 6-1
Balance Sheet of Wang Labs, June 30, 1984
(simplified; millions of dollars)

Assets			Liabilities and net worth		
1. Current assets		$1,128	5. Current liabilities		$542
(*a*) Cash	$ 16		(*a*) Accounts payable and accrued liabilities	$248	
(*b*) Marketable short-term securities	57		(*b*) Notes and commercial paper	192	
(*c*) Accounts receivable	445		(*c*) Other	102	
(*d*) Inventories	563		6. Long-term debt		359
(*e*) Other	47		7. Other liabilities		102
2. Land, plant, and equipment		551	**8. Total liabilities (5 + 6 + 7)**		**1,003**
3. Other assets		573	**9. Net worth (4 − 8)**		**1,249**
			(*a*) Receipts from sale of stock	646	
			(*b*) Retained earnings	603	
4. Total assets (items 1 + 2 + 3)		**$2,252**	**10. Total liabilities and net worth (8 + 9)**		**$2,252**

Source: Wang Laboratories, Inc., *Annual Report, 1984*.

to be machinery and equipment that can be used only to produce buggy whips or other items for which there is no demand, the high book value may not be worth very much; the assets may not earn much income in the future. On the other hand, the stock of a profitable corporation may sell for substantially more than its book value. Between the beginning of 1984 and June 1985, Wang stock sold in the range between $15 and $37.63.

The Income Statement

While the balance sheet shows the assets, liabilities, and net worth of a corporation at a point in time, the income statement shows what has happened *during a period of time*—for example, during a calendar year. A simplified version of Wang's income statement for fiscal 1984 is shown in Table 6-2.

During that year, Wang had $2,185 million in revenues from the sale, leasing, and servicing of office equipment. Costs of $1,924 million must be subtracted from revenues to calculate before-tax profit of $261 million. Corporate income taxes were $51 million, leaving an after-tax profit of $210 million, or $1.52 per share. Of this after-tax profit, $15 million was paid in dividends to stockholders and $195 million was retained by the company. Observe that the retained earnings in Table 6-1 are substantially greater than those shown in Table 6-2. The reason is this: The income statement in Table 6-2 shows only the retained earnings during the one year, fiscal 1984. In contrast, the balance sheet in Table 6-1 shows all retained earnings accumulated over the entire lifetime of the company.

TABLE 6-2
Income Statement of Wang Labs, Fiscal Year 1984
(millions of dollars)

1. Revenues		$2,185
(*a*) Sales	$1,699	
(*b*) Rental and service	486	
2. Less: Costs		1,924
(*a*) Costs, excluding items below	977	
(*b*) Depreciation	140	
(*c*) Selling and administrative costs	619	
(*d*) Research and development	161	
(*e*) Net interest	27	
3. Income (profit) before taxes (1 − 2)		261
4. Less: Income taxes		51
5. Net income (net profit) (3 − 4)		210
(*a*) Dividends	15	
(*b*) Retained earnings	195	

Source: Wang Laboratories, Inc., *Annual Report, 1984*.

Most of Wang's costs are reasonably straightforward. Wang pays wages to its workforce and buys materials from outside suppliers. These costs are included in the large cost subcomponent of $977 million in line 2(*a*) of Table 6-2. However, one cost item, ***depreciation*** [line 2(*b*)], needs to be explained. Depreciation is the way a firm spreads out its costs of plant and equipment over time.

Depreciation

Consider the specific example of a machine acquired by Wang during 1984 for use on its production line. This machine did not wear out during 1984; it will continue to be used in coming years. Therefore, in calculating the cost of production in 1984, it would be misleading to count the full purchase price of the machine. Instead, only a fraction is counted as a cost during 1984, with other fractions being allocated to future years while the machine is still in use.

The most straightforward way to allocate the cost of a machine is to estimate its expected life and then spread the cost evenly over the lifetime. For example, if a $10,000 machine were expected to last 5 years, depreciation would be $2,000 in each of these years.

Depreciation accounting is not an exact science. The useful lifetime of a machine depends not only on physical wear and tear but also on obsolescence, which cannot be accurately forecast. Even if a machine could be permanently maintained in brand-new condition, it would eventually become obsolete; that is, its useful life would end as new and more efficient machines became available. (Obsolescence tends to be greatest for high-technology equipment. An early computer, built in 1946 at the University of Pennsylvania, contained 18,000 vacuum tubes, weighed 30 tons, and occupied a huge room, with other large areas needed for air conditioning. Now, a chip with greater computing capacity may be held on the tip of your finger.)

However, an even greater complication arises because of the tax laws. Note that depreciation is a cost which is subtracted before taxable income is calculated (Table 6-2). As a result, firms have an incentive to take their depreciation as soon as the law permits. The more depreciation they take, the lower is their taxable income, and therefore the lower is their tax. If the government speeds up—or *accelerates*—the rate at which firms are allowed to depreciate plant and equipment, it can encourage them to invest and expand. For example, Congress might reduce the "lifetime" of a machine for tax purposes from, say, 5 years to 3 years. This, in fact, is what the Congress did in 1981, on the recommendation of President Reagan. Such a reduction in the lifetime for tax purposes does not limit the length of time a piece of equipment may actually be kept in service; a company may continue to use it after it has been completely depreciated on the company's books.

***Depreciation* is an element of cost. It is either (1) an estimate of the decline in the value of plant or equipment during the year, because of wear and obsolescence, or (2) the amount which tax laws allow business to count as a cost of using plant or equipment during the year.**

FINANCIAL MARKETS

As we have seen, corporations may finance expansion by retaining their profits or by looking outside for sources of funds. They may borrow from banks, insurance companies, or other financial corporations. Or they may issue additional stocks or bonds. Financial markets and financial corporations perform a strategic role in the economy because they help to determine which businesses will receive the finances for expansion.

Financial corporations, such as banks, savings and loan associations, and insurance companies, are ***financial intermediaries;*** that is, they take small amounts of funds from a large number of people, pool these funds, and lend them in larger amounts to businesses, governments, or individuals. For example, a savings and loan association may receive 100 small deposits with an average size of $300. With the combined total of $30,000, it makes a mortgage loan to someone buying a house. In doing this, the savings and loan (S&L) provides a useful service. The home buyer is saved the trouble of trying to locate the 100 individuals who would be willing to put up small amounts. The people who provide the funds are saved the nuisance of lending directly to the homeowner and of collecting on the loan every month. In addition to handling the paperwork, the S&L investigates the credit-worthiness of the potential home buyer, thus limiting the risk that the loan will not be repaid. Similarly, banks and insurance companies take funds from deposits or insurance policies, pool them, and lend them to businesses, governments, or individuals who meet their standards of credit-worthiness.

Thus, a business that wants to borrow money may go to a bank or an insurance company. But what does a business do if it prefers not to borrow and wants to raise money by selling its common stock instead? It may follow one of two courses. If it is a large corporation that already has many shareholders, it can give the current shareholders the rights, or *warrants,* to buy new stock at a specific price. It normally sets this price below the current market price of the stock in order to give the stockholders an incentive to exercise the rights—that is, to use the warrants to buy stock at the bargain price. Those who already have all the stock they want can sell the warrants to someone who wants to use them to buy the bargain stock. Thus, the corporation ends up by selling the new shares of its stock either to current shareholders or to those who have bought the warrants.

Since a new company does not already have a large number of shareholders, it will use a different method of selling stock. It will approach an ***investment bank,*** a firm that markets securities. The investment bank looks for its profits in the markup between the price it pays to the company for the stock and the price at which it sells this stock to the public. The investment bank may simply undertake to sell as many shares as it can, up to the maximum the company is willing to issue. In this case, the company takes a risk: If buyers are unreceptive, few shares are sold and the company raises only a little money. However, if the investment bank is confident regarding the prospects of the company, it may ***underwrite*** the stock issue; that is, it guarantees the sale of the full issue of stock. If it is unable to find buyers for the whole issue, the investment bank will end up buying the shares itself. In order to limit its risk, the investment bank may bring in other investment banks to form a ***syndicate*** which jointly underwrites the new issue.

Investment banks may also underwrite corporation bonds. As part of their business, investment bankers keep close contact with pension funds and other large-scale purchasers of securities. Among the largest investment banks are Salomon Brothers, Goldman Sachs, First Boston, and Morgan Stanley.

Financial Markets: The Objectives of Buyers of Securities

In some ways, the markets for stocks and bonds are similar to the markets for shirts, shoes, or automobiles. For example, just as the automobile dealer makes profits by the markup on cars, so does the investment banker make profits by the markup on stocks and bonds. Nevertheless, in one very important way, the market for stocks and bonds is quite different from the market for shoes or cars. When you wish to buy a pair of shoes or a car, you can examine the available merchandise and make a reasonably good judgment as to its quality. But when you buy a common stock, you are, in effect, buying a future prospect—something which is clearly intangible and about which it may be very difficult to reach an informed and balanced judgment. Similarly, when you buy a bond, you are buying a set of promises made by the bond issuer to pay interest and principal on schedule.

Because of the uncertainty of the future, purchasers do not simply choose the bond which has the highest interest rate; the likelihood that the company will actually repay is also important. Indeed, purchasers of securities have three objectives to balance: return, risk, and liquidity.

Return is the annual yield, measured as a percentage of the cost of the security. For example, if a bond is purchased for $10,000 and it pays interest of $1,200 per year, then it yields 12%.

Risk is the chance that something will go wrong. For example, the company may go bankrupt, and the bondholder may lose both interest and principal.

Finally, ***liquidity*** reflects the ability of the owner to sell an asset on short notice, with little cost and bother. A passbook account in an S&L is highly liquid. Unless the S&L has run into financial difficulty, the account may be withdrawn at any time for its full dollar value. (Thus, in addition to handling paperwork and evaluating borrowers' credit-worthiness, S&Ls and other financial intermediaries provide their depositors with liquidity.) At the other end of the spectrum, real estate or paintings are very illiquid. If you have to sell your home on short notice, you may have to accept a price which is much lower than you could get with a more lengthy selling effort.

While investors look for a combination of high return, low risk, and high liquidity, they do not all weigh the three objectives equally. Some—particularly those with steady incomes who are saving for the distant future—do not consider liquidity important, while others (perhaps those with children about to enter college) want to keep liquid investments on which they can draw in the near future. Different investors may have quite different attitudes toward risk.

The Objectives of Issuers of Securities

A company raising funds also has three objectives to balance: to obtain funds in such a way as to achieve a high *return* for the corporation's stockholders, to avoid *risk,* and to assure the *availability* of money when it is needed.

A corporation balances risk and return when it chooses whether to issue stocks or bonds. In contrast with the view from the buyer's side, the view of the corporation selling securities is that *bonds* have a *higher risk* than common stock. If the corporation sells bonds, interest payments must be made no matter how badly the company may be doing. Thus, a large outstanding debt can put a corporation in a precarious position. If business slackens, it may be unable to meet large payments for interest and principal and may as a result be driven into bankruptcy. There is no such risk with common stock, since the company can cut dividends in the event of a downturn in business.

While it is safer for a corporation to issue stock, there is a disadvantage. Additional stock involves taking on new part-owners. If the company does well, the rising profits go partially to the new stockholders; the original stockholders must share their bonanza. In contrast, consider what happens if bonds are issued—that is, if the ***leverage*** of the corporation is increased. After the required payment of interest on the bonds, any large profits go only to the original stockholders. Thus, the more highly leveraged a corporation is, the greater is the uncertainty for its owners. Their potential gain is large, but so is their potential loss, including the possibility of bankruptcy.

***Leverage* is the ratio of debt to net worth. If this ratio is large, the corporation is *highly leveraged*.**

As a group, stockholders and corporate managers tend to be optimistic. They consequently may try to maximize their expected gains by a high degree of leverage. Furthermore, limited liability provides an incentive for leverage. If things go well, stockholders can earn many times their original investment. But if things go poorly, they can lose their original investment only once. Thus, a company may be highly leveraged in order to keep the potential gains in the hands of a few stockholders, while much of the risk is borne by bondholders and other creditors. Even though a company takes risk into account when it issues stocks or bonds, it has a temptation to discount the importance of risk, since someone else will suffer much of the possible loss.

If corporate managers were free to leverage to their hearts' content, the economy might be wildly unstable. When businesses go bankrupt, their employees may be thrown out of work and other businesses to whom they owe money may also go bankrupt. Fortunately, however, there are limits to leverage. As leverage increases, the rising risks to bondholders make them cautious. They become increasingly reluctant to buy that company's bonds unless the bonds yield a very high interest. If leverage becomes great enough, the company may find it impossible to sell bonds or to borrow from banks or others. Leverage is limited by the caution of lenders.

The final objective of corporations issuing securities is to ensure the availability of money when it is needed. As a general rule, it is not advisable to finance a new factory with short-term borrowing. It is unwise to have to keep repaying a short-term debt and borrowing money again each year to finance a factory over, say, a 20-year lifetime. In some of those years, funds may not be available to borrowers or may be available only at a very high interest rate. New factories should therefore be financed by long-term borrowing, by the issue of additional stock, or by retained profits.

In order to ensure the availability of money for unpredictable requirements that can arise, a corporation may arrange a ***line of credit*** at a bank. A line of credit is a commitment by a bank to lend up to a specified limit at the request of the company. Similarly, builders may get commitments from savings and loan associations to provide mortgage money in the future. Such commitments allow builders to make firm plans for construction.

The Bond Market

Because security buyers balance risk and return, risky securities generally must have higher yields, or nobody will buy them. This shows up in the bond market yields shown in Figure 6-1. Observe that the highest-grade corporate bonds, classified Aaa by Moody's Investors' Service, have lower yields than the more risky corporate bonds, classified Baa. (In judging the quality of bonds, investors' services consider such things as leverage and the stability of a corporation's earnings.) In turn, U.S. government bonds, which are free from risk of default, have lower yields than even the highest-grade corporate bonds.

Note also that the gaps between these three sets of bonds—the U.S. government, corporate Aaa, and corporate Baa—are not constant. Most conspicuously, the gap between corporate Aaa and Baa yields shot up during the early 1930s. As the economy collapsed into the Depression, bankruptcies mounted; many shaky firms went under. The risks associated with the holding of low-grade corporate bonds rose, and consequently their yields also rose, compared to the yields on high-grade bonds. A similar, but less dramatic, increase in ***risk premiums*** took place during the recessions of 1974 and 1982, when the gap between the yields on corporate Aaa and corporate Baa bonds widened. The gap between risk-free U.S. government bonds and corporate Aaa bonds also widened.

A *risk premium* is the difference between the yields on two grades of bonds because of differences in their risk.

FIGURE 6-1
Long-term bond yields
The differences between yields on different securities reflect primarily differences in risk. (A notable exception is the low yield on state and local government securities, which reflects their tax-exempt status.) The rising trend of all interest rates between 1965 and 1981 was caused primarily by a rise in the rate of inflation.

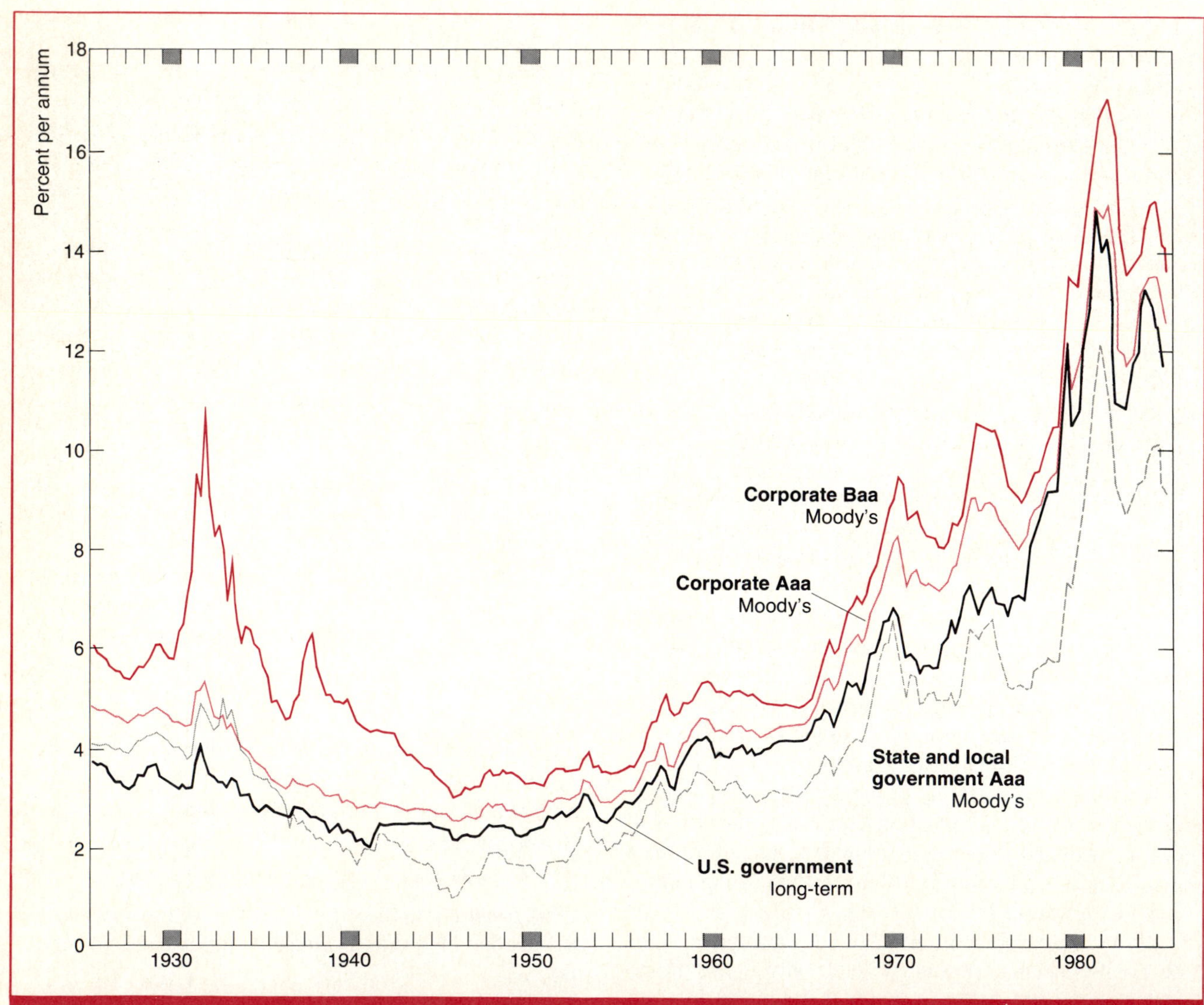

While the most important reason for differences in bond yields is difference in *risk,* several other influences are at work. There are very large quantities of U.S. government bonds outstanding, and the market for these bonds is very active, with relatively small selling costs. (The gap is small between the "bid" price, at which bond dealers are ready to buy, and the "offer" price, at which they are ready to sell.) Thus, U.S. government bonds provide a *liquidity* advantage; less loss results if the buyer has to turn around quickly and sell them. This is a second reason why their yield is low. A third reason is that U.S. government bonds—sometimes simply called U.S. governments—pay interest that is exempt from state income *taxes.*

The biggest tax advantage, however, lies with the state and local government bonds, whose interest is exempt from the large federal income tax, and is in some cases also exempt from state income taxes. This important difference in tax treatment explains why yields on state and local government bonds are lower than on U.S. governments—even though U.S. government bonds are free from the risk of default, while state and local government bonds are not. (In an extreme situation, the federal government has the constitutional right to print money to pay interest and principal on its bonds. State and local governments have no such right and may default on their debt, as the holders of Cleveland and New York City securities found to their sorrow during the 1970s.)

Another notable feature in the bond market was the sharp upward movement of all interest rates between 1965 and 1981. An important reason for this was the acceleration of inflation during that period. When inflation is high, bondholders recognize that interest and principal will be repaid in the future when money is less valuable than at present. They therefore hesitate to purchase bonds unless interest rates are high enough to compensate for the declining value of money. Since 1981, the rate of inflation has declined, and interest rates have receded somewhat.

The Stock Market

Stocks of major corporations already held by the public are usually bought and sold on the stock exchanges, the most famous being the New York Stock Exchange. Stockbrokers throughout the country maintain close contact with the exchanges, buying and selling stocks on behalf of their customers.

A *broker* acts as a representative of a buyer or seller, offering to buy or sell on behalf of clients.

Prices fluctuate on the stock exchanges in response to changes in demand and supply. Stock purchasers are interested in such things as the current and expected future profits of the corporation. Thus, stock prices may rise rapidly during periods of prosperity.

In the 1920s, the desire to "get rich quick" in the stock market became a national mania. With stocks rising, many investors learned that individuals, too, could use leverage to increase their potential gains; they borrowed large sums to buy stocks in the expectation that their prices would rise. Then came the Great Crash of 1929. The Dow-Jones average of 30 major industrial stocks fell from 381 in 1929 to 41 in 1932 (Figure 6-2). Many investors were wiped out. The stocks of the best corporations in America shared in the disaster. From a price of $396 in early September 1929, General Electric fell to $168 in late November and to $34 by 1932. General Motors dropped from $72 to $36 to $8, and AT&T from $304 to $197 to $70.[3]

Another major upswing in stock averages occurred in the 1950s and 1960s, with the Dow-Jones average reaching 1,000 by 1966. During the 1960s, the U.S. economy had the longest continuous expansion on record. Common stocks promised a share in the nation's prosperity. And they were widely looked on as a hedge against inflation. After all, stocks represent ownership of corporations, and in a period of inflation, the dollar value of a corporation's plant and equipment should rise with the general increase in prices. This comforting viewpoint was plausible, but it was not borne out by unfolding events. From its 1966 high, the Dow-Jones average retreated as inflationary pressures accelerated.

During the 1970s, stock market participants came to

[3]For some of the drama of the collapse, see John Kenneth Galbraith, *The Great Crash, 1929* (Boston: Houghton Mifflin, 1961) or Frederick Lewis Allen, *The Lords of Creation* (New York: Harper, 1935), chap. 13.

the view that inflation was very unhealthy for the economy, and signs of accelerating inflation were generally followed by declines in stock prices. As measured by the popular Dow-Jones average in Figure 6-2, the stock market went nowhere during the decade: The average price of stocks was about the same in 1980 as it had been a decade earlier. Then, beginning in 1982, stocks began a substantial advance. One reason was the strong expansion from the recession of 1981–1982. Another was that inflation was under much better control than during the 1970s.

CAPITAL MARKETS: TWO IMPORTANT PROBLEMS

The economic function of the markets for financial capital is similar to the function of markets for goods: These markets help to determine what will be produced in the economy. For example, if a company develops a new

FIGURE 6-2
The Dow-Jones industrial stock average, 1900–1985
The biggest swing in stock prices, in percentage terms, took place during the rising "bull" market of the 1920s and the collapsing "bear" market of 1929–1932. In the first two decades after World War II (1945–1966), average stock prices rose about sixfold. But between 1966 and 1980, there was no further gain; on average, stock prices were no higher in 1980 than in 1966. (Note: The vertical axis is drawn with a ratio or logarithmic scale. As explained in the appendix to Chapter 1, equal vertical distances represent equal percentage changes. For example, the distance from 100 to 200 is the same as the distance from 200 to 400.)

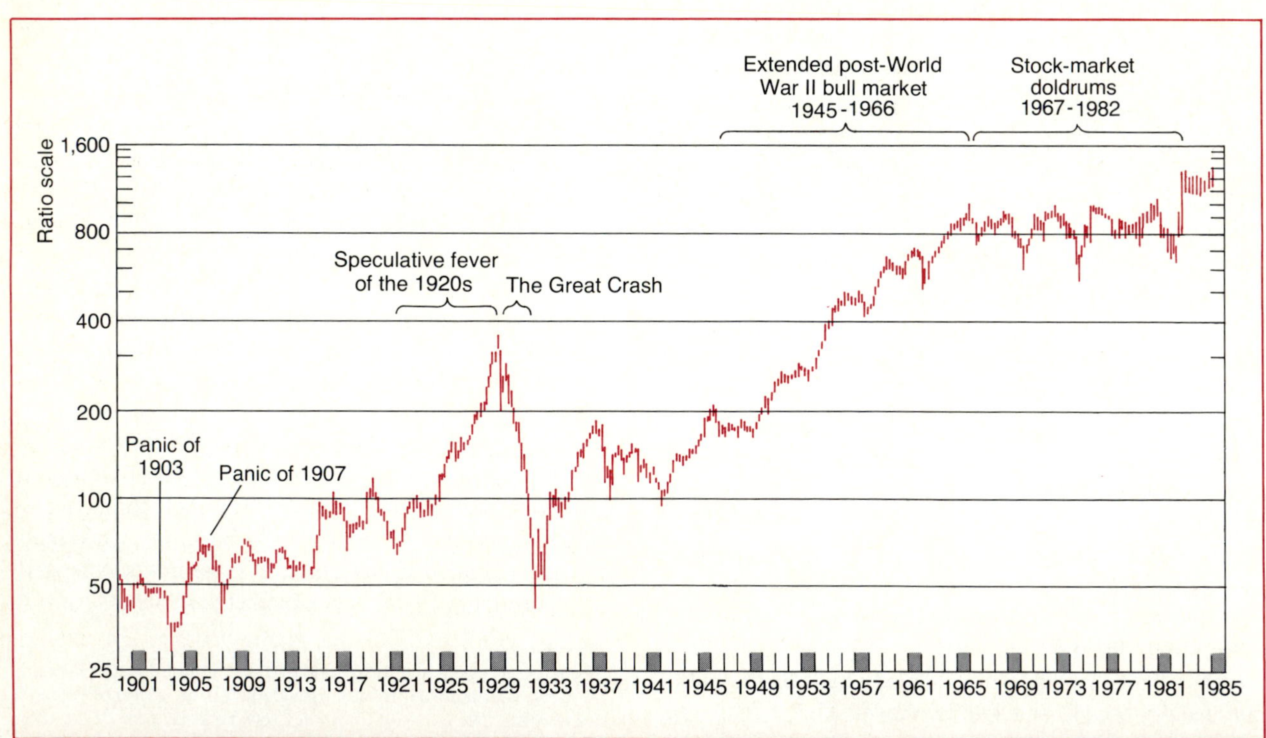

product for which there is a large demand, its profits will likely rise, and it will have relatively little trouble raising funds for expansion by borrowing or by issuing stock. In this way, the company will be able to quickly produce the item in demand.

There are, however, special problems in the capital markets. First, because of difficulty in getting information, money may be directed into the wrong industries or to the wrong firms. Second, private capital markets do not ensure that there will be the right total quantity of investment in the economy.

The Problem of Information: Will Funds Go to the "Right" Industries?

Because securities involve future prospects—a promise of either future interest payments or a share of future profits—they are particularly difficult to evaluate. If promises are being bought, the money may go to the slickest talker. History is full of artful swindlers, ranging from John Law (whose Mississippi Company first provided speculative riches and then financial disaster to its shareholders in eighteenth-century Paris) to Charles Ponzi and to recent con men like Bernard Cornfeld and Robert Trippet. (Ponzi used a masterfully simple scheme to swindle more than $10 million from Bostonians in 1919–1920. His operation declared large fictitious profits, and paid dividends on outstanding stock by selling new stock which investors snapped up because of the high "profits" and dividends. Cornfeld's Investors' Overseas Service separated many Europeans from their savings. Trippet ran a Ponzi-style scheme, notable for the distinguished list of people swindled. It included Walter Wriston of Citicorp, one of the shrewdest bankers in America, from whom Trippet took $211,000.)

Financing that goes into harebrained schemes represents not just a loss to individuals but a loss to society of the alternative projects which could have been financed.

Because it is so difficult for average investors to know whether they are dealing with a Ponzi or with a serious operation, there is a strong case for regulations which require the disclosure of information by those issuing securities. In the United States, such regulations are enforced by the Securities and Exchange Commission (SEC). Before offering securities to the public, companies are required to issue a ***prospectus,*** which is a formal statement presenting information on the current position and the future prospects of the corporation. Publicly owned firms are required to make their accounts public and to announce significant developments which may affect the price of their stock.

The SEC has prevented the type of financial buccaneering which marked the 1920s. (Cornfeld was induced to operate in Canada and Europe because of the strictness of SEC regulations.) Nevertheless, many investment projects are intrinsically risky. It is inevitable that large sums are sometimes channeled into honest projects that fail. In an uncertain world, each investment is an act of faith. The problem is to avoid investment decisions which are acts of *blind* faith.

Capital Markets and the Problem of Instability

When an economy is operating at full employment, it is producing all, or nearly all, that it can with its limited labor force and capital stock. If large additional investment is undertaken in one area, cutbacks must be made elsewhere. Participants in the financial markets evaluate risks and thus tend to channel funds to the companies whose prospects they consider brightest. Consequently, the markets tend to direct funds toward the most productive pattern of new investments.

However, consider the problem when the economy moves down into a recession or a depression. Then, there are large amounts of unemployed labor and unused plant and equipment. The decision to proceed with one investment—such as a factory to build computers—no longer requires that we forego an alternative investment (such as an additional plant for the auto industry). They can *both* be built by putting unemployed labor and unemployed equipment back to work. Indeed, if the downward slide of the economy is severe, there are available resources to produce a lot of additional capital goods of all sorts—and additional consumer goods, too. The important question ceases to be which of the competing investments is better; for example, would it be better to invest in the computer industry or the auto industry? Rather, the central issue becomes: How do we get more investment in *both* the computer industry and the auto industry—and in other industries, too?

The private financial markets do a moderately good job in determining relative risks and rewards and thus do a moderately good job of determing *which* investments will be undertaken. But they suffer major shortcomings in dealing with the question which becomes important during recessions: How can the *total* amount of investment be increased? Consider what happened as the economy collapsed into the Great Depression of the 1930s. Stock market investors became panic-stricken as stock prices plummeted. At the very low prices of the Depression, the stock market was no longer an attractive place for corporations to raise funds. For a corporation to sell stock in those days meant that current stockholders were practically giving away part of their ownership to new buyers. Similarly, with the widespread difficulties of business, risk premiums on bonds rose sharply. For much of the 1930s, there was no overall shortage of funds which banks and others had available for investment. The interest rate on risk-free federal government bonds was very low—between 2% and 3%. But funds were not cheap for many businesses because of extremely high risk premiums. As a result, investment was discouraged, and this deepened the Depression.

Low stock prices and high borrowing costs were not the only reasons that investment dried up during the Depression. Many business executives were so terrified that they would not have undertaken expansion even if funds had been available at very low interest rates. Their pessimism and lack of investment were not the result of a lack of information. During the 1930s, business was indeed faced with appalling prospects; an individual with perfect information would still not have invested.

Because private financial markets do not necessarily result in a stable economy, the responsibility for stability has fallen to the federal government. How the government can fulfill this responsibility is a major topic of Parts 2, 3, and 4 of this book.

KEY POINTS

1. There are three forms of business organization: (*a*) single proprietorships, (*b*) partnerships, and (*c*) corporations.

2. Single proprietorships and partnerships are simple and flexible. On the other hand, the advantages of the corporate form of organization are (*a*) limited liability; (*b*) automatic continuity, even if one or more of the owners should die; and (*c*) better access to funds for financing growth.

3. A corporation can obtain financing by issuing (selling) common or preferred stock, and bonds.

4. There are two main types of business accounts. The *balance sheet* shows assets, liabilities, and net worth at a *point* in time. The *income statement* reports sales, costs, and profits during a *period* of time.

5. A financial intermediary takes funds from individual savers and pools these funds to lend to businesses, governments, or individuals.

6. The purchaser of securities balances three important objectives: *high return, low risk,* and *high liquidity*.

7. A company that issues new securities also tries to find the best balance among three objectives: (1) to keep the *return* of the corporation's stockholders as high as possible, (2) to avoid *risk,* and (3) to ensure the *availability* of money when needed.

8. In general, bonds are less risky than common stocks for buyers of securities and more risky for sellers of new securities. When corporations or individuals increase their debts, they thereby increase their leverage; that is, they increase their ratio of debt to net worth. While this raises their potential gain, it also increases their risk of bankruptcy, since they must make interest and principal payments no matter how bad business is.

9. Because stocks and bonds represent claims to future profits or interest payments, the evaluation of the issuer's prospects are extremely important for anyone buying a security. To help protect the purchaser, the SEC requires corporations to make relevant information available to the public.

10. Financial markets cannot be counted on to ensure the quantity of investment needed for full employment. The maintenance of a high level of employment is a responsibility of the federal government. This role will be studied in future chapters.

KEY CONCEPTS

single proprietorship
partnership
limited liability
corporation

common stock
equity (ownership)
double taxation of dividends
principal (or face value) of a bond
balance sheet
income statement
assets
liabilities
net worth
retained earnings
book value
depreciation
obsolescence
financial intermediary
savings and loan association (S&L)
yield (or return)
risk
liquidity
leverage
line of credit
risk premium

PROBLEMS

6-1. State whether each of the following sentences is true or false, and in each case explain why:

(*a*) If liabilities exceed assets, net worth is negative.

(*b*) If additional stock is issued at a price in excess of the book value, the book value of the corporation's stock will rise.

(*c*) In the United States, dividends plus retained earnings are greater than corporate income taxes.

6-2. In the middle of 1984, the price of Wang common stock was approximately $25 on the American stock exchange. There were approximately 140 million shares outstanding. What was the valuation put on Wang by the stock market? (That is, what was the total value of Wang stock outstanding?) How does this compare with the net worth of Wang, which may be found back in Table 6-1? How do you account for the fact that the stock market's valuation of Wang is different from Wang's net worth, as shown on its balance sheet? By the middle of 1985, the price of Wang stock fell to $16, even though its book value was rising. Can you guess any reason for this?

6-3. Suppose you are an investment adviser and a 50-year-old person comes to you for advice on how to invest $100,000 for retirement. What advice would you give? What advice would you give to a young couple who want to temporarily invest $20,000 that they expect to use for a down payment on a home 2 years from now?

6-4. If a corporation increases its leverage, what are the advantages and/or disadvantages for (*a*) the owner of a share of the corporation's stock; (*b*) the owner of a $100,000 bond of the corporation?

6-5. "While private enterprise does make some mistakes and sometimes invests in losing projects, it is less likely to do so than the government. After all, businesses risk their own money, while government officials risk the public's money." Do you agree? Can you think of any investment projects that the government has undertaken which were particularly desirable? Might they have been undertaken by private businesses? Why or why not? Can you think of any government investment projects which were particularly ill-advised? Can you thing of any investment projects of private corporations that were ill-advised?

6-6. In what ways do the interests of stockholders coincide with the interests of the managers of a corporation? Are there any ways in which their interests are in conflict? (See Box 6-1.)

PART TWO

HIGH EMPLOYMENT AND A STABLE PRICE LEVEL

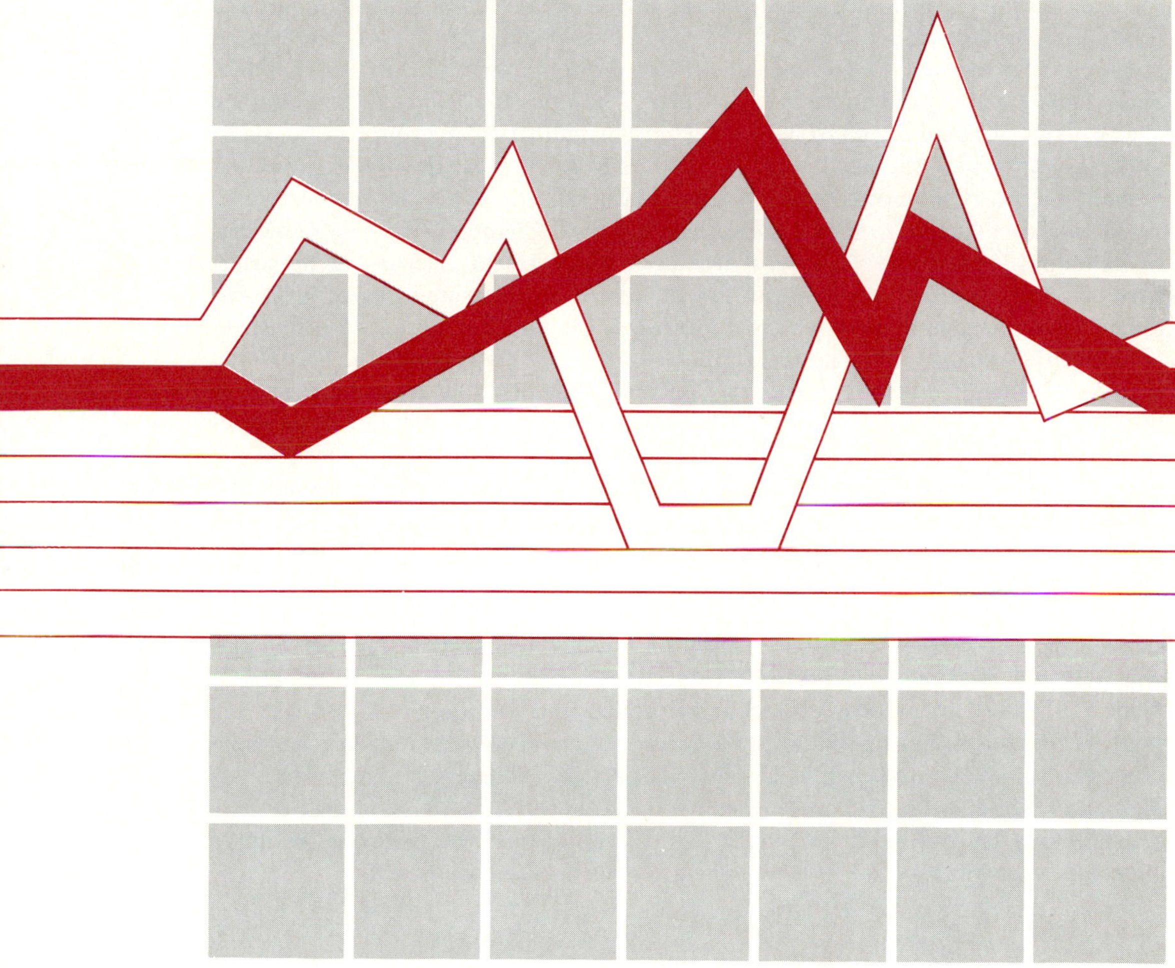

The six chapters of Part 1 have set the stage for the study of economics, providing analytical and institutional background and outlining the major objectives of high employment, price stability, growth, efficiency, and an equitable distribution of income.

The focus of Parts 2, 3, and 4 will be on the goals of *high employment, price stability,* and *growth*. These involve the overall aggregates of the economy. How

many workers are employed in the economy *as a whole?* What is happening to the total quantity of output in the economy? What is happening to the average level of prices? Because they deal with economywide magnitudes, these questions are classified under the heading of *macroeconomics.* (*Makros* means "large" in Greek.) In contrast, the objectives of efficiency and equity, which will be the principal topics of Parts 5, 6, and 7, deal with the details of the economy. What specific goods are produced? Would we be better off if we produced more wheat and less butter? More houses and fewer cars? How is income divided between labor (in the form of wages and salaries) and capital (in the form of interest and profits)? Since these questions deal with the *detailed relationships* among various industries or groups in the economy, they go under the heading of *microeconomics.* (*Mikros,* the Greek word for "small," appears in such words as *microscope.*)

As an introduction to Part 2 on macroeconomics, Chapter 7 describes how national output is measured. Chapter 8 provides an overview of macroeconomic problems of recent decades—how output has fluctuated, how unemployment has risen during recessions, and how prices have increased. Chapter 9 introduces the concepts of aggregate demand and aggregate supply, which are at the core of macroeconomic theory—just as the demand and supply for individual products lie at the center of microeconomic theory. Chapter 10 addresses the question of why high unemployment can exist—and persist—in a market economy. Not surprisingly, much of the basic theory of unemployment can be traced back to the Great Depression of the 1930s and, in particular, to the pen of British economist John Maynard Keynes. Keynes argued that production fell and unemployment rose during the Depression because of *insufficient demand.* With the collapse in demand for automobiles in the early depression, autoworkers were discharged. When the demand for housing slackened, construction workers lost their jobs. When the demand for clothing declined, textile workers were laid off. Thus, the widespread increase in unemployment was caused by an overall decline in the demand for the goods and services produced in the economy; that is, by a decline in *aggregate* demand. When people don't buy, workers don't work. The Keynesian theory of aggregate demand is explained in Chapter 10.

This will lay the basis for Part 3, which will address the policy question: *If aggregate demand is too low or too high, what can be done about it?*

CHAPTER 7

MEASURING NATIONAL PRODUCT AND NATIONAL INCOME

Never ask of money spent
Where the spender thinks it went
Nobody was ever meant
To remember or invent
What he did with every cent.

ROBERT FROST

In our modern economy, we produce a vast array of goods and services: cars, TV sets, houses, clothing, medical care, and food, to name but a few. One way of judging the performance of the economy is to measure the production of all these goods and services. A measure of total production does not, of course, give a complete picture of the welfare of the nation. When we acquire more and more goods, we do not necessarily become happier. Other things are obviously important too; for example, the sense of accomplishment which comes from our everyday work, and the quality of our environment. Nevertheless, the total amount which is produced is one of the important measures of economic success.

THE MARKET AS A WAY OF MEASURING PRODUCTION

The wide range of products poses a problem: How are we to add them all up into a single measure of national product? How do we add apples and oranges?

Market prices provide an answer. If apples sell for $10 per bushel and oranges for $20 per bushel, the market indicates that 1 bushel of oranges is worth 2 bushels of apples. Thus, when market prices are used, oranges and apples can be compared and added, as shown in the example in Table 7-1. In our complex economy, the total value of output can be found in a similar way. By taking the quantity times the market price, we find expenditures on a particular product. By adding up the expenditures for the many goods produced—clothing, food, TV sets, etc.—we can get a dollar measure of national product during the year.

***National product* is the the money value of the goods and services produced by a nation during a specific time period, such as a year.**

TWO APPROACHES: EXPENDITURES AND INCOME

Before looking in detail at the national product, we should look at the overall picture. To do so, let's call once more on the circular-flow diagram introduced in Chapter 3 and repeated here as Figure 7-1. This illus-

TABLE 7-1
Using Market Prices to Add Apples and Oranges

	(1) Quantity (bushels)	(2) Price (per bushel)	(3) Market value (3) = (1) × (2)
Apples	3,000	$10	$30,000
Oranges	2,000	$20	$40,000
		Total	$70,000

Market prices provide a way of adding different goods to get a measure of total production.

trates the simplest of all possible market economies, in which the public consumes all the goods and services being produced.

The performance of this simple economy can be measured by looking at the money payments in either the upper gray loop or the lower gray loop. The upper loop shows expenditures by households buying the goods produced by business. Once business has received these payments, where do they go? The lower loop shows that they go to those who have provided the productive inputs: Wages and salaries go to the labor force, rents to suppliers of land and buildings, and interest and profits to the suppliers of capital. Profits are what is left over after other payments—wages, salaries, interest, etc.—have been made. Thus, in the very simple economy shown in Figure 7-1, both gray loops give exactly the same total. We may look at the upper loop, which shows the *expenditures for national product*. Alternatively, we may look at the lower loop, which measures ***national income.***

FIGURE 7-1
The circular flow of payments
In the upper gray loop are the payments for the goods and services produced. This loop measures national product. In the lower gray loop, we see where the receipts of businesses go: to pay wages, salaries, rents, interest, and profits. This loop measures national income.

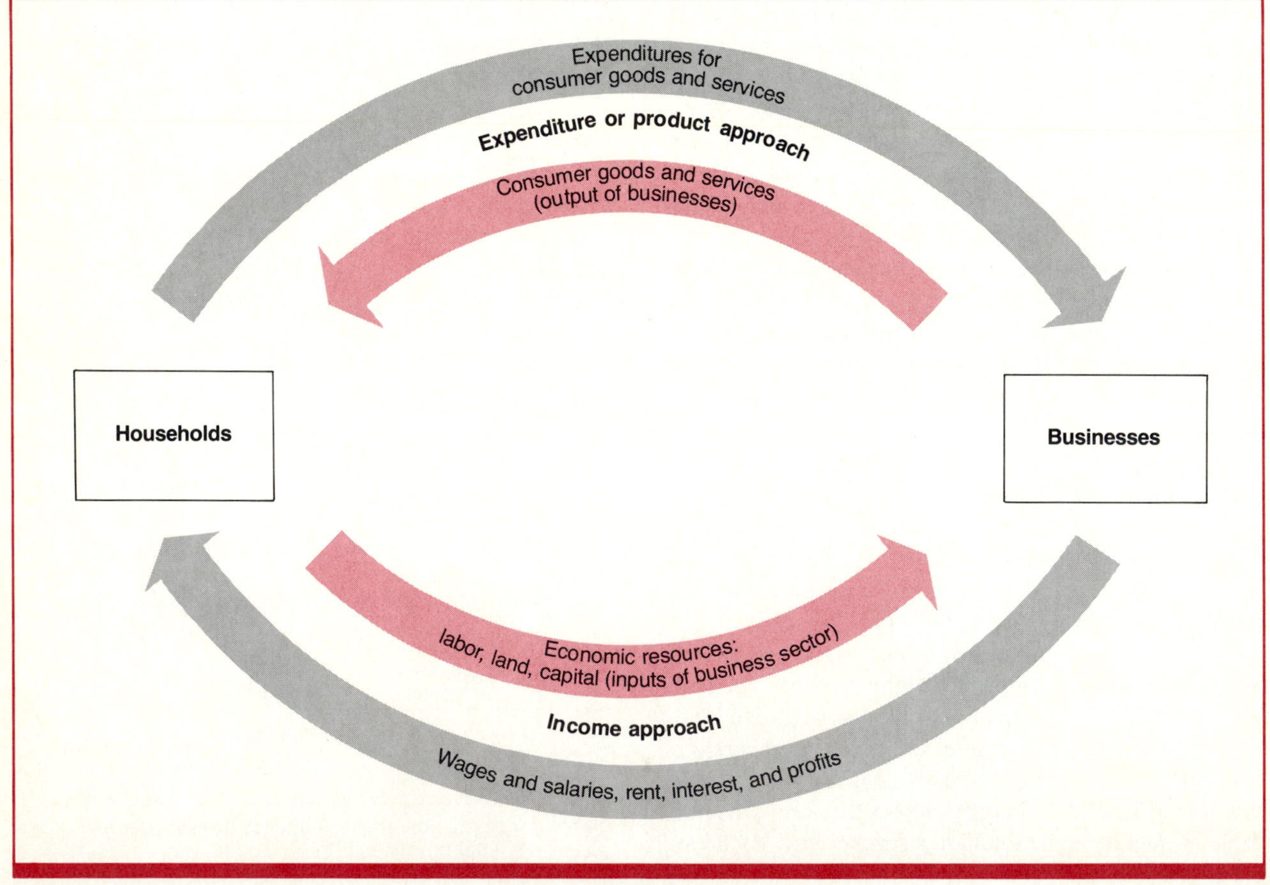

National income **is the sum of all income derived from providing the factors of production. It includes wages and salaries, rents, interest, and profits.**

NATIONAL PRODUCT: THE EXPENDITURES APPROACH

To calculate national product, we look at the upper loop, examining expenditures on the goods and services that have been produced. When we calculate what has been produced, it is important to count everything *once*, but *only once*. Unless we are careful, we may make a mistake and count some things more than once. The reason is that most products go through a number of stages in the process of production; they are sold a number of times before reaching the hands of the final user. For example, copper wiring and silicon chips are sold to electronics companies, which use them to manufacture TV sets. In calculating national product, government statisticians include the TV sets sold to consumers. But they do not also count separately the wiring and chips that went into the sets. Similarly, they count the bread purchased by the consumer. But they do not also count separately the flour that was used in producing the bread. To do so would mean that the flour would be counted twice.

The TV sets and bread bought by consumers are ***final products;*** the wheat that went into the bread and the chips that went into the TV sets are ***intermediate products.*** As a first approximation, national product is found by adding up just the expenditures on *final* products. In this way, double counting is avoided.

A *final product* is a good or service that is purchased by the ultimate user and not intended for resale or further processing.

An *intermediate product* is one that is intended for resale or further processing.

Note that it is the *intended use,* rather than the physical characteristics of a product, that determines whether it is a final good or not. When gasoline is bought by a service station, it is an intermediate good; it is intended for resale to the public. When it is bought by a farmer or trucker, it is also an intermediate product, since it will be used to harvest grain or produce trucking services. However, when it is purchased by a tourist on vacation, it is a final good. Similarly, when I buy a new car for my family's use, it is a final product. But when a taxi company buys an identical automobile, it is an intermediate product, to be used in the production of taxi rides.

The distinction between final products and intermediate products is illustrated in Table 7-2, which shows a simple productive process with only four stages. The first step in the production of a loaf of bread occurs when the farmer grows 20 cents' worth of wheat. The second stage is the milling of this wheat into flour, which is then worth 45 cents. In other words, 25 cents of *value is added* to the 20 cents' worth of wheat when it is made into flour. Similarly, the table shows how value is added at the last two stages, when the flour is baked into bread and when the bread is delivered to the consumer. How much has been produced? The answer: The $1.25 loaf of bread. In calculating national product, we use only the $1.25 value of the bread. We must *not* add up the value of all the transactions in the first column, which would total $2.85.

Value added **is the value of a firm's product minus the cost of intermediate products bought from outside suppliers.**

In the calculation of national product, final products are classified into four categories: (1) personal consumption expenditures, (2) government expenditures for goods and services, (3) private domestic investment, and (4) net exports—that is, exports minus imports. By including government, investment, and net exports, we are now recognizing that the world is more complicated than the simple one in Figure 7-1, where consumers buy all the final goods produced in the economy.

1. Personal Consumption Expenditures (*C*)

Consumption is the ultimate objective of economic activity; we work and produce so that we will have goods and services to consume. Personal consumption expenditures (*C*) constitute the largest component of national product.

They may be divided into three main components: durable goods, such as cars or washing machines; nondurable goods, such as food or clothing; and services, such as medical services or haircuts (Table 7-3).

2. Government Purchases of Goods and Services (*G*)

Consumer goods and services are not the only things produced in the economy. The government hires teachers; educational services are produced. The government spends money for road repairs; better roads are produced. Governments at all levels—federal, state, and local—undertake expenditures for the public good.[1]

While government expenditures on goods and services (*G*) are included in the national product, transfer payments are not. When the government buys an airplane, the airplane is produced. But when the government makes transfer payments—such as social security payments to retirees—the recipients are not required to produce anything in return. Therefore, government expenditures on aircraft are included in national product, but transfer payments are not.

3. Private Domestic Investment (*I*)

Each year, we produce not only goods and services purchased by consumers and government, but also capital goods which help in production in future years. Private domestic investment (*I*) includes three categories: (1) business investment in *plant* and *equipment,* (2) *residential construction,* and (3) *changes in inventories.*

1. ***Plant and equipment.*** This category includes the construction of factories, warehouses, stores, and other nonresidential structures used by businesses, and the acquisition of machinery and other equipment.
2. ***Residential construction.*** The construction of residences is included in the investment segment of national product. The reason for including apartment buildings in investment is straightforward. An apartment building, like a factory or machine, is intended to be an income-producing asset. In future years, the apartment building will produce shelter, for which the owner will charge rent.

There is a substantial advantage in treating all residential construction similarly in the national product ac-

*[1]The inclusion of all government expenditures for goods and services in national product is a problem. While some government purchases are for "final" use, other government spending is for intermediate products. A road, for example, can carry both vacation traffic (a "final," or consumption, type of use) and trucks loaded with goods (an "intermediate" stage in the productive process). Thus, it might be argued that insofar as roads are used for intermediate purposes, this portion of the expenditure for roads should not be included in national product. But national product accountants have ducked this problem. They simply assume that all goods and services purchased by the government are for final use, and they therefore include all such purchases in national product.

TABLE 7-2
Final and Intermediate Products

Stage of production	(1) Value of sales		(2) Cost of intermediate products		(3) Value added (1) − (2) = (3)
Intermediate goods					
Wheat	$0.20	−	0	=	$0.20
Flour	0.45	−	0.20	=	0.25
Bread, at wholesale	0.95	−	0.45	=	0.50
Final good					
Bread, at retail	$1.25	−	0.95	=	0.30
	Total				$1.25

Value is added at the various stages of production. Note that the sum of all the value-added items in the last column ($1.25) is equal to the value of the final product.

counts. When housing of any kind is built, families have shelter; this is true whether they rent the new housing or own it. For consistency, construction of new owner-occupied housing is included in the investment category. More specifically, national product accountants treat owner-occupied housing *as if* the family had originally invested in the home and then, in future years, rented the house to itself. Note that houses are treated differently from consumer durables such as refrigerators. Houses are included in investment; refrigerators are part of consumption expenditures.

3. *Changes in inventories.* We have seen that wheat that goes into bread is not counted separately in the national product because its cost is included as part of the total cost of bread, and is accounted for in the price of the bread. But how about any wheat we produce above and beyond the amount consumed in bread and pastries? What happens to it? The answer is that it is either exported (a possibility that we will consider in just a moment) or it is used to build up our inventories of wheat. Any such increases in our stocks of wheat represent something we have produced this year. Therefore, they are included in this year's national product.

Similarly, increases in inventories of steel are included in national product—for example, the additional inventories of steel held by refrigerator manufacturers or the increase in the inventory of unsold steel held by a steel company. But we do not include the steel which went into the production of refrigerators or machines since it is already included when we count consumer purchases of refrigerators and investment in machines.

Earlier, we said that, as a first approximation, national product is found by adding up only expenditures on final products. That is an acceptable and commonly used generalization. It is 99% right, and that is not bad. But it is not precisely accurate. National product includes not only final products in the form of consumer goods and services, government purchases, and equipment and buildings. It also includes the intermediate products that have been added to inventories. The precisely correct statement is perhaps worth reiterating: We should measure all goods and services *once,* but *only once*.

Changes in inventories can be either positive or negative. In a bad crop year, there may be less wheat on hand at the end of the year than at the beginning. We have taken more out of our stocks than we have put back

TABLE 7-3
The Composition of Personal Consumption Expenditures, 1984

Type	Billions of dollars		Percentage of total	
1. Durable goods		$319		13.6%
(*a*) Automobiles and parts	$150		6.4%	
(*b*) Furniture and household equipment	117		5.0	
(*c*) Other	52		2.2	
2. Nondurable goods		857		36.6
(*a*) Clothing	140		6.0	
(*b*) Food	444		18.9	
(*c*) Gasoline and oil	91		3.9	
(*d*) Other	182		7.8	
3. Services		1,166		49.8
(*a*) Housing	398		17.0	
(*b*) Household operation	164		7.0	
(*c*) Transportation	78		3.3	
(*d*) Others	526		22.5	
Total		$2,342		100.0%

Source: Survey of Current Business.

in. In this case, changes in inventories are negative, and they are subtracted in measuring national product.

Finally, note that the private domestic investment category (I) includes only *private* investment, since government investment—in roads, dams, etc.—is included elsewhere as part of government expenditures for goods and services. Moreover, it includes only *domestic* investment in the United States, since it is U.S. national product that is being estimated. If General Motors builds a factory in Germany, its value is included in German national product, not in U.S. national product. On the other hand, if Volkswagen builds a plant in the United States, that plant is included in U.S. national product.

4. Exports of Goods and Services (X)

Some wheat is exported. It is part of our total production of wheat, and therefore it should be included in national product. Because such wheat does not appear in the first three categories (C, G, I), it is included here—in exports of goods and services (X).

It is obvious how we export a good, such as wheat: We put it on a ship and send it abroad. But how can we export services, such as haircuts and surgical operations? The answer is this. A tourist from Tokyo visiting Hawaii has all sorts of expenditures: for hotel accommodations, for taxi rides, for haircuts, and for medical services. Since these services have been produced by Americans, they must be counted as part of the U.S. national product. Since they are paid for by the foreigner, they are considered exports of services, even though the hotel, the taxi, the barber shop, and the hospital remain in the United States.

Interest paid by foreigners to Americans, and profits of U.S. subsidiaries abroad, are also considered exports of services. They represent income to the United States for the services provided by our capital; that is, they represent returns from our past investments abroad.

5. A Subtraction: Imports of Goods and Services (M)

When the Japanese buy our wheat, this export is included in our national product. What happens, on the other side, when we buy Japanese automobiles? Such purchases of imports are included in the U.S. consumption expenditures category. But these cars were not produced in the United States. Therefore, they should not be counted as part of our national product. Thus, we must take them out. We must subtract imports of cars, and of other goods and services, to complete our calculation of national product.

National Product: A Summary Statement

In summary:

National
product = personal consumption expenditures (C)
plus government purchases of goods and services (G)
plus private domestic investment (I)
plus exports of goods and services (X)
minus imports of goods and services (M)

In symbols, this is written:

$$\text{National product} = C + I + G + X - M \qquad (7\text{-}1)$$

(In this chapter, the equations are numbered—starting here with Equation 7-1—because we want to refer back to them at a later point.)

Finally, several details might be noted. Recall that national product includes only goods and services produced *during the year*. Therefore, it does not include expenditures for used goods, such as cars or houses. They were produced in a previous year and were included in that year's national product. However, renovations of old buildings are included, as are repairs to automobiles. They represent current production. Also included in current national product are the brokerage fees for selling houses and other buildings. They represent payments for a valuable service—namely, assistance in the transfer of the building to someone who wants it.

Common stocks acquired by an individual or institution are not included in national product, since they don't represent production, but only a transfer of ownership. Of course, if a corporation issues stock and finances the construction of a factory with the proceeds, the factory is part of the national product. It has been produced during the current year.

THE COMPLICATION OF DEPRECIATION: GNP AND NNP

The main outline of the national product accounts has now been completed, but we still have a number of details to consider. One of the most important is the measurement of investment.

If we count the full value of buildings and equipment produced during this year, national product is overestimated. Why? Because existing buildings and equipment have deteriorated—or *depreciated*—during the year from wear and obsolescence. After calculating the total value of all new plant, equipment, and residential buildings produced during the year, we should deduct the amount that plant, equipment, and residences have depreciated during the year. Only if we do this will we get a true measure of how much our total stocks of buildings and equipment have increased during the year (Figure 7-2).

Thus, two concepts of investment should be distinguished, *gross investment* and *net investment*.

***Gross private domestic investment* (I_g) is equal to total expenditures for new plant, equipment, and residential buildings, plus the change in inventories.**

***Net private domestic investment* (I_n) is equal to gross private domestic investment (I_g), less depreciation; that is,**

$$I_n = I_g - \text{depreciation}^2$$

*[2] More precisely, to go from I_g to I_n, accountants subtract *capital consumption allowances* (CCA). These allowances include not only depreciation, but also adjustments for the effects of inflation on the measurement of capital. This is a fine point, which we henceforth ignore; we use the simpler concept of depreciation in place of CCA.

FIGURE 7-2

Net investment: A change in the stock of capital

During the year the stock of capital increases by gross investment, less depreciation.

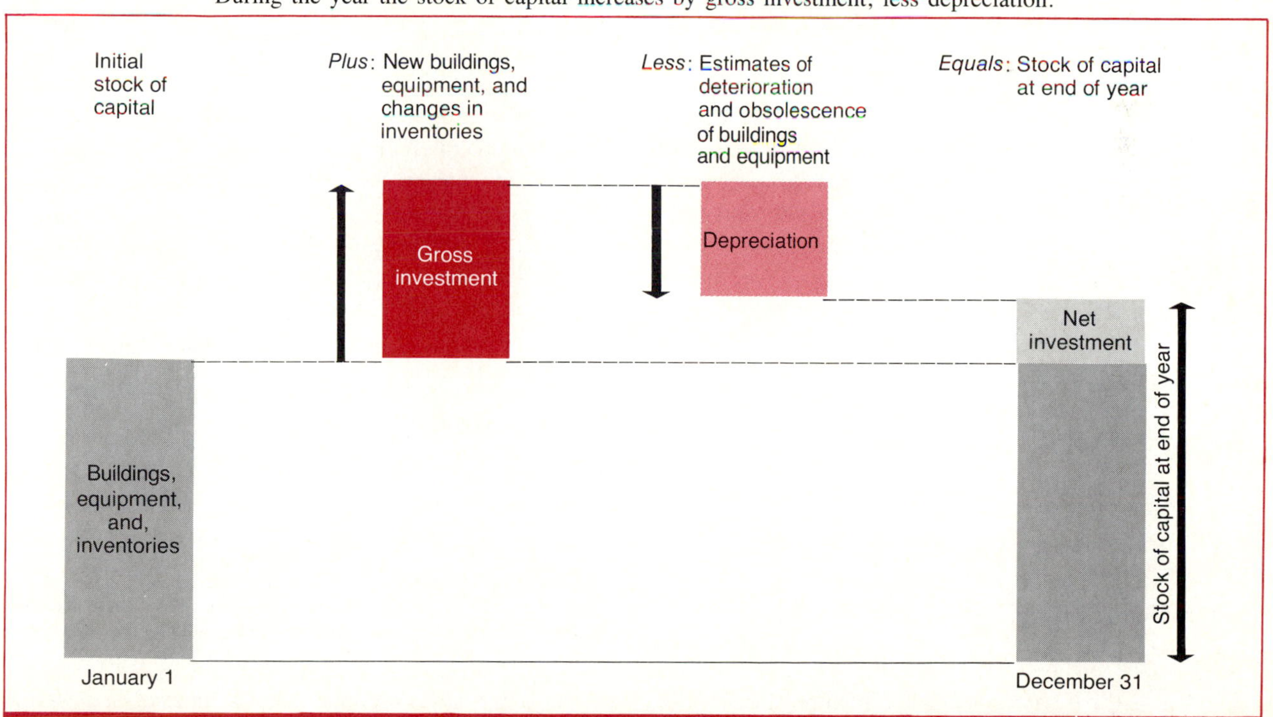

Corresponding to these two concepts of investment, there are two concepts of national product, *gross national product* and *net national product*:

Gross national product (GNP) =

$$C + I_g + G + X - M \qquad (7\text{-}2)$$

Net national product (NNP) =

$$C + I_n + G + X - M \qquad (7\text{-}3)$$

From these two equations, it follows that:

$$\text{GNP} - \text{depreciation} = \text{NNP} \qquad (7\text{-}4)$$

This relationship is illustrated in the first two columns of Figure 7-3, where we follow the common practice of lumping exports and imports together, as net exports; that is, net exports = $X - M$. Observe that in 1984 net exports (X_n) were negative; that is, imports were larger than exports.

In theory, NNP is the measure of national product that we should use because it takes into account the obsolescence and physical deterioration of machinery and buildings during the year. Why, then, is so much more attention paid to GNP than to NNP in the newspapers and economics books? The answer: While NNP is the best measure conceptually, it is difficult to estimate in practice. Gross investment—the value of new buildings and equipment, plus additions to inventories—is relatively easy to measure. But to estimate net investment, we need to measure depreciation, and this raises difficult questions. How rapidly will a machine really wear out? Will it become obsolete before it is physically worn out? If it will be scrapped in 10 years, does its value decline in a "straight line," by 10% each year, or does it lose most of its productive value in the first few years? Because of such questions, we cannot be confident about estimates of depreciation. In practice, therefore, GNP is used *much* more commonly than NNP.

NET NATIONAL PRODUCT AND NATIONAL INCOME: THE COMPLICATION OF THE SALES TAX

Earlier in this chapter, we looked at the circular flow of payments in Figure 7-1, in which upper-loop payments represented national product and lower-loop payments represented national income. In that very simple illustration, the two loops were equal, and net national product and national income were exactly the same size. In our complex real-world economy, they are closely related but not precisely equal.

Net national product (NNP) is the total quantity of goods and services produced during the year, measured at market prices. *National income* is the sum of income earned by those who provide the factors of production. How can they possibly be different? They may be different because the factors of production do not get all the proceeds from the sale of a good. Part goes to the government in the form of sales taxes (and other similar taxes).[3]

To illustrate, consider a package of razors priced at $1.99 plus a sales tax of 10¢. The $1.99 goes into wages and salaries, rents, interest, and profits of those who contribute at various stages to the production of the razors. *This $1.99 is included in national income.* Of course, when you get to the cash register, you will pay the full $2.09. Because net national product is measured at market prices, *it includes the whole $2.09.* Accordingly, net national product exceeds national income by the amount of sales taxes.

This distinction shows up in Figure 7-3, where column 2 measures NNP. We subtract sales taxes (and other similar taxes) in order to get column 3, which shows the national income earned by the suppliers of productive resources.

The tax complication should not obscure a conclusion that is worth emphasizing. With the exception of taxes, the proceeds from the sale of the final product become incomes of the factors of production. Thus:

> **The process of production is also the process of generating income.**

When we examine column 3 of Figure 7-3 in detail, we see all the familiar components of income—wages

*[3]These other similar taxes include customs duties on imports, property taxes, and exise taxes on items such as cigarettes. These taxes are sometimes lumped together under the heading of *indirect taxes*. (This term is based on the assumption that these taxes will not be borne by the producer or importer but will be passed along to the person who buys cigarettes, the imported good, or other item on which a tax is collected.)

FIGURE 7-3

National product and income accounts, 1984 (simplified; in billions of dollars)

GNP = Gross national product
NNP = Net national product
NI = National income
PI = Personal income
DI = Disposable personal income
C = Personal consumption expenditures
G = Government expenditures for goods and services
I_g = Gross private domestic investment
I_n = Net private domestic investment
S = Personal saving

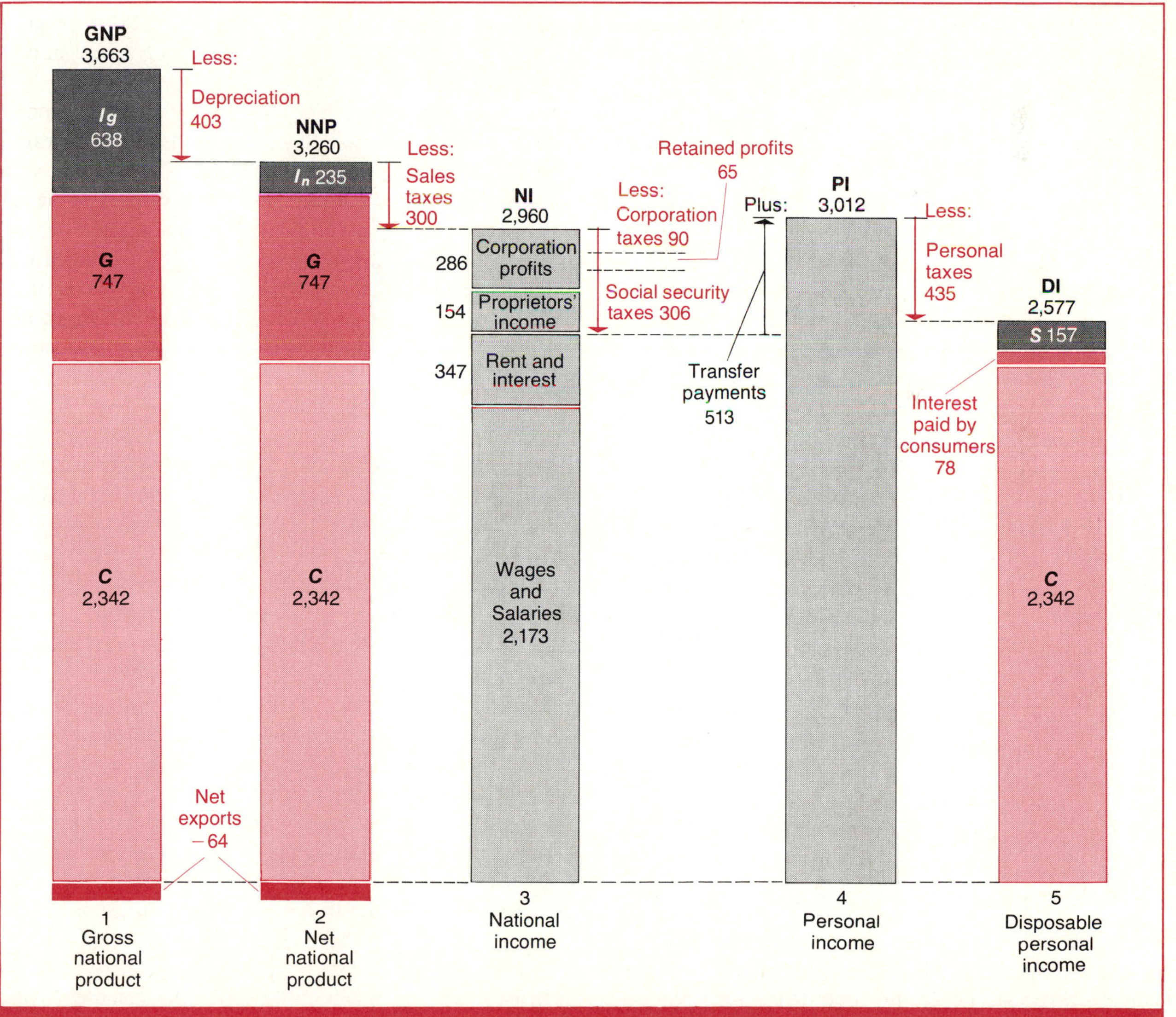

and salaries, rent, interest, and profits—plus a new item we haven't encountered before: "proprietor's income." To understand this item, note that for a corporation such as General Motors, wages are sharply distinguishable from profits. Wages go to the workers, while profits are the return to the owners of the corporation. However, for some businesses—such as a family farm or a mom and pop store—it is not feasible to separate wages, profits, and other income shares. How much of a farmer's income is the result of the family's labor and how much a return on its investment in buildings, equipment, and so on? It is not easy to say. Accordingly, no attempt is made to subdivide such income. It is included as a single sum: proprietors' income.

OTHER INCOME MEASURES

Thus far, we have seen that GNP includes consumption, government purchases of goods and services, gross investment, and exports less imports. The difference between GNP and NNP is depreciation, although this is difficult to measure precisely. We also saw that you have to subtract sales taxes from NNP to get national income, which is the sum of payments for providing factors of production—labor, land, and capital.

Now let's see what happens next.

Personal Income (PI)

Although most of *national income* is received by households as their *personal income* (PI), national income and personal income are not exactly the same.

One reason is that some national income does not flow through the business sector to households:

- Part of corporate profit is taken by the government in the form of corporate income taxes.
- Part of profit is retained by corporations to finance expansion. Thus, dividends are the only portion of corporate profits which *do* flow from corporations to households as personal income.
- Taxes are paid into the social security fund; these taxes have to be deducted from national income before we get personal income.

The other reason that personal income is not the same as national income lies in transfer payments, such as social security pensions and payments to the unemployed. Such transfers *are* a source of personal income to households. But they are not payments to households for providing factors of production. Therefore, they are not included in national income.

Thus, to find personal income (column 4, Figure 7-3), we begin with national income (column 3) and then *subtract* corporation taxes, profits retained by corporations, and social security taxes, and we *add* transfer payments. Personal income is the measure which corresponds most closely to the everyday meaning of "income."

Disposable Personal Income (DI)

Not all personal income is available to the individual or family for personal use, however. The government takes a sizable chunk in the form of personal taxes, mainly the personal income tax. After these taxes are paid, *disposable personal income* (DI) remains. Households can do three things with this income: spend it on consumption, use it to pay interest on consumer debt, or save it. Disposable income is an important concept because consumers look at this income when they decide how much to spend.

Relative Magnitudes

Before leaving Figure 7-3, observe the relative magnitudes of the major boxes. Consumption is by far the largest component of GNP. In 1984, it amounted to 64% of GNP. Government expenditures for goods and services constituted the next largest component. While gross investment was also substantial, most of it went to cover depreciation, leaving a relatively small proportion as net investment.

In the third column, we see that wages and salaries were by far the largest component of national income, 73%. Corporate profits were 10%. (However, remember that there were other "profits" included in proprietors' income.) In the last column, consumption expenditures were 92% of disposable income.

Most of these items are relatively stable, but a few change quite sharply from year to year. Net exports can be either positive or negative; they were usually positive in the years before 1983 but have been negative in recent years. Net investment has been quite volatile, rising sharply during periods of business prosperity and falling during recessions. In the quarter century from 1960 to 1984, gross investment ranged from a high of 17.9% of GNP in 1978 to a low of 13.3% in 1975. Corporate profits are even more responsive to business conditions—reaching a high of 15.2% of national income in 1965 and a low of 6.5% in 1982.

NOMINAL AND REAL GNP

Dollar prices provide a satisfactory basis for calculating national product in any one year; they allow us to add apples and oranges, medical services and cars. But if we wish to evaluate the performance of the economy over a number of years, we face a major problem. The dollar is a shrinking yardstick. Because of inflation, its value is going down. On average, the dollar in 1985 buys only 50% of what it bought in 1975.

As the years pass, the dollar measure of GNP increases for two quite different reasons. First, there is an increase in the *quantity* of goods and services produced. This increase is desirable; we have more and more goods and services at our disposal. Second, the *prices* of goods and services increase. This increase is undesirable; it occurs because we have been unsuccessful in combatting inflation. To judge the performance of the economy, *it is essential to separate the desirable increase in the quantity of output from the undesirable increase in prices.*

To do this, economists use the concept of ***constant-dollar GNP,*** also known as ***real GNP.*** This is calculated by valuing GNP at the prices which existed in a beginning or ***base year,*** not at the prices which actually exist while the GNP is being produced. (The U.S. government uses 1972 as the base year in GNP calculations.) A hypothetical example of an economy producing only two items is given in Table 7-4.

If we looked only at ***nominal*** or ***current-dollar GNP*** in the first two columns, we might come to the erroneous conclusion that output trebled—up from $10,000 in 1972 to $30,000 in 1986. But this clearly misstates the increase in the quantity of goods and services produced. Observe that the quantities of coats and radios both increased by only 20%. By measuring 1986 output at 1972 prices in the final column, we find constant-dollar GNP to be $12,000. Comparing this with 1972 GNP of $10,000, we come to the correct conclusion: Real output increased by 20%.

Obviously, this is a very simplified example. Figure 7-4 shows the actual figures for current-dollar and constant-dollar GNP. Observe how much more rapidly the current-dollar series has risen. Most of the increase in nominal GNP between 1972 and 1984 was caused by a rise in prices (Figure 7-5).

Price Indexes

More specifically, we can use current-dollar and constant-dollar GNP to calculate *how much* the average level of prices has risen since the base year. Returning to the example in Table 7-4, observe that nominal GNP in 1986 is 2.5 times as high as real GNP in that year ($30,000/$12,000 = 2.5). By convention, the average price in the base year is given a value of 100 when calculating a ***price index.*** Thus, in the example in Table 7-4, the index of prices in 1986 is 250 (that is, 2.5 times the base of 100).

An *index* is a number which shows how an average (of prices, or wages, or some other economic measure) has changed over time.

The index calculated from nominal and real GNP

TABLE 7-4
Current-Dollar and Constant-Dollar GNP

(1) 1972 current-dollar GNP	(2) 1986 current-dollar GNP	(3) 1986 constant-dollar GNP
100 coats @ $60 = $6,000	120 coats @ $200 = $24,000	120 coats @ $60 = $7,200
100 radios @ $40 = $4,000	120 radios @ $50 = $6,000	120 radios @ $40 = $4,800
Total $10,000	Total $30,000	Total $12,000

figures is known as the ***implicit GNP price deflator,*** or more simply, as the ***GNP deflator.*** In general, it is calculated as:

$$\text{GNP price deflator} = \frac{\text{nominal GNP}}{\text{real GNP}} \times 100 \quad (7\text{-}5)$$

While the GNP deflator measures the change in the average price of the goods and services we have *produced,* another index—the ***consumer price index*** (CPI)—measures the change in the average price of the goods and services *bought* by the typical household. Specifically, the CPI measures changes in the cost of a basket of goods and services purchased by the typical urban family—food, automobiles, housing, furniture, doctor's services, etc.

When the prices of the goods and services that we produce rise, so generally do the prices of what we purchase—for the simple reason that we consume most of what we produce. Therefore, it's not surprising that the GNP price deflator and the CPI tend to move together, particularly over extended periods of time. However, there may be signficant short-run differences in the behavior of the two indexes—for example, in 1979, when the CPI rose 11.3% while the GNP deflator increased by a more moderate 8.7%. Both indexes were reflecting the steep rise in oil prices during that year. But the effect was stronger on the CPI because it covers all the oil consumed in the United States, including both the oil produced at home *and* the large quantity of imported oil. (On the other hand, the GNP deflator covers only the oil produced in the United States.)

Short-run movements in the two indexes may also differ because the CPI covers only the goods and services bought by the typical urban household. In contrast, the GNP deflator is calculated from the prices of *every* item in GNP—that is, the cost of capital goods and government services, as well as consumer goods and services.

FIGURE 7-4

Gross national product (GNP), measured in current dollars and 1972 dollars

Much of the increase in current-dollar national product has been the result of inflation. Observe that national product has grown much more slowly in constant (1972) dollars than in current dollars.

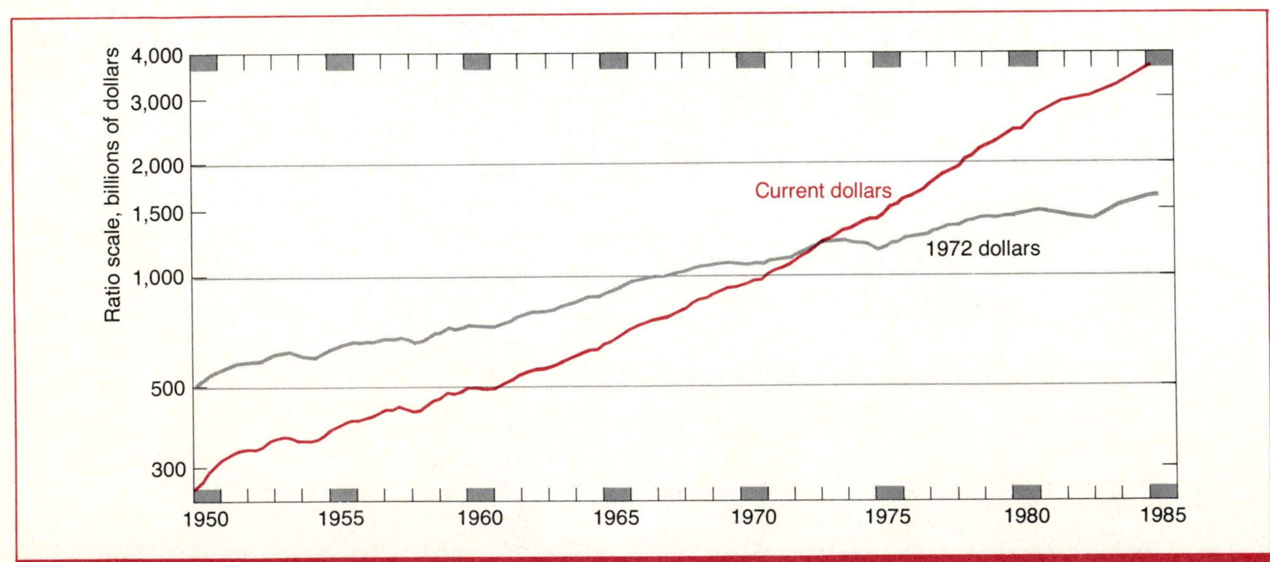

Other Real Measures

Equation 7-5 may be rearranged:

$$\text{Real GNP} = \frac{\text{nominal GNP}}{\text{GNP price deflator}} \times 100 \quad (7\text{-}6)$$

This process—of dividing by a price index—is known as ***deflating.*** Similar equations may be used to calculate other real measures. For example:

$$\text{Real consumption} = \frac{\text{nominal consumption}}{\text{CPI}} \times 100 \quad (7\text{-}7)$$

$$\text{Real wage} = \frac{\text{nominal wage}}{\text{CPI}} \times 100 \quad (7\text{-}8)$$

Suppose the nominal or money wage rises from \$100 to \$107 while the CPI rises by 5%. Then, using equation 7-8, we find:

$$\text{Real wage} = \frac{\$107}{105} \times 100 = \$101.90 \quad (7\text{-}9)$$

The real wage has increased by 1.90%; that is, a worker's wage will buy almost 2% more goods and services.

FIGURE 7-5
The increase in GNP, 1972–1984
Between 1972 and 1984, nominal GNP increased by 209%. However, most of the increase was attributable to inflation. Real GNP increased only 38%.

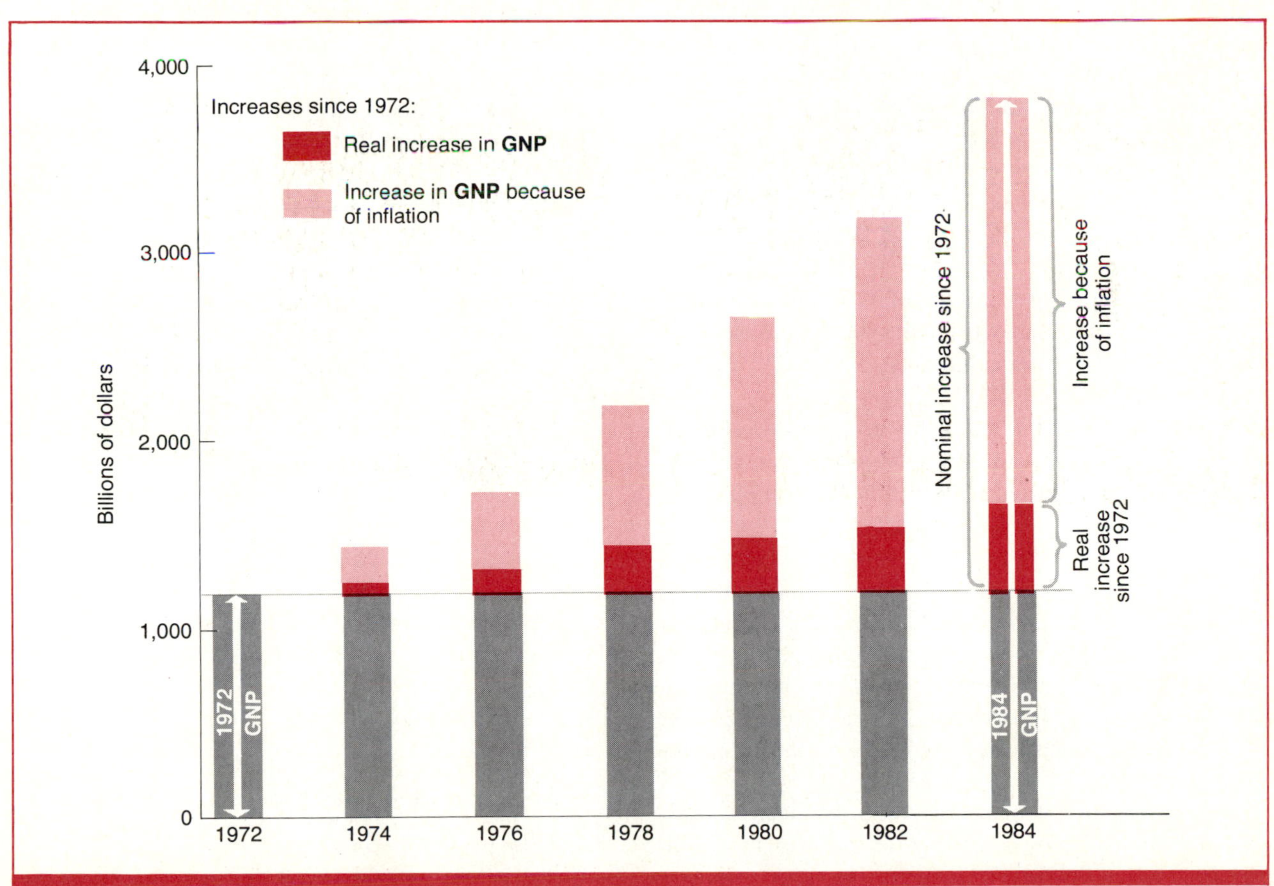

Observe that, in deflating the nominal wage to find the real wage, we use the CPI. This is the most appropriate price index, since it measures changes in the prices of the goods and services that the typical family buys.

While equation 7-9 gives the precise answer, it is cumbersome. A much simpler procedure is often used to find the approximate change:

$$\begin{aligned}\text{Change in real wage} &\\ &\approx \text{change in money wage} - \text{change in CPI}\\ &= 7\% - 5\% = 2\% \qquad (7\text{-}10)\end{aligned}$$

A MEASURE OF ECONOMIC WELFARE

Real GNP is one of the most frequently used measures of economic performance, and large changes in GNP may in fact reflect severe problems or impressive gains. When the nation's real GNP fell by 30% between 1929 and 1933, the performance of the economy was very unsatisfactory. On the other hand, the large increase in real GNP in Japan in recent decades has reflected a rapid rise in the material standard of living.

Yet real GNP cannot be taken as a precise measure of the standard of living. The most obvious difficulty arises because an increase of, say, 10% in real GNP doesn't mean that the average person has 10% more goods and services. The reason is that population is growing. Rather than using total GNP figures, it is appropriate to estimate changes in the standard of living by looking at real GNP ***per capita***; that is, real GNP divided by the population.

Other, more subtle problems arise because market sales are taken as the starting point in calculating GNP. When you hire a professional carpenter to build bookcases, the amount you pay appears in GNP. But if you build bookcases for your home, only the wood and materials are included in GNP; the value of your time as a carpenter is not. Similarly, a restaurant meal appears in GNP. But when you prepare an even better meal at home, only the ingredients bought from the store are included. Thus, GNP does not include some important items, simply because they do not go through the market.

However, in calculating GNP, government statisticians do not adhere mindlessly to the idea that GNP should include all market transactions and nothing else. GNP includes some *imputed* items which do not go through the market. We have already seen that owner-occupied housing is treated *as if* its owners rent to themselves. Imputed rents on such housing are included in GNP, even though people do not actually pay themselves rent. Other imputations include consumption of home-grown food by farmers.

On the other hand, some items which actually do go through the market are excluded from GNP, and quite properly so. Since GNP is taken as a measure of the economy's performance, illegal products—such as heroin—are excluded from GNP on the ground that lawmakers have decided that they are "bads" rather than "goods."

Nevertheless, a number of dubious items remain in GNP. When international relations become more tense, higher expenditures for weapons are included in GNP, but our situation has scarcely improved. If there is an increase in crime, additional expenditures for police, courts, and prisons are included in GNP. Yet society is certainly no better off than it was before the increase in crime.

Furthermore, some goods are included while the "bads" which they create are ignored. For example, GNP includes the production of automobiles and electricity, but there is no downward adjustment for the resulting pollution. Indeed, if people need medical attention as a result, GNP will go up, since doctor's services are included in GNP.[4]

Naturally enough, economists are bothered by the shortcomings of GNP as a measure of well-being. During the past two decades, a number of attempts have been made to deal with some of the inadequacies. These attempts fall under two main headings.

1. Emphasis on Additional Social Indicators

The first approach is to downplay GNP as the measure of how the economy and society are performing, and to realize that it is only one of a number of important indi-

[4]See Kenneth E. Boulding, "Fun and Games with the Gross National Product," in Harold W. Helfrich, Jr., *The Environmental Crisis* (New Haven: Yale University Press, 1962).

cators of performance. Rather than focusing on GNP, policymakers can look at a set of indicators that, taken together, provide both a way of judging performance and a set of objectives for policymakers. In addition to real GNP, important indicators of well-being include such things as life expectancy, infant mortality rates, the availability of health care, education and literacy, the amount of leisure, the quality of the environment, and the degree of urban crowding.

2. A Comprehensive Measure of Economic Welfare (MEW)

The second approach is more ambitious: to provide a comprehensive single measure of economic performance, including not only the standard national product, but also additions for the value of leisure and subtractions for pollution and other disadvantages of crowded urban living. Such a measure of economic welfare (MEW) has been presented by two Yale University economists, William Nordhaus and James Tobin.[5]

The difficulties they encountered were formidable. The most interesting implication of their study is that an entirely satisfactory index *can't* be constructed. To see why, consider the problem posed by leisure. As our ability to produce has increased, the working population has taken only part of the gain in the form of higher wages and other measured incomes; a significant part of the gain has come in the form of a shorter workweek. Specifically, Nordhaus and Tobin calculated that the average number of leisure hours had increased by 22% between 1929 and 1965, while real per capita net national product had risen by 90%.

The question is, What should be made of these facts? Specifically, which of the following conclusions is correct?

1. Production per person went up by 90%, and we had more leisure, too. Therefore, economic welfare improved by more than 90%; it rose *more* than NNP.
2. Production per person went up by 90%. But leisure increased by less than 90%; specifically, by only 22%. Therefore, economic welfare rose by some average of the 90% and the 22%, that is, by *less* than NNP.

It is far from clear which of these conclusions is "correct." Therefore, Nordhaus and Tobin presented two alternative estimates of MEW, reflecting the two alternative assumptions regarding leisure. These alternatives are shown in Figure 7-6, together with the growth of NNP per capita.

The choice between conclusions 1 and 2 is difficult, but it is only the beginning of the problems with evaluating economic welfare in a more comprehensive way. For example, observe that the Nordhaus-Tobin estimates of MEW do not drop during the Great Depression, and indeed, they actually rise between 1929 and 1935. How can this be? Were we really becoming better off as the economy slid into Depression? The explanation for this quirk: Nordhaus and Tobin have included leisure as an element of welfare, and leisure certainly increased as people were thrown out of work. But surely there is something wrong here. Leisure after a good day's work may be bliss, but it's not so pleasant to be idle when you've lost your job.

The ultimate test of economic success is the contribution which economic activity makes to the goal of human happiness. But to seek a single, summary measure of this contribution is surely to set out on an impossible task. In the words of the late Arthur Okun, a former chairman of the Council of Economic Advisers, the calculation of "a summary measure of social welfare is a job for a philosopher king."[6]

Because it seems impossible to develop a single comprehensive measure of welfare, we are stuck with the national product accounts. In spite of all their defects and shortcomings, they do provide an important measure of the health of our economy. Downturns in real GNP act as a signal that we have been unable to prevent recessions, while long-run increases in real GNP per capita are an important indicator of economic progress. GNP is a significant and useful social indicator—but we should not view it as the last word.

[5]William Nordhaus and James Tobin, "Is Growth Obsolete?" in *Economic Growth, Fiftieth Anniversary Colloquium* (New York: National Bureau of Economic Research, 1972).

[6]Arthur M. Okun, "Should GNP Measure Social Welfare?" *Brookings Bulletin* (Washington, Summer 1971).

THE UNDERGROUND ECONOMY: THE CASE OF THE MISSING GNP

The logical question of what GNP statisticians should *attempt* to measure is, however, not the only controversy surrounding the GNP accounts. Another involves what they are able to measure *in practice*. In recent years, a number of economists and government officials have expressed concern that many transactions escape the attention of national product accountants, resulting in a substantial underestimate of GNP.

The reason is that plumbers, carpenters, and doctors—to name but a few—have an incentive to perform services without reporting their income, in order to evade taxes. But, when such income is unreported, it not only disappears from the Treasury's tax records. It also disappears from the GNP accounts. Moonlighting, and the incomes of illegal aliens, are particularly unlikely to be reported. Such "subterranean" or "irregular" activities are by no means confined to the United States: The French have their *travail au noir* ("work in the dark"); the Italians their *lavorno nero* (same thing); the British their "fiddle;" and the Germans their *Schattenwirtschaft* ("shadow economy"). The ***underground economy*** includes not only unreported illegal activities—which, as we have noted, national income accountants intentionally exclude from the GNP—but also such socially desirable services as the work of the moonlighting plumber, whose only illegal act is tax evasion. If we want an accurate measure of the goods and services produced in our economy, we should certainly include such socially desirable services.

FIGURE 7-6
Measures of economic welfare
Nordhaus and Tobin found the measure of economic welfare to be *very* sensitive to the treatment of leisure. Measure 1 is based on the view that welfare has gone up by more than NNP, since we have gotten the increase in output, and more leisure, too. Measure 2 reflects the view that welfare has gone up by an average of the increase in NNP and the (smaller) increase in leisure. (Data for 1929–1965 are from the Nordhaus-Tobin study. We have added our estimates for the period since 1965.)

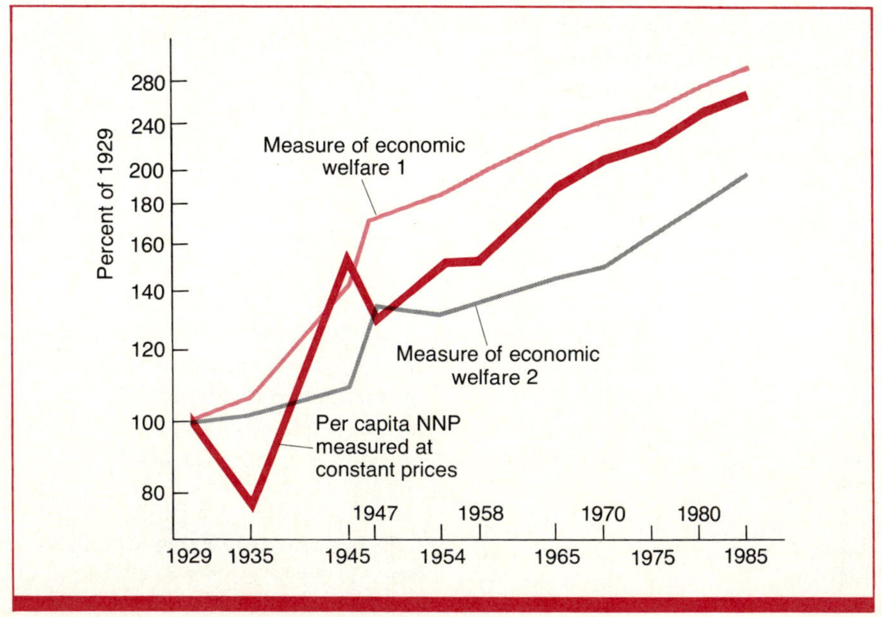

The problem, of course, is to get information, as those in the underground economy are trying to keep their activities secret. Thus, it is difficult to measure the size of the underground economy directly. Rather, economists have looked for the traces left by irregular activities. What might these traces be?

The most obvious way to keep transactions secret is to use currency rather than checks. Thus, economic sleuths looking for traces of the underground economy have usually begun by studying the amount of currency in the hands of the public. For example, in 1979, Peter Gutman of the City University of New York wryly noted that "There is now about $460 of currency in circulation in the United States for every man, woman, and child. . . . [We] may want to ponder . . . what all this currency is used for."[7] Gutman's conclusion was that much of the money was used in a large underground economy, which amounted to about 10% of measured GNP by the late 1970s. Other writers have found evidence that the underground economy is even larger, and growing rapidly.[8] Studies by the Internal Revenue Service (IRS) have supported the conclusion that the underground economy is growing rapidly, but have failed to find evidence that it is substantially larger than 10% of GNP. Using data from its auditing program, the IRS has estimated that unreported income from legal sources grew from 7.1% of GNP in 1973 to 8.5% of GNP by 1981, while illegal income from drugs, gambling, and prostitution grew even faster, from 0.7% to 1.8% of GNP.

If, in fact, the legal segment of the underground economy is not only large but also growing relative to reported GNP, a number of important conclusions follow: (1) Official statistics understate the growth of the economy. (2) Official statistics overstate the true rate of inflation, because those in the rapidly growing underground sector generally charge lower prices to gain customers. (3) Unemployment statistics overstate the true amount of unemployment. People collecting unemployment insurance—but also working "off the record" in the underground economy—are not likely to tell interviewers from the Labor Department that they are employed.

In other words, things may be better than they seem from the official statistics. However, we should not take too much comfort from this conclusion. Because estimates of the underground economy are based on circumstantial evidence, they may contain large errors. Without a doubt, many transactions go unreported. But we do not know just how large the irregular economy really is, nor how much of it represents illegal activities which we do not want to count anyway. Most disturbing is the conclusion of the IRS, which suggests that illegal activities are growing particularly rapidly.

KEY POINTS

1. The market provides a way of adding apples, oranges, automobiles, and the many other goods and services produced during the year. Items are included in national product at their market prices.

2. In measuring national product, everything should be measured once, and only once. Intermediate products (such as wheat or steel) used in the production of other goods (such as bread or automobiles) should not be counted separately since they are already included when we count the final product (bread or automobiles).

3. Net investment equals gross investment minus depreciation. If net investment is positive, more buildings, equipment, and inventories are being produced than are being used up. Thus, the capital stock is rising (Figure 7-2).

4. GNP $= C + I_g + G + X - M$

NNP = GNP − depreciation

Because depreciation is difficult to measure accurately, statisticans have more confidence in the measure of GNP than NNP, and therefore GNP is used more commonly.

5. Receipts from the sale of products are distributed to those who contribute to the productive process by providing labor, capital, or land. In a simple economy, all the proceeds from the sale of goods would be distributed

---

[7] Peter M. Gutman, "Statistical Illusions, Mistaken Policies," *Challenge,* November 1979, p. 16.

[8] Literature on the underground economy includes work by Edgar L. Feige, "How Big Is the Irregular Economy?" *Challenge,* November 1979, pp. 5–13; Richard D. Porter and Amanda S. Bayer, "A Monetary Perspective on Underground Economic Activity in the United States," *Federal Reserve Bulletin,* March 1984, pp. 177–190; Carl P. Simon and Ann D. Witte, *Beating the System: The Underground Economy* (Boston, 1982); and Vito Tanzi, "The Underground Economy in the United States," *International Monetary Fund Staff Papers,* June 1983, pp. 283–305.

in the form of income payments to the factors of production. Net national product and national income would be the same. However, in a real-world economy, national income is less because some of the proceeds from the sale of goods goes to the government in the form of sales taxes. Thus:

$$\text{National income} = \text{NNP} - \text{sales taxes}$$

6. Review Figure 7-3 for the relationships among NNP, national income, personal income, and disposable personal income.

7. Market prices provide a good way for adding up the many different goods and services produced in a *single* year. But they would be a misleading way of comparing the national product in *different* years. The reason is that the value of the dollar shrinks as a result of inflation. A rise in current-dollar national product reflects both an increase in prices and an increase in real production.

8. In order to estimate the increase in real output, constant-dollar figures are used. These are found by measuring GNP at the prices existing in a base year.

9. By "deflating" current data with the appropriate price index, it is possible to get a real measure of other important economic variables, such as the real wage (equation 7-9).

10. Real GNP (or real NNP) per capita is not a good measure of economic welfare. However, when Nordhaus and Tobin tried to calculate a more comprehensive measure of economic welfare, they ran into the insoluble problem of how to deal with leisure.

11. There are two kinds of income in the underground economy:

(*a*) Unreported income of plumbers, carpenters, doctors, farmers, etc. Their failure to report is their only illegal action. The services themselves are legal and socially useful, and they would be included in GNP if government statisticians knew how large they were.

(*b*) Income from illegal activities such as the drug trade. Since Congress has decided that these activities represent social "bads," they would not be included in GNP even if statisticians knew how large they were.

Circumstantial evidence suggests that component (*a*) is growing in proportion to reported GNP. This means that the official GNP statistics understate growth of real GNP. Component (*b*) may be growing even faster.

KEY CONCEPTS

final product
intermediate product
value added
consumption
investment
inventories
government purchases of goods and services
exports of goods and services
imports of goods and services
gross national product (GNP)
net national product (NNP)
gross investment
net investment
depreciation
national income (NI)
personal income (PI)
disposable personal income (DI)
current-dollar GNP
constant-dollar GNP
price index
base year
deflating with a price index
real wage
measure of economic welfare
underground economy

PROBLEMS

7-1. Consider an economy in which the following quantities are measured (in billions of dollars):

Consumption expenditures	$1,000
Value of common stocks purchased	400
Gross private domestic investment	300
Government transfer payments	100
Sales taxes	50
Government purchases of goods and services	200
Corporate income taxes	200
Personal income taxes	100
Exports minus imports	10
Depreciation	75
Purchases of secondhand cars	100

(*a*) Calculate GNP. (Be careful. Not all the items are included.)

(*b*) Calculate NNP.

7-2. The change in inventories can be negative. Can net investment also be negative? Explain.

7-3. Give an example of an import of a service.

7-4. Which of the following government expenditures are included in GNP?

(*a*) The purchase of an aircraft for the Air Force

(*b*) The purchase of a computer for the Treasury Department

(*c*) The payment of unemployment insurance benefits to those who have lost their jobs

(*d*) The salary paid to maintenance workers who mow the grass beside the highways

7-5. Last year a family engaged in the following activities. What items are included in GNP? Explain in each case why the item is, or is not, included.

(*a*) They purchased a used car from their neighbor.

(*b*) They deposited $1,000 in a savings deposit at the bank.

(*c*) They purchased $2,000 worth of groceries.

(*d*) They flew to London for a vacation.

7-6. For 1984 (shown in Figure 7-3):

(*a*) Which was larger: government purchases of goods and services or gross investment?

(*b*) Approximately what percent of NNP was net investment?

(*c*) Approximately how large a percentage of national income were wages and salaries? Corporate profits? Rent and interest?

(*d*) Approximately what fraction of disposable income was saved?

7-7. Of the two measures of economic welfare of Nordhaus and Tobin, do you think one is better than the other? If so, which one, and why? If not, would it be a satisfactory solution to avoid this problem by excluding leisure when calculating a "measure of economic welfare"?

7-8. For each of the following, state whether you agree or disagree. If you agree, explain why. If you disagree, correct the statement.

(*a*) When a trucker buys gasoline, the intended use is to produce trucking services for others, not to take pleasure trips. Therefore, this gasoline is an intermediate product, while the trucking service is a final product.

(*b*) Bread purchased by a household is a final product, but bread purchased by a supermarket or a restaurant is an intermediate product.

(*c*) If new automobiles were treated like new owner-occupied housing in the national product accounts, private domestic investment would be higher and we would be better off.

(*d*) Defense expenditures provide no direct satisfaction to the public. They only protect our freedom to enjoy other goods and services. Therefore, defense expenditures are considered an intermediate product and are not included separately in the calculation of GNP.

(*e*) A road between two manufacturing centers is an intermediate product because it is used to transport goods in the process of production. But a road running to a summer resort is a final good, since it is used primarily for pleasure travel.

7-9. Equation 7-10 shows a simplified way of estimating the approximate change in the real wage. To see how close this approximation is, find the true change in the real wage (from equation 7-8) and compare it to the estimate found with equation 7-10 in each of the following cases:

(*a*) When the money wage increases by 10%, while the CPI increases by 2%

(*b*) When the money wage increases by 30%, while the CPI increases by 22%

(*c*) When the money wage increases by 200%, while the CPI increases by 100%

Do your results from these examples suggest any circumstances under which it would be wise to avoid the use of equation 7-10?

CHAPTER 8

FLUCTUATIONS IN ECONOMIC ACTIVITY:

UNEMPLOYMENT AND INFLATION

A recession is when your neighbor is out of work. A depression is when you're out of work.

HARRY S. TRUMAN

Economic conditions rarely stand still. Moderate expansions often accelerate into inflationary booms, and inflationary booms give way to recessions. This has been true since the beginning of the Republic.

The most obvious way to measure the ups and downs of the U.S. economy is with real GNP figures, which show how aggregate output has expanded and contracted. Unfortunately, however, detailed GNP data are available for only a fraction of U.S. history; it is only since 1929 that the government has collected GNP data on a regular basis. However, by using historical statistics on production and finance (railroad and canal shipments, blast furnace output, banking activity, etc.), we can trace the ups and downs of American business back into the nineteenth century. Figure 8-1 shows fluctuations in business activity since 1835, based on compilations by the AmeriTrust Company of Cleveland.

Of all the fluctuations in our history, the largest took place between 1929 and 1944. First came the collapse into the Great Depression, with real GNP falling sharply between 1929 and 1933. This was followed by a long and painful recovery. It was not until the government

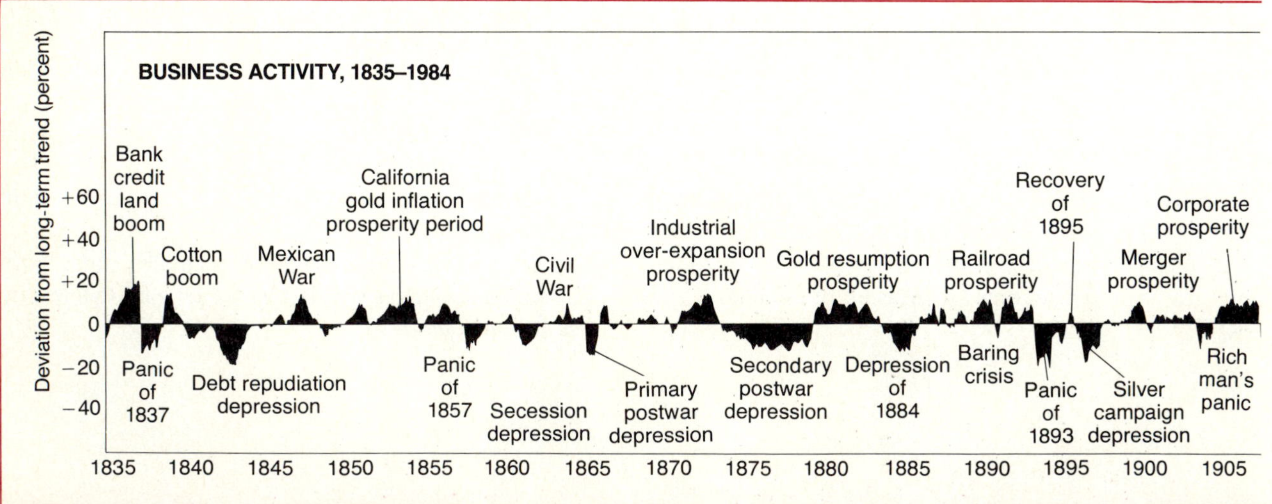

bought huge quantities of munitions during World War II that the economy recovered fully. After the war, there was a temporary drop in output as factories were converted from weapons to peacetime products. Since that time, there has been a series of recessions: in 1948–1949, 1953–1954, 1957–1958, 1960–1961, 1970, 1973–1975, 1980, and 1981–1982.

Fluctuations in economic activity are irregular; no two recessions are exactly alike. Nor are any two expansions. Some last for years, the 1961–1969 expansion being the most notable example. Others are short-lived, such as the expansion of 1958–1960 (which lasted 24 months) and the expansion of 1980–1981, which gave way to a new recession after only 12 months. The economy is not a pendulum swinging regularly at specific intervals. If it were, the analysis of business fluctuations would be simple: The movement of a pendulum is easily predicted.

THE FOUR PHASES OF THE BUSINESS CYCLE

Because business fluctuations are so irregular, it is perhaps surprising that they are called "cycles." However, they all have the same four phases (Figure 8-2).

The key to identifying a business cycle is to identify a ***recession***—the period when economic activity is declining. This immediately raises a problem of definition: How far down does the economy have to go before a recession is declared? There is political as well as economic significance in the answer. No administration wants to be blamed for causing a recession. A private research organization—the National Bureau of Economic Research (NBER)—is the guardian of the keys; it decides what is, and what is not, called a recession. The NBER does not want to call every slight downward jiggle of the economy a recession; the decline should be

FIGURE 8-1
Business activity, 1835–1985
Business activity fluctuates irregularly. The biggest swing occurred between 1929 and 1945, with the economy first collapsing into the Great Depression and then rising to a peak of war production. Earlier booms were associated with such events as the California gold rush and railroad construction. Early recessions generally came in the aftermath of wars or as a result of financial disturbances, such as the panic of 1907.
Source: AmeriTrust Co., Cleveland, with updating and revisions by authors.

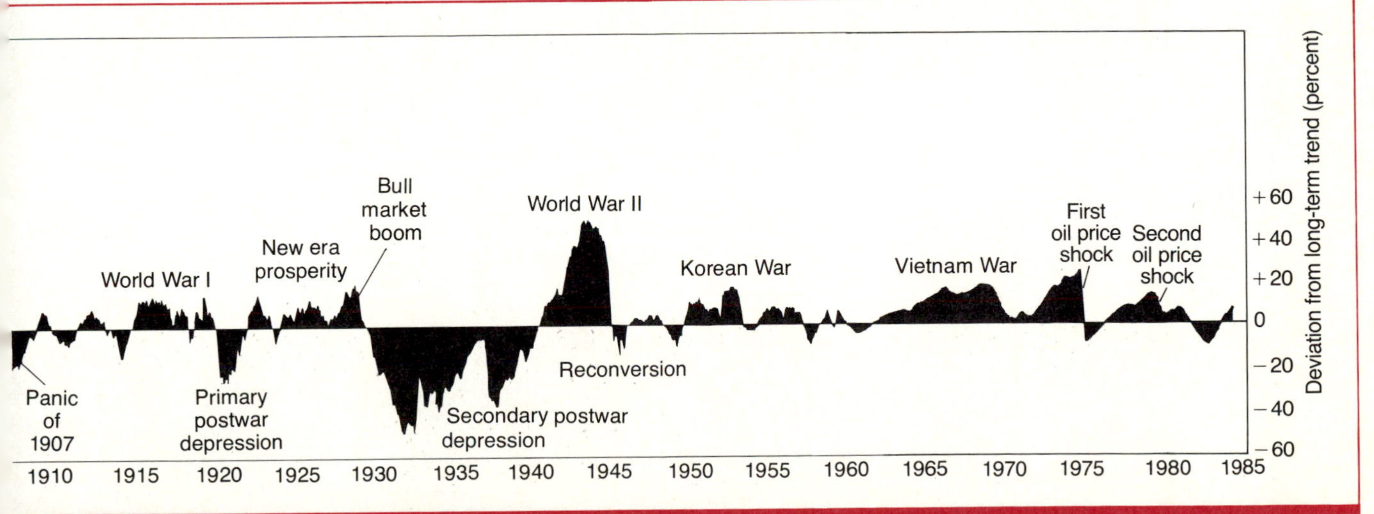

significant. The NBER's major test is historical: Is a downswing as long and severe as declines of the past that have been labeled as "recessions"? (See Box 8-1.) But some simpler definition is needed, since we cannot always pause to review the historical record when using such a common term as recession. Geoffrey H. Moore of Rutgers University—who studied business cycles for many years with the NBER—has offered the summary definition which has already appeared in Chapter 1: A *recession* is a decline in total output, income, employment and trade, usually lasting 6 months to a year, and marked by widespread contractions in many sectors of the economy.[1]

Prior to 1980, a much simpler definition was commonly used: A recession occurs when seasonally adjusted real GNP declines for two or more consecutive quarters. (For an explanation of how GNP and other data are "seasonally adjusted," see Box 8-2.) However, the NBER never accepted this definition, and in 1980, it declared a recession which did not meet this test. Although the recession lasted 6 months, from February to July, real GNP fell in only one quarter—the second quarter, from April to June. (Problem 8-6 at the end of this chapter will help you to see how this apparent paradox is possible. Output may fall for 6 months, even though GNP figures show only one quarter of decline.)

The recession ends with the ***trough***; that is, the ***turning point*** where economic activity is at its lowest. This is followed by the ***expansion*** phase. Output increases, and profits, employment, wages, prices, and interest rates generally rise. Historically, the ***peak,*** or upper turning point, was often associated with a financial

[1]On the problem of defining a recession, see Geoffrey H. Moore, *Business Cycles, Inflation, and Forecasting* (Cambridge, Mass.: Balinger, 2d ed., 1983), Chapter 1.

FIGURE 8-2

Four phases of the business cycle

Periods of expansion and recession alternate, with peaks and troughs in between. The National Bureau of Economic Research identifies each recession, the peak month that precedes it, and the trough month that ends it. Not every expansion reaches a high degree of prosperity with a low unemployment rate: An expansion sometimes ends prematurely and a new recession begins.

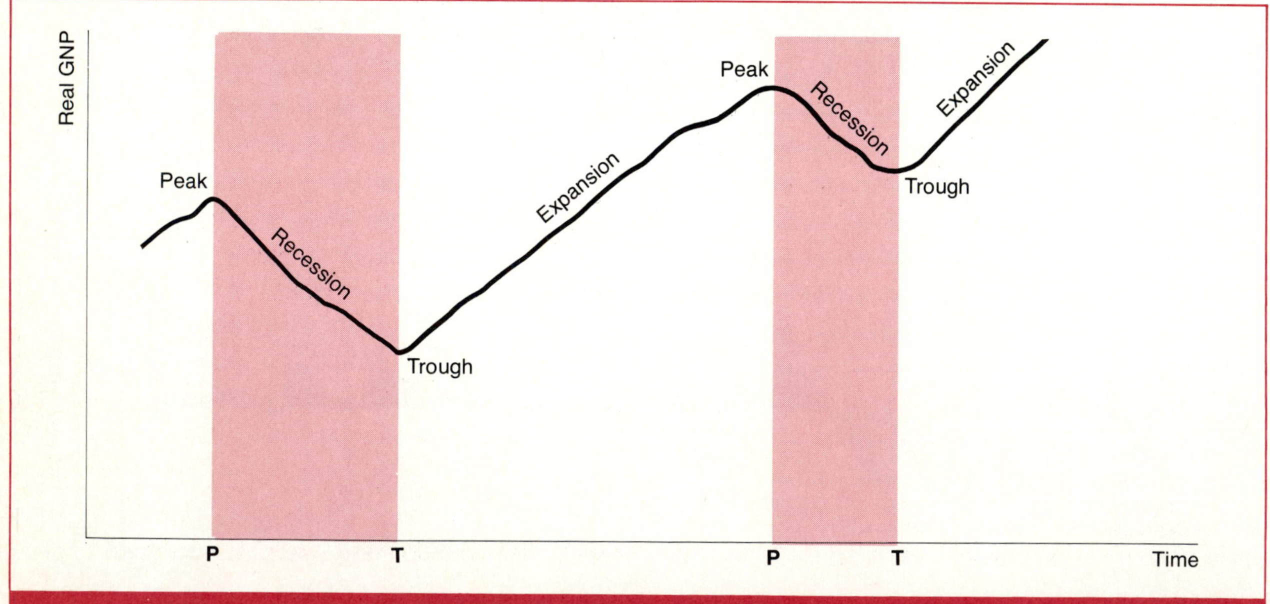

panic, such as the panic of 1907 or "Black Tuesday"—October 29, 1929—when the stock market crashed. Recent peaks have been much less spectacular, with one notable exception. The economic peak in late 1973 coincided with war in the Middle East, an oil embargo, and skyrocketing oil prices.

Not only is it difficult to decide when a downturn becomes strong enough to be classified as a recession. It is also difficult to decide when a serious recession should be labeled a ***depression.*** There is no commonly accepted definition of a depression—except, perhaps, Harry Truman's quip with which we introduced this chapter. Because the depression of the 1930s was so deep and long-lasting, unemployment would have to be severe and persistent before we should talk of a depression. Perhaps the definition should require that unemployment remain at double-digit levels—that is, 10% or more—for a full 2 years. By this criterion, the severe recession of 1981–1982 did not qualify as a depression. Although the seasonally adjusted unemployment rate reached a peak of 10.6% in December 1982, it exceeded 10% for only 8 months.

However, no matter how a depression is defined, there is no doubt that this term should be used to describe the 1930s.

BOX 8-1

WHEN DOES A DECLINE BECOME A "RECESSION"?

The problem of defining a recession has perhaps never been as difficult as it was in the summer of 1970. At that time, the historical approach of the National Bureau of Economic Research failed to provide clear guidance. The problem was that the economy had declined slightly between the last quarter of 1969 and the first quarter of 1970 and then had leveled off. What label should be applied to these conditions? The NBER did not have a good case for declaring a recession, since the slight decline was less severe than anything that had been labeled a recession in the past. But it was *almost* as severe as mild recessions of the past. Furthermore, it was more severe than any of the slight downturns of the past that had been judged too mild to be called recessions.

In other words, the decline fell into an historical gap between past recessions and less severe downturns. The NBER was unsure whether to declare a recession or not, and therefore it compromised. Because the most notable feature of the first half of 1970 was the interruption of growth rather than any substantial decline, Solomon Fabricant of the NBER applied the label "growth recession" to the state of economic activity in the summer of 1970.

The NBER thereby touched a sensitive nerve in Washington. In a speech to the NBER in September 1970, Herbert Stein of the President's Council of Economic Advisers jokingly suggested that, as the Bureau would soon be able to diselect or elect a U.S. president by declaring or not declaring a recession, he foresaw "a drive for direct public election of the members of the board of the National Bureau."

Stein also twitted Fabricant on his declaration of a "growth" recession:

> I was prepared for this finding by a conversation I had with Sol Fabricant a few weeks ago. I met him on Madison Avenue walking a small poodle, or so I thought.
>
> "That's a cute dog," I said.
>
> "That's no dog," he replied; "it's a horse."
>
> "It looks just like a dog to me," I resisted.
>
> "Yes, but it has many attributes of a horse," was his explanation.
>
> "But Sol," I cried, "it's so *small.*"
>
> "I know," he answered. "That's why I call it a growth horse."

Humor soon became irrelevant. After remaining approximately level in the middle two quarters of 1970, real GNP in the fourth quarter fell to a level 1.5% below the high established in late 1969. This was more severe than the declines in a number of previous recessions. By the NBER's standard historical test, a recession had clearly taken place.

THE GREAT DEPRESSION OF THE 1930S

The Great Depression still haunts America. Between the peak of 1929 and and the depth of the depression in 1933, real GNP declined by 30%. The unemployment rate shot up to almost 25% of the labor force. Prices fell, with the GNP deflator declining about 23%. The combination of falling prices and falling real output meant that current-dollar GNP decreased almost 50%.

Nor did recovery come quickly and strongly. Business revived slowly, with the unemployment rate gradually declining to 14.3% by 1937. Then came a sharp setback in 1938—a recession within the depression. It was not until 1941, after the outbreak of World War II in Europe, that the unemployment rate finally fell below 10%. By 1941, the United States was rushing to rearm, buying large quantities of military equipment and supplies. Between 1940 and 1941, defense spending shot up from $2.2 billion (2.2% of GNP) to $13.8 billion (11.0% of GNP). The Great Depression was ended only by an even greater catastrophe—World War II.

The decade of depression was a disaster for many segments of society. Many of those thrown out of work could not find other jobs. In his book, *Hard Times,* Studs Terkel quotes an unemployed San Francisco laborer:

> I'd get up at five in the morning and head for the waterfront. Outside the Spreckles Sugar Refinery, outside the gates, there would be a thousand men. You know dang well there's only three or four jobs. . . .
>
> There'd be this kind of futile struggle, because somehow you never expected to win. We had a built-in losing complex. . . . By now it's one o'clock, and everybody's hungry. These were fathers, eighty percent of them. They had held jobs and didn't want to kick society to pieces. They just wanted to go to work and they just couldn't understand.[2]

[2]Studs Terkel, *Hard Times* (New York: Pantheon Books, 1971).

BOX 8-2

SEASONAL ADJUSTMENT OF ECONOMIC DATA

Not all ups and downs in business activity represent the misbehavior of the economy. Crops grow by the calendar; harvests are gleaned in the summer and autumn months. The month-to-month changes in food production reflect a law of nature with which we learn to live. Retail sales boom during the holiday season in December, only to fall in January.

Such regular month-to-month swings are not our concern. The decline in retail sales in January is the aftermath of the December buying boom; it is not a symptom of an oncoming recession. In order to identify a recession, we must remove the seasonal effects from business activity; that is, we must *seasonally adjust* our data on production, sales, etc. The following technique is used.

From past information, suppose the statistician discovers that December sales of toys typically run at three times the average monthly rate, only to drop to one-half the average monthly rate in January. The raw data for toy sales can then be seasonally adjusted by dividing December's sales by 3 and multiplying January's sales by 2. (In fact, more complicated techniques are used, but this is the general idea.) Similarly, quarterly data for GNP or monthly indexes of industrial production can be adjusted to remove seasonal fluctuations and help to identify fundamental movements in the economy.

The desperation of the long-term unemployed was reflected in a letter written to Eleanor Roosevelt by an Oklahoma woman in 1934:

> The unemployed have been so long without food, clothes, shoes, medical care, dental care, etc.—we look pretty bad, so when we ask for a job we don't get it. And we look and feel a little worse each day. When we ask for food they call us bums. It isn't our fault. . . . We are not bums.[3]

Nor were the unemployed alone in their misery. In the face of slack demand, prices of farm commodities dropped more than 60% between 1929 and 1933. In parts of the country, the plight of farmers was compounded by a natural disaster—a severe drought which turned grain-producing areas into a dust bowl. Business bankruptcies came thick and fast, including the bankruptcies of many banks. In 1933, businesses on average lost money; that is, total profits were negative. However, manufacturing prices did not plummet the way agricultural commodities did. For example, the prices of automobiles and farm implements fell less than 10% between 1929 and 1933.[4]

The depression was worldwide; large-scale unemployment was an international phenomenon. There were immeasurable, but perhaps even greater, political consequences. The depression was one of the factors that brought Hitler to power, with his promises of full employment and military conquest. The world in which we live has been shaped by the events of the 1930s.

The Great Depression laid the foundation for modern macroeconomics. Politicians, economists, and the general public were determined to prevent a repeat of the 1930s. So far, we have been successful. Economic problems in recent decades have been mild compared with those of the thirties.

OUTPUT, UNEMPLOYMENT, AND INFLATION IN RECENT U.S. CYCLES

However, in spite of successes, problems have remained. The economy has continued to fluctuate. Furthermore, and perhaps most disconcerting of all, the performance of the economy does not seem to have improved with time. Recessions have *not* been getting more and more mild. On the contrary, two of the most recent recessions—1973–1975 and 1981–1982—have been the most severe since the Great Depression.

Figure 8-3 shows how output, unemployment, profits, money wages, and inflation have changed since 1959. As is customary, recessions are marked with shaded bars, and the peak and trough months are identified with the letters *P* and *T,* respectively. Although recent recessions have been *much* milder than the collapse of 1929–1933, the recent behavior of the economy is broadly consistent with the 1930s in some important respects. Specifically:

- During recessions, when production is falling, the unemployment rate rises. Likewise, when production rises during an expansion, more workers are needed and the unemployment rate falls.
- During recessions, profits fall by a much larger percentage than output. They rise rapidly during expansions.
- During recessions, when output is declining, inflation generally declines too. When the economy is expanding, the rate of inflation generally accelerates.

Observe that wages and profits behave quite differently during recessions. While profits fall sharply, money wages remain *much* more stable. Indeed, recessions had no readily apparent effect on the wage series shown in Figure 8-3, except for the slowing of the rate of increase in money wages after the severe recession of 1981–1982. Recessions hit workers primarily in the form of unemployment, not lower wages.

Observe, also, that *inflation responds slowly* to changing business conditions. During the first half of the

---

[3]As quoted in Robert S. McElvaine, ed., *Down and Out in the Great Depression* (Chapel Hill: University of North Carolina Press, 1983).

*[4]Technical note: There were two reasons for this difference between the prices of manufactures and basic commodities. (1) Many manufacturers do not operate in perfectly competitive markets; they have some control over their selling prices. (2) During periods of slack demand, manufacturers often do better by reducing production rather than prices. If they cut prices, the price may no longer cover wages, parts, and materials. If they cut production, they can lay off workers, reduce their expenditures on parts and materials, and cut their losses. In contrast, on many farms, the labor is that of the farm family itself. If farmers cut production, they save relatively little on costs. They may feel they have no alternative but to keep producing, and accept what little they get from the sale of their products.

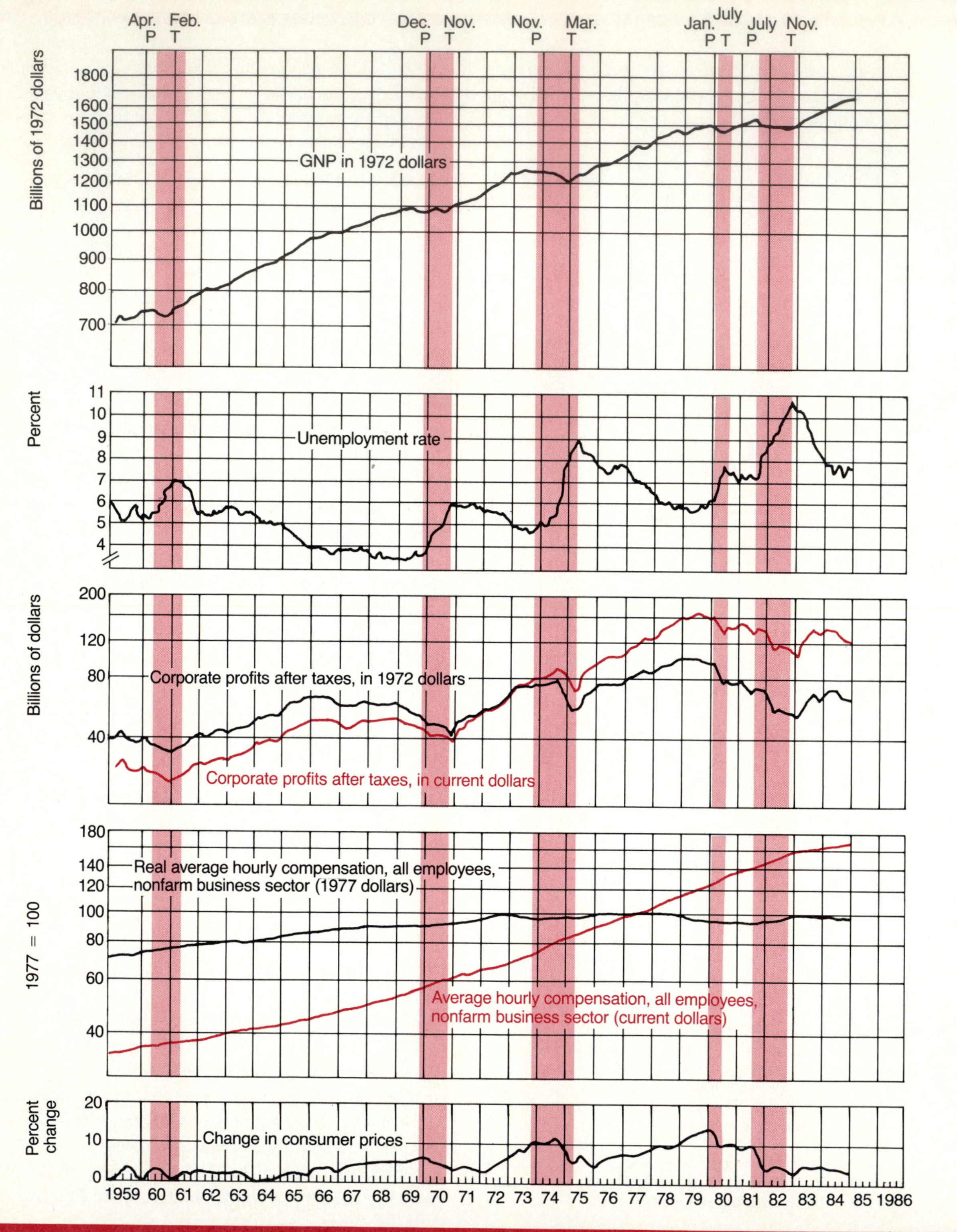

Apr. P
Feb. T
Dec. P
Nov. T
Nov. P
Mar. T
Jan. P
July T
July P
Nov. T
Billions of 1972 dollars
1800
1600
1500
1400
1300
1200
1100
1000
900
800
700
GNP in 1972 dollars
Percent
11
10
9
8
7
6
5
4
Unemployment rate
Billions of dollars
200
120
80
40
Corporate profits after taxes, in 1972 dollars
Corporate profits after taxes, in current dollars
1977 = 100
180
140
120
100
80
60
40
Real average hourly compensation, all employees, nonfarm business sector (1977 dollars)
Average hourly compensation, all employees, nonfarm business sector (current dollars)
Percent change
20
10
0
Change in consumer prices
1959 60 61 62 63 64 65 66 67 68 69 70 71 72 73 74 75 76 77 78 79 80 81 82 83 84 85 1986

long expansion of the 1960s, for example, prices were quite stable. It was only in the latter part of the 1960s that inflation began to accelerate significantly. Similarly, the strong upswings in inflation occurred in the last half of the expansions of 1970–1973 and 1975–1979.

Furthermore, the upward momentum of inflation may continue into the early part of a recession, as it did in 1974. Generally, it is toward the end of recessions that economic slack has its strongest effect in bringing down the rate of inflation. Downward pressure on the rate of inflation sometimes continues into the early recovery—most notably, in 1971 and 1975–early 1976.

The slowness of prices to respond introduces an important complication into the government's task of stabilizing the economy, as we shall see when we get to the more advanced macroeconomic topics of Part 4 (Chapters 14 to 19).

Consumption and Investment during Recession

During recessions, some parts of GNP decline much more than others. This is illustrated in Figure 8-4, which shows the changes in various segments of output between the last quarter of 1979 (which marked the end of the expansion of the 1970s) and the last quarter of 1982 (when the recession reached its trough).

Consumption Over this period, real GNP declined by 0.6%. But real consumption expenditures actually rose, by 4.4%. Expenditures for services and nondurables both increased, while consumers cut back their real spending for durables by 2.1%.

There is a reason for this different behavior of durables, on the one hand, and services and nondurables, on the other. Because durables last, people have the option of postponing purchases during hard times, when they are having trouble paying their bills. For example, as incomes decline, people may decide to fix up their old cars or old refrigerators rather than splurging on new ones. They can continue to enjoy the use of durables, even if they are not currently buying them. This obviously does not apply to services such as medical services: Services are consumed as they are produced. Nor does it apply to nondurable goods: Purchases of food represent one of the last things that people will cut back during recessions.

Investment Much larger fluctuations occur in the investment sector. By the last quarter of 1982, overall investment had fallen by 20.8% from its level 3 years earlier. Residential investment collapsed by no less than 28.4%. Nonresidential fixed investment (which includes both plant and equipment) declined by a less spectacular 6.9%. Inventory accumulation, which had been consistently positive in every quarter from the beginning of 1976 until the third quarter of 1979, had become a large negative figure (−$22.7 billion) by the last quarter of 1982.

Instability of investment has been a continuing feature of business cycles; fluctuations in investment have accounted for a large fraction of overall fluctuations in the economy. Furthermore, the decline in inventories in 1982 was typical for a period of recession. Inventory investment has become negative in every U.S. recession since the Second World War, with only one exception (1970). Moreover, swings in inventory investment have been large. In fact, they have on average accounted for more than half of the total decline in real GNP during the recessions of the past four decades. It is not surprising, therefore, that the declines of the past four decades have frequently been referred to as *inventory recessions*.

UNEMPLOYMENT

The two principal features of a recession are a fall in output and a rise in unemployment. Changes in output are measured by the national product accounts. Changes in unemployment are measured by the unemployment rate.

Calculating the Unemployment Rate

The unemployment rate is estimated each month by the Bureau of Labor Statistics (BLS) using an obvious, direct approach: It asks people. Because it would be prohibitively expensive and time-consuming to ask everybody, a sample of about 65,000 households is surveyed.

← **FIGURE 8-3**
Recent business fluctuations
Source: Department of Commerce, *Business Conditions Digest*.

Questions are asked regarding each member of the household who is over 16, except those unavailable for work because they are in institutions such as prisons or mental hospitals. Each individual is classified in one of three categories: (1) employed, (2) unemployed, or (3) not in the labor force.

The first category includes all those who have worked in the week of the survey, including part-time employees who have worked as little as 1 hour. The second category includes people without work who (1) are on temporary layoff but expect to be recalled, (2) are waiting to report to a new job within four weeks, or (3) say they have actively looked for work during the previous 4 weeks and are currently available for work. The remainder are out of the labor force. This group includes retirees, full-time students without paying jobs, and those who stay out of the labor force in order to look after young children. The unemployment rate is calculated as the number of unemployed as a percentage of the labor force (Table 8-1, line 4*a*).

The BLS also calculates the unemployment rate in an alternative way, as a percentage of the *civilian* labor force (Table 8-1, line 4*b*). To make this calculation, it subtracts the number in the armed forces from the labor force. Until recent years, the unemployment rate was generally quoted in this way, as a percentage of the civilian labor force. However, in line with a recommendation of a commission on unemployment statistics appointed by President Carter and chaired by Sar Levitan of George Washington University, the standard practice now is to

FIGURE 8-4
Percentage change in real GNP and selected components between last quarter of 1979 and last quarter of 1982
The economy reached a cyclical peak in the last quarter of 1979. There were then two quick recessions, with the trough of the second occurring in the last quarter of 1982. This figure shows how some components of GNP declined much more than others. In fact, both consumption and government purchases of goods and services increased in real terms. The recession was concentrated in the investment sector.

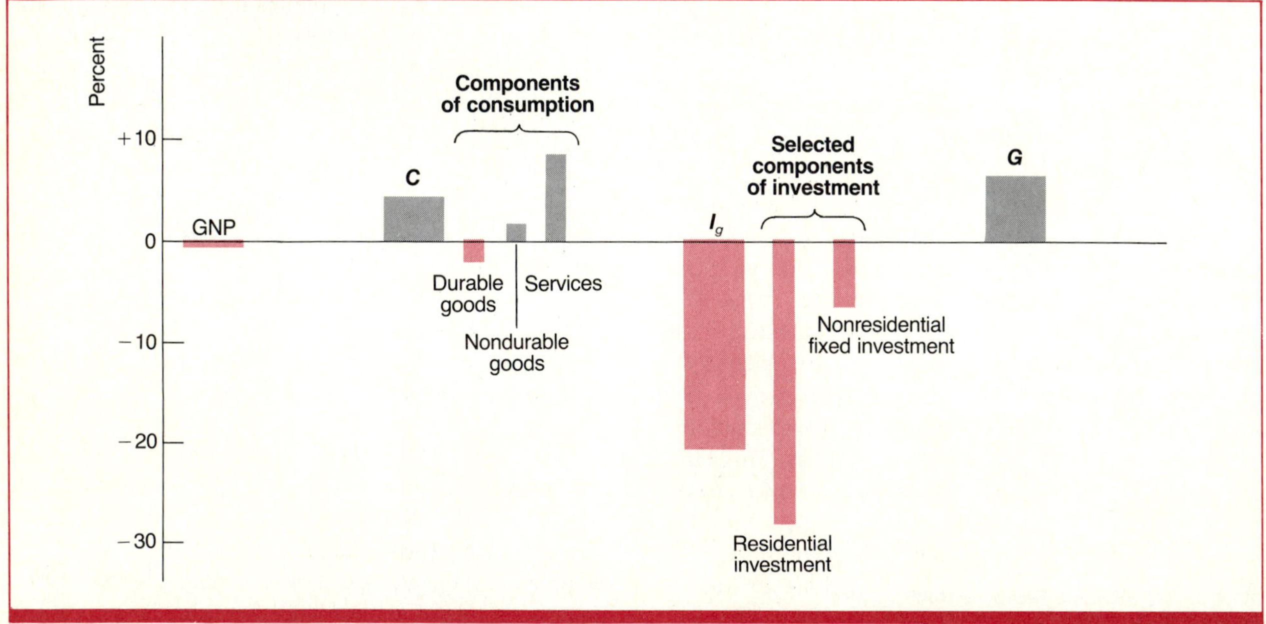

quote unemployment as a percentage of the whole labor force, including the military. When the armed forces are included, the labor force is somewhat larger and the unemployment rate is therefore slightly lower—generally 0.1 or 0.2% less than when just the civilian labor force is used.

The method used in calculating the unemployment rate has caused controversy. (1) Some critics think the official unemployment rate overstates the true figure, pointing out that there is no check on those who say they are looking for work. (2) On the other hand, others observe that, during hard times, workers may become *discouraged* and quit looking for work after they have been repeatedly rebuffed. They thereby drop out of the labor force. Thus, during recessions, the rise in the unemployment rate may not measure the full deterioration in the employment situation. This interpretation is supported by the behavior of the labor force. During recessions, it generally grows very slowly, and sometimes even declines because of the departure of discouraged workers. On the other hand, it grows rapidly during recoveries. When jobs are easier to get, people are more likely to enter the labor force, and those who are in the labor force are less likely to drop out.

***Discouraged workers* are those who want work but are no longer actively looking for it because they think no jobs are available. When they stop looking for work, they are no longer counted either as part of the labor force or as unemployed.**

Finally, during recessions, there is an increase in the number of people who can't get full-time jobs and who are therefore involuntarily limited to part-time work. Such ***underemployment*** does not show up in the unemployment statistics, but information on this point is available. Hours lost for this reason are calculated by the BLS and included in the *labor force time lost* (Table 8-1, line 5). Because this figure includes the hours lost by both the unemployed and the underemployed on a shortened workweek, it is higher than the unemployment rate. Not surprisingly, the gap between the two figures becomes larger during recessions, when more workers are limited to part-time work.

Underemployment

We have just considered one group of the underemployed: those who can find only part-time work when they want full-time jobs. But underemployment also takes a second form, which results from the way in which businesses respond to falling sales.

During recessions, businesses do not change the number of employees quickly. As the economy begins to weaken, businesses are more likely to cancel overtime than to lay off workers. Thus, employment falls less rapidly than output. And, even after overtime has been substantially eliminated, employers are reluctant to lay off workers. One reason is that a person who has been laid off may take a job somewhere else. When sales revive, the business will then have to go to the bother and expense of hiring and training a replacement. Thus, managers often conclude that it is better to keep workers on the job, even if they are not kept busy. Such workers are

TABLE 8-1
The Labor Force and Unemployment
(millions; April 1985)

1. Total population		238
Less: Those under 16, or institutionalized		58
Not in labor force		63
2. Equals: Labor force		117
Less: Armed forces		2
3. Equals: Civilian labor force		115
(*a*) Employed:	107	
(*b*) Unemployed:	8.4	

4. Unemployment rate:

(*a*) As percent of labor force: $\frac{\text{line 3}(b)}{\text{line 2}} = \frac{8.4}{117} = 7.2\%$

(*b*) As percent of civilian labor force:

$$\frac{\text{line 3}(b)}{\text{line 3}} = \frac{8.4}{115} = 7.3\%$$

Addenda:

5. Labor force time lost: 8.2%

6. Labor force participation rates for those over 19:

	Male	*Female*
1950	88.4%	33.3%
1960	86.0%	37.6%
1970	82.6%	43.3%
1980	79.4%	51.3%
1984	78.3%	53.7%

Source: Bureau of Labor Statistics.

underemployed in the sense that they produce significantly less than they could. Thus, as the economy declines into recession, the ***productivity of labor*** generally declines.

Workers are *underemployed* if (1) they can find only part-time work when they want full-time work or (2) they are being paid full time but are not kept busy because of low demand for the firm's products.

The *productivity of labor* is the average amount produced in an hour of work. It is measured as total output divided by the number of hours of labor input.

When the economy finally does recover, labor productivity increases very rapidly. Because many businesses have developed slack during the recession, they have underemployed labor and machinery. Thus, during the early stages of a recovery, businesses can increase their output substantially before they need to add many more workers.

As a result, unemployment fluctuates less than output during the business cycle. Specifically, the unemployment rate moves only 1% for every cyclical change of 2% to 3% in output in the opposite direction. This tendency for unemployment to fluctuate much less than output is known as ***Okun's law,*** after the late Arthur Okun, whose distinguished career included a professorship at Yale University and service as chairman of President Johnson's Council of Economic Advisers.

Who Are the Unemployed?

Unemployment does not fall equally on all members of society. The unemployment rate for teenagers is much higher than for adults (Figure 8-5). The rate for blacks is typically about twice that for whites. The unemployment rate among black teenagers is staggering—almost 51% during the summer of 1982, when the economy was approaching the trough, and almost as high (48.5%) during the early recovery of 1983. Historically, the unemployment rate for women has generally been somewhat above that for men. However, the difference has generally declined during recessions, which hit male-dominated construction and heavy manufacturing jobs particularly hard.[5] During the recession of 1981–1982, the rate for men rose above that of women, and remained above the female rate throughout the recovery year of 1983. However, in 1984–1985 the rate for women was once again above that for men.

Figure 8-6 illustrates two other important features about the unemployed—how they came to be unemployed and how long they are unemployed. Not surprisingly, the duration of unemployment increases sharply during recessions, as unemployed workers experience more and more difficulty in finding jobs. At the end of the prosperous year 1979, less than 10% of the unemployed had been out of work more than 6 months. Following the deep recession of 1981–1982, this figure rose above 25%. This has important implications. Short-term unemployment can be painful, but it is scarcely catastrophic. It is long-term unemployment that is so demoralizing. During recessions, this type of unemployment becomes a larger share of the rising overall unemployment rate. Thus, during recessions, the unemployment situation becomes even worse than it appears in the overall unemployment numbers. For example, while the overall number of the unemployed almost doubled from 6.1 million in December 1979 to 12.0 million in December 1982, the number of long-term unemployed (over 15

[5]Ralph E. Smith, ''Has the Recession been an Equal Opportunity Disemployer?'' in *The Impact of Macroeconomic Conditions on Employment Opportunities for Women* (Washington: Joint Economic Committee, U.S. Congress, 1977), pp. 5–15.

FIGURE 8-5 ⟶

Selected unemployment rates

Unemployment rates vary greatly among different groups in the economy. Blacks consistently have an unemployment rate that is about twice as high as that of whites. Historically, women have had higher unemployment rates than men, but the rate for men rose above the women's rate during the recession of 1982. Teenagers have the highest unemployment rate of all. Even during the relatively prosperous years of 1973 and 1979, the teenage unemployment rate was still about 15%. For the recession year 1982, it was more than 23%.

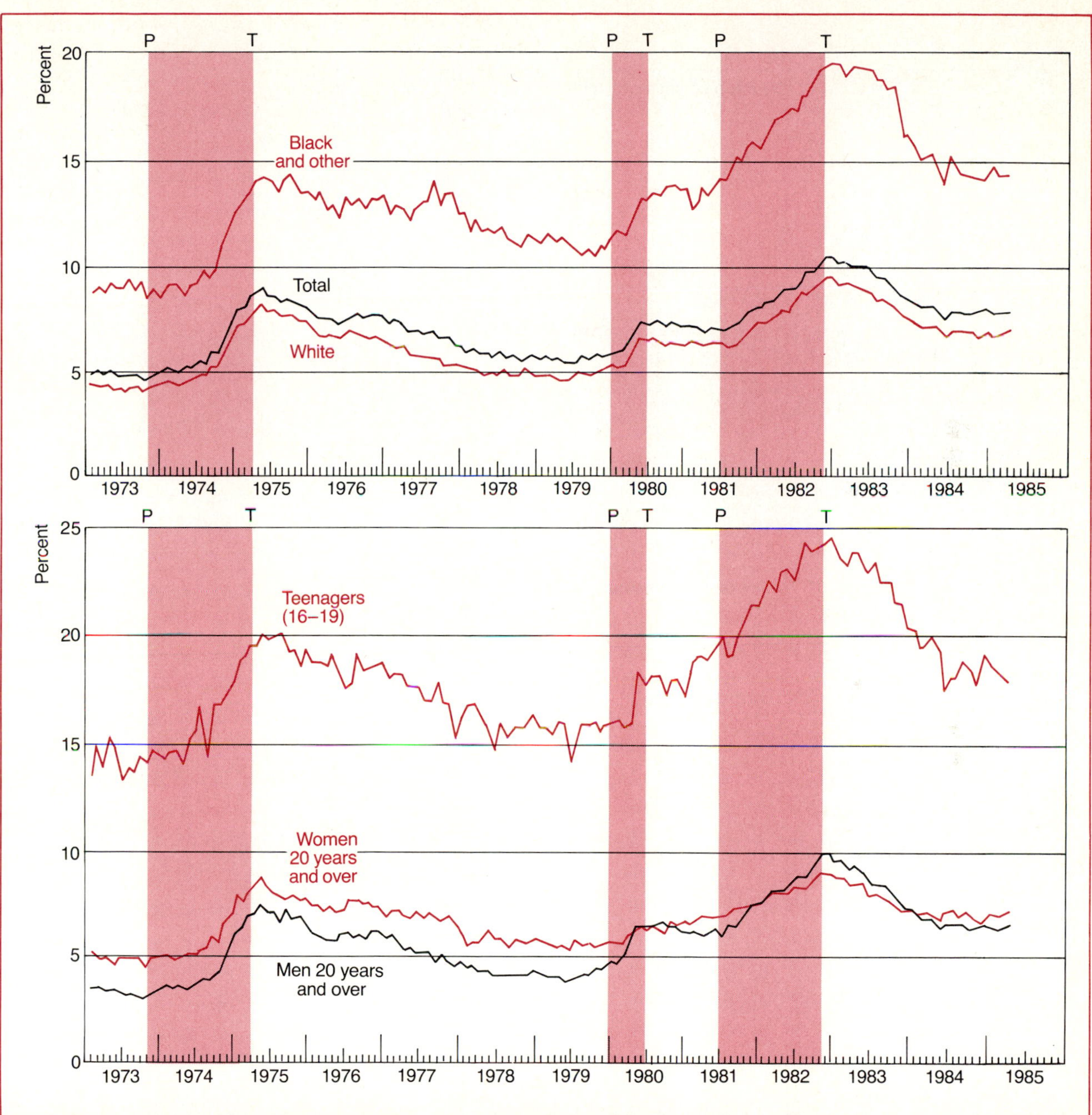
P
T
P
T
P
T
Percent
20
15
10
5
0
Black
and other
Total
White
1973
1974
1975
1976
1977
1978
1979
1980
1981
1982
1983
1984
1985
P
T
P
T
P
T
Percent
25
20
15
10
5
0
Teenagers
(16–19)
Women
20 years
and over
Men 20 years
and over
1973
1974
1975
1976
1977
1978
1979
1980
1981
1982
1983
1984
1985

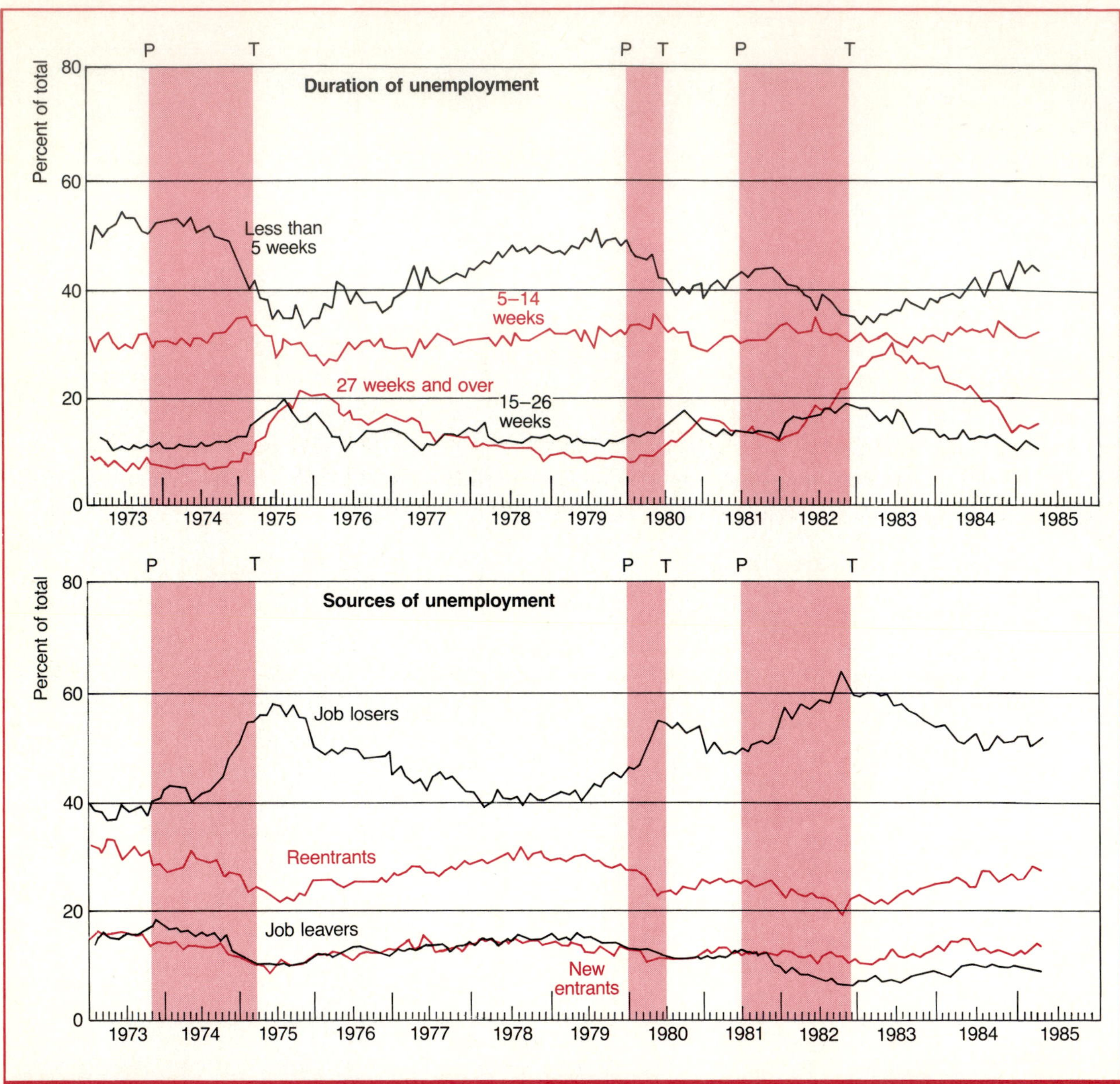

FIGURE 8-6

Duration of unemployment and its sources

The top panel shows how the duration of unemployment increases during recessions and into the early recovery, when people are still having difficulty finding jobs. The lower panel shows the sources of unemployment. During prosperous periods such as 1973 and 1978–1979, most of the unemployed are not people who have lost their jobs through layoff or firing. Rather, the majority are people who have quit their jobs and labor-force entrants who have not yet found work. However, during the recessions of 1980 and 1981–1982, more than half the unemployed had lost their jobs—as many as 60% by late 1982.

weeks) almost *quadrupled,* from 1.2 million to 4.7 million people.

During recessions, people are much more likely to lose their jobs, either through layoff or discharge (Figure 8-6, lower panel). However, even during recessions, it is unusual if more than 60% of the unemployed have actually lost their previous jobs. The other 40% are new entrants (young people who are looking but have not yet found work after leaving school), reentrants (many of whom are reentering the labor force after caring for young families), and people who have quit their last jobs to look for something better. Not surprisingly, people are more reluctant to quit during hard times, when other jobs are scarce. But even as the unemployment rate hit its peak of 10.6% in December 1982, 0.8% of those who had jobs quit during that month.

This illustrates something important about the U.S. labor force. It is quite mobile. Many people are ready to quit their jobs to look for something better. The mobility of the U.S. labor force is illustrated in Figure 8-7. The arrows show the many ways people move into and out of employment and into and out of the labor force. Because of this mobility, it is difficult to define precisely what is meant by "full employment." Clearly, we are not striving for an economy in which the unemployment rate is zero. To accomplish such a goal, we would have to forbid people from leaving one job until they already had another lined up.

Types of Unemployment

Before attempting to define the elusive concept of "full employment," let us consider the various types of unemployment. The first is the one we've talked about so far: *cyclical unemployment*. During recessions, workers are laid off. This is the most important type of unemployment, and the one on which macroeconomic analysis is focused. But there are also other types.

Frictional unemployment There will always be some people between jobs or looking for their first job. Others may be temporarily out of work because of the weather—for example, those employed in construction work.

***Frictional unemployment* is temporary unemployment associated with adjustments in a changing, dynamic economy. It arises for a number of reasons. For example, some new entrants into the labor force take time to find jobs, some workers with jobs quit to look**

FIGURE 8-7

The changing labor force

The labor force is quite fluid. Not only do many people move from job to job, but many move into and out of the labor force and into and out of the pool of unemployed.

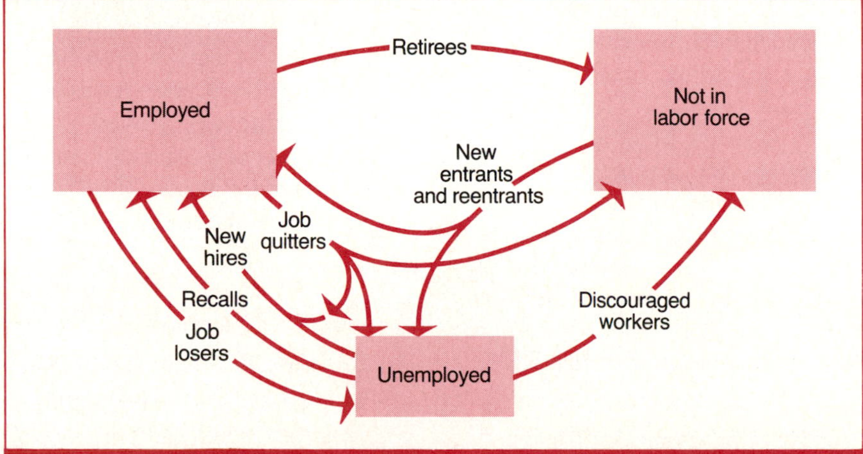

for something better, and some are unemployed by temporary disturbances (for example, bad weather, or a temporary shutdown of an automobile factory to retool for a new model).

Such *frictional unemployment* is practically inevitable. It is difficult to see how it could be eliminated without an oppressive government directing people to the first available jobs. And at least some frictional unemployment is desirable. For example, people often want to spend some time looking for a job. Such time can be well spent, since the first available job may be quite inappropriate. Having people search for high-paying, high-productivity jobs is not only good for them; it also contributes to the overall efficiency of the economy. Similarly, it is desirable to have people engaged in building houses, even though this inevitably results in some unemployment: Some construction jobs can't be done in bad weather.

In our dynamic, changing economy, some industries decline, while others rise. In many cases, when one firm goes bankrupt, others rise to take its place, and the labor force can move to the new jobs quite quickly and easily. Such transitional unemployment is also classified as frictional: People are temporarily between jobs as they hunt for new ones.

Structural unemployment In other cases, the changing pattern of jobs may leave workers stranded. For example, in the 1950s and 1960s, many coal mines shut down in Appalachia because oil was displacing coal. Many of the unemployed miners were unable to find local jobs; to find work, they would have had to move hundreds of miles and learn new skills. Similarly, a loss of part of the market to Japanese cars, combined with automation on the assembly line, has permanently reduced the number of jobs in the automobile industry. Even with the cyclical recovery of automobile sales in 1983–1984, employment in the automobile industry remained about one-third below the peak of 1978, and unemployment remained high in southern Michigan. These are illustrations of *structural unemployment*.

Structural unemployment **results when the location and/or skills of the labor force do not match the available jobs. It can occur because of declining demand for a product, because of automation or other changes in technology, because industry is moving to a different location, or because new entrants into the labor force do not have the training for available jobs.**

It should be obvious that no sharp distinction can be drawn between frictional and structural unemployment. If an auto parts factory closes down and a bicycle factory opens up a mile away, displaced auto workers may quickly and easily find jobs in the bicycle factory. The temporary unemployment is frictional. If the new jobs are 150 miles away, the workers will have to move to take them. During the extended period before they actually do move, they may be classified among the structurally unemployed. But what if the new job is 30 miles away, near the limit of the commuting range? This case is not so clear. The difference between frictional and structural unemployment is one of degree. Structural unemployment lasts longer because, in order to get a new job, a greater change in location or a more extensive acquisition of new skills is required.

Because it is longer-lasting and more painful than frictional unemployment, structural unemployment is a greater social problem. But, once again, it may represent a painful side effect of the desirable flexibility of the economy. After the invention of the transistor, it would have made no sense to protect glassworkers' jobs by requiring radios and computers to use vacuum tubes. However, the pain associated with such structural unemployment does make a case for government assistance to ease the adjustment process—for example, by subsidized retraining for displaced workers. Thus the society that benefits from the new transistor technology can help to reduce the burden that falls on a group of glassworkers who have lost their jobs.

HOW MUCH EMPLOYMENT IS "FULL EMPLOYMENT"?

It is impossible—and undesirable—to eliminate frictional unemployment. Hence, ***full employment*** must be defined as something less than the employment of 100% of the labor force. Over the past quarter century, there has been a lively debate over the unemployment rate which should be considered full employment.

This question arose explicitly in 1961, when the new Kennedy administration was outlining its economic goals. Looking back, members of the administration observed that, in the years following the Second World War, the unemployment rate had generally been just a bit less than 4%, except for the periods (1949–1950, 1954–1955, and 1958–1960) when recessions had pushed the rate up. President Kennedy therefore declared as his "interim goal" the reduction of the unemployment rate to 4%. The administration did not accept this number as full employment, since it hoped to reduce the rate even further after the 4% was actually reached. Nevertheless, the 4% rate came to be the focus of discussions of full employment.

By 1966, the interim goal was reached. In fact, the rate fell even further, to 3.5% in 1969. But during the late 1960s, inflationary pressures were gathering force. There was a widespread agreement that the expansion of the 1960s had become too strong, in part because of the large government expenditures on the war in Vietnam.

During the 1970s, the government found itself struggling to control inflation, even though the annual unemployment rate never fell below 4.9%. A 4% rate of unemployment came to be viewed as an unrealistic objective, in the sense that it could be achieved only during temporary periods when the economy was overheating and inflation accelerating. Frictional unemployment seemed to be higher than it had been in previous decades. Several explanations were suggested:

1. Changes in the composition of the labor force. For example, teenagers had become a larger fraction of the labor force, and teenagers are more likely to drift from job to job than are adults with family responsibilities.
2. Increases in the minimum wage and in the number of people covered. As a result, it was more expensive for employers to hire workers with minimal skills.
3. Reduced pressure on unemployed workers to take the first job available. Family income was being maintained in the face of unemployment by (*a*) improved unemployment insurance and (*b*) increases in the number of families with two or more members in the labor force.

As a result, many economists have argued that the "full-employment rate" should be revised upward—to 5% or 6%, with some suggesting as much as 7%. Because our economy is subject to so many changes, some economists are reluctant to be tied down to a specific figure. However, 6% is now a commonly used number. This was the average unemployment rate during 1978–1979 as the economy approached the end of the expansion of 1975–1979.

ECONOMIC COSTS OF RECESSIONS AND UNEMPLOYMENT

Whenever the economy slips into recession, potential output is lost, never to be recovered. The weeks and months which the unemployed spend in idleness are gone forever.

The substantial economic costs of recessions—in terms of output foregone—are illustrated in Figure 8-8. The black curve represents an estimate of the path the economy would have followed if there had been no business cycles and full employment had been maintained continuously. This path is accordingly labeled ***full-employment GNP*** or ***high-employment GNP*** or ***potential GNP.*** Needless to say, economists are not able to identify this path with precision. Most obviously, there is uncertainty—described in the previous section—over just how much employment should be considered full employment. Nevertheless, this path is useful in estimating the approximate amount of output lost because of recessions.

Lost output is known as the ***GNP gap.*** By far the greatest gap occurred during the Great Depression, prior to the period shown in Figure 8-8. In recent decades, the greatest gap has occurred during the severe recession of 1981–1982 and the early part of the recovery that followed. Table 8-2 indicates that, between 1981 and 1984, over $400 billion in GNP was foregone, measured at 1972 prices, or 6.4% of potential output over those 4 years. In 1984 dollars, this amounts to $935 billion. To put this in perspective, note that $1 billion represents more than $4 for every man, woman, and child in the United States. Thus, the economic slack of 1981–1984 meant a loss of almost $4,000 for every person in the nation. (Note: These numbers can change substantially if different estimates are made of potential output. Problems in estimating the potential path will be studied in detail in Chapter 15.)

The *GNP gap* is the amount by which actual GNP falls below potential GNP.

Observe in Figure 8-8 that actual GNP has on occasion exceeded the estimate of potential—for example, in 1968–1969 and in 1973. This may seem puzzling: How can the economy possibly produce more than its potential? The answer is that the economy is capable of short-term bursts of activity which are unsustainable in the long run because of their cumulative adverse effects on the economy. Most notably, the short bursts of activity can cause the overheating of the economy and an acceleration of inflation.

The economic costs of recession and unemployment illustrated in Figure 8-8 are important; additional goods and services could be put to good use. But it is equally important to recognize the great stresses and hardships on the unemployed. Unemployment is costly not only in terms of the output foregone but also in terms of demoralization of the population (Box 8-3).

INFLATION

The costs of inflation are much less obvious than the costs of unemployment. That may seem surprising, as people are almost unanimous in expressing dislike of inflation. But, in any transaction, there is both a buyer and a seller; when a price rises, the seller gains and the buyer loses. Thus, the analysis of inflation is quite different from the study of unemployment. Unemployment represents a clear loss. When we look at inflation, we have to consider both losers *and* gainers.

FIGURE 8-8
The cost of recession: The GNP gap
During periods of slack in the economy, production is less than the full-employment potential. The GNP gap—the amount by which actual GNP falls below potential—is a measure of output lost because of recessions. (Sources are given in Figure 15-5.)

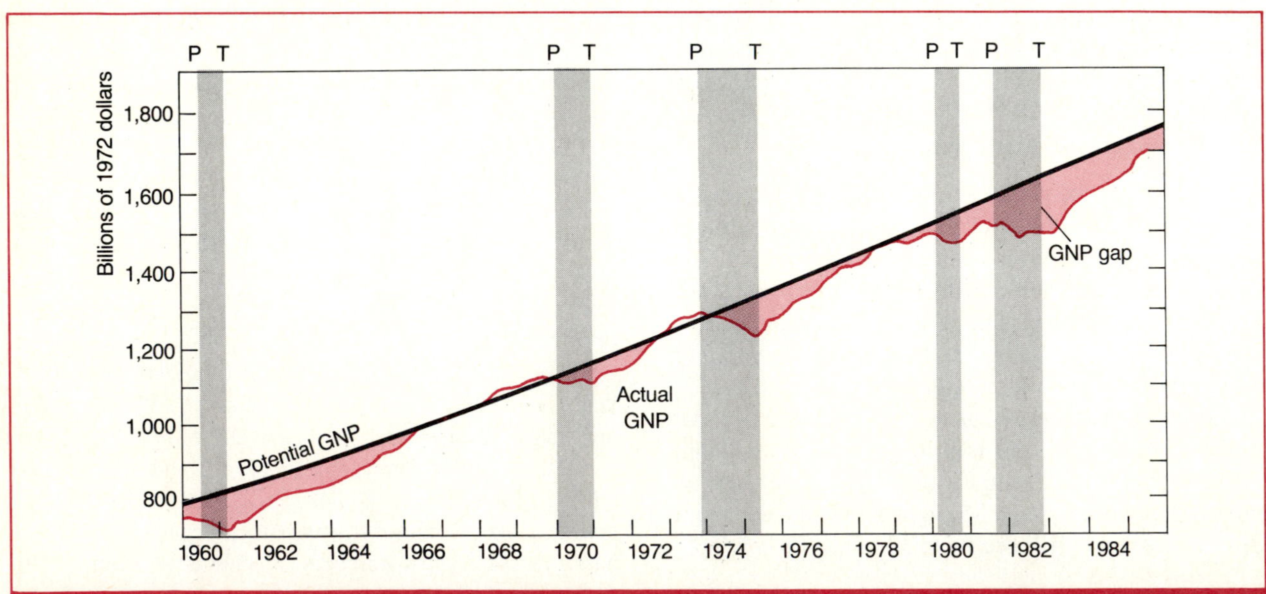

Losers

As a result of inflation, money loses its value. Thus, the most obvious losers are those who own bonds or have lent money in other ways. Consider the individual who purchased a $10,000 government bond in 1962 which came due in 1984. In addition to the interest of 4% per annum, the bond purchaser expected to get $10,000 back when the bond reached maturity. In a formal sense, that expectation was fulfilled: The government did pay the bondholder $10,000 in 1984. But that $10,000 represented a pale shadow of its original value. In 1984, $10,000 bought no more than $2,900 would have bought in 1962. In just 22 years, money had lost over 70% of its value. According to Henry Wallich, inflation represents a "rip-off" of bondholders. (Wallich is a member of the Board of Governors of the Federal Reserve System, a governmental institution whose actions have an important influence over the rate of inflation.)

Some people might say that this doesn't matter much because only wealthy people own bonds. But this is not so. Inflation does not simply steal from the rich and benefit the poor. Many elderly people of moderate means hold bonds or savings accounts, which suffer the same disadvantages as bonds during inflation. During the rapid inflation of the late 1970s, the elderly became so angry over the "rip-off" that one of their organizations—the Gray Panthers—pressured the U.S. Treasury to change its ads for U.S. Savings Bonds. No longer are they touted as the "one sure way to make your dreams come true."

The elderly are also hard-hit by inflation in another way. They have saved through private pension funds, which in turn hold bonds. With inflation, pensions financed by these bonds provide less and less real income for retirees. For the private pension system, the unexpected inflation of the past two decades has been a calamity. (However, social security recipients have not suffered in this way, since their pensions have been increased to compensate for inflation.)

Another group of losers is made up of people whose money incomes do not keep up with inflation. Refer back to Figure 8-3, which shows that hourly earnings fell in real terms during 1973 and 1979. Even though money wages were rising, they did not keep up with accelerating inflation during those 2 years. In fact, there was practically no increase in real income per hour in the nonfarm business sector between 1973 and 1983. Over this decade, the increase in money income did little more than compensate for inflation. In contrast, real income per hour rose almost 25% in the previous decade, from 1963 to 1973.

Winners

While almost everyone understands that there are losers from inflation, it is not so well understood that there also are winners. Businesses that employ workers at stable wages win if the prices of what they sell rise more rapidly than their costs.

Just as bondholders and other lenders lose from inflation, so bond issuers and other borrowers win. When

TABLE 8-2
Output Foregone, 1981–1984
(measured in billions of 1972 dollars)

	(1) Potential GNP	(2) Actual GNP	(3) GNP gap (3) = (1) − (2)	(4) Gap, as percent of potential	(5) Unemployment rate, percent
1981	$1,581	$1,514	$ 67	4.2%	7.5%
1982	1,625	1,485	140	8.6	9.5
1983	1,670	1,535	135	8.1	9.5
1984	1,716	1,639	77	4.5	7.4
			$419	6.4%	

Source for potential GNP: Congressional Budget Office, *The Outlook for Economic Recovery* (Washington, Feb. 1983), updated by authors.

BOX 8-3

WARNING: RECESSIONS CAN BE HARMFUL TO YOUR HEALTH

Harvey Brenner of Johns Hopkins University has found that unemployment and other economic problems have adverse effects on physical and mental health, and shorten life spans. The following excerpts are from his report to the U.S. Congress:†

> In addition to a high unemployment rate, three other factors—decline in labor force participation, decline in average weekly hours worked, and an increase in the rate of business failures—are strongly associated with increased mortality. . . .
>
> Economic inequality is associated with deterioration in mental health and well-being, manifest in increased rates of homicide, crime, and mental hospital admissions.
>
> . . . The report presents new evidence on the relationship between pathological [economic] conditions and . . . per capita alcohol consumption; cigarette consumption; illicit drug traffic and use; divorce rates; and the proportion of the population living alone.

Between 1973 and 1974, the unemployment rate rose from 4.9% to 5.6% of the civilian labor force. Figure 8-9 illustrates Brenner's estimate of the additional stress-related deaths and crimes associated with this increase in unemployment. The statistical relationships found by Brenner do not *prove* that the recession *caused* these results. But the evidence is strong enough to provide a warning: Recessions can be harmful to your health.

†M. Harvey Brenner, *Estimating the Effects of Economic Change on National Health and Social Well-Being* (Washington: Joint Economic Committee, U.S. Congress, June 1984), pp. 2–3.

FIGURE 8-9
The 1974 recession, health, and crime

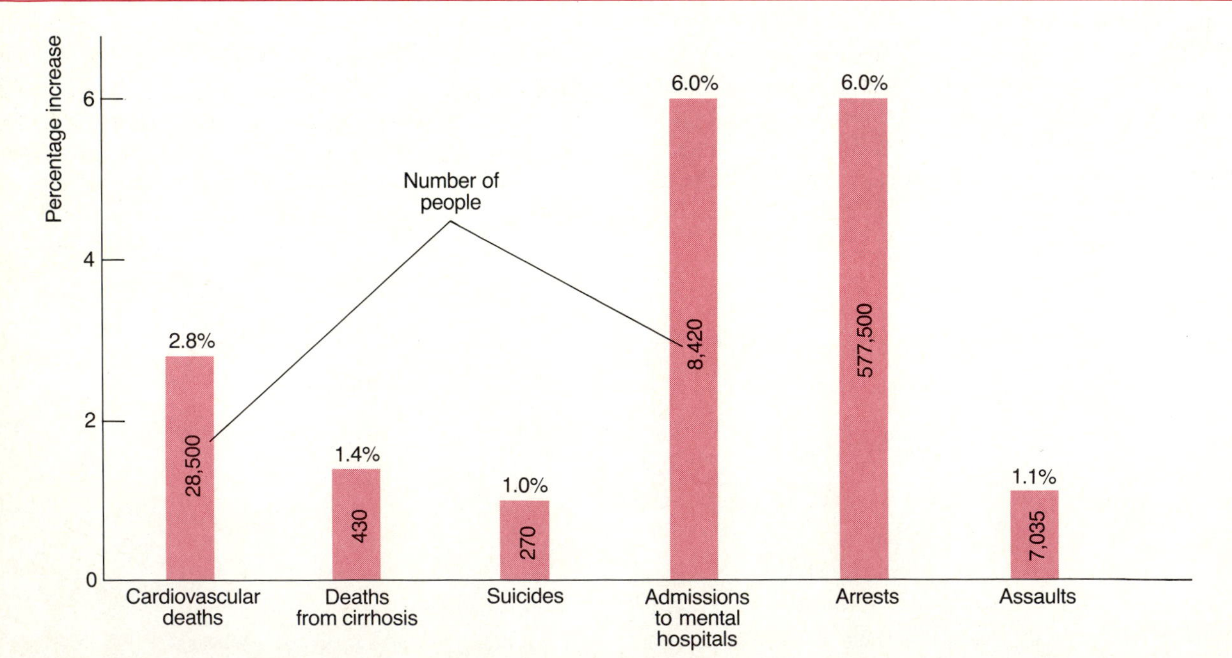

$10,000 is repaid after a period of rapid inflation, we have seen how the lender is worse off: The lender is repaid in dollars whose value has declined. For exactly the same reason, the borrower's position has improved: The dollars that the borrower must repay have decreased in value.

The windfall to homeowners For the average family, the mortgage on their home is by far the largest debt. Consider a typical American family in a small city. In 1967, they bought their dream house for $25,000, paying $5,000 down and borrowing the rest. In 1983, when their youngest child went off to college, they decided to move into something smaller. They sold their house for $70,000. Its dollar value had soared because of the inflation of the 1968–1983 period.

They found that they had a tidy gain, as illustrated in Table 8-3. The original $5,000 of their own money that they had put into the house had grown *tenfold,* to $50,000 (the $70,000 from the sale of the home, minus the $20,000 used to repay the mortgage). Even though the general price level had tripled since 1968, the $50,000 represented much more buying power than their initial $5,000 down payment.

The constant-dollar or real value of the $50,000 can be calculated with an equation similar to those in Chapter 7. Specifically:

$$\text{Real value of an asset (or liability)} = \frac{\text{current dollar value}}{\text{price index}} \times 100 \quad (8\text{-}1)$$

The price index rose from 100 in 1967 to 300 by 1983. Thus, measured in 1967 dollars, the $50,000 was worth:

$$\frac{\$50{,}000}{300} \times 100 = \$16{,}667$$

Thus, the original $5,000 investment had more than trebled in real terms. In 1983, the $50,000 would buy three times as many goods and services as the $5,000 used in 1967 to make the down payment.

This illustration has skipped over some details.[6] But it illustrates an important and valid point: *The inflation of recent decades has provided a windfall to people who borrowed to purchase homes several decades ago.* This has been particularly important for the middle class. Home ownership represents a major fraction of their assets, while home mortgages represent a major fraction of their liabilities. It is not so important for the poor, few of whom own homes, nor for the rich, who have many other assets.

Anticipated and Unanticipated Inflation

Because *inflation can lead to an arbitrary reshuffling of wealth and income,* one of its costs is that it makes the economic system *less fair*.

This is particularly true if inflation is *unexpected*. The inflation beginning in the mid-1960s had strong effects because it came as a surprise to most people.

However, if people anticipate inflation, they can take steps to protect themselves. For example, if people anticipate inflation, (1) they will avoid bonds, unless in-

[6] To simplify, we have assumed that mortgage payments cover only interest. Thus, the whole $20,000 mortgage remains to be paid off when the house is sold. In practice, each mortgage payment normally covers both interest and repayment of part of the principal. The conclusions based on Table 8-3 would not be materially changed by discarding this simplifying assumption.

TABLE 8-3
Inflation and Housing: A Simple Example

1967		1983	
Purchase price	$25,000	Selling price	$70,000
Borrowing (mortgage)	20,000	Repayment of mortgage	20,000
Down payment	$ 5,000	Net	$50,000
		Value in 1967 dollars	= $16,667

terest rates rise to attractive levels; (2) workers will negotiate for higher nominal wages to compensate for the effects of inflation.

These two responses to inflation will be considered in detail in later chapters. For the moment, we note that the damage from inflation rises when it becomes *less predictable*. If people are very uncertain about what is going to happen to prices, they will have difficulty protecting themselves from its effects. Businesses which are very uncertain about inflation will have difficulty making plans. For example, should they borrow to buy machinery now, before its price rises? They cannot make good judgments if they have no clear idea regarding future prices.

One problem with high inflation is that it tends to be *variable* and *unpredictable*. Countries which suffer high rates of inflation find that the inflation rate tends to bounce around by large amounts from year to year; for example, from 100% to 75% to 150%. In contrast, when the average rate of inflation is low—say 2% or 3% per year—it is generally quite stable. Decision making can proceed in a relatively predictable environment.

Because the value of bonds is so strongly affected by inflation, high and unpredictable rates of inflation may cause people to stop buying bonds. The long-term bond market may dry up, making it difficult to raise funds for residential construction or for business expansion.

In summary, rapid inflation creates three problems:

1. An arbitrary redistribution of wealth and income
2. An uncertain environment, in which it is difficult to make business decisions
3. Possibly, the drying up of the long-term bond market.

KEY POINTS

1. The U.S. economy does not expand steadily. From time to time, expansion is interrupted by a recession.
2. During recessions, output declines and the unemployment rate rises. Inflation generally declines. Profits fall sharply.
3. During recessions, the increase in the unemployment rate does not reflect all the pressures on the labor force. Some workers are limited to part-time work when they want full-time employment. Some of the unemployed become discouraged. When they stop looking for work and thus drop out of the labor force, they are no longer counted among the unemployed.
4. During recessions, output declines to a greater extent than employment. Although the unemployment rate rises, it rises by a smaller percentage than the change in output.
5. The unemployment rate for teenagers and minorities exceeds that for the labor force as a whole. Women have generally had a higher unemployment rate than men.
6. Unemployment is classified into three categories: (*a*) frictional unemployment, (*b*) structural unemployment, (*c*) cyclical unemployment. The first represents the smallest problem: people out of work temporarily as they hunt for jobs. Structural unemployment is more serious. Workers have to move or obtain additional skills in order to find jobs. Cyclical unemployment, as the name suggests, is attributable to instability in the economy.
7. There is disagreement over the amount of unemployment which should be considered full employment. While 4% was generally considered full employment during the 1960s, estimates have been substantially increased in the past 15 years, to 5%, 6%, or even 7%.
8. The *GNP gap* measures how much actual output falls short of the full-employment potential. The gap is an important measure of the cost of recessions; it measures how much potential output has been lost. However, it does not include all the social costs, such as the demoralization of those who are out of work.
9. Rapid inflation creates three problems:

   (*a*) An arbitrary redistribution of wealth and income

   (*b*) An uncertain environment, in which it is difficult to make business decisions

   (*c*) Possibly, the drying up of the long-term bond market.

KEY CONCEPTS

recession
trough
expansion
peak

depression
underemployment
discouraged workers
labor force time lost
Okun's law
frictional unemployment
structural unemployment
cyclical unemployment
potential or full-employment output
GNP gap
anticipated and unanticipated inflation

PROBLEMS

8-1. In Figure 8-1, a number of important events have been associated with periods of prosperity. Choose three of these events. Can you explain why each of them contributed to prosperity? (Take one from the period 1835–1865, one from 1865–1900, and one from the twentieth century.)

8-2. Why is it difficult to identify a recession? Why doesn't the NBER just declare a recession whenever real output declines?

8-3. The text notes that inflation may respond slowly to changing economic conditions. For example, the downward pressure on prices may be concentrated in the latter stages of recession, and continue into the early recovery. Why might inflation be slow to respond?

8-4. During business cycles:

(*a*) Why do consumer durable purchases fluctuate more than consumer purchases of nondurables and services?

(*b*) Why does output fluctuate more than the unemployment rate?

8-5. Inflation is generally considered a major economic problem. How is it possible for anyone to gain from inflation?

8-6. In 1980, the NBER estimated that the downward movement of the economy lasted 6 months—February to July, inclusive. Yet real GNP data show only one quarter of decline—the second quarter, from April to June. It seems that there may be something wrong here. We might expect that, if output falls for 6 months, GNP should decline for two quarters.

To show that there is, in fact, nothing wrong, construct a hypothetical set of monthly output figures from October 1979 to September 1980 that satisfy the following conditions:

(*a*) Real GNP reaches a peak value of, say, $1,000 billion in January, 1980.

(*b*) Output declines every month from February until the trough month of July.

(*c*) Quarterly output falls only once: Second quarter output is less than the first quarter of 1980, but the third quarter is above the second, and the first quarter of 1980 is above the last quarter of 1979.

When you have met these conditions, note that you have a series in which GNP does decline for a full 6 months, but the decline shows up in only one quarterly figure.

CHAPTER 9

EXPLAINING UNEMPLOYMENT AND INFLATION:

AGGREGATE SUPPLY AND AGGREGATE DEMAND

I believe myself to be writing a book on economic theory which will largely revolutionize—not, I suppose, at once but in the course of the next ten years—the way the world thinks about economic problems.

JOHN MAYNARD KEYNES

In studying the market for an individual product—such as apples—we illustrated the concepts of demand and supply in a diagram, with the horizontal axis showing the quantity of apples and the vertical axis showing the price of apples. This diagram was very useful. For example, by shifting the demand and supply curves, we could see how price and quantity respond to changing conditions of demand and supply (Figures 4-6 and 4-7).

In macroeconomics, the concepts of ***aggregate demand*** and ***aggregate supply*** are useful in a similar way. Since we are now dealing with the overall magnitudes in the economy, we use the horizontal axis to show the *overall,* or *aggregate,* quantity of output—that is, real national product. On the vertical axis, we put the *average* level of prices.

In drawing the aggregate demand and aggregate supply curves, we must be careful. *We cannot assume that the aggregate demand curve slopes downward to the right simply because the microeconomic demand curve for an individual product slopes this way. Nor can we assume that the aggregate supply curve slopes upward to the right simply because the supply curve for an individual product does.*

To see why, reconsider the earlier explanation of why the demand curve for apples slopes downward to the right. This curve is drawn on the assumption that the price of apples is the *only* price that changes; when we draw the demand curve for apples, we assume that the prices of all other goods remain stable. Thus, when the price of apples falls, it declines *relative to the prices* of all other goods. With apples becoming a ''better buy,'' people are encouraged to *switch* their purchases away from other goods and buy more apples instead. Such switching is the principal reason why the demand curve for an individual product slopes downward to the right.

Now consider what happens when we turn to the macroeconomic demand curve, with total output on the horizontal axis and the average level of prices on the vertical. For the economy as a whole, a fall in the level of all prices cannot cause buyers to switch from ''other goods.'' There are no such other goods. It is not obvious how the aggregate demand curve should be drawn.

A similar problem arises on the supply side. In drawing the microeconomic supply curve for apples, we assume that the prices of all other goods remain stable. Thus, when the price of apples rises, it increases *relative to the prices* of other goods. Farmers therefore have an incentive to *switch* away from the production of other goods and produce more apples instead. When we look at macroeconomics—studying the economy as a whole—producers can't switch away from other goods because there aren't any. We cannot assume that the aggregate supply curve slopes upward to the right just because the supply curve for an individual product does.

How, then, are we to draw aggregate demand and aggregate supply? Historically, there have been two approaches to this problem. The first is the classical approach, which may be traced back several hundred years, to eighteenth-century British philosopher David Hume and beyond. The second is the Keynesian approach, which was introduced during the 1930s as a way of explaining and combatting the Great Depression.

THE CLASSICAL APPROACH

Classical theorists argued that the aggregate quantity of goods and services demanded will increase as the average price level falls, as illustrated in Figure 9-1. The reason is this. Suppose that all prices fall by, say, 50%, as illustrated by the move from P_1 to P_2. Then, each dollar buys more; the ***purchasing power*** of money has increased. Finding that they can buy more with their money, people will step up their purchases. Thus, the aggregate demand curve slopes downward to the right. (But remember: The additional purchases come about, not as a result of *switching* among goods, but because people buy more goods *in total*.)

Furthermore, classical economists went beyond this general statement, to be more specific. With prices only half as high at P_2 as at P_1, each dollar will buy twice as much. Therefore, said classical economists, the quantity of goods and services purchased at *B* will be about twice as great as at *A*. Alternatively, if prices had doubled, from P_1 to P_3, each dollar would buy only half as much as it did originally and people would therefore buy only about half as much at *C* as at *A*. In other words, classical economists believed that we could be more specific about the shape of the aggregate demand curve than about the demand curve for an individual product. (We cannot generalize in the same way about the demand curve for an individual good. If the price of apples falls by 50%, we may expect people to buy more. But there is no reason to believe that they will buy twice as many. They may buy three or four times as many, if apples are good substitutes for other fruit. On the other hand, if the price of gasoline falls by 50%, people may not drive much more; the quantity of gasoline bought may go up only moderately—say, by 10% or 20%.)

In this theory, classical economists *put money at the center of aggregate demand*. In their view, the willingness and ability of people to buy goods *depends on the quantity of money in their possession and on the purchasing power of that money*.

The *purchasing power* of money is the real quantity of goods and services that one dollar will buy. When the price level *rises*, the purchasing power of money *falls*. For example, when the price level doubles, the purchasing power of money falls to half its previous level.

Aggregate Supply: The Classical Approach

Classical economists argued that the aggregate supply

FIGURE 9-1

The classical aggregate demand function

According to classical economists, the aggregate demand function slopes downward to the right. As prices fall, the money in the hands of the public will buy more. As a result, the public does buy more goods and services at *B* than at *A*.

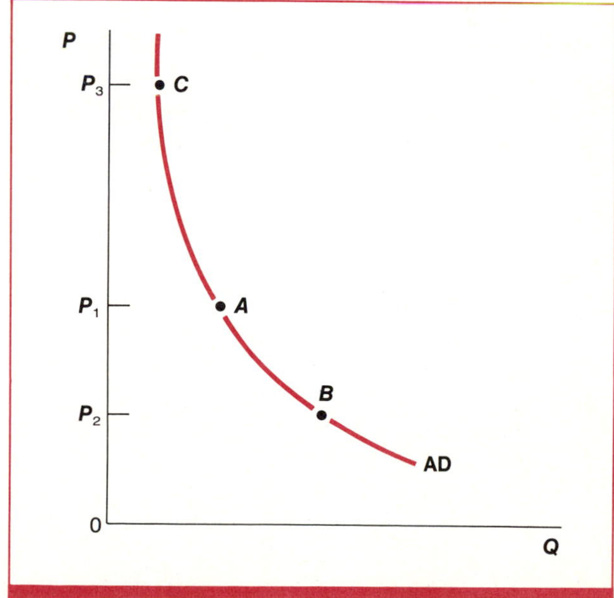

function is vertical at the *potential* or *full-employment* quantity of output, as illustrated in Figure 9-2. Why?

To answer this question, consider what happens if the economy is initially at point *F*, with full employment. Now, suppose that all prices double, including the price of labor (that is, the wage rate). In other words, there is a ***general inflation,*** with *relative* prices and wages being unaffected. Workers are basically in the same position as before. While their money wages have doubled, so have prices. The real wage—the quantity of goods and services which the wage will buy—is unchanged. Therefore, workers' willingness to work remains the same. Businesses also are in basically the same situation as before. Their productive capacity remains unchanged, and the relationship between costs and prices also remains unchanged. As a result, businesses offer the same amount of goods and services for sale. Therefore, point *G* on the aggregate supply curve is directly above point *F*. Similarly, classical economists argued that the quantity of goods and services offered for sale would remain unchanged if all wages and prices fell by 50%, illustrated by the move from P_1 to P_3. Thus, point *H* is directly below point *F*.

FIGURE 9-2

The classical aggregate supply function

According to classical economists, the aggregate supply function is vertical, at the full-employment or potential quantity of national product. A general rise or fall in prices and wages does not make producers any more—or any less—willing to supply goods and services.

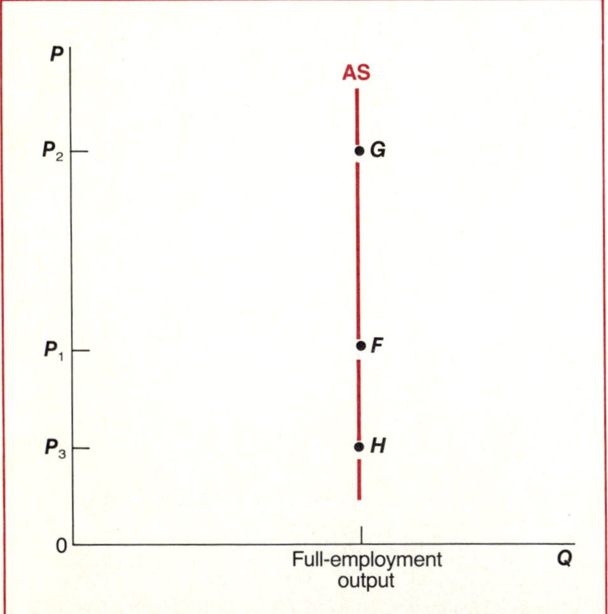

Equilibrium at Full Employment

Bringing together the aggregate demand and aggregate supply curves of classical economics, we find the equilibrium at *E* in Figure 9-3. *Classical economists believed that the economy would be in equilibrium only at full employment,* at a point like *E*, *and that market forces would lead the economy to full employment.*

To explain this classical view, suppose that the economy is initially at a position of large-scale unemployment, such as point *B* in Figure 9-3. The high unemployment rate occurs because, at the initial price level P_1, the quantity of goods and services demanded (at *B*) is substantially less than the full-employment output (at *A*). What will happen, according to classical economists? At P_1, the quantity of goods and services demanded is less than producers are willing to supply. In order to sell more goods, businesses will cut their prices. At the same time, they will reduce the wage they pay, since the large number of unemployed will be so eager to get jobs that they will be willing to work for less than the prevailing wage. Thus, both prices and money wages will fall. With prices falling below P_1, the purchasing power of the money in the hands of the public will increase, and they will buy more. There will be a move along the aggregate demand curve from *B* to *C* to *D*. This process will continue until the economy gets to equilibrium *E*, with full employment. Once this equilibrium has been reached, there will no longer be downward pressures on prices and wages.

The Classical Explanation of the Depression

Since classical economists believed that full employment always exists in equilibrium, how did they explain the Great Depression, with unemployment rates rising above 20%? Their answer: Large-scale unemployment existed only when the economy was in *disequilibrium;* it was the result of *disturbances* to the economy.

Most notably, the economy could be disturbed by a *shift* in the aggregate demand curve. As we have already seen, classical economists focused on money and its purchasing power in their analysis of aggregate demand. In drawing any single aggregate demand function such as AD in Figure 9-3, classical economists assumed that the nominal quantity of money was constant; that is, the number of dollars was fixed. Any change in the quantity of money would cause a shift in the aggregate demand function. It would shift to the right if the quantity of money increased, or to the left if the quantity of money decreased.

Thus, a classical explanation of the Depression goes something like this.[1] In 1929, the economy was close to a full-employment equilibrium at *A* in Figure 9-4, with aggregate demand AD_{1929}. Then, because of disturbances in the banking and financial system, the stock of money in the hands of the public fell substantially between 1929 and 1933. As a result of the decline in the money stock, aggregate demand shifted to the left, to AD_{1933}.

Even with this fall in demand, full employment would still have been possible if prices and wages had fallen all the way to P_E. In this event, full employment would have occurred at new equilibrium *E*. But prices and wages were ***sticky*** in a downward direction; that is, they did not fall quickly in the face of slack demand and high unemployment. One reason for stickiness is that it takes some time for job searchers to realize that they will not find the job they want at the wage they expect. It is only after a frustrating search that they will be willing to settle for a lower wage.[2]

Because of stickiness, prices fell only to P_{1933} by 1933. With prices remaining higher than required for the new equilibrium, the amount of goods and services purchased was far less than the economy's full-employment potential. The economy was in a deep depression at point *B*.

Thus, wage and price stickiness kept the economy from moving directly downward along the aggregate supply function in the face of a collapse in demand. As demand fell, the economy instead moved along the short-run path from *A* to *B*. In the absence of any further disturbance to demand, price and wage adjustments could be expected to gradually restore full employment. Although it would take time, the economy would eventu-

FIGURE 9-3
Equilibrium in classical economics
According to classical economists, large-scale unemployment at *B* would result in an automatic movement back to full employment. Under the pressure of market forces, prices and wages would fall. The economy would gradually move down the aggregate demand curve, toward full-employment equilibrium *E*.

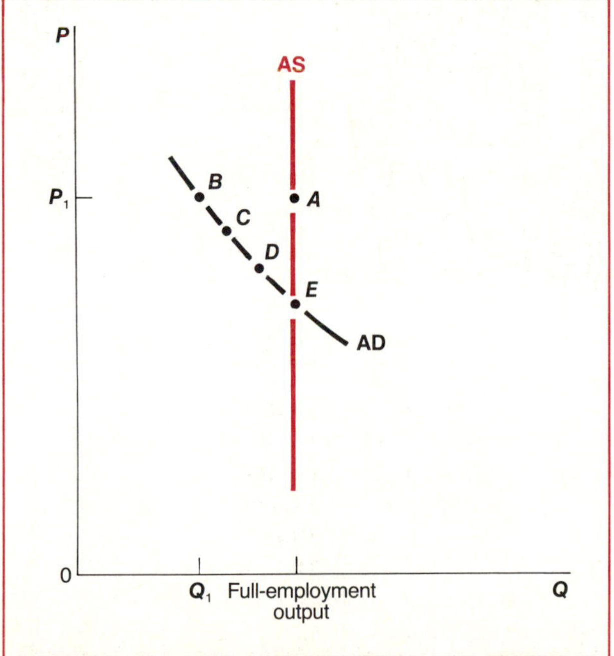

[1]Details may be found in the very readable chapter on the depression in Milton Friedman and Anna Schwartz, *A Monetary History of the United States, 1867–1960* (Princeton: Princeton University Press, 1963).

*[2]Two other reasons for stickiness were explained in Chapter 8, footnote 4, where we considered why the prices of manufactures fell much less than those of agricultural commodities between 1929 and 1933.

Some classical economists argued that distortions among *relative* prices made the depression even more severe. We skip this argument, because it was quite complex. In this section, we consider only the effects of a *general* across-the-board inflation or deflation, in which all prices and wages move by the same percentage and relative prices are accordingly left undisturbed. This allows us to grasp the central points of classical theory.

ally move along the new aggregate demand curve from *B* to *C* to *D* and finally to the new full-employment equilibrium *E*. So argued the classical economist.

In other words, the classical aggregate supply curve illustrated where the economy would *eventually* go. Over the ***long run,*** classical economists were confident that wages and prices would in fact adjust, restoring full employment.

In classical macroeconomics, the *long run* is the period necessary for prices and wages to adjust completely.

This approach led classical economists to suggest two possible solutions for a depression:

FIGURE 9-4
The depression in classical economics
Classical economists believed that principal cause of the Great Depression was a collapse in demand caused by a sharp decline in the money stock. Because of wage and price stickiness, the economy did not move directly to its new full-employment equilibrium *E*, but rather to *B*.

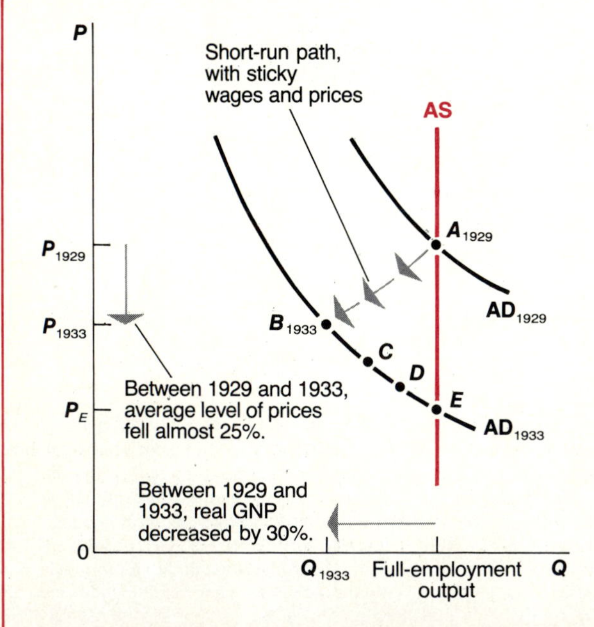

1. The initial source of the disturbance might be eliminated. Steps might be taken to prevent a decline in the quantity of money in the first place, or to restore the quantity of money once it had fallen. If the money supply were increased, and aggregate demand restored to AD_{1929}, the economy might be expected to retrace its path from *B* back toward *A* in Figure 9-4.
2. Workers and businesses might be encouraged to accept lower wages and prices quickly so the economy could move more rapidly to its new full-employment equilibrium *E*. The more willing workers and businesses were to accept lower wages and prices, the shorter would be the temporary period of unemployment. Note that the classical long run is not any fixed number of months or years. It is whatever period is needed for wages and prices to adjust. The faster they adjust, the sooner the economy reaches its long-run equilibrium with full employment.

However, many classical economists were quite skeptical that the government could in practice help much in promoting downward wage and price flexibility. Indeed, many believed that when the government becomes involved in markets, it is likely to keep prices up and increase their stickiness. Thus, many classical economists argued for a policy of *laissez faire*. In macroeconomic as in microeconomic questions, they saw little role for the government, apart from providing a stable monetary system. They believed that the operation of market forces would work to restore full employment.

Classical Macroeconomics: A Preliminary Summary

Before proceeding, let us summarize the main points of classical macroeconomics developed thus far:

1. The aggregate demand curve slopes downward to the right. As prices fall, each dollar will buy more and people accordingly do buy more. A single aggregate demand curve is drawn on the assumption that the nominal quantity of money is constant. If the quantity of money increases, the aggregate demand curve shifts to the right.
2. The aggregate supply curve is vertical at the full-employment output.
3. In the long run, a shift in the aggregate demand

curve causes a change in prices, not in output. The reason is that, in the long run, the economy moves back to the vertical aggregate supply curve.

4. However, in the short run—when wages and prices are sticky—a collapse in aggregate demand can cause a depression. Instead of moving from *A* to *E,* the economy moves from *A* to *B* in Figure 9-4.

5. Although an economy at *B* will eventually move to *E,* a better solution is to increase the money stock, thus increasing aggregate demand back up to AD_{1929}. This will move the economy from *B* back to *A*.

THE KEYNESIAN APPROACH

Prior to the Great Depression, most economists considered unemployment to be a relatively minor and temporary problem, associated with fluctuations in the economy. The decade-long depression of the 1930s shattered this confidence and provided the backdrop for a new theory of unemployment put forward by British economist John Maynard Keynes. His major work—*The General Theory of Employment, Interest and Money*—attacked the prevailing classical view. Specifically, Keynes put forward three major propositions:

1. *Unemployment in the market economy.* In contrast to classical economists, Keynes argued that a market economy might have no strong tendency to move to full employment. On the contrary, a market economy might come to rest in *an equilibrium with large-scale unemployment*—often referred to, more briefly, as an ***unemployment equilibrium.*** Furthermore, even if the economy did temporarily reach full employment, it might be quite unstable and fall back into depression. In other words, Keynes said that the market economy was defective in two important ways:

(*a*) It might lead to a *persistent depression,* such as the depression of the 1930s.

(*b*) It might be quite *unstable,* so that even if we did achieve full employment, this happy state of affairs might be short lived.

2. *The cause of unemployment.* Keynes argued that large-scale unemployment is the result of an *insufficiency of aggregate demand*—that is, too little spending for goods and services.

3. *The cure for unemployment.* To cure unemployment, aggregate demand should be increased. The best way to do that, said Keynes, is by an *increase in government spending.*

This, then, was the main policy message of the *General Theory:* The goverment has the ability—and the *responsibility*—to *manage aggregate demand,* and thus ensure continuing prosperity. Cast aside was the classical view that market forces would solve the unemployment problem, and that the government should strictly limit its interference in the economy. Keynes was particularly impatient with classical economists who argued that, in the long run, market forces would reestablish full employment. "In the long run we are all dead," he retorted.

Keynes held out the promise that the government could increase aggregate demand and thus solve the appalling unemployment problem of the 1930s. His book was a spectacular success; it ranks with Adam Smith's *Wealth of Nations* and Karl Marx's *Das Kapital* as one of the most influential economics books ever written. The *General Theory* led to a sharp change in economic thinking. With its appearance in 1936, the *Keynesian revolution* was under way.

To support his three propositions, Keynes put forward a new theoretical framework, including an approach to aggregate demand and aggregate supply which was quite different from that of classical economists.

The Simple Keynesian Aggregate Supply Function

Classical economists had recognized that prices and wages might be sticky in a downward direction, and had used this stickiness to explain *transitional* periods of large-scale unemployment when aggregate demand decreased. Keynes placed even more emphasis on stickiness. In his view, workers and businesses would *strongly* resist any cut in wages and prices. As a result, wages and prices would remain *rigid* for an *indefinitely* long period in the face of large-scale unemployment.

This meant that there was a horizontal section in the Keynesian aggregate supply function, as illustrated by section *BA* in Figure 9-5. Here's why. If, from an initial position of full employment at point *A,* there were a decline in aggregate demand, prices would remain stable. The fall in demand would show up in terms of a decrease in output, not in prices. This is shown by the movement from *A* to *B*. Furthermore, there would be little tendency, even in the long run, for prices and wages to fall. If aggregate demand remained low, the economy would remain in a depression at *B*.

According to Keynes, the cure was to increase aggregate demand. In response, producers would step up production. Because of the large numbers of unemployed workers and the large quantity of unused machinery, more could be produced at existing prices. Output would increase, and the economy would move to the right along the horizontal range of the aggregate supply function back toward *A*.

Once the economy got to *A*—to a point of full employment—Keynes had no major objection to the classical approach to aggregate supply. Because the economy was already operating at capacity, any further increase in aggregate demand would be reflected in higher prices. The economy would move vertically upward toward *C*. In short, the Keynesian aggregate supply function had two quite different ranges:

1. A *horizontal range,* which was relevant for analysing periods of depression and recession, when inadequate demand resulted in high rates of unemployment. This was the range which most interested Keynes. The major purpose of the *General Theory* was to explain the causes and cures of the Great Depression. Accordingly, this horizontal range of the aggregate supply function is frequently known as the *Keynesian range*.
2. A *vertical range,* which would be reached when aggregate demand was high enough to ensure full em-

FIGURE 9-5

The Keynesian aggregate supply function

There are two main segments of the Keynesian aggregate supply function. In the horizontal section, prices are stable and a change in aggregate demand causes a change in output and employment. In the vertical section, an increase in demand causes an increase in prices.

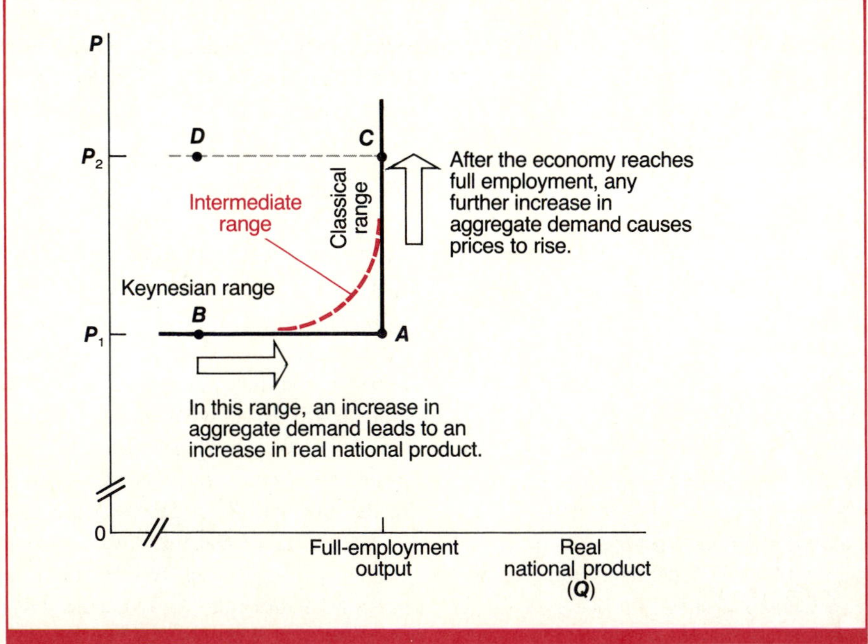

ployment. Further increases in demand would simply cause inflation. Because Keynes had no quarrel with the classical approach once full employment is reached, this vertical section is sometimes known as the *classical range*.

Together, these two ranges give the aggregate supply function *BAC* in Figure 9-5, forming a reversed L. (In this figure, we follow the convention of Keynesian economists, putting "real national product" on the horizontal axis. In previous diagrams, such as Figure 9-4, we followed the convention of classical economists, putting the quantity of real output *Q* on the axis. *Q* is the same as real national product, and the two terms may be used interchangeably.)

According to the approach in Figure 9-5, the average level of prices *ratchets* upward through time. As we have just seen, prices would be downwardly rigid when the economy was at point *B*. An increase in aggregate demand would first lead to an increase in output, to point *A*. But any further increase in demand would lead to higher prices. The economy would move up the vertical portion of the aggregate supply curve to point *C*, with prices rising to P_2. However, once *C* is reached, any reduction in demand would not lead the economy to retrace its path back toward *A* because prices and wages would not move down from the new level established at *C;* businesses and labor would resist such a move. Instead, the response to a fall in aggregate demand would be a decrease in output. The economy would move toward *D* along the lightly dashed line. In short, the simple Keynesian aggregate supply function was a reversed L, with the horizontal part of the L shifting upward every time a new, higher price level was reached.[3]

A complication Unfortunately, the world is more complex than indicated by the simple L-shaped function. From the early days of the Keynesian revolution, economists recognized that there might be no sharply defined point at *A* where the economy suddenly reaches full employment. As the economy expands, all industries don't reach capacity at exactly the same time; some reach it before others. In the industries approaching capacity, prices begin to rise. The overall price index begins to creep up. This occurs while other industries are still operating well below capacity and are still increasing their output as demand increases. Thus, there is a period in which both output and prices are increasing. The economy takes the curved short-cut illustrated in the dashed red curve in Figure 9-5.

While the horizontal range of aggregate supply was used by Keynesians in their explanation of the Great Depression, the sloping *intermediate range* is important in more normal times, when the economy is neither in an inflationary boom (the vertical section) nor in a depression (the horizontal part).

Aggregate Demand: The Keynesian Approach

Keynes proposed that aggregate demand be analysed by studying the demand for the various components of national product:

1. *Personal consumption expenditures*
2. *Investment demand,* that is, the demand for equipment, plant, housing, and additional inventories
3. *Government purchases of goods and services*
4. *Net exports*

Keynes was intent on explaining the Great Depression, and with finding a way to restore full employment. In his view, the Depression was caused by a collapse in aggregate demand, particularly the investment demand component. Keynes stressed the instability of investment demand: Businesses are willing to invest only when they expect the new plant and equipment to add to profits. Expectations are fragile. Once the economy is declining sharply, business executives become pessimistic and therefore cut back on investment. Thus, even though a decline in investment demand may have been the principal *cause* of the depression, it was unrealistic to expect a revival of investment demand to move the economy out of the depression. Rather, it was up to the government to provide a *solution* by increasing the component of aggregate demand directly under its control. That is, it was

[3] Both Keynesian and classical economists recognized a complication that we avoid here. As time passes, the economy grows, with the full-employment or potential output increasing. Therefore, the vertical section of the aggregate supply function shifts gradually to the right with the passage of time.

desirable for the government to increase its spending (item 3) to compensate for the decline in investment demand, and thus restore full employment.

In the coming chapters, we will study the four components of aggregate demand and the forces that cause them to increase or decrease. In these chapters, we will address two of the central questions of Keynesian theory: How large will aggregate demand be? Will it put us near full employment or leave us in a depression?

Before passing on to these topics, we reemphasize: The four components of aggregate demand highlighted by Keynesian theory correspond to the four components of national product studied in Chapter 7. Two major innovations in macroeconomics—the development of national product accounts and the new Keynesian theory of employment—interacted and reinforced one another during the 1930s and 1940s.

Finally, observe that in Figure 9-5 we have drawn no aggregate demand curve. Thus, something is missing from our introduction to Keynesian theory. We have not shown how the demand for goods and services responds to a change in the average level of prices. The rather complicated Keynesian approach to this issue is deferred to the Appendix at the end of this chapter. All we need to note here is the principal conclusion. Except in the special case of a deep depression, Keynesian theory suggests that the aggregate demand curve slopes downward to the right.

CLASSICAL ECONOMICS AND KEYNESIAN ECONOMICS: A SUMMARY

In his *General Theory,* Keynes launched an attack on classical economists on the ground that they had no adequate proposals for dealing with the severe unemployment problem of the 1930s. A heated debate ensued, both over policies and over the proper theoretical framework for studying macroeconomic problems.

Differences between Keynesians and the inheritors of the classical school continue to the present day. These differences attract considerable attention; debates can be interesting. But the fact that differences still exist should not obscure something even more important: On many issues, there is general agreement among macroeconomists, regardless of their intellectual heritage.

Areas of Agreement

Most notably, those in the classical and Keynesian traditions agree:

1. A *sharp decline in aggregate demand* was the principal cause of the collapse into the Great Depression of the 1930s.
2. *Fluctuations in aggregate demand* have been the major cause of fluctuations in real output in recent decades.
3. Accordingly, the *stabilization of aggregate demand* should be an important macroeconomic objective.
4. When the economy is already operating at its full-employment potential, *any large increase in aggregate demand will spill over into inflation.* Both the classical and Keynesian aggregate supply functions are vertical once full employment has been reached. Thus, higher demand causes higher prices.

The second point is worth explaining in more detail. Consider Figure 9-6, with a normal, downward-sloping aggregate demand function, AD_1. The aggregate supply function slopes upward to the right; it corresponds to the intermediate range of the Keynesian supply function in Figure 9-5. Panel *a,* in which aggregate demand shifts, is broadly consistent with the pattern already observed in Chapter 8: During expansions, output increases and inflation generally accelerates. During recession, the opposite happens: Output declines and the upward pressure on prices becomes weaker. If shifts in aggregate supply had been the main cause of business cycles (panel *b*), we would expect strong upward pressures on prices during recessions (as the economy moves from *J* to *K*), with these pressures on prices becoming weaker during expansions (the move back from *K* to *J*). But this is not in fact what usually happens. Therefore, we may conclude that it is not shifts in aggregate supply but rather shifts in aggregate demand that are the major cause of business fluctuations. Not surprisingly, then, we will focus on aggregate demand in our early study of macroeconomics in Chapters 10–13. (Although the outcome in panel *b* is uncommon, it occasionally occurs. For example, both unemployment and the rate of inflation increased between the prosperous year 1973 and the recession year 1974. This unusual case will be studied when we look at shifts in aggregate supply in Chapter 16.)

Areas of Disagreement

1. We have seen how classical economists attributed the depression to a decline in the money stock, and believed that one solution to the depression lay in the restoration of the money stock (a change in monetary policy). In contrast, Keynes emphasized government spending (fiscal policy) as a way of increasing aggregate demand and restoring full employment. There is a continuing difference whether monetary policy or fiscal policy has the stronger and more predictable effect on aggregate demand. Those in the classical tradition focus on ***monetary policy,*** while those in the Keynesian tradition are most likely to think first of ***fiscal policy.*** However, it should be emphasized that *most modern macroeconomists believe that both monetary and fiscal policies are important.*

Monetary policy **involves a change in the rate of growth of the money stock.**

Fiscal policy **involves a change in government expenditures or in tax rates.**

2. While macroeconomists agree that it would be desirable for aggregate demand to be more stable, they differ sharply over *how* stability is best achieved. Those in the Keynesian tradition emphasize the defects and instabili-

FIGURE 9-6
Short-run fluctuations in aggregate demand and supply
In the left panel, aggregate demand fluctuates. During the expansion, output increases and there is upward pressure on prices (the movement from G to H). During recessions, output declines and pressure on prices subsides (H to G). This is the pattern actually observed in most business cycles. In contrast, we do not generally observe the outcome illustrated in the right-hand panel. For example, recessions generally are not accompanied by strong upward pressure on prices, as they would be if the economy were moving from J to K.

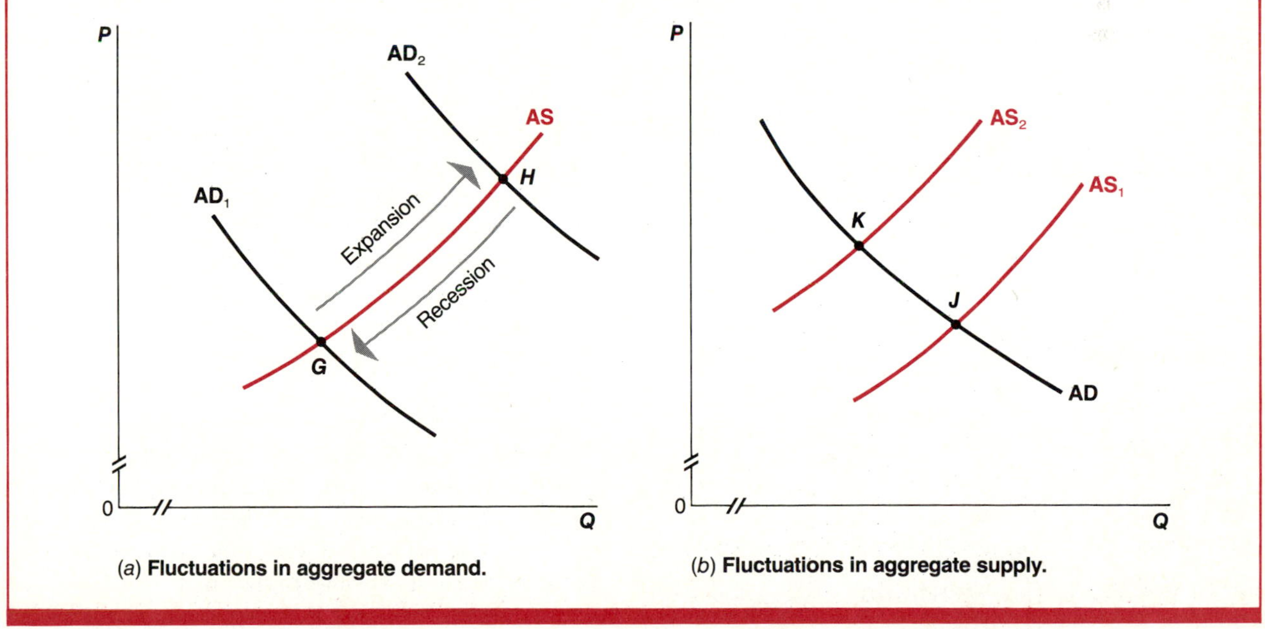

(*a*) **Fluctuations in aggregate demand.**

(*b*) **Fluctuations in aggregate supply.**

ties of a market economy, and believe that the government has the responsibility to *actively manage aggregate demand* in order to reduce the amplitude of business fluctuations.

Those in the classical tradition generally believe that the market economy will be reasonably stable, *if* monetary conditions are kept stable. As a result, they recommend a ***monetary policy rule:*** The authorities should aim for a *steady, moderate increase in the money stock,* at something like 3% or 4% per year. A steady growth is appropriate, since we live in a growing economy. More money is needed to buy the increasing volume of goods and services that can be produced.

Because of their emphasis on money, modern inheritors of the classical tradition are frequently known as ***monetarists.*** They do not argue that adherence to a monetary rule will create a perfectly stable economy, since aggregate demand will not expand in a perfectly stable way even if money does. But they are very skeptical that the government can make things better by active policy management. Like the earlier classical economists, they fear that the goverment is, on average, likely to make things worse. (The reasons for this fear will be explained in Chapter 15.)

This disagreement—between those who argue for *active management* by government and those who advocate a *policy rule*—is probably the most important single dispute among macroeconomists.

3. Because of their belief in the effectiveness of market forces, and because of their skepticism regarding the ability of governments to substantially improve the operation of the economy, monetarists generally believe that the government's role should be narrowly circumscribed.[4] Those in the Keynesian tradition are much more likely to favor a large role for the government. They not only believe in the active management of aggregate demand, but also are generally sympathetic toward other government activities aimed at domestic economic problems—for example, public housing and job training programs. Those who argue for active demand management are not required, by the logic of their case, to argue that the government should also undertake other tasks. But it is not surprising that those who are confident of the government in one area—demand management—also tend to be confident of its abilities in other respects.

4. *The nature of equilibrium* is another area of disagreement. Those in the classical tradition associate equilibrium with full employment. High rates of unemployment represent a *temporary* problem caused by economic fluctuations and short-run *disequilibrium.* In contrast, Keynesian theory puts forward the possibility that the economy might fall into an unemployment equilibrium, involving an *extended* period of inadequate aggregate demand and high rates of unemployment. The economy does not move automatically to full employment.

While the possibility of an unemployment equilibrium remains a point of difference between those in the Keynesian and classical traditions, this issue has become less important with the passage of time. A major reason is that almost a half century has passed since the Great Depression. Keynesians are therefore much less worried about a lengthy depression than they used to be.

KEY POINTS

1. Just as demand and supply are useful in microeconomics, so they are also useful in macroeconomics. However, we cannot assume that the macroeconomic demand and supply curves will necessarily have slopes similar to those of microeconomic demand and supply curves.

2. There are two main approaches to aggregate demand and aggregate supply: the classical and the Keynesian approaches.

3. Classical theory stresses the importance of money as a determinant of aggregate demand. In drawing a single aggregate demand curve, we assume that the nominal quantity of money is held constant. When prices fall, the purchasing power of this fixed nominal quantity increases. Therefore, people purchase more goods and services. Accordingly, the classical aggregate demand function slopes downward to the right.

4. According to classical theory, the aggregate supply

[4]For example, Milton Friedman and Rose Friedman, *Free to Choose* (New York: Harcourt Brace Jovanovich, 1979). The Friedmans would reduce the role of the government in many areas, including education. They recommend that the government support education by giving vouchers to parents to be used in the school of the parents' choice.

function is vertical at potential or full-employment output.

5. Consequently, full employment exists in the classical equilibrium where aggregate demand and aggregate supply intersect.

6. According to classical economists, the depression was the result of a leftward shift in the aggregate demand curve, which in turn resulted from a fall in the money stock. In time—in the "long run"—classical economists believed that wages and prices would fall enough to restore full employment.

7. Keynes emphasized the downward rigidity of wages and prices. In its simplest form, the Keynesian aggregate supply function forms a reversed L, as illustrated in Figure 9-5.

8. According to Keynes, the solution to a depression lay in additional government expenditures, whose purpose would be to increase aggregate demand to the full-employment level. Thus, Keynes rejected the laissez faire conclusions of many classical economists.

9. While Keynesian economists often stress fiscal policy as a tool for managing demand, those in the classical tradition emphasize the importance of money. However, most modern economists believe that *both* fiscal and monetary policies can have an important effect on demand.

10. A significant debate continues over how actively the authorities should manage aggregate demand. Keynesians generally favor active management, while those in the classical tradition generally favor a monetary rule: The authorities should aim for a steady, moderate increase in the quantity of money.

KEY CONCEPTS

aggregate demand
aggregate supply
purchasing power of money
general inflation or deflation
equilibrium at full employment
stickiness of wages and prices
transitional periods of unemployment
long run
Keynesian unemployment equilibrium
reversed-L aggregate supply function
Keynesian and classical ranges of aggregate supply
monetary policy
fiscal policy
active management of demand
monetary policy rule
monetarist

PROBLEMS

9-1. The demand curve for a specific good, such as wheat, slopes downward to the right. Why can't we simply conclude that, as a result, the aggregate demand curve will have the same general shape?

9-2. Draw a diagram showing the classical aggregate demand function. Why does it have the slope you have shown?

9-3. Why is the classical aggregate supply function vertical?

9-4. If the economy starts at a point of high unemployment, explain two ways in which full employment might be restored in the classical system.

9-5. What is the reason for the horizontal section of the Keynesian aggregate supply function?

9-6. According to Keynes, what was the best way to get out of a depression?

9-7. What evidence suggests that fluctuations in aggregate demand, rather than fluctuations in aggregate supply, have been the principal reason for fluctuations in real output?

APPENDIX

THE AGGREGATE DEMAND CURVE OF KEYNESIAN ECONOMICS

In order to complete our story about aggregate demand and aggregate supply, we need to look at what Keynes said about the slope of the aggregate demand function in his *General Theory*. Suppose that in the face of a depressed economy at *B* in Figure 9-7, a general deflation did occur, with prices and wages all falling by, say, 50%. The horizontal segment of the aggregate supply curve would then be at the new prevailing price level; aggregate supply would have shifted down from AS_1 to AS_2. What would the result be? What would happen to the aggregate quantity of goods and services demanded? To answer this, said Keynes, we have to look at what will happen to the major components of demand, particularly consumption and investment.

1. *Consumption demand*. The amount which people consume depends primarily on their incomes. As wages and incomes fall by the same proportion, people find that they are no better off: Their *real wages* remain unchanged. Accordingly, said Keynes, we would not expect any change in the quantity of goods and services they consume. In other words, if we look only at consumption—the largest single component of aggregate demand—we would expect the aggregate demand function to be *vertical,* like AD_2. If it has any tendency to slope downward to the right or left, it will have to be because of the behavior of other components of demand, most notably, investment.

2. *Investment demand*. Investment demand depends in part on what is happening to consumer purchases. For example, a rise in the sales of automobiles will encourage auto manufacturers to invest by buying more plant and machinery. However, if consumption is stable in the face of deflation—for reasons explained in point 1—there is no reason to expect greater investment on this account.

To identify the effects of price changes on investment, we have to look instead at two other forces:

(*a*) *The interest-rate effect*. As prices and wages fall, the amount of money in the system increases in *real* terms—that is, in terms of what it will buy. There are the same number of dollars, but each dollar is worth more. Because individuals and businesses have more real money, they are more willing to lend it; interest rates fall as a result. With lower interest rates, businesses find it cheaper to borrow the money with which to buy equipment. Investment should increase on this account.

(*b*) *The expectations effect*. Investment also depends on people's expectations regarding the future. For example, if prices are expected to rise, businesses have an incentive to buy buildings or equipment as soon as possible, in order to avoid the higher prices later. In extreme cases, there can be strong speculation in real estate—there is a rush to get in while the getting is good. On the other hand, expectations of a fall in prices can cause businesses to put off investment in the hopes of buying the plant or equipment even more cheaply in the future. This, said Keynes, is what makes deflation so dangerous. As prices fall, people may come to expect a continuing deflation. This can cause a weakening of investment demand.

There thus are two opposite forces at work as prices decline—the interest-rate effect, working toward an increase in investment, and the expectations effect, working toward a decrease. Keynes was particularly dubious about the interest-rate effect when the economy was suffering substantial slack. During such periods, interest rates may already be very low. For example, the interest rates on long-term government bonds fell below 3% during the Great Depression. No matter what happens, interest rates can't fall much further. Clearly, interest rates can't become negative; people would simply refuse to buy bonds yielding negative rates and would hold money instead.

Thus, Keynes argued that, during a depression, a weak interest-rate effect is likely to be overpowered by a negative expectations effect. Although it's conceivable that there could be an increase in investment and aggregate demand, with aggregate demand going through point *J* in Figure 9-7, it is much more likely that investment would remain stable or decrease. Therefore, the aggregate demand function is more likely to go through *H* or *G*.

In brief, Keynes presented two reasons for rejecting the classical argument that full employment could be restored by a general fall in prices and wages:

FIGURE 9-7

Aggregate demand in Keynesian economics

If prices and wages fall during a depression, the result may be an increase in the quantity of goods and services demanded, as illustrated by the movement from *B* to *J*. But we cannot count on this. The quantity demanded may remain stable, at *H*, or decrease, to *G*. In other words, we cannot be sure which way the aggregate demand curve will slope. AD_1, AD_2, and AD_3 are all possible.

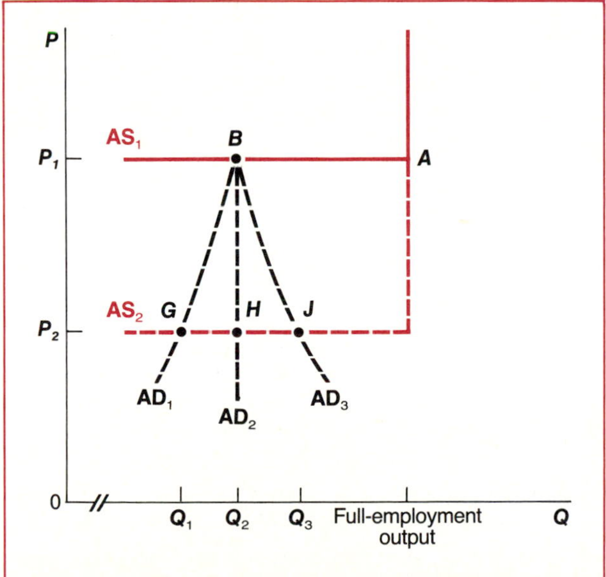

1. In the first place, prices and wages *won't* fall much; they are rigid in a downward direction. The downward shift of the aggregate supply curve illustrated in Figure 9-7 won't in fact occur, according to Keynes.

2. *Even if* prices and wages *did* fall, the market could not be counted on to restore full employment. A more likely outcome would be a movement toward *G* in Figure 9-7; deflation would *worsen* the depression.

Market forces would not lead automatically to full employment, even in the long run. Thus, Keynes came to his central policy conclusion. If the economy is at a point like *B*, the government should not stand idly by while millions remain out of work. It should accept its responsibilities and increase its spending in order to shift aggregate demand to the right and restore full employment at *A*.

Finally, Keynesian theory suggests that the aggregate demand curve should have a normal slope during a period of prosperity; that is, it should slope downward to the right. During prosperity, interest rates are generally much higher than during a depression; they can fall substantially when the real value of the public's money holdings goes up. Thus, the interest rate effect should be relatively strong, outweighing the expectations effect and giving the aggregate demand function a normal downward slope.

As a result, Keynesian and classical theories become quite similar during prosperity. Both suggest a vertical aggregate supply function. Moreover, both foresee an aggregate demand function sloping downward to the right. The sharp differences in the two theories arise when the unemployment rate is high.

PROBLEM

***9-8.** As part of Franklin Roosevelt's program to combat the Great Depression of the 1930s, the National Recovery Act contained provisions to keep prices up. Using Figure 9-4, explain why someone in the classical tradition might consider such legislation a blunder. Using Figure 9-7, explain why a Keynesian would be much more likely to favor such legislation.

CHAPTER 10

EQUILIBRIUM WITH UNEMPLOYMENT:

THE KEYNESIAN APPROACH

The economic system in which we live . . . seems capable of remaining in a chronic condition of subnormal activity for a considerable period without any marked tendency either towards recovery or towards complete collapse. Moreover . . . full, or even approximately full employment is of rare and short-lived occurrence.

JOHN MAYNARD KEYNES,
The General Theory of Employment, Interest and Money

Of all our economic problems, unemployment is perhaps the most vexing. Unemployment represents an obvious waste: The society foregoes the goods and services which the unemployed might have produced. Unemployed people suffer the demoralization, frustration, and loss of self-respect that come from enforced idleness.

As we saw in Chapter 9, the deep depression of the 1930s led to a new theory of unemployment put forward by John Maynard Keynes.[1] This chapter will explain Keynes' major theoretical proposition—that the economy may reach an equilibrium with large-scale unemployment. (The next chapter will outline Keynes' major policy proposals—namely, what the government can do to combat unemployment.)

Equilibrium in an economy is determined by aggregate supply and aggregate demand. To explain Keynesian theory, we begin where Keynes did, focusing on the horizontal section of the aggregate supply function (Figure 9-5), where prices are stable and changes in demand lead to changes in output. To determine how large national output will be, we need to know how big aggregate demand is. Recall from Chapter 9 that Keynes studied aggregate demand by looking at its components:

1. Personal consumption expenditures
2. Investment demand
3. Government purchases of goods and services
4. Net exports

The basic point of Keynesian theory—that the economy may reach an equilbrium with large-scale unemployment—can be illustrated most easily by considering a very simple economy, one with only the first two components of aggregate demand: consumption and investment. Such a simplified economy is studied in this chapter. Government expenditures will be considered in Chapter 11, and net exports in Chapters 11 and 18.

PERSONAL CONSUMPTION EXPENDITURES

Of all the components of total spending, personal consumption is by far the largest. On what do consumption expenditures depend? An individual's consumption is influenced by many factors. Purchases of clothing depend on the weather. The purchase of an automobile depends in part on the price of gasoline and on the state

[1] *The General Theory of Employment, Interest and Money* (London: Macmillan, 1936).

of the roads. We could easily compile an extensive list of factors affecting consumption. But one stands out as the most important: *Consumption depends on the disposable income that people have left after they pay taxes.*

The behavior of American consumers is shown in Figure 10-1, which is based on a survey of families by the Bureau of Labor Statistics in 1980–1981 (with updating and supplementary estimates by the authors). Low-income families on the left confine their spending to little more than the necessities of life—food, clothing, and housing. Even so, they find it hard to make ends meet, and they spend more than their incomes. For example, families at *G* with disposable incomes of $5,000 (measured along the horizontal axis) consume, on average, about $6,500 (measured vertically). But how can low-income families possibly spend more than they have coming in? The answer: by running into debt or by drawing on their past savings. One group of low-income people—those who are retired—are particularly likely to spend more than their current incomes. They draw on the

FIGURE 10-1

Consumption expenditures at different income levels, 1985

Consumption depends on disposable income. Families with higher disposable incomes consume more than families with lower incomes.

Source: Bureau of Labor Statistics, with updating and supplementary estimates by authors.

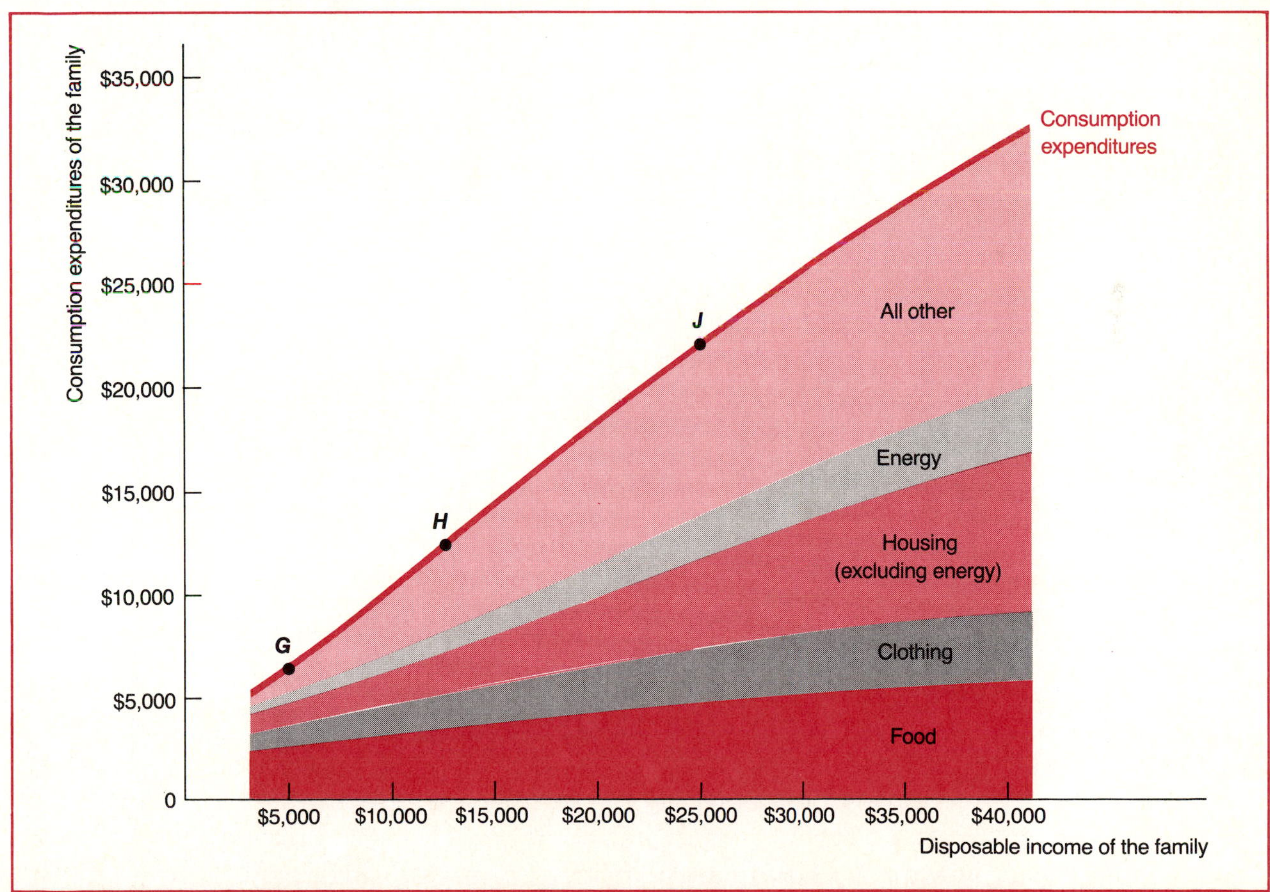

assets, such as savings accounts, that they have accumulated during their working lives.

As the incomes of families rise, they find it easier to live within their current incomes. Thus, the family at *H* with an income of $12,500 spends $12,500 for consumer goods and services. It *breaks even,* spending all its income. As incomes rise further, consumption also rises, but not as fast as income; at incomes above $12,500, families do not consume their full incomes. For example, families at point *J* with incomes of $25,000 consume considerably less than this amount and save the rest.

While Figure 10-1 shows how a family's consumption rises as its disposable income increases, Figure 10-2 illustrates how consumption also rises as disposable income increases for a nation as a whole. Disposable income of the whole nation is shown on the horizontal axis, and expenditures of all consumers on the vertical axis. The numbers corresponding to Figure 10-2 are shown in Table 10-1. For example, the first line of Table 10-1 indicates that, if disposable income is $500 billion, consumption is $600 billion. This is shown at point *A* in Figure 10-2, measured 500 units along the horizontal income axis and 600 units up the vertical consumption axis. Similarly, points *B, C,* and *D* in Figure 10-2 can be derived from the corresponding lines in Table 10-1. Because consumer expenditures depend primarily on real incomes, the incomes and expenditures on the axes of Figure 10-2 are measured in real or constant-dollar terms.

The relationship between consumption and disposable income is known as the ***consumption function.*** It plays a central role in Keynes' theory of unemployment.

The *consumption function* shows how consumption expenditures depend on disposable income.

In Figure 10-2, we may find the ***break-even point***—at which consumption equals disposable income—with the help of a 45° line drawn from the origin. The 45° line has an important property: *Any point on it is the same distance from the two axes.* Consider, for example, an economy in which disposable income is $2,000 billion,

TABLE 10-1
Consumption and Saving
(billions of dollars at constant prices)

	(1) DI Disposable income	(2) C Consumption	(3) Marginal propensity to consume $MPC = \frac{\Delta C}{\Delta DI}$	(4) S Saving (4) = (1) − (2)	(5) Marginal propensity to save $MPS = \frac{\Delta S}{\Delta DI}$
A	$ 500	$ 600		−100	
			$\frac{400}{500} = 0.8$		$\frac{100}{500} = 0.2$
B	1,000	1,000		0	
			$\frac{400}{500} = 0.8$		$\frac{100}{500} = 0.2$
C	1,500	1,400		+100	
			$\frac{400}{500} = 0.8$		$\frac{100}{500} = 0.2$
D	2,000	1,800		+200	

FIGURE 10-2
The consumption function (billions of dollars at constant prices)

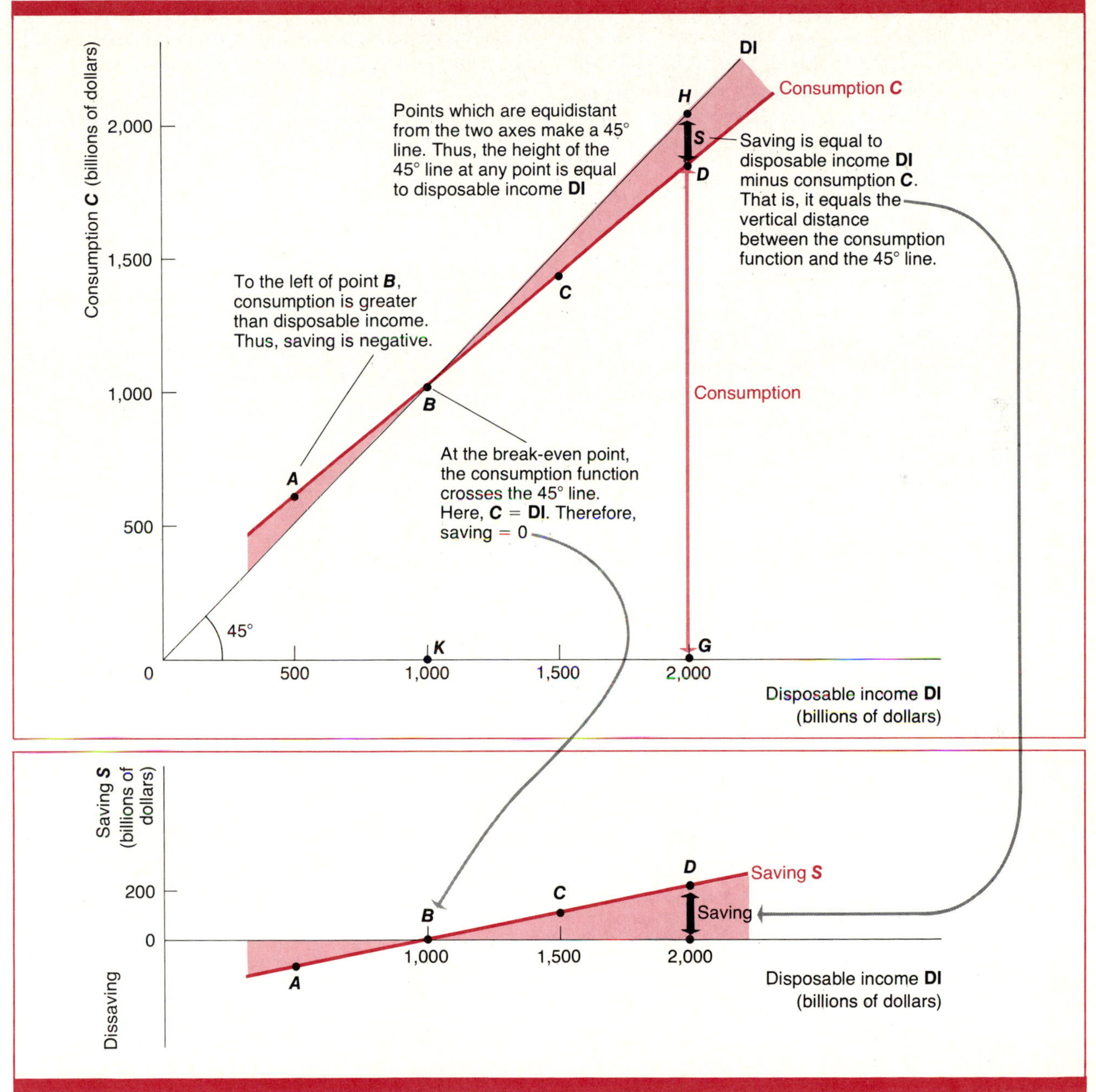

Consumption C (billions of dollars)
2,000
1,500
1,000
500
0
DI
Consumption C
H
S
D
Points which are equidistant from the two axes make a 45° line. Thus, the height of the 45° line at any point is equal to disposable income DI
Saving is equal to disposable income DI minus consumption C. That is, it equals the vertical distance between the consumption function and the 45° line.
To the left of point B, consumption is greater than disposable income. Thus, saving is negative.
C
B
A
Consumption
At the break-even point, the consumption function crosses the 45° line. Here, C = DI. Therefore, saving = 0
45°
K
G
500
1,000
1,500
2,000
Disposable income DI (billions of dollars)
Saving S (billions of dollars)
200
0
Dissaving
D
Saving S
C
B
Saving
A
1,000
1,500
2,000
Disposable income DI (billions of dollars)

FIGURE 10-3
The saving function (billions of dollars at constant prices)
The saving function can be derived from the consumption function. Saving is the vertical distance between the consumption function and the 45° line in Figure 10-2 above.

as shown by the horizontal distance between the origin and point *G* in Figure 10-2. Then the vertical distance from *G* to point *H* on the 45° line is also $2,000 billion. Thus, this $2,000 billion disposable income (DI) may be measured either along the horizontal axis from the origin to point *G* or as the vertical distance from *G* up to the 45° line at *H*.

If disposable income decreases to $1,000 billion and we move to the left along the horizontal axis to point *K*, we can once again measure income as the height of the 45° line—in this case the $1,000 billion vertical distance from point *K* on the horizontal axis to point *B* on the 45° line. But this vertical distance to point *B* also measures consumption; that is, *B* lies on the consumption function. Therefore, point *B*, *where the consumption function and the 45° line intersect,* is the *break-even point*.

At the *break-even point,* consumption equals disposable income; that is, every dollar of disposable income is spent on consumer goods and services.

Saving is what is left of disposable income after consumption expenditures:

$$\textbf{Saving} = \textbf{disposable income} - \textbf{consumption}^2 \qquad (10\text{-}1)$$

Drawing on this equation, we may derive a ***saving function*** (Figure 10-3) directly from the consumption function. For example: Suppose disposable income is $2,000 billion, at point *G* measured along the horizontal axis. Disposable income is also measured by the height of *H* on the 45° line, while consumption is the height of *D* on the consumption function. The difference—distance *HD*—is saving. This distance is used in Figure 10-3 to measure the height of point *D* on the saving function. Similarly, other points on the saving function can be derived by taking the vertical distances between the consumption function and the 45° line in Figure 10-2. Thus, the consumption function (Figure 10-2) and the saving function (Figure 10-3) are *two alternative ways of illustrating precisely the same information.*

The *saving function* shows the relationship between disposable income and saving.

Notice that point *B* in Figure 10-3 corresponds to point *B* on Figure 10-2's consumption function. At this break-even point, where consumption equals income, saving is zero. If we look at points even further to the left, such as point *A* in Figure 10-2, we see that consumption is greater than income; that is, there is negative saving, or ***dissaving,*** as illustrated by corresponding point *A* in Figure 10-3.

The Marginal Propensity to Consume

Keynes was interested in explaining how consumption might change. He therefore introduced an important concept: the ***marginal propensity to consume,*** or MPC. Economists use the term *marginal* to mean "extra" or "additional." (As we shall see in a later chapter, marginal revenue means additional revenue and marginal cost means additional cost.) The marginal propensity to consume is the fraction of additional disposable income that is consumed. Formally,

Marginal propensity to consume =

$$\frac{\textbf{change in consumption}}{\textbf{change in disposable income}} \qquad \textbf{(10-2)}$$

In abbreviated notation, this is written:

$$\textbf{MPC} = \frac{\Delta C}{\Delta \textbf{DI}} \qquad \textbf{(10-3)}$$

where the Greek letter Δ means "change in."

If we think of a small $1 increase in disposable income, this formula reduces to:

MPC = the fraction of a $1 increase in disposable income that is consumed

This is an obvious restatement of the idea: If your in-

[2]More precisely, saving equals disposable income less consumption less interest paid by consumers, as we saw in Chapter 7. However, when explaining the basic Keynesian theory, it is standard practice to ignore the interest complication and use simplified equation 10-1.

come increases by $1 and your consumption increases by $0.80 as a result, then your MPC is $0.80/$1.00 = 0.80.

Similarly,

Marginal propensity to save (MPS)

$$= \frac{\text{change in saving}}{\text{change in disposable income}}$$

$$= \frac{\Delta S}{\Delta \text{DI}} \qquad \textbf{(10-4)}$$

Or:

MPS = the fraction of a $1 increase in disposable income that is saved

In Table 10-1, the MPC and MPS are calculated in columns 3 and 5. Observe that

$$\text{MPC} + \text{MPS} = 1 \qquad (10\text{-}5)$$

This must be the case. If a person gets $1 more in income, whatever is not consumed is saved. In our example, a $1 increase in income results in an increase of consumption of $0.80. Thus, $0.20 is saved and the MPS is 0.20/1.00 = 0.20.

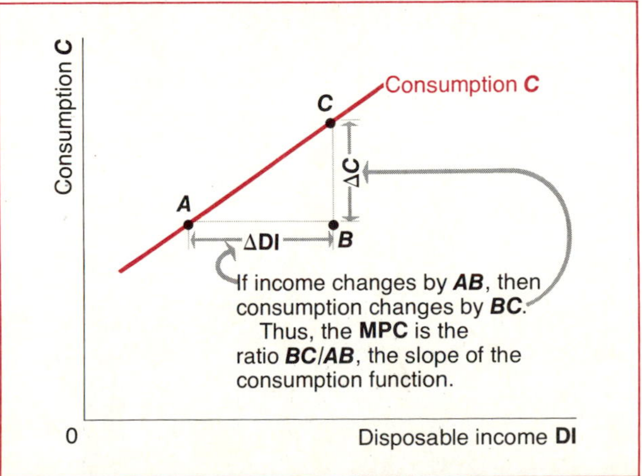

FIGURE 10-4

The marginal propensity to consume

Since the MPC is the slope of the consumption function, the consumption function is a straight line if the MPC is constant.

In Figure 10-4, the MPC is illustrated. It is equal to the vertical change in consumption divided by the horizontal change in income. Thus, the MPC is equal to the slope of the consumption function. Consequently, if the MPC is constant, as it is in our illustration in Table 10-1, the consumption function has a constant slope; it is a straight line. Similarly, the MPS is the slope of the saving function. From equation 10-5 it follows that, if the MPC is constant, so is the MPS. Thus, the saving function is also a straight line, as illustrated earlier in Figure 10-3.

The MPC plays a central role in Keynesian theory. A companion—but *much* less important—concept is also sometimes used, namely, the *average* propensity to consume (APC). This is defined:

$$\text{APC} = \frac{\text{total consumption}}{\text{total disposable income}} \qquad \textbf{(10-6)}$$

The difference between the marginal and average concepts may be seen by referring back to the example in Figure 10-2. Because the consumption function is a straight line with a slope of 0.8, the MPC is a constant 0.8. However, the APC is not constant; it changes along the consumption function. At *B*, for example, consumption equals disposable income, and the APC is therefore 1. At *C*, the APC is less than 1, specifically, 1,400/1,500 = 0.93.

THE SIMPLEST EQUILIBRIUM: AN ECONOMY WITH NO GOVERNMENT

Keynes' objective was to demonstrate that laissez faire market economies contain a fundamental defect: They may come to rest with a very high rate of unemployment. In order to explain this central proposition as clearly and as quickly as possible, we look at a bare-bones economy, in which there is no international trade, no government spending, no taxes, no depreciation, and no retained corporate profits. In this very simplified economy, GNP = NNP = national income = disposable income. In other words, all the receipts from national product pass through the business sector to become the disposable income of the household sector; there are none of the subtractions explained in detail back in Chapter 7. Since GNP and NNP are the same, we can use the abbreviated term *national product,* or NP.

Furthermore, the absence of government and international transactions means that there are only two components of aggregate demand in this very simple economy, namely, consumption expenditures and investment demand. (We reiterate that investment is part of national product. Specifically, investment demand means the demand for new equipment, plant, and houses and additional inventories. When macroeconomists talk of investment demand, they do not include demand for financial assets, such as stocks or bonds, nor the demand for second-hand plant, equipment, or housing.)

To make our task even simpler, we initially assume that investment demand is a constant $200 billion. We do not claim that this assumption is realistic. Indeed, as we have seen in previous chapters, investment is one of the most volatile components of GNP. However, this simple assumption will allow us to complete the main argument as quickly as possible, and then we will be in a position to consider what happens when investment demand does change.

The $200 billion of investment demand can be added to consumption demand to get aggregate demand, as shown in Table 10-2, column 5, and in Figure 10-5. In this diagram, national product NP rather than disposable income DI is shown on the horizontal axis and on the 45° line. We may substitute NP for DI in this diagram because NP = DI in the simple economy we are considering here.

Equilibrium occurs where aggregate demand AD equals national product NP. Comparing columns 1 and 5 in Table 10-2, we see that this occurs at an output of $2,000 billion. The same equilibrium of $2,000 billion is shown in Figure 10-5 at point *E,* where aggregate demand AD cuts the 45° national product line NP.

To see why this is the equilibrium, consider why aggregate demand would not be sufficient to buy a larger quantity of output—say the $2,500 billion measured from the origin to point *L* on the horizontal axis and also vertically from *L* to point *N* on the 45° line. In the right-hand part of Figure 10-5, we show a magnified view of national product *LN*. It is the height of the dark red bar, plus the light red bar, plus the gray bar. But aggregate demand is less than that. It's just the dark red bar (consumption demand) plus the light red bar (investment

TABLE 10-2
Equilibrium National Product
(billions of dollars)

	(1) NP National product (equals disposable income in this simple economy)	(2) *C* Consumption demand	(3) *S* Saving (3) = (1) − (2)	(4) *I** Investment demand (assumed constant)	(5) AD Aggregate demand = *C* + *I** (5) = (2) + (4)	(6) Relation of aggregate demand (5) to national product (1)		(7) Economy will:
H	$1,000	$1,000	0	$200	$1,200	Higher	↓	Expand
J	1,500	1,400	100	200	1,600	Higher	↓	Expand
K	**2,000**	**1,800**	**200**	**200**	**2,000**	**Same**		**Stay at equilibrium**
L	2,500	2,200	300	200	2,400	Lower	↑	Contract
M	3,000	2,600	400	200	2,800	Lower	↑	Contract

FIGURE 10-5

Equilibrium national product

Point *E* represents equilibrium, with output of $2,000 billion. Here, aggregate demand equals national product. A higher rate of production (for example, $2,500 billion) is not stable, as we can see by looking at the magnified version on the right, showing what happens when national product is $2,500 billion. National product equals the vertical distance to the 45° line. For most of this product, there is a market. Consumption demand takes the dark red bar. Investment demand takes the light red bar. But for the gray bar, there is no demand. Unsold goods pile up in the warehouses. Businesses cut back on production. Output falls to its equilibrium of $2,000 billion.

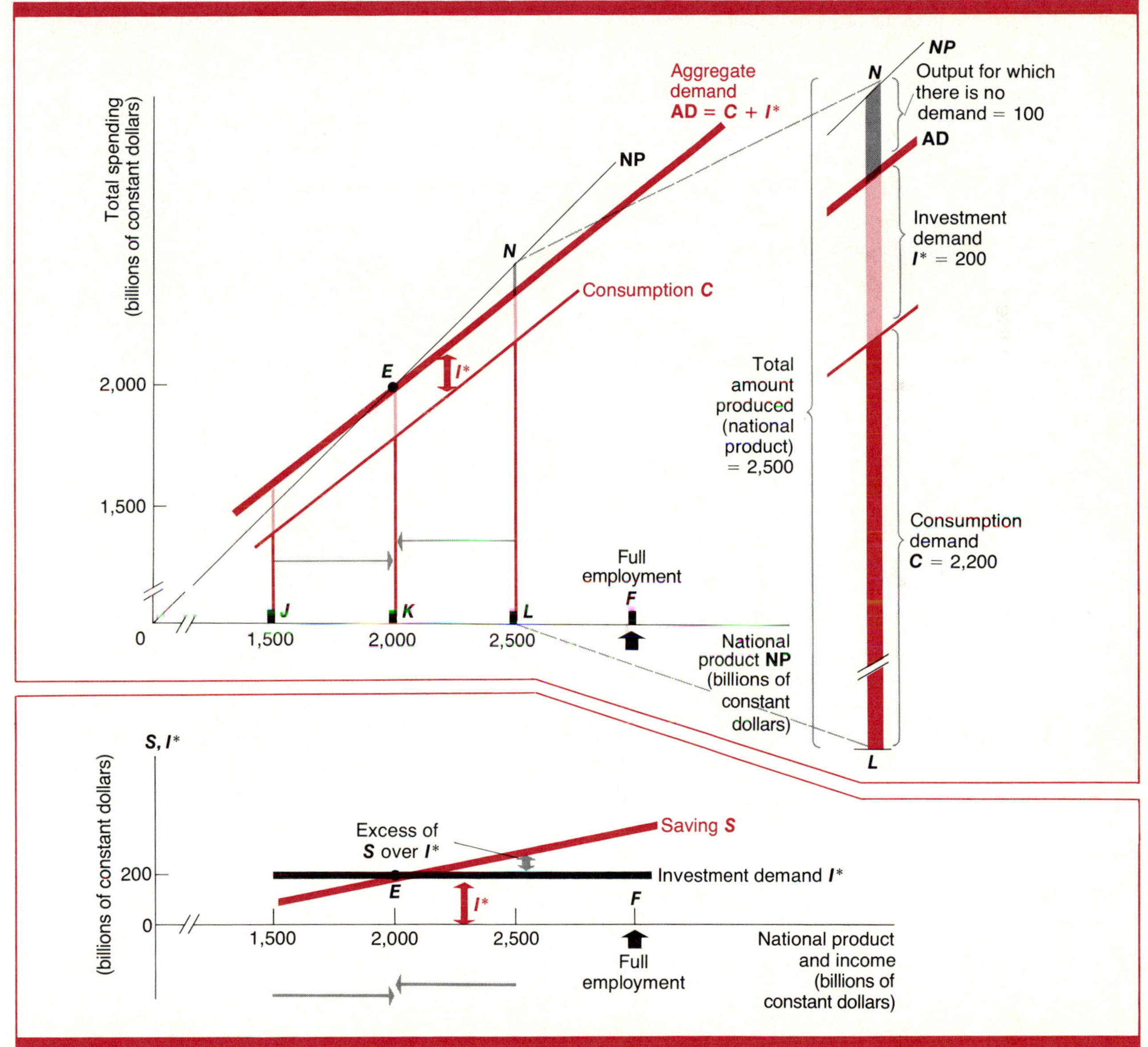

FIGURE 10-6

The equilibrium of saving and investment demand

Equilibrium occurs at output of $2,000 billion, where saving = investment demand. At a greater national product, such as $2,500 billion, disequilibrium exists. Since the leakages from the spending stream (in the form of saving) are greater than the injections (in the form of investment), national product will fall toward its equilibrium at $2,000 billion.

demand). Thus, at an output of $2,500 billion, the amount we produce (national product) exceeds the demand for it (aggregate demand).

What happens to the excess production, shown by the gray bar? It remains unsold; it piles up on retailers' shelves and in warehouses. It represents ***undesired inventory accumulation.*** As unwanted goods accumulate, retailers, wholesalers, and other businesses cut back on their orders. Production falls. Moreover, it continues to contract as long as aggregate demand lies below the 45° national product line. In other words, it continues to fall until the economy reaches equilibrium *E*, where national product NP = aggregate demand AD and there is no further pressure of unsold goods. Therefore, $2,000 billion is the equilibrium quantity of output.

At a disequilibrium quantity of national product, such as $2,500 billion, it is important to distinguish between ***actual investment*** and ***investment demand.*** Actual investment—the quantity which shows up in the official national product accounts studied in Chapter 7—includes all investment in plant, equipment, housing, and inventories, whether that investment is desired or not. Thus, for an economy producing at $2,500 billion, the investment figure that appears in the national product accounts will be the light red bar *plus* the gray bar. ("Gray bar goods," for which there is no demand, and which therefore pile up as *undesired inventory accumulation,* have clearly been produced during the year and must therefore be included in the national product statistics.) In contrast with actual investment, investment demand—also known as ***desired investment*** or ***planned investment***—is only the investment which businesses want; that is, the light red bar. In order to keep straight the important distinction between investment demand and actual investment, we will use the symbol I^* with an asterisk to represent investment demand. As in Chapter 7, a plain I will stand for actual investment; that is, investment as it shows up in the national product accounts.

Actual investment I **is the amount of new plant, equipment, and housing acquired during the year, plus the increase in inventories. All inventory accumulation is included, *whether the inventories were desired or not.***

Investment demand I* **—also known as *desired investment* or *planned investment*—is the amount of new plant, equipment, and housing acquired during the year, plus *additions to inventories which businesses wanted to acquire.* It excludes undesired inventory accumulation.**

Undesired inventory accumulation **is actual investment (I) less investment demand (I^*)**

Just as an output initially greater than equilibrium results in contraction, so an output initially less than equilibrium generates expansion. Consider an output of $1,500 billion, at point *J*. Here, aggregate demand is higher than the 45° national product line. Buyers want to purchase more goods than are currently being produced. Retailers and wholesalers find it difficult to keep goods in stock. Inventories are run down below their desired levels; that is, there is an ***undesired decrease in inventories.*** Because retailers and wholesalers want to meet the large demand and rebuild their inventories, they step up their orders. To fill their larger orders, manufacturers and other producers expand their output toward the equilibrium *E*.

An *undesired decrease in inventories* is equal to investment demand (I^*) minus actual investment (I). It exists when undesired inventory accumulation is negative.

EQUILIBRIUM WITH LARGE-SCALE UNEMPLOYMENT

Now we are in a position to illustrate Keynes' key contention, that the *equilibrium national product need not be at the quantity necessary to ensure full employment.* Equilibrium national product is determined by aggregate demand, as illustrated by point *E* in Figure 10-5. On the other hand, the full-employment national product represents what the economy can produce with its current resources of labor, land, and capital; it is shown at national product *F*. The situation which Keynes feared, and which he believed would be a common outcome of a free-market economy, is the one shown in this diagram. Equilibrium national product at *E* is far less than the full-employment quantity at *F*. (See the quotation from Keynes that introduces this chapter.)

AN ALTERNATIVE APPROACH: SAVING AND INVESTMENT

Figure 10-5 showed how equilibrium national product is determined in the simple economy (with no government, etc.) by putting together consumption expenditures C and investment demand I^*. But we have already seen that the saving function (Figure 10-3) is an alternative way of presenting *exactly the same information* as in the consumption function (Figure 10-2). It is therefore not surprising that, as an alternative to C plus I^*, we can bring saving S together with investment demand I^* to determine equilibrium national product. This is done in Figure 10-6. In the simple economy, *equilibrium occurs when saving equals investment demand,* that is, at point E where national product is $2,000 billion. We may confirm in Table 10-2 that saving (column 3) equals investment demand (column 4) at the same $2,000 billion equilibrium output at which aggregate demand (column 5) equals national product (column 1).

The Circular Flow of Expenditure: Leakages and Injections

To explain *why* equilibrium occurs when saving equals investment demand, we call again on the circular flow of payments previously used in Chapters 3 and 7 and repeated here as Figure 10-7. This figure illustrates a *very*

FIGURE 10-7
The simplest circular flow of payments
(All income is spent for consumer goods and services)
The simplest economy is one in which people consume all their incomes. Incomes are used to buy consumer goods and services. In turn, the receipts from the sale of consumer goods and services are again paid out as incomes in the form of wages, salaries, etc. Once more, people use all their incomes to buy consumer goods and services. Round and round the payments go.

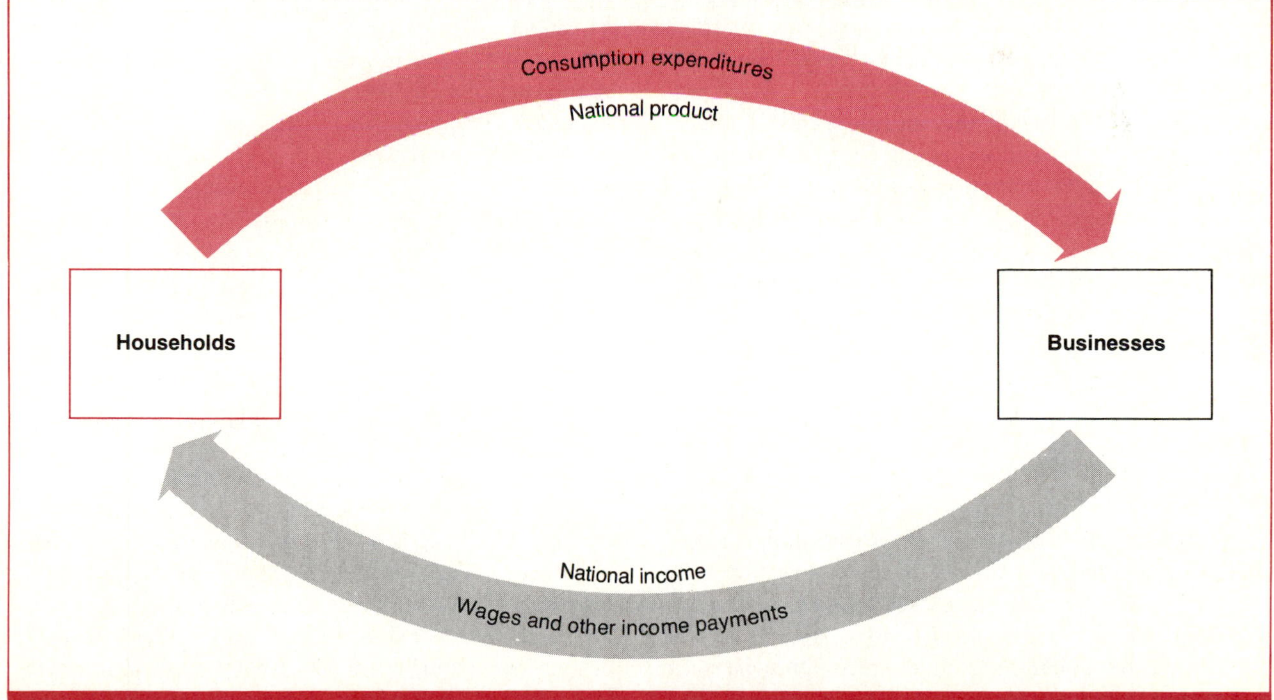

rudimentary economy in which there is no investment demand and in which consumers buy all the goods produced. Suppose that producers sell $1,000 billion of goods during an initial period. In turn, they pay this $1,000 billion to households in the form of wages, salaries, rents, and other incomes, as shown in the lower loop of the diagram. Suppose, further, that the households turn around and spend all their $1,000 billion of income on consumer goods (in the upper loop). Once more the producers sell $1,000 billion in goods and services, and once more they pay out this amount in incomes to the households. Round and round this $1,000 billion of payments goes; national product is stable at this level.

Now let us introduce complications, starting with saving. Suppose that instead of consuming all their incomes of $1,000 billion, people decide that they would like to save $100 billion. They spend only $900 billion on consumer goods. Producers have made $1,000 billion in goods, but they sell only $900 billion. Unsold goods pile up, and producers cut back on production. When they do so, they pay out less in wages and other incomes. The circular flow of national product and income is reduced. Thus, saving represents a leakage from the circular spending stream; it acts as a drag on national product and income.

Now, let us introduce investment demand. Suppose that businesses decide to increase their capital stock and that they order $100 billion worth of machinery. In response to the demand, $100 billion in machinery is produced. The machinery companies pay out the $100 billion in wages, salaries, and other incomes. Incomes rise, people consume more, and the circular flow of national product and income increases. Investment therefore acts as a stimulus to national product and income.

The Equilibrium of Saving and Investment Demand

Thus, in terms of their effect on aggregate demand and output, saving and investment have offsetting effects. Saving is a ***leakage*** from the circular spending stream; an increase in the desire to save leads to a decrease in national product. Investment demand represents an ***injection*** into the circular spending stream; an increase in investment demand leads to an increase in national product. Equilibrium exists when the forces of contraction and expansion are in balance, that is, when saving equals investment demand—as it does in Figure 10-6 at point *E*, where national product is $2,000 billion. At any greater national income, such as $2,500 billion, the leakage from the circular flow of spending—in the form of saving—exceeds the injection of investment spending, and output decreases. If, on the other hand, national product is initially at a point to the left of the $2,000 billion equilibrium, the injection of investment demand exceeds the saving leakage and national product increases. This can be visualized in Figure 10-8: When more is pumped in at the investment end, the income flow becomes larger. This causes more leakages into saving at the other end. The flow stabilizes when the injections and leakages are equal.

Saving and investment decisions are made by different groups. Households save to buy a new car, to send the kids to college, or for retirement. Investment decisions are made principally by business executives; they buy additional plant and equipment when their profit prospects are good. Because of this separation of saving and investment decisions, *there is no assurance that, if an economy begins at full employment, desired investment will be as great as saving*. If it is not—as illustrated at full-employment output *F* in Figure 10-6—national product will decrease and unemployment will result.

The two approaches in Figures 10-5 and 10-6 are exact equivalents; either of those diagrams can be derived from the other. To summarize, we can state the condition for equilibrium in several different ways:

1. Equilibrium exists when national output is equal to aggregate demand—also sometimes referred to as aggregate expenditures. This is the ***output-expenditures approach*** to determining equilibrium, as illustrated by point *E* in Figure 10-5.
2. Equilibrium exists when actual investment *I* equals investment demand I^*, that is, when inventories are at their desired level and there is no undesired accumulation of inventories such as that shown by the gray bar in Figure 10-5.
3. Equilibrium exists when saving and investment demand are equal, as illustrated by point *E* in Figure 10-6. This is the ***leakages-injections approach.***

These three statements are different ways of expressing the same basic point.

The reason for unemployment may be stated in two alternative ways. There will be an *unemployment equilibrium if:*

1. Aggregate demand is too low to buy the full-employment quantity of national product. For example, at full-employment point *F* in Figure 10-5, AD is below NP.

2. The injections of investment demand are less than the leakages into saving when national product is at the full-employment quantity. For example, at full-employment point *F* in Figure 10-6, I^* is below S.

(As we saw in Chapter 9, classical economists be-

FIGURE 10-8

The circular flow, with saving and investment

Investment expenditures work to broaden the spending stream. Leakages into saving narrow it. Equilibrium is reached when leakages from the stream (saving) are equal to injections (investment).

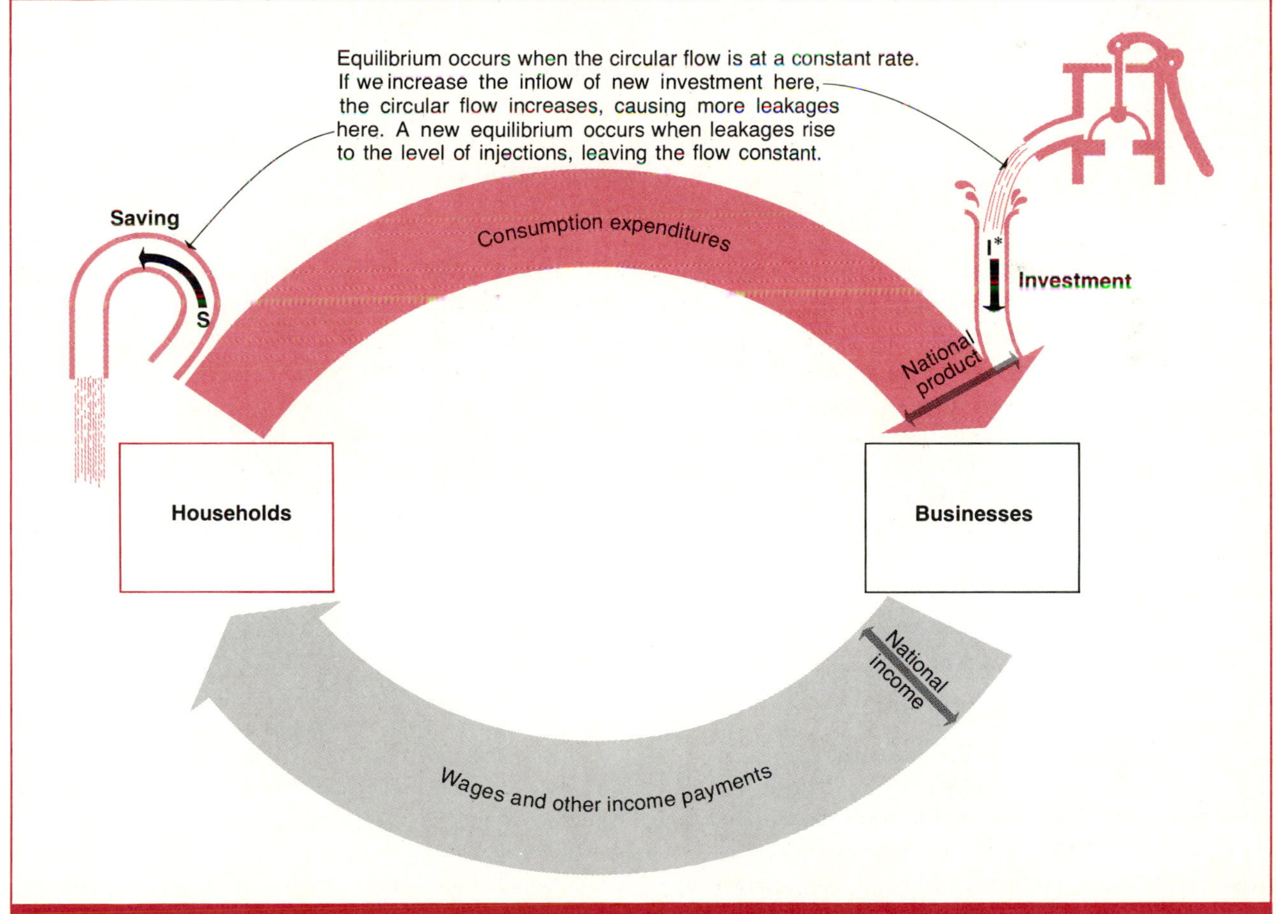
Equilibrium occurs when the circular flow is at a constant rate. If we increase the inflow of new investment here, the circular flow increases, causing more leakages here. A new equilibrium occurs when leakages rise to the level of injections, leaving the flow constant.
Saving
S
Consumption expenditures
I*
Investment
National product
Households
Businesses
National income
Wages and other income payments

lieved that equilibrium would exist only when the economy was at full employment. Appendix 10-A provides more detail on the classical view. Specifically, it explains how classical economists fitted saving and investment into the idea of an equilibrium with full employment.)

CHANGES IN INVESTMENT DEMAND: THE MULTIPLIER

Investment is a flighty bird.

J. R. Hicks

The basic Keynesian diagrams (Figures 10-5 and 10-6) illustrate how the economy can reach an equilibrium at less than full employment. But they can also be used to illustrate how economic activity can change, with the economy periodically moving from boom to recession and back. During the business cycle, investment demand is quite unstable.

Consider what happens if investment demand increases. Suppose that business executives become more optimistic about the future. They will plan to expand their operations, undertaking more investment in plant and equipment. Suppose, specifically, that investment demand increases by $100 billion.

The results are shown in Figure 10-9. When the increase in investment demand is added, the aggregate demand function shifts upward by $100 billion, from AD_1 to AD_2. Equilibrium once more occurs where aggregate demand and national product are equal, that is, where the new aggregate demand function AD_2 cuts the 45° line at H. Thus, the increase in investment demand moves the equilibrium from E to H. Observe that something very important has happened. The equilibrium national product has increased *by $500 billion, which is far more than the $100 billion increase in investment demand*.

How can that be? The answer is this: As businesses build more factories and order more equipment, people are put to work producing the factories and equipment. They earn more wages. As their incomes rise, they increase their consumption expenditures. Thus, the nation produces not only more capital goods, such as factories and equipment, but *also* more consumer goods. National product rises by more than investment. Specifically, as the equilibrium moves from E to H, national product increases by $500 billion. This includes not only the $100 billion increase in investment spending on capital goods (shown as ΔI^* in Figure 10-9) but also an increase of $400 billion in spending on consumer goods (shown as ΔC). These are the additional goods consumers buy as their incomes rise and they accordingly move up the consumption function from G to R.

Thus, the $100 billion increase in investment demand has a *multiplied* effect on national product. The relationship between the increase in national product and the increase in investment demand is known as the ***investment multiplier***, or more simply, as the ***multiplier***. Formally, it is defined:

$$\textbf{Investment multiplier} = \frac{\textbf{change in equilibrium real national product}}{\textbf{change in investment demand}} \qquad \textbf{(10-7)}$$

In our illustration, equilibrium national product rises by $500 billion when investment demand increases by $100 billion. Therefore, the multiplier is 5.

The Multiplier Process: A More Detailed Look

The multiplier process may be better understood by looking in more detail at what happens when there is an additional $100 billion of investment expenditure on capital goods. The *direct impact* is a $100 billion increase in national product; more machines and other capital goods are produced. But this is not the end of the story. The $100 billion spent for plant and equipment goes in the form of wages, rents, profits, and other incomes to those who provide the resources used to produce the capital goods. In other words, disposable incomes are $100 billion higher. (Remember, we are dealing with a highly simplified economy in which there is no government to take a tax bite.) Consumers now spend most of this increase in their disposable income, with the precise amount depending on their MPC. For example, if the MPC is 0.8, consumers are *induced* to spend $80 billion more, as shown in the "second round" increase in the national product in Table 10-3 and Figure 10-11.

But again, this is not the end of the story. When consumers spend \$80 billion more for clothing, food, and other consumer goods, that \$80 billion in spending becomes income for producers. Thus, the incomes of textile workers, farmers, and others who produce consumer goods rise by \$80 billion. With an MPC of 0.8, these people spend \$80 billion × 0.8 = \$64 billion. Once more, national product has risen, this time by \$64 billion. The story goes on and on, with each round of consumer spending giving rise to another, smaller round.

FIGURE 10-9
The multiplier
With an MPC = 0.8, a \$100 billion increase in investment demand causes a \$500 billion increase in national product.

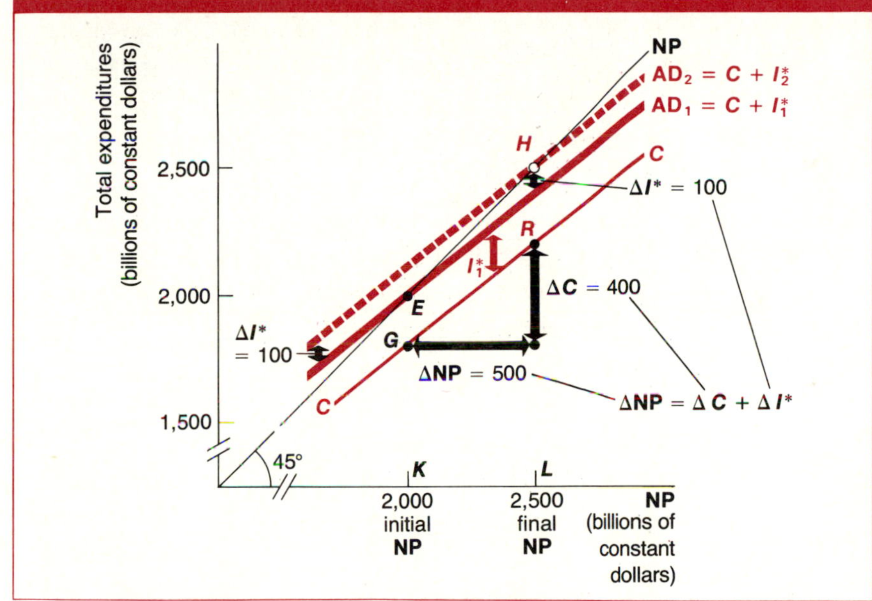

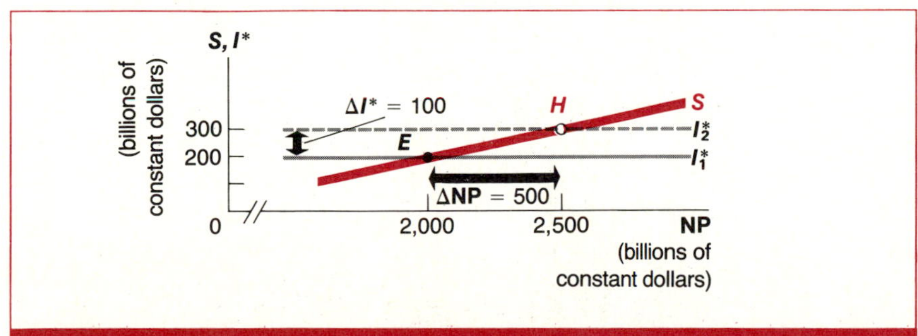

FIGURE 10-10
The multiplier: Saving and investment approach
With an MPS = 0.2, an increase of \$100 billion in investment demand (from I_1^* to I_2^*) causes an increase of \$500 billion in national product.

Observe that, with an MPC of 0.8, the total spending resulting from each dollar of initial investment expenditure forms the series $1 $(1 + 0.8 + 0.8^2 + 0.8^3 \ldots)$. It can be shown[3] that the sum of such a series is:

$$\$1\left(\frac{1}{1-0.8}\right) = \$5 \qquad (10\text{-}8)$$

That is:

$$\begin{pmatrix}\text{initial increase}\\ \text{in investment}\end{pmatrix} \times \begin{pmatrix}\text{multiplier}\\ \text{of 5}\end{pmatrix} = \begin{pmatrix}\text{eventual increase}\\ \text{in national product}\end{pmatrix}$$

In this case, because the MPC is 0.8, the multiplier is 5.

*[3]Let c stand for the MPC. As long as c is less than 1 (in our case, 0.8), then the sum of the series

$$1 + c + c^2 + c^3 \ldots = \frac{1}{1-c}$$

This can be shown by actually doing the division on the right side. In other words, divide 1 by $(1 - c)$, as follows:

$$\begin{array}{r|l} & 1 + c + c^2 \ldots \\ \hline 1 - c & 1 \\ & \underline{1 - c} \\ & \quad c \\ & \quad \underline{c - c^2} \\ & \qquad c^2 \ldots \end{array}$$

More generally:

$$\text{Multiplier} = \frac{1}{1 - \text{MPC}} \qquad (10\text{-}9)$$

Thus, the size of the multiplier depends on the size of the MPC, that is, on the slope of the consumption function. The steeper the consumption function—that is, the higher the MPC—the larger is the multiplier.

Observe also how Table 10-3 and Figure 10-11 correspond to Figure 10-9. Each shows that a $100 billion increase in investment demand causes a $500 billion increase in national product. This $500 billion is made up of the original $100 billion increase in investment, plus $400 billion in *induced* consumption that occurs as people spend more when their disposable incomes rise.

The multiplier works both ways We have just seen how an increase in investment demand (of $100 billion) leads to a multiplied increase in national product (of

TABLE 10-3

The Multiplier Process: Effect on National Product of an Increase in Investment Expenditure

(billions of dollars)

Round	Spending on	Resulting change in aggregate demand and national product	
First	Investment	100.0	Direct initial effect
Second	Consumption	80.0	Induced increase in consumption = 400.0
Third	Consumption	64.0	
Fourth	Consumption	51.2	
Fifth	Consumption	41.0	
.		.	
.		.	
.		.	
Total increase in aggregate demand and national product		500.0	

FIGURE 10-11

The multiplier process: The buildup of national product This figure portrays the various rounds of spending listed in Table 10-3, which result from an initial increase of $100 billion in investment in round 1. Notice how national product builds up toward its equilibrium increase of $500 billion.

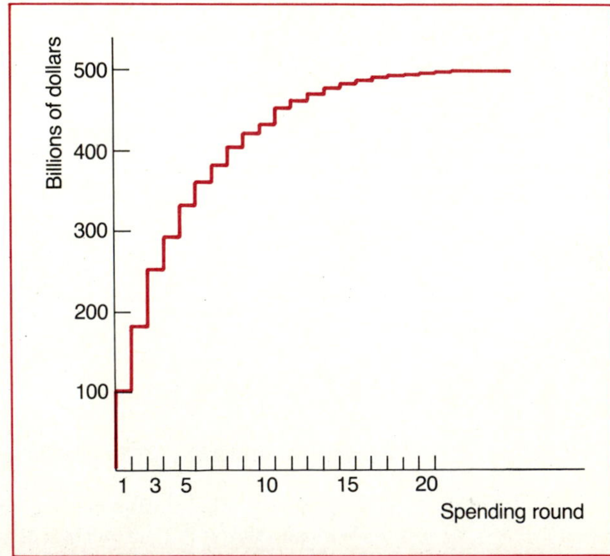

$500 billion). A similar multiplied effect occurs when investment decreases. For example, a "first round" reduction of $100 billion in investment causes a direct reduction of $100 billion in national product and income. With smaller incomes, consumers will cut their spending by $80 billion in the "second round." They will buy fewer books, shirts, or movie tickets. This in turn will reduce the incomes of authors, textile workers, and movie producers. As a result, their consumption will fall. Just as in the earlier example, there will be a whole series of "rounds." The sum of all these rounds will be a $500 billion decrease in national product.

The Multiplier: The Saving-Investment Approach

Just as the saving-investment diagram may be used to show an unemployment equilibrium, so it may also be used to illustrate the multiplier. This is done in Figure 10-10, which once again provides exactly the same information as Figure 10-9. When investment demand increases by $100 billion from I_1^* to I_2^*, equilibrium moves from *E* to *H*. Once again, observe that national product increases by more than the initial increase in investment. Indeed, income increases until people are willing to increase their saving by the full $100 billion injected into the spending stream by the new investment. People are not willing to increase their saving by this $100 billion until their incomes have increased by $500 billion. Remember: their marginal propensity to save (MPS) is 1/5; they save only $1 out of every additional $5 they earn. Thus, from this other perspective, we confirm that equilibrium income rises by $500 billion. (Appendix 10-B provides a further elaboration of the saving-investment approach.)

In this saving-investment approach, it is common to define the multiplier in terms of the MPS rather than the MPC. To do so, first note that income is either consumed or saved. Therefore:

$$\text{MPS} = 1 - \text{MPC} \qquad \text{(10-10, from 10-5)}$$

Thus, equation 10-9 can be rewritten:

$$\text{Multiplier} = \frac{1}{\text{MPS}} \qquad \text{(10-11)}$$

However, it should be stressed that the multiplier takes the value shown in equation 10-11—or in similar equation 10-9—*only if the economy is the very simplifed one we have considered so far*.

In practice, the multiplier will be smaller than indicated by equations 10-9 and 10-11 because of several complications:

1. Part of the increase in demand may show up in terms of *higher prices,* not in terms of larger real national product.
2. *Taxes* and *imports* act as additional leakages from the spending stream. These additional leakages depress the size of the multiplier, even in a world in which prices are stable.

The second point will be explored in Chapter 11. In the present chapter, we will explain the first. However, before we do so, we should bring together the analysis of this chapter—which has thus far been based on the assumption that prices are stable—and the approach of Chapter 9, in which prices were permitted to move.

BRINGING TOGETHER THE TWO APPROACHES

In Figure 10-12, panel *a* repeats the output-expenditures approach of this chapter. Panel *b,* which is based on the aggregate demand and aggregate supply curves of Chapter 9, is drawn directly below it. The two diagrams may be stacked vertically in this manner, because real national product is measured on the horizontal axis of each diagram.

Observe that aggregate demand is shown in both panels. However, the aggregate demand functions in the two panels are quite different. Panel *a* shows how real *output and income* (measured on the horizontal axis) affect the quantity of goods and services demanded (on the vertical axis). Panel *b* shows how the average *price level* (on the vertical axis) affects the quantity of goods and services demanded (on the horizontal axis). This idea—that quantity demanded can depend on more than one thing—is not new. In the analysis of an individual market in Chapter 4, for example, we saw how the quantity of apples demanded was affected by the price of apples,

FIGURE 10-12

Bringing together the two approaches

Panel *a* shows the basic Keynesian approach, in which it is assumed that prices are sticky. Prices remain constant so long as the aggregate supply curve in panel *b* is horizontal, as shown between *E* and *H*.

In panel *a*, the slope of the AD function shows how spending increases when output and income increase. In panel *b*, the slope of the AD function shows how an increase in the price level causes a decrease in the quantity of goods and services demanded.

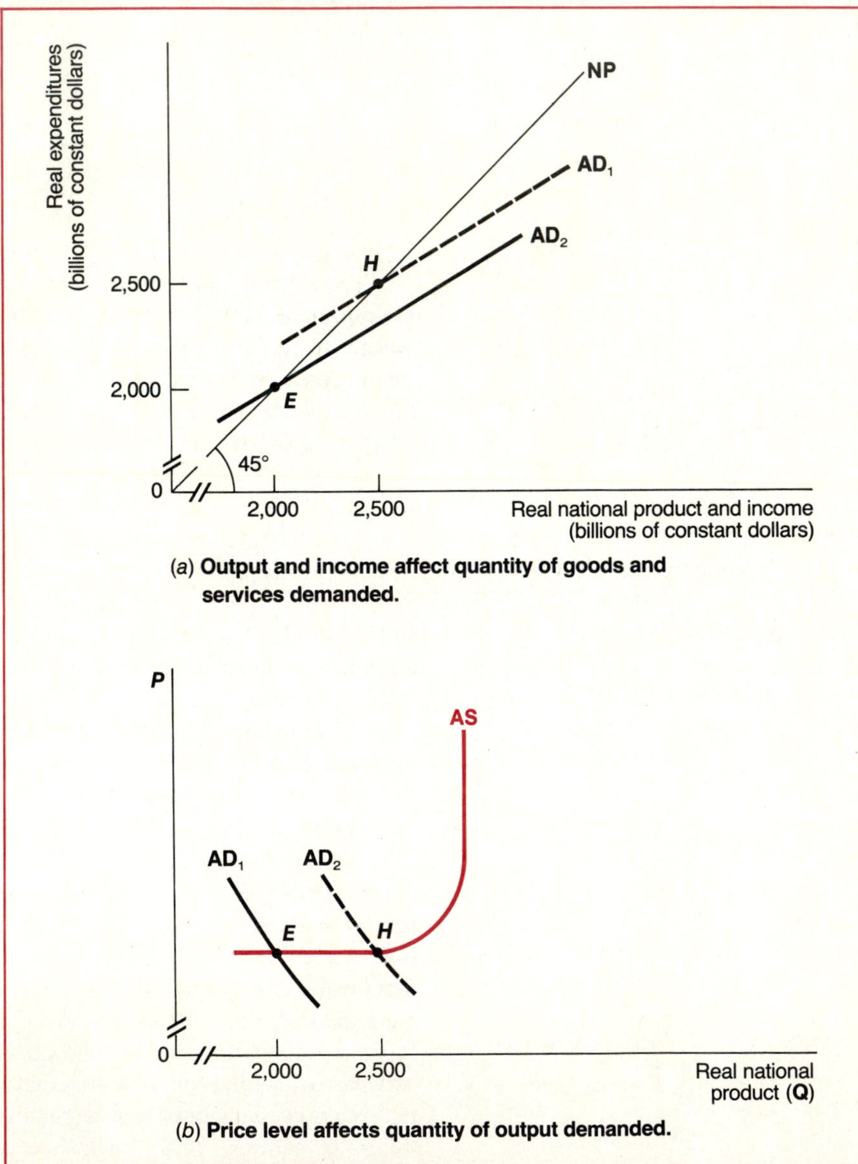

(*a*) **Output and income affect quantity of goods and services demanded.**

(*b*) **Price level affects quantity of output demanded.**

by the income of buyers, and by a number of other influences.

In the basic Keynesian theory outlined in this chapter and illustrated in panel *a,* prices are assumed to remain constant. As investment increases and aggregate demand shifts up, equilibrium moves from *E* to *H*. In panel *b,* the increase in investment also increases aggregate demand. Specifically, it shifts rightward, and equilibrium again moves from *E* to *H,* leaving the price level unchanged. So long as the economy is moving along the horizontal range of the Keynesian aggregate supply curve in panel *b,* with prices remaining stable in the face of an increase in aggregate demand, the fixed-price assumption of panel *a* is valid. We don't need to worry about price changes. It is quite acceptable to show just the upper figure, and skip the lower one, as we have done in the previous diagrams in this chapter.

INFLATION AND THE MULTIPLIER: AN UPWARD-SLOPING AGGREGATE SUPPLY CURVE

However, once we get to the range where the aggregate supply function begins to slope upward, we can no longer ignore price changes. This is illustrated in Figure 10-13. Points *E* and *H* in the upper panel repeat the multiplier analysis in a fixed-price situation. An increase of \$100 billion in investment demand shifts the aggregate demand function up by \$100 billion, from AD_1 to AD_2. This causes an eventual increase of \$500 billion in the quantity of goods and services demanded and in equilibrium national product, as shown by the movement of the equilibrium from *E* to *H*. This increase of \$500 billion in the quantity of goods and services demanded shows up as a \$500 billion rightward shift in the aggregate demand function in the lower panel, from AD_1 to AD_2.

Now, suppose that there is a further increase of \$100 billion in investment demand. Again, the initial investment spending will lead to various rounds of consumer spending. This multiplier process will mean that there will be another rightward shift of the aggregate demand function by \$500 billion in the lower panel, from AD_2 to AD_3. Note that, in this panel, distance $HK = EH =$ \$500 billion. *If* prices were to remain stable, the new equilibrium would be at *K*.

But *K* is not a possible equilibrium because the economy cannot produce that much. As the economy approaches capacity, the aggregate supply function slopes upward. In the face of increasing demand, prices begin to rise. The new equilibrium in the lower panel is at *J,* where the aggregate demand and aggregate supply curves intersect.

Note that, in this move from *H* to *J,* real national product increases by only \$300 billion, from \$2,500 billion to \$2,800 billion. Therefore, the multiplier is no longer 5; it is now only 3. A \$100 billion increase in investment has caused an equilibrium increase in output of only \$300 billion.

How can this be? Why does equilibrium output increase by only \$300 billion? The answer: Part of the increase in demand goes into higher prices. In other words, even though money is being spent at each round of the multiplier, only part of the expenditure results in the production of additional goods and services. Some of it just covers the higher prices that buyers have to pay.

We conclude that, in this range where the aggregate supply curve slopes upward to the right, a formula such as equation 10-9 gives only the *rightward* shift of the aggregate demand function in the lower panel. The increase in real national product is less; point *J* is to the left of point *K*.

This conclusion can be carried back up to the top panel. The shift from AD_2 to AD_3 shows what would happen if prices were to remain stable. But, as part of the spending is dissipated in paying higher prices, there is a drag on the real quantities of goods and services being bought. This effect of inflation brings the aggregate demand curve in the top panel down to AD_4, where the equilibrium at *J* is consistent with the equilibrium in the lower panel. To understand this inflationary environment, the lower panel is essential. Without considering the effects in the lower panel, we cannot tell how much real purchases will be reduced by inflation, and we cannot find the equilibrium at *J*.

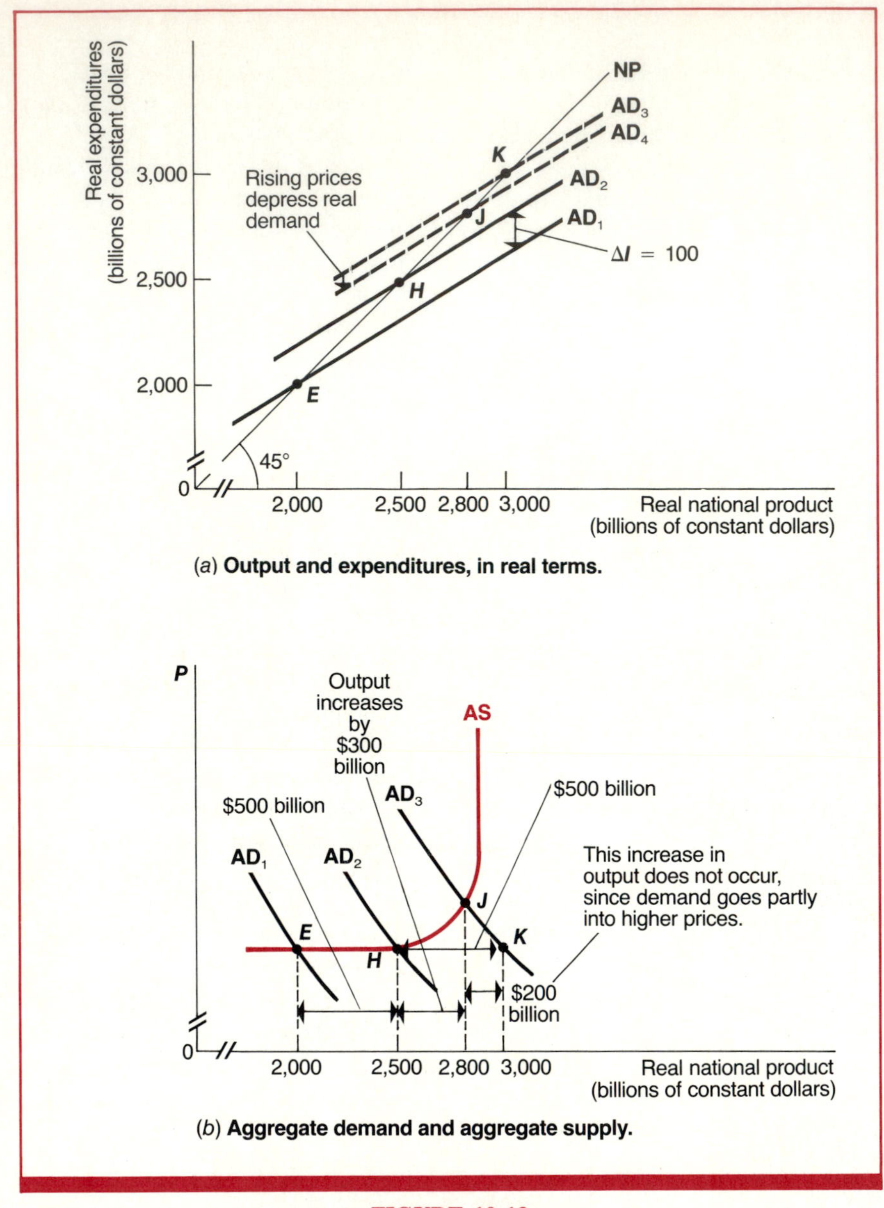

FIGURE 10-13

Inflation reduces the size of the multiplier

Consider first a situation where prices are stable, beginning from equilibrium *E*. A $100 billion increase in investment demand results in an eventual increase of $500 billion in the total quantity of goods and services demanded because of the multiplier process. This is illustrated by the movement of the equilibrium from *E* to *H* in the upper panel. The increase of $500 billion in the quantity of goods and services demanded shows up as a $500 billion rightward shift in the aggregate demand function in the lower panel, from AD_1 to AD_2.

Once the economy enters the upward-sloping section of aggregate supply, a further increase of $100 billion in investment demand will not cause a full increase of $500 billion in real output. Even though the aggregate demand function shifts to the right by a full $500 billion (from AD_2 to AD_3), real national product increases only by $300 billion. Some of the increase in aggregate demand is reflected in higher prices, rather than larger output.

KEY POINTS

1. During the Great Depression of the 1930s, British economist John Maynard Keynes put forward a new theory of unemployment, arguing that:

(*a*) A market economy can come to rest at an equilibrium with large-scale unemployment.

(*b*) The cause of unemployment is insufficient aggregate demand.

(*c*) The most straightforward cure for unemployment is an increase in government spending. (This point will be explained in Chapter 11.)

2. The components of aggregate demand are:

(*a*) Personal consumption expenditures

(*b*) Investment demand, that is, the demand for buildings, equipment, and additional inventories

(*c*) Government purchases of goods and services

(*d*) Net exports (that is, exports minus imports)

3. In this chapter, we analyzed an unrealistic but simple economy, one with only two components of demand, namely, consumption and investment.

4. Consumption expenditures depend primarily on disposable personal income. As incomes rise, people consume more. The change in consumption, as a fraction of a change in disposable income, is known as the *marginal propensity to consume* (MPC).

5. Equilibrium national product occurs where the aggregate demand function cuts the 45° line. A larger national product would be unsustainable, since demand would fall short of production and unsold goods would pile up in inventories.

6. In Keynesian theory, equilibrium national product may be less than the full-employment quantity.

7. There are several alternative ways of stating the condition for equilibrium. It exists when:

(*a*) Aggregate demand and national product are equal, that is, where the aggregate demand function cuts the 45° national product line (Figure 10-5).

(*b*) Inventories are at their desired level, that is, when actual investment equals desired investment and there is no undesired buildup or reduction in inventories (Figure 10-5).

(*c*) Desired investment and saving are equal (Figure 10-6).

8. An increase in investment demand raises national product and income. This induces people to consume more. In the simple economy, national product increases by the rise in investment times the multiplier, where the multiplier is:

$$\text{Multiplier} = \frac{1}{1 - \text{MPC}}$$

Because saving equals income minus consumption,

$$\text{Marginal propensity to save} = 1 - \text{MPC}$$

Thus, the multiplier in the simple economy may alternatively be expressed as:

$$\text{Multiplier} = \frac{1}{\text{MPS}}$$

9. In practice, the multiplier will be smaller than indicated by these two equations because of several complications:

(*a*) Part of the increase in demand may show up in terms of *higher prices,* not in terms of larger real national product.

(*b*) *Taxes* and *imports* act as additional leakages from the spending stream. (This point will be explained in Chapter 11.)

10. Once the economy is in a range where the aggregate supply function slopes upward to the right, only part of any increase in aggregate demand shows up in terms of larger output. Part goes to pay higher prices. In such circumstances, the formulas shown in point 8 represent the rightward shift of the aggregate demand function (for example, from *H* to *K* in Figure 10-13). The increase in real output is less than this rightward shift in demand.

KEY CONCEPTS

consumption function
saving function
break-even point where consumption equals income
45° line
marginal propensity to consume (MPC)
marginal propensity to save (MPS)
investment demand—or desired investment or planned investment (I^*)
actual investment (I)

undesired inventory accumulation
undesired decrease in inventories
unemployment equilibrium
saving-investment approach
circular flow of spending
leakage
injection
output-expenditures approach
leakages-injections approach
multiplier

PROBLEMS

10-1. Draw a diagram showing the consumption function, the aggregate demand function, and the 45° line. What quantity of national product represents the equilibrium? Explain why a larger national product would be unsustainable and would lead to a contraction of production. Explain also why national product will expand if it initially is smaller than the equilibrium quantity.

10-2. The consumption function and the saving function are two alternative ways of presenting the same information. The text explains how the saving function can be derived from the consumption function. Show how the consumption function can be derived from the saving function.

10-3. Draw a diagram showing investment demand and the saving function. What is the equilibrium national product? Explain why a higher national product would be unsustainable. Explain also why national product will expand, if it initially is smaller than the equilibrium quantity.

10-4. The mathematical formula for the multiplier shows that a high MPC causes a high multiplier. By tracing the effects of $100 billion in additional investment through a number of rounds of spending, show that the multiplier is higher with an MPC of 0.9 than with an MPC of 0.8. (Use Table 10-3 to start.)

10-5. On a sheet of graph paper, draw a diagram similar to Figure 10-10. (Make the diagram *large* so that you will be able to see what you are doing.) Following Figure 10-10, show the multiplier effects of a $100 billion increase in investment demand when the MPS = 0.2. Now suppose that the MPS increases to 0.5. In color, draw in a new savings function, going through the same initial equilibrium *E*. When investment demand increases by $100 billion, what now is the new equilibrium NP? What is the size of the multiplier now?

10-6. What is the difference between actual investment (*I*) and desired investment (*I**)? What happens if desired investment is greater than actual investment? Why?

10-7. Consider an economy with the relationship between consumption and income shown in the table below.

(*a*) Fill in the blanks in the Saving column.

(*b*) Investment demand is originally $200 billion. Fill in the blanks in the Initial Aggregate Demand column.

(*c*) What is the equilibrium national product?

(*d*) Now assume that investment demand rises to $300 billion. What does this do to aggregate demand? (Fill in the Later Aggregate Demand column.) What is equilibrium national product now?

(*e*) Comparing your answers to *(c)* and *(d)*, find the multiplier.

Disposable income = NP (billions)	Consumption (billions)	Saving (billions)	Initial aggregate demand (billions)	Later aggregate demand (billions)
$1,000	$ 900	—	—	—
1,100	975	—	—	—
1,200	1,050	—	—	—
1,300	1,125	—	—	—
1,400	1,200	—	—	—
1,500	1,275	—	—	—
1,600	1,350	—	—	—
1,700	1,425	—	—	—
1,800	1,500	—	—	—

10-8. Figure 10-13 showed how the multiplier becomes smaller when the economy enters the upward-sloping section of the aggregate supply curve. Suppose that the economy was initially in the vertical, "classical" range of the aggregate supply curve. Now suppose that businesses spend $100 billion more on plant and equipment. What happens to equilibrium real national product as a result? How large is the multiplier in this case?

APPENDIX 10-A

CLASSICAL ECONOMICS:

EQUILIBRIUM WITH FULL EMPLOYMENT

Chapter 9 described the main difference between Keynesian and classical theories. Although classical economists believed that equilibrium occurs at full employment, they conceded that large-scale unemployment could occur temporarily, as a result of disturbances. However, market forces would move the economy back toward its equilibrium with full employment.

This chapter has explained the revolutionary idea in Keynes' *General Theory*—that there could be an equilibrium with large-scale unemployment. The purpose of this appendix is to look in more detail at the contrasting classical argument.

The main point in the classical case was explained in Chapter 9, especially Figure 9-3. In the face of large-scale unemployment, prices fall, increasing the real quantity of money. Because households have more purchasing power at their disposal, they buy more goods and services. Prices continue to fall, and people consequently continue to buy more, until full employment is reached.

SAVING AND INVESTMENT

There was, however, also a second strand to the classical theory of full employment which is related to the Keynesian theory of saving and investment described in this chapter. Like Keynes, classical economists recognized that desired investment and saving would have to be equal for the economy to be in equilibrium. But, unlike Keynes (Figure 10-6), they did not believe that real national product would have to decrease if investment demand was less than saving.

Rather, classical economists argued that the price mechanism will bring desired investment and saving into equilibrium at full employment. The key price that does this is the interest rate. The interest rate is the reward received by savers, and it is also the price corporations and others pay for borrowed funds with which they construct buildings or engage in other investment projects.

Suppose that investment demand falls short of saving when the economy is at full employment. What happens? According to classical economists, savers have large quantities of funds. In their eagerness to acquire bonds and other earning assets, they are willing to settle for a lower interest rate. As the interest rate falls, businesses find it cheaper to borrow. They are encouraged to undertake more investment projects; in other words, desired investment increases. The rate of interest continues to drop until desired investment and saving are brought into equality, as illustrated in Figure 10-14. The full-employment equilibrium (E) occurs at the intersection of the investment demand curve (I^*) and the curve showing saving when the economy is at full employment (S_{FE}). An increase in the desire to save—that is, a rightward shift in (S_{FE})—causes a fall in the rate of interest, which in turn causes an increase in the quantity of investment. Investment demand doesn't fall short of saving after all. Full employment is maintained.

In other words, classical economists argued that there was something wrong with Keynes' plumbing. Savings do not simply leak from the economy, as they did back in Figure 10-8. Rather, an increase in saving causes a fall in interest rates, which in turn causes an increase in investment. Thus, the financial markets, where savers supply funds to investors, provide a pipe which connects saving and investment in Figure 10-8—that is, a pipe which brings saving leakages back into the spending stream in the form of investment demand.

The Keynesian Rebuttal

In response, Keynes said that classical economists were in error in counting on the interest rate to fall enough to equate saving and investment at full employment. In his *General Theory* (p. 182), he argued that there is ''no guarantee'' that the full-employment saving curve intersects investment demand ''anywhere at all'' when the interest rate is positive. This possibility is illustrated in Figure 10-15. Here, no full-employment equilibrium exists, since I^* and S_{FE} intersect at a negative interest rate. But it is not possible for interest rates to be negative, since people would be unwilling to lend money; they would simply lock it up in a bank vault instead. In fact, Keynes went one step further and argued that the minimum interest rate is not zero but is some small positive rate, shown as i_{min} in Figure 10-15.

Now, if the economy were temporarily at full employment, saving would exceed desired investment by quantity BA.[4] Being at a minimum, the interest rate cannot fall to bring saving and investment demand into equilibrium. Something has to give. According to Keynes, what will give will be output and employment. As leakages into saving exceed injections of investment spending, national product and employment will decrease. With smaller incomes, people will save less; the saving function in Figure 10-15 will shift to the left, all the way to S_2. Now there is an equilibrium because saving and investment demand are equal. However, there is large-scale unemployment at this equilibrium.

Incidentally, Figure 10-15 is based on the only diagram in Keynes' *General Theory,* on p. 180. Clearly, Keynes felt strongly about the errors of classical economists who argued that a change in the interest rate would bring saving and investment into equality at full employment.

The differences between Keynes and the classical economists may be summarized. Classical economists argued that *an increase in saving,* by depressing interest rates, *causes an increase in investment* and thus stimulates growth (Figure 10-14). Saving is a benefit to society; it makes us better off in the future. In contrast, Keynes argued that this isn't necessarily so. Saving may be antisocial. It may decrease national product and employment, a possibility we shall explore in Appendix 10-B. Furthermore, Keynes believed that it is more correct to argue that *a change in investment demand causes a change in saving* (Figure 10-10) than to argue that a change in the desire to save causes a change in investment. Thus, said Keynes, classical economists had gotten the relationship between saving and investment backwards. Because of their confusion, they had overlooked the possibility that the economy might reach an equilibrium with a high rate of unemployment.

In rebuttal, classical economists fell back on their basic argument as to why the economy would reach equilibrium at full employment—an argument already explained in Chapter 9. To recapitulate, they said that prices would fall in the event of large-scale unemployment, when aggregate demand falls far short of the productive capacity of the economy. A fall in the general level of prices would increase the purchasing power of money; the real quantity of money would rise. As a result, people would buy a greater quantity of goods and services. This process would continue until full employment was restored. Because this rebuttal was contained

[4]Keynes' case did not depend on i_{min} being above zero. It could be at zero and still leave a gap between full-employment saving and investment demand, although this gap would be smaller (*GH* rather than *BA*).

FIGURE 10-14

Saving and investment in classical theory

The S_{FE} curve shows how much will be saved at various interest rates in a fully employed economy. The I^* curve shows how much businesses will borrow to finance investment projects at various interest rates. Classical economists argued that if saving exceeds investment demand, the interest rate will fall until saving and investment are equalized—without large-scale unemployment.

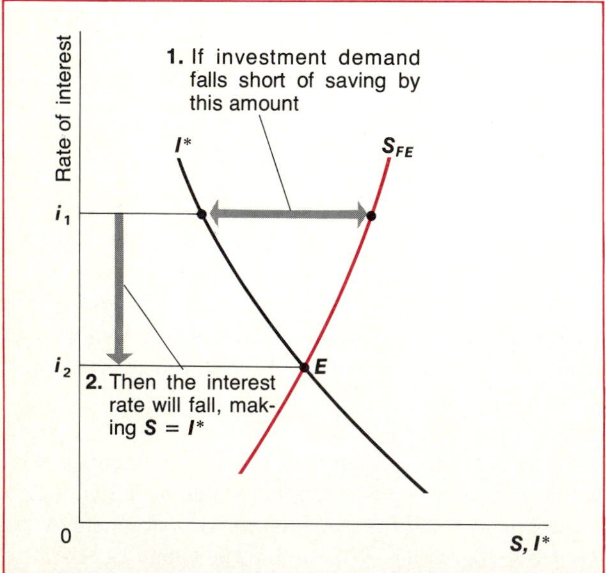

in an article by Cambridge professor A. C. Pigou, the idea that an increase in the real quantity of money will cause an increase in purchases is sometimes known as the *Pigou effect*. Alternatively, it is known as the *real balance effect* because it is the proposition that people will buy more when their real money balances increase.

In summary, classical economists counted on price flexibility to help to restore full employment in *two* ways. First, there was general price flexibility. A fall in the average price of goods and services would increase the purchasing power of money, and thus encourage buying. Second, there was the flexibility of a specific price, namely, the rate of interest. A fall in the interest rate would bring investment demand into line with full-employment saving (Figure 10-14).

SAY'S LAW

There was also a third, less precise proposition in classical theory, known as *Say's law,* after nineteenth-century economist J. B. Say.

Say put forward the disarmingly simple idea that *supply creates its own demand*. When people sell a good or service, they do so in order to be able to buy some other good or service. The very act of supplying one good or service thus creates a demand for some other good or service. There can be too much supply for some specific product, such as shoes, but if so, there is too much demand and not enough supply of some other product. Surpluses and shortages can exist in an *individual* market. Nevertheless, for the economy as a whole,

FIGURE 10-15
The Keynesian rebuttal
Keynes argued that there was something wrong with the classical approach to saving and investment illustrated in Figure 10-14. Specifically, Keynes said that the full-employment saving curve (S_{FE}) might intersect the investment demand curve I^* at an interest rate below the minimum (i_{min}) which can occur in financial markets. In this case, the gap AB between saving and investment demand cannot be closed by a fall in the interest rate. It is closed by a fall in output, causing the saving function to shift to S_2.

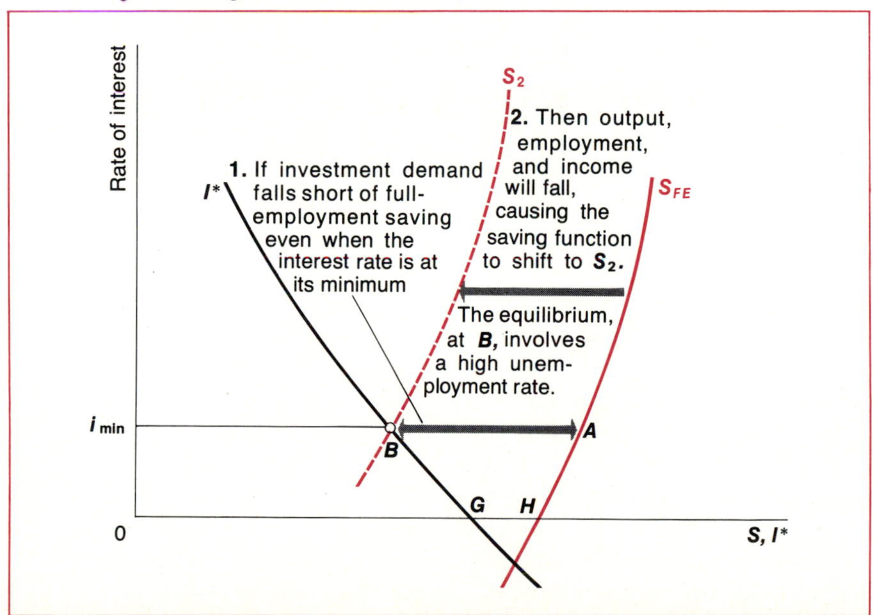

there cannot be an excess of supply over demand.

Keynes put his finger on the problem with Say's simple idea. It is true that, when people create goods and services, they earn income. The income from the production of all the goods and services is sufficient to buy those goods and services. The problem is that people do not spend all their incomes; they save part. Therefore, demand can fall short of production. This shortfall may be offset by investment demand. However, if investment demand is less than full-employment saving, there will be an overall inadequacy of demand and unemployment will result.

Therefore, Say's simple idea is a weak foundation on which to build the idea that the economy will provide full employment. Say's law simply assumes full employment. It provides no mechanism whereby aggregate demand can be brought into equality with aggregate supply at the full-employment quantity of output.

Furthermore, Say's law is inconsistent with the main body of classical economics. According to Say's law, there can be no excess of supply over demand, *regardless of the general price level*. But, according to the more sensible version of classical theory presented in Chapter 9, supply can exceed demand if the average level of prices is above equilibrium (for example, at P_1 back in Figure 9-3).[5]

Although Say's law has been prominent in economic literature, it should not be considered the main idea in classical macroeconomics. In particular, it does not constitute the central pillar of the classical proposition that full employment will exist in equilibrium. Rather, this proposition depends on the two points explained earlier: (1) the increase in the quantity of goods and services demanded that results when the general level of prices falls (the demand curve in Figure 9-3 slopes downward to the right); and (2) the increase in investment demand, and the decrease in saving, caused by a fall in the interest rate (Figure 10-14).

[5]The inconsistency between Say's law and the main body of classical economics is explained in detail in Don Patinkin, *Money, Interest, and Prices* (New York: Harper & Row, 2d ed., 1965).

APPENDIX 10-B

CHANGES IN THE DESIRE TO SAVE:

THE PARADOX OF THRIFT

Keynesian theory explains how equilibrium national product (NP) changes if there is a change in investment demand—as we saw in Figure 10-10. Now let's consider what happens if the saving function shifts upward—or, what amounts to the same thing, if the consumption function shifts downward.

Suppose that people become more thrifty; they save more out of any given income. This causes the saving function to shift upward from S_1 to S_2 in Figure 10-16. Consider what happens at the initial national product A as a result. The leakage into saving (AG) now exceeds the injections in the form of investment demand (AE_1). Aggregate demand falls short of NP and unsold goods pile up. Orders are cancelled, and NP decreases to its new equilibrium, B. In this simple case where investment demand is horizontal, an increase in the desire to save has no effect on the equilibrium quantity of saving or investment. The amount saved and invested is the same at BE_2 as it was originally at AE_1. The only effect is a decrease in output.

However, that is not the worst of it. In order to make the analysis simple, the demand for investment so far has been assumed constant. Clearly that need not be the case. Desired investment can change. Specifically, investment demand may increase as NP increases. As more and more goods are produced, there is a need for more machines and factories. In this case, investment demand is an upward sloping function, as shown in Figure 10-17.

Now a shift in the saving function becomes particularly potent. An increase in the desire to save, moving the saving function from S_1 to S_2, causes a very large decrease in equilibrium national product from A to B. Furthermore, the effects on the equilibrium amount of saving and investment are paradoxical. *As a result of the upward shift in the saving function,* observe that *the amount of saving and investment in equilibrium falls,* from distance AE_1 to BE_2. This is the ***paradox of thrift.***

The *paradox of thrift* occurs when an *increase* in the desire to save (a shift from S_1 to S_2) causes a *fall* in actual saving (from AE_1 to BE_2).

What happens is this: Beginning at the initial equilibrium E_1, an increase in the desire to save causes an increase in leakages from the spending stream. Aggregate demand and NP fall. As they fall, businesses decide that they need fewer machines and factories. There is a decline in the quantity of investment as the economy moves to the left along the investment demand function. Equilibrium is restored only when national product has fallen enough so that people are content to save an amount which is no more than the diminished quantity of investment demand, at point E_2. Because the quantity of investment decreases as national product falls, and because national product must fall by enough to bring saving into equality with investment, saving declines in the move from E_1 to E_2.[6]

[6]When investment changes with national product, the multiplier becomes larger; national product changes more as a result of any vertical shift in the investment or saving function. Thus, for example, national product changes more in Figure 10-17 than in Figure 10-16.

The reason is that, as the economy moves to the left from E_1 (in response to the shift of saving from S_1 to S_2), the gap between S and I^* closes more slowly. (The rate at which it closes depends on the difference between the slopes of the S and I^* functions.) In other words, closing a vertical gap between S and I^* requires a greater change in NP; thus, the multiplier is greater. It can be shown that the multiplier in this case is:

$$\text{Multiplier} = \frac{1}{\text{MPS} - \text{MPI}} \tag{10-14}$$

where MPI, the *marginal propensity to invest,* is the change in investment demand divided by the change in national product. (It is the slope of the I^* function.)

Thus, if the MPS = 0.20, as before, while MPI = 0.15, then the multiplier is 20.

FIGURE 10-16
An increase in the desire to save
An increase in the desire to save does not increase equilibrium saving. Instead, it results in a decrease in output.

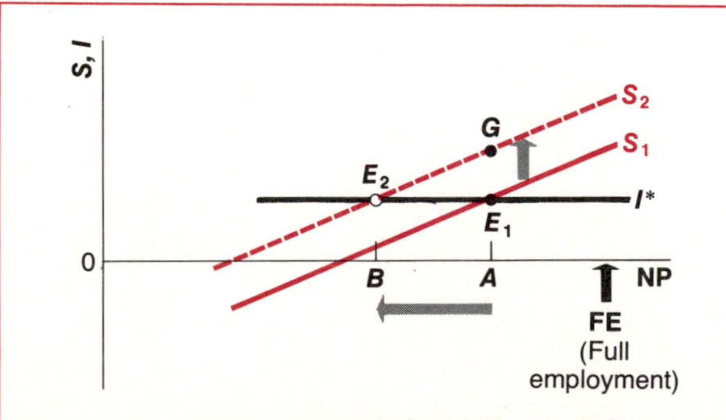

FIGURE 10-17
The paradox of thrift
With the investment demand function sloping upward to the right, an increase in the desire to save results in a movement from E_1 to E_2. In equilibrium, the quantity of saving decreases, since E_2 is not as high as E_1.

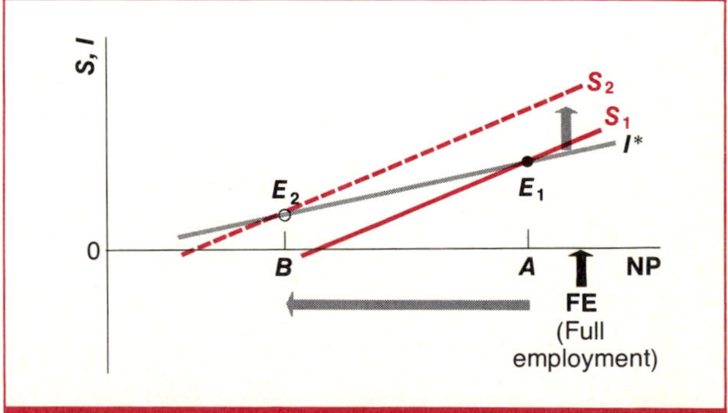

The paradox of thrift is an illustration of one important way in which macroeconomic conclusions—covering the economy as a whole—may be quite different from conclusions for a single individual. If a single individual becomes more thrifty—saving more out of any level of income—then he or she will end up with more saving. But we cannot conclude that, just because this is true for a single individual, it will also be true for the economy as a whole. Such a conclusion would be an illustration of the ***fallacy of composition.*** Figure 10-17 shows a case in which the results for the society as a whole are exactly the opposite from the results for an individual: For the society, a stronger effort to save means less actual saving.

The *fallacy of composition* is the unwarranted conclusion that a proposition which is true for a single individual or single market is necessarily true for the economy as a whole.

The paradox of thrift grows out of Keynesian theory, whose underlying assumptions should be reemphasized at this point. The Keynesian analysis *deals with the situation in which there is large-scale unemployment and prices are downwardly rigid; changes in aggregate demand lead to changes in output and no change in prices.* In short, changes in aggregate demand cause the economy to move along the horizontal section of the aggregate supply function. If, on the other hand, the economy is experiencing booming demand conditions, and is in the inflationary vertical range of the aggregate supply function, the Keynesian analysis of thrift must be completely reversed. The macroeconomic problem is *reduced* by an increase in the desire to save, that is, by a downward shift in the consumption function. As consumption and aggregate demand fall, inflationary forces are weakened. Furthermore, since the economy is at full employment and is therefore fully utilizing its resources, a decrease in consumption releases resources from the production of consumer goods. These resources become available for the production of capital goods. Thus, an increase in the willingness to save indeed adds to the amount of factories and machinery produced; the real saving of society is augmented. ***In a world of inflationary excess demand, the paradox of thrift does not hold.***

PART THREE

AGGREGATE DEMAND POLICIES

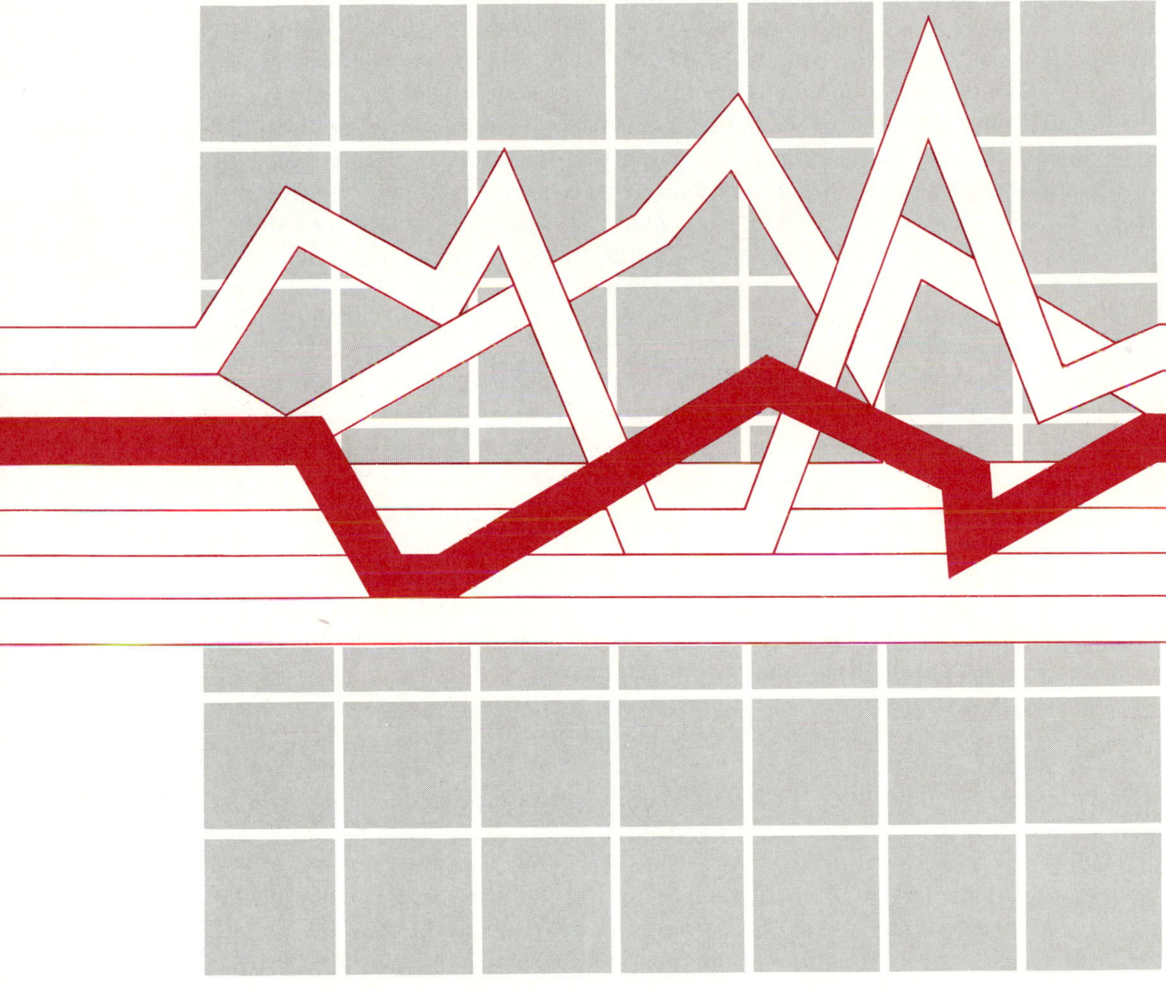

Part 2 has laid the basis for macroeconomics. Chapter 7 explained how we measure national product and changes in the average level of prices. Chapter 8 surveyed the macroeconomic history of recent decades, paying particular attention to fluctuations in economic activity. Chapters 9 and 10 focused on aggregate demand and aggregate supply.

One important message came out of those last two chapters: Recessions and depressions are caused by a fall in aggregate demand. Inflation is caused by too

much aggregate demand. To combat the problems of unemployment and inflation, governments have taken steps to change aggregate demand.

As noted briefly in Chapter 9, the authorities have two policy tools to affect aggregate demand: fiscal policy and monetary policy. Part 3 will explain how these policies work.

Fiscal policy involves changes in (1) *government spending* and (2) *tax rates*. The fine points are explained in Chapter 11, but the main way in which fiscal policies affect aggregate demand and employment may be stated quite simply. If, during a depression, government increases its *spending* for such projects as roads or dams, it thereby increases the demand for cement, steel, and other materials. Some people are put to work producing cement and steel, and others start to work directly on the construction of the roads or dams. As a result, the unemployment rate falls. The *taxation* side of fiscal policy works more indirectly. When the government cuts taxes, people have more income left after taxes, and they tend as a consequence to buy more—more clothing, more washing machines, more vacations, and more of a whole host of goods and services. Again, people will be put to work producing clothing, washing machines, and all the other goods and services that are being bought.

Monetary policy involves changes in the rate of growth of the money stock held by the public. In our economy, there are two types of money. Most obviously, the dollar bills and coins which you have in your pocket are money; you can use them to buy lunch or go to a movie. But many purchases are not paid for with "pocket money." In fact, payment by check is much more important than payment with currency: Most large purchases are made by check. Because checks are commonly used to make purchases, the balances which people hold in their checking accounts are counted as part of the money stock. Because much of our money is held in the form of checking accounts in banks, Chapter 12 explores how the banking system operates, as a background for studying monetary policy.

Chapter 13 presents a detailed explanation of how monetary policy works. Once again, it is possible to summarize the general idea behind monetary policy. When individuals and businesses have more money in the form either of cash or balances in their checking accounts, they are encouraged to spend more. By taking steps to increase the quantity of money, the authorities can encourage spending.

Much macroeconomic theory dates from the Great Depression of the 1930s, when aggregate demand was too low and many workers were consequently unemployed. But problems can also exist on the opposite side. Aggregate demand can get too high. If people try to buy more than the limited available supply of goods, the result is inflation. Again, aggregate demand tools may be used by the authorities. Fiscal and monetary policies can be adjusted, this time to restrain aggregate demand.

Part 3 will explain the basic theory of how fiscal and monetary policies can be used to manage aggregate demand. This is an important topic in macroeconomics. By using aggregate demand tools, we have achieved a much better economic performance during the past four decades than in the years between the two world wars. But we repeat our warning in Chapter 2: *Theory necessarily involves simplification*.

And, when it is presented to beginning students, theory must be especially simple. Thus, the theoretical "road map" of Part 3 has been drawn with the bumps and potholes removed. But bumps and potholes exist.

The bumps and potholes will provide the topics for Part 4 (Chapters 14 to 19). In Part 4, we will look at the real-world complications that make demand management so difficult. We will search for the reasons for a disturbing fact: While the performance of the economy in recent decades has been good by historical standards, it has not become better and better. In particular, the recessions of 1973–1975 and 1981–1982 were more severe than any of the recessions of the 1940s, 1950s, or 1960s. We clearly have not solved the problem of economic instability.

In searching for the reasons for recent macroeconomic problems, we will broaden our horizon. We will go beyond the problems of demand management, with which economists were preoccupied in the decades immediately following the Great Depression. We will also look in more detail at the other side of the picture—aggregate supply. How do producers respond to changes in the average level of prices? What is the capacity of our economy to produce goods and services? Why does capacity grow more rapidly during some periods than it does during others?

But first, we will look at the fundamentals of demand management.

CHAPTER 11

FISCAL POLICY

Fiscal policy has to be put on constant . . . alert. . . . The management of prosperity is a full-time job.

WALTER W. HELLER[1]

In his *General Theory,* Keynes argued that chronic depression might be the outcome of a policy of laissez faire. The market does not ensure full employment. Furthermore, even if the economy were to reach a high rate of employment, this happy situation would probably not last. The market economy tends to be unstable, either slowing down into a recession or speeding up into an inflationary boom.

However, in spite of the defects of the market economy, Keynes was not pessimistic. We are not, said he, inevitably condemned to suffer the economic and social costs of high unemployment or the disruptive effects of inflation. The government can deal with the root causes of these problems. Unemployment is the result of too little aggregate demand: People are thrown out of work when nobody buys the goods they can produce. Inflation is the result of too much aggregate demand: Prices rise when too much demand is chasing the available supply of goods. By taking steps to increase aggregate demand during a recession or depression, the government can increase the amount of national product and put the unemployed back to work. By restraining aggregate demand during periods of inflation, the government can slow down the rate of increase of prices.

This, then, was the policy message of the Keynesian revolution: The government has the ability—*and the responsibility*—to manage aggregate demand and thus ensure a continuing prosperity without inflation. The government can affect aggregate demand with ***fiscal policies***—that is, by changes in government spending or tax rates. The principal purpose of this chapter is to explain how the government can use fiscal policies to manage aggregate demand.

GOVERNMENT PURCHASES

In the bare-bones economy discussed in Chapter 10, the government was completely ignored; there was no government spending or taxation. In order to proceed in simple steps, we will first introduce the effects of government spending and ignore taxes until a later point.

Government expenditures for goods and services are a component of aggregate demand. People are employed building roads, teaching school, and maintaining parks. The roads, educational services, and upkeep of parks are included in national product. When government demand is added to the bare-bones economy of Chapter 10, then:

Aggregate demand (AD) =
consumption expenditures (*C*)
+ investment demand (*I)**
+ government purchases of goods and services (*G*)

Thus, government purchases of goods and services (*G*) can be added vertically to consumption and investment demand to get the aggregate demand line shown in Figure 11-1. Note that when government purchases of $100 billion are added vertically to consumer demand plus investment demand, the equilibrium moves from point *D* to point *E*. The increase in national product, measured by the $500 billion distance *AB* on the horizontal axis, is a multiple of the $100 billion of government spending. *The multiplier process works on government spending* just as it worked on investment expenditures.

[1]*New Dimensions in Political Economy* (New York: W. W. Norton, 1967), p. 69. Professor Heller, of the University of Minnesota, was the chairman of President Kennedy's Council of Economic Advisers.

For example, when workers receive income from building roads, a whole series of spending and respending decisions is set in motion. The workers spend most of their wages for consumer goods such as clothing and cars. Additional employees are hired by the clothing and automobile industries, and these employees also spend more as a consequence of their rising incomes. The process is similar to that illustrated earlier for the investment multiplier in Table 10-3.

In spite of government spending, aggregate demand in our economy may nevertheless still fall short of what is needed for full employment. Such was the case during the Depression of the 1930s. There were some government expenditures, yet the unemployment rate was nevertheless very high—more than 15% of the labor force. This situation is illustrated in Figure 11-2, where equilibrium E is far to the left of the full-employment national product.

FIGURE 11-1
The addition of government spending
Government spending is added vertically to consumption and investment demand in order to get aggregate demand: AD = $C + I^* + G$. Observe that the multiplier process works on government demand. Without government spending, the equilibrium would be at point D (as we saw in Chapter 10). With government spending, the equilibrium is at E. The increase in national product (AB = \$500 billion) is a multiple of the \$100 billion of government spending. As people's incomes rise, they move along the consumption function, consuming \$400 billion more.

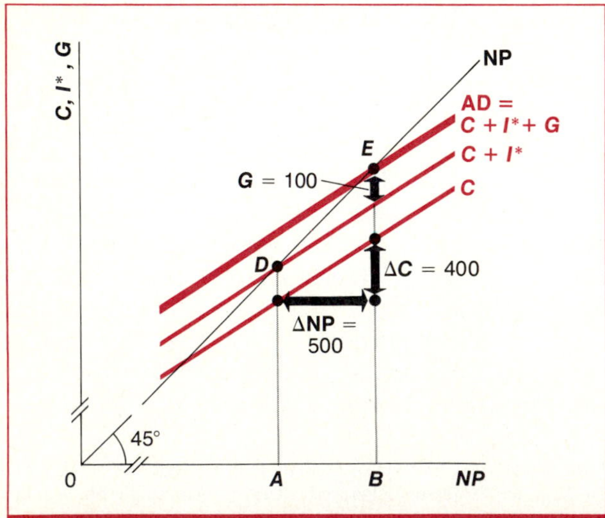

In order to get to full employment, the government should spend more. The question is, how much more? Observe that at the full-employment quantity of national product (F), the aggregate demand function (AD_1) lies below the 45° line. This shortfall of aggregate demand below the 45° line—distance HJ—is known as the ***recessionary gap.***

A *recessionary gap* exists when the aggregate demand function is below the 45° line at the full-employment quantity of national product. The gap is the vertical distance from the 45° line down to the aggregate demand function, measured at the full-employment quantity of national product.

The *output gap*—or *GNP gap*—is the amount by which national product falls short of the full-employment quantity. It is measured along the horizontal axis. The output gap (*BF* in Figure 11-2) is larger than the recessionary gap (*HJ*).

In order to get to full employment, the aggregate demand function must be shifted up by the amount of the recessionary gap (HJ). Thus, HJ is the amount of additional government purchases that are needed. Hence, we come to the first and most important rule of thumb for fiscal policy:

> **By increasing its purchases of goods and services by the amount of the recessionary gap, the government can eliminate the gap and move the economy to full employment.**

When the government increases its spending, once again the multiplier process is put to work. In Figure 11-2, note that an increase of government spending equal to the recessionary gap (HJ) causes output to increase by an even larger amount, BF, that is, by enough to eliminate the ***output gap*** and restore full employment.

One final point should be emphasized. *For the full impact of the multiplier to occur, it is essential that taxes not be increased to pay for the additional government spending.* As we shall see shortly, an increase in taxes would remove purchasing power from the hands of the

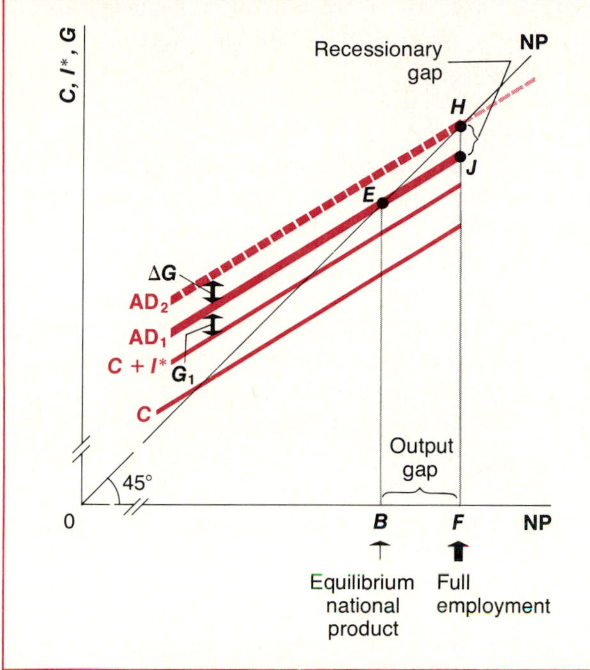

FIGURE 11-2
The recessionary gap, and fiscal policy for full employment
At initial equilibrium *E,* there is large-scale unemployment. (National product *B* falls far short of the full-employment national product at *F*.) To reach full employment, government spending (G_1) should be increased by *HJ,* the amount of the recessionary gap. This will shift aggregate demand up to AD_2 and move the economy to a full-employment equilibrium at *H*. Note that *HJ,* the recessionary gap, is the vertical distance between the aggregate demand line (AD_1) and the 45° line, measured at the full-employment national product.

public and thus act as a drag on consumption. With consumption discouraged in this way, the increase in aggregate demand would be smaller than it would be if tax rates were kept stable.

This, then, is a key policy conclusion of Keynesian economics: During a depression, when a large increase in aggregate demand is needed to restore full employment, *government spending should not be limited to the government's tax receipts*. Spending should be increased without increasing taxes. But if taxes are not raised, how is the government to finance its spending? The answer: by borrowing; that is, by adding to the public debt. Keynes argued that *deficit spending is not unsound during a recession or depression*. On the contrary, it is just what is needed to stimulate aggregate demand and reduce unemployment.

Restrictive Fiscal Policy: The Suppression of Inflationary Pressures

During the 1930s, aggregate demand was too low; the economy was depressed. At other times, aggregate demand has been too high—for example, during the Second World War and early postwar period; during the last half of the 1960s, when the government was spending large amounts on the Vietnam war; and at times during

FIGURE 11-3
The inflationary gap
At the full-employment quantity of output, aggregate demand may exceed the amount that the economy is capable of producing. (*J* is above *H*.) The excess demand will cause inflation. To restrain inflation, aggregate demand should be brought down to AD_2. This can be done by a cut in government spending (ΔG) equal to the inflationary gap.

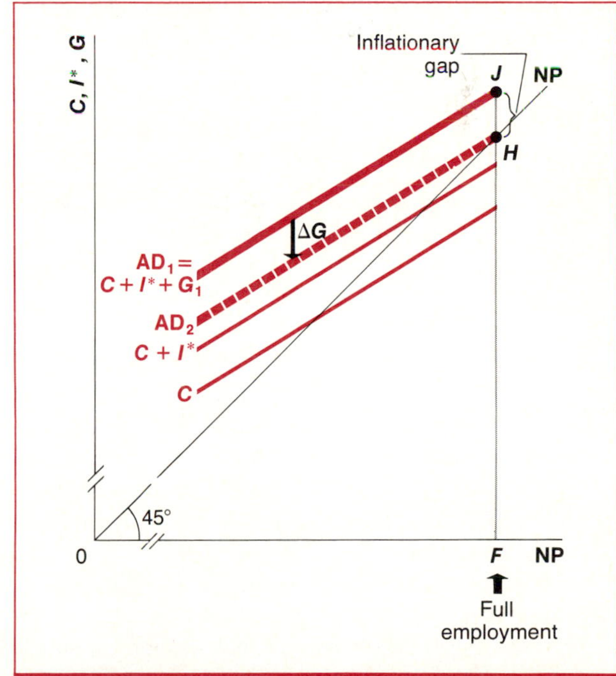

the 1970s (especially 1972–1973 and 1978–1979). In each case, the very high level of aggregate demand caused inflation.

The situation where aggregate demand is too high is illustrated in Figure 11-3. At the full-employment national product, aggregate demand AD_1 is above the 45° line. With existing productive capacity, businesses cannot fill all the orders for goods. There is an ***inflationary gap*** (*HJ*); the excess demand will cause a rise in prices.

An *inflationary gap* exists when aggregate demand is above the 45° line at the full-employment quantity of national product. It is the vertical distance from the 45° line up to the aggregate demand function, measured at the full-employment quantity of national product.

In such circumstances, the appropriate fiscal policy is a sufficient *reduction* in government spending to bring aggregate demand down to AD_2. Specifically, the second rule of thumb for fiscal policy is this:

> **During a period of inflation, excessive aggregate demand can be eliminated by a decrease in government purchases equal to the inflationary gap.**

TAXES

There is one difference between a tax collector and a taxidermist—the taxidermist leaves the hide.

Mortimer Caplin,
former Commissioner of the Internal Revenue Service

Government spending is only one side of fiscal policy—the other is taxation. Although taxes do not show up directly as a component of aggregate demand, they do affect aggregate demand indirectly. When people pay taxes, they are left with less disposable income, and they consequently consume less. Thus, the consumption component of aggregate demand is reduced.

Tax policies can also affect investment. For example, investment may be stimulated by the investment tax credit, which permits those who buy equipment to reduce their taxes by 10% of the cost of the equipment. In this chapter, we concentrate on the effect of taxes on consumption.

A Lump-Sum Tax

In order to introduce tax complications one by one, we initially make an unrealistic but very simple assumption—that taxes (*T*) are levied in a *lump sum*. That is, the government collects a fixed amount—say, $100 billion—in taxes *regardless of the size of national product*.

How does this tax affect consumption? The answer is shown in Figure 11-4. After the tax, people have $100 billion less in disposable income. As a consequence, their consumption declines. By how much? With a marginal propensity to consume (MPC) of 0.8, they consume $80 billion less. They also save $20 billion less. Thus the $100 billion fall in disposable income is reflected in a $20 billion decline in saving and a $80 billion decline in consumption.

This $80 billion decrease in consumption is carried over to Figure 11-5. Point *B* on the after-tax consumption function C_2 is $80 billion below *A*. Similarly, every other point on the original consumption function also

FIGURE 11-4
A tax depresses consumption
If the MPC is 0.8, a $100 billion tax reduces consumption by $80 billion and saving by $20 billion.

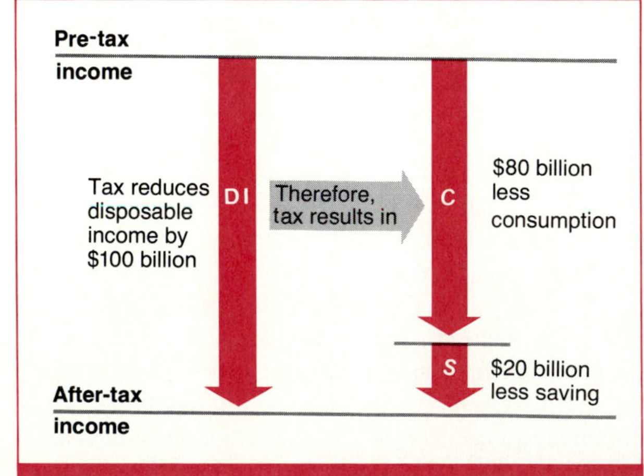

shifts down by $80 billion. The new after-tax function is parallel to the original consumption function but is $80 billion lower. In general:

> **A lump-sum tax causes the consumption function to *shift down by the amount of the tax times the MPC.***

When taxes are increased and the consumption function shifts downward, aggregate demand likewise shifts downward. Thus, when aggregate demand is too high and prices are rising, an *increase* in taxes is the appropriate policy step. On the other side, a *cut* in taxes represents a *stimulative* policy; the reduction in taxes will increase disposable income and shift the consumption function and aggregate demand *upward*.

Note that a change in taxes is almost as powerful a tool for controlling aggregate demand as a change in government purchases of goods and services. Almost, but not quite. An increase of $100 billion in government purchases causes aggregate demand to shift up by the full $100 billion. However, a decrease in taxes of $100 billion shifts aggregate demand up by only $80 billion—that is, $100 billion times the MPC.[2]

FIGURE 11-5
Effect of a $100 billion lump-sum tax
If the MPC is 0.8, a lump-sum tax T of $100 billion causes the consumption function to shift down by $80 billion ($T \times$ MPC).

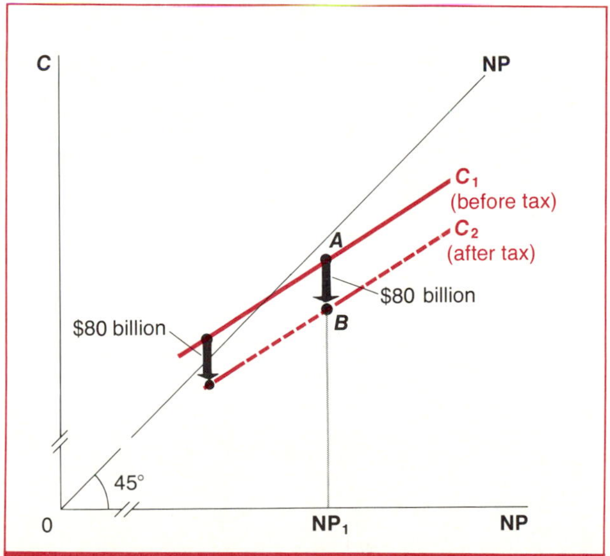

Because government purchases of goods and services are more powerful, dollar for dollar, than a change in taxes, there is reason to turn to government purchases when major changes are desired in aggregate demand. During the early Keynesian period, economists did concentrate on government purchases in their fiscal policy recommendations. However, since 1962, tax changes have become a more prominent way to manage aggregate demand. Thus, President Kennedy's program to "get the economy moving again" included a $10 billion cut in taxes. (This tax reduction was not enacted into law until 1964, after Kennedy's assassination.) Then, in 1968, a temporary tax surcharge was imposed to reduce the inflationary pressures associated with the Vietnam war and Great Society spending programs. In early 1975, taxes were cut in order to stimulate the economy, which was suffering from the worst recession since the 1930s. (However, the tax cuts enacted in 1981 were not aimed primarily at demand management. Rather, they were "supply side" cuts, aimed at increasing the incentives to work and save. The supply side will be considered later.)

There are three reasons why tax changes have become such an important component of fiscal policy:

1. A tax cut is generally ***less controversial*** than an increase in government spending as a way of stimulating the economy. This is true in part because of skepticism over the ability of the government to spend money wisely, and because of fears that the government will grow bigger and bigger.

[2]Like taxes, a $100 billion change in transfer payments is less powerful than a $100 billion change in government spending for goods and services. When the government purchases roadbuilding equipment or other goods or services, it provides jobs directly. However, transfer payments—such as social security pensions—do not provide jobs directly. Like taxes, they affect demand only indirectly, by changing disposable income. Specifically, a $100 billion increase in transfer payments raises disposable income by $100 billion, and thus causes an upward shift of the consumption function by $100 billion times the MPC.

2. Tax changes may be put into effect ***more quickly*** than changes in government spending. For example, an increase in spending for highways, government buildings, dams, or other public works requires considerable planning, and this takes time.

3. Tax changes are ***more easily reversed*** when conditions change. It is true that the public may be unhappy when previously cut taxes are reimposed. However, they may be even more unhappy if government spending programs are eliminated. Furthermore, some government spending—for example, for roads, buildings, or dams—cannot be stopped without considerable waste. A half-finished bridge or dam is no good to anybody.

To summarize our policy conclusions thus far:

1. *To stimulate aggregate demand,* and thus combat unemployment, the appropriate fiscal policy is an increase in government spending and/or a cut in taxes; that is, *steps that increase the government's deficit* or reduce its surplus.

2. *To restrain aggregate demand* and thus combat inflation, the appropriate fiscal policy is a cut in government spending and/or an increase in taxes; that is, *steps that move the government's budget toward surplus.*

> **A government deficit acts as a stimulus to aggregate demand. A surplus acts as a drag.**

Adding Realism: A Proportional Tax

These two important policy conclusions have been illustrated by studying a simple lump-sum tax that was $100 billion no matter what national product might be. But this tax isn't realistic. In fact, tax collections rise and fall with national product. This is obviously true of income taxes. The more people earn, the more taxes they pay. It is also true of sales taxes. If national product and total sales rise, government revenues from sales taxes likewise rise.

We may take a giant step toward realism by discarding the lump-sum tax and studying instead a tax that does rise and fall with national product. The one we consider is a proportional tax, that is, a tax that yields revenues which are a constant percentage of national product.

As we saw in Figure 11-5, a lump-sum tax shifts the consumption function down by a constant amount. However, this is not true of a proportional tax. If national product doubles, tax collections likewise double, and the depressing effects on the consumption function also double. To illustrate, suppose there is a 20% proportional tax. At national product NP_1 in Figure 11-6, this tax depresses consumption from point *B* to *D*. But if national product is twice as great, at NP_2, this 20% tax takes away twice as much of the public's income and therefore depresses consumption by twice as much—from *K* to *L*.

Of course, a 30% tax depresses consumption even more than a 20% tax. Thus, consumption function C_3 lies below C_2. In general, the heavier the tax, the more the consumption function rotates clockwise, as shown in Figure 11-6.[3]

Note two important effects of a proportional tax:

[3]Note that the consumption function rotates around point *A*. Why is this so? By assumption, taxes are proportional to national product. Therefore, in the limiting case where national product is zero, taxes are likewise zero. Consumption is therefore unaffected. Thus, point *A* is on every consumption function, regardless of how high the tax rate is.

FIGURE 11-6
A proportional tax: Effect on consumption
When a proportional tax is imposed, the consumption function rotates clockwise around point *A*. The higher the tax rate, the more the consumption function rotates. As the tax rate rises from 20% to 30%, the consumption function becomes lower and flatter.

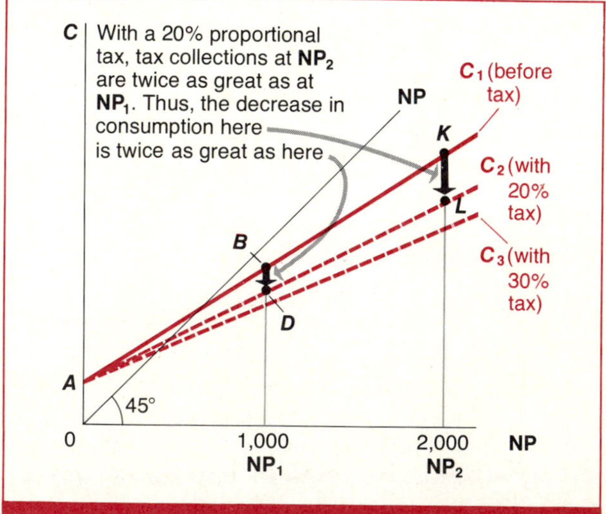

1. The higher the tax rate, the more disposable income is reduced and the more the consumption function is lowered. Thus, an increase in the tax rate lowers the aggregate demand function, and a cut in taxes raises the aggregate demand function. On this first point, then, the effects of a proportional tax are similar to those of the lump-sum tax considered earlier. (But, on the next point they differ.)

2. In an economy with proportional taxes, the consumption function is *flatter* than in a tax-free economy. And the higher the tax rate, the flatter the consumption function becomes. However, as we saw in Chapter 10, the flatter the consumption function, the lower the multiplier. Moreover, the effect of a proportional tax in lowering the multiplier can be very substantial. Recall that with no taxes and an MPC of 0.8 the multiplier was 5. When a 25% proportional tax is introduced, the multiplier drops sharply, to only 2.5. (Appendix 11-A explains why.)

INJECTIONS AND LEAKAGES: AN ECONOMY WITH GOVERNMENT SPENDING AND TAXES

The previous chapter explained a very simplified economy, one with only consumption and investment and no government sector. Such an economy *reaches equilibrium when the injections* into the spending stream, in the form of investment demand, *are just equal to the leakages* from the spending stream, in the form of saving.

When government spending and taxation are introduced, a similar proposition still holds. *Equilibrium exists when injections and leakages are equal.* But now there are *two* injections and *two* leakages (Figure 11-7).

Specifically, *government spending* is an *injection* into the spending stream, similar to investment demand. When the government spends more for roads, buildings, etc., the producers of these roads and buildings earn higher incomes and their consumption consequently rises. The circular flow of expenditures broadens as a result of this government spending.

On the other side, *taxation* is a *leakage,* similar to saving. Income taken in taxes cannot be used by the public for consumption expenditures. As consumption falls, the circular flow of expenditures narrows.

Equilibrium occurs when the injections working to broaden the spending stream are equal to the leakages working to narrow it. Specifically, in an economy with government spending and taxes:

> **Equilibrium occurs when the *injections* (investment demand plus government spending) are equal to the *leakages* (saving plus taxation). That is, equilibrium occurs when**
>
> $$I^* + G = S + T$$

When international transactions are included, the economy is even more complicated, with an additional injection and an additional leakage, as explained in Appendix 11-B.

BUILT-IN FISCAL STABILIZERS

Because taxes lower the size of the multiplier, they add to the stability of the economy. In an economy with high taxes, the multiplier is small. Therefore, a fall in investment demand causes only a moderate decline in national product. On the other side, a runaway boom is less likely in an economy with high taxes, since so much of the increase in income is taxed away before people get a chance to spend it.

Tax revenues that vary with national product are therefore a ***built-in stabilizer*** or ***automatic stabilizer.*** The way taxes act to stabilize the economy is illustrated in Figure 11-8. In this diagram, taxes (*T*) are just adequate to cover government expenditure (*G*) when the economy is at the full-employment national product NP_1; the budget is balanced ($G = T$). Now suppose the economy slips into a recession, with national product decreasing to NP_2. Tax collections fall, and the budget automatically moves into deficit. This fall in tax collections helps to keep up aggregate demand: Disposable income is left in the hands of the public, and consumption therefore falls less sharply. Thus, the downward momentum in the economy is reduced. Similarly, the tax system acts as a restraint on an upswing. As national product increases, tax collections rise. The government's budget moves toward surplus, and the upward movement of the economy is slowed down.

FIGURE 11-7

The circular flow, with government spending and taxes

When the government sector is added, there are two injections (investment and government spending) into the circular stream of spending. And there are two leakages (saving and taxes). Equilibrium is reached when injections are equal to leakages.

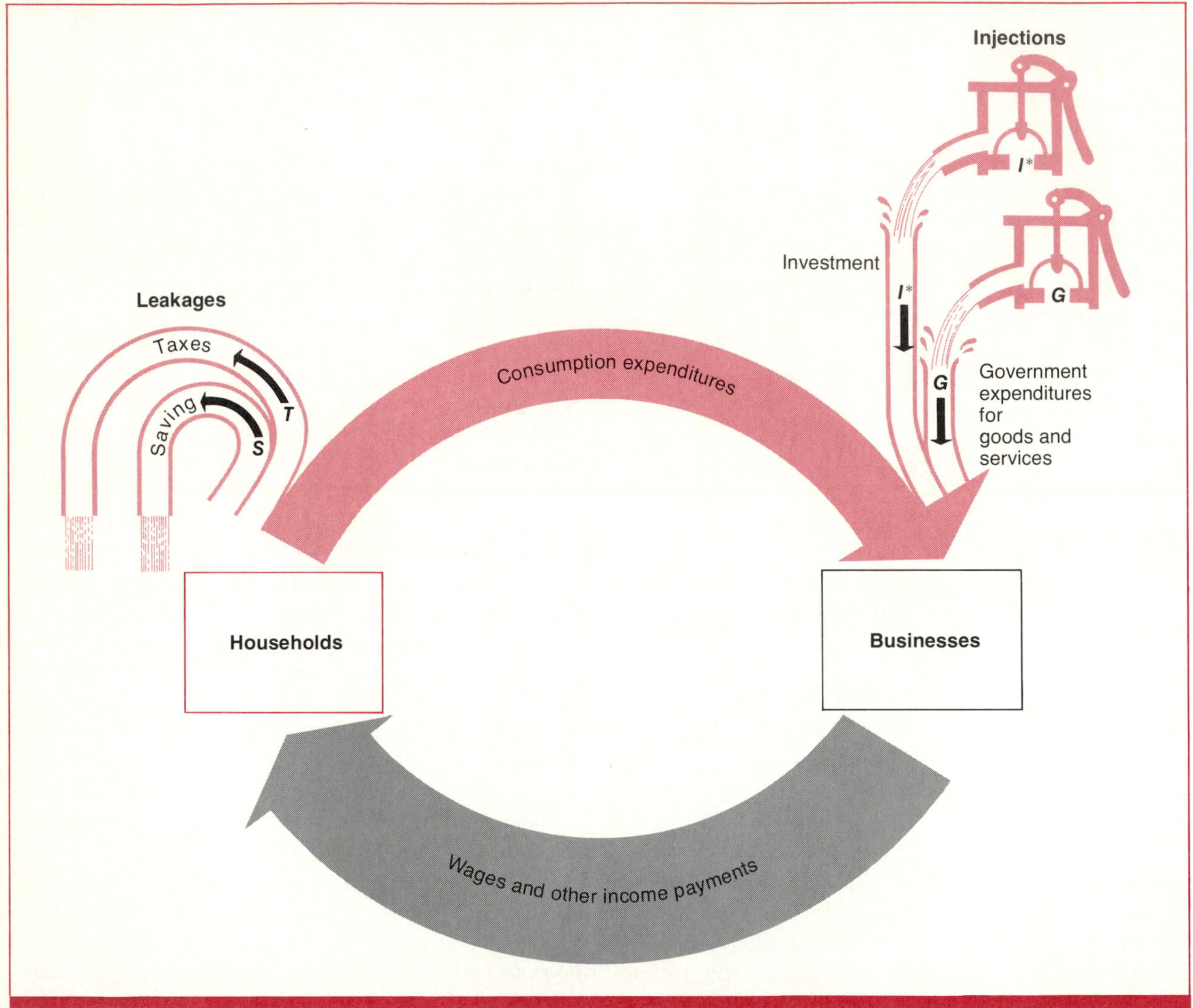

An *automatic stabilizer* is any feature of the economic system that reduces the strength of recessions and/or the strength of upswings in demand without policy changes being made. (Thus, an automatic stabilizer should be distinguished from a *discretionary* policy action, such as a cut in tax rates or the introduction of new government spending programs.)

The degree of automatic stabilization depends on how strongly tax collections respond to changes in national product. That is, it depends on the *marginal tax rate* for the economy as a whole—the fraction of an increase in national product which is paid in taxes. The greater is the marginal tax rate, the steeper is the taxation function (T) in Figure 11-8 and the stronger the automatic stabilization.

There are also automatic stabilizers on the government expenditures side (not shown in Figure 11-8). As the economy slides into a recession, there is an automatic increase in government spending for unemployment insurance benefits and for welfare. The additional government spending sustains disposable income and therefore slows the downswing.

Automatic stabilizers reduce the severity of economic fluctuations. But they do not eliminate them. The objective of discretionary fiscal policy is to reduce the fluctuations even more.

FIGURE 11-8

Automatic fiscal stabilization

As national product increases from NP_1 toward NP_3, the government's budget automatically moves into surplus. This slows down the increases in disposable income and consumption and thus slows down the expansion. Conversely, the budget automatically moves into deficit during recessions as national product decreases from NP_1 toward NP_2. The government deficit helps to keep up disposable income and consumption and thus alleviates the recession.

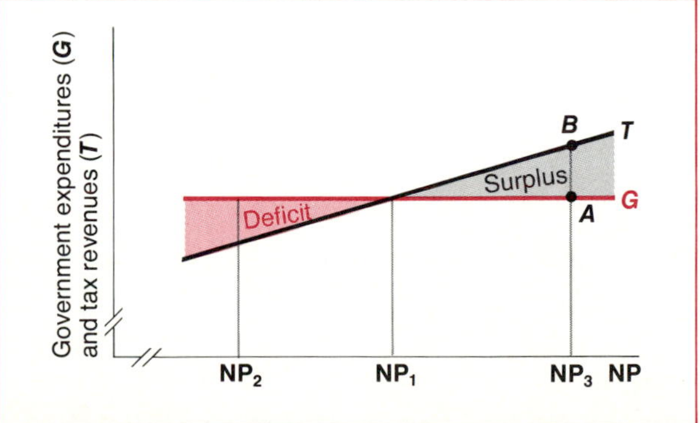

TWO COMPLICATIONS

The tendency for the government's budget to swing automatically into deficit during recessions, and into surplus during inflationary booms, helps to stabilize the economy. It may therefore be looked on as a plus. But it also introduces the following two important complications into fiscal policy.

1. Measuring Fiscal Policy: The Full-Employment Budget

Because the government's budget swings *automatically* toward deficit during recessions and toward surplus during booms, the state of the budget cannot be taken as a measure of how fiscal *policy* has changed. For example, when the budget moves into deficit during recession, this does not demonstrate that policymakers have accepted the teachings of Keynesian economics and have acted to stimulate the economy and offset the recession. They may have done nothing. The deficit may merely reflect a decline in the government's tax revenues as a result of the recession.

In order to determine whether fiscal *policy* is moving in an expansive or restrictive direction, some measure other than the actual budgetary deficit or surplus is therefore needed. The ***full-employment budget*** provides such a measure. The full-employment budget indicates what the surplus or deficit *would be if the economy were at full employment*.

The *full-employment budget* (B_{FE}) is defined:

$$B_{FE} = R_{FE} - G_{FE}$$

where R_{FE} represents full-employment receipts, that is, receipts that the present tax laws would yield if the economy were at full employment

G_{FE} stands for full-employment government expenditures, that is, actual expenditures less expenditures (payments to the unemployed, etc.) that would be avoided if full employment existed. ("Full employment" is currently estimated to exist when the unemployment rate is 6% or thereabouts.)[4]

The point of the full-employment budget is illustrated in Figure 11-9. Suppose the economy starts at NP_1, a position of full employment. With the existing tax rate, represented by line T_1, government revenues are equal to government expenditures *G;* the actual budget is in balance. (So is the full-employment budget. When the economy is at full employment, the two budgets are exactly the same.) Now suppose that the economy slips down into a recession; national product falls to NP_2. Tax revenues decline to *C,* and the actual budget automatically swings into deficit *BC*. To the unwary, it might seem that the government has acted to stimulate the economy by creating a budget deficit. But this is not so. The government has not yet made any policy change. All it has done is to let automatic stabilizers work.

In contrast to the actual budget, the full-employment budget accurately reflects what has happened to fiscal policy: nothing. The full-employment budget is measured at the full-employment national product NP_1, regardless of what the actual national product may be. The full-employment budget is still in balance at *A;* it has not been affected by the onset of the recession.

The full-employment budget *is,* however, affected by a change in fiscal policy. Suppose that, with the economy at NP_2, the government takes discretionary steps to combat the recession by cutting the tax rate to T_2. How does this show up in the full-employment budget measure? At the full-employment national product, NP_1, the new, lower tax rate T_2 would yield revenues of only *E.* Thus, the tax cut causes a full-employment budget deficit of *AE*. (It also causes an increase in the actual budget deficit, from *BC* to *BD*.) Similarly, an increase in government spending—which would be shown by an upward shift of *G*—would cause the full-employment budget to move into deficit and the actual budget to move into greater deficit.

In summary, then:

1. A downward swing in the economy automatically causes the actual budget to move toward deficit. However, the full-employment budget does *not* automatically move toward deficit.

2. A cut in tax rates or an increase in government spending causes *both* the actual and the full-employment budgets to move toward deficit.

3. Because the actual budget responds both to (1) changes in economic activity and (2) changes in policy, it is a misleading measure of policy alone. On the other hand, the full-employment budget is unaffected by changes in economic activity, and it *does* measure policy

[4]Because of uncertainty as to how low the unemployment rate would have to go before the economy should be considered at "full employment," many economists prefer not to use the term "full-employment budget." Instead, they speak of the *high-employment budget* or the *standard-employment budget*. Difficulties in pinning down the concept of full employment will be considered in Chapter 16.

FIGURE 11-9
The full-employment budget
A decrease in economic activity from NP_1 to NP_2 causes the actual budget to move into deficit *BC*. Because the full-employment budget's tax receipts are measured at full-employment national product NP_1, regardless of the actual quantity of output, the full-employment budget is not affected by the recession. However, it does move into deficit (*AE*) as a result of a cut in tax rates, shown by the fall from T_1 to T_2.

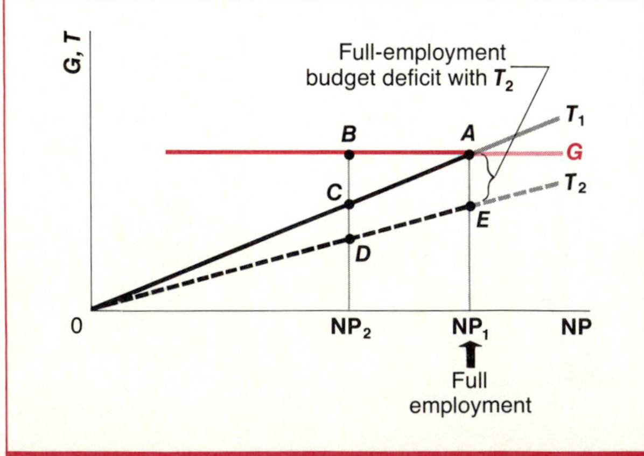

changes. In the example in Figure 11-9, the reduction in tax rates from T_1 to T_2 moved the full-employment budget into deficit *AE*. This movement indicated that the government had changed fiscal policy in an expansionary direction.

The full-employment budget, 1960–1984 We can see how misleading the actual budget would be as a measure of fiscal policy actions by comparing it with the full-employment budget in Figure 11-10. For example, in 1960, 1974, and early 1980, as the economy was slipping into recession, the actual budget moved in a negative direction, toward deficit. But fiscal policy was not strongly expansionary, as the actual budget might falsely have suggested. The stable paths of the full-employment budget in 1960, 1974, and 1980 correctly show that very little change was occurring in fiscal policy.

Moreover, the full-employment budget can be used to identify some important changes in fiscal policy. Observe how the full-employment budget surplus declined in 1964, reflecting the expansionary tax cut of that year. On the other hand, the full-employment budget swung from deficit to surplus in 1968–1969 as a result of the policies designed to reduce inflationary pressures—the

FIGURE 11-10
The full-employment budget and the actual budget, 1960–1984
When the economy is operating below the full-employment level, tax revenues are depressed and the actual budget shows a larger deficit—or smaller surplus—than the full-employment budget. The full-employment budget shows changes in fiscal policy.

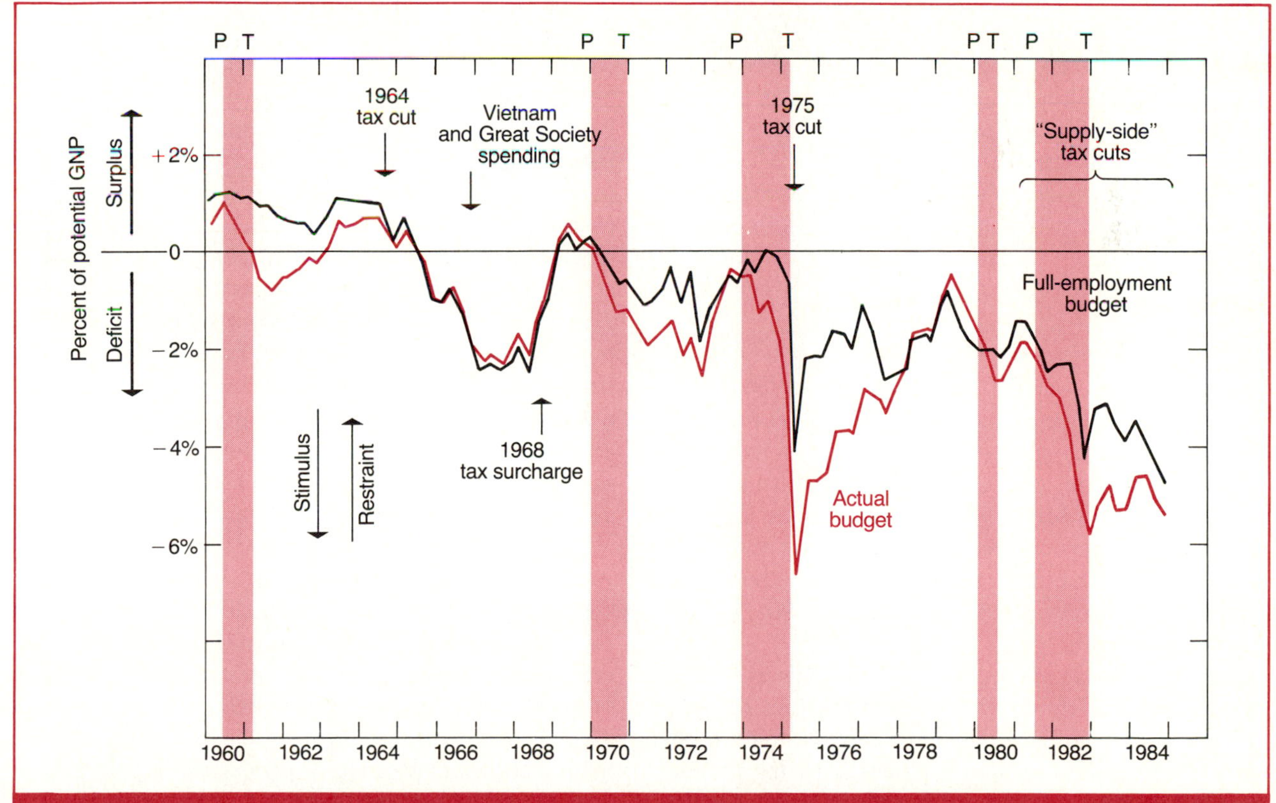

1968 tax increase and restraints on government spending. In 1975, the full-employment budget moved sharply into deficit as a result of the tax cut and increases in government spending designed to lift the economy out of the recession of 1973–1975. In 1981–1982, as the economy slid into a deep recession, the full-employment budget deficits increased sharply as a result of the tax cuts enacted in 1981.

However, Figure 11-10 also shows some disquieting aspects of our fiscal history. Consider what happened from 1965 to 1967. The stagnation of the early sixties was a thing of the past; the unemployment rate was low, and inflation was gaining momentum. The proper fiscal stance was restraint. Yet fiscal policy was moving in the opposite direction. The full-employment budget was moving into deficit, applying more stimulus to an economy that was already overheated. During these years, fiscal policy destabilized the economy, making the inflationary problem worse. In 1972, the increase in the full-employment deficit also acted as a destabilizing force. It added inflationary pressures to an economy already operating close to its capacity. Finally, the full-employment deficit continued to grow in 1984, indicating that fiscal stimulus was being applied even though the economy was already well into the recovery.

Why wasn't fiscal policy used in a more precise way to combat recessions and inflations, in line with the theory of this chapter? There are two major reasons why fiscal policy has not been strongly stabilizing in practice:

1. The government often has ***other objectives*** which take precedence over the stablization of the economy. This was most clearly the case in 1965–1967. President Johnson became caught in the quagmire of an unpopular and frustrating war, and he shied away from an increase in taxes to finance higher government spending. For several years, he overruled the recommendations of his economic advisers that taxes be increased to restrain inflation. The tax increase was not passed until 1968, when it was long overdue.

A second example occurred in 1984. The increasing full-employment deficits of that year were not part of a government program to apply more stimulus to the economy. Instead, the deficits were caused by the government's pursuit of two other objectives, each of which was given higher priority than holding down the deficit: (*a*) increased military expenditures and (*b*) the tax cuts enacted in 1981, which came into effect in stages over the 1981–1984 period. These cuts were not aimed at managing aggregate demand. Rather, they were aimed at reducing the tax burden on the public and increasing their incentives to produce.

Not only does the administration have other objectives which may make it difficult to stabilize the economy with fiscal policy. In addition, the various members of Congress all have their own sets of objectives and priorities. The diffusion of power makes it very difficult to pass stabilizing policies in a timely fashion.

2. Policies may be badly timed or inappropriate because policymakers ***do not fully understand*** the current state of the economy or where it is headed. For example, the government failed to recognize the strength of inflationary pressures in 1972 and erroneously pursued expansive policies. These policies were one of the reasons for the rapid acceleration of inflation in 1973–1974.

2. A Policy Trap: The Annually Balanced Budget

Because the actual budget swings automatically into deficit during recessions, it sets a trap for the unwary policymaker. Suppose that the government tries to balance the actual budget every year. As the economy enters a recession, tax collections decline, causing budgetary deficits. If policymakers are determined to balance the budget, they will have two choices: they can cut government spending or increase tax rates. *Either step will depress aggregate demand and make the recession worse. By raising taxes or cutting expenditures, the government will offset the automatic stabilizers built into the tax system. Trying to balance the budget each year is a policy trap.*

President Hoover fell into this trap during the early years of the Great Depression. He shared the prevailing view that the government should balance its budget. As tax revenues fell and deficits mounted, he was convinced that the elimination of the deficit was essential to restore business confidence and hasten economic recovery. In 1932, he recommended that taxes be increased to get the budget back into balance. Congress agreed. The result was one of the largest peacetime increases in taxes in

U.S. history. Fiscal policy was precisely the opposite of what was need to promote recovery. Rather than the needed stimulus, the country got a large dose of restraint. The stage was set for the collapse into the deepest point of the Depression in 1933. Ironically, the policy did not succeed in its goal of balancing the budget. In part because of the added fiscal restraint, the economy collapsed. As it collapsed, tax revenues fell. The deficit persisted.

Hoover was not alone in falling into the trap; a number of other countries also increased tax rates during the Depression. These blunders set the stage for the Keynesian revolution with its important message: Spending and tax policies should be aimed at the goals of full employment and price stability, and not at the goal of balancing the budget. Keynes argued that *fiscal policy should be designed to balance the economy, not the budget.*

However, the wide acceptance of Keynes' message has left two nagging worries: (1) If the government is not held accountable for balancing the budget, how can it be expected to show restraint in its spending and taxing decisions? (2) If the government runs large deficits, will we not eventually end up with a crushing burden of public debt? Isn't the government in danger of going bankrupt?

THE ISSUE OF RESTRAINT

Keynesian economists attacked the old rule of an annually balanced budget. But to keep the budget under control, many people long for something to put in its place. If the government does not have to live within its tax revenues, its spending may escalate out of control, or it may cut taxes without corresponding restraint on spending. We may warn of the dangers of excess, but can we really expect restraint?

Concerns have grown with the increase in government deficits during the 1980s (Figure 11-10). Particularly worrisome was the very large deficit of 1984, which occurred when the economy was approaching full employment. At that time, there was no need for a large stimulus from fiscal policy.

In recent decades, a number of alternative guidelines have been suggested to provide restraint while avoiding the destabilizing fiscal policies which can occur if the government tries to balance the actual budget every year.

1. Balance the Full-Employment Budget Every Year

Remember why the old balanced-budget rule was destabilizing. As the economy moves into recession and a budget deficit automatically appears, the balanced-budget rule requires an increase in tax rates or cuts in government spending. These can make the recession worse. Such destabilizing actions can be avoided if the government aims at balancing the *full-employment* budget. Since this budget does not automatically swing into deficit during recessions, it does not give a false signal that a tax increase or spending cut is needed. Thus, the full-employment budget has two major uses: as a ***way of measuring*** fiscal policy and as a ***guide*** to fiscal policy.

However, in a severe recession, balancing the full-employment budget may be inadequate. All it does is to allow the automatic stabilizers to combat the recession. It does not allow the government to go one step further and actively fight the recession by introducing fiscal stimulus. (Such stimulus—for example, a cut in tax rates—would violate the rule, since it would put the full-employment budget into deficit. Recall that precisely this case was illustrated in Figure 11-9). Thus, this first rule represents an unambitious strategy. Its aim is to avoid destabilizing actions, not to actively stabilize the economy. It therefore is reminiscent of the doctor's motto: *Primo non nocere,* or "First, do no harm."

2. Balance the Full-Employment Budget, But Only When the Economy Achieves Full Employment

The second approach is more ambitious. It allows a government to take the initiative in managing the economy. During a recession, tax rates *can* be cut or spending increased in order to speed the return to full employment. In other words, the full-employment budget can be shifted into deficit during recessions. But the government is still subject to restraint. It has to return to a balanced budget when the economy reaches full employment.

3. Balance the Budget Over the Cycle

Either of the first two guidelines permits the government to have an *actual* budget which is in deficit on the average. The reason is that, whenever the economy falls short of full employment, either guideline allows a deficit in the actual budget. There is no need for offsetting surpluses during periods of full employment.

More long-term restraint can be provided by *balancing the actual budget over the business cycle*. According to this approach, there should be sufficient surpluses during good times to cover the deficits of the recessions. But, unlike the annually balanced budget, the cyclically balanced budget is consistent with active fiscal management. Tax rates can be cut and spending increased to combat recessions.

4. Limit Government Spending

Another approach is to restrain government spending by *limiting it as a fraction of GNP*. President Carter and President Reagan both subscribed to this objective. In 1976, the year before President Carter came into office, federal government spending was more than 22% of GNP. Carter committed himself to lowering that figure to 21%. This objective was almost reached by 1979, when spending fell to 21.1% of GNP. However, it bounced back up to 22.9% in 1980. A large increase in interest payments pushed up expenditures (the numerator), while the recession kept down GNP (the denominator).

In his first months in office, President Reagan put forward budgetary proposals which would have brought the federal government's percentage of GNP below 20% by 1984. These proposals were based both on a program of restraining domestic expenditures, and on the assumption of a very healthy growth in GNP. Reagan failed even more conspicuously than Carter to reach his objective. Because of substantial increases in expenditures—and lower-than-expected growth—federal government spending actually increased, to 24.0% of GNP by the end of Reagan's first term in 1984. Furthermore, revenues were only 19.2% of GNP, leaving a budget deficit of 4.8% of GNP.

If the government were to follow this fourth guideline and firmly limit its expenditures to a given percentage of GNP, it *might* make recessions worse. During recessions, when GNP falls, expenditures would have to be cut proportionately. Nevertheless, it would still be *possible* for the government to follow this fourth guideline and at the same time pursue a countercyclical policy, in the following ways: (1) Taxes could be cut during recessions or (2) raised to combat inflation. Furthermore, (3) government spending could be restrained even more than required by the guideline during a boom, as a way of fighting inflation.

External Restraints: A Proposed Constitutional Amendment

Some critics of government spending argue that it is unrealistic to expect the government to be restrained by any of the guidelines or rules of thumb listed above. No matter what policy they proclaim, the administration and Congress are likely in practice to choose the line of least resistance. They will give in to those clamoring for bigger spending programs, and cut taxes in order to increase their popularity at the polls. Because the administration and Congress are unable or unwilling to show restraint, these critics argue that restraint should be imposed from the outside, in the form of a constitutional amendment requiring a balanced budget.[5] Not surprisingly, Congress does not look favorably on such an amendment, which would limit its powers. Despite the support of the Reagan administration, Congress has been unwilling to pass a balanced-budget amendment and submit it to the states for ratification. Proponents of the balanced-budget amendment are therefore trying to bypass Congress by having a consitutional convention called. This will happen if two-thirds (34) of the states petition for a convention. By 1984, 32 states had submitted such petitions, and proponents of the amendment were hoping that two more would be added.

Opponents of a balanced-budget amendment put forth a number of objections:

1. As noted earlier, the government would fall into the same trap as President Hoover if it tried to balance the budget every year. As the budget automatically went into deficit during a recession, the government would raise tax rates or cut expenditures, making the recession worse.

2. A balanced-budget requirement would limit the

[5]The case for an amendment is explained by Milton Friedman and Rose Friedman, *Tyranny of the Status Quo* (New York: Harcourt Brace Jovanovich, 1984).

power of Congress to deal with unforseen emergencies in the future.

3. A balanced-budget amendment would raise numerous technical complications. One problem is exactly how to define the budget. The easiest way to balance the budget is to change accounting methods to move deficit items out of the budget.

4. Those who support the amendment are inconsistent. In particular, the Reagan administration has supported the amendment strongly but has nevertheless submitted budgets with very large deficits, far in excess of $100 billion. If the administration believes in a balanced budget, say the critics, it should submit one to the Congress.

Proponents have tried to go at least part way toward meeting the first two of these objections. The proposed amendment would allow a deficit if it were approved by a 60% majority in Congress.

THE PUBLIC DEBT

Whenever the government runs a deficit, it borrows to pay for expenditures in excess of its revenues. When it borrows, its debt increases. Thus, the national debt represents the accumulated sum of all the amounts that the government has borrowed in the past to finance its deficits.

The government has run particularly large deficits—and the national debt has consequently grown very rapidly—during two periods: the Second World War and the period beginning in 1982. The large deficits of recent years have revived an old question: Aren't we passing on a crushing burden of debt to future generations?

In order to explain and weigh the problems associated with a rising government debt, it is helpful to divide the discussion into two parts, looking first at the deficit spending which pushes the debt up, and then at the consequences of the debt itself.

Deficit Spending: Who Paid for World War II?

Consider, first, the very large deficits during World War II. Who bore the economic burden of that war—the people of the time or their children who inherited the large government debt?

The answer is: *It was mostly borne by the people at the time*. To see why, consider what the primary economic cost of that war was. To fight the war, the nation needed thousands of tanks and planes, and millions of troops in the field. This required enormous resources which were no longer available for other uses. Military production in 1943 came *at the opportunity cost of giving up consumer goods in 1943*. For example, when General Motors was making tanks, it couldn't make cars at the same time. It was the people of 1943—and not their children—who had to do without new cars. They were the ones who suffered, not only in terms of lives lost but also in terms of consumer goods foregone.

However, it is only 90% correct to conclude that the burden of the war fell on the people of the early 1940s. Two qualifications are necessary. (1) If the United States had been at peace, we could not only have produced more consumer goods but *more capital goods, too*. Instead of turning out guns, ships, and planes, American industry could have produced more machines and built more factories. If it had done so, the rising capital stock would have benefited not only the people of the 1940s but future generations also. Thus, because our capital stock has been lower than it would have otherwise been, future generations *have* borne some of the burden of the war. (2) The higher debt inherited by the postwar generation created a number of problems, which we will consider in just a moment.

One further clarification is necessary. The major conclusion—that the production of planes and tanks comes at the opportunity cost of giving up consumer goods—is valid only if the economy is at full employment. This was, in fact, the case in 1943. The unemployment rate was low and factories were straining at their capacity. However, we reach quite a different conclusion if we look at deficit spending during a depression like the one of the 1930s, when the economy was operating at a point well inside its production possibilities curve. In such a situation, producing more goods for the government does not require a reduction in consumption and investment. On the contrary, because of the operation of the multiplier, we produce more consumer goods too. As more consumer goods are produced, investment demand is stimulated: To produce more cars and refrigerators, businesses need more machines and factories. Thus, deficit spending by the government *during a depression* generates benefits rather than burdens for both present and future generations. It stimulates the production of more consumer goods for the current generation and more capital stock for future generations.

Deficit Spending in the 1980s: Who Pays?

Both the Great Depression and the Second World War were disasters. But the economic issues which they raised were relatively simple. During the depression, the problem was to get people back to work. During the war, the economic problem was how to increase the production of weapons.

The 1980s, in contrast, raise much more complicated and subtle issues. Nevertheless, the same question should be addressed: What is the cost of deficit spending in the 1980s? Are we creating a burden for future generations?

The first complication is that the economy was in an intermediate position in the early 1980s; we had neither the very large unemployment of the 1930s nor the extreme pressure on productive capacity which occurred in 1943. In 1981–1982, there was a severe recession. This was followed by a a very strong recovery, with the result that the economy was approaching full employment by 1984. It was then that we had to face the question of what we were giving up by deficit spending.

The second complication is that the deficits were a result of several causes. Not only were government expenditures rising, but tax rates had been cut.

The tax cuts raised disposable incomes. Consumers were in a better position to buy. Unlike the situation in 1943, the deficit spending of 1984 did not come out of current consumption. What, then, was adversely affected?

1. First, the large government deficits acted as a *drag on investment*. When the government borrows to finance its deficits, it bids up interest rates. This makes it more expensive for businesses to finance their investment projects. The drag on investment means that a somewhat smaller capital stock will be passed on to future generations. However, the drag on investment was partially offset by the favorable tax treatment granted to those who invested.

2. To finance its deficits, the U.S. government not only borrowed from American citizens, but also *borrowed substantial amounts from foreigners*. As a nation, we were going into debt to foreigners—debt on which we will have to make interest payments in the future.

To see in more detail why the deficits of the 1980s caused problems, we must look at the effects of the rising national debt.

The National Debt: Is It a Burden?

To answer this question, consider the government debt which existed in 1955 because of the deficit of 1943. The first important point is that interest payments on this debt were not made by the people of 1955 to the people of 1943. Rather, they were made by some people in 1955 to other people in 1955. Specifically, the government collected taxes from the general public and used some of the taxes to pay interest to bondholders. Thus, government debt—indeed, any debt—transfers funds from one group *now* to another group *now*. It does *not* transfer funds from people in one time period to people in an earlier period.

However, this transfer from one group to another is neither costless nor unimportant. It causes a number of problems:

1. The transfer may lead to an *undesirable redistribution of income*. This depends on who has to pay the taxes and who holds the bonds and receives the interest. (It also depends on what we consider a ''desirable'' distribution of income.)

2. Foreign-held debt is quite different from domestically held debt. When debt is held domestically, one group of Americans is taxed to pay interest to another group of Americans. When foreigners own U.S. bonds, Americans are taxed in order to pay interest *to foreigners*. In this respect, the budget deficits of the 1980s have been quite different from the budget deficits of earlier periods. Traditionally, foreign holdings of U.S. government bonds and other assets in the United States have been quite small compared with American holdings of foreign assets. We were *net creditors* in the world—foreigners traditionally owed us much more than we owed them. However, during the 1980s, we have been borrowing at a much more rapid rate than we have been acquiring assets abroad, with the result that our net creditor position has disappeared. In 1985, we became *net debtors* in the world for the first time since 1914; that is, we now owe more to foreigners than they owe to us. If the trends of the early 1980s continue, we will soon owe *much* more to foreigners than they owe to us, and we will have to pay much more interest to foreigners than they pay to us. In brief, a *foreign-held debt* is a burden for Americans as a whole; we must make interest payments to foreigners.

3. When the government collects taxes to pay interest on the debt—whether held at home or abroad—there is another cost: the ***excess burden*** of taxation. When taxes are imposed, the public has an incentive to alter its behavior to avoid paying taxes. For example, people have an incentive to hire lawyers to search for tax loopholes and to divert their savings into tax-sheltered investments—that is, investments on which little or no tax is paid. As a result, the efficiency of the economy is reduced.

The *excess burden of taxes* is the decrease in the efficiency of the economy that results when people change their behavior to avoid paying taxes. It should be distinguished from the *primary burden,* which is measured by the amount of taxes people actually pay.

4. The need for the government to make interest payments on a large debt may contribute to *inflation*. For example, inflation may result if the government decides to finance interest payments, not by collecting taxes but instead by borrowing and thus running up its deficit. The rising deficits stimulate aggregate demand and add to inflationary pressures. The inflationary effects are particularly strong if the Federal Reserve (our central bank) creates new money and lends it to the government in order to help the government make its interest payments.

5. The national debt can *feed on itself*. As the debt rises, the government's interest payments also rise. But, as these interest payments are part of the government's expenditures, they make it more difficult to get the expenditures under control in the future.

This fifth problem has caused great concern during the 1980s. Recent deficits have been very different from the large deficits of the early 1940s, which were caused by a temporary wartime crisis. When the war ended, military spending plunged, automatically eliminating the deficits. In contrast, deficits of the 1980s have arisen because the government has committed itself to long-run spending programs that substantially exceed its tax revenues. If the government can't keep deficits down now, how will it be able to do so in the future, when it must make much larger interest payments? Because of a large debt and high interest rates, interest payments are now much larger, compared to GNP, than they have been in the past, and they are growing rapidly (Table 11-1, column 5).

6. The danger of the debt "feeding on itself" has become so severe that some economists fear that *we may have lost our ability to use fiscal policy to combat future recessions*. If the deficit is $186 billion in the relatively prosperous year of 1984, what will happen if we use fiscal policy vigorously to combat the next recession? With even larger deficits, won't we generate an unstoppable tide of debt and even greater interest payments and deficits in the future?

This danger has added urgency to the issue of restraint. If we can't control the budget during reasonably good times, such as 1984–1985, won't we paint ourselves into a corner, where we can't call on fiscal policy when it is needed to fight a recession?

Could the Government "Go Broke"?

If it gets more and more deeply into debt, could the federal government, like a business corporation, go bankrupt? The answer is no, but the reason why it won't "go broke" should be carefully stated.

First, consider one common, but inaccurate, argument. It is frequently asserted that the government cannot go bankrupt because it has the authority to tax. Thus, it has the power to extract from the public whatever amounts are necessary to service the debt. But there is surely something wrong with this argument. State and local governments also have the power to tax, yet they can go broke, as the holders of Cleveland and New York City securities discovered in the 1970s. At times, these cities were unable to make payments on their debt. In a democracy, the government must face elections. Even

TABLE 11-1
The Public Debt and Interest Payments, 1929–1986

Year	(1) Public debt	(2) Gross national product	(3) Interest payments	(4) Public debt, as percentage of GNP (1) ÷ (2)	(5) Interest payments, as percentage of GNP (3) ÷ (2)	(6) Interest payments, as percentage of federal government expenditures	(7) Per capita public debt (current dollars)	(8) Per capital public debt (1972 dollars)
	(billions of current dollars)							
1929	$ 16	$ 103	$ 0.7	16%	0.7%	23.4%	$ 135	$ 412
1940	45	100	1.1	45	1.1	11.6	340	1,172
1945	278	212	4.1	131	1.9	4.3	1,986	5,240
1950	257	287	4.5	90	1.6	10.8	1,689	3,153
1960	290	507	6.8	57	1.3	8.9	1,602	2,358
1970	370	993	13.5	37	1.4	7.1	1,805	1,974
1975	533	1,549	21.7	34	1.4	7.2	2,468	1,962
1980	908	2,627	51.2	35	1.9	8.9	4,009	2,247
1984	1,577	3,661	111.1	43	3.0	13.0	6,665	2,983
1986†	2,074	3,876	142.6	53	3.7	14.6	8,600	3,580

†Estimated.

dictatorships depend on public support. As a result, there are political and practical limits to taxes. The holder of a government bond does not have a guarantee of repayment merely because the government has the right to tax.

The federal government cannot go bankrupt for quite a different reason. It has a power even more potent than the power to tax. Bonds are repayable in money. The government has the power to print money to pay interest or principal—either directly or, more subtly, by pressuring or coercing the central bank (the Federal Reserve) to create money and lend it to the government to avoid default. In other words, a national government does not go bankrupt because bonds are repayable in something—money—which national governments can create.

However, if large quantities of money are created to help make payments on the public debt, the consequence will be a rise in prices. (Recall what happened in the prisoner-of-war camp when large quantities of cigarette ''money'' suddenly came on the scene.) Thus, an excessive national debt has quite different consequences from an excessive corporate debt: It causes excess demand and inflation, not bankruptcy.

However, there is one situation in which even a national government may default on its debts—namely, if it has borrowed in terms of a foreign currency. If the U.S. government issues bonds repayable in dollars, it can, in an extreme case, print the dollars to repay the debt. But suppose that it borrowed large amounts in a foreign currency, such as German marks or Japanese yen. (In fact, the U.S. government has borrowed only small amounts in foreign currencies.) In such circumstances, default would be possibile. No matter how desperate our situation might become, the U.S. government could not print *foreign* currency. Similarly, other national goverments that borrow large amounts of U.S. dollars may run the risk of default. Indeed, in the early 1980s, the danger of default was a severe problem for a number of governments that had borrowed heavily in U.S. dollars—for example, Argentina, Brazil, Mexico, and Poland.

KEY POINTS

1. An increase in government spending causes an increase in equilibrium national product. An increase in taxes causes a decrease in equilibrium national product.
2. When aggregate demand is low and the rate of unemployment is high, fiscal policy should be expansionary; that is, the government should increase spending

and/or cut tax rates. These steps tend to increase the government's deficit.

3. When excess aggregate demand is causing inflation, fiscal policy should be restrictive; the government should cut spending and/or increase tax rates. These steps will move the government's budget toward surplus.

4. Tax collections automatically rise as national product increases and fall as national product falls. Thus, the government budget *automatically* tends to move into deficit during a recession and into surplus during expansions. This tendency helps to reduce the amplitude of cyclical swings in aggregate demand and thus provides *built-in stability* to the economy.

5. Because the government's budget automatically responds to changes in national product, the actual budget cannot be taken as a measure of fiscal policy actions. The appropriate measure is the *full-employment budget,* which indicates what the surplus or deficit would be with current tax and spending legislation, if the economy were at full employment.

6. If the government attempts to balance the actual budget every year, it will fall into a *policy trap* and take destabilizing actions. During a downturn in economic activity, when the budget automatically tends to move into deficit, the government will cut expenditures or raise taxes in an effort to balance the budget, thereby making the downturn worse. The Hoover administration fell into this policy trap in 1932, when it initiated legislation for a large tax increase.

7. This trap can be avoided if the full-employment budget—rather than the actual budget—is used as a policy guide. The full-employment budget has no tendency to swing automatically into deficit during recessions, and therefore it does not erroneously suggest that taxes should be raised. Thus, the full-employment budget has two major functions: (1) as a *measure* of fiscal policy and (2) as a *guide* for fiscal policy.

8. Wars must be fought with the resources available at the time. In a fundamental sense, then, the burden of a war—or other deficit spending by the government—must be borne at the time the expenditures are made. Nevertheless, future generations may be adversely affected. Insofar as deficit spending shifts resources away from investment, future generations will inherit a smaller capital stock.

9. A large government debt involves transfers from one group (taxpayers who finance the interest payments) to another group (bondholders who collect interest). The interest payments on a large government debt can cause a number of problems:

(*a*) They may cause an undesirable redistribution of income within a country.

(*b*) Insofar as the debt is held abroad, people at home will be taxed to pay interest to foreigners.

(*c*) When taxes are imposed to pay the interest, there will be a loss of economic efficiency as people look for ways to avoid taxes. This loss of efficiency is called the "excess burden of taxes."

(*d*) If the government pays interest by borrowing rather than taxing, it can add to inflationary pressures.

(*e*) The debt can "feed on itself." A large debt requires large interest payments. This makes it difficult to avoid future deficits, which add to the size of the debt.

(*f*) Since a large debt requires large interest payments, it can cause such large deficits that the government feels that it has lost the ability to fight recessions with additional deficit spending.

KEY CONCEPTS

aggregate demand management
recessionary gap
output gap or GNP gap
inflationary gap
budget surplus
budget deficit
inflationary gap
lump-sum tax
proportional tax
taxes as a leakage
government spending as an injection
deficit spending
automatic stabilizers
discretionary policy action
actual budget
full-employment budget
full-employment receipts

full-employment government expenditures
annually balanced budget
budget balanced over the cycle
public debt
excess burden of taxes

PROBLEMS

11-1. Using a diagram, explain the difference between the recessionary gap and the output gap. Which is larger? How are these two measures related to the multiplier?

11-2. During the Great Depression, Keynes argued that it would be better for the government to build pyramids than to do nothing. Do you agree? Why or why not? Are there any policies better than pyramid building? That is, can you think of any policies which would give all the advantages of pyramid building, plus additional advantages? Explain.

11-3. During the Great Depression, the following argument was frequently made:

> A market economy tends to generate large-scale unemployment. Military spending can reduce unemployment. Therefore, capitalism requires wars and the threat of wars if it is to survive.

What part or parts of this argument are correct? Which are wrong? Explain what is wrong with the incorrect part(s). Rewrite the statement, correcting whatever is incorrect.

11-4. In 1964 and 1975, when the government wanted to stimulate aggregate demand, it cut tax rates. What are the advantages of cutting tax rates, rather than increasing government spending? What are the disadvantages? When restraint is needed, would you favor increases in taxes, cuts in government spending, or a combination of the two? Why?

11-5. Assume that full employment initially exists and that the actual budget is in balance.

(*a*) If the economy then slips down into a recession and there are no policy changes, will the actual budget and the full-employment budget behave the same? Explain why or why not. (For help with this question, refer to Figure 11-9.)

(*b*) Suppose, as an alternative, that the government takes strong fiscal policy steps to combat the recession. Will there be a difference in the behavior of the actual budget and the full-employment budget? Explain.

11-6. Attempting to balance the budget every year can set a trap for policymakers. It leads to incorrect policies during a depression. Does such a balanced-budget rule also lead to incorrect policies during an inflationary boom? Why or why not?

11-7. In what way is the federal budgetary deficit of 1984 different from that of 1943? Is the deficit of 1984 a problem or not? Explain.

APPENDIX 11-A

THE MULTIPLIER IN AN ECONOMY WITH TAXES

Taxes have a substantial effect on the multiplier process. Consider an economy with a marginal propensity to consume (MPC) of 0.8 and a tax rate of 25%. Each $1 change in investment demand (or in government spending) will then have the following effect on aggregate demand.

	Change in aggregate demand for each \$1 increase in investment demand
1. First round Increase in investment of:	\$1
2. Second round (*a*) Producers of investment goods have earned \$1 more in first round (*b*) Government takes 25¢ in taxes, leaving disposable income of 75¢ (*c*) With MPC = 0.8, consumption as a consequence is 0.8 × 75¢. Thus, in the "second round" of spending, there is an increase in consumption of 0.8 × 75¢ =	\$0.60 = \$1(0.6)
3. Third round (*a*) Producers of consumer goods have earned 60¢ more in first round (*B*) Government takes 25% (or 15¢) in taxes, leaving disposable income of 45¢ (*c*) With MPC = 0.8, consumption as a consequence is 0.8 × 45¢ =	$\$0.36 = \$1(0.6)^2$
4. Fourth round Consumption is	$\$1(0.6)^3$
	⋮

We find the sum of all rounds in a manner similar to equation 10-8:

$$\text{Sum} = \$1(1 + 0.6 + 0.6^2 + 0.6^3 + \cdots) = \$1\left(\frac{1}{1 - 0.6}\right) = \quad \$2.50$$

Therefore, the multiplier is 2.5.

More advanced texts derive the general formula for the multiplier in an economy with taxes:

$$\text{Multiplier} = \frac{1}{s + t - st}$$

where s = the marginal propensity to save

t = the marginal tax rate, that is, the change in tax collections as a fraction of the change in national product

APPENDIX 11-B

INTERNATIONAL TRANSACTIONS AND THE MULTIPLIER PROCESS

In the domestic economy, we have seen that there are two major injections (investment and government spending) and two main leakages (saving and taxes). International transactions make things more complicated. There is one more injection and one more leakage.

Exports are the injection. Larger exports of wheat, or computers, increase U.S. national product. Farmers and workers on the computer assembly-line have larger incomes, and they consequently step up their consumption expenditures. Thus, the multiplier process is set in motion by additional exports, just as it is set in motion by an increase in investment or government spending.

Once we consider international transactions, the multiplier process is more complicated. Consider what happens if IBM exports a computer. This is the initial injection. In the "first round," national product goes up by the full amount of the computer. What is the "second round" effect?

Because the government takes a slice in taxes—of, say, 25%—only 75¢ of each dollar of computer sales gets into the hands of consumers as disposable income. Of this 75¢, consumers save, say, one-fifth (15¢), leaving only 60¢ in consumption. But not all of this is spent on U.S. goods and services. A portion—say, 10¢—goes to purchase imported goods. As a result, the second round increase in national product is only 50¢ for each initial injection of $1.

At this second round, one-half of each $1 in income leaks out into taxes, saving, and imports; only 50¢ is spent by consumers for domestically produced goods. Similarly, one-half is spent on domestic goods, and one-half leaks out of the domestic spending stream in each later round. For each $1 in initial injection, this gives a sum of all rounds equal to:

$$\$1(1 + 0.5 + 0.5^2 + 0.5 + \cdots)$$

Using equation 10-8, we find:

$$\text{Sum} = \$1\left(\frac{1}{1 - 0.5}\right) = \$2$$

Therefore, the multiplier is 2.

In this more complicated economy with international transactions:

1. The multiplier is smaller because of the additional leakage into imports.[6]

2. Equilibrium occurs when total injections (investment plus government spending plus exports) equal total leakages (saving plus taxation plus imports).

Because imports—like taxes—reduce the size of the multiplier, they stabilize national product. For example, when U.S. incomes rise, Americans generally buy more clothing—including more clothing imported from Taiwan and Korea. If imported clothing were not available, Americans would buy domestic products instead. Incomes in the Carolinas and other textile states would rise even more rapidly; the expansion would be even stronger at home. Therefore, imports moderate an expansion. Similarly, they make a recession less severe. As incomes decline, our imports of textiles and other products also decline. Since some of the sales losses fall on Korea and Taiwan rather than on domestic producers, the downswing in U.S. GNP is moderated.

---

[6]In an economy with taxes and international trade, the formula for the multiplier is:

$$\text{Multiplier} = \frac{1}{s + t + m - st}$$

where s = the marginal propensity to save
t = the marginal tax rate
m = the marginal propensity to import, that is, the fraction of national product that is imported

Because one country's imports represent another's exports, international trade has contrasting effects on the two trading partners. An expansion originating in the United States causes an increase in our imports, weakening our upswing. Since these rising imports are exports of another country, such as Korea, the economy of that country expands: Korean employment and output rise because Americans buy more Korean goods. While trade weakens our upswing, it creates an expansion elsewhere. *Prosperity spreads across international boundaries.* Similarly, a recession in one country has a depressing effect on incomes elsewhere. If U.S. income falls, Americans buy less from Korea, reducing output and employment in that country.

CHAPTER 12

MONEY AND THE BANKING SYSTEM

You can't appreciate home till you've left it, [nor] money till it's spent.

O. HENRY

Fiscal policy is the first major tool for managing aggregate demand. Monetary policy is the second. Monetary policy involves control over the quantity of money in our economy. If the quantity of money is increased, spending is encouraged; aggregate demand tends to rise. Similarly, if the quantity of money decreases, aggregate demand tends to fall. By adjusting the quantity of money, the authorities can affect aggregate demand.

However, there is also another reason why money is an important topic in macroeconomics: Money not only provides a way to stabilize the economy; it can also represent a source of problems. Indeed, monetary disturbances have been associated with some of the most spectacularly unstable episodes in economic history. Two examples stand out. One occurred in the years following the First World War, when Germany went through a period of hyperinflation. In December 1919, there were about 50 billion marks in circulation. Four years later, this figure had risen to almost 500,000,000,000 billion marks—an increase of 10,000,000,000 times! Because money was so plentiful, it became practically worthless; prices skyrocketed. Indeed, money lost its value so quickly that people were anxious to spend whatever money they had as soon as possible, while they still could buy something with it. (For a more recent case of hyperinflation, see Box 12-1.)

The second illustration occurred in the United States between 1929 and 1933, when the economy was collapsing into the Great Depression. Economists are still debating how important monetary disturbances were as a cause of the collapse.[1] But there is little doubt that they played some role. As the economy slid downward, the quantity of money fell from $26.2 billion in mid-1929 to $19.2 billion in mid-1933—or by 27%. By the time Roosevelt became President in 1933, many banks had closed their doors, and many people with large deposits had been wiped out.

In the coming chapters, we will investigate the *problems* and *opportunities* which the monetary system presents. Specifically, we will explore the following questions:

1. What are the forces that cause disturbances within the monetary system? What has been done in the past, and what can be done in the future, to reduce the disturbances and make the monetary system more stable?
2. How can money be managed to stabilize aggregate demand and reduce fluctuations in economic activity?

In this chapter, we will explain how the monetary system works and will begin to answer question 1. Future chapters (especially 13 and 14) will provide greater

[1]As we saw in Chapter 9 (especially in Figure 9-4), those in the classical tradition argue that a fall in the quantity of money was a major cause of the collapse into the Depression. For details, see Milton Friedman and Anna Schwartz, *A Monetary History of the United States, 1867–1960* (Princeton, N.J.: Princeton University Press, 1963), Chap. 7. Keynesians tend to be more skeptical. See, for example, Peter Temin, *Did Monetary Forces Cause the Great Depression?* (New York: W. W. Norton, 1976). The disagreements between Keynesians and classicists over the importance of money will be explained in more detail in Chapter 14.

detail on the first point (the problems) and explain the second (the opportunities).

THE FUNCTIONS OF MONEY

Without money, specialized producers would have to resort to barter. Because barter is so cumbersome, a monetary system will naturally evolve, even in the absence of a government—as the development of a cigarette money in the prisoner-of-war camp so clearly illustrated (Chapter 3).

Money has three interrelated functions:

1. First, money acts as the ***medium of exchange;*** that is, it is used to buy goods and services.

2. When money is used as a medium of exchange, it also becomes the basis for quoting prices. For example,

BOX 12-1

WHEN THE INFLATION RATE IS 116,000%, PRICES CHANGE BY THE HOUR.†

In Bolivia, the Pesos Paid Out Can Outweigh the Purchases; No. 3 Import: More Pesos

by Sonia L. Nazario

LA PAZ, Bolivia, Feb. 6, 1985—A courier stumbles into Banco Boliviano Americano, struggling under the weight of a huge bag of money he is carrying on his back. He announces that the sack contains 32 million pesos, and a teller slaps on a notation to that effect. The courier pitches the bag into a corner.

"We don't bother counting the money any more," explains a loan officer standing nearby. "We take the client's word for what's in the bag." Pointing to the courier's load, he says, "That's a small deposit."

At that moment the 32 million pesos were worth only $500. Today, less than two weeks later, they are worth at least $180 less.

Bolivia's inflation rate is the highest in the world. In 1984, prices zoomed 2,700%, compared with a mere 329% the year before. Experts are predicting the inflation rate could soar as high as 40,000% this year. Even those estimates could prove conservative. The central bank last week announced January inflation of 80%; if that pace continued all year, it would mean annual inflation of 116,000%.

Prices go up by the day, the hour, or the customer. Julia Blanco Sirba, a vendor on this capital city's main street, sells a bar of chocolate for 35,000 pesos. Five minutes later, the next bar goes for 50,000 pesos. The two-inch stack of money needed to buy it far outweighs the chocolate.

Bolivians aren't yet lugging their money about in wheelbarrows, as the Germans did during the legendary hyperinflation of the Weimar Republic in the 1920's. But Bolivia seems headed in that direction.

Tons of paper money are printed. Planeloads of money arrive twice a week from printers in West Germany and Britain. Purchases of money cost Bolivia more than $20 million last year, making it the third-largest import, after wheat and mining equipment.

The 1,000 peso bill, the most commonly used, costs more to print than it purchases. It buys one bag of tea. To purchase an average size television set with 1,000 peso bills, customers have to haul money weighing more than 68 pounds into the showroom. (The inflation makes use of credit cards impossible here, and merchants generally don't take checks, either.)

"When it comes to inflation, we're the international champs," says Jorge von Bergen, an executive with a paper-products company, who lugs his money around in a small suitcase. His wife has to take the maid along to the market to help carry the bales of cash needed for her shopping. But all that money buys so little that Mrs. von Bergen easily carries her purchases back home on her own.

Because pesos are practically worthless, dollars now are being demanded for big-ticket purchases. People get their dollars from the 800 or so street-side money vendors who line Avenida Camacho, the Wall Street of La Paz. Banking, in effect, has moved outside.

†Abridged from the *Wall Street Journal*, Feb. 7, 1985, p. 1.

a car is priced at $10,000 and a pair of shoes at $50. Thus, money acts as the ***standard of value.***

3. Finally, money serves as a ***store of value.*** Because it can be used to buy goods or services whenever the need arises, money is a convenient way of holding wealth.

Of course, money is not a perfect store of value because its *purchasing power* can change. As we saw in Chapter 1 (Figure 1-4), prices of goods and services have risen and the purchasing power of money has consequently declined.

MONEY IN THE U.S. ECONOMY

If it waddles like a duck,
And quacks like a duck,
Then it is a duck.

Anonymous

Money is what money does. To define money, we should begin by looking at *what is actually used* to buy goods and services. What is used by the householder paying the electric bill? By the customer at the supermarket? By the child buying candy? By the employer paying wages?

Coins and paper currency (quarters, $1 bills, $10 bills, etc.), which together are known as ***currency,*** are used in many transactions—but certainly not in all. Indeed, most payments are made by check. When you write a check, it is an order to your bank to make payment out of your checking account. Thus, three items—coins, paper currency, and checking deposits—act as the media of exchange. They constitute the most basic and important concept of money, and they are represented by the symbol M1. Unless otherwise specified, this is what economists mean when they speak of ''money.''

M1 = currency plus checking deposits[2]

Checking deposits are by far the largest component of M1, amounting to more than $409 billion in March 1985, compared with $163 billion in currency.

Several complications should be noted about the basic definition of money, M1. M1 has been identified as the items which are *actually used* in making transactions. But something seems to have been left out. When shopping, people often use credit cards rather than either currency or checks. Yet, there is no mention of credit cards in the definition of money. There are two related reasons. First, in a fundamental sense, people don't ''pay'' with credit cards. They simply defer the payment for a few weeks or months. When the credit card bill comes, it must be paid with a check (or, conceivably, with currency). Thus, it is the final payment with a check, rather than the initial charging with a credit card, that represents the fundamental payment. It is the balance in the checking account which is money, not the credit card. Second, people *own* currency and checking accounts. Credit cards, on the other hand, represent an easy way to run up debt. If, as the result of a sudden windfall, I acquire an extra $1,000 which I deposit in my bank account, I will be very much aware of the fact and will clearly be better off as a result. On the other hand, if the credit card issuer informs me that I can charge an extra $1,000, I will not necessarily be better off. Indeed, I may scarcely notice. When we are calculating the quantity of money, we should not mix together *assets*—such as currency and checking deposits—with the *lines of credit* available to holders of credit cards.

A *line of credit* is a commitment by a lender to lend up to a specific amount to a borrower. For example, if I have a $2,000 line of credit with a credit card company, the company is committed to letting me charge up to $2,000.

The second complication is a small, but important, technical point. When the quantity of money is calculated, currency and deposits are counted only when they are held *by the public*—that is, by individuals and nonbank institutions such as manufacturing corporations. Holdings by the federal government, the Federal Reserve, and deposit-accepting institutions are excluded from the money stock, since these are the institutions

[2]Here and elsewhere in the discussion of money definitions, we skip over some of the details. For example, M1 also includes travelers checks. For precise definitions of the various concepts of money, see the footnotes to the table on monetary aggregates in the statistical appendix in any recent *Federal Reserve Bulletin*.

that create money. This exclusion makes sense. For example, if the Federal Reserve has a billion $1 bills printed up and stored in its vaults, it makes little sense to say that the money stock has gone up by $1 billion. That currency gains significance and becomes "money" only when it passes out of the hands of the Federal Reserve and into the hands of the public.

M2, M3, and Liquid Assets

Money is important because it is used in transactions; it makes the exchange of goods and services work much more smoothly and efficiently than a barter system. But money is also important because it can affect aggregate demand. When people have more money, they are likely to spend more.

Once we concentrate on the effect of money on spending, it is not clear that M1 is unique. The line between M1 and other similar assets is a fine one. Consider savings deposits against which checks cannot be written. It is true that such deposits cannot be used directly to make payments. But they can easily be switched into checking deposits, which in turn can be spent. The spending patterns of someone with $10,000 in a noncheckable savings account may not be very different from the spending of a person with $10,000 in a checking deposit.

Thus, when economists are investigating the effects of the banking system on aggregate demand, they frequently broaden their horizons beyond the narrowly defined M1 and also consider the other concepts shown in Figure 12-1. They often use a broader definition of money, M2, which includes noncheckable savings deposits and other close substitutes for M1:

M2 = M1 + noncheckable savings deposits
+ small time deposits (less than $100,000)

A *time deposit* in a bank or S&L is similar to a savings deposit, except that it has a specific time to ma-

FIGURE 12-1
Measures of money and liquidity
(March 1985; billions of dollars)

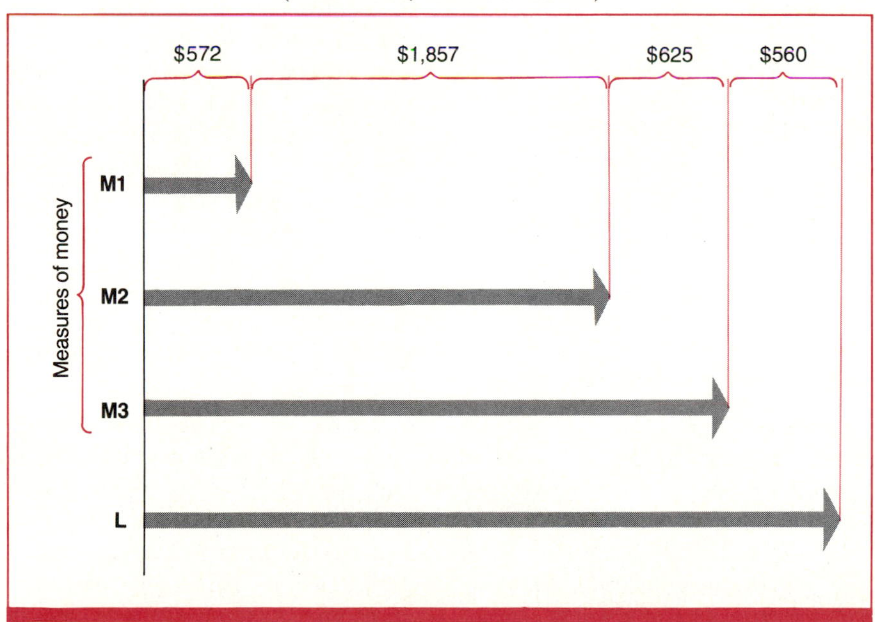

turity. For example, if you have a time deposit that matures in three months, your money is tied up until that date. If you want it sooner, you must pay a penalty.

Large time deposits (over $100,000) are generally held by businesses in the form of "certificates of deposit" (CDs). These can be sold on the financial markets, just as government securities can be sold, thus enabling the depositor to liquidate a CD at any time prior to maturity. These large time deposits are included in an even broader definition of money, M3:

M3 = M2 + large time deposits

In studying what determines spending, it is possible to go beyond M3 to consider other ***liquid assets*** or "near-monies"—such as U.S. savings bonds and short-term marketable government securities—that can be converted quickly into money (M1) with relatively little fuss and cost, and at a stable dollar value. (An example of an asset which is generally *not* liquid is real estate. It may be very difficult to sell, and its price may be quite uncertain, particularly if the owner is eager to sell quickly.)

Thus, macroeconomists also use one additional concept, that of liquid assets, L:

L = M3 + U.S. savings bonds
+ short-term Treasury securities
+ short-term marketable debt issued by corporations

A *liquid asset* is either money or an asset that can be converted easily into money (M1) at a stable dollar value.

BANKING AS A BUSINESS

Because checking deposits in banks constitute a large share of the money used in everyday purchases, banks occupy a strategic position in the economy. Never was this more clear than in the Great Depression, when many banks throughout the country went bankrupt. When Franklin Roosevelt became President in March 1933, the U.S. banking system was in a state of collapse. Monetary disruptions added to the other woes of the economy. Early 1933, with its chaotic banking conditions, marked the depth of the Depression.

However, while banks play a strategic role in the overall operation of the economy, they also have a particular significance to a small fraction of the population: the stockholders of banks. Banks, like manufacturing corporations or retail stores, are privately owned, and one of their major objectives is to make profits for their stockholders. Therefore, two questions are relevant in an analysis of banking operations: (1) How do banks earn profits? and (2) How can banks be used by the authorities to stabilize the economy?

The Goldsmith: The Embryonic Bank as a Warehouse

The quest for profits led to the development of the modern bank. How this happened can be illustrated by dipping briefly into the history of the ancestors of banks—the medieval goldsmiths.

As their name implies, goldsmiths worked and shaped the precious metal. But they also undertook another function. Because gold wares were extremely valuable, customers looked to the goldsmith for safe storage of their treasures. In return for the deposit of a valuable, the goldsmith would provide the customer with a warehouse receipt—the promise to return the valuable to the customer on demand. Thus, the goldsmiths performed a service for a rich elite that was basically similar to the service that a baggage checkroom performs for you or me. They stored packages for a fee and returned them to the owner on demand.

When unique gold ornaments were deposited, the customer naturally wanted to get back precisely the item which had been left with the goldsmith. But not only unique items were held by the goldsmiths for their customers; golden bars and golden coins were also deposited. In these cases, it was not essential to the depositor to get back *exactly* the same gold that had been deposited. Thus the basis for the development of banks was laid.

Fractional-Reserve Banking

To see how the banking business developed, let us look at the goldsmith's business in more detail. To do so, the balance sheet is a useful device. Recall the fundamental balance sheet equation presented in Chapter 6:

Assets = liabilities + net worth

Consider an early goldsmith who had 10,000 "dollars" of his own funds invested in a building. This investment showed up as a building on the left-hand asset side of the goldsmith's balance sheet, and as net worth on the right-hand side (Table 12-1). Now, suppose the goldsmith accepted $100,000 in gold coins for safekeeping. As the coins were in his possession, they appeared on the asset side. But the owners of the gold had the right to withdraw them at any time upon demand. The goldsmith had ***demand deposit liabilities*** of $100,000; he had to be prepared to provide the depositors with this much gold whenever they requested it. Thus, the early goldsmith had the balance sheet shown in Table 12-1.

At this stage, a fundamental question arose regarding the goldsmith's business. If it operated simply as a warehouse, holding the $100,000 in gold coins which the customers had deposited, it would not be very profitable. Its sole source of profits would be the small amount charged for safeguarding gold.

After some years of experience holding gold for many different depositors, the goldsmith might have noticed something interesting. Although he was committed to repay the gold of the depositors on demand, he did not actually repay them all at once in the normal course of events. Each week some of the depositors made withdrawals, but others added to their balances. There was a flow of gold out of the warehouse; but there was also an inflow. While there was some fluctuation in the goldsmith's total holdings of gold, a sizable quantity remained on deposit at all times.

Sooner or later a question therefore occurred to the goldsmith. Why not lend out some of this gold that was just sitting in the vaults, "collecting dust"? Since the depositors did not all try to withdraw their gold simultaneously, he did not need to have all the gold on hand. Some could be put to work earning interest. We can therefore imagine the goldsmith beginning to experiment by making loans. Undoubtedly he started cautiously, keeping a relatively large quantity of gold in his vaults. Specifically, suppose that he kept a large reserve of $40,000 in gold to pay off depositors in the event that a group of them suddenly demanded their gold back. He lent the remaining $60,000 in gold, with the borrowers giving him promissory notes stating their commitment to pay interest and repay the principal after a period of time. Then the goldsmith's balance sheet changed to the one shown in Table 12-2. The only difference was on the asset side: The goldsmith had exchanged $60,000 of gold for $60,000 in promissory notes (shown simply as "Loans").

In making loans, the goldsmith went beyond warehousing and entered the ***fractional-reserve banking*** business; that is, *he held gold reserves that were only a fraction of his demand deposit liabilities.* In normal times, everything worked out well. He kept enough gold to pay off all depositors who wanted to make withdrawals. And he earned interest on the loans he had made.

As time passed and goldsmiths gained confidence in the banking business, they experimented by keeping gold reserves that were lower and lower fractions of their deposit liabilities. Sometimes they had only 20% in reserve, or even less. They had an incentive to reduce reserves, because each additional dollar taken out of reserves and lent out meant that additional interest could be

TABLE 12-1
Balance Sheet of the Early Goldsmith

Assets		Liabilities	
Gold coins	$100,000	Demand deposit liabilities	$100,000
Building	$ 10,000	Net Worth	$ 10,000
Total	$110,000	Total	$110,000

The early goldsmith operated a warehouse, holding $1 in gold for every $1 in deposits.

earned. But, while the entry into fractional-reserve banking allowed goldsmiths to prosper, they faced two major risks in their new banking business:

1. Their loans might go sour; that is, goldsmiths might lend to businesses or individuals who became unable to repay. Clearly, then, the evaluation of credit risks (the estimation of the chances that borrowers would be unable to repay) became an important part of goldsmithing—and of modern banking.

2. Because they kept reserves equal to only a fraction of their demand deposit liabilities, the goldsmith-bankers were counting on a reasonably stable flow of deposits and withdrawals. In normal times, these flows were indeed likely to be stable. But the goldsmith-banker could not count on times being normal. If for some reason depositors became frightened, they would appear in droves to make withdrawals; in other words, there would be a *run* on the bank.

Bank Runs and Panics

During business downturns, people were particularly likely to become frightened and look for safety. What could be safer than holding gold? In crises, then, the public tended to switch into gold—that is, they withdrew gold from their banks. But the banks, operating with gold reserves equal to only a fraction of their deposits, did not have enough gold to pay off all their depositors. A panic, with a run on the banks, was the result. Since banks could not possibly pay off all their deposit liabilities, every individual depositor had an incentive to withdraw his or her deposit before the bank ran out of gold and was forced to close. For all depositors as a group, this was self-destructive behavior: The run could push banks into bankruptcy, with some depositors losing their money forever. But individual depositors could not be expected to commit financial suicide for the common good; they could not be expected to stay out of a lineup of those making withdrawals. Indeed, each depositor had a personal interest to be *first* in line to get back his or her gold.

THE MODERN U.S. BANKING SYSTEM

This account obviously has been an extremely simplified version of the history of banks. But it does help to explain why the U.S. banking system was periodically shaken with crises around the turn of the century. These banking crises added to the instability of the economy. After the panic of 1907, a National Monetary Commission was established to study monetary and banking problems; the Federal Reserve Act of 1913 was the result.

The Federal Reserve

The Federal Reserve—also known informally as the "Fed"—is the central bank of the United States. It is the American equivalent of foreign central banks, such as the Bank of England, the Deutsche Bundesbank of Germany, the Bank of Canada, and the Bank of Japan. As the central bank, the Federal Reserve:

1. Has the responsibility to *control the quantity of money* in the United States.

TABLE 12-2
The Goldsmith Becomes a Banker

Assets		Liabilities and net worth	
Reserve of gold coins	$ 40,000	Demand deposits	$100,000
Loans	$ 60,000	Net worth	$ 10,000
Building	$ 10,000		
Total	$110,000	Total	$110,000

When loans are made . . .
. . . reserves decline . . .
. . . and are now only a fraction of deposit liabilities.

Once the goldsmith had begun to lend the deposited gold and kept gold reserves equal to only a fraction of demand deposit liabilities, the business ceased to be a simple warehouse and became a bank.

2. *Issues paper currency* (dollar bills).

3. *Acts as the "bankers' bank."* While you and I keep our deposits in the commercial banks, commercial banks in turn keep deposits in the Federal Reserve. While you and I—and business corporations—can go to the commercial banks for loans, commercial banks in turn can borrow from the Federal Reserve. The Federal Reserve also helps the commercial banks to make the system of payment by check work smoothly and inexpensively.

4. *Supervises and inspects* commercial banks. (The U.S. Treasury, the Federal Deposit Insurance Corporation, and state banking authorities share this responsibility with the Fed.)

5. Acts as the *federal government's bank*. The government keeps some of its deposits in the Fed, and the Fed administers the sale of government bonds and their repayment when they come due. The Fed also acts on behalf of the government in buying and selling foreign currencies, such as German marks or Swiss francs.

How the Federal Reserve carries out these responsibilities will be major topics in future chapters.

The Commercial Banks

The commercial banks are the most direct descendants of the goldsmiths of old. They perform the two functions of the goldsmith-banker illustrated in Table 12-2; that is, they accept deposits and make loans to businesses and individuals. These two key functions show up clearly in the combined balance sheet of commercial banks shown in Table 12-3. Deposits are shown in items 7 and 8, and loans to businesses and individuals in item 4.

A number of other items on the balance sheet are also worthy of note, beginning with the first entry—reserves. Unlike the goldsmiths and the early banks, modern banks do not hold gold as reserves; gold is no longer the basic money of the United States or of other countries. Instead, banks hold two kinds of reserve: deposits in the Federal Reserve and currency. Banks are *required by law* to keep reserves equal to certain percentages of their deposits, the percentages being specified by the Federal Reserve within the legal limits set by Congress. Note that reserves, which appear on the *asset* side of the balance sheet, must meet the required percentages of the deposits (items 7 and 8) on the *liabilities* side of the bank's balance sheet. For example, with a required reserve ratio of 10%, a bank with \$50 million in deposit liabilities would have to hold \$5 million of its assets in the form of reserves.

TABLE 12-3
Combined Balance Sheet, Commercial Banks, March 1985
(billions of dollars)

Assets		Liabilities and net worth	
(1) Reserves		(7) Checking deposits	457.6
Currency	21.3	(8) Other savings and time deposits	1,167.6
Reserve deposits in Federal Reserve	20.0	(9) Other liabilities	480.7
(2) Deposits held in other banks, and other cash items	142.3	(10) Total liabilities	2,105.9
		(11) Net worth	149.4
(3) Securities			
U.S. government	250.8		
Other	132.8		
(4) Loans			
Commercial and industrial loans	482.7		
Other	989.0		
(5) Other assets	216.4		
(6) Total assets	2,255.3	(12) Total liabilities and net worth	2,255.3

***Required reserves* are reserves that deposit-accepting institutions are required to hold in order to meet their legal obligations. These reserves are specified as percentages of deposits. Required reserves are held in the form of currency or deposits in the Federal Reserve.**

Further down the asset side of the balance sheet, banks hold promissory notes representing loans they have extended to businesses and individuals (item 4). The banks also hold substantial amounts of securities issued by the federal and state governments (item 3).

Other Depository Institutions

Until the early 1970s, commercial banks played a unique role in the U.S. economy. They alone could accept checking deposits from the public. These deposits—known technically as *demand* deposits—paid no interest.

There were, however, a number of other financial institutions which could accept other types of deposits. Most important were thrift institutions such as the savings and loan associations (S&Ls) and savings banks, which accepted *savings* deposits from the public. The public could appear at these institutions and withdraw currency from their deposits, but checks could not be written on such deposits. The thrift institutions used the deposited funds mainly to lend to home buyers. Thus, the most important item on the asset side of their balance sheet was a portfolio of mortgages.

During the 1970s, the distinction between commercial banks and the thrift institutions began to break down. In 1972, a number of New England thrift institutions were eager to attract new deposits, and began to offer a new type of interest-bearing savings account against which a *negotiable order of withdrawal* (NOW) could be written. In effect, such an order was a check, and the thrift insitutions had gotten around the prohibition against checkable savings deposits. At first, the authorities resisted this change. NOW accounts were limited to New England.

However, in 1980 Congress took steps to deregulate financial institutions and encourage competition among them. Thrift institutions throughout the country were permitted to accept checking accounts. Commercial banks, which had previously been prohibited from paying interest on their checking accounts, were now permitted to do so. Thus, the principal distinctions between commercial banks and thrift institutions were eliminated. When we write about "commercial banks" in the following pages, the reader should understand that we mean "commercial banks and other depository institutions, such as savings and loan associations."

Remaining Regulations

In spite of the substantial deregulation of recent years, commercial banks and other depository institutions remain subject to regulations:

1. First, and most important, they are required to hold reserves as a fraction of their deposit liabilities. This regulation is critically important in the ability of the Federal Reserve to control the money stock, as we shall see.

2. Second, they are inspected by a number of agencies, such as the Federal Reserve and the U.S. Treasury. A major purpose of inspection is to prevent unsound practices which might threaten the survival of the institutions. (These inspections are not foolproof. During and following the recession of 1981–1982, the rate of bank failures rose sharply. Among the problem banks was one of the largest in the nation—the Continental Illinois Bank in Chicago—which would have gone bankrupt had it not received special assistance from the government.)

3. Banks have been prohibited from carrying on banking business—the acceptance of deposits and the making of loans—in more than one state. Some states restrict the area within which banks can do business. Illinois is most strict. It prohibits *branch banking*. That is, each bank is permitted to do business at one location only and is not permitted to have branches elsewhere in the state. Other states—such as California—permit state-wide branch banking.

The prohibition against interstate banking is beginning to break down. Some banks have been permitted to take over troubled banks in other states. Some banks have set up subsidiaries in the form of so-called "nonbank banks"—institutions which perform some, but not all, of the functions of banks and thus are permitted to cross state lines. Furthermore, a number of states have passed laws permitting regional banking. Banks from neighboring states would be allowed in, if the neighboring states grant reciprocal privileges letting their banks in. Such regional arrangements are currently subject to law suits, with the outcome in the courts being unclear. However, one conclusion is indisputable: Banking has become a highly competitive and rapidly changing business, and it promises to remain so in the future.

BANKS AND THE CREATION OF MONEY

The public's use of checking deposits as money would be reason enough to look carefully at the operation of banks. But banks require attention for an additional reason—one of great economic importance: In the normal course of their operations, banks create money. Most people have heard of this power in a vague and imprecise way. Banks are consequently looked on with a mixture of awe and resentment. How did they acquire this magical ability, and why should they have such extraordinary power? These attitudes reflect a lack of understanding of banking. There is, in fact, nothing magical in the process whereby money is created. Your local bank does not have a magical fountain pen with which it can create unlimited amounts of money out of thin air.

The operations of banks, and how they create money, can be understood most easily by looking at the balance sheets of individual banks. An individual commercial bank, like the aggregate of commercial banks shown in Table 12-3, has a list of assets and liabilities. To avoid being burdened with detail, we simplify the following tables by showing only the *changes* in the balance sheet of a bank. (Like the whole balance sheet, changes in the balance sheet *must* balance.) To avoid untidy fractions, we assume that the required reserves of banks are a nice round figure—20% of their checking deposit liabilities—even though requirements are not, in fact, this high. To simplify further, we assume that banks initially have just enough reserves to meet the legal reserve requirement.

Now, suppose that you find $100,000 left in a shoe box by your eccentric old uncle when he died. In a state of bliss, you rush to your local bank to put the $100,000 into your checking account. As a result, your bank—call it bank A—has $100,000 more in currency on the asset side of its balance sheet (Table 12-4). It also has

TABLE 12-4
Changes in Assets and Liabilities when Commercial Bank Receives Deposit

Commercial bank A			
Assets		**Liabilities**	
Reserves of currency	+$100,000	Checking deposits	+$100,000
Required $20,000			
Excess $80,000			
Total	$100,000	Total	$100,000

When you deposit $100,000 in currency . . .
. . . bank reserves also rise by $100,000.

Your balance sheet			
Assets		**Liabilities**	
Currency	−$100,000	No change	
Checking deposit	+$100,000		
Total	0	Total	0

When commercial bank A receives your $100,000 deposit, its assets and liabilities both rise by $100,000. But your holdings of money do not change. You have merely switched from one type of money (currency) to another (a checking deposit).

$100,000 more in liabilities, since you have a $100,000 claim on the bank in the form of a checking deposit. (This $100,000 deposit represents an *asset* to you; it is something you own. However, this same $100,000 deposit is a *liability* to the bank; the bank must be prepared to pay you $100,000 in currency if you ask.)

As a result of this deposit, what has happened to the quantity of money? The answer is: nothing. You initially held the $100,000 in currency; you exchanged the currency for $100,000 in checking deposit money. Once the deposit is made, the $100,000 in dollar bills ceases to be counted as part of the money stock, since it is held by the bank. (Remember the technical point regarding the data in Figure 12-1: Currency and checking deposits are included in the money stock only when they are held by the public but not when they are held by the the Federal Reserve, the U.S. Treasury, or deposit-accepting institutions.) The *composition* of the money stock has changed—there is now $100,000 more in checking deposits and $100,000 less in currency in the hands of the public. However, the total amount has not changed.

However, this is not the end of the story, because the bank now has excess reserves. Its checking deposit liabilities have gone up by your $100,000. Therefore, its required reserves have risen by $20,000 (that is, $100,000 times the required reserve ratio of 20%). But its total reserves have risen by the $100,000 in currency that you deposited, and so it now has $80,000 in ***excess reserves***. Like the goldsmith of old, it is in a position to make loans to businesses and other customers.

***Excess reserves* are reserves, in the form of currency or deposits in the Federal Reserve, that are in excess of those required.**

Excess reserves = total reserves − required reserves

Suppose that a local shoe store wants to expand its operations and approaches the bank for a loan of $80,000, an amount that just happens to equal the excess reserves of the bank. The bank agrees. Mechanically, what happens? The bank could, presumably, hand over $80,000 in dollar bills to the store owner, in exchange for the promissory note that commits the store to repay the loan. However, the bank does not normally operate this way. Instead, when it makes the loan, it simply adds $80,000 to the checking deposit of the borrower. This is entirely satisfactory to the borrower, who can write a check against the deposit. As a result of this loan, the balance sheet of the commercial bank is modified, as shown in Table 12-5.

Now, what has happened to the money supply? Observe that *when the bank makes a loan, the stock of money in the hands of the public increases*. Specifically, there now is $80,000 more in checking deposit money. But what has the bank done? Nothing extraordinary. It has merely lent its excess reserves; that is, it has lent *less* than was placed in its safekeeping when you made your original deposit.

TABLE 12-5
Bank A Makes a Loan

Assets		Liabilities	
Reserves of currency	$100,000	Checking deposits	
		of you	$100,000
Loan†	+$ 80,000	of shoe store†	+$ 80,000
Total	$180,000	Total	$180,000

When a bank makes a loan . . .
. . . checking deposits increase.

When the bank lends $80,000, checking deposits increase by $80,000. This represents a net increase in the money stock.

†Items resulting from the loan.

How a Check Is Cleared

So far, so good. However, our story has just nicely begun. The shoe store borrowed from the bank in order to buy inventory, not to leave its money sitting idly in a checking account. Suppose that the shoe store orders shoes from a Boston manufacturer, sending a check for \$80,000 in payment. The shoe manufacturer in Boston deposits the check in its bank (bank B). This sets in motion the process of ***check clearing***—which straightens out accounts between bank A in your home town and bank B in Boston (Figure 12-2). Bank B sends the check along to the Federal Reserve, receiving in exchange a reserve deposit of \$80,000. Bank B's accounts balance, since its assets in the form of reserves have gone up by the same amount (\$80,000) as its checking deposit liabilities to the shoe manufacturer. (The \$80,000 reserve deposit represents an *asset* to bank B and a *liability* to the Federal Reserve.)

The Fed, in turn, sends the check along to bank A, subtracting the \$80,000 from bank A's reserve deposit. Bank A balances its accounts by subtracting the \$80,000 from the deposit of the shoe store that wrote the check in the first place.

FIGURE 12-2
The clearing of a check
In the check-clearing process, the bank in which the check was deposited (bank B) acquires reserves, while the bank on which the check was drawn (bank A) loses reserves.

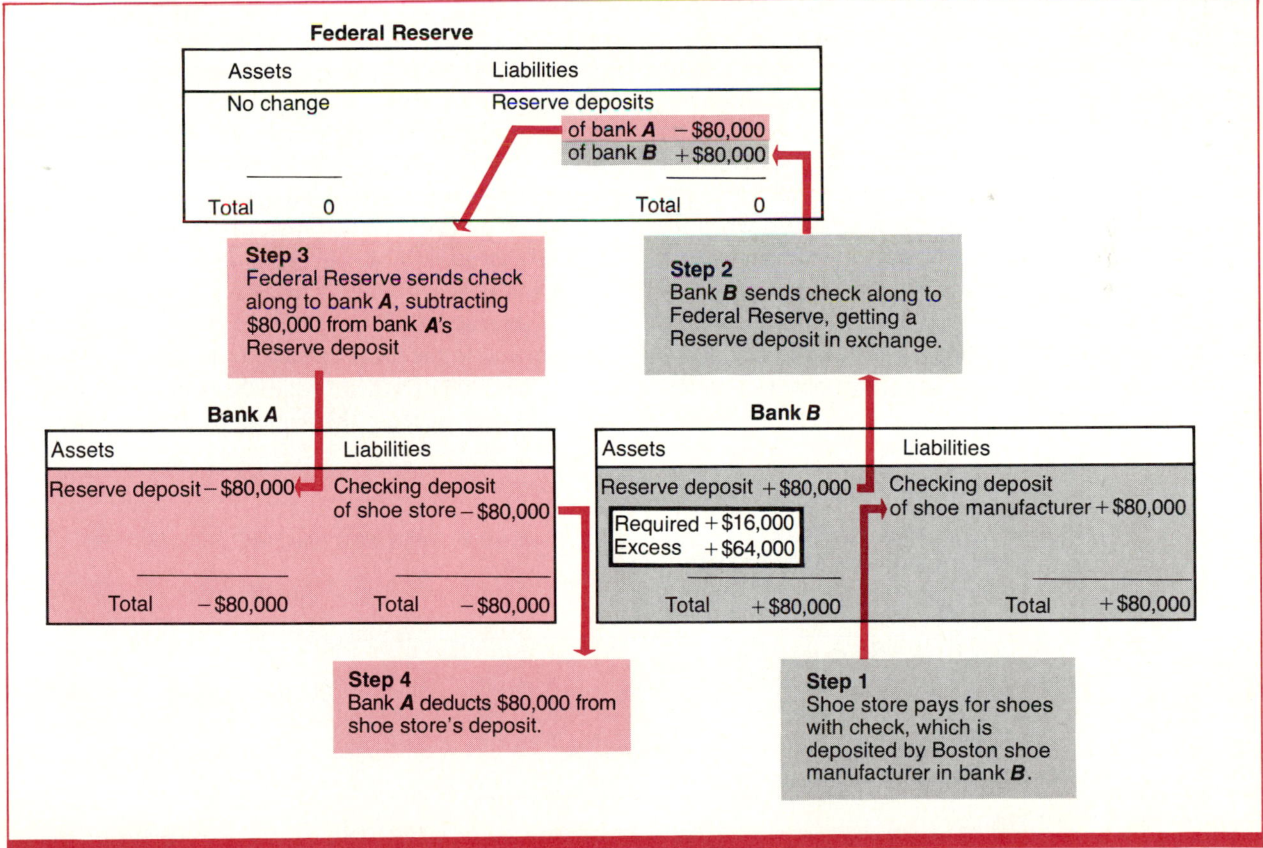

TABLE 12-6
Net Effects on Bank A
(check clearing combined with earlier transactions)

Assets		Liabilities	
Reserves	$ 20,000	Checking deposits of you	$100,000
Required $20,000; Excess 0			
Loan	$80,000		
Total	$100,000	Total	$100,000

This table gives the combined effect on bank A of check clearing (Figure 12-2) and earlier transactions (Table 12-5). After the check is cleared, bank A has no excess reserves.

Why a Bank Can Safely Lend No More than Its Excess Reserves

When the effects of the check clearing (in Figure 12-2) are added to bank A's earlier transactions (shown in Table 12-5), the net effects on bank A's balance sheet may be summarized in Table 12-6. Observe that, as a result of the check clearing, bank A's excess reserves have completely disappeared. (Its currency reserves rose by $100,000 when you deposited the original $100,000. Its reserve deposit in the Fed fell by $80,000 when the shoe store's check cleared. Thus, its net change in reserves is $20,000, just the amount required as a result of its $100,000 checking deposit liability to you.) This was the result of bank A's lending the shoe store an amount equal to its excess reserves. Thus, we come to a fundamental proposition:

A bank may prudently lend an amount up to, but no greater than, its excess reserves.

The Multiple Expansion of Bank Deposits

We have seen how bank A's excess reserves are eliminated when the shoe store's $80,000 check clears. But observe (in Figure 12-2) that bank B now has excess reserves of $64,000, that is, the difference between the $80,000 increase in its actual reserves and the $16,000 increase in its required reserves. ($16,000 = 20% of the $80,000 increase in its checking deposit liabilities.)

Bank B may prudently lend up to the $64,000 of its excess reserves. In Table 12-7, we suppose that it lends this amount to the local camera store. When the loan is made, $64,000 is added to the checking deposit of the camera store. Because the amount of checking deposits

TABLE 12-7
Bank B Lends to Camera Store

Assets		Liabilities	
Reserve deposit	$ 80,000	Checking deposits of shoe manufacturer	$ 80,000
Loan†	+$ 64,000	of camera store†	+$ 64,000
Total	$144,000	Total	$144,000

When bank B lends $64,000 . . .
. . . checking deposits increase by $64,000.

As a result of the second round of lending, the money stock increases by $64,000.

†Items resulting from the loan.

held by the public goes up by \$64,000, *the money stock increases by this amount.*

Suppose that the camera store has borrowed the \$64,000 to buy film, cameras, and equipment from Kodak. To pay for its purchases, it writes a check to Kodak. Kodak deposits the check in its Rochester, New York, bank—bank C. Once again, the check-clearing mechanism is set in operation. When bank C sends the check to the Federal Reserve, it receives a reserve deposit of \$64,000 (Table 12-8). But when the check is sent along to bank B (the camera store's bank), that bank loses \$64,000 in reserves and no longer has any excess reserves.

Observe, however, that bank C now has excess reserves of \$51,200, which it can lend out. When it does so, it will create a new checking deposit of \$51,200, thus increasing the money stock once again. And so the process continues. As a result of your initial deposit of \$100,000, there can be a chain reaction of loans, as shown in Figure 12-3 and Table 12-9. At each stage, the amount of loans that can be made (and the amount of deposits that can thereby be created) is 80% of the amount made in the previous stage. The total increase in deposits is the sum of the series: $\$100{,}000 + \$100{,}000 \times 0.08 + \$100{,}000 \times 0.8^2 \ldots$ If this series is taken to its limit—with an infinite number of rounds—then, by a basic algebraic proposition,[3] the sum is equal to $\$100{,}000/(1 - 0.8) = \$500{,}000$.

Thus, when the banking system acquires additional reserves, it can increase checking deposits by a multiple of the initial reserve increase. The checking deposit multiplier D is equal to the reciprocal of the required reserve ratio R:

$$D = \frac{1}{R}$$

In our example:

$$D = \frac{1}{20\%} = 5$$

[3]Mathematically, this is the same theorem used in the derivation of the multiplier in Chapter 10 (footnote 3). But the economic issues are quite different in the two cases. In the multiplier, the total effects of various rounds of spending are derived. Here, changes in the stock of money are calculated.

TABLE 12-8
The Creation of Money: After the Second Round

Bank B			
Assets		**Liabilities**	
Reserves	\$16,000	Checking deposits of shoe manufacturer	\$80,000
Required \$16,000			
Excess 0			
Loans	\$64,000		
Total	\$80,000	Total	\$80,000

Bank C			
Assets		**Liabilities**	
Reserves	\$64,000	Checking deposits of Kodak	\$64,000
Required \$12,800			
Excess \$51,200			
Total	\$64,000	Total	\$64,000

When bank C receives deposits and reserves of \$64,000, it can prudently lend \$51,200. And so the process continues.

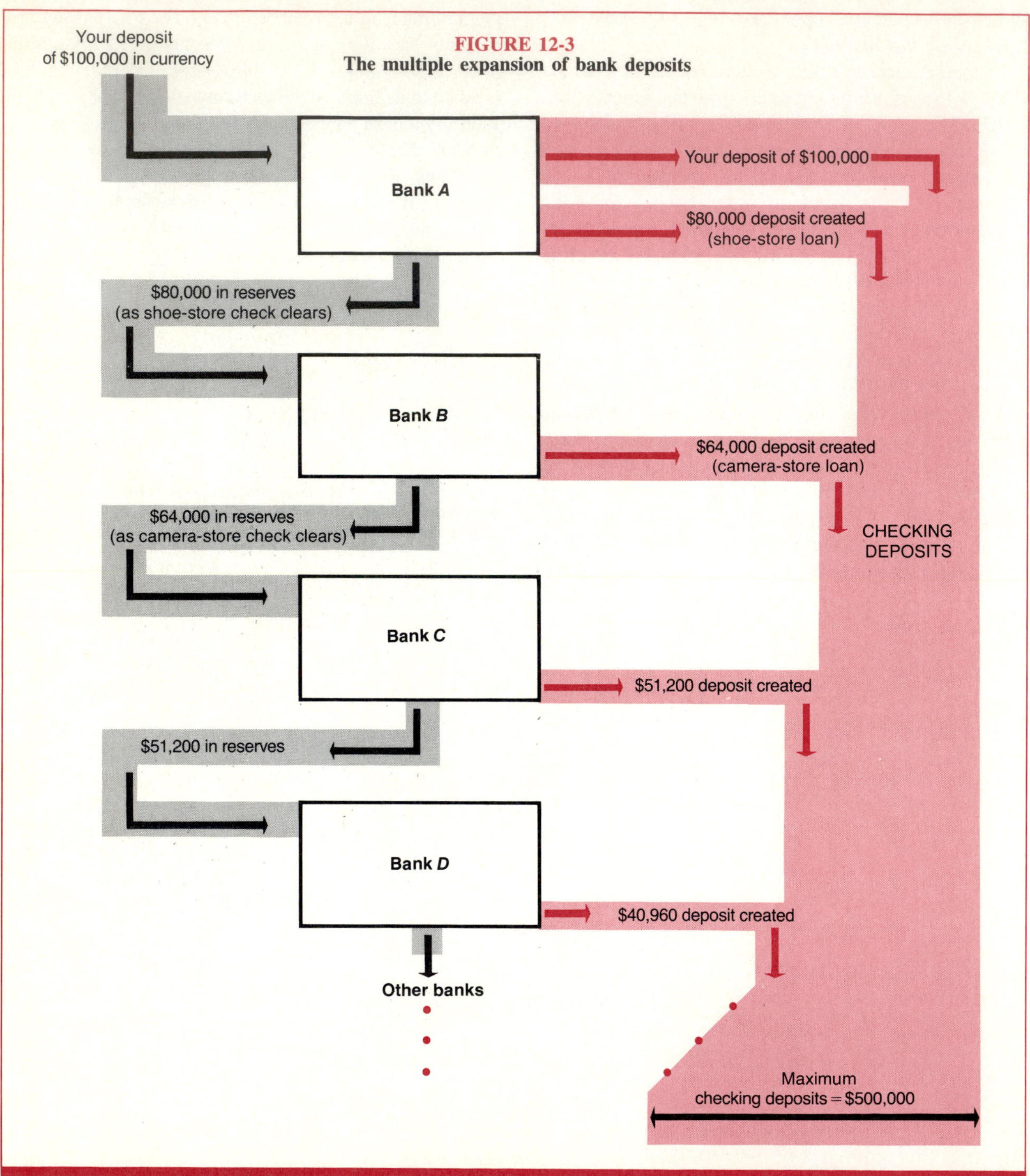

FIGURE 12-3
The multiple expansion of bank deposits

The initial acquisition of $100,000 in reserves made possible an increase in checking deposits of $500,000 (that is, $100,000 × 1/0.2). Alternatively, if the required reserve ratio were only 10%, the banking system would have been capable of creating up to $1,000,000 (that is, $100,000 × 1/0.1) in checking deposits on the basis of $100,000 in reserves. Thus, *when the Federal Reserve changes the required reserve ratio,* as it is permitted to do, *it can have a powerful effect on the amount of loans which the banks can make and on the amount of checking deposits which they can create.*

During the multiple expansion of deposits, the banking system as a whole does something which no single bank can do. *The banking system as a whole can create deposits equal to a multiple of the reserves which it acquires. But any single bank can create deposits* (by lending its excess reserves) *by an amount equal to only a fraction* (80% in our illustration) *of the reserves which it acquires.*

Two Complications

With a required reserve ratio of 20%, $500,000 is the *maximum* increase in checking deposits following a $100,000 acquisition of reserves by the banking system.

TABLE 12-9
The Multiple Expansion of Bank Deposits

A. The chain reaction

Bank	(1) Acquired reserves and checking deposits	(2) Required reserves (2) = (1) × 0.20	(3) Excess reserves = loans which banks can make (3) = (1) − (2)	(4) Changes in money stock (4) = (3)
A	$100,000 (yours)	$20,000	$80,000	$80,000
B	$80,000 (shoe manufacturer's)	$16,000	$64,000	$64,000
C	$64,000 (Kodak's)	$12,800	$51,200	$51,200
D	$51,200	$10,240	$40,960	$40,960
.	.	.	.	.
.	.	.	.	.
.	.	.	.	.
Maximum sum	$500,000	$100,000	$400,000	$400,000

B. Effects on consolidated balance sheet of all commercial banks (with maximum permissible expansion)

Assets		Liabilities	
Reserves	$100,000	Checking deposits	$500,000
Required $100,000; Excess 0			
Loans	$400,000		
Total	$500,000	Total	$500,000

The banking system as a whole can do what no single bank can do. It can transform the original deposit of $100,000 in currency into as much as $500,000 in checking deposit money.

In practice, the actual increase in checking deposits is likely to be considerably less, because of two complications:

1. Banks may decide not to lend out the maximum permitted but to hold some excess reserves instead. During prosperous times, this is not an important complication. Banks receive no interest on their reserves—currency yields no interest, and the Fed does not pay interest on the reserve deposits of banks. Banks have a strong incentive to make loans in order to increase their interest earnings. As a result, the amount of excess reserves they hold is generally very small—much less than 1% of total reserves.

However, during a depression, bankers may be panic-stricken. They may be afraid to make loans because they doubt the ability of borrowers to repay. They may decide to keep their funds secure by holding them as excess reserves rather than lending them out. During the Great Depression, excess reserves skyrocketed, reaching about 50% of total reserves by 1940. This unwillingness of the banks to lend tended to keep down the amount of money in the hands of the public and slowed the recovery. Thus, bank holdings of excess reserves may fluctuate in a perverse manner. Banks may hold large excess reserves during a depression, thereby keeping down the quantity of money. But this is precisely the time when it is most desirable for the quantity of money to expand.

2. As loans are made and people get more checking deposit money, they may want to hold more currency, too. In other words, they may withdraw cash from their deposits. Insofar as this happens, the reserves of the banks are reduced; the initial deposit of currency that started off the expansion is partially reversed. As a consequence, the total amount of monetary expansion is reduced.

When currency is held by the public, it is, in a sense, just ordinary money. The dollar I hold in my pocket is only a dollar. On the other hand, when currency is deposited in a bank, it becomes "high-powered." Although the dollar ceases to count directly in the money stock (since bank holdings of currency are excluded from the definition of money), that dollar bill is a bank reserve. On this reserve base, the banking system can build a superstructure of as much as $5 of checking deposit money if the required reserve ratio is 20%. The large amount of checking deposit money, built on a much smaller base of reserves, can be represented graphically by an inverted pyramid (Figure 12-4).

WHEN BANKS PURCHASE SECURITIES, THE MONEY SUPPLY ALSO INCREASES

Thus far, we have assumed that a commercial bank with excess reserves lends these excess reserves to its customers in order to earn interest. Alternatively, banks can use these funds to purchase securities, such as bonds issued by federal, state, and local governments or by private corporations. The effect on the money stock is similar, whether the banks use their excess reserves to make loans or purchase securities.

To illustrate this point, suppose that, in the *n*th round in the monetary expansion chain, bank N acquires

FIGURE 12-4
The inverted monetary pyramid
On their reserve base of currency and reserve deposits, the commercial banking system can build a superstructure of checking deposits—of as much as $1/R$ times the base.

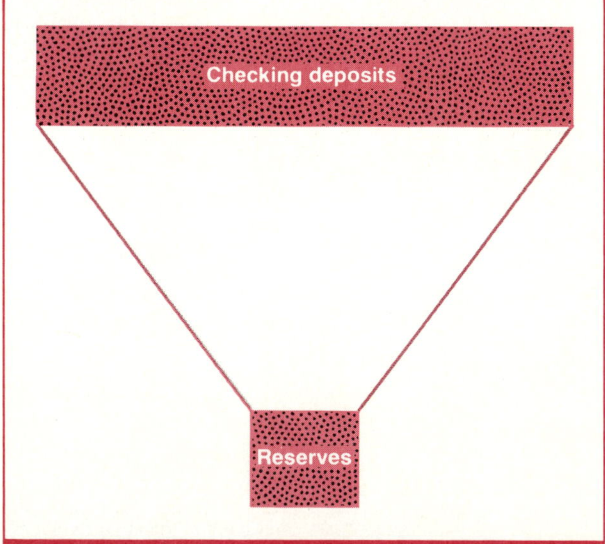

$10,000 in checking deposits and reserves. If the required reserve ratio is 20%, it then has $8,000 in excess reserves. Suppose that it uses these reserves to purchase $8,000 in government bonds owned by the XYZ Corporation. Bank N pays for the bonds by writing a check, which the XYZ Corporation deposits in bank O. Then the money stock as a consequence rises by $8,000, that is, by the $8,000 checking deposit which the XYZ Corporation now owns. The change in the money stock is thus exactly the same as it would have been if bank N had used these excess reserves to make a loan rather than to buy a bond. Moreover, as a result of this transaction, bank N loses its $8,000 of excess reserves, while bank O gains $8,000 of reserves. It is now bank O that finds itself with excess reserves ($6,400, to be precise). When it uses these reserves to make a loan or buy securities, the process of money creation continues.

Thus, it doesn't matter whether banks make loans or purchase bonds. The same multiple expansion of the money supply takes place.

KEY POINTS

1. Money is important in the study of macroeconomics because:

(*a*) The authorities can take steps to alter the quantity of money and thus affect aggregate demand. *Monetary policy* is the second great tool, along with fiscal policy, that can be used to manage aggregate demand. The details of monetary policy will be explained in Chapter 13.

(*b*) At times, strong disturbances have occurred in the monetary system; for example, during the panic of 1907 and the Depression of 1933. Such disturbances can make the economy unstable.

2. Money has three interrelated functions. It acts as (*a*) the medium of exchange, (*b*) the standard of value, (*c*) a store of value.

3. Because currency and checking deposits are used in transactions, they are included in the basic definition of the money stock, M1. Checking deposits constitute by far the larger component of M1.

4. Noncheckable savings and time deposits are close substitutes for M1. When studying how money and the banking system affect aggregate demand, economists thus sometimes focus on an alternative definition of money, M2:

M2 = M1 + noncheckable savings deposits
+ small time deposits (less than $100,000)

A third concept, M3, includes large time deposits.

5. The Federal Reserve is the central bank of the United States. As such:

(*a*) It has the responsibility to control the quantity of money.

(*b*) It issues paper currency.

(*c*) It acts as the "bankers' bank."

(*d*) It supervises and inspects commercial banks.

(*e*) It acts as the federal government's bank.

6. Banks have two principal functions: to accept deposits and to make loans. When a bank makes a loan or purchases a bond, it increases the stock of money.

7. Commercial banks and other depository institutions are required to hold reserves in the form of currency or reserve deposits in the Federal Reserve. These reserves must meet required percentages of the commercial bank's deposit liabilities. The purpose of required reserves is to control the quantity of money that banks can create.

8. When a *single* bank acquires additional deposits and reserves, it can safely lend out only a fraction of these reserves—specifically, its excess reserves. However, the banking *system* (all banks and other depository institutions as a whole) can create deposits that are a multiple of any new reserves that it acquires.

9. The maximum increase in checking deposits that can be created by the banking system is:

$$\frac{1}{R} \times \text{the acquisition of reserves}$$

where R is the required reserve ratio.

10. In practice, the increase is likely to be less than the maximum, since:

(*a*) Banks sometimes hold substantial excess reserves, especially during a depression. During the 1930s, the unwillingness of banks to lend their excess reserves kept down the quantity of money and slowed the recovery from the Great Depression.

(*b*) As people get more checking deposit money, they are likely to want to hold more currency, too. When they withdraw currency from their deposits, the reserves held by the banks are reduced.

KEY CONCEPTS

monetary policy
medium of exchange
standard of value
store of value
currency
Federal Reserve note
checking deposit
savings deposit
time deposit
certificate of deposit (CD)
M1
M2
M3
liquid assets (L)
credit card
line of credit
fractional-reserve banking
balance sheet
checking deposit liability
promissory note
loan
bank run
Federal Reserve
central bank
commercial bank
savings and loan association (S&L)
required reserve ratio
required reserves
excess reserves
check clearing
multiple expansion of bank deposits
checking deposit multiplier
"high-powered" reserves
monetary pyramid

PROBLEMS

12-1. (*a*) Suppose that a corporation that previously paid its workers in cash decides to pay them by check instead. As a result, it decides to deposit $10,000 which it has held in currency in its safe. Show how this deposit will affect the balance sheets of (1) the corporation and (2) its bank (the First National Bank of Buffalo).

(*b*) Does this deposit of $10,000 affect the money stock? Why or why not?

(*c*) How much can the First National Bank of Buffalo now lend, if there is a required reserve ratio of 10%? If it lends this amount to a farmer to buy machinery, show the direct effect of the loan on the bank's balance sheet. Then show the First National Bank of Buffalo's balance sheet after the farmer spends the loan to buy machinery and the farmer's check is cleared.

(*d*) As a result of the original deposit [in part (*a*) of this problem], what is the maximum increase in checking deposits which can occur if the required reserve ratio is 10%? The maximum amount of bank lending? The maximum increase in the money stock?

12-2. Suppose that a bank receives a deposit of $100,000 and decides to lend the full $100,000. Explain how this decision can get the bank into difficulty.

12-3. If all banks are required to keep reserves equal to 100% of their checking deposits, what will be the consequences of a deposit of $100,000 of currency in bank A?

12-4. During the 1930s, banks held large excess reserves. Now they hold practically none. Why? If you were a banker, would you hold excess reserves? How much? Does your answer depend on the size of individual deposits in your bank? On interest rates? On other things?

12-5. Suppose that there is a single huge commercial bank that holds a monopoly on all banking in the United States. If this bank receives $100,000 in deposits, and if the required reserve ratio is 20%, how much can the bank safely lend? Explain. [Hints: (1) Study Table 12-9, part

B. (2) In Figure 12-2, bank A lost reserves to bank B. If there is only one bank, will it lose reserves in this way?]

12-6. During the 1930s, the U.S. banking system did not work well. Banking disturbances contributed to the depth and duration of the depression.

(*a*) Explain how, during a financial crisis, individual bank depositors have an incentive to behave in a manner that makes the crisis worse. Do you think that an educational campaign to teach depositors the dangers of such actions would help to solve this problem? If so, explain how. If not, explain why not.

(*b*) Explain how, during a depression, individual banks have an incentive to behave in a manner that makes the depression deeper and longer-lasting. Do you think that an educational campaign to teach bankers the dangers of such actions would help to solve this problem? If so, explain how. If not, explain why not.

CHAPTER 13

THE FEDERAL RESERVE AND MONETARY POLICY

There have been three great inventions since the beginning of time: fire, the wheel, and central banking.

WILL ROGERS

The Federal Reserve is the central bank of the United States, acting as the federal government's bank and the bankers' bank. As the central bank, it has one responsibility of prime importance. *It controls the quantity of reserves held by the commercial banks* and thereby controls the amount of checking deposit money that they can create. Its responsibility is to see that monetary conditions are consistent with the goals of high employment and stable prices. If too much money is created, inflation will be the result. On the other hand, if the money stock declines, the economy is likely to fall into a recession. In this chapter, we will examine the three principal policy tools used by the Federal Reserve to control the quantity of money:

1. Open market operations, that is, purchases or sales of government bonds or shorter-term securities by the Federal Reserve
2. Changes in the discount rate, that is, changes in the interest rate at which the Federal Reserve lends to banks
3. Changes in required reserve ratios that banks must hold as percentages of their checking and time deposits

Before explaining these tools in detail, let us look briefly at the way the Federal Reserve is organized.

THE ORGANIZATION OF THE FEDERAL RESERVE

When the Federal Reserve Act was passed in 1913, the very concept of a central bank was controversial. Those who opposed the creation of a central bank feared that it would result in a concentration of monetary power, with serious political consequences. This fear was not new. The Second Bank of the United States, which had acted as a rudimentary central bank in the early nineteenth century, had come to an abrupt end at the hands of Andrew Jackson, who attacked its political power. "The bank," said Jackson, "is trying to kill me, *but I will kill it*."[1] And so he did.

The political controversies and compromises that surrounded the establishment of the Federal Reserve show up in its untidy organizational structure. In order to diffuse power, the Federal Reserve was organized with 12 regional Federal Reserve Banks, in Boston, New York, Philadelphia, and other major cities (Figure 13-1). These 12 district banks handle most of the everyday operations of the Fed, including the clearing of checks and the issue of new currency. (If you look to the left of the President's picture on a dollar bill, you will find a seal which identifies the Federal Reserve Bank that issued it.) In Washington, overall coordination is provided by the seven-member Board of Governors of the Federal Reserve System—also known, more simply, as the Federal Reserve Board. During the history of the Fed, there have been numerous power struggles between the Board and the district banks. In the 1920s, the Board was overshadowed by the forceful president of the Federal Reserve Bank of New York, Benjamin Strong. More recently, the Fed has been dominated by the chairmen of the Federal Reserve Board—most notably, William McChesney Martin, who headed the Board from 1951 to 1970; his successor, Arthur F. Burns (1970–1978); and, most recently, Paul Volcker (1979–   ).

[1] Arthur M. Schlesinger, Jr., *The Age of Jackson,* abr. ed. (New York: Mentor, 1949), p. 42.

There have been many revisions in the Federal Reserve Act. The major current powers of the Board and the 12 regional Federal Reserve Banks are those listed in Figure 13-2. Each of the principal tools of the Federal Reserve is treated differently:

1. *Open market operations*. This tool, the most important of all, is controlled by the Federal Open Market Committee (FOMC), which consists of the seven members of the Board of Governors and five of the presidents of the 12 district Federal Reserve Banks. The president of the New York Fed is a permanent member of the FOMC, with the other regional presidents serving on a rotating basis. The FOMC issues directives to the trading desk in the New York Fed, which handles the actual purchase or sale of securities.

2. *Changes in the discount rate*. Proposals for change are made by the regional Federal Reserve Banks, but they must be approved by the Federal Reserve Board.
3. *Changes in required reserve ratios*. Power to change these ratios is held by the Federal Reserve Board in Washington, subject to limits prescribed by Congress.

The members of the Federal Reserve Board are appointed by the President of the United States, subject to Congressional approval. In order to provide the Board with a degree of independence from political pressures and thus to strengthen its ability to fight inflation, members of the Board are appointed for extended 14-year terms, with one position becoming vacant every 2 years. The chairman serves for a 4-year term, which may be renewed.

FIGURE 13-1
The Federal Reserve System
The United States is divided into twelve Federal Reserve districts, each with a Federal Reserve bank. (Alaska and Hawaii are part of the district served by the Federal Reserve Bank of San Francisco.)

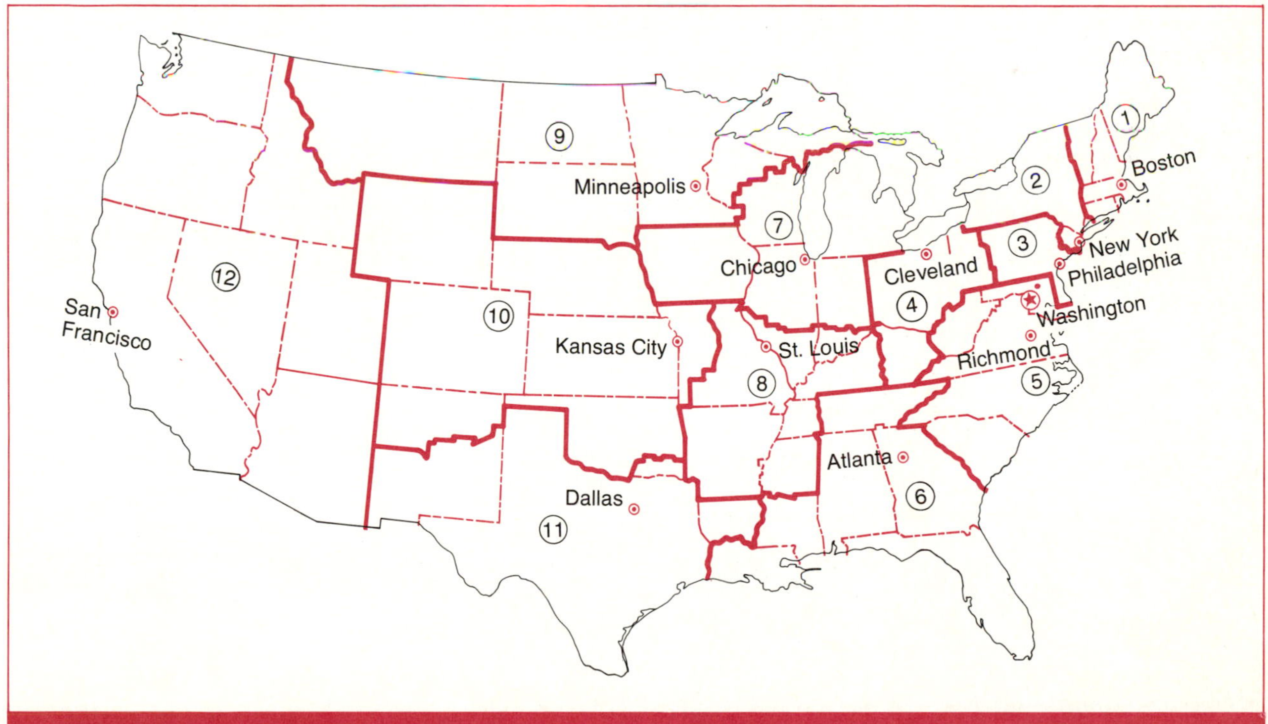

OPEN MARKET OPERATIONS

The Federal Reserve can increase the quantity of commercial bank reserves—and thereby increase the quantity of checking deposit money which the banks can create—by purchasing U.S. government securities on the open market. To make such a purchase, the Fed puts in a bid on the securities market; the seller may be any bank or any member of the general public who holds government securities and is willing to sell. Who the actual seller will be, the Fed does not know. But whether the government security is sold by a bank or by the public, the results are similar.

Suppose the Fed puts in a bid for $100,000 worth of government securities and that General Motors is the seller. General Motors delivers the securities and gets a check for $100,000 in return. GM deposits this check in its commercial bank (bank A). In turn, bank A sends the check along to the Federal Reserve and has its deposit with the Fed increased by $100,000. The changes in the balance sheets of the Fed and commercial bank A are shown in Table 13-1. Observe that, *when the Federal Reserve pays for the government securities, it increases the reserves of the commercial banking system.*

At the initial step shown in Table 13-1, the money supply has gone up by $100,000. Why? The answer is: GM's checking deposit is counted as part of the money stock. (The government security which GM gave up was not part of the money stock.) Furthermore, *the stage is set for an additional expansion* because of the new reserves held by bank A. Specifically, bank A now has $80,000 in excess reserves that can be lent. A whole series of loans, similar to those already described in Chapter 12, can take place. Thus, with a 20% required

FIGURE 13-2
The organization of the Federal Reserve System

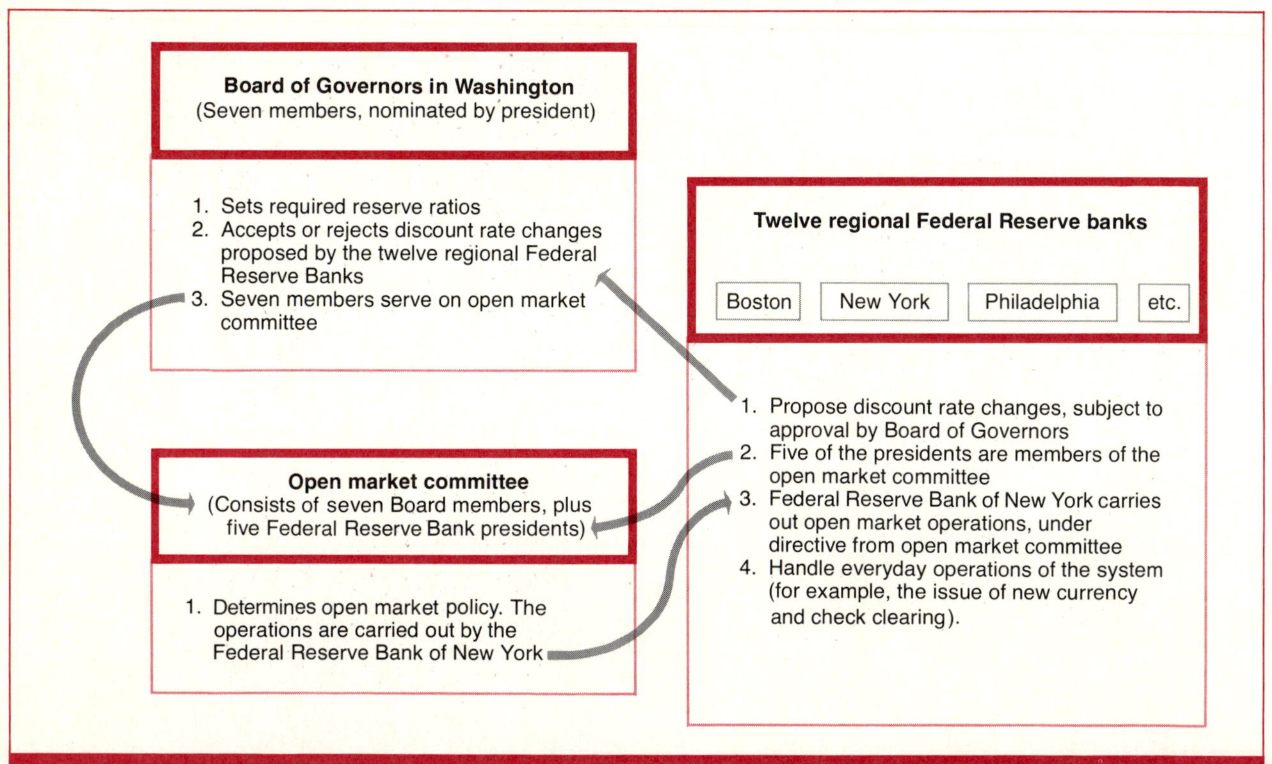

reserve ratio, the $100,000 open market purchase makes possible a maximum increase of $500,000 in checking deposits—that is, an increase of $500,000 in the money stock. (Again, as explained in Chapter 12, this is a maximum. In practice, the actual increase will be less, insofar as the public decides to hold more currency along with its higher checking deposits, and insofar as commercial banks hold excess reserves.)

This, then, is the power of open market operations. The Fed carries out the simple transaction of buying a government security, and the reserves of the banking system increase as a result. Thus, the Fed makes possible an increase in the nation's money supply.

Now suppose that the Fed buys the $100,000 worth of government securities from a commercial bank rather than from General Motors. The end result is the same. The maximum increase in the money stock is once again $500,000, although the mechanics are slightly different. Table 13-2 shows the initial effects of an open market operation if the Fed buys the government securities from the Chase Manhattan Bank. Chase sends the government securities to the Fed. The Fed pays for the securities *by adding $100,000 to the reserves of the Chase Manhattan Bank.* Once again, commercial bank reserves have increased when the Fed pays for its open market purchase. However, observe that, at the initial stage shown in Table 13-2, no change has yet taken place in the money stock. Why? The reason is: Nothing has yet happened to the public's holdings of currency or checking deposits. But note that Chase now has a full $100,000 in excess reserves, since its total reserves have gone up by $100,000 while its deposit liabilities—and therefore its required reserves—have not changed. Chase can safely lend the full $100,000 in excess reserves, creating a $100,000 checking deposit when it does so. Once again, the maximum checking deposit expansion is the series $100,000 + $80,000 + $64,000 + . . . , giving a total of $500,000.

In both examples of an open market purchase (Tables 13-1 and 13-2), note that when the Federal Reserve acquires assets (the government securities), its liabilities also go up. This is scarcely surprising, since the balance

TABLE 13-1

An Open Market Purchase: Initial Effects

(thousands of dollars)

Federal Reserve			
Assets		**Liabilities**	
Government securities	+100	Reserve deposits of bank A	+100
Total	100	Total	100

Commercial bank A			
Assets		**Liabilities**	
Reserve deposit (Required 20; Excess 80)	+100	Checking deposits of GM	+100
Total	100	Total	100

Fed gets government securities.

Commercial bank gets reserve deposit.

GM gets checking deposit.

At this stage, the money supply has increased by $100,000, because GM has a checking deposit of that amount.

Commercial bank A has excess reserves, and therefore a further expansion of the money supply can take place.

TABLE 13-2
An Open Market Purchase: When a Commercial Bank Is the Seller
(initial effects, in thousands of dollars)

Federal Reserve			
Assets		**Liabilities**	
Government securities	+100	Reserve deposits of Chase Manhattan	+100
Total	100	Total	100

Chase Manhattan Bank			
Assets		**Liabilities**	
Government securities	−100	No change	
Reserve deposit	+100		
(Required 0; Excess 100)			
Total	0	Total	0

Government security goes from commercial bank to Fed.
Commercial bank gets reserve deposit.

If the Fed buys the government security from a commercial bank (say, Chase Manhattan), no change takes place in the money stock at this initial stage. However, Chase Manhattan now has a full $100,000 in excess reserves, which it can lend out.

sheet must balance. The increase in Federal Reserve liabilities takes the form of reserve deposits, which act as the reserves of the commercial banks. To summarize briefly:

> **When the Fed wants to increase the quantity of money, it purchases government securities on the open market. When it pays for these securities, it creates new bank reserves. The additional bank reserves make possible a multiple expansion of the money stock.**

Restrictive Open Market Operations

Just as the Fed purchases securities when it wants to increase the money supply, so it sells securities when it wants to decrease the money supply. The numbers on the balance sheets are the same as in Tables 13-1 and 13-2, but the signs are the opposite. For example, when the Fed sells $100,000 in securities to the Chase Manhattan Bank, its holdings of government securities go down by $100,000 and the reserve deposits of Chase also go down by $100,000.

However, an actual open market sale might lead to very tight monetary conditions. We live in a growing economy, in which productive capacity increases. It is appropriate for the money stock to grow through time, in order to encourage aggregate demand to grow and keep the economy at full employment. Thus, restrictive policies by the Federal Reserve normally do not involve actual sales of securities. Rather, *a reduction in the rate of security purchases,* aimed at reducing the *rate of growth* of the money stock, generally provides monetary conditions that are as tight as the Fed wishes in its fight against inflation.

OPEN MARKET OPERATIONS AND INTEREST RATES

When the Federal Reserve goes on the market to buy government bonds or shorter-term securities, it increases the demand for these securities. As a result, it puts upward pressure on their prices.

There is an important relationship between security prices and interest rates. To see why, let us look at U.S. Treasury bills. These are the short-term government securities which the Fed usually purchases in its open market operations. Unlike a government bond, which provides semiannual interest payments, a Treasury bill involves no explicit interest payment. It simply represents a promise by the government to pay, say, $100,000 on a specific date, usually 3 months after the date of issue. The purchaser obtains a yield by purchasing the bill at a *discount,* that is, for less than the full $100,000 face value. For example, a buyer who pays $97,000 for a 3-month bill gets $3,000 more than the purchase price when the bill reaches maturity. Thus, the interest or yield on that bill is approximately 3% for the 3-month period—that is, 12% per annum. (By convention, interest is quoted at an annual rate, even for securities with less than 1 year to maturity.)

Suppose that the Fed enters the market, bidding for Treasury bills and pushing their price up to $98,000. Now, what can be gained by purchasing a bill at this price? Only $2,000, or about 2% for the 3 months; that is, only 8% per annum. Thus, we see that:

> **Security prices and interest rates *move in opposite directions*. A "rise in the price of Treasury bills" (from $97,000 to $98,000 in our example) is just another way of saying "a fall in the interest rate on Treasury bills" (from 12% to 8% in our example). Similarly, a fall in the price of securities represents a rise in the interest rate.**

Thus, when the Federal Reserve purchases government securities on the open market and bids up their prices, it is thereby bidding down interest rates. The proposition that a rise in security prices means a fall in interest yields also holds for long-term bonds, as explained in Box 13-1.

Secondary Effects

The secondary effects of the open market purchase also work toward a reduction of interest rates. As commercial bank reserves rise, the banks will purchase securities and step up their lending activities. The purchase of securities once again tends to push up security prices and push down interest rates. And, in their eagerness to make additional loans, banks may reduce the interest rate they charge. Specifically, they may shave their *prime rate*—that is, their publicly announced interest rate for short-term loans.[2]

To sum up, an open market purchase by the Fed has three important, interrelated effects: (1) it increases the money stock; (2) it makes more funds available for the commercial banks to lend; (3) it lowers interest rates. The way in which these three forces can stimulate aggregate demand will be considered in detail in Chapter 14.

THE FED'S SECOND TOOL FOR CONTROLLING THE MONEY SUPPLY: CHANGES IN THE DISCOUNT RATE

The Federal Reserve acts as the bankers' bank, as we have noted. Just as commercial banks lend to the general public, so the Fed may lend to commercial banks. In exchange for such a loan, the bank gives the Fed its promissory note, secured by acceptable collateral (usually U.S. government securities). For historical reasons, the interest rate on such loans is usually known as the ***discount rate,*** although it is sometimes called the *Federal Reserve Bank interest rate*. (In most other countries, it is known more simply as the *bank rate*.)

The *discount rate* is the interest rate charged by the Federal Reserve on its loans to banks.

In Chapter 12, we saw how a commercial bank provides its customer with a checking deposit when it makes a loan. The transaction between the Fed and a commercial bank is similar. When the Fed grants a loan to a bank, it increases that bank's reserve deposit in the Fed,

[2]Traditionally, the prime rate was defined as the bank's lowest rate, available only to its most credit-worthy customers. However, this is no longer the case. Since 1980, banks have made some loans at rates below the prime. Thus, the prime should now be considered simply the announced rate of a bank, not necessarily its lowest rate.

BOX 13-1

BOND PRICES AND INTEREST RATES

The relationship between bond prices and interest rates can be seen most easily by considering a *perpetuity*—a bond that has no maturity date and is never paid off. It represents a commitment to pay, say, $80 in interest per year forever. Although the U.S. government does not issue such bonds, a number of foreign examples might be cited—the famous British "consols," the "rentes perpetuelles" of France, or the "perps" issued many years ago by the Canadian government. Just as the semiannual interest or coupon payments on an ordinary bond remain fixed regardless of what happens to market interest rates after the bond has been issued, so the government's commitment to pay $80 per year forever to the holder of the perpetuity remains in force, regardless of what happens to current interest rates in the financial markets.

Like other bonds, perpetuities may be sold by their initial owners. A buyer willing to pay $1,000 for such a perpetuity would obtain an interest rate or yield of 8%; that is, $80 per year on the purchase price of $1,000. However, if the price fell, and the buyer could get the perpetuity for $800, the annual $80 payment would provide a yield of 10%. Again, we see that a fall in the price of a security means a rise in the interest rate or yield on the security.

A bond with a specific maturity of, say, 10 years requires a much more complex calculation. As a background, note that if $100 is deposited in an account paying 10% per annum, the deposit rises to a total of $110 at the end of the first year. During the second year, 10% interest is paid on this $110; that is, interest is paid not only on the original deposit of $100 but also on the first year's interest of $10. When interest is paid on interest in this way, we speak of interest being *compounded*. In this example, interest during the second year is $11 (that is, $110 × 10%), raising the deposit to a total of $121 by the end of the second year. This can be expressed:

$$\$100\,(1 + 0.10)^2 = \$121$$

(present value PV; interest rate i; number of years n; future value FV)

In general, this can be rewritten:

$$PV\,(1 + i)^n = FV$$

This relationship is often written in the alternative form:

$$PV = \frac{FV}{(1 + i)^n}$$

In our example:

$$\$100 = \frac{\$121}{(1 + 0.10)^2}$$

This tells us that, if the interest rate is 10%, an asset that has a future value or payoff of $121 in 2 years time is worth $100 today.

For many assets, the payoff is strung out over many years. In other words, there are many terms on the right-hand side of the present value equation. For example, a bond with a 10-year maturity and coupon payments of $8 per year will have a payoff of $8 each year until the tenth year, when the owner receives a final payoff of $8 plus the face value of $100. If the market interest rate is, say, 9%, the present value of this bond (the price at which it can be bought or sold today) is calculated as follows:

$$PV = \frac{\$8}{1.09} + \frac{\$8}{(1.09)^2} + \frac{\$8}{(1.09)^3} + \cdots + \frac{\$8 + \$100}{(1.09)^{10}}$$

$$= \$93.58$$

Or, in general:

Price (PV) of bond

$$= \frac{C}{1 + i} + \frac{C}{(1 + i)^2} + \cdots + \frac{C + \$100}{(1 + i)^n}$$

where C is the coupon payment.

From this equation, we can calculate the price if we know the rate of interest (i), or we can calculate the interest rate if we know the price of the bond. The higher is the one, the lower is the other. Thus, once again we see that the higher is the price of bonds, the lower is the interest rate.

as shown in Table 13-3. Thus, *such loans*—or "discounts"—*add to the total reserves of the banking system.*

Unlike open market operations, Fed lending is at the initiative of the commercial banks rather than the Fed. However, the Fed has two ways of controlling the amount they lend to the commercial banks:

1. It can refuse to lend when the banks ask. Borrowing is intended as a temporary way for banks to bring their reserves up to required levels when they have been run down by unexpected deposit withdrawals or other unforeseen circumstances. Banks are expected to confine their borrowing to periods when it is needed and not simply use it as a way of expanding their operations.

2. The Fed can change the discount rate. A higher discount rate makes it more expensive for commercial banks to borrow from the Fed and thus discourages such borrowing.

A change in the discount rate can also act as a signal of Federal Reserve intentions. For example, a rise in the rate can signal to the banks that the Fed wants to cut back on the rate of monetary expansion. In the years following World War II, the signal sent out by discount rate changes was particularly strong. This was because the discount rate was changed only infrequently, and the changes that did occur were therefore considered as very important indicators of Federal Reserve policy. Since 1955, many small changes have been made to keep the discount rate close to market rates of interest (Figure 13-3), and changes have therefore become less significant. Nevertheless, the discount rate can still be used as a signal by the Fed. For example, in November 1978, when the price of the dollar had been falling sharply in terms of other major currencies, the Fed raised the discount rate by a full percent in order to tell the world that it intended to reduce the rate of U.S. monetary expansion and thereby fight inflation more strongly. On the other side, the Fed cut the discount rate in November 1984, as a signal of easier monetary policy in the face of a slowdown in the growth of GNP.

Criticisms of Discounting

Although the discount rate is one of the major policy tools in the hands of the Fed, the discounting procedure has been the target of two criticisms.

First is the argument that it reduces the effectiveness of open market operations. Suppose, for example, that the Fed wants to restrain the growth of the money stock. In its open market operations, it cuts down on the rate of purchase of securities, or it may even go so far as to sell them. This makes the commercial banks short of reserves; some of them find themselves falling below required ratios. Consequently, they may turn to the Fed, borrowing reserves under the discount procedure. Thus, the Federal Reserve with its left hand (discounting) may pump back the reserves which it is extracting with its right hand (open market operations).

In response to this first criticism, defenders of discounting argue that it acts as a safety valve, allowing the Fed to follow tighter policies than it would otherwise dare. If there were no discounting, the Fed would have to tread lightly in restrictive open market operations, taking care not to put too much pressure on the commercial banks. Even though discounts involve some slippage, they may nevertheless make restrictive policies more feasible: The Fed can safely push harder on the open market lever.

TABLE 13-3

The Federal Reserve Grants a Loan to a Bank

(thousands of dollars)

Federal Reserve			
Assets		Liabilities	
Loan to bank	+100	Reserve deposit of bank	+100
Total	100	Total	100

The Fed makes a loan to a commercial bank.

As a result, bank reserves increase.

FIGURE 13-3

The discount rate and short-term market rates of interest

The Federal Reserve has generally changed the discount rate when necessary to keep it fairly close to market rates of interest. However, the discount rate remained far below the interest rates on federal funds and Treasury bills when those interest rates rose sharply in 1969, 1974, 1979–1980, and 1984. (The federal funds rate is the interest rate at which banks with inadequate reserves borrow from banks with excess reserves.)

Source: Federal Reserve Board, *Historical Chart Book.*

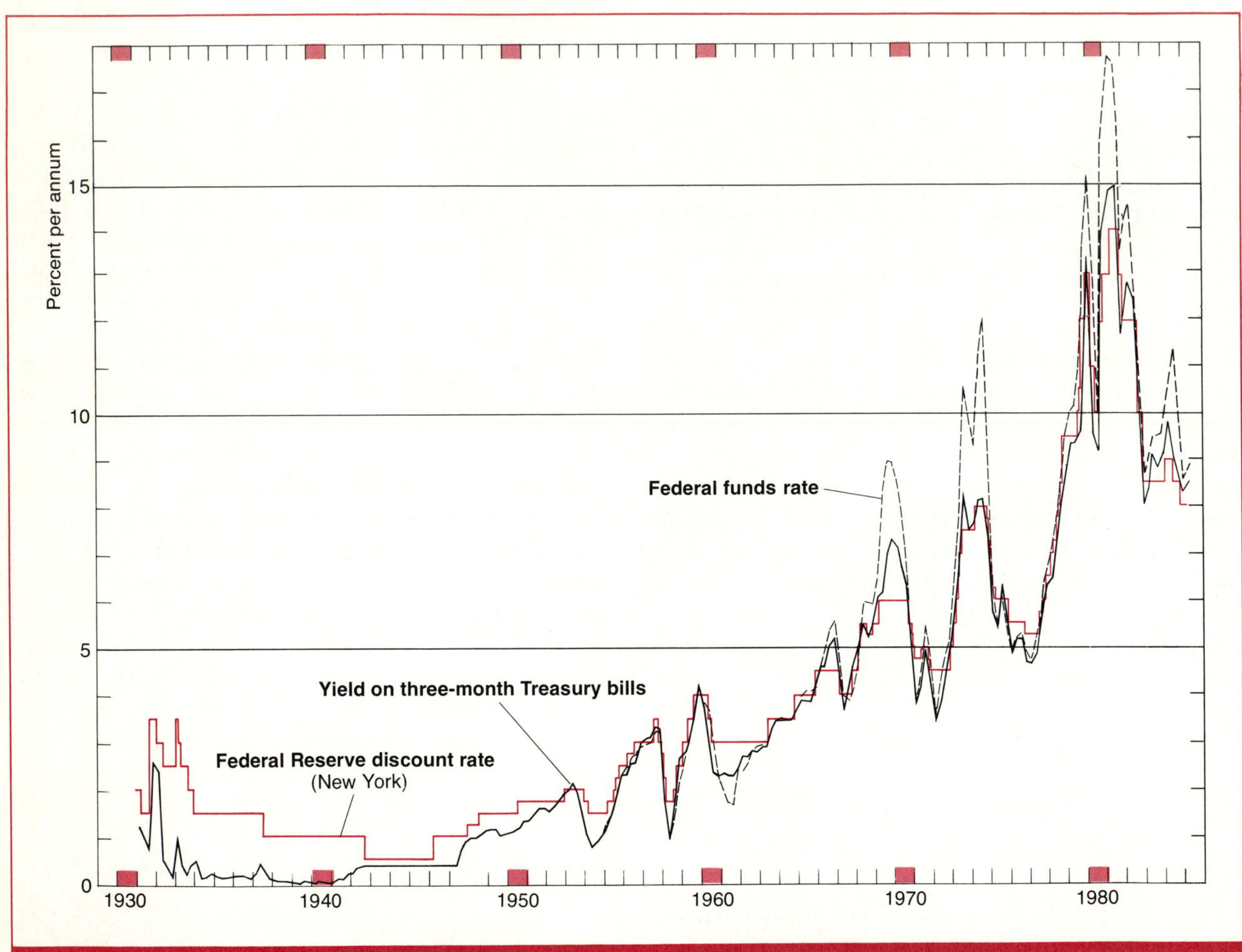

The second criticism is that the discount procedure grants hidden subsidies to banks whenever the discount rate is less than the market rate of interest. In practice, the Fed has been slow to raise discount rates when market rates of interest were rising rapidly, and this has resulted in a discount rate significantly below market rates. In the first half of 1984, for example, the discount rate lagged behind soaring interest rates. Borrowings from the Fed rose from $570 million in February to $8,000 million in August. Banks were being permitted to borrow at a special low rate of interest not available to the general public.

One way of eliminating this problem would be to change the discount rate more frequently in order to keep it from lagging below short-term market rates of interest. Such a proposal was made in a 1970 study by the Fed, but it was not acted upon. The simplest way would be to keep the discount rate at a fixed amount (say, ¼%) above the yield on short-term government bills. Such a ***penalty rate***—that is, a rate in excess of an important market interest rate—would mean that banks would no longer be able to benefit by borrowing at a bargain from the Fed. (Historically, the Bank of England has had a penalty rate, and the Bank of Canada currently uses such a rate.) While the Fed has not kept the discount rate above market rates of interest, it did take steps in 1980–1981 to limit the ability of banks to profit by borrowing from the Fed. Specifically, banks which had borrowed frequently, or for more than one week at a time, were required to pay not only the discount rate but also a surcharge of as much as 4%.

THE FED'S THIRD TOOL FOR CONTROLLING THE MONEY SUPPLY: A CHANGE IN RESERVE REQUIREMENTS

The quantity of deposits that the commercial banks can create depends on the size of their reserves and on the required reserve ratio. In the last chapter, we saw, specifically, that the maximum amount of deposits that can be created is equal to the amount of the reserves times $1/R$. Therefore, an *increase* in R (the required reserve ratio) will *decrease* the amount of deposits that can be created.

Since 1935, the Federal Reserve has had the power to change required reserve ratios within limits set by law. The details of the law are rather complicated, but basically, the Fed is now authorized to set the required reserve ratio on checking deposits anywhere in the range from 8% to 14%. The Fed's power to change required reserve ratios is a potent tool. With total reserves of, say, $100 million, an increase in the required reserve ratio from 10% to 11% would reduce the maximum quantity of checking deposits from $1,000 million to approximately $900 million.

The Federal Reserve learned the power of this tool the hard way, as a result of one of its policy blunders during the Great Depression. Between August 1936 and May 1937, the Fed *doubled* required reserve ratios. The restrictive effects were less strong than they otherwise might have been because banks initially had large excess reserves. (Indeed, the reason for raising the reserve ratios was to mop up excess reserves and put the Fed in a better position to prevent inflation.) The economy nevertheless suffered a severe blow. Banks felt compelled to cut back their loans. This derailed the recovery then in progress; unemployment shot up from 14.3% in 1937 to 19.0% in 1938. Since that unfortunate event, the Federal Reserve has recognized that a change in reserve ratios can act like a sledgehammer. It has therefore been very careful. When changes have been made in recent decades, they have been quite small, usually no more than one-half of 1%.

OTHER MONETARY TOOLS

The Fed's three major weapons—open market operations, changes in the discount rate, and changes in reserve requirements—are *quantitative controls;* they help the Fed control the quantity of money in the U.S. economy. They are supplemented by (1) *selective or qualitative controls,* which can affect the supply of funds to specific markets, and (2) *moral suasion.*

Selective Control on the Stock Market: Margin Requirements

When you buy shares of common stock, you are subject to a ***margin requirement*** set by the Federal Reserve. The objective of margin requirements is to limit speculative excesses in the stock market.

Margin requirements **limit the amount that can be borrowed to purchase stocks or bonds. For example, if the margin requirement on stock is 60%, buyers of stock must put up 60% of the purchase price in their own money and can borrow no more than 40% from banks or stockbrokers.**

The stock market plays an important role in American capitalism. New issues of stock provide corporations with funds for expansion. The owners of outstanding stock have liquidity and flexibility because they can readily sell; they are able to redirect their funds to dynamic new industries. But there is another side to Wall Street: Some view it as Las Vegas East. Periodically, it appeals to the get-rich-quick passion. As stocks rise, people think that they have found the sure way to fortune.

What is the best way to get rich quick, if you ''know'' a stock will rise rapidly? You borrow as much as possible and buy a large number of shares. For example, if you buy $5,000 worth of stock in an unregulated market, you may be able to borrow as much as $4,000 from your bank or broker. Thus, you are required to put up only $1,000 of your own money. If the stock doubles as expected, you can sell it for $10,000. After repaying your loan, you end up with $6,000 (less brokerage and interest costs)—or six times your initial investment of $1,000! The stock purchaser, like the business corporation in Chapter 6, can gain *leverage* by borrowing money.

This was the strategy of the 1920s. The tycoon and the grocery clerk alike became enthralled with the stock market as a shortcut to the good life. However, the speculators of the twenties found that leverage was a two-edged sword. Suppose, in the above illustration, that the unthinkable happens: The stock goes down, not up. It does not have to go down very far before the bank or broker that lent you the money becomes concerned with the safety of the loan. After all, 80% of the original value of the stock has been lent. As the stock falls to 90%, then 85% of the price you paid for it, the stock no longer provides adequate collateral for the loan. Consequently, the lender issues a *margin call:* More money must be put up by the stock owner or the stock will be sold. If the owner has no more funds and cannot meet the margin call, the stock is sold. As a result, it falls further in price. This, in turn, causes other lenders to issue margin calls. Thus, heavy borrowing can make the stock market vulnerable to a cumulative wave of selling. The final act of the great stock market boom of the twenties was the collapse of the Dow-Jones average of industrial stocks from its 1929 peak of 380 to a low of 41 in mid-1932.

If speculators were the only ones to lose, we might dismiss this outcome as some sort of rough justice—they have taken a chance, and lost. But a stock market crash may have repercussions throughout the economy because businesses find it hard to raise the funds they need for expansion. If the prices of their shares have fallen sharply, they can raise very little by a sale of additional stock. Furthermore, as stock prices collapse, the holders of stocks will cut back on their consumption expenditures, adding to a downswing. A healthy stock market bolsters the overall health of the economy. And a healthy stock market requires that stockholders be able to weather temporary setbacks without being forced to dump their shares. They gain staying power by having their own money invested.

Following the great crash of 1929, the Fed was given the power to impose margin requirements, limiting the amount that can be borrowed to purchase stocks or bonds. *Even a constant margin requirement* (of, say, 50%) *adds stability to the financial markets* by providing a significant range over which stocks may fall without triggering margin calls and a cumulative sell-off. But the Fed is also empowered to change the requirements. It can cut margin requirements to revive a low or declining market and raise margin requirements to restrain a speculative burst. (In recent years, the Fed has not used this power. It has kept the requirement on stocks steady at 50% since the last change in early 1974.)

Other Selective Controls

At times in the past, the Federal Reserve has been empowered to use other selective controls. During and immediately after the Second World War, and again during the Korean war, the Fed controlled the amount that could be borrowed to purchase consumer durables. During the Korean war, the Fed also controlled the amount that could be borrowed to buy real estate. At the end of the Korean conflict, the Fed's power to impose real estate and consumer credit was allowed to lapse by Congress.

Acting under temporary authority, the Fed in early 1980 took steps to restrain the growth of credit-card debt. Specifically, it required issuers of credit cards to make special deposits in the Fed amounting to 15% of any increase in the unpaid bills of their cardholders. By discouraging credit-card debt in this way, the Fed hoped to restrain inflation. As the economy slowed down in the summer of 1980, this requirement was eliminated.

Other proposals have from time to time been made for the Federal Reserve to influence the amount of lending in specific markets. Most interesting, perhaps, is the suggestion that the Federal Reserve should positively encourage lending to certain sectors, such as housing or businesses in the ghettos. Banks that make such loans might be rewarded by a lowering of the reserves they are required to keep.

The Federal Reserve has resisted these proposals, arguing that the control of the overall quantity of money is difficult enough, and should not be complicated by also requiring the Fed to perform other, quite different functions. Actions like the encouragement of businesses in the ghetto are political matters, more appropriately handled by Congress and the executive branch than by the partially independent Fed.

Moral Suasion

In addition to its formal weapons—such as open market operations or changes in the discount rate—the Federal Reserve may also attempt to influence the behavior of member banks in less formal ways. Specifically, it may resort to "jawboning," that is, exhorting bankers to refrain from certain actions or encouraging them to take others.

From time to time, for example, the Federal Reserve has recommended that banks reduce the amount of their new loans. The Federal Reserve has also recommended that banks achieve a higher net worth in order to ensure their ability to weather storms. (A bank can increase its net worth by selling additional stock or by retaining more of its profits rather than paying them out in dividends. An addition to net worth increases the amount by which a bank's assets exceed its liabilities. Thus the bank is protected if some of its assets disappear—for example, if some of its loans turn out to be uncollectable.)

There are a number of levers which the Federal Reserve can use in order to fortify its moral suasion and to ensure that the banks do not completely ignore its exhortations. For example, borrowing through the Fed's discount window is a privilege, not a right; if a bank ignores the recommendations of the Fed, it may find the Fed less willing to lend. Also, the Fed must approve certain bank activities, such as the opening of a branch in a foreign country. The Fed can refuse such permission if it feels that the capital position of the bank is inadequate.

Nevertheless, the scope for moral suasion is substantially less in the United States than in a number of other countries. In Britain and Canada, for example, there are only a very few banks, with nationwide service being provided by an extensive network of branches. In those two countries, the head of the central bank can meet face to face with representatives of all the banks in a single room, and moral suasion can be exerted in a more direct and emphatic manner than in the United States.

THE BALANCE SHEET OF THE FEDERAL RESERVE

Some actions of the Federal Reserve do not show up directly on its balance sheet—for example, moral suasion or changes in reserve requirements. But other acts do—for example, its open market operations. Thus, the balance sheet of the Federal Reserve can provide insights into some of the Fed's activities.

The consolidated balance sheet of the 12 Federal Reserve banks is shown in Table 13-4. Two entries on the right side are particularly worth noting. First is the large amount of Federal Reserve notes—the ordinary dollar bills that people hold. This item is very large because of the desire of the public to hold more currency as its overall holdings of money have increased. While open market operations and other Fed policies affect the *amount* of money in the economy, the public is free to choose the *form* in which it holds its money. When the public withdraws currency from the commercial banks, these banks can in turn replenish their currency by withdrawals from their reserve deposits in the Fed.

The second noteworthy item on the right side is the small net worth of the Federal Reserve. If the Fed were a private corporation, this would be cause for alarm. The slightest reversal in its fortunes might cause the value of its assets to dip below the amount of its liabilities, wiping out its net worth and threatening bankruptcy. But the Fed is no ordinary corporation. It is a part of the government, and a very special part, since it has the power to create money. Because of this special power, the Fed need not worry about building up its net worth; it has an assured flow of profits. It earns interest on the large holdings of government securities on the asset side, while it pays no interest on most of its liabilities—in particular, reserve deposits and Federal Reserve notes. The Fed turns most of its profits over to the U.S. Treasury, and as a result, its net worth remains low.

On the asset side of the Fed's balance sheet, U.S. government securities are by far the largest entry; these securities have been accumulated through past open market operations. Loans (discounts) to commercial banks and other depository institutions are not very large—only $2.6 billion at the end of March 1985. Although such loans are generally low, they have shot up at times when banks were short of reserves, such as 1974 and 1984. Finally, the gold entry in the Fed's balance sheet is left over from the historical role played by the Fed in the operation of the gold standard. As part of the gold standard arrangements, the Fed held gold as backing for the U.S. currency and stood ready to buy and sell gold to the public. The gold standard was drastically modified during the Depression of the 1930s and was finally ended in 1971. The Fed and the U.S. Treasury no longer consider gold the ultimate money. Indeed, they view it as similar to any other metal, such as copper or platinum, although the price of gold still retains some special significance as an indicator of conditions in international financial markets.

WHAT BACKS OUR MONEY?

Money is debt. The largest component of the money stock—namely, checking deposits—is debt of the commercial banks and other deposit-accepting institutions. Federal Reserve notes—the currency of everyday use—are liabilities (debt) of the twelve Federal Reserve banks.

In a sense, the money supply is backed by the assets of the banking system. Checking deposits are backed by the loans, bonds, and reserves held by the commercial banks and other depository institutions. Federal Reserve notes are backed by the assets of the Federal Reserve, mainly federal government securities. What, in turn, backs the government securities? The answer is: the government's promise to pay, based in the first instance on its ability to tax, but in the final analysis on its ability to borrow newly created money from the Federal Reserve or to print money directly. (Recall the section in Chapter 11 entitled: ''Could the Government Go Broke?'')

TABLE 13-4
Consolidated Balance Sheet of the 12 Federal Reserve Banks, March 29, 1985
(billions of dollars)

Assets		Liabilities and net worth	
U.S. government securities	$161.0	Deposits	
Loans to depository institutions	2.6	Reserve deposits of depository institutions	$ 27.0
Gold certificate account	11.1	U.S. Treasury	3.1
Other assets	32.1	Foreign and other	0.6
		Federal Reserve notes	163.7
		Other liabilities	8.3
		Total liabilities	202.7
		Net worth	4.1
Total	$206.8	Total	$206.8

In the Federal Reserve's balance sheet, U.S. government securities are the main asset, and Federal Reserve notes the largest liability.

Clearly, we have gone in a circle. Currency is backed with government debt, and government debt is ultimately backed by the ability of the federal authorities to print more currency. In a sense, the whole game is played with mirrors; money is money because the government says it is. Until a few years ago, Federal Reserve notes boldly proclaimed that "the United States of America will pay to the bearer on demand" the face value of the Federal Reserve note. What would happen if an individual submitted a $1 bill and demanded payment? He or she would receive another $1 bill in exchange. This does not make much sense, and the bold proclamation has been eliminated from Federal Reserve notes. Now, we can say simply: A dollar is a dollar is a dollar.[3]

What, then, determines the value of a Federal Reserve note? Dollar bills have value because of (1) their scarcity compared to the demand for them and (2) their general acceptability. So long as the Federal Reserve keeps the supply of money in reasonable balance with the demand for it, money retains its value even though it has no explicit backing with precious metal or any other tangible commodity.

Dollar bills are generally acceptable by such diverse people as the taxi driver, the house painter, and the doctor. They all know they can turn around and buy other goods and services with the dollar bills. In part, general acceptability is a matter of convention—as in the case of cigarettes in the POW camp. But convention and habit are reinforced by the status of Federal Reserve notes as ***legal tender.*** Creditors *must* accept them in payment of a debt. Coins are also legal tender, but only up to reasonable limits. The electric company is not obliged to accept 4,562 pennies if a customer offers them in payment for a bill of $45.62. (The items which are legal tender can change through time. For example, beginning in 1985, the British halfpenny was no longer legal tender at all. Because of inflation, this small coin had become a nuisance.)

[3]The correspondence between the U.S. Treasury and an irate citizen, who asked for redemption of a $10 bill and got two $5 bills in exchange, is reproduced under the title "A Dollar Is a Dollar Is a Dollar," *American Affairs,* April 1948; also reprinted in Lawrence S. Ritter (ed.), *Money and Economic Activity: A Selection of Readings* (Cambridge, Mass.: Houghton Mifflin, 1952), pp. 45–46.

Legal tender **is the item or items that creditors must accept in payment of debts**

What Backs Checking Deposits?

How about checking deposits? What protects their role as part of the money stock? Unlike currency, checking deposits are not legal tender. A gas station is not obliged to accept a personal check and usually won't do so.

People are willing to hold money in the form of checking deposits because of the convenience of paying by check, and because they are confident that they can get currency for the deposits when they want it. But what assurance do depositors have of actually being able to get $100 in currency for every $100 they hold in checking deposits?

The first assurance lies in the assets of the banks—their reserves and earning assets of loans and securities. If a bank finds that people are withdrawing more than they are depositing, it may cover the difference by liquidating some of its assets—for example, by selling some of its bonds or by using the proceeds of its loans as they are repaid. However, bank assets may not always be enough; indeed, they proved to be woefully inadequate during the Depression of the 1930s. As the economy collapsed, many businesses could not repay their bank loans, and the value of bank assets shrank. As their assets fell to less than their deposit liabilities, the banks were driven into bankruptcy, and many depositors suffered heavy losses.

This situation clearly was dangerous because bank runs are contagious. In early 1933, the contagion spread like wildfire, and the banking system collapsed. In order to prevent a repetition of the 1930s, an important additional backing was provided for depositors. The government set up the *Federal Deposit Insurance Corporation* (FDIC) to insure bank deposits up to a sizable limit, currently $100,000 per deposit. For this insurance, the banks pay premiums to the FDIC. A similar institution—the Federal Savings and Loan Insurance Corporation, or FSLIC—guarantees deposits in savings and loan associations up to the same limit. Because deposits are now guaranteed by the government, people no longer have the same incentive to run on their banks, and the U.S. banking system is much more secure than it was in the early 1930s. Nevertheless, those with more than $100,000 in deposits are still exposed to possible loss and have an incentive to run on banks in trouble. (Details are provided in Box 13-2.)

An even greater danger of runs exists for state-chartered institutions that are not required to belong to the FDIC or FSLIC. A few states permit state-chartered institutions to choose privately operated insurance, which is not backed by the full faith and credit of the state government. In 1985, this led to trouble, first in Ohio and then in Maryland. When a number of state-chartered S&Ls suffered substantial losses, doubts arose regarding their ability to meet their obligations to depositors, and of the ability of the private insurance to cover any losses. The result was a run on the S&Ls. In a scene reminiscent of the depth of the Depression in 1933, Ohio and Maryland each declared an S&L ''holiday''—the S&Ls were closed to provide an opportunity to sort out the situation. Meeting in a crisis atmosphere, the state legislatures decided that state-chartered S&Ls would be required to get federal insurance. This episode demonstrated the wisdom of federal insurance, backed by the financial resources of the U.S. government.

Why Not Gold?

There is an obvious problem with ***fiat money***—paper currency that is money solely because the government says it is. The government or central bank can create such money at will. What, then, is to restrain the authorities from creating and spending money recklessly, generating a runaway inflation?

It is this question that provided a rationale for the ***gold standard.*** If the currency issued by the government and/or the central bank is convertible into gold, then the authorities will not be able to create money recklessly. Like the goldsmith of old, they will have to keep a gold backing equal to a reasonable fraction of their currency liabilities. This was the original design of the Federal Reserve when it was established in 1914. The Fed was required to keep gold reserves to back its currency and deposit obligations. Under the old gold standard, the Fed itself was a ''fractional-reserve'' bank. It could create liabilities—in the form of currency and reserve deposits—that were a multiple of its gold reserves. But it did not have the power to create an unlimited amount of such liabilities.

As in the case of the commercial banks (illustrated earlier in Figure 12-4), the Federal Reserve's ability to create liabilities may be illustrated by an inverted pyramid, as shown in Figure 13-4. In this case, however, the reserves are gold. The liabilities created on the basis of those reserves are not the ordinary bank accounts which

BOX 13-2

THE CONTINUING PROBLEM OF FINANCIAL INSTABILITY

Bankers aren't supposed to be smart. They're supposed to be safe.

ELLIOT BELL
Former Superintendent of Banking, New York State

As a result of the collapse of 1933, a number of major steps were taken to protect the banking system, such as the establishment of the Federal Deposit Insurance Corporation. Nevertheless, a number of banks have run into deep trouble in recent years.

One of the reasons for trouble has been the very dynamic nature of banking during the past two decades. Banks have discovered new ways of raising money and doing business. For example, they now compete more actively for funds by offering certificates of deposit (CDs)—large time deposits with attractive interest rates.

Unlike the small deposits which you or I have in our banks, CDs tend to be volatile or "footloose." A corporation with a CD worth several hundred thousand dollars may be quite likely to take its money when the CD matures, and put it in another bank at a higher interest rate. The volatility of CDs is heightened because they often exceed the amount covered by insurance. Thus, CD holders can lose their money if the bank goes bankrupt. When questions arise regarding the stability of a bank, CD depositors have a particularly strong incentive to take their money out. If they don't, they may lose it.

The volatility of CDs has become an increasingly severe problem as banks have come to depend more and more heavily on them as a source of funds. By the end of 1984, the value of CDs had become about 60% as large as total checking deposits. Furthermore, CDs are spread unevenly—they are a particularly important source of funds for banks in financial centers such as New York and Chicago, and relatively unimportant for institutions such as the Bank of America, whose numerous branches provide a stable base of small deposits. In addition, some banks depend on sizable amounts of very short-term borrowing—some of it just overnight—in the federal funds market and elsewhere. (In the federal funds market, banks with excess reserves lend to banks in need of funds.)

In fact, the refusal of CD holders to roll their deposits over (that is, their refusal to redeposit the funds when the deposits matured) and the drying up of other short-term funds contributed to the quick, well-publicized collapse of three banks—Franklin National, a large New York bank (1974); Penn Square (1982), an Oklahoma bank; and Continental Illinois (1984), a very large bank in Chicago. In each case, the bank was unable to keep short-term funds when major problems appeared. Franklin National was having difficulty in the highly competitive New York market, and had suffered losses speculating on the foreign exchange markets. It had bought foreign currencies when it expected their prices to rise, but they had fallen instead. Penn Square made huge loans to the oil industry, many of which became uncollectable when the price of oil declined. Continental Illinois made the mistake of buying some of Penn Square's loans to the oil industry, so it also suffered losses when the price of oil declined.

These banking problems have raised three major policy questions:

1. Has banking deregulation gone too far, too fast? One form of deregulation has been the relaxation of ceilings on interest rates that banks can pay depositors. As a consequence, have banks competed too strongly for business, offering interest rates higher than they can afford to pay? The debate over deregulation has been quite spirited, particularly since the troubles of Continential Illinois may be attributable to too *much* regulation, of a different kind. Specifically, the prohibition against branch banking in Illinois means that a Chicago bank cannot become big by attracting large numbers of small depositors. It is forced to rely on large CDs and borrowings from short-term financial markets for a large fraction of its funds. This might be contrasted with the situation in California, which allows statewide branch banking.
2. When banks are in trouble, should the Fed ease the pressure on the banking system as a whole by introducing a more expansive monetary policy, which will provide banks with more funds and therefore more elbow room at a critical time? This question came to the fore in 1984, when bank failures were rising in spite of the strong economic recovery. Ten federally insured banks had failed in each of the years 1979, 1980, and 1981, but 48 failed in 1983 and 76 in 1984. Some students of monetary policy feared that the Fed might have to pursue an expansionary policy in order to save the banks, even at the risk of rekindling inflation.
3. Should the Fed and the FDIC bail out specific banks that get in trouble? In fact, Franklin National and Continental Illinois were bailed out, with even the largest depositors being paid in full. Penn Square was allowed to go under, apparently as a signal to large depositors that they could not chase high interest rates without giving some thought to the risks they were running. However, it was considered too dangerous to allow Continental Illinois to fail, since this might cause a run on other large banks in the major financial centers. The different treatment of relatively small Penn Square and huge Continental Illinois is troubling. Do we have a double standard, with "socialism for the rich" but no similar rescue for smaller banks? (In spite of the bailouts, banks still have a strong incentive to manage their affairs competently. While the depositors of Continental Illinois were protected, its stockholders suffered huge losses and many of its managers were fired.)

The question of a "double standard" also arose when the government guaranteed loans to large firms like Lockheed (during the 1970 recession) and Chrysler (1980) in order to prevent their collapse, even though hundreds of smaller companies were allowed to fail. One reason for this double standard is easy to find. If a very large corporation is allowed to fail, it can create a major shock to the economy.

you or I hold. Instead, they are rather special liabilities—currency and the reserve deposits which commercial banks own.

By combining the Federal Reserve pyramid and the commercial bank pyramid, we can see how the monetary system formed a two-layered pyramid in Figure 13-5. The Fed could create liabilities that were a multiple of its gold reserves, shown as the "first multiple" in the lower left part of the diagram. The commercial banking system could create checking deposits equal to a multiple of its reserves, shown as the "second multiple" in the middle of the top layer. As a result of the two multiple expansions, a very large quantity of money could be created on the basis of the nation's holdings of gold.

A country is on the *gold standard* when its currency is convertible into gold, that is, when the treasury and/or central bank stands ready to buy or sell gold at a fixed price (for example, 1 ounce of gold = $20.00).

FIGURE 13-4

The Federal Reserve under the old gold standard

Under the old gold standard, the Federal Reserve itself was a fractional-reserve bank. It was required to keep gold reserves equal to a fraction of its liabilities of currency and deposits. This figure might be compared to the inverted monetary pyramid created by commercial banks (Figure 12-4).

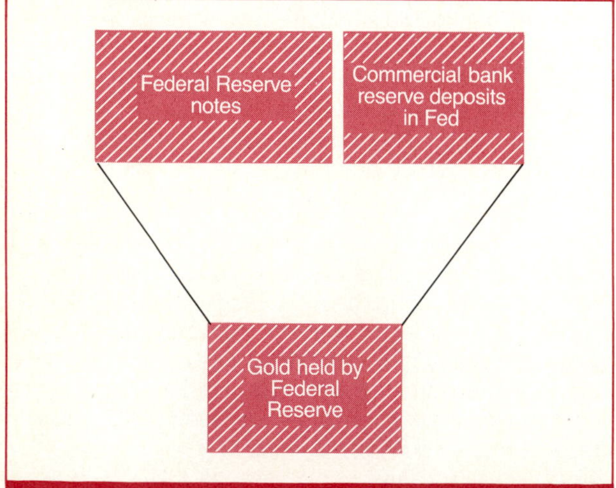

When a country is on the gold standard, gold coins may circulate as part of the money stock.

While the gold standard fulfilled its objective of restraining reckless money creation, it had two serious flaws. First, the quantity of money tended to fluctuate as a result of changes in the quantity of gold. When the Fed bought gold flowing into the country from abroad or from U.S. gold mines, the effects were similar to those of an open market operation: Commercial bank reserves increased. (The effects on the Fed's balance sheet were similar to those from the open market operation shown in Table 13-1, except that the asset acquired by the Fed was gold rather than government securities.) Moreover, the gold improved the reserve position of the Fed itself. Therefore, the Fed was able to lend more to the commercial banks or buy more government securities on the open market. Thus, commercial bank reserves could be increased in this way as well. Consequently, a gold inflow could lead to a large increase in the money stock. Similarly, a gold outflow could have a very powerful contractionary effect. There was no assurance that a monetary system that responded to gold flows in this manner would provide the quantity of money needed for a full-employment, noninflationary economy.

The second difficulty was even more serious. Indeed, it was the reason for the collapse of the gold standard during the Depression. Because of the fractional-reserve system applying to both the commercial banks and the Federal Reserve, any tendency for the public to demand items lower in the pyramid had a powerful contractionary effect on the size of the money stock. We saw in Chapter 12 how a deposit of $100,000 in currency permitted a monetary expansion. A withdrawal of currency by the public likewise has a contractionary effect. But if the public withdraws gold, it is withdrawing the item at the base of the whole pyramid. In this case, the contractionary effect is particularly severe. Reserves have been removed from the Federal Reserve itself, and the Federal Reserve itself must take restrictive steps—such as reducing its loans to commercial banks—in order to meet its own required reserve ratios. In short, when the public withdraws part of the gold base, there is a multiple shrinkage of the money stock.

FIGURE 13-5

The gold standard pyramid (simplified)

This diagram combines Figures 12-4 and 13-4. The parts marked in diagonal lines, taken from Figure 13-4, show how the Fed can create liabilities that are a multiple of its gold reserves. The dotted parts illustrate how the commercial banking system can create liabilities that are a multiple of its reserves of gold and deposits in the Fed. As a result of this two-layered pyramid, the money stock can be very large compared to the underlying stock of gold.

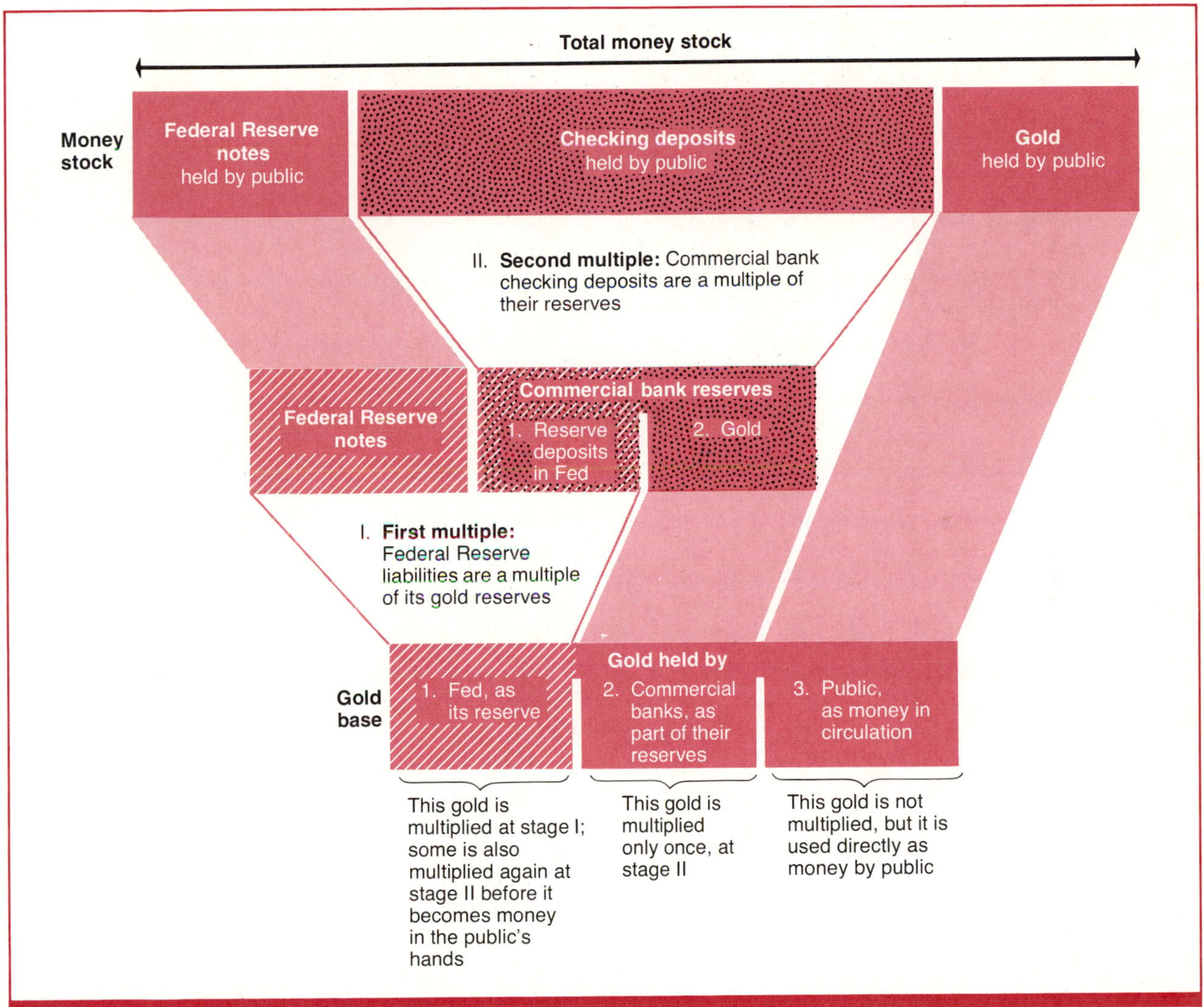

During the Great Depression, people became frightened as unemployment and business bankruptcies shot upward. Being frightened, they tried to switch their assets into safer forms. They switched out of bank deposits into paper currency and gold. Foreign holders of dollars were particularly anxious to exchange them for gold after the British suspended the convertibility of the pound into gold in 1931. The monetary system thus came under strong contractionary pressures when the economy was already headed downward. As the economy collapsed into the deepest part of the Depression, the rules of the game were changed to prevent the public from withdrawing more gold. Under legislation recommended by President Franklin Roosevelt, the American public was forbidden to hold gold (with a few exceptions, such as for dental work). It wasn't until the beginning of 1975 that the public was allowed to hold gold again, and by then gold no longer played an important role in the monetary system.

The problem with the gold standard, then, is that it does not provide a *steady* and measured restraint. Rather, it exerts restraint in the form of a *threat of disaster*. If a crisis of confidence occurs, the public will switch away from paper money and into gold, and the monetary structure will collapse. So long as the authorities are lucky, with gold flowing in steadily from mines or from foreign countries, and so long as they follow farsighted policies that prevent any crisis of confidence, it is possible that the system may work reasonably well. But in the period between the two world wars, the authorities were neither farsighted nor lucky. The gold standard added to the disaster of the 1930s. Any system that "kicks an economy when it is down" is basically destructive and should be discarded. This was done in stages between 1933 and 1971.

The Great Depression of the 1930s not only revealed fundamental flaws in the gold standard. It also illustrated the faulty assumptions of those who designed the Federal Reserve System. The Fed was established in 1914 in response to earlier financial panics, including that of 1907. During those early panics, banks were under severe pressure; there was a danger that they would run out of reserves and be unable to meet their obligations. The problem—or so it seemed—was that reserves were scattered among many, many banks. In order to make the most of the nation's overall reserves of gold and have them available for emergencies, it seemed that what was needed was a centralized *federal* reserve. This was one of the ideas behind the establishment of the Fed. But the fundamental problem was *not* a scattering of gold reserves. The fundamental problem was the fractional-reserve system built on gold. With fractional reserves, it was *impossible* for the banking system to meet a general run—whether the reserves were scattered or not. There simply wasn't enough gold to let everybody switch out of deposits and into gold. The centralization of gold reserves enabled the Fed to help a single bank in trouble. But it provided no protection at all against a simultaneous run on the whole banking system. The Fed had been established in the hope of ending panics. But, measured by that objective, it was a colossal failure. By far the worst panic of all came two decades after the Fed was established.

The history of the gold standard, and, in particular, the role of gold in the early Depression, gained in importance in the late 1970s as inflation accelerated into double digits (above 10%). Because governments and central banks appeared unwilling or unable to exercise enough restraint to control inflation, some observers concluded that the only way to restore a sound monetary system was to reestablish some link to gold, and thus impose an external constraint on monetary policy. While interest in the gold standard has waned with the decline in inflation in the early 1980s, it still remains strong.

While we grapple with the inflationary problem of our time, we should be aware of the problems in some of the proposed solutions—including a return to the gold standard. In particular, we should remember how the gold standard contributed to the Depression of the 1930s. We might also remember the words of British economist D. H. Robertson, looking back at the economic wreckage of the period between the two world wars:[4]

> The value of a yellow metal, originally chosen as money because it tickled the fancy of savages, is clearly a chancy and irrelevant thing on which to base the value of our money and the stability of our industrial system.

[4]D. H. Robertson, *Money*, rev. ed. (Cambridge: Cambridge University Press, 1948), p. 144.

DESTABILIZING MONETARY POLICIES: THE TRAP OF AN INTEREST RATE OBJECTIVE

At the beginning of Chapter 12, two reasons were given for studying money:

1. Monetary policy is one of the two major tools for managing aggregate demand.
2. Sharp changes in the quantity of money have been a source of economic instability. Rapid increases in the quantity of money have caused inflation, and a substantial decline in the quantity of money made the Great Depression worse.

Much of this chapter has been devoted to the first point, explaining how the Federal Reserve can change the quantity of money in an effort to stabilize the economy. Then, in the section on the gold standard, attention was turned to the second subject. We saw how the money stock might contract in a perverse way during a depression if people switch out of bank deposits and into gold as times become worse.

Although the end of the gold standard removed one source of monetary instability, others remain. Some are quite subtle and are deferred to Chapter 15. But one potential source of instability lies at the very center of the way in which central bank policy is made.

The ultimate objectives of the Federal Reserve are full employment and price stability. However, the Fed does not control employment or the level of prices directly. Rather, it adjusts the levers of monetary policy and, in particular, open market operations. It is only by affecting the quantity of money and interest rates that the Fed affects employment and prices.

In formulating policy, the Federal Open Market Committee (FOMC) has a decision to make. Should it give the trading desk at the New York Fed instructions to aim for a certain level of interest rates? Or should the trading desk be ordered to concentrate on the quantity of money? Or some combination of the two? A controversy has raged over this question for decades. Critics of the Fed argue that it has generally concentrated on interest rates and that, as a result, it has sometimes destabilized the economy.

To see why, suppose that the Federal Reserve has decided to keep the interest rate near the existing rate of 8% per annum. Then suppose that an upturn in the economy occurs. Business executives become more optimistic and undertake additional investment; aggregate demand rises. To finance their new plant and equipment, they borrow. The additional demand for funds creates pressures for interest rates to rise and bond prices to fall. If the Fed wants to keep interest rates from rising—that is, to keep bond prices from falling—it now has to buy bonds on the open market. However, such open market purchases increase bank reserves and lead to an increase in the money stock. As a consequence, there is an additional increase in aggregate demand. As demand rises, businesses are encouraged to revise their investment plans upward once more; the expansion gathers momentum. There is a *cumulative upward movement,* with changes in aggregate demand and in the money stock feeding back and reinforcing one another.

The Fed cannot control both the money stock and the interest rate. If it wants to control the money stock, it must let interest rates rise in the face of a large increase in the demand for loans.

If it decides to control interest rates, it loses control of the money stock. The result can be a vicious circle, with higher demand initially causing an increase in the money stock, and the increase in the money stock in turn causing a further increase in demand, and so on.

A substantial upswing in the economy is not necessarily bad. Indeed, if the economy is bumping along with very high rates of unemployment, a strong expansion is desirable. In this case, a decision by the Fed to keep interest rates from rising can contribute to a recovery. But a policy of interest rate stabilization may also cause a healthy expansion to run away into an inflationary boom.

Thus, an attempt to stabilize interest rates can be a trap for monetary policy, just as an attempt to balance the budget every year represents a trap for fiscal policy. We saw earlier that, if the government attempts to balance the budget every year, it will cancel out the automatic fiscal stabilizers. The interest rate can also act as an automatic stabilizer. The large demands by businesses to borrow during an investment boom will bid up interest rates. The higher interest rates will discourage some potential borrowers. Because they find it so expensive to finance new equipment or other investment, they will shelve some of their investment projects. Thus, a rising interest rate will slow down the growth of aggregate demand and prevent a rapid buildup of inflationary pressures. If the Fed takes steps to keep interest rates from rising, it will prevent them from acting as an automatic stabilizer in this way.

Illustrations

Perhaps the simplest and clearest example of interest rate stabilization occurred during the 1940s. In order to help the Treasury borrow cheaply to finance the war debt, the Federal Reserve promised to keep interest rates pegged (fixed) at a low level. To do so, it had to buy securities, thus losing control over bank reserves and the money supply. This lack of control contributed to the inflation of the 1940s and became a particular problem during the Korean war. In order to regain control over the money stock and restrain inflation, the Federal Reserve argued that it should be released from its commitment to the Treasury to keep interest rates low. The Treasury at first objected, but finally agreed in the *Treasury-Federal Reserve Accord* of 1951.

A second, but somewhat more complex example occurred in 1972. This case requires some background. In the face of continuing inflation, President Nixon introduced wage and price controls in August 1971. One problem with controls is that they may be considered unfair. Unions, in particular, fear that controls will be used to limit wages but not profits and other incomes. Therefore, if controls are to have broad public support, they must be applied to all forms of income, including interest and dividends. The responsibility for supervising interest and dividends was assigned to Chairman Arthur Burns of the Federal Reserve, who had been an early advocate of government restraints on wages and prices.

This was an unfortunate choice. Burns was now wearing two hats, and the two jobs were in conflict. In support of the wage-price program, his responsibility was to keep down interest rates. On the other hand, as chairman of the Federal Reserve, his responsibility was to control the money supply, even if this meant an increase in interest rates. What actually happened? The Federal Reserve held interest rates down, and the money supply rose rapidly during 1972. This contributed to the rapid increase in inflation in 1973.

Because of this episode and other similar experiences, the Federal Reserve announced in 1979 that it was changing its procedures. In the future, it would focus more on the quantity of money and less on interest rates.

The Great Depression

Finally, this discussion would be incomplete without an additional word about the decline in the money stock that accompanied the greatest macroeconomic catastrophe of all—the 1929–1933 collapse into the Great Depression. One reason for the decline in the money stock has already been noted—the gold standard. A second important reason was the set of policies followed by the Fed, which made the decline in the money stock even more severe.

When the Fed was established, monetary theory was not understood very well. An influential idea was that the banking system should *meet the needs of trade*. Its very plausibility made this idea particularly dangerous. After all, what seems so wrong with the idea that banks should be willing to provide funds to businesses when they "need" them—that is, when they are eager to borrow? The not-so-obvious but important answer is this: Businesses are eager to borrow during periods of prosperity. However, large bank lending will cause large increases in the money stock and turn prosperity into an inflationary boom. On the other hand, business demand for loans is slack during recession. If banks simply respond to the demand for loans, the money supply will decline, making the recession worse. Under the monetary policies followed in the early 1930s, the quantity of money did in fact decline in response to a decline in the demand for loans.

It is important for the Federal Reserve to have an idea of how it wants the money stock to change. The Fed is inviting disaster if it responds passively, creating more money whenever the demand for borrowed funds is high and creating less whenever the demand is slack.

It is unfortunate that the authorities fell into the two great policy traps at the beginning of the 1930s, making the Depression worse. On the fiscal side, President Hoover fell into the trap of trying to balance the budget; taxes were raised sharply in 1931. On the monetary policy side, the Fed allowed the money supply to decline in the face of the worsening Depression.

However, in one sense, this sad history is somewhat reassuring. By avoiding such policy blunders, we should be able to prevent a repeat of the 1930s. If the depression had occurred in spite of good policies, this really would be alarming, since it would leave an unanswered question: Can we prevent a repeat?

KEY POINTS

1. The Federal Reserve is responsible for controlling the quantity of money in the U.S. economy. It has three major quantitative tools at its command: (*a*) open market operations, (*b*) changes in the discount rate, and (*c*) changes in required reserve ratios.

2. The Federal Reserve's untidy organizational chart is the result of an early controversy over the desirable degree of centralization. There are 12 regional Federal Reserve Banks and a Board of Governors in Washington. For monetary policy, the most important body is the Federal Open Market Committee, which is made up of the seven members of the Board of Governors plus five presidents of the regional Federal Reserve Banks.

3. When the Federal Reserve purchases securities on the open market, it increases bank reserves; when it sells securities, it reduces reserves. Changes in reserves affect the amount of checking deposit money that commercial banks and other depository institutions can create.

4. A purchase of securities by the Federal Reserve tends to bid up security prices. When this happens, the yields (interest rates) on securities are bid down.

5. A decrease in the discount rate encourages bank borrowing from the Fed. Such borrowing creates bank reserves.

6. When it reduces required reserve ratios, the Fed increases the quantity of checking deposits the banks can create on any given reserve base.

7. Less important tools of the Federal Reserve include selective or qualitative controls (most notably, margin requirements for purchases of stocks) and moral suasion.

8. In the last analysis, there is nothing backing our currency: ''A dollar is a dollar.'' Money retains its value because it is scarce. Even though it doesn't cost the Federal Reserve anything to create reserve deposits, and the costs of printing currency are small, the Fed does not create money recklessly. If it did so, there would be a wild inflation.

9. Under the old gold standard, the Fed was required to hold gold reserves equal to a fraction of its deposit and note liabilities. Since this system is based on gold, and gold ''can't be printed,'' there was a restraint on irresponsible money creation. However, the gold standard had two enormous defects. First, the amount of money that could be created on the available gold base was not necessarily the quantity needed for full employment with stable prices. The second defect was even worse. In a crisis of confidence, people exchanged other forms of money for gold. This caused a sharp contraction of the money supply. Because of its defects, the gold standard was abandoned. The ability of the Fed to expand the money supply is no longer limited by its gold holdings.

10. Chapter 11 explained how the makers of fiscal policy could fall into a trap if they followed a policy of balancing the budget every year. The central bank also faces a policy trap. If it stabilizes interest rates, it may lose control of the money stock. The result can be a vicious circle, with higher demand causing an increase in the money stock, and the increase in the money stock in turn causing a further increase in demand.

KEY CONCEPTS

open market operation
discount rate
required reserve ratio
12 regional Federal Reserve Banks
Board of Governors of the Federal Reserve System
Federal Open Market Committee (FOMC)
Treasury bill
prime rate
penalty rate
quantitative controls
qualitative controls
margin requirement
margin call
moral suasion (jawboning)
legal tender
fiat money

Federal Deposit Insurance Corporation
gold standard
monetary pyramid
monetary policy trap
interest rate stabilization
needs of trade

PROBLEMS

13-1. What are the three major tools of the Federal Reserve for controlling the quantity of money? Which of these tools affect the quantity of reserves of the commercial banks?

13-2. Suppose that the Federal Reserve purchases \$100,000 in Treasury bills from commercial bank A. Explain how the balance sheets of the Fed and commercial bank A are affected. How much can commercial bank A now safely lend? (Assume that bank A's reserves were just adequate prior to the purchase by the Fed.)

13-3. Table 13-1 shows the changes in the balance sheets of the Fed and a commercial bank when the Fed purchased a government security from General Motors. Show how the balance sheet of GM changed as a result of this open market purchase.

13-4. Suppose that the price of a 3-month \$100,000 Treasury bill is \$96,000. What is the approximate yield on this bill? (Following the conventional practice, quote the yield at an annual rate.) Now suppose that the price of 3-month bills falls to \$95,000. What happens to the yield?

13-5. The Fed makes discounts at the initiative of the commercial banks and other depository institutions. In what way do discounts reduce the control of the Federal Reserve over the money supply? In what way might the power of the Fed to grant or refuse discounts increase its control over the money stock?

13-6. "Counterfeiting is generally an antisocial act. But when there is a depression, all counterfeiters should be let out of jail." Do you agree or disagree? Explain why.

13-7. What backing do Federal Reserve notes have? Why are these notes valuable?

13-8. Why can the Fed fall into a "policy trap" if it tries to stabilize interest rates? For review, also explain the policy trap which faces the makers of fiscal policy.

PART FOUR

GREAT MACROECONOMIC ISSUES OF OUR TIME

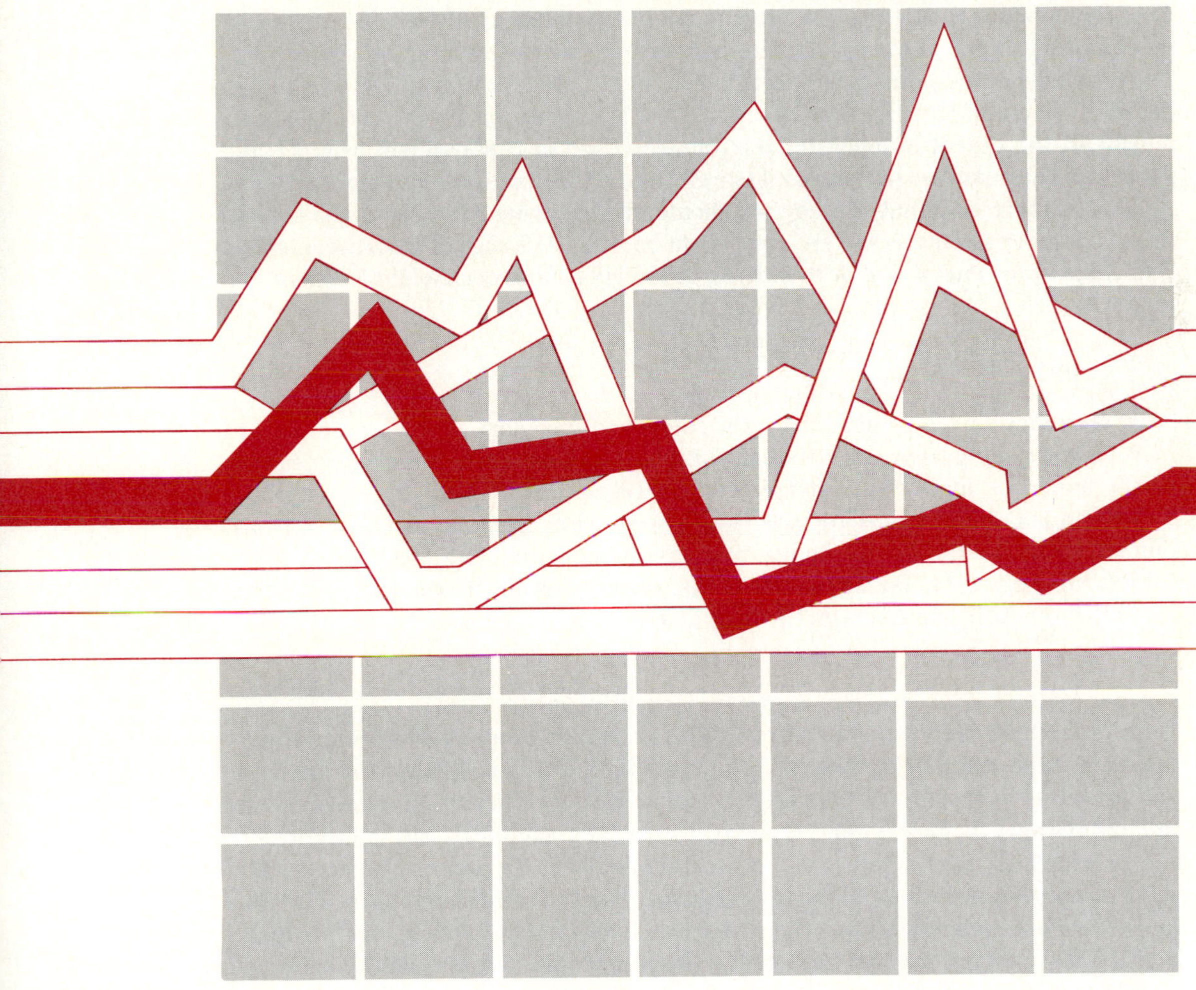

Part 3 of this book has introduced the two major tools of demand management: fiscal policy (involving changes in government spending and in tax rates) and monetary policy (open market operations, changes in required reserve ratios, and changes in the discount rate). By changing monetary and fiscal policies, the authorities can influence aggregate demand, aiming for the objectives of full employment and stable prices.

In the introduction to Part 3, the reader was warned that an effort would be made to keep the explanations simple. The "potholes" in the road map of economic policy were left out. But, while theory may be simplified, the real world remains complex. Although substantial progress has been made during the past 40 years in managing the economy to provide for full employment and stable prices, there have also been failures in the form of periodic recessions and stubborn inflation. We have done much better than our grandparents did in the decades between the two world wars. But we do not seem to be moving on from one success to ever greater successes. The problem of recession has not been licked. In fact, the recession of 1981–1982 was the most severe in the past four decades. Whether measured by the rate of unemployment, the rate of inflation, or the rate of growth of real national product, the American economy has performed less well since 1970 than it did during the 1960s.

Nor is there unanimity on how we should proceed from here. On the contrary, there are sharp controversies on some of the most basic issues of macroeconomics. The chapters of Part 4 will deal with six of the great macroeconomic issues of our time.

1. Monetary Policy and Fiscal Policy: Which Is the Key to Aggregate Demand?

Most economists believe that *both* fiscal policy and monetary policy are important tools for controlling aggregate demand. But there are substantial disagreements over which should be made the centerpiece of aggregate demand policy. Those in the Keynesian tradition often emphasize fiscal policy, while those in the classical tradition see money as the key to changes in aggregate demand. This controversy is the subject of Chapter 14. We will conclude that the best approach generally involves a combined, cooperative use of both fiscal and monetary policies.

2. How Actively Should Aggregate Demand Be Managed?

Some economists are very concerned with the instability of aggregate demand, particularly the investment component. They believe that it is important for the fiscal and monetary authorities to manage demand actively in order to combat recessions and inflationary booms. Other economists are very skeptical that policymakers know enough to stabilize aggregate demand. They believe that, in practice, active policy management is more likely to destabilize than to stabilize aggregate demand. They therefore recommend that the authorities follow a set of stable policy settings. In particular, they argue that the Federal Reserve should aim at a stable, moderate rate of growth of the money stock. This controversy, which is perhaps the most important single macroeconomic debate of our time, is studied in Chapter 15.

3. Aggregate Supply: How Can Inflation and Unemployment Coexist?

Chapter 9 introduced a relatively simple set of aggregate supply functions: (1) the vertical aggregate supply function of classical theory; (2) the aggregate supply function of basic Keynesian theory, which forms a reversed L; and (3) the curved, upward sloping aggregate supply curve which is useful in explaining how an increase in aggregate demand may be reflected partly in an increase in real output and partly in an increase in prices.

However, in order to explain some of the puzzles of recent years, it is necessary to consider aggregate supply in more detail. In particular, none of the three simple aggregate supply functions is adequate to explain an important puzzle of the past 15 years: How can a high rate of inflation and a high rate of unemployment exist *together*? This question is considered in Chapter 16.

4. How Do We Adjust to Inflation?

The problems created by high unemployment are obvious: With many people out of work, the society foregoes the goods and services that otherwise could have been created. The loss of a job often brings both economic hardship and demoralization.

The problems with rapid inflation are less clear. But they are important because of the rapid inflation both here and abroad during the past decade. They are studied in Chapter 17. One of the major, lasting consequences of our inflation has been that people trying to buy their first homes find great difficulty in doing so.

5. Supply-Side Economics: Productivity Problems and Policies

Traditionally, macroeconomics has concentrated on the "demand side"—that is, on aggregate demand policies designed to achieve high employment and stable prices. But there also is a "supply side," involving the productive capacity of the economy.

The supply side has attracted increasing attention over the past decade, in part because of the poor productivity performance of the U.S. economy in the 1970s, and in part because one of the main economic objectives of the Reagan administration has been to increase productivity. The supply side will be the topic of Chapter 18.

6. Fixed or Flexible Exchange Rates?

The countries of the world are interdependent; prosperity in one country affects its trading partners. The Depression of the 1930s caused worldwide distress. The prosperity of recent decades has likewise been an international phenomenon. The subject of Chapter 19 will be the ways in which inflation and employment in one country can be affected by its transactions with other countries.

An important facet of this topic is the exchange rate system. Should exchange rates be pegged by governments, or should they be allowed to fluctuate in response to changes in supply and demand? (An exchange rate is the price of one national currency in terms of another. For example, the price of the British pound in terms of U.S. dollars is an exchange rate. An exchange rate is pegged when it is kept fixed by one or more national governments.) Between 1971 and 1973, the system of pegged exchange rates set up at the end of World War II came apart at the seams. Since 1973, most important exchange rates have been flexible; that is, governments have allowed them to fluctuate in response to changing demand and supply conditions. In Chapter 19, we will consider the relative merits of pegged and flexible exchange rates.

CHAPTER 14

MONETARY POLICY AND FISCAL POLICY:

WHICH IS THE KEY TO AGGREGATE DEMAND?

Nothing in excess

ANCIENT GREEK PROVERB (DIOGENES)

In the previous chapters, we have dealt with the two major tools with which aggregate demand can be controlled: fiscal policy and monetary policy. When we have two tools, the question naturally arises: ''On which one should we rely?''

Views on that question have changed considerably in recent decades. The Keynesian revolution not only emphasized the responsibility of government to manage aggregate demand. It also identified fiscal policy as the primary tool to do so. Monetary policy was considered much less important. Keynes and his followers argued that, in the deepest pit of a depression, expansive monetary policies might be completely useless as a means of stimulating aggregate demand. An increase in the money stock might have no effect on spending. In more normal times, Keynes was less skeptical regarding the effects of monetary policy. In fact, he emphasized the importance of money in his earlier works, especially *Monetary Reform* (1924) and *A Treatise on Money* (1930). Nevertheless, the *General Theory* left a strong legacy in favor of fiscal policy as the primary tool to control aggregate demand.

In the two decades between 1945 and 1965, when Keynesian theory dominated macroeconomic analysis in the United States, fiscal policy was at the center of attention, with monetary policy being considered much less important. Some Keynesians went as far as Warren Smith, who in 1959 dismissed the control of aggregate demand through monetary policy as ''a mirage and delusion.''[1]

During the 1960s, there was a resurgence of interest in monetary policy and in the classical theory which had identified money as the key determinant of aggregate demand. The most prominent role in this revival of classical economics was played by Milton Friedman, then a professor at the University of Chicago (now retired). Friedman summarized his position: ''Money is extremely important for nominal magnitudes, for nominal income, for the level of income in dollars. . . .'' Furthermore, Friedman was skeptical about the effectiveness of fiscal policy as a tool for controlling aggregate demand. He of course recognized that the government budget has an important influence on the allocation of resources: The budget determines how much of national product is spent by the government and how much is left for the private sector. But Friedman doubted that fiscal policy has an important effect on aggregate demand: ''In my opinion, the state of the budget by itself has no sig-

[1]*Staff Report on Employment, Growth, and Price Levels* (Washington: Joint Economic Committee, U.S. Congress, 1959), p. 401. Smith was writing about general monetary controls, such as open market operations, that affect the quantity of money. He was less skeptical of the effectiveness of selective controls, such as those on consumer installment credit. (Smith was a professor of economics at the University of Michigan and a member of President Johnson's Council of Economic Advisers.)

nificant effect on the course of nominal income, on inflation, on deflation, or on cyclical fluctuations.''[2]

While Friedman and other neoclassical macroeconomists have had a profound effect, neoclassical theory has not attained the predominant position enjoyed by Keynesian theory in the decades following the Second World War. Most macroeconomists are eclectic, agreeing with some parts of Keynesian analysis and with some parts of classical economics. In response to the question posed back in the first paragraph, most present-day macroeconomists would answer: ``Both monetary and fiscal policies are important. We should not rely exclusively on either.''

To understand current thinking on monetary and fiscal policies, it is important to study both Keynesian and classical theories. Each theory provides a sensible framework for the orderly investigation of macroeconomic developments. Each can heighten our understanding of how the economy works. Chapter 11 explained the Keynesian view of how fiscal policy can affect aggregate demand. To complete our discussion of fiscal and monetary policies, this chapter will explain:

1. The Keynesian view of how monetary policy can affect aggregate demand, and the circumstances in which the effect may not be very strong

2. The classical view on how monetary policy can affect aggregate demand, and why those in the classical tradition expect the effects of monetary policy to be both strong and predictable

3. The reasons why some of those in the classical tradition have doubts about fiscal policy, specifically, why they doubt that fiscal policy has the strong and predictable effect on aggregate demand suggested by the Keynesian theory outlined in Chapter 11

4. The advantages of using a *combination* of monetary and fiscal policies as part of an overall strategy of stabilizing aggregate demand

5. Why monetary policy has in fact been the predominant demand-management tool since the late 1970s, in spite of the widely recognized advantages of using a balanced combination of monetary and fiscal policies

[2]Milton Friedman and Walter Heller, *Monetary vs. Fiscal Policy: A Dialogue* (New York: W. W. Norton, 1969), pp. 46, 51.

THE EFFECTS OF MONETARY POLICY: THE KEYNESIAN VIEW

Keynes identified a three-step process by which a change in monetary policy could affect aggregate demand (Figure 14-1):

1. An open market operation and a change in the money stock can affect the rate of interest. For example, an open market purchase of bonds by the Fed will raise bond prices; that is, lower the interest rate.

2. A change in the interest rate can affect investment demand. With a lower interest rate, business executives are encouraged to borrow money to buy new machines or to build new factories.

3. Higher investment demand will have a multiplied effect on aggregate demand and national product.

The third step involves the familiar multiplier explained in Chapter 10. Here, we will look at steps 1 and 2.

Step 1: Monetary Policy and the Interest Rate: The Stock of Money and the Demand for It

The first step in the process—how an open market operation can affect interest rates—was discussed briefly in Chapter 13. Because this step is important in the Keynesian evaluation of monetary policy, we consider it in more detail here.

In Keynes' theory, the interest rate reaches equilibrium when the demand and supply of money are equal; that is, *when people are willing to hold the amount of money that exists in the economy*.

People hold money in order to buy goods and services. As a result, the demand for money *depends on national income*. The reason is straightforward. The higher is income, the more purchases people will plan to make, and the more money they will consequently want to hold.

The demand for money also *depends on the interest rate*. Whenever money is held rather than used to buy a bond or other interest-bearing security, the holder of money gives up the interest that could have been earned on the security. Suppose that interest rates are high. The treasurers of corporations will try to keep as little money on hand as is conveniently possible, putting the rest into interest-bearing securities. At an interest rate of 15% per annum, for example, $10 million earns $30,000 in interest per week—a tidy sum. On the other hand, if interest rates are very low, people do not need to be so careful about cash management; they do not forego much interest by holding money rather than securities. Therefore, more money will be held.

This willingness of people to hold more money at a lower rate of interest is illustrated by the downward-sloping demand curve in Figure 14-2. Suppose that $200 billion of money has been created by the banking system. S_1 illustrates this money supply. The equilibrium interest rate is 8%, at the intersection of the demand and supply curves.

Consider next what happens if the Federal Reserve purchases securities on the open market, causing an expansion of the money stock to $300 billion, as shown by S_2. At the old 8% interest rate, there is a surplus of money shown by the gray arrow; people have more than they are willing to hold at this interest rate. What do they do with the excess? They buy interest-bearing securities. Bond prices are bid up; that is, interest rates are bid down. The interest rate falls to its new equilibrium, 6%.

Step 2. The Interest Rate and Investment Demand: The Marginal Efficiency of Investment

Having seen how an increase in the stock of money can lead to a fall in the interest rate, we now turn to the second step: How a fall in the interest rate can lead to an increase in investment. But, before we take this step, we should consider how the decision to invest is made.

Business executives are interested in acquiring equipment or buildings because of the stream of returns such investments will provide. Consider a very simple illustration, an imaginary machine costing $100,000 that will last forever. With it, a manufacturer expects to produce and sell $50,000 more in goods each year. If the wages paid to workers to run the machine, plus the cost of material inputs, plus administrative costs, add up to $40,000 per year, the machine will provide a return (R) of $10,000 per year. In other words, the machine will

FIGURE 14-1
How monetary policy affects aggregate demand and national product: The Keynesian approach

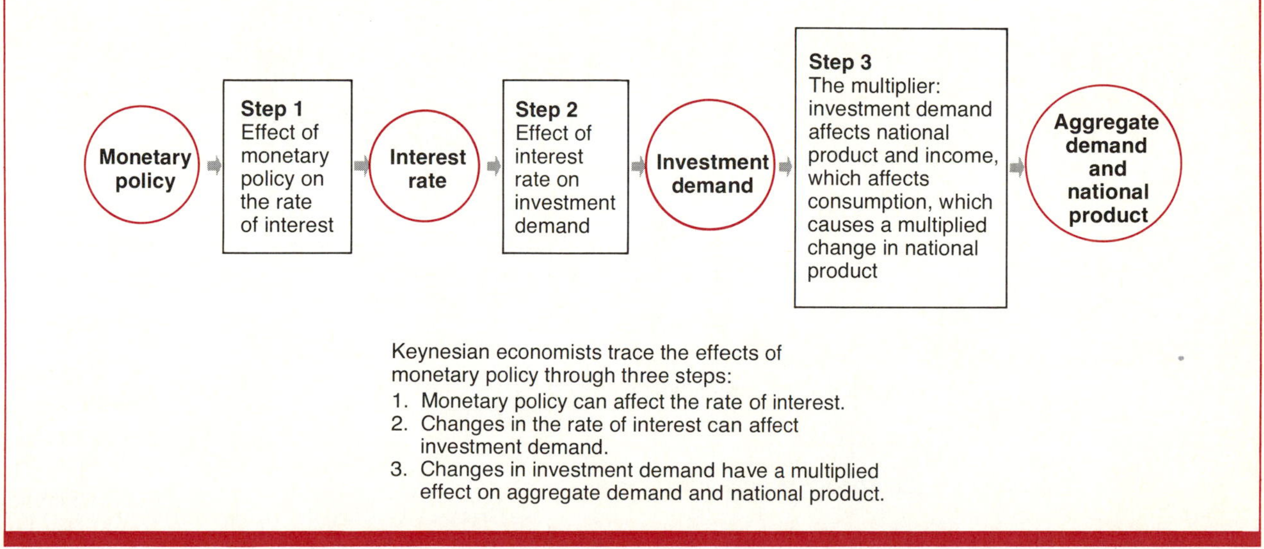
Monetary policy
Step 1
Effect of monetary policy on the rate of interest
Interest rate
Step 2
Effect of interest rate on investment demand
Investment demand
Step 3
The multiplier: investment demand affects national product and income, which affects consumption, which causes a multiplied change in national product
Aggregate demand and national product
Keynesian economists trace the effects of monetary policy through three steps:
1. Monetary policy can affect the rate of interest.
2. Changes in the rate of interest can affect investment demand.
3. Changes in investment demand have a multiplied effect on aggregate demand and national product.

provide a ***rate of return*** (r), or *yield,* of 10% per annum on the initial investment of $100,000.

Alternatively, consider quite a different machine, which also costs $100,000 but completely wears out in 1 year. Suppose that this machine generates enough in sales to cover labor, material, and administrative costs, plus an additional $110,000. Then this machine also provides a rate of return of 10%. That is, it provides enough to cover the $100,000 purchase price of the machine and leave 10% over.

Both these illustrations are very simple. But they do provide examples of how the percentage rate of return may be calculated by taking into account:[3]

1. The initial price and expected life of the machine
2. The addition to sales expected as a result of the machine
3. Costs associated with running the machine, for labor, materials, etc.[4]

FIGURE 14-2

The stock of money, and the demand for it

The quantity of money demanded increases as the interest rate falls. The equilibrium interest rate occurs where the quantity of money demanded is equal to the stock in existence.

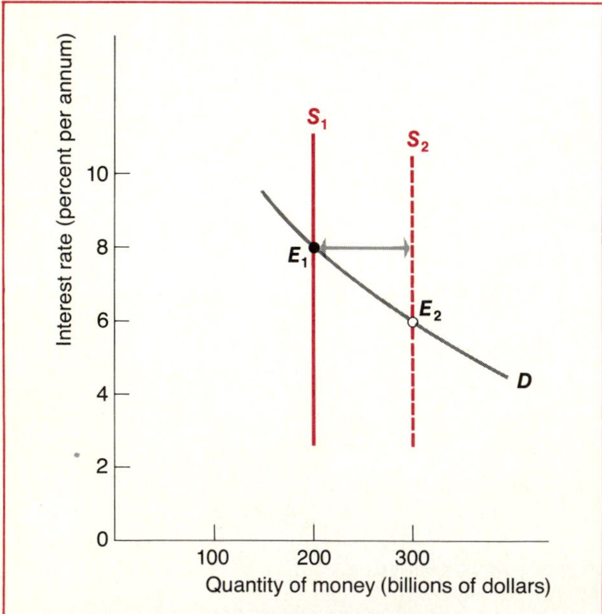

In making plans for capital expenditures for the coming year, the business executive will look first at the equipment or building that provides the highest expected rate of return. For a dynamic company in a growing industry, this rate may be very high—20% or 30% per annum, or even more. In such cases, a corporation that is able to borrow will find it profitable to do so to acquire the new equipment.

It will be profitable to continue to borrow and invest, *as long as the rate of return (r) from the investment exceeds the rate of interest (i) paid on the borrowed funds.* As long as this is so, the new plant or equipment will provide a flow of returns sufficient to cover the interest payments and leave something over to add to profits. On the other hand, it would be a mistake to invest in plant or equipment with an expected rate of return below the rate of interest. More would be paid out in interest than would be contributed by the machine or building, and profits would suffer as a result. Even if the firm has excess funds from retained profits and has no need to borrow to finance new plant and equipment, it would be a mistake to undertake investments with low rates of return. The money could more profitably be used to buy

*[3]The formula for calculating the rate of return r is a close cousin of the bond formula in Box 13-1. Specifically, if a machine has a life of n years, then:

$$\text{Price of machine} = \frac{R_1}{1+r} + \frac{R_2}{(1+r)^2} + \cdots + \frac{R_n + S}{(1+r)^n}$$

where R_1 = the return in the first year, measured in dollars; R_2 = the return in the second year; etc.

S = the scrap value of the machine at the end of its life in year n

r = the rate of return (measured as a percentage or fraction)

If we know the price of the machine and estimate the R's and S, we can solve for r.

In the simple example of a machine with a 1-year life (in which we implicitly assumed a scrap value of zero at the end of the first year), this calculation is:

$$\$100{,}000 = \frac{R_1}{1+r} = \frac{\$110{,}000}{1+r}$$

Therefore,

$$r = 0.1 = 10\%$$

[4]Interest paid on funds borrowed to buy the machine is not included in these costs. Interest comes into the decision-making calculation at a later point, as we shall see.

bonds and earn interest. Thus, to determine whether to undertake an investment project, the business executive calculates *whether the expected rate of return on the plant or equipment is greater than the rate of interest.*

Of course, the executive lives in an uncertain world and cannot be confident that the estimated rate of return will prove accurate. Therefore, the prudent executive will adjust expected yields downward by some amount to compensate for risks and be on the safe side in making investment decisions.

Other businesses make similar calculations. Thus, for the economy as a whole, those investment projects will be undertaken whose risk-adjusted rates of return (r) exceed the rate of interest (i).

This decision-making process is illustrated in Table 14-1 and Figure 14-3. In Table 14-1, all investment projects for the economy are ranked according to their expected rates of return. For example, the highest-ranked $65 billion in projects are expected to yield returns of 12% or higher, and so all these projects will be undertaken if business can borrow at 12% or less. The next $15 billion in projects (for a cumulative total of $80 billion = $65 billion + $15 billion) are expected to yield at least 10%, and so on. This schedule, commonly called the ***marginal efficiency of investment*** (MEI), is graphed in Figure 14-3. It shows how investment increases as the interest rate falls. For example, if the interest rate is 8%, $100 billion of investment is undertaken. (The first $100 billion of investment yields a return of at least 8%.) Then, if the interest rate falls to 6%, investment will increase to $125 billion at point *D*. Thus, a drop in the interest rate from 8% to 6% causes a $25 billion increase in investment.

TABLE 14-1
Expected Return on Investment

	(1) Expected rate of return (r) (percent per annum)	(2) Amount of investment expected to yield at least the return in (1) (in billions of dollars)
A	12%	$ 65
B	10	80
C	8	100
D	6	125

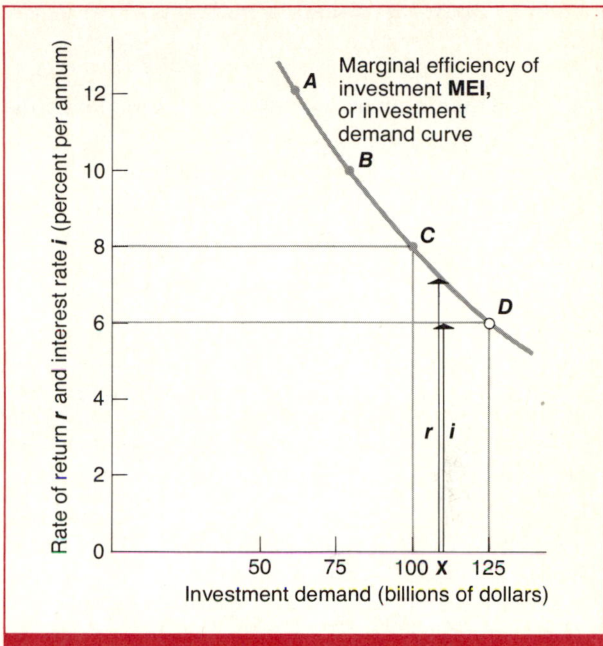

FIGURE 14-3
The marginal efficiency of investment: The investment demand curve
The investment demand (or marginal efficiency of investment) curve slopes downward to the right. At a lower interest rate, more investment projects are undertaken.

The advantage to businesses of undertaking additional investment when the interest rate falls from 8% to 6% may be seen more precisely by considering a specific project that ranks between *C* and *D;* for example, project *X,* which ranks in the 110th billion dollars of investment. The rate of return (r) on this project is just over 7%, as shown by the height of the MEI curve. When the interest rate was 8%, this project was not undertaken, because the 8% cost of borrowing money exceeded the 7% return. However, when the interest rate falls to 6% (arrow i), the project is undertaken. It adds to profits because the 7% return now more than covers the interest cost. Similarly, the other projects between *C* and *D* become profitable when the interest rate falls from 8% to 6%.

We may now summarize how monetary policy affects aggregate demand:

Expansive monetary policy:

	Step 1	Step 2	Step 3
Open market purchase →	**Interest rate down →**	**Investment up →**	**National product up by a multiplied amount**

Restrictive monetary policy:

	Step 1	Step 2	Step 3
Open market sale →	**Interest rate up →**	**Investment down →**	**National product down by a multiplied amount**

The *marginal efficiency of investment* is the schedule or curve that shows possible investment projects, ranked according to their expected rates of return. It shows how much businesses will want to invest at various interest rates. It is also sometimes known as the *investment demand* schedule or curve.

Problems with Monetary Policy

By this three-step process, shown in detail in Figure 14-4, open market operations can affect aggregate demand. Why, then, were early Keynesians skeptical regarding the possible effectiveness of monetary policy as a tool for managing demand? The answer is: We cannot be certain that the effects at either of the first two steps will be very strong.

Keynes himself was particularly concerned that an expansive monetary policy might be ineffective at the very first step, and therefore could not be counted on as a way of getting out of the deep Depression that existed when the *General Theory* was written. During a deep depression, interest rates may be very low—for example, in the 2% to 3% range that prevailed during much of the Depression of the 1930s. In such circumstances, the ability of the Fed to push the rates down even further is not very great. Clearly, interest rates cannot be pushed all the way down to zero. (At a zero interest rate, nobody would be willing to hold bonds. They would be giving up the use of their money and getting nothing in return. It would be better to hold money in the bank instead.) Thus, when interest rates are already very low, it may become impossible for the Federal Reserve to move them much lower. Expansive monetary policy cannot have much effect on interest rates; it fails at step 1.

In more normal times, open market operations can significantly affect the interest rate, and the second step becomes the principal concern in the operation of monetary policy.

The Responsiveness of Investment to a Change in the Interest Rate

As Figure 14-3 is drawn, investment is quite responsive to a change in the rate of interest. For example, a fall in the interest rate from 8% to 6% will cause a 25% increase in investment demand, from $100 billion to $125 billion. An alternative possibility is illustrated in Figure 14-5. Here, the investment demand (MEI) curve falls much more steeply than it did in Figure 14-3. Now, even with a sharp drop in the interest rate from 8% to 6%, investment does not increase very much—only by $5 billion. This, then, is the second reason why monetary policy may be ineffective.

During the 1940s and 1950s, economists were concerned over this possibility, that businesses might not increase their investment much when the interest rate fell. Early studies of the MEI schedule suggested that it might, in fact, be almost vertical. Thus, in contrast with Keynes, who believed that monetary policy might be ineffective during a depression because of the central bank's inability to lower interest rates (step 1), some of

FIGURE 14-4

How monetary policy works: Details on the Keynesian approach

This figure fills out the details in Figure 14-1. In step 1, the fall in the interest rate depends on the amount of additional money and the slope of the money demand function. In step 2, the amount of extra investment that is generated by a reduction in the interest rate depends on the MEI curve. In step 3, the investment has a multiplied effect on aggregate demand. In the simple economy, the multiplier equals 1/MPS.

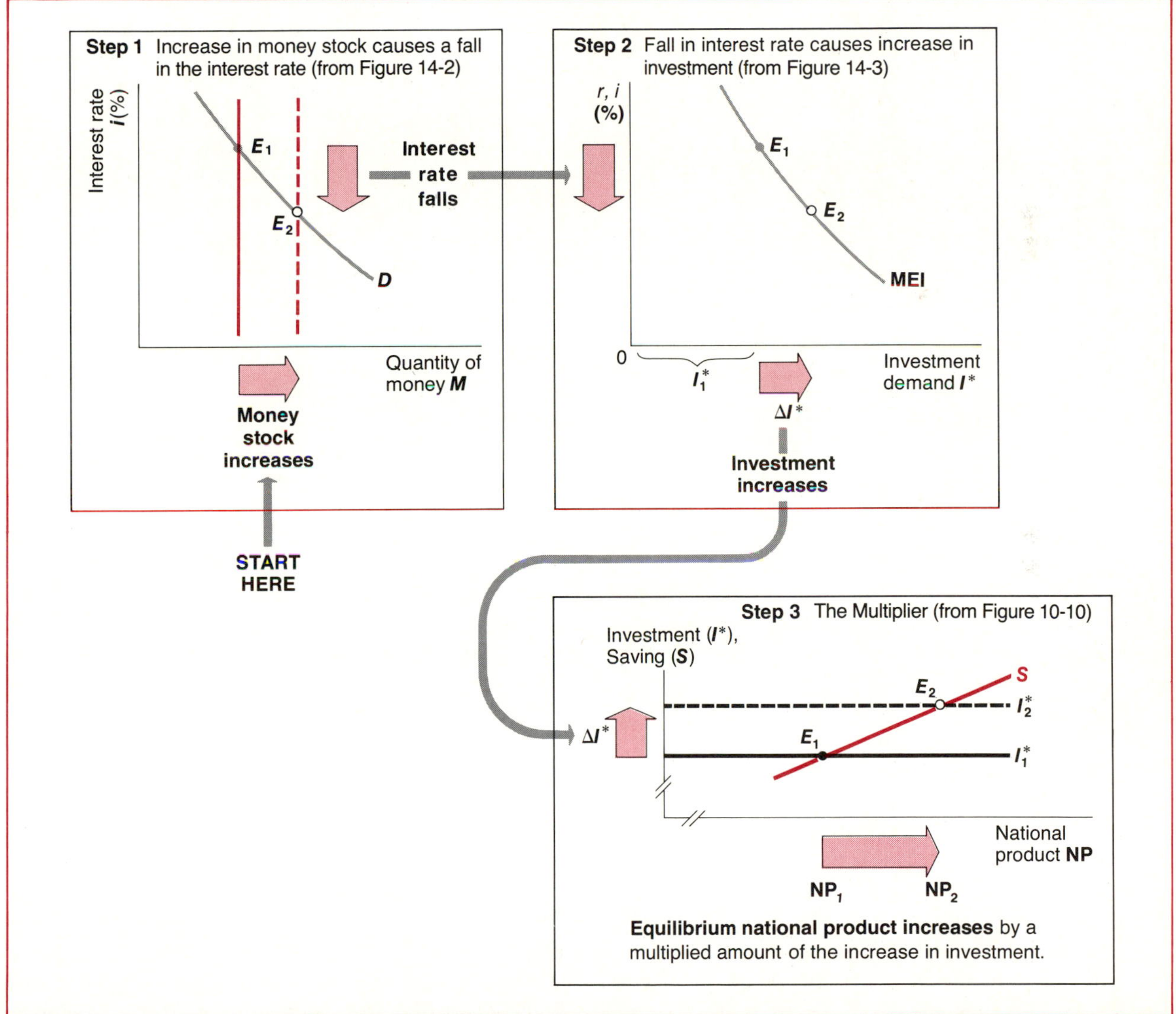

his followers developed even broader skepticism regarding monetary policy. Even if interest rates could be changed, they doubted that investment would be greatly affected (step 2). Thus, they doubted that monetary policy could be counted on to play much more than a secondary, supporting role to the main tool, namely, fiscal policy.

An Effective Monetary Policy

During the last two decades, there has been a movement back toward a more central position. The early fears—that monetary policy is ineffective—have dissipated. As we have seen, these fears were partly based on the early evidence that investment does not respond much to changes in interest rates. However, the early studies did not provide a conclusive case for believing that monetary policy is ineffective, for two major reasons:

FIGURE 14-5

Monetary policy is ineffective at step 2 if an interest rate reduction has little effect on investment

If the MEI curve is steep, investment will not increase much when the interest rate falls. Therefore, the effect of monetary policy on aggregate demand is not very powerful.

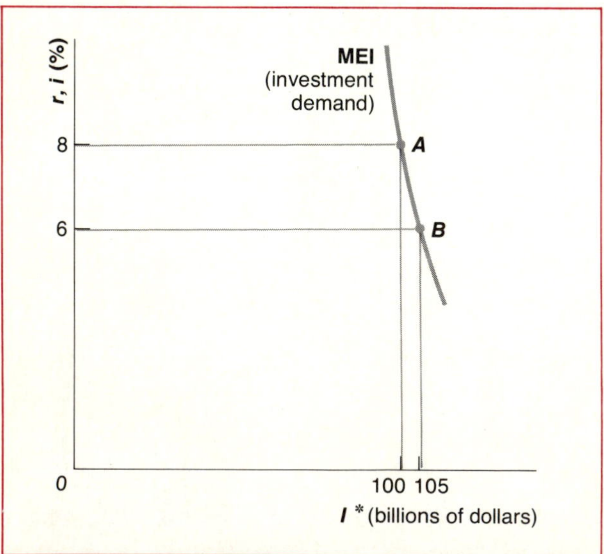

1. Statistical problems in measuring how much investment responds to changes in interest rates First, it is not clear that the early studies were correct in concluding that interest rates do not affect investment demand very much.

It is surprisingly difficult to identify the effects of interest rates on investment because so many other important changes are occurring at the same time. If investment doesn't fall much as the interest rate rises, there are two possible explanations: (1) The interest rate has little effect on investment—as the early studies concluded; or (2) investment is influenced by the interest rate, but there are other offsetting influences. For example, investment may remain high or even rise during a period when rising interest rates are tending to depress it, because at the same time investment is being stimulated by increasing business optimism. More recent statistical work indicates that the early studies did not adequately deal with such complications, and consequently did not provide good estimates of how much investment responds when the rate of interest changes.

2. Credit rationing: The availability of loanable funds It is possible that investment might be affected by monetary policy even when investment demand is very unresponsive to changes in the rate of interest. This is illustrated in Figure 14-6, which repeats the steep MEI curve of Figure 14-5.

Suppose that the initial equilibrium is at point *A*, with $100 billion in investment. The central bank introduces a restrictive monetary policy. By selling securities on the open market, it pushes up interest rates and reduces commercial bank reserves. If banks initially have little or no excess reserves, they will be forced to cut back on their loans and other earning assets.

However, we are assuming that even with higher interest rates—of, say, 10% rather than the original 8%—businesses are still quite eager to borrow and to invest. At *B*, businesses want to invest almost as much as at *A*. However, this is what businesses want, not what they get. Banks can't lend as much as businesses want. To protect their reserve positions, banks ***ration*** their available funds, lending less than credit-worthy customers want to borrow.

***Credit rationing* occurs when banks and other lenders are short of loanable funds. They lend less than they would like if they had the funds, and less than credit-worthy borrowers want to borrow.**

When this happens, investment decreases from *B* to *C*, to the *left* of the marginal efficiency of investment (MEI) curve. Investment declines, not because of a lack of desire to invest, but because businesses are unable to obtain financing. The distance *CB* reflects investment that doesn't occur because of the *unavailability of funds*. Thus, restrictive monetary policy works not only because of (1) the discouraging effect of higher interest rates on investment (shown by the movement from *A* to *B*) but also (2) the inability of businesses to invest because they cannot get funds (the movement from *B* to *C*).

However, a question arises as to why credit rationing can occur in the first place. If there are eager borrowers and limited funds, why doesn't the price of funds (the interest rate) rise to bring demand and supply into equality? In other words, why doesn't the price rise in this market, just as the price of wheat would rise if the quantity demanded exceeded the quantity supplied?

Historically, the major reason has been government-imposed ceilings on the interest rates which banks and other financial institutions could charge. Rising demands for credit therefore showed up only partly in terms of higher interest rates, and partly in terms of shortages and rationing.[5] For example, ***credit crunches***—periods of severe rationing—occurred in 1966 and 1973–1974. However, beginning in the late 1970s, there was a major movement toward deregulation of financial insitutions, and interest rates have become much freer to move up. In recent years, credit rationing has consequently become *much* less important, and high interest rates have become much more important as a mechanism for discouraging borrowers during periods of tight money.

FIGURE 14-6
Credit rationing

When the Federal Reserve reduces the quantity of bank reserves by an open market sale, commercial banks *must* reduce their loans or other earning assets to meet reserve requirements. As a consequence, they may ration credit, lending less than borrowers want and less than the banks would be willing to lend if they had ample reserves. Because of an inability to borrow, businesses are forced to cut back on investment. The effects of credit rationing are shown by distance *BC*.

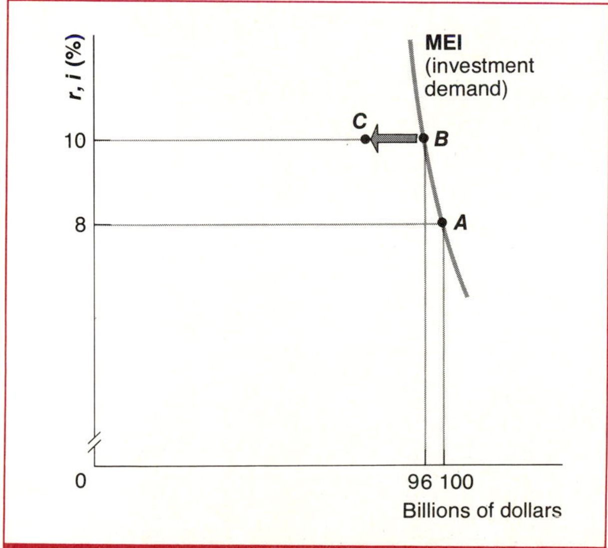

A *credit crunch* occurs when funds suddenly become much scarcer and credit rationing becomes very severe.

Whether it is better for restrictive monetary policy to work through high interest rates or credit rationing has been a matter of heated debate, particularly during 1982 when interest rates were very high. Unfortunately, this debate is quite complex. The case for allowing interest rates to rise to their equilibrium levels—that is, the case against interest rate ceilings—will be explained in detail in Chapter 35. The main point is that high interest rates

[5]In the earlier discussion of rent controls (Box 4-1), we already saw how a government-imposed price ceiling can cause a shortage. In that example, buyers could not rent all the apartments they wanted at the controlled market price, and they therefore ended up at a point to the left of their demand curve. For similar reasons, borrowers can end up to the left of their demand curve, at point *C* in Figure 14-6, when there is a shortage of funds and credit is rationed.

allocate the available funds in the most efficient manner, to the borrowers who are most willing to pay. These are generally the borrowers with the most productive investment opportunities. On the other side, it may be argued that credit crunches are preferable. It is true that crunches can be acutely painful, but they do help the Fed to suppress demand effectively and quickly. Consider, in contrast, what happens when interest rates are free to move up and little or no credit rationing takes place. Some financial analysts fear that interest rates might have to reach "murderous" levels, threatening mass bankruptcy, before effective monetary restraint could be achieved.[6] According to this view, rising interest rates work more slowly and more dangerously than restraint through credit rationing.

We repeat the main points. Credit rationing is a controversial topic. However, until the end of the 1970s, it provided an important way in which restrictive monetary policy could suppress aggregate demand.

The Asymmetrical Effect of Monetary Policy

While credit rationing can contribute to the effectiveness of monetary policy, it also adds to the list of reasons why *restrictive* monetary policies may have a stronger and quicker effect on aggregate demand than do *expansive* policies. Specifically, there are three reasons why restrictive monetary policies may be more effective than expansive policies:

1. The Fed can be more confident of its ability to push interest rates up than of its ability to push them down. If interest rates are already low, the Federal Reserve may be unable to push them down further. On the other hand, there is no limit on the height to which interest rates can be pushed by restrictive monetary policies.

2. When the Federal Reserve follows an easy money policy by purchasing securities on the open market, it increases bank reserves and thus makes additional bank loans and an increase in the money stock *possible*. But the Fed cannot force the banks to lend. Indeed, when banks were frightened during the depression of the 1930s, they held large quantities of excess reserves. On the other hand, consider a restrictive policy of open market sales. Bank reserves are reduced below the legal minimum. In this case the banks *must* respond by reducing their holdings of loans and securities, thus cutting back on the money stock.

3. A tight monetary policy can work by causing credit rationing. Businesses may be unable to borrow to finance investments, and thus may be pushed to a point to the left of the MEI curve (Figure 14-6). However, the opposite is not true. No matter how expansive monetary policies become, businesses cannot be forced to borrow more than they want; they cannot be forced to a point to the right of the MEI curve.

Because of these asymmetries, monetary policy is sometimes compared to controlling aggregate demand with a string. If restrictive policies are adopted, the string tightens; investment is firmly drawn back. However, the effects of expansive policies are much less certain. An expansive "push on the string" makes an increase in investment possible. If the demand for investment is strong, investment in fact does respond, keeping the string taut. In this case, monetary policy is powerful. However, if business executives are pessimistic, they may not respond much to easier monetary conditions. They borrow little more, if any. Investment remains stagnant. The string goes limp. Monetary policy aimed at stimulating aggregate demand has little effect. In short, monetary policy may be more effective as a tool for restraining aggregate demand during periods of inflation than it is for stimulating the economy during periods of recession or depression.

MONETARY POLICY: THE CLASSICAL VIEW

In contrast to Keynes, who started his analysis of aggregate demand by looking at its components (consumption,

---

[6] For details of this view, see the paper by Albert Wojnilower of the First Boston Corporation, "The Central Role of Credit Crunches in Recent Financial History," *Brookings Papers on Economic Activity* 2:1980, pp. 277–327.

Rising interest rates can increase the danger of collapse of financial institutions in at least two ways. (1) Rising interest rates cause a decline in the prices of bonds and other securities (as explained in Box 13-1). This depresses the value of the assets of banks and other financial insitutions. (2) High interest rates increase the difficulties which developing countries face in meeting their debt payments to banks. Particularly in 1983–1984, banks had trouble collecting on their large foreign loans.

investment, government purchases of goods and services, and net exports), classical economists began from quite a different starting point. Their analysis was based on the ***equation of exchange:***

$$MV = PQ \qquad (14\text{-}1)$$

where M = quantity of money in the hands of the public

P = average level of prices

Q = quantity of output, that is, real national product or real national income[7]

Thus, PQ = national product, measured in nominal (dollar) terms

and V = ***income velocity of money,*** that is, the average number of times that the money stock (M) is spent to buy final output during a year. Specifically, V is defined as being equal to PQ/M.

Suppose that the money stock is $100 billion. Assume that, in the course of a year, the average dollar bill and the average checking deposit are spent six times to purchase final goods and services. In other words, V is 6. Then, total spending for final output is $100 billion times 6, or $600 billion. In turn, this total spending (MV) equals the total quantity of goods and services (Q) times the average price (P) at which they were sold.

But how can the same dollar be used over and over to purchase final goods? Very simply. When you purchase groceries at the store, the $50 you pay does not disappear. Rather, it goes into the cash register of the store. From there, it is used to pay the farmer for fresh vegetables, the canning factory for canned goods, or the clerk's wages. The farmer or the clerk or the employee of the canning factory will in turn use the money to purchase goods. Once more, the money is used for final purchases. The same dollar bill can circulate round and round.

The Quantity Theory of Money

The equation of exchange, by itself, does not get us very far because it is a ***tautology*** or truism; that is, it *must* be true because of the way the terms are defined. Note that velocity is defined as $V = PQ/M$. Thus, by definition, $MV = PQ$. (Just multiply both sides of the first equation by M.)

However, in the hands of classical economists, the equation of exchange became more than a tautology; it became the basis of an important theory. This theory—the ***quantity theory of money***—was based on the proposition that *velocity (V) is stable*.

The *quantity theory of money* is the proposition that velocity (V) is stable. Therefore, a change in the quantity of money (M) will cause nominal national product (PQ) to change by approximately the same percentage.

If, for example, the money stock (M) increases by 20%, then nominal national product (PQ) will also rise by about 20% as a consequence. In other words, the old classical economists and their modern neoclassical followers put forward the following central proposition:

1. A change in the quantity of money (M) is the key to changes in aggregate demand. When people have more M, they spend more on the nation's output.[8] Specifically, an increase in M will cause an approximately proportional increase in nominal national product (PQ).

In Chapter 9, we encountered several other important classical propositions:

2. *In the long run,* real output (Q) moves to the full-employment, capacity level. Therefore, the long-run effect of a change in M is on P, not on Q. Most notably, a rapid increase in the quantity of money causes a rapid inflation.

[7]In basic theoretical discussions, the distinction between national product and national income is ignored and the two terms are used interchangeably.

Besides equation 14-1, there is another version of the equation of exchange. This alternative version focuses on total transactions, including intermediate sales, rather than just on the final transactions included in national product. Here we concentrate on the final-payments, or *income,* version of the equation of exchange, as it leads to the simplest comparisons between classical and Keynesian theories.

[8]In other words, the aggregate demand curve shifts when the money stock changes, as already illustrated back in Figure 9-4.

3. *In the short run* (over periods of months or quarters), a change in M can have a substantial effect on both P and Q. For example, a decline in the quantity of money can cause a decline in output (Q) and the onset of a recession. During a recession, a growth of M can cause a short-run increase in Q, moving the economy back toward full employment.
4. Monetary disturbances are a major cause of unstable aggregate demand and of business cycles. If M is kept stable, a market economy will be quite stable.
5. Thus, the major macroeconomic responsibility of the authorities is to provide a stable money supply. Specifically, the money supply should be steadily increased at a rate that is adequate to buy the full-employment output of the economy at stable prices. The authorities should adhere to a *policy rule,* increasing the money stock at a slow, steady rate of about 3% per year.

Why Should Velocity Be Stable? The Demand for Money

The quantity theory may be traced back over 200 years, at least as far back as the writings of philosopher David Hume in the eighteenth century. The early quantity theorists attributed the inflation of the time to the inflow of gold and silver from the New World. The exact mechanism by which money affected aggregate demand and prices was not spelled out in detail by these early theorists. They believed that it was self-evident that, when people have more money, they spend more. When they spend more—with more money chasing a relatively fixed quantity of goods—prices rise.

More recently, particularly in response to the criticisms of Keynesians, neoclassical economists have been more explicit about their theory. Velocity is stable, they argue, because *the demand for money is stable*. The demand for money arises because of the usefulness of money in purchasing goods and services. Money is held only temporarily, from the time people receive income until they spend it to purchase goods and services. The higher are people's incomes, the more money they will need to make purchases. Therefore, the quantity of money demanded depends on the size of national income. And it is national income in current dollars (that is, PQ rather than simply Q) that is important in determining the demand for money: If prices rise, people will need more money to pay for the more expensive goods and services. Thus, neoclassical economists focus on nominal national income as the principal determinant of the demand for money.

Figure 14-7 illustrates this relationship. The higher is current-dollar or nominal national product (measured up the vertical axis), the greater is the quantity of money demanded (measured along the horizontal axis). Suppose that the actual amount of money in the economy is initially at S_1 and that the current-dollar national product is at A_1. Then the supply S_1 and demand for money will be in equilibrium, at point E_1. The quantity of money demanded, measured by the distance A_1E_1, will be equal to the quantity of money (S_1) actually in existence.

FIGURE 14-7

The demand for money: A classical view

Those in the classical tradition argue that the demand for money is stable and depends primarily on current-dollar national product. If the stock of money which people hold exceeds the demand for money, then people will increase their spending.

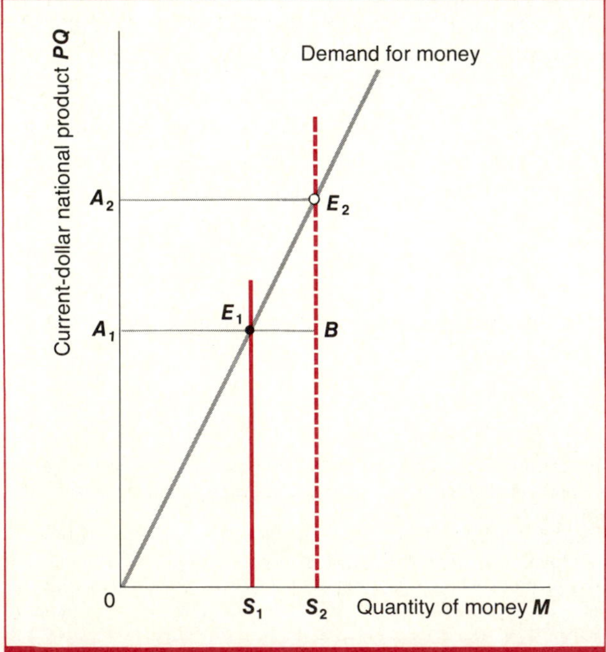

Now, suppose that an expansive monetary policy is followed, with the money supply increasing to S_2. At the existing national product (A_1), the stock of money that people have (A_1B) is greater than the amount they want to hold (A_1E_1); there is a temporary surplus of money of E_1B. With more money than they want, people spend it to buy more goods and services. In other words, aggregate demand goes up. If the economy is initially in a depression, with large amounts of excess capacity, output (Q) will respond strongly to the increase in money. But if the economy is already at or near full employment, Q can't increase substantially, and higher aggregate demand will cause a rise in prices (P). In either case, current-dollar national product (PQ) will increase. As this happens, people become willing to hold more money. The process continues until current-dollar national product rises to A_2, where the quantity of money and the demand for it are again in equilibrium at E_2. In this way, a change in the quantity of money causes an approximately proportional change in national product PQ. But this in turn means that V is stable. (If a 10% increase in PQ occurs whenever there is a 10% increase in M, the ratio PQ/M is constant; that is, V is constant.)

Thus, the theoretical underpinning of the quantity theory of money—the proposition that V is stable—is this: There is a stable demand for money, similar to the straight line shown in Figure 14-7.

CLASSICAL DOUBTS ABOUT FISCAL POLICY: CROWDING OUT

Classical economists were united in emphasizing the importance of money as a determinant of aggregate demand. However, their views on fiscal policy were less unanimous. During the Great Depression of the 1930s, some of them recommended substantial increases in government spending as a way of increasing demand, output, and employment. Others were quite skeptical about the effects of fiscal policy. For example, the British Treasury opposed additional government spending on the ground that it would do no good, since it would merely displace, or ***crowd out,*** an equivalent amount of private investment demand. (One of Keynes' principal objectives in writing the *General Theory* was to combat this British Treasury view.)

Expansive fiscal policies may crowd out investment demand in the following way. When the government increases its expenditures or cuts taxes, its deficit rises. To finance its deficit spending, the government sells new bonds or shorter-term securities; that is, it borrows from the financial markets. The additional borrowing pushes up interest rates. Higher interest rates, in turn, cause a movement along the marginal efficiency of investment (MEI) curve; the amount of investment decreases (Figure 14-8).

***Crowding out* occurs when an expansive fiscal policy causes higher interest rates and these higher interest rates in turn depress investment demand.**

There is little doubt that some crowding out takes place. The question is how much. Keynesian economists—particularly early Keynesians—have often argued that investment is not very responsive to interest

FIGURE 14-8

Crowding out: The monetarist view

Government deficits may push up the interest rate—from i_1 to i_2, for example. This causes a movement along the MEI curve from C to D, and investment demand decreases from I_1^* to I_2^*.

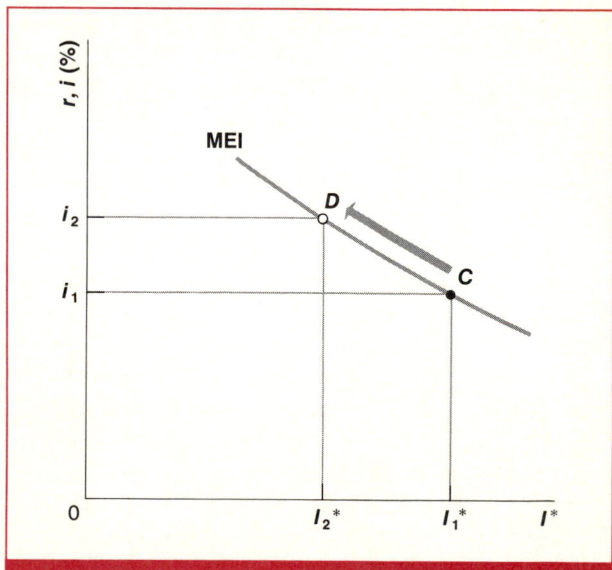

rates. This view is illustrated back in Figure 14-5, where investment decreases only a little in a move from B to A. As a result, not much crowding out of investment takes place. Consequently, fiscal policy is a powerful tool for controlling aggregate demand (and monetary policy is weak). Monetarists, on the other hand, generally believe that the MEI curve is quite flat (as shown in Figure 14-8) and that deficit spending by the government tends to crowd out a relatively large amount of private investment.

In casting doubt on the effectiveness of fiscal policies, monetarists make one important qualification: If the central bank buys any of the additional bonds being issued by the government, it will be engaging in an expansive open market operation. New money will be created and this will have a powerful expansive effect on aggregate demand. But monetarists attribute the higher demand to a change in the money stock, not to the government deficit itself. They see ***pure fiscal policy*** as having little effect on aggregate demand.

Pure fiscal policy **involves a change in government spending or tax rates unaccompanied by any change in the rate of growth of the money stock.**

RECENT DOUBTS ABOUT FISCAL POLICY: NET EXPORTS

In this chapter, we have thus far summarized the long-lasting debate which began with Keynes' attack on classical economics in the 1930s. ''Crowding out'' was part of that debate.

In recent years, and particularly with the ballooning of government deficits during the Reagan presidency, another reason has arisen for doubting a strong stimulative effect from deficit spending. Specifically, an increase in the government's deficit can have a negative effect on net exports. To see why, we must follow through the detailed effects of the government deficits caused by an expansive fiscal policy. Again, we will be considering a *pure* fiscal policy, with no change in the money stock.

Once more, we start with the higher interest rates which the government deficits cause. The higher U.S. interest rates encourage foreigners to buy U.S. bonds. In order to buy these bonds, they need dollars. To buy the dollars, they offer their own currency in exchange, for example, Japanese yen. As they buy dollars, they bid up the price of the dollar in terms of yen; for example, the price of the dollar is bid up from 200 yen to 220 yen.

Now consider how this affects Japanese wishing to buy American goods, such as a computer selling for $1 million. Initially, when a dollar was worth 200 yen, this $1 million computer would cost the Japanese buyer 200 million yen. After the price of the dollar was bid up, the same computer would cost the Japanese 220 million yen. Because computers have thus become more expensive to foreign buyers, they buy fewer; U.S. exports of computers fall. For similar reasons, other U.S. exports also decline.

The change in the price of the dollar also affects U.S. imports. When the dollar becomes more expensive in terms of yen, it takes more yen to buy one dollar. But that is just another way of saying that it takes fewer cents to buy 100 yen; the price of yen has fallen. This makes Japanese goods cheaper to American buyers, who consequently buy more imports.

With rising U.S. imports and declining exports, the net export component of U.S. aggregate demand decreases. This partially cancels out the stimulative effects of budgetary deficits.

This argument may be summarized:

> Taxes down or government spending up → Government deficit up → Interest rate up → Purchase of U.S. bonds by foreigners → Rise in price of dollar in terms of foreign currencies → Fall in exports and rise in imports

In both these cases—the crowding out of investment and the decline in net exports—government deficit spending has an effect on the *composition* of output. There are negative effects on investment and the production of exports. In addition, the U.S. production of import-competing goods—such as cars—declines when Americans buy imports instead.

This change in the composition of output was a cause of concern to Martin Feldstein of Harvard University, who served as President Reagan's Chairman of the Council of Economic Advisers from 1982 to 1984. Feldstein was worried that the large government deficits would cause the economic expansion of 1983–1984 to become ***lopsided,*** with undesirably low exports and investment.

A Caution

One caution is necessary regarding the two ways in which fiscal policy can be weakened—namely, by crowding out of investment and by a decline in net export demand. These two negative forces are not independent. *We cannot simply add them together* and come to the conclusion that fiscal policy has little chance of success. The reason is this: The more net exports decline, the smaller will be the crowding out of investment.

To see why, consider what happens when foreigners buy U.S. bonds. As we have just seen, they thereby bid up the price of the U.S. dollar and depress net exports. But, as they bid for U.S. bonds, they help to maintain U.S. bond prices and keep U.S. interest rates from rising as high as they otherwise would go. Because of this moderating effect on interest rates, the crowding out of investment is less strong. In brief, when foreigners buy U.S. securities, they indirectly cause a decline in our net exports. But they also help to finance U.S. investment, reducing the amount by which investment is crowded out.

In recent years, financial capital has become more mobile among nations. Foreigners are more willing to buy U.S. bonds when U.S. interest rates are high. They are also more able to do so because of the relaxation of foreign legal restraints on capital flows. As a result, the effect of deficits on net exports has become more important, and crowding out of investment less important. In fact, U.S. domestic investment was quite strong in the recovery of 1983–1984, when federal government deficits totalled just over $350 billion. It was net exports that were conspicuously weak. In those 2 years, foreigners acquired a total of $170 billion of U.S. assets, and U.S. merchandise imports exceeded exports by $170 billion.

DOUBTS ABOUT FISCAL POLICY: AGGREGATE DEMAND AND AGGREGATE SUPPLY

The two complications we have just studied—regarding crowding out and net export demand—explain why fiscal policy may have a weak effect *on aggregate demand.* However, insofar as fiscal policy is aimed at affecting real output, we should also look at the limits on fiscal policy because of the nature of *aggregate supply.*

This will be illustrated in Figure 14-9, which represents an elaboration of earlier Figure 10-13*b*. Consider first the simplest case, where fiscal policy has its maximum effect. There are no complications to detract from its strength. Specifically, (1) there is no crowding out of investment; (2) there is no negative effect on net exports; and (3) the aggregate supply curve is horizontal, which means that any increase in aggregate demand will show up entirely in terms of an increase in output and not at all in terms of higher prices. In this simple case, an expansive fiscal policy causes a strong rightward movement in aggregate demand, from AD_1 to AD_2 in Figure 14-9 (left panel). Equilibrium moves from E to H, with real national product increasing sharply from Q_1 to Q_2.

The left panel also illustrates what happens when some investment demand is crowded out and net exports decline. In this case, the effect of fiscal policy on aggregate demand is weakened. The aggregate demand function shifts only from AD_1 to AD_3, with equilibrium national product increasing to Q_3. Thus, distance Q_3Q_2 shows the combined effect of crowding out and a decline in net exports.

Finally, the right panel also includes complications on the supply side. Now, as aggregate demand increases from AD_1 to AD_3, both prices and real national product increase. The economy moves upward along the aggregate supply curve AS_2 to the new equilibium K, where output is Q_4. The distance between Q_4 and Q_3 represents the output that isn't produced because of a rise in prices.

This last complication—the failure of output to rise because of the upward slope of the aggregate supply function—*applies equally to monetary policy.* Thus, the debate studied in this chapter—over the relative effectiveness of monetary and fiscal policies—has to do only with their relative effectiveness *in changing aggregate demand.*

STATISTICAL EVIDENCE

To summarize the major debate in this chapter: Monetarists argue that velocity is stable. Money is the key to changes in aggregate demand. An increase in the quantity of money causes an increase in national product, measured in dollars. Some monetarists are skeptical about pure fiscal policy, arguing that it will have little effect on aggregate demand. In contrast, Keynesians believe that fiscal policy has a powerful impact on aggregate demand. Some Keynesians argue that monetary policy is less effective, particularly as a way of getting an economy out of a depression or recession.

It would seem easy to settle this dispute—simply look at the facts and see which theory is more in line with the observations of the real world. Unfortunately, this is easier said than done, for reasons that may be best understood by considering the full-scale counterattack which monetarists launched against Keynesian economics during the 1960s.

This counterattack was supported by two major statistical studies, the first by Milton Friedman and David Meiselman, and the second by a group of economists at the Federal Reserve Bank of St. Louis.[9] Friedman and Meiselman argued that Keynesian economics had been accepted, and classical economics rejected, on the basis

[9]Milton Friedman and David Meiselman, "The Relative Stability of Monetary Velocity and the Investment Multiplier in the United States," in Commission on Money and Credit, *Stabilization Policies* (Englewood Cliffs, N.J.: Prentice-Hall, 1963), pp. 168–268; and Leonall C. Andersen and Jerry Jordan, "Monetary and Fiscal Actions: A Test of Their Relative Importance in Economic Stabilization," *Federal Reserve Bank of St. Louis Review,* November 1968, pp. 11–16.

FIGURE 14-9

The effects of fiscal policy

In the left panel, aggregate supply is horizontal. In the absence of crowding out and a decline in net exports, expansive fiscal policy has a strong effect on real output. However, if crowding out occurs and net exports decline, aggregate demand shifts only to AD_3 rather than AD_2. The effect of fiscal policy is weaker.

The right panel introduces an upward-sloping aggregate supply curve. In this case, some of the increase in demand goes into higher prices, rather than greater ouptut. With aggregate demand AD_3, the new equilibrium is at *K,* not *J.*

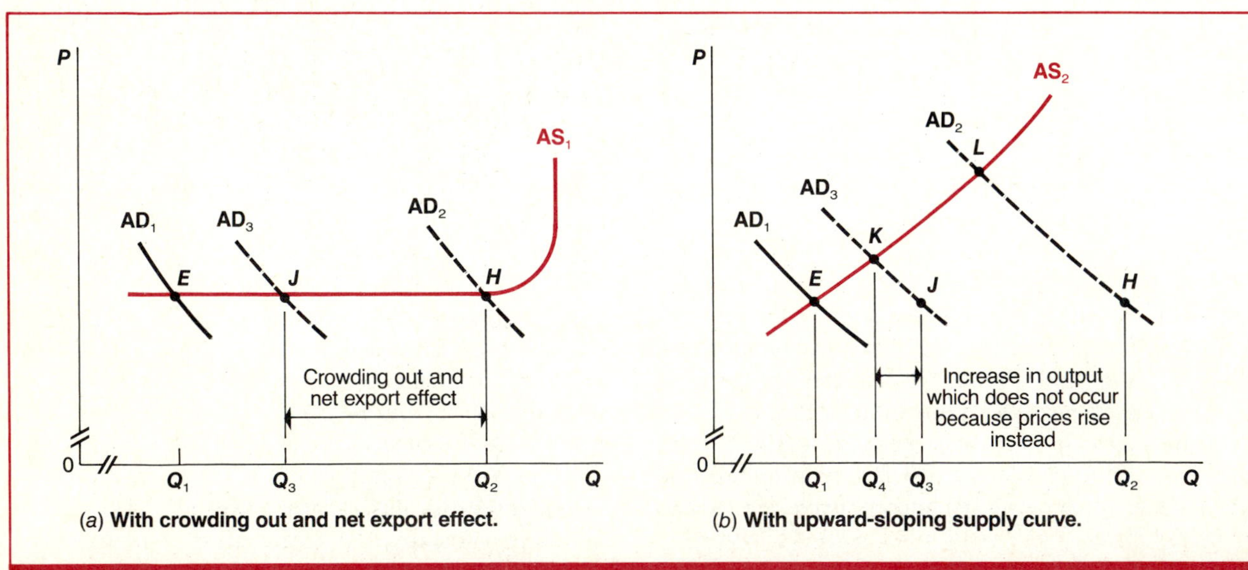

of the theoretical case put forward by Keynes in his *General Theory*. Yet nobody had stopped to study the facts seriously. Nobody had done a *comparative* study to find out which was more consistent with the facts—the classical theory or the Keynesian theory. The time had come, said Friedman and Meiselman, to conduct such a study.

The centerpiece of classical theory was the velocity of money; classical theory was based on the premise that velocity is stable. The central theoretical tool of Keynesian analysis was the marginal propensity to consume (MPC) and its algebraic cousin, the multiplier. For Keynesian demand-management policies to be useful, the MPC and the multiplier must be reasonably stable and predictable. According to Friedman and Meiselman, therefore, the debate came down to a basic question: Which is more stable, velocity or the multiplier?

Looking at the statistical evidence for 1897 through 1958, they found the results to be "remarkably consistent and unambiguous." The velocity of money was found to be decidedly more stable than the multiplier throughout that six-decade period—with one notable exception: the decade of the depressed 1930s. The conclusion indicated by the Friedman-Meiselman results: Keynes' theory was not a "general" theory at all. Rather, it was a special theory with relevance to the thirties. (Keynes had called his theory "general" because it dealt not only with conditions of full employment but also with those of large-scale unemployment. In contrast, he considered the classical theory "special," since it applied only to a fully employed economy.)

In the test between Keynesian and classical economics, Friedman and Meiselman declared the classical theory to be the clear winner. Similar results were obtained by the St. Louis Fed.

Problems of Interpretation

Needless to say, these results did not persuade Keynesian economists to give up the contest; the monetarist studies were themselves vulnerable to attack. Most important, perhaps, was a fundamental problem that bedevils *any* statistical test of a theory. A theory is usually in the form of a cause-and-effect statement: "If the money stock is increased, this will cause an increase in aggregate demand;" or, to take an illustration from simple microeconomic theory, "If the price of a good rises, consumers will, as a consequence, buy a smaller quantity." Yet, statistical evidence is merely a series of observations. The observed facts regarding money, aggregate demand, prices, and quantities purchased tell us simply *what* has happened, not *why* it has happened. Statistics do not show what caused what; they show only what things have happened together.

For example, if we observe that two items (A and B) are closely related, both rising and falling together, this observation does not, in itself, permit us to decide whether (1) A caused B, or (2) B caused A, or (3) both A and B were caused by a third item, C.

Now consider the Friedman-Meiselman and St. Louis statistical results, which indicated that changes in the quantity of money (*M*) and changes in nominal national product (*PQ*) moved together closely. Friedman and Meiselman concluded that the quantity theory was upheld, that changes in the stock of money *cause* a powerful and predictable change in aggregate demand. What was the response of their critics? That no such powerful causal relationship had been demonstrated. While aggregate demand and changes in the quantity of money do indeed move together, the reason is not just because money influences aggregate demand (the monetarist explanation). It is also because aggregate demand influences the quantity of money. In other words, cause and effect can operate in the *opposite* direction to the one emphasized by monetarists.

How could that be so? How could a change in demand cause a change in the quantity of money? We have already answered this question in Chapter 13. If the Federal Reserve responds passively, allowing the money supply to rise when business are clamoring for loans during boom conditions, then rising aggregate demand can indeed cause a rise in the quantity of money. Because of this complication, it is difficult or impossible to tell from simple statistical tests just how strong the effect of money is on aggregate demand.

THE UNCERTAIN LESSON OF RECENT HISTORY

The difficulty of deciding which theory is more correct is

increased by the conflicting lessons that may be drawn from recent history.

From the viewpoint of their proponents, the monetarist studies appeared at a good time. The events of the late 1960s tended to confirm the quantity theory and to cast doubts on the Keynesian view. In mid-1968, Congress imposed an income tax surcharge and placed a limitation on federal government spending in order to cool down the inflation generated by the Vietnam conflict. Economists using the Keynesian approach expected a powerful restrictive effect on aggregate demand. In fact, there were fears that the Congress had engaged in "fiscal overkill" and that a recession would be caused by the sharp shift toward fiscal restraint. In order to soften the expected recession, the Federal Reserve eased monetary policy, allowing a rapid rate of growth of the money stock. Thus, monetary policy was expansive, while fiscal policy was restrictive. What happened? The economy followed the path set by monetary policy and continued to boom throughout late 1968. Indeed, the boom continued until after monetary policy was shifted sharply toward restraint in early 1969. Monetarists seemed vindicated, and Keynesians were shaken in their beliefs. In the words of Alan Blinder and Robert Solow, the events of the late 1960s threatened to send Keynesian economic advisers "scurrying back to their universities with their doctrinal tales [sic] between their legs."[10]

However, the monetarist triumph was short-lived. By the mid-1970s, the economy was not behaving the way the quantity theory said it should. In 1975, a strong upswing in GNP began in spite of a slow growth in the money stock. According to the quantity theory, this strong upswing should not have occurred with so little increase in the quantity of money—"the case of the missing money," in the words of Princeton's Stephen Goldfeld.[11] Because GNP grew more rapidly than the money stock, velocity rose.

Then, during the severe recession of 1982, velocity fell sharply (Figure 14-10). The recession was *much* more severe than could be explained on the basis of what was happening to the money stock. In other words, something other than changes in the money stock caused aggregate demand to rise so strongly in the late 1970s and to fall so strongly in 1982.

Because of these changes in velocity, the relationship between money and GNP has been much less close during the past decade than it was previously. In a recent study, Ronald McKinnon of Stanford University found that 63% of the changes in GNP between 1958 and 1969 were attributable to changes in the quantity of money, but only 33% of the changes between 1972 and 1982 were.[12]

The history of the past two decades has not been kind to doctrinaire economists, whether monetarist or Keynesian.

The Recent Reliance on Monetary Policy

Changes in velocity have weakened the case for monetarism in the past decade. Nevertheless, the emphasis on monetary policy has been substantially greater in the past decade than in previous years.

Particularly notable was the policy announcement of the Federal Reserve in October 1979, which took a significant step toward the monetarist policy position. In the future, said the Federal Reserve, it would place greater emphasis on bank reserves and on the money stock, and less on interest rates. But if stable money growth is to be counted on to stabilize aggregate demand, velocity will have to be stable. Why did the Fed take this step when velocity seemed to be getting less stable?

The answer lies primarily in the policy problem facing the Fed. Inflation had been accelerating rapidly, from about 5% in 1976 to 9% in 1978 and more than 13% in 1979. People were wondering how far the inflationary spiral would go. Fears of even higher inflation in the future were themselves contributing to inflation. For example, unions were demanding higher wages in the expectation that prices would continue to rise. In turn, businesses were raising prices further in order to cover their higher wage costs. The Fed believed that the cooling of inflation, and the breaking of inflationary expecta-

[10]Alan Blinder and Robert Solow, "Analytical Foundations of Fiscal Policy," in Blinder, Solow, and others, *The Economics of Public Finance* (Washington, D.C.: The Brookings Institution, 1974), p. 10.

[11]Stephen Goldfeld, "The Case of the Missing Money," *Brookings Papers on Economic Activity* 3:1976, pp. 683–730.

[12]McKinnon, *An International Standard for Monetary Stabilization* (Washington: Institute for International Economics, 1984), p. 37.

tions, constituted the most important goal of macroeconomic policy.

Monetarism, with its focus on price stability as a policy goal, provided an appropriate framework for a campaign against inflation. By declaring its intention to lower the rate of growth of the money stock, the Fed hoped to convince the public that it meant business in its fight against inflation. Furthermore, emphasis on the supply of money could reduce the Fed's political problem. An anti-inflationary tight monetary policy would lead to an increase in interest rates, at least in the short run. This would cause attacks on the Fed. By emphasizing its responsibility for controlling the money supply, the Fed hoped to reduce the political pressures on it to buy bonds in order to keep interest rates down. (If it caved in to such pressures and bought bonds, it would increase bank reserves and the money stock, and perpetuate the inflationary spiral.) With regard to inflation, the Fed's policies were a success. By 1982, the rate of inflation had been reduced below 4%—although the econ-

FIGURE 14-10
The income velocity of money
The income velocity of money is the ratio of national product to the quantity of money. If M1 (currency plus checking deposits) is taken as the definition of money, there has been an upward trend in velocity (V1) since the late 1940s. If M2 is taken as the definition of money, velocity (V2) has been quite stable for the past three decades, although it fluctuated considerably between 1910 and 1950.

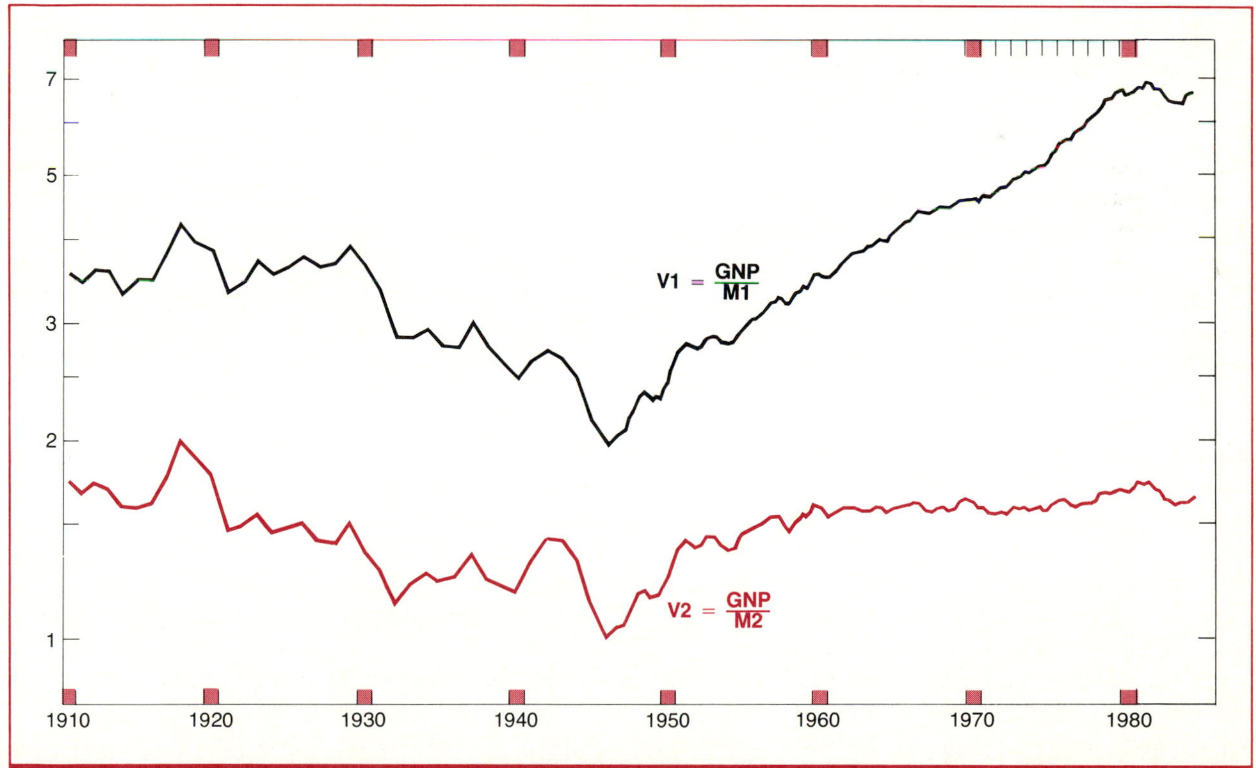

omy had been put through a severe recession in the process.

Since 1981, there has been another reason for the emphasis on money and monetary policy. The tax cuts and increases in military spending, which provided the cornerstone of President Reagan's economic policy, resulted in very large deficits in the federal budget. Although many political leaders believed that it was important to reduce deficits, there was little agreement on how to do so. Each spending program had its supporters, and tax increases were unpalatable. Fiscal policy was caught in a political gridlock: Conflicting pressures made it very difficult to cut spending or raise taxes substantially. Because it was so difficult to make major adjustments in fiscal policy, monetary policies seemed to be the only macroeconomic "game in town." Monetary policy was left at the center of the stage by default.

THE CASE FOR USING MONETARY AND FISCAL POLICIES TOGETHER

This concentration on monetary policy has not, however, been a desirable outcome. A substantial case can be made that the best macroeconomic policy includes both fiscal and monetary policies, used cooperatively.

The controversy covered in this chapter provides the first reason. Although the profession has moved away from the extremes and toward the center, there is still a difference of opinion over the relative strengths of monetary and fiscal policies. Statistical evidence does not provide a sharp, clean resolution to this dispute. Continuing uncertainties over the effectiveness of monetary and fiscal policies provide a case for using both. It's unwise to put all our eggs in one basket, especially when we're not sure which basket it should be.

Furthermore, there are other reasons for favoring a combined monetary-fiscal strategy. During a boom in aggregate demand, restrictive steps are desirable. Such steps are painful. Cuts in government spending hurt various groups in the economy. Nobody wants an increase in their taxes. A tighter monetary policy and higher interest rates can put a squeeze on housing construction and other types of investment. By using a combination of policies, the effects of each may be kept moderate and the adverse impacts diffused. Thus, we may avoid placing a very heavy burden on any single segment of the economy.

KEY POINTS

1. Most present-day economists take a central position, believing that both fiscal and monetary policies have substantial effects on aggregate demand. However, some economists have taken polar positions. Early Keynesians not only focused on fiscal policy; some also believed that monetary policy might have little effect on aggregate demand. On the other side is the monetarist view that money is the predominant force determining aggregate demand, and that fiscal policy has little effect.
2. Keynes proposed that the effects of monetary policy be analyzed by looking at three steps: (*a*) the effect of monetary policy on the rate of interest, (*b*) the effect of the interest rate on investment, and (*c*) the effect of a change in investment on aggregate demand (the multiplier).
3. Keynes himself believed that expansive monetary policies could not be counted on to get the economy out of the Depression of the 1930s because of a problem at the very first step. Interest rates were already very low and could not be pushed down much further by an expansive monetary policy.
4. Some early followers of Keynes had more general doubts about the effectiveness of monetary policies—not just in a depression but also in more normal times. Specifically, they argued that a problem would arise at step 2 because investment is not very responsive to changes in the rate of interest. That is, the MEI schedule is steep, as illustrated in Figure 14-5.
5. However, even if the MEI schedule is steep, restrictive monetary policies may reduce investment and aggregate demand by forcing banks to ration their loans.
6. Monetary policy may be more effective in restraining aggregate demand than in raising it. Monetary policy has been compared to controlling aggregate demand with a string.
7. Classical macroeconomics is based on the equation of exchange ($MV = PQ$) and on the proposition that velocity V is stable (the quantity theory). If velocity is

stable, a change in money M will cause current-dollar national product (PQ) to change by approximately the same percentage.

8. Classical economists believe that, in the long run, the principal effect of a change in the rate of growth of M will be a change in the price level P. In the short run, however, changes in the growth of M can also affect real national product Q.

9. Indeed, those in the classical tradition believe that monetary disturbances are one of the principal causes of fluctuations in real output.

10. The view that velocity is stable is based on the belief that there is a stable demand for money. If, after a period of equilibrium, people get more money, their holdings of money will exceed their demand for it (Figure 14-7). They will use the surplus to buy goods and services, thus increasing current-dollar national product (PQ).

11. Some of those in the classical tradition doubt that fiscal policy will have a substantial effect on aggregate demand, unless the fiscal policy is accompanied by changes in M. That is, they have doubts about the effectiveness of *pure* fiscal policy. These doubts are based on the belief that an increase in deficit spending will push up interest rates and therefore crowd out private investment.

12. There is also a second way in which the expansive effects of an increase in deficit spending may be partially offset. Higher interest rates may encourage foreigners to buy U.S. bonds, raising the price of the U.S. dollar in terms of foreign currencies and consequently depressing net exports. This complication was important during the expansion of 1983–1984.

13. Statistical evidence does not give a clear, unambiguous confirmation of either the strong Keynesian or the strong classical view. At times—1968, for example—the evidence supports the quantity theory, and at other times—such as 1975 and 1982—the evidence tends to contradict it.

14. Because of this—and for other reasons, too—it is undesirable to place exclusive reliance on either monetary or fiscal policy. Instead, it is wiser to use a combined monetary-fiscal strategy.

15. Nevertheless, there has been a very heavy reliance on monetary policy since 1979. One reason has been the desire of the Fed to control the rapidly accelerating inflation of the late 1970s. Another has been the great difficulty in changing fiscal policy during the 1980s.

KEY CONCEPTS

demand for money
marginal efficiency of investment (MEI)
rate of return
investment unresponsive to a change in the interest rate
credit rationing
credit crunch
availability of loanable funds
pushing on a string
equation of exchange
income velocity of money (V)
quantity theory of money
monetary rule
crowding out
investment responsive to a change in the interest rate
pure fiscal policy
cause-effect relationship

PROBLEMS

14-1. (*a*) In the Keynesian framework, there are three separate steps in the process by which monetary policy affects aggregate demand. What are these three steps?

(*b*) Keynes argued that expansive monetary policy would be ineffective in getting the economy out of the Depression of the 1930s because of a problem at one of these three steps. Which step? What was the nature of the problem?

(*c*) Some of the followers of Keynes argued that monetary policy is generally a weak and ineffective tool for controlling aggregate demand. They foresaw a problem at another one of the steps. Which step? What was the nature of the problem?

14-2. The Keynesian theory of the demand for money

(shown in Figure 14-2) was developed at a time when no interest was paid on checking deposits. There was an obvious cost in holding money: namely, the interest which could otherwise have been earned by buying a security.

Now banks and other institutions are permitted to pay interest on checking deposits, as we saw in Chapter 12. When banks pay interest on such deposits, how would you expect the demand for money to be affected as a result?

14-3. Suppose that a machine that will last forever costs $100,000 and yields a return of 10%. Now suppose that the price of the machine doubles to $200,000, while the amount that such a machine will produce remains the same and the prices of outputs and inputs also remain unchanged. What happens to the yield on the machine?

14-4. The marginal efficiency of investment shows the expected rates of return of possible investment projects. For what reasons might expected rates of return on investment projects change through time? How would each of these reasons affect the MEI curve?

14-5. How do strong Keynesians and strong monetarists disagree on the way in which the MEI curve should be drawn? How does the way a strong Keynesian draws the MEI curve cast doubt on the effectiveness of monetary policy? How does the way a strong monetarist draws the MEI curve cast doubt on the effectiveness of fiscal policy in controlling aggregate demand?

14-6. Why might a restrictive monetary policy have more effect on aggregate demand than an expansive monetary policy?

14-7. "I accept the equation of exchange as valid. But I do not accept the quantity theory of money." Is it consistent for an economist to hold such a position? Why or why not?

14-8. Explain how a budget deficit might cause a trade deficit. (A trade deficit is an excess of imports over exports.)

CHAPTER 15

FINE TUNING OR STABLE POLICY SETTINGS?

If something works, don't fix it.

AMERICAN PROVERB

In the study of macroeconomics, better policies are the ultimate goal. No matter how elaborate our theories, and no matter how much progress we make in understanding detailed macroeconomic relationships, our work has not succeeded if it cannot be translated into better policies. The ultimate test of macroeconomic policies is the degree to which they help in the achievement of high employment and stable prices.

It is not clear whether we should judge the policies of the past 25 years as a success or a failure. In part, the answer depends on the question: Successful compared to what? Certainly, compared to the depressed decade of the 1930s, the economy has performed very well during the past quarter century. The unemployment rate has never gotten anywhere near the 24.9% of 1933. However, we have not been doing better and better as time passes. The recessions of 1974 and 1982 were much more severe than any during the 1940s, 1950s, or 1960s. During the recession of 1982, the unemployment rate rose to 10.6%, the highest rate since the Great Depression. With respect to inflation, the U.S. experience of the past two decades has also been worse than that of the preceding period. Bursts of inflation occurred during the late 1960s and the 1970s, with inflation hitting a peak of 13.3% by 1979. Although inflation was brought under much better control in the early 1980s, it still remained about 4% per year in 1982, 1983, and 1984, substantially above the average annual rate of 1.6% between 1955 and 1965.

The mediocre performance of the economy in the past two decades has revitalized an old debate which goes back to the early days of the Keynesian-classical controversy in the 1930s. On the one side are those in the Keynesian tradition, who argue that aggregate demand policies should be *actively managed* in pursuit of the goals of high employment and stable prices. As the economy heads toward recession, expansive policies should be adopted. As the economy heads toward an inflationary boom, restraint should be exercised. On the other side are the monetarists, who argue that activist, discretionary policies are more likely to do harm than good, no matter how well-intentioned policymakers might be. Consequently, they argue that ***discretionary*** policies should be avoided. Instead, permanent policy settings should be chosen and maintained regardless of the short-term fluctuations in economic activity; that is, a ***policy rule*** should be followed. It is of course important that the rule be chosen carefully and, in particular, that it be consistent with economic stability. For example, it would be a mistake to adhere to the rules of the old gold standard. Because banks under that system kept fractional reserves in the form of gold, a large superstructure of money could be built on a relatively small base of gold reserves. This made the banking system vulnerable to runs.

However, monetarists suggest that there is a policy rule which *is* consistent with a high degree of economic stability. Specifically, they suggest that the Federal Reserve should aim at a slow, steady increase in the money supply, at something like 3% or 4% per year. This increase would provide the money needed to purchase the expanding national output at stable prices.[1]

[1]The appropriate percentage would depend on the definition of money. If M1 is chosen, the increase should be kept low, at about 2% per year. The reason is that aggregate demand has risen more rapidly than M1; there has been an upward trend in V1 (illustrated back in Figure 14-10). If past trends in V1 continue, aggregate demand would hit its target growth of 3% to 4% with a increase of only 2% in M1. Because of the lack of trend in the velocity of M2, an appropriate growth rate for M2 would be in the 3% to 4% range.

Discretionary **fiscal and monetary policies are policies that the government and the central bank adjust periodically in order to deal with changing conditions in the economy.**

As in Chapter 14, the sharp contrast between Keynesians and monetarists may be illustrated by comparing the statements of Keynesian Warren Smith and monetarist Milton Friedman. The flavor of the activist, hands-on-the-helm Keynesian view was given by Smith:[2]

> The only good rule is that the budget should never be balanced—except for an instant when a surplus to curb inflation is being altered to a deficit to fight deflation.

Friedman explicitly criticized the activist policy of attempting to "fine-tune" the economy:[3]

> Is fiscal policy being oversold? Is monetary policy being oversold? . . . My answer is yes to both of those questions. . . . Monetary policy is being oversold. . . . Fiscal policy is being oversold. . . . Fine tuning has been oversold.

We introduce this debate over the active management of demand by looking more closely at the Keynesian approach, in which aggregate demand policies are adjusted in pursuit of the goals of full employment and stable prices. In later sections of this chapter, we will explain criticisms of that policy and problems with the alternative of following a monetary rule.

AIMING FOR A STABLE HIGH-EMPLOYMENT ECONOMY: THE ACTIVE KEYNESIAN APPROACH

As we have seen—especially in Chapter 10—Keynes believed that a market economy would suffer from two major diseases. The economy would move toward an equilibrium where there would probably be inadequate aggregate demand and high unemployment. And, even if the economy did get to a position of full employment, it would be unlikely to stay there, primarily because of the instability of investment demand. In short, demand would tend to be both *inadequate* and *unstable*.

In the early days of the Keynesian revolution, inadequate aggregate demand was considered a more important problem than instability. This was scarcely surprising, because of the depth and persistence of the Great Depression. However, since the late 1940s, the emphasis of Keynesian thinking has shifted away from the problem of stagnation and toward the problem of instability. The economy did not lapse back into depression in the period after World War II, as many economists feared it would. In the past four decades, it has gone through bouts of inflation as well as periodic recessions. There has been no long-run lack of aggregate demand, although demand has been unstable.

Nevertheless, concern continued over both the adequacy and the stability of aggregate demand. Therefore the policy problem, as seen by Keynesian economists, was (1) to stimulate aggregate demand to the full-employment level and then (2) to adjust or *fine-tune* it whenever needed to combat business fluctuations.

This Keynesian strategy is illustrated in Figure 15-1. Suppose that the economy in year 1 begins at a position of high unemployment. The actual production of the economy, at *A*, is well below the potential at full employment (*B*). Of course, the potential output of the economy does not remain constant. As time passes, the labor force grows, the capital stock increases, and technology improves. Thus, the path of full-employment or potential GNP trends upward. The objective of policy in

[2]Warren Smith, statement to a meeting of Treasury consultants, as quoted by Paul A. Samuelson, *Economics,* 11th ed. (New York: McGraw-Hill, 1976), p. 222.

[3]Milton Friedman and Walter Heller, *Monetary vs. Fiscal Policy* (New York: W. W. Norton, 1969), p. 47. Many other passages might be cited to illustrate the disagreement, whether economic performance can be improved with active demand management policies. For example, shortly after leaving his position as chairman of the Council of Economic Advisers under President Kennedy, Walter W. Heller proclaimed that "The significance of the great expansion in the '60s lies not only in its striking statistics of employment, income, and growth but in its glowing promise of things to come." (*New Dimensions of Political Economy,* New York: W. W. Norton, 1967), p. 58. In contrast, in his paper entitled "Have Fiscal-Monetary Policies Failed?" (*American Economic Review,* May 1972, p. 17), Friedman wrote: "I believe that we economists in recent years have done vast harm—to society at large and to our profession in particular—by claiming more than we can deliver." His skeptical view is also made clear by the title of his recent book, *Bright Promises, Dismal Performance* (New York: Harcourt, Brace, Jovanovich, 1983).

year 1 should be to aim the economy toward the full-employment path. However, full employment cannot be achieved immediately; there are lags in the implementation and effect of policy. Thus, policy in year 1 should be aimed at stimulating the economy so that it approaches full employment at some time in the reasonably near future, as shown by the arrows in Figure 15-1.

An Example

By going back to the early 1960s, we can find a very clear and explicit illustration of this Keynesian strategy. The black parts of Figure 15-2 were presented by the Council of Economic Advisers (CEA) in its *Annual Report* in early 1962. The thin dashed lines show three possible outcomes. *A*, the most favorable, would eliminate the GNP gap within 2 years. On the other hand, a growth path toward *C* would not represent any improvement; the GNP gap would remain just as wide in 1963 as it was in 1961. The policy problem was to try to make the economy follow path *A*, or close to it.

The outcome in the following years is shown in the red parts of Figure 15-2, which are taken from a diagram in a later CEA report.[4] The red curve showing actual GNP traces out a very impressive performance. Although the GNP gap was not eliminated within 2 years, it was eliminated within 4. By the end of 1965, the economy was right on target. What remained now was to fine-tune the economy, keeping it as close as possible to the potential growth path.

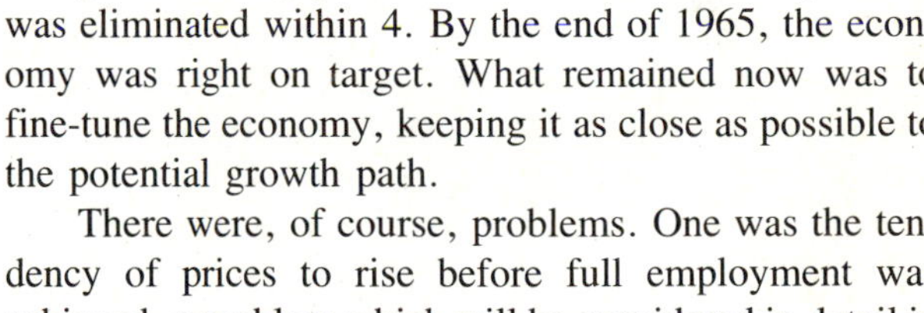

There were, of course, problems. One was the tendency of prices to rise before full employment was achieved, a problem which will be considered in detail in the next chapter. The second was the well-recognized problem of lags: How do you adjust policies when the actions taken today do not affect the economy until some future time, when they may no longer be appropriate?

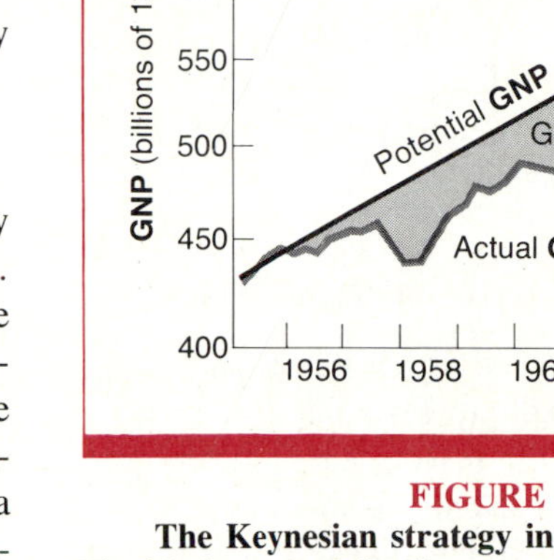

FIGURE 15-2

The Keynesian strategy in practice, 1962–1966

The black parts of the diagram are taken from the Council of Economic Advisers' *Annual Report, 1962,* p. 52. They show the gap between the actual and potential GNP, and illustrate how various future paths (*A, B,* and *C*) would affect the gap. The red parts of the diagram show the outcome; they are taken from the CEA report 5 years later. Although the economy had not moved quickly back to its potential path, the gap had been eliminated by late 1965.

FIGURE 15-1

The Keynesian strategy: An active policy

The activist Keynesian strategy is to move to the potential GNP path. Fiscal and monetary policies should then be fine-tuned to combat instability and keep the economy as close as possible to potential GNP.

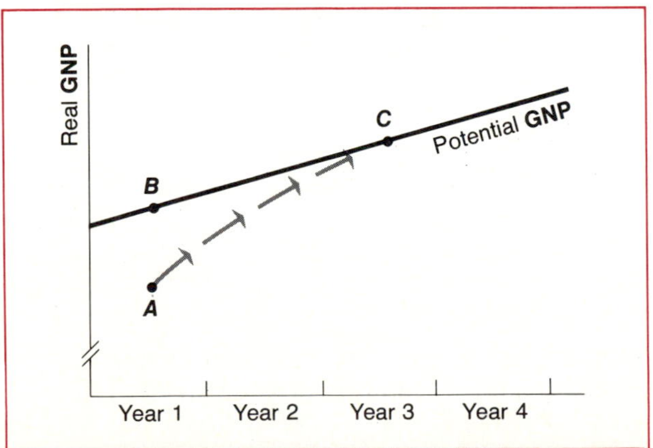

[4]CEA *Annual Report, 1967,* p. 43. Students are encouraged to look at the annual reports of the CEA, which provide some of the best discussions of economic issues. (One tip is necessary, however. It may be difficult to find these reports listed under the Council of Economic Advisers in a card catalogue. The reason is that they are printed in the same volume as the *Economic Report of the President* and may be listed under this title instead.)

Keynesians believed that they had an adequate—although far from perfect—answer. By forecasting, policymakers can get a fairly good idea of where the economy is headed. Thus, they should be able to "lead" their moving target.

Details of economic forecasting are deferred until a later section in this chapter. Here, we turn to the way in which lags are used as an argument against an active demand-management policy.

THE CASE AGAINST ACTIVISM: LAGS

The core of the case against activism is the argument that active policies are more likely to destabilize than to stabilize the economy. The first reason that monetary and fiscal policies may cause instability is that they may be badly timed. They may fight the battles of last year, and be inappropriate to deal with the problems of the present and, more important, those of the future.

There are *three lags* between the time that aggregate demand should be changed and the time when the change actually occurs. Suppose that the economy begins to slide down into a recession. This fact may not be recognized for some time. It takes time to gather statistics on what is happening. Initial signs of weakness may be dismissed as temporary disturbances; not every little jiggle in economic activity grows into a recession or boom. Thus, the first lag is the *recognition lag,* which occurs between the time the weakness in the economy begins and the time when it is recognized. Furthermore, even after the decline is recognized, policymakers take some time to act; this is the *action lag*. For example, congressional hearings must be held before taxes are cut. Spending programs must be designed before they can be implemented. Finally, after action is taken, there is some delay before the major *impact* on the economy is felt. For example, when government spending finally is increased, the various rounds of consumer spending in the multiplier process take time. For monetary policy, there is a lag between the open market purchase that pushes down interest rates and the actual investment that is stimulated as a consequence. These, then, are the lags which occur before aggregate demand actually changes: the ***recognition lag,*** the ***action lag,*** and the ***impact lag.***

Consider how these lags can lead to incorrect policies and add to the instability of the economy. Suppose, for example, that the ideal path of aggregate demand is shown by the solid line in Figure 15-3. But actual demand follows the dashed curve. Starting at point A, aggregate demand starts to slip below the desired level; the economy begins to move into a recession. However, this problem is not recognized for some time—not until point B. Even then, taxes are not cut immediately; action does not take place until point C. By this time, it may be too late. There is a further lag before the action affects demand (between points D and E), and by then the economy has already recovered. Fuel is added to the inflationary fire. Then, as the severity of inflation is recognized, policies are shifted in a restrictive direction. But once again there are lags; the policies can come too late, making the next recession worse. Rather than trying to adjust to changing conditions, it might be better to follow a stable set of policies. So argue those in the classical tradition.

The Helmsman's Dilemma

The slowness of the economy to respond and the momentum that can accumulate in the downswing or upswing mean that the problem of the policymaker can be compared with that of the helmsman of an ocean-going ship. The helmsman may turn the wheel, but a large ship does not respond immediately. Suppose a ship heads out of New York harbor with plans to go due south past the eastern tip of Cuba on the way to the Panama Canal. If the helmsman finds his course drifting to the east, he can correct it by turning the wheel to starboard.

The problem is, how much? If he turns the wheel just slightly, the ship will continue on its easterly course for some time; it does not respond quickly. In his anxiety, he may then turn the wheel more sharply. Clearly, the more sharply the wheel is turned, the more quickly the ship will return to its course of due south. But, if the wheel is swung hard to starboard, a new problem will arise. Once the ship points due south, it will be turning with considerable momentum; the ship will move in a westerly direction. In his panic, the helmsman may be tempted to swing the wheel back hard to port. We can imagine the voyage of the anxious mariner—zigzagging down the Caribbean.

Of course, ships do not zigzag all over the ocean.

With some practice, the helmsman learns not to lean too hard on the wheel. He learns to move the wheel back to the center *before* the ship gets back to its intended course; the ship's momentum will complete the turn. Policymakers face the same type of problem. They must try to switch toward restraint *before* an economic expansion turns into an inflationary boom. William McChesney Martin, who served as the chairman of the Federal Reserve for most of the 1950s and 1960s, sadly observed that the Fed has an unpopular task—to take away the punch bowl just when the party really gets going.

Not only do policymakers have the helmsman's problem; they also face a few more which provide extra excitement. One of the additional complications is that the helm and the rudder of the economic ship are connected by elastic bands and baling twine. Unlike the mechanism connecting the ship's wheel to the rudder, the mechanism connecting monetary and fiscal policies to aggregate demand does not work in a precise, highly predictable manner. Furthermore, the economic policymaker may have to chart a course across turbulent and stormy seas. Between 1965 and 1980, there were large shocks to the U.S. economy: first the war in Vietnam, then the oil embargo and the quadrupling of oil prices in 1973 and 1974, then the second big jump in oil prices in 1979–1980. If the ship is being guided across placid seas, the policymaker has the luxury of turning the wheel meekly and slowly so as not to overcorrect. But in stormy waters, this is not good enough. A meek application of policies will be overwhelmed by other forces. This, then, is the helmsman's dilemma: How hard should the wheel be swung, and how soon should it be moved back toward center?

THE CASE AGAINST ACTIVISM: THE OVERESTIMATION OF POTENTIAL

The danger of overreaction is increased by a fourth type of lag. The three lags in the previous section represented delays *before* aggregate demand changes. The fourth lag occurs *after* aggregate demand changes. It involves the differing speeds with which real GNP and prices respond to changes in demand. Specifically, when aggregate demand rises, the short-run effect on real output is generally powerful. Unless producers are already straining hard against their capacity limitations, they respond to an

FIGURE 15-3
Lags and economic instability
Because of the recognition, action, and impact lags, it is possible that policy changes will make things worse. Expansive steps aimed at fighting the recession at point *C* may add to a later inflationary boom at *E*. Similarly, policies aimed at restraining an inflationary boom may make the next recession worse.

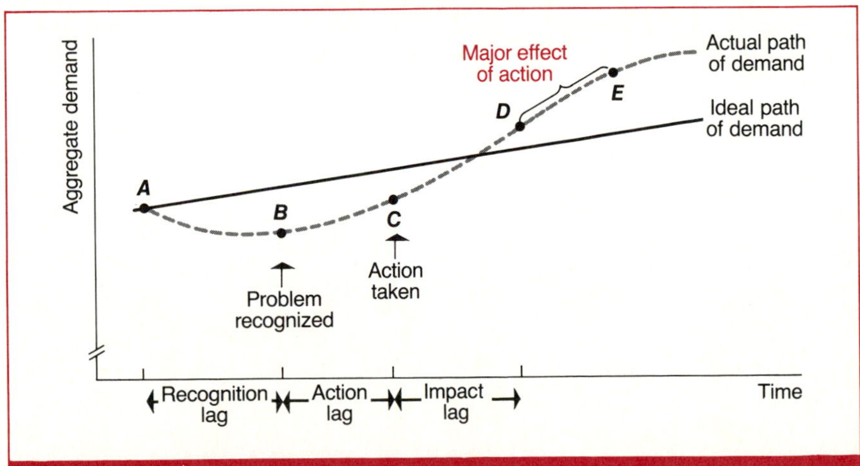

increase in demand by producing more. However, as time passes, the higher demand is reflected more and more in terms of higher prices and less and less in terms of real output. Thus, *when aggregate demand is stimulated, the favorable output effects come quickly; the unfavorable price effects are delayed*. This creates a temptation to stick with expansive fiscal and monetary policies too long in order to gain their short-term benefits in terms of higher output.

Figure 15-4 illustrates this lag. Note that the response of prices in the lower panel comes after the change in output shown in the top panel. Figure 15-4 also illustrates some of the criticisms directed at the activist Keynesian approach. The first step in the Keynesian approach is to estimate potential GNP. Policymakers tend to be optimistic, overestimating potential GNP and the amount by which unemployment can be reduced by expansive demand policies. Such an overly optimistic estimate is shown by the black potential GNP line in Figure 15-4. The red line shows the true potential path

FIGURE 15-4

Policy activism: The case against

Because of delayed response of prices and overly ambitious goals, aggregate demand will be overstimulated, say the critics of active demand management. When inflation finally does become an obvious problem, then policymakers will overreact.

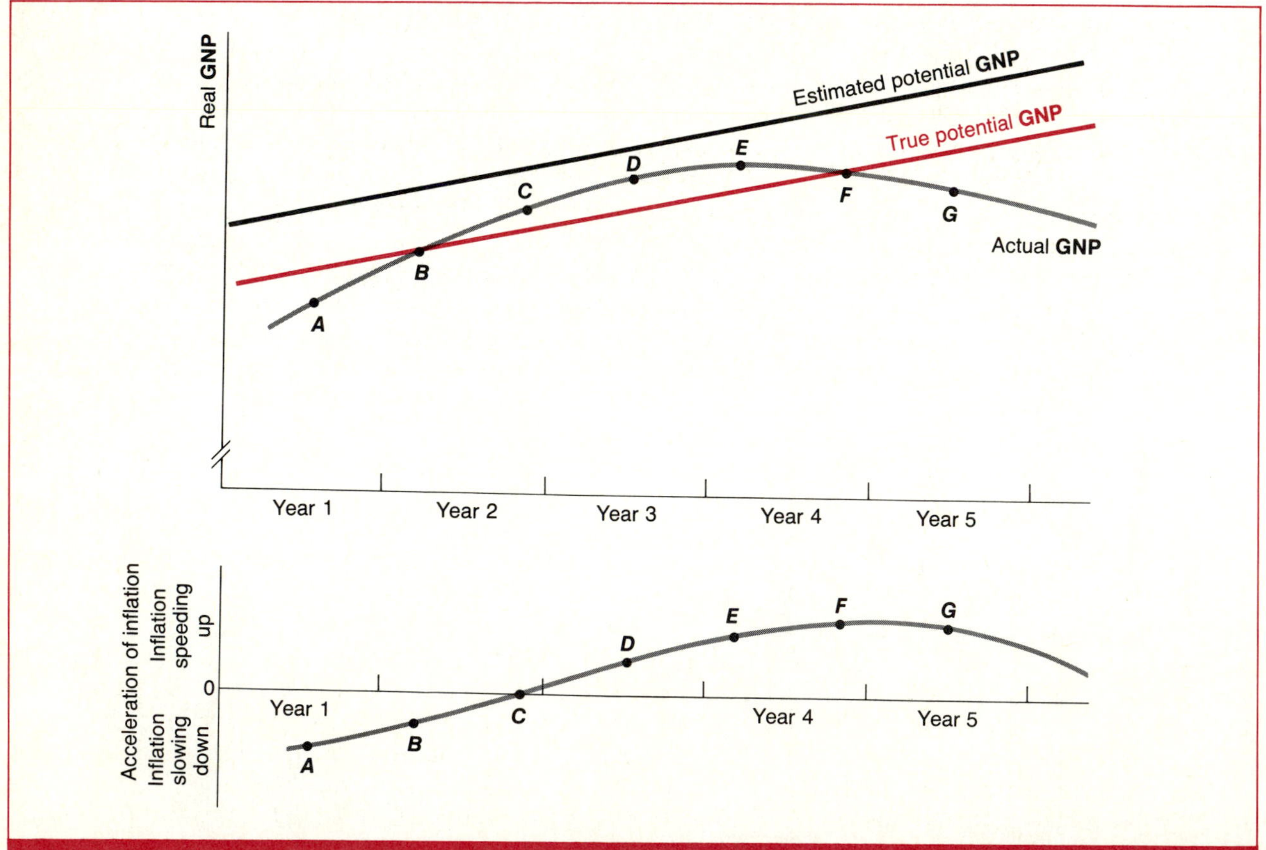

which can be followed without causing an overheating of the economy and an acceleration of inflation.

Now let us see what the critics fear if activists are in charge. Beginning at *A*, the economy is recovering from a recession. Monetary and fiscal policies are set for the expansion of aggregate demand. Real output is rising briskly, the unemployment rate is falling, and inflation—with its delayed response—is still slowing down because of the previous period of slack. Everything seems to be going well. The expansive policy settings are retained. But, without anyone noticing, the economy moves past *B*, crossing the true potential path. The error in estimating the potential path means that policymakers incorrectly believe that aggregate demand is still too low. (GNP is still below the optimistic black estimate of potential.) As a result, expansive policies are continued. In reality, however, aggregate demand is too high, since the economy is above the true potential path shown in red. Therefore, a less expansive policy is appropriate.

As the economy crosses the true potential path, the seeds of a more rapid inflation are being sown, although the inflationary result does not appear for some time. As the curve in the lower diagram illustrates, inflation does not begin to accelerate until time *C*.

If the error in estimating the black potential GNP path has been large, the economy may never actually reach it. The expanding demand shows up increasingly in terms of inflation, and less and less in terms of real output. The expansive fiscal and monetary policies cause an increase in aggregate demand, but they do not control the extent to which the higher demand will cause higher output and the extent to which it will show up in the form of higher prices.

Between *C* and *D*, a sharp policy debate is likely. Those focusing on the optimistic black path argue that to reach it, aggregate demand should be increased even more. But, as inflation is by now accelerating (to the right of point *C* in the lower part of the diagram), others urge caution. As time passes and inflation gets worse and worse, those urging restraint eventually win the debate. With inflation by now rising rapidly, the policy adjustment may be abrupt.

As a result, the economy may fall into a sharp recession. But, as always, inflation responds with a lag. *It remains serious even though tight policies have been introduced. As a consequence, everything seems to be going wrong during the period between E and G*—just as everything went right during the expansion between *A* and *B*. The economy is headed into a recession and unemployment is rising, yet inflation is still getting worse. As the unemployment rate rises higher and higher while inflation continues stubbornly, more and more people argue that demand restraint simply won't stop inflation. Inflation has become "built in," and skeptics charge that nothing much can be done about it with monetary and fiscal policies. Aggregate demand policies are therefore turned in an expansive direction quite quickly, in order to increase output and reduce unemployment. A new upswing begins. But inflation has accelerated more as a result of the extended period of excess demand than it has fallen as a result of the shorter period of slack. Thus, each upswing begins with a higher rate of inflation than the previous one. This, then, is the case against activism.

Just as the case in favor of activism can be supported with real-world evidence (most notably from the early 1960s, as shown in Figure 15-2), so the critics can point to evidence of failures of discretionary policies. First, they note that most recent recoveries have in fact begun with higher and higher rates of inflation. The inflation rate was less than 1% in the early recovery year of 1961; between 3% and 4% in the early recovery of 1971 and 1972; about 7% in the early recovery of 1975; and over 10% as the economy started coming out of recession in late 1980. (A notable exception was the recovery starting at the end of 1982, when the inflation rate was about 4%. The previous expansion of 1980–1981 had been unusually short, and the recession of 1981–1982 severe.)

Second, the 1970s and early 1980s provide a real-world illustration of the principal point of Figure 15-4; that is, how an overestimation of potential GNP can lead to policy problems. Specifically, consider Figure 15-5, which includes estimates of potential GNP by the CEA and the Congressional Budget Office (CBO). The original estimate of the potential GNP path—made in the late 1960s and shown in black—indicated that actual GNP in 1972 was still well below potential. Accordingly, expansive monetary and fiscal policy settings were maintained through 1972 to stimulate the economy. Even at the peak of the expansion in 1973, GNP was still below the current estimate of potential shown in black.

But in fact GNP was not still below its potential. Later, more realistic estimates of potential GNP presented by the CEA in 1977—shown as the solid red path in Figure 15-5—indicate that actual GNP had reached the potential path by the end of 1972. If the authorities had known this at the time, less expansive policies would presumably have been followed in 1972–1973. Instead, they acted on the mistaken belief that there was still slack in the economy, and continued to increase aggregate demand. This caused an inflationary burst in 1973–1974, which resulted in a sharp shift toward a tighter monetary policy in early 1974. In turn, the tighter policy contributed to the depth of the 1974 recession.

Potential GNP was again overestimated in 1977–1978. Although the estimates of potential had already been revised downward in early 1977 (from the original black estimates to the solid red path in Figure 15-5), even this revised series was too high. In 1979 and 1982, the potential was again adjusted downward, as shown by the dashed red paths in Figure 15-5.

FIGURE 15-5
Actual and potential GNP, 1968–1984
According to estimates of potential GNP available at the time, shown in black, actual GNP still fell short of potential in 1973, suggesting that aggregate demand was still too low. Later (1977) revisions of potential GNP, shown in solid red, indicate that the economy had reached potential by the end of 1972, and that aggregate demand was too high by early 1973. In 1977–1979, available estimates of potential (solid red) indicated that actual GNP was far below the potential, suggesting that strongly expansive aggregate demand policies were in order. Later revisions of potential, shown in the dashed red, indicate that the GNP gap was much less than originally believed, and that the appropriate policy was for a less rapid expansion of aggregate demand.
Source: Except for lowest dashed curve, estimates for potential are taken from Council of Economic Advisers, *Annual Report,* 1979, p. 75. The 1982 estimate of potential is based on the curve in Congressional Budget Office, *The Outlook for Economic Recovery,* February 1983, p. 56.

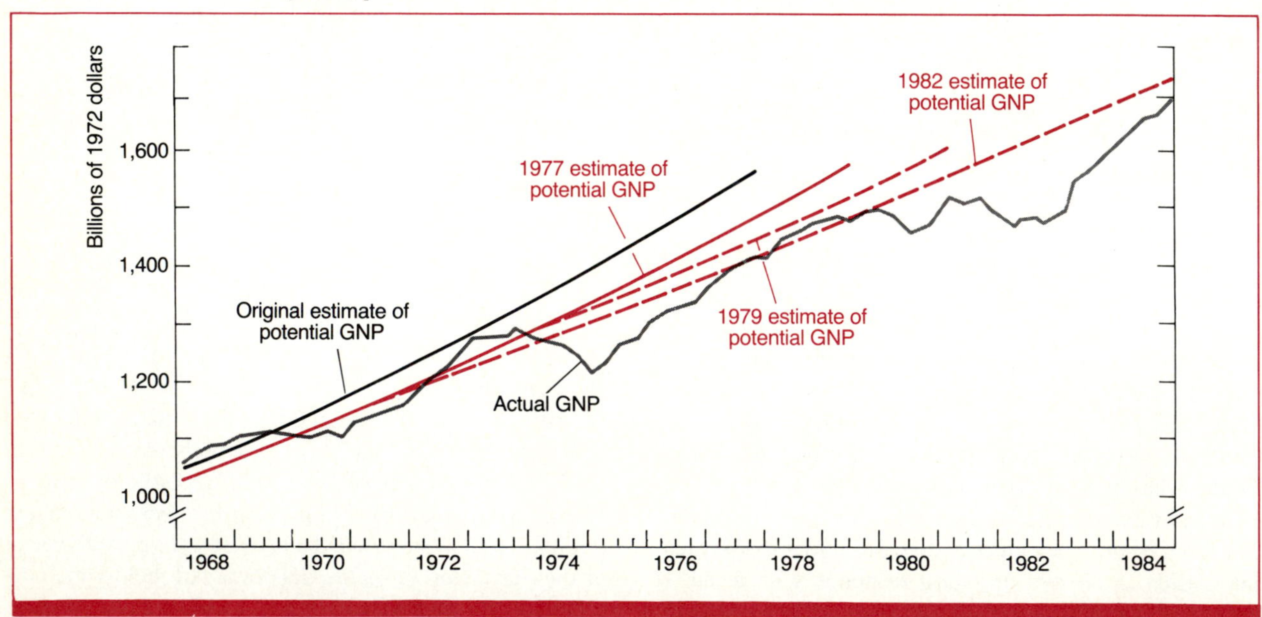

Again, these overestimates resulted in policy errors. Because the authorities thought that potential GNP was the solid red line rather than the lowest dashed path, they once more overestimated the slack in the economy. They therefore followed an overly expansive aggregate demand policy in 1977–1978. They compounded the problem by maintaining the policy too long, until inflation was accelerating strongly. Then tighter aggregate demand policies were instituted. But these tighter policies did not come until 1979, when the economy was on the threshold of recession. In short, the overestimation of potential GNP again contributed to a set of policies which made economic instability worse.

The question arises as to how the potential GNP could have been overestimated so much. Some monetarists argue that Keynesians generally overestimate both potential GNP and their ability to stimulate high levels of production and employment without causing inflation. But surely there is more to it than this broad generalization. After all, there was no similar overestimate of potential GNP in the 1960s. In the 1970s, fundamental changes were occurring in the economy which misled the CEA.

In simplified terms, here's how the CEA estimated potential GNP. It took as a starting point a recent period when there was a low rate of unemployment and a high rate of utilization of plant and equipment. This gave an initial point on the path of potential GNP. Then the growth in the productive capacity of the economy was estimated. This depends on (1) the expected increase in the quantity of labor available and (2) the expected increase in ***labor productivity***—that is, the increase in output per labor hour. The greater the productivity increase, the more rapid will be the rate of growth of potential GNP. During the 1970s, it turned out that the actual rate of increase in productivity declined sharply. However, before the fact, the CEA expected past rates of productivity growth to continue, and consequently it overestimated the rate of growth of potential GNP. (The poor productivity performance in the 1970s will be studied in Chapter 18.)

The CEA summarized its experience in its *Annual Report, 1980* (p. 76): "Projecting potential GNP growth into the future is subject to large errors." But this conclusion throws into question the whole strategy of active aggregate demand management, which is based on the assumption that potential GNP can be accurately forecasted and taken *as a target* at which aggregate demand policy should be aimed. (For other problems with policy targets, see Box 15-1.)

THE CASE FOR A MONETARY RULE

There are many doubts about how well discretionary demand-management policies have worked. However, discretionary policies cannot be considered in a vacuum. We should also look at the alternative suggested by monetarists, that the quantity of money be increased at a steady, moderate rate. There are several elements in this monetarist case:

1. The desirable path of aggregate demand is one of steady, moderate growth, which will make possible the purchase of the growing output of the economy at approximately stable prices.

2. The best way to ensure a steady, moderate increase in aggregate demand is with a steady, moderate increase in the money stock. Velocity is, of course, not perfectly constant, and therefore even a perfectly stable growth of money would not lead to a perfectly stable growth in demand. But, say the advocates of a monetary rule, the amount of instability would be less than the instability caused by discretionary policies. Furthermore, a rule involving a slow growth of the money stock would avoid the strong inflationary tendencies which have resulted from discretionary policies during the past two decades. That is, monetarists have two objectives: to reduce the *instability* of aggregate demand, and to avoid an inflationary *trend* in demand.

3. Some of the proponents of a policy rule base their case on political as well as economic considerations. They believe that a policy rule will result in less interference by government officials in the free-enterprise system. Several decades ago, Henry C. Simons of the University of Chicago made rules a cornerstone of his *Economic Policy for a Free Society*:[5]

In a free enterprise system we obviously need highly

[5]Henry C. Simons, *Economic Policy for a Free Society* (Chicago: University of Chicago Press, 1948), p. 169.

definite and stable rules of the game, especially as to money. The monetary rules must be compatible with the reasonably smooth working of the system. Once established, however, they should work mechanically, with the chips falling where they may. To put our present problem as a paradox—we need to design and establish with the greatest intelligence a monetary system good enough so that, hereafter, we may hold to it unrationally—on faith—as a religion, if you please.

THE CASE AGAINST A MONETARY RULE

On behalf of discretionary policy-making, we will examine four major criticisms of a fixed monetary rule: (1) In practice, there cannot be a rigid rule that is followed regardless of the consequences. (2) The proponents of a monetary rule generally aim for a slow rate of increase in aggregate demand, in order to ensure price stability. The critics argue that, in practice, the result may be an unnecessarily high rate of unemployment. That is, the *trend* of demand may be too low if the monetarist proposal is followed. (3) Paradoxically, efforts to follow stable policy settings can, in practice, lead to abrupt changes in policies. (4) Even though there is much to be said for a stable rate of growth of aggregate demand, a monetary policy rule will not provide it. Velocity is not stable. In other words, there are substantial nonmonetary sources of disturbance in the economy. Policies should be

BOX 15-1

THE PROBLEM OF GOALS: IS THERE A POLITICAL BUSINESS CYCLE?

In the past several chapters, we have seen how the economy can be destabilized when policymakers pursue what seem to be plausible goals. To sum up thus far:

1. Chapter 11 explained how policymakers can fall into a trap and destabilize the economy if they attempt to balance the budget every year.
2. Chapter 13 explained how policymakers can similarly fall into a trap if they attempt to stabilize interest rates.
3. This chapter has explained the problems which arise if policymakers aim at an unattainable estimate of potential GNP.

However, these are not the only cases in which the pursuit of certain goals can lead to economic instability. Most notably, government expenditures during wartime are generally so high that they cause rapid inflation. But inflation in such circumstances does not necessarily mean that the government is making a mistake. The inflation of the 1940s was not too high a price to pay for the defeat of Hitler.

A "Political" Business Cycle?

Another objective of policymakers—namely, the desire to get reelected—may also contribute to economic instability. Officeholders want the voters in a mellow mood when they enter the polling booths; the economy is an important determinant of voting behavior. Unemployment was a major factor in Herbert Hoover's defeat, and inflation in Jimmy Carter's. Moreover, the evidence suggests that the recent *trend* of the economy is more important than its *position*. Consider, for example, Roosevelt's landslide victory in 1936. The economy was still in miserable shape, with the unemployment rate averaging 16.9%. Nevertheless, unemployment was down from the 24.9% of 1933. Things were improving; Roosevelt had given the public hope.

This suggests that, if a president wants to maximize the chances of reelection, a rather cynical strategy can help. The political game is not simply to create sustained prosperity. Even though times will be good, they will not be noticeably improving, and there is a danger that extended prosperity will eventually push the rate of inflation upward. In its crudest form, the game is to have an election during the *early* recovery, when everything will be going well. The unemployment rate will be falling, while the inflation rate may still be coming down as a result of the earlier period of slack demand. But, of course, an early recovery requires a preceding recession. Thus, in the words of Yale's Raymond Fair, a vote-maximizing strategy "requires that the economy be first brought into a recession. From the recession trough, the policy is then to stimulate the economy strongly until election day."[†]

The evidence is inconclusive as to whether such a strategy is actually followed. Sometimes the economy is in an early recovery during an election year; sometimes it is not. Three historical cases are particularly interesting.

The first was the four-year term of President Nixon, from 1969 to 1972. In the first year of his administration, monetary policy was adjusted in a restrictive direction, while fiscal restraint continued. As a result, a recession began late in 1969, with recovery starting about a year later. In 1971–1972, policies were expansive. By the election year, the recovering was proceeding nicely. There were widespread rumors that the White House was pressuring the Fed to keep monetary conditions easy. However, even though the events fit the vote-maximizing strategy, we cannot be sure that policies were in fact motivated by a desire to maximize votes. There were other plausible explanations. As we have seen earlier in this chapter, GNP was still substantially below existing estimates of potential in 1971–1972. It is possible that this, and not the desire to maximize votes, was the reason for the expansive policies of those years.

The second case was the presidency of Jimmy Carter, from 1977 to 1980. Early in his administration, stimulative steps were taken. Then, as the expansion increasingly put upward pressures on prices, policy was moved in a restrictive direction in 1979, leading to a recession in the election year 1980. Thus, presidents do not always follow the vote-maximizing strategy; indeed, policy was directly the opposite between 1977 and 1980. Of course, Carter's experience—as the first elected president since Hoover to be defeated in a bid for reelection—is unlikely to be ignored by other presidents. It may be taken as a lesson in what not to do, and it may therefore increase the chances of a political business cycle in the future.

Finally, events in the Reagan administration were consistent with a political business cycle. There was an early recession in 1981–1982, followed by a strong expansion in the 2 years preceding the 1984 election. But, as we read the evidence, the recession was not the result of a vote-maximizing strategy. It seems to have come as a genuine surprise to the President.

To the question of whether a political business cycle exists, the most we can say is, "perhaps."

[†]Raymond Fair, "Growth Rates Predict November Winners," *The New York Times,* January 25, 1976. See also L. Laney and Thomas Willett, "Presidential Politics, Budget Deficits, and Monetary Policy in the United States, 1960-76," *Public Choice,* 1, 1983.

changed from time to time to combat these disturbances and smooth out aggregate demand. (Nonmonetary sources of instability are studied in the appendix.)

We now consider each of these four points in detail.

1. Can There Be a Rigid Rule?

Monetarists argue for a policy rule that should be followed regardless of current conditions. In Simons' view, it should be followed regardless of how the chips fall. However, this rigid position can scarcely be taken literally. After all, evidence regarding economic institutions and economic behavior should be taken into account in establishing any rule; not to do so would be foolish. Yet these institutions and patterns of behavior change. When they do, any rule based on them should be reconsidered—not held steadfastly, like a religion. There used to be a monetary "religion" based on the gold standard. However, it contributed to the disaster of the 1930s. As Simons himself observed, "The utter inadequacy of the old gold standard, either as a definite system of rules or as the basis of a monetary religion, seems beyond intelligent dispute."[6] But that is exactly the point—the evidence indicated that the gold standard was a bad rule. Rules should not be maintained regardless of the evidence, regardless of how the chips fall.

As MIT's Paul Samuelson has observed, a set of rules is "set up by discretion, is abandoned by discretion, and is interfered with by discretion."[7] It is impossible to establish a rule that will prevent a repetition of the

[6]*Economic Policy for a Free Society,* p. 169.

[7]"Principles and Rules in Modern Fiscal Policy," *Collected Papers of Paul A. Samuelson* (Cambridge, Mass.: MIT Press, 1966), vol. 2, p. 1278.

greatest destabilizing acts of governments in the past. In the midst of military conflicts, governments will bend or discard rules. *No religion of finance will stand in the way of the religion of victory*. Monetary rules do not exist in a vacuum. They involve questions of alternatives, of evidence, of analysis—not of theology.

2. Insufficient Aggregate Demand?

Monetarists generally propose a monetary rule designed to allow aggregate demand to rise no more rapidly than the productive capacity of the economy. If successful, the rule would result in long-run price stability.

It is not altogether clear whether it is desirable to have a trend in aggregate demand which is just barely adequate to buy the growing output of the nation at stable prices. It depends in part on the nature of aggregate supply. If the aggregate supply curve slopes upward before full employment is reached—as illustrated by the intermediate range of the Keynesian aggregate supply curve shown back in Figure 9-5—a case can be made for increasing aggregate demand somewhat more rapidly than the rate that would leave prices constant. By accepting a moderate upward movement in prices, we can achieve greater output and employment.

If, on the other hand, the aggregate supply curve is vertical, as in the classical theory illustrated in Figure 9-3, a noninflationary trend is just fine. Output and employment will be just as high as with an inflationary trend. Thus, the monetarist proposals for aggregate *demand* depend in part on their belief in the vertical aggregate *supply* of classical theory.

A detailed study of aggregate supply must be deferred until the next chapter. However, the main point can be summarized. Critics of a monetary rule fear that monetarists would keep the trend of aggregate demand too low, creating high unemployment. Monetarists believe that discretionary policymakers will create too much demand, causing a persistent inflation.

3. Abrupt Changes in Practice?

No government can commit itself to follow policy rules regardless of how the chips fall; governments are elected to use their best judgment. But, even though the supporters of a monetary rule might concede that no rule can be adhered to for all time, regardless of the evidence, an important issue remains: Should policymakers attempt to fine-tune the economy, adjusting aggregate demand policies frequently in an attempt to stabilize the economy? Or should they make policy adjustments infrequently and gradually, keeping an emphasis on the long-run performance of the economy?

Paradoxically, an attempt to move toward more stable policies can in practice lead to abrupt shifts in policy. Consider two examples.

The paradox of gradualism: The Nixon years Some of the problems of gradualism were illustrated during the Nixon administration. During the preceding Kennedy-Johnson years, Keynesianism had been at its zenith. Kennedy spoke of getting the country moving again; fiscal stimulus was proposed as a means for doing so; and as full employment approached, fine tuning became the order of the day. Then, when Nixon took office, a significant change in emphasis took place. The Chairman of the Council of Economic Advisers, Paul McCracken, spoke of gradualism. In early 1971, George Shultz, the Director of the Office of Management and Budget, characterized current policy: "Steady as you go."[8] Certainly there was at least a hint of stable policy settings.

But what happened? As the economy recovered slowly from the trough of the recession in November 1970, the unemployment rate remained high, at least by the standards of the time. By the middle of 1971, the seasonally adjusted unemployment rate was still what it had been in late 1970—about 6%.

Pressures mounted to "do something." The result was a very abrupt shift, with a new economic policy being introduced in August of 1971. Wages and prices were frozen. Taxes were cut to stimulate domestic spending. Steps were taken to lower the price of the dollar in terms of other currencies in order to stimulate exports.

Thus, we face dangers on either hand. If we attempt to fine-tune the economy, we may overreact to small and transitory disturbances. But, if "steady as you go" becomes our watchword, very strong political pressures may build up as problems persist. The result may be a very abrupt change in policy indeed. The Nixon adminis-

[8]Shultz later became Secretary of State under President Reagan.

tration fell victim to the second danger. Although it advocated gradualism, it ended up with one of the sharpest policy shifts of recent decades.

The change in monetary policy in 1979 During the 1970s, a number of steps were taken toward the monetarist position. At the beginning of the decade, the Fed began to adopt targets for monetary growth, in addition to interest rate targets. Following the deep recession of 1973–1975, which was accompanied by a very slow growth in money, Congress urged the Fed to pay more attention to money growth targets. Then came the announcement in October 1979 that the Fed would focus more on money growth targets and less on interest rates.

The 1979 announcement was intended to restrain the inflationary spiral and calm fears of ever-escalating inflation. Once again, an issue arose as to how a transition to a new policy would take place. There is an inherent problem in adopting the monetarist prescription in an inflationary period like 1979, with high inflation and rapid increases in the money stock. (M1 was increasing at about 8% per year.) If the objective is to have money grow at a slow, steady rate of, say, 3% per year, how is this new policy to be introduced? If the Fed immediately moves to a 3% money growth path, a sharp change will have occurred: The growth of the money stock will have been very unstable during the transition. On the other hand, if the Fed simply stabilizes money growth at the existing rate of 8%, the anti-inflationary goal will never be achieved.

In practice, the Fed compromised, picking a goal somewhat less than the prevailing 8%. By the middle of 1980, M1 was only 5% higher than a year earlier. Thus, a rather sharp change in policy had taken place—although not so sharp as would have occurred by moving immediately to a money growth rate of 3%. The sharp deceleration in the rate of growth of money was accompanied by the 1980 recession.

Although very substantial progress was made toward the goal of lower inflation, two problems arose following the Fed's policy announcement of 1979. Although interest rates were high and volatile—as might be expected during a transition period when the Fed disclaimed responsibility for interest rates—the money stock did not in fact grow in a more stable way than it had earlier. Thus, monetarists could argue that, in spite of what the Fed said, the stable-policy prescription was still not being followed.

More important, however, was the erratic behavior of velocity, particularly in 1982, when it plunged during the recession. In the equation $MV = PQ$, nominal output PQ was much less than would be expected by looking at what was happening to M. In other words, that recession was not simply a "monetary phenomenon," caused by a decline in the rate of growth of money. Other, nonmonetary factors were at work. Because of the weakness of velocity and the depth of the recession, the Fed took steps to increase the rate of growth of the money stock in the summer and fall of 1982. By increasing M, the Fed was compensating for a fall in V.

As we have already seen in Chapter 14, the monetarist case was weakened by this fall in velocity and by the earlier changes in velocity in the 1975–1978 period. As compared to a decade ago, economists now have less reason to expect that stable money growth will lead to stable increases in aggregate demand.

4. Would a Monetary Rule Make the Growth of Aggregate Demand More Stable?

Although recent changes in velocity have weakened economists' confidence in the quantity theory of money, we should be very careful not to come to sweeping conclusions. In particular, we should recognize that the debate is over the *relative* merits of two options: (1) a monetary rule and (2) discretionary demand management policies. The evidence of the past 15 years suggests a rather disconcerting conclusion. As compared to where we were fifteen years ago, we can have less confidence in a good macroeconomic performance *regardless of whether* option 1 *or* option 2 is chosen. We have just seen that, because of recent changes in velocity, we have less reason to be confident that stable money growth will lead to a stable growth in aggregate demand. The early pages of this chapter showed why we have less reason to be confident about discretionary policies. In the early 1960s, discretionary policies seemed successful. The period since 1970 leads to harsher judgments, as explained in the discussion of Figure 15-5.

With both options looking rather unattractive, it is not clear what has happened to the *relative* merits of the two. It's not clear whether discretionary policies or a monetary rule will make aggregate demand more stable. We seem to be left with only one straightforward conclusion, which we don't much like. It's less fun to be a macroeconomist now than it was in 1970.

THE OUTCOME OF THE DEBATE

While monetarist rulemakers remain in the minority, significant changes in attitude have occurred during the 1970s as a consequence of their criticisms of activist policies and as a consequence of the disappointing results with aggregate demand management:

1. There has been increased awareness that demand management itself may be a cause of economic instability. Overly ambitious demand management may cause accelerating inflation. Furthermore, substantial lags may result in actions which are too late and which add to the magnitude of cyclical swings.
2. There is more widespread recognition of the importance of paying attention to the long-term consequences of policies. In particular, because aggregate demand has a lagged effect on prices, there is a general recognition that anti-inflation policies should be made with the long run in mind.

FORECASTING

If a little knowledge is dangerous, where is the man who has so much as to be out of danger?

Thomas Huxley

The proponents of rules have made significant contributions to macroeconomic policy debates, but they have not swept the field. Monetary and fiscal policies are still adjusted from time to time. However, the debate over discretionary policies has highlighted the dangers of managing aggregate demand.

In particular, lags mean that policies adopted today will not have their full effect until some months in the future. The problem is: Will the effects of the policy be appropriate at that time? In deciding whether to change policy, the Fed and fiscal policymakers have *no alternative but to forecast*. The question is not *whether* to forecast, but *how*. Anyone who thinks that forecasting can be avoided is, in fact, forecasting in a naive way. By implying that policy be designed for the needs of the moment, such a person is making the simple forecast that the problems of the future will be the same as those of today. Even the proponents of a monetary rule are forecasting in a sense. Their case is based on the forecast that velocity will be stable in the future.

Forecasting with a Model

In developing a forecast for the coming months, economists in and out of government use a number of techniques, most of them using computers. Typically, past information on consumption, income, etc., is used to estimate how the economy behaves. For example, how is consumption related to income? Based on past relationships, future consumption is estimated. Typically, forecasters also estimate future investment, government expenditures, and net exports. The path of investment is forecast on the basis of current and expected future interest rates and other important influences. The President's budget and spending authorizations by Congress are used to estimate the probable course of government spending. Exports are estimated on the basis of expected economic activity abroad; the more prosperous are foreign economies, the more likely they are to buy our exports. Such pieces are fitted together to make a statistical—or *econometric*—model of the economy. With such a model, it is possible to make a projection of GNP.

A simple example will give a general idea of how this is done. We begin by repeating a fundamental equation that appeared earlier as equation 7-2:

$$\text{GNP} = C + I_g + G + X - M \qquad (15\text{-}1)$$

Suppose that statistical evidence indicates that consumers in the past have spent 90% of their disposable incomes, and that two-thirds of GNP flows through to consumers in the form of disposable income. That means that consumption is 60% of GNP (that is, 90% × ⅔):

$$C = 0.6\text{GNP} \qquad (15\text{-}2)$$

Suppose, also, that businesses are expected to invest $600 billion in the coming period:

$$I_g = \$600 \qquad (15\text{-}3)$$

The budgets of the federal, state, and local governments commit them to $800 billion in purchases of goods and services:

$$G = \$800 \qquad (15\text{-}4)$$

Exports are expected to amount to $400 billion:

$$X = \$400 \qquad (15\text{-}5)$$

Finally, past experience indicates that imports are about 10% of GNP:

$$M = 0.1\text{GNP} \qquad (15\text{-}6)$$

Substituting the last five equations into equation 15-1, we can solve:

$$\begin{aligned} GNP &= 0.6\text{GNP} + \$600 + \$800 + \$400 - 0.1\text{GNP} \\ &= 0.5\text{GNP} + \$1{,}800 \end{aligned}$$

That is:

$$\text{GNP} = \$3{,}600 \qquad (15\text{-}7)$$

We thus forecast GNP to be $3,600 billion.

In practice, of course, economists use substantially more complicated equations. For example, consumption expenditures depend not only on consumers' disposable income but also on their wealth (such as stocks and bonds). When forecasting, economists pay particular attention to the time element, for example, *how quickly* consumption responds to changing levels of disposable income. Taking these two complications into account, we get a more sophisticated consumption function:

$$C_t = 0.5\text{DI}_t + 0.2\text{DI}_{t-1} + 0.05W_t \qquad (15\text{-}8)$$

where DI stands for disposable income, W stands for wealth, and the subscripts stand for time periods; specifically, $t - 1$ is the quarter before t. In plain English, equation 15-8 says that consumption expenditures in any quarter (C_t) depend upon disposable income in that quarter (DI_t) and in the previous quarter (DI_{t-1}), and also upon wealth in that quarter (W_t).

Although equation 15-8 is still relatively simple, it is beginning to resemble the consumption function used in actual econometric models. The appendix to this chapter will introduce some of the basic ideas used to explain investment in such models.

Well-known econometric models include the MPS model (of the Massachusetts Institute of Technology, the University of Pennsylvania, and the Social Science Research Council), the model of Data Resources, Inc. (DRI), and Lawrence Klein's model at the University of Pennsylvania's Wharton School, to name a few.

These models provide a useful starting point for forecasts and are particularly helpful in cross-checking the various components of aggregate demand (consumption, investment, government spending, and net exports) to make sure that they are consistent. However, models have a major limitation. Essentially, they project the future on the basis of relationships which have held in the past, but which may change. The future of the economy depends on many forces, some of which are not easy to incorporate into formal econometric models. Thus, forecasters generally adjust the initial results of their econometric models to allow for additional factors that they consider important. The final result is a "judgmental" forecast—using the results of models, but with modifications.

In adjusting the raw output of econometric models, forecasters use the results of various surveys of future intentions, for example: Commerce Department questionnaires regarding investment intentions; Conference Board surveys of capital appropriations by businesses; and surveys of consumer attitudes, including those done by the Survey Research Center at the University of Michigan.

Turning Points

One of the hardest problems in forecasting is to tell when a turning point will take place—when an expansion will reach a peak and a decline will begin, or when a recession will hit the trough and a recovery begin. One of the weakest features of econometric models is that they do not forecast turning points very accurately. But turning points are *very* important. If an upswing will end in the next several months, now is the time to consider more expansive policies.

What is needed, then, is something that will signal a coming turn. The search for ***leading indicators*** has been centered in the National Bureau of Economic Research. A number of leading indicators have been identified; they include such items as common stock prices, new orders for durable goods, and the average number of hours worked per week. An index of leading indicators is published monthly by the Department of Commerce in *Business Conditions Digest*.

A *leading indicator* is an economic variable that reaches a turning point (peak or trough) before the economy as a whole does. (New orders for durable goods are an example.)

As Figure 15-6 shows, leading indicators have been helpful: They have predicted every recession since 1948. However, even when they correctly signal a future recession, they don't tell *when* it will occur; they don't provide the same period of advance warning each time. Note that the leading indicators provided a 23-month warning of the 1957 recession, but only a 3-month warning of the very severe recession of 1981–1982. Worse still, they sometimes send false signals, indicating a recession even though the economy in fact continues to

FIGURE 15-6
Index of leading indicators
The curve shows the behavior of the leading indicators. The *P* and *T* notation along the top dates the peaks and troughs of the economy; the recessions in between are shaded. Note that a signal from the leading indicators usually means a coming turn—but not always. For example, the indicators turned down in early 1984, but there was no recession on the horizon. The figures show the number of months by which the indicators led the turning points in the economy. Sometimes there is a long warning: 23 months elapsed between the time when the indicators turned down in 1955 and when the economy as a whole began to decline in 1957. But in 1981, the indicators gave only 3 months warning of a very severe recession.
Source: Department of Commerce, *Business Conditions Digest*.

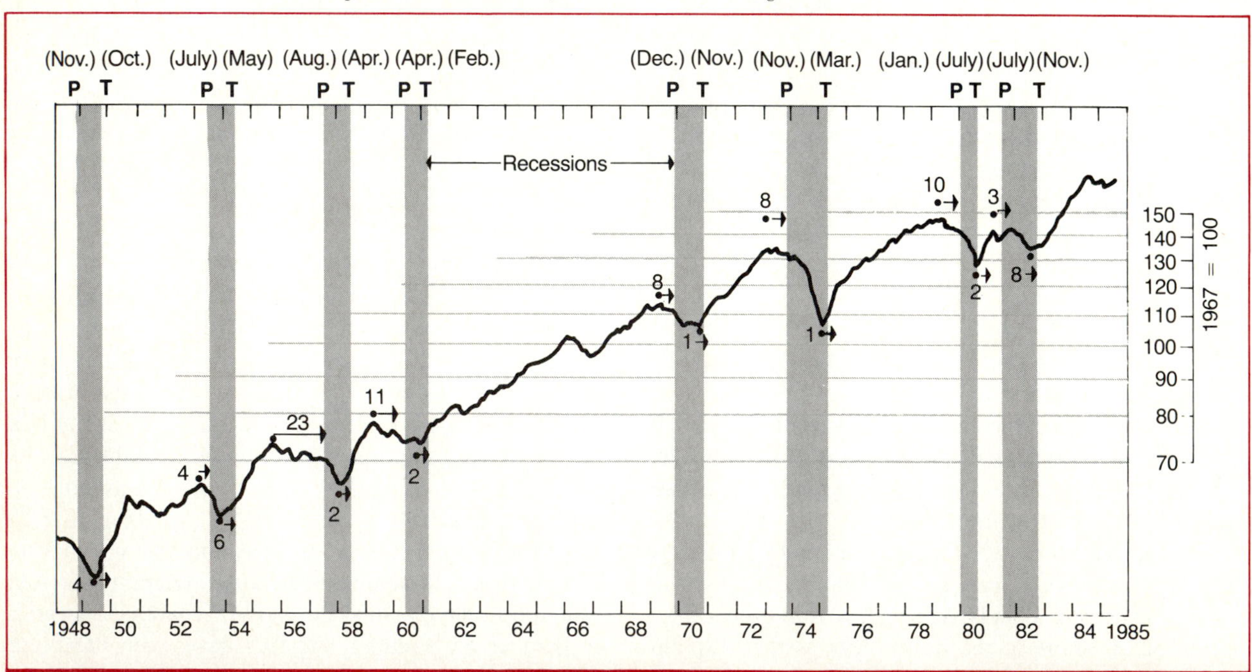

expand. For example, there was no recession following the downturn in the indicators in 1966 and 1984 (although the expansion did slow down in each case). The false signals have led to a common quip: Leading indicators have signaled seven of the last five recessions.

The Proof of the Pudding

Figure 15-7 gives the results of five well-known forecasts, one government and four private. The red lines show how much GNP was expected to change over a period of 1 year according to the *median* forecast (the middle of the five forecasts). The black lines show the actual changes over the year. The difference between the two is thus the amount by which forecasters missed the mark. The average size of the error in predicting nominal GNP was 2.2%, while the average error in predicting real GNP was 1.6%.

An inspection of Figure 15-7 indicates that there is a tendency for actual changes in GNP and predicted changes to move together. Thus, it is much better to use the median forecast than to rely on a simple procedure, such as extrapolating from recent trends or assuming that

FIGURE 15-7

The forecasting record

Most of the time, forecasts are reasonably accurate. The biggest problems in forecasting arise during recessions. Note in particular how forecasters underestimated the fall in real GNP during the recessions of 1973–1975 and especially 1981–1982.

(The dates on the horizontal axis show the *end* of the year-long forecasting period. For example, the forecast for real GNP for the first quarter of 1982 is shown as +2.2%. This means that, in the first quarter of 1981, forecasters predicted a 2.2% increase for the coming year. The actual change for the year, shown in black, was −2.0%.)

Source: Stephen K. McNees and John Ries, "The Track Record of Macroeconomic Forecasts," *New England Economic Review*, December 1983, p. 10.

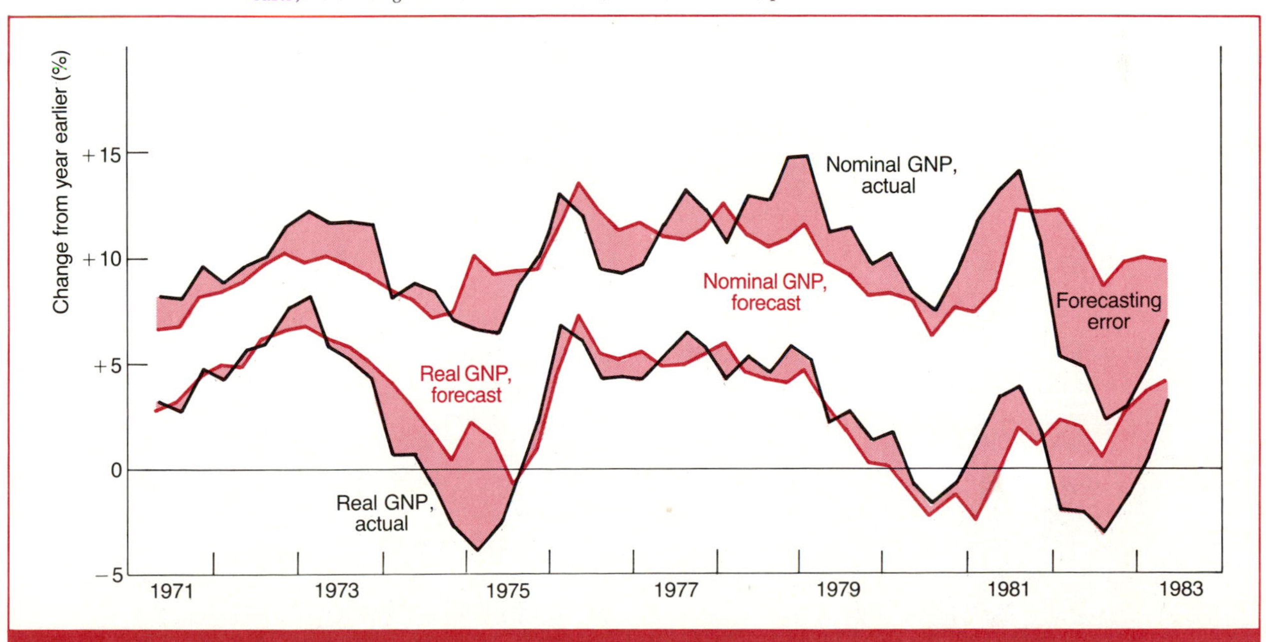

the increase over the next year will be the same as the average increase for the past few years. This conclusion is reassuring. Businesses and governments pay millions for forecasts. They are not wasting their money.

Less reassuring, however, is the record of forecasters during the three recessions of 1973–1975, 1980, and 1981–1982. In only one of these cases (1980) did forecasters anticipate the strength of the downturn in real GNP. During the recession of 1973–1975, the record of forecasters was mixed. Although they anticipated the weakening of the economy in late 1973, they greatly underestimated how much real GNP would fall. They also underestimated how long the recession would last, forecasting a rebound by early 1975. The worst record came in 1981–1982, when forecasters failed to anticipate the worst recession of recent decades.

Forecasting was particularly difficult during 1981–1982, because fiscal policy was moving sharply in an expansive direction, while monetary restraint was being exercised. This reinforces the point made at the end of Chapter 14: When monetary policy is pushed in one direction, and fiscal policy in another, the path of the economy becomes particularly uncertain. It is wise not to put all our policy eggs in one basket. Howard Baker, the Republican leader in the Senate, was right on the money when he referred to the large tax cuts enacted in 1981 as a "riverboat gamble."

It is worrisome that forecasters are not able to anticipate recessions better. If discretionary policies are to be successful, it is particularly important that policy be moved in an expansive direction as the economy is approaching a recession.

KEY POINTS

1. The mediocre record of monetary and fiscal policies in recent years has enlivened an old debate: Should aggregate demand policies be actively adjusted in the quest for high employment and stable prices? Or should monetary and fiscal rules be followed?

2. The activist Keynesian approach involves several steps. First, the full-employment or potential path of GNP is estimated. Second, if actual GNP is significantly below potential GNP, aggregate demand should be expanded until the potential path is approached. Thereafter, fiscal and monetary policies should be adjusted as needed to combat fluctuations.

3. This strategy was followed with success during the first half of the 1960s. However, aggregate demand became too high and inflation accelerated in the last half of the decade.

4. The existence of time lags makes it difficult to design countercyclical policies. Actions taken today may not be appropriate to the economy of tomorrow, when they will have their major effect.

5. There are *three lags* between the time that aggregate demand should be changed and the time when the change actually occurs. The *recognition lag* is the interval before changes in economic conditions are recognized. The *action lag* is the interval between the time a problem is recognized and the time when fiscal and monetary policies are adjusted. The *impact lag* is the interval between the time when policies are changed and the time when the major effect on aggregate demand occurs. Because of lags, policies implemented today will have their effects in the future, when they may be too late.

6. There is also another important lag. When aggregate demand changes, the effects on prices lag behind the effect on output. That is, when aggregate demand increases, output generally responds quickly, with inflation increasing only after a lag. When aggregate demand falls, output generally falls quickly, with the economy sliding into a recession. Inflation begins to fall only after a lag.

7. Monetarists believe that discretionary policies are likely to do more harm than good. They recommend a *policy rule*—that the money stock be increased by a fixed percentage, year after year, regardless of current economic conditions. Monetarists believe that discretionary adjustments in aggregate demand policies are likely to do more harm than good because:

(*a*) There are lags before aggregate demand can be adjusted, and between changes in demand and the effect on prices.

(*b*) People tend to be overly optimistic in estimating the potential path of real GNP (Figure 15-5).

(*c*) Expansive policies are generally continued too long as a result of the lags and overoptimism. Then, when inflation becomes a clear and present danger, policymakers generally overreact, causing a fall in aggregate demand and a recession. However, inflation does not respond quickly to the lower aggregate demand. The restrictive policies are therefore deemed a failure, and another round of expansive policies is begun. Consequently, discretionary policies are likely to cause instability and an inflationary bias in the economy. Each recovery tends to begin with a higher rate of inflation than the previous one.

(*d*) Policy rules will result in less interference by the government and therefore in more economic freedom.

8. The economy can be destabilized when policymakers pursue what seem to be plausible goals. A number of examples have been provided:

(*a*) Chapter 11 explained how policymakers can fall into a trap and destabilize the economy if they attempt to balance the budget every year.

(*b*) Chapter 13 explained how policymakers can similarly fall into a trap if they attempt to stabilize interest rates.

(*c*) This chapter has explained the problems which arise if policymakers aim at an unattainable estimate of potential GNP.

9. A number of arguments can be made against a monetary rule and in favor of discretionary policies:

(*a*) In practice, no government will follow a policy rule regardless of the short-run consequences (how the chips fall) and competing objectives (such as wartime finance).

(*b*) Rulemakers tend to propose a rule that will keep the trend of aggregate demand too low. An unnecessarily high rate of unemployment will be the result. [Compare this with key point 7(*c*), the monetarist view that activist policies will give the economy an inflationary bias.]

(*c*) Efforts to follow stable policies may paradoxically lead to abrupt policy shifts.

(*d*) A monetary rule does not ensure a stable increase in aggregate demand.

10. In spite of these counterarguments, important changes in attitudes have occurred as a consequence of the monetarist criticisms of fine tuning and the disappointing results with aggregate demand management:

(*a*) The problem of lags is more clearly recognized.

(*b*) The importance of keeping long-term objectives in mind is more widely recognized.

11. Because policies have their major effect on aggregate demand some months in the future, a forecast of future conditions must be made—explicitly or implicitly—whenever policy is changed. To forecast, economists use econometric models, supplemented with survey data and ''judgmental'' adjustments. The experience of recent years suggests that it is particularly difficult to forecast recessions.

KEY CONCEPTS

policy activism
discretionary policy
policy rule
fine tuning
potential GNP
GNP gap
recognition lag
action lag
impact lag
lag between output changes and price changes
productivity of labor
gradualism
econometric model
turning point
leading indicator

PROBLEMS

15-1. Explain the steps in the activist Keynesian strategy.

15-2. What case do monetarists make against the activist approach?

15-3. If discretionary policies are followed, what are the consequences of overestimating potential GNP? Use the U.S. experience since 1970 in your answer.

15-4. What case can be made against a monetary policy rule?

15-5. Why do Samuelson and others argue that a policy rule is impossible?

15-6. In the section describing the possible overestimation of potential GNP, we observed that output and prices do not respond at the same rate to changes in aggregate demand. In such circumstances, why do the statistics sometimes give policymakers conflicting signals about the appropriate way to adjust aggregate demand? How do the conflicting signals add to the "recognition lag?"

15-7. Why must future economic conditions be forecast when monetary or fiscal policies are changed? If policymakers do not believe they are forecasting, why may we conclude that they are in fact using implicit forecasts? If someone argues for no change in monetary and fiscal policies, is he or she making any forecast about the future? Why is it particularly important to forecast turning points? Can you think of any reason why it is difficult to forecast turning points accurately?

APPENDIX

THE ACCELERATOR:

A NONMONETARY EXPLANATION OF BUSINESS FLUCTUATIONS

If business cycles were primarily the result of monetary disturbances, a smooth growth in the money stock would make the economy more stable. However, the stronger are nonmonetary disturbances, the less the economy can be smoothed by a monetary policy rule, and the stronger is the case for discretionary policies to offset the disturbances—provided that the authorities can act quickly enough in the presence of lags.

Separating monetary from nonmonetary disturbances is not a simple matter. "Nonmonetary" theories of business cycles generally focus on the investment sector of aggregate demand, since this is the most unstable. The theory of investment presented in this appendix will be nonmonetary in the sense that money is not an integral part of the theory. However, we cannot demonstrate that it is completely nonmonetary. In fact, we will see later that monetary issues are lurking in the background.

INVESTMENT DEMAND: THE SIMPLE ACCELERATOR

Suppose we put ourselves in the business executive's shoes. Why should we want to invest? Why, for example, should we want to acquire more machines?

The simplest answer is that businesses want more machines because they want to produce more goods. *The desired stock of capital depends on the amount of production.* This fundamental proposition lies behind the ***acceleration principle,*** illustrated in Table 15-1 and Figure 15-8. In the first 2 years of this example, a bicycle manufacturer sells 200,000 bicycles per year. Suppose that one machine is needed for every 10,000 bicycles produced. Assume also that the manufacturer initially has the 20 machines needed to produce the 200,000 bicycles. So long as the demand for bicycles remains stable (as shown in Table 15-1, phase I, years 1 and 2), there is no need for additional machines; there is no net investment.

That does not mean, however, that machine production is zero. Suppose that a machine lasts for 10 years, with 2 of the original 20 machines wearing out each year. So long as the demand for bicycles remains constant at 200,000 per year, gross investment will continue to be 2 machines per year. (That is, 2 machines will be purchased to replace the 2 that wear out each year.)

Now, suppose that the demand for bicycles starts to grow in phase II. In the third year, sales increase by 10%, from 200,000 to 220,000. As a consequence, the manufacturer needs 22 machines; 2 additional machines must be acquired. Gross investment therefore rises to 4 machines—2 replacements plus 2 net additions. An increase in sales of only 10% has had an *accelerated* or magnified effect on investment. Gross investment has risen from 2 to 4 machines, or by no less than 100%. (This magnified effect on investment provides an important clue as to why investment fluctuates so much more than GNP.) Then in the fourth year, with the growth of sales remaining constant at 20,000 units, gross investment remains constant at 4 machines per year.

Next, see what happens in phase III. In the fifth year, demand begins to level out. As growth slows to 10,000 bicycles, only 1 additional machine is needed. Both net and gross investment *decline* as a result of *slowing* of the growth of bicycle sales. We emphasize: *An actual decline in sales is not necessary to cause a decline in investment*. (Sales did not decline in the fifth year; they merely grew more slowly than in the fourth year.) Then, when the demand for bicycles levels out in the sixth year, there is no longer a need for any additional machines; net investment drops to zero, and gross investment falls back to 2. Then, if bicycle sales begin to decline in phase IV (year 7), the number of machines which the manufacturer needs will decline; the machines which are wearing out will not be replaced. Net investment becomes negative, and gross investment can fall to zero.

This example of the acceleration principle (or ''accelerator'') illustrates a number of important points:

1. Investment (in machines) fluctuates by a much greater percentage than output of the goods for which capital is used (bicycles).
2. Net investment depends on the *change* in the production of the goods for which capital is used.
3. Once output begins to rise, it must continue to grow by the same amount if investment is to remain constant. A reduction in the growth of output will cause a *decline* in investment (year 5). But a very rapid growth of sales may be unsustainable. Therefore, a rapid upswing in economic activity contains the seeds of its own destruc-

TABLE 15-1
The Acceleration Principle

Time	(1) Yearly sales of bicycles (in thousands)	(2) Desired number of machines (column 1 ÷ 10,000)	(3) Net investment (change in column 2)	(4) Gross investment (column 3 + replacement of 2 machines)
Phase I: Steady sales				
First year	200	20	0	2
Second year	200	20	0	2
Phase II: Rising sales				
Third year	220	22	2	4
Fourth year	240	24	2	4
Phase III: A leveling off				
Fifth year	250	25	1	3
Sixth year	250	25	0	2
Phase IV: Declining sales				
Seventh year	230	23	−2	0
Eighth year	210	21	−2	0
Phase V: A leveling off				
Ninth year	200	20	−1	1
Tenth year	200	20	0	2

Investment fluctuates much more than consumption. Net investment depends on the *change* in consumption.

tion. As the growth of consumption slows down, investment will fall.

4. It is possible for gross investment to collapse, even though there is only a mild decline in sales (as shown in year 7).

5. For investment to recover, it is not necessary for sales to rise. A smaller decline in sales is sufficient (year 9). Thus, a decline in economic activity contains the seeds of recovery.

This illustration is simplified, but the validity of its major points may be shown in a few examples. If business slackens off and fewer goods are shipped, the amount of trucking declines. Consequently, the demand for new trucks will decline sharply. Or consider what happens when the birthrate declines. Construction of schools is cut back. (New schools are needed primarily to accommodate an increase in the student population.) Note how the accelerator applies not only to machines, but also to other forms of investment such as school buildings and factories.

The accelerator can also apply to inventory investment, and this can add to the instability of the economy. Merchants may attempt to keep their inventories in proportion to sales. Thus, if sales increase by, say, 10%, orders to the factory may be increased by perhaps 20% in

FIGURE 15-8
The acceleration principle

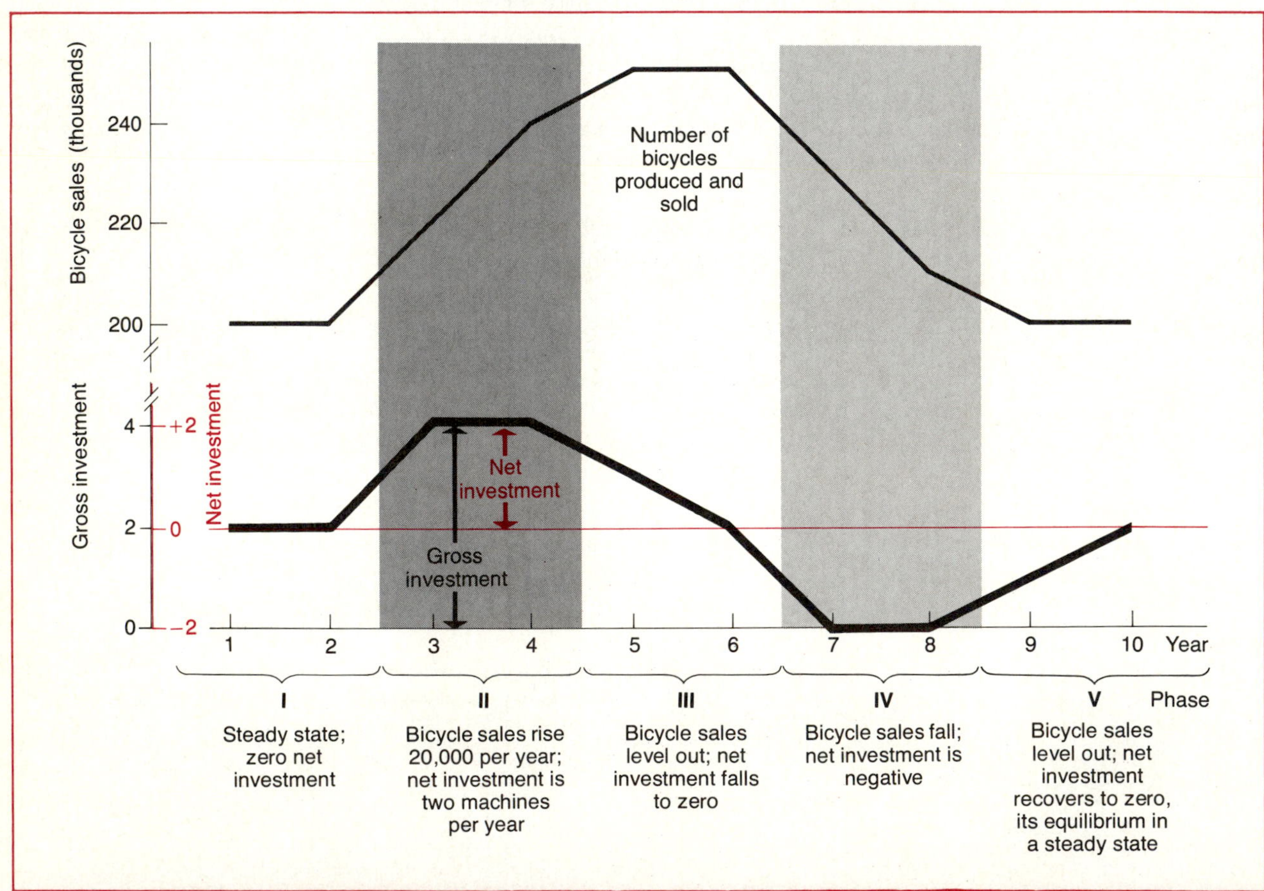

order to bring inventories up into line with the higher sales. Nevertheless, inventory investment does not always act as a destabilizing force. There is no need for retailers to keep any rigid relationship between their sales and inventories. On the contrary, the effects of temporary spurts in sales may be cushioned by the existence of inventories: Retailers may meet the increased sales by running down their inventories.

MODIFICATION OF THE SIMPLE ACCELERATOR: LAGS IN INVESTMENT

Even in the case of a manufacturing operation, it is an oversimplification to assume that a rigid relationship exists between sales and the number of machines. In practice, the firm does not need exactly one machine for every 10,000 bicycles produced. Instead of acquiring new machines, a firm can run its factories overtime when demand increases. In this way, it can change its ***capital/output ratio***. Furthermore, at the end of 10 years, an old machine does not suddenly disintegrate; it wears out gradually. During a boom, older machines can be kept in use beyond their normal retirement age.

The *capital/output ratio* is the value of capital (machines, factories, etc.) divided by the value of annual output.

What should be taken into account by businesses in deciding whether to buy new machinery or to "make do" by patching up old machinery or scheduling overtime? One important consideration is how long an increase in sales is expected to last. If it is just a temporary spurt and will quickly subside, expensive new machines should not be ordered. They may not be received quickly enough to meet the bulge in demand, and may add to idle capacity during the next downturn. Thus, the immediate response to increases in sales may be to schedule overtime and to wait and see before ordering new machines. As a result, there are significant delays in the response of investment to changes in sales.

In the short run, these delays add to stability. Businesses do not rush out to buy new machines with every little increase in sales. However, over longer periods, lags can add to the force of an upswing or a downswing. If high sales continue for some time, businesses conclude that prosperity is permanent. Orders for new machines are placed. Once this happens, competitors may become concerned. If they don't jump on the bandwagon, they may lose their place in a growing market. A boom psychology can develop. Although investment demand is initially slow to respond, it can gain momentum.

INTERACTIONS BETWEEN THE ACCELERATOR AND THE MULTIPLIER

Interactions between consumption and investment add to the momentum of the economy. As more machines are ordered, incomes rise in the machinery-producing industries. As incomes rise, people consume more. As they buy more consumer goods, business optimism is confirmed—the rising sales are "for real." As a consequence, orders for plant and equipment increase even more. Once again, the higher incomes resulting from higher investment stimulate consumption; the multiplier process makes the expansion stonger. Thus, increases in investment demand and increases in consumer demand reinforce one another.

Eventually, however, a strong expansion must slow down. Economic resources—labor, land, and capital—are limited, and national output cannot expand indefinitely at a rapid pace. Output begins to increase more slowly. Because of the accelerator principle, investment turns down. Because of the multiplier, national product declines by several times as much as the decrease in investment. A recession is under way. Thus, the interaction of the accelerator and multiplier helps to explain not only (1) the *strength* of cycles but also (2) *why turning points occur*—why, for example, a boom does not continue indefinitely, but instead reaches a peak and turns into a recession.

However, an expansion does not *inevitably* turn into a recession. If the increase in demand and output can be kept moderate and steady, the natural rebound into recession may be avoided. For this reason, *moderate growth can be more healthy and lasting than a business boom.*

The Downswing and Lower Turning Point

When the lessons of the simple accelerator model (listed

earlier as points 1 through 5) are modified to take account of time lags and the interaction between the multiplier and accelerator, the following sequence occurs as a result of a reduction in the growth of sales:

1. In the short run of a few weeks or months, there is little if any decline in investment in plant and equipment. This is because investment in plant and equipment is cushioned from the effects of changing sales in a number of ways: (*a*) Inventories are temporarily allowed to increase, with the result that factory orders hold up better than final sales; (*b*) overtime is reduced; and (*c*) the opportunity is taken to retire machines that have been kept in service past their normal lifetimes.
2. If sales continue to be weak, business executives begin to fear the worst. Rather than accumulate higher and higher inventories, firms cut back sharply on their orders. As production falls, factories slash new orders for machines. (These are the effects of the accelerator.) Momentum is added to the downswing as laid-off workers reduce their consumption (the multiplier).
3. However, consumption demand does not continue to decline indefinitely. While some purchases may easily be postponed, consumers try to maintain their expenditures for food and other necessities. Furthermore, as automobiles and other consumer durables wear out, consumers become increasingly anxious to replace them. As the decline in consumer spending moderates, investment in machinery and buildings begins to recover. (However, the recovery may be delayed by the desire of retailers, wholesalers, and manufacturers to work off excessive inventories.)

Each of these three stages is important, and each contains its own valuable lesson. These lessons are, respectively:

1. Investment is not volatile in the face of small and temporary reductions in the rate of growth of sales.
2. If sales remain weak for some time, investment falls. The downswing gathers momentum because of feedbacks between falling investment and falling consumer demand—that is, because of the interaction of the multiplier and the accelerator.
3. However, the downward movement does not continue forever. Even in the worst depressions, economic activity does not collapse toward zero. The accelerator process generates natural forces of recovery even before consumption bottoms out.

In deciding whether to invest, business executives compare the advantages of new machinery with the alternative of "making do" by scheduling overtime and keeping old machines in production. In this decision, a relevant consideration is the cost of new machines. There are two important costs: (1) the price of the machine itself and (2) the price of the financing—that is, the interest rate. Here is an important place where money comes into the picture. For example, open market purchases can be used to push down interest rates and thus lower the cost of acquiring new machines, buildings, and inventories. Thus, the Federal Reserve can encourage the recovery from a recession. Similarly, open market sales (or less-than-normal purchases) and higher interest rates discourage investment, and thus can help prevent a healthy expansion from turning into an unhealthy boom.

KEY POINTS

12. Investment fluctuates more widely than other segments of GNP. The accelerator principle illustrates why. Investment depends on the change in output, and investment demand can change by a large percentage in the face of relatively small percentage changes in sales. The accelerator also helps to explain why turning points occur in the business cycle. Investment can fall even in a growing economy, if the *growth* of sales slows down. An actual decline in sales is not necessary. During a recession, investment can recover when sales decline at a slower rate. An actual upturn in sales is not necessary.
13. While the acceleration principle illustrates important forces that help to determine investment demand, it represents a simplification. In practice, there may be delays in the response of investment to changes in sales. These delays contribute to the stability of the economy in the face of small disturbances. However, they mean that, once an expansion or contraction gets going, it can gather momentum.
14. The interaction between the accelerator and the multiplier also adds to the momentum of an upswing or downswing. When investment demand falls, incomes

and consumption demand also fall, causing a further decline in output (the multiplier). This decline in output in turn depresses investment (the accelerator).

PROBLEMS

15-8. Complete the table below illustrating the acceleration principle. Assume that one machine is needed to produce every 1,000 automobiles, that a machine lasts 10 years, and that one-tenth of the initial number of machines is scheduled for retirement in each of the next 10 years.

Year	(1) Yearly sales of autos	(2) Desired number of machines	(3) Net investment	(4) Gross investment
1	100,000			
2	100,000			
3	90,000			
4	80,000			
5	80,000			
6	80,000			
7	90,000			
8	100,000			
9	100,000			

15-9. Suppose, alternatively, that there is a lag in investment. The number of machines desired in any year is calculated by taking the average number of autos produced in that year and the previous year. In other respects, follow the assumptions of problem 15-8. Then recalculate the table in problem 15-8. Does this change in the assumption make investment demand more or less stable?

15-10. Suppose you are in business, and demand for your product has recently increased. You now have to choose among (1) turning away some of your new customers, (2) scheduling overtime, (3) adding a new shift, or (4) expanding your factory and the number of your machines. Explain the important considerations in choosing among these four options.

CHAPTER 16

AGGREGATE SUPPLY:

HOW CAN INFLATION AND UNEMPLOYMENT COEXIST?

The first panacea for a mismanaged nation is inflation of the currency; the second is war. Both bring a temporary prosperity; both bring a permanent ruin. But both are the refuge of political and economic opportunists.

ERNEST HEMINGWAY

In the three decades following the Great Depression, macroeconomists were preoccupied with aggregate demand. How could we prevent a repeat of the the depression, with its decade-long inadequacy of demand? How, and to what extent, could we hope to manage aggregate demand in order to reduce short-run fluctuations in the economy? Then, beginning in the 1960s, macroeconomists also began to pay close attention to aggregate supply. Any study of macroeconomics is now incomplete without an investigation of *both* demand and supply.

The last five chapters dealt in detail with the demand side and, in particular, with the use of monetary and fiscal policies to affect aggregate demand. In this chapter, we turn to aggregate supply.

Chapter 9 introduced the aggregate supply function of Keynesian theory, repeated here as Figure 16-1. According to this view, if there initially is a deep depression at *A*, with output falling far short of the economy's full-employment potential, an increase in aggregate demand will cause the economy to move toward *B*. In the horizontal range *AB*, the increase in demand will be reflected entirely in an increase in output, while prices will remain stable. At the other end, if an economy begins on the vertical section at *F*, an increase in demand will be reflected entirely in terms of higher prices, as the economy moves upward from *F*. Finally, there is an intermediate range, between *B* and *F*. As the economy approaches full employment, an increase in demand will be reflected partly in terms of higher output and partly in terms of higher prices.

(We reemphasize a point already encountered several times: A change in *demand* causes a movement *along* a *supply* curve. For example, an increase in aggregate demand causes a movement along the aggregate supply curve from *B* to *F* in Figure 16-1. In Chapter 4, we similarly saw how a shift in demand for an individual product would cause a movement along the supply curve for that product.)

In all probability, the reader has become increasingly uncomfortable with the view of the world represented by Figure 16-1. It doesn't seem to fit the facts very well. In particular, it suggests that, whenever inflation rates are high, the economy should be at full employment, at *F* or above. On the other hand, prices should be stable whenever the unemployment rate is high, to the left of *B*. Yet there have been times when *both* the unemployment rate and inflation have been high. In 1980, for example, the inflation rate exceeded 12%, at a time when unemployment averaged 7%. In 1981, the inflation rate was almost 9%, while unemployment averaged 7.5%. While Figure 16-1 has been useful as an introduction to the idea of aggregate supply, it is too simple. It is not consistent with what has happened in recent decades. The time has come to look closely at the facts.

To do so, economists use a slightly different approach from Figure 16-1. Instead of looking at how prices and output change, they use a diagram with the two central macroeconomic problems—inflation and unemployment—on the axes, as shown in Figure 16-2. This alternative approach to aggregate supply illustrates the three general ideas behind Figure 16-1:

1. First is the idea that prices will be stable in a deep depression. This is illustrated by points *A* and *B*. When *prices* are *stable,* the *rate of inflation* is *zero*. Thus, points *A* and *B* are on the horizontal axis of Figure 16-2. If, starting from a point of severe depression at *A*, aggregate demand rises, output will increase and the rate of unemployment will fall. The decrease in the unemployment rate shows up as a *leftward* movement from *A* to *B* in Figure 16-2. This corresponds to the *rightward* movement when output increases in Figure 16-1.

2. Second is the idea that, whenever there is rapid inflation, the economy is at full employment. This idea is illustrated by the vertical range above *F* in Figure 16-2. Because of frictional unemployment, there is some unemployment—of something like 5% or 6%—even at points of "full employment." In the range above *F*, a faster growth in aggregate demand will mean more inflation, with no change in output or employment.

3. Third is the intermediate range, between *B* and *F*. An increase in demand is reflected partly in higher prices, and partly in terms of rising output and falling unemployment.

THE FACTS

Historical observations are plotted in Figure 16-3, where each point shows the inflation rate and the unemploy-

FIGURE 16-1

The Keynesian aggregate supply function

This figure repeats the aggregate supply function of earlier chapters. If the economy begins at a point of depression, such as *A*, an increase in demand will increase real output. The economy will move from *A* toward *B*, with prices remaining stable. Once full employment has been reached at point *F*, a further increase in aggregate demand will cause inflation, with the economy moving upward from *F*.

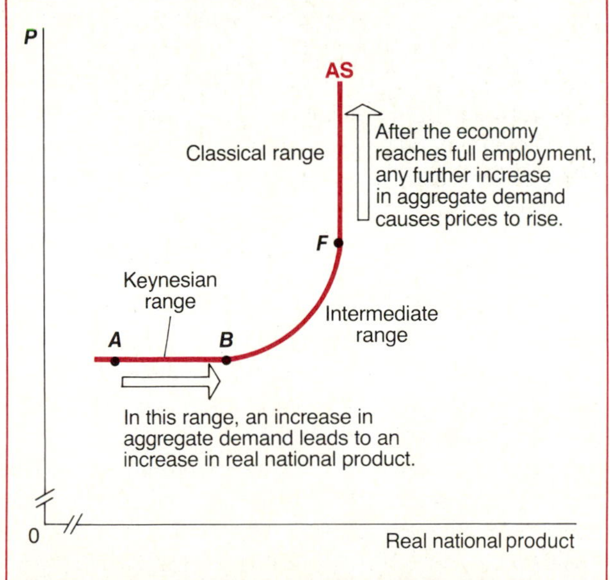

FIGURE 16-2

The aggregate supply function: An alternative presentation

The major ideas in Figure 16-1 are repeated in this diagram. Starting from a point of depression, such as *A*, an increase in demand will leave prices stable. The rate of inflation will be zero. Output will increase. Unemployment will fall, as illustrated by the leftward movement to *B*. In the intermediate range from *B* to *F*, an increase in aggregate demand is reflected partly in inflation and partly in output and employment. Once full employment has been established at *F*, a more rapid growth in aggregate demand is reflected entirely in terms of inflation with no change in the unemployment rate.

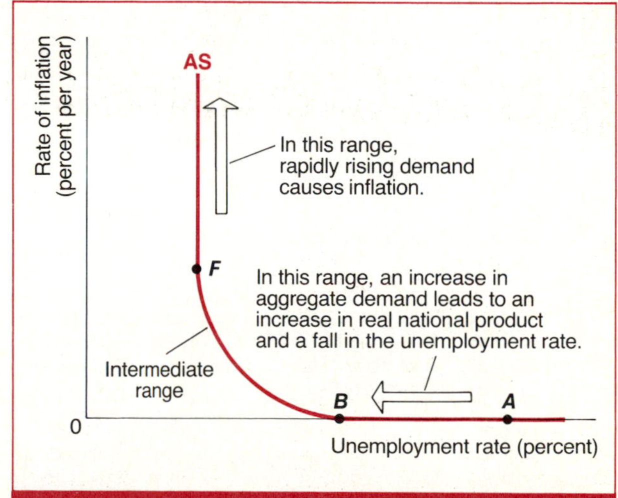

ment rate in one of the years since 1961. When these points are joined chronologically, two major conclusions stand out:

1. Between 1961 and 1969, the data form a smooth curve, similar to the intermediate range of the aggregate supply function in Figure 16-2. Such a curve is known as a ***Phillips curve,*** after British economist A. W. Phillips, who found that British data for 1861–1957 fitted a similar curve.[1]

When the rate of inflation (or the rate of change of money wages)[2] is put on the vertical axis and the rate of unemployment on the horizontal axis, historical data sometimes trace out a smooth curve bending upward to the left—for example, the curve traced out by U.S. data for the 1960s. Such a curve is known as a *Phillips curve*.

2. The observations since 1969 are above and to the right of the Phillips curve traced out by the 1960s. Since 1969, we have frequently suffered from high rates of both inflation and unemployment. To use an inelegant but common term, we have suffered from ***stagflation.***

***Stagflation* exists when a high rate of unemployment (stagnation) and a high rate of inflation occur at the same time.**

In the rest of this chapter, we will look closely at these two points. First, we will look at why the economy might move along a Phillips curve, as it did during the 1960s. Second, we will look at the puzzle presented by the 1970s and 1980s. Why did things get worse after 1969, with higher inflation *and* higher unemployment?

The importance of answering the second question can scarcely be exaggerated. Suppose we cannot figure out what is happening. Suppose the economy does not behave in a predictable manner—it does not move along a predictable aggregate supply curve or Phillips curve in response to a change in aggregate demand. Then the basis for the demand management policies discussed in earlier chapters is undercut. If expansive fiscal and monetary policies are introduced during a recession, can we count on an increase in output? Or will we get more inflation instead? On the other hand, if we apply restraint during an inflationary boom, can we count on a reduction in the rate of inflation? Or will we merely get less output? In other words, demand management policies require *both* a knowledge of how monetary and fiscal policies affect aggregate demand, and a knowledge of how the economy responds to changes in aggregate demand. Making sense of what has happened since 1969 is therefore one of the major tasks of macroeconomic theorists. But, before turning to this central question, we lay the background by looking at the Phillips curve traced out in the 1960s.

THE PHILLIPS CURVE OF THE 1960s

During the 1960s, available empirical evidence—including the red curve traced out by the U.S. data in Figure 16-3 and Phillips' similar British curve—pointed strongly toward the conclusion that increases in aggregate demand move the economy along a smooth, stable Phillips curve. Increases in aggregate demand had an effect partly on output and employment, and partly on prices. And, as the economy moved further and further to the left up the Phillips curve, this curve became steeper and steeper. In other words, each additional increase in demand caused more and more inflation and a smaller and smaller decline in the unemployment rate. Why might the economy move along such a curve in response to changes in demand?

Consider, first, the position of businesses. When there is large-scale unemployment of the labor force, plant and equipment are also likely to be used at much less than capacity. If demand increases in these circumstances, the primary response of businesses is to increase

[1]A. W. Phillips, "The Relation between Unemployment and the Rate of Change of Money Wages in the United Kingdom," *Economica,* November 1958, pp. 282–299. For a readable account of the controversies over the Phillips curve (on which this chapter concentrates), see Robert M. Solow, "Down the Phillips Curve with Gun and Camera," in David A. Belsley and others (eds.), *Inflation, Trade and Taxes* (Columbus: Ohio State University Press, 1976), pp. 3–32.

[2]The original Phillips curve showed the rate of change of money wages—rather than inflation—on the vertical axis. Since money wages rise rapidly during periods of high inflation, a similar curve is traced out whichever measure is put on the vertical axis.

output rather than prices. An increase in output will allow the fuller utilization of plant and equipment and result in rising profits. Furthermore, businesses may be skeptical about their ability to make price increases stick. If they raise prices rapidly, their competitors—who also have excess capacity—will be only too eager to capture a larger share of the market.

As the expansion continues and plant and equipment are used more fully, businesses respond differently to an increase in demand. They have less excess capacity. Therefore, as demand increases, they have less opportunity to raise profits by increasing output rapidly. At the same time, they are increasingly in a position to raise prices. Higher prices involve less risk of a loss of markets to competitors, since the competitors are also approaching capacity and are in no position to expand output rapidly to capture additional sales. Furthermore, as the unemployment rate falls, businesses find it harder to hire and keep workers. As the labor market tightens, businesses become increasingly aggressive in their bidding for workers, offering higher wages. As wage rates move upward, the costs of production rise. Businesses respond by raising the prices of their products.

Similarly, labor responds differently to increases in

FIGURE 16-3
Inflation and unemployment
The 1960s trace out a *Phillips curve*. Points for the years 1970 are higher and further to the right, reflecting higher inflation *and* larger unemployment rates.

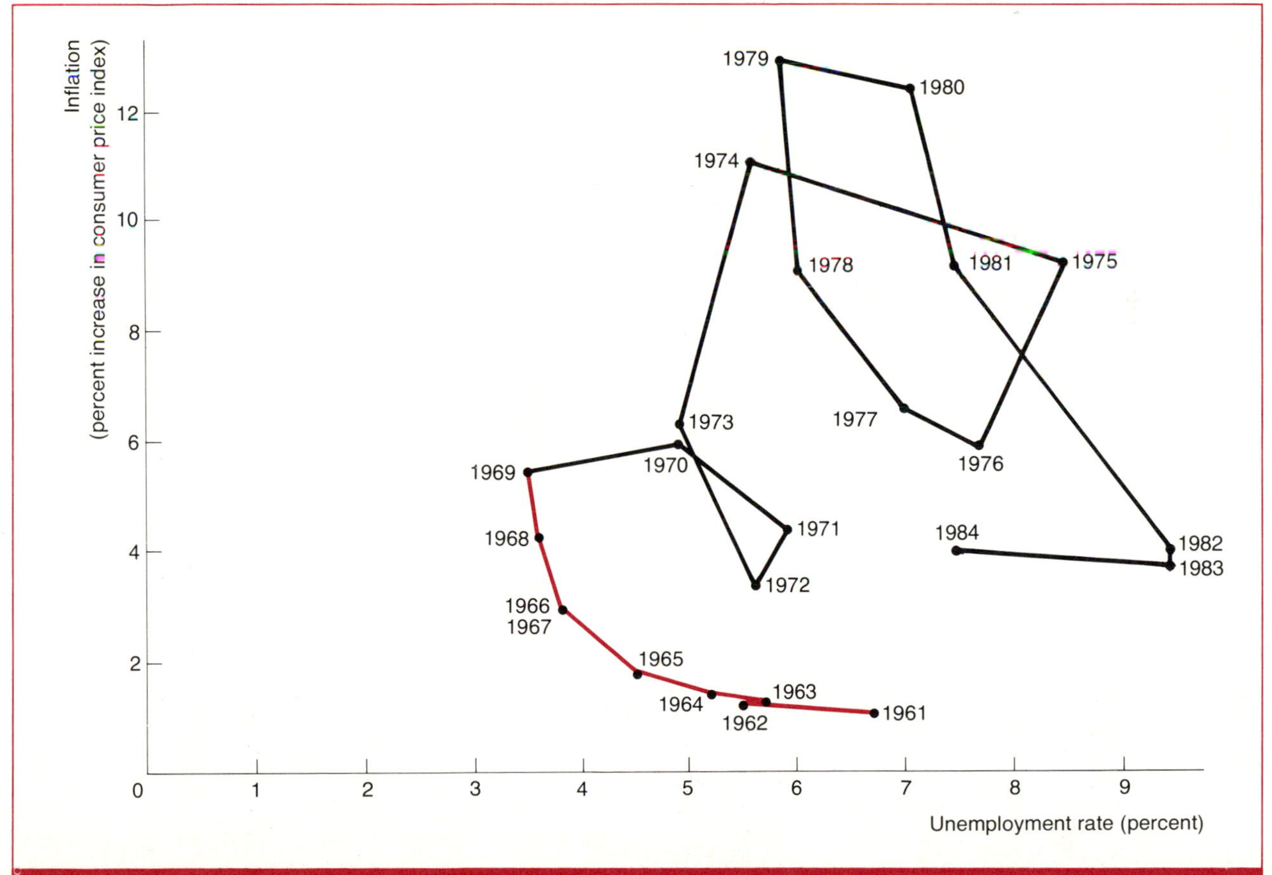

aggregate demand as employment increases. When the unemployment rate is high, the first concern of workers is with jobs. If they are offered work, they are generally quick to take it without too much quibbling over pay. However, as economic expansion continues, the situation gradually changes. Workers become less concerned with getting and keeping a job and more aggressive in demanding higher pay.

These changing conditions, which affect both business and labor, do not come about suddenly at some well-defined point of full employment. On the contrary, they occur gradually. When demand increases, the economy may consequently move smoothly up a Phillips curve like the red curve in Figure 16-3, with successive increases in demand being reflected more in terms of inflation and less in terms of output and employment.

Thus, there were two reasons for policymakers to believe that they faced a well-defined, stable Phillips curve during the 1960s. (1) It conformed to the facts—most notably, Phillips' historical study, and the unfolding situtation in the United States. (2) It seemed plausible from a theoretical viewpoint.

The Policy Dilemma of the 1960s: The Trade-off between Inflation and Unemployment

This belief by policymakers—that they faced a well-defined Phillips curve—presented them with a ***policy dilemma.*** By adjusting aggregate demand policies, they could move the economy along the Phillips curve. But what point should they try to pick? A point like *G* in Figure 16-4, with low inflation and a high rate of unemployment? Or a point like *H,* with low unemployment but a high rate of inflation? Or some point in between? Facing a ***trade-off*** between the goals of high unemployment and price stability, what relative importance should they attach to the two objectives?

Faced with this dilemma, the government responded in two ways. One was to emphasize the objective of high employment. After all, unemployment represents a clear and unambiguous loss to the economy, whereas the costs of inflation are much more difficult to identify. Thus, the Kennedy administration undertook a policy of expanding aggregate demand, aimed at reducing the unemployment rate toward a target of 4%. By itself, such a policy would move the economy from its 1961 position at *G* toward *H* in Figure 16-4.

The second response was to try to figure out a way to do even better. The problem posed by the Phillips curve was that inflation would creep up before the 4% unemployment target was achieved. To prevent this, President Kennedy introduced *wage and price guideposts*. By directly restraining wages and prices as the economy expanded, he hoped to move to a point such as *B* in Figure 16-4, where the economy would reach *both* goals of full employment and stable prices.

The details of the wage-price guideposts are deferred until the end of this chapter. For the moment, it is enough to note that they did not work as well as hoped.

FIGURE 16-4

The problem of the sixties: The inflation-unemployment trade-off

The Phillips curve presents policymakers with a dilemma. By adjusting aggregate demand, they can choose a point on the Phillips curve. But what point should they choose? *G* provides a low rate of inflation but high unemployment. *H* provides high employment but at the cost of substantial inflation. In 1961, the economy was at point *G*. The objective of the Kennedy and Johnson administrations was to reduce unemployment—but without increasing inflation. By restraining wage and price increases as aggregate demand expanded, they hoped to move the economy toward point *B*.

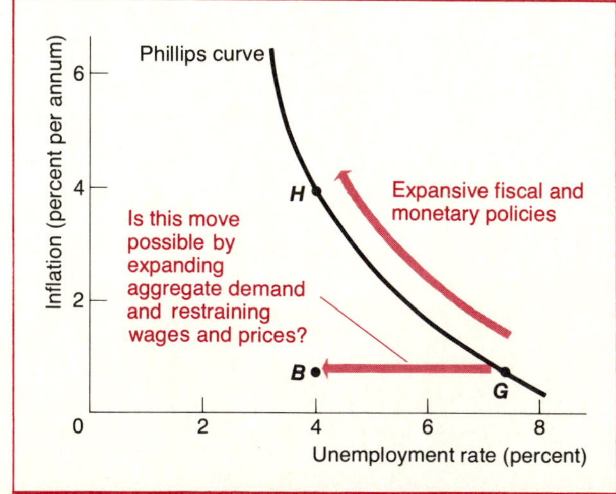

The economy did not in fact move toward *B* during the 1960s. As we have already seen in Figure 16-3, it moved instead along a Phillips curve which became steeper as the economy expanded and the rate of unemployment declined.

THE RECORD SINCE 1970: HIGHER INFLATION AND HIGHER UNEMPLOYMENT

Since 1970, the behavior of the economy has been disconcerting. The previous decade began with high hopes that we could get the best of both worlds, achieving full employment together with price stability. But since 1970, we have suffered the worst of both worlds. High rates of unemployment and inflation have occurred simultaneously. What went wrong? Two principal explanations have been offered.

Cost-Push vs. Demand-Pull Inflation

The age of Keynesian economics is over; the macroeconomic revolution in fiscal and monetary management we owe to Keynes has run afoul of the microeconomic revolution in trade union and corporate power.

John Kenneth Galbraith

The first explanation involves the distinction between ***demand-pull*** and ***cost-push*** inflation. This distinction can be illustrated most easily with the simple aggregate demand and aggregate supply curves in Figure 16-5. The left panel shows what happens when aggregate demand increases—that is, when the aggregate demand curve shifts to the right. Output increases, and unemployment declines. But the rising demand also pulls up prices. The economy moves upward to the right, from *G*

FIGURE 16-5
Demand-pull inflation vs cost-push inflation

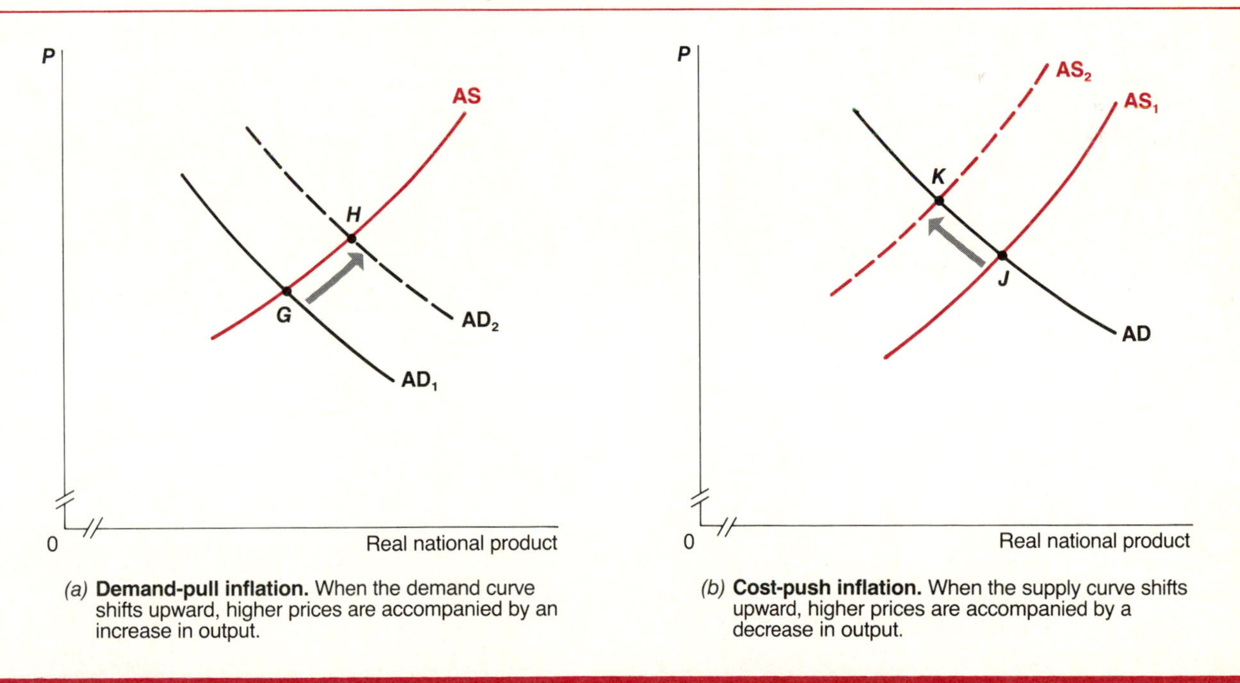

(a) **Demand-pull inflation.** When the demand curve shifts upward, higher prices are accompanied by an increase in output.

(b) **Cost-push inflation.** When the supply curve shifts upward, higher prices are accompanied by a decrease in output.

to *H*. This is the typical inflation—rising prices are accompanied by rising output.

***Demand-pull* inflation occurs when demand is rising rapidly. Buyers bid eagerly for goods and services, "pulling up" their prices.**

Now suppose that strong labor unions and monopolistic companies have the power to influence wages and prices. Even during a period of slack in the economy, when the demand for labor is low and the unemployment rate is high, a strong union may be able to use the threat of a strike to negotiate higher wages. Furthermore, a firm with few competitors may raise its prices even though demand is sluggish. If this firm is producing basic materials, parts, or other intermediate goods, its higher prices will push up the costs of other companies using its products. Businesses with higher costs of labor and material inputs may pass them along to the consumer in the form of higher prices. In other words, there is *cost-push* inflation.

***Cost-push,* or *supply-side,* inflation occurs when wages or other costs rise and these costs are passed along in the form of higher prices. Prices are "pushed up" by rising costs. Cost-push inflation is also sometimes known as *market-power* inflation.**

This possibility is illustrated in the right-hand panel of Figure 16-5. As costs rise, the aggregate supply curve shifts upward, from AS_1 to AS_2. As the economy moves from *J* to *K,* rising prices are accompanied by a *decline* in output and a rise in the unemployment rate.

In the late 1950s, cost push was used to explain why inflation and unemployment were both increasing. This early round in the cost-push debate was heated. In particular, it invited a search for culprits. Business executives blamed inflation on the aggressive and "irresponsible" bargaining of labor unions for higher wages that had forced businesses—so they claimed—to pass along their higher labor costs in terms of higher prices. On the other hand, labor blamed powerful corporations for pushing up prices in their greed for "fantastic profits."

Oil While labor and management blamed each other for cost-push inflation during the late 1950s, one cost-push culprit stood out in the 1970s: the Organization of Petroleum Exporting Countries (OPEC). In a brief period during 1973 and 1974, OPEC doubled and then redoubled the prices which importers had to pay for oil. In 1979–1980, oil prices more than doubled again.

Because of the importance of oil as a source of power for industry, as a fuel for our transportation system, and as a source of heat for our homes and factories, the skyrocketing price of oil had a powerful effect on the United States and, indeed, on all oil-importing countries. Businesses with higher costs for power, heating, and transportation tried to pass these higher costs along to consumers in the form of higher prices. The economy was subjected to severe cost-push pressures, with inflation soaring into the "double-digit" range—that is, above 10%—in 1974, 1979, and 1980.

The cost-push idea can be illustrated by an upward shift of the aggregate supply curve in Figure 16-5*b* or, alternatively, by an upward shift of the Phillips curve from PC_1 to PC_2 in Figure 16-6. Earlier, we saw that even a stable Phillips curve—such as PC_1 in Figure 16-6—presents the authorities with a dilemma. They can choose low inflation, but this will mean high unemployment (at point *G*). Alternatively, they can choose low unemployment, but this will mean high inflation (at point *H*). Or they can pick an intermediate point, such as *J*. Observe how much more difficult the situation becomes when cost-push forces are strong, and the Phillips curve shifts upward. If the authorities keep aggregate demand growing at a stable rate, both unemployment and inflation will increase, as illustrated by the move from *J* to *K*. If they decide to prevent any increase in inflation, regardless of the cost, they will have to restrain aggregate demand. The result will be a move from *J* to *L*. While inflation will be no higher at *L* than it was at *J*, there will be a large increase in unemployment. On the other hand, if the authorities aim at preventing any increase in unemployment, they will stimulate aggregate demand and the rate of inflation will go even higher as the economy moves to *M*.

The sharp upward shift of the Phillips curve led to a major policy disagreement in 1974 and 1975. On the one hand, the Ford administration and the Federal Reserve were worried at the prospect of runaway inflation, and leaned toward tight aggregate demand policies. The rate of increase in the money stock was reduced, and the President recommended a tax *increase* in late 1974. Thus, the Fed and the President apparently were aiming at a point between *K* and *L* in Figure 16-6. However, congressional concern over this strategy grew as the recession of 1974–1975 deepened, and Congress moved to expand aggregate demand by *cutting* taxes in early 1975. During 1974 and 1975, the net result of the oil price shock and the policy response was a combination of high unemployment rates—averaging more than 7%—and high inflation rates, averaging more than 10% per year.

Between 1975 and 1978, oil price increases were much more moderate than in 1973 and 1974. This helped to reduce inflation during the sustained economic recovery that began in mid-1975. But then, when the revolution in Iran interrupted Iranian oil supplies in 1979, OPEC took the opportunity to jack up prices once more.

FIGURE 16-6

Cost-push inflation: The policy problem

Cost-push shifts the Phillips curve upward, from PC_1 to PC_2. If demand is restrained in order to fight inflation, the unemployment rate will increase, from *J* to *L*. If demand is expanded in order to keep the unemployment rate from rising, the rate of inflation will increase, from *J* to *M*.

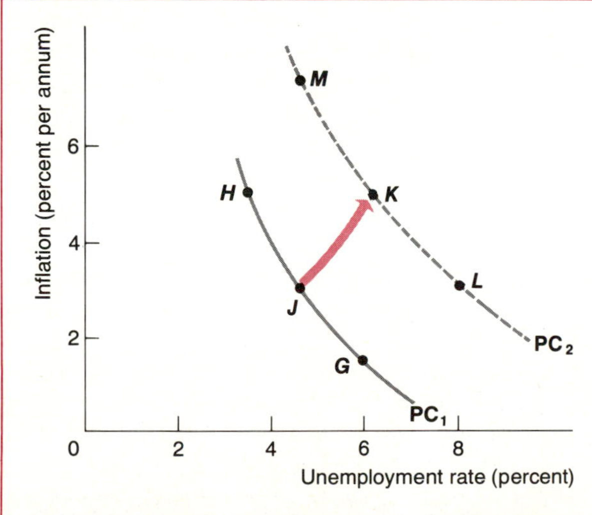

Again the result was a combination of high inflation and recession.

In summary, this first explanation of stagflation depends on disturbances from the cost side. The Phillips curve can be shifted up by aggressive wage and pricing activities by unions and businesses or by shocks from abroad, such as the increase in the price of imported oil. When such a shift occurs, the economy is likely to suffer an increase in both inflation and unemployment, with the mix depending on aggregate demand policies.

PRICE EXPECTATIONS AND THE WAGE-PRICE SPIRAL: THE ACCELERATIONIST ARGUMENT

The second explanation of simultaneous high rates of inflation and unemployment goes further, throwing into question the whole concept of a permanent curve such as the one discovered by Phillips. According to this line of argument, the Phillips curve is inherently unstable. It *shifts whenever people's expectations of inflation change*. In particular, it shifts upward as inflation gathers momentum. If the managers of monetary and fiscal policies aim for a low rate of unemployment, inflation will accelerate to higher and higher rates. Hence, this is known as the ***accelerationist*** argument.

The easiest way to explain this argument is to assume initially that prices have been stable for a long period of time. On the basis of past experience, they are expected to remain stable into the indefinite future. The economy rests at a stable equilibrium at *G* on the initial Phillips curve (Figure 16-7), where the inflation rate is zero. Now suppose that the government decides that the unemployment rate at *G* is unacceptable. Expansive fiscal and monetary policies are introduced in order to increase aggregate demand and reduce the unemployment rate to a target of U_T.

What happens? To meet the higher demand, producers need more workers. Job vacancies increase, and those looking for jobs get them easily and quickly. Production increases and unemployment falls. In the face of higher demand, producers gradually begin to raise prices. But in the early stages of inflation, little change takes place in money wages. Most collective bargaining contracts are for 3 years, and union wages change only slowly as a result. Nonunion wages are also sticky. People may work on individual contracts that run for 1 year or more. Even where there is no written contract, it is customary to review wages only periodically—say, once a year. Thus, the initial reaction to the increase in demand is a relatively large increase in output, only a moderate increase in prices, and an even smaller increase in wages. The economy moves along the Phillips curve to point *H* (Figure 16-7).

FIGURE 16-7

The acceleration of inflation: The wage-price spiral

If demand is continuously increased by whatever amount is necessary to maintain the low target rate of unemployment U_T, then the result is an ever-increasing rate of inflation. The economy moves successively to points *H, J, K,* and higher. (The original Phillips curve PC_1 shows how the economy responds to changes in aggregate demand during the short-run period *when the initial wage contracts remain in force*.)

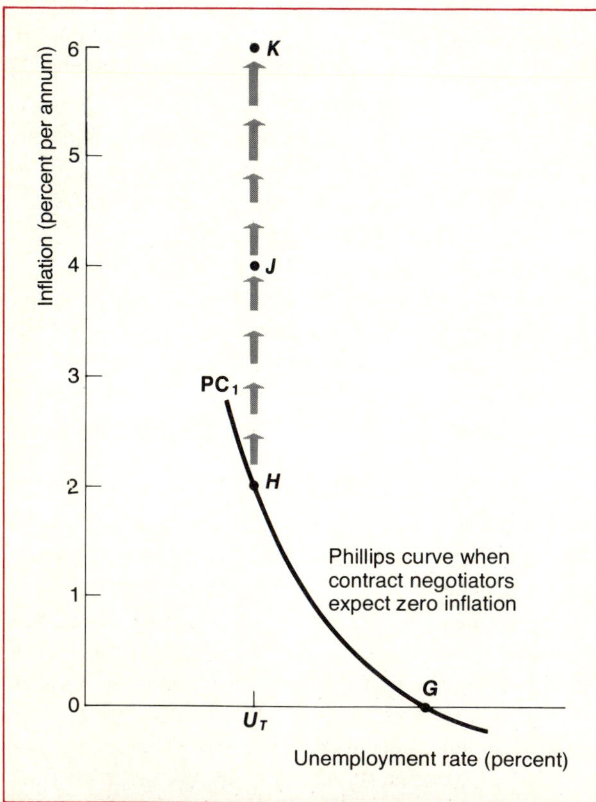

However, *point H is not stable*. The initial Phillips curve (PC_1) reflects wage *contracts that were negotiated on the assumption of stable prices*. But prices are no longer stable, and the contracts do not last forever. As new contract negotiations begin, workers observe that their real wages—the amount of goods and services their wages will buy—have been eroded by inflation. They demand a cost-of-living catch-up. So long as aggregate demand rises rapidly enough to keep the economy operating at full blast, the unions are in a good position to get their demands. With booming markets, employers capitulate to strike threats. Nonunion employees are likewise granted raises to keep them from quitting to look for more highly paid work. Because demand is high and rising, businesses can easily pass along the higher wages in the form of higher prices, and they do so. The rate of inflation accelerates; the economy moves to point *J*, above the original Phillips curve. But, with a higher rate of inflation, workers find that once again they have been cheated by inflation; once again their real wages are less than expected. At the next round of wage negotiations, they demand a larger cost-of-living catch-up. The ***wage-price spiral*** gathers momentum. So long as demand is expanded enough to keep unemployment at the low target rate of U_T, inflation will *continue to accelerate,* from *H* to *J* to *K,* and so on.

Thus, the Phillips curve gives the wrong impression. It creates the illusion that there is a simple trade-off between inflation and unemployment, that a low rate of unemployment can be ''bought'' with a moderate, steady rate of inflation. But, in fact, the cost of trying to achieve a low rate of unemployment is much more serious: *an ever accelerating rate of inflation*. Wages and prices spiral upward, with higher prices leading to higher and higher wage demands, and higher wages being passed along in the form of higher and higher prices.

Limiting the Rate of Inflation

An ever-accelerating rate of inflation is intolerable. If prices rise faster and faster, sooner or later the whole monetary system will break down and the economy will revert to an inefficient barter system. (The rate required for a complete breakdown is very high indeed—

thousands of percent per annum. Nevertheless, severe disruptions may be caused even by rates of inflation of 10% or 20%.) At some time, therefore, the monetary and fiscal policymakers will decide to draw the line; they will refuse to increase aggregate demand without limit.

To keep this illustration simple, assume that (1) the monetary and fiscal line is drawn sooner rather than later and (2) aggregate demand policies can be adjusted quickly and precisely. As soon as the economy gets to point H, the government recognizes the danger of an ever-accelerating inflation. It therefore switches aggregate demand policies. Instead of increasing aggregate demand by whatever amount is necessary to maintain a low target rate of unemployment, the authorities limit aggregate demand to whatever degree is necessary to prevent inflation from rising above the 2% level reached at H. In other words, the authorities *change the policy target*. Their objective no longer is to keep the unemployment rate low at U_T, but instead is to keep inflation from rising above the 2% target level I_T (Figure 16-8).

What happens? Workers still push for higher wages because the 2% rate of inflation is still eroding their purchasing power. But employers are now in a bind. They cannot easily pass along higher wages because of the restraint on demand. Furthermore, the restraint on demand means that output begins to fall and unemployment rises. The economy moves to the right.

FIGURE 16-8
Limiting the rate of inflation
If the managers of monetary and fiscal policies switch targets, limiting demand to prevent inflation greater than I_T, the economy will begin to move to the right.

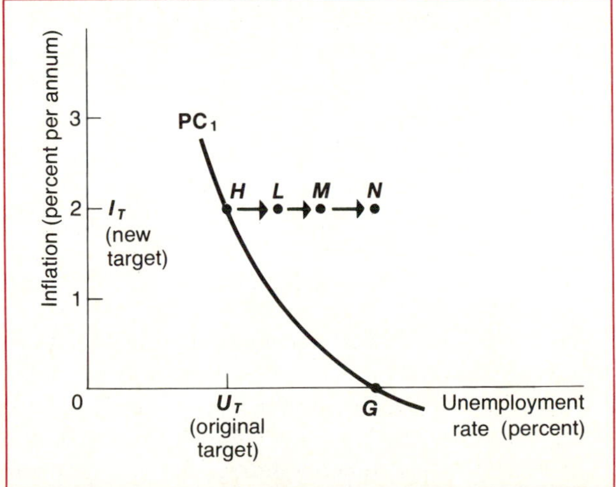

The Vertical Long-Run Phillips Curve

As demand is restrained, the economy moves to the right. But how far? Suppose demand is controlled in such a way as to keep inflation permanently at a rate of 2%. Where will the ultimate equilibrium be in Figure 16-8? At L? At M? Farther to the right? There are reasons to believe that the economy will stop at N, directly above the original equilibirium G.

To see why, let us go back to the initial point, G. This represented a stable equilibrium. It was the result of an extended experience with a zero rate of inflation. Both businesses and labor had a chance to adjust completely to the stable price level. If they now get a chance to adjust completely to a 2% rate of inflation—with a 2% yearly increase being added to prices and wages—the new equilibrium should be at N, where both labor and business are in the same *real* position as at G. At G, prices were stable. Now, at N, prices are rising by 2%. However, workers are just as well off as they were at G because they are receiving enough additional money income to compensate for the inflation. Their real wage is unaffected by the inflation. Consequently, they should be neither more nor less eager to work. Businesses are also in the same real situation at N as at G. They pay 2% more for labor and for material inputs each year than they would have paid at G, but they are compensated by the average increase of 2% in their prices. Their profits are the same in real terms. Therefore, they should hire the same number of workers at N as they did at G. Thus, N lies directly above G, and the unemployment rate is the same at N as at G.

With a steady 2% rate of inflation, the economy moves eventually to N, where the unemployment rate, real wages, and real profits are the same as at G. Alternatively, if the rate of inflation rises to 4% before monetary and fiscal policy makers draw the line to prevent more rapid inflation, the economy eventually moves to R (Figure 16-9) or, with a steady 6% rate of inflation, to T. All these are points of stable equilibrium. In each case, employers and employees have adjusted completely to the prevailing rate of inflation. (In contrast, point *H* was unstable because workers had not yet had a chance to renegotiate their wages to reflect the new inflation.)

In other words, the points of long-run equilibrium trace out a vertical line; the ***long-run Phillips curve*** (PC_L) is *perfectly vertical. In the long-run, there is no trade-off* between inflation and unemployment. By accepting more inflation, we cannot *permanently* achieve a lower rate of unemployment. Expansive demand policies cause a lower rate of unemployment only during a temporary period of disequilibrium—at *H*, for example. During the temporary disequilibrium, workers and others are committed to contracts they would not have accepted if they had correctly anticipated the rate of inflation. As people have time to adjust, unemployment gravitates toward the equilibrium or ***natural rate.***

FIGURE 16-9

The vertical long-run Phillips curve

The economy gravitates toward the vertical long-run Phillips curve PC_L as the negotiators of wages and all other contracts adjust to the prevailing rate of inflation. There is no long-run trade-off between unemployment and inflation.

However, the short-run Phillips curve is *not* vertical. For example, once contracts have adjusted completely to a 4% rate of inflation at *R*, then an unexpected disturbance in aggregate demand will cause the economy to move along the short-run Phillips curve $PC_{4\%}$ running through *R*. Thus, a spurt in demand will cause an increase in output, a fall in unemployment, and an increase in inflation as the economy moves from *R* to *S*.

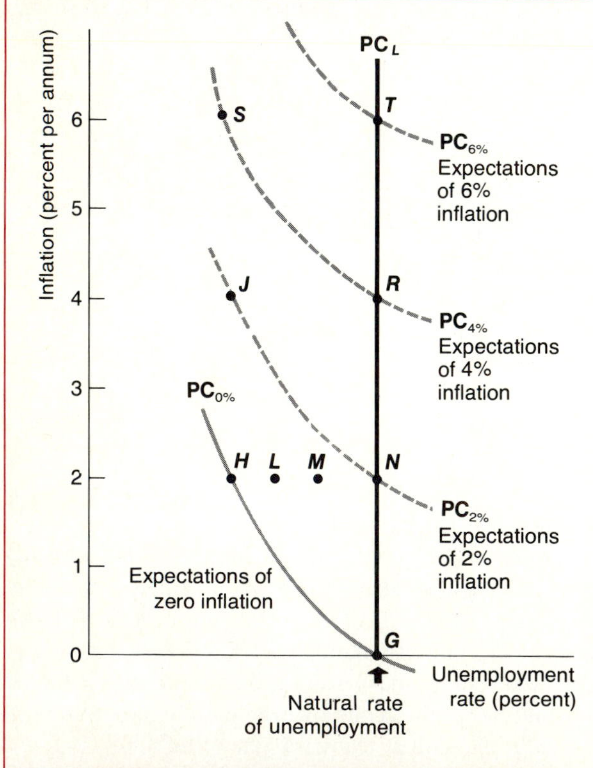

The *long-run Phillips curve* is the curve (or line) traced out by the possible points of long-run equilibrium, that is, the points where people have adjusted completely to the prevailing rate of inflation. At such points, actual inflation is the same as expected inflation.

The *natural rate of unemployment* is the equilibrium rate that exists when people have adjusted completely to the prevailing rate of inflation. (Alternatively, it may be defined as the equilibrium rate that exists when the inflation rate is accurately anticipated by the public.)

The *accelerationist* argument includes the following related propositions:

1. The long-run Phillips curve is vertical. There is an equilibrium or "natural" rate of unemployment which is independent of the rate of inflation.

2. If demand is stimulated by however much is needed to keep the unemployment rate below the natural rate, the result will be a continuous acceleration of inflation.

Through each of the long-run equilibrium points—such as *N*, *R*, or *T* in Figure 16-9—there is a *short-run Phillips curve,* each reflecting contracts based on the prevailing rate of inflation. For example, the short-run Phillips curve ($PC_{4\%}$) running through *R* is based on the expectation by contract negotiators that there will be a continuing rate of inflation of 4% per year. Suppose that after a number of years at *R,* the authorities adjust monetary and fiscal policies to make aggregate demand grow more rapidly. Faced with a high demand, businesses increase output, hire more workers, and begin to raise prices by more than 4% per annum. Their profits temporarily shoot up because workers are committed to the old labor contracts, based on expectations of 4% inflation. The economy moves along the short-run Phillips curve $PC_{4\%}$ to a point such as *S,* with a low rate of unemployment. But *S* is unstable for the same reason that *H* was unstable. Point *S* results from wage contracts that were agreed to when inflation was expected to be 4%. But actual inflation is 6%. Therefore, contracts will be adjusted during the next round of negotiations. When wage contracts are adjusted upward, an accelerating wage-price spiral will result if the authorities continue to follow expansive aggregate demand policies. Alternatively, if demand managers take steps to prevent any further increase in inflation, the economy will move to the right, back toward the long-run Phillips curve and the natural rate of unemployment at *T.*

Note that there is a similarity between this accelerationist, or natural rate, theory and the earlier explanation of inflation based on cost-push. In each case, the Phillips curve shifts upward, and in each case higher wage contracts can play an important role in the shift. But here the similarity stops. While cost-push theorists see higher wages as a major *cause* of inflation, accelerationists believe that *both* wage and price increases are the result of a *single* underlying cause: excess demand. The government should not go looking for culprits in the form of powerful unions or powerful businesses or OPEC. Rather, the culprit is right in Washington: the government itself (including the Federal Reserve), which has generated the inflationary demand in the first place with excessively expansionary policies.

The vertical long-run Phillips curve brings us back to the view of classical quantity theorists. *In the long run,* changes in aggregate demand affect prices (*P*) and not the quantity of output (*Q*) or employment. Thus, the vertical long-run Phillips curve turns out to be the same as the vertical aggregate supply curve of classical economics (originally shown in Figure 9-2), but in another guise.

Because we are brought back to the classical view, it is not surprising that the case for the vertical long-run Phillips curve—together with other aspects of the accelerationist argument—came from the pen of one of the leading monetarists, Milton Friedman. (Another early proponent was Edmund Phelps of Columbia University.)[3] Friedman wrote, "There is *always* a *temporary tradeoff* between inflation and unemployment; there is *no permanent tradeoff.*" The short-run Phillips curve slopes downward to the right; the long-run Phillips curve is vertical.

During the 1970s, the idea of a vertical long-run Phillips curve became widely accepted by those in the Keynesian and classical traditions alike. Now, it would be difficult to find any economist who believes that the original curved Phillips curve represents a stable long-run relationship. By 1975, Arthur Okun was willing to concede on behalf of the original Phillips curve school: "We are all accelerationists now."[4]

Nevertheless, two matters of controversy remain:

1. Some economists in the Keynesian tradition argue that the long-run Phillips curve bends to the right as the rate of inflation gets very low, even though it may be vertical throughout most of its length. This view is explained in Box 16-1. Furthermore, some Keynesians argue that the acceleration of inflation in the 1970s had little to do with excess demand, as the accelerationists claimed. Instead, it resulted primarily from "supply shocks," most notably the two major increases in the international price of oil.

2. At the other end of the intellectual spectrum, some go beyond the views of Phelps and Friedman to argue

[3]Milton Friedman, "The Role of Monetary Policy," *American Economic Review,* March 1968, pp. 1–17; and Edmund S. Phelps, "Phillips Curves, Expectations of Inflation and Optimal Unemployment over Time," *Economica,* August 1967, pp. 254–281.

[4]Okun, "Inflation: Its Mechanics and Welfare Costs," *Brookings Papers on Economic Activity* 2:1975, p. 356. Okun was paraphrasing an earlier concession of Friedman: "In one sense, we are all Keynesians now." [Friedman had, however, tacked on the qualification that "in another [sense], no one is a Keynesian any longer." From Milton Friedman, *Dollars and Deficits* (Englewood Cliffs, N.J.: Prentice-Hall, 1968), p. 15.]

Okun pointed out that the data fit a Phillips curve "like a glove" during the 1960s. However, he observed that, since 1970, "the Phillips curve has become an unidentified flying object."

BOX 16-1

A CURVED LONG-RUN PHILLIPS CURVE?

"We are all accelerationists now." At least, we are all accelerationists during periods such as the past two decades, when inflation has consistently been above 3%. Most economists acknowledge that even more expansive demand policies would not reduce the unemployment rate in the long run. Above an inflation rate of 2% or 3%, the long-run Phillips curve is vertical.

However, some economists—particularly those in the Keynesian tradition—still believe that the long-run Phillips curve bends to the right as the economy approaches and crosses the horizontal axis. If aggregate demand were held to little or no increase, year after year, the result would be a high rate of unemployment, year after year. This is illustrated by point *B* in Figure 16-10.

There are two grounds for this belief. First is a theoretical argument which can be traced back to Keynes' *General Theory*. Second is the evidence of the Great Depression.

Consider first the theoretical argument. As we have already seen, the case for the vertical Phillips curve can be explained by looking at what happens as inflation begins to rise. Workers are concerned with their *real* wages and demand additional money wages to compensate for the inflation. As a result, the short-run Phillips curve shifts upward.

Suppose, however, that demand is slack, creating downward pressures on wages. In such circumstances, said Keynes, workers are concerned not only with their real wages but also with *money* wages. If prices are falling, then workers would be able to maintain their real standard of living even if they accepted cuts in their money wages. However, they will resist such cuts. In his *General Theory* (p. 14), Keynes suggested a reason: People who accept an outright cut in money wages will find their *relative* positions deteriorating, compared with those who do not accept cuts. A cut in the money wage represents a humiliation that workers will resist strongly, regardless of what is happening to the level of prices and to real wages.

Why should this unwillingness to accept lower money wages matter? After all, we live in a growing economy. In most years, productivity increases and the trend of real wages is upward. Thus, even in an economy with zero inflation, the average nominal wage should increase.

However, not all industries are average. Even in a growing economy, some industries decline. As their demand falls, they will discharge workers, adding to the rolls of the unemployed. This process may be slowed down if the industry cuts its prices relative to other prices. Its ability to do so depends in part upon the wage it pays. If the rate of inflation is zero and average wages in the economy are going up by 1% per annum, the declining industry gains a wage advantage of only 1% by giving its workers no increase at all. On the other hand, if the inflation rate is 2% and the average money wage increase is 3%, the declining industry may gain a 3% advantage by keeping nominal wages constant. The workers will not like their declining real wages. They may grumble. But they will go along rather than face unemployment. However, they would not have acceded to a cut in nominal wages.

Thus, by permitting workers to accept some decline in real wages gracefully without the humiliation of a nominal wage cut, a modest rate of inflation tends to maintain employment in declining industries. Consequently, there may be a less serious unemployment problem with a 2% rate of inflation (at point *A* in Figure 16-10) than with a stable price level (at *B*). In short, the unwillingness to accept lower nominal wage rates provides a reason for believing that the long-run Phillips curve bends to the right as it approaches the axis.

It also means that, in the face of a collapse in demand, the unemployment rate may rise very high and may stay for an extended time at a point such as *C*. Because firms find that they can cut nominal wages very little, if at all, they resist cuts in their prices. The very low aggregate demand shows up primarily in terms of low output and high unemployment, and very little in terms of falling prices.

Some fragmentary evidence from recent decades suggests that money incomes as well as real incomes may indeed be important. For example, during the 1970s the real incomes of many professors fell, since their salaries failed to keep pace with inflation. If prices had been constant, and if administrations had tried to bring about exactly the the same real cuts by reducing dollar salaries, it is likely that professors would have objected much more strongly.

However, it is to the Great Depression that we

must go for comprehensive evidence regarding downward wage rigidity. Suppose, for the moment, we assume that prices and wages *do* adjust downward and that the long-run Phillips curve as a consequence is vertical right down to the axis and beyond. Suppose, then, that aggregate demand is slack, causing temporary unemployment in excess of the "natural rate." Not only should inflation be rung out of the economy, but prices should start to fall *at an accelerating rate.* (The argument is similar to that in Figure 16-7, except that prices are now falling rather than rising. Workers are willing to accept lower and lower money wages as prices fall.) In fact, nothing of the sort happened during the depression. Prices did fall between 1929 and 1933. However, they then stabilized. Between 1933 and 1937, prices actually rose, even though the unemployment rate consistently exceeded 10%. This evidence is flatly inconsistent with the accelerationist hypothesis. If that hypothesis were correct, prices should have fallen faster and faster, as long as unemployment remained above the natural rate.

Not surprisingly, this complication has not been a major preoccupation of economists in the past quarter century, when the pressure on prices has been upward, not downward. But it is of considerable historical interest. Moreover, if anti-inflationary policies are successful, it may become relevant once more. The implication of a diagram such as Figure 16-10 is that, once inflation has been reduced to 1% or 2%, we should be satisfied and declare victory. Any attempt to stabilize prices further may raise the problem of a trade-off, in terms of higher unemployment.

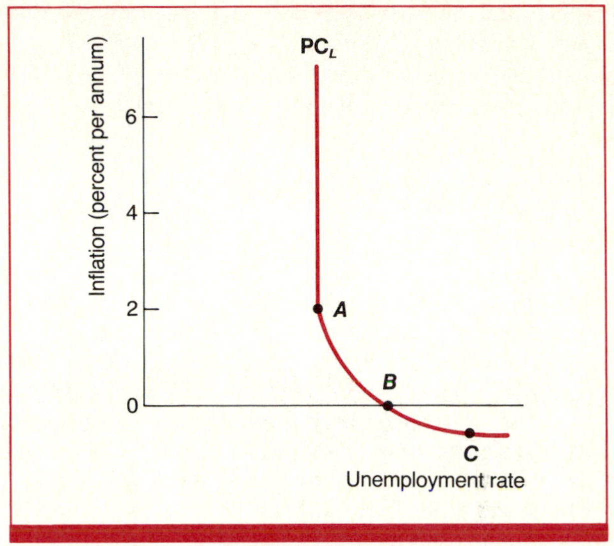

FIGURE 16-10
A curved long-run Phillips curve?

that there is no tradeoff between inflation and unemployment at all, *even in the short run*. This will be explained later, in Box 16-2.

THE PROBLEM OF UNWINDING INFLATIONARY EXPECTATIONS

The short-run Phillips curve represents another trap for policymakers. Those who decide on monetary and fiscal policies may think that they can achieve low rates of unemployment to the left of the long-run Phillips curve by expansive demand policies. In fact, they will be able to maintain such a low rate of unemployment only if they allow inflation to spiral higher and higher.

Furthermore, the problem is even worse than that. Once inflation becomes engrained in negotiators' expectations, it can be eliminated with demand-management policies only at the cost of a high rate of unemployment, to the right of the long-run Phillips curve.

This is shown in Figure 16-11. Suppose the economy has reached point *T*, with inflation consistently running at 6% year after year. This point is stable; inflation will neither rise nor fall and the unemployment rate remains steady. Now, suppose that policymakers decide that an inflation rate of 6% is too high. They are determined to reduce it by restrictive monetary and fiscal policies.

As aggregate demand is restrained, businesses find their sales falling. Production is cut back and workers are laid off. The unemployment rate rises. Because of intensifying competitive pressures as businesses scramble to make sales, businesses no longer insist on such high price increases and the rate of inflation begins to slacken off. However, this does not happen quickly. Businesses are still committed to pay the hefty wage increases under the old labor contracts; their costs continue to rise even though demand is slack. As a result, the short-run effect of the restrained demand shows up most strongly in a fall in output and a rise in unemployment, and only to a limited extent in lower inflation. The economy moves to point *V*.

The high short-run costs of an anti-inflationary aggregate demand policy—in terms of greater unemployment—have been emphasized by many economists. For example, Arthur Okun presented the following grim prospect to Congress:

> Each dollar trimmed from [nominal] GNP means a loss of about 90¢ of output, and the saving of about a dime on price level. Any anti-inflationary proposal that relies solely on balancing the budget and tightening money is, in reality, a proposal for an encore of that experience. And it should carry a truth-in-packaging label.[5]

Because point *V* is off the long-run Phillips curve, it is unstable. It is on the short-run Phillips curve running through point *T*, reflecting wage contracts negotiated on the expectation that inflation would continue at 6% per year. But actual inflation is now only 4%. Because of the lower inflation rate, workers are willing to settle for more moderate wage increases at the next round of wage negotiations. This willingness is reinforced by their desire to protect their jobs during a period of high unemployment. Furthermore, employers take a strong bargaining stance because of disappointing sales and low profits.

When wage settlements become more moderate, the economy moves from point *V*. If monetary and fiscal policies are kept tight, the rate of inflation will continue to drop. The economy will move down from *V* to progressively lower points. The argument here is similar to that in Figure 16-7, except that everything is operating in the opposite direction.

On the other hand, if monetary and fiscal restraint is eased as the economy reaches 4% inflation, sales will begin to revive, the unemployment rate will fall, and the economy will move back toward the long-run Phillips curve at point *R*. This argument corresponds to the earlier one in Figure 16-8, again operating in the opposite direction.

This theory provides part of the explanation for the simultaneous high rates of unemployment and inflation in the period from 1974 to 1981. (Part of the explanation also may be found in the cost-push forces arising in the international oil market.) During the late 1960s, demand inflation was allowed to gather steam, both because of the desire to get unemployment down and because of government spending for the Vietnam war. The inflationary momentum was accelerated by the expansive aggregate demand policies of 1971–1973 and 1977–1979. Then, when high and rising rates of inflation became a matter of grave concern, demand was restrained in 1974 and at the beginning of the 1980s. The anti-inflationary policies led to major recessions in 1974–1975 and in 1981–1982. In each case, the inflation rate was driven down, but at the cost of a very high rate of unemployment.

FIGURE 16-11

High unemployment while inflation is being unwound

Once inflation becomes built into contracts, it is painful to unwind. The short-run Phillips curve shown here reflects contracts based on the expectation of 6% inflation. It takes a period of high unemployment at *V* before wage contracts are adjusted downward.

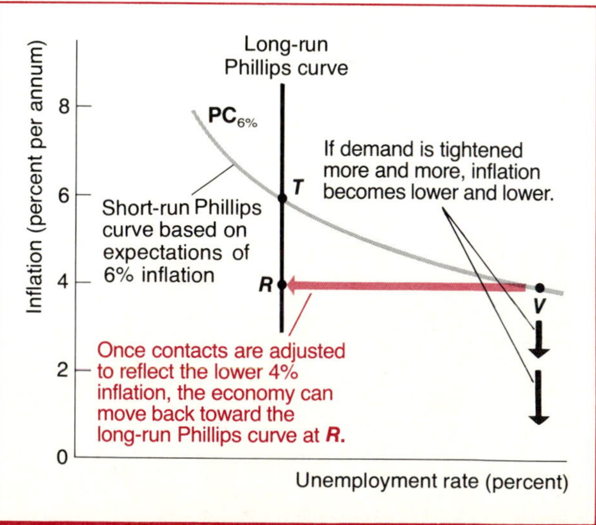

[5]Testimony before the Joint Economic Committee, U.S. Congress, April 30, 1979. Okun served as the chairman of the Council of Economic Advisers under President Johnson.

BOX 16-2

THE THEORY OF RATIONAL EXPECTATIONS: NO TRADE-OFF, EVEN IN THE SHORT RUN?

Friedman and Phelps argued that the long-run Phillips curve was vertical, and thus cast doubt whether there is a *long-run* trade-off between inflation and unemployment. Recently, some economists have taken an even stronger position, casting doubt on whether policymakers face a trade-off *even in the short run*. The chief doubters are members of the ***rational expectations*** school, an offshoot of monetarism.

To introduce the general idea of rational expectations, we consider the accelerationist argument in more detail. We have already seen that, according to this argument, an attempt to hold unemployment at U_T—less than the natural, or equilibrium, rate U_N—leads to an ever-accelerating inflation. To summarize briefly: From initial point of equilibrium *G* in Figure 16-12, an increase in aggregate demand causes unemployment to decrease and prices to rise. The economy moves to *H*. But *H* is not a stable equilibrium. *H* is on the short-run Phillips curve $PC_{0\%}$ which is based on the expectation of zero inflation. However, actual inflation is running at 2% per annum. Contracts are adjusted upward to compensate for the 2% inflation, causing the short-run Phillips curve to shift up to $PC_{2\%}$. If the government wants to keep unemployment at the low target rate of U_T, it will have to increase aggregate demand more rapidly, moving the economy from *H* to *J* in the next period.

Suppose we have gotten to *J* in this manner, with actual inflation at 4%. The question is, on what rate of inflation will the next round of contracts be based? What rate of inflation will people expect in the next period?

The answer, according to the original accelerationist argument, is that the expected rate for the future will be the same as the *actual* rate today—in our example, the 4% rate of inflation at point *J*. (This is an example of *adaptive expectations;* people's expectations adapt to past inflation.) If people adjust to inflation in this way, the short-run Phillips curve will shift up to $PC_{4\%}$. By increasing aggregate demand enough, the authorities can move the economy to *K*, keeping unemployment at the low rate U_T.

However, this is not necessarily the correct answer. Rational expectations theorists point out that the public has already been fooled twice. They expected zero inflation, but got 2% inflation at *H* instead. Then they expected 2% inflation and were wrong again. Inflation was 4% as the economy moved to *J*. It is therefore not rational for people to expect that they will necessarily get the same inflation next period that they have today. Once people figure out the authorities' strong commitment to a low rate of unemployment, they will come to expect that future inflation will be *worse* than inflation today. Hence, when the economy is at *J*, a *rational expectation* would be that inflation in the future will be higher than the 4% that exists today; it will be all the way up to, say, 6%. This high expected future rate—not the existing 4%—becomes the basis for renegotiating contracts. In other words, when the economy is at *J* and people have a chance to renegotiate contracts, the short-run Phillips curve shifts up from $PC_{2\%}$, not to $PC_{4\%}$, but rather all the way up to $PC_{6\%}$.

Rational expectations are based on available information, including information about the policies being pursued by the authorities. The public does not make systematic mistakes. (In this example, they learn not to keep underestimating future inflation.)

There are now two possibilities:

1. The authorities remain determined to keep unemployment at the small percentage U_T, and expand aggregate demand at an increasingly rapid rate in order to do so. The economy moves from *J* to *M*, leapfrogging over *K*. The rate of inflation has jumped from 4% at *J* all the way to 8% at *M*. The public has once again been fooled. (They expected 6% inflation, but got 8%.) No matter what inflation they have anticipated in the past, they have gotten more. Next time, how much inflation will they anticipate? 15%? 20%? More? The next jump in the inflation rate may be huge.

   Thus, so long as demand-management authorities attempt to keep unemployment less than the natural rate U_N, *rational expectations make inflation even more severe.* Indeed, the lid may be blown right off the inflation rate *as soon as the public figures out what the authorities are up to.*

2. The second possibility at point *J* is that the author-

ities recognize the danger of runaway inflation and accordingly do not expand aggregate demand so rapidly. In this case, the economy moves from *J* to *L*, where the inflation rate is at least stable. At *L*, equilibrium exists: The public expects 6% inflation and gets it.

Rational Expectations Make It Easier to Unwind Inflation

Now consider what happens if the authorities take a further step and try to unwind inflation by following restrictive demand policies. We shall see that rational expectations make it *easier* to lower inflation.

Suppose the economy is initially at point *L*, where inflation is 6%, and the authorities are determined to reduce that rate. Let us reconsider the traditional argument, based on the assumption that people expect the current rate of inflation to continue; that is, the short-run Phillips curve is $PC_{6\%}$. When the authorities tighten aggregate demand policy, the economy moves from *L* to *R*, where inflation has dropped from 6% to 5%. With people expecting current inflation to continue, contracts are now written on the expectation of a 5% inflation rate. Thus the short-run PC curve shifts down to $PC_{5\%}$. If the authorities continue to pursue tight enough policies to keep the unemployment rate at U_R, substantially greater than the natural rate, the economy will move to *S* in the next period, then to

FIGURE 16-12
Rational expectations and the acceleration of inflation

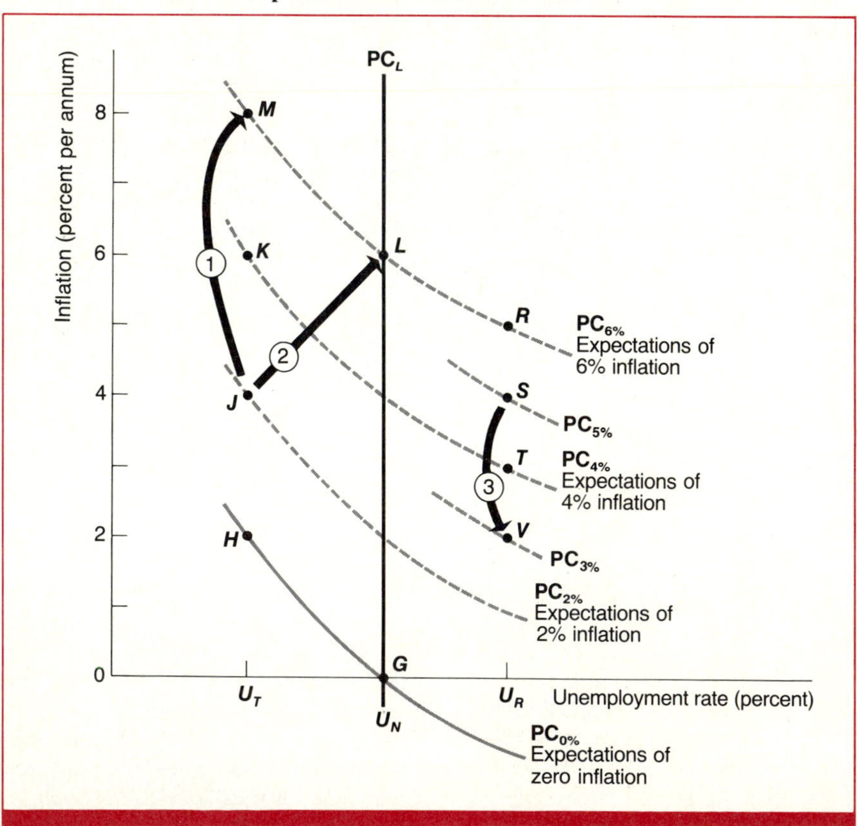

T, and so on. Thus, the inflation rate is reduced—but very painfully. The unemployment rate is high, while inflation comes down only 1% each time period.

However, this traditional argument is once more based on irrational expectations. People expect that inflation will be the same in the future as it is now. But that's not what's happening. The inflation rate is coming down each period.

Once people learn that the authorities are firmly committed to reducing inflation, even at the cost of heavy unemployment, they develop the rational expectation that inflation will be *less* in the future than it is now. When they sign contracts based on this assumption, the PC shifts down even more rapidly. Therefore, if the economy is at *S*, they will sign contracts based not on the assumption that inflation will stay at its current rate of 4% but that it will instead be lower, say 3%. Thus, just as rational expectations caused inflation to leapfrog up from *J* to *M* in response to continuing expansionary policies, so rational expectations will cause the economy to leapfrog from *S* to *V* (arrow 3) in response to continuing policies of restraint. In short, rational expectations make it possible to bring inflation down more rapidly. *Long periods with high unemployment may not be necessary to unwind inflation.*

Note that the ***credibility*** of an anti-inflationary policy becomes its key to success. Paradoxically, the way to stop inflation *without* long periods of high unemployment is to convince the public that you *will* tolerate long periods of high unemployment. They will be willing to sign contracts based on lower inflation rates only if they believe that inflation will, in fact, come down.

Rational Expectations and Discretionary Policy

Let us sum up the rational expectations argument thus far:

1. A consistently expansionary policy can quickly lead to very rapid inflation.
2. A consistent, credible policy of restraint can lead to a rapid unwinding of inflation.

In other words, a policy aimed at a low unemployment rate can lead to an inflationary disaster. But a policy aimed at stable prices can be successful without an unemployment disaster. The best choice: Follow a consistent policy aimed at stable prices. Since rational expectations theorists are an offshoot of monetarism, they argue that the way to do this is with a steady increase in the quantity of money.

However, this is not the end of the case which rational expectations theorists make against discretionary policies. Thomas Sargent and Neil Wallace of the University of Minnesota also claim that it is *useless to follow a policy of fine tuning the economy by introducing expansive aggregate demand policies each time the economy goes into a recession.* Briefly, the argument is this. The ultimate effect of more demand is higher prices. If demand is increased each time the economy moves into a recession, people will come to *anticipate* the inflationary consequences. Anticipating higher prices, they will press for higher wages. Eager borrowers will bid up interest rates. Businesses will increase the prices of their products. Thus, the increase in aggregate demand will go into higher prices, not higher output and employment. *When the public anticipates the effects of expansive demand policies aimed at reducing unemployment, it renders these policies ineffective.* Systematic fine tuning of aggregate demand is useless. The Federal Reserve can affect output and employment only by trickery, that is, by following erratic policies. (The economy may move from *G* to *H* during a brief period if the Fed tricks the public by a sudden, unexpected increase in the money stock.) Whenever the Fed follows a consistent policy, the public will figure it out; the only effect will be on prices, not output. In effect, the authorities *face a vertical Phillips curve* in either the long run or the short. No consistent policy will have any effect on output. (Output may, however, still deviate from the natural rate because of random disturbances which the public can't anticipate.)

This argument has attracted much attention among economists because it may help to explain the disappointing results from the stabilization policies of the 1970s. Even though the authorities frequently attempted to reduce unemployment with expansive policies, the unemployment rate remained high and inflation accelerated. It may also help to explain the speed with which the rate of inflation declined during the recession of 1980–1982.

However, the rational expectations argument has been challenged by advocates of demand management, such as MIT's Franco Modigliani. In his presidential address to the American Economics Association, Modigliani observed that the rational expectations model is inconsistent "with the evidence: if it were valid, deviations of unemployment from the natural rate would be small and transitory—in which case [Keynes'] *General Theory* would never have been written."[†]

Modigliani's point is this. Within the rational expectations framework, the unemployment rate departs from the natural rate only when there are surprises. According to the rational expectations theory, people are perceptive; they do not consistently make the same mistake. Therefore, while the unemployment rate might fluctuate around the natural rate because of random disturbances, the theory suggests that the unemployment rate should not be *consistently* above or consistently below the natural rate for any extended time. In fact, it was far greater than the natural rate *throughout* the 1930s. The rational expectations theory is inconsistent with the facts.

[†] "The Monetarist Controversy, or, Should We Foresake Stabilization Policies," *American Economic Review*, March 1977, p. 6.

POLICIES TO DEAL WITH UNEMPLOYMENT AND INFLATION

The accelerationist theory raises three important policy issues:

1. What are the implications of this theory for demand management policies?
2. What can be done to reduce the natural or equilibrium rate of unemployment in the economy? That is, what can be done to shift the long-run Phillips curve to the left?
3. Can anything be done to ease the transition to a lower rate of inflation? That is, are there other policies which can be used to reduce inflation without causing the high unemployment which normally accompanies a tough restrictive demand policy (illustrated by *V* in Figure 16-11)?

1. Aggregate Demand: The Importance of Steady Growth

The vertical long-run Phillips curve implies that the *trend* of aggregate demand has no effect on the unemployment rate. A consistent inflation will lead to no gains in terms of lower unemployment. However, there is a strong advantage in a *stable* rate of growth of aggregate demand.

This point is illustrated in Figure 16-13, which brings together the argument of Figure 16-11 and the top part of Figure 16-9. With a stable increase in aggregate demand, we would expect to stay at a point—such as *R*—on the long-run Phillips curve, with a stable rate of inflation (4% in this example). Consider, now, the unstable situation, where periods of rapid expansion in aggregate demand alternate with periods of recession.

During the period of rapid expansion of demand, output increases, the unemployment rate falls, the inflation rate accelerates, and the economy moves to a point such as *S*, to the left of the long-run Phillips curve. (This repeats the argument we have already covered in Figure 16-9.) If, then, the rapid expansion of demand is slackened, the economy moves back toward the long-run Phillips curve, to a point such as *T*. But the higher rate of inflation (6%) has gotten built into the economy: *T* is on short-run Phillips curve $PC_{6\%}$ reflecting expectations of 6% inflation. Now, suppose that the growth of aggregate demand is restrained in order to bring inflation back down to its original 4% rate. The economy slides down $PC_{6\%}$ to point *V*, with a high rate of unemployment. (Again, we have already encountered this argument in Figure 16-11.) As contracts are renegotiated to recognize the 4% inflation, the economy can revive toward *R* with a stable 4% rate of inflation—provided, of course, the growth of aggregate demand also revives.

Which pattern is better—an economy consistently at *R* or one that moves consecutively from *R*, to *S*, *T*, *V*, and back to *R* in the face of unstable demand? The answer is: the stable pattern. *Because the short-run Phillips curves are curved,* the unemployment penalty in moving to *V* (2% in our example; that is, 8% − 6%) is greater than the amount by which unemployment is eased in moving to S (1% in the example; that is, 6% − 5%). Thus, we come to an important conclusion: *Instability causes a higher average rate of unemployment*. It further follows that if we want to avoid the necessity of fighting inflation with points such as V, we should also be careful not to let aggregate demand expand so rapidly as to push the economy to points such as S. We have already noted Okun's grim analysis of points such as V. As the other half of the argument, he warned against overexpansion of demand (that is, points such as S):

> We should set our fiscal and monetary policies to accept some down-side risks on output and unemployment in the short run. We didn't accept enough of these risks in 1977–1978. It turned out in retrospect that fiscal-monetary policy was too stimulative. We must do better in the future to establish a safety margin against overly strong markets.[6]

[6]Testimony before the Joint Economic Committee, U.S. Congress, April 30, 1979.

FIGURE 16-13

Instability and the average rate of unemployment

In a stable economy, equilibrium remains at R, at the natural rate of unemployment (shown here as 6%). In an unstable economy, moving from R to S, T, V, and back to R, the average rate of unemployment is greater. This is because the reduction in unemployment (1% less than the natural rate) in moving to S is less than the unemployment penalty (2% greater than the natural rate) while inflation is being unwound at V.

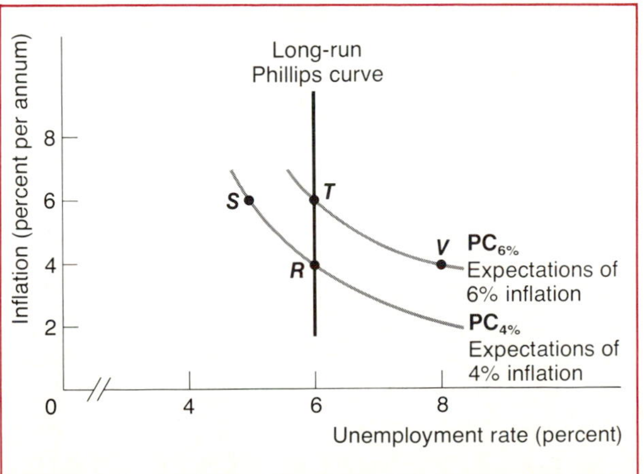

2. What Can Be Done to Reduce the Equilibrium Rate of Unemployment?

Even if we were to achieve a perfectly smooth growth of aggregate demand, our macroeconomic problems would not be solved. Although cyclical unemployment would be eliminated, there would still be a sizable amount of "natural" unemployment due to frictional and structural causes. Not all of this represents voluntary unemployment while people search for appropriate jobs. Some workers—particularly teenagers—have trouble finding jobs no matter how hard they look. Accordingly, it is appropriate to study ways of reducing the natural rate—that is, ways of shifting the long-run Phillips curve to the left. The problem is that we have been going in the opposite direction.

The increase in the natural rate in the past 25 years

The equilibrium or natural rate of unemployment—below which inflation will begin to accelerate—has increased substantially during the past 25 years. In the early years of the Kennedy administration, an unemployment target of 4% was considered achievable without unleashing inflationary pressures. By the middle seventies, the Council of Economic Advisers was suggesting that the natural rate had risen at least as high as 5%.[7] By the end of the seventies, the evidence suggested that the natural rate of unemployment was even higher—perhaps 6% or maybe even more. Particularly disconcerting was the increase in inflation from 4.8% in 1976 to 9.0% in 1978, even though international oil prices were relatively stable and unemployment was high, averaging 7% in 1977 and 6% in 1978. In 1984, when the rate of inflation stabilized close to 4%, the unemployment rate was between 7% and 8%. These events would suggest that, if anything, the natural rate of unemployment exceeds 6%.

Such changes in the natural rate do not conflict with the accelerationist theory that the long-run Phillips curve is vertical. According to that theory, *demand management* does not affect the equilibrium rate of unemployment; the rate of unemployment cannot be permanently reduced by a more inflationary policy. However, the natural rate of unemployment *can* be changed if conditions

[7]Council of Economic Advisers, *Annual Report, 1962*, pp. 44–47; and CEA, *Annual Report, 1975*, pp. 94–97.

in the labor market change; that is, the whole long-run Phillips curve can shift to the right or left.

Three explanations have been put forward for the apparent increase in the natural rate of unemployment; that is, the rate to which unemployment can be reduced without causing an acceleration of inflation.

The first is based on the change in the composition of the labor force. Compared with the 1960s, the labor force in the 1970s contained a larger percentage of teenagers, who have higher unemployment rates than adults. As teenagers became a larger fraction of the labor force, the overall unemployment rate tended to rise. However, this should be a smaller problem in the future. Because of past changes in the birthrate, the percentage of teenagers in the labor force has been declining since 1977, and this drop should help to reduce the overall rate of unemployment.[8]

Second, increases in the height and coverage of the minimum wage have worked toward a higher equilibrium rate of unemployment because employers are discouraged from hiring low-productivity workers. This is particularly true of teenagers with limited training and work experience.[9] Because the minimum wage can make it difficult for teenagers to get that first job and acquire work experience, proposals have been made to exempt teenage employment from the minimum wage or, alternatively, to have a lower minimum for teenagers than for adults. (These proposals have been opposed by those who fear that employers would simply replace adults with lower-wage teenagers.)

The third explanation is that improvements in unemployment insurance and welfare help to maintain the incomes of the unemployed. As a consequence, they are less desperate to take the first job that comes along. Frictional unemployment rises as those out of work engage in a more leisurely search for jobs. It is not clear what, if anything, should be done about this, since there is a conflict of objectives. It is desirable to reduce the hardship of the unemployed by providing unemployment insurance. But their incentive to take unattractive jobs is thereby lessened, and this makes it more difficult to achieve the goal of lower unemployment. However, one thing is clear. Government programs should be designed, insofar as possible, to maintain incentives to get a job. In particular, care should be taken to avoid programs that allow people to be better off by not working.

[8]For a readable analysis of teenage unemployment, see Bernard E. Anderson and Isabel V. Sawhill (eds.), *Youth Employment and Public Policy* (Englewood Cliffs, N.J.: Prentice-Hall for the American Assembly, Columbia University, 1980). See especially the first essay by Richard B. Freeman, "Why Is There a Youth Labor Market Problem?"

[9]For example, Edward Gramlich of the University of Michigan found that the 25% increase in the minimum wage in 1974 caused a rise of 2 percentage points in the unemployment rate of teenagers. Gramlich, "Impact of Minimum Wages on Other Wages, Employment, and Family Incomes," *Brookings Papers on Economic Activity,* 1976, 2, pp. 409–451.

Steps to reduce the equilibrium rate of unemployment In addition to the two measures just suggested—exempting teenagers from the minimum wage and taking care to retain incentives when designing unemployment insurance—what else might be done to reduce the equilibrium rate of unemployment? First, a reduction in discrimination against minorities would help to reduce the high rates of unemployment of those groups. Second, government training programs might help the chronically unemployed prepare themselves for useful work. The Comprehensive Employment and Training Act (CETA) was aimed specifically at this objective, and programs under this act expanded rapidly during the 1970s. However, these programs were controversial. Critics argued that they were expensive and not very successful. In particular, CETA programs provided relatively little training; their major effect was to provide jobs directly. They were one of the domestic programs to come under the budget-cutting axe when President Reagan came into office.

The government as the employer of last resort? Government programs—such as CETA—which provide jobs for the unemployed might be made more ambitious. The government might act as the ***employer of last resort;*** that is, the government might stand ready to provide jobs to all those who want work but are unable to find it in the private sector.

The government has no such commitment to provide last-resort jobs, and the Reagan administration has been moving in the opposite direction, to reduce employment programs as part of an overall program to limit the goverment's role in the economy.

The most explicit proposal in favor of a broad program of public employment was included in the original 1976 draft of the Humphrey-Hawkins bill, officially known as the *Full Employment and Balanced Growth Bill*. That bill would have committed the government to offer whatever jobs were needed to get the unemployment rate down to a target of 3% per annum. However, the last-resort provisions were dropped from the later version of the Humphrey-Hawkins bill that was actually passed.

Proponents of public employment programs point out that government projects might give the unemployed something useful to do. For example, the unemployed might do maintenance jobs in the cities or carry out conservation and public works projects similar to those of Roosevelt's recovery program in the 1930s.

On the other side, opponents object that such programs would be expensive. Just how expensive was indicated during 1977–1978, when the Carter administration more than doubled the size of the Public Service Employment Program to 725,000 jobs at a cost of $8.4 billion. That works out to more than $11,500 per job. (The average worker got considerably less than that—about $7,200. The rest went into administration and supporting services.)

It might seem that, if people are unemployed, it is obviously worthwhile for the government to hire them for, say, $4 to produce $3 worth of output. Society at least gets the $3 worth of additional output rather than the zero output that they would produce if they remained jobless. However, critics of public employment programs argue that this isn't necessarily so. Without last-resort jobs, people might look harder for jobs in the private sector. Thus, over time, public employment could come to include some people who would otherwise have been employed in the private sector, where workers typically produce at least as much as they earn. Consequently, public employment could be a drag on the overall output of the economy.

There seems to be no simple, painless, and uncontroversial way to lower the high natural rate of unemployment.

3. Bringing the Inflation Rate Down: Proposals to Ease the Transition

A high natural rate of unemployment can be painful. But even more painful are the transitional periods when the inflation rate is being wound down and the unemployment rate exceeds the natural rate (for example, at point *V* back in Figure 16-11). It is only through the hardship of unemployment—or the threat of it—that the market persuades individuals and institutions to reduce their demands.

A number of suggestions have been made to reduce wage and price increases in a less painful manner: (1) direct restraints on wages and prices; (2) the ***indexation*** of labor contracts, that is, providing for changes in wages during the contract period in response to changes in the level of prices; (3) steps to increase productivity and thus lower the cost of goods and services; this was an element of the "supply side" strategy of the Reagan administration; and (4) the pursuit of a strong, definite, credible anti-inflation policy so that expectations of inflation will be quickly adjusted downward. Each of these proposals is controversial. The issue of credibility was raised in Box 16-2. Indexation is deferred to Chapter 17 and supply side economics to Chapter 18. Here we look at direct restraints.

DIRECT RESTRAINTS ON WAGES AND PRICES: INCOMES POLICIES

Policies aimed at controlling inflation by direct restraints on money wages and prices are sometimes known as ***incomes policies***. Wage restraints affect the money incomes of workers. Price restraints affect other incomes, such as profits and rent.

Price and wage controls have often been introduced during wartime to suppress the inflationary pressures unleashed by excess demand. For example, they were used during World War II, when aggregate demand rose rapidly because of huge increases in military spending. More recently, the government has used incomes policies on a number of occasions: the guideposts of the Kennedy and Johnson administrations, the wage-price freeze introduced by the Nixon administration in 1971, and the guideposts of the Carter administration. The circumstances and objectives of these policies were somewhat different. The objective of the Kennedy-Johnson guideposts was to prevent inflation from gaining steam in the first place, while the purpose of the Nixon freeze was to roll back existing inflation.

The Kennedy-Johnson Guideposts

To restrain wages and prices as expansive fiscal policies were applied, the Kennedy administration announced two guideposts:

1. On average, prices should not rise.
2. In general, money wages should not rise by more than the increase in labor productivity in the economy as a whole, estimated at 3.2% per year in the early 1960s.

These two guideposts are consistent. If wages increase by no more than productivity, no inflation need result. Labor can be paid more because labor produces more. Employers can afford to pay the higher wages and still keep prices constant on average.

According to the guideposts, the increase in wages should be no more than the 3.2% increase in productivity in the economy *as a whole*—not the increase in productivity in a specific industry. In some industries—such as computers—productivity rises very rapidly, by as much as 20% per year. Such industries do not have to pay workers 20% more each year; they can get all the workers they want with much more moderate wage increases. With productivity rising much more rapidly than wages, costs per unit of output fall and prices should accordingly be adjusted downward. On the other side, industries with little or no increase in productivity have to pay wage increases in line with the economy as a whole. Otherwise, they are unable to hire and retain workers. Because the wages they have to pay are rising while their productivity is not, these industries find their costs rising. They have to raise their prices. Thus, the Kennedy guideposts recommended that prices *on average* remain stable, but prices were expected to rise in industries with small increases in productivity, while prices should fall in industries with large gains in productivity.

The idea of the guideposts was that restraint by labor and management would contribute to the general good; the economy could expand without inflation. The guideposts were to be enforced by public pressure on offenders and by exhortations or ''jawboning.'' There were no legal teeth to back them up.

The guideposts came under severe strain in the mid-1960s, when the rapid expansion of aggregate demand began to pull prices and wages up strongly. So long as the inflation rate was very low, the wage-price guideposts constituted a consistent package. Labor could settle for an increase of 3.2% in money wages and still enjoy rising real incomes. However, by 1966–1967, consumer prices were rising about 3% per year. In these circumstances, workers could scarcely be expected to stick to a 3.2% wage increase. If they did so, their real wages would remain approximately constant. They would not get a share of the rising national product.

One way to deal with this problem would be to protect labor's real income by permiting the money wage to increase by the estimated 3.2% productivity increase *plus* the rate of inflation. But this larger wage increase would have perpetuated inflation, not cured it. After 1965, less and less attention was paid to the guideposts. They became irrelevant.

The Wage-Price Freeze of 1971

During the first half of 1971, the economy was suffering from stagflation, with unemployment (at 6%) and inflation (at 4%) running well above their averages for the previous decade. Demand restraint was being used to combat inflation. But inflation had been built into contracts; the economy was at a point like *V*, to the right of the long-run Phillips curve back in Figure 16-11.

President Nixon sharply shifted gears in August of 1971, introducing his *New Economic Policy*. To shortcut the painful process of reducing inflation, a 90-day freeze on wages, prices, and rents was imposed, followed by less rigid controls. Demand policies were shifted in an expansive direction to stimulate output and employment.

Like other experiments with incomes policies, these controls were controversial. In one way, they seemed to work very well. The inflation rate dropped sharply in late 1971 and 1972, and the unemployment rate declined slightly. However, inflation soon spiraled up again after the controls were relaxed. By 1973, the rate of inflation was 6.2%, more than in 1971. By 1975, inflation was

9.1% and unemployment 8.5%—both far above their 1971 levels. Consequently, there are two conflicting views of this episode:

1. The wage-price controls worked, breaking the inflationary momentum without going through the costs of an extended period with high unemployment. However, the successes of late 1971 and early 1972 were wiped out when inflation was reignited by excess aggregate demand and by the increases in the price of oil.
2. The controls were not really a success at all, but merely a short-run illusion. They temporarily suppressed price increases but did not improve underlying trends. When the controls were eliminated, inflation quickly regained lost ground.

Incomes Policies in the Carter Administration: Pay and Price Standards

When President Carter came to office, he lacked legislative authority to impose wage and price controls. (The authority used by Nixon had lapsed.) In his first year in office, he therefore confined himself to low-keyed statements that he hoped business and labor would show restraint. ''Wishboning,'' the critics called it. It was not very effective; the rate of inflation accelerated in 1977. Then, in 1978, the President announced pay and price standards, somewhat similar to those of the Kennedy-Johnson administrations. However, prices were already rising at almost 7% per year. Therefore, it was obviously unreasonable to use the increase in productivity as the wage guidepost. The Carter standard for wage increases was set at 7%, with those earning less than $4.00 per hour being exempted. Price increases were also to be limited.

A novel aspect of Carter's program was a ***real wage insurance*** proposal, whereby workers who agreed to the 7% money wage increase would get tax rebates in the event that prices rose by more than 7%. This was designed to protect them against a fall in the real wage in the event of rapid inflation. However, an important objection to the proposal was that, if prices in fact rose by more than 7%, the automatic tax cuts would act as a stimulus to demand and increase inflation even more. Notice that the automatic tax cuts would be the opposite of the ''automatic fiscal stabilization'' explained in Chapter 11, whereby tax collections automatically increase in the event of booming demand and inflation. Partly because of this objection, this part of Carter's program never came into effect; Congress refused to enact it.

During the 1970s, other proposals incuded the ***tax-based incomes policy,*** or TIP. According to this concept, the government would use tax incentives or tax penalties to encourage businesses to comply with guideposts. Critics doubted that TIP would be effective enough to justify the complications it would introduce into the tax system. In response, President Carter's Council of Economic Advisers, in its last *Annual Report* in January 1981 (p. 60), referred to TIP as an ''important untried innovation'' and argued that, ''While TIPs may impose administrative and efficiency costs, those costs appear to be far less than would be incurred by reducing inflation solely through restraining aggregate demand.''

President Reagan was unimpressed by the idea of an incomes policy. In his view, wage and price guideposts represented an unwarranted intrusion of the government. One of his early acts was to abolish the Council on Wage and Price Stability, which had administered pay and price guideposts.

Incomes Policies: Controversial Issues

The desirability of guideposts or more formal controls on wages and prices has been the subject of continuing and heated debate in the United States and other countries. Four main points are at issue:

1. *Workability*. Skeptics point to the breakdown of the Kennedy-Johnson guideposts, to the inflation which followed Nixon's price freeze, to the failure of Carter's guideposts to prevent double-digit inflation, and to disappointing experiences with incomes policies in foreign countries during the past quarter century.[10] Proponents

[10]See Robert J. Flanagan, David W. Soskice, and Lloyd Ulman, *Unionism, Economic Stabilization, and Incomes Policies: European Experience* (Washington: Brookings Institution, 1983).

On the United Kingdom's experience, see also Hugh Clegg (a member of the early British Prices and Incomes Board), *How to Run an Incomes Policy, and Why We Made Such a Mess of the Last One* (London: Heinemann Educational Publishing, 1970).

point to the substantial successes of the 1960s. During the period when the wage-price guideposts were in force, the United States had an unusually long period of steady expansion. And, until excess demand was generated by Vietnam war spending, prices were reasonably stable; until 1966, the rate of inflation remained below 2%.

In more detail, the case against an incomes policy goes as follows. If the government proclaims guideposts, business and labor leaders can scarcely be expected to cooperate voluntarily. Labor leaders have to answer to union members who want higher wages, and business executives have to answer to their stockholders who want higher profits. Indeed, guideposts may be counterproductive. If the government has approved a 3.2% wage increase, how can any self-respecting labor leader settle for less? The 3.2% may thus become the floor from which bargaining begins. Furthermore, guideposts may also be counterproductive on the price side. Fearing that guideposts may simply be a warning of more stringent controls to come, businesses may decide to "jump the gun." If prices are about to be frozen, won't a business try to raise them now, while there is still time? There is some evidence that they may do so. After the election of 1976, but before the inauguration, President-elect Carter announced his intention to ask Congress for standby authority to impose wage and price controls. Soon thereafter, steel companies announced price increases. Many observers came to the conclusion that they wanted to "jump the gun" and establish a high price in case prices were in fact frozen.

Furthermore, price controls require a major bureaucracy. But even a large bureaucracy can't keep up with the complex interactions among markets. If costs of inputs rise, businesses may quit producing goods if they are not allowed to raise prices. Thus, price controls may result in shortages. Goods in high demand may be channeled into *black markets,* where prices are above the legal limits. Because sellers are breaking the law, they may charge higher prices to compensate for their risk of being fined or imprisoned. In such circumstances, price controls might make the inflation worse.

Finally, governments that use incomes policies may suffer from the illusion that they can indeed control prices in this way and are therefore free to increase aggregate demand rapidly. If they do so, the incomes policies will collapse under the intense pressures of excess demand, and prices will shoot up. This is one interpretation of the events of 1971–1974 and 1977–1980.

On the other side, the case in favor of incomes policies has been neatly summarized by John Kenneth Galbraith (a retired Harvard professor): "Any idiot can argue the case against controls in the abstract. It is only that there are no alternatives." If direct action is not taken to restrain wages and prices, there is only one way to stop inflation: restrain aggregate demand and allow a painfully high rate of unemployment. For example, inflation was brought down in 1981–1982 without wage and price controls, but only at the cost of a very severe recession in which the unemployment rate rose to 10.8%.

2. *Allocative efficiency*. Opponents of guidelines and controls point out that they interfere with the function of the price system in allocating production. As we saw in Chapter 4, prices provide information and incentives to producers. When goods are scarce, prices rise, encouraging producers to make more. If prices are controlled, they no longer can perform this important role.

A particular problem arises because controls or guideposts may be enforced erratically. Responding to political pressures, the government may enforce price restraints most vigorously for goods that are considered essential. As a result of the relatively low prices, businesses will switch to the production of more profitable items. Thus, *price controls may end up by creating shortages of the very goods the society considers particularly important*. (Recall the discussion of rent control in Box 4-1.)

Proponents of incomes policies recognize this danger, but believe that it can be dealt with. Advocates of guideposts or controls generally propose that a government agency be given the authority to grant exemptions, permitting higher wages and prices in industries where there is a threat of shortages.

3. *Economic freedom*. The proposal for a powerful government agency is viewed with alarm by the opponents of incomes policies. If officials are allowed to decide whether a firm will be able to raise its prices, they may thereby gain the power to decide whether the firm will survive or not. Price and wage controls restrict the freedom of businesses and labor.

Proponents of controls tend to downplay these dangers and argue that they must be put in perspective. If no restraint is applied to wage and pricing decisions, the control of inflation will involve high rates of unemployment. The unemployed will be used as "cannon fodder" in the war against inflation. Thus, the freedom of business executives and labor leaders to do as they please must be weighed against the right of workers to have jobs.

4. *Equity*. Price guideposts tend by their very nature to be complicated; it is difficult to impose any general standard on all prices. Prices must be allowed to rise in industries with small increases in productivity, as we have already seen. Wage guideposts, on the other hand, can be more specific and applied across the board. For example, a guidepost of 3% may be proclaimed for all workers. Labor leaders in the United States and other countries have complained that, as a consequence, wage-price guideposts tend to be unfairly enforced. Most of the attention is directed toward the relatively simple wage guideposts. Thus, labor leaders sometimes argue that they don't object to a general policy covering *all* incomes, but they do object to a policy that controls only wages. Incomes policies should not be used to redistribute income away from labor and toward profits.

The enforcement of price guideposts may also lead to complaints of unfair treatment of specific businesses. In pressing for compliance, the government may find politically unpopular businesses—such as steel—to be especially inviting targets for public ridicule and official harrassment.

The first two of these issues become particularly important when we address the question of how long incomes policies should last. Some proponents argue that such policies should be used only temporarily to slow down specific inflationary spurts. If they are soon removed, allocative problems are unlikely to be severe. (Again, recall from the discussion of rent control in Box 4-1 that the shortage of apartments becomes more acute as time passes.) However, if controls are removed quickly, prices may simply bounce up to where they would have been in the absence of restraint; there may be no lasting effect. Some economists—most notably John Kenneth Galbraith—argue that the problem of reconciling high employment and stable prices is a permanent one. Therefore, *permanent* restraints on wages and prices should be imposed.

Incomes policies: A final word A discussion of incomes policies would be incomplete without noting that governments also follow policies that *raise* prices. For example, agricultural price supports keep up farm prices, while restraints on imports reduce competition and raise the U.S. prices of products such as steel and autos. In the face of strong political lobbies, it is easy for the government to take the line of least resistance and extend such price-raising policies. But to do so is to sabotage its fight against inflation. Thus, in evaluating an administration's anti-inflationary policies, we should keep in mind two related questions: What policies have they been following to benefit specific industries or specific groups of workers? To what extent have these policies raised prices and wages?

KEY POINTS

1. Data for the 1960s trace out a *Phillips curve*. Observations since 1969 are above and to the right of this curve.

2. Two major explanations have been offered for the simultaneous high rates of inflation and unemployment of the 1970s—that is, for the upward shift in the short-run Phillips curve: (*a*) cost push, particularly in the form of higher oil prices and (*b*) higher wage settlements, which workers demand in order to compensate for higher prices. (In other words, a wage-price spiral causes an upward shift in the short-run Phillips curve.)

3. Because inflation affects wage and other contracts, the short-run Phillips curve is unstable. There is a different curve for every expected rate of inflation.

4. Phelps and Friedman argue that people adjust completely to a steady, expected rate of inflation. As a consequence, there is *no long-run trade-off* between inflation and unemployment. The long-run Phillips curve is a vertical straight line.

5. The equilibrium rate of unemployment, where the Phillips curve is vertical, is known as the *natural rate* of unemployment. The natural rate has increased in the past quarter century.

6. Proposals to bring the natural rate of unemployment back down include: (*a*) steps to combat discrimination against minorities, (*b*) training programs for the unemployed, and (*c*) a program in which the government acts as the employer of last resort.

7. When restrictive monetary and fiscal policies are used to bring down the rate of inflation, the result can be a very high rate of unemployment. Several proposals have been made to ease the transition to a lower rate of inflation: (*a*) *incomes policies,* in the form of wage-price guideposts or controls, (*b*) the pursuit of a firm, *credible* policy (Box 16-2), (*c*) indexation of labor contracts (to be studied in Chapter 17), and (*d*) steps to increase productivity (Chapter 18).

8. Incomes policies have been used in an attempt to ease the transition to a lower rate of inflation and to prevent inflation from gathering momentum in the first place. Presidents Kennedy and Johnson used wage-price guideposts in an effort to keep the average level of prices stable as the economy expanded. President Nixon imposed a wage-price freeze to break inflationary expectations. President Carter used wage-price guideposts in an attempt to contain inflationary pressures. President Reagan has not used such incomes policies.

9. Incomes policies are controversial on four principal grounds: (*a*) Are they effective? (*b*) Do they adversely affect allocative efficiency? (*c*) Are they consistent with economic freedom? (*d*) Are they fair?

KEY CONCEPTS

Phillips curve
stagflation
policy dilemma
the trade-off between inflation and unemployment
demand-pull inflation
cost-push inflation
shift in the Phillips curve
acceleration of inflation
accelerationist theory
wage-price spiral
long-run Phillips curve
natural, or equilibrium, rate of unemployment
government as employer of last resort
incomes policies
guideposts
jawboning
wage-price freeze
tax-based incomes policies (TIP)

PROBLEMS

16-1. Why does the (short-run) Phillips curve bend more and more steeply upward as it goes to the left? That is, why isn't it a straight line?

16-2. Explain why expansive demand policies aimed at a low rate of unemployment might cause a wage-price spiral and an accelerating rate of inflation.

16-3. A steady increase in aggregate demand will result in a lower average rate of unemployment over an extended period of time than will a stop-go policy, which involves alternate periods of restrictive and expansive policies. Why?

16-4. For each of the following statements, state whether you agree or disagree and explain why. If the statement is incorrect, fix it.

(*a*) On each short-run Phillips curve, there is one and only one stable point, namely, the point at which the short-run Phillips curve intersects the long-run Phillips curve.

(*b*) According to the Phelps-Friedman theory of the vertical Phillips curve, there is no trade-off between the objectives of high employment and stable prices in the short run. Such a trade-off occurs only in the long run, after the economy has had a chance to adjust to the prevailing rate of inflation.

(*c*) The Kennedy-Johnson wage guidepost provided for an increase of wages of approximately 3%. The objective of this wage increase was to provide labor with a gradually increasing share of national product in order to make up for past exploitation of workers.

16-5. Guideposts and wage-price controls are often opposed both by labor unions and by business executives. Why do labor leaders oppose them when their objective is to make possible a combination of low inflation and low unemployment? Why do business executives oppose them when one of their main objectives is to restrain nominal wage increases without having to put the economy through a period of recession and falling profits?

16-6. In late 1976, when president-elect Carter announced his intention to ask Congress for standby authority to impose wage and price controls, he gave people an incentive to "jump the gun." Why? Would people have an incentive to jump the gun before the Kennedy-Johnson guideposts were imposed? Before the Nixon freeze?

***16-7.** If the Phillips curve—such as that shown in red in Figure 16-3—is stable only in the short run, how was it possible for Phillips to find a curve for Britain that was stable for almost a full century?

***16-8.** President Carter's proposal for real wage insurance might have destabilized fiscal policy, since it would have provided for automatic tax cuts when inflation was high. Does the same criticism apply to tax-based incomes policies, whereby the tax rates of corporations depend on whether they adhere to guideposts? Explain why or why not.

***16-9.** Would you favor the government's acting as the employer of last resort? Why or why not? If you are in favor, what jobs would you give to those hired under a last-resort program? How much would you pay them? Would you place any time limit on how long they can work for the government under this program?

---

*Questions marked with asterisks are more difficult than the others.

CHAPTER 17

HOW DO WE ADJUST TO INFLATION?

Inflation is the time when those who have saved for a rainy day get soaked.

Together with unemployment, inflation is one of the two major macroeconomic diseases. Each trip to the supermarket or department store is a nagging reminder of how much the value of the dollar has shrunk.

Just a few years ago, inflation was considered a problem of secondary importance—and with good reason. It is true that there had been an inflationary burst in the 1940s and early 1950s, associated with the Second World War and the conflict in Korea. But, following the end of the Korean war in 1953, the price level remained quite stable for more than a decade. In 1965, prices on average were only 18% higher than in 1953, reflecting an average rate of inflation of less than 2% per year.

Furthermore, from a longer historical viewpoint, rapid inflation had been an exceptional disease associated with war, as Figure 17-1 illustrates. During wars, the U.S. government typically resorted to the printing press, creating money to help finance its military expenditures. As a consequence, prices shot upward. During the Revolutionary War, the quip "not worth a continental" reflected the sharp decline in the value of the currency issued by the new "continental" government of the United States. During peacetime, in contrast, there was no strong upward trend of prices. In 1914, the average level of prices was no higher than in 1875. On the eve of the Second World War in the late 1930s, the average level of prices was *below* the peak of 1920.

In the 1970s, a fundamental change took place. The rapid inflation of the period from 1973 to 1981 was new; it cannot be attributed to military spending. Although the initial round of inflation in the late 1960s was touched off by the military escalation in Vietnam, inflation subsided to 3.4% per year in 1971 and 1972 as the United States was extricating itself from the conflict in Southeast Asia. During the next 9 years, 1973–1981, when the rate of inflation exceeded 6.5% in every year except one (4.8% in 1976), defense expenditures shrank as a percentage of GNP. Furthermore, other countries with economies somewhat similar to the United States—such as Britain and Canada—also suffered high rates of inflation in spite of extended peace and low military expenditures. It is true that the U.S. rate of inflation was brought down below 4% in 1982–1983, largely as a result of a severe recession. Nevertheless, we seem to have entered a new era. Rates of inflation above 5% can no longer be considered abnormal events, associated simply with war (Box 17-1).

In the early discussion of inflation in Chapter 8, we emphasized the distinction between ***expected*** and ***unexpected inflation.*** When inflation is unexpected, it causes an arbitrary redistribution of income and wealth. Debtors gain. Bondholders lose, as do people working for fixed money wages. But when inflation persists, people come to expect it and they adjust their behavior to protect themselves. In Chapter 16, we studied one of the ways in which people adjust to continuing, expected inflation. Specifically, inflation is taken into account by wage negotiators, who may be able to adjust money wages in such a way as to leave workers with the same real wages that they would have achieved in the absence of inflation. The argument that there is a vertical long-run Phillips curve is based on the view that negotiators will in fact adjust completely to continuing, steady rates of inflation.

In this chapter, we will consider some of the other ways in which individuals and the government respond to persistent inflation. We will also look at the ways in which markets—particularly those for bonds—*may fail to adjust* even over extended periods, with the result that inflation has a continuing impact on real incomes and other real variables. While unexpected inflation has the strongest effects on people's real incomes and wealth, there can be continuing effects even when people come to anticipate the inflation. Finally, we will look at the complications which inflation creates for a government trying to develop a coherent macroeconomic strategy.

Specifically, in this chapter we shall:

1. Illustrate the ways in which the bond market may adjust to a continuing inflation, and the ways in which this market may not adjust completely even in the event of a steady, perfectly anticipated inflation.

2. Illustrate how *taxes* can be a major reason why inflation has a substantial, continuing effect on the bond market, even when the inflation is anticipated perfectly.

3. See that *when inflation is rapid,* it tends to be *highly variable* from year to year. Consequently, it is *difficult to anticipate* what the inflation rate will be during a rapid inflation. This is one reason why rapid inflation has serious consequences.

4. Study the causes and effects of *indexation*—the provision in contracts for automatic adjustments (in wages, etc.) in response to inflation. In particular, we will see how indexation can have unpredictable effects, sometimes making it easier to reestablish price stability, but often contributing to high and volatile inflation.

5. Study the effects of high inflation on the government's budget, and see why it becomes so difficult to determine which macroeconomic policies are most appropriate during periods of rapid and changing inflation.

Throughout this chapter, one recurring theme will be the effects of inflation on the cost of home ownership. Housing not only represents a major expenditure for the typical American family; it also is the most important way most families save. (The largest asset the typical family acquires is its home, and paying off the mortgage is one way to save.) The significance of the housing

FIGURE 17-1
Prices, 1800–1985

Rapid inflation has usually been associated with wars or their immediate aftermath. The rapid inflation during the last half of the 1970s was a notable exception.

This figure shows both the familiar consumer price index (CPI) and the producer price index (PPI), which is an index of the prices of goods produced in the economy. The CPI includes the prices of services, but the PPI does not.

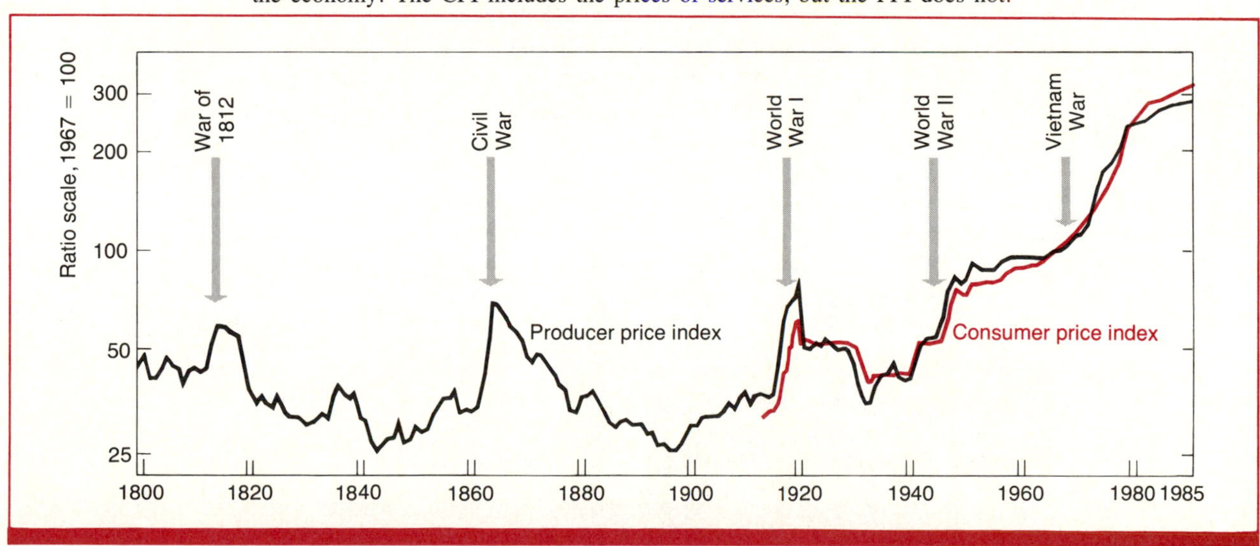

market scarcely needs to be emphasized to undergraduates. During the next decade, many of you will acquire your first homes. The more rapid is inflation, the more difficult will it be for you to buy a home—even if your money income completely keeps up with inflation.

ADJUSTING TO STABLE, CONTINUING INFLATION

Consider first a stable, continuing, predictable inflation. Such inflation is a nuisance: Workers, bondholders, homeowners, and others have to adjust dollar amounts for inflation if they want to calculate their real incomes or wealth. However, it is not obvious how the fundamental performance of the economy is changed. In fact, there is a traditional argument in economics that the real quantities in an economy—such as real incomes and real wealth—will be affected little, if at all, by a steady, predictable inflation. We have already seen in Chapter 16 how real wages may remain unaffected by steady inflation.

A similar argument suggests that the *relative* prices of various goods may be unaffected by *stable, predictable* inflation (of, say, 6% per annum). Typically, with a zero rate of inflation—where prices *on average* are stable—some prices will rise while others will fall. To the degree that a steady, predictable inflation leaves fundamental conditions in the economy unchanged, then relative prices need not be affected. The price of a good which, for a variety of reasons, would have risen in the noninflationary situation by 2%, will in this inflationary situation rise by 8%—that is, 6% to compensation for

BOX 17-1

POCKET MONEY

RUSSELL BAKER[†]

A curious side effect of inflation is the psychological change that occurs in the human attitude toward money. Recently, for example, without even noticing it, I abandoned the habit of carrying all paper money in my wallet and took to stuffing bills of $1 and $5 denominations into my trouser pocket, which in the past had been habitually reserved for items of small value, like coins.

In my rigidly organized psychological system, the wallet was the repository for things of value—paper money, credit cards, permits issued by the more terrifying bureaucracies, and so forth. The pants pocket, more easily, more thoughtlessly accessible to the right hand, has always been the place for things whose loss would not be a disaster. Toothpicks collected from the delicatessen counter, coins, chewing gum wrappers, lint, and messages to telephone editors, lawyers, and agents immediately.

A year or so ago, I began noticing dollar bills turning up among the coins and lint. Then, a couple of months ago, reaching in the pocket for a dollar to buy a magazine that used to cost 25 cents, I was startled to come up with a $5 bill. At first, somewhat alarmed, I stuffed the big bill into the wallet, but it left me uncomfortable. What, after all, was a $5 bill any more? Did it deserve the dignity of a wallet? At the rate people were demanding $5 bills, you could wear out a wallet in two weeks if you had to manhandle it for each demand.

The $5 bill went permanently to the pants pocket along with the lint, toothpicks, the ridiculous pennies and quarters, and the wretched, bloodless, decaying, unworthy one-dollar bills.

This created immense psychological relief. When one stopped thinking of $5 bills as "real money," the pain and outrage occasioned by being charged $1.25 for a copy of Newsweek and $6 for a pound of veal became almost tolerable. I no longer look with awe upon fellow New Yorkers who pay $110 a month for parking space for their cars. The people across the street who rent two-bedroom apartments for $2,200 a month still leave me agape in such wonder as will be dispelled, I suppose, only when I shift the $20 bills from wallet to pocket.

[†]Abridged from his column in *The New York Times*, Feb. 14, 1979.

inflation, plus 2% for the other reasons. Similarly, prices which would have fallen in the noninflationary situation will rise by less than the rate of inflation.

The Real Rate of Interest

Because inflation has such a strong effect on borrowers and lenders, it affects the interest rate that lenders charge and borrowers pay. We've already seen in Chapter 8 how inflation harms lenders; they are repaid in money whose value has declined. Consequently, inflation makes lenders reluctant to make loans. The supply of loanable funds decreases, as illustrated by the shift from S_1 to S_2 in Figure 17-2. At the same time, inflation benefits borrowers. People are therefore eager to borrow, and the demand for loanable funds by businesses, home buyers, and others increases from D_1 to D_2. Equilibrium moves from E_1 to E_2. There is an increase in the price of loans (the interest rate).

The question is, how much does the interest rate rise? One common argument—traced back a half century to the work of Irving Fisher of Yale—is that the interest rate will rise by the amount of inflation, thus leaving borrowers and lenders in the same real position as before. That is, borrowers and lenders will face the same ***real rate of interest*** as before, with this real rate calculated in a manner similar to that used for the real wage in Chapter 7. Specifically:[1]

Real rate of interest ≈
nominal rate of interest −
expected rate of inflation **(17-1)**

Figure 17-2 illustrates the reason for believing that the nominal rate of interest will include a full compensation for inflation, bringing the real interest rate back to its original level. The noninflationary equilibrium is at E_1, with a nominal rate of interest of 3%. With zero inflation, the real rate of interest is likewise 3%.

With a steady, expected inflation of 5% per year, how much does the supply of loanable funds (S_1) shift? Point A on supply curve S_1 shows us that, *before inflation,* lenders had to receive 2% interest to induce them to provide C units of loanable funds. This suggests that, once there is an inflation of 5%, those lenders will be willing to lend the same C units only if they receive an interest rate of 7%, at point B. This provides them with a 5% compensation for inflation—shown by arrow f—and the same 2% real rate of interest as before. No matter what point we consider on S_1, the corresponding point on S_2 is 5% higher. Thus, the entire supply curve shifts up by the amount of the inflation arrow f.

A similar argument applies to borrowers. With inflation, their enthusiasm for borrowing increases, since

FIGURE 17-2
Inflation and the demand and supply of loanable funds
As a result of inflation, people are eager to borrow; the demand for funds increases to D_2. Lenders are reluctant, causing the supply of loanable funds to decrease to S_2. As a result, the rate of interest rises.

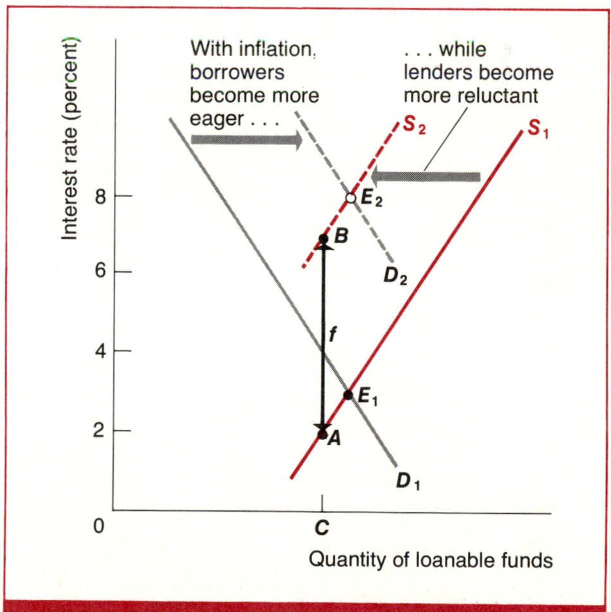

[1]As in the case of the real wage (equation 7-10), this is only an approximation. Once again, we have to divide to get the *precise* answer:

$$1 + i_r = \frac{1 + i_n}{1 + \text{expected rate of inflation}}$$

where i_r = the real rate of interest
i_n = the nominal rate of interest

they will repay with money whose value has declined. Their demand for loans shifts up by 5%: No matter how much they borrow, they will be willing to pay 5% more for it, because this is the benefit they get from inflation. With both curves shifting up by the same 5%, new equilibrium E_2 is 5% above original equilibrium E_1. In this simple case of a stable, predictable inflation, the nominal rate of interest therefore should rise to 8% to compensate for the 5% inflation, leaving the real interest rate unaffected at 3%. Of the 8% total, 3% can be looked on as a net payment to lenders, while the other 5% compensates them for the decline in the value of the money they have loaned (Figure 17-3).

INFLATION AND INTEREST RATES IN THE UNITED STATES

In Figure 17-4, we can see how nominal rates of interest have risen substantially during the past two decades. This is broadly consistent with the theory just explained, since the rate of inflation has also increased during these two decades.

Unfortunately, it is difficult to go further and determine whether the nominal interest rate includes a full compensation for inflation. The problem is that people look to the *future* when they borrow or lend; the theory says that nominal interest rates should include compensation for *expected* inflation. The difficulty is that we do not live in the simple world we have thus far assumed, where the rate of inflation is stable and perfectly predictable. In the real world, we don't know the *expected* rate of inflation with any degree of precision, and therefore we have no straightforward way to calculate the real rates of interest which bond buyers and other lenders expect to receive.

The situation is not hopeless, however. Expected future inflation surely depends in part on what is happening currently. One very simple approach is to assume that people expect the current rate of inflation to continue into the future. This rate of inflation can then be used in equation 17-1 to estimate the real rate of interest.

This has been done in Figure 17-4. When calculated in this way, long-term real interest rates were quite stable, between 2% and 3%, until 1973. Until that time, economists were quite confident that real long-term interest rates would remain quite stable in the face of inflation.

However, the estimates of real yields on bonds became very low during the middle 1970s, actually falling below zero; that is, nominal yields were less than the current rate of inflation. The most plausible explanation of the negative rates is that there is something wrong with the assumption that people expected current inflation to continue. In the mid-1970s, the public did *not* seem to expect the high prevailing inflation to continue. The high inflation could be attributed in part to the oil price shock, whose inflationary effects might be expected to peter out through time. Because expected future inflation was less than current inflation in 1974–1975, real interest rates were in fact higher than the naive estimates shown in Figure 17-4. The puzzle of 1974–1975 can be solved.

FIGURE 17-3

Nominal and real rates of interest, with 5% inflation

On a $100 loan, $5 is required to compensate the lender for the yearly loss of value of the $100 loaned. With a nominal payment of $8, this leaves the lender ahead by $3. Thus, the real rate of interest is 3%.

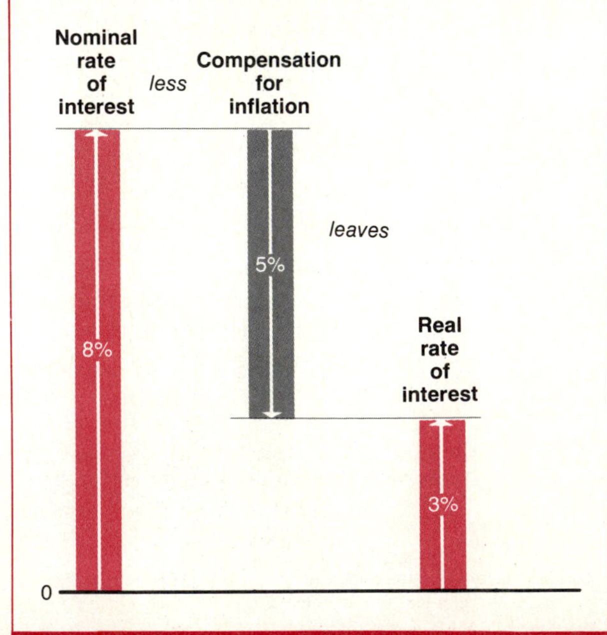

It is less easy to explain the high estimates for the real rate of interest since 1980. Nominal interest rates remained very high, even though the rate of inflation declined from 12.4% to less than 4%. One logical possibility is that people considered the low rate of inflation an aberration and were skeptical that inflation would be kept down in the future. As in the mid-1970s, the rate they expected may have differed from the current rate of inflation. Another possibility is that real interest rates were in fact very high, in part because of the large deficits of the federal government. At any rate, economists now are much less confident than they were a decade ago that nominal interest rates will compensate fully for inflation, leaving the real rate stable. Lawrence H. Summers of MIT has concluded that "the data suggest some tendency for interest rates to adjust to changes in expected inflation, but far less than is predicted by theory."[2] In other words, inflation *may* have some continuing effect on the *real* rate of interest. If this is so, inflation can have substantial and continuing effects on borrowers and lenders.

We now turn to three complications: (1) how inflation causes a "front loading" of debt, (2) how inflation and taxation interact, and (3) why high inflation is gener-

[2] Lawrence Summers, "The Nonadjustment of Nominal Interest Rates," in James Tobin (ed.), *Macroeconomics, Prices and Quantities* (Washington: Brookings Institution, 1983), p. 232.

FIGURE 17-4

Yields on corporate bonds

Market yields have risen sharply in the past two decades. However, until 1981, the increases could be fully explained by more rapid inflation. Estimated real rates of interest did not exceed 3% until the early 1980s.

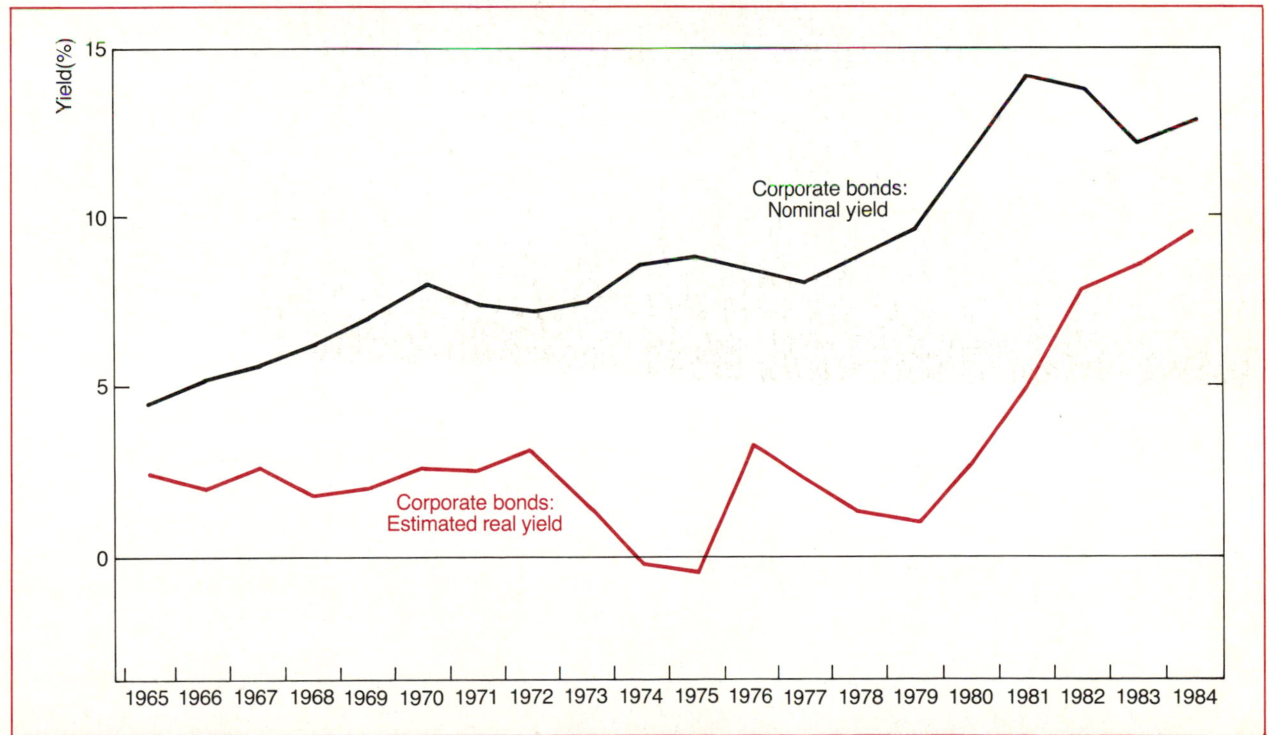

ally variable and unpredictable inflation. In each case, we consider how bond contracts may be adjusted in an effort to reduce the effects of inflation—and how and why these efforts may not be completely successful.

HOW INFLATION CAUSES A "FRONT LOADING" OF DEBT

Even if nominal interest rates rise enough to completely compensate for inflation, the inflation may still have real consequences. Borrowers face a problem. To see why, suppose a family buys a home. They take out a mortgage of $100,000 to be repaid over a 30-year period.

First, consider their situation in a noninflationary world, with nominal and real interest rates at 4%. Their payments are approximately $475 per month for 30 years. This monthly payment covers both interest and the repayment of the $100,000 loan. Because there is no inflation, the burden of the debt is spread evenly over the 30-year period. The $475 they pay in the last month has the same purchasing power as the $475 paid in the first month.

Now, consider what happens with 10% inflation. If the real interest rate remains at 4%, the nominal rate will be 14%. This will mean payments of approximately $1,500 per month over the 30 years. This $1,500 represents a *huge* burden at first, since prices have not yet risen very much. However, by the final year, the $1,500 will be trivial. It will represent less purchasing power than $100 in the first year. (With 10% inflation, prices double every 7 years. Prices will therefore increase by more than 16-fold within the 30-year period. See Box 17-2.)

Thus, inflation and high nominal rates of interest result in the burden of mortgages being shifted forward to the early years. The mortgages are ***front-loaded.***

A debt is *front-loaded* if the payments, measured in real terms, are greater at the beginning than at the end of the repayment period.

Many people who could buy a home in a noninflationary situation find they cannot do so if inflation is rapid, because of the heavy burdens they face during the early years. This is an important real effect of inflation—*even if the real interest rate remains unchanged and inflation is correctly anticipated.*

Following the rapid increase in inflation and the escalation of interest rates, the percentage of households owning their own home declined in 1981 and 1982, thus reversing a long upward trend. Home ownership had become more difficult for three reasons: (1) high interest rates, (2) high house prices, and (3) the recession of 1981–1982, which dragged real incomes down. Even after the strong recovery of 1983–1984, high interest rates and high house prices made it very difficult to buy a home. In 1950, 7 out of 10 American families could afford to buy the average new home. By 1984, fewer than 3 in 10 could.

Graduated Payment Mortgages

Why not remove front loading by starting with low payments, increasing them gradually as prices rise? In our example in which prices rise steadily at 10% per annum, home buyers would have an initial payment of approximately $480 at the end of the first month, when prices have risen only a little. The monthly payment would then rise gradually, in line with inflation, to reach $8,300 by the time the final payment was made at the end of the thirtieth year. In this way, the burden would be the same in every month—*provided that inflation continued at a steady 10% per year*. (The figures are correct. With 10% inflation, $8,300 at the end of 30 years has the same purchasing power as $480 at the end of the first month.)

However, if inflation slowed down, a family would be in trouble if it had a mortgage whose payments rose in this way. With money retaining much of its value, the rising dollar payments would become a larger and larger burden, and home owners might be unable to meet their payments. A rapid inflation may indeed slow down, as it did in the early 1980s. This means that potential home owners cannot risk borrowing, nor can savings institutions risk making loans with ***fully graduated*** payments; that is, loans whose payments will remain constant in real terms if the present rate of inflation continues.

A *graduated-payment mortgage* is one whose money payments rise as time passes. A *fully graduated* mortgage is one whose money payments will rise enough to

keep real payments constant if the present rate of inflation continues. (Such fully graduated mortgages are not available.)

While some lending institutions have experimented with mildly graduated mortgages, the graduation falls *far* short of the amount which would be needed to level out the real burden. As a consequence, home buyers continue to face front-loaded mortgages, and many therefore have to settle for smaller homes than they could afford if there were no inflation.

(A graduated-payment mortgage, whose payments increase *gradually* to *stabilize* real payments, should not be confused with a common type of mortgage that has in fact been offered by lending institutions—one whose payments are low for the first year but then increase *abruptly*. Home buyers, beware! Such mortgages are dangerous. People often move into homes and, after the first year, find that they cannot afford the mortgage payments, which have risen sharply in real terms. The fact that lending institutions have responded to high nominal interest rates by offering such mortgages represents one of the not-so-obvious costs of inflation.)

To sum up: Full graduation of mortgages does not occur. Therefore, inflation results in the front loading of mortgages to some degree. This means that, even after inflation has continued for some time and has been built into people's expectations, it continues to have an effect on real aspects of the economy. Most notably, it increases the real burden faced by home owners in the early years. In this important way, our economy fails to adjust to an inflationary environment.

BOX 17-2

THE RULE OF 70: HOW LONG DOES IT TAKE FOR PRICES TO DOUBLE?

Consider the effects of a steady inflation at 10%. During an initial base year, the index of prices is 100; in the second year, it becomes 110. During the third year, the index rises again by 10%. That is, it rises to 110% of the previous year's height, or to 121 (110 × 110%). Because the index grows at a compound rate, it increases by a larger number each year. As a result, the index reaches 200 in less than 10 years. But how long does it take? The answer is: about 7 years.

This answer is found by using the ***rule of 70:***

$$\text{Approximate number of years required to double} = \frac{70}{\text{percentage rate of growth per year}}$$

In our example, where the rate of growth was 10% per year:

$$\text{Approximate number of years required to double} = \frac{70}{10} = 7$$

Because it is a general formula, the rule of 70 has broad applicability. It can be used to estimate not only how long prices take to double, but also how long your interest-bearing bank account takes to double, or how long a GNP growing at a constant real rate takes to double. For example, if GNP grows at 3.5% per year, it will double in about 70/3.5 = 20 years.

The rule of 70—reflecting the underlying phenomenon of compounding—would lead to spectacular results if inflation were to continue at 7%, the average annual rate during the decade from 1975 to 1985. Between 1985 and 1995, prices would double, then redouble by year 2005. By 2015, they would be 8 times their 1985 level; by 2025, 16 times. If you wanted to earn $32,000 in 1985 dollars by the time of your retirement in 2035, you would have to bargain for a million bucks a year. But that would be just a hint of things to come. If all prices were to rise at the same average rate, by 2060 your grandchildren would be paying $80 for a cup of coffee. It would cost them $2.5 million to send one of their kids to a private college for 1 year!

INFLATION AND THE TAX SYSTEM

Inflation can introduce three major complications into the tax system: (1) inflation has pushed people into higher tax brackets; (2) inflation greatly complicates the taxation of interest; and (3) inflation introduces quirks and inequities into the taxation of businesses.

1. Tax Bracket Creep: Inflation and the Increasing Burden of Taxes

Until recently, inflation has meant that, as dollar incomes rose, taxpayers were pushed up into higher and higher tax brackets. The general idea may be illustrated by referring back to the 1984 tax schedule in Table 5-2 (page 82). A couple earning $20,000 pays a federal income tax of $1,741, or 8.7% of their income. Suppose that the average level of prices doubles, and so does the couple's pretax income. It is now $40,000, which barely keeps up with inflation. If the tax schedule remains unchanged, taxes now take $6,538, or 16.3% of their income. Although they are earning no more income in real terms, taxes take a larger share. Similarly, inflation can cause taxes to rise for other families, both rich and poor, whose incomes barely keep up with inflation. While all are affected, the problem is most severe for the middle class. The poor do not pay much income tax. The rich are already in the highest marginal tax bracket. It is the middle class whose taxes rise most.

Thus, inflation has generally raised the real burden of taxes. In order to eliminate this effect, the 1981 tax act provided for the income tax to be ***indexed,*** beginning in 1985. Indexation means that tax brackets and exemptions rise with inflation. If prices double, so does the nominal income at which the the various tax brackets begin. For example, the 18% bracket begins at $40,000 instead of $20,000. Thus, if your money income doubles when prices double, you stay in the same place in the tax table. Your income remains the same in real terms, and so does your tax.

If the income tax is *indexed,* the law provides for exemptions, tax brackets, and other dollar measures in the tax code to increase automatically, in the same proportion as the increase in the price index.

Indexation was not part of the Reagan administration's early tax proposals; it was included in the 1981 tax act at the initiative of Congress. However, President Reagan became a staunch supporter, resisting suggestions in 1983 and 1984 that indexing be deferred or eliminated as a way to reduce the large budget deficits. He summarized the case for indexing:

> Let's not kid ourselves. Government has found inflation a very handy method for getting additional revenues without having to face the public and demand a tax increase. It is a tax. Government gets a profit from inflation. And I would like to see indexing put in place to permanently take away from government the incentive to create inflation in order to get more money.

In any country without indexing—or with an indexing system that adjusts only partially for changes in prices—inflation has a real effect on the economy, since it increases the percentage of the nation's income that is paid in taxes.

2. Inflation and the Taxation of Interest

Inflation has another real effect on taxpayers—it imposes a tax penalty on bondholders. To illustrate, consider a noninflationary situation where the interest rate is 3% in both nominal and real terms. A bondholder in the 50% tax bracket pays one half of the interest in taxes, leaving an after-tax return of 1½% in both nominal and real terms.

Now suppose that there is a continuing rate of inflation of 5%, which gets built into the interest rate. The results are shown in Figure 17-5. The nominal interest rate rises to 8%, leaving a constant pretax real rate of interest of 3%. The bondholder in the 50% tax bracket pays half the 8% interest in taxes, leaving 4% after taxes. Note what has happened to the ***real after-tax return.*** Subtracting the 5% inflation rate, we find that the real after-tax return has not only disappeared; it has in fact become negative. The reason is that the tax is collected, not just on the 3% real rate of interest but rather *on the whole 8% of nominal interest.*

However, while the tax system adds to the woes of bondholders and other lenders, it lessens the interest burden borne by borrowers. The reason is that interest payments reduce the taxable incomes of many borrowers. (Interest payments represent a business expense for corporations; they are subtracted as a cost in calculating taxable profits. Similarly, households may deduct interest payments on mortgages and other debt in calculating taxable income.) Just as the lender includes the full 8% of nominal interest as part of income, so the borrower can subtract the full 8% in nominal interest in calculating taxable income. Thus, the calculations of Figure 17-5 also apply to a borrower in the 50% tax bracket. With 8% paid in nominal interest, half of this is saved in taxes, leaving a net nominal cost of 4%. But this is less than the rate of inflation. The after-tax real burden on the borrower is negative.

This advantage to the borrower depends on the tax bracket. The higher the income of the taxpayer, the higher the tax bracket and the greater the advantage in borrowing during a period of inflation. This introduces another problem into the housing market. Upper income people have a particularly strong incentive to buy homes. They view housing "primarily as an investment rather than as necessary shelter."[3] As a result, we may get the wrong *combination* of housing—too many oversized houses to provide tax advantages to the wealthy, and not enough housing for lower-income people. Thus, the tax treatment of interest means that inflation has another real impact on the economy.

Because inflation and high nominal interest rates increase both the tax advantages to borrowers and the tax penalties on lenders, why aren't the shifts of demand and supply in Figure 17-2 even greater? Why doesn't the nominal interest rate rise by even more than the rate of inflation, in such a way as to stabilize the *after-tax* real rate of interest? The problem is that it is not clear just how this could happen. While borrowers and lenders are all affected by inflation, not all are subject to tax. For example, pension funds pay no tax on interest earnings. Other borrowers and lenders are subject to widely different marginal tax rates. If nominal interest rates were to

[3]Anthony Downs, *Rental Housing in the 1980s* (Washington: Brookings, 1983), p. 33.

FIGURE 17-5

Effect of 50% tax, with 3% real rate of interest

When inflation is 5% per year, the individual or corporation in the 50% tax bracket is not left with enough to compensate for inflation. The real after-tax interest rate is negative.

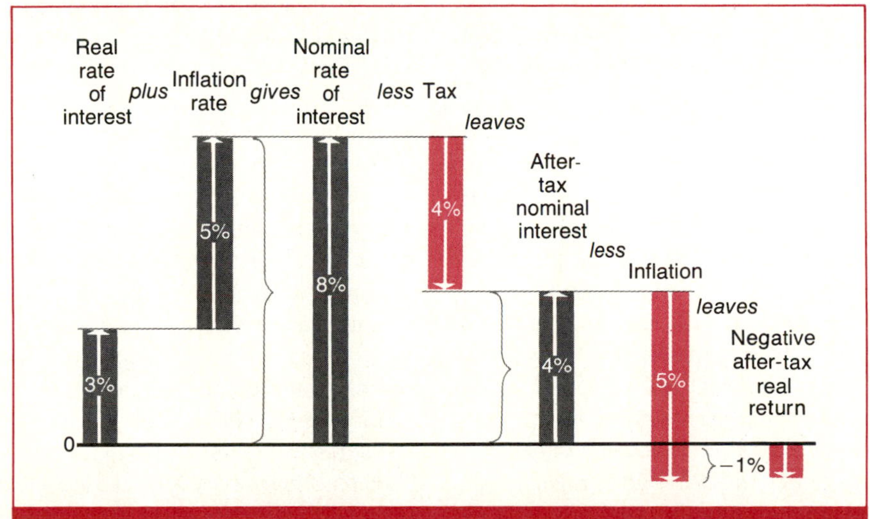

respond to taxes, it is not clear to *which* tax rate they would respond.

In fact, statistical investigations have turned up little evidence that interest rates do respond to taxes. Recall that, until 1981, interest rates had risen by no more than enough to compensate for inflation (Figure 17-4). There was no additional increase left to be explained by taxes. Since 1981, nominal rates have in fact been high, and it is possible that one reason is that the tax system has raised interest rates by encouraging borrowers and discouraging lenders. However, it is not clear that this provides the correct explanation for high interest rates. In particular, it is not clear why the bond market should have begun for the first time to adjust to the inflation-taxation combination in 1981, especially as the inflation rate was beginning to come down. There was a much more plausible explanation for the high real interest rates after 1981—namely, the ballooning deficits of the federal government.

3. The Inflation-Taxation Combination: The Effects on Business

In some respects businesses lose from inflation, while in other respects they gain.

How businesses lose: They pay taxes on artificial profits Consider what happens when a business uses materials bought several years ago in producing goods today. Their accounting cost—that is, the cost at which the materials were acquired—is less than the current cost of similar materials. Thus, the costs of production tend to be understated and profits consequently overstated. Some of the profits that appear on the business statement are artificial. But they are still taxed.

What is true of material inputs is also true of machinery. Of course, a machine is not used up all at once. Rather, it is "used up"—depreciated—over a number of years. Suppose a machine is depreciated over, say, 5 years. According to present tax law, the price at which the machine was originally acquired is used in calculating depreciation. But, after several years of inflation, the price of the machine is higher. When the original price is used to calculate depreciation, the current costs of production are once more understated. Profits are accordingly overstated. Once again, artificial profits are taxed.

These artificial profits can be very large, particularly during periods of rapid inflation such as 1979–1980. In 1979, many companies began recalculating their profits after figuring their expenses in constant dollars. The results were striking. General Motors estimated that $1.1 billion of its total profits of $2.9 billion were the result of inflation. AT&T estimated that *over half* its 1979 profits were artificial. In 1980, Bethlehem steel found that, when account was taken of inflation, its reported profit of $121 million became a *loss* of about $200 million.

Many business executives suggest that they be allowed to depreciate buildings and equipment more heavily, to take account of inflation, so that there will be fewer artificial profits for the government to tax. Specifically, they advocate ***replacement-cost depreciation.*** Depreciation would be calculated using the current replacement cost of the machine, rather than its original price. The Treasury's proposals for tax reform in 1985 included a provision for replacement-cost depreciation.

With *replacement-cost depreciation,* the current replacement costs of buildings and equipment—rather than the original acquisition costs—are used in calculating depreciation.

How businesses gain from the inflation-taxation combination: They borrow If inflation is unexpected, businesses get a windfall because the funds they have borrowed at low interest rates can be repaid with lower-valued money. If inflation is expected, interest rates are higher in compensation. But businesses still get the tax advantage—explained earlier—which comes to borrowers in the event of inflation. This advantage is particularly great for businesses with large real estate holdings. Real estate can often be mortgaged for a large percentage of its value. Furthermore, land and buildings generally rise in price during inflationary periods.

Because inflation offers this advantage to business, the proposal to allow replacement-cost depreciation is controversial. Critics charge that it would give an unfair break to business by removing the disadvantages while leaving the advantages they gain from inflation. The case for replacement-cost depreciation is further weakened by the other tax breaks enjoyed by businesses that invest—

for example, accelerated depreciation and the investment tax credit. When the Treasury proposed replacement-cost depreciation in 1985, it balanced this proposal with the recommendation that the investment tax credit be repealed.

Inflation introduces many quirks and peculiarities into the tax system, which was developed on the assumption that the average level of prices would remain reasonably stable. It would be *very* complicated to rewrite the tax laws to remove the effects of inflation. One of the best ways to limit tax inequities is to keep the rate of inflation down.

INFLATION AND UNCERTAINTY

The chief evil of an unstable dollar is uncertainty.
Irving Fisher

Thus far, the main focus has been on the effects of continuing, stable, anticipated inflation and on the ways in which the economy does and does not adjust to such inflation. We have seen that, even in this case, inflation has real effects. But when it is unexpected, inflation has much stronger effects. These can be very serious when the average rate of inflation is high, because rapid inflation generally has a large erratic, unexpected component. A country with a very rapid inflation may, for example, find that inflation bounces from 100% one year to 50% the next and to 90% the next. On the other hand, a country with a low average rate of inflation will find that the inflation rate is also quite stable from year to year. Thus, observe in Figure 17-6 that the year-to-year change in the U.S. rate of inflation was quite small during the late 1950s and early 1960s, when the average rate was low. Between 1968 and 1982, U.S. inflation was more rapid *and* more erratic. Let us consider the effects of erratic inflation on the issuers and buyers of bonds and on wage earners and employers.

Erratic Inflation and the Debt Market

Bonds are generally bought by people interested in a stable income; those who are are willing to take risks are more likely to go into the stock market. While increases in nominal interest rates help compensate bond buyers for *predictable* inflation, unpredictable inflation makes the real return on bonds very uncertain. If the rate of inflation shoots up above the nominal interest rate, the bond holder will be "soaked;" the interest won't even cover the dollar's loss of value through inflation. On the other hand, if the inflation rate unexpectedly comes down, the bond holder will receive a windfall.

Because bond buyers (lenders) are generally interested in stability and safety, they tend to withdraw from the market if inflation becomes erratic. Similarly, potential issuers of bonds (borrowers) are reluctant to bring out new bonds; they also are uncertain whether erratic inflation will make them winners or losers. Thus, erratic inflation tends to dry up the traditional long-term bond market. Bond buyers are reluctant to buy, and corporations are reluctant to issue bonds. For example, in 1980, there was great uncertainty whether inflation would accelerate and, if so, by how much. For this reason (and also because of the recession), the number of new bonds issued in the United States fell sharply. Because uncertainty over the future rate of inflation disrupted the bond market, businesses found it more difficult to finance long-term projects. The resulting reduction in investment represented a real cost to the economy.

Innovation in the mortgage market Bond contracts may be adjusted to reduce the effects of uncertainty, but once more the adjustment is likely to be imperfect and incomplete. One way of altering corporate bonds, home mortgages, or other debt is to provide for periodic changes in the nominal rate of interest during the term of the loan. The interest payable can be tied to a current rate of interest, such as that on U.S. Treasury bills or newly issued bonds. In this way, interest payments can be adjusted in the face of changing conditions. With the large changes in inflation and interest rates in the United States, savings and loan associations have put increasing emphasis on such ***adjustable-rate mortgages,*** also known as ***variable-rate mortgages.*** The majority of newly issued mortgages now have adjustable rates.

An *adjustable-rate mortgage* (ARM) has an interest rate that is adjusted periodically in response to changes in the market rate of interest.

Note that the adjustable-rate mortgage is aimed at a

different problem than the graduated-payment mortgage. The adjustable-rate mortgage is designed to deal with the problem of *variable* inflation and interest rates. The graduated-payment mortgage is aimed at reducing the problem of front loading, which arises when inflation and interest rates are *high*. As we have seen, graduated-payment mortgages are not appropriate when inflation and interest rates are erratic. Because variable-rate mortgages have become common, while graduated-rate mortgages are rare, the mortgage market has dealt much better with the problem of *variable* inflation and interest rates than with *high* rates and front loading.

INDEXED WAGES

Inflation is like toothpaste. Once it's out, you can hardly get it back in again.

Karl-Otto Pohl
President of the West German Central Bank

Unforeseen changes in the rate of inflation also affect the real returns from other contracts, such as wage contracts. As already noted, the real wages of workers on long-term contracts decline when inflation accelerates unexpectedly.

FIGURE 17-6
The changing rate of inflation
When inflation was low, in the late 1950s and early 1960s, there was little change in its rate from year to year. Between 1968 and 1981, the average rate of inflation was higher on average, and it also varied considerably from year to year.

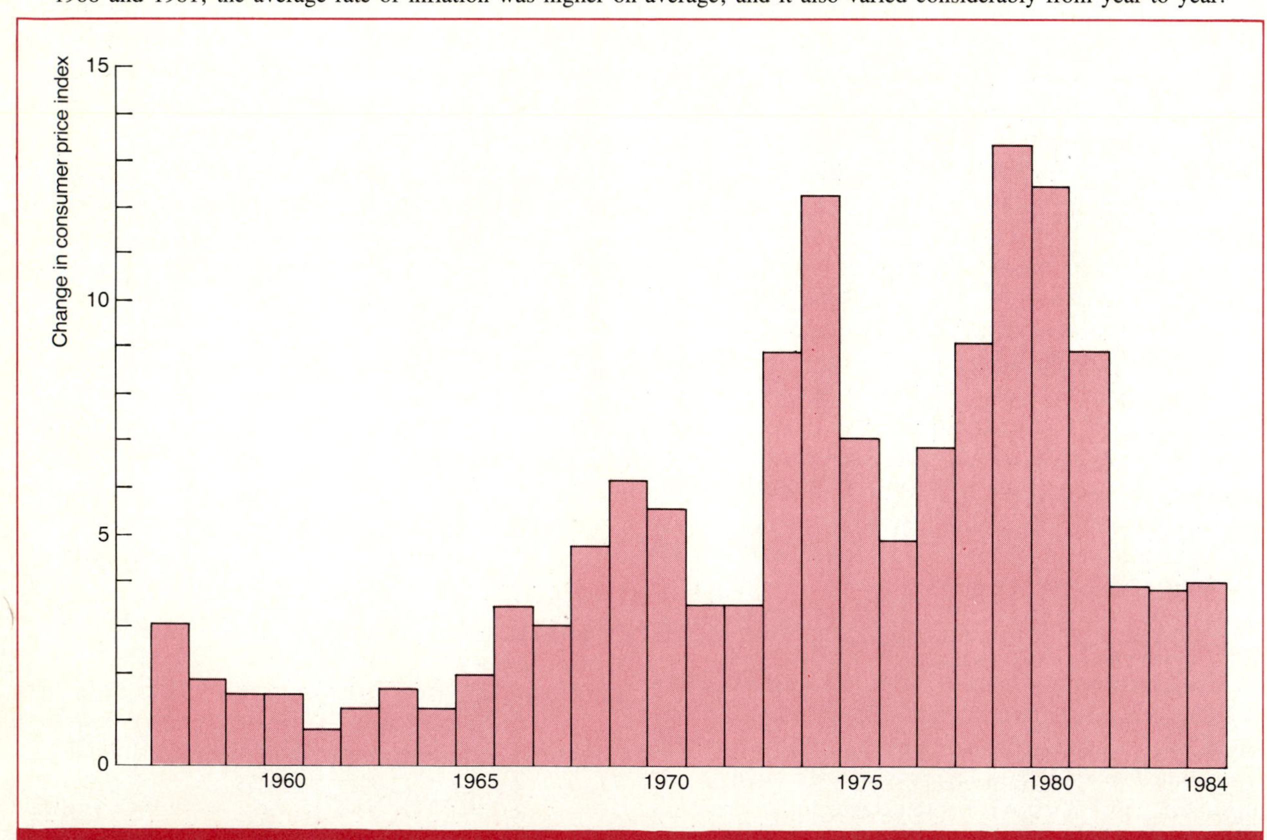

One way for workers to protect themselves during periods of erratic inflation is to negotiate shorter-term contracts; for example, contracts covering 1 year rather than the 3 years that are standard for union contracts in the United States. However, frequent negotiation is time consuming for business executives and labor leaders. Furthermore, it raises the possibility of more frequent strikes.

An alternative is to arrange in the contract for increases in the money wage to compensate for inflation. In other words, wage contracts can be ***indexed.*** During the 1970s, when the rate of inflation was accelerating rapidly, indexed contracts became quite common in the United States. In 1970, only 25% of the workers covered by major collective bargaining contracts were protected from inflation by ***escalator clauses.*** By the end of the decade, that figure had risen to 60%.

An *indexed* wage contract contains an *escalator clause* that provides workers with additional money wages to compensate for inflation, generally as measured by the consumer price index (CPI). The additional wage is often referred to as a *cost of living allowance* (COLA).

Often, there is a *cap* on the indexation, which limits indexation to no more than a specified percentage.

Indexed Wages: A Way of Easing the Transition to Lower Inflation?

The primary reason for wage indexation is to reduce workers' uncertainty over their real wage. But it is also sometimes recommended as a help in unwinding the inflationary spiral discussed in Chapter 16. We noted there that a vicious cycle can exist. Because people expect inflation, they build it into their wages and other contracts. As a consequence, costs continue to rise and continuing upward pressure is exerted on prices. To a considerable degree, inflation exists because people expect it, and people expect it because it exists. Karl-Otto Pohl's toothpaste has gotten out of the tube.

If wage contracts are not indexed, the process of unwinding inflation may be very slow and painful, as we noted in Chapter 16. It may take a number of years of abnormally high unemployment (at points such as *V* in Figure 16-11) before expectations of inflation can be reduced and inflation sweated out of the system. Some economists have suggested indexing wages as a way of breaking the inflationary spiral. Instead of negotiating a 10% wage increase during a period of 8% inflation, workers might settle for a 2% real wage increase; that is, an increase of 2% plus the increase in the price index. If initial success were achieved in reducing the rate of inflation (by, say, 3%), indexing would *automatically* reduce the increase in nominal wages (from 10% to 7%). Upward pressures on prices would be reduced further and the inflationary spiral broken in a relatively rapid and painless way.

However, two *major* difficulties arise when indexed contracts become common:

1. If inflation gets worse, indexation makes the spiral even worse still. Wages respond more quickly, generating even faster price increases. Thus, while indexing means that inflation can be wound down more quickly, it also means that inflation can accelerate more quickly. Prices become more erratic. (The natural tendency of negotiators to index contracts during periods of high inflation is one reason why high inflation tends to be erratic. Put another way, the desire of people to protect themselves from erratic inflation makes inflation even more erratic.)

The danger of indexation causing an acceleration of inflation is particularly great if the increase in productivity slows down. Consider an extreme example. Suppose that all wage agreements and other contracts (such as bonds and contracts for the delivery of materials and parts) are fully indexed, with no caps. In other words, all contracts are set in real terms. Suppose that productivity has in the past been rising at 3% per annum and that labor contracts include a 3% real wage increase for the future. Then suppose that the growth in productivity slows down to 1%. Something has to give. Contracts promise people 3% more per year in real terms. These contracts cannot be fulfilled, since only 1% more is being produced each year. Money wages will be continuously increased in a vain attempt to provide the 3% real wage increase. The result of such unfulfillable contracts will be an explosion of money wages and prices.

In fact, as indexation increased in the 1970s, the rate of productivity growth declined (for reasons which will be studied in Chapter 18). The combination of indexation and weak productivity added to the acceleration of inflation during that decade.

2. Indexing leads to a quick response of wages and other prices to an external shock, such as an increase in the price of oil. Somebody has to pay the higher cost of imported oil. If wages and other incomes are stable in dollar terms, each of us will bear the burden of higher prices at the gas pump. But if we are protected by indexing, our wages and the prices of what we sell will increase automatically. The burden will be passed along to someone else at the end of the line—such as a retired person with a pension fixed in dollar terms. Thus, in the face of an external shock, indexing leads to two problems: a speeding up of the inflationary effect, and an even heavier burden on those "at the end of the line" who are not protected from inflation.

In this regard, Britain had a particularly unfortunate experience with indexation. In 1973, Prime Minister Edward Heath's Conservative government encouraged inclusion of escalator clauses in wage contracts, in the belief that they would make it easier for labor leaders not to demand overly large nominal wage increases. The timing could not have been worse. The new indexation clauses added to the inflationary effect of the first explosion in the international price of oil in late 1973 and 1974.

Because of such problems, some early advocates of indexing (such as Milton Friedman) have become less enthusiastic in recent years. While indexing undoubtedly contributed to the rapid fall in the rate of inflation in the United States in 1981–1982, indexing generally seems to have made inflation worse, not better. Most sobering, perhaps, has been the experience of Israel, where indexing is widespread. Inflation increased from about 40% in 1974 to 130% in 1980 and 425% in 1984. Ezra Sadan, of the Finance Ministry, compared indexation to a drug: "Once you've got used to it, you have to keep it up." Of course, indexing is not solely, or even primarily, responsible for the acceleration of inflation. Israeli problems are compounded by very high military expenditures. Like high oil prices, they must be borne by somebody.

In a number of countries, attempts have been made to reduce inflationary pressures by moving away from indexation or by avoiding it in the first place. West Germany has had legal prohibitions against wage indexation. In Greece, Andreas Papandreou's government combined a wage freeze with a delay in the indexing of pensions. Some countries—such as Brazil, France, and Italy—have tried to reduce the inflationary spiral by changing the indexes used to compensate workers and others for inflation. In Brazil, the cost of imported oil was excluded from the index, thus reducing the inflationary effects when oil prices were rising and dealing with problem 2 above. In order to combat inflation, the French government of François Mitterand in 1982 decided to link wages and pensions, not to the actual rate of inflation (14% in 1982), but to the *target* rate for the coming year—8% for 1983 and then 5% for 1984. In this way, the indexing system was transformed into a method of restraining wages and pensions. Such moves sometimes meet severe resistance. In Italy, where Prime Minister Cossiga took office in 1978 with the announcement that he would fight inflation by adjusting the wage escalator (*scala mobile*) downward, the reaction of the unions was so strong that he quickly backed down. However, this was just one round in a continuing struggle. In 1984, Prime Minister Craxi took steps to curb the *scala mobile,* and his actions were upheld in a national referendum in 1985.

MACROECONOMIC POLICY IN AN INFLATIONARY ENVIRONMENT

Inflation not only creates problems for home buyers, businesses, and labor negotiators. It also means that policymakers have difficulty in figuring out what is going on and what policies are most appropriate. In particular, inflation changes the value of outstanding government debt, and therefore complicates the measurement and evaluation of fiscal policy.

To see why, let's reconsider some of the major facts about the federal government's finances in a recent year. At the beginning of fiscal 1984, the government's total outstanding debt was $1,382 billion. During that year, government expenditures were $842 billion, receipts were $666 billion, and the deficit was accordingly $176 billion. The deficit necessitated additional government borrowing, which raised the national debt to $1,558 billion by the end of the fiscal year; that is, the debt rose by the amount of the deficit. Of the government's expenditures, $111 billion were interest payments on the national debt. The inflation rate was approximately 4%.

Calculating the "Real" Deficit

Here's one possible interpretation of these facts. With 4% inflation, the beginning debt of $1,382 billion could grow by a similar 4%—or by $55 billion—without its real size changing at all. Thus, the first $55 billion of the deficit is not really a deficit. It does not add to the government's obligations in real terms; it simply offsets the effects of inflation. Thus, the true deficit was not the $176 billion commonly reported. Rather, it was $55 billion less, or only $121 billion. That is, the ***real deficit*** was only the amount by which the real debt of the government rose. According to this line of argument, the standard figures greatly overstate the real deficit, and therefore greatly overstate the stimulus coming from the fiscal side.

The *real deficit* of the government is measured by the increase in the real debt of the government. If the debt falls in real terms, the government has a *real surplus*.

Proponents of this view include Robert Eisner of Northwestern University and Paul Pieper of the University of Illinois, who argue that "in government accounts as in private accounts, inflation plays vast tricks." They recalculate the government deficit as the increase in the real value of the debt, and find that this greatly alters the picture of fiscal policy. Rather than sizable deficits—as shown in the standard figures—Eisner and Pieper estimate that the real budget was in *surplus* between 1978 and 1980 (Figure 17-7). They argue that many economists have been mistaken in concluding, on the basis of the standard figures, that the federal budget became perversely expansionary after 1966, when inflation was increasing. On the contrary, "the federal budget may properly be viewed as more frequently in surplus than in deficit. . . . The view that fiscal policy has generally been too easy and overstimulatory is contradicted." Furthermore, "the 1981–1982 recession cannot be properly interpreted as the triumph of all-powerful monetary constraints over relatively ineffective fiscal ease." Why not? Because, say Eisner and Pieper, the real inflation-adjusted budget was not very stimulative at that time. Particularly in 1981, the real deficit was quite small.[4]

An Alternative View

An alternative view is that it is a great mistake to measure fiscal policy in real terms, even though it is of course perfectly correct that inflation decreases the real value of outstanding government debt.

According to this alternative view, it is reasonable and desirable for individuals and corporations to recalculate their debt and other liabilities and assets in real terms, to get a better idea of how they are doing. Individuals and corporations may *adjust* and *respond* to inflation in this way. However, the government is fundamentally different. The government should not simply respond to inflation. Through its monetary and fiscal policies it is primarily *responsible* for inflation. If it keeps its accounts in real terms, it is not only more likely to ignore inflation. It is also likely to make inflation worse. By keeping accounts in real terms, it can *destabilize the economy*.

To see why, consider what happens if the economy enters a period of inflation. As a result, the real value of the debt falls. As calculated by Eisner and Pieper, the real budget automatically swings into surplus. Measured in this way, fiscal policy is becoming more restrictive. To offset this unexpected restraint, the government may cut taxes or increase spending. But this will add to the inflation.

Similarly, if the government focuses on the real deficit or surplus, it may destabilize the economy during a deflationary period, such as the early 1930s. Between 1929 and 1933, prices fell approximately 25%. As a result, the real value of the goverment debt rose. In real terms, the government's budget was moving into deficit.

[4]Robert Eisner and Paul J. Pieper, "A New View of the Federal Debt and Budget Deficits," *American Economic Review*, March 1984, pp. 11–29. The quotations are from pp. 11 and 23. In addition to taking into account price changes, Eisner and Pieper adjust the budget figures for a number of other items, including increases in the value of gold owned by the government.

If the government focused on this real deficit, it might erroneously assume that it was already providing a large stimulus, and fail to make the needed shift toward expansion. It might even introduce budget cuts to limit the increase in the real debt. But such cuts would make the depression worse.

Monetary Policy in an Inflationary Environment

Similar issues arise with respect to monetary policy. The real quantity of money in the economy is important; it helps to determine the quantity of goods and services that people will buy. What would happen if the Fed were to concentrate on the real quantity of money? To make things simple, suppose that the Fed follows a policy of slowly increasing the real money stock, in line with the slow increase of the productive capacity of the economy.

Again, the focus on real magnitudes could have destabilizing results. Consider again an economy entering a period of inflation. The nominal quantity of money has undoubtedly been rising. However, when we adjust it for inflation, we may find that the real amount of money has not been rising much. It may even have been falling.[5] If

*[5]This is a likely outcome if the inflation is rapid. Because money is losing much of its value, people have an incentive to spend it more quickly. This will drive prices up even more. Prices may rise more than the nominal quantity of money, resulting in a decline in the real quantity.

FIGURE 17-7

Adjusting the federal budget for inflation

Federal deficits add to outstanding government debt. Calculated in the standard way, as an increase in the nominal debt outstanding, the federal budget has been substantially in deficit in recent years. However, when the deficit is recalculated as the increase in the real value of the debt outstanding, then some of the deficits of recent years are transformed into *surpluses*. Because of inflation, the real value of government debt declined in 1978, 1979, and 1980.

Source: For 1976–1980, R. Eisner and P. J. Pieper, "A New View of the Federal Debt and Budget Deficits," *American Economic Review,* March 1984, p. 16. Updated by authors, 1981–1984.

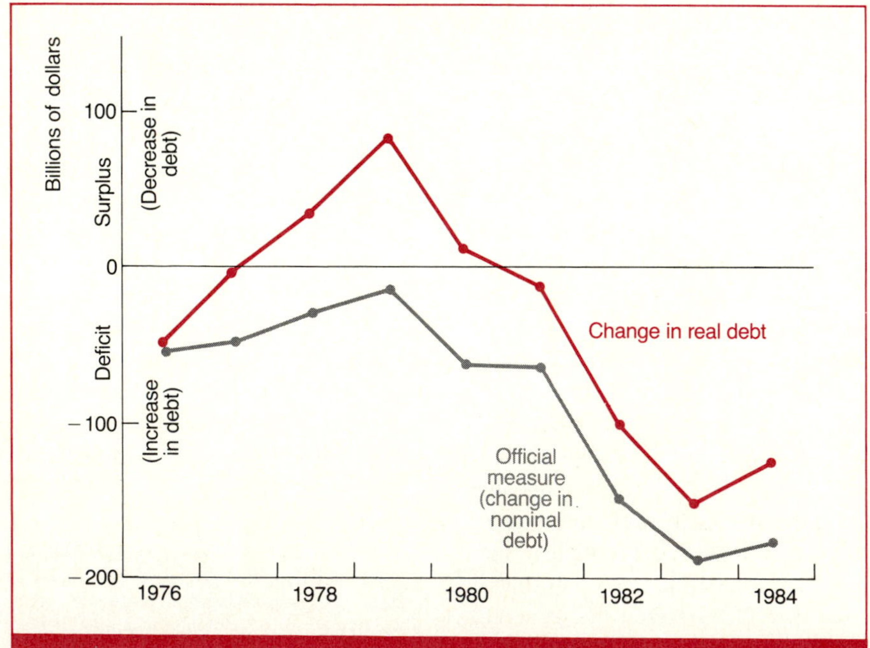

the central bank is focusing on the real quantity, it may conclude that monetary policy is too tight and create more money. This is precisely the wrong way to respond to inflation.

Similarly, concentrating on the real quantity of money can be the wrong thing to do during a period of deflation. Again, consider what happened between 1929 and 1933. Prices fell approximately 25%, while the nominal quantity of money fell about 27%. Thus, in real terms, the quantity of money declined only slightly. A central bank focusing on the real quantity might conclude that there was only a small problem with monetary policy. But, in fact, the large decline in the nominal quantity of money was having catastrophic effects. The central bank should not focus on the real quantity of money. Furthermore, outside observers should not use changes in the real quantity of money as the primary way of judging the tightness or looseness of monetary policy.

In brief, real accounting—which makes sense for individuals and corporations—does not make nearly as much sense for the government and central bank, since they are responsible for the overall operation of the economy. Real accounting can lead to destabilizing actions. A somewhat similar point may be made about indexation. For individuals or unions, it makes sense; it provides some protection from the uncertainty of inflation. But the government is fundamentally different. It has responsibility for the system as a whole. It may reasonably oppose indexation because of the destabilizing effects on the price level.

It is going too far to argue that real magnitudes are not important. They are. But the use of real magnitudes as guides for macroeconomic policy is problematic, to say the least. Even in the best of times, policymakers face difficulties in determining the best macroeconomic policies. When inflation is rapid, it greatly adds to their difficulties.

KEY POINTS

1. During periods of inflation, people are eager to borrow and reluctant to lend. This causes nominal rates of interest to rise.

2. The *real* rate of interest is (approximately) the nominal rate less the expected rate of inflation. Real interest rates cannot be calculated precisely because we do not have direct observations of the *expected* rate of inflation. However, they may be estimated by assuming that the expected rate of inflation equals the current rate.

3. When real rates are calculated in this way, we find that the real rate of interest has been much more stable than the nominal rate, which has risen with inflation. However, real interest rates have not remained perfectly stable in the face of inflation. For example, real rates were low in the middle 1970s.

4. When inflation pushes up nominal rates of interest, the effect is that borrowers have to repay loans more quickly. For example, the normal mortgage, with the same dollar payment each month, becomes "front-loaded." This makes it more difficult to buy a home, since higher real payments are required in the early years.

5. One way to deal with this problem would be with graduated-payment mortgages, whose money payments rise over the life of the mortgage, thus lessening the front loading. However, graduated-payment mortgages are very rare, and even in the few cases where they are available the amount of graduation falls far short of the amount that would be needed to level out the real burden on the borrower.

6. Inflation generally causes people to move into higher income tax brackets, even if their real incomes are stable. To eliminate this effect of inflation, the U.S. income tax has been indexed, beginning in 1985.

7. The combination of high inflation and taxation means that lenders in high tax brackets end up with negative after-tax returns. Borrowers in high tax brackets end up gaining in real terms. Thus, during periods of rapid inflation, well-to-do people are discouraged from lending and encouraged instead to borrow—for example, by purchasing large houses with big mortgages.

8. Inflation complicates the taxation of businesses. For example, it raises the question of whether historical costs or current replacement costs should be used as the basis for depreciation.

9. High inflation tends to be erratic inflation. One way that people have to protect themselves from erratic inflation is with indexed contracts. However, such contracts make inflation even more erratic. It is possible that indexation might aid in a relatively painless unwinding of inflation. In practice, it has more frequently been associated with accelerating inflation.

10. If the government's deficit or surplus is measured as the increase or decrease in the *real* value of government debt outstanding, the government has been running surpluses, not deficits, during many of the past 20 years.

11. It is, however, questionable whether fiscal policy should be measured in this way, as the change in the real debt. In particular, governments that focus on this real measure may engage in destabilizing fiscal actions. Similarly, a central bank may destabilize the economy if it focuses on what is happening to the real quantity of money.

KEY CONCEPTS

nominal rate of interest
real interest rate
front-loaded mortgage payments
graduated-payment mortgage
tax-bracket "creep"
indexation of the income tax
real after-tax return from bonds
replacement-cost depreciation
variable-rate mortgage
indexed wages
escalator clause
cost of living allowance
cap on indexation
government's real debt
real quantity of money

PROBLEMS

17-1. How does inflation make it difficult for people to acquire their first homes, even if they have assurance that their future incomes will rise with the general price level? Why are the problems less severe for those who already own a home but are selling it to move into a larger one?

17-2. Suppose that, after a period of stable prices, inflation rises gradually to a rate of 10% per annum. At 10%, it hits a peak and then gradually disappears.

(*a*) How will this affect homeowners who acquired their homes before the inflation began?

(*b*) How will those who acquire homes when inflation peaks at 10% be affected as inflation decreases?

17-3. What problem can be reduced with graduated-payment mortgages? What problem with variable-rate mortgages?

17-4. Do you favor "indexation" of the income tax code? Why or why not? What is the best case to be made on the other side?

***17-5.** Would indexation make the income tax a more or less powerful "automatic stabilizer?" (Refer back to the section on built-in stabilizers in Chapter 11. And be careful. This is not an easy question. You should consider what happens both during a strong upswing and during a recession.)

17-6. In the early 1970s, the maximum marginal tax rate on unearned income (including interest) was 98% in Britain. (Top marginal rates have since been reduced.) During that period, the rate of inflation in Britain rose to more than 20% per annum.

(*a*) With 20% inflation and 98% tax rates, what would the nominal interest rate have to be to leave the high-income bondholder with a zero real after-tax return? With a 3% real after-tax return?

(*b*) Without looking up the facts, can you make an educated guess whether nominal interest rates in Britain rose by enough to leave high-income individuals with a positive after-tax real return? If you looked at the list of holders of bonds of a British corporation, would you expect to find many high-income individuals?

17-7. Explain why the government's deficit or suplus may be calculated as the change in the real value of the debt. Calculated in this way, is the government more or less likely to have a deficit than it does with standard calculations? Why?

17-8. What difficulties arise if the government's deficit or surplus, as calculated in problem 17-7, is used as a guide in the making of fiscal policies? Does the same problem arise if the real stock of money is used as a guide by the central bank? Why or why not?

***17-9.** Do you favor allowing businesses to use replacement-cost depreciation in calculating taxable income? Why or why not?

CHAPTER 18

PRODUCTIVITY AND GROWTH:

WHY HAVE THEY BEEN DISAPPOINTING?

Not to go back, is somewhat to advance,
And men must walk, at least, before they dance.

ALEXANDER POPE

In previous chapters, we focused on the goals of high employment and price stability. There is also a third important macroeconomic objective: growth.

PRODUCTIVITY AND ECONOMIC GROWTH

The key to growth is an increase in productivity. When the typical worker produces more in an hour—that is, when the ***average productivity of labor*** increases—then total output grows. This follows from the basic relationship:

Total output (Q) =
labor hours (L) ×
average productivity of labor (Q/L) (18-1)

In other words, total output depends on:

1. The total number of hours worked.
2. The average productivity of labor. This is often known as "labor productivity" or, even more simply, "productivity."

The solid lines in Figure 18-1 show the average annual rates of change of the three items in equation 18-1, namely, the quantity of output, labor hours, and labor productivity.

In this figure, we can see clearly the rapid increase in labor productivity until well into the second half of this century. Between 1948 and 1966, productivity increased by more than 3% per year, well above the historical average. In contrast, the performance between 1973 and 1981 was poor, with labor productivity increasing by less than 1% per year. Observe also the more rapid increase in productivity in the 1981–1984 period.

These big changes in the rate of productivity improvement raise four major questions:

1. Why did productivity increase so rapidly in the period following the Second World War?
2. Why was productivity performance so poor between 1973 and 1981?
3. Are the productivity problems of the 1970s behind us? Do the figures for the early 1980s represent a short-run fluke, or are they the beginning of a new upward trend?
4. Is it desirable for the government to promote productivity and growth? What policies has the government used?

These questions will provide the main topics for this chapter. But before looking at them in detail, we will consider the relationship between labor hours and productivity.

Increases in Labor Hours and Productivity

Observe in Figure 18-1 how the increase in labor productivity generally has moved in the opposite direction to the increase in labor hours. When the input of labor hours has risen slowly, productivity has generally increased rapidly. In particular, the most rapid increase in productivity (1948–1966) coincided with the slowest rate of increase in labor hours. The long upward trend in productivity growth from 1800 into the 1960s corresponded with a long downward trend in the rate of growth of labor hours.

There is a good reason for this inverse relationship. The fewer workers entering the labor force, the more capital each one has to work with. With more capital, each worker can produce more.

Therefore, one of the explanations for the slow increase in productivity in the 1970s is straightforward: The labor force grew rapidly. As a result, there was only a slow increase in the amount of capital at the disposal of the average worker, and productivity likewise increased slowly.

The two reasons for the rapid growth in the labor force were:

1. The "baby boom" after World War II. Following a long depression and war, many people felt free for the first time to have children. By the late 1960s, these children were reaching working age.

2. The increasing participation of women in the labor force. In 1965, less than 40% of women over 16 were in the labor force. By 1980, the figure had risen to more than 50%.

As a result, *employment increased rapidly during the*

FIGURE 18-1

Average annual rates of change of output, labor hours, and productivity in the United States, 1800–1984

Between 1800 and the middle 1960s, there was a long upward trend in the rate of growth of labor productivity (*Q/L*). This coincided with a downward trend in the rate of growth of total labor hours worked (*L*). Between 1966 and 1980, the long-term trends were reversed: The input of labor hours grew rapidly, and productivity grew very slowly. Since 1981, productivity has shown signs of recovery. (This figure includes only output in the private domestic sector; the government sector is excluded. The dates on the horizontal axis indicate the beginning and end of each period. Thus, the point at the top left of Figure 18-1 shows that total output rose at an average annual rate of 4.2% over the period from 1800 to 1855.)

Source: John W. Kendrick, "Survey of Factors Contributing to the Decline in U.S. Productivity Growth," in Federal Reserve Bank of Boston, *The Decline in Productivity Growth* (1980), p. 3, updated by authors.

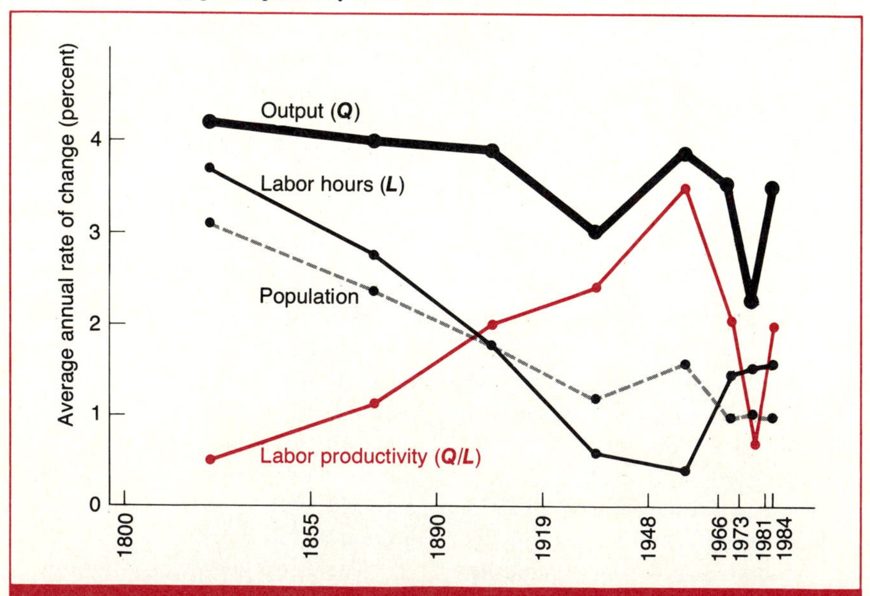

1970s. The number of civilians with jobs rose from less than 80 million in 1970 to almost 100 million in 1980.

Thus, the slower increase in productivity in the 1970s was partly attributable to the normal working of the economy. More people wanted jobs. On the whole, the economy was successful in providing these jobs. The result was less capital for each worker than there otherwise would have been and, consequently, a less rapid increase in productivity. To the extent that this was the explanation for the slower growth in productivity, there is no cause for alarm. On the contrary, the economy worked well because it provided jobs for new entrants into the labor force. However, a rapid growth in employment was *only partly* responsible for disappointing productivity performance. There were other, less reassuring, forces at work, as we shall see later in this chapter.

THE INCREASE IN PRODUCTIVITY, 1948–1973

Why does productivity increase? Some of the most notable work on this topic has been done by Edward F. Denison of the Brookings Institution, a policy-oriented think-tank in Washington, D.C. Denison's findings for the period 1948–1973 are summarized in the first column of Table 18-1.

Between 1948 and 1973, there was an average annual increase of 2.5% in output per worker.[1] Of this increase, Denison attributed 0.3% to changes in the labor force. The average worker put in fewer hours per week, and this, by itself, would have depressed output per worker by 0.2%. However, Denison found that an improvement in the quality of the labor force, as measured by education, more than made up for the decline in the workweek. The increase in schooling of the U.S. labor force is illustrated in Figure 18-2. Over the past three decades, the percentage with a high school diploma has risen steadily, and so has the percentage with at least 8 years of schooling.

Denison found that the increase in physical capital contributed 0.4% to the increase in output per worker, or slightly less than the amount attributable to education. An improved allocation of resources—primarily from reduced discrimination against minorities and lower barriers to international trade—added 0.3%. Economies of scale added another 0.4%. Even though our economy is

[1]Denison studied output per *worker*, while Figure 18-1 shows output per *hour*. As a result, Table 18-1 does not correspond precisely to Figure 18-1. However, output per worker does change in much the same way as output per hour.

TABLE 18-1
Changes in Output per Person Employed
(nonresidential business sector)

	(1) 1948–73		(2) 1973–81		(3) Difference (2) − (1)	
Average annual change in output per person employed		2.5%		−0.2%		−2.7%
Percent attributable to:						
Labor:		0.3		0.2		−0.1
Divided into changes in:						
Hours at work	−0.2		−0.4		−0.2	
Education	0.5		0.6		0.1	
Physical capital		0.4		0.2		−0.2
Improved allocation of resources		0.3		0.0		−0.3
Economies of scale		0.4		0.3		−0.1
Legal and human environment		0.0		−0.2		−0.2
Advances in knowledge and not elsewhere classified		1.1		−0.7		−1.8

Source: Edward F. Denison, "The Interruption of Productivity Growth in the United States," *Economic Journal*, March 1983, p. 56.

already large, we have not yet exhausted all the advantages of size.

Finally, advances in knowledge—plus a residual not explained elsewhere—accounted for 1.1%, or almost half of the total increase. A significant source of growth is an *improvement in technology,* that is, inventions, better designs of machinery, and better methods of production.

The most important conclusion of Denison's study was that growth resulted from a *combination* of causes. *No single determinant held the key to growth,* nor could any simple strategy—such as increasing the investment in plant and equipment—hold out hope for a major acceleration of growth. Observed Denison: "The tale of the kingdom lost for want of a nail appears in poetry, not in history."

THE PUZZLE OF 1973–1981: WHAT WENT WRONG?

The last two columns of Table 18-1 show the results of Denison's effort to explain why output per worker became stagnant between 1973 and 1981. The most striking feature of these columns is that Denison's "explanations" *don't explain most of this change.* Between the earlier period and 1973–1981, the change totaled 2.7% per year (shown in column 3)—that is, the swing from +2.5% to −0.2% in the annual growth of output per worker. Denison's detailed estimates account for only a third of this swing; the remaining 1.8% is in the unexplained residual (the final item in Table 18-1). Ruefully, Denison concludes: "What has happened is, to be blunt, a mystery."[2] Other researchers have likewise been unable to explain most of the change.

Changes Identified by Denison

Before we investigate this large, mysterious residual, let us consider the changes which Denison does identify. During the 1973–1981 period, the *decline in the average number of hours at work* became more pronounced. It accounted for a 0.4% decline in output per worker, com-

[2]E. F. Denison, *Accounting for Slower Economic Growth: The United States in the 1970s* (Washington, D.C.: Brookings Institution, 1979), p. 4.

FIGURE 18-2
The educational attainment of the labor force
The percentage of the labor force with high school and college diplomas has been rising steadily, while those with less than 8 years' schooling has been falling.
Source: Statistical Abstract of the United States.

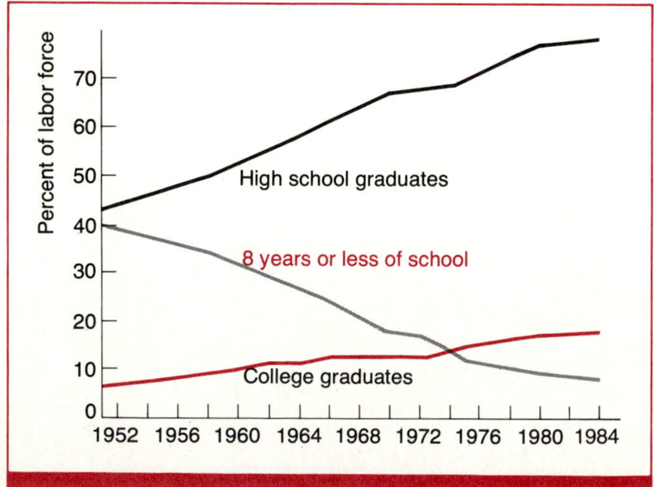

pared with the more moderate 0.2% decline during the earlier period. The large decline of 1973–1981 was due primarily to an increase in part-time employment.

A *slowdown in investment* provided Denison's second explanation. Although physical capital per worker increased between 1973 and 1981, it did so at a slower rate than in the previous period.

Of the remaining estimates, most interesting is the *legal and human environment,* to which Denison attributes a 0.2% decline. This category includes government regulations which have required the diversion of a growing share of the nation's labor and capital to reducing pollution and increasing safety. (The benefits of a better environment do not show up in measured GNP. Thus, our productivity in creating the good life may be increasing, even though our productivity in terms of measured GNP is not.) Also included are the depressing effects of more crime, which has forced businesses to divert resources to crime prevention. Thefts of merchandise have also reduced measured output.

The Mysterious Residual

Because of the very large (1.8%) unexplained residual, Denison looks in some detail at frequently mentioned possibilities which are not identified in Table 18-1. These include a decrease in *research and development* (R&D) expenditures, and the rise in *energy prices*.

Denison is skeptical that lower R&D explains much of the disappointing performance. As a percentage of GNP, R&D expenditures did decline, from a peak of 3.0% in 1964 to 2.3% in 1977. But this decline was gradual, and it is hard to see how it could account for the abrupt deterioration in output per worker in 1973–1974. Furthermore, the decline in R&D was concentrated in the government category, mostly for weapons and space research.

On the other hand, F. M. Scherer of Swarthmore College points out that, if R&D had continued to grow at its rate of the 1960s, it would have been 30% to 40% higher than it actually was in the mid and late 1970s. Scherer estimates that this shortfall in R&D expenditures accounted for between 0.2% and 0.4% of the decline in the productivity performance of the U.S. economy. Because R&D expenditures provide a payoff over an extended period, Scherer concludes that the low R&D expenditures will continue to exert a similar drag on productivity—amounting to 0.2% to 0.4%—for some time.[3]

The Increase in Energy Prices

The rise in energy prices is perhaps the most interesting of the possibilities left out of Table 18-1. Energy prices are an obvious scapegoat. The first oil price shock occurred in 1973–1974, and could thus explain the timing of the sharp deterioration in 1974. Moreover, higher oil prices might explain why the growth rate declined abruptly in 1973–1974 in *many* countries.

Nevertheless, Denison is again skeptical that higher oil prices account for much of the decline. He points out that oil consumption did not fall much, particularly in the 1973–1976 period, when output per worker was very weak. If oil consumption had fallen sharply, this would have indicated the adoption of different and probably less productive methods of doing business. But, since oil use did not fall much, it is difficult to explain the deterioration in this way.

There are several reasons for believing that oil prices could have had a more damaging effect on productivity than Denison estimated. Considerable new investment has been required in response to the higher oil prices—for example, in the automobile industry, which undertook a complete retooling to produce smaller cars. Such investments did not show up in large current reductions in oil consumption by industry, the measure which Denison used to estimate the disruptive effects of oil price increases. Yet they did make a major claim on capital resources. Furthermore, business executives have spent much time and effort trying to figure out how best to respond to higher energy prices. Dale Jorgenson of Harvard concludes that the oil price increases, and the related increases in the price of electricity, "contributed to a marked slowdown in productivity growth."[4]

In summary, we have a fair idea of some of the

---

[3]F. M. Scherer, "R&D and Declining Productivity Growth," *American Economic Review,* May 1983, p. 216.

[4]Dale Jorgenson, "The Role of Energy in Productivity Growth," in John W. Kendrick (ed.), *International Comparisons of Productivity and Causes of the Slowdown* (Cambridge, Mass.: Balinger, 1984), p. 309.

causes of the poor productivity performance of the 1973–1981 period. Denison has been able to account for about one third of the decline. Furthermore, R&D and oil prices may have been more important than Denison believes. But *we simply do not know with any degree of precision the reasons for the drastic deterioration* in the productivity performance of the U.S. economy after 1973.

THE 1980s: A RENEWAL OF VIGOROUS GROWTH?

If we had a more precise idea of what happened a decade ago, we would be in a better position to interpret the recent signs of an upturn in productivity, shown in Figure 18-3. For example, if we knew that spiralling oil prices really were the major culprit in the productivity slowdown, we would expect productivity to rebound in the face of more stable oil prices.

However, it is not just our lack of knowledge of what happened in the 1970s that makes it hard to tell whether the early 1980s mark the beginning of a new period of vigorous growth. We should avoid coming to firm conclusions from *any* brief period because year-to-year changes in productivity can be strongly affected by the business cycle.

Cyclical Swings in Productivity

During cyclical recoveries, productivity generally increases very rapidly. During recessions, it generally increases very slowly, or even declines. Why?

A major reason is that employment is sticky in the face of fluctuating demand. Many white-collar workers are on annual salaries and cannot easily be laid off during recessions. Nor is it costless to lay off production-line workers. They may get jobs elsewhere and be unavailable when the company wants to expand. Because of the costs of hiring and training, a company's labor force represents an investment which may be lost if workers are laid off. As the economy slides into a recession, firms therefore reduce their employment less than their output. Because underemployed workers are retained, produc-

FIGURE 18-3

Labor productivity, 1970–1984

During recessions, productivity is weak. Notice how productivity actually declined during the recessions of 1974 and 1980. On the other hand, productivity expands rapidly during cyclical expansions. (The data in this figure apply only to the nonfarm business sector.)

Source: Council of Economic Advisers, *Annual Report, 1985,* p. 279.

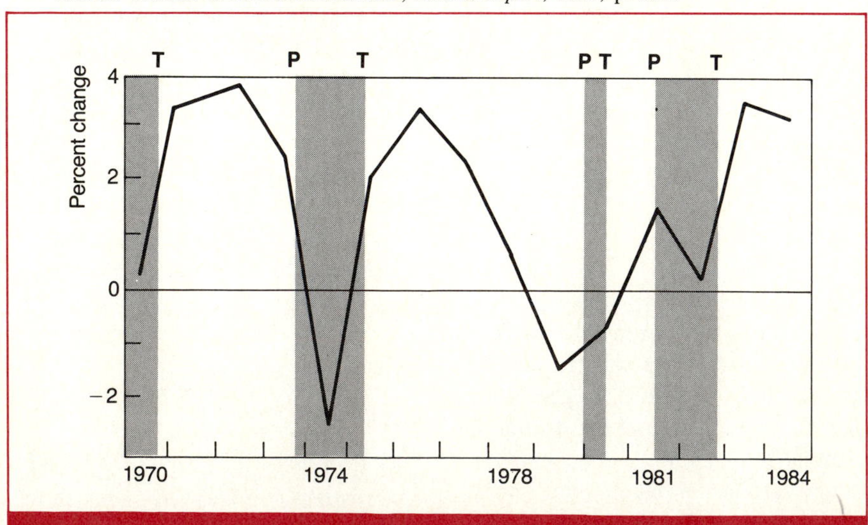

tivity suffers. Then, as economic conditions improve and output recovers, the slack is picked up. Firms can increase their output rapidly without adding many new workers. As a result, productivity rises rapidly during the recovery from a recession.

Figure 18-3 shows how productivity declined during the recessions of 1974 and 1980. Not all recessions have an equal effect on productivity, however. The recession of 1982 was much more severe than that of 1980. Yet productivity actually increased during 1982.

One reason was that many firms had already been weakened by the recession of 1980. In order to survive in the face of the severe recession of 1982, they felt that they had to give up their practice of retaining underutilized workers; they cut their work force. The 1982 recession was tough for white collar workers, as well as those on the production line. Many lost their jobs. There were two major results. The unemployment rate rose unusually rapidly. However, because labor input was being cut drastically, productivity was stronger than usual for a deep recession. In brief, business cycles can have strong, but uneven, effects on productivity.

What, then, are we to make of the large increase in productivity during 1983 and 1984? Is it just the result of the cyclical expansion from the depths of the recession? Or should we come to the more optimistic conclusion that it is the beginning of a new upward trend? John W. Kendrick takes the optimistic view in his presidential address to the Southern Economic Association, "Long-term Economic Projection: Stronger U.S. Growth Ahead."[5] But it still seems too early to tell. Caution is particularly appropriate because of what happened in late 1984 and early 1985. By that time, productivity was increasing much more slowly than it had in the previous 2 years.

INTERNATIONAL COMPARISONS

The slowdown in the 1970s has not been the only reason for concern. In addition, productivity improved more slowly in the United States than in most other advanced countries between 1950 and 1981, as shown in Figure 18-4. (However, fragmentary evidence suggests that productivity has been increasing more rapidly in the United States than in most European countries in recent years.)

Three principal explanations have been offered for the slower productivity improvement in the United States between 1950 and 1981: (1) U.S. investment is low by international standards, (2) countries that are catching up can copy U.S. technology, and (3) cultural differences give an advantage to some countries, particularly Japan.

Low Investment

Investment is one of the major sources of growth, and low investment is frequently cited as a major reason for lagging U.S. productivity. As a percentage of NNP, net investment in the United States is only half as large as in France or West Germany, and only a third as large as in Japan. One secret of Japan's success is really no secret at all. The Japanese have put 20% of their NNP into investment.

Borrowed Technology

In some ways, the most advanced country has a difficult time. If its technology is to improve, it must have a consistent flow of new inventions. Although some ideas come in a brilliant flash, most research and development is painstaking and expensive. How much easier it is to borrow technology from a more advanced country! This, then, provides a second explanation for the relatively higher growth in productivity in other countries. They have U.S. technology to copy.

However, this explanation was much more valid 20 years ago than it is today. Although the United States retains the lead in many areas of technology, other countries have closed much of the gap. Japan is ahead in robotics, and productivity in Japanese automobile factories surpasses that in the United States. It is American car manufacturers who are now copying the Japanese.

Recent trends in R&D expenditures are shown in Figure 18-5. As the leading country, the United States has had to rely primarily on domestic technology, and R&D expenditures have been relatively high. Twenty years ago, other countries could copy American technology and grow rapidly in spite of their lower R&D expenditures. However, as the technology gap has closed,

[5]J. W. Kendrick, *Southern Economic Journal,* April 1984, pp. 945–964. Kendrick is a professor at George Washington University.

foreign R&D has grown rapidly, particularly in Germany and Japan. These countries are counting more and more on domestic technology to maintain their high rates of growth.

Cultural Differences

The Japanese, it is sometimes argued, have a major advantage because of their strong cultural traditions. In their crowded islands, individuals are continually reminded of their duties to society. This gives Japanese businesses an advantage because they have a committed labor force which is willing to pay meticulous attention to quality.

It is hard to know how much of the Japanese reputation for quality is the result of cultural differences and how much is due to management practices. Major Japanese firms are committed to provide lifetime employment to many of their workers. Workers have a greater stake in their company's future, and this may explain their attention to quality. In its U.S plant, Honda has been able to maintain Japanese-level quality, suggesting that it is management, rather than culture, which provides the primary explanation for quality. This conclusion is reinforced by changes in the U.S. automobile and electronics industries. In response to Japanese competition, they have been able to close some of the quality gap.

Furthermore, some cultural differences give the United States an advantage over its competitors. U.S. workers are much more willing than European workers to move in order to take advantage of new employment opportunities.

FIGURE 18-4

Productivity changes: International comparisons

Productivity increases in the United States have been substantially less than those in France, Germany, and particularly Japan.

Source: Angus Maddison, ''Comparative Analysis of the Productivity Situation in the Advanced Capitalist Countries,'' in John W. Kendrick (ed.), *International Comparisons of Productivity and Causes of the Slowdown,* p. 71.

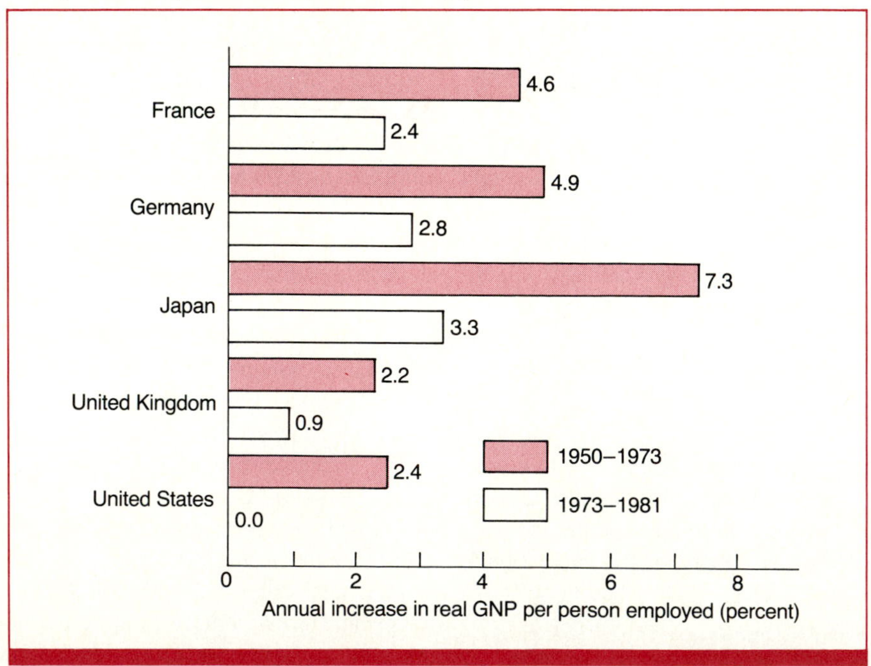

WHY GROW?

Slow U.S. growth has led to a search for ways to promote growth. But, before turning to policies designed to increase productivity and growth, we consider an even more fundamental issue: *Should* we strive for a higher rate of growth?

A Rising Material Standard of Living

At first glance, it might seem obvious that growth is desirable. Higher output makes possible a higher material standard of living. Even small changes in rates of growth can compound into large differences over long periods of time. If output increases by 1% a year, it doubles every 70 years. But if it rises by 2% per year, it doubles every 35 years and *quadruples* every 70.

However, we should not simply assume that the faster the economy grows, the better. If our overriding goal is faster growth, we may sacrifice other important goals, such as *current consumption,* a *cleaner environment,* and *leisure*.

FIGURE 18-5
Expenditures on research and development
Until the late 1970s, the United States spent a larger percentage of its GNP on R&D than did other countries.
Source: National Science Foundation, *International Science and Technology Data Update,* January 1985, p. 3.

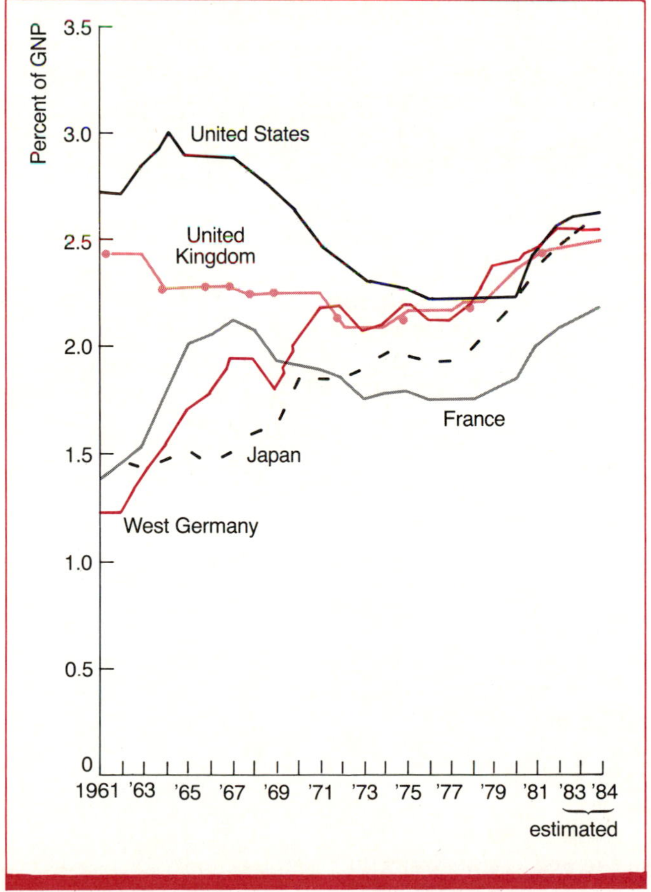

1. *Current consumption foregone.* As we noted in Chapter 2, one way to grow faster is to invest more. But when we invest more in the production of capital goods, we give up the consumer goods we alternatively could have produced today. Even though investment now will make it possible for us to produce more consumer goods in the future, there is a limit to how far we should pursue a high-growth policy. At some point, it makes no sense to reduce our current consumption further, just so our children or grandchildren can live in splendor in the future.

2. *The environment.* E. J. Mishan, formerly of the London School of Economics, has argued that growth—as usually measured by GNP—is a mirage, since goods and services are included, but the degradation of the environment and the "uglification" of the countryside are ignored.[6]

One way to increase the rate of growth of GNP would be to eliminate government regulations to improve the environment and increase safety. The expenditures on these objectives could then be used for investment, thereby increasing our output. But, while GNP would grow faster, we would not necessarily be better off. Even though clean air is not included in GNP, it is nevertheless important.

3. *Leisure.* As we saw in Chapter 7, GNP also excludes leisure. During the twentieth century, the average work week has gone down about 25%. We could have had more growth by taking less leisure. But we would not necessarily have been better off.

POPULATION AND GROWTH

Growth may result from an increase in production *per capita*—an increase which makes possible a rising standard of living. It may also result from an increase in population. In examining how population and growth are related, we should consider, at least tentatively, the issue of whether there is an "optimal" population. Clearly this involves fundamental social values which go well beyond economics, but the size of the population also has economic implications.

[6]E. J. Mishan, *Technology and Growth* (New York: Praeger, 1969).

The population issue is quite different for the advanced countries and the very poorest of the less developed countries, whose people struggle to find enough to eat. Here, we consider a country which is sufficiently affluent that physical survival is not the central economic problem.

If the population grows, there are two conflicting effects on per capita output. Most obviously, there is a depressing effect. With more people and a larger labor force, there is less capital and fewer natural resources at the disposal of the typical worker. On the other hand, a larger population and a larger market may raise the standard of living by making possible economies of large-scale production.

For some countries in some periods of history—for example, the United States in its early history—population was small, while resources were abundant. In these cases, economies of scale were the more important influence. A rising population contributed to an increase in per capita income. But such cases are rare. In most countries, certainly in modern times, population is large enough to be pressing on resources. Resource restraints are the more important of the two influences. While a 10% increase in population causes an increase in production, the increase is less than 10%. Therefore, the additional population depresses *per capita* output.

Hence, a question arises: Do we want a larger population if it holds down per capita output and income? In, say, 50 years, is it desirable to have a larger population than today, even though our standard of living may be held in check by the population growth? Or would it be better to have about the same population as today, with a much higher income per capita? Or would it be better yet to have a declining population, with a *very* much higher income per capita? This is not a question for an economist, but for a moral philosopher. There is nothing in economic analysis that allows us to answer the question of whether one life is "worth" more or less than two lives with a lower income per capita.

It is occasionally argued that there is an optimal population, where *per capita income is at a maximum.* But this argument is based on the implicit judgment that additional lives have no value whatever if they depress per capita income ever so slightly. It is not clear what the basis for this judgment might be. Most families reject it whenever they decide to have a child, since their per capita income is reduced as a result. And this judgment may be attacked by showing how absurd it becomes when pushed to its logical conclusion. The United States might have the highest possible per capita income with a population of only 10,000,000, or perhaps even as few as 1,000,000. Just think of the raw materials this small group would have at its command. These resources could be sold to foreign countries for a fortune!

CHANGING ATTITUDES TOWARD GROWTH

During the early history of the United States, the prevailing view was that the government should assist in the opening up of the new land. The Homestead Act of 1862—which provided 160 acres to anyone who would till it—reflected this view. During the nineteenth century, the government granted substantial blocks of land to the railroads, providing not only the right of way needed for their lines, but also additional lands whose value would rise as new territories were developed.

The prevailing view into the twentieth century was that the government should provide a favorable milieu for growth, without necessarily becoming a direct participant in development projects. There were, of course, some obvious and noncontroversial exceptions, such as the government's responsibility for roads. Then, under President Hoover, the Boulder Dam project was initiated. But the biggest change came while Franklin Roosevelt was president. The government departed from its primarily supportive role, and undertook such major development projects as the Tennessee Valley Authority (TVA). However, the government's objective at that time was as much to create jobs as to have the projects themselves.

With the inauguration of President John F. Kennedy in 1961, growth became a major government objective. In promising to "get the country moving again," Kennedy—like Roosevelt—was motivated by a desire to reduce unemployment. But now there was an emphasis on growth as a principal objective in and of itself. Growth was considered essential to meet pressing national needs.

First, and perhaps foremost, was the perceived need to grow in order to maintain the international standing of the United States. To use the catchwords of the time, the United States was in a race to "keep ahead of the Russians." Not only was the Soviet Union considered a clear and present military danger, requiring a long-term increase in U.S. military expenditures which could best be borne by a growing economy. The Soviet Union was also considered a threat to win the international popularity contest because of its impressive growth. How, asked the Kennedy administration, could we expect newly freed colonial peoples to shun the Soviet way of life if their economic system held out hope for more rapid advancement than ours? In retrospect, much of this argument seems odd. It was based on the assumption that the developing countries might choose a Soviet-style system because of growth, with little concern for its other consequences. And it was based on an exaggerated estimate of Soviet growth. In spite of the fears of 1960, the mixed economies of Western Europe, Japan, and North America remain substantially ahead of the Soviet Union, particularly in the production of huge quantities of consumer goods, in the development of high-technology products, and in agriculture.

Second, Kennedy and his advisers considered a rapid rate of growth highly desirable for domestic reasons. Not only would greater investment promote high employment. But also, some of the increase in production could be used to improve the lot of "The Other America"[7]—that is, the relatively invisible Americans who remain in poverty. Furthermore, a rising productive capacity could be used to construct schools, hospitals, and other needed projects.

By the 1970s, many Americans were having doubts that faster growth was desirable. In part, this seemed to be a tired reaction to the enthusiasms of the 1960s. Our overconfidence had gotten us into the mess in Vietnam, and had led to the overheating of the economy with its inflationary consequences. But there were also more direct doubts that growth should be a prime economic objective. Increasing attention was given to the environment and other competing goals. After the first great increase in the price of oil in 1973–1974, there was con-

[7] *The Other America*, by Michael Harrington (Baltimore: Penguin Books, 1962), described the bleak existence of the poor.

cern that a growth in output might put intolerable pressures on natural resources.

However, as the 1970s drew to a close, the pendulum swung back toward productivity and growth as national objectives. Once again, the desire for greater growth and productivity was related to both international and domestic objectives. There was a common—although far from universal—view that high Soviet military expenditures required greater spending for weapons on our part. If GNP were growing rapidly, additional defense expenditures would be less painful. On the domestic side, faster growth was desired not only for the additional goods and services which would be available, but also because the greater supply of goods and services would reduce inflationary pressures.

"SUPPLY-SIDE" ECONOMICS: A NEW GROWTH POLICY?

The new concern with growth in the late 1970s and early 1980s represented a major change in emphasis in macroeconomics. Since the "Keynesian revolution," the major preoccupation of macroeconomists had been with demand management—that is, with the adjustment of fiscal and monetary policies to provide enough aggregate demand to ensure a low unemployment rate, but not so much as to cause inflation. However, the poor productivity performance of the late 1970s drew attention to the fact that output depends not only on aggregate demand, but also on the ability of the economy to supply goods and services.

At the beginning of the Reagan administration, a number of "supply-side" tax cuts were enacted. These tax cuts were aimed at promoting growth in three ways: (1) by encouraging saving and investment, (2) by encouraging people to work more, and (3) by promoting the efficient use of resources. Important tax changes included the following:

1. Personal income tax rates were cut almost one-quarter. The objective was not only to reduce the tax burden on the public, but also to encourage people to work hard and to save.

2. Corporate income taxes were cut. Because corporations were left with more profits after tax, they had more funds to invest. They also had greater incentives to invest because the after-tax profitability of capital was increased.

3. Depreciation was speeded up and simplified. The "useful life" of an investment is no longer the basis for its depreciation. Most investments are now put in one of four broad categories and depreciated in 15, 10, 5, or 3 years. By reducing taxes, this acceleration of depreciation also raised the profitability of investment.

4. Businesses were given tax credits for research and development. By encouraging R&D, the government hoped to speed up innovation and technological change.

Proponents of these tax changes not only expected that they would increase the capacity of the economy to supply more goods and services. They also hoped that the tax changes would enable the government to control inflation in a relatively painless way.

Reducing Inflation without Recession?

As we saw in Chapter 16, the Federal Reserve faces a cruel dilemma, at least in the short run. If demand is suppressed in order to fight inflation, the unemployment rate may shoot up. Figure 18-6 illustrates how supply siders hoped to escape from this dilemma. By cutting taxes, they hoped to encourage production and shift the aggregate supply curve to the right, from AS_1 to AS_2. The economy would move from *A* to *B*. Rising output would go hand in hand with success in fighting inflation.

There is no doubt that a rightward shift in aggregate supply makes it easier to suppress inflation without causing unemployment. The question is, how strong is this favorable effect? How much can the aggregate supply curve be shifted? Over any short-term period, the answer is: not much. It is very difficult to raise the growth rate by as much as 1% per year. Yet this causes only a small shift in aggregate supply in any one year.

In practice, shifts in aggregate supply were completely overshadowed by shifts in demand during the early 1980s. Inflation was reduced substantially, from 12.4% in 1980 to 3.8% in 1983. However, the major reason for the lower inflation was not a shift in aggregate supply. Instead, the major reason was a decline in aggregate demand and the deep recession of 1981–1982.

Cutting Taxes without Losing Revenue?

Some of the more enthusiastic supply-side economists not only believed that inflation could be reduced without causing unemployment. They also believed that tax rates could be cut without the government losing revenue.

This idea was put forward most explicitly by Arthur Laffer of the University of Southern California, who drew the ***Laffer curve*** shown in Figure 18-7. This curve illustrates the relationship between tax rates and total government revenues. If the tax rate is zero, no revenues are collected. On the other hand, if the tax rate is 100%, once again revenues are zero; nobody will work to earn income if the government taxes it all away. People will either loaf or, more likely, spend their time finding ways—legal or otherwise—to avoid the tax.

At some intermediate tax rate, T_m, revenues are at a maximum. If the tax rate is below this level, say at T_1, a tax increase will cause little change in work effort and tax avoidance. Therefore, a tax increase will cause a rise in government revenues. For example, as taxes rise from T_1 to T_2, revenues increase from R_1 to R_2. On the other hand, if taxes are initially *above* T_m—at T_3, for example—a further increase in the rate to T_4 will cause enough idleness and tax evasion that the total taxes collected by the government will decrease, from R_3 to R_4.

The question is whether the initial tax rate is above or below the maximum revenue rate T_m. Although we know that revenues are zero if the tax rate is either zero or 100%, we do not know how high T_m is. For example,

FIGURE 18-6
A supply-side tax cut
Supply-side economists expect that a cut in taxes will lead to a rightward shift in the aggregate supply curve, as illustrated by the shift from AS_1 to AS_2. If aggregate demand remains stable, equilibrium will move from *A* to *B*. Output will be increased without causing inflation.

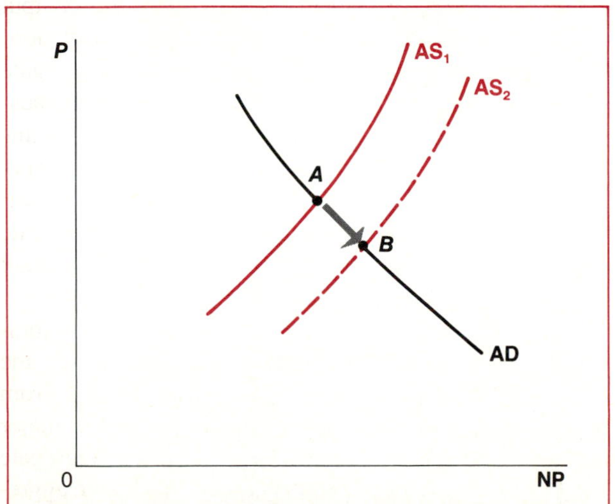

FIGURE 18-7
The Laffer curve
The Laffer curve illustrates the relationship between tax rates (*T*) and government revenues (*R*). If the tax rate is zero, no revenues are collected. If the rate is 100%, revenues are likewise zero, since nobody will earn income for the government to confiscate. At some intermediate point, *M*, tax revenues are maximized.

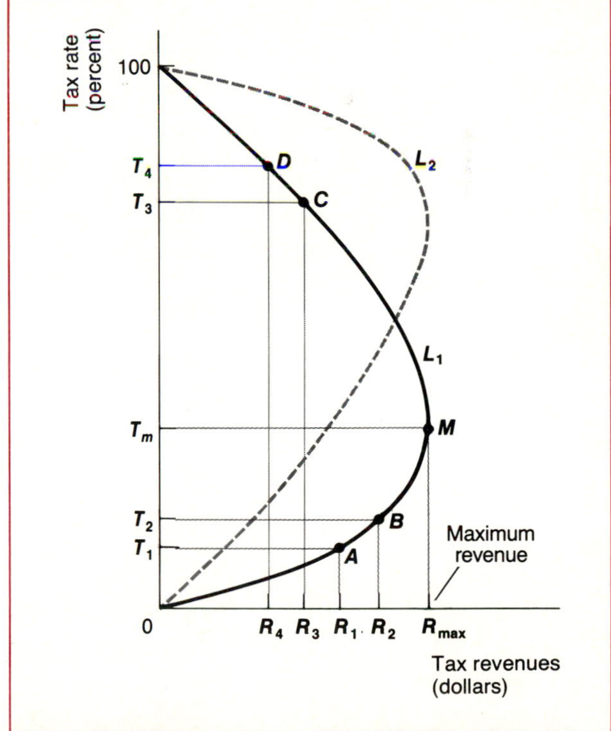

the curve could be the dashed L_2 rather than L_1. Laffer believed that we were already above T_m in 1980, in the range where a tax increase leads to a fall in government revenue. In other words, a *cut* in the tax rate would lead to an *increase* in revenues. Thus, a tax cut would be a painless policy, benefiting the public while reducing the government's deficits.

Again, things did not turn out as supply-siders hoped. The tax cuts of 1981 did not generate additional tax revenues. Government deficits ballooned.

Do Tax Cuts Promote Growth? Incentives vs. Crowding Out

When supply siders predicted that tax cuts would lower inflation and generate more revenues, they touched off a lively debate. But there is an even more fundamental issue: Do supply-side tax cuts in fact promote investment and growth?

At first glance, the answer would seem to be an obvious yes. Tax incentives—such as accelerated depreciation—promote investment, and investment promotes growth. But unfortunately, the answer is not quite so simple. Tax cuts set in motion other forces that can depress the rate of growth.

Specifically, the larger deficits caused by the tax cuts can ''crowd out'' investment, as explained in Chapter 14. In order to finance its deficit spending, the government borrows on the financial markets. This creates upward pressures on interest rates. In turn, higher interest rates discourage investment.

Thus, tax cuts create two conflicting forces. The direct effect of tax incentives is to increase investment. But investment is discouraged by the indirect effects, working through higher deficits and higher interest rates. It is not clear which of these effects is stronger. On balance, we cannot be sure whether the 1981 tax cuts encouraged or discouraged investment.

INDUSTRIAL POLICY

Part of the reason for the poor performance of the U.S. economy, it is widely believed, is the adversary relationship which developed between business and government in the 1970s. One way to stimulate growth is to have closer cooperation between the government and business, similar to that in Japan. Proponents of a new ***industrial policy*** suggest that the government establish a planning agency to identify the most promising products for future development. Research grants or other government programs could then be used to encourage resources to move into the future ''winners'' and away from declining industries. In this way, productivity and growth could be promoted.

Although the proposal to pick winners seems attractive, such a policy runs substantial risks. It may be as difficult for governments as for racetrack bettors to pick winners. Governments may in fact be less able than capital markets to pick winners. Before investing in a company, private individuals or firms have a great incentive to investigate it carefully, until they are convinced that it is a likely winner. But, in deciding how to invest the public's money, a politician has two separate objectives: to pick winners with a high economic payoff and the promise of *future* jobs, and to pick firms that provide many votes. Often these firms are the ones with a lot of *present* employment, but poor future prospects; that is, these firms are economic losers. Thus, rather than picking the economic winners (as the Japanese sometimes—but not always—do), the U.S. government might end up picking losers, as the British and Italian governments sometimes do. The government might come to the aid of corporations in danger of collapse. Consequently, a U.S. industrial strategy might lead to ''lemon socialism''—that is, government ownership and support of dying companies.

Thus, a central problem in developing an industrial policy is that its proponents are motivated by two quite different objectives: (1) to encourage new, high-productivity industries and (2) to help declining industries. Those who focus on the second objective express alarm that the United States is ''deindustrializing,'' as fewer and fewer workers find employment in the older heavy industries (Box 18-1). A number of business leaders have jumped on the industrial policy bandwagon, hoping that it will lead to protection from foreign competition. But the more attention is paid to propping up declining industries, the less likely it is that an industrial policy would add to the dynamism and productivity of the U.S. economy.

CONCLUSION: UNCERTAINTIES ABOUT GROWTH AND PRODUCTIVITY

If one thing stands out in this chapter, it should be this: Growth and productivity are complex phenomena. We understand their causes only imperfectly—as illustrated by Denison's large, mysterious residual. And there is great uncertainty about the best policies to stimulate productivity. In particular, the relatively simple policies offered by some supply-side economists and industrial policy advocates seem to be based on weak foundations. There is no single, simple key to unlock the door to higher productivity; there is no ''horseshoe nail'' to save our ''kingdom.''

BOX 18-1

THE DEBATE OVER INDUSTRIAL POLICY†

The following are excerpts from a debate on industrial policy. Arguing for an industrial policy were Barry Bluestone (Boston College) and Bennett Harrison (MIT). The opponents were Robert Lawrence and Charles Schultze of the Brookings Institution.

Bluestone: It seems we're going to be holding steady at an unemployment rate of 7½%. But more important is some of the occupational skidding in the economy. A large number of workers, many of them in basic industries, are being dislocated and are moving down the the occupational hierarchy.

Our institute at Boston College recently completed a survey of unemployed auto workers [who subsequently got new full-time jobs]. On average they have suffered a 30% loss in real earnings. . . . The new jobs that have been created have been disproportionately in low-wage industries.

Lawrence: When steelworkers or automobile workers lose their jobs, it's very likely that they will suffer a 30% decline in their living standard. The crucial question is: should the state be guaranteeing individuals their current income levels?

The answer ought to be no. To ask people who are earning $13,000 or $15,000 to subsidize employment of those who earn $26,000 or $28,000 seems to me to be inequitable.

Harrison: Employment of production workers has fallen by 7% since July 1983. All of the growth of manufacturing in the 1970s has been managers, salaried professionals, technicians, and their secretaries.

Displaced blue-collar factory workers are not about to be retrained for the service jobs inside their companies. They're not going to become managers, accountants, lawyers, engineers, or clerical workers. The dislocation problem is much greater than one would believe. . . .

In July of this year, the average manufacturing wage for production workers was $370 a week. For nonsupervisory service-sector workers, the average was $248. Our standard of living is being threatened by structural changes in the world economy.

Schultze: There is a common thread to recommendations about industrial policy—that the government ought to correct the allocation of investment among industries, localities and firms.

Neither Bluestone nor Harrison or, in fact, any industrial-policy proponent has come up with specific objective criteria which government might use to substitute for the forces of the market in determining where private investment and other resources ought to go. If the whole industrial-policy operation is not to be one vast pork barrel, government must have objective criteria. You can't stop all plant closings. You can't protect all declining industries. Which ones should you protect, and how much? You can't support all new ventures. Which ones?

Finally, the whole thrust of the industrial policy recommendations is terribly dangerous to democratic government. The more political power is turned over to producer groups organized by industry—and that's inherent in all this—the more we invite the domination of politics by economic power groups.

†Abridged, from the *Washington Post*, Nov. 11, 1984.

KEY POINTS

1. The growth of output depends on the combined effect of increases in (*a*) the number of hours worked, and (*b*) labor productivity.

2. Productivity grew most rapidly in the 1948–1966 period. This corresponded to the slowest rate of growth of labor hours. Productivity growth was slow during the late 1970s, when labor hours were increasing rapidly.

3. Denison found that there were a number of important causes for the rapid growth between 1948 and 1973. No single cause was the ''key'' to rapid growth.

4. Denison was unable to explain about two-thirds of the deterioration in the productivity performance of the U.S. economy in the 1973–1981 period. He may have underestimated the effects of R&D and the increase in the price of oil.

5. Productivity improved rapidly in 1983–1984, and the economy grew vigorously. It is unclear how much of this was due to the recovery from the recession, and how much was due to an increase in the underlying growth trend of the economy. It is too early to say if we are on a new, vigorous growth path.

6. We should not simply assume that the faster the growth rate, the better. If we single-mindedly pursue the growth objective, we may give insufficient attention to other goals, such as current consumption, a clean environment, and leisure.

7. There has been a cycle in attitudes toward growth. The Kennedy administration emphasized growth. Then doubts about growth grew in the late 1960s and early 1970s. By the the late 1970s and early 1980s, growth again became the center of attention.

8. Supply-side economists advocate tax cuts as a way of increasing the capacity of the economy to supply goods and services. They believe that tax cuts will shift the aggregate supply curve to the right by promoting saving, investment, hard work, and efficiency. They also suggest that tax cuts provide an escape from difficult trade-offs. When the supply curve shifts to the right, inflation may be reduced without creating unemployment. Some enthusiastic supply siders suggest that tax rates may be cut without losing any government revenue; the lower rates may be offset by higher incomes on which taxes are collected. The deficits of recent years suggest that this view is too optimistic.

9. Tax cuts increase the profitability of investments, and thus encourage businesses to invest. However, there is also a force working in the opposite direction. Tax cuts increase government deficits. When the government borrows, it puts upward pressure on interest rates, and the higher interest rates discourage investment (the ''crowding-out'' effect). It is not clear whether the net effect of these two forces is an increase or decrease in investment.

10. Another proposal for stimulating growth is for government to adopt an industrial strategy to help ''winners.'' One risk in this policy is that the government might in practice slip into ''lemon socialism,'' helping losers and keeping resources in low-productivity industries.

KEY CONCEPTS

average productivity of labor
technological improvement
supply-side tax cuts
Laffer curve
industrial policy
lemon socialism
deindustrialization

PROBLEMS

18-1. Why might a rapid increase in population cause a drag on productivity? Are there any circumstances in which a rapid increase in population might encourage a rapid increase in productivity?

18-2. Observe in Figure 18-1 that the rate of growth of labor hours in the 1919–1948 period was almost as slow as in 1948–1966. But the rate of growth of productivity was substantially less rapid. That is, productivity did not grow as rapidly between 1919 and 1948 as we might expect simply by looking at the low rate of growth of labor hours. Were there any events during this period that acted as a drag on productivity? Explain how they acted to keep productivity from increasing more rapidly.

18-3. During recessions, productivity generally expands very slowly, or even declines. On the other hand, it generally expands very rapidly as the economy recovers from recession. Explain why. The 1982 recession was more severe than that of 1980, but productivity nevertheless held up better in 1982 than in 1980. How can this be explained?

18-4. Explain how supply-side policies might make it possible to achieve both higher output and lower rates of inflation at the same time. Illustrate your answer with a diagram.

18-5. One of the ideas behind supply-side economics is that, if taxes are cut and people are left with more disposable income, they will work more. Some evidence on this point is provided in Figure 1-1 in Chapter 1, which shows how the workweek has changed as living standards have risen. Since 1900, has the workweek increased or decreased as incomes have risen? Is this also true in the period since 1950? How do you explain the way in which the workweek has changed? What tentative conclusion can we come to about the relationship between people's incomes and their willingness to work?

(Supplementary note: The length of the workweek is only one way in which willingness to work can change. A rise in after-tax incomes may encourage more people to enter the labor force. Statistical evidence indicates that this in fact happens. The income tax cuts of 1981 are estimated to have increased the labor force by about 2%.)[8]

[8]Robert H. Haveman, "How Much Have the Reagan Administration's Tax and Spending Policies Increased Work Effort?" in Charles R. Hulten and Isabel V. Sawhill (eds.), *The Legacy of Reaganomics* (Washington: Urban Institute, 1984), p. 115.

CHAPTER 19

FIXED OR FLEXIBLE EXCHANGE RATES?

As for foreign exchange, it is almost as romantic as young love, and quite as resistant to formulae.

H. L. MENCKEN

Economic efficiency requires specialization. It is efficient to grow wheat and corn in the midwest and to grow cotton in the south. The scope for specialization goes far beyond the boundaries of any single country. Even such a large nation as the United States can gain by international specialization. The United States exports products such as wheat, aircraft, and computers. In return, we import cameras, cars, oil, and coffee.

The way in which international specialization can contribute to a high standard of living fits into the study of economic efficiency in Part 6; we therefore defer a detailed consideration of international trade and efficiency to Chapter 31. In this chapter, we will study the monetary and macroeconomic aspects of international transactions. What happens if the United States spends more abroad than foreigners spend here? What complications are introduced into monetary and fiscal policies by international transactions? What can be done to minimize international disturbances to the U.S. economy?

EXCHANGE RATES

In many ways, international trade is like domestic trade. It adds to economic efficiency because of comparative advantage and economies of scale. But there are two major complications that make international transactions different from domestic trade:

1. With domestic trade, there's just one currency. For example, when a New Yorker purchases Florida oranges, the consumer pays in dollars, and that's the currency the seller wants. But international trade involves *two currencies*. Consider a British firm importing U.S. cotton. It has British pounds (£) to pay for the cotton. But the U.S. exporter wants to receive payment in dollars. Therefore, the British importer will go to the ***foreign exchange market*** in order to sell pounds and buy the dollars needed to pay for the cotton, as illustrated in Figure 19-1. Foreign exchange markets are located in major financial centers, such as London and New York.

Foreign exchange **is the currency of another country. For example, British pounds or Japanese yen are foreign exchange to an American. U.S. dollars are foreign exchange to a Briton or German.**

A ***foreign exchange market*** **is a market in which one national currency (such as the U.S. dollar) is bought in exchange for another national currency (such as the Japanese yen, ¥).**

An ***exchange rate*** **is the price of one national currency in terms of another national currency. For example, the price £1 = $1.20 is an exchange rate, and so is $1 = ¥250.**

2. International trade is complicated by *barriers* that do not exist in trade between states, provinces, or cities within the same country. Most notably, national governments impose ***tariffs*** (also known as *duties*) on many imports. Tariffs protect domestic producers by giving them an advantage over foreign competitors. However, consumers suffer: Prices of imports are increased by tariffs.

A *tariff* is a tax imposed on a foreign good when it enters the country.

Tariffs and other restrictions on trade will be studied in Chapter 32. Here, we concentrate on the first point—foreign exchange transactions and the complications they raise for domestic stabilization policies.

THE FOREIGN EXCHANGE MARKET

MISS PRISM: Cecily, you will read your political economy in my absence. The chapter on the fall of the rupee you may omit. It is somewhat too sensational.

Oscar Wilde
The Importance of Being Earnest

Like the market for wheat or oranges, the market for foreign exchange can be studied by looking at demand

FIGURE 19-1
International trade and the foreign exchange market
International trade normally involves more than one national currency. The British importer wants to pay in pounds, while the U.S. exporter wants to receive payment in dollars. Consequently, the British import results in a transaction on the foreign exchange market, with pounds being sold for dollars.

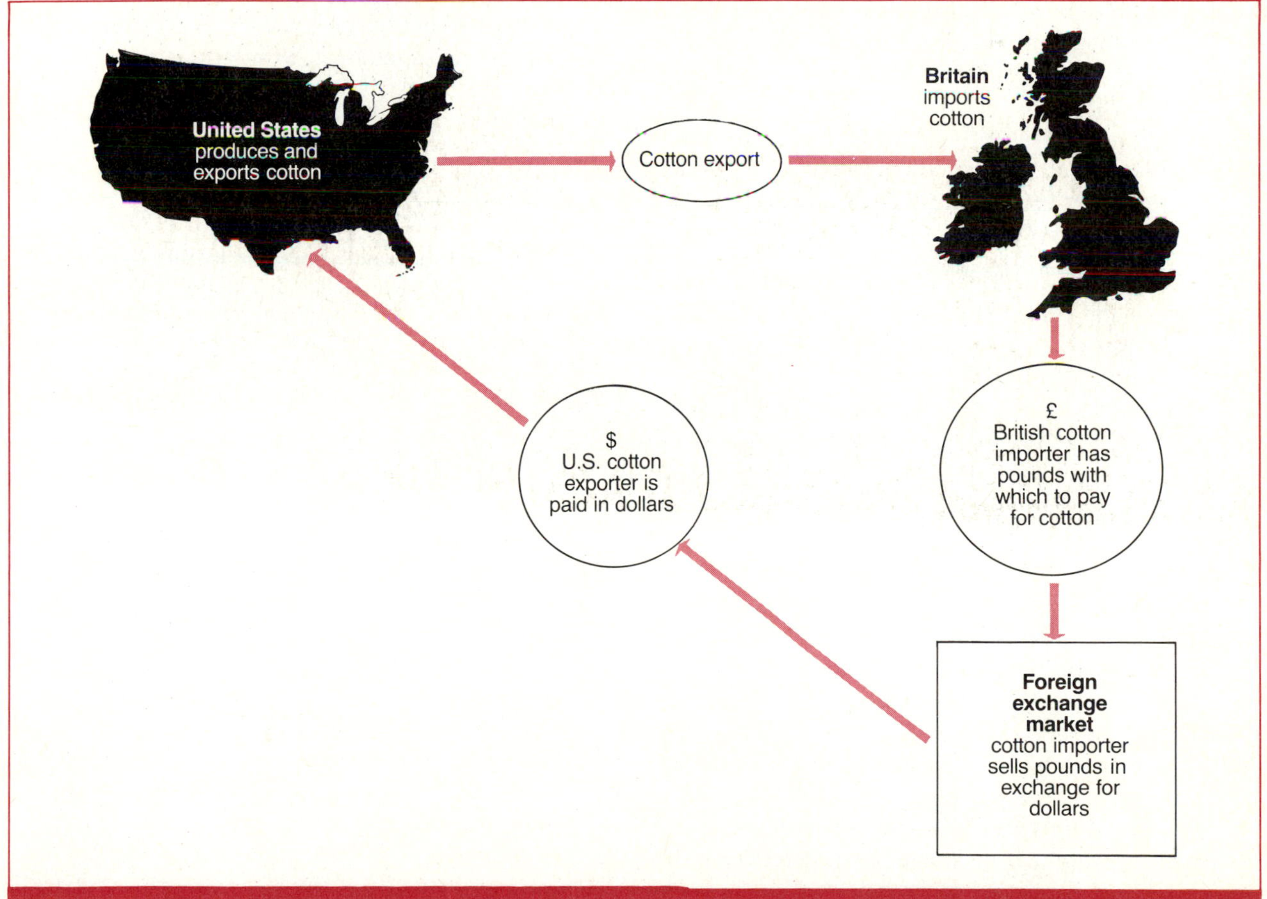

and supply. The demand for British pounds by those now holding dollars arises from three types of transactions:

1. *American imports of British goods.* For example, when Americans buy British textiles, they create a demand for British pounds. In order to pay for British textiles, the American importer buys the pounds which the British textile manufacturer wants.

2. *American imports of British services.* For example, an American tourist may stay in a British hotel and eat in a British restaurant. In order to pay the hotel or restaurant, the American first buys pounds with dollars. Thus, the tourist creates a demand for pounds.

What is the difference between an import of a good and an import of a service? The good physically enters the United States; the textiles are unloaded at an American port. In the case of a service, there is no such physical transfer of a good to the United States. Obviously, the hotel room and the restaurant stay in London. But in either case, Americans are buying from the British, and this creates a demand for pounds.

3. *American acquisitions of British assets.* For example, if an American corporation wants to invest in Britain by building a new factory, it will buy pounds to pay the British construction firm.

The demand for pounds, like the demand for wheat, depends on the price. Suppose that, instead of being worth $2, the British pound had the much lower price of $1. What would this mean? British goods and services would be less expensive to Americans. If the price of the pound were $2, a British hotel room costing £50 would cost an American $100. But if the price of the pound were $1, that same room would cost only $50 in U.S. money. As a result, Americans would be more likely to buy British textiles or cars, and American tourists would be more likely to go to Britain. (In fact, the pound did fall close to $1 in early 1985, and there was a rush of tourists to Britain. Some wealthy Americans even flew to Britain to shop.) Thus, when £1 costs $1, the quantity of pounds demanded is greater than when a pound costs $2, as illustrated by the demand curve (*D*) in Figure 19-2.

Observe in this example that the price which an American pays for a British hotel room depends on two things: (1) the British price of the room (£50 in the example) and (2) the exchange rate between the pound and dollar.

Now consider the other side of the market, the supply of pounds to be exchanged for dollars. When British residents want to buy something from the United States, they pay for it in dollars. They offer pounds in order to get dollars; they create a supply of pounds. Thus, the supply of pounds depends on: (1) British imports of U.S. goods, (2) British imports of U.S. services, (3) British acquisitions of U.S. assets, that is, British investment in the United States.

DISEQUILIBRIUM IN THE EXCHANGE MARKET

The demand for pounds may exactly equal the supply at the existing exchange rate. It is possible, for example, that at an existing exchange rate of £1 = $2, the demand and supply curves intersect, as shown at the initial equilibrium *E* in Figure 19-3.

However, we live in a changing world. Even if the demand and supply are initially in equilibrium, one or

FIGURE 19-2

The demand and supply for British pounds

The equilibrium exchange rate is determined by the intersection of demand and supply. The demand for pounds in terms of dollars depends on U.S. purchases of British goods, services, and assets. The supply of pounds depends on British purchases of U.S. goods, services, and assets.

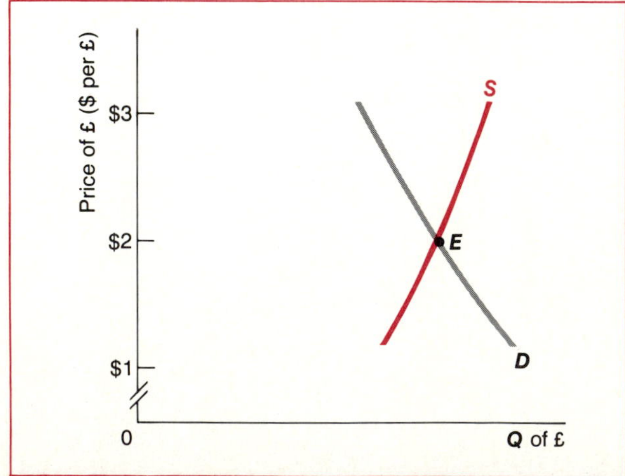

both curves may shift as time passes. Suppose that the demand for pounds decreases from D_1 to D_2. It might do so for any of a number of reasons; anything that decreases the U.S. demand for British products will cause a leftward shift of the demand for pounds. An example has been the switch by Americans away from purchasing British cars to buying Japanese cars instead.

As a result of the shift in the demand curve, the initial price of $2 per pound is no longer an equilibrium. In the face of this change, the British government has the option of taking any one—or a combination—of the following steps:

1. *Intervening in the foreign exchange market.* The British government can keep the price of the pound at $2 by selling some of the U.S. dollars it owns to buy the excess supply of pounds, *GE*. In order to be able to stabilize exchange rates in this manner, governments and central banks hold ***reserves*** of foreign currencies.

2. *Imposing direct restrictions on international transactions.* In order to maintain the price of £1 = $2, the British government may reduce the supply of pounds so that it shifts leftward and passes through point *G*. This can be accomplished by direct restrictions on international transactions. For example, the British government can increase tariffs and thus reduce British purchases of U.S. goods; the British therefore supply fewer pounds to buy dollars.

3. *Altering domestic monetary and fiscal policies.* The British government may reduce the supply of pounds more indirectly by adopting restrictive monetary and fiscal policies. Such policies will reduce British imports—and consequently the supply of pounds on the foreign exchange market—for two reasons. First, tighter policies will slow down British economic activity and reduce incomes. As a result, consumption will fall, including the consumption of imports. Second, the tighter policies will reduce British inflation. As British goods become more competitive in price, British consumers will switch away from imports and buy less expensive domestic goods instead.

4. *Allowing the exchange rate to adjust.* The British government may allow the exchange rate to move to the new equilibrium *F*.

FIGURE 19-3

A shift in the demand for pounds

If the demand for pounds shifts to the left from D_1 to D_2, there will be an excess supply of pounds (*GE*) at the old exchange rate. The British can eliminate this excess supply by one or a combination of the following steps: (1) The purchase of pounds in exchange for dollars by British authorities. (2) Restrictions on imports and other international transactions. (This will reduce the supply of pounds so that the supply curve shifts to the left to pass through point *G*.) (3) Restrictive aggregate demand policies in Britain, which also will reduce British imports and the supply of pounds. (4) A change in the exchange rate to its new equilibrium.

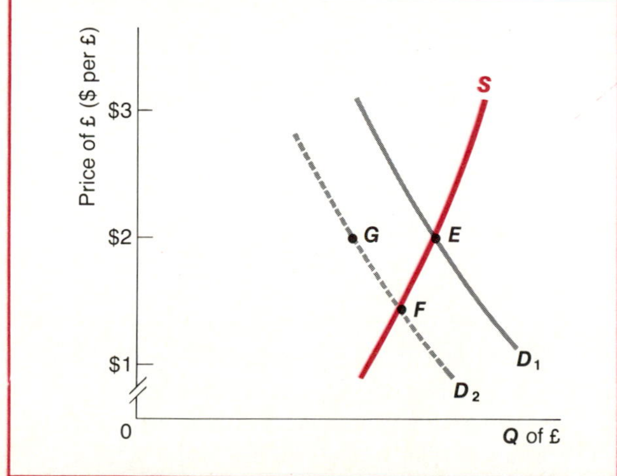

Since the end of the Second World War in 1945, the central debate in international finance has been over the relative merits of these four options. But before studying recent developments, we will look at the historical gold standard, where reliance was placed on the third option. The idea underlying the gold standard was that exchange rates would be kept stable and international equilibrium would be maintained by changes in aggregate demand.

THE CLASSICAL GOLD STANDARD

Prior to the First World War, and again briefly in the period between the two world wars, a number of countries adhered to the international gold standard. Gold coins circulated as part of the money supply, and paper currency was convertible into gold. The dollar was worth a fixed quantity of gold—approximately 1/20th of an ounce. Similarly, the British pound was worth a fixed quantity of gold—about one-quarter of an ounce.

As a result, exchange rates were stable. One British pound was worth about 5 times as much gold as the U.S. dollar—4.86 times as much, to be precise. Consequently, nobody would pay much more than $4.86 for a pound, or take much less. The exchange rate stayed close to £1 = $4.86.

The Adjustment Mechanism of the Gold Standard

The international gold standard provided an automatic ***mechanism of adjustment.*** It worked to prevent a continuing flow of gold from one country to another. Here's how.

Suppose that Britain begins to import much more than it exports. Britain pays for the extra imports with gold; gold flows from Britain to the United States and other countries. The U.S. money stock automatically rises, since gold itself is money. Furthermore, gold flowing into U.S. banks adds to their reserves, since gold also is a bank reserve. With the additional reserves, banks can expand their loans, thereby causing a further increase in the money stock. With more money, Americans spend more. Prices are bid up in the United States.

On the other side, Britain is losing gold. As a result, its money stock automatically falls. Aggregate demand declines, and so do prices. As British goods become cheaper compared with U.S. goods, British exports rise and imports fall. The British stop losing gold.

An *international adjustment mechanism* is a set of forces that operate to eliminate balance of payments surpluses or deficits. That is, an adjustment mechanism works to ensure that one country won't continuously lose large amounts of gold or other reserves to other countries.

A country has a *deficit* when its foreign expenditures exceed its foreign receipts.

A country has a *surplus* when its foreign receipts exceed its foreign expenditures.

Problems with the Gold Standard

The international gold standard provided exchange-rate stability during much of the nineteenth century, when international trade and investment grew rapidly. But the gold standard had two major defects:

1. The process of adjustment could be very painful. For example, gold sometimes flowed out of a country that was already in a recession. The gold standard caused an automatic reduction in the money supply, further depressing aggregate demand and increasing unemployment. In other words, there sometimes was a ***conflict*** between the *expansive* policies needed for domestic prosperity and the *decrease* in the money stock required by the gold standard to drive down prices and strengthen the country's ability to compete on world markets.

From time to time, gold flows also made the domestic situation worse in the country *receiving* gold. This happened when there already were strong inflationary pressures. The automatic increase in the quantity of money made the inflation worse.

2. As we saw in Chapter 13, the gold standard could lead to very ***unstable*** monetary conditions. Under the fractional-reserve system of banking, a large quantity of money was built on a relatively small base of gold. The monetary system was therefore vulnerable to a crisis of confidence and a run on the gold stock. Such a crisis of confidence came during the Great Depression of the 1930s, and the gold standard collapsed. One country after another announced that it would no longer convert its currency into gold.

THE ADJUSTABLE PEG: THE IMF SYSTEM, 1945–1971

In 1944, toward the end of the Second World War, senior financial officials from the allied countries met at Bretton Woods, New Hampshire. This conference designed an *adjustable peg* system of exchange rates for the postwar world and established a new organization, the International Monetary Fund (IMF), to help make the new system work. The Bretton Woods conference also established a second important international organization, the World Bank, to provide financial assistance for postwar reconstruction and for economic development.

The adjustable peg system was designed to provide some of the exchange-rate stability of the old gold standard, while avoiding its major defects. Specifically, under the Bretton Woods system, exchange rates were to be kept stable within a narrow band (±1%) around an officially declared ***par***. For example, between 1949 and 1967, the pound was pegged at an official price or par value of £1 = $2.80.

Under the IMF system prior to 1971, the *par value of a currency* was the official price of the currency, specified in terms of the U.S. dollar or gold.

The founders of the IMF recognized that some provision would have to be made for international adjustment in the event of deficits or surpluses. Recall from the discussion at the beginning of the chapter that there are only four major ways for Britain to deal with a disturbance in the foreign exchange market. It may:

1. Keep the price of pounds stable by buying surplus pounds with dollars, or selling pounds in the event of a shortage.
2. Change tariffs or other restrictions on imports or other international transactions.
3. Change domestic aggregate demand policies in order to shift the supply curve for pounds.
4. Change the exchange rate.

The IMF system represented a compromise, with each of these steps playing a part. Increases in tariffs or other restrictions on imports (option 2) were considered undesirable, since they reduced international trade and made the world economy less efficient. However, they were permitted in emergencies, including the severely disrupted period after World War II. The main reliance was intended to be on the other three options.

Exchange market disturbances might be temporary, reflecting such things as strikes, bad weather that affects crops, or other transitory phenomena. In such circumstances, changes in exchange rates were considered undesirable. A fall in the price of the currency would be reversed in the future when the transitory events passed, and such swings in exchange rates were judged to perform no useful function. Rather than allow exchange rates to move, countries should fill temporary deficits by using foreign exchange reserves to intervene in the foreign exchange market (option 1). Because temporary swings might be quite large, the IMF was empowered to lend foreign currencies to deficit countries in order to help them stabilize their currencies on the exchange markets. Thus, "Fund" is an important part of the title of the IMF. The member countries of the IMF provided it with the funds to lend to deficit countries.

However, no country has unlimited quantities of foreign exchange, and there are limits to the amount the IMF is willing to lend. Therefore, a country can intervene in the exchange market to support the price of its currency only as a temporary stopgap measure to deal with short-run disturbances. *Sales of foreign exchange cannot be a permanent solution to a continuing deficit*.

Some disturbances in the exchange market are not transitory; some shifts in the demand or supply curves for foreign exchange will not reverse themselves in the future. In such cases, more fundamental steps than exchange market intervention must be taken, such as changes in domestic aggregate demand (option 3). For example, if a country is following excessively expansive aggregate demand policies, the resulting inflation may price its goods out of world markets and cause international payments deficits. In such cases, there is no conflict between domestic and international objectives. A more restrictive demand policy is appropriate in order to restrain inflation at home *and also* to improve the international payments position. The IMF can require a country seeking a loan to introduce such restraint in its monetary and fiscal policies.

However, an adjustment in domestic demand is not always a desirable way of dealing with an international payments problem. As we have seen in the discussion of the gold standard, a deficit country might already be suffering from domestic recession. Restrictive aggregate demand policies to solve the international payments problem would just make the recession worse.

In such circumstances, where the first three options had been ruled out or proved inadequate, the country was in a ***fundamental disequilibrium***, and the Bretton Woods system approved the only remaining option: Change the exchange rate. For example, the British ***devalued*** the pound from £1 = $4.03 to a new par of £1 = $2.80 in 1949, and again lowered the par value to $2.40 in 1967. On the other side, the Germans ***revalued*** their currency (the Deutsche Mark, or DM) upward in 1961 and 1969.

A country *devalues* when it lowers the par value (the official price) of its currency.

A country *revalues* when it raises the par value of its currency.

In brief, exchange rates were *pegged, but adjustable*.

THE IMF SYSTEM: THE PROBLEM OF ADJUSTMENT

For several decades, the IMF system worked reasonably well—well enough to provide the financial framework for the recovery from the Second World War and for a very rapid expansion of international trade. But it contained major flaws that caused a breakdown in the early 1970s.

In practice, there were defects in the policy of changing the par value of a currency to deal with a "fundamental disequilibrium." When a country begins to run a deficit or surplus, it is uncertain whether the deficit or surplus is only temporary—in which case it can be dealt with by buying or selling foreign currency rather than by changing the exchange rate—or whether it represents a fundamental disequilibrium, in which case a change in the par value is appropriate. The IMF agreement itself provided no help in this regard. At no place did it define a fundamental disequilibrium.

Since a fundamental disequilibrium involves a surplus or deficit that will persist, one simple test is to wait and see whether in fact it does persist. But waiting can be a nerve-wracking experience. In particular, deficits cause the loss of foreign exchange reserves. And, as reserves dwindle, ***speculators*** add to the problem. As soon as speculators become convinced that the deficits will continue—and that the British, say, may eventually be forced to devalue—they have an incentive to sell pounds. For example, if a speculator sells pounds when the price is $2.80 and the British do devalue the pound to $2.40, the speculator can buy the pounds back for $2.40, making a profit of 40¢ on each pound. Speculators may stampede into the market because the pound is such a fat target. Speculators win if the pound goes down. If the crisis passes without a devaluation, they don't win. But they don't lose, either. In such circumstances, the speculator looks on the foreign exchange market as a great place to bet: Heads I win; tails we're even.

A *speculator* is anyone who buys or sells a foreign currency (or any other asset) in the hope of profiting from a change in its price.

Thus, speculators may add a flood of pounds for sale on the foreign exchange market. To keep the pound from dropping in price, the British authorities have to buy up these excess pounds, using their reserves of U.S. dollars to do so. Consequently, the entry of speculators into the market speeds up the loss of British foreign exchange reserves, and puts increased pressure on the authorities to devalue. This may then become a case of ***self-fulfilling expectations***. The expectation by speculators that the pound will be devalued leads them to take an action (selling pounds) that increases the likelihood that the British authorities will, in fact, have to devalue.

In our example, speculators reap a windfall gain of 40¢ per pound when the British devalue. But this 40¢ represents a transfer from the British authorities, who lose exactly the same amount by fighting the speculators. (When a speculator sells pounds, the British authorities buy these pounds at $2.80. After the devaluation, they sell them back at $2.40, for a loss of 40¢.) Ultimately, the British taxpayer bears this loss. Why, then, do the authorities fight speculation as it builds up? Why don't they devalue quickly? The answer is that they are still unsure whether a devaluation is really necessary. They hope to end speculation by restoring confidence that the pound will not be devalued.

To restore confidence, the authorities firmly proclaim their determination to defend the pound. Even if they are almost sure that they will have to devalue the pound tomorrow, they must declare today that they will *not* do so. What choice do they have? If they admit that a devaluation is possible—or even if they refuse to comment—speculators will pour pounds into the market and reap even greater profits at the expense of the government when the devaluation does occur.

Once government leaders have staked their reputations on the defense of the currency, it is very difficult for them to back down and change its par value. Therefore, in practice, devaluations tended to be infrequent and long delayed under the IMF system. And, once they came, they tended to be large, so that the government would not have to go through the painful experience again in the near future. Thus, the system of adjustable pegs did not work out as hoped. For long periods the system was one of rigid pegs as officials committed themselves firmly to the existing exchange rates. Then, when pressures became intolerable and changes had to be made, jumping pegs were the result, with drastic adjustments being made.

When countries clung desperately to their existing par values, they were pushed back toward the old gold standard system, using domestic aggregate demand as a way to adjust. The British, for example, engaged in a series of ***stop-go*** domestic policies, restricting aggregate demand when they were losing foreign exchange reserves, and turning policies to "go" when their international position improved. Thus, a strong destabilizing force was introduced into domestic economic policy.

The lack of a smooth and effective adjustment process was not the only shortcoming of the old IMF system. In that system, the U.S. dollar played a central role, and this created special problems for the United States.

THE U.S. DOLLAR AND THE ADJUSTABLE PEG: THE PROBLEMS OF LIQUIDITY AND CONFIDENCE

Under a pegged exchange-rate system, not all countries are equal. It is not possible for every country to have control over its exchange rate. The reason is that there are fewer independent exchange rates than there are countries. In a very simple world of two countries, say the United States and Britain, there is only one exchange rate. (Of course, this rate may be quoted either way. For example, $1 = £0.50 is just another way of stating that £1 = $2.) In general, in a world of n countries, there are only $n - 1$ independent exchange rates.[1]

This fundamental fact posed two interrelated questions for the designers of the IMF system:

1. If an exchange rate—such as the rate between the British pound and the U.S. dollar—begins to rise or fall, does Britain or the United States have the responsibility of intervening in the foreign exchange market to keep it close to the official par value?

2. In the case of fundamental disequilibrium, the par value might have to be altered. Does the United States or Britain make the decision to alter the par value? And which country chooses the new par?

The IMF solution to the first question was as follows. Other countries tied their currencies to the U.S. dollar, and the United States in turn undertook to keep the dollar convertible into gold.[2] This determined the entire set of exchange rates between countries (Figure 19-4). As far as exchange rates were concerned, the United States was the odd man out. Every other country was responsible for an exchange rate. As the nth country, the United States had no such responsibility.

The answer to the second question followed from the answer to the first. Since Britain was responsible for keeping the pound pegged in terms of dollars, the ball

---

[1]In a three-country world—Britain, France, and the United States—it may seem that there are three independent exchange rates: one between the pound and the dollar, another between the franc and the dollar, and another between the franc and the pound. But in reality, there are only two (that is, $n - 1$). Any two exchange rates determine what the third will be. For example, if the price of the pound is $2 and the price of the franc is 20¢, it follows that the pound is worth 10 times as much as the franc; that is, £1 = 10 francs.

[2]That is, the United States undertook to buy or sell gold to foreign central banks or treasuries at the official price of 1 ounce = $35. In technical terms, the IMF system was an example of the *gold exchange standard,* which exists when countries peg their currencies either to gold or to another currency—like the dollar—that in turn is pegged to gold.

Although all currencies were thus pegged to gold either directly or indirectly, the old IMF system was a far cry from the classical gold standard. The U.S. government made no commitment to sell gold to the public. Indeed, between the Great Depression and 1975, U.S. citizens were forbidden by law to hold gold. Furthermore, exchange parities were to be adjustable, not fixed firmly as under the gold standard.

was in the British court when the decision came to change the parity. However, Britain was to consult other members of the IMF regarding the new parity.

Thus, the United States had a unique role in the IMF system. The dollar was the ***key currency.*** Other countries kept their currencies pegged to the dollar, and they took the initiative in choosing new parities when exchange rates were adjusted. The United States was thus placed squarely in the center of one of the thorniest problems of the IMF system—that of ***international liquidity.*** What volume of reserves should there be, and how should additional reserves be created?

International liquidity **is the total amount of reserves held by the various nations.**

International Liquidity

Under the old adjustable peg system we are now describing, a country held its international reserves in the form of:

1. Gold.
2. Foreign exchange.
3. The country's reserve position in the IMF, that is, the contributions that the country had made to the IMF. Each country had an unconditional right to withdraw its past contributions.

For the United States—with its responsibility to keep the dollar convertible into gold—gold formed the primary reserve. Other countries had the responsibility of stabilizing their currencies relative to the dollar, and

FIGURE 19-4
The old IMF adjustable peg system
Each of the $n - 1$ countries set its exchange rate with the U.S. dollar (black arrows). These $n - 1$ exchange rates determined all exchange rates, including those in gray. The United States, as the nth country, set the price of gold.

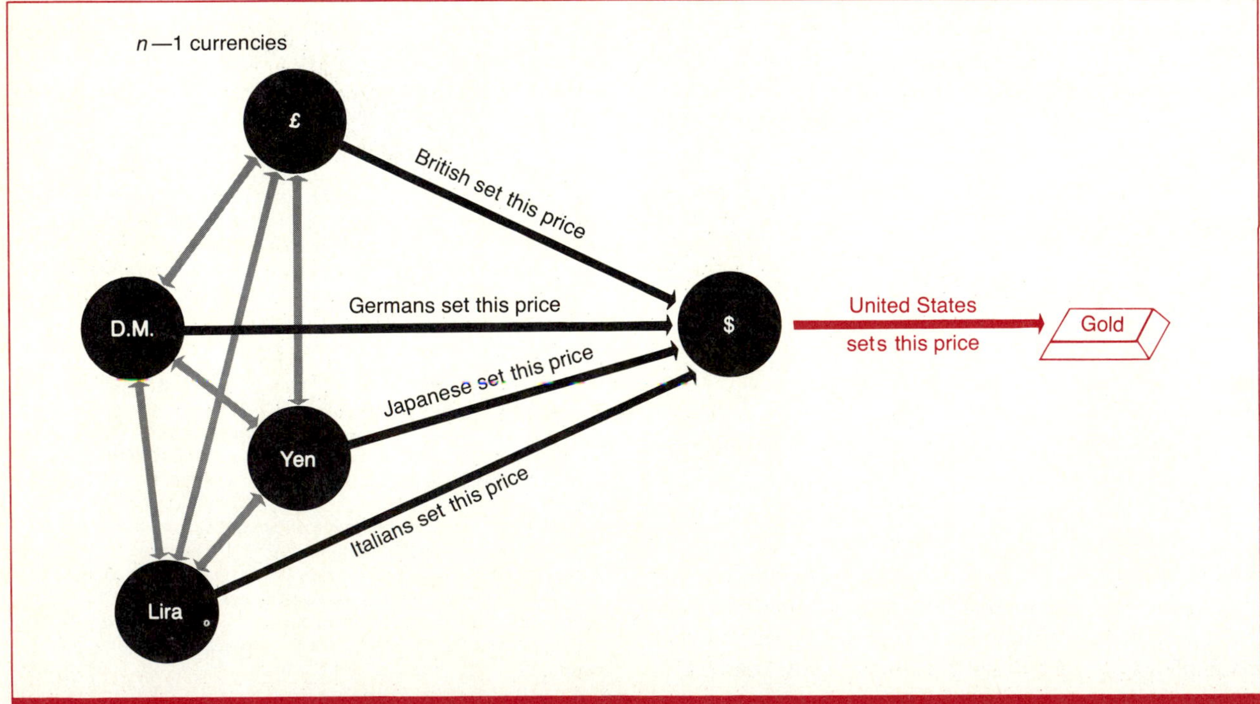

they therefore kept sizable amounts of dollars to be used as needed to intervene in the exchange markets.

In his 1960 book, *Gold and the Dollar Crisis,* Robert Triffin of Yale University argued that there was a fundamental problem with the IMF system. As international trade expanded, countries would want more reserves. How could reserves be increased? By digging more gold, or by increases in foreign holdings of U.S. dollars.

The prospects for large increases in the supply of gold were not promising. Furthermore, it is not very sensible to dig gold out of one hole in the ground—a mine in South Africa, the Soviet Union, or Canada—merely to bury it in another hole in Fort Knox or the vaults of the New York Fed. Thus, if countries were going to get the reserves they needed, their foreign holdings of dollars would have to increase. But how does a foreign country get more U.S. dollars? By running a surplus with the United States. In other words, *if other countries were to accumulate dollar reserves, the United States would have to have deficits.* But, as American deficits continued and foreign dollar holdings became larger and larger compared with the relatively stable U.S. stock of gold, the ability of the United States to convert the dollar into gold would increasingly come into question. There would inevitably be a crisis of confidence, a run on U.S. gold by foreign governments, and a collapse of the IMF system.

In brief, the IMF system could not last. The United States could eliminate its deficit, giving the world a *liquidity crisis,* with inadequate reserves. Or the United States could continue to run deficits, with the predictable result of a *crisis of confidence* and a run on U.S. gold. Triffin suggested a solution. The IMF should be turned into an international central bank, capable of creating an international reserve that would supplant the U.S. dollar. This reserve could be methodically created to meet growing needs for liquidity.

Special Drawing Rights

Toward the end of the 1960s, an international consensus developed that something had to be done about the problem outlined by Triffin. Another reserve had to be created as an alternative to dollars, so that the United States would no longer have to run deficits to provide reserves for the rest of the world. After a series of hard negotiations, the IMF was empowered to create special drawing rights (SDRs), which could be used by nations to cover balance-of-payments deficits.

SDRs consist of bookkeeping accounts in the IMF owned by national governments, somewhat similar to the deposits that individuals hold at commercial banks. But the mechanism for creating SDRs is much simpler than the open market operations by which a central bank creates money within a domestic economy. The IMF creates SDRs in the easiest possible way: It directly adds SDRs to the accounts of the various nations with the IMF. Nothing is received in exchange. The SDRs are simply *allocated* to the various member nations of the IMF. SDRs can be used by a nation to cover an international deficit.

According to the initial design, the SDR was equal to a specific amount of gold. Thus, the SDR was frequently referred to as "paper gold." However, gold is no longer at the center of the international economic system and the SDR is no longer tied to gold. Instead, it now has a value equivalent to a basket of five major currencies—the dollar, the franc, the mark, the pound, and the yen. This basket is more diversified than any single currency. As a result, some private transactions are now expressed in terms of SDRs rather than a national currency.

THE BREAKDOWN OF THE ADJUSTABLE PEG SYSTEM, 1971–1973

In 1971, the old adjustable peg system came apart. During the early part of that year, the U.S. economy was recovering from recession. But the recovery was painfully slow, in part because of the large leakage of U.S. demand into imports. (Recall that expenditures on imports increase production and employment in foreign countries rather than in the United States.)

There was a growing concern in Washington that imports were increasing so rapidly because the value of the dollar was too high. Some American goods had been priced out of world markets. Yet, as the *n*th country, the United States had little control over this situation. Instead, the value of the dollar was determined when other countries pegged their currencies to it—as we saw in Figure 19-4. In spite of substantial U.S. deficits during the 1960s—and foreign complaints about these deficits—other developed countries had on average devalued their currencies with respect to the dollar. That is, they had raised rather than lowered the exchange value of the dollar, making it even more difficult for the United States to reduce its deficit. Indeed, the U.S. deficit mushroomed in early 1971, and doubts grew regarding the ability of the United States to maintain the convertibility of the dollar.

In August 1971, the United States suspended the convertibility of the dollar into gold, and imposed tariff surcharges in order to pressure foreign countries into raising the prices of their currencies—that is, into lowering the value of the dollar. In the uncertainty that followed, a number of countries abandoned their fixed pegs and allowed their currencies to ***float*** on the exchange markets.

A *floating,* or *flexible,* exchange rate is one that is allowed to change in response to changing demand or supply conditions.

If governments and central banks withdraw completely from the exchange markets, the float is *clean.* A float is *dirty* if a nation's government or central bank intervenes in exchange markets by buying or selling foreign currencies in order to affect its exchange rate.

In December 1971, an attempt was made to patch up the pegged exchange-rate system at a conference at the Smithsonian Institution in Washington. The new pegged rates chosen by most of the participants involved higher prices of their currencies. Thus, the United States achieved its goal of dollar devaluation. But the Smithsonian patchwork did not last. In 1972, the British let the pound float. Stresses on the exchange-rate system increased. There were such large amounts of internationally mobile money that an exchange rate could not be held in the face of speculation. In an unsuccessful attempt over a 4-day period to keep the mark from rising, West German authorities sold enough marks to speculators to buy 2 million Volkswagens. In early 1973, countries abandoned the pegs of the Smithsonian Agreement and most major currencies were allowed to float.

FLEXIBLE EXCHANGE RATES

A flexible exchange rate system has several advantages:

1. The principal alternative—a pegged exchange rate system—broke down in the early 1970s, in part because of an inadequate adjustment mechanism and in part because of huge currency transactions by speculators. Today, it would be even more difficult to maintain pegged rates because the pools of internationally mobile funds are now even larger. The main argument for flexible exchange rates is the *lack of a good alternative*.
2. When exchange rates are allowed to fluctuate, countries do not have to defend the existing exchange rate by selling their foreign exchange reserves. And they are not forced by a loss of reserves to adopt restrictive domestic policies. In other words, flexible exchange rates give domestic authorities *more freedom* to follow the policies needed to stabilize the domestic economy.
3. A country following stable domestic policies is *insulated from foreign inflation*. We will see why in just a moment, when we come to the idea of a "virtuous circle."

However, flexible exchange rates have been critized on a number of grounds:

1. Changes in exchange rates may *disrupt international trade and investment*. It is a matter of dispute whether this disruption is greater with flexible exchange rates than under the crisis-prone IMF system, with its infrequent but large changes in parity.
2. Critics point to the *large fluctuations* in exchange rates since 1973 (Figure 19-5), arguing that the back-and-forth movements have served no useful purpose. Exchange rates have in practice responded to short-run, transitory disturbances. Many of the changes have not been necessary to correct fundamental disequilibrium. However, supporters of flexible rates respond that the post-1973 period has been unusual in terms of the size of disturbances. For example, increases in the international price of oil caused huge changes in the pattern of interna-

tional payments. While the flexible exchange rate system might not have responded as smoothly as we might have liked to these shocks, it's not clear that a pegged rate system could have survived them at all.

3. When exchange rates are allowed to float, an important *discipline* over monetary and fiscal policies is lost. Under the IMF adjustable peg system, the fear of balance-of-payments deficits and losses of reserves provided a restraint on inflationary domestic policies.

This is the other side of the freedom argument put forward by proponents of flexible exchange rates. What one person considers "freedom" another may consider a "lack of discipline." Proponents of flexible exchange rates emphasize advantages of freedom. Monetary and fiscal policies can be used to stabilize the domestic economy, not the exchange rate. Opponents of exchange rate flexibility argue that such freedom is undesirable because weak and indisciplined governments will be more likely to follow inflationary policies.

4. Exchange rate movements can contribute to domestic problems. For example, if a country has a weak international payments position, its currency will ***depreciate.*** True, the depreciation contributes to international adjustment. As the price of the home currency falls, imports become more expensive and people buy fewer foreign goods as a result. But, it is precisely this increase in the price of imports that causes a problem. It *adds to domestic inflation.* A country can become caught in a ***vicious circle,*** with domestic inflation causing a depreciation, the depreciation in turn adding to the domestic inflationary spiral, and the higher inflation leading to even more depreciation.

A floating currency *depreciates* when its price falls in terms of other currencies. (Note that a pegged currency is *devalued;* a floating currency *depreciates.*)

A floating currency *appreciates* when its price rises in terms of other currencies.

FIGURE 19-5

Selected exchange rates, 1971–1985

Exchange rates have fluctuated over a wide range since 1971. In early 1973 and again in 1977–1978, most currencies rose in terms of the dollar. In the early 1980s, the prices of most currencies fell in terms of the dollar.

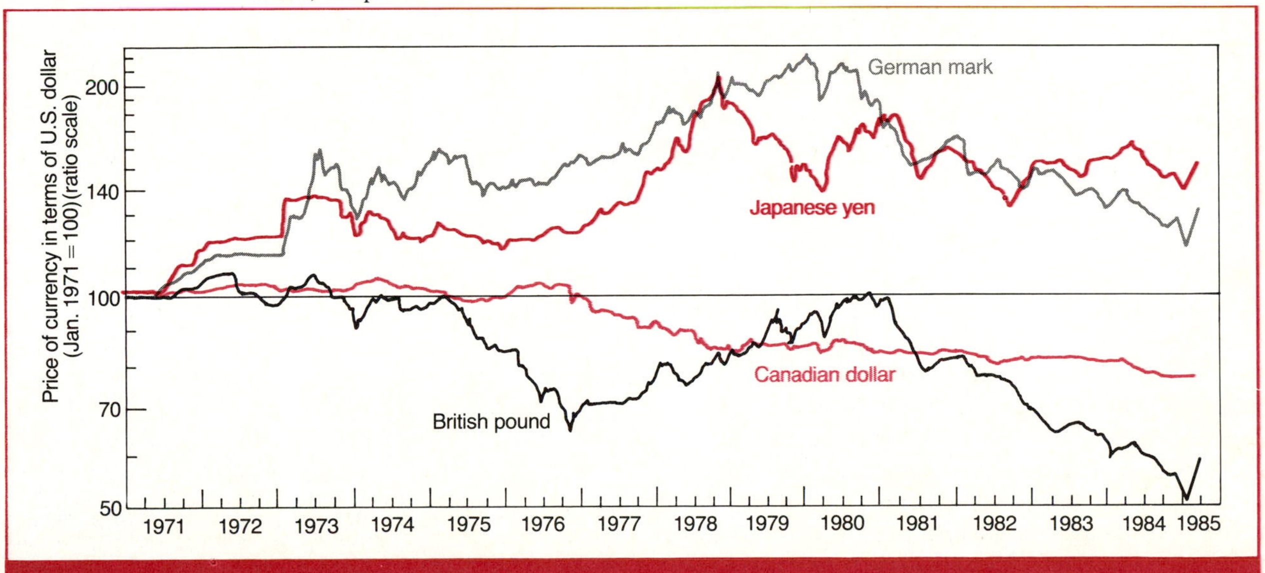

There is, however, another side to this argument, too. A country following stable domestic policies is insulated from inflationary disturbances originating abroad. Suppose, for example, that Germany follows restrained policies, keeping its domestic prices stable. Then its goods become more and more attractive as prices rise in foreign countries. As foreigners eagerly buy German goods, they bid up the price of the mark; that is, they bid down the prices of their own currencies. As a result, imports into Germany remain inexpensive in spite of the foreign inflation. Germany benefits from a ***virtuous circle.*** Stable domestic prices lead to an appreciation of the mark, keeping import prices down and making it even easier to keep prices stable in Germany.

The Fluctuating U.S. Dollar

Figure 19-6 shows how the average price of the dollar has changed since 1971 in terms of foreign currencies. Between the middle of 1971 and mid-1973—as the IMF system was coming apart at the seams—the U.S. dollar fell almost one-quarter in terms of other currencies. Observe, however, that the dollar *rose* about 10% at the time of the first oil shock in late 1973. This may seem surprising, but the reason is straightforward. Many other countries—particularly Japan and the major industrial countries of continental Europe—import an even greater percentage of their oil than the United States, and were even more adversely affected by higher oil prices. As a result, their currencies fell with respect to the dollar—which is just another way of saying that the dollar rose.

Since 1975, there have been two major movements in the dollar—a sharp downward slide between 1976 and 1979 and an even stronger upswing between 1980 and 1984.

The collapsing dollar, 1976–1978 Between 1976 and 1978, aggregate demand expanded rapidly in the United States, partly because of expansive fiscal and monetary policies. Output rose, and the rate of inflation accelerated from less than 5% in 1976 to 9% in 1978 and to more than 13% in 1979. Soaring inflation made U.S. goods less attractive on world markets. As foreigners backed away from U.S. goods, they demanded fewer dollars, and the dollar fell sharply. In turn, this made inflation worse in the United States. In the fall of 1978, the administration and the Federal Reserve became concerned that the United States was being caught in a vicious circle. If something were not done, would inflation escalate to 15% or 20% or even more? Alarmed by this prospect, President Carter announced a "dollar rescue package," including tighter fiscal and monetary policies and intervention in the exchange markets to buy dollars and thus keep the price of the dollar up.

Note that, in spite of flexible exchange rates, the United States did not feel completely free from international complications. Domestic policy was shifted in response to the collapse of the dollar. What can we con-

FIGURE 19-6
The fall and rise of the dollar, 1971–1985
In 1971, 1973, and 1977–1978, the average price of the dollar moved lower in terms of other currencies. With tighter monetary policy and growing government deficits, the dollar moved sharply higher between 1981 and 1984. To calculate this average, the currency of each country is weighted according to the amount of trade of that country with the United States.

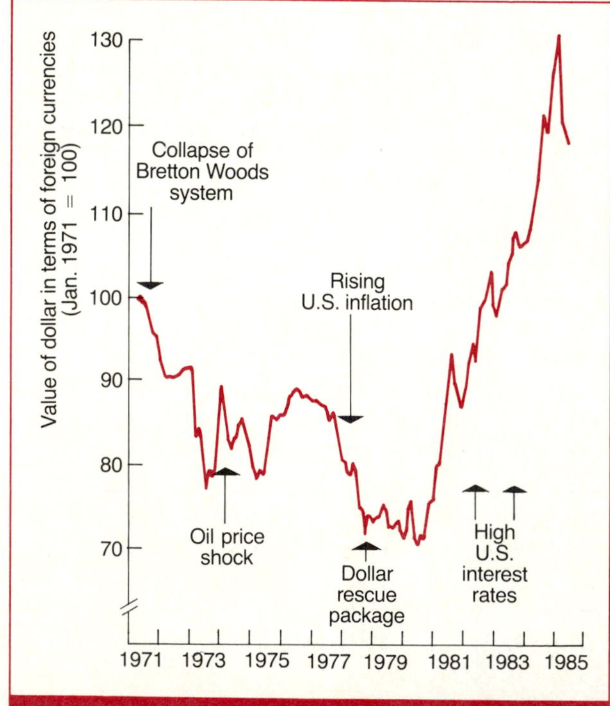

clude? It may be true that flexible exchange rates provide more independence than do pegged rates. However, they don't provide complete independence. Even the United States is strongly influenced by international economic developments.

The soaring dollar, 1980–1984 Further steps toward monetary restraint were taken in 1979, when the Fed announced a new policy of limiting monetary growth to fight inflation. The rate of inflation responded strongly, falling below 4% by 1982. Success in fighting inflation strengthened the dollar on the international exchanges.

Other forces contributed to the upsurge of the dollar. The tax cuts enacted in 1981 led to large government deficits. Government borrowing, combined with monetary restraint, caused very high interest rates in the United States. As a result, foreigners flocked to buy U.S. bonds, thereby increasing the demand for dollars and driving the value of the dollar upward. This trend was reinforced by economic disturbances in developing countries and lackluster performance in Europe. The United States became a "safe haven" for restless foreign investors. Why take chances abroad, particularly when American bonds paid such high rates of interest?

The result of the rush to buy dollars was striking. Observe in Figure 19-6 that the dollar shot up about 70% between 1980 and 1984. By early 1985, the dollar had not only recovered all the ground lost during the 1970s but had risen 30% above the heights of early 1971, prior to the collapse of the Bretton Woods system. In spite of U.S. success in fighting inflation, foreigners had to pay more for American goods because the dollar had become so expensive. At the same time, foreign goods became cheaper to American buyers. The consequence was a profound change in the U.S. economic position in the world. American imports soared, while exports remained stagnant. The U.S. trade deficit, which had hovered near $30 billion a year between 1977 and 1981, shot up to $61 billion in 1983 and $107 billion in 1984. The United States was selling bonds and other assets to foreign countries and using the proceeds to buy huge quantities of foreign goods. (The appendix to this chapter provides details on the U.S. balance of payments.)

Deindustrialization? The surge of imports led to difficulties in a number of basic U.S. industries, such as automobiles, steel, and textiles. Some observers feared that the U.S. economy was in the process of *deindustrialization*. We might lose the manufacturing core of our economy and become a nation committed to services. Pressures grew to "do something" to protect basic industries, with uneven results. Restrictions on imports of steel were tightened. But the administration seized the opportunity provided by the strong domestic recovery and record profits in the automobile industry. Restraints on Japanese car exports to the United States were relaxed in early 1985.

Foreign nations were quick to point out that one of the reasons for the large U.S. trade deficit was the huge budgetary deficit of the U.S. government, which kept real interest rates high and led to the high value of the dollar. Although the strong dollar helped their economies in one way—by making it easier to sell to the United States—it created problems in other ways. In particular, the high U.S. interest rates sucked funds out of their economies, pulling their interest rates up, too. High world interest rates created particularly severe problems for countries with large foreign debts.

THE INTERNATIONAL DEBT CRISIS

Between 1973 and 1982, the developing nations borrowed heavily from foreign countries. As a result, their external debt expanded at a very rapid and unsustainable rate, increasing almost fivefold. In 1982, a crisis shook the international financial system when Mexico became unable to make payments of interest and principal to foreign lenders. After tense negotiations, Mexican debt was ***rescheduled***—that is, repayment was postponed. In the following months and years, a number of other developing countries went through similar rescheduling exercises, which reduced the immediate pressures to repay. However, many third world countries are still saddled with staggering foreign debts—totalling over $800 billion in 1985. (This is enough to buy 100 million cars.) The long-run ability of these countries to pay interest on their debts remains in doubt, to say nothing of the repayment of principal.

Borrowing from foreign nations can play an important and constructive role in the development process.

By borrowing, countries—like business firms—can obtain the funds needed to buy machinery and equipment. When such capital is put to good use, it not only results in greater production and higher living standards at home. It can also be used to produce goods for export, thus providing the funds to service the debt.

Unfortunately, the developing nations expanded their debt not only to finance investment and growth, but also for less productive purposes. When the price of oil skyrocketed in 1973–1974, most countries felt unable to cut back oil consumption quickly. In order to pay for expensive oil imports, many went deeply into debt. They were borrowing to finance current consumption—something that could not continue indefinitely.

Paradoxically, the oil-importing countries were not the only ones to borrow more when the price of oil increased rapidly. Some of the oil *exporters*—such as Mexico—also incurred large new debts. The Mexicans expected that the real price of oil would continue to rise; that is, they expected the price of oil to go higher and higher compared with the average price of other products. If the future promised large and growing oil revenues, why not benefit now by borrowing? Furthermore, Mexicans were actively encouraged to borrow by U.S. bankers who looked on international loans as relatively safe—especially loans to foreign governments. If problems arose, the banks counted on the U.S. government, the IMF, or other official bodies to step in to prevent a default.

The recession in the United States and elsewhere caused a sharp reduction in the demand for the exports of the developing countries. As a result, they found it more difficult to earn the foreign exchange needed to make payments on their debt. Monetary conditions in the United States also had adverse effects on the developing world. When U.S. interest rates rose, so did the interest which the developing countries had to pay on their debt. Furthermore, many of the loans were denominated in dollars. This meant that the burden of the debt increased as the dollar rose on the international exchange markets. There was, however, one bright spot in this generally bleak picture: It became easier to export to the U.S. market because the U.S. dollar was appreciating.

A number of events precipitated the crisis of 1982. Argentina waged an expensive war with Britain in the South Atlantic. Mexico was shocked by the decline in the price of oil.

Although the rescheduling of the debt of Mexico and other countries has eased the immediate crisis, the international economy remains vulnerable. Many developing countries see as their major hope a further decline in the price of oil, which would ease their balance-of-payments problems. But Mexico and some other oil exporters are counting on a higher price of oil to get them out of *their* financial bind. No matter what happens to the price of oil, somebody will have to be disappointed.

In a study for the Brookings Institution, Thomas O. Enders and Richard P. Mattione come to a conclusion that is "sobering for both debtors and creditors." The debt reschedulings, and the accompanying policies of demand restraint, have been built on the assumption that a few years of tough adjustment will be sufficient to get out of the crisis and lay the basis for a new period of rapid growth. However, they find little basis for such optimism. Rather, the huge foreign debts are likely to act as a continuing drag on growth, with potentially catastrophic results:

> When the crisis in some countries drags on, . . . it is easy to imagine resentment and frustration turning against governments when they fail to persuade the United States and other industrial countries of the need for more generous terms. Not only would the current broad but weak trend toward democracy falter, but public order and national security could also be at risk.[3]

THE EUROPEAN MONETARY SYSTEM

Because of their desire for closer economic relations, the members of the European Economic Community—made up of most of the Western European nations—established the *European Monetary System* (EMS) in 1979. One objective of this system is to reduce fluctuations in the exchange rates between the European currencies and thus provide a more stable basis for trade. However, the European leaders were mindful of the rigidities which had brought down the IMF's pegged exchange

[3]Thomas O. Enders and Richard P. Mattione, *Latin America and the Crisis of Debt and Growth* (Washington: Brookings, 1984), pp. 55–56. (Enders is the U.S. ambassador to Spain.)

rate system and had also led to the breakdown of an earlier attempt at stabilizing European exchange rates in the early 1970s. They therefore allowed for significant flexibility in the EMS. Countries can let their currencies move in wide bands, of as much as 6% around par. Member nations are encouraged to change their par rates more quickly than they did under the old IMF system.

The objective of the European countries is to progressively reduce the degree of flexibility among their currencies, perhaps ultimately moving to a single, unified currency. However, such a step is unlikely in the near future. For the time being, considerable exchange rate flexibility has been retained. The EMS currently represents a significant experiment with an intermediate system, part way between freely flexible exchange rates and the pegged exchange rates of the old IMF.

KEY POINTS

1. International trade is different from domestic trade because (*a*) imports are often subjected to special taxes (tariffs) and (*b*) international trade involves more than one national currency.

2. A foreign exchange market is a market for one national currency in terms of another. The demand for a foreign currency depends on (*a*) imports of goods, (*b*) imports of services, and (*c*) acquisitions of foreign assets.

3. Similarly, a nation's supply of a foreign currency depends on: (*a*) exports of goods, (*b*) exports of services, and (*c*) acquisitions of its assets by foreigners.

4. The price which an American pays for a British good depends on (*a*) the British price of the good, measured in pounds, and (*b*) the exchange rate between the pound and the dollar.

5. Suppose that after a period of equilibrium in the foreign exchange market, the demand for pounds in terms of dollars shifts to the left. At the existing exchange rate, the quantity of pounds demanded will be less than the quantity supplied. The British government can deal with the surplus of pounds by one or a combination of the following steps:

(*a*) Intervening in the exchange market, that is, selling U.S. dollars to buy up the surplus pounds

(*b*) Devaluing the pound or permitting it to depreciate in response to market forces

(*c*) Reducing the supply of pounds through restrictions on imports or other international transactions

(*d*) Restricting aggregate demand in Britain and thus reducing the supply of pounds originating from British imports

6. Under the classical gold standard, the adjustment mechanism worked through changes in aggregate demand. Suppose, for example, that a country had a competitive advantage with low-priced goods, and consequently exported a lot and imported only a little. Gold would flow in. This flow would automatically increase the quantity of money. Aggregate demand would be stimulated and prices would rise. With higher prices, the country would lose its competitive advantage. Its exports would fall and its imports would rise.

7. There were two major defects in the classical gold standard:

(*a*) The change in aggregate demand caused by an international gold flow might make it more difficult to meet the domestic objectives of full employment and stable prices.

(*b*) Because domestic currency was convertible into gold, the monetary system was vulnerable to a crisis of confidence and a run on the available gold stock. This defect contributed to the collapse of the international gold standard during the Great Depression of the 1930s.

8. At the end of the Second World War, the IMF system was established, with pegged but adjustable exchange rates. In the event of a fundamental disequilibrium, a country could devalue or revalue its currency. There were three major problems with this system: the confidence problem, the adjustment problem, and the liquidity problem.

(*a*) There could be a crisis of *confidence* when a devaluation was expected. Speculators had an incentive to sell the currency before its official price was reduced (that is, before the currency was devalued).

(*b*) In order to discourage speculation, authorities generally denied that devaluation was being considered. Once they had made a commitment not to devalue, exchange rates tended to be rigid, leaving the system without an adequate *adjustment* mechanism. Deficit countries tended to have continuing deficits, and surplus countries tended to have continuing surpluses.

(*c*) Until the first special drawing rights (SDRs)

were created in 1970, increases in *liquidity* depended on U.S. deficits. When the United States ran deficits, foreign countries acquired reserves in the form of U.S. dollars.

9. The adjustable peg system broke down in the 1971–1973 period, leading to the present system of flexible, or floating, exchange rates.

10. Flexible exchange rates have a number of advantages and a number of disadvantages. There are two main arguments for flexible exchange rates:

(*a*) It is not clear that there is a good alternative. The gold standard collapsed in the 1930s, while the pegged system broke down in the 1970s.

(*b*) With flexible rates, countries gain freedom to tailor their aggregate demand policies to the domestic objectives of full employment and stable prices, rather than to the balance of payments.

Criticisms of flexible exchange rates are that:

(*a*) Changes in exchange rates may disrupt trade.

(*b*) There have been large fluctuations in exchange rates since 1971. Many of the exchange rate changes do not seem to have been necessary to correct fundamental international disequilibrium.

(*c*) Central bankers and governments may follow inflationary policies if they don't have to worry about keeping the exchange rate pegged.

(*d*) A depreciation of the currency will make imports more expensive and thus add to inflation. In turn, this will reduce the ability of the country to compete on international markets, and that will lead to a further devaluation. Thus, a country may be drawn into a vicious circle of inflation-depreciation-inflation-depreciation.

11. Between 1982 and 1984, large U.S. budgetary deficits contributed to high U.S. interest rates, a soaring dollar, and a rapidly increasing U.S. deficit in international trade.

12. Between 1973 and 1982, the external debt of the developing nations grew at a rapid, unsustainable rate. In 1982, a number of countries were unable to meet their commitments to pay interest and principal, and debts were rescheduled.

13. An objective of the European Monetary System is to reduce fluctations in exchange rates among the European currencies.

KEY CONCEPTS

tariff
exchange rate
foreign exchange
foreign exchange market
imports of goods
imports of services
acquisition of foreign assets (investment in foreign countries)
foreign exchange reserves
official intervention in the exchange market
adjustment mechanism
deficit
surplus
gold standard
adjustable peg
IMF
par value
fundamental disequilibrium
devalue
revalue
speculator
rigid peg
adjustment problem
''stop-go'' policy
***n*th country**
key currency
liquidity problem
special drawing right (SDR)
confidence problem
flexible, or floating, exchange rate
clean float
dirty float
depreciation of a currency
appreciation of a currency
vicious circle
virtuous circle
deindustrialization

rescheduling of debt
European Monetary System

PROBLEMS

19-1. Suppose that after a period of equilibrium, the demand for the British pound falls on the exchange markets. What choices does the British government have in dealing with this change?

19-2. Under the old gold standard, what prevents a country from continuously losing gold?

19-3. In a system of adjustable pegs, why does there have to be an *n*th country? Why did the United States end up as the *n*th country? What special problem or problems does the *n*th country have?

19-4. Why might a country follow a "stop-go" policy under a pegged exchange-rate system?

19-5. The text explains why the finance minister of a deficit country would be unwise to admit that a devaluation was being considered under the old IMF adjustable peg system. Would the finance minister of a surplus country be similarly unwise to admit that a revaluation was under consideration? Explain why or why not.

19-6. Explain how speculators who bought marks worth "2 million Volkswagens" gained at the expense of the German goverment when the mark was finally allowed to rise on the exchange markets.

*__19-7.__ The text states that the rapid buildup of external debt in the 1973–1982 period was "unsustainable;" that is, it could not rise indefinitely at that rapid rate. Might a slower buildup be "sustainable," or will any steady buildup of debt lead to a financial crisis sooner or later? If you believe that a slow rate of growth of debt (say 1% or 2% per year) might be sustainable, explain why. If you think that it must lead to a crisis sooner or later, explain why.

APPENDIX

THE BALANCE-OF-PAYMENTS ACCOUNTS

The U.S. balance-of-payments accounts provide a record of transactions between residents of the United States and other countries. A system of ***double-entry bookkeeping*** is used. That is, a set of accounts with two sides (+) and (−) is constructed, and any single transaction results in equal entries on both sides (or offsetting entries on the same side). Consequently the accounts logically *must* balance. We have already run into this concept of double-entry bookkeeping in our study of banks in Chapters 12 and 13. For example, if the Fed purchases a $100,000 bond from a commercial bank (Table 13-1), the Fed's assets increase by $100,000 (the bond), while exactly the same change takes place in its liabilities (in the form of the reserve deposit of the commercial bank).

With *double-entry bookkeeping*, each transaction results in equal entries on both sides (or offsetting entries on the same side), so that the two sides of the accounts must balance.

To illustrate how double-entry bookkeeping works with international transactions, consider a simple example where a U.S. company exports a $100,000 computer to Germany. The export is entered on the positive—or "credit"—side of the U.S. balance of payments. But something else also happens. The German importer has to pay for the computer. Suppose, to make things easy, that the importer pays with a check, which the U.S. computer company deposits in its Frankfurt bank account. (For convenience, a business engaged in international trade may keep accounts in a number of foreign banks.) Table 19-1 shows the effects of this single transaction on the U.S. balance-of-payments accounts. Note that an increase in U.S. assets (bank accounts) in Germany appears as a negative item. This must be so, to make the accounts balance.

The overall U.S. balance of payments is subdivided into two main accounts. In one category—the ***capital account***—statisticians enter changes in U.S.-owned assets in foreign countries and changes in foreign-owned assets in the United States. For example, the increase in the computer company's deposit in Frankfurt is a U.S.-owned asset in a German bank, and accordingly it is a capital account item. Other capital account items include increases in ownership of foreign stocks or bonds, or of property such as factories and capital equipment. In other words, *international investment* shows up in the capital accounts.

All other items—that is, those which do not represent changes in the ownership of foreign assets—are put in the ***current account,*** shown at the top of Table 19-2.

THE CURRENT ACCOUNT

Item 1(*a*), merchandise exports, includes the products such as wheat, computers, and aircraft exported by the United States in 1984. Americans receive income—principally dividends and interest—from past investments abroad, entered as item 1(*b*).

Note that *returns from investments appear in the current account,* even though the investments themselves are included in the capital accounts. The reason is this: If General Motors buys a German company, U.S.-owned assets abroad rise; therefore, this investment belongs in the capital account. But when GM receives dividends from this German company, there is no change in ownership. GM receives the dividends but still owns the German company. Thus, dividends go in the current account, in item 1(*b*). Similarly, interest from a foreign bond is put in the current account. (However, when a foreign bond is paid off, that represents a change in asset holdings and appears in the capital account.) Interest and dividend receipts are considered an export of services; that is, they represent payments by foreigners to Americans for the *use of the services of American capital.*

U.S. exports of goods and services appear on the positive side of the U.S. balance of payments. Our imports of goods and services appear on the negative side.

Unilateral transfers are the final item in the current account. Included in this item are payments immigrants send back to their families in the "old country," grants by the U.S. government and private charities to foreigners, and payments made to those drawing pensions from the United States while living abroad.

THE CAPITAL ACCOUNTS

The capital accounts are divided into three main subcategories: *A,* changes in nonreserve assets; *B,* changes in reserve assets; and *C,* the statistical discrepancy.

TABLE 19-1
An International Transaction
(effects on the U.S. balance of payments)

Positive items (credits)		Negative items (debits)	
U.S. export of computer	$100,000	Increase in U.S.-owned bank account in Germany	$100,000

Each international transaction—such as this export to Germany—affects both sides of the U.S. balance of payments equally. As a consequence, the two sides of the balance of payments sum to the same total.

A. Changes in Nonreserve Assets

Direct investment in the United States occurs when there is an increase in ownership by foreigners who control a business in the United States. For example, when Honda establishes production facilities in the United States, that appears as direct investment, item 2(*a*). Similarly, on the other side, when Ford builds a plant in Mexico, that also appears as direct investment, 7(*a*). Other investment, 2(*b*) and 7(*b*), does not involve control: Individuals or corporations are acquiring foreign bonds or stocks of companies they do not control, or short-term foreign assets such as bank accounts.

Note that, when foreigners increase their assets in the United States, the increase is entered as a *positive* item in the U.S. balance of payments. An increase in U.S.-owned assets abroad is entered as a negative item. (We already saw in Table 19-1 why an increase in U.S. bank deposits in Germany is a negative entry.)

The fact that a *negative* entry is made for an increase in U.S.-owned assets abroad is worth emphasizing. It is advantageous for the United States to own large assets abroad. [Specifically, item 1(*b*) shows that in 1984 we received $88 billion in interest and dividends from our earlier investments abroad.] Therefore, *we should resist the temptation to consider a negative item as necessarily ''bad'' or a positive item as necessarily ''good.''*

B. Changes in Reserves

Increases in foreign official assets in the United States, item 3, represent dollars held by foreign governments and central banks, mostly in the form of U.S. Treasury bills.

On the other (debit) side of the accounts, increases in U.S. reserves of foreign currencies are entered; these reserves are owned by the U.S. Treasury or the Federal Reserve. When gold holdings of the U.S. Treasury or

TABLE 19-2
U.S. Balance-of-Payments Accounts, 1984
(billions of dollars)

Positive items (credits)			Negative items (debits)		
		I. Current account			
1. Exports of goods and services		362	5. Imports of goods and services		453
(*a*) Merchandise exports	220		(*a*) Merchandise imports	328	
(*b*) Receipts from U.S. investments abroad	88		(*b*) Payments for foreign investments in United States	70	
(*c*) Other	54		(*c*) Other	55	
			6. Unilateral transfers, net		11
		II. Capital accounts			
		A. Changes in nonreserve assets			
2. Increase in foreign nonreserve assets in United States		90	7. Increase in U.S. nonreserve assets abroad		18
(*a*) Direct investment in the United States	21		(*a*) Direct investment	6	
(*b*) Other	69		(*b*) Other	12	
		B. Changes in reserves			
3. Increase in foreign official assets in United States		3	8. Changes in U.S. reserve assets		3
(*a*) U.S. government securities	5		(*a*) Gold	0	
(*b*) Other	−2		(*b*) SDRs	1	
			(*c*) Reserve position in IMF	1	
			(*d*) Foreign currencies	1	
		C. Statistical discrepancy			
4. Statistical discrepancy		30			
Total		485	Total		485

Federal Reserve increase, the transaction is also included in reserves. (Gold is considered an international asset and is included in the capital accounts even though it does not represent a claim on any foreign country.) Note that an acquisition of gold by the United States appears as a *negative* or debit item in this nation's balance of payments. (Remember our earlier warning: Positive doesn't necessarily mean "good" or negative, "bad.") By considering a very simple transaction, we can see why this must be so. Suppose that an American manufacturer exported $1 million of machinery and that the foreign country paid with $1 million in gold. The machinery export appears on the positive side of our balance of payments. To make the accounts come out right, our acquisition of gold must appear on the negative side.

C. The Statistical Discrepancy

Theoretically, there should be no statistical discrepancy. If government statisticians had a perfect knowledge of international transactions, the sum of the positive items considered thus far would be exactly equal to the sum of the negative items. But they aren't equal. The statistical discrepancy is whatever number is necessary to make them equal. From the size of this discrepancy—$30 billion in 1984—it is obvious that international transactions are measured *very* imperfectly. Because the government has a better record of current account transactions than capital account transactions, it is assumed that most of the errors and omissions occur in the capital accounts; thus, the statistical discrepancy is included in the capital accounts.

THE BALANCE OF PAYMENTS

If the two sides of the balance of payments must be equal, what do we mean when we talk of the balance of payments being in "deficit" or "surplus"? When such terms are used, *we must be excluding certain items from the calculations*. One standard way of calculating the balance of payments is to exclude changes in reserves (category II*B*), taking the net amount of all other items. This concept of the balance of payments—known as the ***official reserve transactions balance,*** or ***official settlements balance***—measures the surpluses or shortages that would occur in foreign exchange markets at existing exchange rates in the absence of official intervention. That is, in terms of Figure 19-3, it represents the amount of reserves *GE* bought or sold by governments and central banks to keep the exchange rate from reaching the intersection of demand and supply (*F*). By this definition, U.S. international payments were in balance in 1984. That is, our acquisitions of reserves ($3 billion) were the same as the increase of reserves held by foreign governments and central banks in the United States (also $3 billion).

A country has an *official settlements surplus*—or, more simply, a *balance-of-payments surplus*—if it is acquiring net international reserves. (That is, if its international reserves are increasing more rapidly than foreign countries' reserve claims on it.)

A *balance-of-payments deficit* occurs when a country is losing reserves on a net basis.

Two other balances are also commonly calculated. The ***current-account balance,*** as the name implies, includes only the items in the current-account (category I). In 1984, the United States had a current-account deficit of $91 billion. In other words, we spent more abroad than we earned. As a result, foreigners accumulated more assets in the United States than we accumulated abroad.

A country has a *current-account surplus* if its exports of goods and services are greater than the combined sum of its imports of goods and services plus its net unilateral transfers to foreign countries.

Finally, we may subtract merchandise imports ($328 billion) from merchandise exports ($220 billion) to find the ***trade balance,*** or ***merchandise-account balance***—a deficit of $108 billion in 1984.

A country has a *trade surplus*—or *merchandise-account surplus*—if its merchandise exports exceed its merchandise imports.

As recently as 1981, the United States ran a small current-account surplus (Figure 19-7). A sizable merchandise deficit was offset by large receipts of interest and dividends from past U.S. investments abroad. Because of the small current-account surplus, the U.S. was acquiring more assets abroad than foreigners were acquiring here. However, international payments have changed a great deal in recent years. By 1984, when the United States was running a current-account deficit of $91 billion, foreigners were acquiring many more assets in the United States than we were aquiring abroad.

FIGURE 19-7
International payments of the United States
The U.S. trade balance and current-account balance moved in a negative direction in 1976 and 1977. As the economy recovered and inflation began to accelerate, imports rose rapidly. It was not until 1978 that the dollar had depreciated enough to restore U.S. competitiveness and cause a rebound in the U.S. trade balance.

The trade balance deteriorated even more sharply between 1982 and 1984. The soaring U.S. dollar meant that U.S. products were less and less competitive on world markets.

(The current account and merchandise accounts are seasonally adjusted, quarterly figures, at annual rates. The official settlements balances are annual figures.)

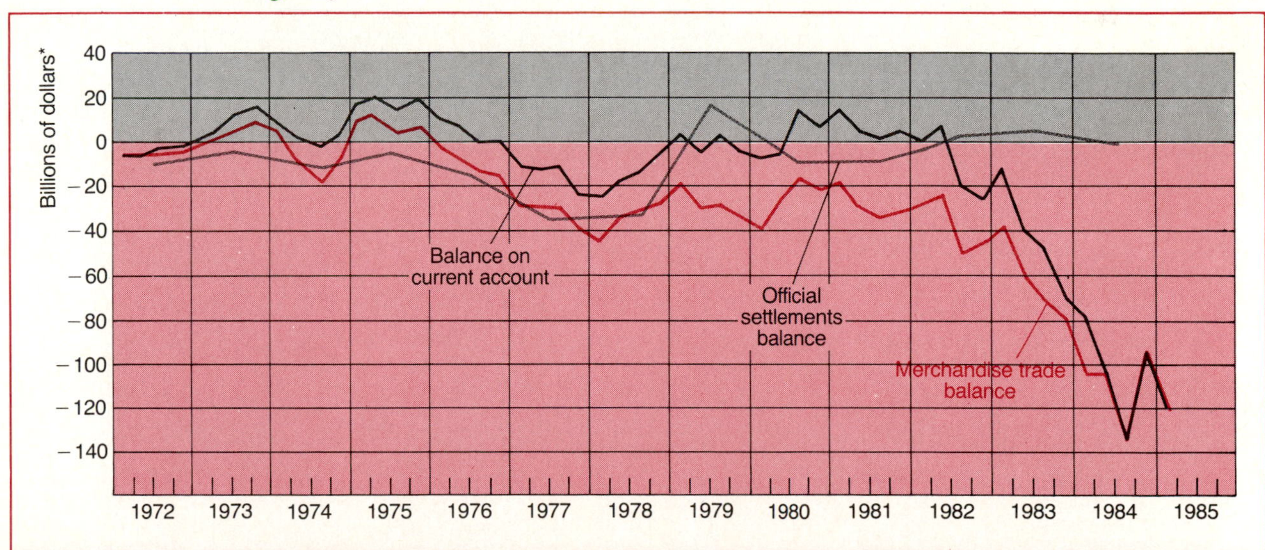

PART FIVE

MICROECONOMICS:

IS OUR OUTPUT PRODUCED EFFICIENTLY?

Parts 2, 3, and 4 have focused on unemployment and inflation, the two great problems in macroeconomics. Now that we have taken this broad overview of the economic "forest," we turn to a more detailed examination of the "trees." Thus, the microeconomic analysis that follows in Parts 5, 6, and 7 will involve an examination of the individual producers of goods and services—such as Ford Motor Company or the Florida orange grower—and the individual consumers who purchase cars and oranges. This study of the economy "in the small" is directed to the three questions introduced in Chapter 4: *What* is produced? *How* is it produced? *For whom* is it

produced? In Parts 5 and 6 we will deal with the first two questions, just introducing the question of *for whom,* which will be taken up in detail in Part 7.

In Part 5 our focus will be on efficiency. One might well ask: "Because Parts 2, 3, and 4 were concerned with unemployment, were they not also devoted to the question of efficiency?" The answer is a clear yes. Historically, unemployment has been a major source of economic inefficiency. Idle labor and idle capital have meant the loss of output that could have been produced. We have also seen that severe inflation causes inefficiency. If the price system breaks down because of inflation and no longer gives the clear signals on which business planning must be based, decision making deteriorates and the nation's output is less as a consequence.

Recognizing that these sources of inefficiency are important, we now turn our attention in Part 5 to the additional reasons why our economy is inefficient. To isolate these new sources of difficulty, we shall assume away the two great macroeconomic problems of inflation and unemployment. In other words, we now assume that there is no general rise in prices nor large-scale unemployment. Even if these extremely favorable assumptions were realized, there would still be reasons why we might not be making the most of our productive ability. Specifically, we might be producing too much of one good and not enough of some other. That is one of the major problems to be studied in Part 5.

In this study of microeconomics, we begin by picking up the demand and supply curves developed in Chapter 4. A brief review of those curves is provided in the following box, entitled "Remember?" If you don't remember, we strongly recommend that you reread Chapter 4.

REMEMBER?

Demand . . .

The quantity of apples demanded depends on the price of apples . . .

. . . and other influences such as the price of bananas, changing tastes, or changing consumer income.

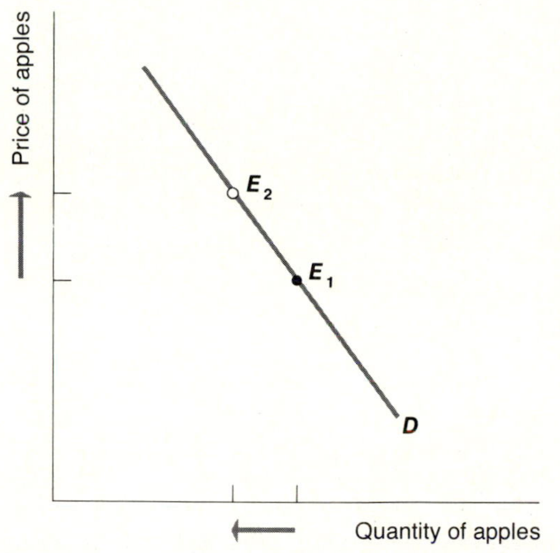

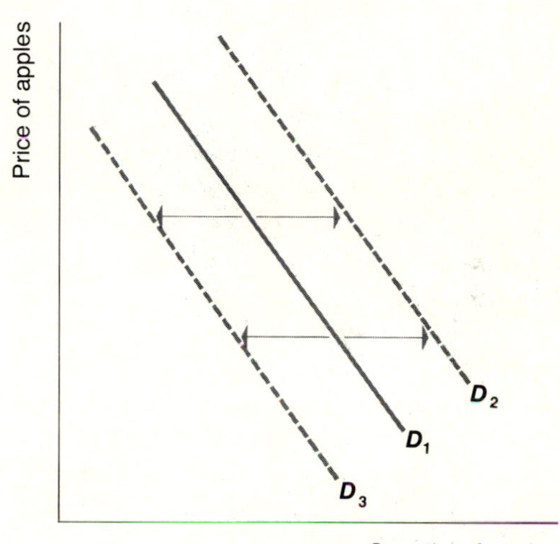

In this panel, we see that if the price of apples rises, the quantity demanded becomes smaller. Such a movement along a given demand curve is described as a "decrease in the quantity demanded."

In this panel, we see that if one of the *other* influences changes, the demand curve shifts. For example, if income rises, the demand curve shifts from D_1 to D_2. On the other hand, if income falls, the demand curve shifts to D_3. This leftward shift in the curve is described as a "decrease in demand."

Supply . . .

The quantity of apples supplied depends on the price of apples . . .

. . . and other influences such as the weather, the price of fertilizer and other inputs, changing technology, and the prices of alternative outputs like wheat.

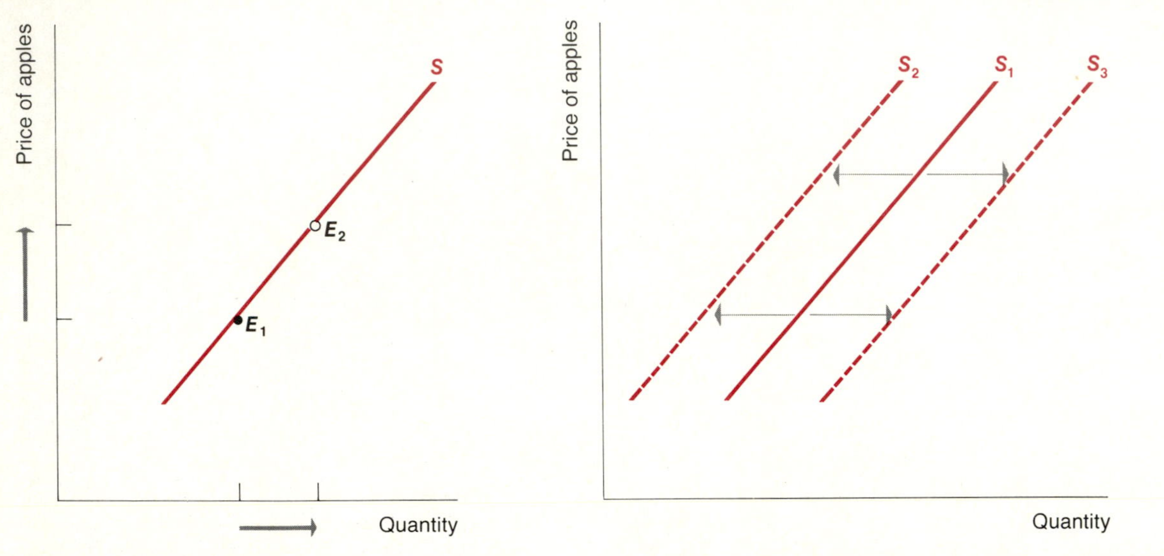

In this panel, we see that if the price of apples increases, equilibrium moves up the supply curve. Such a movement is referred to as an "increase in the quantity supplied."

In this panel, we see that if one of these other influences changes, the supply curve shifts. For example, if the price of fertilizer or some other input rises, the supply curve shifts from S_1 to S_2.

On the other hand, if there is particularly good weather, then the supply curve shifts to S_3. Such a shift in the supply curve is described as an "increase in supply."

Supply and Demand Together Determine Price
Equilibrium price and quantity occur at *E*, where the supply and demand schedules intersect.

Note: Neither curve shifts so long as other influences on supply and demand do not change ("other things remain equal"). However . . .

. . . suppose that other influences do change. For example, suppose that consumer income rises, so that demand shifts from D_1 to D_2. Then equilibrium moves from E_1 to E_2, with more sold at a higher price.

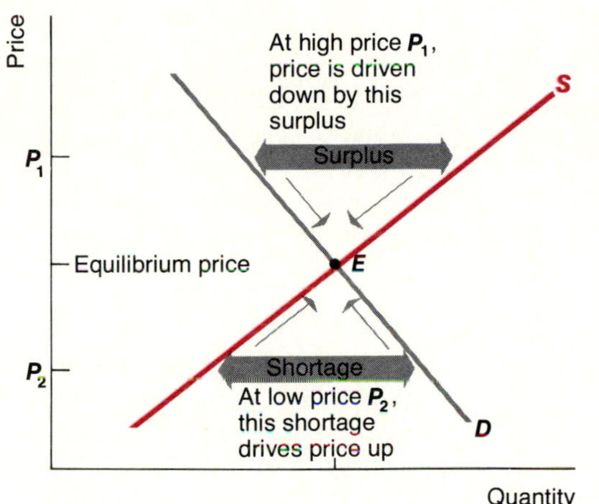

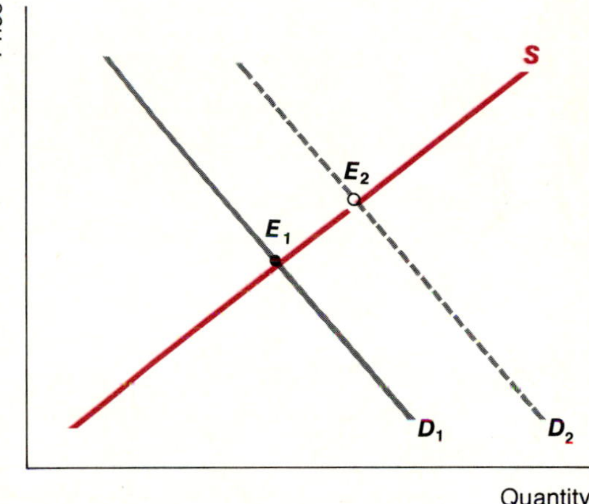

CHAPTER 20

DEMAND AND SUPPLY:

THE CONCEPT OF ELASTICITY

Good theory is usually trying to tell you something, even if it is not the literal truth.

ROBERT M. SOLOW

There isn't a farmer in the country who complains when he has a good crop. But some thoughtful ones may be concerned if everyone else has a good crop too. The reason is simple: A good crop nationwide will reduce the price, and that may hurt farmers more than the benefit they get from increased sales. Whether or not they will benefit or lose on balance depends on the ***elasticity of demand.*** This chapter is devoted to developing this concept and showing how important it is in answering such widely diverse questions as: Will a bumper crop result in higher or lower farm income? Does the consumer or the producer bear the burden of a sales tax? Why are agricultural prices unstable?

THE ELASTICITY OF DEMAND: HOW MUCH DOES THE QUANTITY DEMANDED RESPOND TO A CHANGE IN PRICE?

Suppose you are managing the university drama club. Your play has a week to run, and the theatre is running half empty for each performance. You consider lowering the ticket price by 20%, from \$10 to \$8. This policy will be a great success if it fills a lot of those empty seats. But it will be a failure if the public doesn't respond and you get very few extra sales.

These two possibilities are illustrated in Figure 20-1. To explain this diagram, we must first identify total revenue geometrically. For example, if the initial equilibrium is at E_1 in panel *a,* what is total revenue? The answer is \$10,000, that is, the base Q of 1,000 tickets times the height P of \$10 a ticket. However, base times height is the area of a rectangle—in this case, rectangle 1, shaded in red. Similarly, we can sketch in gray rectangle 2 that measures the total revenue at the different point E_2 on the demand curve.

> ***Essential idea for future chapters:*** **The *total revenue* of sellers is the area of the rectangle to the southwest of the point of equilibrium on the demand curve. It is the quantity sold (the base of the rectangle) times the price (the height of the rectangle). This rectangle also represents the total cost of this good to buyers, that is, their total expenditure on this good.**

Now let us return to the original question: Can you increase your total revenue by lowering the price? If you face the demand curve shown in panel *a,* the answer is yes. The quantity demanded is very responsive to the reduction in price; demand is described as ***elastic.*** As you lower price from \$10 to \$8 and move down the demand curve from E_1 to E_2, total revenue rises from the \$10,000 of area 1 to the \$12,800 of area 2. (This \$12,800 is 1,600 tickets at \$8 each.)

On the other hand, if you face the demand curve shown in panel *b,* the price cut fails. Attendance increases very little as you lower price. As you move down the demand curve from E_1 to E_3, total revenue decreases from \$10,000 to \$8,800. Because the quantity demanded is relatively unresponsive to the change in price, demand is described as ***inelastic.*** Thus elasticity is a measure of how strongly the quantity responds to a change in price:

Elasticity of demand, ϵ_d

$$= \frac{\%\text{ change in quantity demanded}}{\%\text{ change in price}} \quad (20\text{-}1)$$

If ϵ_d is greater than 1, demand is *elastic*.
If ϵ_d is less than 1, demand is *inelastic*.
If ϵ_d is equal to 1, then demand has *unit elasticity*.

Reconsider, now, the theater example in Figure 20-1. In both panels, the price reduction is the same: \$2, or 20%. In panel *a*, quantity increases sharply, from 1,000 to 1,600. Since this represents a larger percentage increase in quantity than the 20% decrease in price, demand is elastic. Furthermore, the large increase in quantity more than offsets the reduction in price, resulting in an increase in total revenue. This leads us to a rule of thumb for judging whether a demand curve is elastic or not: If a fall in price causes an increase in total revenue as in panel *a*, demand is elastic. However, if a fall in price causes a reduction in total revenue—as in panel *b*—demand is *inelastic*. Finally, if revenue remains unchanged in the face of a change in price, elasticity is 1.

A number of calculations of elasticity are provided in Box 20-1. Less formal illustrations are provided in the demand curves shown in Figure 20-2. In panel *a* the elasticity of the completely vertical demand curve is zero. The reason is that price has no effect whatsoever on the quantity demanded, which remains 10 regardless of how the price may change. Thus the elasticity ratio in equation 20-1 is zero because the change in the quantity

FIGURE 20-1
Pricing theatre tickets: The elasticity of demand and total revenue.

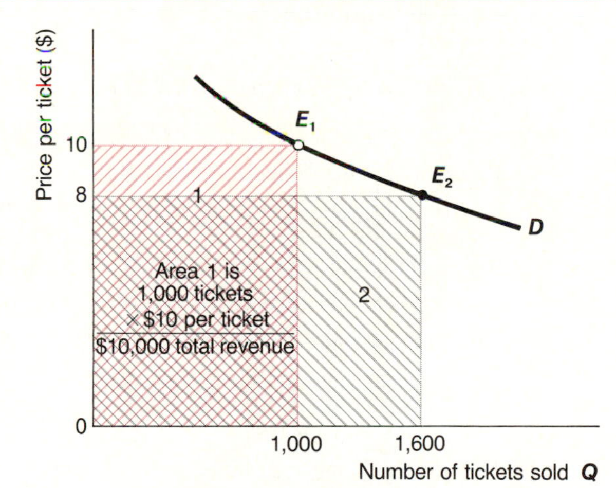

(*a*) **Elastic demand.** If lowering the price raises total revenue, demand is elastic and the reduction in ticket price is successful.
At original equilibrium E_1, there is a \$10 price, 1,000 tickets are sold, and total revenue is \$10,000, shown as area 1. When price is reduced to \$8, 1,600 tickets are sold at E_2, and total revenue rises to \$12,800, shown as area 2.

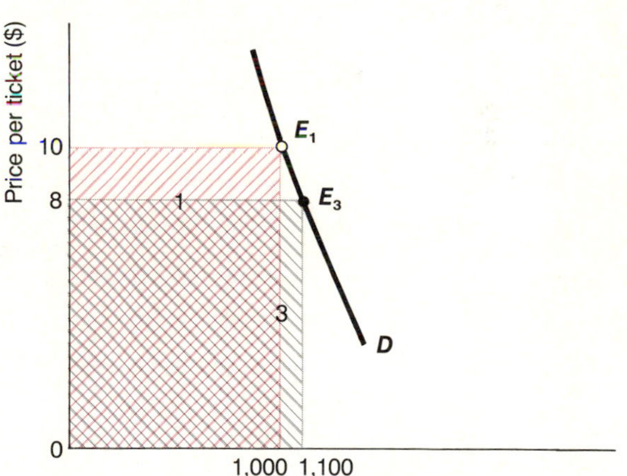

(*b*) **Inelastic demand.** If a lower price reduces total revenue, demand is inelastic and the policy fails.
Starting from the same initial equilibrium E_1 with \$10,000 total revenue, a price reduction produces a quite different result. Since ticket sales respond very little to the price reduction, total revenue *falls*—specifically, to 1,100 × \$8 = \$8,800.

BOX 20-1

CALCULATION OF ELASTICITY

In this box, we show how elasticity between two points on a demand curve can be calculated. If we let ΔQ represent "change in Q," then the percentage change in quantity in equation 20-1 may be written $(\Delta Q/Q)(100\%)$. If we similarly rewrite the percentage change in price as $(\Delta P/P)(100\%)$, our elasticity formula becomes

$$\epsilon_d = \frac{(\Delta Q/Q)(100\%)}{(\Delta P/P)(100\%)} = \frac{\Delta Q/Q}{\Delta P/P}$$

Applying this formula in a straightforward manner to the move from E_1 to E_2 in panel *a* of Figure 20-1, we get a first approximation of the elasticity of demand:

$$\epsilon_d = \frac{600/1{,}000}{2/10} = 3.0$$

(Actually, ϵ_d is negative since the change in quantity is positive while the change in price is negative. However, the negative sign on ϵ_d is often omitted.)

Unfortunately, there is a problem with this straightforward "first approximation." We used the initial E_1 values of $Q = 1{,}000$ and $P = 10$. But now suppose we had moved in the reverse direction along the demand curve, from point E_2 to E_1. The initial values would now be those at E_2; that is, $Q = 1{,}600$ and $P = 8$. You can confirm that this would result in the different calculation of $\epsilon_d = 1.5$. This raises a problem because we would like an elasticity measure that is the same whether we start at E_1 or E_2. Therefore, rather than taking either E_1 or E_2, we take the average of the two; that is, we use the average quantity $\overline{Q}$ and average price $\overline{P}$. Thus, elasticity of demand is calculated to be

$$\epsilon_d = \frac{\Delta Q/\overline{Q}}{\Delta P/\overline{P}} \qquad (20\text{-}2)$$

$$= \frac{600/[(1{,}000 + 1{,}600)/2]}{2/[(10 + 8)/2]} = 2.1$$

As we expected, this falls between our two previous calculations of 3.0 and 1.5. Because this value is more than 1, demand is elastic.

Since equation 20-2 provides a way of calculating elasticity between two points separated by an arc of the demand curve, it is commonly referred to as the *arc elasticity* formula.

---

demanded in the numerator is zero. At the other extreme, the completely horizontal demand in panel *e* has infinitely large elasticity because even the smallest drop in price would result in an unlimited increase in the quantity demanded.

In the intermediate case in panel *c*, quantity increases at the same rate as price falls. Hence, the numerator and denominator in equation 20-1 are the same and elasticity is 1. Note how total revenue remains constant in this case.

In Figure 20-2, as we move farther to the right, the slope gets smaller. (For a review of the concept of slope, see page 25.) While the slope is getting smaller and smaller, the demand curve is becoming more and more elastic. Can we conclude that this relationship between slope and elasticity always holds? The answer is yes, *if the curves being compared pass through the same point,* such as E_1 in the two panels of Figure 20-1. Thus, we have another rule of thumb for elasticity: *If* two demand curves pass through the same point, the one with the smaller slope is more elastic.

This idea is important. However, it is also important to recognize that when two demand curves do *not* pass through the same point, elasticity *cannot* be judged merely by slope. An illustration is provided in Figure 20-3, which shows the demand for bananas in the small Canadian economy and the large U.S. economy. Although U.S. demand has less slope, both curves have exactly the same elasticity. In both cases, the quantity demanded increases by 100% when price falls by 20%.

Another example where slope is not a good measure of elasticity is provided in panel *c* of Figure 20-2. As we move down this curve, its slope changes. However, its elasticity does not; it remains constant at 1. A further illustration is provided in problem 20-5, where it is shown that as we move along a demand curve that is a straight line—and therefore has constant slope—its elasticity keeps changing.

ELASTICITY OF SUPPLY

Just as elasticity of demand describes the responsiveness of buyers to a change in price, so elasticity of supply describes the responsiveness of sellers. Supply is elastic if producers respond strongly to price changes by drastically altering the quantity they supply, or inelastic if they respond weakly. More precisely, the formula for supply elasticity is similar to the formula for demand elasticity in equation 20-1:

Elasticity of supply, ϵ_s

$$= \frac{\%\text{ change in quantity supplied}}{\%\text{ change in price}} \qquad (20\text{-}3)$$

Figure 20-4 shows five examples of supply elasticity. They range from the completely inelastic supply in panel

FIGURE 20-2
Varying degrees of elasticity

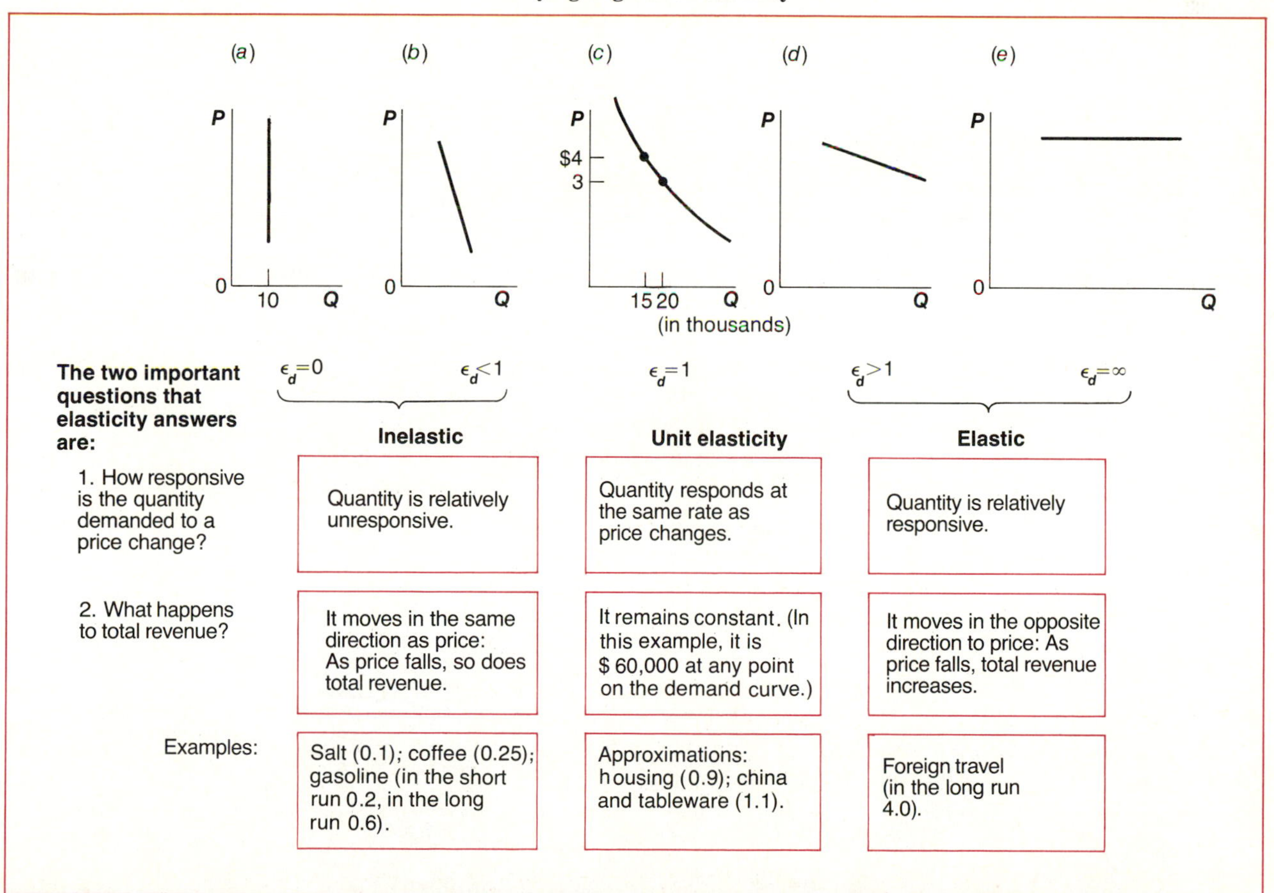
(a)
(b)
(c)
(d)
(e)
P
0
10
Q
$4
3
15 20
(in thousands)
$\epsilon_d = 0$
$\epsilon_d < 1$
$\epsilon_d = 1$
$\epsilon_d > 1$
$\epsilon_d = \infty$
The two important questions that elasticity answers are:
Inelastic
Unit elasticity
Elastic
1. How responsive is the quantity demanded to a price change?
Quantity is relatively unresponsive.
Quantity responds at the same rate as price changes.
Quantity is relatively responsive.
2. What happens to total revenue?
It moves in the same direction as price: As price falls, so does total revenue.
It remains constant. (In this example, it is $ 60,000 at any point on the demand curve.)
It moves in the opposite direction to price: As price falls, total revenue increases.
Examples:
Salt (0.1); coffee (0.25); gasoline (in the short run 0.2, in the long run 0.6).
Approximations: housing (0.9); china and tableware (1.1).
Foreign travel (in the long run 4.0).

a to the completely elastic response in panel *e*.[1] Once again, as in the case of demand, there is a simple rule of thumb for relating slope to elasticity: *If two supply curves pass through the same point* (such as the common point at the lower left end of each supply curve in Figure 20-4), *the one with the smaller slope is the more elastic.* But otherwise, elasticity cannot be judged merely by slope.

In contrast with demand—which traces out a curve if the elasticity is one—supply with unit elasticity is a straight line. If extended, it would pass through the origin 0. Note that this is true of the supply curve with unit elasticity in panel *c* of Figure 20-4. On such a line, P always changes by the same percentage as Q; in our example, when P doubles, Q also doubles. Since the numerator and denominator in equation 20-3 are equal, the elasticity of supply is 1.

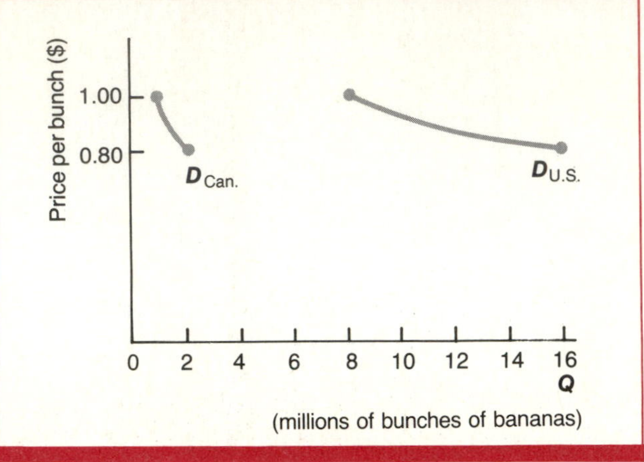

FIGURE 20-3

Why slope alone does not indicate elasticity

The U.S. demand curve for bananas has less slope than the Canadian demand, but the elasticity of the two curves is identical. The reason is that if the price falls by 20%, the quantity doubles in both cases. In Canada, it increases from 1 to 2, whereas in the United States, it increases from 8 to 16.

[1] To calculate the arc elasticity of supply between two points A and B in panel *d*, we use the same approach as in the calculation of the arc elasticity of demand in Box 20-1:

$$\epsilon_s = \frac{\Delta Q/\overline{Q}}{\Delta P/\overline{P}} = \frac{100/[(100 + 200)/2]}{2/[(5 + 7)/2]} = 2$$

Thus, this supply is confirmed to be elastic.

Despite the similarity in the calculations, there is one respect in which elasticity of supply and demand are quite different. Elasticity of demand indicates whether or not total revenue rises when we move to a new equilibrium on a demand curve. However, there is no similar interpretation for supply. If we move to a higher-priced equilibrium on a supply curve—say, from A to B in Figure 20-4*c*—price and quantity both increase. Hence, total revenue rises *regardless* of the elasticity of supply.

FIGURE 20-4

Different elasticities of supply

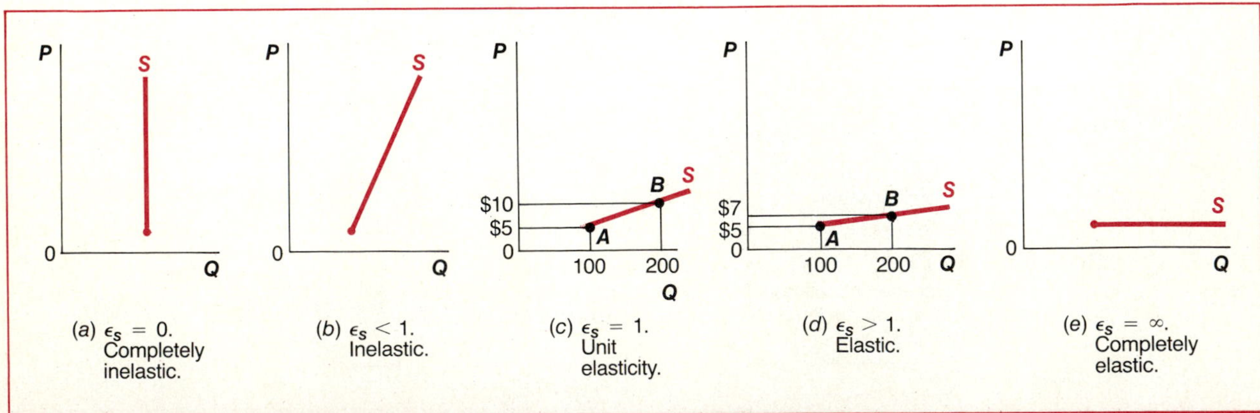

So far we have calculated elasticity assuming that the location and slope of the demand and supply curves are known However, usually they are not; the problems involved in estimating them are described in the appendix to this chapter.

We now turn to the broad influences that determine elasticity of demand and supply.

THE DETERMINANTS OF ELASTICITY

Why is the demand for some products highly elastic while demand for others is inelastic?

Elasticity of Demand

1. *Importance in the budget.* Big items in a budget tend to have a more elastic demand than small items. For example, the demand for cars is more elastic than the demand for salt. Car purchasers may spend hours trying to negotiate a 3% price reduction on a new car; if they don't get it, they may not buy the car. But they won't even notice a 30% drop in the price of salt. For such a small item, consumers are very insensitive to price.

2. *Substitutability.* Items that have good substitutes generally have a more elastic demand than those that do not. To illustrate, consider sugar and salt, both of which are small items in any budget. Yet sugar has a more elastic demand than salt because its substitutes—like honey—are better than the substitutes for salt.

3. *Luxuries versus necessities.* Whereas essentials such as electric power or bread have an inelastic demand because purchasers can scarcely avoid buying them, luxuries generally have a more elastic demand. For example, luxuries such as foreign vacations have an elastic demand because purchasers can stop buying them if their prices rise. (However, if we go all the way up to the category of superluxuries, demand may become inelastic again. The reason is that these goods are bought by those who are so rich that they aren't affected by a change in price—indeed, they may not even notice it. There is no better illustration than John Pierpont Morgan's comment that anyone who has to ask the cost of a yacht can't afford one.)

4. *Time.* Over time, demand becomes more elastic. For example, if the price of gasoline rises, there is very little immediate reduction in the amount the public purchases. It takes some time for drivers to switch to smaller cars and longer yet for the auto companies to design and build more fuel-efficient cars. However, when they do, the public's purchases of gasoline are reduced. Thus demand is more elastic in the long run than in the short.

Elasticity of Supply

Supply is elastic if producers are able to back away from the market if prices fall, and are able and willing to expand sales if prices rise. Thus, elasticity of supply depends upon:

1. *The feasibility and cost of storage.* Goods that rot quickly must be put on the market regardless of price; their elasticity of supply is low. The same tends to be true of goods that are costly to store.

2. *The characteristics of the production process.* Does an item have a close substitute in production? That is, can the labor, land, and equipment used to produce the item be readily switched into the production of another good? If the answer is yes, supply will be elastic. For example, the elasticity of supply is greater for an individual grain—such as corn—than for all grains taken together. The reason is that, in the face of a fall in the price of corn, a producer is able to shift production into a substitute grain such as wheat or barley. This ability of producers to respond to a change in price makes the supply of corn elastic. On the other hand, if the price of *all* grain falls, a farmer will have much more difficulty in shifting out of grain production altogether because there aren't close substitute activities. For example, if the farmer were to try to move into, say, dairy farming instead, this would be a very costly switch because it would require different kinds of capital equipment. Thus, with farmers less able to respond to a change in price, the elasticity of supply of grain will be less. In short, products like corn with a close substitute in production have a more elastic supply than products without a close substitute in production.

In contrast to substitutes in production—like corn and wheat—other goods may be *joint products,* like beef and hides: When you produce one, you get the other. The decision to butcher a steer is influenced by the price of beef but hardly at all by the price of hides. Once the steer has been butchered, the relatively unimportant hide will be sold regardless of its price. In other words, the supply of hides is inelastic because hides are a relatively unimportant joint product.

3. *Time*. Just as time makes demand more elastic, it also makes supply more elastic. In fact, this idea has already been encountered in our discussion of rent control in Chapter 4. It is only with the passage of time that the supply of apartments becomes more elastic. Figure 20-5 provides another example used by the English economist Alfred Marshall in his discussion of the influence of time on supply almost a century ago.

Suppose demand for a perishable commodity like fresh fish suddenly rises from D_1 to D_2. The immediate effect on the first day in panel *a* is that price rises to P_2. Note that the quantity supplied is not influenced by price. Whatever quantity has been caught that day—in our example, Q_1—is put on the market, regardless of price. (In Marshall's day, refrigeration was inadequate. Thus, there was no way suppliers could respond to a changed price by putting more or less on the market.) Consequently, the immediate supply S in panel *a* is completely inelastic.

However, in the days that follow, the higher price induces fishing boat captains to increase their crews and bring retired boats back into service. The quantity of fish caught and offered for sale increases. Thus, supply becomes more elastic in panel *b*, and price settles down somewhat to P_3. But this is not the long-run equilibrium. As more time passes, new boats can be built and even more fish caught. Thus, in the long run, supply is even more elastic, as shown in panel *c*. The result is a further moderation of price, to P_4.

With this discussion of the elasticity of demand and supply in hand, let's show how useful elasticity can be in answering two important policy questions: First, who bears the burden of a commodity tax? Second, what are the special problems of agriculture?

APPLYING ELASTICITY: WHO BEARS THE BURDEN OF A SALES TAX?

To answer this question, consider the supply and demand for a good shown in panel *a* of Figure 20-6. The initial equilibrium before the tax is at E_1, with 10 million units

FIGURE 20-5
How the elasticity of supply changes over time

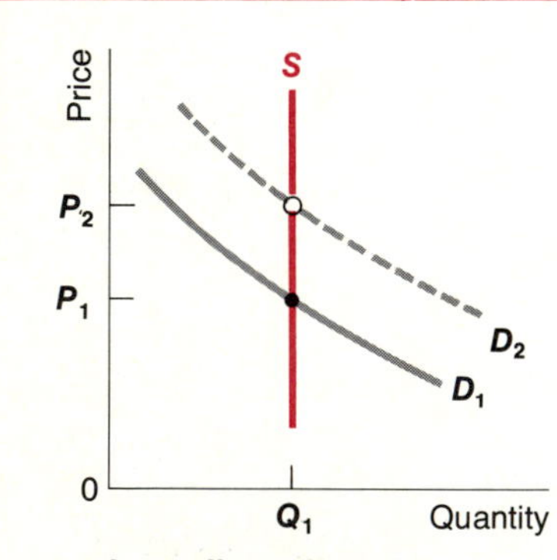

(a) **Immediate effect.**

On the first day, supply is completely inelastic. Thus, the shift in demand from D_1 to D_2 results in a very large price increase, to P_2.

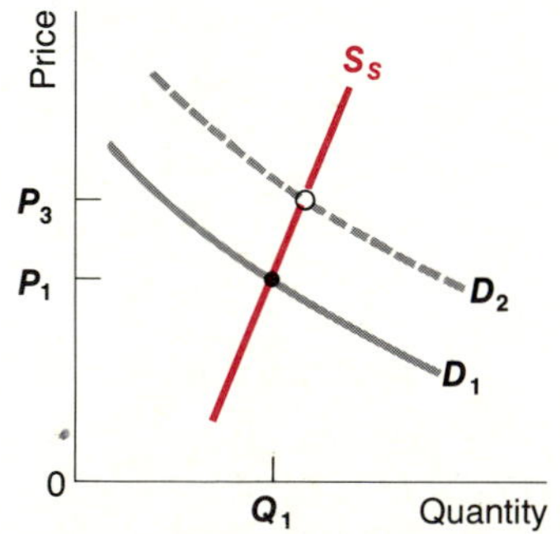

(b) **Short-run effect.**

Supply now has some elasticity, since the catch of fish can be increased by hiring larger crews and using existing boats more heavily. Thus the price rise is moderated to P_3.

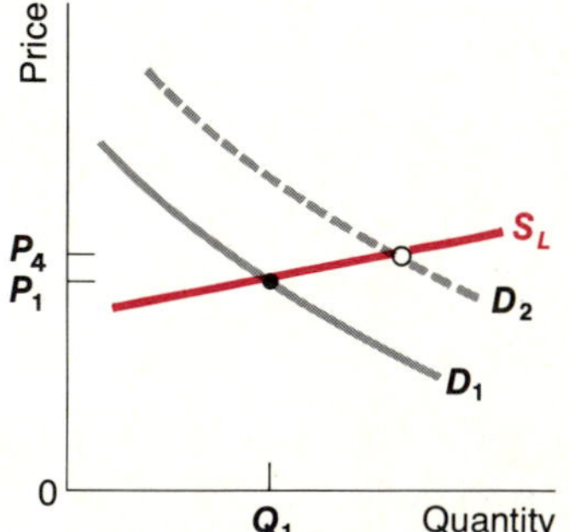

(c) **Long-run effect**

Supply now has even greater elasticity, since there is now time for new boats to be built. As a result, more fish are sold and the price settles down further to P_4.

sold at a price of $3. Suppose that the government now imposes a sales tax of $1 per unit, to be collected from sellers. Who bears the burden of this tax?

The effect of this tax is to shift the supply curve upward from S_1 to S_2 by the full $1 amount of the tax. To confirm this, consider any quantity supplied—say, 12 million units. Point *A* on the supply curve S_1 shows that before the tax, sellers would have to receive $4 per unit to induce them to sell these 12 million units. This means that *after* the tax, they must receive $5—at point *B*—in order to enable them to pay the government the $1 tax and still have the same $4 left. Thus, point *B* is on the new after-tax supply curve S_2. And no matter what point we consider on S_1, the corresponding point on S_2 is always $1 higher. Thus, the entire supply curve shifts upward by the amount of the tax.

As a result of the tax, the equilibrium moves from E_1 to E_2, and the price rises from $3 to $3.20. Thus, buyers bear 20 cents of the burden; they pay 20 cents more per unit. What happens to sellers? The price they receive rises by 20 cents—from $3 to $3.20; but $1 of this must go to the government, so the seller gets only $2.20 after tax. Because the seller ultimately receives $2.20 rather than the original $3, the seller bears 80

FIGURE 20-6

How the burden of a sales tax depends on the elasticity of demand and supply

In part *a*, equilibrium of S_1 and *D* results in before-tax price of $3. When the $1 tax is imposed, supply shifts from S_1 to S_2 and the new equilibrium price is $3.20. Buyers pay 20 cents more; this is the burden of the tax that they bear. Sellers receive $2.20—that is, the $3.20 market price less the $1 tax that they must pay the government. Thus they receive 80 cents less than the original $3, and this 80 cents is the burden they bear. In part *b*, supply is more elastic than demand, and the after-tax price rises to $3.80. In this case, buyers bear 80 cents of the burden and sellers only 20 cents.

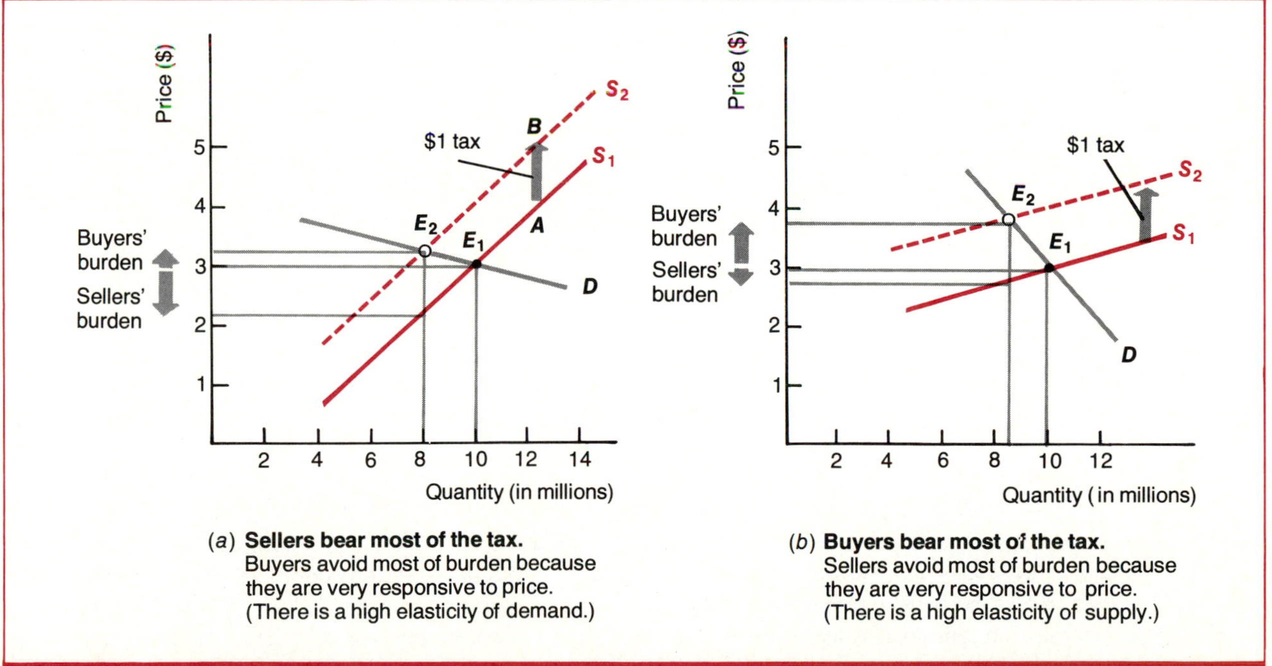

(*a*) **Sellers bear most of the tax.** Buyers avoid most of burden because they are very responsive to price. (There is a high elasticity of demand.)

(*b*) **Buyers bear most of the tax.** Sellers avoid most of burden because they are very responsive to price. (There is a high elasticity of supply.)

cents of the burden. To sum up, the two gray arrows on the far left show how the $1 tax is split up into the 20 cent burden on buyers and the 80 cent burden on sellers.

The reason that buyers bear a lighter share of the burden in this case is because they respond more to changes in price than do sellers; that is, demand is more elastic than supply. However, in panel *b* the reverse is true. Here, sellers are more responsive to changes in price; supply is more elastic than demand. As a result, sellers bear the lighter burden of the tax.

These conclusions can best be summarized if we think of two groups in a market, one buying, the other selling. Suppose one group—it doesn't matter which—takes the view: "We aren't keen to stay in the market. If the price moves against us, we can back away. In responding to price changes, we're flexible, sensitive, *elastic*." Suppose the other group feels: "We have no choice; we must stay in the market. Even if price moves against us, we can't back away. We're inflexible, unresponsive, *inelastic*." It is no surprise that this second group will bear most of the burden of a tax and will, in other situations as well, be in the more vulnerable position.

APPLYING ELASTICITY: WHAT ARE THE SPECIAL PROBLEMS OF AGRICULTURE?

The two decades between World War I and World War II were times of distress for U.S. agriculture. Farm prices and land values fell sharply and bankruptcies were common. During the 1930s, income per family on American farms fell to less than half the depressed income in the city. In response, the government greatly expanded its policies of assistance to farmers—policies which, in some cases, had dated back to the Civil War. Over the decades that followed, these policies have been modified and extended and new ones added. Consequently, by 1985, the U.S. government had become heavily committed to a wide range of policies designed to support farm income.

Unfortunately, these policies had become very expensive; between 1980 and 1983, government outlays for farm support programs almost tripled. The Reagan administration, faced with an increasing deficit, decided that farm assistance was one of the areas in which it had to make drastic cutbacks, and this caused great concern on America's farms. Many farmers had borrowed heavily to buy inflated land or expensive equipment in the prosperous days of the late 1970s, and then discovered that it was nearly impossible to make payments on their loans when interest rates rose. In many instances, farmers simply went bankrupt. There were predictions that many more would follow if the government were to cut back its support of their incomes. In short, the Reagan administration argued that it could not afford such costly farm support policies, while many farmers argued that, without them, they would not be able to survive.

One element of the farm program is a system of government supports for the prices that farmers receive for a number of commodities, including wheat, cotton, sugar, and peanuts. Under this policy, the government announces a support price. If the market price falls to that support level, farmers can sell any amount they wish to the government. Thus the government's policy of stepping in and buying whenever necessary prevents the price from falling below the support level. (In practice, the government actually uses a complicated loan scheme to keep prices up. However, we skip the complications because the loan scheme is so similar to a simple program of price supports.)

Why has the government made this guarantee to farmers, but not to other producers? One reason is that agriculture has historically suffered from two special problems. Agricultural prices have been *unstable,* fluctuating up and down from year to year; and they have shown a tendency to *fall,* compared to the price of other goods. To understand each of these problems, we first ask: "What would happen to agricultural prices if there were no government intervention in these markets?" As we shall see, the concept of elasticity is very important in providing an answer.

Year-to-Year Price Instability

In Figure 20-7, we show the problems that arise because agricultural demand and supply are inelastic in the short run. Demand for farm products is relatively inelastic because people must satisfy their appetite for food no matter what happens to price. Supply is also inelastic in the short run for several reasons. In some cases the product is perishable; in other cases, the crop is already planted and it is too late for farmers to respond much to a change in price.

In a normal year with demand D and supply S_1, equilibrium is at E_1 with price P_1. However, with a bumper crop, supply shifts to S_2, equilibrium moves to E_2, and price falls all the way to P_2. In this example, a bumper crop cuts price by a third! Worse yet for farmers: The inelasticity of demand has meant that their income has been reduced, from the rectangle enclosed to the southwest of E_1 to the smaller rectangle to the southwest of E_2. (It was this income reduction resulting from a bumper crop that worried the thoughtful farmer in the introduction to this chapter.) Similarly, you can confirm that a *poor* crop that results in equilibrium at E_3 will *raise* farm income. In short, because demand and supply are inelastic, relatively small variations in crop yield result in large price fluctuations. Moreover, the better the crop, the lower farm income may be as a result. This point is illustrated further in Box 20-2.

FIGURE 20-7

Short-run instability of farm price and income

In a normal year, inelastic demand D and supply S_1 result in equilibrium at E_1. However, if there is a bumper crop and Q_2 is put on the market, equilibrium is at E_2 and price falls from P_1 to P_2. Because demand is inelastic, farm income is lower at E_2 than at the normal equilibrium E_1. But if there is a poor crop Q_3, equilibrium is at E_3 and farm income is higher than normal.

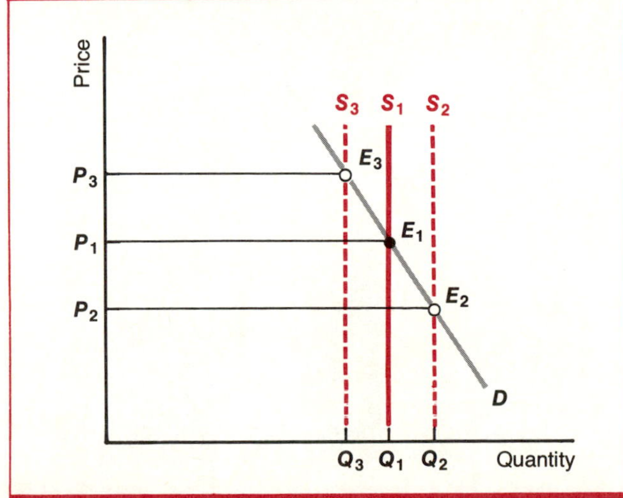

Long-Run Downward Trend in Price

The second farm problem is best understood by considering our economic history. If we go back far enough, farming was our largest activity, with the majority of the population working on the soil. With old-fashioned techniques of agricultural production, an individual family could do little more than produce enough for itself.

However, with improvements in agricultural methods and technology, productivity increased. A typical farm family could produce more and more food: enough for two familes, then three, then four, and so on. As that happened, the number of people required on the farm to produce food fell to a smaller and smaller fraction of the population. This decline has had effects that have reached far beyond agriculture. In fact, one of the essential requirements of our industrial development has been the ability of farmers to produce more food than they consume. Without this capability, the labor force necessary for a developing industry would never have been released from the task of grubbing a bare living out of the soil. It was no accident that the industrial revolution in Britain in the eighteenth century was preceded by a revolution in agricultural productivity. And that agricultural revolution has continued at a rapid pace: The average American farm family in 1930 supplied food for itself and 4 city families; today it supplies food for itself and about 40 city families here and abroad. Moreover, U.S. farmers would be producing even more were it not for government programs that have taken acreage out of cultivation.

However, this huge increase in agricultural productivity has been a mixed blessing for the farmers who have achieved it. Once again, elasticity is the key to understanding why. In panel *a* of Figure 20-8, E_1 represents the initial equilibrium in an earlier period, at the intersection of long-run supply S_1 and demand D_1; demand is relatively inelastic because food is a necessity. Over many decades, D has been shifting to the right from D_1 to D_2 because of (1) the increase in the total food-consuming population and (2) the rising income of that population. However, the effects of rising income have been fairly modest. Although consumers purchase more of almost everything as their incomes rise, their expenditures on food rise less rapidly than their expenditures on many other goods. With rising income, people may double their expenditures on clothes and triple their expenditures on vacations, but they increase their food consumption by only a small amount. After all, how much more can anyone eat? Technically, we say that the ***income elasticity*** of demand for food is low; that is, food purchases respond weakly to an increase in income. (For more on income elasticity and other kinds of elasticity, see Box 20-3).

On the other hand, over these same decades there has been an even greater shift in supply (from S_1 to S_2 in panel *a* of Figure 20-8) because of rapid improvements in farm productivity. With supply shifting to the right more rapidly than demand, price has fallen to a new equilibrium at E_2. However, as price falls, farmers—and even more important, their children—leave the farm to pursue more highly paid careers in the city. Because they do, the proportion of the population on the farm falls. This outflow of people from the farm also means that there is a less rapid increase in farm output than would otherwise occur. In other words, agricultural supply S_2 shifts less rapidly to the right. In turn, this means a less severe price reduction.

This, in a nutshell, is the history of American agriculture: Because productivity has outrun demand, the proportion of the population on the farm has fallen. By becoming more and more productive, American farmers are doing a great service to the public in terms of provid-

BOX 20-2

TO FLORIDA CITRUS GROWERS, A FREEZE IS A BLESSING

Cold Eases the Fears of a Bumper-Crop Surplus Resulting in Money Loss

> The freezing weather in Florida's citrus belt will reduce this year's previously predicted bumper crop . . . but ironically it will ease the worries of growers who had feared they would lose money because of the surplus.
>
> "Nature has bailed us out of a bumper crop," a spokesman for the Florida Citrus Commission said yesterday in a telephone interview. "The growers were going to lose money, but now the problem has been taken care of and an oversupply situation has been corrected."

This was the story[†] in 1977; and in 1981, 1983 and 1985, history repeated itself. For example, in 1981 a freeze destroyed about 20% of the Florida orange crop. The wholesale price of concentrated orange juice immediately rose by 30%.

What do these events imply about the elasticity of demand for citrus fruit, and oranges in particular?

[†] Rona Cherry in *The New York Times*, Jan. 23, 1977, reproduced with permission.

ing large quantities of food at a very low price. But their very success has meant that farmers are producing themselves—or their neighbors—out of jobs.

Will the Future Bring Food Scarcity?

A number of observers contend that although the American farmer in the early 1980s was producing far more than we could consume or sell abroad, this situation will not persist. Instead they predict a chronic food shortage.

As an omen of things to come, they cite our experience in the early 1970s when, as a result of crop failures in the Soviet Union and other countries, there was a world shortage of agricultural goods and prices rose rapidly. For example, the average price of wheat rose from \$2.20 a bushel in 1972 to over \$5 a bushel in 1974. The American farmer responded to this high price with larger than usual export sales. Thus America became "the world's breadbasket"—the source of food supply to a world suffering from a severe shortage.

The question is: Was this period of scarcity and high price just an early warning of a new era of food shortage rather than surplus? Specifically, will the traditional problem of supply outrunning demand and downward pressure on price shown in panel *a* of Figure 20-8 be replaced by the new problem shown in panel *b*, where supply shifts less than demand and food prices rise?

Some of the reasons put forward for expecting food supply to lag behind demand are not very convincing—for example, the claim that we are facing a food crisis because the world is running out of land. In fact, studies

FIGURE 20-8
The long-run trend in agriculture
The classic problem of agriculture in part *a* has been that supply has shifted to the right more rapidly than demand. Hence, price has fallen. This situation may repeat itself in the future or it may, as some people predict, change to the situation shown in part *b*. There, shifts in supply do not keep pace with shifts in demand and price rises.

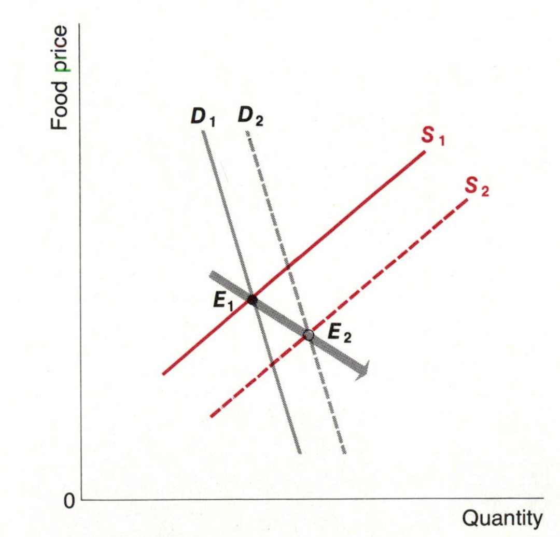

(*a*) Will the traditional problem of agriculture continue, or . . .

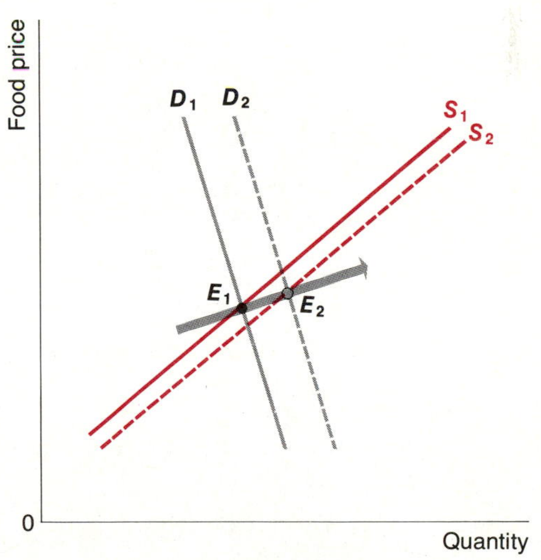

. . . (*b*) will the situation change?

BOX 20-3

OTHER ELASTICITY MEASURES

The demand for any good is affected not only by its price but also by many other influences, such as consumer income. In this box we show how the elasticity concept can be used to measure the strength of these other influences as well.

Income Elasticity of Demand

Just as price elasticity measures how the quantity demanded responds to price changes, income elasticity measures how the quantity demanded responds to income changes. Formally,

$$\text{Income elasticity of demand} = \frac{\text{\% change in quantity demanded}}{\text{\% change in income}} \qquad (20\text{-}4)$$

Notice how this definition is similar to that of price elasticity in equation 20-1. (Incidentally, when economists use the simple term "elasticity," they generally mean "price elasticity.")

The American automobile is an example of a good with a high income elasticity of demand. Various estimates place its value between 2½ and 3; in other words, a 1% increase in income results in an increase in auto purchases of 2½% to 3%. On the other hand, the income elasticity of gasoline is about 1 and of tobacco is considerably less—about 0.6. Thus the demand for tobacco is described as "income inelastic"; when income rises, tobacco purchases rise less rapidly.

Income elasticity has another important interpretation. Recall that income is a "demand shifter"; when income rises, the demand—for autos or tobacco—shifts to the right. Income elasticity of demand measures the magnitude of that shift. In the case of automobiles, the shift is important, while in the case of tobacco it is far less so. (For a small category of goods—inferior goods—an increase in income shifts the demand curve to the *left*: Purchases decline as income rises. In such cases, the income elasticity of demand is negative. An example is low-quality food: When incomes rise, people buy less, since they are now able to afford better food.)

Cross elasticity of demand

The quantity of a good demanded depends not only on its own price but also on the prices of other goods. For example, the demand for cars depends on the

price of gasoline. The **cross elasticity of demand** measures the strength of this effect. Specifically:

$$\text{Cross elasticity of demand} = \frac{\%\text{ change in quantity demanded of } X}{\%\text{ change in the price of } Y} \quad (20\text{-}5)$$

If the cross elasticity is positive, the goods are **substitutes.** For example, beef and pork are substitutes: A 1% increase in the price of pork causes an increase of about 0.3% in the quantity of beef demanded; that is, it causes the demand curve for beef to shift to the right by 0.3%. As another example, a 1% increase in the price of butter causes an increase of about 0.8% in the quantity of margarine demanded. Thus, butter and margarine are even closer substitutes than beef and pork.

On the other hand, if cross elasticity is negative, the goods are **complements.** For example, as a result of an increase in the price of gasoline, people drive less; the demand for cars is reduced. Thus the price of gasoline is a demand shifter, moving the demand for cars to the left. Cross elasticity—which is negative in this case—measures the magnitude of this shift.

To sum up: The *sign* of cross elasticity determines whether goods are substitutes or complements, that is, whether an increase in the price of one shifts the demand for the other to the right or left. The *numerical value* of cross elasticity measures the strength of this effect.

indicate quite the contrary: Only about half of the world's arable land is now being used, and much of the unused acreage has good agricultural potential. Moreover, recent advances in technology have allowed us to increase output by expanding our use of other inputs—like fertilizer—rather than land. For example, during the past three decades, the U.S. acreage of land in peanuts has remained the same, but our output of peanuts has gone up about five times. If this trend continues, our future requirements for additional land may not be as great as is often supposed.

However, there are other reasons that food supply may lag behind demand that are not so easy to dismiss. For example, there is the continuing question of how much damage is being done to the environment by the heavy use of fertilizers and pesticides. Moreover, there is a problem of the depletion of ground water because so much has been drawn off for irrigation purposes. The deforestation of many areas—particularly in the developing world—has interfered with a steady supply of water and made soil erosion worse. Finally, some observers believe that the serious crop failures in foreign countries in the last 15 years have been the result of unfavorable trends in the world's climate.

To decide whether the future situation will be the one shown in panel *a* or panel *b* of Figure 20-8 requires projecting not only world food supply but also demand. This projection requires an answer to the difficult question: Will the rapid population increase in the developing countries continue, or will these countries begin to show the lower birthrate patterns observed in the industrialized parts of the world?

In the mid-1980s, it is impossible to predict whether, in the next century, we will face a continued surplus in agriculture or a severe world scarcity. All we can say for sure is that by the mid-1980s, the major agricultural problem facing governments both in North America and Europe was not food scarcity. Quite the contrary: The problem was what to do about large surpluses.

The problems of agriculture, and the various policies that the government has introduced in response, are so important that we examine them in more detail in Box 20-4 and return to them in Chapter 24.

BOX 20-4

ANOTHER PERSPECTIVE ON AGRICULTURE: IS FALLING PRICE THE SIGN OF A SICK INDUSTRY?

In some cases, a falling price is a sign of a sick industry. In other cases, it is the sign of a very healthy industry indeed. For example, consider IBM. As already noted, computer technology has recently been developing at an exceptionally rapid rate. A computer that once filled a room has now been replaced by a tiny chip that can be fitted into the eye of a needle. As a result, IBM and other computer manufacturers have been able to cut prices drastically. Yet, in spite of rapidly falling prices, IBM's profits have increased. Lower prices and higher profits have *both* been possible because of the large increase in productivity. Thus, what matters is not simply prices. It is the relationship between prices and productivity. In fact, the health of an industry is affected by three major variables—productivity, the prices of outputs, and the prices of inputs.

For American agriculture, the relationship between the price of outputs and the price of machinery

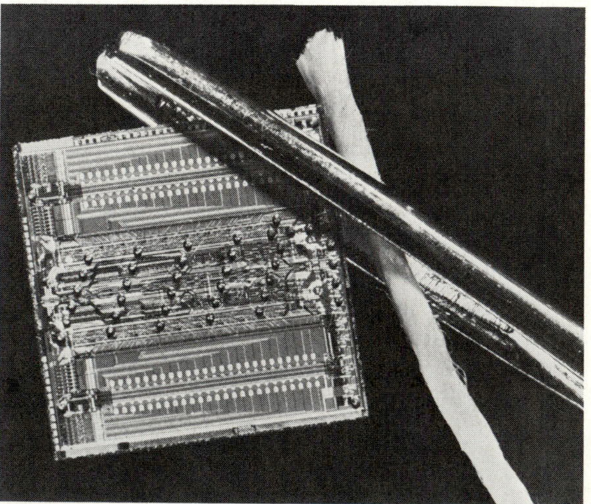

and other inputs has long been a matter of concern—at least since the 1930s, when farm prices plummeted while machinery prices remained more stable. During and after the Second World War, the relative price of farm goods rose sharply. But, since 1950, farm prices have been under downward pressure. As a result, the ratio of prices farmers received to the prices they paid fell by 1985 to less than 60% of the 1910–1914 average—that is, to less than 60% of ***parity.*** Details on the parity ratio are shown in Figure 20-9.

Parity is the ratio of prices received by farmers divided by the prices paid by farmers, expressed as a percentage of the 1910–1914 figure.

The rapid increase in farm productivity has worked to keep farm incomes up. Nevertheless, farm incomes have fluctuated substantially. During the early 1970s, farm incomes rose as a result of continuing improvements in productivity, combined with an upward spurt in farm prices and in sales to foreign countries. At other times, farm incomes have been under severe downward pressure. For example, in 1984–1985, sluggish demand for U.S. farm products on world markets caused a fall in farm incomes. This put many farmers in a severe squeeze, and contributed to the bankruptcies that were taking place at that time. Thus most of the farm community was left out of the recovery that was taking place in the rest of the economy.

FIGURE 20-9
The parity ratio, 1910–1984
The farm parity ratio, which nosedived during the depression in the early 1930s, recovered to above its original 100% level during the 1940s. However, since then it has been on a downtrend.

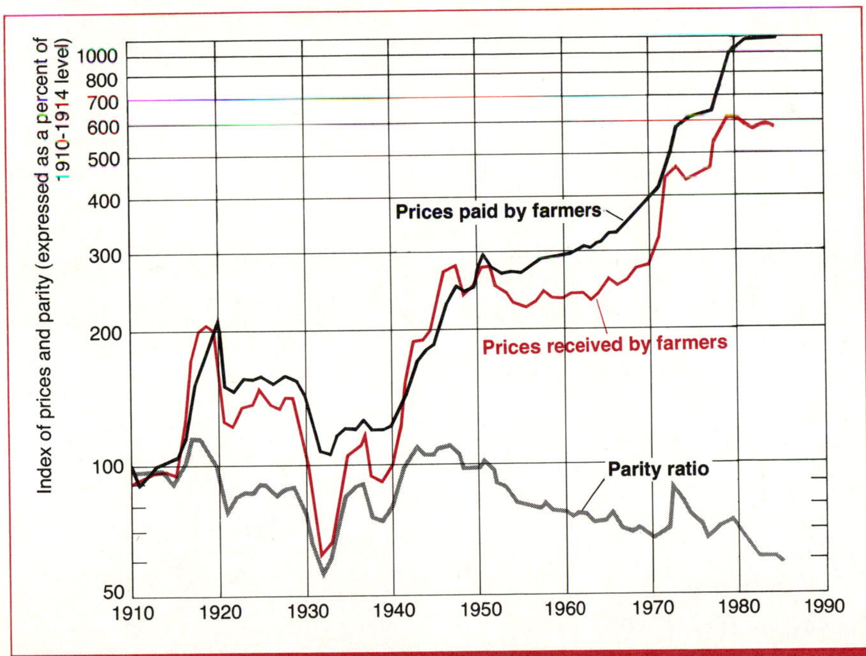

KEY POINTS

1. Elasticity of demand is a measure of the responsiveness of quantity demanded to price: the more responsive, the more elastic.

2. Elasticity of demand also indicates what happens to total revenue as price changes. If demand is elastic, a reduced price will raise total revenue. However, if demand is inelastic, a reduced price will lower total revenue. Goods with high demand elasticity include large-budget items and items with close substitutes.

3. If two curves pass through the same point, the one with less slope is the more elastic. However, if they do not pass through the same point, there is no such simple relationship between slope and elasticity.

4. Elasticity of supply measures the responsiveness of quantity supplied to a change in price; again, the more responsive, the more elastic. Goods with high elasticity of supply include items that can be easily and cheaply stored and goods with close substitutes in production.

5. The elasticities of demand and supply are less in the short run than in the long run.

6. Year-to-year fluctuations in food prices are made more severe by inelasticity of demand. This same inelasticity means that a bumper crop may lower farm income, while a poor crop may raise income.

7. The downward trend in farm prices relative to other prices has occurred in the past because of rapidly improving farm technology and our relatively stable demand for food. As a consequence, supply has tended to outrun demand. It is not clear whether this will continue or whether the situation will be reversed, with food prices rising in the future.

KEY CONCEPTS

elastic demand
inelastic demand
unit elasticity of demand
total revenue as a $P \times Q$ rectangle
relationship of elasticity to total revenue
elasticity of supply
burden of a sales tax
joint products
why low elasticity leads to price instability

PROBLEMS

20-1. At a time when the price of gasoline was $1 a gallon, a *New York Times* editorial stated that a 50 cent increase in its price would lower gasoline consumption by an estimated 10%. What does this imply about the elasticity of supply or of demand?

20-2. Suppose you are the manager of Fenway Park, home of the Boston Red Sox. You have been selling tickets for $8 each, but because of the huge salaries that two of your star outfielders have negotiated you are losing money. The owners who have employed you may be millionaires, but they are concerned, and they press you to take action to increase your total revenue. Specifically, they suggest that you raise the ticket price to $10. This suggestion bothers you—particularly when it leaks out to the press. Not only do the sportswriters denounce the ''greed'' of the owners; they also argue that higher prices will backfire, causing fans to stay away in droves. As a consequence, gate receipts will be lowered, or so the sportswriters say.

In this controversy, what role does the elasticity of demand play? What assumptions are the owners making about elasticity? What assumptions are the sportswriters making?

20-3. Fill in the blanks below.

The curve with greatest elasticity is ____________.

The next greatest elasticity is ____________.

The next greatest is ____________.

The lowest elasticity is ____________.

Unit elasticity is ____________.

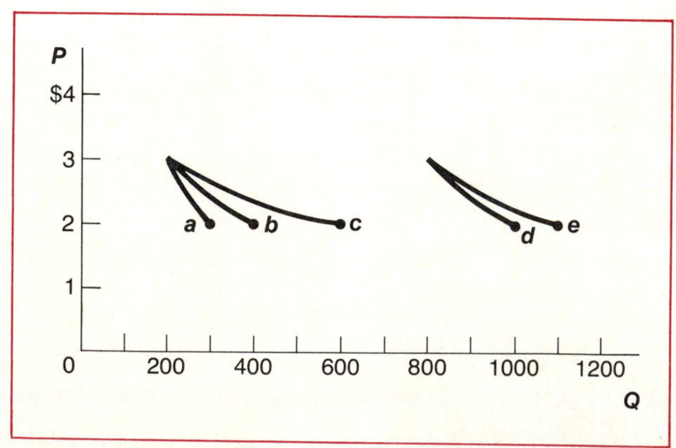

20-4. (*a*) Why don't we define elasticity much more simply, as just the flatness of a curve; that is, elasticity = the change in Q/the change in P? *Hint:* Plot exactly the same demand curve as in Figure 20-1*a* but change the scale in which you measure price. Specifically, measure price in quarters, not dollars, so that the height of E_1 and E_2 are now four times as great. What happens to the flatness of D?

(*b*) "Slope is a poor measure of elasticity because it depends on the arbitrary scale in which P (or Q) is measured." Is this statement true or false?

20-5. Using equation 20-2, calculate the elasticity of section AB in the demand curve shown below. Do the same for section CE. Consider the following statement: "Since AB and CE have the same flatness, but different elasticity, this shows once again that flatness does not necessarily reflect elasticity." Is this true or false?

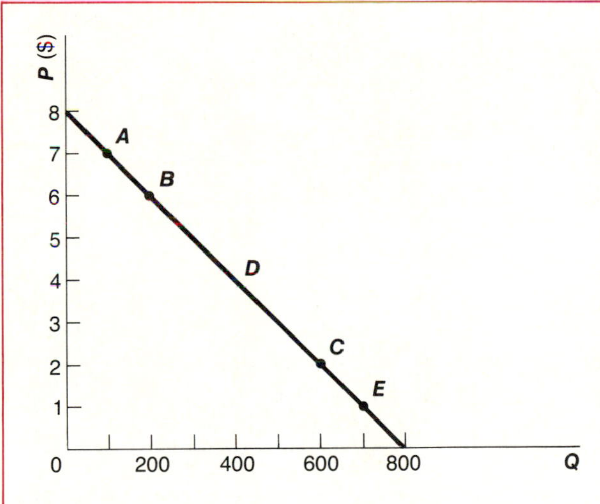

20-6. "Heating oil for homes has a greater elasticity of demand in the long run than in the short." Do you agree? Explain.

20-7. The supply curve in panel *c* of Figure 20-4 is reproduced as S_1 in the diagram below. Its elasticity has already been calculated to be 1. Which of the other two supply curves—S_2 or S_3—also has an elasticity of 1? What is the elasticity of the other? Does this confirm our statement that slope does not necessarily measure elasticity? Extend S_3 downward and to the left. Which axis—the P or the Q axis—does it intersect? Is the following statement correct? If not, correct it.

If a straight line supply curve, when extended, passes through the P axis, it is inelastic. If it passes through the Q axis, its elasticity exceeds 1.

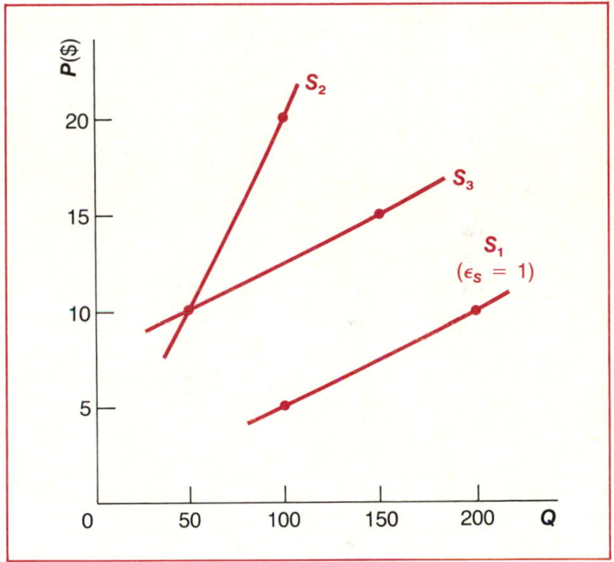

20-8. Would you expect the income elasticity of food to be higher or lower than that of restaurant meals? Explain.

***20-9.** Redraw Figure 20-6*a* on the assumption that buyers, rather than sellers, initially pay the tax. Does this change affect the way the two groups bear the eventual burden?

20-10. This problem is based on Boxes 20-1 and 20-4. In the diagram below:

(*a*) What is the elasticity of demand curve D_1 as price falls from \$20 to \$10? As price rises from \$10 to \$20?

(*b*) How does the elasticity of D_1 compare with that of D_2?

(*c*) Now suppose income has doubled and that demand has consequently shifted from D_1 to D_2. Calculate the income elasticity of demand.

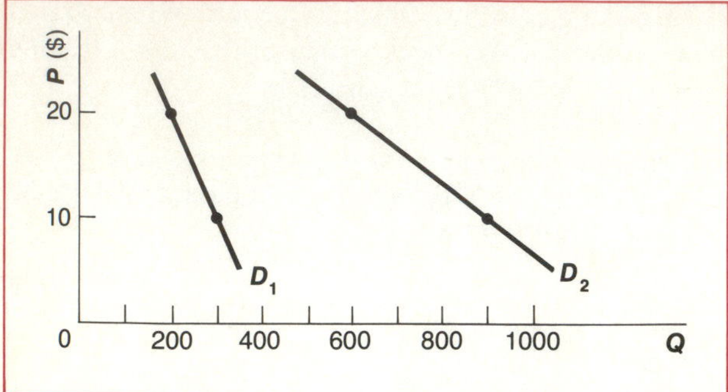

APPENDIX

STATISTICAL DIFFICULTIES IN ESTIMATING DEMAND AND SUPPLY:

THE IDENTIFICATION PROBLEM

To understand the problem of discovering the shape and location of demand and supply curves, first consider demand. One method of estimating it is to observe how much of the good has been purchased in the past at various prices. For example, the 1985 dot in panel *a* of Figure 20-10 tells us that quantity Q_1 was purchased in that year at price P_1. If we are lucky we will observe a "scatter" of observations like the one shown in this diagram. A straight line fitted to these observations provides our estimated demand curve.

In panel *b*, we examine the underlying demand and supply curves that gave rise to these four "lucky" observations. Through the entire period of observation, the demand curve remained stable at D. But the supply curve shifted. For example, the 1982 observation was the result of the intersection of the demand curve and the 1982 supply curve S_{82}, while the 1983 observation was the result of the intersection of that same demand curve and supply, which had now shifted to S_{83}.

The reason that we were lucky in our scatter of observations in panel *a* was because they were generated in panel *b* in precisely this way—by the intersection of a *stable* demand curve and a *shifting* supply curve. We have been able to "identify" demand because of shifts in supply. (As an exercise, set up an example where supply is identified by shifts in demand.)

In the more typical case shown in Figure 20-11 we are not so fortunate. Since both supply and demand have shifted from year to year in panel *b*, the resulting scatter of observations in panel *a* gives us neither demand nor supply but some apparently incomprehensible combination of both.

To emphasize the difficulty in this problem, in panel *c* we show a completely bogus supply and demand system that could have equally well generated the scatter in panel *a*. When all we have to work with is what we see in panel *a*, how can we decide whether this scatter has been generated by the true, inelastic supply and demand system in panel *b* or the completely bogus elastic system in panel *c*? Or by some other bogus system?

The answer is that the problem is indeed hopeless unless we can get more information. Specifically, we require information on how supply shifts and on how demand shifts. The way in which such information can be used is illustrated in the highly simplified example in Figure 20-12—a figure which initially seems just as puzzling as Figure 20-11. (As an exercise show how this scatter could have been generated by several supply and demand systems.)

Now let us see how we *can* identify the true underlying supply and demand system if we have additional information on how each curve shifts. First, suppose we know that an increase in income causes a parallel shift to the right of the demand curve. We examine the figures on income and discover that it was the same in 1983 and 1984, but indeed did increase in 1985. This implies that the demand curve remained in the same position in 1983 and 1984, but shifted to the right in 1985.

Next consider supply. What might have caused it to shift? On investigation, we discover that there was a strike in 1984; this reduced the quantity supplied, shifting the supply curve temporarily to the left in 1984. Accordingly, we conclude that the supply curve was in the same position in 1983 and 1985 (when there were no strikes) but temporarily shifted to the left in 1984.

This additional information allows us to eliminate all bogus supply and demand systems from further consideration. There is now only one supply and demand system that could have generated the observations in Figure 20-12, and that is the true one. As an exercise, you should try to discover it yourself before looking at the solution in Figure 20-13.

To sum up: We started out with an apparently incomprehensible scatter of observations that seemed to reveal neither demand nor supply. However, with some additional information on what causes demand and supply to shift, we were able to estimate both in Figure 20-13.

FIGURE 20-10
Special case when demand is easily estimated

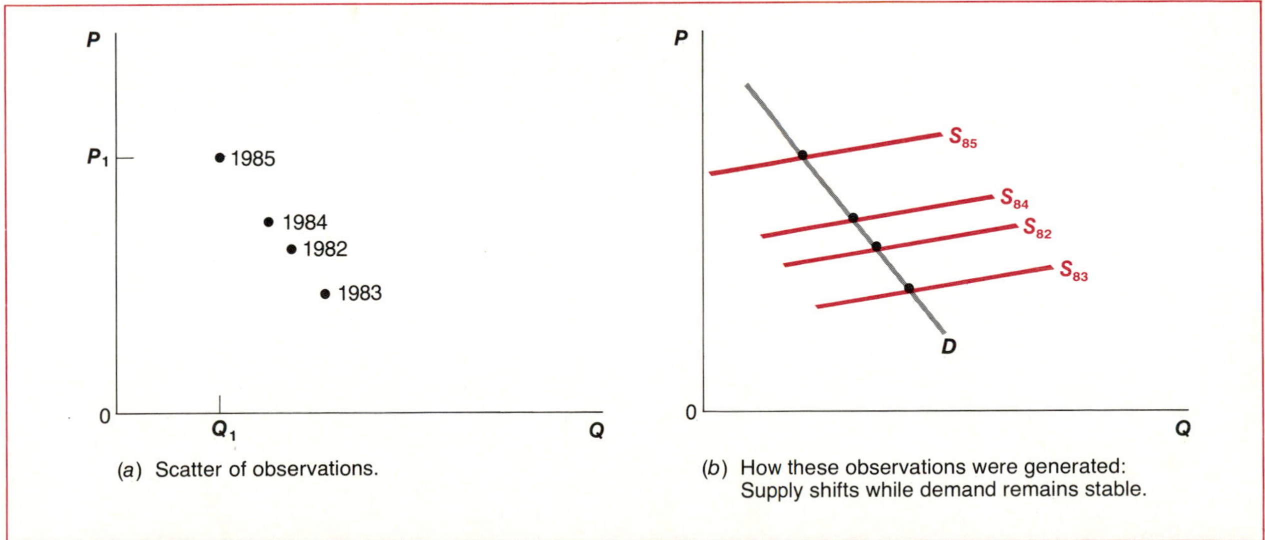

(*a*) Scatter of observations.

(*b*) How these observations were generated: Supply shifts while demand remains stable.

Of course, this simplified illustration can provide only a "feel" for the identification problem. In practice, estimating supply and demand—like estimating most other economic relationships—involves additional complications. For example, each curve may shift in response to several influences rather than just one. Thus, the demand for beef shifts not only with income but also with the price of pork. This sounds like "too much" information. But it isn't: All of it can be used to estimate demand and supply by an econometrician (economic statistician) using the appropriate statistical techniques.

PROBLEM

20-11. Using Figure 20-13, illustrate our claim that shifts in supply identify demand and that shifts in demand identify supply. In particular, show graphically the

FIGURE 20-11
When demand estimation requires a special approach

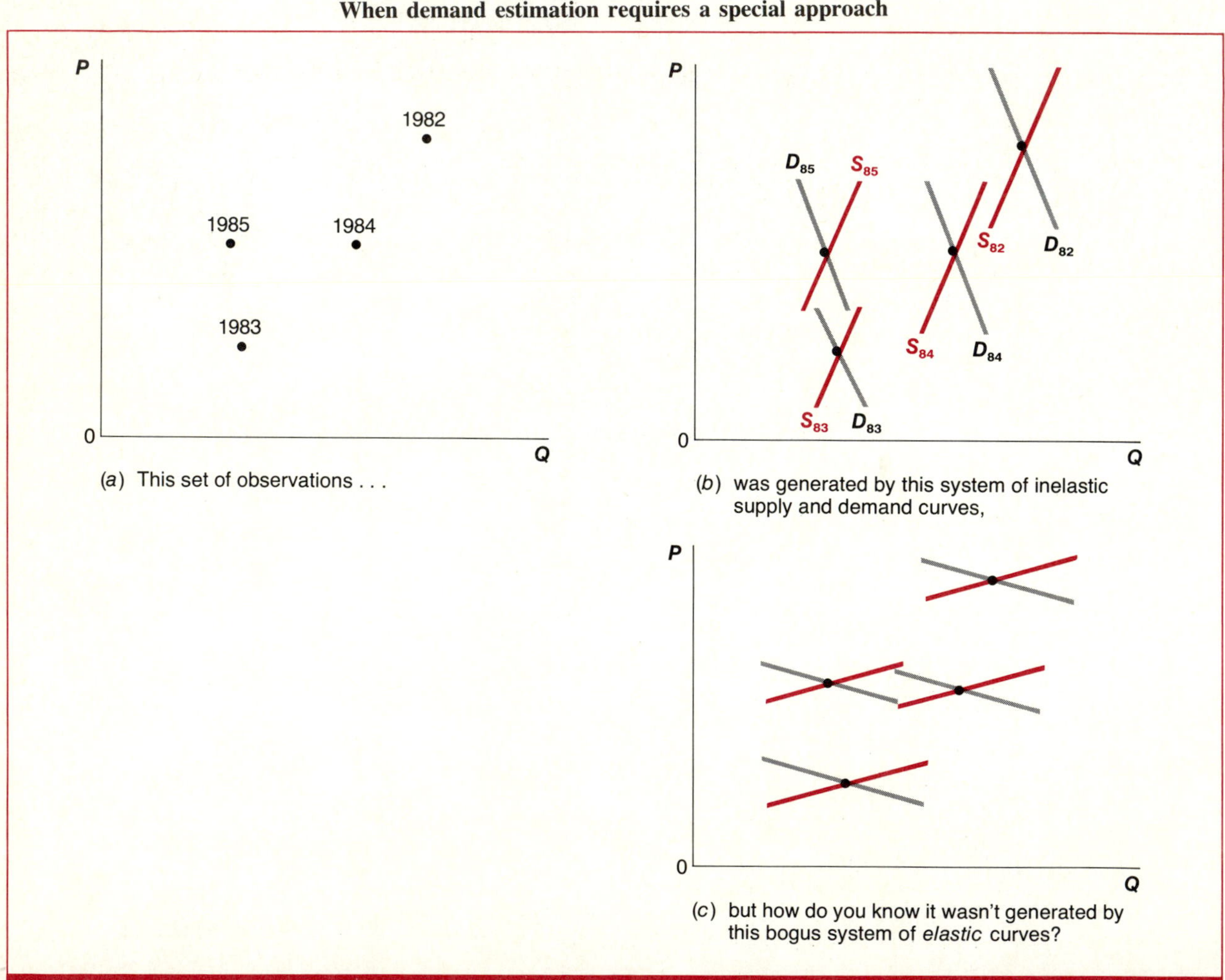

(*a*) This set of observations . . .

(*b*) was generated by this system of inelastic supply and demand curves,

(*c*) but how do you know it wasn't generated by this bogus system of *elastic* curves?

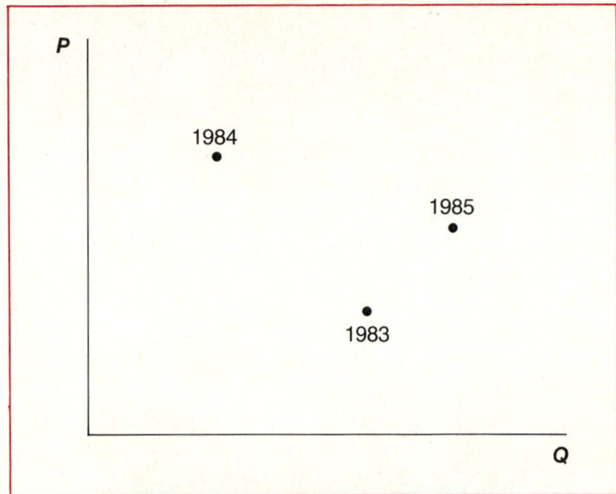

FIGURE 20-12
Can demand be identified?
This scatter seems hopeless. Without further information, it is.

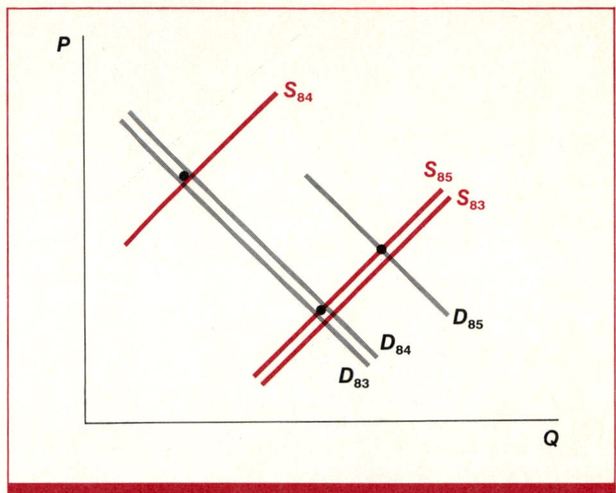

FIGURE 20-13
How demand (and supply) can be identified
With knowledge that there was a parallel shift to the left in supply in 1984 and a parallel shift to the right in demand in 1985, this supply and demand system is the only one that can be fitted to the three observations in Figure 20-12.

scatter we would have observed, and what we would—or would not—be able to identify if (*a*) there had been no income increase in 1985; (*b*) there had been neither an income increase in 1985 nor a strike in 1984.

CHAPTER 21

DEMAND

Producers dance to the consumers' tune.

REPRISE FROM CHAPTER 4

What is the tune that consumers play? Why do they demand certain products but not others? In this chapter we will examine the demand curve in detail in order to clarify what it tells us about consumers' behavior. While we will be developing many important ideas, there will be several that we will emphasize in boldface type as being essential for an understanding of future chapters. For example, we will show graphically how much consumers are hurt when the price of a good rises. To illustrate, we will demonstrate the damage to U.S. consumers from an increase in the price of oranges following a Florida freeze.

In Chapters 4 and 20 we described and used the *market* demand curve. In this chapter, we will go behind this curve to examine its fundamental characteristics. The first step is to see how the market demand curve is related to the *individual* demand curves of the many consumers who buy a product.

MARKET DEMAND AS THE SUM OF INDIVIDUAL DEMANDS

The total market demand for a good or service is found by summing the demands of all individual consumers, as illustrated in Figure 21-1. (In this example, two individuals represent the millions of consumers in the economy.) Bill Jefferson's demand, illustrated in panel *a,* shows how much he is willing and able to buy at various prices. Similarly, Barbara Washington's demand is shown in panel *b,* indicating her quite different willingness to buy the same product. At any given price, say $1, we horizontally add the quantities demanded by each consumer in order to get the corresponding point on the market demand schedule in panel *c*. Observe that individual demand curves are labeled with a small *d,* and the market demand with a capital *D*.

Let us now consider the behavior of an individual consumer in detail.

THE INDIVIDUAL CONSUMER'S DECISION: THE CHOICE BETWEEN GOODS

The consumer chooses between goods: for example, food and clothing. Should the consumer use a given income to buy more clothing and less food, or more food and less clothing? This choice between goods is a key decision, and we will return to it later.

However, it is also useful to view the consumer as choosing, not between food and clothing, but between food and *all* other goods; in other words, choosing between food and money (since money can be used to buy all other goods). This decision between food and money is described by the individual's demand curve: At each price, the demand curve tells us how much food the consumer will choose.

BEHIND THE DEMAND CURVE: SUBSTITUTION AND INCOME EFFECTS

Consider a very simple example: an individual's demand for apples. The demand curve indicates that the consumer will buy more apples when their price falls. There are two reasons for this:

1. Apples become a better buy, compared to other goods. Remember from Chapter 4: When we draw a demand curve for a good, we assume that "other things" remain unchanged—including the prices of all other goods. Thus, a fall in the price of apples means that they become cheaper relative to other items. Consequently, the consumer *switches* from other goods—such as pears and oranges—and buys more apples instead. The increase in the number of apples bought because of such switching is called the ***substitution effect.***

2. The other reason concerns income. When we draw a demand curve, we assume not only that the prices of other goods remain unchanged but also that *money* income is constant. For example, the consumer continues to have an income of, say, $10,000. But when the price of apples falls, money goes further. More can be bought with the $10,000; that is, the consumer's *real* income rises. The consumer is now able to buy more goods, *including* more apples. This is called the ***income effect.***

The substitution effect and the income effect combine to make the consumer willing and able to buy more of a good when its price falls.

For most goods, there is little income effect. For example, items like pepper, apples, or even shoes are such a small part of the consumer's budget that a fall in the price of any of these would have little or no discernible effect on anyone's real income. Thus, for most goods, we do not have to pay much attention to the income effect. However, there are a few items—such as cars, college tuition, and houses—that are such an important part of people's budgets that a reduction in their price would significantly increase the real income of consumers. Furthermore, if we deal with a broad class of goods—for example, all food rather than just a single item like apples—this becomes a large part of our budget and the income effect becomes more important. (At the same time, the substitution effect becomes less important: There is no good substitute for food as a whole.)

In the balance of this chapter we will examine specific, relatively small items such as apples, where the income effect is not very important, and defer to the appendix the analysis of broad classes of goods—such as food and clothing, where the income effect is more important.

FIGURE 21-1
How individual demands combine to make up market demand
To find total quantity demanded at each price—for example, $1—horizontally add the quantities demanded by all individual consumers.

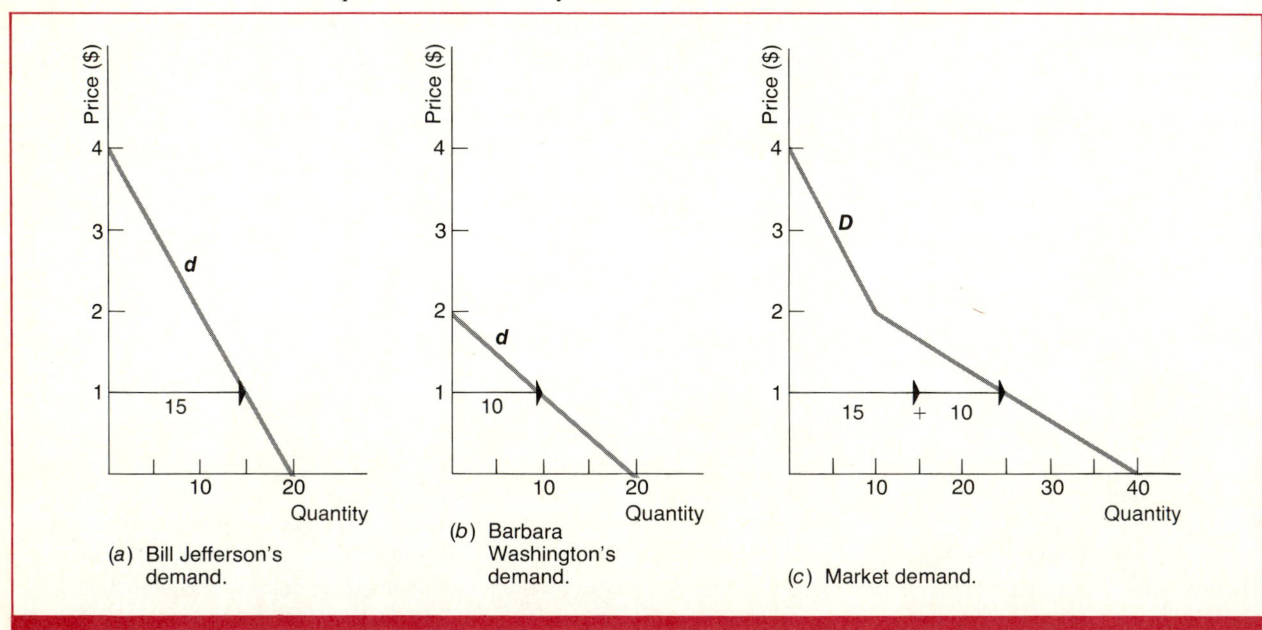

HOW THE DEMAND CURVE REFLECTS MARGINAL BENEFIT

Thus far, we have viewed the demand curve in the way it is shown in panel *a* of Figure 21-2. We considered the various possible prices of apples. For each of these prices, a *horizontal* arrow indicates how much the consumer will buy.

In panel *b* we reproduce *exactly the same demand curve* with exactly the same points on it. However, we now take a slightly different point of view. In this case, we begin by considering the various possible quantities that may be purchased. For each of these quantities, a *vertical* arrow indicates the maximum price the consumer is willing to pay. For example, the arrow on the left indicates that the consumer is willing to pay $7 for the fourth box of apples. If the price is above $7, the consumer won't buy that fourth box.

The reason it is important to examine demand from this slightly different viewpoint is that the consumer's willingness to pay in panel *b* reflects how much benefit or satisfaction he or she gets from this good. For example, we've seen that a consumer who already has three units will pay a maximum of $7 for a fourth unit. In other words, $7 is the consumer's own evaluation of the additional benefit—that is, the ***marginal benefit***—derived from that fourth unit. (The word ''marginal'' is frequently used in economics to mean *additional* or *extra*.) Similarly, the marginal benefit from the fifth unit is $6.

The *marginal benefit* (MB) to a consumer is the additional benefit from consuming one more unit. It is measured by how much the consumer is willing to pay for that unit (the height of the individual's demand curve).

In later chapters, we will be drawing on this basic idea, expressed in slightly different form:

> *Essential idea for future chapters:* **When you see a demand curve, you should visualize the marginal benefit arrows enclosed beneath it.**

Notice how the individual's marginal benefit de-

FIGURE 21-2
Two views of a demand curve

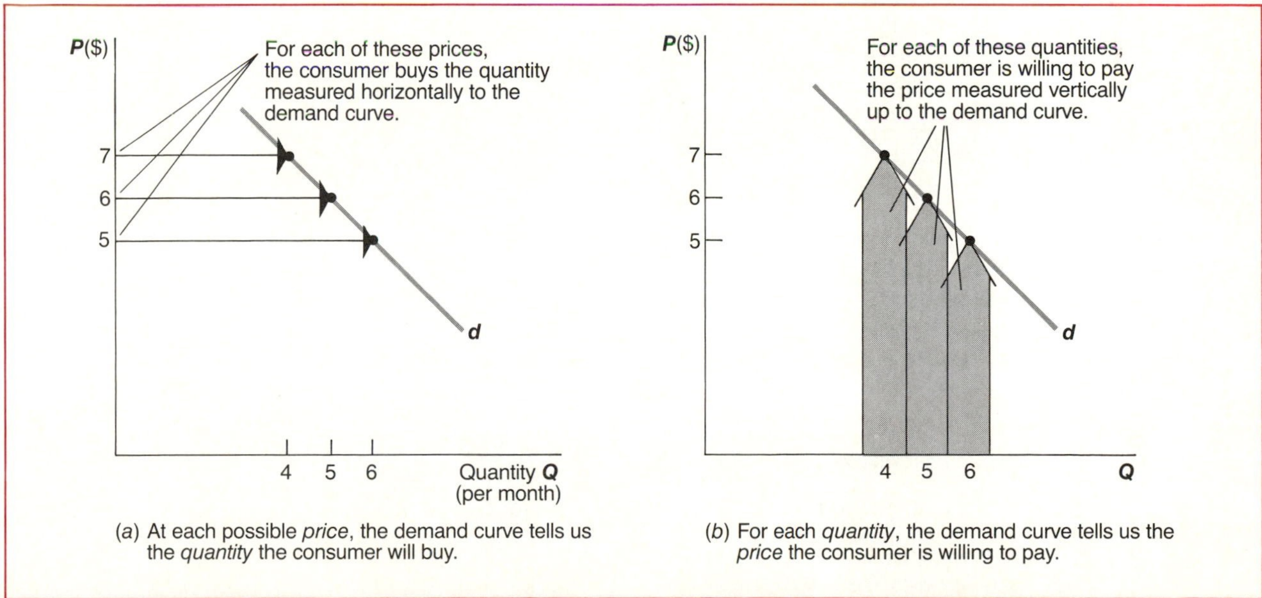
P($)
For each of these prices, the consumer buys the quantity measured horizontally to the demand curve.
7
6
5
d
4 5 6
Quantity Q (per month)
P($)
For each of these quantities, the consumer is willing to pay the price measured vertically up to the demand curve.
7
6
5
d
4 5 6
Q

(*a*) At each possible *price*, the demand curve tells us the *quantity* the consumer will buy.

(*b*) For each *quantity*, the demand curve tells us the *price* the consumer is willing to pay.

clines as more and more is acquired. This makes sense. An individual might get a lot of benefit from the first box of apples. But with more and more apples, the consumer's appetite for apples is satisfied; that is, the consumer gets less satisfaction—or *utility*—from each additional box. Since eventually this must be true for any good, it is called the ***law of diminishing marginal utility,*** or the ***law of diminishing marginal benefit.***

Be careful with this "law." Although marginal utility must *ultimately* fall, it may rise at first. For example, if the apples are an exotic variety, for which a taste is acquired only slowly, the consumer may get more pleasure out of a second box than the first. But eventually, as more and more apples are acquired, the individual's desire for these apples must decline.[1]

CONSUMER EQUILIBRIUM: HOW MUCH OF A GOOD TO BUY?

In Figure 21-3, the consumer's demand schedule is reproduced from the previous diagram, with more detail added. If the market price is $6 as shown, the demand curve tells us the individual will decide to buy five units. Another way of describing this decision is to note that the first unit will obviously be purchased, since the consumer values it at $10 (the first marginal benefit arrow), while its price is only $6. Since the second, third, and fourth units are also valued above their price of $6, the consumer will also buy them. The fifth will be the last one purchased because the $6 benefit it provides is just equal to its $6 price. The consumer will then be picking the best point and will be in equilibrium.

> ***Essential idea for future chapters:*** **A consumer does best—that is, reaches equilibrium—by buying additional units of a good until the marginal benefit it provides falls to the level of its price, that is, until**
>
> $$\mathbf{MB} = P \qquad (21\text{-}1)$$

It is easy to confirm that the consumer should not go beyond this point to purchase more. For example, it would be a mistake to purchase the sixth unit because the $6 price of that unit exceeds the $5 benefit from it.

In Box 21-1, equilibrium for a consumer is examined using an approach that emphasizes how the consumer chooses *between* goods.

WHY MARGINAL AND TOTAL BENEFIT MUST BE CLEARLY DISTINGUISHED: ADAM SMITH'S PARADOX OF VALUE

We've seen the importance of *marginal benefit* MB to the consumer making a decision on how much to pur-

FIGURE 21-3

Diminishing marginal benefit and consumer equilibrium
Willingness to pay—as shown by each arrow under the demand curve—reflects the marginal benefit the consumer receives from this good. Eventually, as more is bought, this marginal benefit must decline.

The consumer continues to buy more of this good as long as the marginal benefit from it exceeds the price. Equilibrium occurs at *E*, where marginal benefit equals price.

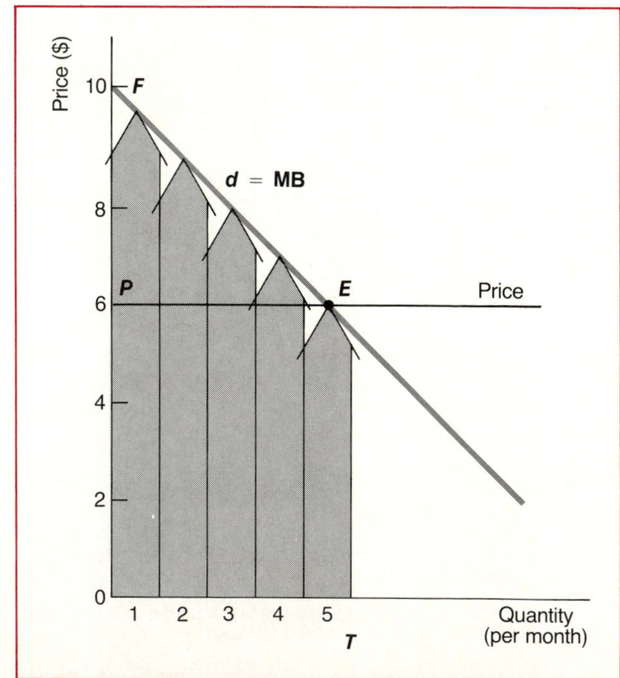

*[1]Strictly, we should not use dollars as the yardstick to measure "utility" or benefit. The reason is that the utility obtainable from a dollar can change. Because of this logical problem, most advanced theoretical work uses a different approach, explained in the appendix.

BOX 21-1

EQUILIBRIUM FOR THE CONSUMER: HOW TO CHOOSE BETWEEN GOODS

Figure 21-3 shows how much of a single good a consumer buys. An important alternative approach addresses the question at the beginning of the chapter: How does a consumer choose *between* goods? How should a consumer's food budget be divided between oranges and cherries? The answer is: The quantities of the two goods should each be adjusted (either increased or decreased) until a dollar's worth of oranges yields the same marginal utility as a dollar's worth of cherries. To see why, suppose that the consumer is initially out of equilibrium. Specifically, the marginal utility of $1 of cherries is greater than $1 of oranges. In this case, income will provide more satisfaction or utility if the consumer buys $1 more of cherries and $1 less of oranges. The utility received from the additional cherries will exceed the utility lost on the oranges. The total satisfaction obtained from the consumer's income will continue to increase if purchases are switched in this way until the marginal utilities are equalized. And they will indeed equalize because the law of diminishing marginal utility tells us that eventually the marginal utility of cherries will fall as more are bought, while the marginal utility of oranges will rise as fewer are bought.

We can state this theorem in general:

A consumer will be in equilibrium if purchases of each good are adjusted to the point where *the marginal utility from the last dollar of expenditure on one good is the same as the marginal utility from the last dollar spent on each of the other goods.* In this way, the individual maximizes the total utility from a given income.

If you wish, you may pursue this basic idea further. This conclusion may be restated: Consumer equilibrium requires that

$$\frac{\text{Marginal utility from a basket of cherries}}{\text{Price of cherries}} = \frac{\text{marginal utility from a basket of oranges}}{\text{price of oranges}} \qquad (21\text{-}2)$$

In symbols:

$$\frac{MU_{\text{cherries}}}{P_{\text{cherries}}} = \frac{MU_{\text{oranges}}}{P_{\text{oranges}}} \qquad (21\text{-}3)$$

To illustrate, suppose a basket of cherries is twice as expensive as a basket of oranges; for example, suppose P_{cherries} is $8 while P_{oranges} is $4. Then equation 21-3 tells us that in equilibrium the consumer will get twice as much marginal utility from the last basket of cherries as from the last basket of oranges. Suppose this is indeed the case: The last basket of cherries provides 24 units of utility, and the last basket of oranges provides 12 units. Then we confirm that equilibrium exists because equation 21-3 checks out:

$$\frac{24 \text{ units of utility}}{\$8} = \frac{12 \text{ units of utility}}{\$4}$$

Note from the left side of this equation that the consumer is spending $8 on the last basket of cherries to get 24 units of satisfaction. In other words, each dollar spent on the last basket of cherries yields a marginal utility of $24/8 = 3$ units. On the right side, each dollar spent on the last basket of oranges provides the same utility; specifically, $12/4 = 3$ units. Thus, we confirm that equation 21-3 is just a recasting of the basic principle in boldface. In equilibrium, the consumer gets the same amount of utility—in this example, three units—from the last dollar spent on cherries as from the last dollar spent on oranges.

Alternatively, we can rearrange equation 21-3 to get another statement of the consumer's equilibrium:

$$\frac{MU_{\text{cherries}}}{MU_{\text{oranges}}} = \frac{P_{\text{cherries}}}{P_{\text{oranges}}} \qquad (21\text{-}4)$$

In our example:

$$\frac{24 \text{ units of utility}}{12 \text{ units of utility}} = \frac{\$8}{\$4}$$

This is just a restatement of the same simple idea. In equilibrium, the consumer must get twice as much marginal utility from the last basket of cherries (on the left side of this equation) because cherries are twice as expensive (on the right side). The appendix confirms in a more formal way that equation 21-4 does indeed describe consumer equilibrium.

chase. Now we consider the *total benefit* the consumer gets from the *entire* purchase. For example, the total benefit for the consumer who purchases five units in Figure 21-3 is the shaded area *FETO*. The first arrow shows the benefit from the first unit; the second arrow shows the benefit from the second unit; and so on, giving a sum equal to the shaded area.

The *total benefit* a consumer receives from a good is the sum of the marginal benefits it provides—that is, the shaded area under the demand curve and to the left of the quantity purchased.

This distinction between marginal and total benefit is essential to solve a puzzle posed by Adam Smith in the *Wealth of Nations*. One of the most valuable commodities in the world is water; we simply cannot do without it. If necessary, we would be prepared to sell everything we own to acquire it. Yet it sells at a very low price. In contrast, we could easily do without diamonds or champagne; yet they sell for very high prices. Is the world upside down?

To show why the answer to this question is no, we bring together the supply and demand curves for water and champagne in Figure 21-4. In the case of water in panel *a*, the price P_W is very low because water is so plentiful; a huge quantity can be supplied at a very low price. We consume a huge quantity of it, using it even in ways in which it has very little value, such as washing the car or watering the lawn. Thus its low price reflects the low *marginal* benefit it provides, shown by arrow Q_1E.

On the other hand, in panel *b,* we see that the demand for champagne is far less than the demand for water. But champagne sells at a high price because it is very scarce and costly to produce; that is, it can be supplied only at a relatively high price. Consequently, only the most enthusiastic buyers consume it, and on the last unit they consume they enjoy a marginal benefit *GE*—shown by the higher arrow—equal to the price P_C. We conclude that the higher price of champagne is telling us that, *at the margin*—where we look at only the last unit consumed—*champagne has higher value than water*.

However, this is only part of the story. The *total* benefit from water includes not only the value of the last glass we use, but of *every* glass, and the ones that keep us from dying of thirst are very valuable indeed. In fact, the marginal benefit of one of those first glasses of water, say at Q_2, is so high that we don't have enough room at the top of the diagram to show it. In other words, the total benefit from water—the shaded area in panel *a*—is so large that there isn't room to show it in full. Compare this to the relatively small total benefit from champagne—the shaded area in panel *b*. Thus we conclude that, *overall,* water is much more valuable to us than champagne, even though its price is lower; that is, even though its value *at the margin* is less. The paradox is resolved.

Throughout our study of microeconomics we'll be looking at what happens when people decide to consume or produce one more unit; that is, we will be focusing on what's happening "at the margin." Looking at the margin is the best way to evaluate *how well markets are working*. However, this champagne/water example should remind us that the units *before* we get to the margin may be very important.

Finally, observe that the total shaded area of benefit people get from champagne in panel *b* exceeds the rectangle OP_CEG that they pay for it. (This rectangle to the southwest of *E* is the quantity *OG* that consumers buy times the price OP_C that they pay per bottle.) The excess of consumer benefit over cost—that is, the triangular area P_CAE—is sometimes referred to as ***consumer surplus.***[2] As an exercise, you should return to Figure 21-3 and explain the consumer surplus that the individual in that diagram is receiving.

HOW IS THE CONSUMER AFFECTED BY A CHANGE IN PRICE?

In Figure 21-5, we reproduce the consumer's demand for apples from Figure 21-3, along with the equilibrium at *E* if the price is $6. Now suppose the price of apples falls to

*[2]Robert Willig of Princeton University discusses this traditionally controversial concept in "Consumer's Surplus Without Apology," *American Economic Review,* September 1976, pp. 589–597. He points out that consumer surplus is an important concept in evaluating changes in public policy. However, estimating its size is more complicated than our simple analysis suggests.

$2 with the new equilibrium at E_2. How much does the consumer gain because the price is lower?

To answer this question, first note that the consumer saves $4 on each of the first five units because the price is $2 rather than $6. This gain is shown by the first five shaded segments in Figure 21-5—that is, by the rectangle $PERP_2$. However, there is also a second source of gain because, in response to the lower price, the consumer increases purchases from five to nine units; and the consumer enjoys a gain on these additional units as well. For example, the sixth unit yields a gain of $3. This is the $5 the consumer would have been *willing* to pay for this unit—as given by the height of the demand curve—less the $2 *actually* paid.

There are similar shaded gains on other new units purchased. Thus the gain from the additional purchases is shown as the triangle EE_2R. Taking both these sources of gain into account, we conclude that a decrease in price from P to P_2 yields a consumer gain equal to the entire shaded area.

FIGURE 21-4

How can the price of a necessity like water be so low while the price of an unnecessary luxury like diamonds or champagne is so high?

In panel *a*, *D* and *S* result in equilibrium at *E*, with price at P_W and the low marginal benefit of water shown by the arrow Q_1E. On the other hand, in panel *b* the high cost of supplying champagne means that its price and marginal benefit are at the much higher level P_C. Thus, if we consider *only the last unit consumed*, champagne has a higher value. However, if we consider *all units consumed*, this conclusion is reversed. The total benefit from water—the shaded area in panel *a*—greatly exceeds the total benefit from champagne, the shaded area in panel *b*.

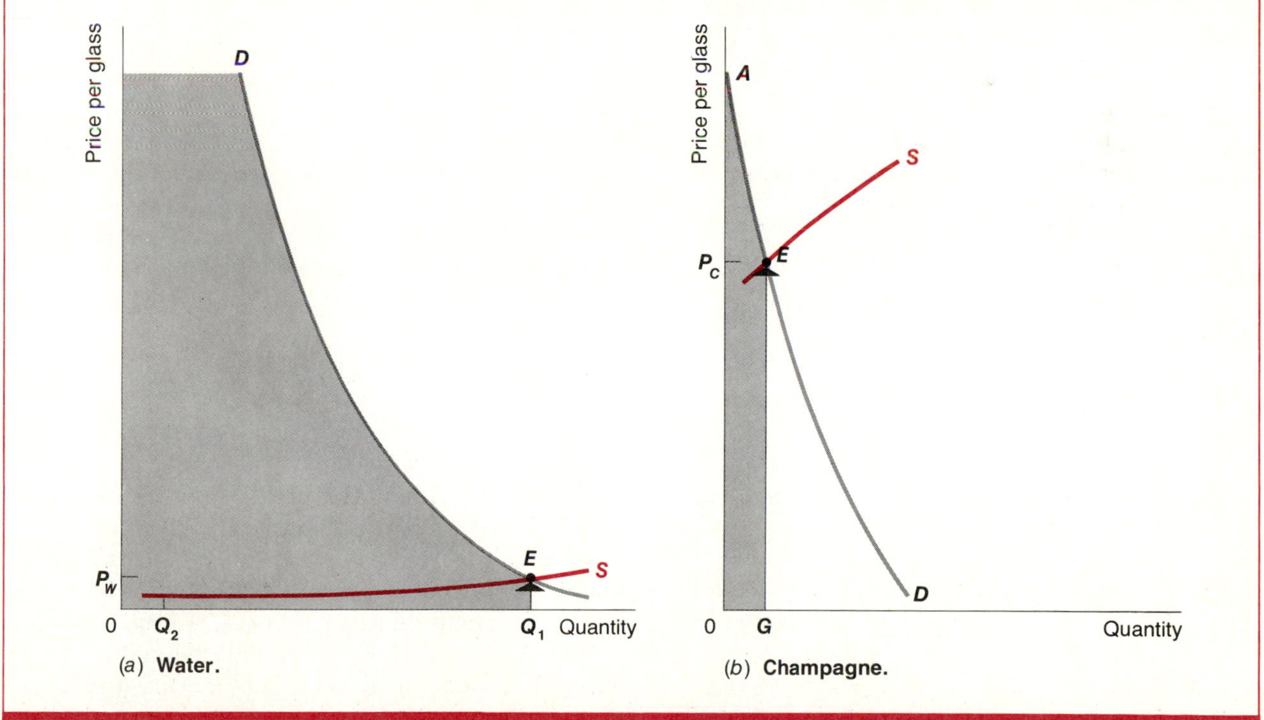

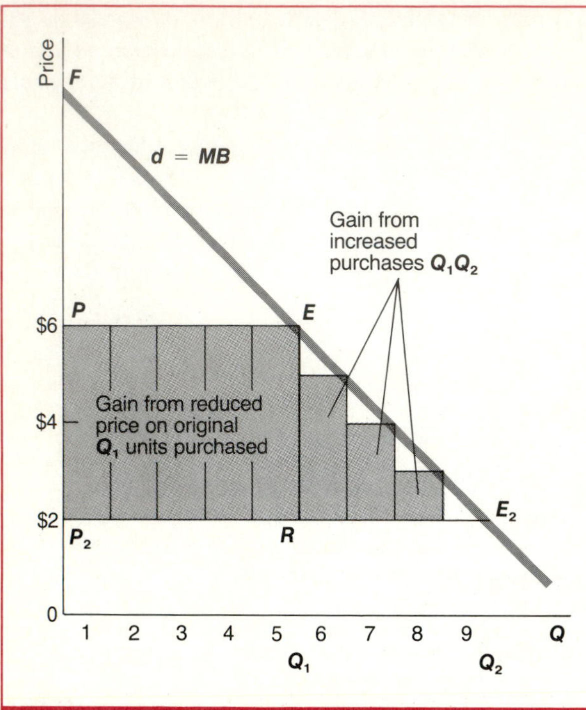

FIGURE 21-5

If market price falls from \$6 to \$2, the consumer gain is the shaded area

At the initial \$6 price, the consumer purchases 5 units at E. When price falls by \$4, the consumer gains by being able to obtain these 5 units more cheaply. The gain on these 5 units is \$4 × 5 = \$20, shown as the shaded rectangle P_2PER.

However, the consumer also obtains a second gain. Because of the price reduction, more units are purchased, as shown by the movement from E to E_2. On these additional units, there is a gain of shaded triangle REE_2. To illustrate, consider one of these additional units, the sixth. The \$5 the buyer would be willing to pay for this unit is shown by the height of the demand curve. But since this unit costs only \$2, the buyer enjoys a shaded gain of \$3. All similar shaded areas in triangle EE_2R represent gains on the *new* purchases.

When both of these source of gain are considered, the consumer's benefit from the price reduction is the entire shaded area.

Essential idea for future chapters: **If the market price falls, the consumer gain is shown by the horizontal area between the old and new price and to the left of the demand curve. (If market price increases from P_2 to P, the consumer is worse off by this amount.)**

This area of gain may also be looked on as the *increase* in consumer surplus. Initially, consumer surplus is the triangular area PFE. With the lower price, it becomes the larger triangle P_2FE_2. The difference in these two is the shaded area. This increase in consumer surplus is the consumer gain from the price reduction.

THE FLORIDA FREEZE: APPLYING THE ANALYSIS OF CHAPTERS 20 AND 21

As noted in the previous chapter, cold waves in 1977, 1981, 1983, and 1985 froze part of the Florida citrus crop. The effects of a freeze are illustrated in Figure 21-6. (To simplify this illustration, picking, shipping, and other costs of getting the oranges to market are ignored.) The harvest coming onto the market is reduced from the normal supply S to S_2. This in turn means that prices are higher, with equilibrium at E_2 rather than E_1. Several groups of Americans are affected, as follows:

- *Producers benefit*. Because demand for citrus fruit is inelastic, producers' revenue increases. As a group, they gain more from the higher price than they lose from the reduced harvest. Of course, those who lose their entire crop are worse off, but their loss is less than the gain of the other producers who can sell their crop at a higher price.
- *Consumers lose*. Because the price rises, consumers lose areas 1 + 2.

With producers benefiting and consumers losing, it is not immediately obvious how the nation as a whole is affected, on balance. However, a moment's reflection leads us to the following conclusion:

- *On balance, the nation loses*. When oranges freeze, we have fewer to eat; as a nation, we are worse off.

The various effects of a crop loss may be summarized. Because demand is inelastic, producers as a group gain; their total revenues increase. (If demand were elas-

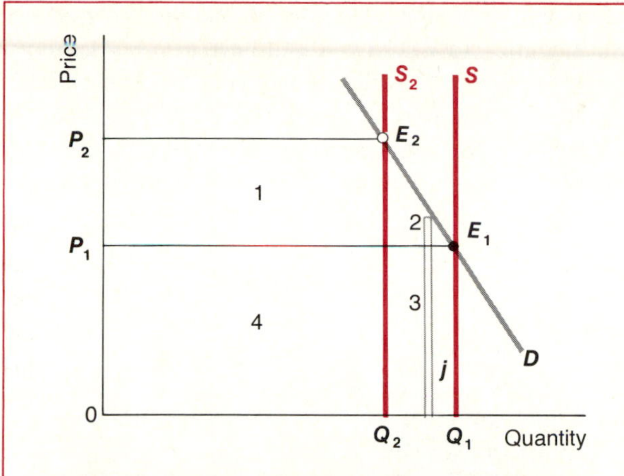

FIGURE 21-6

How Florida citrus freeze benefits producers but damages consumers and the nation as a whole

The normal crop of S would have resulted in equilibrium E_1 with price P_1. But because of a freeze, the supply coming to the market is reduced to S_2. Consequently, equilibrium is at E_2 with price P_2.

Without the freeze, producers' total revenue would have been the rectangle 4 + 3 to the southwest of E_1, that is, the number of units sold Q_1 times the price of each P_1. However, with the freeze shifting equilibrium to E_2, revenue is area 1 + 4 instead. Since area 4 is common to both, producers gain area 1 from the freeze but lose area 3. Consumers lose area 1 + 2 as a result of the increased price. For the nation overall, we must consider the effect on both groups:

Consumers	lose 1	lose 2	
Producers	gain 1		lose 3
Sum indicates nation will		lose 2	lose 3

This overall loss to the nation of area 2 + 3 is easily confirmed. Consider j, one of the cases of fruit that freezes. The marginal benefit it would have provided is the height of the thin bar at j. If we sum all the similar bars throughout the range of lost output between Q_2 and Q_1, the result is area 2 + 3, the total damage to the nation as a whole because those oranges froze.

Warning: Area 1 is a loss to consumers and a gain to producers. In cancelling it out in the tabled calculations above, we assume that area 1 is valued similarly by the consumers losing it and the producers receiving it—or at least similarly enough not to upset our conclusions. Although this is a reasonable enough assumption, it represents a complication that we will return to in Chapter 25.

tic, total revenues would fall, and producers as a group would be worse off.) However, regardless of demand elasticity, consumers and the nation overall lose.[3]

Now let us examine more carefully our conclusion that producers benefit from a freeze. If you are an individual producer, it will not be in your interest to let your crop freeze. Nothing you can do as an individual affects price. Whatever the price may be, the more you have to sell, the better. However, a freeze benefits producers as a group, because the resulting scarcity *does* affect price. This raises the question: If producers cannot get Mother Nature to restrict their supply, is it not in their interest to work together to do it themselves? The answer is yes. However, in practice they may have difficulty in organizing to restrict supply. In turn, this may lead them to look instead to the government to introduce and enforce collective supply restrictions—for example, a government restriction on the number of acres that a farmer may plant. Such a limitation raises price and may also raise farm income, but what it does to consumers and the nation as a whole is quite another matter.

EXTENSIONS OF DEMAND THEORY: TRANSACTIONS AND TIME COSTS

Time is Money.
Ben Franklin

In deciding to buy another unit of a product, the consumer compares the benefit the unit provides with its cost. However, cost is a broad term, covering more than just the purchase price. For example, someone consider-

[3]If a good is produced for export, it is possible for the nation as a whole to gain from a damaged crop. For example, if damage to a coffee crop in Brazil reduces supplies, Brazil as a nation may gain. The reason is that prices soar, to the benefit of Brazilian producers. True, consumers lose, but they are mostly in foreign countries, not Brazil. In such cases, it may be in the national interest to restrict supply, as Brazil did during the 1930s by dumping coffee into the ocean.

Such supply restrictions should, however, be approached cautiously, even if a narrow national viewpoint is taken. In the long run, the elasticity of demand may be much higher than in the short run. In other words, if coffee prices are kept high for a long period, people may switch to tea and decide that they prefer it. Furthermore, competing producers in other countries may be encouraged to increase production in response to higher prices.

ing the purchase of a car will be concerned with not only its price but also the expected cost of gasoline, insurance, service, and repairs. Informed buyers also take account of ***transactions costs.***

Transactions Costs

To illustrate such costs, suppose that, after careful consideration of the profit prospects of International Business Machines, you buy 100 shares of IBM stock from a "discount" broker. In addition to the cost of the stock itself, you incur two transactions costs:

1. *The commission charged by the broker.* Discount brokers provide only one service: buying or selling stocks. For this, they charge a fee or commission. They do not give advice or provide information on companies. As a consequence, you also face a second cost.
2. *Search cost,* also called *information cost*. This is the cost in collecting the information necessary to make a sensible decision. This cost includes not only the time you spend in your study of IBM, but also any out-of-pocket expenses you may incur. For example, you may subscribe to publications which provide information on corporations. The cost of gathering information may be larger than the commission you pay the broker.

You may, of course, play your cards differently the next time by going to a traditional broker. You will pay more, but you will get more in return. The broker will not only buy the stock for you, but also provide you with information on corporations and suggestions on what stocks to buy or sell.

***Search cost,* or *information cost,* is the time and money spent in collecting the information necessary to make a decision to buy or sell stocks or any other item.**

The Business of Providing Information

It's not just traditional stockbrokers who are in the information business. As another example, real estate agents provide information to both buyers and sellers. They give buyers information about houses that are available. They provide sellers with advice on pricing of a home and information on possible buyers.

If you are selling a house, should you go to a real estate agent—to whom you will have to pay a commission if the house is sold—or should you place an ad in the paper and try to sell the house on your own? You will usually do better by going to an agent; agents are in the business of making contact with potential buyers. Specialization in marketing may be just as important as specialization in other skills, such as law or medicine.

Nevertheless, you should beware. Whenever you deal with people who provide information or advice, it's important to ask: Is the information or advice really in *your* interest, or are the agents being influenced—consciously or subconsciously—by quite different interests of their own? For example, is your real estate agent suggesting that you accept a low price on you home in order to make the sale and earn a commission? Does your stockbroker have the same motive in encouraging you to buy or sell stocks?

How Do Search Costs Influence Market Price?

The more information auto buyers have, and the more willing they are to bear search costs by seeking out alternative sellers, the less car dealers will be able to overcharge; that is, the less dealers will be able to raise their prices above the level of their competitors. Thus search tends to reduce the average price the public pays and also the variation in prices. Moreover, the percentage variation in price will be less for expensive items like cars—where it pays the consumer to search hard for the best buy—than for small-ticket items where it's not worth the trouble. A grocer may be able to raise the price of salt by 10% without anyone noticing, but a car dealer who tries to charge 10% more than the competition will soon be out of business.

Search efforts undertaken by the public provide several benefits. Individuals who search generally purchase products which better satisfy their requirements. Moreover, the benefits go beyond the individual. As the public searches and acquires more information, it becomes less likely that a poor product will survive in the marketplace. In addition, as we've already seen, prices tend to be lower and have less spread. If all these things happen, it becomes less necessary for a single buyer to incur large search costs. There will be less risk of being overcharged or ending up with a poor product. Thus, paradoxically, the more searching the public does, the less any individual buyer needs to search.

Time represents a major part of search costs—for example, the time a consumer spends shopping around at various car dealers. But time can be expensive, not only in searching for products, but also in consuming them after they have been purchased.

Time Costs in Consumption

Examples abound. Car or TV buyers seek out a reliable product because, once they have made their purchase, they don't want to waste a lot of time getting it repaired. Time may be a critical consideration in deciding not only on goods but also on services. For example, a day-long bus trip from Buffalo to Boston may cost less than an airline ticket, but most people don't take the bus because it takes more time. In particular, people with high incomes incur high time costs in traveling by bus; the time they waste is very valuable. Consequently the rich fly.

Time cost helps to explain consumption patterns, not only within the United States but also among countries. In North America we buy costly home appliances because they save valuable time. In poorer countries, the laundry is more likely to be done by hand; the time required is of little consequence where incomes are low and time is therefore less valuable.

Throughout the balance of this book, we refer simply to price; but remember that "price" should be interpreted broadly to include transactions and time costs.

KEY POINTS

1. Marginal benefit is the satisfaction derived from consuming one more unit of a good or service. It is measured by the height of the demand curve, which shows how much the consumer is willing to pay for an additional unit.
2. When you see a demand curve, you should visualize the vertical marginal benefit bars beneath it.
3. To reach equilibrium, a consumer increases the purchase of a product until its marginal benefit falls to the level of its price.
4. When price falls, consumers gain by the horizontal area to the left of the demand curve and between the old and the new price.
5. When a crop is damaged (by spoilage, frost, or whatever), producers may be better or worse off, depending on whether demand is elastic or not. But consumers and the nation as a whole lose.
6. Price should be interpreted broadly, to include transactions and time costs.

KEY CONCEPTS

individual demand
market demand
choice among goods
substitution effect
income effect
marginal benefit (MB)
law of diminishing marginal utility
relationship of demand to marginal benefit
consumer equilibrium, where marginal benefit equals price
consumer surplus
gain to consumers from a fall in price
effect of lost output on consumers, producers, and the nation as a whole
transactions cost
time cost
search cost (information cost)

PROBLEMS

21-1. Suppose each of three individuals has unit elasticity of demand for a particular good. Without drawing any diagrams, can you guess what the elasticity of the total market demand for this good will be?

Now draw diagrams showing each of the individual demands, and how the market demand should be constructed. How does the slope of market demand compare with the slope of the individual demands? Is market demand therefore more elastic? Explain.

21-2. Using your own example, explain why marginal benefit must eventually fall.

***21-3.** If the price of oranges rises and of cherries remains constant, show in either equation 21-2 or 21-3 why the consumer is no longer in equilibrium. What action does the consumer take to get to a new equilibrium?

21-4. Suppose that a substantial part of a lettuce crop spoils en route to market because of the producers' negligence. Will these producers suffer a loss as a consequence? Explain. How will consumers and the nation as a whole be affected? Would your conclusion be changed if the producers were insured?

21-5. (*a*) Suppose that, without even looking at the new products available, a buyer has decided to purchase a new camera rather than a new TV. Show how this decision might be reversed if, for the first time, the buyer realizes that these two alternative purchases involve different search costs.

(*b*) Repeat question (*a*), replacing search costs with time costs in consumption.

21-6. What do you estimate the time cost of your education to be?

21-7. Consider two individuals—one who is retired and one who is not. Both are wealthy and therefore equally able to purchase the world's most reliable and most expensive car. Which one is more likely to do so? Why?

APPENDIX

THE THEORY OF CONSUMER CHOICE:

INDIFFERENCE CURVES

In this appendix, we develop an important principle introduced in Chapter 2 and emphasized in Box 21-1: Economic behavior involves a *choice between alternatives*. To illustrate, consider an individual consuming unit—a single individual or household. Suppose for simplicity that the household is consuming only two goods, food and clothing. To analyze the decision it faces, we introduce the concept of an ***indifference curve*** in Figure 21-7 and Table 21-1.

To illustrate this concept, suppose that the household begins at a point chosen at random in Figure 21-7; say, point *A*, where it is consuming three units of clothing and two units of food. Then, to draw the indifference curve through *A*, we ask the following question: What other combinations of clothing and food would leave the household equally well off?

The household may inform us that it would be equally satisfied at point *B*, with two units of clothing and three units of food. In other words, if the household starting at *A* were asked if it would give up one unit of clothing in return for one more unit of food, it would respond that it doesn't care whether such a change takes place or not: The household is indifferent between points *A* and *B*.

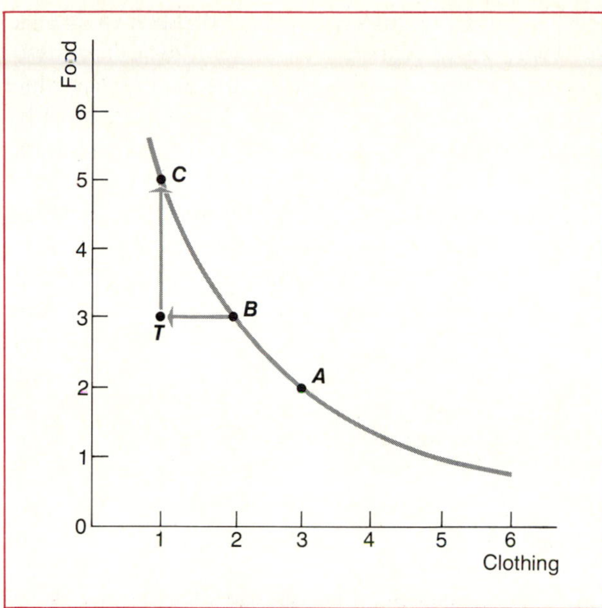

FIGURE 21-7
An indifference curve
An indifference curve joins all points where the household has the same level of total utility or satisfaction.

On an *indifference curve,* each point represents the same level of satisfaction or utility. A household is indifferent among the various points on its indifference curve.

Now let us continue the experiment, asking the household under what conditions it would be willing to give up one more unit of clothing. In moving upward and to the left from point *B*, the household recognizes that it is getting short of clothing and already has a lot of food. It states that it is willing to give up another unit of its very scarce clothing only in return for a large amount (two units) of food. Consequently point *C*, representing one unit of clothing and five of food, is on the same indifference curve as *A* and *B*. Because the household is increasingly reluctant to give up clothing as it has less and less, the indifference curve has the bowed shape shown.[4]

THE MARGINAL RATE OF SUBSTITUTION: THE SLOPE OF THE INDIFFERENCE CURVE

In moving from *B* to *C*, notice that the slope of the indifference curve is 2.[5] This geometric concept has an important economic meaning. It is the amount of food ($TC = 2$) that is required to compensate for the loss of 1 unit of clothing ($BT = 1$); that is, it is the ***marginal rate of substitution of food for clothing.***

[4]Although indifference curves usually have a changing slope, this need not always be the case. For example, a two-car family might be indifferent among the choices of (*A*) two Chevys, no Ford; (*B*) one Chevy, one Ford; or (*C*) no Chevys, two Fords. Then, with Chevs on one axis and Fords on the other, the indifference curve joining points *A*, *B*, and *C* would be a straight line. The reason is that this particular family considers the two cars to be *perfect substitutes* for each other.

[5]Actually the slope of a line between *B* and *C* is −2. (The vertical change is +2, while the horizontal change is −1.) For simplicity, we ignore the negative signs that apply to all slopes in this appendix.

TABLE 21-1
Combinations among Which the Household Is Indifferent

Combination	Clothing	Food	Amount of additional food required to induce household to give up 1 unit of clothing (the marginal rate of substitution of food for clothing)
A	3	2	
			1
B	2	3	
			2
C	1	5	

***The marginal rate of substitution* (MRS) of food for clothing is the amount of food required to compensate for the loss of one unit of clothing, while leaving the consuming unit equally well off. Geometrically, it is the slope of the indifference curve.**

THE INDIFFERENCE MAP

The indifference curve in Figure 21-7 is reproduced as u_1 in Figure 21-8. Recall that our starting point, *A,* was a point chosen at random. We might equally well have started at point *F* or *G;* there is an indifference curve that passes through each of these points as well. In other words, there is a whole family of indifference curves which form the ***indifference map*** in Figure 21-8.

While all points on a single indifference curve represent the same level of satisfaction, points on another indifference curve represent a different level of satisfaction. Observe that, at point *G,* the family has more clothing and more food than at *F*. Thus, the family prefers *G* to *F*. Because other points on u_3—such as *H*—are equivalent to *G,* they must also be preferred to *F* and to every other point on u_2. Therefore, indifference curve u_3 represents a higher level of satisfaction or utility than u_2. The farther the indifference curve is away from the origin (to the northeast), the greater the level of satisfaction.

FIGURE 21-8
An indifference map
There is a whole set of indifference curves for the household, each curve representing a different level of utility. Thus u_2 represents a higher level of utility than u_1, and u_3 a still higher level.

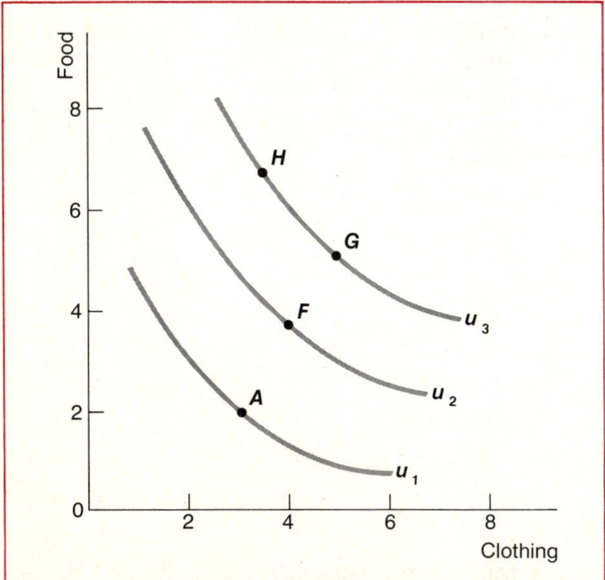

Incidentally, this illustrates how three variables can be shown in a diagram with only two dimensions. The three variables are the quantity of food, the quantity of clothing, and the household's utility. We can visualize this system of indifference curves as mapping out a utility hill, with each curve representing a contour line showing points with equal utility, just as a geographer's contour line shows points of equal height above sea level. A geographer's contour lines do not cross, and the indifference curves of a household do not cross either.

As the household moves from the origin to the northeast, it moves up the utility hill to higher and higher levels of satisfaction.[6]

THE BUDGET LIMITATION

As we have seen, the indifference map reflects the household's *desires;* the household prefers *G* to *F* in Figure 21-8 and is indifferent between *H* and *G*. However, the household's behavior depends not only on what the household *wants,* but also on what it is *able* to buy.

[6]One advantage of the indifference curve approach is that we don't have to worry about the units of measurement as we move up the utility hill. We know that curve u_3 represents more utility than curve u_2, but we don't need to know *how much* more. Specifically, with indifference curves, we are only making statements such as: "*F* is preferred to *A, G* is preferred to *F,* and *G* and *H* are equally desirable."

Thus, the indifference map involves simply an *ordering* of various consumption packages. This is called ***ordinal measurement*** (for example, *F* is better than *A*) in contrast to ***cardinal measurement*** (for example, *F* is 25% better than *A*). Cardinal measurement is not necessary with the simple ordering represented by indifference curves.

Avoiding the problems in cardinal measurement of utility was one of the main reasons why Nobel prizewinner J. R. Hicks developed the indifference curve approach in his *Value and Capital* (London: Oxford University Press, 1939).

What the household is able to buy depends on three things: its money income, the price of food, and the price of clothing If the household's income is \$100, while the price of food is \$10 per unit and clothing is \$20, the various options open to the household are illustrated by the ***budget line*** *KL* in Figure 21-9.

The *budget line*—sometimes called an *income line* or *price line*—shows the various options of a household with a given money income and facing a given set of prices.

FIGURE 21-9

The equilibrium of a household with a budget limit
KL represents the household's budget limit. Each point on this line represents a combination of food and clothing that can be purchased, and that just barely exhausts the household's budget. Equilibrium involves moving along this budget line to the point *E* of tangency with the highest achievable indifference curve.

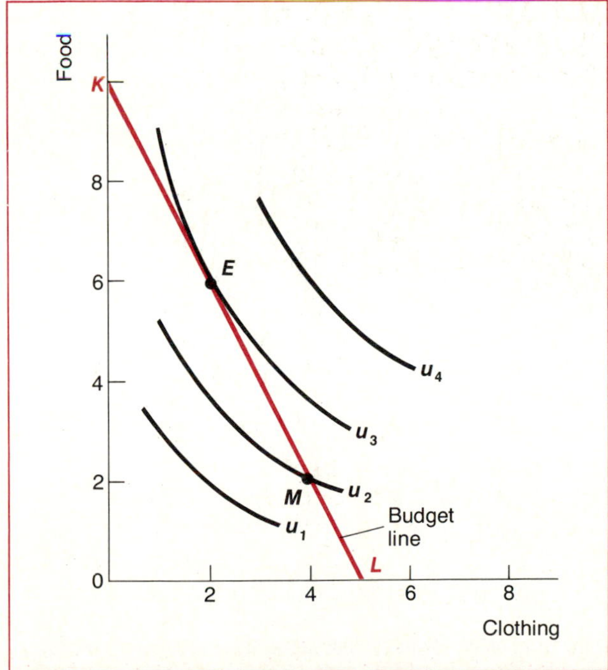

If the whole \$100 is spent on food at \$10 per unit, the household can buy 10 units, as shown by point *K*. At the other extreme, if the household spends its whole \$100 on clothing at \$20 per unit, it can buy five units, as shown by point *L*. Similarly, it can be shown that any other point on the straight line *KL* will exactly exhaust the budget of \$100. (As an exercise, show that this is true for point *M*.)

The slope of the budget line between K and L is

$$\frac{\text{Vertical distance } OK}{\text{Horizontal distance } OL} = \frac{10}{5} = 2$$

This is the same as the price ratio of the two goods, that is,

$$\frac{P_{\text{clothing}}}{P_{\text{food}}} = \frac{\$20}{\$10} = 2 \qquad (21\text{-}5)$$

Since this is always true,

The slope of the budget line is equal to the price ratio of the two goods.

THE HOUSEHOLD'S EQUILIBRIUM

Faced with the budget limit *KL,* the household purchases the combination of food and clothing shown at *E;* that is, it moves along the budget line to the point where that line touches the highest possible indifference curve, in this case u_3. Any other affordable purchase, like *M,* is less attractive because it leaves the household on a lower indifference curve—u_2 rather than u_3.

Consumers maximize their satisfaction or utility by moving along their budget line to the highest attainable indifference curve. This is achieved at a point of tangency such as *E* in Figure 21-9.

A point of tangency, of course, is a point where the slope of the indifference curve (MRS) is equal to the slope of the budget line (the price ratio of the two goods). That is,

$$\text{MRS} = \frac{P_{\text{clothing}}}{P_{\text{food}}} = 2 \text{ in this example}^7 \quad (21\text{-}6)$$

In conclusion, we reemphasize that the budget line and the indifference map are independent of one another. The indifference map shows the household's preferences; in defining the indifference map, no attention is paid to what the household can actually afford. What it can afford is shown by the budget line. When the indifference map and the budget line are brought together, the choice of the household is determined.

DERIVING A DEMAND CURVE FROM AN INDIFFERENCE MAP

The indifference curve/budget line analysis is used in panel *a* of Figure 21-10 to show how the household responds to a fall in the price of clothing. When clothing was originally priced at $20 per unit, we have seen that the budget line was *KL* and the equilibrium was E_1—both reproduced from the previous figure. Now suppose that the price of clothing falls to $10, but the price of food remains unchanged. Because the price ratio has changed, the slope of the budget line changes. Specifically, the budget line rotates from *KL* to *KR*. (If all $100 is spent on clothing, the household can now buy 10 units at point *R*. But because the price of food does not

[7]For readers who have studied marginal utility in Box 21-1, it can be shown that MRS—with its value of 2 in this case—is also the ratio of the marginal utilities of these two goods. That is,

$$\text{MRS} = \frac{\text{MU}_{\text{clothing}}}{\text{MU}_{\text{food}}} = 2 \quad (21\text{-}7)$$

We can see why from our example. Since the household is willing to give up only one unit of clothing to get two units of food, it values clothing twice as highly as food; that is, its marginal utility of clothing is double its marginal utility of food.

When we substitute equation 21-7 into 21-6, the result is

$$\frac{\text{MU}_{\text{clothing}}}{\text{MU}_{\text{food}}} = \frac{P_{\text{clothing}}}{P_{\text{food}}} \quad (21\text{-}8)$$

which is a confirmation of the basic relationship, equation 21-4, introduced in Box 21-1.

FIGURE 21-10
The effect of a fall in the price of clothing
As the price of clothing falls from $20 to $10, the budget line rotates counterclockwise from *KL* to *KR*. As a result, the quantity of clothing purchased increases from 2 to 5 units. In panel *b* we graph exactly this same information about price and quantity; again we move from point E_1 to E_2. However, in panel *b* these points define the consumer's demand curve.

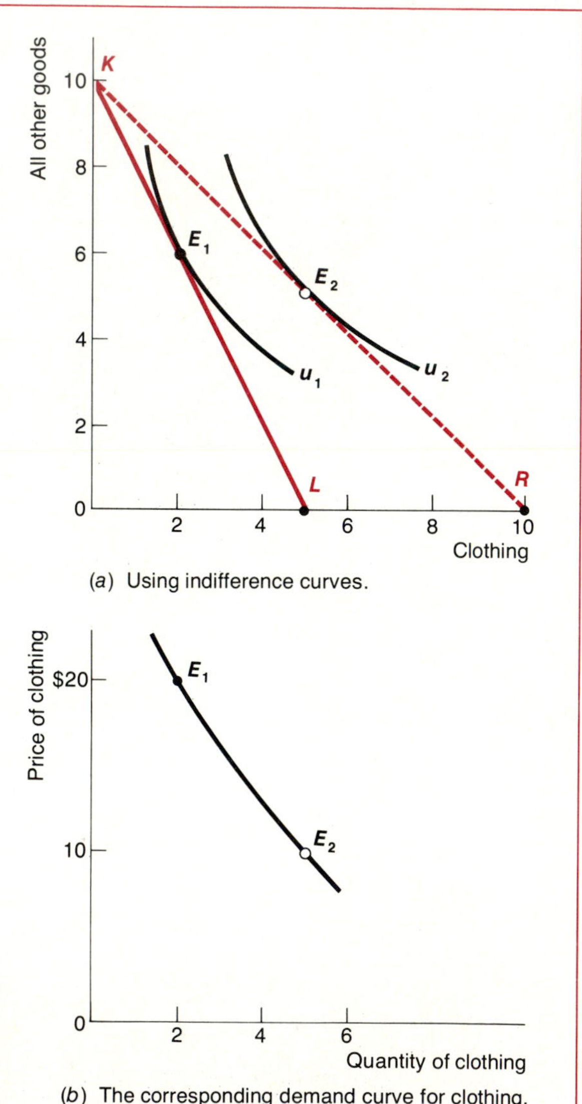

change, the new budget line still ends at point K, as before.[8])

Faced with the new budget line KR, the household again searches for its highest possible indifference curve, finding it at the point of tangency E_2. The two points of equilibrium, E_1 and E_2, define the two points on the demand curve of the household, shown in panel *b* of Figure 21-10. Thus, the individual's demand curve can be derived from his or her indifference map.

The *substitution effect* is the change in the quantity purchased which would occur as a result of a change only in relative prices, with real income held constant. In Figure 21-11, it is the distance from Q_1 to Q_3.

THE RESULTS OF A PRICE CHANGE: SUBSTITUTION AND INCOME EFFECTS

We have already seen that, in the event of a decrease in the price of clothing, the consumer will increase purchases because of the substitution effect and the income effect. In Figure 21-11 we begin with a decrease in price that moves the consumer from E_1 to E_2—thus increasing clothing purchases from Q_1 to Q_2. We shall now show how this increased purchase can be broken down into a substitution and income effect. To look at the effects of substitution alone, we keep the consumer on the original indifference curve u_1. This means that we are holding real income constant. At the same time, we allow the slope of the price line to change to reflect the lower price of clothing. Thus, we find a new price line ST parallel to KR—thus reflecting the new price—but tangent to the original indifference curve u_1 at point V. The *substitution effect* is the quantity change Q_1Q_3 associated with the move from E_1 to V, as shown by arrow 1.

However, the consumer does not actually move from E_1 to V, but from E_1 to E_2. The rest of the move—from V to E_2, shown by arrow 2—represents the *income effect*. Observe that a shift in the price line from ST to KR results from a change in real income alone; that is, it involves no change in relative prices, since the slope of ST and KR are the same.

FIGURE 21-11
The substitution and income effects of a price reduction: A detailed description of the move from E_1 to E_2 (in Figure 21-10a)

With the fall in the price of clothing, there is a move from equilibrium E_1 to E_2, which can be decomposed into two parts:

Move 1 from E_1 to V shows the substitution effect by holding real income constant. (V is on the same indifference curve as E_1).

Move 2 from V to E_2 shows the income effect by holding relative prices constant. (The slope at V and E_2 are the same.)

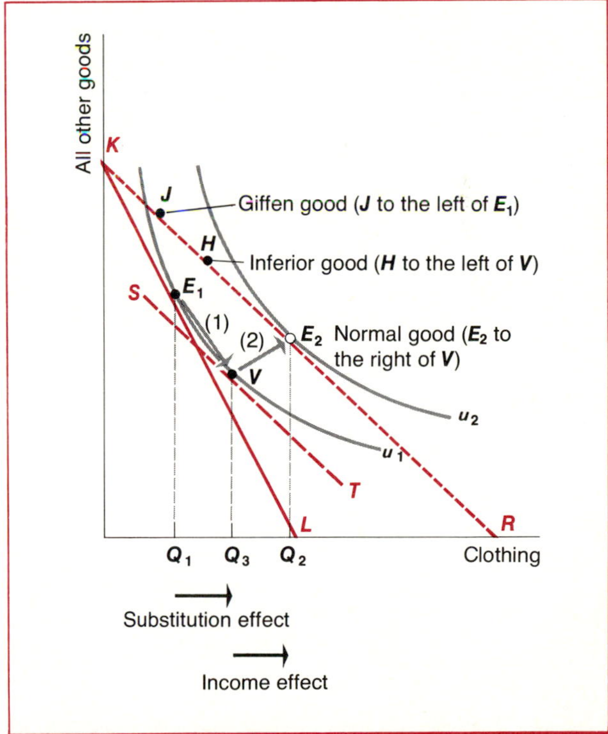

[8]Because our simple example has only two goods—food and clothing—food may be interpreted as representing all goods other than clothing. In showing the relationship between the indifference curve diagram and the demand curve for clothing, it is customary to write "all other goods" on the vertical axis, as we have done in panel *a* of Figure 21-10.

The *income effect* is the change in the quantity purchased which would occur as a result of a change only in real income. In Figure 21-11, it is the distance from Q_3 to Q_2.

When the price of clothing falls, the shape of the indifference curve guarantees that the substitution effect will lead an individual to buy more clothing and less of other goods; that is, arrow 1 points to the southeast in Figure 21-11. However, the sign of the income effect is not certain. For the vast majority of goods—the normal goods—the income effect will lead an individual to buy more of both clothing and other goods; arrow 2 points to the northeast, as shown in Figure 21-11. However, for the few goods which are *inferior,* the income effect is different; an increase in income alone—that is, a move from budget line *ST* to *KR*—*reduces* the quantity purchased. In such a case, the tangency of an indifference curve to *KR* occurs not at E_2 but instead at a point such as *H, to the left of V*. (To illustrate this possibility, erase u_2 and draw in this other indifference curve, ensuring that it is tangent to *KR* at *H*.) Note that in this case, arrow 2 no longer points to the northeast but instead points to the northwest: The increase in income reduces the quantity of clothing purchased.

Economists have been fascinated with the logical possibility that this sort of unusual income effect might be sufficiently strong to more than offset the substitution effect; in other words, that an indifference curve might be tangent to *KR* at a point such as *J, to the left of* E_1. Then the reduction in the price of the good would lead to a move from E_1 to *J* and a *reduction* in the purchase of that good. Such a case would be extremely rare. One example has been attributed to Victorian economist Giffen, involving the purchase of potatoes in a very poor economy. In such a special case, a fall in the price of the basic staple—potatoes—would so increase people's real income and their purchases of meat and other expensive foods that they would buy *fewer* potatoes. Notice that such a peculiar good—a so-called *Giffen good*—would have a strange demand curve; it would slope downward and *to the left*.

PROBLEM

21-8. Gasoline is a normal good. Show the substitution and income effects of a price increase.

CHAPTER 22

COSTS AND PERFECTLY COMPETITIVE SUPPLY:

THE SHORT RUN

"and consumers dance to the producers' tune"

REPRISE FROM CHAPTER 4

In the last chapter, the consumer was king, deciding which goods would be produced and which would not. But in fact, it's a joint regency: The producer is also a king. Goods aren't produced unless the consumer wants them *and* the producer can deliver them at a price acceptable to the consumer. In this chapter, we begin our study of producers. Just as in our study of consumers, we will highlight the concepts that will be essential for you to understand fully before reading the rest of this book.

In the last chapter, we stressed the *choices* open to consumers, specifically, the choice of which goods to consume. The producer likewise faces fundamental choices:

1. *Which* goods will the firm produce? And *how many* units of each?
2. *What combination of inputs* will the firm use in the production of these goods? For example, will a manufacturer of home appliances use a highly automated assembly line that can be operated by only a few workers or use less automated equipment and more workers? Will a wheat farmer use a great deal of fertilizer on each acre or produce the wheat using more land and less fertilizer?

While these are the fundamental choices, in practice producers are constrained by their decisions of the past. For example, General Motors is committed to auto production by its huge investment in plant and equipment, most of which can be used only to make cars. Thus GM does not have the choice next month of producing aircraft or shoes instead. Furthermore, GM's short-term committment for next month is not only to the *kind* of equipment it will have—that is, equipment to produce automobiles. GM is also committed to the existing *quantity* of equipment; it is now too late to order new machines or build new factories to use in next month's production. With its stock of plant and equipment already determined, GM has only a narrow set of production decisions for next month: *How many vehicles* will it produce and *how many workers and how much material will it use* to produce these vehicles?

THE SHORT RUN AND THE LONG

Those narrow decisions face GM in the ***short run,*** when it cannot change the quantity or type of capital it has inherited from past investment decisions. However, if GM is deciding what it will be doing 5 or 10 years from now, it will have far more flexibility. It will have time to acquire more capital. Or, it can contract its capital stock by deciding not to replace its worn-out plant or equipment. Thus in the ***long run,*** the firm can pick from a wide range of choices. It can choose to produce in a ***capital-intensive*** manner—with many machines and few workers—or in a ***labor-intensive*** manner, with many workers and few machines. It can enter new businesses or drop certain products altogether.

The *short run* is the period during which the firm cannot change the quantity or type of its plant and equipment.

The *long run* is the period during which the firm is able to change the quantity or type of its plant and equipment.

The short run is *not* defined as any specific number of weeks, months, or years. Instead, it is whatever time period plant and equipment are fixed. In some industries, the short run may last many years. That much time is needed to design and construct a large electric power plant, for example. In other industries, the short run may be just a matter of days. To illustrate, a college entrepreneur can quickly buy a word processor and thereby acquire the capital equipment to set up business typing term papers. Furthermore, the short run may be briefer for an expanding firm than for a contracting firm. An expanding firm may be able to acquire new equipment quickly, while a contracting firm may be able to reduce its capital stock only slowly. There may be no market in which it can sell its used machinery, and its capital stock may take years to wear out.

In the next few chapters, we will be looking at the decisions of producers. We begin in this chapter by considering a specific case. How many units will a firm produce if (1) it is making a *short run* decision and (2) it is in a *perfectly competitive* industry? In Chapter 23, we will turn to the long run, still looking at a perfectly competitive industry. Chapters 24 through 26 will consider monopolies, oligopolies, and other types of imperfectly competitive industries. Through all these chapters, we will assume that business executives try to maximize their firm's profits. Of course, executives may also have other motives—for example, ensuring the security of their jobs or increasing their own importance by expanding their operations and the number of people who work for them. However, to keep things simple, we focus on the important objective of profit maximization. Specifically, we assume that if a firm can increase its profits by making more of a good, it will do so. Or, if it can increase profits by producing less, that's what it will do.

If it is trying to maximize profits, how much output will a firm produce and supply in the short run? That's the central question in this chapter. We begin with production costs, which have a major influence on supply.

COSTS IN THE SHORT RUN

A firm's total costs of production may be subdivided into two components: (1) ***fixed costs*** and (2) ***variable costs.***

1. ***Fixed costs*** or ***overhead costs.*** Fixed costs (FC) are the costs that do not vary as output changes. Indeed, they are incurred *even if no output is produced at all*. This is illustrated in Table 22-1, which shows the costs of a hypothetical manufacturer of shoes. Observe that fixed costs in column 2 are constant at $35, regardless of the quantity of output q in column 1.

Because the firm cannot change the quantity of plant and equipment in the short run, many of the costs associated with such capital are fixed. For example, *interest* must be paid on the funds originally borrowed to buy the equipment, and *depreciation* occurs whether or not any output is produced. Similarly, buildings must be protected with *fire insurance* regardless of how much is produced.

2. ***Variable costs.*** On the other hand, variable costs (VC) *do* change as the firm increases the quantity of output. For example, the firm hires more labor and buys more electricity, leather, and other materials. In Table 22-1, column 3 illustrates how variable costs rise as quantity increases.

***Fixed costs* are those costs that do not change as output increases.**

***Variable costs* are those costs that *do* increase as output increases.**

Total cost (TC) in column 4 of Table 22-1 is the sum of fixed and variable costs. For example, we see that, if the firm is producing eight pairs of shoes, it incurs $35 of fixed costs and $295 of variable costs, for a total cost of $330.

Marginal cost (MC) is the *additional* cost as output increases by 1 unit. Business executives often refer to marginal cost as ''incremental cost.''

***Marginal cost* is the increase in total cost because one additional unit is produced.**

In Table 22-1, marginal cost is calculated in column 5. For example, if the firm increases its output from seven to eight units, its total cost in column 4 increases from $245 to $330; that is, its total cost increases by $85. This is the marginal cost of the eighth unit.

The costs in Table 22-1 are illustrated in panel *a* of Figure 22-1. As output increases and we move to the right in this panel, we see that fixed cost remains the same. However, variable cost—shown as the upper white arrow—rises. Total cost also increases since it is the sum of the two—that is, it is the combined height of the two white arrows.

Observe that each red bar or ''stairstep'' in this diagram represents marginal cost MC because it shows how total cost rises with each additional unit of output.

The red marginal cost bars in panel *a* are shown separately in panel *b*. For example, the first marginal cost bar in panel *b* is $24 high. This is just a reproduction of the first red bar in panel *a,* which shows total cost rising by $24—from $35 to $59—when output increases from zero to one unit. Similarly, the second bar in panel *b* is a reproduction of the second red bar in panel *a,* with its value being $75 − $59 = $16. Thus the whole set of MC bars in panel *b* can be viewed as ''what would be left'' if the supporting gray bars in panel *a* were removed and the red MC bars were allowed to settle down to the base line.

THE LAW OF DIMINISHING RETURNS

As output increases, marginal cost may fall at first, but eventually it *must* rise (as indeed it does in Figure 22-1*b*). The reason is the ***law of (eventually) diminishing returns.*** To understand this law, consider the short-run situation of the firm producing shoes with a given stock of capital. Suppose it has only one variable factor, labor. As it initially hires more labor, each additional worker increases the firm's output by a substantial amount. But ultimately, as its labor force grows and its capital equipment is operated closer and closer to capacity, an additional worker will add only a small amount to the firm's output. All the new employee can do is work on odd jobs or stand around waiting for one of the machines to be free. In other words, the ***marginal product of labor*** must eventually decrease. This illustrates the law of eventually diminishing returns.

The *marginal product of labor* is the number of additional units of output which result from using one more worker.

TABLE 22-1
Short-Run Costs of a Hypothetical Firm Producing Shoes

(1) Quantity produced (pairs) q	(2) Fixed cost FC	(3) Variable cost VC	(4) Total cost TC = FC + VC = (3) + (2)	(5) Marginal cost MC = change in total cost
0	35	0	35	
1	35	24	59	59 − 35 = 24
2	35	40	75	75 − 59 = 16
3	35	60	95	95 − 75 = 20
4	35	85	120	120 − 95 = 25
5	35	115	150	150 − 120 = 30
6	35	155	190	190 − 150 = 40
7	35	210	245	245 − 190 = 55
8	35	295	330	330 − 245 = 85

The *law of (eventually) diminishing returns:* If more of one factor (labor) is employed while all other factors (like capital) are held constant, eventually the marginal product of that one factor (labor) must fall.

This law is easily confirmed in agriculture. As more and more workers are added to a constant amount of land—say, 100 acres—the marginal product of labor *must* eventually fall. If it did not, the entire world could be fed from this single farm—or, for that matter, from your back garden.

FIGURE 22-1
Short-run costs of the shoe manufacturer in Table 22-1
In panel *a*, total cost is the sum of fixed cost and variable cost. Marginal cost indicates how much total cost is increasing, and is shown by the set of red bars in panel *a* or in panel *b*.

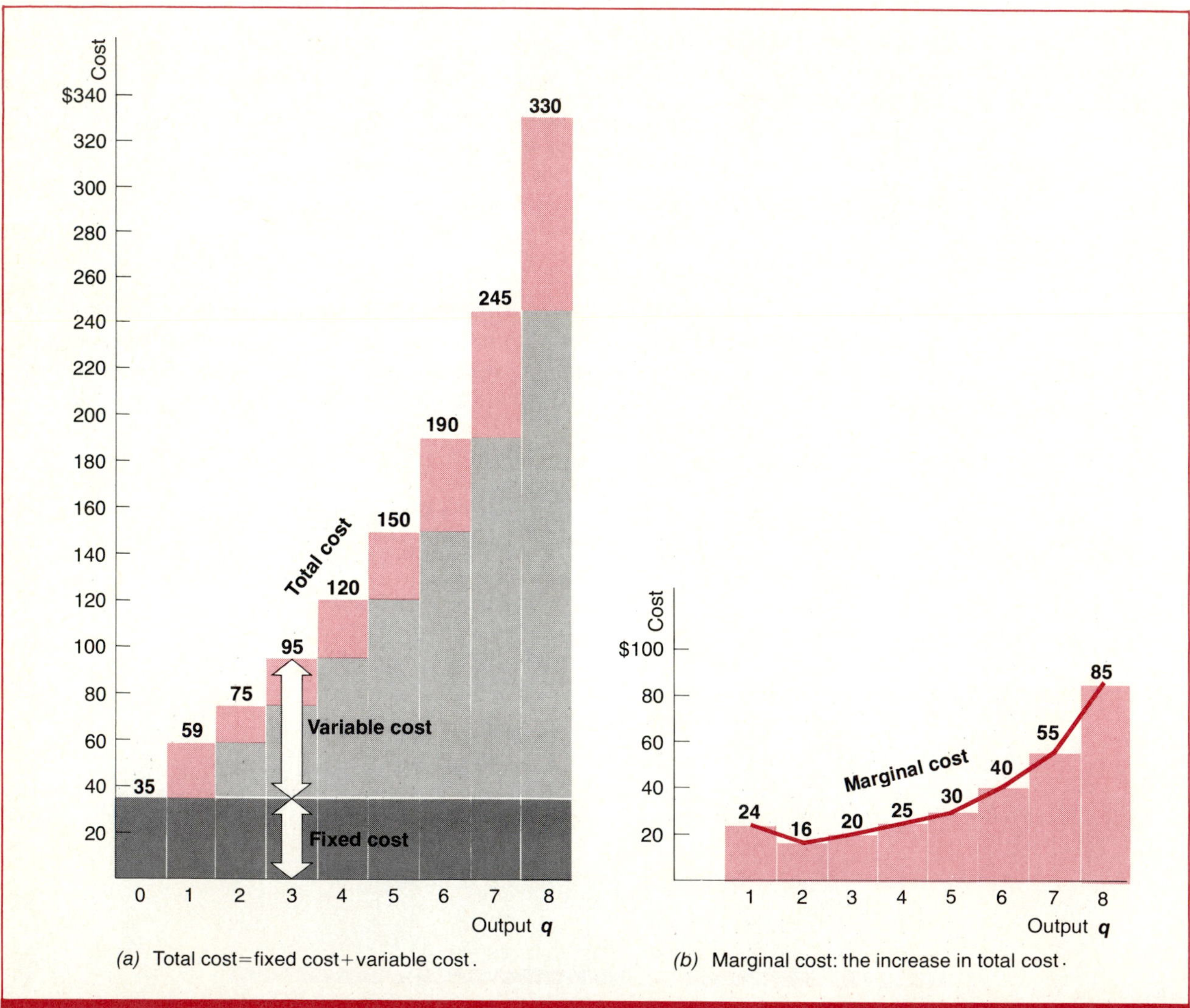

(a) Total cost=fixed cost+variable cost.

(b) Marginal cost: the increase in total cost.

In Part 7 of this book, we shall see that the law of diminishing returns is a key to explaining wages and other income payments. For now, it is important because it explains why marginal costs must ultimately rise. In our example, the law of diminishing returns means that eventually an extra worker in the shoe factory is able to do only odd jobs and produce very little. Most of his time is wasted. True, the firm can still produce another unit of output; but when it's done by a worker like this who is wasting most of his time, this unit of output comes at a very high marginal cost.

The law of diminishing returns ensures that marginal costs must eventually rise.

The law of diminishing returns is illustrated in more detail in Box 22-1.

BOX 22-1

DIMINISHING RETURNS: THE SHORT-RUN PRODUCTION FUNCTION

To study the idea of diminishing returns in more detail, it is helpful to look at the ***short-run production function,*** which shows how physical output increases because of an increase in variable input. As an example, Table 22-2 shows the short-run production function of a hypothetical bicycle producer whose only variable input is labor. Because we are looking at the short run, the quantity of capital is fixed.

The first line in this table shows the number of workers this firm may employ, while the second line shows the resulting number of bicycles produced in a week. For example, if the firm uses three workers, it is able to produce 18 units of output. Line 3 shows the marginal product of labor, that is, the number of additional bicycles produced when one more worker is added. For example, when the fifth worker is added, production increases from 21 to 23 bicycles, and the fifth worker's marginal product is therefore two bicycles. Finally, the fourth line shows average product—that is, total product TP in line 2 divided by the number of workers in line 1. The data from this table are illustrated in Figure 22-2.

This example illustrates the law of eventually diminishing returns. Although marginal product rises at first—the marginal product of the second worker (seven bicycles) is greater than that of the first worker (five bicycles)—marginal product then begins to fall, to six bicycles, three, two, and then one. Again, the explanation is that the firm's machinery becomes more and more fully used, and the new workers therefore don't have much machinery at their disposal.

The marginal product MP for the fourth, fifth, and sixth workers in Table 22-2 is reproduced in line 2 of Table 22-3. This can now be used to calculate the marginal cost of bicycles in line 4—provided we know the wage rate; suppose it is $300 per week, as shown in line 3. To illustrate how marginal cost can be calculated, note that the fourth worker has a marginal prod-

TABLE 22-2
The Short-Run Production Function for a Bicycle Manufacturer
(The quantity of capital is fixed. Product is measured in number of bicycles per week.)

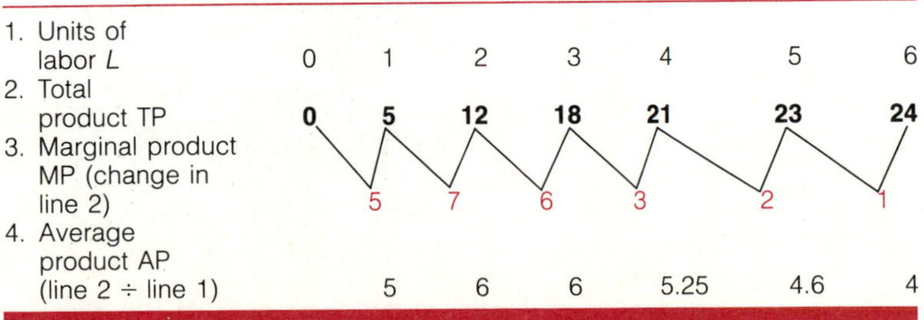

1. Units of labor L	0	1	2	3	4	5	6
2. Total product TP	**0**	**5**	**12**	**18**	**21**	**23**	**24**
3. Marginal product MP (change in line 2)		5	7	6	3	2	1
4. Average product AP (line 2 ÷ line 1)		5	6	6	5.25	4.6	4

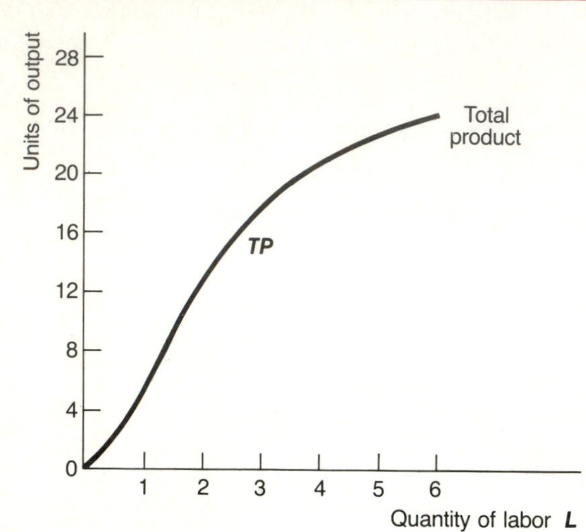

(*a*) **Total product.**

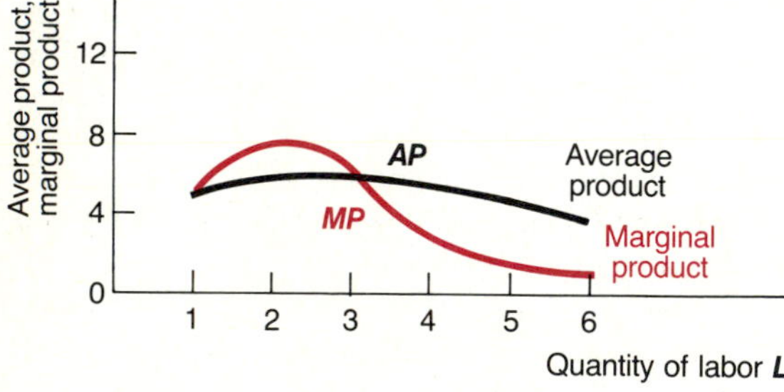

(*b*) **Average and marginal product.**

FIGURE 22-2

Total and marginal product curves for the bicycle firm

The curves in this diagram correspond to the data in Table 22-2. The marginal product MP curve must eventually decline because of the law of eventually diminishing returns.

TABLE 22-3

Declining Marginal Product and Rising Marginal Cost

1. Units of labor *L*	4	5	6
2. Marginal product MP	3	2	1
3. Wage per worker	\$300	\$300	\$300
4. Marginal cost (line 3 ÷ line 2)	\$100	\$150	\$300

uct of three bicycles. Since it cost \$300 to hire that worker, and he produces three bicycles, the marginal cost of each of those bicycle is \$100, as shown in line 4. Continuing these calculations, we see that when the fifth worker is hired at \$300 cost, the result is only two more bicycles, for a marginal cost of \$150 per bicycle. Observe how diminishing returns—that is, the declining marginal product of labor in line 2—results in rising marginal cost in line 4.

Finally, once we calculate marginal cost in this way, and if we know fixed cost, we can calculate other costs. Returning to our earlier example of the shoe company in Figure 22-1, we see that knowledge of marginal cost in panel *b* plus knowledge that fixed cost is \$35 is all that is needed to reconstruct the *complete cost diagram in panel a*. To confirm this, cover panel *a* and reconstruct if for yourself. All that is necessary is to start with the dark gray \$35 of fixed cost as a base, and build up the red marginal cost "stairsteps" on top of this, one by one.

We can therefore sum up, for any such firm whose only valuable input is labor. All its costs can be derived from its short-run production function, once its wage and fixed costs are known.

Figure 22-3 reproduces the rising portion of the marginal cost curve from Figure 22-1*b*. We shall show that this is the key to deriving the firm's supply curve. However, in order to do so, we must first answer the important question: How will the firm maximize its profits?

PROFIT MAXIMIZATION: MARGINAL COST AND MARGINAL REVENUE

To determine how much the perfectly competitive firm will produce to maximize its profit, we must also know the price at which it can sell. Suppose this price is $40, as shown in Figure 22-3. Because the perfectly competitive firm has no control over price, the $40 price is shown as a horizontal line: Price remains at $40, regardless of what this firm does. This price line is also the firm's marginal revenue, which, as you can by now guess, is defined:

***Marginal revenue* (MR) is the increase in total revenue from the sale of one more unit.**

It is easy to confirm that marginal revenue will be this constant $40 price. The reason is that total revenue will be $40 from the sale of one unit, $80 from the sale of two, $120 from three, and so on. No matter how many units the firm may be selling, its total revenue will always increase by $40 if it sells one unit more.

Given this $40 price and the marginal cost schedule shown in Figure 22-3, how many units will the firm produce? The answer is six. The reason is that any decision to produce at a greater output, say seven, would be a mistake, since the $55 marginal cost of producing that seventh unit exceeds the $40 in additional revenue which it brings in. On the other hand, if the firm is at an output below six, say four, expansion will be in its interest. Why? The marginal cost of the fifth unit is $30, and it can be sold for $40; consequently, it's in the firm's interest to produce that unit. But at six units, there is no tendency to expand or contract production because marginal cost MC has risen to the level of price (that is, marginal revenue). This is the equilibrium output for the firm because at this point its profit is at a maximum.

***Essential idea for future chapters:* To maximize profits, a firm will expand its production until it reaches the output where its marginal cost has risen to the level of its marginal revenue, that is, to the point where**

$$MC = MR \qquad (22\text{-}1)$$

For a perfectly competitive firm, MR = price *P*. Such a firm will maximize profit where

$$MC = MR = P \qquad (22\text{-}2)$$

FIGURE 22-3

A perfectly competitive firm produces where MC = price (marginal costs are for the shoe producer shown in Figure 22-1)

Marginal cost MC is equal to price *P* at an output of six units. This is the amount that will be supplied by the profit maximizing firm if the price is $40.

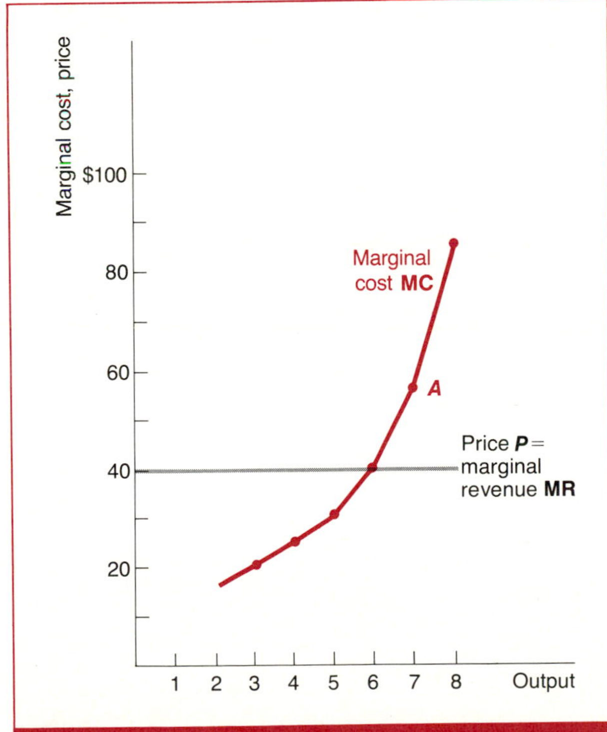

This can be confirmed in Table 22-4. The first three columns show some of the costs of the perfectly competitive shoe producer described earlier. Column 4 shows how the firm's total revenue rises $40 for each additional unit sold, giving the constant marginal revenue of $40 shown in column 5. Profits are calculated in the last column as total revenue minus total cost. We confirm that this firm's maximum profit is $50, and this is realized if its output is six. The arrow on the right marks this as the output the firm will produce. (Profit is also a maximum at five units of output, but in cases like this economists typically assume that the firm produces the larger output.) Note that, at this profit maximizing output of six, marginal cost in column 3 is equal to the $40 of marginal revenue (price) in column 5. This confirms our conclusion that this firm maximizes its profit where its marginal cost is equal to its marginal revenue. For an alternative view of profit maximization, see Box 22-2.

THE SHORT-RUN SUPPLY OF THE PERFECTLY COMPETITIVE FIRM

While the firm facing a $40 price in Figure 22-3 responds by producing six units, what does it do if the price rises to $55? To answer this question, visualize the horizontal price line shifting up from the $40 shown to this new, higher $55 level. The firm will respond to this higher price by increasing its output to seven units, where MC is again equal to price. Or, if price falls to $30, it will supply five units (as confirmed in Table 22-7 in the appendix to this chapter).

Notice that, in showing how much output the firm will supply at various prices, we are defining the firm's supply curve. As price rises, the firm simply follows its marginal cost curve up; or if price falls, it follows it MC curve down. Thus, MC defines the supply curve of the individual firm—subject to one important qualification.

The Shutdown Point

The qualification is that it is not certain the firm will produce anything at all. If it does, MC does indeed determine the quantity supplied. However, if the price falls low enough, the firm will close down. The next important question therefore is: How far can price fall before the firm closes down and stops producing altogether?

To throw light on this question, more information on costs is required. In Table 22-5 we reproduce, for reference only, the earlier cost calculations for the shoe firm in Table 22-1 and now add three additional columns of cost calculations, as follows:

TABLE 22-4
Profit Maximization by a Perfectly Competitive Shoe Producer Facing a $40 Price†

(1) Quantity of output q	(2) Total cost TC	(3) Marginal cost MC	(4) Total revenue TR	(5) Marginal revenue MR = price P	(6) Profit or loss (6) = (4) − (2)
0	35		0		−35
		24		40	
1	59		40		−19
		16		40	
2	75		80		5
		20		40	
3	95		120		25
		25		40	
4	120		160		40
		30		40	
5	150		200		50
		40		40	
6	190		240		50 ⇐
		55		40	
7	245		280		35
		85		40	
8	330		320		−10

†The first three columns in this table are cost figures reproduced from Table 22-1.

BOX 22-2

ANOTHER VIEW OF PROFIT MAXIMIZATION: TOTAL REVENUE AND TOTAL COST

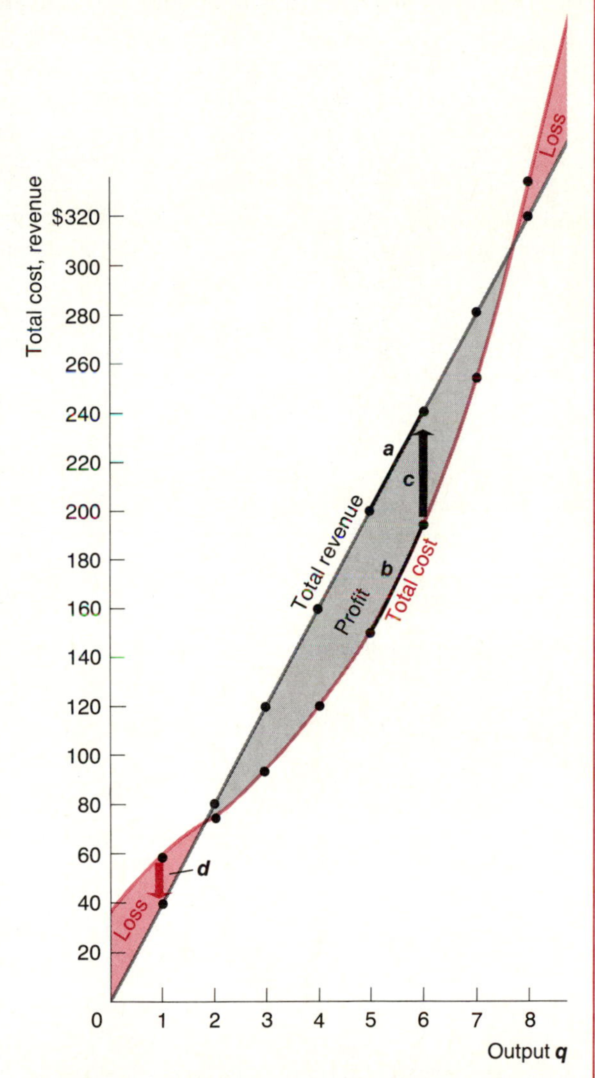

FIGURE 22-4
Another view of profit maximization by the perfectly competitive shoe producer

Graphing a firm's marginal revenue and marginal cost curves in Figure 22-3 is not the only way we can visualize its profit maximization. We can alternatively graph its *total* revenue and *total* cost curves in Figure 22-4, and show its profit maximizing output on this diagram. Specifically, we first plot the firm's red total cost curve, taken directly from Figure 22-1*a*. (In that figure, it was plotted as a series of bars, but here we draw it as a curve.) The firm's total revenue is also plotted. Note that it is a straight line from the origin because of our earlier observation: Given the $40 price the firm faces, the first unit it sells yields $40 of total revenue, the first two units yield $80, and so on. Note that the slope of this line is equal to the price—that is, to the firm's marginal revenue.

Initially, if the firm produces only one unit of output, it operates at a loss of $19, shown by arrow *d* in Figure 22-4: Its $59 total cost exceeds its $40 total revenue. However, as it increases its output, the firm moves upward to the right out of the red loss area into the black profit range where total cost is below total revenue. Finally, at eight units or more of output, total cost rises above total revenue, and the firm again operates at a loss.

Where in the range between two and seven units of output does the firm maximize profits? The answer is at six units, the output where its profit—the vertical distance *c* between the total revenue and total cost curves—is greatest.[†]

This is also the output where the slopes of the total revenue and total cost curves—specifically, the slopes of line segments *a* and *b*—are the same. We have already seen that the slope of the total revenue line is marginal revenue. Likewise, the slope of the total cost curve is marginal cost.[‡] Thus equating these two slopes is, in fact, equating marginal cost and marginal revenue—just as we did in Figure 22-3.

[†] As noted earlier, profits are also at a maximum at five units, but in such cases, economists assume that the larger output is sold. We also assume here that the firm can't produce a fraction of a unit; for example, it can't produce 5½ units.

[‡] This is easily confirmed by referring back to Figure 22-1. Each marginal cost stairstep in that diagram becomes the slope of the corresponding segment of the total cost curve in Figure 22-4. Readers familiar with calculus will now see why it is a valuable tool in economics. Marginal cost is simply the first derivative—that is, the slope—of the total cost curve.

1. ***Average cost*** (AC) or ***average total cost*** (ATC), defined as total cost divided by output. For example, suppose the firm produces five units of output; reading over to column 4, we see that its total cost is \$150. Therefore its average cost is \$150/5 = \$30, as shown in column 6.
2. ***Average variable cost*** (AVC), defined as variable cost divided by output. For example, if the firm produces five units of output, its variable cost is \$115 in column 3. Therefore, its average variable cost is \$115/5 = \$23, as shown in column 7.
3. ***Average fixed cost*** (AFC), defined as fixed cost divided by output. If the firm is again producing five units of output, its fixed cost is \$35 in column 2; therefore its average fixed cost is \$35/5 = \$7 in column 8.

Each of these concepts, along with the MC curve, is graphed in Figure 22-5. Note that the MC curve cuts the AC curve where AC is at a minimum. This must be so for reasons explained in Box 22-3, where we also explain the significance of AFC.

Now consider what happens if the price falls to \$30. To identify its best output, the firm finds the point where MC equals the \$30 price; this is *H*, where five units are produced. Observe that, at this point, average cost AC is at a minimum and is equal to price. Since the price received for selling each unit barely covers the average cost AC, the firm's profit is zero. The best the firm can do is ***break even.***

The *break-even point* is the lowest point on the AC curve. When the price is at this height, the firm makes zero profit.

Next, suppose price falls below \$30, to say \$25. If the firm produces at all, its output will be four units, at point *J* where MC equals the \$25 price. At this point, the firm will suffer a loss, since *J* lies below the AC curve: The \$25 price does not cover the \$30 average cost of producing each unit. It sounds as though this firm will close down. But it does not. *Even though it is operating at a loss, it continues to produce at J in the short run.* The reason is that its \$25 selling price more than covers its average *variable* cost; that is, point *J* is above AVC. Therefore, the firm can completely cover its variable cost and still have some revenue left over to cover part of

TABLE 22-5
Short-Run Costs of a Hypothetical Firm Producing Shoes†

(1) Quantity produced (pairs) q	(2) Fixed cost FC	(3) Variable cost VC	(4) Total cost TC = FC + VC = (3) + (2)	(5) Marginal cost MC = change in total cost	(6) Average cost‡ AC = TC ÷ q = (4) ÷ (1)	(7) Average variable cost‡ AVC = VC ÷ q = (3) ÷ (1)	(8) Average fixed cost‡ AFC = FC ÷ q = (2) ÷ (1)
0	35	0	35				
				59 − 35 = 24			
1	35	24	59		59 ÷ 1 = 59	24 ÷ 1 = 24	35 ÷ 1 = 35
				75 − 59 = 16			
2	35	40	75		75 ÷ 2 = 38	40 ÷ 2 = 20	35 ÷ 2 = 18
				95 − 75 = 20			
3	35	60	95		95 ÷ 3 = 32	60 ÷ 3 = 20	35 ÷ 3 = 12
				120 − 95 = 25			
4	35	85	120		120 ÷ 4 = 30	85 ÷ 4 = 21	35 ÷ 4 = 9
				150 − 120 = 30			
5	35	115	150		150 ÷ 5 = 30	115 ÷ 5 = 23	35 ÷ 5 = 7
				190 − 150 = 40			
6	35	155	190		190 ÷ 6 = 32	155 ÷ 6 = 26	35 ÷ 6 = 6
				245 − 190 = 55			
7	35	210	245		245 ÷ 7 = 35	210 ÷ 7 = 30	35 ÷ 7 = 5
				330 − 245 = 85			
8	35	295	330		330 ÷ 8 = 41	295 ÷ 8 = 37	35 ÷ 8 = 4

†The first five columns are reproduced from Table 22-1.
‡Rounded to the nearest dollar.

its fixed costs. It is better to cover part of these fixed costs than to shut down and cover none at all. (To confirm this conclusion, note that if it closes down, its loss will be equal to its fixed cost of $35. However, if it produces four units, its loss will be only $20—that is, the difference between its total revenue of $100 and its total cost of $120.)

Thus, so long as a firm is at least covering its variable costs, it continues to produce. That remains true so long as price is above the ***shutdown point,*** *K*. If the price falls below this, the firm will close down because it will not even be able to cover its variable costs. For example, suppose the price falls to $16. If the firm produces at all, it will be two units at point *L*. But at this point the $16 price is below AVC. Since the firm can't cover even its variable costs, it will shut down. If it were to insist on producing two units, its revenue would be $32, its cost $75, and its loss $43. This is more than the loss it incurs by closing down—namely, the $35 of fixed cost it still must pay. Therefore, the firm does better by shutting down.

The *shutdown point* is the point where the MC curve cuts the AVC curve. If price is below this point, the firm produces nothing.

FIGURE 22-5

The firm's cost curves and how they define its short-run supply

Marginal cost is reproduced from Figure 22-3. Average cost AC, average variable cost AVC, and average fixed cost AFC are taken from the last three columns in Table 22-5. The firm's short-run supply curve is shown as the heavy curve. It is that portion of its MC curve that lies above its AVC curve.

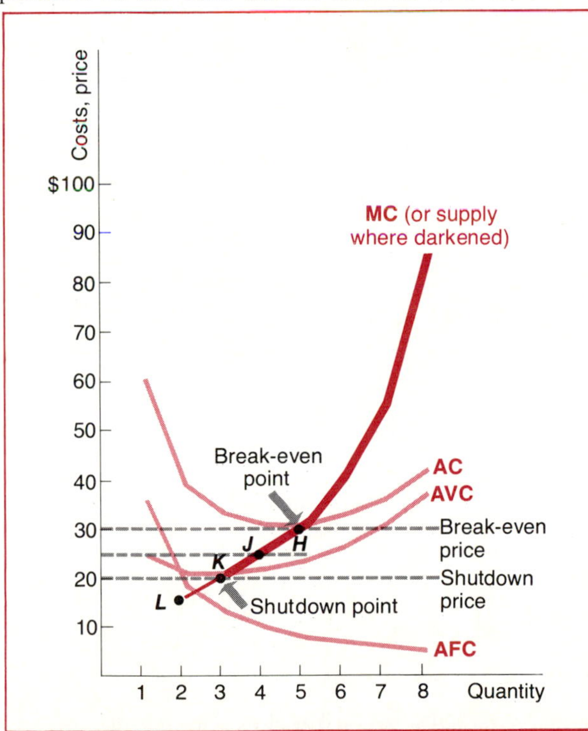

By trying various prices we have established that the firm will supply the quantity given by its MC curve—*unless* the price falls below the shutdown point *K*, in which case the firm will supply nothing. In other words: *In the short run*—in the period when the firm is working with a fixed capital stock—the firm reacts to any given price by supplying a quantity that can be read off its marginal cost curve, *provided it is at a point above AVC*. This then allows us to specify the firm's short-run supply curve:

The firm's *short-run supply curve* is that part of its marginal cost curve MC that lies above its average variable cost curve AVC.

The idea that supply is derived from the marginal cost of the producer is just as important as the idea in Chapter 21, that demand represents marginal benefit to the consumer. Just as we visualized a set of marginal benefit bars or arrows beneath the demand curve, so we arrive at a similar idea on the supply side:

> ***Essential idea for future chapters:* Whenever you see a supply curve, you should visualize the set of marginal cost bars enclosed beneath it.**[1]

[1]Just as a set of marginal cost bars is enclosed beneath the curve in panel *b* in Figure 22-1.

THE ECONOMIST'S CONCEPT OF COST: OPPORTUNITY COST

Before we turn in detail to the long run in the next chapter, there is one important final point to clarify: The economic definition of cost is not the same as the accounting definition. To illustrate the broader economic definition, suppose a friend who operates a store has asked you to analyze her business. Her breakdown of costs in column *a* of Table 22-6 seems to confirm her view that she is being successful. With revenue of $122,000 and costs of $74,000, she is earning an accounting profit of $48,000.

However, you dig more deeply. You discover that she could earn a $44,000 salary by accepting a job from an insurance company. This is an *implicit cost*—or *imputed cost*—because it is not paid out of pocket. However, we must include it, as we have done in column *b;* otherwise, we would not have an adequate picture of the

BOX 22-3

TWO IMPORTANT INFLUENCES ON AVERAGE COST

In this box we examine how a firm's average cost curve is influenced by its marginal cost curve and its average fixed cost curve.

The Influence of Marginal Cost: Why a Firm's Costs Are Like a Baseball Player's Average

Late in the 1980 season, Kansas City's George Brett had the best chance to hit the magic .400—that is, 40 hits in each 100 times at bat—since the Boston Red Sox' Ted Williams did it with .406 in 1941. The numbers on the right show Brett's batting performance during 1 week in September. In the first three games against Chicago and Detroit he batted a disappointing .250 (one hit in each four times at bat). Since this marginal performance shown in red was below his average in the .380s, it pulled his average down. However, in the next three games, his fortunes improved: He batted .500 or better. Since this marginal performance was above his average, it pulled his average up.†

So too with marginal and average costs. Until they reach their point of intersection *H* in Figure 22-5, marginal cost is below average cost; hence, it is pulling AC down. But to the right of *H,* MC is above AC and hence is pulling AC up. Since AC is falling until it reaches *H* but rising beyond, it must be at a minimum at *H,* where it meets MC.

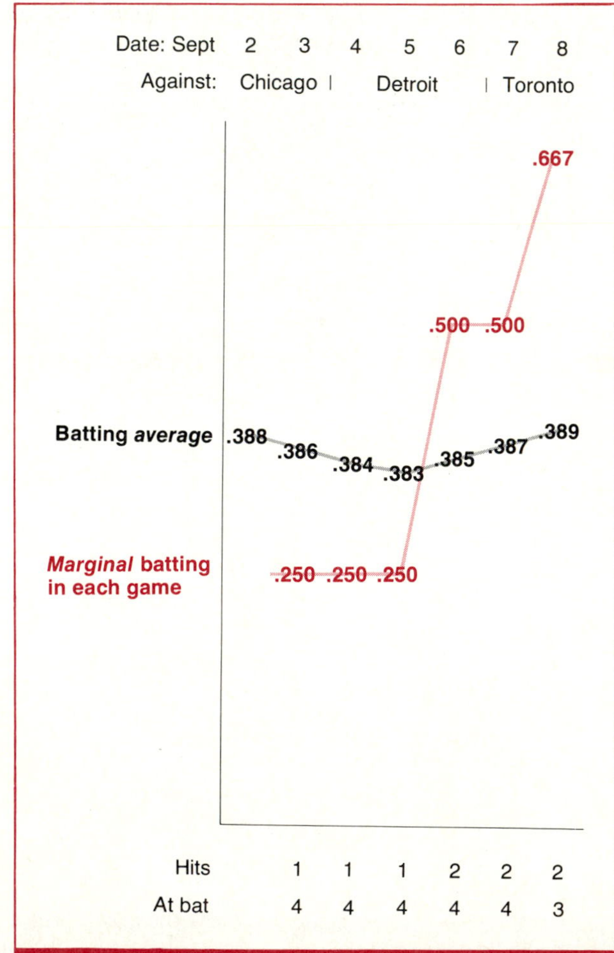

The Influence of Average Fixed Cost

To show how average cost is influenced by average fixed cost AFC, note that as output increases and we move to the right in Figure 22-5, AFC gets smaller and smaller. It must; after all, a fixed overhead cost—in this case the constant $35—is being divided by a larger and larger output. As business executives know, increased volume means that overhead can be spread over a larger number of units of output. Consequently, the overhead cost that has to be charged to each unit shrinks.

This is important because average cost AC in column 6 of Table 22-5 is the sum of two components: average variable cost AVC plus average fixed cost AFC in columns 7 and 8.[‡] When AVC ceases to fall—in our example, at two units of output—AC continues to fall for a while because it is pulled down by its other component, the always-falling AFC. Moreover, the larger are fixed costs, the more influential AFC will be; that is, the longer it will continue to pull AC down. (To confirm, do the simple calculations in problem 22-2 at the end of this chapter.) Thus high overhead industries—such as the telephone companies that require very heavy investment—tend to have falling average costs over a wide range of output.

[†] Did Brett hit .400? Although the last three games shown here started him on a hitting streak that carried him over .400 for a week in late September, he couldn't maintain the pace and finished the season with .390.

[‡] This is easy to confirm: Just divide all terms in the equation TC = VC + FC by the quantity of output *q*.

TABLE 22-6
The Evaluation of Costs and Profit

(*a*) By accountants			(*b*) By economists		
Total revenue		$122,000	Total revenue		$122,000
Costs (out-of-pocket)			Explicit (out-of-pocket) costs		
Labor	$10,000		Labor	$ 10,000	
Materials	59,000		Materials	59,000	
Rent	5,000		Rent	5,000	
Total	$74,000	$ 74,000			
			Implicit costs (income foregone)		
			Owner's salary	$ 44,000	
			Interest	1,000	
			Normal profit	2,000	
			Total costs	$121,000	$121,000
Accounting profit		$ 48,000	Economic (above-normal) profit		$ 1,000

true economic costs in operating this business—that is, the cost of all the resources used, including her own time. And we would not be able to judge whether she is doing as well in this business as she could in another activity, namely, working for the insurance company.

This implicit cost for her own time illustrates the concept of ***opportunity cost,*** that is, the alternative foregone.

The *opportunity cost* of an input is the return that it could earn in its best alternative use.

Opportunity cost also indicates *how much an input must be paid to keep it in its present use*. For example, if your friend doesn't earn her opportunity cost—that is, her potential salary in insurance—she has an incentive to shift out of her present activity into the higher-return insurance business. This illustrates a point made early in this chapter. Producers make a *choice* as to what goods or services to produce. In this case, your friend chooses between retailing and insurance services. (Incidentally, if your friend has strong nonmonetary reasons for preferring her own retail business—such as the freedom she gets from self-employment—she may *not* take the other higher-paying job after all. Such nonmonetary motives are often important. However, in the simplified story described here, we ignore such motives.)

You also discover that your friend has other opportunity costs which must also be included in column *b*. For example, she has a substantial amount of her own funds tied up in this business. What would be her best alternative use of these funds? She indicates that she would lend out part, getting $1,000 in interest. She would use the rest to buy part ownership of a company in which she could reap a $2,000 profit. This last item—the opportunity cost of capital—is called ***normal profit.***

We emphasize that whenever we draw a cost curve in this book, we include not only explicit out-of-pocket accounting costs, but also implicit costs such as normal profit. Therefore, in our example, costs are the full $121,000 shown in column *b* of Table 22-6. This broad definition means that costs tell us how much all the resources employed by the firm could be earning elsewhere. Since her $122,000 of revenues exceed this $121,000 cost, she has earned above-normal profit of $1,000. (In economics, the word "profit" means *above-normal* profit unless otherwise stated.) It is this $1,000 "bottom-line" profit that allows you to judge that your friend is indeed successful. Her business not only provides her an appropriate $44,000 income for her own time, and an appropriate return for the capital she has invested. It also provides her an additional $1,000. If present firms in an industry are making such above-normal profits, there is an incentive for other enterpreneurs to move their capital into this business to get in on a good thing.

***Economic profit* is above-normal profit; that is, profit after the opportunity costs of capital have been taken into account.**

Now suppose that salaries in other jobs increase. Specifically, suppose the insurance company increases its offer to your friend from $44,000 to $47,000. This increases the $44,000 owner's salary item by $3,000; and when column *b* is accordingly recalculated, the $1,000 of (above-normal) profit becomes a $2,000 loss. Your friend is no longer able to earn as much in this enterprise as in her best alternative activity. So long as she views this alternative line of work as equally interesting, she has an incentive to move.

Thus, *economic profit* (or loss) *provides a signal, indicating whether resources will be attracted to* (or repelled from) *an activity*. Accordingly, economic profit exerts pressure on the firm, directing it toward "what" to produce.

KEY POINTS

1. The producer has a number of fundamental choices: (*a*) which good should be produced, (*b*) how many units should be produced, and (*c*) what is the best combination of inputs to use?
2. In this chapter we have described the short run, when the firm can change only the quantity of labor it uses. It cannot change its quantity of plant and equipment; it is committed by past decisions. In the next chap-

ter we will consider the long run, when the firm can change its capital stock.

3. *For any firm,* profits are maximized at the output where MC = MR.

4. *For a perfectly competitive firm,* the price is given; price is not affected by how much the firm produces. For such a firm, MR = *P* and the firm will maximize its profits at the output where MC = *P*, as shown in Figure 22-3.

5. In turn, this means that a firm's short-run supply is determined by its short-run marginal cost curve—provided the price is at least high enough to cover the firm's variable costs.

6. By cost, economists mean ''opportunity'' cost. Thus, economists include not only explicit accounting costs, but also implicit costs such as the normal profit on capital invested in the enterprise.

7. After all such opportunity costs have been covered, any remaining profit—that is, above-normal profit—provides an indication of how much more is being earned in this activity than in the next best alternative. If present firms are making such a profit, resources are attracted into this industry. On the other hand, if present firms are not covering their opportunity costs—that is, if they are suffering an economic loss—resources are encouraged to move out.

KEY CONCEPTS

short run
long run
fixed cost
variable cost
total cost
marginal cost
law of diminishing returns
marginal product of labor
marginal revenue
average cost
relationship of marginal cost to average cost
average variable cost
average fixed cost
break-even point
shutdown point
how supply is determined by marginal cost
economic versus accounting definitions of cost
explicit versus implicit costs
opportunity cost
normal versus above-normal (economic) profit

PROBLEMS

22-1. Recalculate Table 22-4 and find the profit-maximizing output for the firm if the price is: (*a*) $50, (*b*) $35.

22-2. Suppose the fixed cost of the firm in Table 22-1 were $10,000 instead of $35, while variable cost remained the same. What happens to MC? to AC? Is it correct to say that, as fixed overhead costs increase in importance, AC tends to fall over a wider range of output?

22-3. To understand the problem of operating at a point like *J* in Figure 22-5, suppose you have inherited a house in another city which you wish to rent. You have to pay $80 a week of fixed costs such as taxes whether or not it's rented, and another $40 a week of variable costs such as utilities if you do rent it. If you can get only $100, should you rent the house or leave it vacant? Explain why.

22-4. Explain why economists define costs to include normal profit. If additional profit exists, what does this tell us?

22-5. Suppose a farmer in Kansas provides a statement of his costs to his income tax accountant. Are there any opportunity costs he may miss? Explain.

22-6. ''In the long run, all costs are variable.'' Do you agree? Explain, using machinery as an example of a fixed cost.

***22-7.** In Box 22-1, we claimed that once you know marginal costs in panel *b* of Figure 22-1, along with fixed cost of $35, you can cover up panel *a* and reconstruct it. As an alternative demonstration, cover up all the figures in Table 22-5 except the fixed cost in columns 1 and 2 and the MC figures—24, 16, 20, etc.—in column 5. Can you then fill in columns 3 and 4? If so, can you go on to fill in columns 6, 7, and 8? If not, what addititonal information would you require?

APPENDIX

SHORT-RUN PROFIT CALCULATIONS FOR A PERFECTLY COMPETITIVE FIRM

The costs of the hypothetical firm in Table 22-1 are reproduced in the first five columns of Table 22-7. In the other columns we show how this firm selects its output to maximize profit—or minimize loss—if it is faced with various market prices such as $40, $30, $25, and $20.

Columns 6 and 7 repeat our earlier calculation in Table 22-4 of how the firm responds to a $40 price. Total revenue is shown in column 6 as the $40 price times the number of units. Profit is calculated in column 7 from the figures in columns 4 and 6. For example, if output is two units, total revenue is $80 in column 6, and total cost is $75 in column 4. Thus, profit is $5. Alternatively, if output is one unit, total revenue is $40 and total cost is $59, resulting in a loss of $19—that is, a profit of −$19. The result of all such calculations in column 7 confirms our conclusion in Figure 22-3 that an output of six units maximizes profit.

If price is $30, the arrow in column 9 shows that the firm will produce five units of output at a zero profit: Its total cost in column 4 is $150, exactly the same as its total revenue in column 8. Since the firm facing a $30 price can do no better than break even with a zero profit, $30 is its break-even price.

If the price is $25, the best the firm can do is to minimize its loss at $20 by producing four units. It does not close down because its total revenue of $100 more than covers its variable cost of $85 in column 3, thus leaving $15 to partly cover its fixed cost. This result is better than shutting down and not covering *any* of its fixed cost.

If price is $20, the firm has two equally unattractive options. It can produce three units at a loss of $35, with its $60 in revenue just barely sufficient to cover its $60 of variable costs. Or it can close down completely, in which case it would run the same $35 loss—that is, the $35 of fixed cost that it cannot avoid. Twenty dollars is its "shutdown" price. At any price below this, it cannot even cover its variable costs and it will close down.

TABLE 22-7
How a Perfectly Competitive Firm Will Select Its Profit-Maximizing (or Loss-Minimizing) Output in Response to Four Hypothetical Prices

(1)	(2)	(3)	(4)	(5)	(6)	(7)	(8)	(9)	(10)	(11)	(12)	(13)
					Best output (shown by arrow) if:							
					Price = $40		Price = $30		Price = $25		Price = $20	
Quantity *Q*	Fixed cost FC	Variable cost VC	Total cost TC	Marginal cost MC	Total revenue TR	Profit (+) or loss (−) TR − TC	Total revenue TR	Profit (+) or loss (−) TR − TC	Total revenue TR	Profit (+) or loss (−) TR − TC	Total revenue TR	Profit (+) or loss (−) TR − TC
1	35	24	59	24	40	−19	30	−29	25	−34	20	−39
2	35	40	75	16	80	5	60	−15	50	−25	40	−35
3	35	60	95	20	120	25	90	− 5	75	−20	60	−35 ←
4	35	85	120	25	160	40	120	0	100	−20 ←	80	−40
5	35	115	150	30	200	50	150	0 ←	125	−25	100	−50
6	35	155	190	40	240	50† ←	180	−10	150	−40	120	−70
7	35	210	245	55	280	35	210	−35	175	−70	140	−105

†Profit is also at a maximum at five units of output. In cases like this, we assume that the firm selects the larger output.

CHAPTER 23

COSTS AND PERFECTLY COMPETITIVE SUPPLY:

THE LONG RUN

Variability is the law of life.

SIR WALTER OSLER

Chapter 22 explained costs and supply in the short run, when there is no opportunity to change the quantity of plant and equipment. In the long run, the quantity of capital can change for two reasons:

1. Existing firms may acquire new plant and equipment, or decide not to replace plant and equipment that wears out.
2. *New* firms may enter the industry, bringing in additional plant and equipment, or old firms may leave.

In this chapter, we will explore how these two changes in the capital stock can affect costs and supply. First, we will look at how an existing firm's decision becomes more complicated in the long run. It has to decide not only on how much labor it will employ, but also how much capital it will install. Its plant and equipment which were *fixed* in the short run, become *variable* in the long run.

This presents business executives with one of their most important and challenging questions: Should they expand by acquiring new machines and building new factories, or should they contract by deciding not to replace old capital as it wears out and becomes obsolete?

LONG-RUN COSTS OF A FIRM

To find the firm's long-run costs, we begin with the short-run cost curves AC and MC in Figure 22-5 and reproduce them here as SAC_A and SMC_A in Figure 23-1. *S* designates the short run, and the subscript *A* represents the fixed amount of capital the firm has been using in the short run.

Suppose this firm has been producing shoes at output q_1 and it wishes to produce a larger number, say q_3. It could do so by hiring more labor while continuing to use its present small capital stock *A*. In other words, it could continue to operate on cost curves SMC_A and SAC_A. However, if it does this, the cost of producing shoes would become very high. As we saw earlier, the new workers would spend a lot of their time standing around waiting for one of the available machines to become free. This problem is shown in Figure 23-1 as the extremely high marginal cost of producing a pair of shoes at point *c*—and the very high average cost at point *d*.

This strategy doesn't make sense. If the firm wants to produce quantity q_3, it has an incentive to install more equipment and perhaps build a new factory. By providing workers with more machines, the firm will be able to cut costs. In other words, the firm makes the *long-run* decision to expand its capital to a new larger amount *B*. Then it will be able to operate on the new short-run average cost curve SAC_B. (Each short-run AC curve applies to a specific amount of capital. When the firm's stock of capital changes, so does its short-run AC curve and the corresponding MC curve.) Note how successful this is. Since the firm is now operating on SAC_B rather than SAC_A, its average cost of producing q_3 units is only *e*, rather than *d*.

If the firm expects to produce any output greater than q_2, the larger capital stock *B* is better than *A;* it will mean lower average costs. That is, for any output exceeding q_2, SAC_B lies below SAC_A. However, for a small output less than q_2, it is *not* desirable to have large

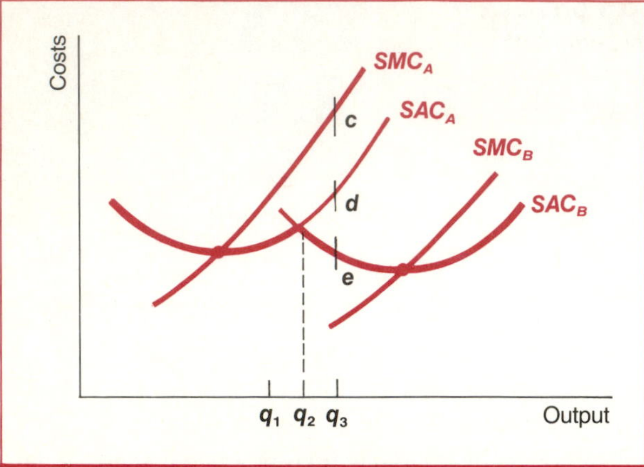

FIGURE 23-1
Costs in the short and long run
SAC_A shows short-run average cost with a given fixed capital stock *A*. If the firm wishes to produce more than q_2 in the long run—say q_3—it can reduce its average cost by expanding its capital stock and moving to short-run average cost curve SAC_B. This reduces its average cost from *d* to *e*.

capital stock *B*, because in this range SAC_B lies *above* SAC_A. The reason is that a large capital stock means high overhead costs. If very little output is produced, the high overheads will be spread over few units; average costs will be high. Unused capacity is expensive.

To sum up so far: A firm starting with capital stock *A* follows SAC_A as it expands output. However, when output expands beyond q_2, the firm acquires more capital and moves to SAC_B. Thus the lowest average cost it can achieve in the long run—when it can choose between capital stock *A* and stock *B*—is given by the heavily shaded, scalloped curve in Figure 23-1.

The Envelope Curve

In Figure 23-2 we reproduce SAC_A and SAC_B and add two more cost curves, SAC_C and SAC_D, that apply when the capital stock is even larger. If the firm making a long-run decision wishes to produce output q_4, it chooses capital stock *C* and operates on short-run curve SAC_C at point *R*. This is the lowest possible average cost at which the firm can produce q_4. Alternatively, if it wishes to produce q_5, it chooses larger capital stock *D* and operates on SAC_D at point *S*—the lowest average cost at which it can produce q_5. If we join all points like *R* and *S*, the result is the heavy long-run average cost curve LAC. This is called an ***envelope curve*** because it encloses all the short-run SAC curves from below. (While it seems quite easy to draw this curve, the economist who introduced the idea had difficulty, as explained in Box 23-1.)

To draw the smooth envelope curve LAC, we assume that there are many quantities of capital from which the firm can choose, not just the four illustrated. You can imagine many intermediate SAC curves in Figure 23-2. (Nevertheless, it should be recognized that in some cases, capital may be "lumpy." For example, a firm can't acquire half a machine. The "lumpy" case was illustrated in Figure 23-1, where there were no feasible quantities of capital between *A* and *B*, and where the envelope curve was scalloped, not smooth.)

We emphasize that LAC shows the *lowest* average cost at which each output, such as q_4 or q_5, can be produced in the long run, when producers have the opportunity to adjust their quantity of capital. Because the decision to acquire capital depends on expectations regarding future sales, LAC is sometimes called a *planning curve*. Points in the light area below LAC cannot be achieved with present technology and with present factor prices. Points in the darker area above LAC can be chosen. However, a technically efficient firm rejects any such point in favor of a lower-cost point on the LAC.

ECONOMIES OF SCALE

Observe that, until point *R* in Figure 23-2 is reached, long-run average cost falls as output increases. The question arises: How can that be? How can the cost per unit fall when output is increased from, say, 1,000,000 units to 2,000,000?

The answer lies in ***economies of scale.*** Recall from Chapter 3 that economies of scale exist if an *X*% increase in the quantity of *all* inputs results in an increase of more than *X*% in the quantity of output.

The way in which economies of scale lead to falling average costs may be illustrated with an example. Suppose that a firm faces fixed input prices: It won't bid up the wage rate, regardless of how many workers it hires, nor will it bid up the price of any other input like steel or machinery, no matter how much it buys. Because input prices are constant, an increase of, say, 100% in the quantity of all inputs raises total costs by the same 100%. However, because of economies of scale, output rises by more than 100%; that is, output rises faster than total costs. Consequently, there is a decrease in the cost per unit; in other words, average cost falls.[1] Thus we arrive at an important conclusion: Economies of scale mean falling long-run average costs—as long as input prices are constant.

In turn, another question arises: Why do economies of scale exist? There are a number of reasons. Improvements in technology, such as the development of the word processor, may create economies of scale if this new equipment is very expensive. For example, in a very small office with a small output, it may be impossible to justify the expense of a word processor; one ordinary typewriter will do. In a much larger office with much larger output, a word processor may replace several typewriters, at a substantial cost savings. In a factory, greater output may mean that workers can become adept at specialized tasks—like the workers in Adam Smith's pin factory in Chapter 3. It also means that more highly specialized machinery can be used in an assembly-line operation. Furthermore, with a greater output, a firm may be better able to use its talent. If a production line supervisor is able to direct 20 workers but is in charge of only 10, output and the number of workers employed can be doubled without requiring another supervisor. Similarly, the firm's executives may be able to handle more work and responsibility; as the firm grows and output increases, new managers are initially not required.

[1]To illustrate, suppose it initially costs $3,000 to produce two units of output; average cost (LAC) is $3,000 ÷ 2 = $1,500. Now suppose costs double to $6,000, and because of economies of scale, output increases even faster—it triples to six units. LAC falls to $6,000 ÷ 6 = $1,000. In short, LAC falls because output increases faster than cost.

FIGURE 23-2

The long-run envelope cost curve

The SAC curves are the short-run average cost curves that apply if capital stock is fixed at various levels, *A*, *B*, etc. LAC is the long-run average cost curve that encloses all of them from below. It is the appropriate curve for a firm in its long run planning when it is free to select any quantity of capital. For example, to produce q_4, it would select capital stock *C*, thus operating on SAC_C at point *R* and keeping its average cost down to the lowest possible level—that is, the height of *R*. Similarly, to produce q_5, it would select capital stock *D*, thus operating on SAC_D at point *S* and keeping its cost down to the lowest possible level at *S*.

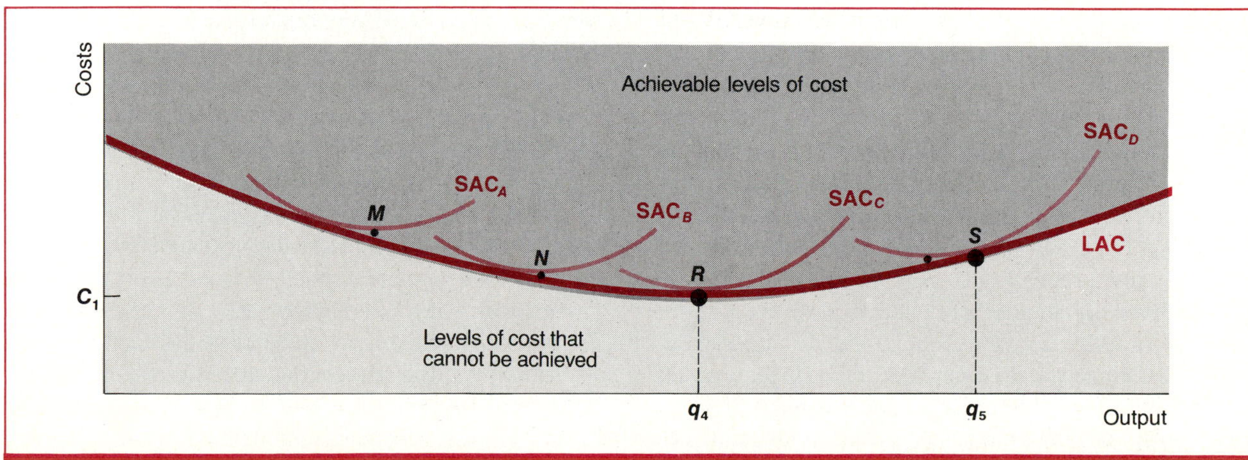

BOX 23-1

IF YOU HAVE HAD TROUBLE DRAWING CURVES IN ECONOMICS, YOU ARE NOT ALONE

The discerning reader will notice in Figure 23-2 that LAC touches the lowest short-run curve (SAC_C) at its minimum point. However, it doesn't touch any other SAC curve at its minimum. For example, it touches SAC_A slightly to the left of its minimum point *M*.

This is such a subtle problem that it was missed by Jacob Viner, the economist who first developed the idea of the "envelope" curve. He asked his draftsman to draw an envelope curve to pass through the minimum point on each SAC curve. His draftsman knew that this couldn't be done, and said so. Viner insisted. So the draftsman presented him with a long-run curve which went through the minimum points on each SAC. But it clearly wasn't an envelope curve. (To confirm this, sketch a curve through the minimum points such as *M* and *N*, and you will see that it is not the envelope curve LAC at all.) Viner permitted the erroneous diagram to appear in his article, complaining that his obstinate draftsman "saw some mathematical objection . . . which I could not succeed in understanding."†

There was a sequel. In the 1930s, Viner was unimpressed by Keynes's new theory of unemployment and income. On his arrival in North America, Keynes was asked to name the world's greatest living economist. He reportedly replied that modesty prevented him from naming the greatest, but the second greatest was surely Viner's draftsman.

†Jacob Viner, "Cost Curves and Supply Curves," 1931; reprinted in George J. Stigler and Kenneth E. Boulding, *Readings in Price Theory* (Homewood, Ill.: Richard D. Irwin, 1952), p. 214.

Therefore, there is less management cost for each unit of output and average costs tend to fall.

With all these reasons for economies of scale, why are there ever ***diseconomies of scale?*** Why does LAC ever begin to rise, as it does at point *R* in Figure 23-2? The supervisor example provides a clue. Suppose output and employment, which have already doubled, now increase by another five times. In addition to the original supervisor, five new ones must now be hired. So far, it seems that average cost need not change, since there has been the same proportionate increase in both output and costs. However, another person may now be required just to coordinate activities among the six supervisors. Thus as a company grows, new tiers of management may have to be created. Eventually a point is reached where management becomes too costly and unwieldy, and decision making becomes too cumbersome and slow. There are just too many people between the vice president who makes the final decisions and the workers on the line who carry them out. Consequently, average costs tend to increase.

The point where decision making becomes unwieldy generally occurs much earlier in agriculture than in industry. Therefore point *R*, where LAC begins to rise, is encountered in agriculture at a relatively small output. One reason is that, on a relatively small farm, the owner-operator has the opportunity and incentive to make crucial decisions with great speed. When the sun shines, the farmer makes hay. When crops are ripe and the weather is threatening, the farmer drops secondary activities and works very hard to harvest the crop. On the other hand, if the farm were part of a huge company, the crop could be lost by the time decision making worked its way through several echelons of management.

Economies of Scale and Diminishing Returns

We shall now show that it is possible for a firm to be facing both economies of scale—as described here—*and* diminishing returns, as described in the last chapter. Since economies of scale mean falling costs and diminishing returns mean rising costs, we might well wonder: How is this possible?

The answer is that the law of diminishing returns is a short-run concept that applies if only one factor (labor) can change, while economies of scale is a long-run concept describing a situation where *all* factors are variable.

In Figure 23-3 we show a firm that is facing both diminishing returns and economies of scale. *In the short run,* as more and more labor is applied to the constant capital stock, marginal costs rise, as shown by arrow *f*. These rising cost are a reflection of diminishing returns. However, as capital increases *in the long run,* costs fall as the firm moves down along LAC (arrow *e*). There are economies of scale. (Economies of scale and diminishing returns are considered in further detail in Appendix 23-A, where we examine the firm's long-run and short-run production functions. Its long-run production function is then used in Appendix 23-B to provide more detail on how a firm maximizes its long-run profit.)

FIGURE 23-3

How a firm can face both economies of scale and diminishing returns

This firm faces diminishing returns, as shown by arrow *f*; its marginal cost curve SMC_A rises in the short run, so long as its capital stock is fixed at level *A*. For this firm, there are also economies of scale, as shown by arrow *e;* its average cost LAC falls in the long run as it is able to increase its use of *all* factors.

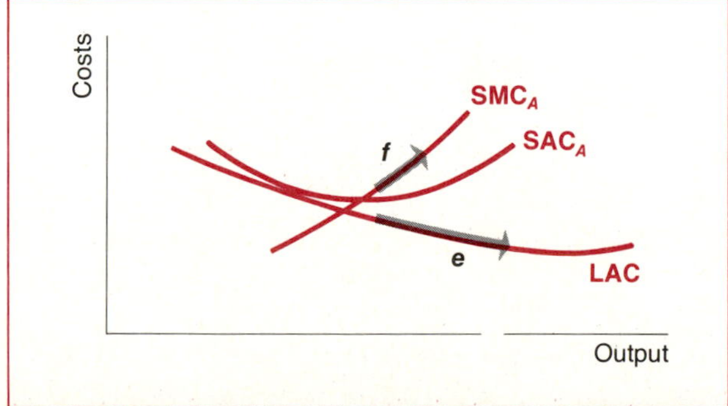

SUPPLY IN THE LONG RUN: THE PERFECTLY COMPETITIVE INDUSTRY

The discussion of long-run costs in the previous section applies in general to firms selling in any type of market—whether it be monopoly, perfect competition, or any other form of market. However, when we come to drawing a supply curve, we must narrow our focus and look at perfectly competitive suppliers.

The Definition of Perfect Competition

The time has come for a more precise description of perfect competition. Thus far, we have emphasized only one of its characteristics:

1. ***Each individual buyer and seller is a price taker.*** That is, no firm can influence the price by deciding to increase or decrease its production, and no buyer can influence the price by deciding to increase or decrease purchases. Because each buyer and seller takes the market price as given, each concentrates on the *quantity* to buy or sell; there is no pricing decision for the individual market participant to make.

This first characteristic follows from two underlying assumptions:

(*a*) ***There are many buyers and sellers,*** with each buying or selling only a trivial fraction of the total market transactions.

(*b*) ***The product is standardized;*** that is, the product is the same regardless of where or by whom it is produced. For example, one farmer's wheat is the same as another's; it doesn't matter to buyers whether wheat is produced in Minnesota or in Montana. In contrast, autos are not standardized. It makes a lot of difference whether you get a Volkswagen or an Oldsmobile. This is one reason why the auto industry is not perfectly competitive.

The second characteristic of a perfectly competitive market is important in any study of long-run supply:

2. ***An absence of barriers to entry.*** That is, firms are free to enter the industry. An example of a barrier to entry has existed in the trucking industry. Until recently, truckers were required to have licenses, and the government granted new licenses only reluctantly. Other examples of barriers to entry will be explained in later chapters.

In a *perfectly competitive industry,* there are many buyers and sellers of a standardized product, with no single buyer or seller having any influence over its price. New firms are free to enter the industry because there are no barriers, such as restrictive government licensing.

The Importance of Entry

Figure 23-4 shows how the entry of new firms affects supply. Initially, with 200 similar firms in the industry, each supplying 10 units at price P_1 in panel *a,* there are 2,000 units supplied to the market in panel *b*. Indeed, at any price such as P_1, the quantity supplied to the market is found by multiplying the supply *s* of the individual firm in panel *a* by 200. In other words, to derive the industry's supply curve S_{200} in panel *b,* we horizontally sum the 200 supply curves of the individual firms in panel *a*. (At the beginning of Chapter 21, a market demand curve was derived in a similar manner, by summing individual demand curves.)

If 100 similar new firms enter, increasing the number to 300, then 3,000 units are supplied at price P_1; the supply curve shifts from S_{200} to S_{300}. Finally, if the number of firms increases to 400, industry supply shifts to S_{400}.

Supply in the Long Run

As price rises in a perfectly competitive industry, new firms are encouraged to enter, increasing the quantity

FIGURE 23-4

With no barriers to entry, industry supply shifts as new firms enter

In a perfectly competitive industry, suppose there are 200 firms like the one shown in panel *a;* then industry supply in panel *b* is S_{200}. If the number of firms increases to 300, the supply becomes S_{300}; and so on.

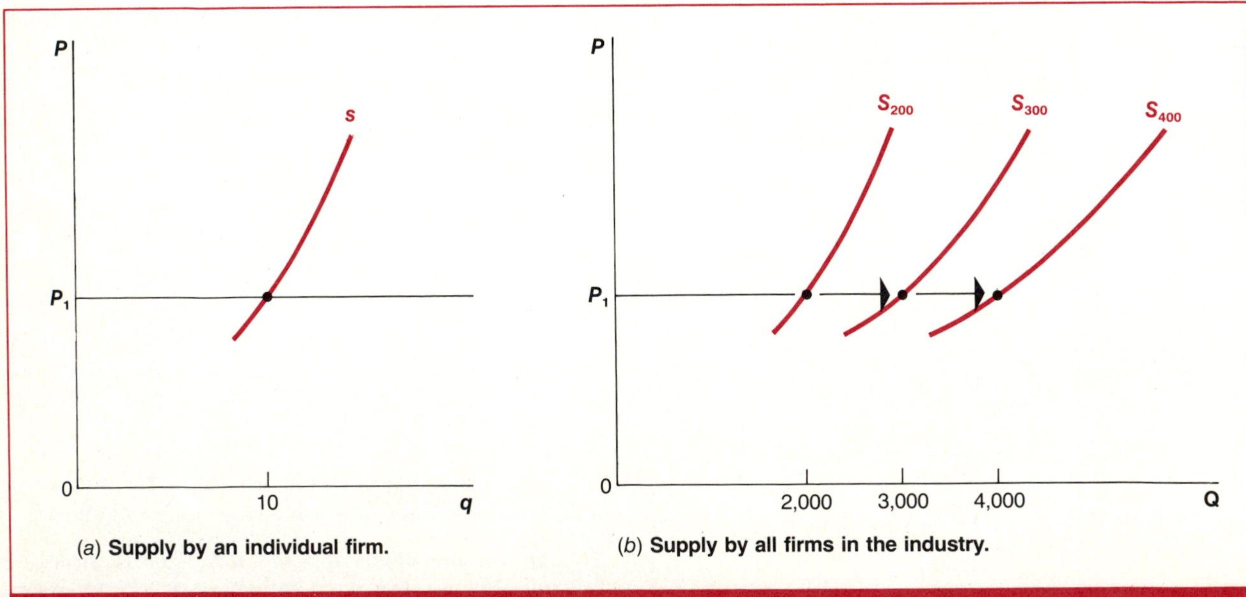

(*a*) **Supply by an individual firm.**

(*b*) **Supply by all firms in the industry.**

supplied. We now ask: How many firms will enter, and what will the equilibrium price be in the long run? Two possibilities should be distinguished.

Case A: Perfectly elastic long-run supply In this first case, every input is uniform, or *homogeneous*. All land is identical, all entrepreneurs are equally skillful, all workers have the same talents, and so on. In addition, the industry is not very large in the economy. As a result, the expansion or contraction of the industry causes no change in the prices of its inputs. In other words, new entrants can obtain the same quality of inputs as existing firms, and inputs are available at stable prices. In these circumstances, the long-run supply curve will be perfectly horizontal.

Figure 23-5 shows why. Panel *a* describes an individual firm while panel *b* shows the demand and supply for the whole industry. Initially, the industry is at point E_1 in panel *b;* price is P_1, and output is 5,000 units. There are 1,000 firms, each producing an output of five units at breakeven point *H* in panel *a*.

Since the individual firm is producing at its breakeven point, P_1 is just sufficient to cover the firm's average cost. Because existing firms are earning no (above-

FIGURE 23-5

Long-run adjustment to an increase in demand

In this diagram, both the individual firm and the industry are initially in equilibrium at price P_1. The firm in panel *a* is at *H*, producing 5 units. The industry in panel *b* is in equilibrium at E_1, with 5,000 units sold. (There are 1,000 firms like the one in panel *a*.)

Now suppose that demand increases from D_1 to D_2. In the short run, the price rises to P_2 and firms make temporary profits shown by the shaded area in panel *a*. New firms enter, shifting supply to the right in panel *b*. The price falls. In the long run, the number of firms in the industry increases to 2,000, with supply shifting to S_{2000}. The new equilibrium is at E_3, with price dropping all the way back to P_1. Faced with price P_1, the individual firm in panel *a* moves back to *H;* it no longer makes profits, and there is no further incentive for new firms to enter. With each of the firms in panel *a* producing 5 units, the 2,000 firms in the industry produce the 10,000 units shown in panel *b*.

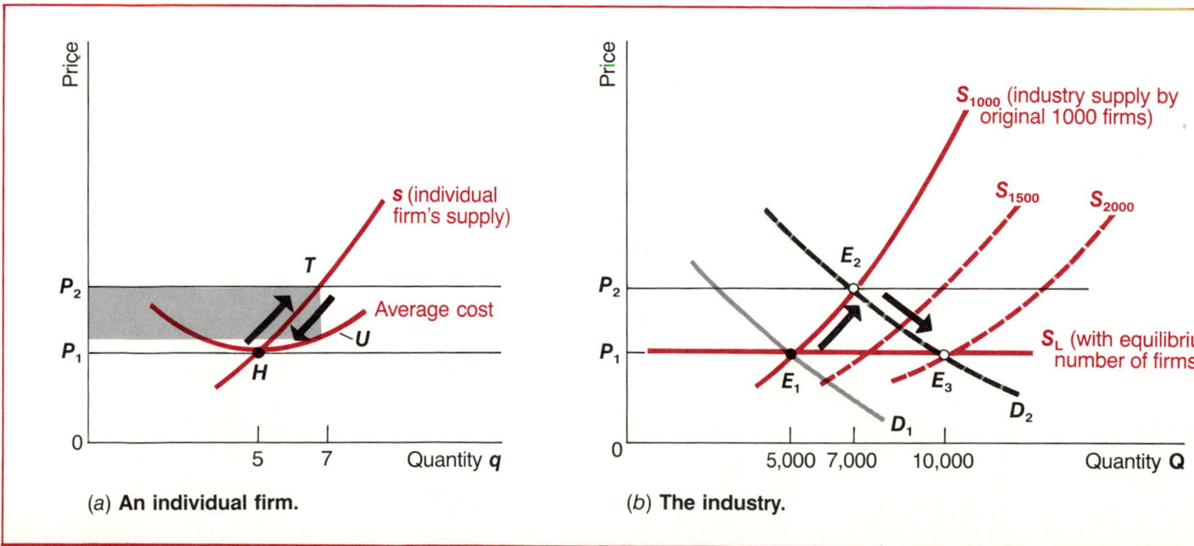

normal) profit, there is no incentive for new firms to enter. Thus, point H in panel *a* is a long-run equilibrium for the firm, and point E_1 in panel *b* is the corresponding long-run equilibrium for the industry.

Now consider what happens in panel *b* if demand increases to D_2. In the short run, the higher demand causes equilibrium to move to E_2, with price rising to P_2. In response to this higher price, each firm in panel *a* moves up its supply curve to *T*, where it is producing seven units and making a temporary profit shown by the shaded gray rectangle.

To explain this profit rectangle, note that the firm's profit *per unit* is *TU*—the difference between its selling price at *T* and its cost per unit at *U*. Its *total* profit is this per unit profit of *TU*—the height of the rectangle—times the seven units it sells—the base of the rectangle. That is, its total profit is the area of this rectangle. (We reemphasize that this is *above-normal* profit. Remember, normal profit is included in the average cost curve.)

Because of the absence of any barriers to entry, this profit will attract new entrants. As the number of firms increases from 1,000 to 1,500, supply in panel *b* shifts from S_{1000} to S_{1500}. This influx of new firms continues until there are 2,000 firms in the industry, with the new supply curve S_{2000} moving the industry to new equilibrium E_3. In the process, price drops all the way back to P_1, and the individual firm in panel *a* responds by moving back to H. Since it no longer makes a profit, there is no longer any incentive for new firms to enter. Thus, E_3 is the new long-run equilibrium for the industry in panel *b*, and H is the long-run equilibrium for the individual firm in panel *a*.

FIGURE 23-6

Long-run adjustment to a decrease in demand

In this diagram, the initial long-run equilibrium (H for the firm, E_1 for the industry) is the same as in Figure 23-5. Now, however, demand decreases from D_1 to D_3 in panel *b*. In the short run, the price falls to P_3, and each firm in panel *a* suffers a loss because this price is too low to cover its average cost. Some firms leave the industry, shifting supply to the left in panel *b*. The price recovers. In the long run, the price rises all the way back to P_1 at new long-run equilibrium E_5. Each of the individual firms that remains in the industry moves back to H in panel *a* and no longer suffers losses. Therefore, there is no further tendency for firms to leave.

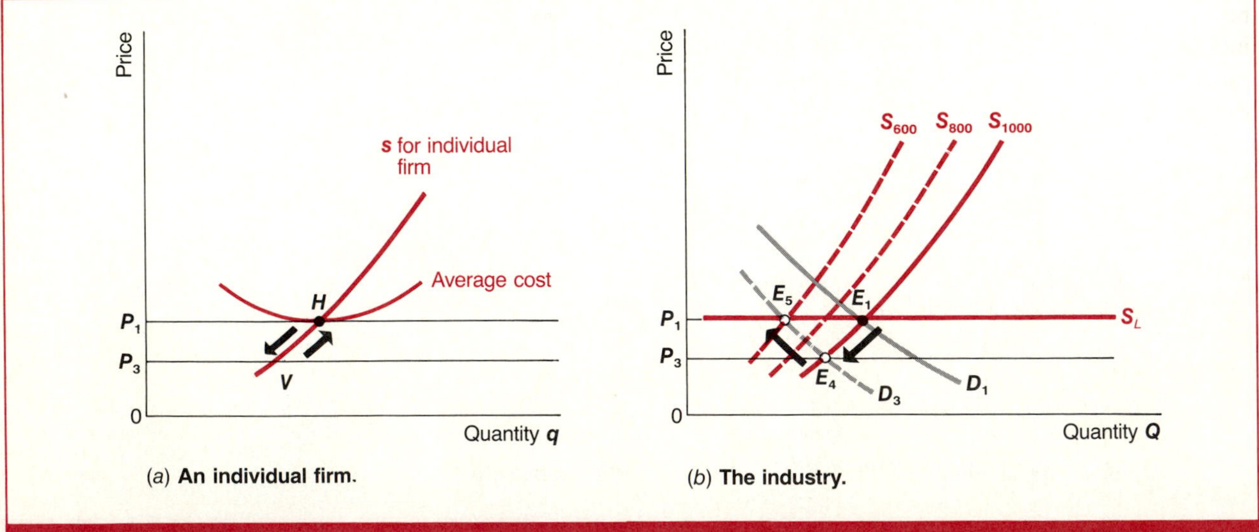

We now construct the long-run supply curve S_L in panel *b* by joining points of long-run equilibrium like E_1 and E_3. Unlike supply curves S_{1000}, S_{1500}, and S_{2000}—each of which is drawn on the assumption of a specific number of firms—the supply curve S_L applies to the long run when there is time for the number of firms to change. Observe that this long-run supply S_L is horizontal—that is, perfectly elastic; in the long run, price doesn't rise at all. Increased demand doesn't raise price because any increase in demand can be satisfied by new firms entering the industry, producing at the same cost as existing firms. It is possible for new firms to produce at this same cost because they have access to inputs of the same quality, at stable prices.

A similar argument applies if demand declines from D_1 to D_3 in Figure 23-6. The industry in panel *b* moves from E_1 to a new short-run equilibrium at E_4, with price depressed to P_3. In response to this lower price, each individual firm in panel *a* moves down its supply curve from *H* to *V*, where it suffers a loss because the new price P_3 is less than its average cost. Therefore, in the long run, firms leave the industry. As a consequence, the supply curve in panel *b* shifts to the left from S_{1000} to S_{800} and eventually to S_{600}, at which point the number of firms in the industry has been reduced from 1,000 to 600. E_5 is the new long-run equilibrium; price has gone back up to P_1, and each individual firm in panel *a* has responded by moving back up to *H*. At this point the firm no longer suffers a loss and there is therefore no further incentive for firms to leave. Again, we see that the long-run industry supply, defined by joining long-run equilibrium points E_1 and E_5, is the horizontal line S_L.

Case B: A rising long-run supply curve The long-run supply curves S_L of many industries are not horizontal; they slope upward to the right. This happens if costs rise as new firms enter, either because these firms bid up the prices of inputs or because they have to use inputs of lower quality. As an example, new wheat growers may find that the highest quality land is already being used by existing producers; the only land still available may be less productive.

Such a case is illustrated in Figure 23-7, where the initial long-run equilibrium is at E_1. An increase in demand from D_1 to D_2 causes a move to a new short-run equilibrium at E_2. At high price P_2, profits of existing firms encourage new entrants. As the number of firms increases from 100 to 150, supply shifts from S_{100} to S_{150} and the new long-run equilibrium is established at E_3. In this case, price does *not* drop all the way back to P_1. Instead, it falls only part way, to P_3. At this price, a new firm producing on the best land that's left—relatively poor land on which costs of production are relatively high—is just able to cover its costs. There is no further incentive for firms to enter. This is why E_3 is the new long-run equilibrium. Therefore, the long-run supply curve S_L, constructed by joining long-run equilibrium

FIGURE 23-7

Long-run adjustment with a rising supply curve

In this diagram, factors of production are not uniform in quality; some land is more suitable for growing wheat than other land. When demand increases from D_1 to D_2, the price rises to P_2 in the short run. The resulting profits to existing producers encourage new entrants into the industry. As the number of firms increases from 100 to 150, the industry supply moves from S_{100} to S_{150}. As a result, equilibrium moves from E_2 to E_3 and price declines from P_1 to P_3. However, it does not fall all the way back down to P_1 because the new entrants are using land less well suited to wheat, and their costs are accordingly higher than P_1.

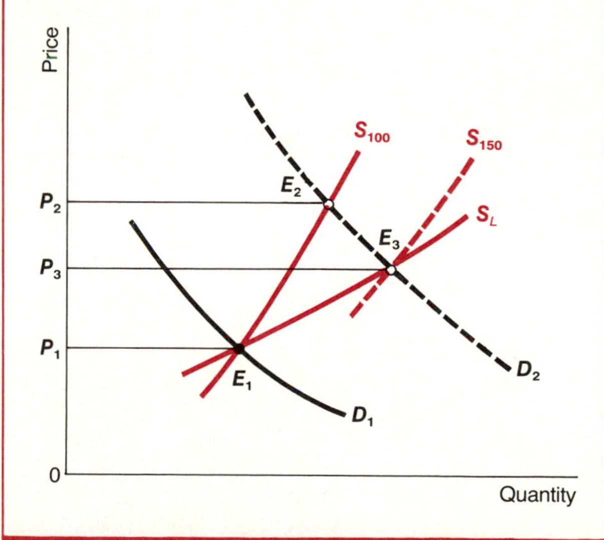

points E_1 and E_3, slopes upward. It is not perfectly elastic. (Another view of the adjustment of the industry in this case is provided in Appendix 23-C.)

HOW MUCH DO PRODUCERS GAIN FROM A HIGHER PRICE?

Just as we examined how a price change will affect consumers in Chapter 21, we now consider how a price change will affect producers.

In Figure 23-8, suppose price is initially $500, with producers responding by producing 30 units at *R*. Their total revenue is rectangle 1—that is, the 30 units (the base of the rectangle) times the $500 price for each unit (the height of the rectangle). If price increases to $700, producers move to new equilibrium *T* with their total revenue increasing to rectangle *OPTQ,* that is, area 1 + 2 + 3. In this move, their total revenue increases by areas 2 + 3. However, only area 3 is a net gain because area 2 represents increased costs. To clarify area 2, note that it is made up of a whole set of marginal cost bars enclosed under the supply curve. For example, the marginal cost of the 34th unit is bar *AB*. Area 2 is simply the sum of all such marginal cost bars as output is increased from 30 to 40 units. It represents the increase in total cost. Therefore, in this case we confirm that area 3 is the net gain to producers.

> ***Essential idea for future chapters:*** **If price rises, the gain to producers may be estimated as the horizontal area to the left of the supply curve between the old and the new prices.[2] If market price falls, producers are worse off by a similar amount.**

(Appendix 23-D explains why this sort of area may be only an approximate measure of the effect on producers.)

This conclusion applies either in the long run or the short—depending on whether we draw the long- or short-run supply curve[3] in Figure 23-8.

FIGURE 23-8

As price rises, producers gain the shaded area

At initial price $500 and equilibrium *R*, 30 units are supplied for a total revenue of 30 × $500 = $15,000, shown as area 1. At a price of $700, equilibrium moves from *R* to *T* and 40 units are sold, for a total revenue of $28,000, or areas 1 + 2 + 3. Total revenue thus increases by areas 2 + 3. Of this increase, area 2 represents the additional cost of producing the 10 more units, while area 3 is the gain to producers.

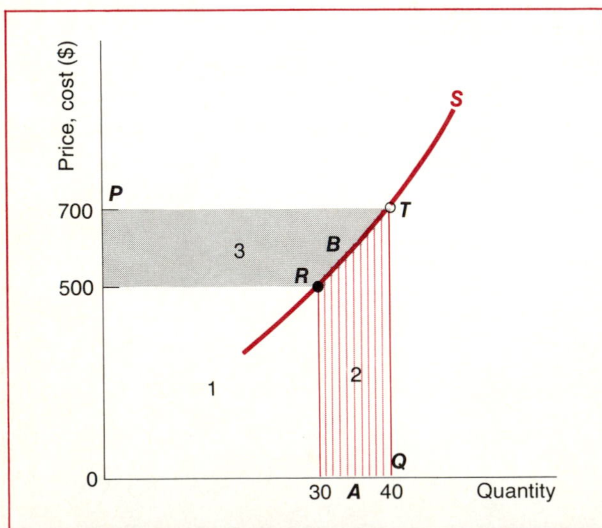

KEY POINTS

1. In the long run, a firm's average cost curve is the "envelope" of all its short-run average cost curves. The long-run envelope curve indicates how average costs change as the firm changes its capital stock.
2. If input prices are constant, economies of scale

[2]This gain is sometimes spoken of as an increase in *producer surplus*. It is analogous to the increase in consumer surplus when the price falls.

[3]However, those who ultimately receive this gain may be quite different in the short and long run. In the short run, the firms already in the industry—for example, the original wheat farmers—capture most or all of this gain in the form of profits. This is true whether they own or rent the land. But in the long run, this gain goes to the owners of the wheat land. The reason is that, as new farmers enter wheat production, they have to use less suitable land. Farmers therefore bid up the rent on the more productive original wheat land. (It doesn't matter to them whether they pay a high rent for productive land or less rent on lower-productivity land.) Owners of the original highly productive land therefore get a windfall in the form of higher rental income—or a higher price when they sell the land. Thus, in the long run, the gain from an increased price goes to factors—such as land—which are particularly suited to the good being produced. These ideas will be developed in more detail in Chapter 35.

cause the long-run average cost curve to slope downward.

3. It is possible for a firm to face both economies of scale (that is, a falling long-run average cost curve) and diminishing returns (a rising short-run marginal cost curve).

4. In a perfectly competitive industry, there are so many buyers and sellers of a standardized product that none can affect price. In addition, there is an absence of barriers to entry by new firms.

5. An industry's long-run supply is more elastic than its short-run supply. One important reason is that, in response to a higher price, new firms enter. As a result, industry output increases.

6. If new firms can enter an industry without facing higher costs, long-run supply is horizontal. However, if new firms face higher costs, long-run supply slopes upward.

7. A price increase provides a gain to producers roughly equal to the area to the left of the supply curve between the old and the new price. A price decrease makes producers worse off by a corresponding amount.

KEY CONCEPTS

envelope cost curve
economies of scale
diseconomies of scale
economies of scale occurring with diminishing returns
standardized product
barriers to entry
homogeneous inputs
long-run supply
entry and exit of producers
effect of a price change on producers

PROBLEMS

23-1. (*a*) Consider a firm operating at point R on the SAC_C and LAC curves in Figure 23-2. Does its short-run supply extend below R? If so, how far? Why?

(*b*) Suppose price falls below C_1 on the left axis. Explain how the firm, with the benefit of hindsight, would view its original decision to enter this industry. What would its output be in the short run? in the long run? Is this another illustration of why supply is more elastic in the long run than in the short run?

23-2. "A firm that is facing diminishing returns (rising costs) cannot be facing economies of scale (falling costs)." Do you agree? Explain.

23-3. In Figure 23-5, the shaded gray area measures the temporary profits which firms make as a result of an increase in demand. In Figure 23-6, demand decreases, and each firm suffers a short-run loss, which was not shown in this diagram. Redraw this figure, showing this temporary loss area.

23-4. Suppose demand increases from D_1 to D_2 in Figure 23-7 and the industry moves from E_1 to new equilibrium E_3. Since new P_3 is above the original P_1, does this mean that all new entering firms will earn an excess profit? Explain.

***23-5.** At new equilibrium E_3 in Figure 23-7, would you expect that the original firms renting the most productive land would be able to hang onto their excess profit? Or might at least some of it be captured by the owners of that very productive land?

APPENDIX 23-A

THE LONG-RUN PRODUCTION FUNCTION

Because the firm can change the quantity of capital in the long run, the options open to it are much broader than in the short run. The broader options are shown in its ***long-run production function.*** An example is given in Table 23-1.

Because the firm is varying the quantity of capital as well as labor, this production function has two dimensions. From left to right, the quantity of labor increases. In the upward direction, the quantity of capital increases. For each combination of capital and labor, the corresponding number in the production function table indicates the maximum quantity of output that the firm can produce. For example, if the firm uses 3 units of capital (*K*) and 5 units of labor (*L*), it can produce 39 units of output. (For the moment, ignore the fact that some numbers in Table 23-1 are shown in color. The reason for this is explained in Appendix 23-B.)

Table 23-1 is the long-run production function of the firm whose short-run production function was shown in Table 22-2. That earlier table now appears as the bottom row of Table 23-1. In fact, the long-run production function is made up of a *whole set* of rows, with each representing a different short-run production function. Once the firm chooses how much capital it will use, it is confined in the short run to operate along the corresponding row of this table. For example, if it chose six units of capital, it is confined in the short run to the top line of the production function. However, in the long run, it can move anywhere in Table 23-1.

***The long-run production function*—or, more simply, the production function—shows various combinations of inputs and the maximum output which can be produced with each combination of inputs. For a simple firm with only two inputs (labor and capital), the production function can be shown by a two-dimensional table like Table 23-1.**

The production function in Table 23-1 can be used to illustrate economies of scale. To do so, we look at what happens when *both* inputs are increased in the same proportion. Suppose the firm doubles its input of labor from 1 to 2 workers, and also doubles its capital from 1 to 2 units. As a result, its output more than doubles, from 5 to 19. Since its output increases by a greater percent than its inputs, it enjoys economies of scale in this range.

However, in the short run, the same firm faces di-

TABLE 23-1

A Hypothetical Firm's Production Function

This simplified production function shows the number of units of output a firm can produce from various combinations of inputs. For example, if it combines 2 units of labor with 1 unit of capital, the second element in the bottom row indicates that it can produce 12 units of output.

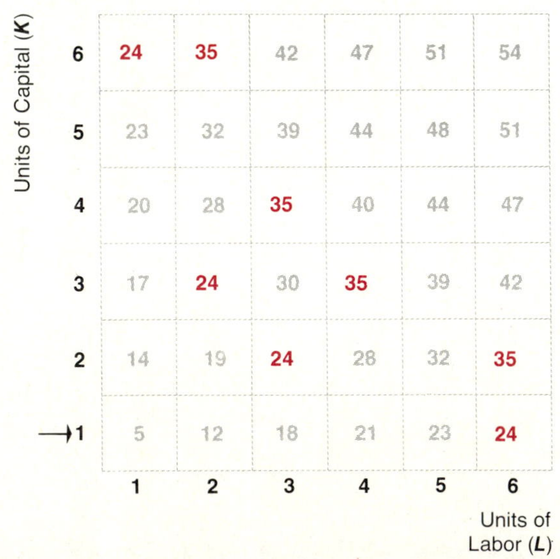

Units of Capital (*K*)						
6	**24**	**35**	42	47	51	54
5	23	32	39	44	48	51
4	20	28	**35**	40	44	47
3	17	**24**	30	**35**	39	42
2	14	19	**24**	28	32	**35**
→1	5	12	18	21	23	**24**
	1	2	3	4	5	6
						Units of Labor (***L***)

minishing returns. To see this, consider what happens when only *one* input—labor—is increased, while the quantity of capital is fixed at, say, 1 unit. The firm is therefore confined to the bottom row in the production function. As it increases the input of labor, the second worker has a marginal product of 7 units (that is, 12 minus 5 units) while the third has a marginal product of 6 units (18 minus 12). Since marginal product is falling, the firm is facing diminishing returns. We therefore conclude that a firm enjoying economies of scale may also face diminishing returns; this confirms the point made in Figure 23-3.

APPENDIX 23-B

THE FIRM'S LONG-RUN PRODUCTION FUNCTION AND ITS PROFIT-MAXIMIZING CHOICE OF INPUTS

In this appendix we study in more detail a question posed at the beginning of Chapter 22: How does a profit-maximizing firm decide which combination of inputs to use? For example, does it use a great deal of labor and little capital, or a great deal of capital and only a small amount of labor? Put this way, the decision applies to the long run, since it is only in the long run that the firm's capital can be changed. The question is: What is the best point for it to select in its long-run production function in Table 23-1? (The same type of decision is made in the short run when there are several variable inputs; for example, if the farmer is deciding on whether to use a lot of fertilizer and only a little labor, or vice versa.)

To decide what combination of inputs to use, the first step it to graph the production function.

STEP 1. GRAPHING THE PRODUCTION FUNCTION: EQUAL-OUTPUT CURVES

First, note that several input combinations in Table 23-1 yield 24 units of output. These appear in color and are reproduced to form the "output = 24" curve in Figure 23-9. Similarly, the "output = 35" curve is also extracted from Table 23-1. These equal-output curves—often called *isoquants*—are similar to the indifference (or equal-utility) curves that were shown earlier in Figure 21-8. Just as the indifference map in that earlier diagram showed a whole family of indifference curves, each representing a higher level of utility as the household moved northeast from the origin, so the production function provides a whole set of equal-output curves that also forms a hill. As the firm moves to the northeast, using more inputs, it reaches higher and higher output levels.

In one respect, however, the equal-output curves of the producer contain more information than the indifference curves of the consumer: Each equal-output curve represents a *specific number* of units of output. On the other hand, all we know about indifference curves is whether they represent "higher" or "lower" levels of satisfaction. We don't know how many "units of utility" they represent.

STEP 2. GRAPHING THE PRICE OF INPUTS: EQUAL-COST LINES

Maximizing profits requires not only the production function information we have just graphed but also information on the price of inputs. How is this graphed? If the price of labor is \$20 per unit, and the price of capital is \$30, straight line c_2 in Figure 23-10 is an *equal-cost line*. This shows all the combinations of labor and capital that can be purchased for a total cost of \$120. (For example, this is the cost the firm will incur at *A* if it buys four units of capital at \$30 per unit and no labor. For more detail, see the legend to Figure 23-10.) Similarly, c_1 represents the input combinations that would cost the firm \$60. You can visualize a whole family of parallel lines showing successively higher costs for the firm as it moves to the northeast.

MAXIMIZING PROFIT

Figure 23-11 brings the previous two diagrams together. Curves q_1 and q_2 are from the firm's production function in Figure 23-9, while the straight lines are equal-cost lines of the type drawn in Figure 23-10. If the firm wishes to produce 24 units of output it will do so at least cost by using the input combination shown by E_2—that is, two units of capital and three of labor. In general:

The firm selects the point on its equal-output curve that is tangent to an equal-cost line.

Any other way of producing this quantity is rejected because it would be more costly. For example, the firm does not use input combination E_4 because this lies on higher cost line c_4.

FIGURE 23-9
The production function in Table 23-1 graphed as a set of equal-output lines
To graph the production function, we extract the red numbers from Table 23-1. For example, each of the input combinations that yield 24 units of output in Table 23-1 is graphed in this diagram. When joined, they become the "output = 24" curve.

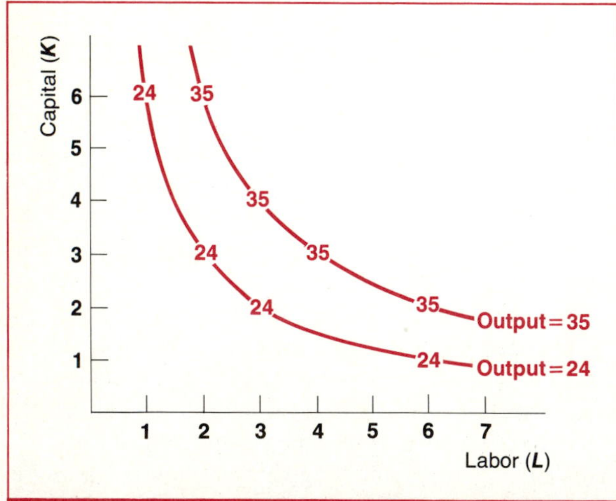

FIGURE 23-10
Equal-cost lines
If the price of labor is \$20 per unit and the price of capital is \$30, c_2 is the equal-cost line that shows all combinations of these two inputs that can be purchased for \$120. For example, combination *D* of 3 units of labor and 2 of capital costs 3(\$20) + 2(\$30) = \$120. Similarly, combination *B* costs 6(\$20) + 0(\$30) = \$120. Parallel line c_1 is also an equal cost line, but it shows all input combinations that would cost \$60. There is a whole family of similar parallel lines, each representing a different cost. If the price of labor relative to capital changes, there is a whole new family of parallel lines with a different slope.

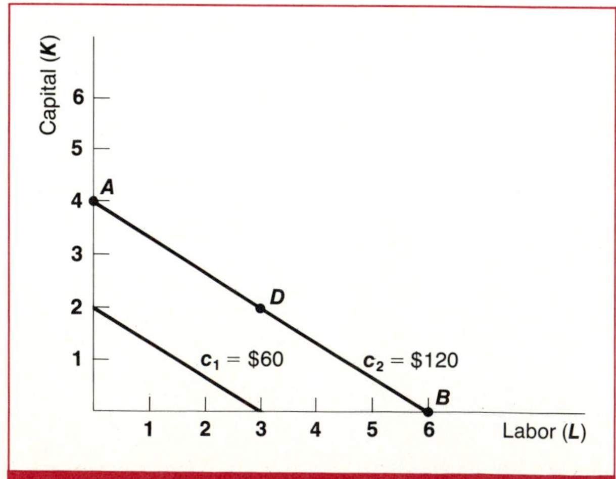

Just as E_2 is the best point for a firm wishing to produce 24 units of output, so E_5 is the best point if it wishes to produce 35 units of output. The final step for the firm is then to examine all points such as E_2 and E_5 and select the one that will maximize its profits. This, then, is the way one can answer our original question: "What point in Table 23-1 does the firm select to maximize its profit?"

FIGURE 23-11
The firm's equilibrium is determined by its equal-output curves and its equal-cost lines
The least cost way of producing 24 units of output is to select input combination E_2 where the equal-output and equal-cost lines are tangent. The firm then calculates its profit at E_2 by comparing its $120 cost with its revenue (24 units of output times whatever its selling price may be). Similarly, to produce 35 units of output, the firm selects tangency point E_5 and evaluates its profit there. Of these tangency points, it selects the one with the greatest profit.

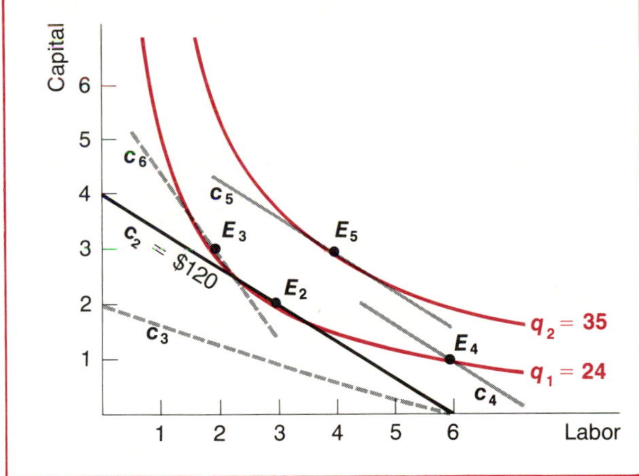

THE EFFECT OF A CHANGE IN THE PRICE OF INPUTS

If the relative price of labor and capital changes, there is a new family of equal-cost lines with a different slope. For example, if the price of capital rises from $30 to $60 while the price of labor is unchanged, flatter line c_3 is now the new $120 equal-cost line. You can visualize the whole family of new equal-cost lines parallel to it. Thus:

The slope of the family of equal-cost lines depends on the relative price of the firm's inputs.

Thus, an equal-cost line for the firm is similar to a consumer's budget line; its slope depends on the relative price of the items being purchased.

Now suppose that capital has become *less* (rather than more) expensive relative to labor, and the equal-cost lines have therefore become steeper. Specifically, suppose the new set of equal-cost lines is c_6 and the family of lines parallel to it. To produce 24 units of output, the firm no longer uses input combination E_2. Instead it picks E_3, the point of tangency with one of its new equal-cost lines. This type of move to the northwest will also occur along q_2 and all the other equal-output lines. Thus, no matter what its initial profit maximizing point, the firm moves northwest, substituting an input that has become relatively less expensive (capital) for the one that has become relatively more expensive (labor).

PROBLEM

23-6. With capital at $30 and labor at $20, how much less is the cost incurred by the firm that operates at E_2 rather than E_4 in Figure 23-11?

With capital at $20 and labor at $30, how much less is its cost if it operates at E_3 rather than E_2?

APPENDIX 23-C

LONG-RUN SUPPLY IN A PERFECTLY COMPETITIVE INDUSTRY WITH NONUNIFORM FACTORS OF PRODUCTION

The first three panels of Figure 23-12 display the long-run marginal cost curves of three wheat-producing firms. (For every long-run average cost curve, we may draw a corresponding marginal cost curve.) These three firms represent the large number which are either producing wheat or are willing to start producing if the price rises enough.

At price P_1, the only firm willing to produce wheat is firm *A*. It is the firm with the land that is most suitable for wheat and is the only one which can produce with an average cost as low as P_1. Thus total industry supply in the last panel is just arrow *f*, the quantity supplied by firm *A*.

Although price P_1 is not high enough to induce firms *B* and *C* to enter the industry, suppose price rises. At P_2, industry supply is substantially augmented as firm *B* starts to produce and supplies the quantity indicated by arrow *g*. As price rises above P_2, market supply becomes the horizontal sum of the individual supplies of firms *A* and *B*. Finally, at price P_3, firm *C* is attracted into production, and market supply is shown by the three arrows representing the supplies of all three firms. Thus the industry supply curve is the heavy line in the last panel, representing the horizontal sum of the supplies of the individual firms. It has an upward slope because differences in the quality of wheat land cause differences in the costs of the three wheat-producing firms.

FIGURE 23-12

A rising long-run industry supply

At P_1, market supply is arrow *f* from firm A, the only firm able to produce at that low price. At P_2, A's supply is augmented by arrow *g* from firm B, since B is barely induced into production. At price P_3, firm C also starts to produce (arrow *k*). Thus, at any price, industry supply *S* in the last panel is the horizontal sum of the supplies of all individual firms.

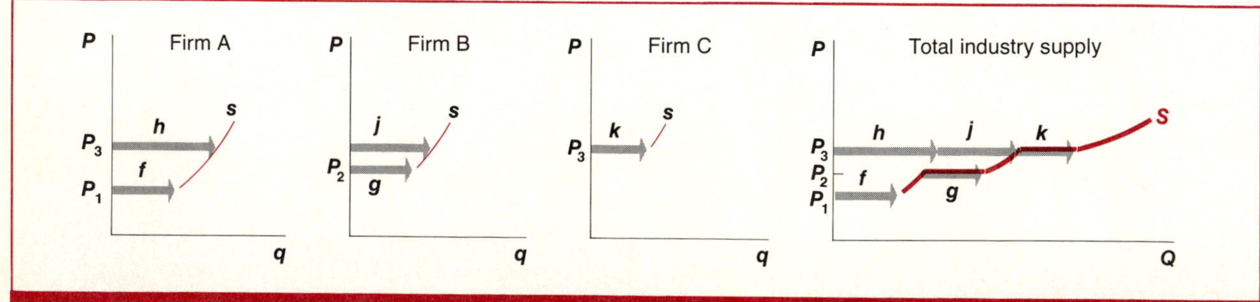

APPENDIX 23-D

USING THE INDUSTRY SUPPLY CURVE TO MEASURE THE GAIN TO PRODUCERS:

SOME COMPLICATIONS

As we have seen in Figure 23-7, the long-run industry supply curve may slope upward because of different qualities of factors of production, such as different qualities of wheat land. In this case, a rise in the price of the product results in a gain for those who provide the factors of production. Specifically, the owners of the better qualities of land receive higher rents. These gains were measured in Figure 23-8 by the area to the left of the supply curve between the old and the new price. In this appendix, we consider other forces that may affect the long-run slope of the supply curve, and may therefore make this area of gain to producers an imperfect measure. For example:

Case 1. First, the long-run supply curve may slope upward even if all factors of production are of uniform quality. To illustrate, the supply of trucking services may slope upward even if the factors of production (drivers, trucks, etc) are of equal quality. The reason is that, as more and more trucks are operated, the roads become congested. Trucks move more slowly, and as a consequence the costs of the trucking companies rise. This makes the supply curve of trucking services slope upward.

In this case, an increase in the demand for trucking may cause an increase in the long-run equilibrium price *without* any gain for producers—in particular, without any benefit to *any* factor of production in the trucking industry. The higher price may simply be dissipated in the higher costs resulting from road congestion.

Case 2. It is even possible for the long-run supply curve to slope *downward* if all factors of production are of uniform quality. Consider the case of a metal-fabricating industry made up of a number of competitive firms located in a small city near Chicago. As the industry grows, the costs facing each firm may fall. This may occur, for example, because the Pittsburgh supplier who is shipping unprocessed steel to this industry is now delivering much more. There are economies of scale in shipping, and the resulting savings may be passed along to the firms buying steel.

Case 3. Finally, there may be a combination of forces at work. For example, the long-run supply curve of the metal-fabricating industry may be horizontal because two sets of forces are balanced: As this industry expands, the fall in the price of unprocessed steel may be just offset by the rise in rents on land being used by this industry. In this case, an increase in output does provide a gain to those who supply factors of production—specifically, a gain to the owners of land. This gain occurs even though the supply curve is horizontal and therefore provides no indication whatsoever of any gain for producers from expansion of this industry.

To sum up: Case 1 shows that the area to the left of the supply curve may *exaggerate* the gain for producers in an expanding industry; it may suggest a gain where none exists. On the other hand, case 3 illustrates how the area to the left of the supply curve may *understate* the gain to producers. In that case, there *was* a gain, but it couldn't be shown to the left of the supply curve because the supply curve was horizontal.

Because of such complications, the supply curve can be used only as a rough first approximation in measuring how producers gain from an increase in price.

CHAPTER 24

PERFECT COMPETITION AND ECONOMIC EFFICIENCY

Under perfect competition, the business dodoes, dinosaurs and great ground sloths are in for a bad time—as they should be.

R. H. BORK AND W. S. BOWMAN, JR.

In Chapter 21, we examined how consumers in a perfectly competitive market respond to the price they face. In Chapters 22 and 23, we studied how producers on the other side of such a market respond. In this chapter, we bring these two sides together in order to ***describe how a perfectly competitive market operates***. This will then be used to ***evaluate its performance*** from the point of view of society as a whole. How well does a perfectly competitive market deliver the goods and services the public wants?

We shall see that, if two important assumptions are satisfied, a perfectly competitive market does provide an efficient result: Neither too much nor too little output is produced. In future chapters, we shall see why other market structures typically do not result in allocative efficiency. For example, we shall see in the next chapter that monopoly is not efficient: Too little output is produced.

Two Important Assumptions

Thus far, we have made no distinction between the *private benefit* a good provides to those who buy it, and the benefit it provides to society as a whole—its *social benefit*. Often the two are the same. For example, when someone buys beefsteak, the only benefit that goes to society is the benefit received by that individual. There is no additional benefit to anyone else. However, private and social benefit don't always coincide in this way. For example, the benefit to society of services provided by professional gardeners may include not only the benefit enjoyed by those who buy these services, but also some benefit to other individuals in the neighborhood.

But for now, we assume away this complication. We assume that the purchaser gets all the benefit from the good; that is, the benefit received by the purchaser represents the total benefit to society. Thus:

Assumption 1. **Social benefit is the same as private benefit. More precisely, the marginal benefit of a good to society as a whole—which we shall call MB_S—is the same as MB, its marginal benefit to those who consume it. Either can be measured by the height of the market demand curve.**

$$MB_S = MB \text{ to consumers} \quad (24\text{-}1)$$

We make a similar assumption about cost:

Assumption 2. **The cost of a good to society is the same as the private cost incurred by producers of this good. More precisely, the marginal cost of a good to society as a whole—which we shall call MC_S—is the same as MC, its marginal cost to producers. Either is shown by the height of the market supply curve.**

$$MC_S = MC \text{ to producers} \quad (24\text{-}2)$$

For example, the cost to society of producing wheat is generally just the cost incurred by wheat farmers. However, there are again exceptions. The cost to society of paper may be not only the private cost incurred by the firms producing it, but also the cost to those people living downstream who suffer if these firms dump polluting wastes into the river.

Exceptions to these two assumptions are important and will be the focus of attention in Chapters 28, 29, and 30. But until then, we will limit ourselves to the large number of cases where these assumptions are valid.

With these assumptions in hand, we now turn to a detailed description of a perfectly competitive market.

HOW A PERFECTLY COMPETITIVE MARKET WORKS

Figures 24-1 and 24-2 illustrate the decisions of many consumers and many producers in a perfectly competitive market. In the middle panel of Figure 24-1, note that supply and demand are equal at an equilibrium output of 100 units and a $10 price. At this equilibrium, the quantity purchased by each consumer is shown in the panels on the left, while the quantity sold by each producer is shown in the panels on the right. (As always, we use only a few consumers to represent the very large number who participate in this market, and we do the same for producers.)

In Figure 24-1, the central panel showing *S* and *D* is so important that it is reproduced in Figure 24-2. In panel *a* we show what's happening to consumers, as originally described in Figure 21-3. Consumers make the decision that is best for them by continuing to purchase until *their marginal benefit equals their marginal cost.* Their marginal cost is what they have to pay for each additional unit of the good, that is, its price *P*. Thus consumers purchase 100 units where their marginal benefit equals the price.

For consumers: $$\text{MB} = P \tag{24-3}$$

FIGURE 24-1

Individual consumers and producers in a perfectly competitive market

In panel *b*, market demand *D* reflects the individual demands in panel *a*, while market supply *S* reflects the supplies of individual firms in panel *c*. The perfectly competitive solution, where *S* and *D* intersect, is at a price of $10 and an output of 100 units. The bars in panel *a* show how each consumer continues to purchase until marginal benefit MB equals the $10 price, and the bars in panel *c* show how each firm produces to the point where its marginal cost *MC* is equal to this $10 price. Since each consumer's MB is therefore equal to each producer's MC, any change in production or consumption would result in an efficiency loss.

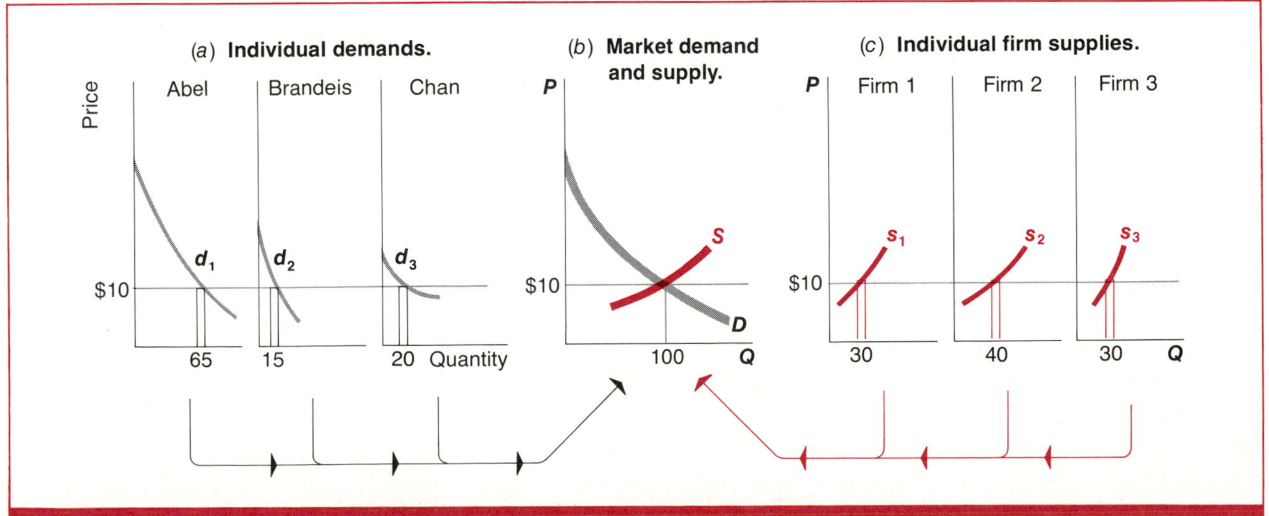

In panel *b* we show what's happening to producers, as originally described in Figure 22-3. Producing firms make the decision that is best *for them* by continuing to produce and sell this good until *their marginal benefit equals their marginal cost*. In perfect competition, the marginal benefit which they get from selling one more unit is the price *P*. Therefore they produce 100 units.

For producers: $P = \text{MC}$ (24-4)

From these two equations, it follows that

$$\text{Consumers' MB} = \text{MC to producers} \quad (24\text{-}5)$$

as we see in panel *c*. Finally, recall the two key assumptions introduced earlier (equations 24-1 and 24-2). Because of these two assumptions, the equation above becomes:

$$\text{MB}_S = \text{MC}_S \quad (24\text{-}6)$$

That is, the marginal benefit to society equals the marginal cost to society. This is the condition that provides an efficient outcome for society as a whole, as we will confirm in the next section.

The efficient outcome for society is where

$$\text{MB}_S = \text{MC}_S$$

This occurs in perfect competition, if social benefits are the same as benefits to consumers and social costs are the same as costs to producers.

FIGURE 24-2
The competitive market: The equalization of marginal benefit and marginal cost
This is an elaboration of panel *b* in Figure 24-1.

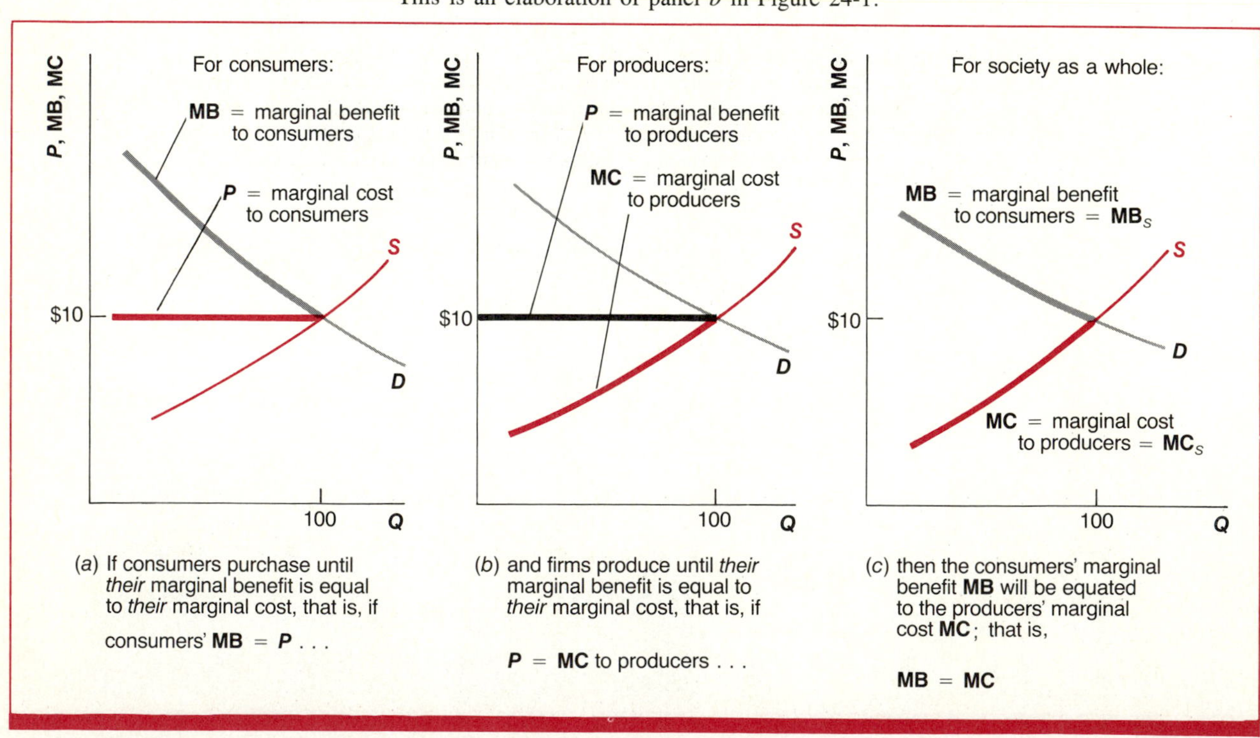

P, MB, MC
For consumers:
MB = marginal benefit to consumers
P = marginal cost to consumers
S
$10
D
100
Q
(a) If consumers purchase until their marginal benefit is equal to their marginal cost, that is, if
consumers' MB = P . . .
P, MB, MC
For producers:
P = marginal benefit to producers
MC = marginal cost to producers
S
$10
D
100
Q
(b) and firms produce until their marginal benefit is equal to their marginal cost, that is, if
P = MC to producers . . .
P, MB, MC
For society as a whole:
MB = marginal benefit to consumers = MB_S
S
$10
D
MC = marginal cost to producers = MC_S
100
Q
(c) then the consumers' marginal benefit MB will be equated to the producers' marginal cost MC; that is,
MB = MC

To sum up so far: Under perfect competition, with consumers making *their* best decision by equating *their* marginal benefit and marginal cost in panel *a*, and producers making *their* best decision by equating *their* marginal benefit and marginal cost in panel *b*, the result in panel *c* is an efficient output for society as a whole.

This is such an important conclusion in economics that we emphasize it in Box 24-1 and now illustrate it with two examples.

DEMONSTRATING WHY PERFECT COMPETITION IS EFFICIENT

It has been shown that, under specified conditions, perfect competition equates the marginal benefit to society MB_S and the marginal cost to society MC_S. We will now demonstrate that, because $MB_S = MC_S$, this outcome is efficient; we can't do better.

In Figure 24-3 we reproduce the market supply and demand curves from panel *c* of Figure 24-2. Now suppose output is expanded beyond the perfectly competitive quantity of 100 units where marginal benefit to society equals marginal cost to society. Specifically, suppose the quantity is the 140 units shown in panel *a*. This outcome is inefficient, as we can see by considering a single unit, *c*, of this additional output. The benefit it provides to society is shown by the empty bar, the height of the demand curve. However, its cost is even larger, as shown by both the empty bar and the red bar—that is, the height of the supply curve. Thus the cost of this unit exceeds the benefit it provides; there is a net loss to society shown by the red bar. The sum of all similar losses on all the other excess units of output in the range between 100 and 140 is shown by the red triangle. This is the efficiency loss from producing too much.

On the other hand, suppose that for some reason output is less than 100 units—say, the 60 units shown in panel *b*. This outcome is also inefficient, as we can see by considering one of the units that is not longer pro-

BOX 24-1

CONDITIONS THAT RESULT IN AN EFFICIENT SOLUTION

Since MB and MC represent marginal private benefits and costs, and MB_S and MC_S represent marginal social benefits and costs, then:

If social and private benefits are the same,	$MB_S = MB$	(24-1)
and if consumers in a perfectly competitive market act in their own self-interest by purchasing up to the point where their marginal benefit equals price	$MB = P$	(24-3)
and if producers in a perfectly competitive market act in their own self-interest by producing up to the point where their marginal cost equals price,	$P = MC$	(24-4)
and if private and social costs are the same,	$MC = MC_S$	(24-2)
then Adam Smith's "invisible hand" works; the pursuit of private interest by both consumers and producers yields a result that is in the interest of society as a whole	$MB_S = MC_S$	(24-6)

That is, there is an efficient solution.

duced, say *d*. Since its cost would have been the empty bar under the supply curve, and its benefit the empty bar *plus* the red bar under the demand curve, the net benefit to society of producing it would have been the red bar. Or to put the same point another way, society incurs the loss of this red bar because this potentially beneficial unit is not produced. The sum of all such losses through the range of restricted output from 100 down to 60 is the red triangle. This is the efficiency loss from producing too little. An example is the rent control program described earlier in Box 4-1. When the government sets a low price, suppliers reduce their output. This decline in quantity results in an efficiency loss from producing too little, just like in panel *b*.

Since there is an efficiency loss if either more or less is produced then the perfectly competitive output where marginal benefit and cost to society are equal—in our example, 100 units—this is the output that is efficient. Only if output is at this level do we avoid a red efficiency loss.

This idea of an efficiency loss—sometimes called a "deadweight" loss—is so important in the study of microeconomics that you should be sure you have mastered Figure 24-3 before proceeding. In particular, we emphasize:

> ***Idea essential for future chapters:* An efficiency loss—or deadweight loss—occurs whenever there is a move away from the output where the marginal benefit to society is equal to the marginal cost to society. Such an efficiency loss from producing too much or too little can be shown graphically by one of the red triangles in Figure 24-3.**

Finally, as an alternative demonstration of why effi-

FIGURE 24-3
Inefficient quantities of output

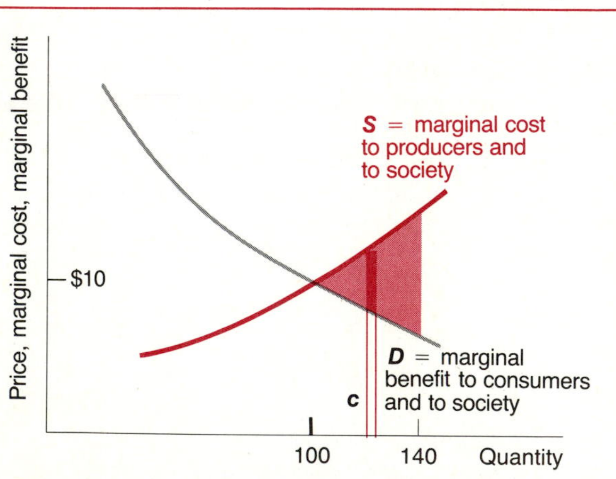

(*a*) **Too much.** Output is 140, which is greater than the perfectly competitive equilibrium of 100 where marginal benefit to society is equal to marginal cost to society. On each of these 40 additional units there is an efficiency loss because marginal cost (the height of the supply curve) exceeds marginal benefit (the height of the demand curve). The total efficiency loss from all such units of excess output is the shaded red triangle.

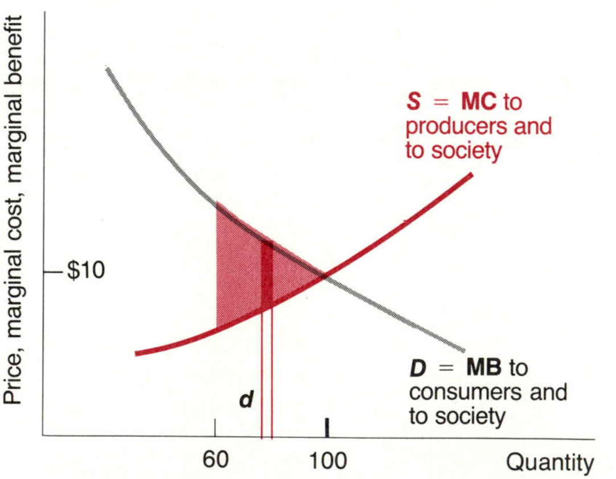

(*b*) **Too little.** Output is restricted to only 60 units, less than the perfectly competitive level of 100. On each of these 40 units foregone, marginal benefit (the height of the demand curve) would have exceeded marginal cost (the height of the supply curve). There is therefore an efficiency loss because these potentially beneficial units are not produced. This loss is shown as the shaded red triangle.

ciency occurs at the perfectly competitive output—where marginal benefit and cost to society are equal—return to Figure 24-1, where we first described the market we have been studying so far in this chapter. Suppose you are an all-powerful bureaucrat or czar and think you can do better than this perfectly competitive solution. Specifically, suppose that you arbitrarily order that, instead of the equilibrium quantity of 100 units, 40 more units are to be produced. Try as you like, you cannot avoid a social loss on those additional units. On the one hand, they must cost more than $10 to produce. Regardless of the firms you select to produce them in panel *c*, those firms will have to move to the right, *up* their supply curves to a higher marginal cost. At the same time, those additional units will be consumed by individuals in panel *a* who value them at less than $10. No matter who gets to consume these units, those individuals will move to the right, *down* their demand curves to a lower marginal benefit. Because the cost of each additional unit is greater than $10, and the benefit it provides is less than $10, there is a net social loss, that is, an efficiency loss. You thought you could do better. In fact, you did worse.

A further discussion of efficiency is provided in Box 24-2 and in Appendix 24-A at the end of this chapter.

FREE ENTRY AND ECONOMIC EFFICIENCY

In defining perfect competition, one of the key requirements is the absence of barriers to entry. We shall now show that, if this condition is not met, inefficiency may result. To illustrate, suppose that the third firm in Figure 24-1 has been blocked out of this market for some reason; for example, suppose it's a firm that needs a government license, and it has been turned down. Because its supply s_3 would not exist, total market supply in the center panel would be less, that is, it would lie to the left of *S*. You can visualize (or sketch in) this new supply

BOX 24-2

PARETO AND THE ELIMINATION OF DEADWEIGHT LOSS

With a bit of extra effort and imagination, we can increase our understanding of the important idea of efficiency.

A change that will make one individual better off without hurting anyone else is called a *Pareto-impovement,* after Italian Vilfredo Pareto, who originated the idea. If we have made all such Pareto-improvements, we arrive at a ***Pareto-optimum.*** This is exactly what economists mean by an efficient solution. It means that all deadweight losses have been eliminated—that is, all possible Pareto-improvements have been made.

The idea of a Pareto-improvement can be illustrated by referring back to Figure 24-1. Suppose that initially Brandeis gets one less unit than we have shown there (namely, 14 units), while Chan gets one more (21 units). A Pareto-improvement is now possible because we can make Chan better off without hurting anyone else—that is, without hurting Brandeis, the only other person involved. Here's how. Let Chan sell that one unit to Brandeis for $10. Chan benefits from this transaction: Because he values his twentieth unit at $10, he values his twenty-first unit—the one he is giving up—at less than $10; so he benefits when he receives $10 for it. At the same time, Brandeis has not been hurt because he values the unit he receives—his fifteenth—at exactly the same $10 that he pays for it.

This Pareto-improvement is possible because, initially, all producers and consumers did not value their last unit equally. But with this transaction, we have reached the perfectly competitive solution in Figure 24-1, where all consumers and producers *do* value their last unit equally, at $10. That is, the marginal benefit MB for every consumer is equal to the MB for every other consumer, and is also equal to the marginal cost MC for every producer. Consequently, any further Pareto-improvement is impossible. Therefore this perfectly competitive solution is Pareto-optimal, that is, efficient.

curve. Note that the equilibrium output where this new supply intersects D is less than the efficient output level of 100, and a triangular efficiency loss would therefore result: Potentially beneficial units of output would not be produced because this third firm would have been unable to enter this market and produce them.

OTHER TYPES OF EFFICIENCY

Thus far we have shown only how a perfectly competitive market can provide *allocative efficiency*. How does this market measure up in terms of *technological* and *dynamic* efficiency?

Technological, or Technical, Efficiency

Technological, or technical, efficiency means avoiding outright waste. Thus a restaurant is technically inefficient if it produces a standard meal using twice as much labor as other restaurants. A construction firm is technically inefficient if it destroys its machinery because it fails to keep it oiled. In brief, technical inefficiency exists if there is poor management and unnecessarily high costs. To illustrate in panel *a* of Figure 24-4, technical inefficiency raises the firm's average cost curve up to AC_2, compared with the average cost curve AC_1 of a technically efficient firm.

Perfect competition works toward technical efficiency as well as allocative efficiency. If a firm is inefficient and is therefore producing at a high-cost point, such as F, it won't be able to survive in competition with technically efficient firms that produce with average costs at G. Thus, there is a tendency for inefficient old firms to go the way of the dinosaurs—to be driven out of business by their existing competitors or by new firms with lower costs. (Note how perfect competition puts pressure on firms to produce at the lowest point on their

FIGURE 24-4
How perfect competition promotes technical and dynamic efficiency

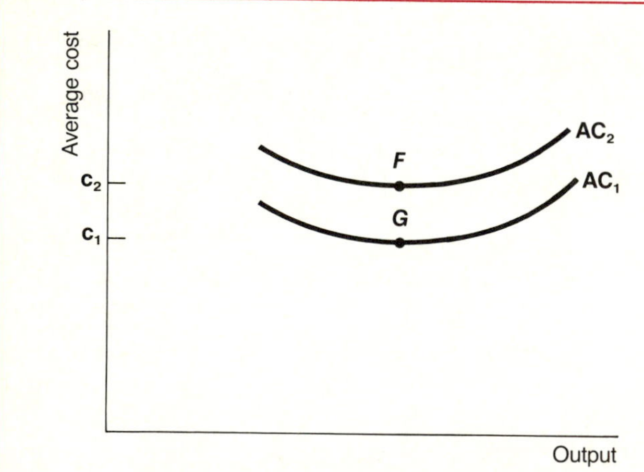

(*a*) Perfect competition results in technological efficiency because it forces inefficient firms operating on AC_2 (at a point like *F*) down to AC_1 to a point like *G*.

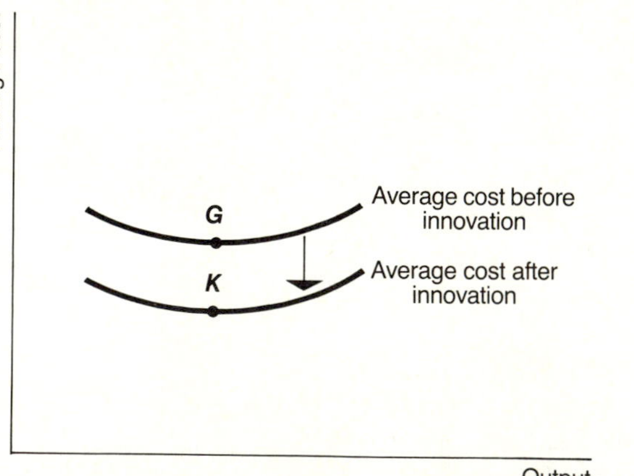

(*b*) In this case an innovation has shifted the average cost curve down. Under perfect competition, firms at a point like **G** are now forced down to a "new technology" point like ***K*** or are driven out of business. In this sense, perfect competition induces dynamic efficiency—although in some other respects other market forms may be superior.

average cost curves. We also saw this in our earlier example in Figure 23-6, where the firms that survive in the long run all produce at the lowest point, *H*.)

In contrast to the firm in perfect competition, a monopoly firm may be protected from the pressures of competition. If it has a stranglehold on a market—because of a patent, for example—it can survive even if management is sloppy; it doesn't have to worry about facing new competitors. But even though monopoly does not *have* to achieve technical efficiency, it still has an incentive to do so; greater technical efficiency means greater profits. Therefore, in later chapters we will generally show monopoly firms producing on their technically efficient average cost curves.

Dynamic Efficiency

Dynamic efficiency exists when changes are occurring at the best rate—for example, when new technology is being developed and adopted at the best rate. While a competitive market gets high marks for promoting allocative efficiency and technical efficiency, its superiority is less clear in terms of dynamic efficiency.

In some ways, perfect competition does indeed promote dynamic efficiency. Suppose, for example, that a new process or new invention has been discovered that reduces costs. This shifts the average cost curve down as shown in panel *b* of Figure 24-4. Firms that do not lower their costs by adapting to this new technology will be left producing at a point such as *G*, at a disadvantage in competing with firms using the new technology and producing at a point such as *K*. Thus, firms that ignore new technology and are consequently unable to compete will also go the way of the dinosaurs. We conclude that, by forcing firms to *adopt* new technology, perfect competition generates dynamic efficiency.

However, let's go one step further and ask the question: What sort of market does the best job of *creating* new technology in the first place? There is considerable debate over this question, with many contending that, in this respect, some other market forms are superior. One argument is that it is easier for a large monopolistic firm to finance the research necessary for many innovations. Furthermore, a large firm has more incentive to engage in research, since it is large enough to reap many of the gains. In contrast, no individual farmer has much incentive to try to develop a new strain of wheat; most of the gains would go to other farmers.

In conclusion, the competitive market scores high in two of the three aspects of efficiency—including allocative efficiency, which will be our focus in the next few chapters.

MARKET PRICE AS A SCREENING DEVICE

Every economy must have some device to determine who will consume a scarce good and who will not. In our economy, market price plays that role by acting as a barrier that must be overcome by buyers. In panel *a* of Figure 24-5, we see a competitive market in which 1,000 units are sold at a $15 price. In panel *b*, we see that this price has blocked out consumers who aren't willing to pay at least this $15 price. In panel *c*, we see that this same price also acts as a barrier, blocking out all high cost producers who are unable to sell this good for $15. Thus a perfectly competitive price screens out unenthusiastic buyers and high-cost sellers; both groups are excluded from the market because of one simple criterion—they are unwilling or unable to meet the market price.

PREVIEW: PROBLEMS WITH THE COMPETITIVE MARKET

Thus far, we have provided a very rosy picture of how well perfectly competitive markets work. The examples of inefficient outcomes occurred when the government intervened to overrule the workings of a competitive market. When the government czar dictated output, too much was produced. When the government set a rent ceiling, too little housing was produced. Indeed, up to this point, the analysis has had a strong laissez faire message: The government should leave the market alone, its wonders to perform.

However, this gives a distorted view of the American economy. In particular, all four basic conditions listed in Table 24-1 must be met if the free market is to lead to an efficient outcome.

In practice, these conditions are often violated; in Table 24-1 we show how they may be violated, and the chapters that deal with each case. When they are violated, a laissez faire economy will operate inefficiently. In this case, government intervention may make the economy work more efficiently, not less. Furthermore, *even when all four conditions are met,* the outcome will not necessarily be quite as good as this chapter has so far suggested, as we shall now see.

FIGURE 24-5
Price as a barrier that screens buyers and sellers in a competitive market

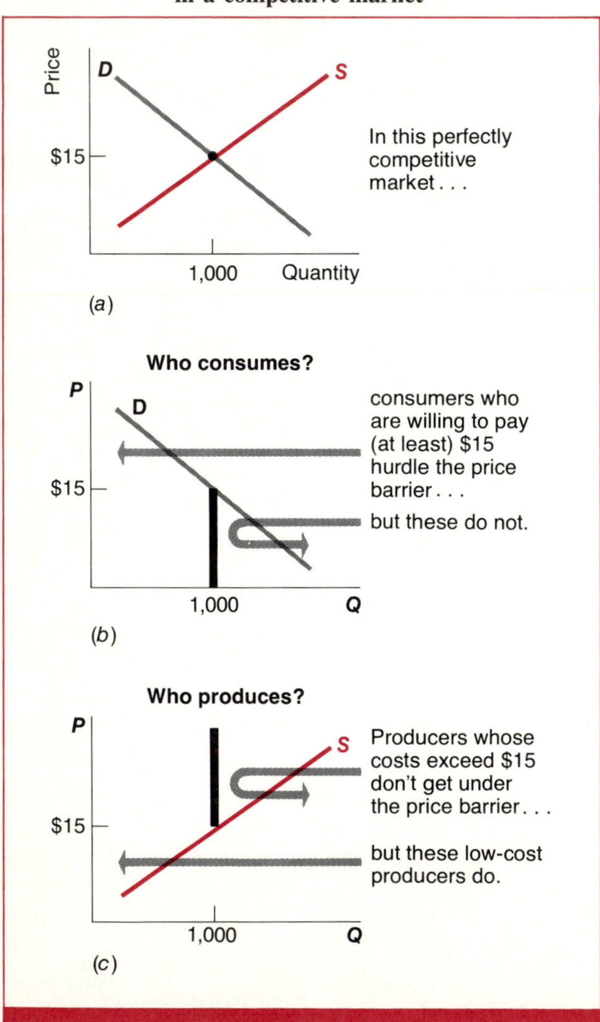
Price
D
S
$15
In this perfectly competitive market . . .
1,000
Quantity
(a)
Who consumes?
P
D
$15
consumers who are willing to pay (at least) $15 hurdle the price barrier . . .
but these do not.
1,000
Q
(b)
Who produces?
P
S
$15
Producers whose costs exceed $15 don't get under the price barrier . . .
but these low-cost producers do.
1,000
Q
(c)

A RESERVATION ABOUT THE PERFECTLY COMPETITIVE SOLUTION: IT DEPENDS ON THE DISTRIBUTION OF INCOME

Let's now return to Figure 24-1. Suppose that Abel has a higher income than Brandeis and this is the reason why he has greater demand for this good. (Remember, demand depends both on desire for the product *and* ability to pay. And with his higher income, Abel has a greater ability to pay.) In Figure 24-6 we reproduce Figure 24-1, making only one change: We suppose that the incomes of Abel and Brandeis are reversed. Brandeis now has the high income and hence high demand, while Abel has the low income and low demand, as shown in the first two panels in this diagram. Since nothing else need change,[1] the rest of Figure 24-6 is the same as before. In this diagram, just as in Figure 24-1, a perfectly competitive market yields an efficient solution. However, it is a quite different solution. There is no way that economists can judge which of the two solutions is better. All we can say is that both are efficient.

Abel and Brandeis, of course, will each have a clear opinion on which is better: Abel prefers Figure 24-1, where he gets most of this good (65 units), while Brandeis will prefer Figure 24-6, where *he* gets the lion's share. However, from the overall point of view of society as a whole, there is no way to judge. True, if we could meter the heads of these two individuals and thus be able to say that, in moving from Figure 24-1 to Figure 24-6, Brandeis's gain in satisfaction or utility exceeds Abel's loss, we might judge the pattern in Figure 24-6 superior. But this we cannot do, since *there is no known way of comparing the utility or satisfaction one person gets from a good with the utility someone else gets.*

To sum up: For each possible distribution of income, there is a different perfectly competitive solution. Each of these solutions is efficient, but we cannot demonstrate that one is better than the rest. The question of how income should be distributed is one that economists alone cannot answer, although we will shed more light on it in Chapter 36.

[1]Market price need not be exactly the same $10 as in Figure 24-1, but this is an unimportant detail that does not affect the argument.

TABLE 24-1
How the Four Basic Conditions that Lead to Efficiency Can Be Violated

	Condition	Will be violated if:	Considered in Chapter(s):
(24-1)	$MB_S = MB$	There are benefits to others than purchasers; for example, neighbors enjoy a well-kept garden	30
(24-2)	$MC = MC_S$	There is pollution or other costs not borne by producers	28, 29
(24-3)	$MB = P$	A single buyer has some influence over price. This may occur if there are only a few buyers	34
(24-4)	$P = MC$	A single seller has some influence over price. This may occur if there are only a few sellers	25, 26

FIGURE 24-6
Another efficient, perfectly competitive solution
This figure is similar to Figure 24-1, except that Brandeis now has a greater income and demand than Abel, and consequently consumes the greater quantity (60 units). This diagram also shows a perfectly competitive solution just like the one in Figure 24-1. Both solutions are efficient, but which is better? The individuals concerned will have conflicting views. Abel prefers Figure 24-1 and Brandeis prefers this figure. However, an economist examining this from the point of view of society as a whole cannot judge, because in the move from Figure 24-1 to this figure it is impossible to compare Brandeis' utility gain with Abel's utility loss.

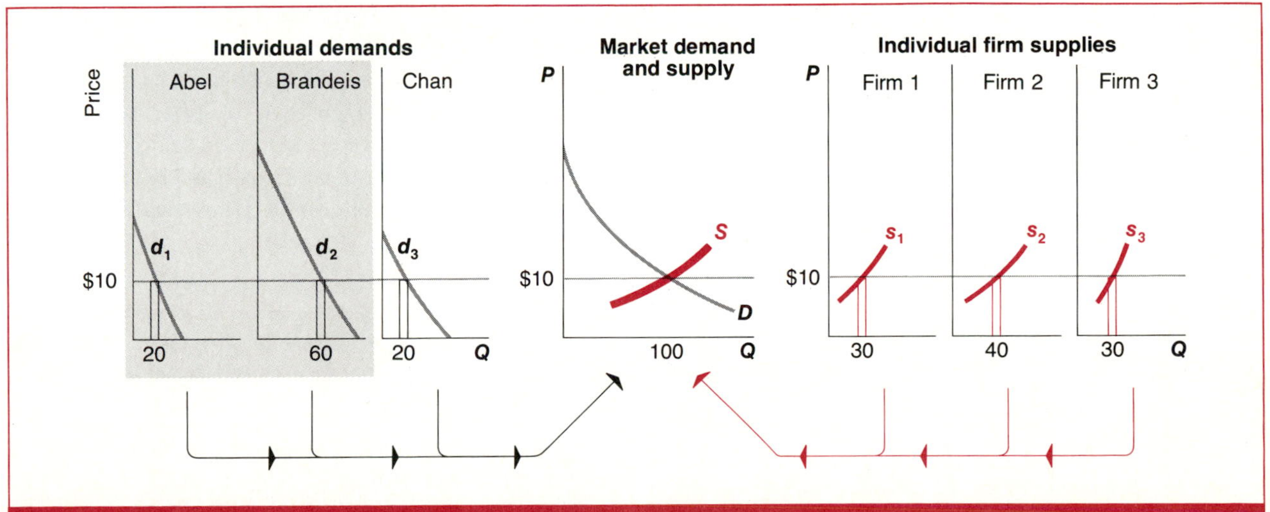

ANOTHER RESERVATION: WHEN BUYERS OR SELLERS ARE MISLED BY PRICE SIGNALS

We have now dealt with the basic features of perfectly competitive markets. However, there are a number of additional complications. For example, a market price acts as a signal to which both consumers and producers react. But what happens if they get the wrong message?

To illustrate this problem, we consider a case where producers may misread the price signal. Recall from Figure 20-7 how a small shift in the supply of an agricultural product—perhaps because of crop failure or disease in a herd—will result in a substantial change in price. We shall now show that this instability may be made worse if there is a time lag between the decision to produce an agricultural good and its eventual delivery to the market. There are many examples of this sort of delay: Wheat must be planted in the fall or spring for harvest in the summer, and the decision to breed cattle is made several years before the beef is eventually sold.

In such situations, an initial disturbance may set off a cycle of price fluctuations, with price high one year, low the next, high the next, and so on. To illustrate, suppose that, due to some initial disturbance, hogs become very scarce; perhaps a large number are lost because of disease. As a result, the price of hogs is unusually high. Seeing this high price, farmers are induced to expand hog production. When these hogs come to market at a later date, the result will be an oversupply, and the price will fall. In turn, this depressed price will induce farmers to switch out of hogs, and this shift will create a scarcity in the next period that will lead once again to an abnormally high price. Thus the cycle continues as long as producers misread the market price signals and erroneously use today's price in making their production decisions. Even though this market is perfectly competitive, it follows a cyclical pattern and therefore does not work well, as we shall see in more detail in the next section.

*SPECULATION AND PRICE INSTABILITY

There are several ways in which a cycle of fluctuating prices may be broken. First, after perhaps two or three sharp changes in price, more and more farmers recognize what is happening and accordingly stop making the erroneous assumption that today's price provides a good prediction of tomorrow's price. As they do, the price cycle is moderated. The second way that price fluctuations may be reduced is if others in the economy—speculators—recognize what is happening and take action.

Speculation as a Stabilizing Influence

The public often views speculators as gamblers who take risks, whose profits or losses have little or no effect on the general well-being. However, the actions of speculators may be beneficial to the economy as a whole, as we will now demonstrate. Then, in the next section we will show how speculation can be damaging.

To illustrate how speculation works, suppose that price in a hog cycle was high last year and is accordingly low this year. Now a number of people realize: "This has happened before. This is that hog cycle again. Because price is low this year a lot of farmers will be getting out of hogs. Next year pork will be scarce and the price will go way up again. Let's buy some of this year's cheap pork, refrigerate it, and sell it next year."

This will be a profitable venture—if the costs of storage, etc., are not too high—because it puts into practice the advice any stockbroker will give: Buy cheap and sell dear. The remarkable thing is that this action benefits not only those who undertake it, but also society as a whole, because it moderates the price cycle. Why? The speculators' purchase of pork when it is cheap creates an additional demand that prevents its price from falling quite so far. And when the speculators sell pork later at a high price, this creates an additional supply that prevents the price from rising quite so far. Thus the cycle is moderated by ***speculation.***

***Speculation* is the purchase of an item in the hope of making a profit from a rise in its price, or the sale of an item in the expectation that its price will fall.**

Basically, the case for speculation is as simple as that. But the argument isn't complete until we show that stabilizing price is beneficial from the viewpoint of soci-

*Note to instructors. Although starred sections include important material, they can be omitted from a short course without loss of continuity.

ety as a whole. We demonstrate this by considering the case where speculators buy pork this year when its price is low, and then sell it next year when its price is high.

Panel *a* of Figure 24-7 shows the demand curve for pork. In the absence of speculation, initial equilibrium is at E_1, with low price P_1 because of high output Q_1. Panel *b* shows next year with the same demand curve but with lower production Q_2. In the absence of speculation, equilibrium is at E_2 and the price is a high P_2.

Now consider the behavior of speculators. This year in panel *a,* they buy $Q_1'Q_1$ units when the price is low, store them, and sell them next year when the price is high. This year their purchases reduce the available supply from Q_1 to Q_1'. Therefore price is raised from P_1 to P_1'. Next year, their sales increase the supply from Q_2 to

FIGURE 24-7

How speculation may have the beneficial effect of stabilizing price

Without speculation, equilibrium this year is at E_1 and next year at E_2. Speculation involves reducing the available supply on the market this year from Q_1 to Q_1' (as shown by the arrow) and transferring it to next year, thus increasing the supply then by this same amount, from Q_2 to Q_2'. This raises price this year and lowers it next year until the two are almost equal. The loss from reduced consumption this year is the light red area in panel *a*. However, the gain from increased consumption next year will be the gray area in panel *b*. The difference in these two areas is the beneficial effect of this speculation.

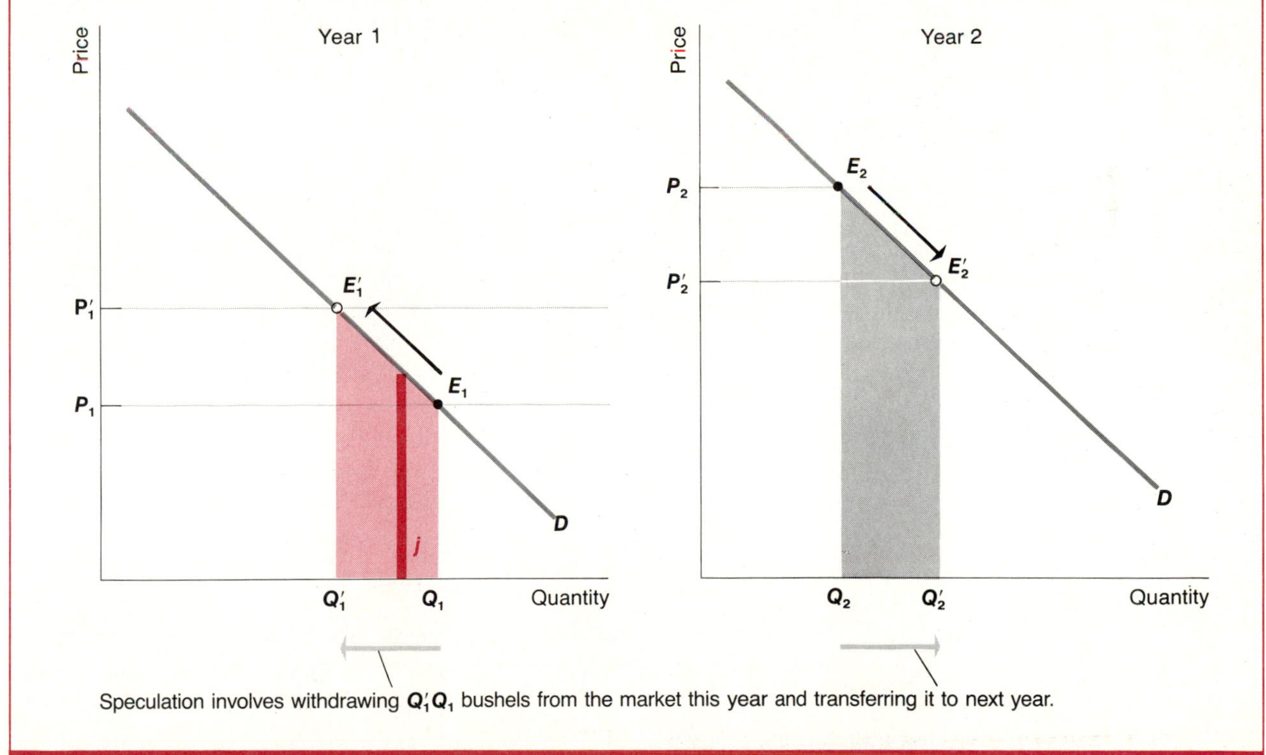

Q_2'. This lowers the price from P_2 to P_2'. Note that the cyclical swing in price has been almost eliminated: Speculation has changed price in the 2 years to P_1' and P_2', and there is very little difference between the two. The only reason that there is a difference at all is that speculators have to earn a return to cover their storage and interest costs[2]—and to compensate them for the risk they have to run in a situation in which a wrong guess can cost them dearly.

This sort of speculation not only provides an adequate return for speculators; it is also beneficial for society as a whole. True, reduced consumption this year takes away benefits from the public now, as shown by the red area in panel *a* of Figure 24-7. To confirm this loss, note that since typical unit *j* is no longer consumed, the marginal benefit to consumers shown by the dark red bar is eliminated. The total loss because all such benefits are eliminated in the range $Q_1'Q_1$ is the total red area. However, this year's loss to consumers in panel *a* will be more than offset by an even greater gray increase in benefit to consumers next year in panel *b*.

The reason for this difference is that, in this year of plenty when there is a glut, the public is losing units that it doesn't care that much about because its appetite is already reasonably satisfied. But next year when there is a scarcity, a "relatively hungry" public will be getting back these units when they mean a lot. The difference between the red and gray areas therefore indicates the net benefit to society from this speculation.

In short, speculation reduces the fluctuation in price. It also reduces the fluctuation in the quantity consumed: Without speculation, different quantities—Q_1 and Q_2—would be consumed each year; with speculation, roughly the same quantities are consumed—Q_1' and Q_2'. By ironing out the fluctuation in quantities—that is, by moving some of this good from a year of glut to a year of scarcity—speculation provides a benefit to society.

[2]The necessity of earning a return in order to cover interest and storage costs explains why speculators stop when they do; any more speculation would further reduce the price difference in the 2 years and thus no longer leave them with an adequate return.

For an examination of how storage can benefit not only consumers—as we will demonstrate here—but also producers, see Brian D. Wright and Jeffrey C. Williams, "The Welfare Effects of the Introduction of Storage," *Quarterly Journal of Economics*, February 1984, pp. 169–192.

Moreover, this conclusion—that there is a benefit from eliminating a price cycle—means that there is a loss from having a price cycle in the first place. A pattern of stable prices would be better for society. This then leads us to our second major reservation about a perfectly competitive market: It may lead to unstable prices if there is a failure in the timing and signaling mechanism. If this unstable price pattern is not ironed out by speculators, the public loses; the free movement in price allowed by a perfectly competitive market becomes a disadvantage. This is true *even though a free movement in price can offer advantages in other circumstances.* For example, when an unexpected freeze drives up the price of oranges, people are encouraged to use the scarce oranges carefully.

Speculation as a Destabilizing Influence

So far, speculators emerge from this discussion very much the heroes of the piece, but only because we have assumed that they predict the future correctly. However, they may guess wrong, and if they do, their actions can result in a loss both to themselves and to society. For example, suppose they purchase and store pork this year on the expectation that there will be a greater shortage and higher price next year, and they are wrong; there is a glut and lower prices instead. In this case, speculators lose because the pork they hold falls in price. Moreover, society as a whole also loses, because speculators move some of today's supply into next year's period of plenty, when pork is needed even less. Thus, the individual success of speculators *and* their potential benefit to society depend on their ability to predict the future correctly.

There is another possible problem with speculation. The speculators we have described so far operate in a perfectly competitive way. Although all of them together influence price, none of them individually can. The story is quite different for a speculator who attempts to ***corner a market.***

A market is cornered **when someone buys enough of the good to become the single (or at least dominant) seller, thus acquiring the power to resell at a higher price.**

To see why cornering a market is quite different from perfectly competitive speculation, note that the perfectly competitive speculators who buy today to sell next year are *hoping* for a future shortage and higher price. On the other hand, the speculator who tries to corner a market is trying to *create* a future shortage and higher price: If he can succeed in becoming the only seller, he can then create a future shortage by, say, cutting his sales in half. In this case, society loses. Because of the artificially created shortage, there is less of this good for the public to consume.

Even if the speculator doesn't succeed in cornering the market, heavy purchases or sales may be damaging for society because of the price gyrations that result. An example was provided by Bunker Hunt and his brothers, who bought silver heavily, contributing to the rise in its price from about $10 an ounce in the summer of 1979 to a record level of more than $50 in January 1980. By that time, the Hunt group held an estimated *one-sixth* of the western world's stock of silver. Improbable though it might seem—and although the Hunts still had a long way to go—it appeared they might be trying to corner the world market in silver. (One investigator later was not so sure; he suggested that they were just playing a game of monopoly with real money.) In any case, their adventure turned into disaster. The silver market turned down, in part because of the slack demand caused by the 1980 recession. A wave of selling drove the price back down below $10 an ounce. Estimates of the Hunt's losses during this collapse ran as high as $1 billion. No one would pretend that such price gyrations were beneficial to the economy as a whole; indeed, they dislocated industries such as photography that use silver. Thus we conclude that this type of speculation is costly to society, *whether or not* the speculator succeeds in cornering the market.

*GOVERNMENT AGRICULTURAL PRICE SUPPORTS

One of the arguments for agricultural price supports is that the government thereby acts like the stabilizing speculators in Figure 24-7, preventing the severe fluctuations in price that would otherwise occur. The problem of price instability is particularly serious in agriculture for two reasons noted earlier. (1) Producers may misread price signals—as we saw in our earlier example of a pork cycle; (2) prices may be unstable because agricultural goods are sold in perfectly competitive markets where supply and demand are relatively inelastic, and supply may shift dramatically because of changes in the weather. Thus without government intervention, the price of wheat could rise by 50% in a year of drought, and fall by 50% in a year of glut. This does not happen elsewhere in the economy: The prices of cars or clothing simply do not gyrate in this way. Moderating such fluctuations in price is desirable not only for farmers, but for the economy as a whole.

It is, however, difficult to evaluate farm price supports because they can have two quite different objectives.

Objective 1. To Stabilize Price and Consumption

And let them gather all the food of those good years that come, and lay up corn under the hand of Pharaoh, and let them keep food in the cities.

And that food shall be for store to the land against the seven years of famine, which shall be in the land of Egypt; that the land perish not through the famine.

Genesis 41:35-36

To see how a government price support program can have the same favorable effect as the successful, perfectly competitive speculation in Figure 24-7, suppose that the government commits itself to maintaining price at a support level of P_1' in panel *a*. In a bumper-crop year, it buys up quantity $Q_1'Q_1$, thus keeping price up to the P_1' support level. Then in the poor crop year in panel *b,* when there is a shortage, the government sells the accumulated stock, thus keeping price down. In short, the government moderates price fluctuations just as stabilizing speculators might, by moving goods from a period of plenty in panel *a* to a period of crop failure in panel *b*. As a consequence, the nation realizes an efficiency gain.

Although this provides a case for government price guarantees, difficult questions remain. For example: Since the government price guarantee to farmers has much the same effect in stabilizing price and quantity as successful private speculation, why can't private speculators do the job? If they can see a future shortage developing, why wouldn't they buy at low prices now in order to sell at high prices in the future period of scarcity—in the process moderating the fluctuation in price and quantity consumed?

To some degree, the question of who can do the better job of stabilizing price—private speculators or the government—reduces to the question of whether the government can predict future price as well as speculators can. If it can, a government price support is the better way to stabilize price. The reason is that a government guarantee to farmers at planting time of the price they will eventually receive is the best way to induce the right production response—and private speculators cannot provide such a guarantee. However, many doubt that the government can predict as well as private speculators. After all, those in government are good at winning elections, whereas private speculators are good at predicting future price. (Those who aren't, lose money and go out of business.) Furthermore, there is another problem with a government price guarantee: It frequently involves a second objective in addition to stabilizing price.

Objective 2: To Raise Average Price

To isolate one issue at a time, assume that the problem of price instability does not exist; food is being produced at an efficient output, and the government has already stored enough to cover the risk of bad crops here or abroad. In these circumstances, suppose the government introduces a price guarantee designed to *raise price rather than stabilize it*. Farmers respond to this higher price by producing more. There are two major effects. First, farm output has been increased beyond its initial perfectly competitive, efficient level, so that there is an efficiency loss. At the same time, there is also a transfer of income to farmers who receive a higher price, from taxpayers who must pay the subsidy necessary to raise the price.

By the early 1980s, this transfer from American taxpayers to U.S. farmers was growing rapidly. Between 1981 and 1983 government spending on farm price and income supports rose from $6.6 billion to $18.9 billion[3]—a remarkably large figure, given the fact that 1983 net cash income on the farm was only $43 billion.

As detailed in Appendix 24-B, one problem was that the government had set the price guarantees too high. Farmers responded by producing more. At the same time, consumers were deterred by the high price and bought less. The resulting large excess supply had to be purchased by the government—at the high guaranteed price it had itself set. Some relief was provided by a government program to get farmers to withdraw some of their acreage from circulation. Farmers responded by taking a huge amount of land out of production—an area estimated to be equal to three Virginias. But despite this, surplus production continued—and with it, the drain on the U.S. Treasury. This drain was reduced in 1983–1984, but only because of drought.

Few economists were prepared to justify this costly program of farm support. But suppose the guaranteed price had been set at a less expensive level for the taxpayer. Could it then be defended? One argument used by supporters of this policy is that it helps to ease farm poverty. However, a price guarantee that subsidizes a bushel of wheat rather than a poor farmer is a very ineffective way of curing poverty, since it subsidizes the wealthy high-volume farmer much more than the poor low-volume farmer. For example, in 1982 the 30% of the farmers with the largest sales received almost 80% of the government subsidy payments; they would have received even more, except for the $50,000 limit on the subsidy that any one farmer could receive. As a consequence, most of the government subsidy went to farmers who were already wealthy, with average assets of about $1 million and net worth of about $800,000. Moreover, the problem is not just that wealthy farmers get more income from the government than poor farmers. They have often got a much larger *percentage* of their income from the government. This raises the question: Wouldn't it be far better to subsidize farmers, *not* according to how many bushels of wheat they produce, but instead accord-

[3]Council of Economic Advisers, *Annual Report, 1984,* p. 112. The chapter on Food and Agriculture provides a very good summary of the various programs the government uses to assist farmers; it has been drawn on heavily in this discussion.

ing to their degree of poverty? (Care would have to be taken to design such a program in such a way that it wouldn't destroy the incentive to work—a problem we return to later.)

We conclude that in government farm policies, the reason for a price guarantee is a key issue. If the price guarantee is designed only to stabilize price by accumulating grain in bumper years to cover years of drought, a substantial argument can be made in its favor. However if it is also designed to raise average farm prices, it becomes more difficult to justify. Moreover, this issue is complicated by the fact that the real objective of price supports is often to raise price, but they are promoted on the grounds that they would stabilize price. How, then, does one determine which objective is being pursued? While there is no sure-fire way of answering this, here's one important clue. If the government surplus grows beyond the amount that is necessary to cover future crop failures, price guarantees have been raising farm income. But if farm income is judged a desirable objective, shouldn't we be developing far more appropriate policies—policies that would more successfully cure farm poverty without further enriching the already affluent farmer?

KEY POINTS

1. The efficient quantity of output from the point of view of society as a whole is where marginal social cost is equal to marginal social benefit.
2. If social costs are the same as private costs and social benefits the same as private benefits, a perfectly competitive market results in an efficient output. Thus, perfect competition eliminates deadweight loss; it allocates resources efficiently.
3. While the first two points above relate to allocative efficiency, perfect competition also tends to encourage technological efficiency by putting pressure on firms to operate on their lowest possible average cost curve.
4. In terms of dynamic efficiency, perfect competition may or may not be the best market form to induce new innovations. However, it does rate highly in ensuring that, once new innovations exist, they will be rapidly introduced.
5. For each distribution of income, there is a different perfectly competitive result. Economics cannot tell us clearly which one is best.
6. Another problem with a perfectly competitive market is that its price signals may be misread, and price may fluctuate as a result. An example is the hog cycle that occurs if producers erroneously assume that price this year is a good indication of what price will be next year.
7. Private speculation or government price guarantees may be beneficial in a perfectly competitive market if on balance they reduce price fluctuations. Competitive speculators, if successful, tend to stabilize price. However, those with larger resources who attempt to "corner a market" can have a destabilizing influence.
8. If government price supports are designed to raise, rather than just stabilize price, they become more difficult to justify. They introduce inefficiency into the system, and they are a high-cost, relatively ineffective way of curing farm poverty.

KEY CONCEPTS

private versus social benefit
private versus social cost
allocative efficiency
technological efficiency
dynamic efficiency
why perfect competition provides allocative efficiency
why perfect competition provides technological efficiency
efficiency loss (deadweight loss)
how price rations scarce goods
efficiency and the distribution of income
when market signals mislead
***speculation**
***when speculation is efficient, when not**
***cornering a market**
***agricultural price supports**
***how farm subsidies transfer income**

*An asterisk indicates that material is drawn from optional parts of the chapter.

PROBLEMS

24-1. By showing what happens to individual consumers and producers in panels *a* and *c* of Figure 24-1, confirm that a reduction of output to below 100 units must result in an efficiency loss.

24-2. "A perfectly competitive price that all buyers and sellers take as given is the key link in orchestrating production and consumption in an efficient way." Do you agree? If so, illustrate. If not, explain why not.

24-3. According to Adam Smith, the pursuit of private gain leads to public benefit. Under what circumstances is this not true?

24-4. Suppose existing firms in a perfectly competitive industry are all producing in panel *a* of Figure 24-4 at technologically inefficient point *F*, with price also at this level. Show how they will be driven out of business by technologically efficient new entrants producing at *G*. In your answer make sure you address the following questions: Is there initially a profit to be made by new entrants producing at *G*? Why? Do new firms therefore enter? What does this do to industry supply? What then happens to industry price? Can the old firms at *F* remain in business?

24-5. In our discussion of speculation, we stated that, if speculators guess wrong, they lose and so does society. Using a diagram like Figure 24-7, confirm that this statement is correct. In answering this, assume that speculators buy a good in one year, but that, in the next year when they sell it, it is even more plentiful and cheap.

24-6. What are some of the pros and cons of government-guaranteed prices for farmers?

APPENDIX 24-A

ILLUSTRATING THE EFFICIENCY OF PERFECT COMPETITION WITH INDIFFERENCE CURVES

This chapter has shown that perfect competition results in efficiency—provided that social and private benefits are the same and social and private costs are equal. To illustrate this point, demand and supply curves have been used. The same conclusion can be shown in an alternative way, using the indifference curves explained in the appendix to Chapter 21 and the production possibilities curve (PPC) introduced in Chapter 2.

Figure 24-8 illustrates how producers maximize their income. Suppose that they are initially at point *A* on their production possibilities curve, making 500 units of clothing and 1,300 units of food. Suppose also that the prices of food and clothing are both $10 per unit. Then producers' income totals $18,000; that is, ($10 × 500) + ($10 × 1,300). Producers are now on the $18,000 income line L_1, whose slope reflects the relative prices of the two goods, just like the slope of the equal-cost lines in Figure 23-10. Just as there was a whole family of equal-cost lines in that earlier diagram, we can visualize a whole set of parallel-income lines such as L_1 and L_2 in Figure 24-8, each indicating successively higher income levels as producers move to the northeast. The objective of producers is to reach the highest one possible. To illustrate, producers operating at point *A* on the $18,000 income line can do better by moving along the PPC to point *E*, which is on the $20,000 income line.

(At *E*, they produce 1,000 units of each good for a total income of $20,000.) This is the best they can do—it is the highest income line they can reach.

Producers maximize their income by producing at the point on the production possibilities curve that is tangent to the highest attainable income line.

In Figure 24-9, we put this theory of producer behavior together with our earlier theory of consumer behavior, in which we described consumer preferences with a set of indifference curves. In a perfectly competitive economy, in which every producer and every consumer takes prices as given, equilibrium is at *E* in Figure 24-9. On the one hand, producers maximize their income by selecting point *E* on the production possibilities curve because this point is tangent to the highest attainable income line *L*. At the same time, consumers maximize their utility by also selecting point *E*—because this is the point of tangency between their highest attainable indifference curve U_2 and the income line *L*. Thus the community as a whole achieves an efficient solution, because at *E* it is producing the combination of food and clothing that lifts it to its highest attainable level of utility U_2. Given the community's ability to produce, as shown by its PPC, there is no way it can reach a higher level of satisfaction than U_2. For example, it's not possible to reach U_3.

This, then, is our alternative illustration of the prop-

FIGURE 24-8

How producers maximize their incomes

The line representing producers' income goes through the point (*A*) at which production is taking place. The slope of this line depends on the relative prices of the two goods. Producers attain the highest income line by producing at tangency point *E*, where the slope of the production possibilities curve is the same as the slope of the income line.

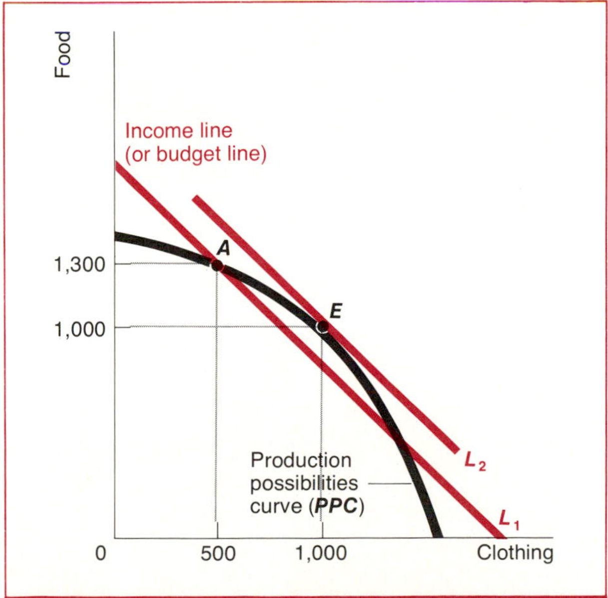

FIGURE 24-9

The competitive equilibrium

The competitive equilibrium occurs at *E*. Producers pick the point where the PPC is tangent to the highest attainable income line. Consumers pick the point where the income line is tangent to the highest attainable indifference curve. At this point, *E*, the production possibilities curve and the indifference curve are tangent. The maximum level of utility U_2 is achieved, given the productive capacity of the economy as shown by the PPC.

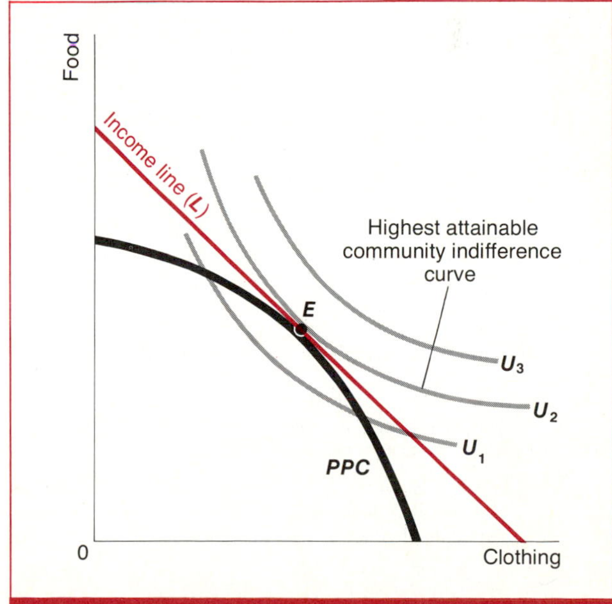

osition established in Figure 24-2: A competitive economy leads to an efficient solution.[4]

We emphasize again that this efficient solution results from producers on the one hand and consumers on the other responding independently to the competitive market prices reflected in the slope of the income line L.[5] This in turn raises the final question: Why does the competitive market generate the relative prices shown by L? To answer this question, suppose that initially the relative prices are different; specifically, suppose that they are shown by line L_1 in Figure 24-10. (The lower slope of L_1 reflects a lower relative price of clothing.) Facing these relative prices, producers maximize their income by producing at A, the point of tangency between the PPC and income line L_1. But consumers try to consume at B, the point of tangency between income line L_1 and indifference curve U_3. However, they are in fact unable to reach point B, since the economy is incapable of producing this combination of food and clothing. (B is outside the PPC.) As a consequence, markets are out of equilibrium. The quantity C_B of clothing demanded by consumers exceeds the quantity C_A supplied by producers; the price of clothing consequently rises. At the same time, the quantity F_B of food demanded is less than the quantity F_A supplied; the price of food falls. As the relative prices of food and clothing change, the income line moves from L_1 toward L. In response, producers move from A toward E, while consumers move from B toward E. This movement continues until the income line actually becomes L, and producers and consumers have moved all the way to E. It is only then that demand and supply are brought into equilibrium. Thus, the equilibrium prices are indeed those reflected in line L.

FIGURE 24-10

How markets adjust from an initial point of disequilibrium

If the relative price of clothing is originally below its equilibrium—that is, if prices are those reflected in L_1 rather than L—producers will want to produce at A and consumers will want to consume at B. As a result, there will be a shortage of clothing equal to $C_B - C_A$ and a surplus of food equal to $F_A - F_B$. Consequently, the price of clothing will rise and the price of food will fall until these prices reach their equilibrium values, reflected in the slope of the income line L.

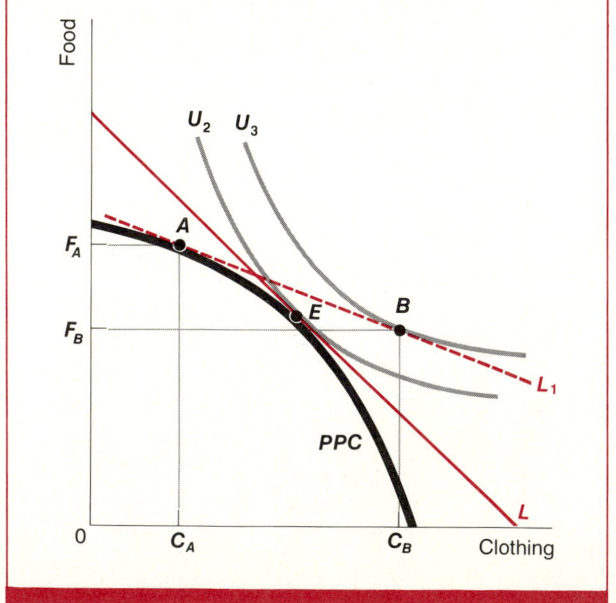

*[4]It may seem that there must be a catch somewhere. According to this analysis, there seems to be a single (unique) efficient solution at E—and we have already seen in Figure 24-6 that there is not: For each income distribution there is a different efficient solution. This puzzle is resolved by noting that in Figure 24-9 we have drawn a set of indifference curves for the *community as a whole,* rather than for an individual household. There are problems in defining such a community indifference system; there is no simple way of ''adding up'' the preferences of all the individuals in the nation. To illustrate, consider the simple, extreme case of a two-person economy. If I have all the income, my preferences are the ones that count; if you have all the income, it is your preferences that count. In other words, a community's preferences depend on who has the income. This means that there is no unique community indifference system; the community's indifference map can change every time there is a change in the distribution of income. Nor, as a consequence, is there any unique efficient equilibrium; the equilibrium depends on how the nation's income is distributed. This is exactly the conclusion we reached earlier.

*[5]To illustrate what can go wrong if producers do not act as perfect competitors, suppose that the producers of clothing form a monopoly and restrict the supply of clothing. In other words, the economy moves to the left of E in Figure 24-9 and it is no longer possible to reach indifference curve U_2. Consequently, the nation's utility is less than a maximum, that is, less than U_2.

APPENDIX 24-B

FORMS OF FARM ASSISTANCE

During the depression of the 1930s, when incomes everywhere were low, those on the farm were particularly disappointing. The income of the average farm family was only 40% of the income level elsewhere in the economy. However, by the decade 1973–1983, the gap had been almost closed. According to the Council of Economic Advisers, average farm income had risen to 88% of income elsewhere. (However, poverty was still much more severe on the farm. The percentage of the 1983 farm population below the poverty line was still almost double the percentage elsewhere.)

Part of the reason for the improvement in farm income was a wide variety of government assistance programs. Most important were programs aimed directly at raising farm prices.

In the absence of any government action, equilibrium in the wheat market is shown at E_1 in each of the panels of Figure 24-11. Farm income is equal to the rectangle to the southwest of E_1—that is, price P_1 times quantity Q_1. The three panels illustrate three different ways the government may raise the price the farmer receives.

PRICE SUPPORTS

In panel *a* the government supports the price of wheat at a higher level P_2. Farmers respond to this price incentive by moving up their supply curve from E_1 to E_2.

At the same time, consumers are discouraged by this higher price, and move back up their demand curve from E_1 to E_3. Thus, at this higher price there is now an excess supply equal to E_3E_2 which must be purchased by the government at a cost to the taxpayer equal to the shaded area. This taxpayer cost is the number of bushels the government must buy up—the base of the rectangle—times the price it must pay for each bushel—the height of the rectangle. However, this government program has increased farm income from the original rectangle to the southwest of E_1 to the larger rectangle to the southwest of E_2; that is, farmers now receive price P_2 on the Q_2 bushels they sell.

DEFICIENCY PAYMENTS

An alternative policy, shown in panel *b,* is of equal benefit to the farmer. In this case, the government again guarantees the same price P_2 to farmers, who again respond in the same way by moving up their supply curve from E_1 to E_2. Thus, as before, they produce Q_2. However, in this case the government makes no attempt to maintain the market price at P_2 by buying up the surplus. Instead, it lets the market price "find its own level." Because Q_2 is coming onto the market, price falls to P_4. (Point E_4 on the demand curve tells us that large quantity Q_2 will be purchased only at low price P_4.)

Farmers are guaranteed P_2 per bushel by the government, but they are getting only P_4 from the market. The government must therefore put up the difference; in other words, it must pay a subsidy P_2P_4 to farmers for each bushel they sell. Multiplying this by Q_2, the number of bushels sold, yields the shaded area—the total subsidy paid by the government to farmers.

HOW DO THE TWO POLICIES COMPARE?

Note that each of these policies involves an efficiency loss because the government is inducing farmers to produce Q_2, which is more than the efficient, perfectly competitive quantity Q_1. (We reemphasize: Here we are considering policies which permanently increase the price received by farmers, not policies which smooth out fluctuating prices.) As a consequence, there is triangular efficiency loss E_1E_2T in panel *a*—exactly the same as the triangular loss $E_1E_2E_4$ in panel *b*. Note that these are the same sort of losses that were first illustrated in Figure 24-3*a*.

FIGURE 24-11
Alternative farm assistance programs

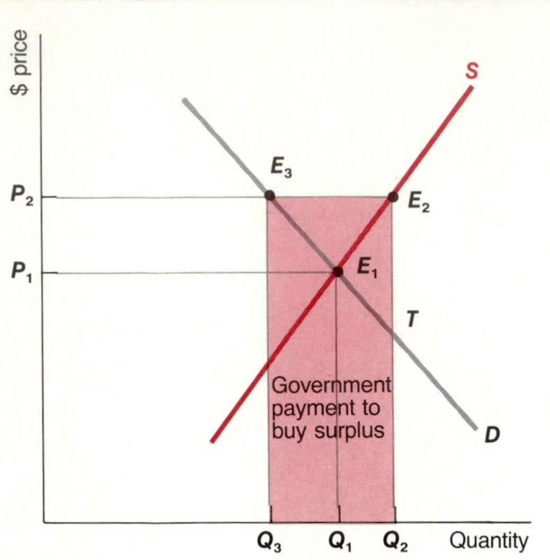

(*a*) **Price support at P_2.** The government must buy this surplus.

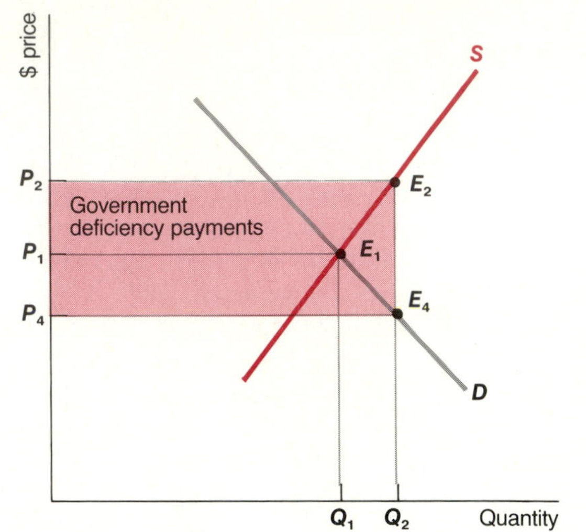

(*b*) **Deficiency payment.** The government pays farmers P_2P_4 for each bushel sold.

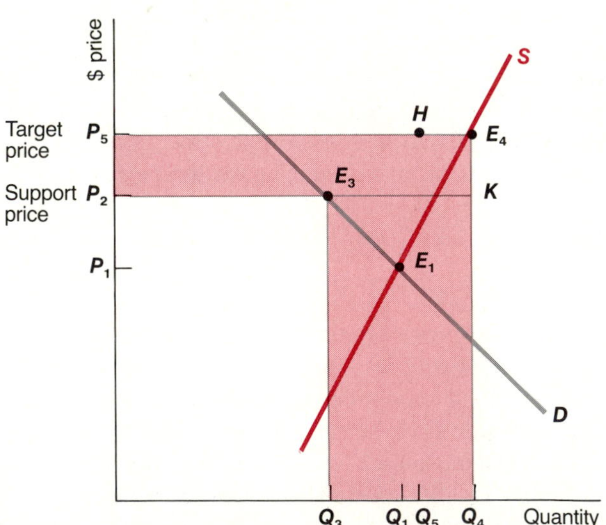

(*c*) **Policies *a* and *b* combined.** The government makes deficiency payment P_2P_5 and buys surplus Q_3Q_4.

Under either program *a* or *b*, the government guarantees that farmers will receive P_2 per bushel. They consequently move up their supply curve from equilibrium E_1 to E_2.

In panel a, the government provides a *price support* by fixing the market price at P_2. Consumers move up their demand curve from E_1 to E_3. The difference in the amount produced at E_2 and consumed at E_3 must be purchased by the government, at a cost shown by the shaded area.

In panel b, the government still guarantees farmers price P_2, but makes no attempt to keep up the price paid by consumers. As a consequence, this price falls to P_4, the highest price consumers will pay to buy the large quantity Q_2 that is produced. Since farmers have been guaranteed a price P_2 and are receiving only P_4 from buyers, the government pays them the difference, that is, a *deficiency payment* of P_2P_4 on each bushel. Since farmers are producing Q_2 bushels, the total payment they receive from the government is the shaded area.

Thus in either panel *a* or *b,* the large unshaded rectangle is what consumers pay when they buy the wheat, while the shaded rectangle is the cost to taxpayers. In either case, the taxpaying-consuming public pays the same total amount for wheat—that is, the entire area to the southwest of E_2.

In panel c, the government combines the two policies. The *support price* is set at P_2; this becomes the market price. In response, consumers buy Q_3. The government then makes a deficiency payment to farmers of P_2P_5 to reach the *target price* of P_5 that farmers receive. In response, farmers produce Q_4. The government must purchase the resulting surplus of Q_3Q_4 at P_2 per bushel, with this part of the program therefore costing the taxpayer rectangle $E_3KQ_4Q_3$. In addition, the government makes a deficiency payment of P_2P_5 on Q_4 bushels of wheat, for an additional cost to the taxpayer of rectangle $P_5E_4KP_2$.

Which policy do farmers prefer? The answer is that they generally favor the price support policy. They view it as providing a fair price for their wheat, whereas they sometimes regard the deficiency payment in panel *b* as a subsidy from the public purse. However, in fact the two policies benefit farmers equally: Under either scheme their income increases from the area to the southwest of E_1 to the area to the southwest of E_2. Moreover, under either scheme, the large area to the southwest of E_2 also represents the total cost of wheat to the public. This includes both the shaded rectangle that the public pays in taxes for the government support program and the unshaded rectangle that consumers pay when they buy wheat. (Specifically, consumers pay the unshaded area to the southwest of E_3 in panel *a* and the unshaded area to the southwest of E_4 in panel *b*.) In short, under *either* program, farmers receive the same amount for their wheat, while the taxpaying-consuming public pays the same amount for wheat.

There is, however, one good reason for the public to prefer the deficiency-payment policy: The public gets more wheat—Q_2 in panel *b* rather than the Q_3 in panel *a*. Public preference for this policy clearly holds so long as the government has already accumulated enough to cover years of crop failure—as assumed in this appendix—and any additional agricultural produce it may accumulate will accordingly either spoil or be sold at give-away prices. To illustrate a give-away: Faced with the prospect that an accumulated butter surplus would spoil, the European Common Market sold it to the Soviet Union for *one-quarter* the support price its own citizens were paying. European butter consumers were not amused. The U.S. government has provided less spectacular, but still substantial, subsidies for U.S. agricultural exports.

Which policy does the government use? Historically, price supports in panel *a* have been the favored policy. Moreover, in 1984 they were still being used for some products, such as peanuts. However, for many other products—including cotton, rice, wheat, and a number of other feed grains, the government was using both price supports and deficiency payments.

COMBINING PRICE SUPPORTS AND DEFICIENCY PAYMENTS

In panel *c* of Figure 24-11, the government guarantees a *support price* of P_2. This becomes the price at which wheat is bought and sold on the market. Consumers respond to this by moving up their demand curve from E_1 to E_3, purchasing Q_3. At the same time, the government guarantees an even higher *target price,* P_5, to farmers. To do this, the government has to provide farmers with a deficiency payment of P_2P_5 per bushel. (Added to the price P_2 that farmers receive on the market, this gives a total price of P_5.) Faced with target price P_5, farmers respond by producing Q_4; that is, they move up their supply curve to E_4. With consumers buying Q_3 and farmers producing Q_4, there is a surplus—an excess supply—of Q_3Q_4. To prevent this from depressing the market price, the government has to buy up this surplus, at a cost of area $E_3KQ_4Q_3$. The government also incurs a cost of area $P_5E_4KP_2$, the deficiency payment it has to make directly to farmers; this is a payment of P_2P_5 per bushel on the Q_4 bushels that farmers sell. Thus the total combined cost to the government—that is, the cost to the taxpayer—is the entire shaded area.

As already noted, this drain on the public treasury grew rapidly in the early 1980s. The reason was that the target price—that is, the inducement to farmers to produce—had been set to increase automatically each year with inflation, at a rate that turned out to be unrealistically high, and that therefore induced an unexpectedly large supply. In addition, demand was disappointing because export markets were less than expected. Thus in the early 1980s, the government purchased large surpluses, illustrated by distance Q_3Q_4. Moreover, the annual increases in the target price led to increasing deficiency payments. These were two reasons, then, why the cost to the government of its farm subsidies almost tripled between 1981 and 1983. In an attempt to limit the costs, the government used the following form of market intervention.

SUPPLY MANAGEMENT: TAKING LAND OUT OF CULTIVATION

In the face of large surpluses, the government used two incentives to induce farmers to retire acreage out of production and thus cut back their output to less than Q_4. (1) Farmers couldn't qualify for deficiency payments unless they did reduce production, and (2) farmers were also paid for reducing production. While some of this payment was in the form of cash, the administration didn't like the idea of paying farmers cash for not producing. Therefore, beginning in 1983, the government introduced *payments in kind* (the PIK program). Instead of money, the government paid farmers bushels of wheat—or bushels of whatever else they had previously been producing.

Superficially, this looked like an attractive way of dealing with two difficult problems at once. Because farmers reduced their output from Q_4 to, say, Q_5, the government no longer had to accumulate such a large surplus. With subsidized farm output reduced by Q_4Q_5, the shaded drain on the treasury was reduced by rectangle $HE_4Q_4Q_5$. Moreover, because the government was giving away wheat, it was reducing the mountain of surplus wheat it had accumulated in the past.

Unfortunately, it wasn't this simple. Farmers who received this PIK wheat from the government eventually resold it. When they did, this wheat again created a surplus that the government once again had to buy. Thus PIK became a far less attractive solution than the government had hoped, and in 1984 it was abolished.

PROBLEM

24-7. If you are working for the U.S. government, and your only concern is to minimize the money the government has to pay to farmers, would you prefer the program in panel *a* or panel *b* of Figure 24-11: (*a*) if the demand curve passing through *E* is very elastic? (*b*) if demand is very inelastic?

CHAPTER 25

MONOPOLY

The monopolists, by keeping the market constantly understocked . . . sell their commodities much above the natural price.

ADAM SMITH
Wealth of Nations

At one end of the market spectrum, there is perfect competition, with many sellers. At the other end of the spectrum, there is monopoly, with only one seller. (The Greek word *monos* means ''single,'' and *polein* means ''to sell.'') Chapter 24 showed that, under certain conditions, perfect competition is efficient. This chapter will demonstrate why monopoly is not. A case can therefore be made for government intervention in the marketplace. But in what way should the government intervene?

To begin, consider the conditions that lead to monopoly.

WHAT CAUSES MONOPOLY?

There are four major reasons why there may be only one firm selling a good:

1. *Monopoly may be based on control over an input or technique*. A firm may control something essential that no other firm can acquire. One example is the ownership of a necessary resource; an oft-cited illustration was Alcoa's control over bauxite supplies that allowed it to monopolize the sale of aluminum before World War II. Another example is the ownership of a patent, which allows the inventor exclusive control over a new product or process for a period of 17 years. (Patents are designed to encourage expenditure on research by allowing the inventor to reap a substantial reward.) When an existing firm owns an essential patent or exclusive control over a resource, new firms might like to enter the industry but they cannot; the industry remains monopolized.

2. *Legal monopoly*. It is sometimes illegal for more than one company to sell a product. For example, a private bus company is sometimes given the exclusive right to service a community.

3. *Collusive monopoly*. If permitted by law, several producers may get together to form a single firm or a single unified marketing operation in order to charge a higher price and increase their profits. However, once these firms have created a monopoly, it may not be easy to maintain. They may have difficulty in keeping out new firms attracted by the high price.

4. *Natural monopoly*. A natural monopoly exists when economies of scale are so important that one firm can produce the total output of the industry at lower cost than could two or more firms. An example is the local telephone service. It obviously costs less to string one set of telephone wires down a street than two.

The prevalence of monopoly depends partly on how narrowly a market is defined. When the jumbo jet was first introduced, Boeing had a temporary monopoly; other companies had not yet developed their jumbos to compete with the 747. However, Boeing did not have a monopoly in the broader market for airliners, since it still had to compete with McDonnell-Douglas in the sale of smaller aircraft. As another illustration, the local gas company has a monopoly in providing natural gas, but not in the broader market of heating homes where it must compete with firms supplying oil and electricity. Indeed, in the very broadest sense, every producer competes with every other producer for the consumer's dollar. If you buy a new TV, you may help to pay for it by turning down your thermostat and thus reducing your gas bill. Therefore, in a very broad sense, the gas company is in competition even with the producer of TVs.

However, if markets are defined in a reasonably limited way, significant areas of monopoly exist—in water, local gas service, and local electrical service, to name a few. Nonetheless, the importance of monopoly should not be overstated. ***Oligopoly***—where the industry is dominated by a few sellers—is much more important in the U.S. economy. Some of the largest industries in our economy are oligopolies, including automobiles, large computers, aircraft, heavy construction equipment, large electrical generators, and steel. Moreover, long-distance telephone service, which used to be the monopoly of AT&T, is now an oligopoly. In spite of the importance of oligopoly, it is appropriate to consider monopoly first. Monopoly is the simpler form, and it provides a necessary background for the study of oligopoly.

NATURAL MONOPOLY: THE IMPORTANCE OF COST CONDITIONS

When discussing the problems that arise from the monopolization of an industry and the appropriate government policy, it is essential to answer the question, "Is this industry a *natural* monopoly?" In other words, "Can this good be produced less expensively by one firm than by two or more firms?" As we shall see, many of the questionable decisions by the government and the courts in dealing with monopoly have been the result of a failure to address this question.

The cost conditions which lead to natural monopoly are shown in panel *b* of Figure 25-1, and are contrasted with conditions which do not in panel *a*. The two products shown are assumed to have identical demand curves in order to highlight the difference in their costs—the central issue in explaining natural monopoly.

In the industry shown in panel *a*, a typical firm's long-run average cost curve AC reaches a minimum at

FIGURE 25-1
How cost conditions can lead to natural monopoly

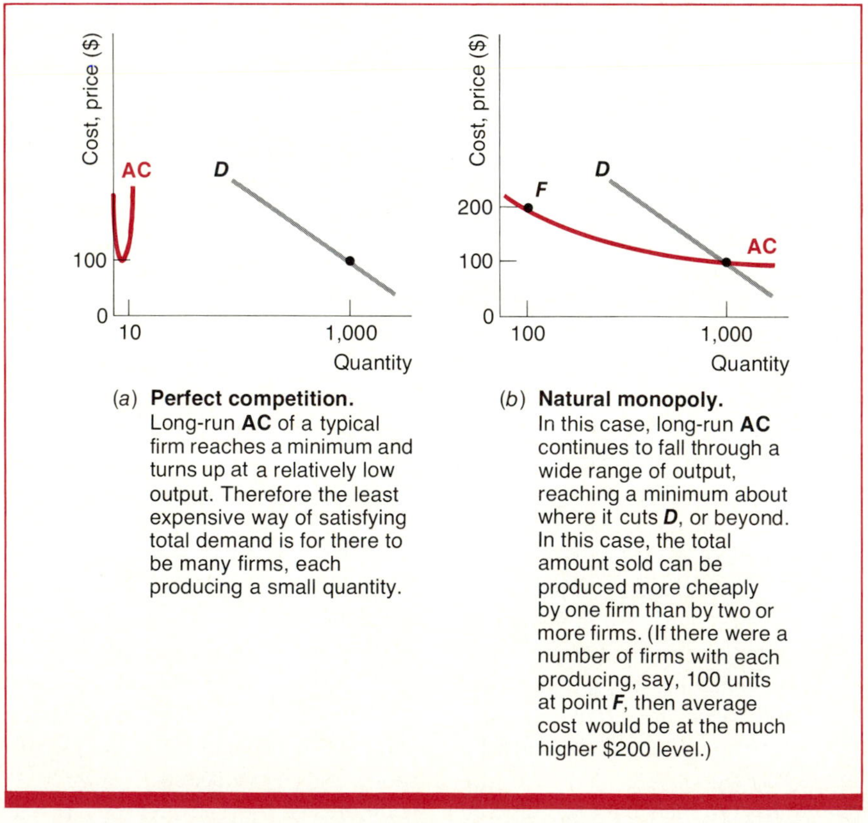

(*a*) **Perfect competition.** Long-run **AC** of a typical firm reaches a minimum and turns up at a relatively low output. Therefore the least expensive way of satisfying total demand is for there to be many firms, each producing a small quantity.

(*b*) **Natural monopoly.** In this case, long-run **AC** continues to fall through a wide range of output, reaching a minimum about where it cuts ***D***, or beyond. In this case, the total amount sold can be produced more cheaply by one firm than by two or more firms. (If there were a number of firms with each producing, say, 100 units at point ***F***, then average cost would be at the much higher $200 level.)

only 10 units of output, a very small portion of the total market. As a consequence, total demand cannot be satisfied by one firm operating at its minimum cost. Instead, the least costly way of servicing this market is to have many small firms producing just 10 units each. If a firm tries to produce at higher volume, say 20 units, it will incur a relatively high cost that will leave it unable to compete with smaller, lower-cost firms. With many small firms surviving, the result is perfect competition.

In panel *b,* AC reaches the same minimum value of $100, but the big difference is the much larger volume of output necessary for a firm to achieve this low cost. Unlike the AC curve in panel *a* that reaches a minimum and turns up at a very small volume, AC in panel *b* continues downward. The least expensive way of servicing the market is with one firm, and the stage is set for monopoly.

***Natural monopoly* occurs when the average cost of a single firm falls over such an extended range of output that one firm can produce the total quantity sold at a lower average cost than could two or more firms.**

Why might costs continue to fall through much or all of the range needed to satisfy total market demand? The answer may be: high fixed cost, that is, high overhead. Local electric, telephone, water, and gas services are all natural monopolies, because the fixed cost in running electric or telephone wires, or in laying water or gas pipes, is very high relative to variable cost. To illustrate what happens when fixed costs dominate, set fixed cost in Table 22-5 at $1,000, rather than just $35, and recalculate average cost. Notice how AC continues to fall as this $1,000 of fixed overhead is spread over a larger and larger number of units of output.

To verify that the cost curve in panel *b* in Figure 25-1 leads naturally to a monopoly, suppose that initially a few firms are each producing 100 units at point *F*. This low volume results in a high average cost of $200 for each firm. An aggressive firm will discover that by increasing its output, it can lower its cost, and hence offer its product at a lower price than its competitors. Thus it can squeeze them out of business. In such a case of natural monopoly, competition tends to drive all firms but one out of the market. Small firms, with their relatively high costs, simply cannot compete with the single large firm operating at—or near—minimum costs.

There is an obvious attraction to the consumer of such price competition during the period in which the industry is being ''shaken down'' and the number of firms reduced. However, this favorable situation for the consumer is likely to disappear once the successful firm has eliminated all its competitors and has emerged as a monopoly. It now has to worry little about the entry of new competitors: With its high volume—and therefore low cost—the monopoly can greet any new entrants with whatever price cutting is necessary to drive them into bankruptcy. With little fear of present or future competition, the monopoly can then raise its price. Thus consumers of this product are at the mercy of the monopolist, except insofar as they are prepared to cut back their purchases in the face of a higher price—or insofar as the government regulates price. The question is: If the monopoly is free to set its price, how high will the price be? But before we answer it, we need to make one more distinction between perfect competition and monopoly.

THE DIFFERENCE IN THE DEMAND FACING A PERFECT COMPETITOR AND A MONOPOLIST

A perfectly competitive firm must take the market price as given. For example, an individual farmer never thinks of asking 1¢ a bushel more for his wheat, because he knows he won't get it; and he never offers to sell his wheat for 1¢ less, since he can sell all of it for the going market price. The farmer has no ***market power:*** As an individual producer among many, he is unable, by reducing the quantity he supplies, to have any noticeable influence on price.

The *market power* of a firm is its ability to influence its price, and thereby its profit.

To confirm that a farmer has no market power, suppose that the price of a bushel of wheat is $2, as determined by market supply and demand in panel *b* of Figure 25-2. In panel *a* we show the response of the individual

FIGURE 25-2

The difference in the demand facing the monopolist and the perfect competitor

On the left-hand side, the demand facing an individual firm is shown with a light line and marked with a small *d*. Market demand is shown on the right hand side with a heavy line and is marked with a capital *D*.

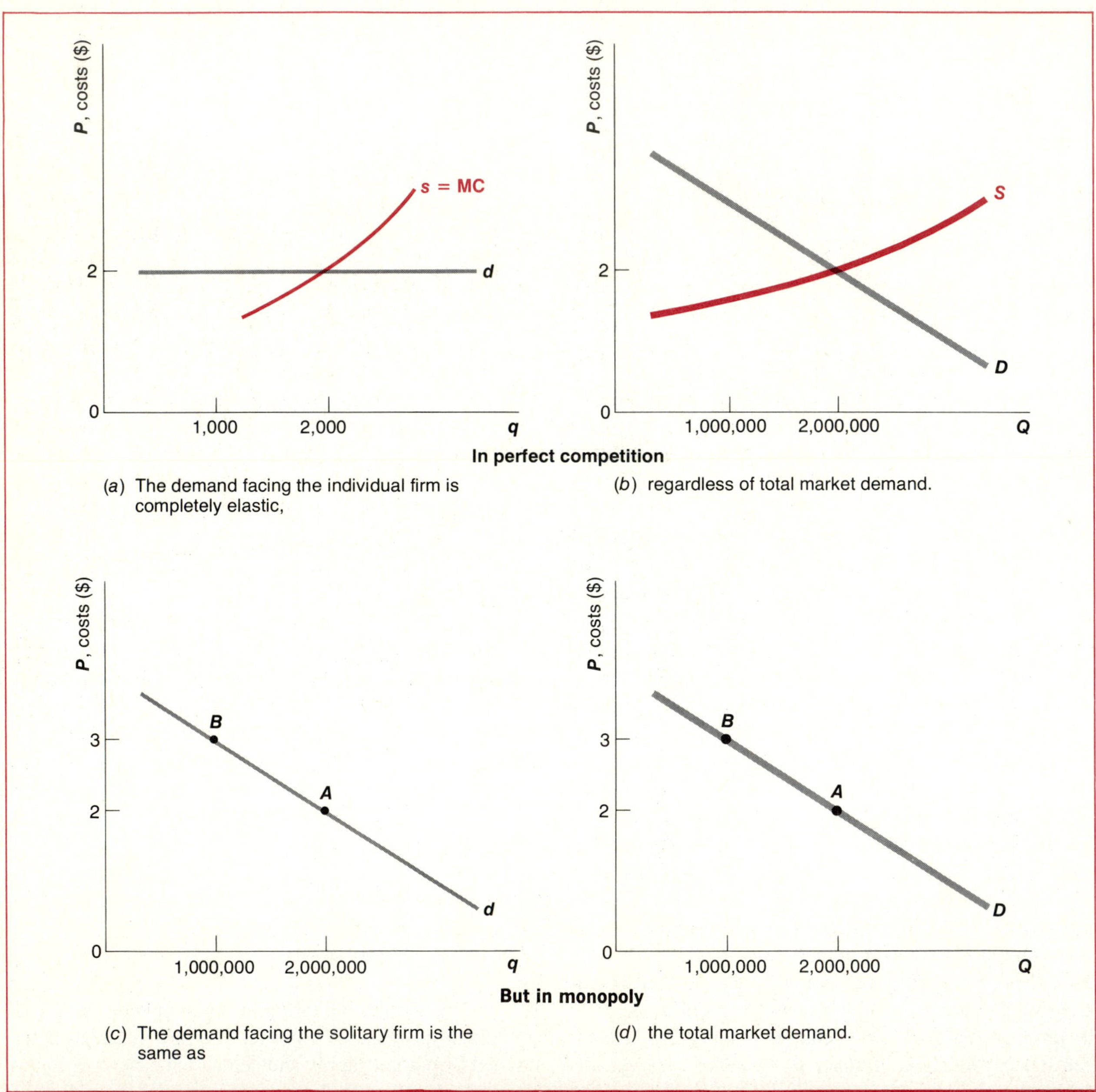

(*a*) The demand facing the individual firm is completely elastic,

(*b*) regardless of total market demand.

(*c*) The demand facing the solitary firm is the same as

(*d*) the total market demand.

farmer to this price. Because his supply curve is *s*, he produces 2,000 units. Now suppose he tries to influence the price. Specifically, suppose he cuts his supply in half from 2,000 to 1,000 units in the hope of making wheat scarce and raising its price. His move will reduce market supply in panel *b*, shifting *S* to the left, but by such a trivial amount—only 1,000 units—that this action won't even be noticed in the market; if you try to draw the new supply curve, you will find that you are essentially just drawing a line over the old supply *S*. Consequently market price, as determined in panel *b*, will remain the same. The farmer has tried to raise the price, but this attempt to exercise market power has failed miserably. As an individual seller, he has no influence whatsoever over price, and this is reflected in the completely elastic demand curve he faces in panel *a*. In short, he has to take the market price as given.

The situation facing a monopoly is quite different, as shown in panels *c* and *d*. In panel *d*, total market demand is exactly the same as in the competitive case above. The only difference is that this market demand is now satisfied by a single monopoly firm. In other words, *the demand facing the individual firm in panel c is exactly the same as the total market demand in panel d.*

As a result, the monopoly can indeed affect price. To confirm this, suppose that it is initially selling at a $2 price. Because it is the only seller, this firm alone is supplying all the 2 million units sold, shown at point *A* in both panel *c* and panel *d*. Now suppose the monopoly tries to influence price by cutting its sales in half, from 2 million to 1 million units. The demand curve tells us that the firm can sell these 1 million units at a price of $3. Thus the firm moves from *A* to *B* on the demand curve. By restricting its output, the monopoly *is* able to make this good scarce and thus raise its price.

In short, the monopoly firm has market demand within its grasp. It can move along the market demand curve from a point like *A* to *B*, selecting the one that suits it best. On the other hand, the perfect competitor has no control over market price; instead, the individual firm faces its own completely elastic demand curve, and all it can do is select the quantity to sell. While the monopolist can raise the price, the perfect competitor must take price as given. The monopolist is a ***price maker;*** the perfect competitor is a ***price taker.***

WHAT PRICE DOES THE MONOPOLIST SELECT?

As we saw in Chapter 22, *any* firm—whether a monopolist or perfect competitor—maximizes profit by selecting the output where its marginal cost MC equals its marginal revenue MR. (See statement 22-1 on page 459.) In that earlier chapter we also saw that *marginal revenue for the perfectly competitive firm is the given market price at which it sells.* In our present example, marginal revenue for the perfectly competitive firm in panel *a* of Figure 25-2 is the $2 selling price; no matter how many units the firm sells, its revenue will increase by $2 if it sells one more. In other words, its marginal revenue schedule is identical to its completely elastic demand curve. *However, for the monopolist, marginal revenue is not equal to the selling price, and the marginal revenue curve is different from the demand curve.* This is such an important point that it deserves a detailed explanation.

What Is the Marginal Revenue of a Monopolist?

Suppose the monopoly firm in Figure 25-3 moves from *B* to *C* along its demand curve. At *B* it was selling 1 unit at a $50 price, but now at *C* it is selling 2 units at a price of $45 each; in other words, at *C* its average revenue AR is $45. What is its marginal revenue for that second unit, that is, the additional revenue it receives because it is selling 2 units rather than 1? To calculate the answer, note that the monopoly's total revenue from selling 1 unit was $50; but when it sells 2, its total revenue is $90. Thus, its revenue has risen by $40; this is its marginal revenue from the sale of the second unit. We conclude that the firm's marginal revenue of $40 is less than the $45 price. This point is worth emphasizing:

> **For a monopolist, marginal revenue MR is *less than price P.***

Table 25-1 shows the monopolist's calculation of marginal revenue at each output. Total revenue is given in column 3, while column 4 shows how this total revenue changes for each successive unit sold. This is the marginal revenue schedule MR that is graphed along with the demand curve in Figure 25-3. This diagram emphasizes how the monopoly's marginal revenue curve lies below its demand curve.

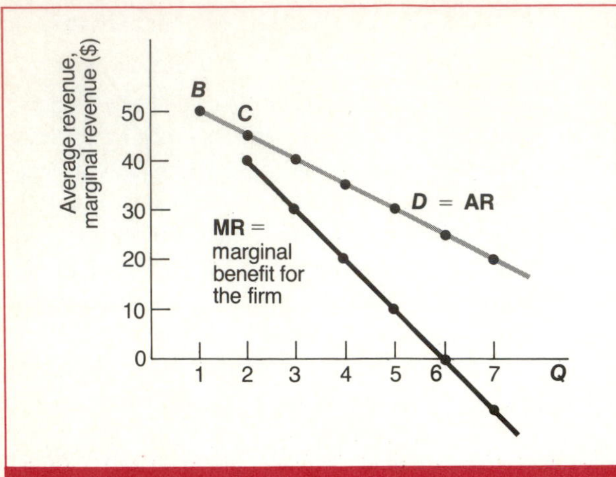

FIGURE 25-3

Why a monopolist's demand (AR) and marginal revenue (MR) differ

Numbers are drawn from Table 25-1. At point *B*, the monopoly sells 1 unit for \$50. At point *C*, it sells 2 units for \$45 each, for a total revenue of \$90. The sale of the second unit increases its total revenue by \$90 − \$50 = \$40. Thus its marginal revenue from increasing its sales from 1 to 2 units is \$40. Another way to calculate this is to note that the monopoly receives a \$45 price on the sale of the second unit, but from this it must deduct the \$5 "loss" it must take on the first unit because it is getting only \$45 for this rather than the original \$50.

The demand and marginal revenue curves now become the stepping stones needed to answer the following question: How high does a profit-maximizing monopoly set its price?

Monopoly Output and Price

Like any other firm, the monopoly maximizes profit by equating marginal cost MC with marginal revenue MR. An illustration is provided in panel *a* of Figure 25-4, where the monopolist's *D* and MR curves are reproduced from the preceding diagram, along with its MC and AC curves. The monopoly selects output Q_1 where MC and MR intersect. This is the output that maximizes its profit. If the firm selects any other output—whether greater or smaller—its profit will be less, as confirmed in the legend to this diagram.

A monopolist—like a perfect competitor—maximizes profit by selecting output where

Marginal cost MC = marginal revenue MR

However, for the monopolist—unlike the perfect competitor—MR is *not* the same as price.

With its output thus determined at Q_1, what price does the firm then charge? In other words, what is the maximum price the monopoly can charge and still sell quantity Q_1? The answer is given by the demand curve,

TABLE 25-1

How Marginal Revenue for a Monopolist Is Derived from Demand (Average Revenue) Information

Demand			
(1) Quantity (*Q*)	(2) Price *P* (average revenue)	(3) Total revenue (*P* × *Q*)	(4) Marginal revenue (MR)
1	\$50	\$ 50	
			(90 − 50) = \$40
2	45	90	
			(120 − 90) = 30
3	40	120	
			(140 − 120) = 20
4	35	140	
			(150 − 140) = 10
5	30	150	
			(150 − 150) = 0
6	25	150	
			(140 − 150) = −10
7	20	140	

which indicates at point (E) that the firm can charge a price as high as P_1 and still sell those Q_1 units. This choice by the monopolist of output Q_1 and price P_1 is often referred to as its selection of the *profit-maximizing point* (E) on its demand curve.

A monopoly, like any other firm, must address another important question: Should it be in business at all? For the firm shown in this diagram, the answer is yes. In selling Q_1 units, it makes an above-normal or monopoly profit of EV on each unit. This is the difference between the price it gets for selling each unit—the height of E on the demand curve—and its average cost of producing each unit, that is, the height of V on the AC curve. The monopoly will remain in business as long as it can cover

FIGURE 25-4

Two equivalent views of the profit-maximizing equilibrium of a monopoly

A third view is illustrated in problem 25-4. This uses the *total* revenue and *total* cost curves in the same way that they were used to show the profit maximization of a perfect competitor in Figure 22-4.

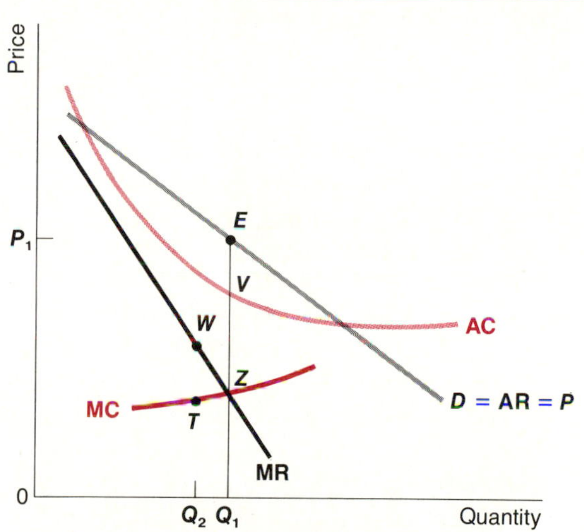

(*a*) **The firm examines marginal revenue and marginal cost, and equates the two.** To confirm that profit is maximized at output Q_1, where **MR** = **MC**, we use the familiar method of showing that any other output is inferior. For example, suppose the monopoly is producing at smaller output Q_2. It can increase its profit by producing one more unit, since the additional cost of this unit is only ***T***, while it provides a marginal revenue of ***W***. Consequently, the monopolist produces this additional unit—and continues for the same reason to expand output so long as **MR** lies above **MC**; in other words, up to output Q_1, where **MR** and **MC** are equal. Similarly, if the monopoly is producing an output greater than Q_1, it will contract. Only at Q_1, where **MC** = **MR**, is there no incentive to expand or contract.

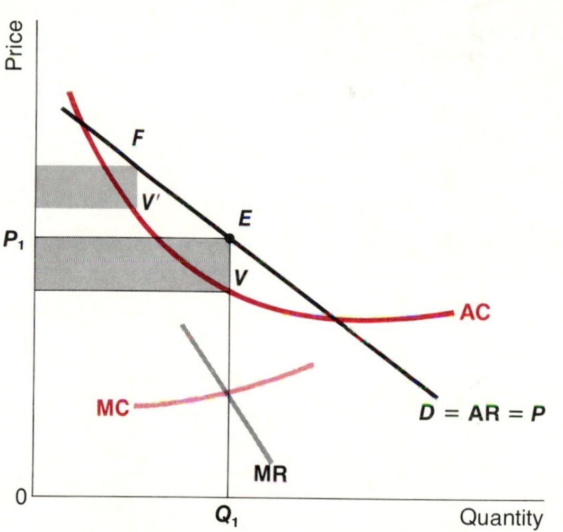

(*b*) **The firm examines average revenue and average cost, and maximizes the gray profit area.** This is exactly the same firm as in part *a*. In this case its average curves are darkened, because it is concentrating on these. At ***E***, the firm earns the profit shown by the gray area, because it is producing P_1E units at a profit of ***EV*** on each. (Since average revenue is ***E***, and average cost is ***V***, average profit is ***EV***.) The firm selects the point ***E*** on its demand curve that maximizes this gray profit area; the selection of any other point, such as ***F***, leads to a smaller profit area.

its costs, including a normal profit; that is, as long as its selling price E is at least as high as its average cost V. (Recall from Chapter 22 that the average cost curve includes normal profit.) However, if the demand curve lies below the average cost curve throughout its range, it is not possible for the monopoly to cover its costs, and it will leave this business in the long run.

If distance EV is the firm's profit per unit, what is its total profit? The answer is the large shaded area in panel b—that is, the per unit profit EV times P_1E, the number of units sold. This area is shaded in gray to represent above-normal profits, in contrast to losses which will appear later in red.

These two panels show in two equivalent ways how the monopoly firm maximizes profit: In panel a, it equates MC and MR. Alternatively, in panel b, it arrives at the same output Q_1 by selecting the point E on its demand curve that maximizes the shaded profit area; that is, it selects the point E that creates a larger profit rectangle than would be created by selecting *any* other point on its demand curve, such as F.

We shall use these two approaches interchangeably. For now, we concentrate on the MC = MR approach in panel a; however, we will later use the approach in panel b because it clearly shows the profits which the firm is attempting to maximize. Moreover, panel b demonstrates both conditions that a firm must satisfy: It ensures (1) that the marginal condition MC = MR is met and (2) that the firm is operating at a profit—or, more precisely, that the firm is not operating at a loss that would drive it out of business in the long run.

Although the monopoly's decision to equate MC and MR results in the profit-maximizing output *for the firm,* a question remains: Is this the efficient output for *society as a whole?*

IS MONOPOLY EFFICIENT?

No one can argue that a monopolist is impelled by "an invisible hand" to serve the public interest.

R. H. Tawney

The answer is no. The analysis developed so far will allow us to show that monopoly results in *allocative* inefficiency: The firm produces too little output, and the nation's resources are misallocated as a consequence. However, before we show this, let us consider monopoly from the viewpoint of technological and dynamic efficiency.

A monopoly may be *technologically* inefficient; the firm may not be operating on its lowest possible cost curve. Because it has no competition, a monopoly may be careless in its cost controls, and resources may be wasted as a consequence. In drawing our diagrams, we have been assuming away this kind of inefficiency. However, in doing so we should not forget: *Technological inefficiency in monopoly industries may be a very important cost to society.*

The relationship between monopoly and dynamic efficiency is less clear. As noted in the previous chapter, large, profitable monopolistic firms may have a greater financial capacity and incentive to engage in research and development than smaller, perfectly competitive firms. This research and development may lead to new techniques of production that will lower the firm's cost curves. Or it may lead to distinctive new products. For example, when AT&T was still a monopoly, its Bell Labs developed the transistor, which made the vacuum tube obsolete and opened up the enormously important field of solid-state electronics. The next chapter will deal with the dynamic effects of monopoly in more detail.

Consider now the central concept of efficiency studied by economists: *allocative efficiency*—or just "efficiency," for short. As we saw earlier, a good is being produced efficiently if its marginal social benefit is equal to its marginal social cost. To see whether or not monopoly passes this test, we extract the demand curve D from Figure 25-4 and reproduce it in Figure 25-5. It is now labeled the marginal benefit to society, since it shows the benefit this good provides to consumers. (We continue to make the assumptions from the last chapter that the marginal benefit to society MB_S = MB to consumers, and the marginal cost to society MC_S = MC to the producer.) We also reproduce the monopoly's marginal revenue curve MR and its marginal cost curve MC. With MC being the marginal cost of this good to the only firm producing it, it is also the marginal cost of this good to society as a whole. Since this curve intersects society's marginal benefit curve at R, the efficient quantity of output is Q_1.

However, this is not the output that the monopoly produces. Instead, as we have seen, it produces the smaller and therefore inefficient output Q_2, where MC = MR. The reason that it produces too little is that the firm equates marginal cost MC not with the marginal benefit to *society* (D) but instead with MR, the marginal benefit to the *firm itself*. Thus Adam Smith's invisible hand goes astray. The pursuit of benefit by an individual firm does *not* result in the best output for society.

The efficiency loss that results because monopoly produces too little (Q_2 rather than Q_1) appears as the red triangle. Note its similarity to the triangle in Figure 24-3*b*, which also showed the efficiency loss from too little output.

FIGURE 25-5
Monopoly results in allocative inefficiency: The invisible hand goes astray
Monopoly results in output Q_2, which is less than the efficient output Q_1; each of the units of reduced output between Q_1 and Q_2, offer a higher marginal benefit to society (shown by the height of the D curve) than their marginal cost to society. It would therefore be beneficial to produce these units, and the efficiency loss from monopoly occurs because these potentially beneficial units are not produced. This loss is shown by the red triangle.

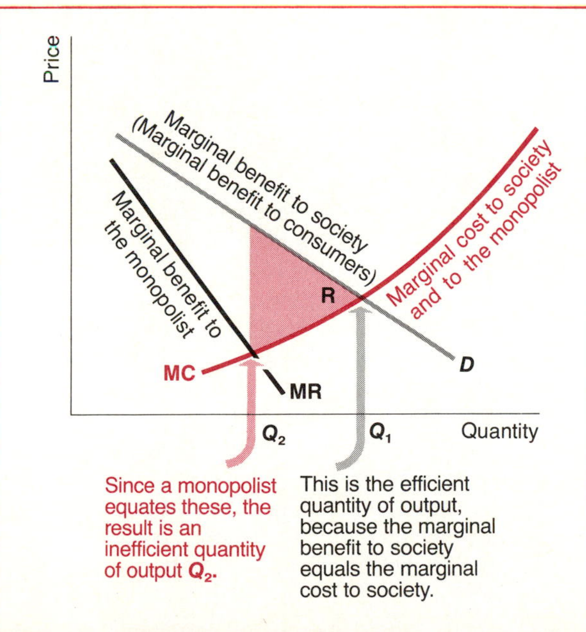
Price
Marginal benefit to society (Marginal benefit to consumers)
Marginal benefit to the monopolist
Marginal cost to society and to the monopolist
R
MC
MR
D
Q2
Q1
Quantity
Since a monopolist equates these, the result is an inefficient quantity of output Q2.
This is the efficient quantity of output, because the marginal benefit to society equals the marginal cost to society.

An Example: Collusive Monopoly

The analysis above applies to any profit-maximizing monopoly, that is, any of the four types described at the beginning of this chapter. Now let us consider in more detail one of these types—a collusive monopoly.

Figure 25-6*a* illustrates an industry that is perfectly competitive: The least expensive way of producing this good is with many small firms. As long as this industry remains perfectly competitive in panel *a*, total output of the industry is the efficient quantity Q_1 where supply—reflecting marginal costs—is equal to demand, reflecting marginal benefits. The price of the product is P_1.

Now suppose in panel *b* that these small firms get together to form a monopoly. Specifically, suppose they collude to form a single marketing agency to raise price. (An example is the marketing of dairy products described in Appendix 25-A.) Further suppose that the marketing arrangement leaves costs and demand unchanged; in other words, the MC and demand curves in panel *b* are the same as in panel *a*. What price and quantity does the marketing agency select in order to maximize the profits of the producers?

The agency will follow the monopolist's strategy of calculating its marginal revenue curve MR from its demand curve D. It then restricts output from Q_1 to Q_2, where MC = MR, and raises price from P_1 to P_2. In other words, as a monopoly, the agency will select point E_M on the demand curve.

> **The monopolization of a perfectly competitive industry raises price from P_1 to P_2 in our example, and reduces output from Q_1 to Q_2. This reduction in output means that too little is being produced, and there is the red triangular efficiency loss shown in panel *b*.**

The monopolist's policy of restricting output is designed to make the good scarce so that its price can be raised. For producers who form a monopoly, it is this ability to raise price that provides them with an opportunity for profit that wasn't available to them when they were perfect competitors.

THE TRANSFER EFFECT OF A MONOPOLY

The previous discussion seemes to lead to the clear judgment that society is harmed if a perfectly competitive industry is monopolized. While this conclusion is generally correct, it's not absolutely airtight, for two reasons. One is described in Box 25-1. The other arises because of the ***transfers*** associated with monopoly.

To illustrate, when monopoly raises price from P_1 to P_2 in panel *b* of Figure 25-6, consumers suffer while the monopolized producers benefit. In other words, there is a transfer from consumers to producers, equal to the $1 million area of the gray rectangle. (The price increase that consumers pay and producers receive is $10 per unit on each of the 100,000 units purchased.)

This gray area cancels out in dollar terms; the monopolized producers gain this $1 million while consumers lose it. However, it may not cancel out in terms of satisfaction; that is, the gain in satisfaction to producers who receive this extra $1 million may conceivably be greater than the reduction in satisfaction to consumers who lose it. For example, suppose that the item is something like the grapes from which champagne is made; the farmers who produce the grapes get together to set up a marketing board that raises the price. The consumers of champagne are so wealthy they hardly notice the increase in price. However, if the farmers who produce the grapes have low incomes, they may get very great satisfaction from the additional $1 million they receive. In

BOX 25-1

THE THEORY OF THE SECOND BEST

The conclusion that the monopolization of an industry results in inefficiency—that is, a misallocation of resources—is generally correct, but not always.

To understand why, consider industry X in an economy where all other industries are perfectly competitive. If X is monopolized, not enough of X's output is produced, and there is too much output of all the other goods. There is allocative inefficiency: Too few of the nation's resources are going into the production of X. This is the standard conclusion.

However, now suppose that all the other industries are themselves monopolized, but X is perfectly competitive. In this case, there will be too little output of all the other goods; in other words, there will be too much X. What happens if industry X is now monopolized? This will reduce its output, moving it in the right direction by bringing it back closer into line with the other industries. Thus, the allocation of the nation's resources may actually be *improved.*

This is known as the *problem of the second best.* The first best economy is one in which all industries behave in a competitive way. If one industry is then monopolized, the economy becomes less efficient. However, in a second best world—one in which some industries are *already* monopolized—it is unclear whether monopoly in yet another industry will make the economy more or less efficient. There is no simple answer to this question; the theory of the second best is quite complex.

The *theory of the second best* is the theory of how to get the best results in remaining markets when one or more markets have monopoly or other imperfections about which nothing can be done.

A second best argument is sometimes made in support of government policies to monopolize an agricultural industry; an example is the milk-marketing agency described in Appendix 25-A. Since the rest of the economy is pervaded by monopoly influences, so the argument goes, monopolizing agriculture may improve the nation's resource allocation. By and large, economists remain unimpressed with this argument and continue to recommend that we aim at the "first best" solution by reducing monopoly influence wherever it may be found. Hence, the theory of the second best is introduced here, not as a reason for encouraging monopoly in any specific sector, but rather as a warning that the economic world is seldom as simple as we might hope.

this case, most people would conclude that the act of transferring income provides a net benefit. Moreover, it is conceivable that such a benefit might offset the red efficiency loss which arises because output declines from Q_1 to Q_2. In this case, one could argue that the monopolization of the industry would be desirable.

While this argument is logically possible, it is also somewhat strained; we have picked a very special case. Therefore, most economists would be prepared to stick with the conclusion that the monopolization of an industry typically results in a net loss to society.[1]

Note that this problem of whether the $1 million is of equal benefit to buyers and sellers arises in evaluating almost every economic policy, whether it is controlling monopoly price, limiting pollution, or opening trade with foreign countries. Most policies result in a change in some market price, and hence a transfer of income between buyers and sellers. Thus, any normative conclusion on whether the policy is desirable or not requires a reasonable working assumption of how people compare

[1]Any full evaluation of monopoly involves examining several other issues as well. For example, to the degree that firms hire lawyers to help them establish or strengthen a monopoly position, then it's reasonable to argue that, from society's point of view, these legal resources are being wasted. For a discussion of this and other costs of monopoly not discussed here, see for example, Anne Krueger, "The Political Economy of the Rent-Seeking Society," *American Economic Review*, June 1974, pp. 291–303; and Richard Posner, "The Social Costs of Monopoly and Regulation," *Journal of Political Economy*, August 1975, pp. 807–828.

FIGURE 25-6

When a perfectly competitive industry (panel *a*) is monopolized (panel *b*), the result is a red efficiency loss and a gray transfer of income

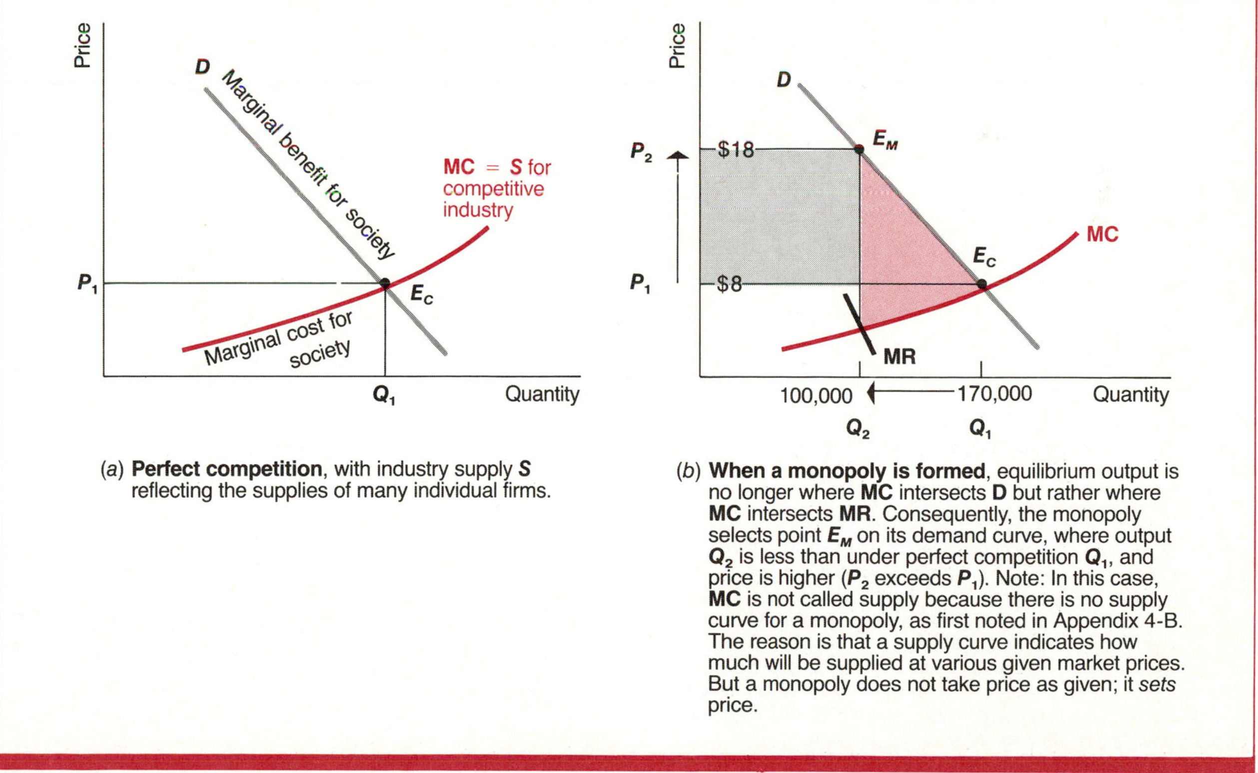

(*a*) **Perfect competition**, with industry supply ***S*** reflecting the supplies of many individual firms.

(*b*) **When a monopoly is formed**, equilibrium output is no longer where **MC** intersects **D** but rather where **MC** intersects **MR**. Consequently, the monopoly selects point E_M on its demand curve, where output Q_2 is less than under perfect competition Q_1, and price is higher (P_2 exceeds P_1). Note: In this case, **MC** is not called supply because there is no supply curve for a monopoly, as first noted in Appendix 4-B. The reason is that a supply curve indicates how much will be supplied at various given market prices. But a monopoly does not take price as given; it *sets* price.

in their valuation of income.[2] Anyone unprepared to make such an assumption is restricted to positive economics—to an analysis of economic events, policies, and institutions, without any judgment on whether or not they have been beneficial to the community as a whole

GOVERNMENT POLICIES TO CONTROL MONOPOLY

We shall now explain our earlier claim that, in formulating policies to protect the public from monopoly, the government should begin with the question: "Is the industry in question a natural monopoly or not?" Suppose it is not; suppose the monopoly is the result of collusion. In this case, we've already seen that there is a strong argument for preventing monopolization—or if it has occurred, for breaking it up. To achieve this objective, "antitrust" laws have been passed. They will be considered in Chapter 27.

In the balance of this chapter we will concentrate on the other case, where the industry is a natural monopoly. Because of economies of scale, the average cost curve AC keeps falling over a wide range of output, as illustrated in Figure 25-7. The least expensive way for market demand to be satisfied is by one large producer. Breaking the monopoly up into a number of smaller firms would be counterproductive. We don't need more than one set of electrical wires running down a street; nor do we need more than one set of gas pipes. If we had several firms in any of these activities, they would be duplicating the investment—that is, the fixed costs—of the existing monopoly, and this would involve a waste of resources. Graphically, breaking the natural monopoly in Figure 25-7 up into a number of small firms, each with output Q_3, would raise average cost to C; the benefits from economies of scale would be lost. In the case shown here, everyone would lose. The monopoly would lose its monopoly profit. Moreover, consumers would also be damaged: Even if the new, perhaps highly competitive firms were to earn no economic profit, they would still have to sell at a high price C just to cover their high costs, and that price would be higher than the price P_1 that consumers were paying before the monopoly was broken up.

Thus breaking up a natural monopoly is no solution at all. Indeed, reducing the output of the firm by break-

FIGURE 25-7
Natural monopoly: Regulating price rather than breaking up the firm
Without price regulation, the monopoly firm maximizes its profit by selecting point E_1 on its demand curve: At this point, output is Q_1, where the firm's MR = MC. If the government sets maximum price at P_2, the firm is forced down its demand curve to point E_2, with its output increasing to Q_2. This is the efficient output where the marginal benefit to society (D) is equal to marginal cost MC. The efficiency gain from this policy comes from the elimination of the original "triangle" of monopoly inefficiency E_1E_2T; this triangle is the same sort of efficiency loss as the red triangle in Figure 25-5. This policy also reduces monopoly profit: Since initially the monopolist maximized profit by selecting point E_1, any other point on the demand curve—including E_2—involves less profit.

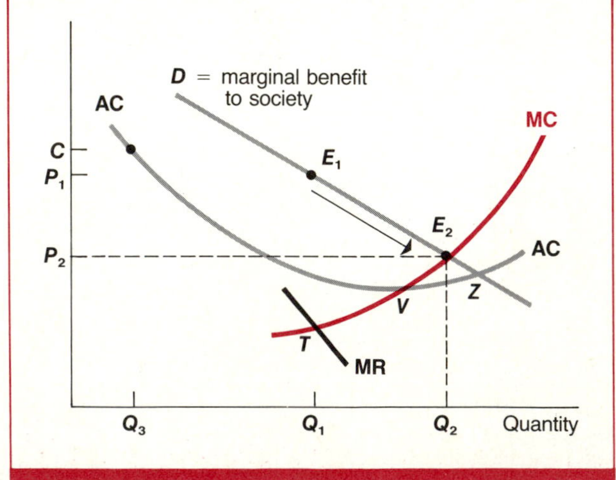

[2]The same issue arises in macroeconomics. During any period in which the nation's per capita income increases, most Americans benefit, but a few are hurt. Any judgment that such an income increase has been of benefit to the nation overall involves a reasonable assumption about how people compare in their valuation of income. The assumption normally used is that losers get roughly the same satisfaction from $1,000 of income as winners do. For more detail, see Arnold Harberger, "The Three Basic Postulates for Applied Welfare Economics: An Interpretive Essay," *Journal of Economic Literature*, September 1971, pp. 785–797.

ing it up is a move in the wrong direction because this raises costs. Instead, the government should force the firm to *expand*. Specifically, it should force the firm to move from E_1 down its demand curve to the efficient point E_2, where the marginal benefit to consumers (and to society) is equal to the marginal cost to producers (and to society).

How does the government force the monopoly to do this? The answer is: Set the maximum price that the firm can charge at P_2, the price at which its MC curve intersects the demand curve. This is called ***marginal cost pricing***.

***Marginal cost pricing* is setting price at the level where MC intersects the demand curve.**

Since the monopoly is now prohibited from raising price, it is forced to act like a perfectly competitive firm, taking price P_2 as given. Like the perfectly competitive firm, it will produce to point E_2, where its MC curve rises to the level of its given price P_2. Because E_2 is the efficient output where MC intersects demand, this policy has eliminated the original efficiency loss due to monopoly.[3]

We emphasize that, in forcing the move to the efficient point E_2, the government has *not* broken up this natural monopoly. It has simply *removed the monopoly's market power*—that is, the power of the monopoly to set a high price. In practice, there are two ways the government can do this:

1. It may take over and operate the monopolized activity, setting the price of its output at P_2. This is generally the case with water services.

2. Alternatively, the government may let the monopoly continue as a privately owned firm but will set up a regulatory agency to control its price. This agency then dictates price P_2. This is generally the case with electric companies.

In summary, consider how well marginal cost pricing solves the monopoly abuse of producing too little at too high a price. The monopoly is forced to reduce its price, and consequently it sells more; that is, its output increases. In addition, its monopoly profit has been reduced, though not necessarily eliminated; in our example, a per unit profit of E_2Z remains.

Unfortunately, dealing with monopoly in practice is often not so easy. Although marginal cost pricing still allows a profit in the example shown in Figure 25-7, in other circumstances it may lead to a loss. In such a case, marginal cost pricing is not a satisfactory policy, since the government would be setting the price too low to allow the firm to stay in business. Such a monopoly requires some other form of price regulation. This more difficult situation is dealt with in Box 25-2.

THE SPECIAL CASE OF DISCRIMINATING MONOPOLY: LETTING A MONOPOLIST ACT LIKE A MONOPOLIST—IN SPADES

The argument so far is that a monopolist should not be allowed the freedom to set a high price. However, this general rule has an interesting exception which can be illustrated in the special case of the only doctor in a small town.

Figure 25-8 shows the demand she faces; some individuals are willing to pay more than others for the service she offers. The diagram also shows her average costs, which, as always, include her opportunity costs—the income she could earn elsewhere. If she must quote a single price to all patients, she will not stay in this com-

[3]The original efficiency loss under uncontrolled monopoly was triangle E_1TE_2, because the monopoly chose equilibrium E_1 rather than the efficient equilibrium E_2.

This example presents a puzzle: A government price ceiling increases efficiency here, but in other circumstances a government price ceiling—such as the ceiling on rents described earlier—*reduces* efficiency. How is this possible? The answer: The ceiling on rents moved an industry *away* from an efficient, perfectly competitive equilibrium. On the other hand, the price ceiling in Figure 25-7 moves an inefficient monopoly at E_1 *toward* an efficient equilibrium at E_2.

Clearly, government intervention can be a powerful tool, since it can move a market away from its free-market equilibrium. While this can be damaging if the free market is initially competitive, it can be beneficial if the free market is initially monopolized. For this reason, economists oppose price regulation in some circumstances but favor it in others.

munity. The reason is that the average cost curve AC is always above the demand curve *D*, regardless of the price charged. Consequently, there is no single price she can select that will cover her costs. The best she can do is to select a point like *E* on the demand curve, setting her fee at P_1 and selling quantity Q_1. However, she still suffers a loss. Specifically, her total loss, compared with what she could earn elsewhere, is areas 1 + 2; that is, Q_1 units sold at a loss of CP_1 on each.

Under such circumstances, this community loses its doctor. The question is: Isn't there some way she could be allowed to charge more and thus find this town attractive after all? The answer is yes. Indeed she can charge more in a way that will not only benefit her but the community as well. Here's how: by discriminating among patients, selling her service at a higher price to some than to others. To illustrate, suppose she starts at initial position *E*, charging one price P_1 to all her patients and incurring losses 1 + 2. She can do better by charging her wealthy patients a higher fee P_2 for the Q_2 of services they require. This increases her income by areas 1 + 3, more than offsetting her original losses 1 + 2. Therefore, she is now able to more than cover her costs. With a higher income here than she could earn elsewhere, she decides to stay in town.

In short, if she cannot discriminate, she won't be able to earn as much here as elsewhere, and will leave. However, if she is allowed to discriminate, she will be able to earn a higher income and will stay in town. This is beneficial not only for her but for her patients as well. They get area JEQ_1O of benefit from her services, which is more than the area 3 + 1 + 4 + 5 that they pay for these services. (Her wealthy patients pay price P_2 for Q_2 of her services, for a total of area 3 + 1 + 4. At the same time, her less wealthy patients pay price P_1 for Q_2Q_1 units, for a total of area 5.) Price discrimination is justified in this case because it benefits everyone concerned.

However, even when price discrimination is desirable, it may not be possible. To make different prices stick, the discriminating monopolist must be able to divide the market, thus preventing individuals who buy at the low price from turning around and selling to those who are charged the higher price. In our example, the doctor is able to divide her market: A poor patient who is able to buy an operation at a bargain price cannot turn around and sell it to a rich friend. On the other hand, a bus company may not be able to divide its adult market, charging some customers $10 and others $20. The reason is that those who are able to buy cheap $10 tickets

FIGURE 25-8

When discriminating monopoly may be justified

If the doctor—the potential monopolist—can charge only one price, she will leave this town, because the demand *D* is not substantial enough to overlap AC. Any point such as E_1 that she might select on *D* would thus leave her operating at a loss, shown by area 1 + 2. On the other hand, she will stay if she is allowed to discriminate, charging low fee P_1 to the poor and high fee P_2 to the rich. On her Q_2 of services sold to the rich, she increases her income by area 1 + 3, which is more than enough to offset her original loss 1 + 2. Thus she can earn a profit—her benefit from discriminatory pricing. At the same time, her patients also benefit because they keep their doctor.

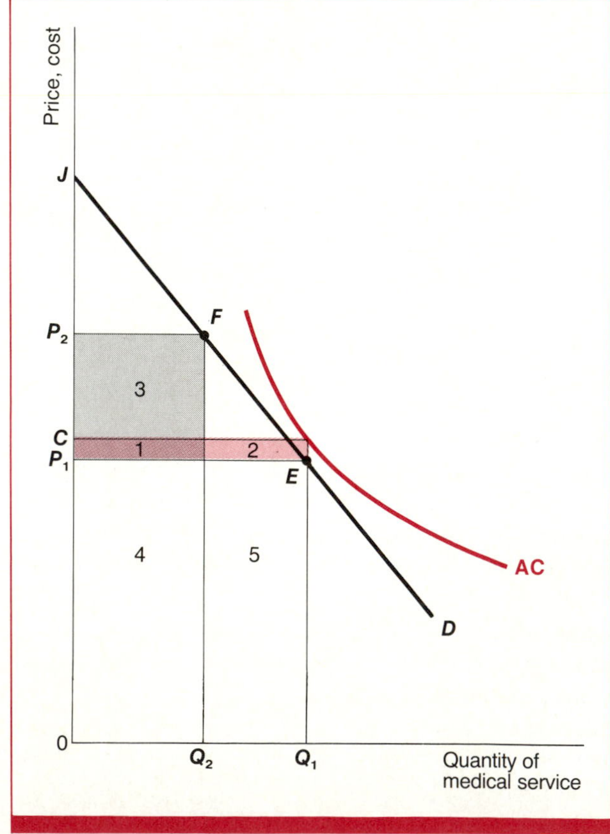

may sell them to the others for a price like $15 that benefits both groups. (However, the bus company *can* divide its market between adults and children, since an adult can't buy a cheap ticket from a child and use it on a bus. The company may also give a discount to senior citizens, since they are also relatively easily identified, and those who are not 65 usually don't want to pretend that they are.)

Finally, it should be reemphasized that it is possible to defend price discrimination by the monopolist in Figure 25-8 because *D* does not overlap AC, and she would leave otherwise. However, price discrimination cannot be similarly justified in the normal case of monopoly, where *D* does overlap AC and the monopolist can therefore at least cover costs by quoting a single price. This is the type of monopoly that we shall concentrate on hereafter in this book.

DO FIRMS REALLY MAXIMIZE PROFITS?

The best of all monopoly profits is a quiet life.
J. R. Hicks

So far, it has been assumed that producers maximize profits. However, they may occasionally pursue quite different objectives. Sometimes, they may decide on a policy because it makes them look good to their stockholders. Sometimes, with the objective of expanding their market share, they may increase output beyond the profit-maximizing point, provided they achieve some reasonable level of profit. (It is often not clear whether this is simply expansion for its own sake, or whether firms are giving up profit in the short run in order to increase it in the long run. For example, firms may want to grow in order to generate public confidence and thereby made it easier to sell their products in the future.) Alternatively, in order to avoid risk, producers may swing in the other direction and "think small," only undertaking expenditures that will yield an assured high profit. Or they may follow a policy of "no change" solely because they enjoy the quiet life. For example, if they are earning large profits, why should they worry about changing their output and price just because their cost curves have shifted slightly? Or why should they worry about the small extra cost if they hire a few relatives?

Why not construct our economic theory using one of these other assumptions instead? The answer, in some cases, is that these other assumptions would not be specific enough. For example, 10 business executives in identical circumstances, each pursuing the quiet life, might come up with 10 different decisions on output and price; you can't construct much of a theory with that. Even in those cases where a theory can be constructed, it will have the same flaw as profit maximization: It will not describe all economic decision making. Accordingly, we use profit maximization because this assumption is simple and precise enough to allow us to "get off square one" and construct a theory, and because it generally describes economic decision making at least as well as any alternative simple assumption. However, we recognize that in some cases it may not be as accurate a description of reality as we would like. And it is often only part of the story, since other objectives may also influence the decision-making process.[4] Therefore, we should be appropriately guarded in making claims for our conclusions.

Of course, if we have evidence that certain firms are pursuing some other objective such as rapid growth, we may be able to adjust our profit-maximization conclusions in some reasonable way. For example, since high-growth firms tend to produce a larger output than profit-maximizing firms, we might ask: What does this greater output imply about price to the consumer? What are its effects on efficiency? How would producers respond to price regulation? And so on. The answers to some of these questions are straightforward, but others are not so clear. If we wanted to clarify them, we might even go one giant step further and construct a whole new theory from scratch, based on some other assumption than profit maximization. But that's a story for a more advanced course.

---

[4]For more detail on alternative theories of decision making by the firm, see H. A. Simon, "Rational Decision-Making in Business Organizations," *American Economic Review,* September 1979, pp. 493–513; and Robin Marris, *The Economic Theory of Managerial Capitalism,* (New York: Basic Books, 1968).

BOX 25-2

UNFORTUNATELY, DEALING WITH NATURAL MONOPOLY IS OFTEN NOT SO SIMPLE

In Figure 25-7, average cost reached a minimum and turned up at point V *before* it reached the demand curve; that is, it turned up to the left of the demand curve. In Figure 25-9 we now consider the case where the average cost curve AC keeps falling until *after* it has crossed the demand curve. In this instance, the regulation of monopoly price involves substantial problems.

To see why, suppose that we try to apply the policy that worked so well in Figure 25-7, and again try to drive the monopoly firm down its demand curve from its original profit-maximizing equilibrium at E_1 to the efficient point E_2, where marginal cost intersects demand. As before, suppose we attempt to do so by regulating price at P_2. This policy will not work here because it will turn the monopoly into a money loser and eventually drive it out of business. The reason is that at E_2 it is operating below its average cost curve AC. Thus the price P_2 that the firm receives is not enough to cover its average cost at G. The firm's per unit loss is GE_2, and its total loss is the red area.

A different approach is required; we now consider three possibilities.

Average Cost Pricing

The lowest price the government can set without eventually forcing the firm out of business is P_3, which will result in a new equilibrium at E_3. Here price is barely high enough to cover average cost; the firm just breaks even. This policy is called ***average cost pricing.*** Once again, the regulatory agency takes away the monopoly's power to select a point on its demand curve; the agency makes the decision on the appropriate point and makes it stick by regulating price.

Average cost pricing is setting price at the level where AC intersects the demand curve.

In theory, break-even price P_3 should be easy for the agency to find. If the firm is earning an (above-normal) profit—as it would, for example at E_1—price is too high; so lower it. If the firm is operating at a loss, at a point like E_2, price is too low; raise it. This simple rule of thumb will bring the regulators to P_3, the price that just covers costs, including a fair return on the capital the owners have invested. *In practice,* however, P_3 is very difficult to determine, largely because of problems in defining (1) a fair percentage return to capital and (2) the amount of capital invested—problems examined in Appendix 25-B.

Finally, the effect on efficiency of average cost pricing is shown in panel b of Figure 25-9. If it were possible to move the monopoly all the way down its demand curve from E_1 to E_2, the result would be the now familiar triangular efficiency gain shown as areas 4 + 5. However, average cost pricing allows us to move this firm only part way, from E_1 to E_3. Therefore the gain is limited to area 4.

We conclude that since this policy of average cost pricing increases monopoly output from Q_1 to Q_3, it results in a *gain in allocative efficiency.* (Remember that unless we state otherwise, the word "efficiency" means "allocative efficiency.") Unfortunately, however, this policy, and any of the others discussed in this box, may lead to a *loss in technical efficiency*—that is, the firm may not operate on its lowest possible cost curve. After all, why should the firm in Figure 25-9 strive hard to lower its costs, when a reduction in costs will cause the regulatory agency to correspondingly lower price? Why shouldn't the firm's executives be allowed generous expense accounts, since such costs are simply passed on to consumers in the form of higher prices? No matter what the firm does, it isn't allowed to make an above-normal profit; so why should it tightly control its costs? (At best, the firm can earn an above-normal profit only temporarily, between the date it reduces its costs and the date the regulatory agency gets around to reducing its price.)

Government Subsidy (with Marginal Cost Pricing)

Another possible government policy to deal with the monopoly in Figure 25-9 is to force it all the way down its demand curve from E_1 to efficient point E_2 by marginal cost pricing, while at the same time paying the firm whatever lump-sum subsidy is necessary to cover its loss. In other words, a regulated price of P_2 drives the firm down its demand curve to point E_2 (thus cap-

FIGURE 25-9

Regulating monopoly price: The difficult case

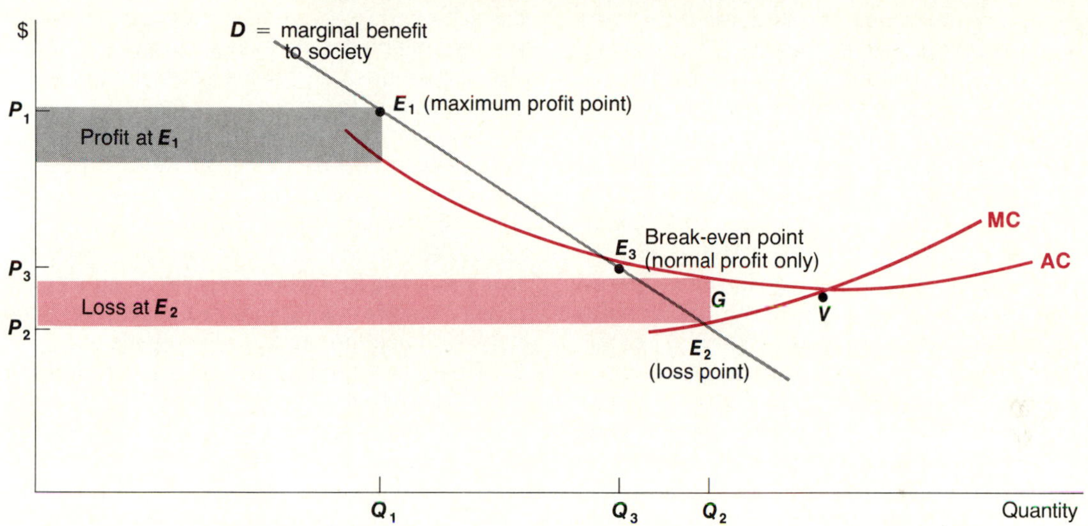

(*a*) **Average cost pricing.** An unrestricted monopoly would maximize profit by selecting point E_1 on its demand curve. (The profit it would earn is shown by the gray area.) Average cost pricing involves driving the monopoly down its demand curve to E_3, by setting a price ceiling at P_3. At this point the firm just breaks even, earning only the normal profit necessary to keep it in business.

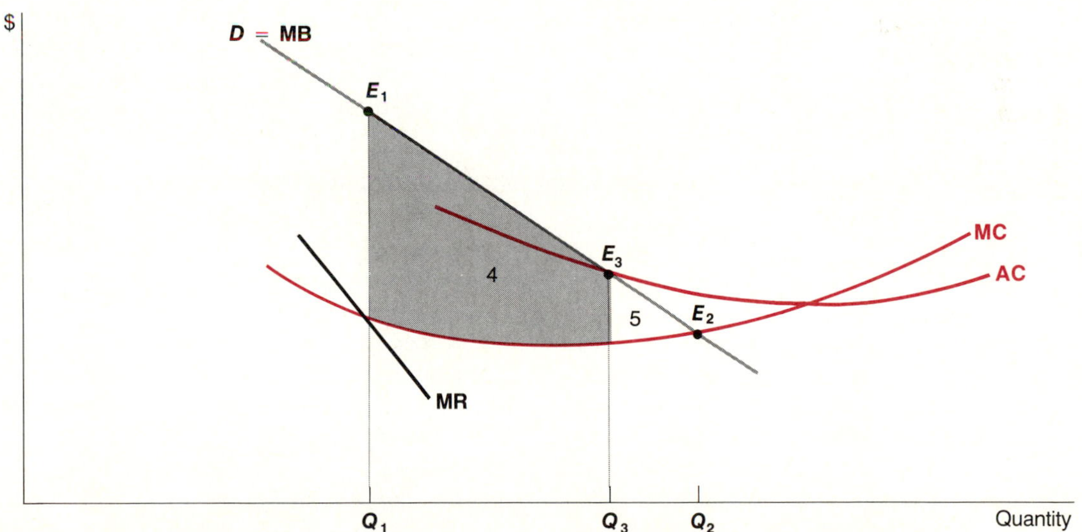

(*b*) **Efficiency gains that are achieved (4), and those that are not (5).** If it were feasible to drive the monopoly firm all the way down its demand curve from E_1 to E_2, then there would be an efficiency gain 4 + 5. But since the firm can be driven down only to E_3, the efficiency gain is limited to area 4.

turing the entire possible efficiency gain 4 + 5), while a subsidy equal to the red area in panel *a* keeps the firm in business.

Although this policy may be attractive in theory, it raises such serious problems in practice that it is seldom used. One reason is that it is difficult for the public to understand why a government committed to controlling the market power of monopoly should end up subsidizing it. The point that the government is also regulating price—and thus eliminating the profit of the monopoly—is difficult to explain to the public. Moreover, the policy of taking money out of the monopolist's pocket with one hand (the regulated price) while putting it back with the other (the subsidy) may strike the public as being inconsistent, even though it is not. In addition, the general problem in price regulation reappears here. So long as the government is committed to subsidizing the costs of a monopolist, how can those costs be controlled? A firm may be very successful in holding costs down so long as it has to meet the test of the marketplace where failure means bankruptcy; but it may be far less successful in controlling its costs if it knows it will receive a subsidy for any loss it incurs. Finally, a government that has to get a subsidy passed by a log-rolling Congress ("I'll vote for the subsidy in your district if you'll vote for the subsidy in mine") may end up with a compromise subsidy that has little relationship to the original efficiency objective.

Government Ownership

The political problems involved in granting a subsidy are less severe if the government owns the monopoly, which it can then operate in the public interest at efficient point E_2. Again, taxpayers must subsidize the loss that results. Government-owned mass transit systems are often cited as examples; government subsidies cover more than half the costs of the typical large urban public transportation system.

However, there is no guarantee that such a publicly owned enterprise will be operated at the most efficient point E_2, since the objective of the government-appointed management may not be to increase efficiency so much as to redistribute income. For example, the government may be trying indirectly to provide income—in the form of low-cost fares—to those who use the urban transport system.

Finally, we reemphasize that the same problem arises here as with the other policies discussed in this box: So long as the firm's management receives whatever subsidy is necessary to cover its costs, it has inadequate incentive to keep costs down. There is a good reason why this may become a particularly serious problem in a public enterprise. Even in a private enterprise, the owners (stockholders) may have problems in controlling a management that is inefficient, wasteful, or pursuing its own interests at the expense of the owners' interests. However, in a public enterprise this is even more difficult because of the layers of government bureaucracy separating the managers of the enterprise from its owners—in this case, the taxpayers. (Problems of a bureaucracy are examined further in Chapter 30.)

KEY POINTS

1. Monopoly means that there is a single seller. This situation may occur when a firm controls something essential to the production or sale of a good—such as a patent, resource, or government license. Or it may occur if a number of firms collude in order to be able to quote a single industry price.

2. Another important reason for monopoly is that a firm's costs may fall over such a wide range of output that total market demand can be most inexpensively satisfied by a single firm. This is a *natural monopoly*. Even if there are initially many firms in such an industry, they will tend to be eliminated by competition, with the single large firm that emerges able to undercut any present or future competitors.

3. A monopoly can do something a perfectly competitive firm cannot: Because it faces a demand curve that slopes downward to the right, it can quote the price at which it will sell.

4. Whereas marginal revenue MR for a perfect competitor is the same as price, MR for a monopoly is less than price; that is, a monopoly's MR curve lies below its demand curve.

5. A monopolist maximizes profit by equating MC with MR, not with price. As a consequence, monopoly results in an inefficiently low output. It also results

in a transfer of income from consumers to the monopolist.

6. If the firm is not a natural monopoly—but instead is, say, the result of collusion—a strong case can be made for breaking it up. The government has antitrust laws to do this, or to prevent such a monopoly from being formed in the first place. These laws will be described in Chapter 27.

7. If the firm *is* a natural monopoly, breaking it up would raise costs. A preferred government policy is to set the maximum price the monopolist can charge. Facing this given price, the monopolist is forced into the price-taking role of the perfect competitor, and consequently increases output to a more efficient quantity.

8. A case can sometimes be made for allowing a monopoly to price-discriminate, that is, to charge a higher price to one group than to another. Our example was a doctor in a small town who charged a higher price to her wealthy patients. Such discriminatory pricing may be justified if the good or service could not otherwise be produced.

KEY CONCEPTS

patent
legal monopoly
collusive monopoly
natural monopoly
oligopoly
market power
price maker
price taker
monopolist's demand
monopolist's marginal revenue
inefficiency from monopoly
how monopoly raises price and reduces output
transfer effect of monopoly
marginal cost pricing
average cost pricing
discriminating monopoly (when justified, when not)
objectives other than maximizing profit

PROBLEMS

25-1. Which is closer to being a monopoly, American Motors or Rolls Royce? Answer the same question for the producer of pastries in a small town or the producer of the wheat used in it. In each case, explain your answer.

25-2. Consider an industry in which the discovery and development of advanced machinery and technology mean that, as time passes, average costs for a firm tend to drift lower and lower; that is, through time the average cost for an individual firm moves from AC_1 to AC_2 in the following diagram. What do you think would happen in such an industry? Explain why. From the point of view of society as a whole, does the falling cost involve any advantages? Any disadvantages? In your view, how do these compare?

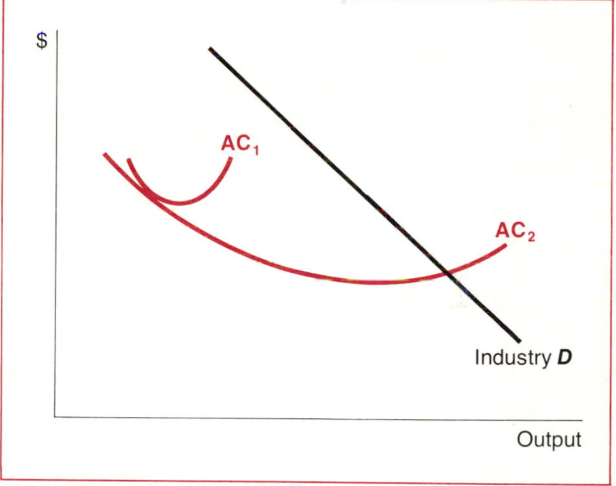

25-3. (*a*) If the firm with AC_2 in the diagram above is not regulated, would you expect that all the monopoly profits would go to the firm's owners? If not, who else do you think might eventually capture a share of these profits?

(*b*) Draw in the marginal cost curve that corresponds to AC_2. Show the best level at which to set regulated price. Explain why it is best.

***25-4.** This problem provides another way of viewing a monopolist's profit maximization, in addition to the two set out in Figure 25-4. In the next diagram, note that the

TC and TR curves for a monopolist are the same as for a perfect competitor on page 461, except for one important difference: Because a monopoly faces a downward sloping demand curve, its TR is a curved rather than a straight line. Using that earlier approach, describe how the profit-maximizing output of this monopolist is determined. In particular, show geometrically why MC = MR.

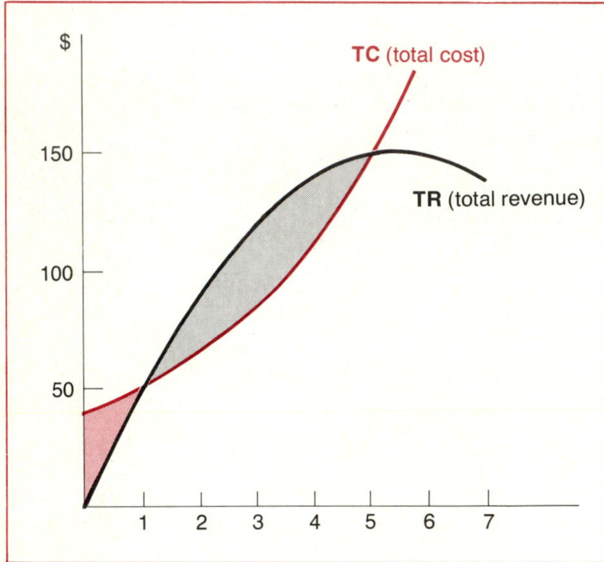

25-5. Given the cost conditions in the diagram at the top of the next column, name the price that would be set by a monopoly that is: (*a*) maximizing its profit, (*b*) operating as a nonprofit organization, (*c*) being run by the government at an efficient output. If (*a*) and/or (*b*) are not efficient, explain why.

25-6. Does output Q_1 in Figure 25-4*b* yield the monopolist the largest *profit per unit of output?* Explain why or why not.

25-7. Consider the following statement: ''Monopolies should be subject to price control. Competitive industries should not. Every owner has a monopoly in the renting of his or her building. Therefore, the government should control rents.'' Do you agree in part or in whole with this statement? Explain.

25-8. We have seen that the uncontrolled monopoly operating at E_1 in Figure 25-7 is inefficient. Which of the

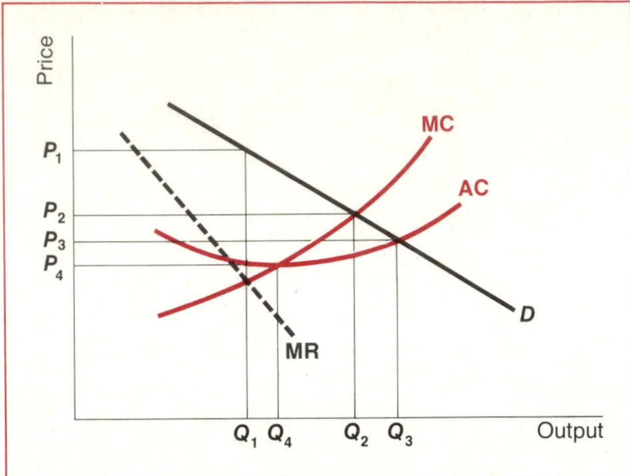

conditions for efficiency in Box 24-1 has been violated? Hint: What is the marginal cost of the uncontrolled monopoly? What is its price?

25-9. The following diagram shows the demand and the costs the government faces in providing a public utility service (say electricity) in a certain city.

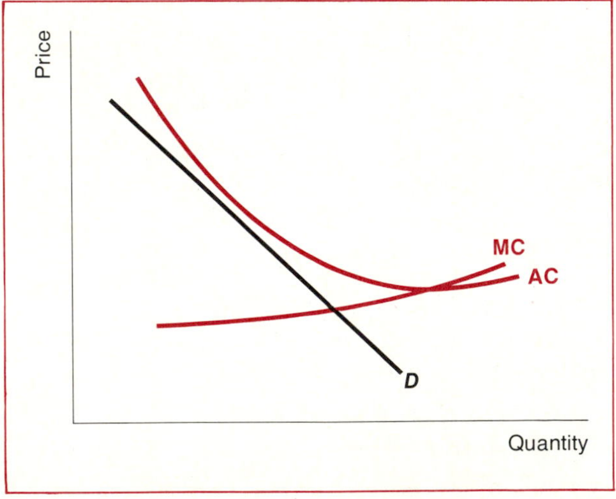

(*a*) If the government is interested only in maximizing the utility's profit—or minimizing its loss—show the price it will set and how much it will produce and sell. Also show its profit or loss.

(*b*) Is this output the best from the viewpoint of allocative efficiency? If so, explain why. If not, show what the most efficient output is and explain why. What price does the firm set to achieve this output, and what is its profit or loss at the efficient output?

(*c*) Suppose that this public utility is allowed to set discriminatory prices. It decides to charge the public a higher rate for its initial purchases while, for any additional purchases, it continues to charge the rate it set in question (*b*). Could the public utility sell an efficient output and still make profits by following a policy of price discrimination?

(*d*) Do you see now why public utilities are sometimes allowed to set discriminatory rates?

(*e*) In the section "The Special Case of Discriminating Monopoly," it was observed that for successful discrimination, a firm must be able to segregate its market and prevent resale among buyers. The doctor has no great problem in segregating her market. How about the public utility selling electricity?

***25-10.** Suppose the government owns the two monopolies shown in Figures 25-7 and 25-9. In the interests of efficiency, how should their prices be set? Would each firm operate at a profit or a loss? What government subsidy(ies) would be required? Would two such monopolies taken together necessarily require a subsidy? Explain.

***25-11.** Evaluate the following policy recommendation: "The sole objective in dealing with monopoly is to eliminate excess profits. And this is easy to do. Just examine the firm's current operations, calculate its average cost (including normal profit), and set price at this level."

APPENDIX

GOVERNMENT MARKETING PROGRAMS:

HELPING COMPETITORS TO ACT LIKE A MONOPOLIST?

Things are seldom what they seem,
Skim milk masquerades as cream.

Gilbert and Sullivan,
H. M. S. Pinafore

We have seen how a government agency set up to regulate a monopoly will force the firm to act like a perfect competitor, in the process driving it down its demand curve. However, in some cases, the government has acted in the opposite direction. A competitive industry has been provided with a marketing organization—that is, a single agency that can quote price for all the firms and thus allows these competitive firms to act like a monopolist. Specifically, by quoting a higher price the agency can move these firms *up* their market demand curve—something they cannot do by acting individually.

In panel *a* of Figure 25-10, point E_1 is the equilibrium in a competitive industry before any attempt is made to create a monopoly. The market price is $80, with 1,000 units being sold. At the same time, the situation of one of the 100 individual firms in the industry is shown in panel *b*. The firm is in equilibrium at F_1, producing 10 units and just covering its costs. (As an aside, note that panel *a* will be picking up much of the argument developed for the industry in Figure 25-6, while panel *b* will be detailing what happens to an individual firm.)

When a marketing association is formed, all producers speak with one voice and quote a higher price. Suppose the price the association decides on is $140, well above the competitive $80 level. The industry consequently moves up its demand curve in panel *a* from E_1 to E_2. To make this higher price stick, the association must, like any monopolist, reduce sales from 1,000 units to 600. This cut implies that the individual firm in panel *b* must decrease its output from 10 to a quota of 6. Therefore, the firm moves from F_1 to F_2. Despite the fact its output has been reduced, its increased price now allows it to earn the profit shown as the shaded gray area.

FIGURE 25-10

Effect of a producers' association or government marketing program on an industry and on an individual firm

Panel *a* illustrates a competitive industry. Market equilibrium is at E_1 where $D = S$. When this industry is monopolized by a producers' association or government marketing agency, equilibrium moves from E_1 to E_2. The association raises price from $80 to $140, and this reduces industry sales from 1,000 units to 600.

In turn, the sales of the individual firm in panel *b* must be reduced from 10 units to a quota of 6. This means that the firm moves from F_1 to F_2, where it makes the $240 profit shown by the gray area: On each of its 6 units, it earns a $40 profit. Although this reduction in output has generated profits, each firm facing the given $140 price would like to *increase* its output by moving from F_2 to *B*, where MC = price. However, such additional output would drive market price down; the industry in panel *a* would slide down its demand curve from E_2 toward E_1, with the individual firm in panel *b* moving from F_2 to the no-profit point F_1.

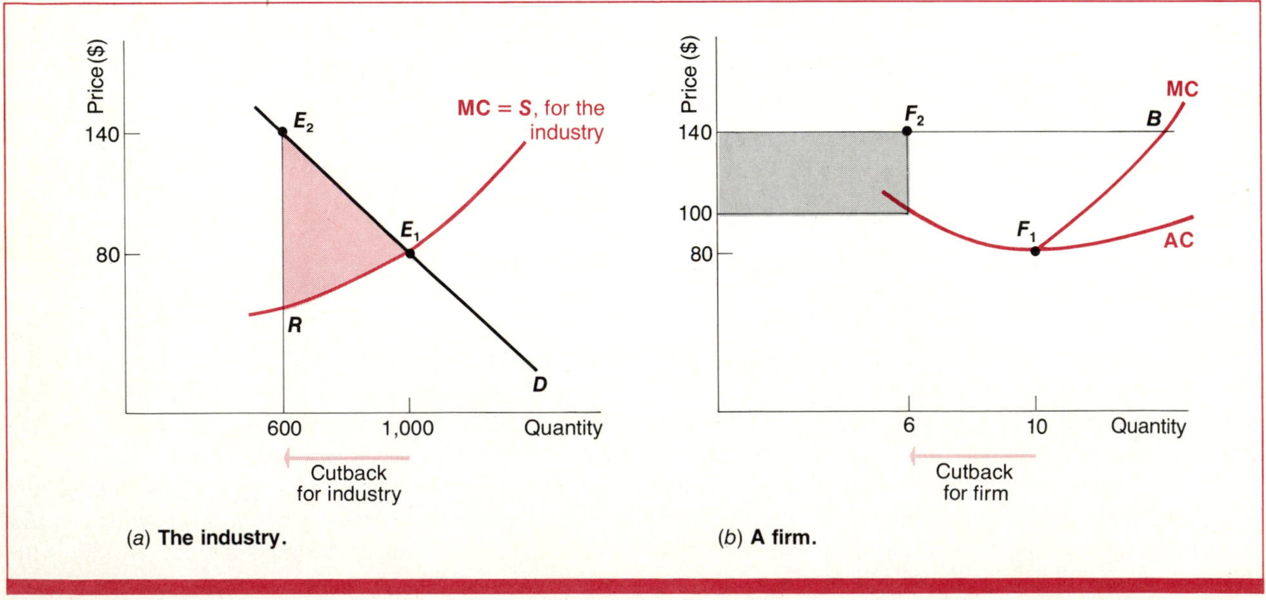

The monopolization of this industry has had the expected results. Producers benefit from their newfound profit, while consumers lose because of increased price. On balance, there is an overall efficiency loss shown by the red area in panel *a*.

However, there are strong pressures for such associations to come apart. While it is in the collective interest of all firms to restrict their output in order to raise price to $140, at this high price it is in the interest of the individual firm to *expand* output. In fact, at the $140 price set by the association, the firm in panel *a* has an incentive to produce, not at F_2, but at *B*, where MC intersects the given price. The problem, then, for the industry association is how to compel each individual firm to operate in the collective interest at F_2 rather than attempt to pursue its own interest at *B*. This discipline is essential: If some firms start to produce more than their quota, more than 600 units will come onto the market and price will fall. Moreover, getting existing firms to stick to their quotas is not the only problem: The entry of new firms, attracted by the gray above-normal profits, would also drive price down.

The problem of enforcing quotas and restricting entry often leads perfectly competitive producers of agricultural goods in the United States and elsewhere to seek a government marketing agency to do what a private producers' association may not be strong enough to accomplish. Since even a government agency may have difficulty in enforcing a quota on output, limitations are often placed instead on the acreage a farmer can plant—as in the case of U.S. tobacco producers—or on the number of hens that a poultry farm can maintain, as in the case of Canadian egg producers. However, such a quota system, even when enforced by government regulations, may spring leaks. For example, a number of Canadian egg producers were found with more hens than their quotas allowed. In fact, two of these individuals who "came up with egg on their face" were members of the board of directors of the marketing board that had set the quotas! There can be no clearer illustration of the problems of restricting output when producers' collective and individual interests are in conflict.

In the United States, there have been a number of examples of voluntary producers' associations. To cite one: By 1910, milk producers in certain regions of the country had privately banded together to gain bargaining power over their price. Their success was always limited by their inability to firmly control output coming onto the market, so that by the early 1930s they had become relatively ineffective. Under the pressure of very low milk prices in 1935, the government introduced a system of "milk marketing orders," which guaranteed the farmer a minimum price, depending on the use of the milk and the location. (Except for California, the price in any U.S. location depended on its distance from Eau Claire, Wisconsin, the heart of the U.S. dairy industry.) In addition to an efficiency loss, there were unfortunate side effects when the government thus became involved in propping up price for a group of producers: The milk suppliers had an incentive to make political campaign contributions to politicians with potential influence over their marketing program. Promises of large campaign contributions by milk producers before the 1972 Nixon election were followed by a price increase for the industry, and this action became the subject of a special Watergate-related investigation.

PROBLEMS

***25-12.** Show the profit that the firm in Figure 25-10*b* would capture if it could get away with producing at point *B*. Is this an equilibrium if all firms try to do the same? Explain.

***25-13.** How might an agricultural marketing association be defended by using the theory of the second best?

***25-14.** The British Columbia Milk Board sells milk at a price more than 10% above the free-market level. The board has also made it illegal to sell reconstituted milk, that is, powdered milk mixed with water and fresh milk. The reason given for this action is to protect the consumer from an inferior product. Yet, in tests, many consumers cannot distinguish this milk from fresh milk, and it would cost far less. Is the marketing board protecting consumers or some other group?

APPENDIX

AVERAGE COST PRICING:

PUBLIC UTILITY REGULATION

Several problems arise when the theory of average cost pricing is put into practice in regulating a ***public utility***.

A *public utility* is a natural monopoly in which many decisions—particularly pricing decisions—are regulated by a government agency. (Some public utilities are owned by the government.) A public utility typically provides an essential service to the public, and often has high overhead costs because of the heavy equipment it requires to deliver its product to the consumer. Examples include the companies that supply natural gas via pipelines, and those that supply electricity via transmission lines.

HOW IS AVERAGE COST CALCULATED?

Recall from Figure 25-9 that average cost pricing involves setting a price that will barely cover average costs, including normal profit. In other words, the objective is to keep the price low enough to prevent excessive monopoly profits but high enough to provide the normal profit that will keep the firm in business. Estimating a fair or normal profit for the owners involves estimating the amount of capital they have invested and a fair percentage rate of return to be applied to that capital.

1. What is a fair percentage rate of return on capital invested? The answer to this should be: the opportunity cost of capital—the percentage rate of return it could earn elsewhere in the economy. Although regulatory agencies have given some consideration to earnings in other sectors of the economy, their rates of return have not matched rates elsewhere, perhaps because of tradition and a feeling that it is their responsibility to the public to keep their prices down. This problem of a relatively low rate of return in public utilities has been made worse by a squeeze that results from inflation. It raises the costs of inputs to utilities, but there is a regulatory time lag before the utilities are allowed to compensate by raising their price. Because of their relatively low rate of return, it has been difficult for the utilities to attract capital.

It is sometimes argued that this lower return is a reflection of the lower risk involved in public utility investment. True, there is no risk that the public utility will be driven bankrupt by competitors, since there are none. However, a utility may be driven bankrupt by costs that get out of control. Although by 1985 no public utility had gone bankrupt since the Depression, there was a real risk that it might occur again. Moreover, public utility investment involves its own special kind of risk: the risk that the regulators will not adequately or quickly enough protect the investors' return from being eroded by inflation. Finally, there is another substantial risk involved in investing in a public utility using nuclear power: At any point, the government or the courts may force the firm to suspend or terminate its operations. Because of all these considerations, public utilities are far from being a risk-free form of investment; therefore, the relatively low rate of return earned on this investment does discourage the inflow of capital.

2. What is the value of the capital invested (the "rate base")? Should it be the *original cost* of the machinery and other capital bought by the firm, or the *present replacement cost* (less depreciation in either case)? Because of inflation, this makes a lot of difference. The cost of replacing most equipment far exceeds its original cost years ago. Thus far, there is no clear consensus among the regulatory agencies on which method to use.

OTHER PROBLEMS AND REFORM PROPOSALS

Few would argue that regulation of a public utility

should be abolished. Such regulation is the most reasonable way of getting the low costs offered by a natural monopoly while avoiding the worst monopoly abuses. However, it is far from being problem-free; it can be argued that regulation can be improved, both by making it more consistent[5] and by speeding up regulatory decisions (so capital-starved utilities are caught less in an inflation squeeze).

[5]The problem of conflicting regulations is further illustrated by the comical situation in which telephone companies operating in California were caught. Their Californian regulating agency insisted that they pass on to their customers (via a price reduction) some federal tax savings. But then the IRS (Internal Revenue Service in Washington) ruled that they could not get these tax savings if they passed them on. (One reason for the tax break was to encourage investment, and the phone companies wouldn't have an incentive to invest if they had to pass the savings along to the users.) Thus, the companies were caught in a Catch 22 situation. They were receiving a benefit from IRS that they had to pass on to the Californian consumers; but as soon as they passed it on, the IRS wanted it back. The companies' solution: Don't take the benefit from IRS in the first place; just forget the whole thing. But then the California regulators, annoyed that phone users in the state weren't getting a reduced price after all, forced the companies to lower their price. The phone companies then went to work lobbying in Washington to have the tax law changed. This is only the beginning of the story, but it illustrates the administrative and legal tangle that a firm can find itself in when it is caught in the conflicting regulations of two or more government agencies.

PROBLEM

***25-15.** Some recently installed nuclear power plants have been so expensive to build that covering this cost would require the regulatory agencies to raise electricity prices by 40% to 60%. Moreover, this 40 to 60% price increase has been calculated on the assumption that even this sort of ''rate shock'' would not change the quantity demanded of electricity. Explain why a regulatory agency that passed this full 40% to 60% price increase on to the public might find that the utility could *still* not cover its costs.

CHAPTER 26

MARKETS BETWEEN MONOPOLY AND PERFECT COMPETITION

People of the same trade seldom meet together, even for merriment and diversion, but the conversation ends in a conspiracy against the public, or in some contrivance to raise prices.

ADAM SMITH,
Wealth of Nations

Monopoly represents the clearest form of market power; the monopoly firm is alone in the marketplace and has the power to choose its selling price. However, if we look at such giants of American business as General Motors, IBM, and General Electric, we find that most of them are not monopolists. General Motors competes with Ford, Chrysler, and foreign producers; IBM has to compete with Apple in personal computers and with Digital Equipment in business computers; General Electric competes with Westinghouse in electrical generators, and with Pratt and Whitney in jet engines. ***Oligopoly***—where a market is dominated by a *few* sellers—is more significant in the U.S. economy than outright monopoly.

This chapter initially deals with oligopoly, concentrating on the difficult policy questions it raises and the various measures the government can use to control it. In addition, this chapter describes another of the many kinds of market that lie between monopoly and perfect competition: monopolistic competition, which has been used to describe firms engaged in retail trade. This will complete our discussion of the basic market forms.

OLIGOPOLY

The degree to which an industry is dominated by a few sellers is measured by a ***concentration ratio.*** Two such ratios are in common use: The four-firm concentration ratio measures the percentage of an industry's output produced by its four largest firms, while the eight-firm ratio measures the output of its eight largest firms. Figure 26-1 shows that the auto and breakfast food industries are dominated by large firms. However, also notice that there are some industries, like petroleum and refining, which are not.

Have these concentration ratios been getting larger or smaller over time? The answer is: larger for some industries, smaller for others. For example, Figure 26-1 shows that by 1977 greeting cards and boats differed dramatically. Yet 30 years earlier, they had essentially the same degree of concentration: Between 1947 and 1977, the four-firm concentration ratio rose from 39% to 77% for greeting cards, while it fell from 31% to 11% for boats. At the same time, in many other industries such as concrete block and bricks, there was little change.

If we look at the average for all industries, there is little evidence of any dramatic increase or decrease over time. In the words of MIT's Morris Adleman in 1951, any tendency for change, even if it does exist "must be at the speed of a glacial drift." In the next two decades, concentration in manufacturing seems to have increased, but by a barely discernible amount, according to a study by Mueller and Rodgers. They estimated that, over the period from 1947 to 1972, the four-firm concentration ratio for 167 U.S. manufacturing industries rose, on average, from 41% to 43%.[1] There seems to be no strong

[1]See Willard F. Mueller and Richard T. Rogers, "The Role of Advertising in Changing Concentration of Manufacturing Industries," *The Review of Economics and Statistics,* February 1980, p. 90. Using 1947–1972 data, Mueller and Rogers also provide estimates indicating that the slight increase in the overall average was the net result of a small decline in concentration in producer goods industries, and a more marked increase in concentration in consumer goods industries—in part because TV advertising made it easier for the few largest firms in a consumer goods industry to dominate their market.

tendency for America's largest firms to eliminate their competition and emerge as monopolists.

Indeed, in the past decade, the overall competitiveness of the U.S. economy seems to have been getting somewhat *greater* because of the rise of new industries such as microcomputers, with many small highly competitive firms, and because of the increasing importance of service industries, where firms are often small. In addition, U.S. manufacturing has been faced with greater competition from imports. For example, import competition has made the U.S. auto industry far more competitive than its high concentration ratio in Figure 26-1 suggests. (However, in some cases the government has limited this competition by barriers to international trade, such as the quotas imposed in the past on the imports of Japanese cars.) Failure to take imports into account limits the validity of any measure of concentration, including the two shown in Figure 26-1 or the somewhat more complicated "Herfindahl index" discussed in Box 26-1.

Because there is no strong tendency for industries to become monopolized, oligopoly seems to be a stable form of market organization. It is not merely a temporary stop on an inevitable road to monopoly. What accounts for this stability? Why do a few firms grow so large, while none goes all the way to become a monopolist? In other words, why are there several firms in an industry rather than just one?

Part of the answer lies in the nature of costs. In many industries, there are advantages of large-scale production; there is a decline in average cost as output rises. A plant designed to produce 500,000 cars per year can operate at a much lower average cost than a plant designed to produce 50,000. But costs do not continue to fall forever. Once a plant is producing a million units, doubling its output won't significantly reduce its costs

FIGURE 26-1

Importance of "big four" and "big eight" in selected industries, 1977

Source: Bureau of the Census, U.S. Department of Commerce, *1977 Census of Manufacturers: Concentration Ratios in Manufacturing,* MC 77-SR-9, Table 7.

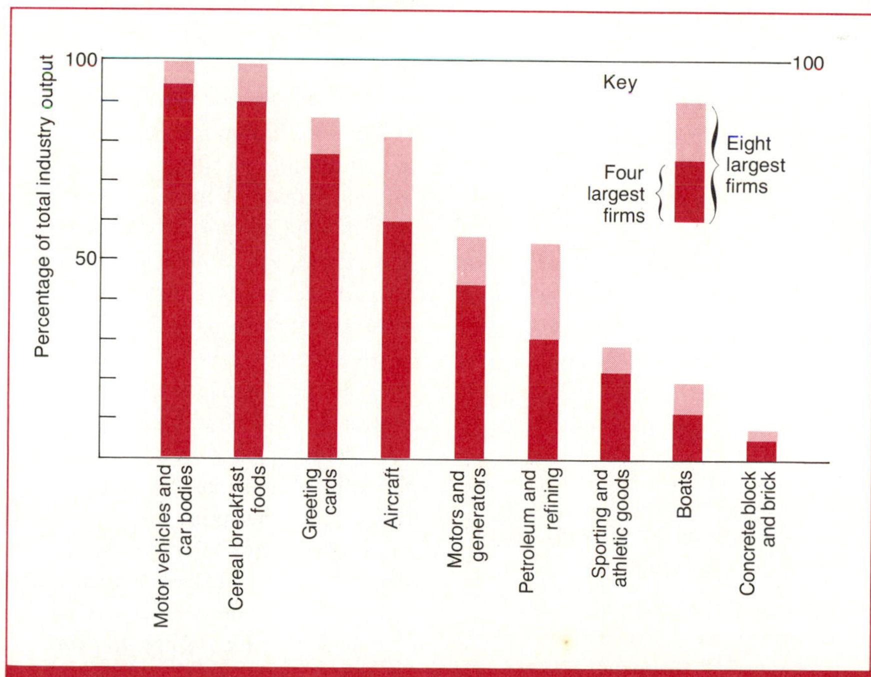

BOX 26-1

ANOTHER MEASURE OF INDUSTRY CONCENTRATION: THE HERFINDAHL INDEX

To understand this index, first consider a monopoly—an industry with the maximum possible degree of concentration. One hundred percent of the industry's output is sold by one firm; that is, the market share of this firm is 100% = 1.0. In this case, the Herfindahl index value is

$$(1.0)^2 = 1.0, \text{ the largest value the index can take}$$

Next, consider a nearly monopolized industry. One firm produces 90% of the output, while the only other firm produces 10%—that is, their market shares are .9 and .1. In this case, the index becomes

$$(.9)^2 + (.1)^2 = .82, \text{ still a very high value}$$

Notice that the value of the Herfindahl index falls as the number of firms in the industry increases.

As our final example, suppose that there are again two firms in the industry, but the first one no longer dominates. Instead, they both sell the same amount; their market shares are .5 and .5. Following our procedure of squaring market shares, we get a Herfindhal index of

$$(.5)^2 + (.5)^2 = .50$$

Thus the index also falls as the market shares of the firms become more equal.

Formally, the Herfindahl index is defined as the *sum of the squared market shares of all the firms.* It does a good job of taking into account the number of firms in an industry, and the degree of equality in their market shares. These are two characteristics that are critical in any evaluation of the concentration of an industry.

Although the Herfindahl index is slightly more complicated, the Justice Department has recently been using it rather than the four-firm concentration ratio in making its decisions on whether an industry is too concentrated.

further. When costs cease to fall, there is no longer this incentive for firms to continue to grow into a monopoly position.

The result is ***natural oligopoly.*** In panel *b* of Figure 26-2 we see that this market form falls somewhere between the extremes of perfect competition and natural monopoly. Note that average costs for an individual firm continue to fall over a considerable range, up to an output of 300 units. If existing firms are producing less than this, there is a tendency for them to expand. However, at an output of 300 units—still far short of satisfying total market demand of 1,000 units—costs stop falling. At this point, existing firms no longer have a "falling cost" incentive to expand into a monopoly position.

***Natural oligopoly* occurs when the average costs of individual firms fall over a large enough range so that a few firms can produce the total quantity sold at the lowest average cost.**

However, it is not just cost conditions that account for the persistence of oligopoly. Oligopoly represents a balance of forces that encourage concentration and those that work against it.

One of the strongest forces working toward larger and larger corporations is the incentive such firms have to acquire market power. The larger a firm becomes by internal growth or by buying out and absorbing its competitors, the greater its power to set price. (The fewer and smaller its competitors, the fewer sales they will be able to take away if the firm raises its price.) For this reason, a firm in natural oligopoly, with no further opportunities to cut costs by expanding, may nonetheless still seek to expand in order to push competitors out of the market and thus acquire more power to set price.

On the other side, the government provides a countervailing force that deters the expansion of firms and discourages the monopolization of an industry. Specifically, the desire to protect consumers and competitors has led Congress to pass antitrust laws that prevent firms from establishing a monopolylike position.

The ***product differentiation*** which exists in many oligopolistic markets also discourages monopolization.

A car is not just a car; there are many kinds—it's a differentiated product. For many years, American Motors has been very successful in the production of a very special kind of vehicle—a four-wheel-drive Jeep. The profits it obtained by its strength in producing this highly differentiated product saved it from bankruptcy, and thus prevented the broader auto industry from becoming even more concentrated. Likewise, product differentiation is important in many other oligopolistic industries. Control Data builds computers that are similar but not identical to giant IBM's. McDonnell-Douglas builds planes that are similar but not identical to those of Boeing. However, the product differentiation that is so important in many oligopolistic markets may not be significant in others. In the basic steel industry, for example, one company's product is much the same as another's.

THE OLIGOPOLIST AS A PRICE SEARCHER

We have seen that oligopoly lies in the broad area between the extreme cases of monopoly and perfect competition. At either of these two extremes, the firm does not have to worry about how its competitors will react if it changes its price or output. By definition, the monopolist has no competitors worth worrying about. On the other hand, the perfectly competitive firm has so many competitors that none will even be aware of any change it may make in its price or output. Since it provides such a miniscule part of the total market supply, its competitors won't even notice if it reduces the amount it is supplying. In contrast, in an oligopoly, each firm is very much aware of the other firms. Each recognizes that the others will notice any action it takes, and it must there-

FIGURE 26-2
Natural oligopoly compared with perfect competition and natural monopoly

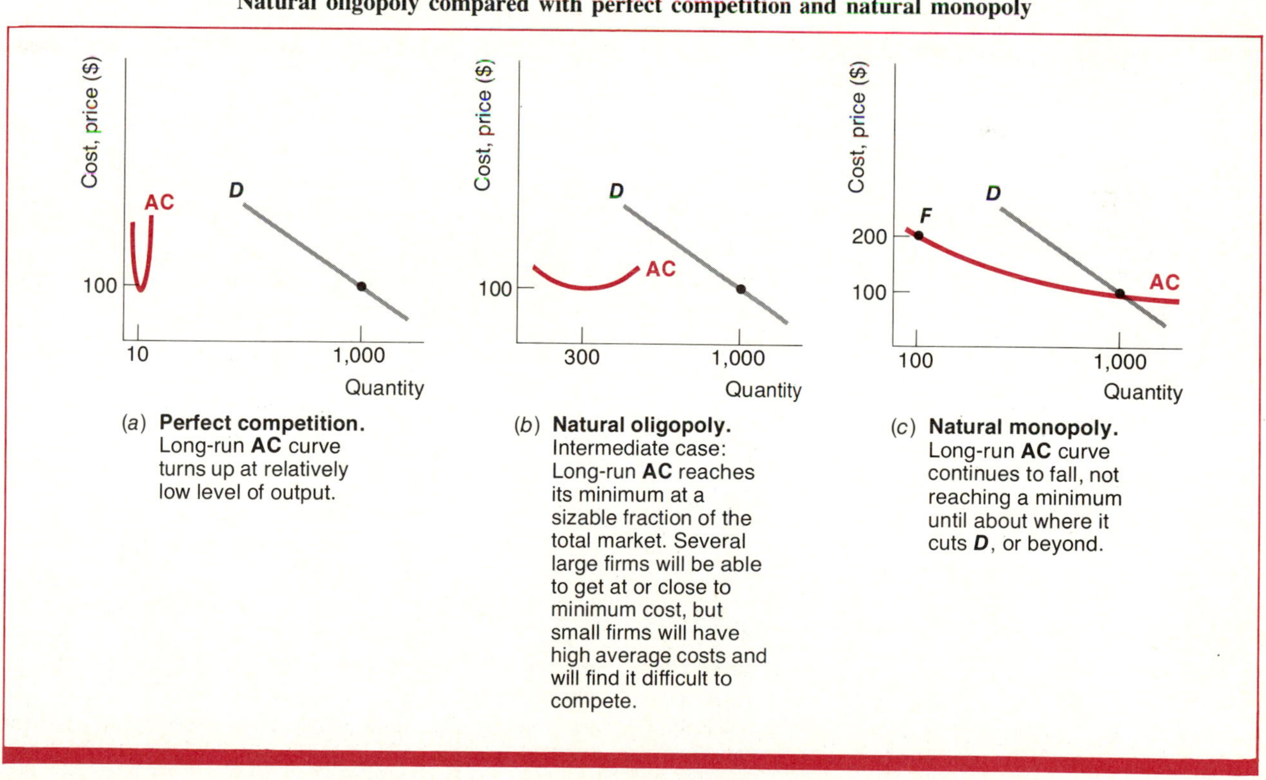

(*a*) **Perfect competition.** Long-run **AC** curve turns up at relatively low level of output.

(*b*) **Natural oligopoly.** Intermediate case: Long-run **AC** reaches its minimum at a sizable fraction of the total market. Several large firms will be able to get at or close to minimum cost, but small firms will have high average costs and will find it difficult to compete.

(*c*) **Natural monopoly.** Long-run **AC** curve continues to fall, not reaching a minimum until about where it cuts ***D***, or beyond.

fore be concerned about how they will react. If it reduces price, will its competitors follow? Will its action set off a price war? Where might this lead? In an oligopoly, the firms are mutually *interdependent;* each is very sensitive to the reactions of its competitors.

The three different types of market can be distinguished in a simple way. In *perfect competition,* firms are ***price takers.*** The individual firm has no influence over price, since it is determined by the impersonal forces of demand and supply. In *monopoly,* the firm is a ***price maker.*** It is able to select a point on the market demand curve; that is, it is able to choose the price at which it will sell. In *oligopoly,* the firm is a ***price searcher.*** Although it has some influence over price, it can't set a price in the simple way that a monopolist can. Instead, in its pricing decisions it must take into account a major complication: How will its competitors react?

Because an oligopolistic firm is in competition with several other large firms capable of vigorously responding to its actions, it must develop a marketing strategy. The world of oligopoly can resemble a chess game, with move and countermove. And, like a chess game, the outcome may be unpredictable. Once we enter the world of oligopoly, we leave behind the simple, definite solutions of both monopoly and perfect competition. Ever since Augustin Cournot's nineteenth-century study of duopoly (two sellers), it has been recognized that, when there are just a few sellers, the search for an equilibrium price can be quite complex. Oligopoly is one of the least satisfactory areas of economic theory.

For this reason, it is not possible here to do more than emphasize a few highlights. The first topic involves the situation where oligopolists recognize their common interest in raising prices, and collude to act as though they were a monopoly. The second topic is the case where oligopolists abandon this common interest in pursuit of their own individual interests and the collusive arrangement comes apart.

Collusion

In the United States, collusion is against the law. The reason for such laws may be seen by looking at the economic effects of a ***cartel,*** the most formal type of collusion, where firms get together to gain the advantages of monopoly.

A *cartel* is a formal agreement among firms about price and market sharing.

As a simple example, consider a market in which there are three similar firms. Suppose that, while maintaining their separate corporate identities with their own plants and sales forces, they get together to agree on a common price. In their collective interest, what is the best price to choose? The answer: the price which a monopolist would pick, that is, the price which will maximize their combined profits. Specifically, this price is determined in Figure 26-3 as follows. The horizontal arrows show how the marginal cost curve for the industry in panel *b* is derived, as always, from the marginal cost curves of the individual firms. The highest profit in panel *b* is earned at an output of 600 units, where the MC curve for the industry cuts the industry's marginal revenue curve MR. (MR may be calculated from the demand curve for the industry, just as it was for the firm in Table 25-1). Point *E* on the demand curve indicates that the profit-maximizing output of 600 units can be sold at a price of $100.

Thus, the collusive oligopoly maximizes profits by behaving as if it were a monopoly. However, it faces a problem which the monopolist doesn't have to worry about: How is the restricted production of 600 units to be divided among the three firms? The simplest solution is to set a quota of 200 units for each, as shown in panel *a*. Each firm sells at point *F,* where it makes a profit of $4,000, illustrated by the gray area; that is, it sells 200 units at a profit of $20 each. (The $20 profit is the difference between the $100 selling price and the $80 average cost.)

While this collusive arrangement benefits the three firms, it is harmful to the economy as a whole. Just as in the case of monopoly, too little is produced, as we see in panel *b*. For an efficient allocation of resources, output should not be 600 units. Instead it should be 900, where marginal cost equals the marginal benefit to society, that is, where the marginal cost curve intersects the demand curve. The efficiency loss from collusion is shown by the red triangle—another example of the triangular loss from producing too little. In a cartel, just as in a monopoly, Adam Smith's "invisible hand" fails, as Smith himself recognized in the quotation at the beginning of this chapter.

There are a number of ways that participants in a cartel can agree to limit sales, in addition to the equal division just described. For example, in the 1930s, an agreement between General Electric and Westinghouse effectively limited Westinghouse to a small share of the market for light bulbs. (Westinghouse agreed to pay General Electric a 2% royalty for the right to produce an improved light bulb, provided Westinghouse confined itself to selling only one-third as many bulbs as GE. If Westinghouse sold more, it would have to pay a prohibitively high royalty of 30%.) Another way to divide the market is to use historical market shares—or, even more simply, geographical areas. For example, two European firms agreed in the 1920s to carve up the market for

FIGURE 26-3
Collusion by three oligopolists

In panel *b*, MC for the industry is shown as the horizontal sum of the MC curves for the three individual firms on the left, and MR for the industry is calculated from the industry's demand *D*. The maximization of industry profit requires that output be set at 600 units (where the industry's MC = MR) and that price be set at $100. In other words, the colluding firms select point *E* on the market demand curve. Each firm is then allowed a quota of 200 units of output in panel *a*, where it earns the gray profit area. The problem is that the individual firm facing the given $100 price would prefer to sell more than its 200-unit quota. (It can sell an additional unit for $100, while its cost of producing it is only $40.) If it does so, more than 600 units will be produced and the industry's price in panel *b* will begin to fall. If firms thus forget their *collective* interest in favor of pursuing their *individual* interest, the price-fixing arrangement comes apart.

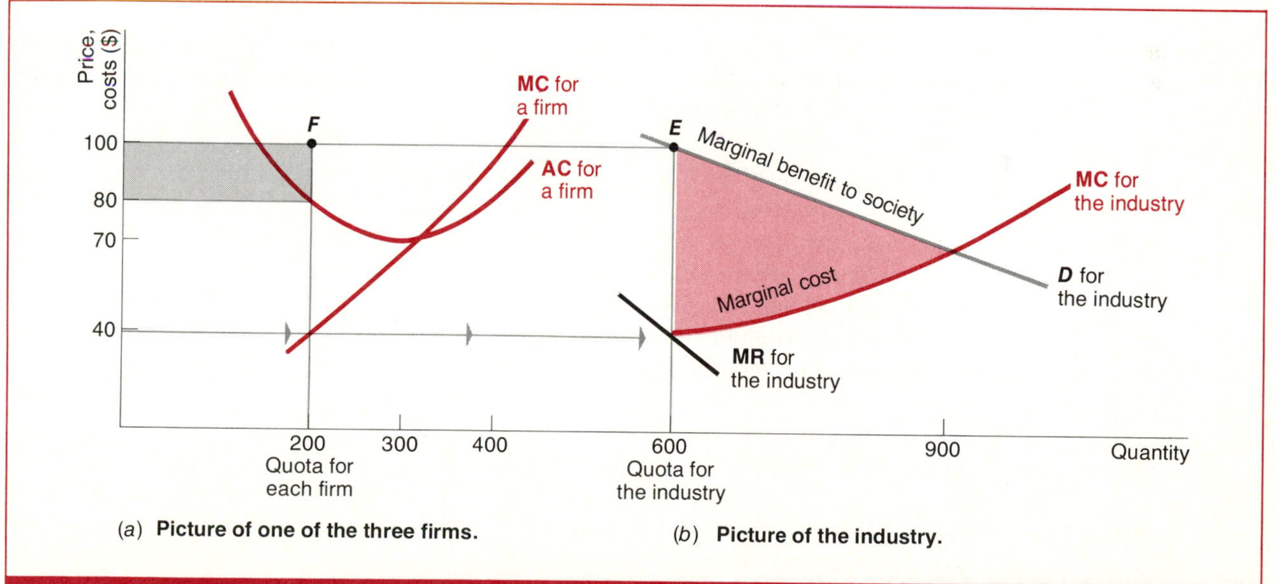

(*a*) **Picture of one of the three firms.**

(*b*) **Picture of the industry.**

explosives. Dynamite was allowed exclusive rights in certain continental European markets, in exchange for leaving British Empire markets to Nobel—the same Nobel who became famous for the peace prize.

Another form of collusion is a *bidding cartel*. For example, in isolated cases, some antique dealers in Britain have met together before the auction of a valuable item to set the price at which all of them but one would drop out of the bidding. This meant that their designated member who was left in the bidding was able to buy the antique for a bargain price at the expense of the seller. Why were the other dealers prepared to stop bidding at a low price? The answer: They knew that they would get their turn to make a bargain purchase.

The Breakdown of Collusion: The Incentive to Cheat

Market-sharing arrangements tend to be unstable, whether the firms have agreed on equal shares or not. Each firm in the cartel has an *incentive to cheat* by producing more than its alloted share.[2] To see why, note in panel *a* of Figure 26-3 that an individual firm producing 200 units of output could produce another unit at a marginal cost of only $40. If it could sell it for the going price of $100 by stealing away a sale from one of its competitors, the firm's profit will increase by $60. Thus, it has an incentive to step up sales efforts or give secret price rebates in order to win customers. (Even if a firm grants a 30%, 40%, or 50% rebate on the selling price of $100, it will still receive more from this sale than its marginal cost.) Thus, the cartel's problem is this: The members have a *collective* interest in restricting sales in order to keep the price up; however, each member firm has an *individual* interest in selling more than its allotted share. If individual interests come to dominate, with firms producing beyond their quotas, industry output in panel *b* will increase beyond 600 units, and there will be a move down the demand curve to a lower price. In other words, a struggle by firms to increase their market share will destroy the cartel. Because of the strength of the individual interest, cartels have often collapsed after short and stormy histories.

Moreover, when there is a complete breakdown in a cartel, the struggle over markets may intensify. This is particularly true if the cost advantages of large-scale production have been increasing as a result of technological change. In this case, a natural oligopoly may be evolving into a natural monopoly. In the absence of government intervention, only one firm will ultimately survive. The question is, which one? Each firm wants to be the victor; each has an incentive to try to gain an advantage over its rivals by expanding rapidly to gain the lower costs from large-scale production. Excess production is likely, with firms pushing frantically for sales. The result may be ***cutthroat competition,*** that is, selling at a price below cost in order to drive rivals out of business. In this struggle, the prize sometimes goes to the firm with the "deepest pockets" (the largest financial resources), which enable it to sustain the short-term losses while it is cutting the throats of its rivals.

[2]It is "cheating" as viewed by the other members of the cartel, but not as viewed by the public. More production will lower price and reduce the red efficiency-loss triangle.

A CASE STUDY OF COLLUSION: OIL

The most conspicuous collusive arrangement of recent decades has been the Organization of Petroleum Exporting Countries (OPEC), made up of many major oil exporters, including a number of Middle Eastern nations, along with Indonesia, Nigeria, and Venezuela. The prime objective of OPEC was to raise the price of oil, and in less than a decade—between 1973 and 1982—that price rose from less than $3 a barrel to $34, as shown in Figure 26-4. The result was far and away the greatest peacetime transfer of wealth among nations in history. Why was OPEC this successful in the 1970s? And why did it seem to be losing control, as the price of oil began to fall in the 1980s?

OPEC's success in 1973–1974 was particularly surprising because a number of experts thought it would fail. However, in those early days, OPEC had one great strength: Oil buyers had to deal with its members, since they were by far the largest international source of oil, as Figure 26-5 illustrates. In particular, note the preeminent position held by Saudi Arabia. Because OPEC supplied most of the internationally traded oil, it was able to set the world price.

However, OPEC had an apparent weakness: While it was raising the price, it had no formal system of production quotas to restrict its output and supply. How then was it able to make its high prices stick? There were several special reasons; one of the most important is described in the next section, while the others are discussed in Box 26-2.

The Rising Price in the 1970s: The Key Role of the Saudis

Although the OPEC countries collectively had no effective way of controlling production, one OPEC member—Saudia Arabia—was such a large supplier that it was able to keep the oil price up during the early years of OPEC success. Specifically, whenever it appeared that a price-depressing glut was developing on the world oil market, Saudi Arabia would cut back its own production. This maintained the world oil shortage that kept the price from falling. Thus OPEC was able to maintain a high price during the 1970s without resort to production quotas.

Saudi Arabia was willing and able to cut back its production of oil because of its very special circumstances. With its small population, it had accumulated huge assets from past oil sales. Therefore, unlike some of the heavily populated OPEC countries such as Nigeria, Saudi Arabia wasn't desperate to raise money by large-scale oil production; it could comfortably "keep its black gold in the ground." To illustrate, by early 1975, Saudi production was little more than half of capacity, and it was this production restriction that helped make the rapid price increase of 1973–1974 stick. Then, in

FIGURE 26-4
How OPEC raised world oil price

There have been two periods of very rapid increases in the price of oil—1973–1974 and 1979–1980. In between, oil price rose by less than the rate of inflation, and OPEC's real income per barrel of oil declined. By the early 1980s, the dollar price of oil had started to decline.

Source: World Oil, Aug. 15, 1980, p. 55, and the *Petroleum Intelligence Weekly.*

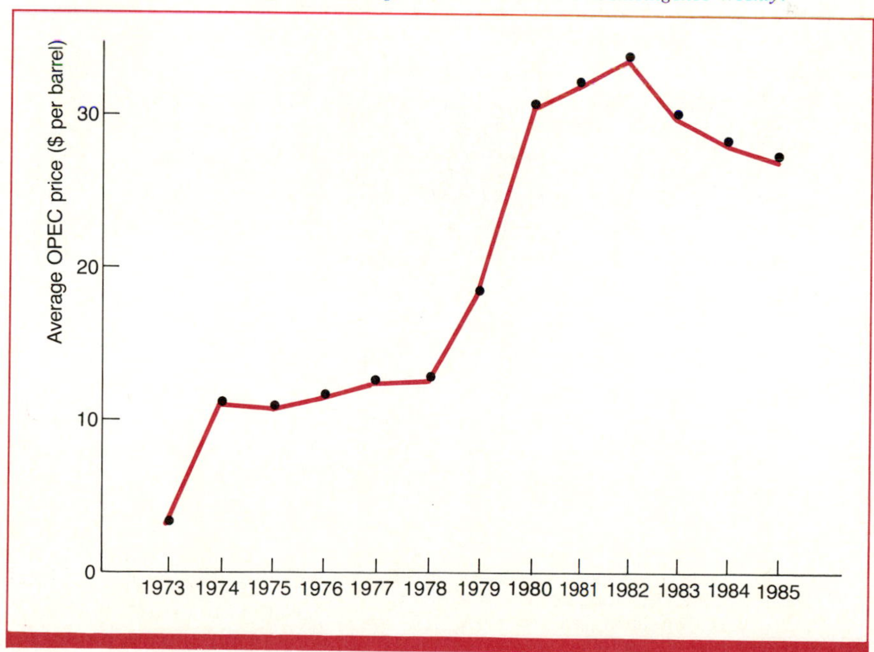

1979–1980, OPEC seized the opportunity provided by the interruption of Iranian supplies to raise the price sharply again.

Thus, during the 1970s, OPEC was a cartel in the sense that its members fixed price. But it was not a cartel in the sense of fixing and enforcing formal production quotas to limit the sales of each member country. Instead, the price was generally maintained by Saudi Arabia, which, as the dominant supplier, was prepared to adjust its *own* sales. For this reason, some experts view OPEC in the 1970s as not so much a traditional cartel as a market characterized by Saudi leadership.

The Falling Price in the 1980s: The Attempt to Set Production Quotas

By the early 1980s, however, there was strong downward pressure on the price OPEC could charge because demand for OPEC oil was falling. There were several reasons:

1. The deep international recession of 1981–1982 reduced the demand for oil.

2. Substitute supplies of energy, whose production was stimulated by the high price of oil, came on the market in substantial volume. These substitutes included coal and

FIGURE 26-5

If you wanted to buy oil on the international market in the 1970s, OPEC was the place to go

This map illustrates how important the OPEC countries were in determining the supply of oil on the international market. The width of arrows indicates the volume of international flows of oil in 1978. (This figure shows only international flows and does not include domestic flows. Two of the largest domestic flows were from producers to users within the United States, and within the U.S.S.R.)

Source: Energy Information Agency, Department of Energy, Annual Report to Congress, 1979, vol. 2, pp. 37, 72.

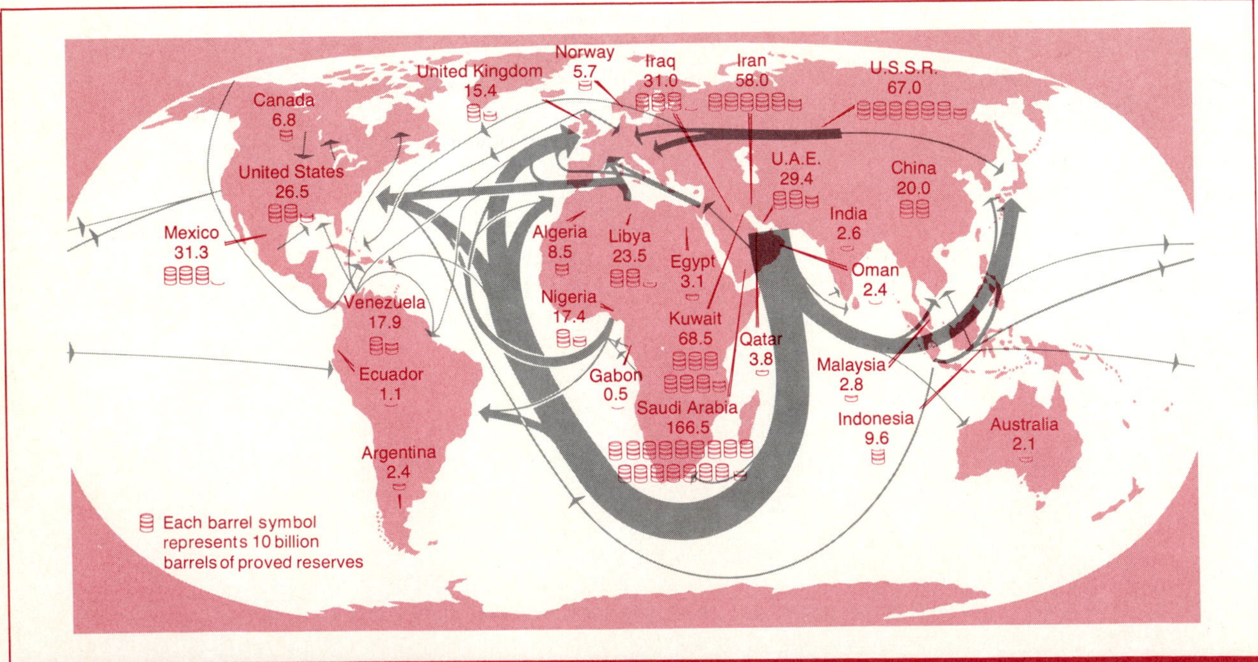

natural gas. The production of nuclear power also rose significantly in some countries, such as France.

3. Conservation efforts, also stimulated by the high oil price of the seventies, began to have substantial effects by the early 1980s. For example, aging gas-guzzlers were replaced on the road by smaller cars, and fuel efficient equipment was introduced in industrial plants.

4. The process of conservation was accelerated by the removal of U.S. price controls on oil and gasoline. This decontrol meant that Americans had to pay the high world price of oil, and they responded by buying less.

Figure 26-6 shows how oil use in the United States, which had been tied closely to economic activity, began to drop in the late 1970s.

BOX 26-2

WHY OPEC WAS ABLE TO RAISE PRICE WITHOUT SETTING PRODUCTION QUOTAS

When everything went wrong for OPEC in the 1980s, it was a severe shock because in the 1970s everything had gone right. There were several reasons for OPEC's good fortune in those early days.

1. International oil companies such as Exxon and Royal Dutch Shell were very concerned about the future scarcity of oil. Therefore, in order to ensure their own future oil supplies, they made a major effort to maintain good relations with OPEC members. In particular, they were hesitant to encourage price cutting by switching away from a country with a high price to one with a somewhat lower price (although they did this to some degree).

Furthermore, the major oil companies had no strong incentive to encourage price cutting and a breakup of OPEC, since their profits soared as a result of higher oil prices. At the same time that the OPEC countries were getting a price increase on the oil they were producing in the Middle East, the oil companies were getting a price increase on the oil they were producing within the United States.

2. Oil demand was inelastic in the short run; that is, it was insensitive to price. It is true that, in the long run, oil demand *is* sensitive to price; for example, the high oil price has induced the development of fuel efficient cars and thereby reduced the quantity demanded. However, in the early 1970s, there wasn't yet time for such long-run adjustments. This meant that OPEC could raise price without a large short-run reduction in the quantity demanded; thus, its total revenues increased sharply when its price was raised. Because of the huge increases in their revenues, the members of OPEC had relatively little temptation to "rock the boat" by undercutting OPEC's price.

There were several reasons why the short-run demand for OPEC oil was inelastic. For many users, oil and gasoline were necessities. Factories were willing, if necessary, to pay a much higher price for oil rather than shut down. The person who had to drive to work continued to buy gasoline, even when its price rose sharply.

Another reason why the demand for OPEC oil was insensitive to price was that the U.S. government kept the domestic U.S. price of oil from rising as fast as the world price quoted by OPEC. Therefore U.S. oil buyers faced less "price shock." It was no surprise that they responded less strongly, in terms of cutting back their consumption of oil. In other words, because of the U.S. government's price controls, it seemed—at least from OPEC's point of view—that Americans were willing to keep on buying oil without being sensitive to the price OPEC was charging. So why shouldn't OPEC raise price further?

3. Not only was the short-run elasticity of demand for oil low. In addition, during the critical 1973 period when OPEC began its rapid price increases, the demand curve for oil was shifting out rapidly because of the boom conditions that existed then. Accordingly, when OPEC began hiking the price, demand was both inelastic and growing.

4. At the same time, the quantity of oil sold by OPEC was curtailed for noneconomic reasons. Because of the Arab embargo on sales to the United States and other countries supporting Israel in the 1973 Yom Kippur war, OPEC's oil exports fell by about 25%. This "political" restriction in supply helped to make the price increase stick in 1973.

5. Americans, Europeans, and other oil importers not only used less oil. The oil they did import increasingly came from new non-OPEC sources, such as Mexico and the North Sea; it was less risky to buy from these sources than the war-torn Persian Gulf. Moreover, these non-OPEC countries were frequently willing to sell at a price below that of OPEC. Thus the Persian Gulf tended to become the residual source of supply. U.S. purchases of Persian Gulf oil fell about 75% between January 1981 and May 1983. Although Japanese purchases remained relatively strong, the massive flow of oil out of the Persian Gulf shown in Figure 26-5 had fallen by about 50%. In early 1985, more oil was being pumped out of the North Sea than Saudi Arabia, and OPEC's sales had fallen from two-thirds of the world trade in oil to one-third.

In the face of falling sales, each OPEC member came under increasing pressure to cut its price to prevent its sales from falling further. For example, Iran and Iraq were desperate for funds to finance their war; they couldn't afford to lose oil sales. Even the Saudis felt that they had to keep their sales from falling further, because of the need to finance their rapidly increasing imports.

In these circumstances, one, or both, of two things had to happen: (1) The world price of oil had to fall or (2) OPEC had to convert itself into a bona fide cartel by setting and enforcing production quotas on its members. In the early 1980s this was the key question: Could OPEC, a loose price-fixing organization that had prospered in the 1970s when market demand was moving in its favor, now turn itself into a disciplined price and output-fixing cartel as market pressures turned against it?

FIGURE 26-6
The oil bond broken
For many years, U.S. oil consumption was linked to GNP. However, during the large price increase in 1978–1980, this link was broken and oil consumption fell dramatically.
Source: Reprinted with permission of Terry C. Allen from *Fortune*, Dec. 26, 1983, p. 114.

The first set of OPEC quotas, introduced in March 1982, was not very successful. There was widespread cheating; Iran and Libya simply disregarded their quotas. With OPEC unable to control supply, competitive price cutting began. In less than a year, the world price of oil fell from $34 to less than $30. There then followed a series of meetings in which new agreements were reached, only to be broken. By 1985, OPEC agreements were no longer unanimous; it was not clear how they could be enforced when the previous unanimous agreements had failed. With Saudi production reduced to far less than one third of capacity, OPEC's problem of maintaining price could no longer be solved by a large reduction in Saudi output. (Even if the Saudis had reduced their output to *zero,* the other OPEC countries would still have been able to oversupply the world market.)

OPEC had become a classic case study in the two problems that make it so difficult to hold a cartel together: (1) How can the cartel keep individual members from producing more than their quota? (2) How can the cartel prevent outside producers—in this case, producers such as those in the North Sea and Mexico—from expanding production and undercutting the cartel's price?

PRICING BY AMERICAN OLIGOPOLIES

We have seen that one of the ways oligopolists can try to avoid price wars is to form a cartel and agree formally on price and market shares; we have also seen how difficult this is to enforce. In the United States and many other countries, there is an additional problem: Collusion is illegal. American producers can't even discuss prices with their competitors without risking a jail sentence. How, then, do American oligopolists reduce the pressure of price competition? How do they avoid price wars and arrive at a reasonably profitable price?

One explanation is that each firm faces a "kinked demand curve." Although this concept is controversial, it provides important insights into how each oligopolist must take the others' responses into account.

The Kinked Demand Curve

The best way to understand this idea is to put yourself in the position of one of the three large oligopolists in an industry. The demand you face will have a kink if your competitors behave in the following way:

1. If you cut your price, the firms competing with you take your act as a challenge. They will not want you to take customers away from them, and therefore they will meet your price cut with a price cut of their own.
2. On the other hand, if you raise price, your competitors consider this a golden opportunity. By keeping their own selling price stable, they will be able to capture a share of your sales.

In short, your competitors behave in a nonsymmetric way: If you drop your price they will follow you, but if you raise your price they will not.

Figure 26-7 shows how this behavior leads to a kinked demand curve and to price stability. This figure illustrates an industry with three firms of similar size. Each initially has one-third of total sales, with point E_1 showing your initial price and sales. If you change price and *if* your competitors follow, you may expect to retain your present one-third of the market. Thus you will move along the relatively steep demand curve labeled d_F. (Note that at any price, say P_2, the quantity you sell on d_F is one-third of the total sales shown on the market demand curve D.)

However, d_F is relevant only if you quote a price *below* the existing price at E_1. If you quote a price *above* this—say P_3—your competitors will *not* follow. Instead, they will stand pat. Because you will now be quoting a higher price than they are, you will lose part of your market to them, as shown by the red arrow.

Therefore, if you drop your price below E_1, you face demand d_F, while if you raise your price above E_1, you face demand d_N. In other words, the behavior of your competitors presents you with the kinked demand curve shown by the heavy lines.

The kinked demand curve shown by the heavy lines in Figure 26-7 is the demand the oligopolistic firm faces *if its competitors follow its price down but not up.*

Faced with this demand curve, how do you maximize profit? The likely answer: Select point E_1, where the kink occurs. Thus, you don't rock the boat. You continue to quote the price P_1 that you and your competitors have been quoting, and you retain your safe, traditional share of the market. Your profit is shown as the shaded rectangle. (Experiment with other points on the kinked demand curve above and below E_1; note that in each case the resulting profit rectangle is less. Moreover, also shift your cost curve AC up or down a bit and notice that E_1 remains your profit-maximizing point. Thus you tend to keep your price stable at P_1 even if your costs change.)

The idea of a kinked demand curve was first developed in the 1930s, and it has had continuing appeal as a

FIGURE 26-7

A kinked demand curve

Suppose that you have two equally large competitors and your initial position is at E_1. If your competitors were to follow any price change you might make, you would face demand curve d_F. Regardless of the price you might quote, you would retain one third of the market. (For example, if you were to quote price P_2, you would sell 10 units.) Unfortunately, you do not face d_F throughout its entire range because your competitors will follow you only if you reduce price. Thus, the only portion of d_F that is relevant is the heavily lined section below E_1. If you raise price, your competitors will not follow and you will face demand curve d_N. (Since they don't raise their prices, your competitors will cut into your share of the market, as shown by the red arrow). In short, if your competitors follow your price change down but not up, you will face the heavy kinked demand curve.

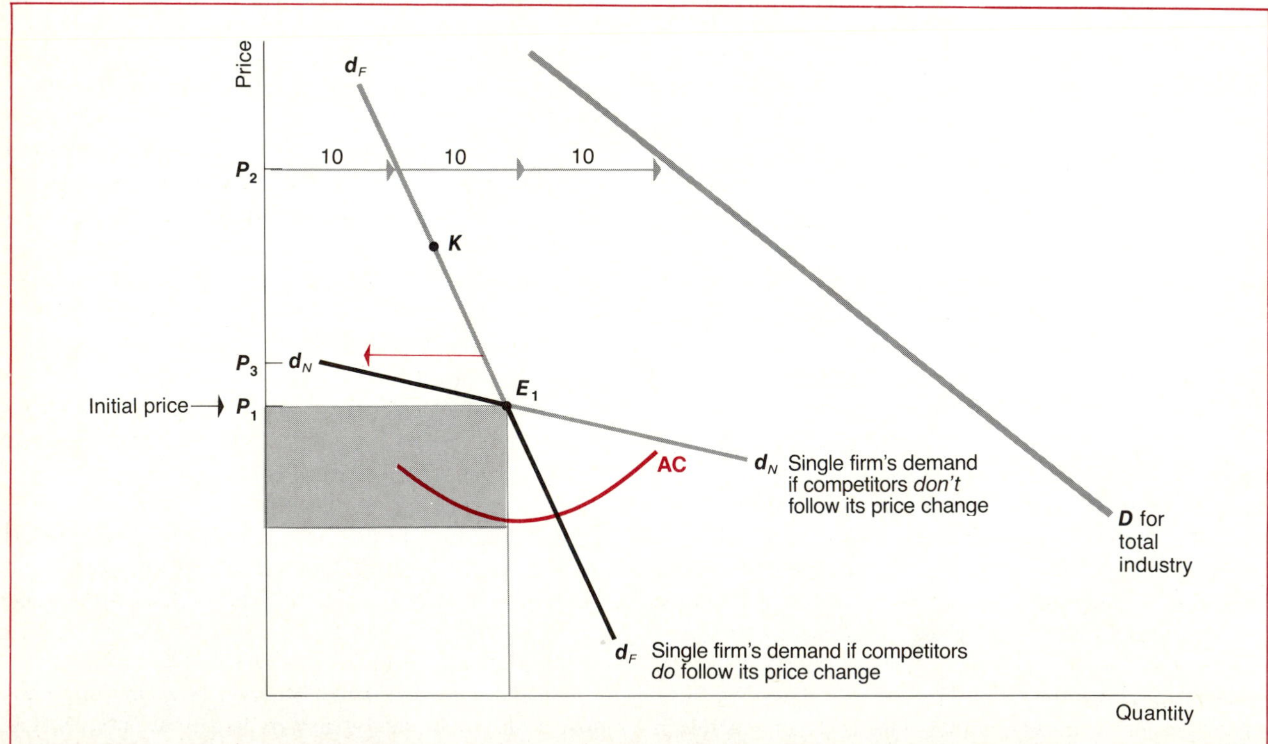

way of explaining why oligopoly prices are stable, and in particular, why they often remain firm during recessions when demand declines. There are, nevertheless, important exceptions. In 1974, 1980, and 1982, auto manufacturers offered rebates—in effect, price reductions—in order to increase their lagging sales.

The theory of the kinked demand curve is controversial. In the first place, it is incomplete. While it may explain price stability, it does not explain how price is established in the first place. For example, in Figure 26-7, price remains at P_1 because it started out at P_1 and that is where the kink occurs. But how did price get to be P_1 in the first place? It has no explanation, like the "smile without the cat" in *Alice in Wonderland*. The second difficulty is that prices are not nearly as rigid as the theory suggests. As already noted, automobile prices have occasionally fallen. And they have frequently risen. The same is true of steel prices. Over the years, the prices of computers have been cut many times, leaving them at a small fraction of their earlier level.

Thus, the theory of the kinked demand curve explains too much; it explains something (price stability) that frequently does not exist. Rather than try to explain why oligopoly prices are stable—when often they are not—it makes more sense to ask why oligopoly prices change in a reasonably orderly way. One answer is provided by the theory of *price leadership*.

Price Leadership

Where collusion is illegal—as in the United States—the simplest way for firms to achieve an orderly change in price is for one firm to take the initiative with the others following.

To illustrate this price leadership concept in Figure 26-7, suppose that you are the price leader, in the sense that you know that you can quote a different price and your competitors will follow you. Then the demand curve you face is no longer kinked. Instead, *it is the line d_F throughout its entire length* because your competitors will follow your price change either down *or* up. In these circumstances, you will be able to lead the industry up to a new, higher price at a point like *K*, provided you are correct and the other firms will indeed follow your lead.

If your leadership is thus assured, the result may approach that of a cartel. As leader, you will have selected the price at point *K* that will maximize your own profits. Moreover, this price should be approximately the one that will maximize profits for the industry as a whole; this is why the other firms may be willing to accept your leadership. The outcome at *K* is the same monopolylike solution that would result from collusion. Therefore, although collusion does not formally exist, the result may be the same: Firms arrive at the collusive profit-maximizing price, not by illegally agreeing on it beforehand but by simply following the leader. This is sometimes called "tacit collusion."

However, because there is no formal agreement, your leadership may *not* be assured after all; the problem of "cheating" may be substantial. The leader may find others shaving prices—or providing rebates—in order to increase their market shares. For example, during this century, giant U.S. Steel has sometimes acted as price leader and has not reacted to under-the-table price cuts by some smaller firms. (It was better to ignore them than to retaliate and risk leading the whole industry into a round of price cutting.) Consequently, these smaller firms were able to take advantage of U.S. Steel's price umbrella to cut into its markets: In 1910, U.S. Steel held almost half the market, but by the 1950s, its share had fallen to about one-third. Thus, while the giant in an industry may have a decided advantage from lower costs, the smaller firms may also have a major advantage: They may be able to compete aggressively without provoking competitive responses from the giant.

In practice, it may be quite difficult to identify any clear pattern of price leadership. There may be no consistent price leader; first one company may take the initiative in changing prices, then another. General Motors does not always announce its new model prices first; the initiative is sometimes exercised by Ford. Furthermore, price leadership may be quite tentative. One firm may announce a price increase to see if others follow. If they don't, the price change may be rescinded. This sort of "trial and error" pricing may just be a way for the firm to test whether or not it can in fact act as a price leader.

Finally, even when oligopolists follow a pattern of price leadership, we cannot be certain that they are exerting monopoly power. If costs have generally risen by, say, 10%, an oligopolist may raise price by about 10% in the expectation that others will follow. Price leadership

BOX 26-3

THE DETERMINATION OF OLIGOPOLY PRICE

In this box, we consider several other ways in which oligopoly price may be determined. Summing up the discussion so far, we have seen how a firm will stay at E_1 in Figure 26-7 if its executives believe that other firms will follow its price down, but not up. We have also seen how a price leader—that all other firms will follow in either direction—will move up d_F to K, raising price above the "kinked value" P_1.

1. Cournot-Nash Equilibrium

Now suppose, at the other extreme, that the firm assumes that *none* of its competitors will react at all to *any* price change it makes, in either direction. Such a firm is assuming that it will face demand curve d_N throughout its entire length, with the subscript N meaning "No response by competitors." If this firm starts at E_1, it will attempt to move down d_N to the southeast in order to increase its sales and profit. That is, the firm will increase its output and reduce its price.†

If all firms make the same assumption that competitors won't react, they will behave in the same way; they will reduce their price and increase their quantity. At the new ***Cournot-Nash equilibrium*** output will be greater and price lower than at E_1.

A *Cournot-Nash equilibrium* is the equilibrium that results when each firm assumes that none of its competitors will react to any change it makes.

In fact, the Cournot-Nash equilibrium is a more complicated concept than this single example suggests, with possible applications beyond an analysis of oligopoly. In its application to oligopoly, it has been criticized because it is often unrealistic for a firm with only a few competitors to assume that they will ignore a change in its policy. For example, if Zenith lowers the price of TV sets, is it reasonable to assume that RCA won't respond? If Remington offers a discount on its razor, won't Phillips be under pressure to follow?

2. Conjectural Variation

A broader approach to the problem of oligopolistic pricing is to assume that a firm's decisions are based

on ***conjectural variation.*** The firm makes an assumption (a conjecture) on how its competitors will respond. One example is the firm with the kinked demand curve in Figure 26-7; it conjectures that its competitors will follow its price change down, but not up. Another example is the price leader that assumes its competitors will follow its price change in either direction. Still another is the firm we've just described that moves to a Cournot-Nash equilibrium. The problem, of course, is that there is a whole multitude of such conjectures. Another example would be a firm that assumes that half of its competitors will follow it down, but none will follow it up. (You can sketch this case in Figure 26-7. The firm's demand curve is d_N down to point E_1, and thereafter a demand curve lying midway between d_N and d_F.) In short, the concept of conjectural variation is useful, but *only if* the firm can make a reasonable and specific assumption about its competitors' reactions.

3. Focal Point Pricing

Harvard's Thomas Schelling gives the following noneconomic example to illustrate how independent firms may end up quoting the same price even though there is no price leadership, nor any collusion, nor even a preexisting price:

> You are to meet someone in New York City. You have not been instructed where to meet; you have no prior understanding with the person on where to meet; and you cannot communicate with each other. You are simply told that you will have to guess where to meet and he is being told the same thing and that you will just have to try to make your guesses coincide. You are told the date but not the hour of this meeting; the two of you must guess the exact minute of the date for meeting. At what time will you appear at the chosen meeting place?‡

Of the thousands of possible choices, Schelling discovered that most people selected the information booth at Grand Central Station, at high noon. Both are "focal points" because they provide the best guess of what the other person will do. So too with price: A retailer who wants to guess the price that competitors will charge for a new product in the range of say, \$11.20 to \$12.40, may well select the focal point \$11.98. This price is based on the familiar tradition of "charging \$12 but making it seem like \$11." Thus, without any communication whatsoever between firms, this focal point of \$11.98 becomes the industry price.

4. Cost-Plus Pricing

With cost-plus pricing, a firm determines its price by adding a specified markup of, say, 20% to its average cost. Economists have been uncomfortable with this concept because it raise a couple of nagging questions: Why does the firm pick 20% rather than some other figure? How does the firm know its average cost without first knowing its output? (In Figure 26-7, observe how the firm's average cost AC changes as its output increases.) In practice, firms that use this approach may solve this problem by arbitrarily specifying a target output of, say, 80% of capacity; then at this specified output level, their average cost is determined by the height of the AC curve. Finally, by adding on their fixed percentage markup, they arrive at a price.

This approach presumes that a firm pricing this way will be able to sell roughly its target quantity, using the target markup. However, if it is under pressure from price-cutting competitors, it may have little hope of doing so. To prevent its sales from falling substantially, it may have to reduce its markup. Although such a firm may view itself as engaged in fixed-markup (cost-plus) pricing, it is not doing this at all. Instead, it is adjusting its price in response to market pressures like any other profit-maximizing firm. Its percentage markup isn't fixed at all.

†Why will it move in this direction? To answer this, note that we are considering a firm that selected point E_1 when it faced the kinked demand curve. But now it is facing d_N; that is, it can move to a point anywhere on d_N. To maximize its profit, which way will it move? It won't move to the left; it could have done that when it faced the kinked demand curve, and it chose not to do so. Therefore it will move to the right. (There is also a very slight chance that E_1—the firm's profit-maximizing point when it faced the kinked demand curve—is also its profit-maximizing point when it faces d_N. In this case, the firm won't move at all.)

‡Thomas C. Schelling, *The Strategy of Conflict* (Cambridge: Harvard University Press, 1960), p. 56.

has apparently occurred; yet the firms may merely be defending themselves against rising costs, rather than exploiting monopoly power at the expense of the public.

There are many ways in which oligopoly price may be set, with no single pattern followed in all cases. For a sample of several other patterns of oligopoly price determination, see Box 26-3.

NONPRICE COMPETITION

Price is not the only way in which oligopolistic firms compete; they also compete, for example, by advertising and by attempting to provide a better product. These ways of competing are often preferred to price competition because they don't risk setting off a price war in which all participants lose.

Advertising

The firm that advertises has a simple objective: to make people want its product and buy more. That does not mean, however, that the more advertising the better. Since advertising must be paid for, it also shifts up the cost curve. At some point, the firm will find that enough advertising is enough; any further advertising would involve a cost that can no longer be justified by increased sales.

In an oligopoly, the primary goal of advertising is often to capture the competitor's market. Thus, for example, the primary objective of Ford's advertising is to take sales away from General Motors and other auto companies. For its part, General Motors advertises to take sales away from Ford and the Japanese.

Advertising also increases the total market demand for the product. A monopoly firm will sometimes advertise, not to take sales away from competitors (since it has none) but instead to increase the demand for its product. For example, AT&T used to advertise its long-distance services, even when it still had a monopoly. Some associations of perfect competitors also advertise to increase total market demand, even though no single producer would find it profitable to do so. For example, the milk producers' association advertises to encourage people to drink milk. However, the most heavily advertised products lie in the battleground between perfect competition and monopoly, where a firm like General Motors may benefit from advertising both because it increases the total demand for automobiles and, more particularly, because it takes sales away from its rivals.

There is some controversy over the social value of advertising. On behalf of their industry, advertising agencies make the following points:

1. Advertising helps the consumer to make better decisions. It informs the public of new products and of improvements in old ones. By informing consumers of what is available, it reduces search costs. For example, advertising may tell consumers where the bargains are, so they can save time and effort in shopping.

2. Advertising helps new producers to compete. By informing the public of a new product, it helps the producer to expand sales toward a high-volume, low-cost level.

3. Advertising stimulates research. If new products could not be advertised and sold in huge quantities, the cost of their research and development could not be covered.

4. Advertising supports the communications industry. Radio and TV are financed by advertising revenues. If we didn't pay for our entertainment this way, we would have to pay for it in some other way. Even the mundane classified ads play a significant role in the support of newspapers.

5. Advertising results in higher-quality products. The goodwill built up from past advertising of a brand may be an asset of great value for a firm—an asset it will be careful not to damage by turning out a shoddy product.

On the other side, critics respond:

1. Most advertising represents a waste. The heaviest advertising takes place in oligopolistic markets where firm A's major motive is to steal customers from firm B, and B advertises to cancel out the effects of A's advertising. After advertising, A and B share the market in roughly the same way as before. Little has changed, except that costs have gone up. Consumers pay more for this product merely because it is advertised. (Firms can't opt out of this wasteful game because then they *would* lose market share to competitors.)

2. Where advertising is not a self-canceling waste, it is often pernicious, creating frivolous wants, distorting tastes, and increasing the materialism of a materialistic society. (Recall Galbraith's skepticism over the satisfaction of "created" wants, discussed in Chapter 4.)

3. Advertising often misinforms and leads to lower-quality products. This occurs, for example, if firms are able to sell inferior products by falsely implying in their advertising that they are better. In this case, the cost of advertising includes both the waste in resources that go into making this claim *and* the cost to the public because it gets an inferior product.

4. Much advertising is offensive. We cannot listen to radio or TV without being bombarded with tasteless ads. Worse yet, advertising may lead to distorted news coverage. It may be difficult for a newspaper to provide a balanced treatment of a labor dispute if it is getting a great deal of advertising revenue from the firms involved, but none from the labor union. (However, if a lot of workers buy the paper, the pressures may even out.)

Since it is difficult to compare these conflicting claims, our conclusion is that the statement that advertising involves "*all* loss" is too extreme, and so is the statement that advertising involves "*no* loss whatsoever." What do you think?

Other Ways in Which Firms Compete

In addition to advertising, there are other forms of nonprice competition. A firm can hire a larger sales staff in order to beat the bushes for customers. Or it can spend more on research, development, or design to improve the quality or attractiveness of its product. The typical oligopoly, such as an auto or appliance company, is locked in a struggle to match its competitors' price, *and* advertising, *and* sales force, *and* improvements in design and quality. Little wonder that the world of the oligopolist seems more competitive than that of the farmer, who may operate in a "perfectly competitive" market but who never even thinks of a neighbor as a competitor. (But remember: According to the economist's definition, farming is the more competitive industry, since a single farmer has no influence whatsoever over price.)

BARRIERS TO ENTRY

Nonprice competition often creates barriers to entry. For example, if several large oligopolistic firms such as the auto companies have been competing in the past by making huge expenditures on advertising, it may be almost impossible for a new firm to break into the industry unless it too has vast sums to spend. Existing producers may be associated with widely recognized brand names, either because of past advertising or because their product has been used for many years. In some countries, the brand name "Kodak" is almost synonymous with "camera," and it is difficult to compete with that.

There are also other barriers to entry. Existing producers may get more favorable treatment from retailers. A new entrant may be caught in a vicious circle: It can't sell unless retailers give it shelf space; but retailers won't give it shelf space until it can prove it can sell. This is a particularly serious problem for the large number of new manufacturers of microcomputers. How do they get their products into the stores when most stores can comfortably stock no more than eight or ten models? (Sales staffs find it difficult to keep track of the detailed performance of more models.) One option is to sell through their own stores, as Tandy (Radio Shack) does. However, this is very expensive, and the large financing required is itself a barrier to small entrants. (Tandy was already in the retail business, selling CB radios and other electronics before it developed its computer.)

But the single most important barrier to entry is the fact that, in most oligopoly industries, costs fall over a wide range of output. In other words, economies of large-scale production make it very difficult for a small firm to compete. In order to get started, a new firm must have "deep pockets"; it must have the financial resources to set up a productive facility large enough to move it quickly into the high-volume, low-cost range of production. For this reason, new competition in oligopolistic markets often comes, not from struggling new firms but rather from giants in other industries. For example, Xerox was faced with new competition when IBM, Kodak, and several Japanese firms entered the market for office copiers. And IBM's big concern is not with new computer firms. It is that AT&T may come into the computer market with full force now that regulatory restraints on AT&T have been lifted.

If such barriers to entry are low or nonexistent, new firms freely enter. The result is no longer oligopoly (with a few sellers), but instead a quite different market form: monopolistic competition. This is the last type of market we will describe. As we do so, you can compare it with other markets in summary Table 26-1.

MONOPOLISTIC COMPETITION: LOW BARRIERS TO ENTRY

If the average cost curve stops falling and starts to rise when the firm is producing only a small fraction of the total sales of the industry, there is no cost advantage in being a giant and many competitors enter the industry. This situation sounds like perfect competition, but it is not if firms are producing a ***differentiated product.*** In this case, the result is ***monopolistic competition.*** Because each firm is selling a somewhat different product, it has some control over price; if it raises its price slightly, it won't lose all its customers. Thus, it does not face the perfect competitor's perfectly horizontal demand curve. Instead, its demand curve slopes downward to the right. But because of the existence of many competitors, its control over price is not great. In other words, the demand curve facing the individual producer is quite elastic, as illustrated in Figure 26-8.

Monopolistic competition **exists when there are many sellers of a differentiated product in an industry without barriers to entry. The demand curve facing the individual competitor is quite elastic, but not completely so.**

Even if products are physically identical, they can still be differentiated in other respects. As an example, consider tubes of Crest toothpaste sold in stores in different locations. Although the products are physically the same, the consumer will view the closer store's toothpaste as "better" and will consequently be willing to pay a few cents more for it. Thus location gives each store some control over its price; it can charge a few cents more and not lose all its customers. However, it doesn't have much control. If it charges a much higher price, buyers will bypass it to go to one of its less expensive, though less convenient, competitors.

Small retail stores in a large metropolitan area are often viewed as monopolistic competitors. They have very little control over price, and don't need to be greatly concerned about the responses of their competitors. However, the three grocery stores in a small village are local oligopolists; each has to consider carefully the responses of its competitors if it cuts prices. Similarly, Sears-Roebuck and J. C. Penney are local oligopolists rather than monopolistic competitors, because each is a significant participant in the local retail market, and each has to give some thought to how the other will respond.

It is relatively easy to get into small-scale retailing; a vast pool of funds is not necessary to buy a single drugstore. Where existing firms are making above-normal profits, new entrants will come in, tending to eliminate these excess profits, as illustrated in Figure 26-8. Initially, the typical firm shown in panel *a* is operating at E_1 and earning a profit shown by the shaded area. But, as new competitors enter and capture some of its sales, the

TABLE 26-1
Types of Market Structure

Type of market	Number of producers and type of product	Entry	Influence over price	Advertising	Examples
Monopoly	One producer; product with no close substitute	Difficult or impossible	Substantial (price maker unless price is regulated by government)	Only to increase market demand	Local telephone service
Oligopoly	(*a*) Few producers; little or no product differentiation	Difficult	Some (price searcher)	Yes, although less than if there is product differentiation, as in case (*b*)	Steel Aluminum
	(*b*) Few producers; differentiated product	Difficult	Some (price searcher)	Heavy	Autos Computers Cigarettes
Monopolistic competition	Many producers; differentiated product	Easy	A little	Yes	Retail trade
Perfect competition	Many producers; undifferentiated product	Easy	None (price taker)	None, except perhaps through a collective association	Some agricultural products

demand curve it faces shifts to the left. (It gets a smaller share of the total market.) This process continues until its demand becomes tangent to the average cost curve, as shown in panel *b*. Faced with this new demand curve, the best the firm can now do is to select the point of tangency E_2, where it earns no excess profit. (Any other point on the demand curve would leave it operating at a loss.) Thus, free entry tends to eliminate above-normal profits for the run-of-the-mill firm in monopolistic competition.

Observe in panel *b* of Figure 26-8 that monopolistic competition seems to be inefficient. At the firm's output of 80 units, MC ($70) is not equal to price ($90), so there is no reason to expect an efficient allocation of resources. It is often claimed that there is "excess capacity," that is, too many firms in the industry. Consumer demand could be satisfied at lower cost if there were fewer firms, each producing more—that is, if the typical firm in panel *b* were to move from E_2 to E_3 by increasing its output from 80 units to 100 and thus lowering its average cost to the the minimum of $85. If the industry were reorganized in this way, wouldn't the result be a more efficient allocation of resources?

The answer is: not necessarily. True, cost would be lower, and this would be an advantage for society. However, there would also be a disadvantage: Since there would be fewer firms, consumers would have less choice. For example, a reduction in the number of retail stores would mean that those remaining could sell a larger volume, thus reducing their costs (and prices). But it would also mean that some customers would have to travel further to shop. Perhaps the convenience of local stores is worth the slightly higher price we have to pay.

In short, if you drive the typical firm down from E_2

FIGURE 26-8
Equilibrium for a typical firm in monopolistic competition

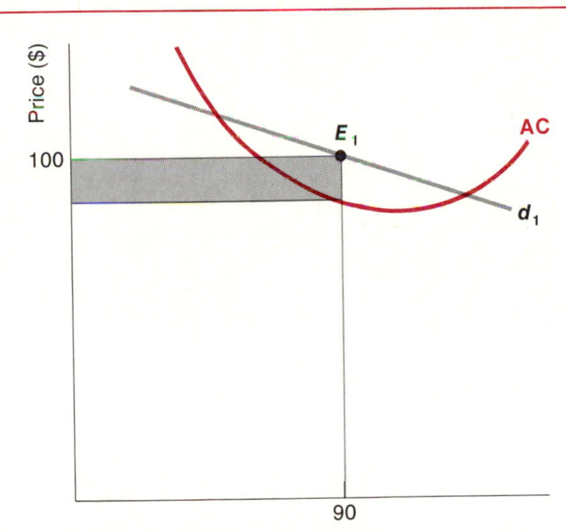

(*a*) **In the short run.** The firm faces a sloping demand $\boldsymbol{d_1}$ because its product is differentiated. Short-run equilibrium is at $\boldsymbol{E_1}$, with the above-normal profit shown in the shaded area. This attracts new firms into the industry, shifting this firm's ***d*** to the left until a new equilibrium is reached at $\boldsymbol{E_2}$ in panel *b*.

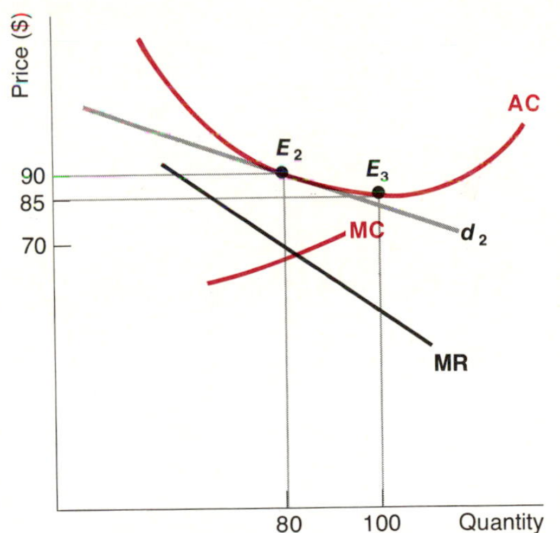

(*b*) **In the long run.** This is a long-run equilibrium because above-normal profits have been eliminated by the entry of new firms. (Note: In these two panels, **AC** is the same. The only thing that changes is demand, which shifts to the left from $\boldsymbol{d_1}$ to $\boldsymbol{d_2}$ as a result of the new entrants.)

to E_3 in Figure 26-8, it would produce at lower cost and this would be a benefit to society. However, because its output would be increased, the number of firms would be reduced and consumers would get less variety; this would be a loss. On balance, it is not clear that this move would be beneficial. Thus, when a product is differentiated, it becomes difficult to pin down the idea of efficiency as simply as we did with an undifferentiated product (in Box 24-1). As a practical matter, no economist argues that the government should undertake broad regulation of firms operating in monopolistic competition. It is difficult to make a federal case out of the inefficiences—if any—that arise from monopolistic competition.

But this is not true of monopoly or oligopoly. According to the estimate of one authority,[3] the cost of inefficiency in such markets is between 0.5% and 2.0% of the value of the nation's GNP. In 1985, that represented between \$20 and \$75 billion of lost output. Here a federal case can be made, as we explain in the next chapter.

As already noted, Table 26-1 provides a summary of market structures, with perfect competition and monopoly on the two extremes and monopolistic competition and various forms of oligopoly in the broad spectrum in between. In reviewing this table, there is an important word of warning:

DON'T JUST COUNT NUMBERS: THE CONCEPT OF CONTESTABLE MARKETS

When one observes an activity in which there is only a single firm, there is a natural tendency to conclude that it is a monopoly, with all the problems that this raises. For example, how much does it restrict output below the efficient quantity? How much is its product overpriced? Should this firm be split up, or should its price be controlled? And so on.

However, even though a firm is technically a monopoly—in the sense that it's a single seller—it may not be able to *behave* like one by raising its price and restricting its output. In this case, the problems of monopoly may not arise.

As an example, consider a route between two cities which is now serviced by only one airline. It may appear that this airline has monopoly power. But in fact it may not, because it is operating in a *contestable market*. If it tries to exercise monopoly power by raising its price, another airline will begin to fly this route; that is, another airline will "contest" this market. This potential competition forces the airline to behave like a competitor even though it's a single seller. The moral is this. In analyzing any market—and in particular, in analyzing what appears to be a monopoly—don't just count the number of *actual* sellers. Emphasis must also be placed on freedom of entry, that is, on the number of *potential* new sellers. How contestable is the market?

An airline route perhaps provides the best example of a contestable market, because it is so easy to shift planes from one route to another. But other examples might be cited. There may be only two or three contractors building houses in a small town. If they can restrict entry of new competitors in some way—for example, by getting special zoning restrictions or acquiring all the available land—an oligopoly model with long-run profits may be the best way to describe their behavior. But if they can't restrict entry and local carpenters can start to build houses, there may be enough potential competition to keep the two or three existing firms from earning above-normal profits. Similarly, the only carpenter in a village may not be able to charge high prices because this will simply cause somebody else to take up carpentry. In contrast, people can't simply "take up" medicine; they must go to medical school and be licensed. Thus, the doctor has more market power than the carpenter. Once again, we see the importance of ease of entry. It is not only existing competition, but also *potential* competition that matters.

KEY POINTS

1. Many American markets are oligopolies, dominated by a few firms. In any such market, there is an incentive for firms to collude so that they can act like a monopolist in raising price and restricting output. Such monopolylike behavior would lead to an inefficient allo-

---

[3]F. M. Scherer, *Industrial Market Structure and Economic Performance*, 2d ed. (Chicago: Rand McNally, 1980), p. 464.

cation of resources. One deterrent to such collusive behavior is the difficulty of establishing and enforcing the production quotas or market sharing that is typically required to maintain a high price. Even more important are the legal prohibitions against collusion in the United States.

2. An important example of a collusive agreement is OPEC, the Organization of Petroleum Exporting Countries. Between 1973 and 1981, OPEC increased the world price of oil more than 12-fold. The result was the greatest peacetime transfer of wealth in history. OPEC was remarkable because for very special reasons it did not require formal production quotas during the 1970s when it was raising price. However, during the 1980s, in an attempt to resist downward market pressure on price, it established a quota system. By 1985 it was not clear whether or not this system would survive.

3. Antitrust laws prohibit American firms from engaging in overt collusion that restricts competition. Nevertheless, there are forms of tacit collusion—such as price leadership—that are difficult to prosecute but may allow oligopolists to exercise some degree of monopolylike power.

4. Oligopolists often prefer to compete in ways other than cutting price. They may try to capture sales from rivals by extensive advertising campaigns, or by expenditures on research to develop better products.

5. When there are no barriers to entry—such as patents or economies of large-scale production—and many small firms enter an industry, the result is monopolistic competition. This is similar to perfect competition except that each firm is selling a differentiated product. For this reason, each firm has some small control over price: It faces a slightly sloping demand curve rather than the completely flat demand facing a perfect competitor. Because of free entry, above-normal profits for the run-of-the-mill firm tend to disappear in the long run.

6. Price *could* be reduced below the level that occurs in monopolistic competition, but only at the cost of providing consumers with less choice. Therefore, little case can be made for government regulation.

7. In analyzing any market, counting the number of competitors is not enough. One must also examine the freedom of entry; is the market "contestable"? If it is, even a single producer may have little monopoly power.

KEY CONCEPTS

concentration ratio
natural oligopoly
differentiated product
collusion
cartel
bidding cartel
incentive to cheat
cutthroat competition
Organization of Petroleum Exporting Countries (OPEC)
kinked demand
price leadership
tacit collusion
focal point pricing
cost plus, or markup, pricing
competition by advertising
competition in product quality
barriers to entry
monopolistic competition
contestable markets

PROBLEMS

26-1. Suppose there is a monopoly in the production of good X.

(*a*) For this firm, what will be the four-firm concentration ratio, like the dark red bars shown in Figure 26-1? What will the Herfindahl index be? (See Box 26-1.)

(*b*) Repeat question (*a*) for an industry in which there are three equal-sized firms.

(*c*) Do the four-firm concentration ratio and the Herfindahl index both take account of all firms in the industry? In your view, which does a better job of describing the degree of industry concentration? Why?

26-2. If there are only four large firms in your industry, explain why collusion would be in your economic interest as a producer. Explain how consumers of your product would be affected. Describe the problems involved in arranging a collusive agreement and in making it stick. Would the agreement be legal?

26-3. What do you think would happen to the world price of oil if:

(*a*) OPEC countries were able to enforce a quota system?

(*b*) Non-OPEC producers were to reduce their production?

(*c*) The North Sea producers were to cut price by $5 a barrel?

(*d*) Large new deposits of oil were discovered off the California coast?

(*e*) Large new deposits of oil were discovered off the Saudi Arabian coast?

(*f*) Saudi Arabia were to withdraw from OPEC?

(*g*) There were major developments in nuclear technology, with fusion power expected to become a major source of electricity by 2010?

(*h*) The U.S. government were to impose an additional tax of $1 per gallon on gasoline?

26-4. ''In 1985, when the Saudis were operating at less than one third of their oil-production capacity, they could no longer hold oil price up by reducing their supply. However the Saudis *were* able to keep oil price up by forcing the other OPEC members to restrict *their* supplies. The Saudis did this by threatening to drive the price lower.'' Explain. Could the Saudis really have driven price lower? If not, why? If so, how?

26-5. ''Agricultural prices are unstable, but other prices are stable.'' Evaluate this statement in the light of our discussion of kinked demand and our earlier analysis of agriculture in Chapter 20. To what degree do you believe this quotation justifies agricultural price supports?

26-6. On balance, do you think that advertising is beneficial or damaging to society?

26-7. Manufacturers of cigarettes and producers of perfume both advertise. Do you think waste is involved in either case? In one more than the other? Discuss the possible benefits from advertising and the possible damage in each case.

26-8. In this chapter, we noted that some people have tried to justify advertising because it helps new competitors enter the market. However, others have argued that advertising provides a major advantage to established firms and thus is a barrier to entry. Is it possible for both these views to be correct? If so, explain how. If not, which case do you think is the stronger, and why?

26-9. At one time, lawyers who cut their fees below the level allowed by their state bar association could be disbarred. How would you evaluate this regulation from an economic point of view? If you were a lawyer, how would you view it?

***26-10.** What is the difference between the monopolylike collusion of the cartel in Figure 26-3 and the monopolization of the milk industry in Figure 25-10? Why should the monopolization of an industry be outlawed in the first case, yet condoned—in fact, organized—by the government in the other?

PART SIX

ECONOMIC EFFICIENCY:

ISSUES OF OUR TIME

Part 6 will deal with a number of microeconomic issues, such as the best way to protect the environment and the effects of barriers to international trade. While studying these issues, we will continue to ask the fundamental questions addressed in Part 5: When do free markets work well, and when do they work badly? When they work badly, what forms of government intervention should be considered?

In Chapter 27, some of the ways government intervenes to regulate business are examined. Through its antitrust laws, the government discourages the monopolization of industry and forbids price-setting conspiracies among oligopolists. While

such antitrust policies have often made the economy more competitive and efficient, the government has also used policies that have had the opposite effect. For example, it has *reduced* competition and efficiency in some industries by restricting the entry of new firms.

The government also intervenes in the marketplace to improve the quality of life by regulating safety, health, and working conditions. In Chapter 28 we examine in detail one of the major quality-of-life issues—controlling pollution of the environment. What policy is the government now using to control pollution, and what alternative methods are available?

Chapter 29 deals with a quality-of-life issue of particular importance to future generations: At what rate should we use our natural resources? At some time in the future, will our expanding resource requirements outrun our shrinking resource supplies?

The focus of Chapter 30 will be on ''public goods''—those goods and services which cannot be adequately delivered by a free market. One example is police protection: A privately owned, profit-maximizing firm cannot be relied upon to protect the public at large. If we are to have adequate police protection, it must be provided by the government. However, special problems arise. One of the most important is the problem of determining how much the government should spend on each of the goods and services it provides. The public has much more difficulty in signaling to the government what it wants—via the ballot box—than in telling private firms what it wants when it ''votes'' in the marketplace, purchasing certain goods and ignoring others.

The last two chapters in this part deal with international trade. Chapter 31 describes how countries benefit from such trade. For example, the United States gains by specializing in such products as wheat and computers, exporting these items in exhange for coffee, TV sets, and oil. Other countries likewise gain from specialization. Trade also makes our economy more efficient by increasing competition. The U.S. auto market is more competitive because of imported Japanese and European cars. In addition to showing how trade increases efficiency, this chapter also explains how trade redistributes income. Who are the winners and losers?

Finally, Chapter 32 describes the ways in which the government has intervened in the international marketplace by imposing barriers to trade. For example, it has restricted the imports of foreign steel and automobiles, and this has made U.S. markets for these products less competitive. Such restrictions have generally reduced the income of the nation as a whole, although they have benefited certain groups, such as the producers of steel and autos.

CHAPTER 27

HOW MUCH SHOULD THE GOVERNMENT REGULATE BUSINESS?

Government . . . promotes our happiness . . . by restraining our vices.

THOMAS PAINE
Common Sense

One of the principal ways the government influences the economy is by regulations on private business. Not only does the government act to limit the exercise of market power by large firms. It has also imposed regulations to promote safety and health in our workplaces, highways, and the environment.

In the 1960s and 1970s there was a rapid growth in government regulation. What forms of regulation developed? How successful were they? During the 1970s, did we attempt to regulate too much? During the late 1970s, and especially in the Reagan years since 1980, there has been a slowing and, in some cases, a reversal in this trend. Is there now some risk that the government will regulate too little?

Government regulations on business fall into three major categories:

1. Antitrust laws to prevent firms from reducing competition by such acts as collusion or cutthroat pricing.
2. Regulatory controls over an industry's price and conditions of entry. Within this broad category, two quite different kinds of regulation should be distinguished:

(*a*) Regulation of a natural monopoly such as a power company. Since this form of regulation has already been studied in Chapter 25 (especially Box 25-2 and Appendix 25-B) we will concentrate here on type *b*.

(*b*) Regulation of a naturally more competitive industry, such as trucking.

3. Quality-of-life regulation of health, safety, and working conditions. This type of regulation grew rapidly during the 1970s.

Each of the three types of regulation will be examined in turn, beginning with antitrust. Before studying the antitrust laws themselves, we look at the difficult economic questions that must be considered in developing an antitrust policy.

I. ANTITRUST POLICY: SOME PROBLEMS

In order to prevent the accumulation of market power, antitrust laws make the takeover of one firm by another illegal if it can be established that this would substantially reduce competition. On the same grounds, large existing firms can be broken up. However, setting precise guidelines for taking such action is not an easy task. A number of problems complicate the life of the policymaker. For example, it is not certain that breaking up large firms will improve the performance of the economy. In business, big isn't *necessarily* bad.

Are There Advantages of Large Size?

In a number of industries, there are advantages of large size, for several reasons:

1. Large firms can better afford research and development Because of their very large sales, big firms may be able to finance large research and development (R&D) projects that could not be undertaken by small firms. These expenditures benefit not only the firms that are thereby able to develop the profitable new products. Society as a whole also benefits as these new products become available. In his classic defense of large firms, Joseph Schumpeter wrote:

As soon as we go into details and inquire into the individual items in which progress was most conspicuous, the trail leads not to the doors of those firms that work under conditions of comparatively free competition but precisely to the doors of the large concerns—which, as in the case of agricultural machinery, also account for much of the progress in the competitive sector—and a shocking suspicion dawns upon us that big business may have had more to do with creating that standard of life than keeping it down.[1]

Although large firms with their heavy R&D expenditures are often the source of innovation, their role should not be exaggerated. Many innovations come, not from firms that are already large, but from firms that are small and seeking to become large. For example, the personal computer was introduced by upstart Apple, not by the giants of the computer industry. The oxygen furnace was invented, not by a giant U.S. firm, but by a small Austrian firm which was less than one-third the size of a single plant of U.S. Steel.

2. Large firms can capture economies of scale In many industries, economies of scale can be fully realized only by very large firms. As already noted in Chapter 25, in any decision on whether or not a monopoly should be broken up, an important question arises: Is this a natural monopoly based on economies of large-scale production? If the answer is yes, breaking it up will raise average costs; a better policy generally is to regulate its price. On the other hand, if the firm is not a natural monopoly, it is appropriate to consider breaking it up.

This simple principle—that costs should be considered before a firm is broken up—has not always been recognized by the courts in antitrust judgments. Most notably, in the Alcoa case of 1945, Judge Learned Hand stated that the purpose of the antitrust laws is to "perpetuate and preserve, for its own sake and *in spite of possible cost,* an organization of industry in small units which can effectively compete with each other." (Italics are added.)

How can we resolve the conflict between Judge Hand's view that "small is good" and the view that, in the face of economies of scale, "big is better?" The proper answer may be a compromise. One can agree with Judge Hand that competition is beneficial. At the same time, costs in the form of economies of scale should also be considered—a point he rejected. If economies of scale are very important—as in the case of many public utilities—monopoly should be allowed, but in regulated form. In short, dealing with monopoly involves assessing several influences, with costs being one. One of the important changes in antitrust policy in recent years has been the growing recognition that economies of scale should be taken into account before any decision is made to break up a large firm or block a merger.

There has also been a growing recognition of the importance of foreign competition. In those industries which are now subject to intense competition from abroad, large U.S. corporations are far less objectionable than they would be in an isolated U.S. economy. There are two reasons: (1) U.S. producers may be unable to compete with imports unless they are large enough to capture economies of scale. With the flood of Japanese auto imports in recent years, nobody has been talking about breaking up General Motors anymore. (2) Because of competition from imports, the market power of U.S. giants is reduced. They are not as free to raise prices since they risk losing markets to foreign firms.

What Is "Unfair" Competition?

In order to protect small competing firms, antitrust legislation is designed to limit a number of unfair practices, such as ***cutthroat competition.*** This occurs when a large firm attempts to drive its competitors out of business by pricing at less than cost. The large firm takes a loss in the short run, but it has the financial resources to do so. Its ability to outlast its smaller competitors may be particularly strong if the large firm has many products. In this case, the sale of the other items may provide more than enough profit to cover its losses on the products it is selling at cutthroat prices. Once the cutthroat firm emerges as a monopolist, it can raise prices enough to more than recoup any earlier losses.

***Cutthroat competition*—sometimes called *predatory pricing*—is pricing below cost in order to drive competitors out of business.**

[1]Joseph Schumpeter, *Capitalism, Socialism and Democracy* (New York: Harper, 1942), 3d ed., p. 82.

In practice, it is difficult to draw a line between fair competition and unfair cutthroat competition. One might think that a fair price is one that covers total costs, including a normal profit. But there may be problems in calculating total costs, particularly for a large firm producing many goods: It's not clear how some costs—such as overhead—should be allocated among its various products. Furthermore, even if a firm is pricing below costs, this doesn't necessarily mean that it is engaged in cutthroat pricing to eliminate competitors. In the early 1980s, both GM and Ford suffered large losses; that is, they priced below average costs. But they weren't trying to "cut Chrysler's throat." Rather, they were frantically trying to hold their shares of the market in the face of stiff Japanese competition. Because of such real-world complexities, it is very difficult even to identify—let alone control—unfair competition.

What Constitutes Collusion?

In order to protect the consuming public, the antitrust laws prohibit collusive agreements by oligopolists to raise price. However, collusion may be as difficult to identify as unfair competition. There may be exceptional cases where collusion has clearly taken place. For example, competitors may get together with the specific intention of fixing price and splitting up the market. In such cases, they can be sent to jail for their efforts (Box 27-1). But what action should be taken in more complex cases, where oligopolists with a common interest arrive at the same price without even so much as a wink or a nod because all firms follow a price leader? Certainly we cannot make it illegal to quote the current market price. If a firm's price "meets the competition," how can it be condemned? After all, doesn't a perfectly competitive producer—such as the wheat farmer—sell at the going market price? If everybody sells at the same price, this does not *prove* collusion.

A further complication is that collusion, like bigness, isn't *necessarily* bad. For example, if automobile firms were allowed to collude on research, they might develop pollution-control and safety equipment more quickly and cheaply. However, they have been hesitant to engage in such joint activities because of fears that they might be prosecuted under antitrust laws.

ANTITRUST LEGISLATION IN THE UNITED STATES: A SUMMARY

Because of the complexities of antitrust laws, it is not feasible to do more than note the most important ones below.

The Sherman Antitrust Act (1890)

In response to the wave of mergers and the growing concentration of industry in the late nineteenth century, Congress passed the Sherman Act. It was direct and to the point. "Every contract, combination in the form of a trust[2] or otherwise, or conspiracy in restraint of trade" was declared illegal. It was likewise illegal to "monopolize, or attempt to monopolize, or combine or conspire . . . to monopolize" trade.

Teddy Roosevelt became the first "trust-busting" president. The surge of legal activity initiated during his presidency led to the breakup of Standard Oil and the American Tobacco Company in 1911.

The Clayton Act (1914)

The Clayton Act spelled out some of the missing details of the Sherman Act. Among its provisions, the Clayton Act:

1. Prohibited ***interlocking directorates*** designed to lessen competition. An interlocking directorate exists when a director sits on the board of two or more competing firms.

2. Prohibited ***tying contracts,*** sometimes called ***full-line forcing.*** Such a contract requires purchasers to buy other items in a seller's line in order to get the one they really want. Thus it helps a firm with a particularly appealing product to use it to monopolize the sale of other products.

3. Prohibited corporations from taking over another company by purchasing its common stock, if the takeover "substantially lessens competition." However, this provision was evaded by some firms that purchased the

[2]The word *trust* has a long history. Before the Sherman Act, a favorite way to limit competition was to put common stock of different firms into a trust, with an agreement for collective action and profit sharing. The word *antitrust* is now used broadly, to refer to any action against a powerful firm or group of firms.

BOX 27-1

THE GREAT ELECTRICAL EQUIPMENT CONSPIRACY AND OTHER MISDEEDS

The classic case of price fixing occurred more than two decades ago, when the manufacturers of heavy electrical equipment illegally conspired to set prices, thereby raising the cost of almost every power-generating station built in the United States. Senior officials from General Electric, Westinghouse, and 27 other firms ended up in court. Two million dollars in fines were eventually paid, and seven executives each spent 30 days in jail. Moreover, they faced an even greater personal cost. Almost as soon as the Justice Department began its investigation, the salary of one GE vice-president was cut from $127,000 to $40,000. While he was recovering from that shock, he was fined $4,000 and sent to prison for 30 days. When he got out, GE eased him out of the company altogether.

Here is how *The Wall Street Journal* (Jan. 10, 1961) described the conspiracy in a passage that strangely echoes the words of Adam Smith, written over two centuries ago and quoted at the beginning of Chapter 26.

> Many of the meetings took place at the conventions of the National Electrical Manufacturers Association and other trade groups. Rather typically, after a conventional and perfectly lawful meeting of some kind, certain members would adjourn for a rump session and a few drinks in someone's suite. It seemed natural enough that mutual business problems would be discussed—specifications, for example—and like as not prices would come up. In time it was easy enough to drift from general talk about prices into what should be done about them—and finally into separate meetings to fix them for everyone's mutual benefit.

One scheme they used was a form of bidding cartel. The firms agreed in advance on a complicated system in which each firm knew from the phase of the moon whether it should bid low or high on a contract. Thus each firm waited for its turn to be the winning low bidder. When its turn came, it knew that it would have no competition, so it could set its "low" bid substantially above the bid it would have otherwise made.

More recently, bid rigging has also been used on a much wider scale by U.S. roadbuilders to raise prices by up to 20% on highway construction. The resulting extra cost to taxpayers who have had to foot the bill has run as high as several hundreds of millions of dollars per year. This triggered the largest single antitrust investigation in U.S. history; between 1979 and 1983, federal prosecutors in 20 states obtained 400 criminal convictions with 141 jail sentences and fines totaling about $50 million. Notice that the major effort in this case was not against the giants of U.S. industry, but was instead against many small firms.

Even more surprising was the following report of an apparent attempt by American Airlines Robert Crandall to fix price in a phone call to Braniff Chairman Howard Putnam. This excerpt—taped by Putnam without telling Crandall—picks up a discussion of how difficult it was for the two airlines to make a profit when they were both flying the same routes and cutting prices.

> *Crandall*:. . . there's no reason I can see, all right, to put both [our] companies out of business.

Putnam: But if you're going to overlay a route of American's on top of . . . every route that Braniff has—I can't just sit here and allow you to bury us without giving our best effort.

Crandall: Oh, sure, but Eastern and Delta do the same thing in Atlanta and have for years.

Putnam: Do you have a suggestion for me?

Crandall: Yes, I have a suggestion for you. Raise your [expletive] fares 20%. I'll raise mine the next morning.

Putnam: Robert, we. . . .

Crandall: You'll make more money and I will too.

Putnam: We can't talk about pricing.

Crandall: Oh [expletive] Howard. We can talk about any [expletive] thing we want to talk about.

In this case, no price fixing actually occurred because Putnam didn't take the bait. However, if he had, this tape could have put them both in jail.

physical assets of the other company instead. This loophole was not closed until the ***Celler-Kefauver Antimerger Act*** in 1950.

The Federal Trade Commission Act (1914)

The Federal Trade Commission (FTC), a board of five members, was set up in 1914 to deal with "unfair methods of competition." Like the Justice Department, the FTC can enforce the Sherman or Clayton Acts by taking alleged violators to court. In addition, the FTC was given some powers normally reserved to the courts; for example, it could issue cease-and-desist orders where it found unfair competition. However, the law did not define what "unfair" meant, and the courts made it clear that they, and not the FTC, would pass judgment on this question. Nevertheless, the FTC still has a role in deciding whether agreements among firms will be permitted. For example, it was the FTC that approved the 1983 agreement between GM and Toyota to produce cars in California. In addition, the FTC has responsibility for curbing misleading advertising and misrepresentation of products.

These three acts, the Sherman Act, the Clayton Act, and the Federal Trade Commission Act, have formed the cornerstone of antitrust policy.

The Other Side: Legislation That Tends to Reduce Competition Rather than Increase It

Congress has passed several laws that have encouraged restraints on trade; they have put the interests of the producer above those of the consumer.

1. *The Capper-Volstead Act (1922)* provides immunity from antitrust laws to farmers who form cooperatives—provided these agencies do not engage in "undue price enhancement."

2. *The Robinson-Patman Act (1936)*—sometimes called the Chain Store Law—was designed to protect small firms in an industry from larger competitors. In the words of cosponsor Wright Patman, the act's objective was to "give the little business fellows a square deal" by curbing price cutting by large discount and chain stores. It was designed to prevent large stores from buying from suppliers at quantity discounts, unless such discounts were justified on the basis of actual cost economies. It also prohibited stores from selling to the public "at unreasonably low prices." Its major effect was to impede, though not prevent, the efficient development of retail trade.

3. *The Miller-Tydings Act (1937)* exempted ***fair trade*** contracts from antitrust laws when such contracts are permitted by state law. Under a fair trade contract, the manufacturer of a name-brand good could fix the price that retail stores charge the public. During the 1960s and 1970s, manufacturers found it increasingly difficult to enforce such contracts, and under heavy public attack, the fair trade exemption was ended.

MERGERS AND BREAKUPS

Antitrust policy has not only been aimed at controlling collusion and unfair practices of large firms, but has also been designed to limit bigness in cases where there would otherwise be substantial adverse effects on competition. Mergers may be forbidden and large existing firms broken up.

Preventing Mergers That Would Damage Competition

How should the authorities decide whether or not a proposed merger will significantly restrict competition? Before trying to answer this question, three different types of merger should be distinguished. The merger that is most likely to be anticompetitive is a ***horizontal merger,*** involving firms which previously competed with each other. However, a ***vertical merger***—in which a firm merges with one of its suppliers—may also suppress competition by making it difficult for other suppliers to sell to that firm.

Both of these kinds of merger were illustrated in a 1962 case in which the Supreme Court disallowed a merger between the Brown Shoe Co. and T. R. Kinney. This was a vertical merger because shoe manufacturer Brown became a supplier to Kinney's retail stores. At the same time, it was a horizontal merger for two reasons: (1) both firms manufactured shoes, and (2) both firms had retail shoe stores. The government lawyers were unable to make a convincing case that the merger would restrict horizontal competition in shoe manufacturing. However, they did successfully argue that the merger would restrict horizontal competition in shoe retailing, since the new merged firm became the dominant seller in some markets. Moreover, the government lawyers also successfully argued that the merger had unfavorable vertical effects. In the 2 years following the merger, manufacturer Brown increased its supply of shoes to Kinney's retail stores from zero to 8% of Kinney's purchases. Thus, the court concluded that Brown was using its relationship to Kinney to limit the sales by other shoe manufacturers to Kinney.

In the third type of merger—a ***conglomerate merger***—a firm joins another in a completely different activity. International Telephone and Telegraph grew into a huge conglomerate by acquiring firms in unrelated activities: Avis (rent-a-car), Sheraton (hotels), Grinnel (automatic fire sprinklers), Continental Baking, Hartford Fire Insurance, and many others.

A *horizontal merger* is a union of firms in the same competing activity.

A *vertical merger* is a union of a firm and its supplier.

A *conglomerate merger* is a union of firms in unrelated activities.

Whether conglomerate mergers adversely affect competition—and if so, by how much—is a controversial issue. A conglomerate merger may invigorate a weak company in an industry by providing it with new capital and more aggressive management. In such cases, competition can be enhanced. On the other hand, a merger may help an already strong company to increase its dominance of an industry.

Between 1950 and 1980, the antitrust authorities exercised a substantial degree of restraint over vertical and horizontal mergers, but were much more relaxed in allowing conglomerate mergers. The result was successive waves of conglomerate mergers.

From 1980 to 1985, there was a relatively permissive attitude not only to conglomerate mergers but also to vertical and horizontal mergers. These were allowed, provided they did not give new firms enough market power to raise price. Further evidence of the government's permissive policy was its more helpful attitude in working with companies to ensure that their merger plans were consistent with antitrust law and its decision not to contest the GM/Toyota agreement to build small cars in California.

As Figure 27-1 illustrates, the result was a series of record-breaking mergers. (See also Box 27-2.)

Breaking Up an Existing Firm to Make an Industry More Competitive

As the song goes: "Breaking up is hard to do." On its last business day in early 1969, the outgoing Johnson administration filed suit against IBM for trying to monopolize the computer business. The case dragged on and on. The government didn't even begin to present its case until 1975, and then took 3 years to complete it; one witness alone was on the stand for 78 days. Two judges observed that the case was lasting longer than World War

II and jokingly suggested that it might cost more. Little wonder that lawyers referred to the case as a ''black hole'' into which their careers might disappear without a trace. In 1982, the government dropped its case on the grounds that it was ''without merit.''

The outcome was different in an antitrust action initiated in 1974 against another giant: AT&T (American Telephone and Telegraph), a company that held a monopoly in the provision of some phone services. AT&T was a huge company with assets greater than those of Exxon, Mobil, and General Motors combined.

Specifically, the Justice Department sued AT&T to force it to divest itself of Western Electric, its manufacturer of telephone equipment. Because of serious delays, such as the death of the first judge, the case didn't go to trial until 1981. Because both AT&T and the Reagan administration wished to reduce the uncertainty surrounding the future of the company, they reached an out-of-court settlement in 1982 to split up AT&T, not into two companies but into eight. Seven of the new companies—with names like Pacific Telesis and Bell Atlantic—now provide local phone service to a U.S. region. As a local monopoly, each continues to have its rates regulated. The eighth company—the new, leaner (and meaner?) AT&T—still retains Western Electric to produce telephone equipment, along with divisions that provide research and long distance service. An AT&T executive described the breakup as the ''largest corporate event in history, like taking apart a 747 and putting it back together again while it is still in the air.''

Telephone users who previously dealt with only one phone company—the old AT&T—often found their service deteriorating. Moreover, the rates on local phone services were increased to cover their costs more fully. On the other hand, rates were reduced on long distance services, where AT&T faced competition and where

FIGURE 27-1

The targets have been getting larger and larger (selected takeovers, 1977–1984)

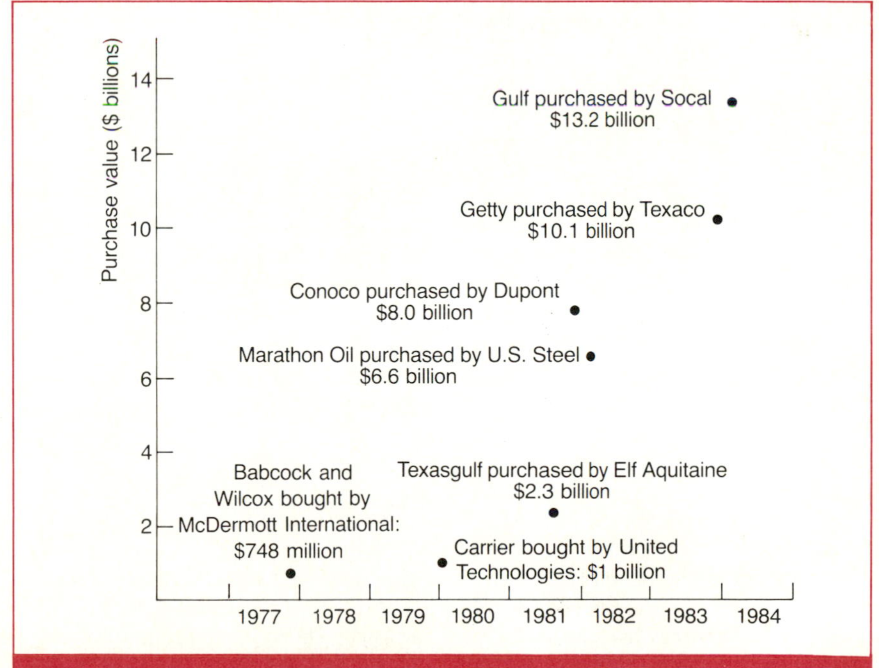

BOX 27-2

WHY THAT URGE TO MERGE?

In this box we consider the advantages and disadvantages of a merger to (1) the acquiring firm, (2) the "target" firm that is being taken over, and (3) society as a whole.

The Interests of the Acquiring Firm

Tax laws provide two incentives for firms to merge. First, tax laws provide an incentive to retain profits rather than pay them out as dividends to stockholders. As we saw in Chapter 6, dividends are subject to tax twice—once when they are earned as corporate profit, and once when they are paid out as income to the dividend recipient. On the other hand, profits that are not paid out as dividends but are instead held as retained earnings are taxed only once, as corporate profits. If firms with large retained earnings cannot use them effectively in their current business, they have an incentive to "conquer new worlds" by purchasing another firm. The second tax incentive occurs if a corporation has a loss. Profitable firm A may have an incentive to take over a firm B which has suffered losses, because B's losses can then be used by A to reduce its taxable profit.

In the case of a horizontal merger, such as the purchase by one steel company of another, the new higher-volume company may be able to achieve economies of scale because its output of steel has increased. In the case of any of the three kinds of merger, the acquisition of another business may be a challenging way for a firm to use underutilized management talent; that is, expanding the firm may be a way of achieving economies of scale in management. There may also be economies of scale in R&D. To illustrate, Saab-Scandia, a Swedish conglomerate, produces aircraft, trucks, and automobiles, thereby reducing the design and engineering costs of each. Another incentive for a merger is to diversify by expanding into a new business. For example, if a firm is producing ski equipment with profits in the winter, its management may be interested in acquiring a tennis equipment company to provide profits in the summer.

Changing prices on the stock market provide firms with another reason to merge. Surprisingly, mergers may be encouraged both by high stock prices and by low ones. During the go-go days of the 1960s, high-flying companies with stocks selling at fancy price-earnings ratios could use their own overpriced stock as a way of paying for a new acquisition. Because their own stock was so highly priced, they often could buy the other firm's shares with relatively few shares of their own company. On the other hand, the mergers of the late 1970s and the huge oil mergers in the 1980s were quite different. Typically, the incentive of the acquiring firm was that the price of the stock of the *target* firm was *low,* often far below book value. Thus a target firm could be acquired by purchasing its stock at a bargain price. Often the acquiring firm paid for the purchase with borrowed cash.

An example was the record-breaking 1984 purchase of Gulf by Standard Oil of California (Socal). Since Gulf's stock was worth far less than the value of its oil reserves, it was cheaper for Socal to buy the whole Gulf company than to drill for new reserves. To acquire Gulf, Socal paid an awesome $13.2 billion, borrowed from a consortium of banks. The resulting debt load left Socal in a much more leveraged position. Socal's management was basically "betting the company" on the gamble that there would be no dramatic rise in interest rates or fall in oil price—either of which could put the company in deep trouble. On the other hand, if interest rates and oil price moved in a favorable direction, Socal would be a big winner.

The Interests of the Target Firm

Stockholders of a firm may welcome a takeover bid by another firm, since they are typically offered more than the current market price of their stock. Thus, one game in the stock market is to try to identify and buy the stock of potential target companies before they actually receive takeover bids.

While the stockholders of a target firm may welcome a takeover bid, a quite different view may be taken by its *management*—the president, vice-presidents, etc., who run the company. Why would managers object? After all, they are frequently also large stockholders, and this gives them an incentive for welcoming a takeover. However, *in their role as managers* they often oppose a takeover because the corporate reorganization that follows may place their jobs in jeopardy. In order to protect managers in the event of a merger, they are sometimes offered a "golden parachute" contract—that is, the right to a large financial settlement if they decide to "bail out" of the merged firm or if they are fired.

If the management of a target firm agrees, the takeover is a "friendly" one, and there may be little fanfare in the press. The highly publicized struggles occur when the takeover is contested. Management decides to resist the acquiring firm, which is then called a "shark" or a "black knight."

White Knights, Greenmail, and Other Forms of Shark Repellant

Here are some of the strategies the management of a target firm may use to resist an unfriendly takeover:

1. The target firm may accuse the acquiring firm of violating the antitrust laws by seeking to accumulate monopoly power. This is an easier charge to make if the two firms are already in the same business—that is, if the takeover is a horizontal one. But even if it is not, a farsighted management fearing a takeover may *put* itself in the same business by taking over a third firm.
2. When a target firm realizes its stock is being accumulated by a "shark," the target firm can buy back this stock by offering the shark a premium price for it, that is, a price above its current market value. Because some view this payoff in the face of a threat as a legal form of blackmail, it is called "greenmail."

Who bears the cost of this greenmail? The answer is the other shareholders who don't get paid off; they are left with a company of diminished value because money has been wasted in this payoff. Thus, the payment of greenmail is a way for top executives to save their jobs by using shareholders' money to pay off the sharks. Sometimes smaller shareholders become so infuriated that they sue the executives for making this payment.

A recent example of greenmail might well be subtitled "Mickey Mouse in High Finance." June 1984 was Donald Duck's 50th birthday, and it should have been a joyous occasion in Disney World. It was anything but. Takeover artist Saul Steinberg had been accumulating Disney stock and was threatening a takeover. Disney's management dealt with this threat by paying Steinberg over $70 a share for his Disney stock, which was then worth $65 on the market. When the remaining Disney stockholders heard the news and realized that they would be footing the bill, the market value of the stock immediately fell to $60—and soon thereafter to less than $50.

3. Another way of dealing with a shark is the Pac-Man strategy of eating it before it eats you. When Bendix attempted to acquire Martin Marietta by purchasing its stock, Martin Marietta retaliated by attempting to take over Bendix by purchasing Bendix' stock. Because a surprised Bendix lacked "second strike capability" it was suddenly hard pressed to defend itself. To do so, it turned to the fourth kind of defense.
4. This form of defense is to find a "white knight"—in this case Allied, a "friendly" company with compatible goals that was invited to take over Bendix to prevent it from falling into unfriendly hands. It was all quite bizarre—a battle among corporate executives high on adrenelin and short on sleep. Strangest of all, perhaps, was the way in which William Agee profited. As the head of Bendix, he had fired the initial shot in this corporate war. Even though his attempt to take over Martin Marietta was a fiasco, he did very well indeed. When Allied took over Bendix, he became the president of the new, larger Allied. Unsatisfied with his new job, he took only 8 days to pull the cord on his $4.1 million golden parachute.

The Interests of Society

Benefits of mergers The basic argument for allowing mergers is that they are the result of a search for business profit, and *provided that competition is not restricted,* this profit is likely to result in an economic gain for society. There are exceptions. For example, the payoff to greenmailers represents a transfer from present stockholders, with no additional income or wealth created. A second example occurs when lower taxes constitute the only gain from a merger.

To illustrate the economic gains from mergers, consider a merger that does not restrict competition or reduce employment in the target company. If it increases efficiency in some way—say, by reducing costs because of economies of scale—someone in society benefits: either the owners of the firm in the form of higher profits, or the labor force in the form of higher wages, or consumers of the product in the form of lower prices—perhaps all three.

Another view of a possible benefit to society is this: An inefficient firm that is earning a low return on its assets—with its stock therefore selling at a low price—will be a target for takeover by another firm that may be able to earn a higher return on those assets. The benefit to society is any increased earnings on these assets. However, there is a problem in this. To avoid becoming takeover targets, managers may become so preoccupied with keeping their earnings up in the short run that they damage their earnings in the long run.

Cost of mergers If a merger does restrict competition, then, like any form of monopolization, it is likely to result in private profit for the firms but an efficiency loss to society. This is why the antitrust authorities, in evaluating a merger, ask: "Would this merger increase the monopolization of a market?"

For several additional reasons, it has been argued that mergers may be damaging on balance. Size itself may be considered objectionable, especially if one considers the political implications of the concentration of power in the hands of very large firms. For example, International Telephone and Telegraph (ITT) became involved in schemes to influence a presidential election in Chile.

Mergers may also have a long-term deterrent effect on entrepreneurship. The fear of an eventual takeover may discourage entrepreneurs from setting up and developing their own businesses. While this may be true in some cases, in others it is not. Some entrepreneurs set up a business in the *hope* it will be taken over; they view an attractive takeover offer as their eventual financial reward. They will particularly welcome a takeover if their business has reached a point where it is worth more to sell than to continue to operate themselves.

A final observation While the Reagan administration has allowed some horizontal mergers, it is instructive to consider one that it initially blocked: the proposed 1984 merger between LTV and Republic Steel—a merger to create a steel company second only to U.S. Steel in size. One reason for the unfavorable decision was that the steel industry was protected from foreign competition by government barriers to imports of steel. These barriers increased the market power of American steel firms, and made it possible for them to raise prices. The merger was turned down because it would have created even more market power.

Critics charged that the trade barriers were a mistake in the first place, and that blocking the merger simply compounded the error. Both policies should be reversed. Reducing the barriers would allow competition from foreign firms that would prevent U.S. firms from raising price. Allowing mergers would provide U.S. steel firms with greater volume and hence the lower costs necessary to match the competition of foreign steelmakers in the U.S. market and in other markets as well.

Within a few months the government did indeed reverse itself. It allowed the merger to take place, and in addition, ruled against the steel industry on its appeal for stricter barriers against imported steel. However, government policy is not always consistent; the government went on to impose a different set of trade barriers to protect the industry.

costs had been falling as technology improved. The price of much phone equipment fell as Western Electric now had to face increased competition.

Because the old AT&T had been one of the world's most efficient telephone systems, breaking it up was a clear rejection of the guideline "If it works, don't fix it." It wasn't immediately clear whether the new system would work better or worse than the old. This depended on the answers to a large number of questions, such as: Would economies of scale be lost because of the breakup? On the other hand, would new, more intense competition *reduce* costs? Would Bell Labs, the research wing of AT&T, lose or retain the excellence that had led to such inventions as the transistor?

ANTITRUST POLICY: FINAL OBSERVATIONS

During the late nineteenth century, antitrust legislation was launched on a wave of hostility toward giant corporations and their predatory, anticompetitive methods. But, since the days of the nineteenth-century "robber barons,'' there have been relatively few black and white situations. Antitrust history is largely the story of difficult gray areas.

At an early stage, in the 1920 U.S. Steel case, the Supreme Court put forth the rule of reason. The Court held that mere size was no offense, and that giant U.S. Steel had not actually exercised monopoly power. But standards change. By 1945, the Court held that guilt does not require any overt act. In the Alcoa case of that year, the Court decided that even if a firm's actions might be otherwise reasonable, these actions are nevertheless illegal if they help the firm to maintain a monopoly position. For example, one reasonable business policy is to expand plant capacity in anticipation of increased demand. But the court decided that such increases in capacity represented a violation by Alcoa, since they tended to block out potential new firms:

> [Alcoa] insists that it never excluded competitors; but we can think of no more effective exclusion than progressively to embrace each new opportunity as it opens, and to face every newcomer with new capacity already geared into a great organization, having the advantage of experience, trade connections and the elite of personnel.

With the permissive U.S. Steel decision in 1920 at the one extreme and the much tougher Alcoa decision in 1945 at the other, the courts have interpreted the antitrust laws in a wide variety of ways. There has also been a wide variation in the approach of different presidents. Theodore Roosevelt's administration aggressively took firms to court. The Reagan administration has not, preferring to get business to follow its guidelines and avoid court cases.

In the face of the need to balance the complex considerations of market power, tacit collusion, economies of scale, and the other issues which monopoly and oligopoly raise, it is too much to hope for a simple solution. Perfect competition is the perfect answer only in textbooks. In the real world, we must settle for *workable competition,* by which we gain many of the advantages of large-scale business but curb the more flagrant abuses. Harvard's Richard Caves has compared antitrust laws with traffic laws. Drivers can usually get away with 38 miles an hour in a 35-mph zone; the police are there to catch the speeder who goes 45 or 50. The fact that we *might* get caught makes most of us drive a little more carefully. Similarly, the electrical machinery and road construction cases described in Box 27-1 remind business executives that there is a jail cell awaiting the flagrant offender; they are likely to be more careful as a result.

Moreover, fear of prosecution by the government is not the only discipline a business faces. A firm may also be sued by a competitor that has been damaged by anticompetitive practices. In such a civil antitrust suit, the court may award the injured party up to *three times* the amount of the damage. For example, after the electrical equipment executives were sentenced to jail for *criminal* price fixing, their companies were also taken to court in almost 2,000 *civil* suits. As a consequence, they had to pay about $500 million in damages. Obviously, this ***treble damage clause*** acts as a deterrent to antitrust violations.

II. REGULATION OF PRICE AND ENTRY

. . . [In the] airlines it appears that the prime obstacle to efficiency has been regulation itself and the most creative thing a regulator can do is remove his or her body from the market entryway.

Alfred Kahn,
former Chairman of the Civil Aeronautics Board

In Chapter 25, we examined in detail the case for regulating a natural monopoly, such as an electric company. Such regulation can force the firm to act more like a perfect competitor facing a given market price. Here we discuss a policy that is much more difficult to justify: government regulation of a naturally more competitive industry, such as the airline or trucking industry. As will become evident, regulation in this case typically allows firms to act in a *less* competitive way. For example, regulation may reduce competition by blocking the entry of potential new firms. Therefore it is no surprise that this form of regulation is often welcomed by the firms that are already in the industry. (See Box 27-3.)

A Case History: The Airlines

Until 1978, the Civil Aeronautics Board (CAB) regu-

BOX 27-3

THE PARABLE OF THE PARKING LOTS

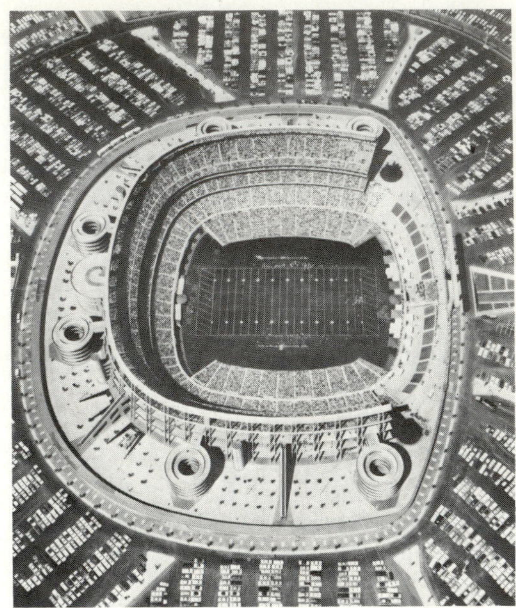

Producers have a natural interest to narrow the market and raise the price.

ADAM SMITH

Henry Manne, professor of law at the University of Miami, tells a simple parable to illustrate the problems of government regulation which protects existing firms by blocking the entry of new firms.[†]

Once upon a time in a city not far away, thousands of people would crowd into the local football stadium on a Saturday afternoon. The problem of parking was initially solved by a number of big commercial parking lots whose owners formed the Association of Professional Parking Lot Employers (APPLE). But, as time passed and crowds grew, every plumber, lawyer, and schoolteacher who owned a house in the neighborhood went into the parking business on Saturday afternoon, and cars appeared in every driveway and on most lawns. Members of APPLE viewed the entry of these "amateurs" into their business with no great enthusiasm, especially since some were charging a lower fee. Stories began to circulate about their fly-by-night methods, and the dents they had put in two cars (although, on investigation, it was discovered that denting was an equally serious problem in the commercial lots).

At a meeting of all members of APPLE, emotions and applause ran high as one speaker after another pointed out—in some cases, in a very statesmanlike way—that parking should be viewed, not as a business, but as a profession governed by professional standards. In particular, cutthroat price competition with amateurs should be regarded as unethical. The one concrete proposal, quickly adopted, was that APPLE members should contribute $1 per parking spot "to improve their public image, and put their case before the proper authorities."

No accounting was ever made of this money, but it must have been spent wisely, since within a few months the city council passed an ordinance to regulate industry price and to require that anyone parking cars must be licensed. However, it turned out to be difficult for an independent house owner to get a license; it required passing a special driving test to be "professionally administered" by APPLE, a $27,000 investment in parking facilities, and $500,000 in liability insurance. Since every commercial lot found its costs consequently increasing by 20 percent, the city council approved a 20 percent increase in parking fees. (Within a year, APPLE had requested that the city council guarantee the liability insurance, so that people would have no fear of parking in commercial lots. One argument put forward by an APPLE spokesman was that this idea was similar in its intent to recent congressional legislation setting up an insurance scheme for stockbrokers.)

On the next football afternoon, a funny thing happened on the way to the stadium. Since police were out in large numbers to enforce the ordinance, driveways and lawns were empty and long lines of cars were backed up waiting to get into each commercial lot. The snarl was even worse after the game. Some people simply gave up waiting for their cars and had to return to retrieve them next day. (There was even a rumor that one car was never found.) In response, APPLE decided to go ahead with a "statistical-logistic study of the whole socioeconomic situation" by two computer science professors at the local university.

Their report cited the archaic methods of the industry and pointed out that what each firm needed was fewer quill pens and more time on a computer.

As the parking lots began to computerize their operations it became quite clear that in the face of these rising costs, a further increase in parking fees was required. The increase was quickly approved by city councillors relieved that, in the modernization of the industry, they had finally found a solution. But, unfortunately, it was no solution after all. The problem, it turned out, was not so much deciding which car should be moved where, as actually moving it—and that continued to be done by attendants who had become surly and uncooperative because of the pressure they were facing.

Relief, however, did appear in two forms. First, many people got so fed up with the hassle that they started watching the game on TV. Second, small boys who lived in the houses closest to the stadium went into the car wash business on Saturday afternoon. They charged $5, but it was worth the price, since they guaranteed a top-quality job. (In fact, they guaranteed that they would spend at least 2 hours on it.) And they always had as many cars as they could handle, even on rainy days—in fact, especially on rainy days.

†"The Parable of the Parking Lots," *Public Interest*, no. 23 (Spring 1971), pp. 10–15. Abbreviated with the author's permission.

lated airline ticket prices and the routes serviced by each airline. By controlling routes, the CAB controlled entry. Between 1938 and 1978, the CAB turned down all requests by new carriers to serve long distance "trunk" routes between major cities. Thus it restricted the competition along these routes. This led to the charge that the CAB was regulating the industry more in the interests of the regulated firms than of the general public. In effect, the regulatory agency had taken on some of the responsibilities of a cartel manager by restricting entry, setting price, and dividing up the market (the routes each airline serviced). True, it did not set the high monopoly price of a private cartel. On the other hand, this special kind of "public cartel" offered two advantages not available to a private cartel: (1) Because it was administered by a government agency, there wasn't the problem of cheating that arises in a private cartel; the airlines were *forbidden* by the government to undercut the prices set by the CAB. (2) It was immune from the danger of prosecution under the antitrust laws.

At the same time, there were several ways in which regulations limited the profits of the airlines. One of the most important was the CAB requirement that forced airlines to continue service to smaller cities, even at a loss. Thus regulation resulted in ***cross-subsidization,*** that is, one group of passengers being subsidized by another. Specifically, small-city travelers—who got service they would not have otherwise enjoyed—were being subsidized by travelers on trunk lines who paid more for their tickets. One of the chief arguments of those who supported regulation was that it provided small-city passengers with convenient and safe service that would be dropped if regulation were to end.

Deregulation In 1978, Congress passed the Airline Deregulation Act. By the end of that year, passengers were benefiting from lower fares. In turn, lower prices resulted in more airline travel. In 1978, passenger travel increased by 40% as airline fares fell by 20%. At the same time, the airline industry was entering a state of competitive flux. The major airlines did indeed drop some of their service to small cities. However, between 1978 and 1983, 14 new airlines moved into the industry, not only to "fill the gap" by serving the small-city routes discontinued by the major airlines, but also to provide the majors with severe competition on the big-city trunk routes. In the shakeout that often occurs when an industry becomes more competitive, several long-established airlines faced bankruptcy. While some narrowly escaped, one notable casualty was Braniff. With deregulation, Braniff had gone deeply into debt to buy new planes, in the hope of gaining a much larger share of the market.

The airline shakeout was complicated by a combination of unlucky events. Jet fuel prices doubled in 1979–1980. Following a crash, DC-10s were grounded for more than a month in 1979 by the Federal Aviation Administration. Airline travel was further disrupted by a strike of air traffic controllers in 1981. The recessions of 1980 and 1981–1982 reduced airline travel.

In response to these external pressures, the airlines—now free to compete—tried to fill the empty seats by cutting prices. This was beneficial to travelers. It became possible to travel one way between New York and Los Angeles for $99. Moreover, passengers were now taking advantage of a much wider variety of discount fares; three out of four passengers traveled on a discount, compared with one in three before deregulation. However, this discounting added to the losses for the airlines.

Consequently, during this shakeout period the question arose: ''How much of the financial difficulty of the airlines is due to deregulation, and how much is due to other pressures on the industry?'' A number of airline executives, including some who originally had opposed deregulation, expressed the view that the airline companies—as well as passengers—had benefited on balance from deregulation. For example, deregulation was allowing the airlines to move their equipment around quickly into more efficient routing patterns. Moreover, with the recovery during 1983 and 1984, and with some of the shakeout complete, the airlines profit-and-loss statements improved.

However, not all problems were solved. Deregulation allowed airlines to fly whenever and wherever they wished. Many of them scheduled flights for the rush hours along the trunk routes. The resulting traffic jams at the major airports left travelers late and angry. A simple market solution—auctioning off the right to each specific landing time—was resisted because it would make it prohibitively expensive for private planes to land and take off. Pressures were finally eased when the airlines were permitted to get together to discuss their scheduling problems. Some observers—including Alfred Kahn, who had led the struggle for deregulation and was now back at Cornell University—argued that this was much inferior to an auction of landing rights. There was a danger that the airlines might use an agreement over schedules as a way of limiting competition and working toward a private cartel.

Deregulation of Trucking

In 1980, Congress enacted legislation to remove many of the regulations on the trucking industry. The Interstate Commerce Commission (ICC) had already been allowing easier entry into the industry, and had been dropping many of its costly regulations, such as those that had restricted trucks from carrying certain items. For example, one company had been permitted to carry empty ginger ale bottles, but not empty cola or root beer bottles. Another had been allowed to haul 5-gallon cans but not 2-gallon cans. Such regulations had been causing inefficiency and were in direct conflict with the government's desire to conserve fuel.

As deregulation proceeded, the experience of the trucking industry paralleled that of the airlines in a number of ways. Prices were driven down by the recessions of 1980 and 1981–1982, and by competition from the 10,000 new firms that entered the industry. At the same time, fuel prices were rising. The result was severe financial difficulty for many firms; more than 300 went bankrupt, including some sizable firms. Labor came under pressure, since the high earnings in this industry could no longer be passed on to the consumer in the form of a high price. Wages in some cases were frozen for 3 years, and in other cases were reduced.

By 1983, the Reagan administration had prepared a bill that would have eliminated the ICC and completed the deregulation of trucking initiated under the Carter administration. However, the bill was sidetracked, allegedly as a result of pressure from the teamsters, the most important union in the trucking industry.

III. QUALITY-OF-LIFE REGULATION TO IMPROVE HEALTH, SAFETY, AND WORKING CONDITIONS

Whereas the price-entry regulation we have just discussed is imposed on a single industry—such as the airlines—quality-of-life regulation is usually imposed economy-wide on all industries. There is another significant difference in the two kinds of regulation: Whereas price-entry regulation often promotes the interests of the firms being regulated, quality-of-life regulation is often opposed by regulated firms because it raises their costs and is considered a nuisance. Thus quality-of-life agencies tend to reflect the views, not of the regulated firms, but instead of those who worked hard to have the regulations imposed. For example, OSHA (the Occupational Health and Safety Administration) tends to reflect the view of organized labor, and EPA (the Environmental Protection Agency) the views of environmental groups. (Pollution and the role of the EPA in controlling it are studied in the next chapter.)

Since quality-of-life agencies are pursuing important social objectives such as health and safety, we might assume that they operate in the public interest. They should, and often do; but not always.

Evaluating Quality-of-Life Regulations with Benefit-Cost Analysis

The improved health and safety standards that are designed to provide obvious benefits to society can also involve substantial costs. For example, when firms are required to purchase safety equipment, their costs rise. While the economywide evidence is that some of these higher costs are borne by the firms' owners or labor force in the form of lower income, much of this burden is passed on to customers in the form of higher prices. However, in one way or another, the public pays for the health and safety benefits it receives.

Under what circumstances are we buying too little safety, and when are we buying too much? The answer is: We are buying too little whenever there are additional safety regulations that would cost less than the benefits they would provide. We are buying too much whenever the costs exceed the benefits. Examples of too little safety may be found by going back to the 1950s, when there were few restrictions on the disposal of dangerous chemicals or radioactive wastes. An example of too much regulation (referred to as a ''regulatory absurdity'' by Charles Schultze, the Chairman of the Council of Economic Advisers under President Carter) was the 21 pages of fine print regulations imposed some years ago by OSHA on how to build a ladder, including such trivialities as how far the screws must be indented. While a number of unnecessary regulations have been eliminated in the last decade, this example nonetheless still illustrates an important point: *A regulation cannot be justified simply because it is pursuing a desirable goal such as health or safety.* Instead, it should be subjected to a ***benefit-cost*** test.

***Benefit-cost analysis* is an estimate of the benefits and costs of a policy and a comparison of the two. *A benefit-cost test* is the requirement that the benefits of a policy exceed its costs.**

All too often, the benefits of a new regulation are not estimated, and costs are almost entirely ignored. Sometimes the fault does not lie with the agency that sets the regulations, but instead with the Congress that established the agency. For example, in the Clean Air Act and the Delaney Amendment to the Food, Drug and Cosmetic Act, Congress *prohibits* agencies from considering the costs of their regulations.

Costs of Quality-of-Life Regulation

1. *The payment of salaries and other costs of operating the agencies.* By 1985 these costs were about $4 billion. Although this was a significant sum, it was relatively unimportant compared with the other costs of regulation.
2. *The costs firms incur in complying with the regulations.* These include the costs to business of health and safety equipment, and the cost of the paperwork that firms must supply to the agencies. At one point General Motors estimated that the documents it had to file to get its cars approved for 1 year would have made a stack 15 stories high.
3. *Efficiency cost of regulation.* There are many subtle effects of regulation on efficiency and productivity: The more time and effort a firm's management spends in satisfying government regulations and in trying to influence its regulatory agency, the less time it has to develop, produce, and market its products.

However, some of the effects are not so subtle. Regulations frequently lead to serious delay. For example, the testing and approval of a new drug by the Food and Drug Administration (FDA) has typically taken 5 to 7 years. The reason is that people in such an agency often develop a defensive ''seige'' mentality. They are faced with two conflicting objectives: (1) Get a drug out as quickly as possible so that it can begin to *save* lives but (2) delay its release until it can be tested sufficiently to ensure that it is safe so that it doesn't *take* lives. Faced with this choice, regulators often delay. They will be criticized less for delaying too long—and failing to save lives—than they will be for releasing a drug too soon, in which case its fatal effects may raise a political storm.

The FDA has recognized the cost of unnecessary delay—a particularly serious issue for anticancer drugs—and as a consequence has set up a ''fast track'' for particularly promising drugs.

A final observation on costs Regulation affects investment: The more resources channeled into safety and antipollution equipment, the less that remain for equipment that produces more output. Thus, lost output in the future is the opportunity cost of investment in antipollution and safety equipment today.

While the estimates of these effects are subject to considerable uncertainty, they suggest that the costs of quality-of-life regulation are now substantial. The question is: Have these regulations provided benefits sufficient to justify this high cost?

Benefits of Quality-of-Life Regulation

When benefits are measured one agency at a time, they have sometimes turned out to be disappointing. Early statistical evaluations of OSHA suggested that, at best, it had reduced accident rates by only a small amount.

On the other hand, EPA's regulations have generated considerable benefits, not only in resisting the trend toward a more polluted environment, but in even reversing it in some cases—as we shall see in the next chapter. Moreover, the introduction of safety requirements such as seat belts and stronger doors and bumpers by the National Highway Traffic Safety Association (NHTSA) has apparently provided substantial benefits, since these regulations were followed by a reduction in auto injuries and fatalities. This is even more impressive because, during this period, cars were becoming smaller and lighter—and for this reason less safe. Thus, just preventing the safety record from getting worse represented substantial success. However, it is hard to sort out how much of this success was due to NHTSA regulations, and how much to other influences, such as the reduction in the speed limit and the decrease in the proportion of the population in the low-age category where accident rates are high.

In brief, the benefits of quality-of-life regulations have been mixed: substantial in some cases, disappointing in others.

An example where benefits apparently fell short of costs and where there consequently may have been too much regulation was the banning of saccharin, a very mild carcinogen. Under the law, the FDA is required to ban artificial carcinogens, *regardless* of the overall costs and benefits. The benefit of this ban was less cancer. But its cost was the increase in heart disease of overweight people who were driven back to sugar. Thus, the ban on saccharin may have saved a few lives from cancer but lost as many—or perhaps more—from overweight.

Why Benefit-Cost Analysis Is Not the Last Word

Benefit-cost analysis is not easy. For example, it is difficult enough to estimate that the cost of a certain regulation will be $10 million and its benefit will be the saving of 20 lives. But there is an even greater problem: Before these two figures can be compared, it is necessary to put a dollar value on the human lives that are saved. And how do you do *that*? Box 27-4 provides some suggestions. Since each of these involves problems, the benefits and costs of regulations protecting human life cannot be compared in a very precise way.

This leads to another problem. In its attempt to limit the regulatory reach of the government, the Reagan administration has subjected regulations to benefit-cost tests. On the face of it, this sounds like major progress. However, critics charge that a benefit-cost test sets an almost impossible standard for any new regulation, not only because benefits and costs are so difficult to measure, but also because benefits like saving a life are often more difficult to measure than costs. Hence in any formal evaluation, benefits may get less weight than they deserve, and desirable regulations are therefore not introduced. Thus, critics contend, insisting on a rigid benefit-cost test is no more justified than the other extreme position that *any* regulation that improves human health or safety is desirable, no matter what its costs may be.

The Need for Consistency

In the last analysis, a *judgment* must be made. It may not

BOX 27-4

THE ETERNAL PUZZLE: WHAT IS A HUMAN LIFE WORTH?

Thief (holding a gun): "Your money or your life."
Jack Benny (pausing): ". . . I'm thinking. . . . I'm thinking."

The simple answer to the question in the title is: Any life is worth an infinite amount. The miner trapped underground has a life which is priceless. Yet, we don't value our own lives this way. Were they to have infinite value, safety concerns would dominate all others. We would live as close as possible to our work and never drive a car, let alone take a trip to earn something as trivial as a few thousand dollars.

Society doesn't place an infinite value on a life either. To illustrate: Lives can be saved by installing crash barriers down the middle of roads. Yet we don't do this on every country road. We simply aren't willing to spend the billions of dollars this would cost. This then raises the critical question "How much *are* we willing to spend to save a human life?" This is really just a recasting of the original question: "What is a human life worth?" However, this new question is one that everyone—including even those who philosophically refuse to place a money value on a human life—will recognize should be asked if we want to make a sensible decision on, say, whether a crash barrier will be built or not.

Why not then just ask people: "What would you be willing to pay to save *your* life?" Unfortunately, we wouldn't be able to get a sensible reply to this question because almost everyone would say "An infinite amount if I could get may hands on it." However, we *can* estimate how much people value their lives by observing those who actually "put their lives on the line." Thus we may ask, for example: "How much more than the average wage must be paid to induce a worker to take a high-risk job like that of a lumberjack?"

Although this is probably the most promising way of evaluating a human life,† several difficulites remain. For example: (1) This estimate includes only the valuation of the person's *own* life. But isn't an additional value placed on this life by family and friends? (2) The

higher wage paid in high-risks jobs indicates only how the workers who actually take these jobs value their lives. But isn't this far less than the valuation of the vast majority of the population who won't take such risky jobs because they value their lives more highly? (3) How much of the higher wage is compensation for the risk of death, and how much for the risk of injury? The higher wage compensates for both, but we are interested only in evaluating the risk of death. (4) These estimates are only meaningful if the people taking these jobs understand the risks they are taking.

In a recent study, Martin Bailey of the University of Maryland looked at how workers act in risky situations. Their behavior suggests that they estimate the value of their own lives somewhere in the $200,000 to $700,000 range.‡ The imprecision of this estimate illustrates how difficult it is to place a value on a human life.

† It is certainly an improvement over one of the early methods which has frequently been used in legal judgments—namely, evaluate a life by asking: "How much would the individual have earned over the rest of his or her lifetime?" This yields a poor measure because it implies that the value of the life of a disabled person is zero. The error is basically the same as the one made in the more extreme statement (in *Technology Review*, July 1981, p. 11) that a clean air standard for Montana is uneconomic because "some of the people who will die from air pollution are unemployed and therefore have no economic value."

‡ Martin J. Bailey, *Reducing Risks to Life: Measurement of the Benefits* (Washington: American Enterprise Institute, 1980).

Rachel Dardis uses a different approach, examining how much consumers are willing to pay for fire detectors that reduce the risk to their lives. She concludes that the value of a human life is between $200,000 and $500,000—that is, in the bottom half of Bailey's range. See Dardis, "The Value of Life: New Evidence from the Marketplace," *American Economic Review*, December 1980, pp. 1077–1082.

be as difficult as we have so far suggested; we may sometimes be in a position to identify a desirable policy change, even when only fragmentary evidence is available. For example, the cost of an OSHA emission standard for coke ovens is estimated to lie somewhere between $4.5 million and $158 million for each life it saves. Although this estimate is terribly imprecise, it is still good enough to allow us to reject this policy, because there is an alternative way of saving lives—by eliminating railroad crossings—that would only cost $100,000 each.[3]

Note that in this case we can arrive at an important conclusion—even though we have information only on the *cost* of saving a life, but none whatsoever on the *benefit* of saving a life. Specifically, we can conclude that government policy is inconsistent. It makes no sense to engage in *any* activity—saving lives or anything else—in an exceedingly expensive way (at least $4,500,000) when one can achieve the same objective at far less cost ($100,000).

Moreover, if we have even the roughest sort of estimate of the benefit of saving a life—for example, if we know that this benefit falls anywhere between the $200,000 to $700,000 cited in Box 27-4[4]—we can go one large step further to a policy recommendation: Coke-emission standards should be relaxed in favor of eliminating railroad crossings. Or, to put the same point in a different way: We will be able to save more lives at the same cost.

There are many other illustrations of regulatory inconsistency. For example: Why should the law require the FDA to ban saccharin because it is a food additive suspected of causing cancer, when there is no ban against *natural* foods with similar risks of cancer?

However, the problem of regulatory inconsistency goes far deeper than this. Agencies have often been established with objectives that are in direct conflict. For example, in pursuing its desirable goal of protecting the environment, the EPA encouraged the conversion of the nation's power plants from coal to less polluting fuels such as natural gas. But in pursuing its desirable goal of conserving scarce forms of energy, the Federal Energy Administration reversed the EPA's guidelines and urged the conversion from gas back to coal because coal is our most plentiful energy source.

CONCLUDING OBSERVATIONS

Members of Congress are faced with a wide array of problems which involve large expenditures of their own time and public funds. It is no surprise, therefore, that when they have encountered a problem that can *apparently* be solved by setting up a regulatory agency, they have often done so.

Because of the growth of regulation, by 1980 there had been a long-term shift in decision making away from the marketplace. Business decisions that had been determined in the marketplace a few decades earlier were being influenced by regulatory agencies, with disputes being settled in the courts. To reverse this trend, and to reduce the cost to business of complying with regulations, the Reagan administration (1) essentially halted the introduction of major new regulations and (2) rolled back some existing ones. However, it encountered resistance in its pursuit of this second objective. Critics charged that, in its attempts to reduce regulation, the administration was focusing too heavily on the costs of regulation to business, and was not concerned enough about the benefits, such as protection of the environment or greater safety in the workplace. Moreover, critics pointed out that the administration exaggerated the savings from relaxing regulations. For example, the National Highway Safety Administration lowered the requirement on auto bumpers so that they had to withstand an impact of only 2.5 miles per hour rather than the previous 5 miles per hour. This reduced the initial cost of the auto. While this was correctly claimed as a savings, no account was taken of the increased cost of maintaining and insuring a car with a weaker bumper. (Some estimates indicated that this cost exceeded the savings.)

In evaluating regulations, it is important to ask not only whether their benefits exceed their costs. It is also important to ask whether we are using the most effective

[3]For these and other estimates, see Martin Bailey, *Reducing Risks to Life* (Washington, D.C.: American Enterprise Institute, 1980), p.26.

[4]Actually, our argument still holds for an even wider range of values—specifically, so long as a human life is worth anything between the $100,000 railroad crossing estimate and the $4,500,000 coke oven estimate.

method for reaching our objective. This is a question we will address in the next chapter. Specifically, in order to reduce pollution, should we rely on a regulatory authority that sets a physical limit on emissions? Or should we modify the market in an appropriate way, so that businesses have an incentive to reduce pollution?

KEY POINTS

1. The government regulates business in three ways:

(*a*) Antitrust laws are designed to keep markets competitive by limiting the accumulation and exercise of market power.

(*b*) Regulatory agencies control price and conditions of entry into certain industries, including both natural monopolies—such as public utilities—and naturally more competitive industries such as the airlines.

(*c*) Other agencies regulate health, safety, and working conditions economywide across all industries.

2. Antitrust laws raise difficult questions. For example, when is price cutting unfair? How do you know when firms are colluding? Nonetheless, antitrust laws have improved the competitive tone of American business, because violations can lead to jail sentences, to fines, or to civil suits from competitors for triple damages.
3. The three main laws in the governments' antitrust arsenal are the Sherman Antitrust Act, the Clayton Act, and the Federal Trade Commission Act.
4. To protect competition, the government may take legal action to break up large firms, or to prevent the merger of existing firms into a new, larger enterprise.
5. Although government regulation may be the appropriate policy to deal with a natural monopoly, it is more dubious in industries such as the airlines. In such cases, the regulatory agency can be viewed as a legal way of "cartelizing" the industry by raising its price and dividing up its market.
6. A quality-of-life regulation cannot be justified simply because it is pursuing a desirable goal—even if this goal is saving lives. Instead, regulations should pass a benefit-cost test. However, estimating benefits and costs is often difficult, and judgment must sometimes be substituted when good estimates are not available.
7. With the growth of regulation, economic decision making is shifting from the marketplace to the government and courts.

KEY CONCEPTS

antitrust policy
advantages of size
how imports make an industry competitive
cutthroat competition
collusion
Sherman Antitrust Act (1890)
Clayton Act (1914)
Federal Trade Commission Act (1914)
laws that restrict competition
horizontal merger
vertical merger
conglomerate merger
workable competition
price-entry regulation
a regulatory agency as a "cartelization" device
cross-subsidization
benefit-cost analysis

PROBLEMS

27-1. It sounds like a good idea to forbid any firm from predatory price cutting—that is, pricing to drive its competitors out of business. However, consider the two examples below. In each case, do you think that the price-cutting action should be judged illegal (as it sometimes has been)?

(*a*) An efficient firm with lower cost than any of its competitors charges a lower price, and thus drives the less efficient firms out of business. This is an example of how our competitive system works: The more efficient take business away from the less efficient. Do you think this is a good system? If the less efficient are not driven out of business, what happens to the cost of producing goods?

(*b*) In a natural monopoly with economies of scale, the large expanding firm finds its costs are falling;

hence, it lowers its price and drives its small competitors out of business.

Do you see now why enforcing antitrust laws is difficult?

27-2. Recently, the wealthy Bass brothers bought up almost 10% of the shares of oil giant Texaco. Although the brothers made no public statements about their intentions, Texaco's managers became so nervous that they bought back these shares from the Basses for $400 million more than their market value. Why were they nervous? How would you describe this "payoff"? If you were a Texaco stockholder, how would you view this?

27-3. Which of the following agreements among firms in an industry do you judge desirable? Undesirable? (*a*) An agreement to reduce output by 10% to end a glut on the market; (*b*) an agreement to quote the same price; (*c*) an agreement by the railroads to lay the same width of track.

27-4. Does government encourage or discourage takeovers with (*a*) its tax laws? (*b*) its antitrust laws? Explain your answer.

27-5. Suppose that, for the last 10 years, a government agency had regulated the prices of hotel rooms, thus preventing price competition among the big companies like Hilton and Sheraton. Suppose, also, that in return, these companies had maintained hotels in many smaller cities. Suppose the government is now considering an end to this regulation. (*a*) As an adviser to this industry, draw up a brief on how dangerous this action would be. (*b*) Now, switch roles and criticize the brief. In your view, which is the stronger case? Do you think this example is similar to airline regulation?

***27-6.** To understand cross-subsidization better, consider a simplified example in which there are two individuals: A lives in a large city, B in a small one. Draw a diagram showing what the demand curve of each individual for airline services might look like.

(*a*) Suppose that in the initial unregulated situation, A gets airline service at price P_1, while B gets no service. Show the consumer surplus—if any—for each individual.

(*b*) Suppose the following policy of cross-subsidization is introduced: A is forced to pay a price above initial price P_1—and has consumer surplus reduced—in order to allow B for the first time to have airline service and thereby enjoy a consumer surplus. Show how this policy may provide a collective benefit, that is, an increase in the combined consumer surplus of both individuals taken together.

***27-7.** Suppose that landing rights at airports were auctioned off, as suggested by Alfred Kahn and others. There are two ways in which small private jets might be treated.

(*a*) Their owners might be treated the same as airlines and be required to pay the same amount as a large commercial jet.

(*b*) A certain number of slots at each airport might be reserved for small jets. There would be a separate auction for these slots, with only the owners of private planes being allowed to bid.

Which of these proposals would be better? Why?

27-8. During the debate over trucking deregulation, the *Washington Post* (March 2, 1980) quoted C. R. Looney, the traffic manager of PPG Industries, as follows:

> I grant you some of these [truck] rates are a little higher than they should be, . . . but it is a trade-off we shippers should accept. There are so many different products [on which different rates might be set by truckers] that I just don't see how we could "keep up" if rates were deregulated.

(*a*) Has this problem of confusing prices arisen in the airline industry since it has been deregulated? On balance, how would you weigh this problem against the gains of deregulation to the traveling public?

(*b*) Would you expect this problem of confusing prices to be greater or less in trucking than in airlines? How would this confusing array of trucking rates compare with the confusing array of prices consumers face on the many items they buy in a department store? Does this make a case for regulating department store prices? Why or why not?

(*c*) Looney's bosses at PPG told Congress they favored deregulation. How do you explain the different views of Looney and top management?

27-9. Supporters of more strict government regulation of the economy have on occasion used the following argument: "A clean environment is a necessary precondition for any economic activity. Similarly, safety for the labor force is a necessary precondition for manufacturing. Thus these objectives must be achieved regardless of what their benefits and cost may be.'' Do you agree? Explain why or why not.

27-10. Should a driver who is careless and runs into a railroad train be able to sue the automaker for producing a car that involves an unreasonable safety risk? Should he be able to sue the auto company if he has bumped into another car at very slow speed and his engine has exploded as a consequence? If your answer differs in these two cases, how do you draw the line?

CHAPTER 28

PROTECTING THE ENVIRONMENT IN A GROWING ECONOMY:

HOW SHOULD POLLUTION BE LIMITED?

The difference between inefficient and efficient . . . policies [to control pollution] can mean scores, perhaps hundreds, of billions of dollars released for other useful purposes over the next several decades.

ALLEN V. KNEESE and CHARLES L. SCHULTZE

During recent decades, the nation has been releasing an alarming amount of waste into the environment. U.S. industry has been annually producing an estimated 90 billion pounds of toxic waste, including well-known poisons like arsenic and mercury—and only 10% of this has been disposed of properly. Because of air pollution, the life expectancy of the residents of big cities is estimated to be 2 years less than it would otherwise be.[1] Ground pollution, caused by past dumping of poisonous chemicals, has made Times Beach, Mo., a ghost town. Since its 2,000 inhabitants left because of potentially dangerous levels of dioxin, its houses have been boarded up and the wind has been whistling through its empty streets. According to a 1982 study by the Environmental Protection Agency, 30% of the nation's drinking water is contaminated, primarily because of seepage from chemical waste dumps. As waste dumps and other dangerous forms of disposal are outlawed, the question arises: How *will* we get rid of toxic material? Even the least dangerous method—burning it at sea—can have adverse effects on the oceans and coastlines.

By the mid-1980s it was clear that the government's task of limiting pollution in its various forms will involve heavy expense. There will be few easy answers; difficult choices will have to be made. In this chapter, we shall be seeking general principles that can be applied in making these choices.

We begin by considering the controls on pollution that are now in place.

POLLUTION: THE COSTLY JOB OF CONTROL

In order to reduce pollution, Congress has passed laws such as the Water Pollution Control Act and the Clean Air Act. These laws:

1. Limit the pollutants a firm may discharge into the water, air, or earth. The Environmental Protection Agency (EPA) has the responsibility for setting and enforcing these limitations.
2. Limit the pollutants discharged by a product, such as the exhaust emissions discharged by automobiles.
3. Provide subsidies to municipalities for building waste disposal plants, and provide tax reductions to firms installing pollution control equipment.

The result has been substantial progress in certain areas in cleaning up the environment. There are now boutiques in Cleveland along the Cuyahoga, a river that used to be so contaminated with oil and debris that it twice caught fire. The Great Lakes are cleaner and clearer, and fish are returning. In Maine, salmon have come back to the Penobscot River: People in Bangor claim to be catching 20-pounders during lunch hour.

[1]Lester B. Lave and Eugene P. Seskin, "Air Pollution and Human Health" (Washington: Resources for the Future, 1977).

But these tales tell only half the story. The EPA is to be judged not only by such instances where the environment has improved, but also by a number of instances where the environment has *not* improved—where EPA's sole "success" has been to keep the environment from getting worse. It is important to recognize that pollution will be a continuing problem because we will never be able to eliminate it completely. Even if we were to bring U.S. industry to a standstill by closing down every plant that did any polluting whatsoever, pollutants from millions of country barnyards and city streets would still wash into our streams. Since it is not possible to eliminate pollution, the practical questions are:

How far should pollution be cut back?
What costs should we be willing to bear?

Before answering these questions, we should understand the various costs involved in controlling pollution. No matter how the cleanup is initially financed, the public eventually bears the burden in one of the following four ways.

1. As taxpayers, we pay higher taxes because of the subsidies granted to firms installing pollution control equipment.
2. Since these subsidies cover only part of the cost of that equipment, some must also be borne by the firms that install it. In turn, they pass on much of this burden to the public by charging more for their products.
3. Alternatively, to the degree that firms "pay for" pollution-control equipment by investing less in other types of capital equipment, our growth of productivity and output is reduced. Thus the public pays in the future.
4. The most highly publicized cost occurs when jobs are lost because pollution-control standards force a plant to close down. Even those who live closest to sources of industrial pollution—such as steel mills—often prefer pollution to the loss of jobs. Comments from those who live close to a U.S. steel mill in Clairton, Pennsylvania are typical: "We're not against clean air, but we do need jobs and we do need U.S. Steel. . . . When the day

BOX 28-1

WHY NOT CONTROL POLLUTION BY ENDING ECONOMIC GROWTH?

A no-growth policy would do no more than *stop an increase* in pollution; it would provide no reduction whatsoever in *existing* pollution. Thus, as a way of reducing pollution, a no-growth policy would be inferior to our present policies, which have allowed us to reduce some kinds of pollution by an estimated quarter or a half. To have achieved such a reduction in pollution simply by reducing output would have required a massive reduction in GNP. Instead, we have achieved this reduction while the economy has been growing.

Thus, as a way of reducing pollution, a limit on output would be extraordinarily expensive, yet ineffective. It is like killing a rat by burning your house down. Even if you cure the problem, the side effects are appalling. Better by far to find a cure specifically designed to deal with the problem: If the problem is a rat, get a trap; if the problem is pollution, find a policy that directly reduces it.

comes that smoke stops coming out of those stacks, we'll all have to find another town.''

Thus, in one way or another, the cost of controlling pollution touches us all. It is a large tab—no one really knows how large. Just to achieve the original cleanup standards set in the early 70s would have cost an estimated \$40 to \$60 billion a year. Moreover, since then we have become aware of new problems such as acid rain. David Stockman, who was budget director from 1981 to 1985, has estimated that a substantial reduction in this one problem could cost more than \$20 billion.

Because it is so costly to control pollution, we should use the least expensive methods. Unfortunately, we have often not used these methods in the past; one of the major criticisms of the EPA has been that its pollution-control policies have often been far too expensive. This chapter will explain why and outline a better approach. (A worse policy, but one that is sometimes recommended, is described in Box 28-1.) But first, we consider why government intervention is necessary in the first place. Why does the private market fail? Why can't we count on Adam Smith's ''invisible hand'' to limit pollution?

POLLUTION: AN EXTERNAL COST

When pollution exists, *private and social costs differ*. To understand why, consider a pulp and paper factory located on a river. The costs of paper to society include not only the private or ***internal costs*** of production faced by the pulp and paper firm, but also the cost to those who live downstream and must put up with the wastes that the firm releases into the river. While the pulp and paper firm has to pay for internal production costs, any cost downstream is ***external*** to its operation, since this cost must be borne by others.

Internal **or** ***private costs*** **are the costs incurred by those who actually produce or consume a good.**

External costs**—also known as** ***neighborhood costs*** **or** ***cost spillovers*****—are costs borne by others. Pollution is an example.**

Consider a simple illustration. Suppose that each unit of a product is treated with an ounce of a fluid that is then released as a waste into a river. Suppose also that each of these ounces of fluid imposes a constant damage to those downstream. Then each unit of output imposes a constant external pollution cost, shown as the short, dark red arrow in Figure 28-1. When it is added to the internal cost borne by producers (the black arrow MC), the result is the tall arrow MC_S, the marginal cost of this good to society. MC_S is a constant height above MC because of our assumption of a constant external cost for each unit of output.

CONTROLLING POLLUTION: THE SIMPLE CASE

When there is such an external cost, even a perfectly competitive market results in a misallocation of resources, as shown in Figure 28-2. In this figure, MC and MC_S are reproduced from Figure 28-1, and demand D represents this good's marginal benefit—both private and social. S_1 shows what firms are willing to supply. This curve measures internal private costs—the only costs faced by firms making supply decisions. With demand D and supply S_1, the perfectly competitive equilibrium is E_1.

FIGURE 28-1

With pollution, private and social costs differ

The marginal cost to society of a good, shown by the longest arrow MC_S, includes both the marginal *internal* cost to the producing firm (the black arrow MC) plus a marginal *external* cost not borne by the producing firm (the dark red arrow).

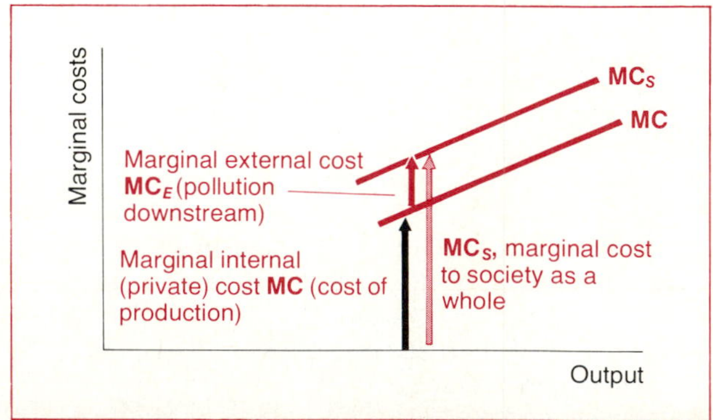

For society, E_1 is not an efficient outcome, because it equalizes marginal benefit and marginal *private* cost only. An efficient solution requires that marginal benefit be equal to marginal *social* cost MC_S. This occurs at E_2, at the smaller output Q_2. We conclude that in a free, competitive market, *firms produce too much of a polluting good*—Q_1 rather than the efficient amount Q_2.[2] It is in society's interest to cut back production of this good and use the resources to produce something else.

To confirm that Q_1 is an inefficient output, note that the benefit from the last unit produced is the light red arrow under the demand curve. However, its cost is even greater, since it includes both its private cost (this same arrow) and its external cost shown by the dark red arrow. Hence, this dark red arrow represents the net loss in producing this last unit Q_1. Since there is a similar sort of loss in the production of each of the other "excess" units between Q_2 and Q_1, the total efficiency loss is measured by the red triangle.

In this instance, a relatively simple cure is possible: Levy a per-unit tax on producers equal to the marginal external cost shown by the dark red arrow. Such a tax imposes a cost on producers equal to the cost of their pollution on others. Thus, the tax "internalizes" the externality: The producer is forced to face the external cost along with the internal cost. As a result of the tax, the supply curve shifts up from S_1 to S_2; to confirm, recall that supply reflects marginal cost, and this has risen by the amount of the tax that must be paid. The new equilibrium is at E_2, where demand and new supply S_2 intersect. The new output of Q_2 is efficient because marginal benefit equals marginal *social* cost. Finally, the efficiency gain from this tax policy is the red triangle, the original efficiency loss that has now been eliminated. In brief, as a result of this tax, society gets a benefit that the market would otherwise not deliver—cleaner water.

Several other ways have been suggested for reducing pollution. One is discussed in Box 28-2. Another is to set a limit on the output of polluting firms.

Such a limit may or may not help to solve the problem; in fact, it may even be worse than doing nothing at all. For example, suppose output is limited to Q_3. As an exercise (problem 28-1) you can show that too little will be produced, and there will be a loss to society of triangle FE_2G. Since this loss will exceed the original loss, the cure in this case will be worse than the original problem. You should also be able to show that an even more severe restriction on output will result in an even greater efficiency loss. Thus, an arbitrary limit on output may be an inefficient policy. A much better approach—if the costs of pollution can be estimated—is to impose a tax of this same amount. Then the correct degree of pressure will be applied to the market to push it back from the initial Q_1 to the efficient output Q_2.

FIGURE 28-2

Free-market efficiency loss when there is an external cost

Before the antipollution tax, industry supply is S_1, reflecting only the private internal costs of production facing sellers. This supply equals demand at E_1, with output at Q_1. This output is inefficient because marginal social cost exceeds benefit for all units between Q_2 and Q_1. For example, the last unit Q_1 is not worth producing; its benefit, shown by the light red arrow under the demand curve, is less than its two costs to society (the light red arrow plus the dark red arrow under the MC_S curve). The efficiency loss is the sum of all such dark red arrows—that is, the red triangle. *After the tax r,* producers are forced to face both the internal *and* external costs, so that their supply curve shifts up from S_1 to S_2. *D* and S_2 now yield an equilibrium at E_2, with output Q_2. This is efficient because marginal social cost and benefit are equal. The efficiency gain from reducing output from Q_1 to Q_2 is the elimination of the red triangle.

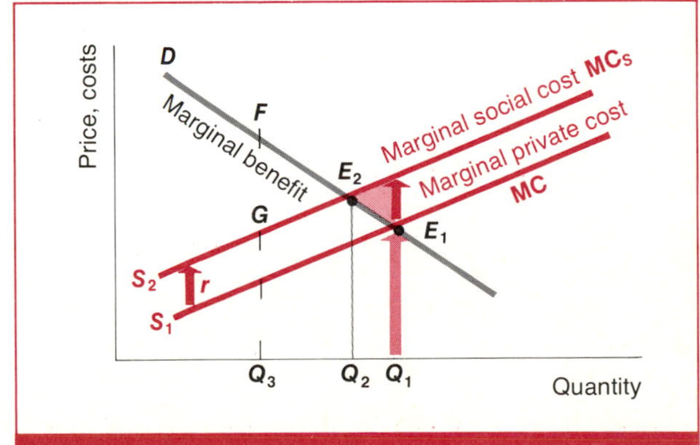

[2]In terms of our earlier analysis, the market does not lead to an efficient solution because marginal private cost MC is not equal to marginal social cost MC_S, and condition 24-2 on page 489 is violated.

BOX 28-2

THE POSSIBLE ROLE OF PROPERTY RIGHTS IN DEALING WITH AN EXTERNAL COST

It has been suggested that the problem of too much pollution by upstream firms could be cured by assigning those who live downstream the property right to clean water. Suppose, for example, that they can sue or charge any polluting firm an amount that exactly compensates them for any damage they incur. For example, in Figure 28-2, suppose that those living downstream can charge firms \$*r* per unit of pollution that these firms emit. Polluting firms are now in exactly the same position as they were when the government imposed a tax of \$*r*; the only difference is that they are now paying this "tax" to the residents downstream instead of to the government. In either case they will voluntarily reduce their output from Q_1 to Q_2, where inefficiency has been eliminated. It seems as though proper assignment of property rights over the water is the key.

In an article on "The Problem of Social Cost" (*Journal of Law and Economics,* October 1960), Ronald Coase of the University of Chicago went one step further. He argued that, strictly from the point of view of economic efficiency, it does not matter who holds the property rights. In our example, it does not matter whether those downstream have the property rights and are compensated \$*r* per unit by the upstream polluting firms, or if the upstream firms have the property rights. True, if the upstream firms have the rights, they are free to dump waste into the river. However, those living downstream will be willing to pay them \$*r* for each unit that pollution is reduced, and the upstream firms will therefore find it profitable to cut back their pollution.[†]

Thus, according to Coase, a problem such as pollution arises because there is something valuable—in this case, clean water—over which there are no property rights. Consequently, there is no market; that is, clean water can't be bought and sold. Create property rights, and you create a market that makes it possible for Adam Smith's invisible hand to work to reduce or eliminate inefficiency. Some other form of government intervention is not necessary; all the government needs to do is to establish a market and then let it work.

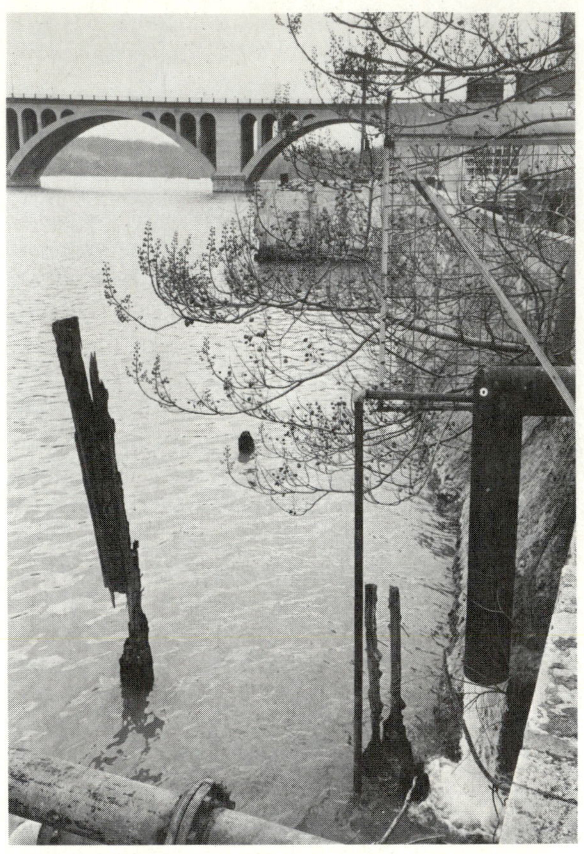

It is enlightening to consider this analysis from another point of view. The problem with pollution is that something that used to be in unlimited supply—clean water—has now become scarce. Unless someone owns it and charges for its use, it will be used in wasteful ways; for example, the water will be used to carry off pollutants and the river will become a public sewer. On the other hand, if someone does own the water and charges for it, its price will act as a monitoring device to direct it into its most productive uses.

The conclusion that property rights and free bargaining may eliminate inefficiency is a very interesting one. It follows—subject to a number of reservations that will be considered directly—because the existence of inefficiency means that the two parties collectively lose. Therefore, it is in their collective interest to get together and make a deal to eliminate this inefficiency. However, this raises an even broader question: Why can't free bargaining remove any *other* form of inefficiency as well, such as monopoly? Since inefficiency makes the two parties collectively worse off, why don't they make a deal to avoid it? Specifically, why can't buyers compensate the monopoly firm to get it to stop acting like a monopolist, that is, to get it to lower its price and increase its output?

The answer is that there are problems ("transactions costs") in making such deals. How do a million buyers of a monopoly product organize themselves to make a payment to the monopolist? How do a thousand residents on a river and the hundreds of polluting firms upstream organize themselves to make and receive payments? To illustrate, suppose the property rights to the water are owned by the polluting upstream firms. How do downstream residents get together to pay these firms to reduce their pollution? Specifically, how do the downstream residents keep some of their members from becoming "free riders," that is, people who are happy to have a payment made—and their pollution thereby reduced—but who won't contribute themselves?‡

Another problem is: How do downstream residents know which firms are polluting the river and which are not? Moreover, if the downstream residents do reach an agreement with the polluting firms, how do they know that these firms have indeed reduced their pollution? Even attempting to solve these problems may involve substantial transactions costs.

For this reason, the existence of property rights and free bargaining would not always lead to an efficient result. Even if it did, the question of equity would not be resolved: Who should pay the fee necessary to achieve efficiency and who should receive it? Nonetheless, Coase's ideas are important because they help us to understand more clearly why externalities are a problem, and how it may be possible to deal with them in a wide variety of ways.

†Those living downstream will be willing to pay this $\$r$ per unit because this is what pollution costs them; it is therefore what they would be willing to pay to get rid of it. Moreover, since the polluting firms receive a payment of $\$r$ per unit for reducing pollution, they will cut back to Q_2—for the same reason that they cut back that far in the face of the government's $\$r$ per unit tax. (It doesn't matter whether firms are paid $\$r$ per unit for cutting back, or are taxed $\$r$ per unit if they do *not* cut back. In either case they have the same incentive to cut back.)

‡These problems may be far less serious if the property rights are held, not by the upstream firms but by the downstream residents, and if the payment (fine) to be paid to them by the upstream firms is set by the courts. Polluting firms would then respond to this fine just as they did to the tax in Figure 28-2. In fact, this policy is effectively the same as the pollution tax in that earlier diagram—except for one important respect. The residents downstream, rather than the government, receive the payment from the polluting firms. This sounds very equitable: The people downstream who are hurt by pollution are compensated for it. Unfortunately, this provides an example of why the objectives of equity and efficiency are often in conflict. This very equitable solution introduces a *different* source of inefficiency. Because of the compensation people receive if they locate downstream, more decide to do so, and the pollution they consequently absorb represents a loss to society. In their location decision, people should take pollution into account and—other things equal—locate away from the river. But they won't take pollution into account if they are fully compensated for it by the polluting firms. Thus too many people locate downstream, and there is an efficiency loss.

CONTROLLING POLLUTION: A MORE COMPLEX CASE

In practice, policymakers face a number of complications omitted from our earlier example. First, in any particular airspace—say, over Los Angeles—or any particular body of water, such as Lake Erie, the problem is not just a single polluting industry, as shown in Figure 28-2, but many. Second, pollution and output are not locked together in the fixed way assumed in the earlier diagrams, in which each additional unit of output generated a constant amount of pollution. In the more typical case, the amount of pollution may vary. A good may be produced with a large amount of pollution if wastes are dumped without restriction into the water or air. However, if wastes are treated, or if less polluting fuels are used, there will be only a small amount of pollution.

Consider a firm that begins to treat its wastes, or uses cleaner but more expensive fuels. This firm reduces pollution, but at a cost. This cost of reducing pollution for all firms in an area is shown in Figure 28-3 as the curve MCR. (*R* stands for reducing pollution.) It is drawn by first graphing point Q_1, the amount of pollution that will occur if it is not restricted in any way. As pollution is cut back, firms move to the left up the MCR curve. At first, cleanup costs are low as the easy battles are won. For example, pollution unit Q_2 can be eliminated at the low cost shown by the short red bar. However, the more pollution is reduced, the higher becomes the cost of further cleanup; that is, the MCR curve becomes higher and higher as firms move to the left in this diagram.

Until the last few decades, there were few restrictions on pollution. Therefore, firms generally dumped pollutants rather than going to the expense of treating them. The result was pollution Q_1. Some of our lakes and rivers became public sewers.

FIGURE 28-3

The cost of reducing pollution and the effect of a tax

Q_1 is the amount of pollution that would occur in the absence of any control measure. As we move from this point back to the left along MCR, we see the cost of reducing pollution by one more unit—for example, by installing pollution-control equipment. Thus if pollution has been restricted all the way back to Q_4, any further reduction would involve very expensive pollution-control measures, involving a cost shown by the tall red bar.

If pollution tax T is imposed, firms voluntarily reduce pollution, moving from Q_1 to Q_3. So long as they are still to the right of Q_3, they will continue to reduce pollution because the cost of doing so (for example, the short red bar) is less than the cost of paying the tax. However, they would not move to the left of Q_3. In this range, it costs them more to reduce pollution (the tall red bar) than to continue to pollute and pay the tax T.

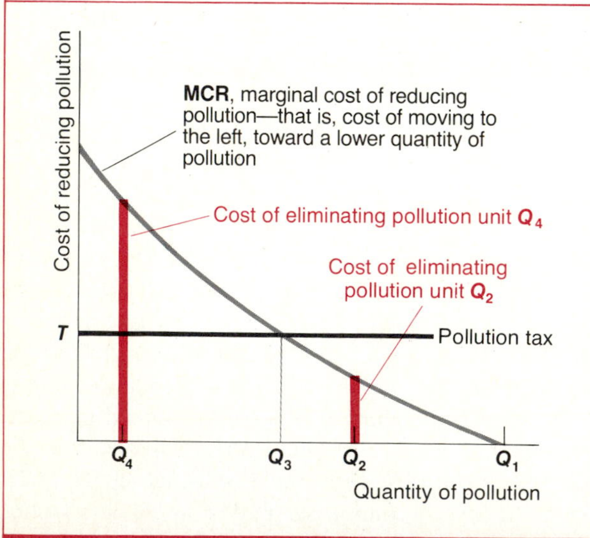

To prevent this, suppose the government wishes to reduce pollution dramatically. Specifically, suppose it wants to cut pollution in half—from Q_1 to Q_3. Consider the policies which might be used.

Option 1. A Pollution Tax

Assume that the government levies an *effluent fee*—that is, a tax on each unit of pollution discharged into the environment. Specifically, in Figure 28-3, suppose that tax T is charged for each unit of pollution. Then firms eliminate pollution in the right-hand tail of the MCR curve, where it costs less to stop polluting (for example, the short red bar) than to continue to pollute and pay the tax T. However, pollution is reduced only to Q_3, where the tax line intersects MCR. To the left of this point, the costs of reducing pollution are high, as illustrated by the tall red bar. In fact, they are higher than the tax T. Thus, in this range, firms have an incentive to pay the tax and continue to pollute.

Although effluent fees have long been advocated by economists, they are still not widely used. However, in a similar approach, there have been some attempts to make polluting firms pay—although not with a payment tied specifically to each unit of pollution. For example, the EPA's Superfund, a multibillion-dollar program to clean up hazardous chemical dumps, was initially financed by a tax levied on firms that were heavy polluters. There has also been a proposal to have coal-burning utilities that create acid rain finance the cost of limiting its damage.

Option 2. A Physical Limit on the Pollution by Each Firm

One might well ask: Why go to all the trouble of setting the pollution tax in Figure 28-3 when pollution could be cut by the same amount by a simple, direct control—specifically, by requiring every firm to cut its emissions by half? The answer is that although this approach would achieve the same reduction in pollution, it would involve heavier cleanup costs, as we shall now show.

Not all firms face the same costs in reducing pollution. With a tax, pollution is cut back by firms that can do so *at the lowest cost,* that is, by firms to the right of Q_3. Firms to the left of Q_3 continue to pollute. However, if all firms are required to cut their pollution in half, firms to the left of Q_3 must now also participate—at the high cost illustrated by the tall red bar.

Therefore the advantage of a pollution tax is that it "lets the market work." With firms reacting to the tax, pollution is reduced by those firms that can do so in the least expensive way. Thus society devotes fewer real resources to the cleanup task.[3] The savings can be substantial. Based on a number of recent estimates, Wallace Oates of the University of Maryland has ventured the rough guess that *a pollution tax would cost society 75% to 80% less than a policy of requiring all firms to reduce pollution by the same fraction*.[4]

Which of these two policies have governments used? The answer is suprising: Instead of letting the market work with some form of pollution tax, governments have instead relied principally on regulatory controls. Physical limits on pollution have been set for individual firms—a policy, as already noted, that has involved unnecessarily large cleanup costs.

Recently, however, there have been encouraging signs that governments may be moving toward a third compromise solution that allows them to set physical limits on pollution, but also "lets the market work" and hence avoids unnecessarily large cleanup costs.

Option 3. Physical Limits on Pollution with Trade Allowed in Emissions Permits

The third option is for the authorities to set a specific limit on the amount of pollution that each firm is permitted. For example, each firm may be given a permit to pollute just half as much as in the past. So far, this is just like option 2. But now a twist is added to let the market work: Firms are allowed to buy and sell pollution permits. It can be shown that in a perfectly competitive market, permits will sell for price T. Firms to the right of Q_3 gain by selling their permits for T and cleaning up pollution at the low cost illustrated by the short red bar. For firms to the left of Q_3, it is cheaper to buy permits costing T and continue to pollute, than to undertake the even higher cost of reducing pollution shown by the tall red bar.[5] Thus pollution is reduced by those firms to the right of Q_3 which can do so at the lowest cost. Accordingly, under option 3 with marketable permits, pollution will be reduced in the same low-cost way as in option 1 with a pollution tax. Therefore, options 1 and 3 are superior to option 2. It is only under the second option—in which all firms are required to reduce pollution by a fixed amount—that high-cost cleanup is undertaken by firms to the left of Q_3.

The general principle is this:

> **Pollution can be reduced at lower cost if the government enlists the power of the market. It can change incentives by imposing a tax, or introducing marketable permits and then letting private firms respond. The firms are the ones that know best what their costs are, and thus are best able to select the response that will minimize those costs.**

This then is our basic conclusion: Because option 2 does not use the market, it is more costly than options 1 or 3. But in comparing option 1 and 3, which is preferable?

A Comparison of Options 1 and 3

These two options differ in one important respect. Under option 1, firms are penalized. If they continue to pollute they are required to pay a tax. If they stop polluting, they

---

[3] To simplify this illustration, we have assumed that any firm is either completely to the left of Q_3, or completely to the right. In fact, firms typically have some units of pollution on each side. High-cost firms have most of their units to the left of Q_3, and low-cost firms have most of their units to the right. Nevertheless our conclusion still holds: The least costly way of cutting pollution in half is with a tax, with every firm eliminating only its pollution to the right of Q_3. Low-cost firms will be cutting their pollution by more than half, while the high-cost firms will be cutting it by less than half.

[4] "Markets for Pollution Control," *Challenge*, May-June, 1984, p. 12. One of the studies on which Oates based his estimate was that of Allen V. Kneese and Charles L. Schultze, *Pollution, Prices, and Public Policy* (Washington: The Brookings Institution, 1975).

Although a tax is generally preferable, there are exceptions. For example, in the case of radioactive wastes that would damage the environment far into the future, it may be simpler and just as effective to impose a physical limit—namely, an outright ban on emitting such materials. If a tax were used to eliminate such wastes, it would have to be set at a prohibitively high level and thus be equivalent to a ban.

*[5] Why would the price of permits be T? If this is the price, then firms have the same incentive to reduce pollution as if they faced a tax T. In either case, they respond by reducing their pollution to Q_3. Thus if the permit price is T, Q_3 will be the quantity of permits firms will want. This is exactly equal to the Q_3 of permits supplied by the government. Therefore, T is the equilibrium price.

are required to pay the costs of cleanup. In either case, they are adversely affected by the introduction of a pollution tax.

However, with the marketable permits of option 3, firms need not lose. Indeed, those with low cleanup costs actually gain. They can sell their pollution rights for a price T that is higher than their cleanup costs. While high-cost firms *are* adversely affected, they don't lose as much as under tax option 1.[6]

The fact that polluting firms have a strong preference for option 3 makes it, in one sense, a more attractive policy for the government to introduce. Business won't lobby so hard against it, and it may therefore be much easier to get through the legislature. Pollution may be controlled without interminable delays.

However, option 3 raises a problem. Why should businesses that have polluted in the past be granted valuable emission permits, some of which they may sell? In other words, why should some firms be allowed to profit from their past pollution? This suggests that, on equity grounds, option 1 may be preferred because it punishes—rather than rewards—past polluters.

Thus far, we have assumed that the government has set as its target a reduction in pollution by one-half, to Q_3. Why not by one-third, or three-quarters, or some other figure? Box 28-3 describes how the target should be set.

LOCAL POLLUTION: SAG POINTS AND BUBBLES

The damage done by pollution depends on where it is emitted. Smoke discharged in a city affects more people than smoke emitted over a desert; pollution dumped into a river above a city is more harmful than pollution below the city. A location where pollution is particularly harmful is sometimes known as a ***sag point.*** It is especially desirable to reduce pollution in such locations. This may be done by imposing higher taxes on emissions or by having particularly strict emission controls at sag points.

[6]Why? Under option 1 they have to pay tax T on *all* the polluting they do. Under option 3 they incur no cost for *some* of the polluting they do—namely, the pollution that is covered by the free permits they have been granted.

Thus, for example, some states inspect the pollution-control equipment of cars in and around large cities, but not in rural areas.

Local pollution problems are sometimes dealt with by placing on imaginary ***bubble*** over a sensitive area, with pollutants being controlled strictly within the bubble. New sources of pollution are permitted only if the firm arranges for an equal reduction of pollution—that is, an ***offset***—elsewhere within the bubble.

THE RECORD SO FAR: A MIXED ONE

There has recently been some progress in developing market-oriented forms of control. For example, by 1982 an estimated 1,900 offset transactions had taken place. However, despite such progress, a number of serious problems remain. The most common method of controlling pollution is still inefficient, high-cost option 2, with physical limits set on the pollution by individual firms and no trading or sale of permits allowed. Furthermore, air and water standards are often set with little regard for the cost of reducing pollution. Indeed, in some cases the courts have interpreted the law as *prohibiting* the EPA from even considering costs when setting standards. Instead, the EPA tends to concentrate on what is technologically possible with existing pollution-control knowledge, and some of these measures are extremely expensive. Furthermore, the Clean Air Act, as amended, is designed to "protect and enhance" the quality of the nation's air—a worthy objective, except that the legislation has been interpreted to mean that the air should not be allowed to deteriorate significantly *anywhere*. Consequently, even the states with the cleanest air have encountered problems attracting new firms. This has blocked one avenue for reducing the overall pollution problem, namely, shifting firms from overloaded, highly polluted areas where the pollutants they add are particularly damaging, into regions with low pollution levels where much of their pollutants could be "washed away" by natural processes.

Moreover, some firms have expended more effort in fighting air or water standards in the halls of Congress and the courts than in cleaning up the environment. In some cases, firms seem to be counting on the government to provide an eleventh-hour exemption from the law. For example, a threat to close down seven plants, employing 24,000 workers in Ohio's Mahoning Valley, induced the EPA to exempt the companies from water-emission restrictions. Such flip-flops have tended, at a minimum, to erode the credibility of the control programs. This has meant that standards have not been set in an even-handed way, but have instead been defined by a government under pressure to make last-minute changes.

AN ALTERNATIVE POLICY? SUBSIDIZING POLLUTION-CONTROL EQUIPMENT

To supplement its other efforts, the federal government has provided large grants to municipalities installing waste treatment plants. It has also provided subsidies in the form of tax reductions to firms installing pollution-control equipment. How effective are such subsidies?

In the first place, such subsidies are effective only if the equipment that is installed does a good job of reducing pollution. One of the problems has been that, after the government subsidizes the new installation, it pays little or no attention to how efficiently it is operated—that is, how effectively it reduces pollution. In some cases, the municipalities that have been subsidized to install expensive equipment have not even been able to cover its operating costs, and the equipment is no longer used at all.

The second problem is that this form of subsidy puts all the emphasis on *end-of-pipe treatment*—that is, on the reduction of pollution as it is about to be discharged into the environment. However, if a subsidy is justified for end-of-pipe treatment, it should be similarly justified for *any* reduction in pollution, regardless of how it may be achieved—for example, by the use of less powerful chemicals or cleaner fuels. Such alternatives may be far less costly. For instance, at a cost of only $1 million, the 3M Company introduced a less polluting process that saved the company over $10 million in waste disposal and other costs.

It may be concluded, therefore, that an end-of-pipe subsidy is too narrow an attack on the problem. Firms may not use the lowest-cost method to control pollution but instead may switch to the end-of-pipe method solely because it is subsidized. The principle is a simple one: It is better to tell firms what to do than to give them detailed instructions on how to do it. A regulation made as far back as the eighteenth century B.C. illustrates this principle. Hammurabi, King of Babylonia, set a very simple building code. If a house collapsed and killed an occupant, the builder was put to death. All details for meeting this regulation were left to the builder.

An even narrower approach is a regulation that requires firms to install a *specific kind* of end-of-pipe equipment. For example, consider the requirement that coal-burning electrical utilities install ''scrubbers'' to clean the smoke they emit. This tends to divert them from the more sensible solution of using cleaner coal; so long as the government requires scrubbers, there is no incentive to use the more expensive, cleaner fuel. In turn, the continued heavy use of dirty coal creates a new problem in the form of a liquid sludge generated by the scrubbers. Thus, reducing air pollution creates water pollution. Again we conclude: The lowest-cost policy is to provide firms with a sufficient incentive to clean up and let them, in the pursuit of profit, decide on the least expensive way of doing it.

FUTURE PROBLEMS IN PROTECTING THE ENVIRONMENT

By the mid-1980s, the EPA was an embattled agency. It was under pressure from business because it was too harsh and from environmentalists because it was too lenient. In many cases its solutions caused new problems. Its regulations to clean the air induced firms to build higher chimneys that just moved their polluting smoke on high wind currents into more distant locations. We have seen that when the EPA reduced air pollution by requiring scrubbers, the result was water pollution; in turn, when the EPA regulated water pollution, firms sometimes responded by dumping their pollutants into the ground. Thus while the EPA was succeeding in some of its attempts to clean up, some of its policies were simply transforming pollution from one form to another.

No sooner did the EPA get a handle on one problem than it became aware of another. Moreover, many of the

BOX 28-3

POLLUTION CONTROL: PROBLEMS AND PERSPECTIVE

In Figure 28-3, the target amount of pollution is assumed to be Q_3. In fact, it is not a simple task to determine the target amount.

How Far Should Pollution Be Reduced?

In Figure 28-4 we reproduce MCR from Figure 28-3 and also show MCP, the marginal cost of pollution to society. These two curves should not be confused. MCR is the cost of *reducing* pollution—for example, the cost of pollution-control equipment. On the other hand, MCP is the cost of *having* pollution—that is, the cost to us of foul air and contaminated water. As long as there is only a small amount of pollution—at, say, Q_4—the marginal cost of having this pollution (the height of MCP) is low. The first units of waste that are dumped into a stream generally break down and are absorbed by the environment. Similarly, the smoke from a campfire in a deserted area has no perceptible effect on the air. However, as pollution builds up, additional emissions become increasingly noxious and damaging; that is, as we move to the right in this diagram, the MCP curve rises.

FIGURE 28-4

Efficiency loss from leaving pollution uncontrolled

MCR is reproduced from Figure 28-3. We also show MCP, the environmental cost of additional units of pollution. The best target is to restrict pollution to Q_3, where MCR = MCP.

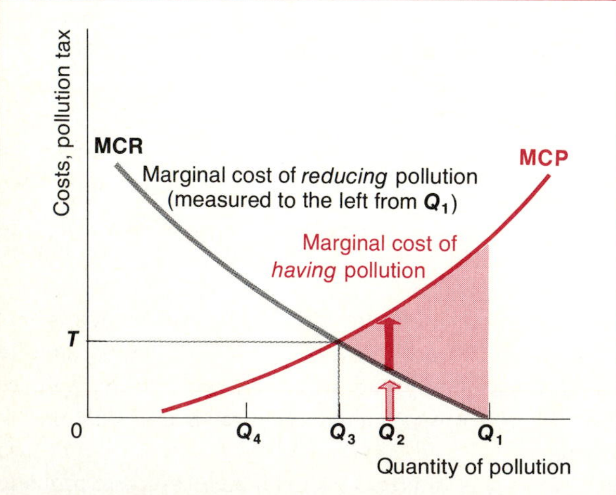

With these two curves, the best target is to reduce pollution to point Q_3, where MCP = MCR. Any other quantity is less desirable, as we can illustrate with the case where pollution is left completely uncontrolled and consequently reaches Q_1. For all units of pollution to the right of Q_3, MCP is greater than MCR, so it is a mistake to let this pollution continue. To evaluate the social cost of this mistake, consider one typical unit of this excess pollution, say unit Q_2. The cost of eliminating this unit of pollution is the height of the MCR curve, as shown by the light red arrow. This is less than the cost of letting this pollution continue (the height of the MCP curve, as shown by both red arrows). Therefore, the net cost of allowing this unit to continue is the dark red arrow. If we sum the similar costs on all such units through the range Q_3 to Q_1, the result is the triangular red area—the loss to society from allowing pollution to continue at its uncontrolled level of Q_1 rather than limiting it to Q_3.

On the other hand, a policy of cutting pollution back to the left of Q_3 also causes a loss. For example, if pollution is reduced to Q_4, the cost of the last unit is just the height of the MCP curve above Q_4. However, this last unit is exceedingly costly to eliminate (the height of the MCR curve). Eliminating it is therefore a mistake. We conclude that the best target, Q_3, can be found only by taking into account both the cost of having pollution MCP and the cost of removing it MCR.

Unfortunately, in practice it is not that easy to estimate the target Q_3 because of the difficulties in estimating MCP and MCR. For example, in trying to estimate the marginal cost of pollution MCP, we simply do not know with any precision how dangerous many pollutants really are. Furthermore, there are many pollutants, and the damage that any one pollutant does may depend on the presence of other types. For example, asbestos in the air is more likely to cause cancer when other pollutants are present or when people smoke.

Pollution in Historical Perspective

Why are we so concerned now with pollution, while a few decades ago we were almost totally unconcerned? Is the problem worse, or have we just awakened? If it is getting worse, what can we expect 20 or 30 years from now?

Figure 28-5 illustrates how the MCR curve shifts to the right as the economy grows. MCR_{1960} cuts the baseline at Q_{1960}, the level of pollution that would have occurred had it been left completely unrestricted at that early date. Similarly, the other MCR curves indicate uncontrolled pollution levels Q_{1980} and Q_{2000} at those later dates. The red triangle marked 1980 shows the loss from a policy of leaving pollution uncontrolled at that time. It is defined just like the red triangle in Figure 28-4.

Now consider our situation in 1960. At that time, there were fewer factories clustered along any river and fewer cars spewing fumes into the air. Therefore, pollution was less severe. The result of leaving pollution uncontrolled was the relatively small loss shown as the red triangle marked 1960. In those days, people did not think much about this problem.

Now let us look ahead to the future, to the year 2000. If industrial activity keeps growing, unrestricted pollution would grow to Q_{2000}, and the loss from failing to deal with it would be the very large red triangle 2000. There are several reasons why this loss builds up so rapidly. First, as output grows, so too does pollution. Second, pollution may grow even faster, since more powerful chemicals and other materials may be used as technology changes. Thus MCR shifts rapidly to the right. In addition, in the view of many experts, the MCP curve becomes steeper and steeper: The cost of pollution not only rises, but it does so at an increasingly rapid rate.

We emphasize that Figure 28-5 is not a prediction of the future; it is merely a picture of what the future would have looked like *if* we had not taken action—or what it will look like if we give up our efforts to control pollution. In this respect, pollution is similar to the public health problem in the nineteenth century. With the increase in urban population, lack of adequate sanitation produced a growing health problem that could equally well have been described by a diagram like Figure 28-5. The response to this challenge was the public health programs that prevented the "prophecy" in such a diagram from coming true. Similarly, pollution-control legislation can help to ensure that the prophecy in Figure 28-5 does not come true.

FIGURE 28-5

Pollution in perspective

If no attempt had been made to deal with this problem, unrestricted pollution would have increased (with growing GNP) from Q_{1960} to Q_{1980}, and eventually to Q_{2000}. As a result, the loss to society of leaving pollution unchecked in each of these years would have been the rapidly growing set of triangles marked 1960, 1980, and 2000.

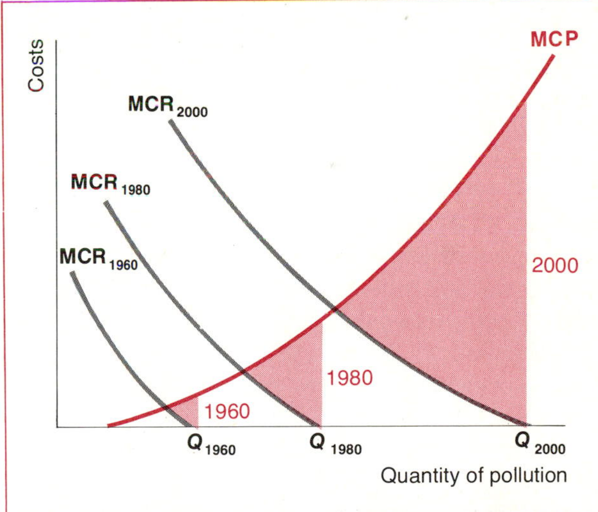

problems were completely new. For example, consider two that have recently come to our attention: Is the world's outer atmosphere being damaged by air pollutants? What can be done about the natural oil leaks in the ocean floor that wash tar onto some Californian beaches?

As we become increasingly aware of the problems that pollution can create, it becomes difficult to keep them in perspective and concentrate on the important ones. One reason is that the EPA operates in an area of relative scientific ignorance. We simply don't know how dangerous many pollutants are. This raises a conflict between the EPA and the nation's industries. Who should bear the burden of proof? (1) Should the EPA have to prove that a waste product is harmful before restricting it? If so, we may today emit wastes which are in fact dangerous but have not yet been proved so. Or (2) should business have to prove that a waste product is *not* harmful before emitting it? If this rule were applied, waste disposal would become such an enormous problem that many firms would be unable to survive, and many of those that did would be charging the public far higher prices.

Acid rain provides an example of this conflict. Although we know that, in the face of prevailing winds, the coal-burning utilities in the midwest produce the acid rain that falls on the lakes and forests to the east, by 1984 we still didn't yet know *for sure* how damaging it was. The decision of the Reagan administration was for further study: How could one justify a costly attack on a problem until we could be sure it was serious? The reply by critics was: Something is severely damaging those lakes and forests, and acid rain is the likely candidate. If we wait for these studies to provide final confirmation, we may incur severe damage that could have otherwise been prevented.

One thing is certain. As pollution limits continue to be imposed on business by the EPA, there will be continued conflict between the two. This is a further reason for the government to impose fewer of its own regulations and rely more on the marketplace—that is, replace detailed regulations with a market-oriented system of incentives that requires business to worry about the details. In other words, the government should be spending more of its effort in designing and building ''better dams to control pollution'' (such as tax incentives or marketable permit systems) and less on ''putting a regulatory finger into every leak.''

However, when we criticize the government for not always using the most effective pollution-control method, we should not lose perspective. Control should be improved, yes; but abandoned, no. ''Where would we be without an agency such as the EPA?'' is an important question to keep in mind. (See Figure 28-5 in Box 28-3.)

RECYCLING

One of the most promising ways to deal with pollution is to recycle wastes rather than dump them into the environment. Beer cans do not deface the landscape if they are reprocessed and used again. Wastes that are recycled into the production process do not foul our rivers.

Figure 28-6 illustrates the potential benefits from recycling. The basic idea behind this diagram is the concept of *material balances*. On the left, production draws in the materials it requires. Included are both new materials drawn up through pipe *a,* and recycled materials

FIGURE 28-6
Recycling and the environment
The economic system in the upper half of this diagram uses the environment in the bottom half by extracting resources from it through pipe *a,* and returning residuals back to it through pipe *b*. For any given level of production and consumption, increased recycling—that is, diverting materials from pipe *b* to pipe *c*—provides two benefits: It reduces the residuals dumped into the environment through pipe *b, and* it reduces the natural resources that must be drawn out of the environment through pipe *a*.

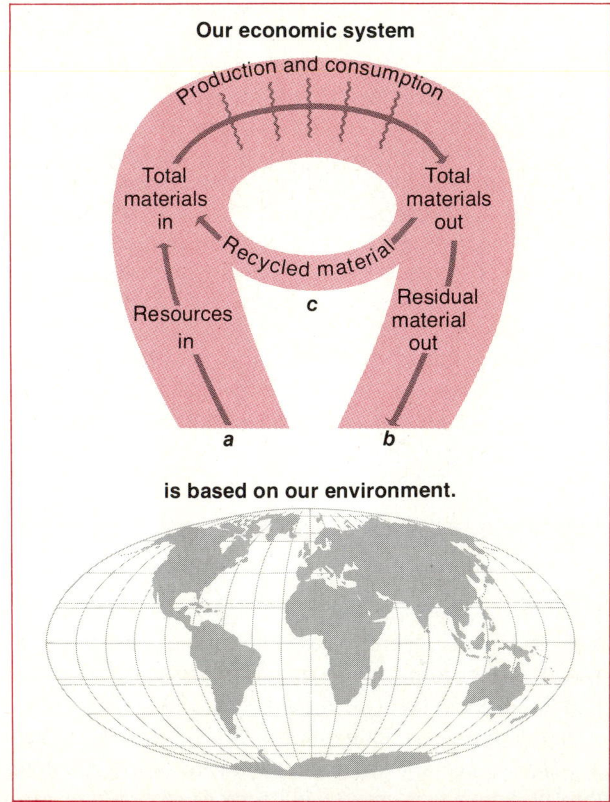

returned to the production process through pipe *c*. These materials pass through the production/consumption process and reappear in different form as "total materials out" on the right side of the diagram. Some of these leftover materials, such as chemical wastes, are the result of production. Others—like beer cans—are residuals from consumption.

This figure provides a framework for thinking about two important issues:

1. As our economic system expands, strains on the environment tend to increase, both because more material is drawn up through pipe *a*, and because more pollutants are dumped back into the environment through pipe *b*.

2. The pollution problem can be reduced by more recycling, that is, by directing more of the leftover material on the right into pipe *c* rather than pipe *b*. Moreover, any success on this score will have a highly desirable side effect. The more our production/consumption requirements on the left can be satisfied by materials recycled through pipe *c*, the fewer natural resources will have to be drawn from the environment through pipe *a*. In brief, recycling helps to solve two important problems at once: the problem of pollution and the problem of conserving natural resources. In the next chapter we will turn to a detailed analysis of the conservation of natural resources.

KEY POINTS

1. Pollution is an example of an external cost, a cost that is borne not by the individual or firm directly involved in the activity, but by somebody else instead.
2. With the Clean Air Act and the Water Pollution Control Act, the government has imposed controls on the amount of pollutants firms can release into our air or water.
3. However, there are two alternative market-oriented systems of control that are more efficient: (*a*) charging a tax on polluters or (*b*) issuing marketable permits to polluters. Both are designed to encourge the reduction in pollution by those firms that can do so at the lowest cost.
4. Either a marketable permit system or a tax is superior to another government policy that has been used: subsidizing firms or municipalities for installing pollution-reducing equipment. Such a subsidy is too narrow an approach to the problem because it attacks pollution only at the "end of the pipe." Hence, opportunities to reduce pollution in less costly ways may be missed.
5. Recycling wastes from production or consumption back into the production process helps solve two problems: First, less polluting waste is dumped into the environment. Second, fewer natural resources need to be extracted from the environment to support our present production and consumption levels.

KEY CONCEPTS

internal (private) cost
external cost
social cost
inefficiency of free market
how a tax may increase efficiency
internalizing an externality
marginal cost of reducing pollution (MCR)
pollution tax
Superfund
pollution limits for individual firms
marketable pollution permits
sag points
bubbles
offsets
subsidization of pollution-control equipment
end-of-pipe treatment
recycling
material balances
how recycling helps to solve the problems of pollution *and* resource conservation

PROBLEMS

28-1. Is output Q_3 in Figure 28-2 efficient? If not, explain why, showing the triangular efficiency loss.

28-2. In 1977, after almost a week of oil spill, an oil blowout in the North Sea was finally capped by a high-priced, high-living American named Red Adair. Draw a diagram like Figure 28-1 to show the various costs involved in offshore drilling for oil. Determine whether the following costs are external or internal: (*a*) the expenditure by the oil companies on installing and operating drilling rigs; (*b*) the cost to the companies of hiring Red Adair; (*c*) the loss of marine life and the damage to beaches if oil spills occur and cannot be capped in time.

28-3. "When faced with a problem, economists have a natural inclination to suggest a solution that somehow utilizes the power of the price system; thus their solution for pollution control is a tax. On the other hand, lawyers have a natural inclination to set up regulations, and pass judgment on a case-by-case basis. And because lawyers make our laws, this is what has happened." Explain why this case-by-case approach has increased the cost of pollution abatement.

28-4. Critically evaluate the following statements:

(*a*) "Pollution taxes are immoral. Once a firm has paid its tax, it has a license to pollute. And no one should have this license."

(*b*) "Imposing a physical limit on the emission of a pollutant is like saying that you can do just so much of a bad thing and pay no penalty, but the moment you step over this line you will pay a large penalty."

(*c*) "There is no point in insisting on crystal-clear discharges into a river as muddy as the Mississippi."

(*d*) "Since it is impossible (and in any case, undesirable) to eliminate all polluting activities, the cost of pollution can be reduced if some polluting activities are moved into geographic regions where the environment can absorb most of the pollutants without noticeable effect."

(*e*) "Whereas a tax discourages a polluting activity, a subsidy to install pollution-control equipment does not. Therefore a subsidy should not be used."

***28-5.** Redraw Figure 28-4 to illustrate the two special cases where a pollution tax is not appropriate: (*a*) where pollution is no problem and (*b*) where pollution is so costly (as noted in footnote 4) that it should be banned outright.

28-6. Use Figure 28-6 to explain the various effects on the environment when cars were made smaller during the decade of the 1970s.

28-7. We have seen that the target rate of pollution is not zero. Do you think that the target rate of crime should be zero, or not? In other words, do you think we should expand crime prevention and hire police until the crime rate is driven to zero?

***28-8.** Suppose that, instead of issuing marketable permits to polluting firms, the government sells these permits in an auction sale. Is the following statement true or false? Wherever false, correct it.

Under an auction sale of permits, the result would still be an efficient one. Pollution would still be cut back to its target level, because this is the number of permits the government would auction off. The big difference is that there would be no windfall to past polluters. All proceeds from the auction would go to the public treasury (just like the proceeds from the tax in option 1). In other words, an auction of permits would be as equitable as a tax on polluters, because either would channel the funds raised from pollution control into the public treasury, and thus prevent any of these funds from falling into the hands of past polluters.

***28-9.** (Based on Box 28-2.) The most equitable solution for air pollution is to have polluting firms pay a tax, not to the government but instead to the nearby residents who suffer from pollution. Is this also likely to be the most efficient solution? Why or why not?

APPENDIX

CONGESTION AND THE AUTOMOBILE

Parking is such sweet sorrow.

SID CAESAR

Congestion can be analyzed in much the same way as pollution, since both represent an external cost. An individual who decides to drive a car during congested periods takes into account costs such as gasoline as well as aggravation and delay. Since the driver must face these costs, they are internal costs. However, the driver does not take into account the external costs—the increased aggravation and delay that *other* drivers encounter because one more car is on the road, making traffic jams a little more dense and parking spots a bit harder to find.

The problem is illustrated in Figure 28-7. During nonrush hours, drivers equate the marginal costs (MC) and marginal benefits of driving (MB_1). Forty-five trips are taken, at equilibrium E_1. Traffic moves smoothly, and drivers face no congestion problems. But during rush hours, drivers put a much higher value on using the highway because they have to get to work, and driving is the most convenient way. Accordingly, the marginal benefit curve shifts up to MB_2, and equilibrium moves from E_1 to E_2, where drivers take 90 trips. Congestion is now a problem for two reasons. First, congestion results in a loss of time and gasoline, and consequently increases each driver's own *private cost* of taking a trip; that is, E_2 is on the rising portion of the MC curve. Second, since each additional car makes the congestion worse, other drivers also face an additional burden of aggravation and delay. This is the *external cost* of the trip the driver is taking; it is shown as the dark red arrow in Figure 28-7. When this cost is added to the private cost MC, the result is the marginal cost to society of having one more car on the road (MC_S).

The rush-hour problem is this: The decision by any driver to take a trip is based only on *private* cost MC rather than *social* cost MC_S. Thus equilibrium is at E_2, with too many cars on the road and with an efficiency loss shown by the red triangle (as detailed in the diagram's caption). The way to avoid this loss is to reduce the number of trips being taken from 90 to the efficient number, 80; in other words, move equilibrium from E_2 to E^*. This can be done by imposing a tax or toll T on each trip equal to the gap at E^* between MC and MC_S. Such a toll will raise the private cost MC up to MC*, with each driver then taking into account not only his or her own private costs but also the external cost on other drivers. Private decisions equating MC* with MB_2 will then result in efficient equilibrium E^*. This will eliminate the efficiency loss shown by the red triangle.

This general conclusion should, however, be qualified. This toll will provide a net gain only if the benefit it provides—that is, the elimination of the triangular efficiency loss—exceeds the cost of collecting the toll, including traffic delays at toll booths. To reduce the cost and delays of toll collection, it has been suggested that toll booths be replaced with an electronic device or a TV camera that would read off the license plate of each passing car, along with the time of day. Then drivers would be sent a bill—like a phone bill—at the end of each month.

Note that, as in the case of pollution, the efficient solution does not require the elimination of congestion but only its reduction. In Figure 28-7, traffic is reduced only to 80 cars, not to 60. Also note that the appropriate toll varies with the time of day: When MB_2 is high, reflecting the desire to travel in rush hours, the efficient toll is T. But when MB_1 is lower, reflecting the more limited desire to travel in nonrush hours, no toll is required. Thus, the appropriate toll is determined by the pressure of drivers to use the highway. Once set, the toll then relieves that pressure.

FIGURE 28-7
Traffic congestion
During nonrush hours, equilibrium is at E_1, with 45 trips being taken. There are no external costs; MC and MC_S coincide. However, during rush hours, drivers put a higher value on using the highway, so that the marginal benefit MB_1 increases to MB_2, with drivers taking more than the 60 trips where congestion begins to be a problem. Because the highway is now crowded, traffic is delayed and private MC rises; each driver wastes his or her *own* time and gasoline in the traffic jam. In addition, *other* drivers also suffer increased delay whenever one more car is added to the traffic. This external cost must be added to private MC to get marginal social cost MC_S. Private decisions by drivers equating MB_2 and private MC result in equilibrium at E_2, with 90 trips being taken. This is 10 more than the efficient number (80) where MB_2 equals social cost MC_S. The cost of congestion because of these 10 excess trips is the red triangle, for the following reasons: The last trip (the ninetieth) provides the benefit shown by the light red arrow under MB_2. However, the cost of this trip is the height of the MC_S curve—that is, the private cost shown by the light red arrow, *plus* the external cost to the other drivers, shown by the dark red arrow. Thus, the net cost of this excess trip is the dark red arrow. When similar costs for the other 10 excess trips are summed, the result is the red triangular efficiency loss. This can be eliminated by a toll *T* that moves equilibrium from E_2 to E^*.

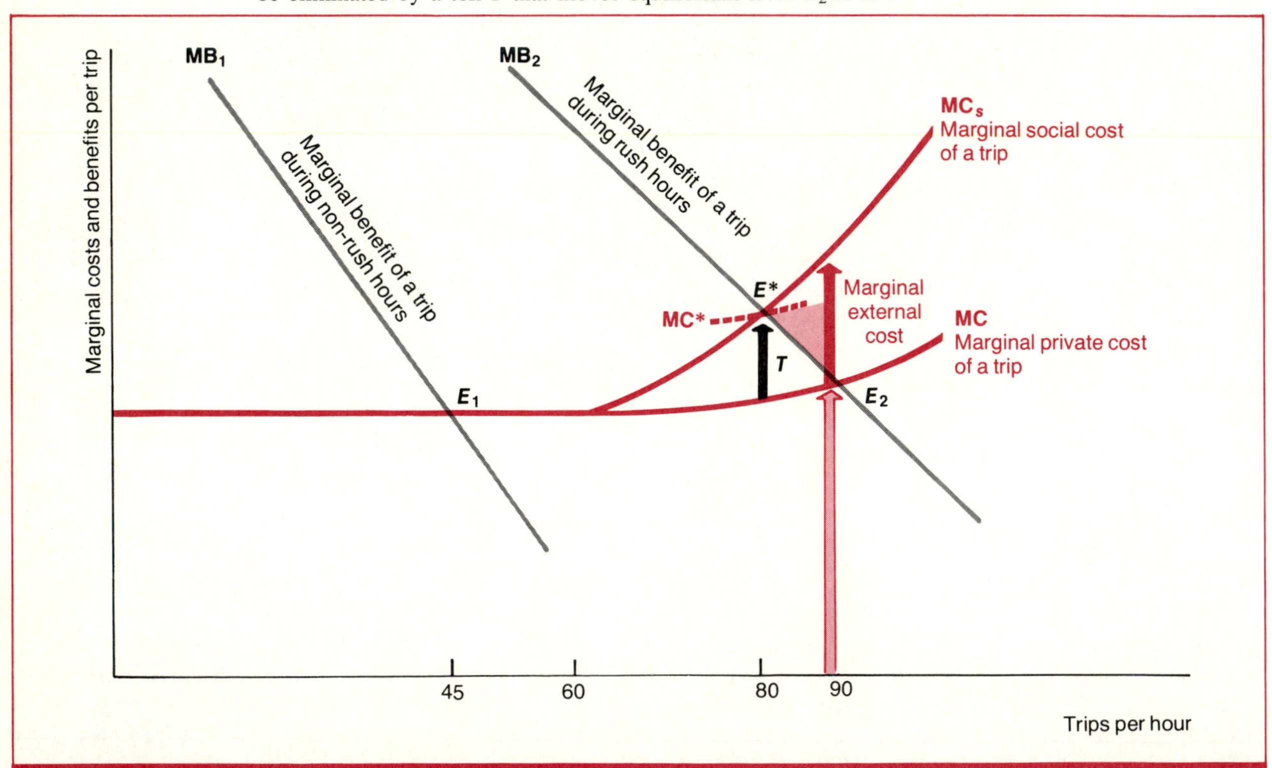

In describing such a toll, we have considered only the objective of efficiency. Of course, another objective of a toll may be to raise money to pay for the road. But in a congested area, the toll should not be set just for this money-raising reason. An example will illustrate why: Suppose that there are two bridges into a city and that they are just barely able to handle the traffic without tie-ups. If a toll is set on each bridge to raise the money to cover its costs, there will be no toll on the old bridge that has already been paid for, but a high toll on the new bridge. As drivers consequently switch from the new to the old bridge, a traffic jam will be created where none existed before.

Finally, there have been a number of other suggestions for reducing auto congestion. Each would reduce the problem, although generally in a somewhat less efficient way than a toll. These include proposals to:

1. Increase the tax on gasoline. This would reduce congestion by reducing the cars on the road anywhere, at any time. But this policy is less effective than a toll because it does not deal directly with the problem of congestion on specific highways at specific times.
2. Induce people to form car pools by levying a toll not on the car but rather on the empty seats in it.
3. Provide a further incentive for car pools by reserving fast lanes for cars with more than, say, two passengers.
4. Reserve fast lanes for buses, so that some of the people in a hurry will stop driving their cars in favor of a faster trip by bus.
5. Tax downtown parking lots to discourage drivers from entering the congested area.
6. Charge people a monthly flat-rate license fee to drive in a congested area, with police imposing fines on nonlicensed cars caught in these areas.

PROBLEMS

28-10. Show why completely eliminating congestion by cutting traffic back to 60 cars in Figure 28-7 would be worse than taking no action at all. Is it always true that the complete elimination of an externality is worse than no action whatsoever?

28-11. Do you see any similarity between rush-hour tolls and peak-load (rush-hour) increases in the price of electricity? What do you think the efficiency effect of setting a high price for peak-load electricity would be?

CHAPTER 29

NATURAL RESOURCES:

ARE WE USING THEM AT THE RIGHT RATE?

The . . . economy of the future might be called the "spaceman economy," in which the earth has become a single space ship, without unlimited reservoirs of anything.

KENNETH BOULDING

Natural resources are the endowments of nature. Examples include metals, fish, timber, and oil. While natural resources are an important factor of production, they are typically quite different from another essential factor of production—labor. The amount of labor that will be available next year will be little affected by whether or not it is used (employed) today. However, the same thing is not true of natural resources such as iron ore and timber, where the amount available next year *does* depend on how much is used today. For this reason, questions of conservation are important. Are we adequately conserving these resources, or are we using them too rapidly? Do the expanding industrial requirements of a growing economy, along with our finite and shrinking resource supplies, put us on a collision course that will eventually bring about a collapse of the economy, as some observers have predicted? And what can economics tell us about when and how the government should intervene to limit our use of natural resources?

THE INEFFICIENT USE OF A COMMON-PROPERTY NATURAL RESOURCE: FISH

To illustrate why we may use a resource too rapidly without adequate concern for conservation, consider fishing. The main reason that too many fish are caught is this: Nobody owns the oceans, rivers and lakes, nor the fish that swim there; that is, fish are a ***common-property*** resource. The result is shown in Figure 29-1. D is the market demand for fish. The height of this curve, as usual, reflects the marginal benefits these fish provide to the public that consumes them. S is the supply of fish. The height of this curve reflects the marginal cost faced by those who "produce" (catch) the fish. This cost includes, for example, the expense of hiring crews and mending nets, and is shown by the light red arrow on the left. But S does *not* take into account another important cost, shown by the dark red arrow. This is the *external* cost of fishing done today. The more fish are caught today, the fewer fish will be available for those who fish in the future. Individual boat captains who fish today do not take this into account in calculating this cost. After all, any fish an individual boat catches today will not affect the number it will be able to catch in the future. Thus, each captain has an incentive to respond to supply curve S, taking no account of how fishing today affects the future fish population. The result is an equilibrium at E, where $D = S$ and the catch is Q. However, this is not efficient. Instead the efficient equilibrum is at E^*, with a smaller catch Q^*, where marginal benefit D equals marginal social cost S'. The efficiency loss from the overfishing that occurs at E is shown as the familiar red triangle, reviewed in detail in the caption to the diagram.

Similar problems arise for other common-property resources. For example, commonly owned pastures, or ***commons,*** are likely to be overgrazed.

Note how this problem of overfishing or overgrazing is analytically similar to the problem of overpolluting described in Figure 28-2. In each case, decision-makers do not take an important external cost into account. In the case of pollution, the external cost is the damage to those who live downstream or downwind. In the case of fishing, the external cost is the damage to those in the future who have less of the resource available. (For more detail on how fishing today may reduce future catches, see Box 29-1.)

MEASURES TO INDUCE APPROPRIATE CONSERVATION

There are three approaches that may be used to provide better conservation of a common property resource. That is, there are three ways to reduce the catch in Figure 29-1 from the inefficient overfishing quantity Q to the effi-

FIGURE 29-1

Market for a common-property resource: Fish

The marginal social cost curve includes the light red arrow of marginal private cost incurred by those who fish today (the cost of labor, mending nets, etc.) and the dark red arrow of external cost because there will be fewer fish available in the future. The efficient equilibrium is at E^*, where marginal benefit is equal to marginal social cost. However, this is not the equilibrium that occurs, because this natural resource is not privately owned. Those who fish take into account only their marginal private cost of fishing today; they ignore the external future cost. Therefore, their supply curve is S and the actual equilibrium is at E, where $S = D$. The result is an inefficiently large catch Q, with an efficiency loss shown by the red triangle. This efficiency loss is easily confirmed by considering a, one of the "excess" fish caught. The hollow bar under the demand curve represents the marginal benefit of catching a, while its marginal cost—including the effect on future catches—is shown as the hollow bar plus the red bar. Thus the net loss from catching this fish is the red bar, and the sum of the losses on all the other "excess" fish caught over the range Q^*Q is the red triangle.

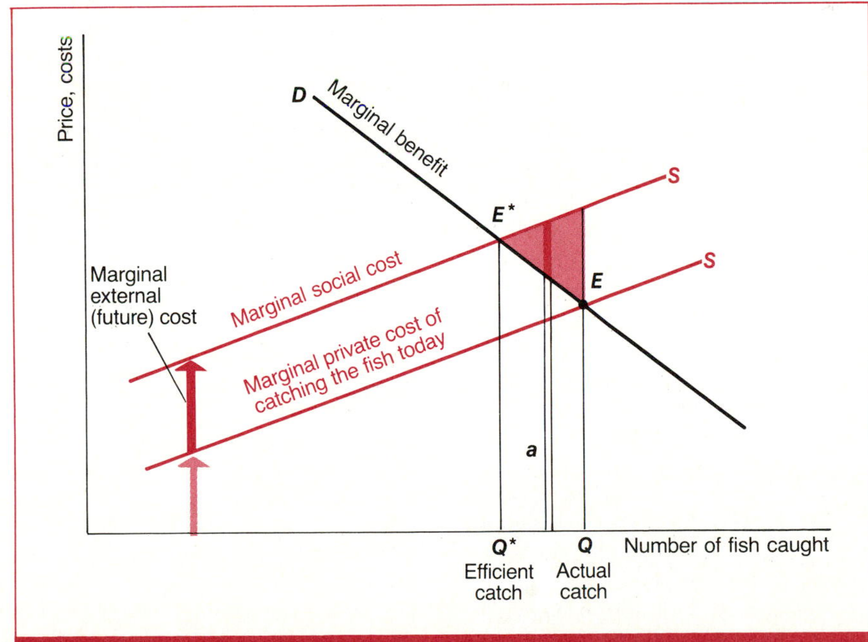

BOX 29-1

THE IDEA OF MAXIMUM SUSTAINABLE YIELD

Our statement that "The more we fish today, the less there will be to catch in the future" is generally true, but it lacks precision. We will now make this idea much more precise.

To begin, note that in certain circumstances, fishing today may have a disastrous effect on future catches; in other cases, it may have little effect. As an example of the disastrous possibility, suppose the fish population is so reduced in number that it can barely survive. Reducing that population further by fishing today may extinguish the species. In this case, our fishing today would reduce *all* future catches to zero. At the other extreme, suppose the fish population is so large it cannot grow further. There are no further natural food sources to sustain it, and for every fish that is hatched, another must die. Then fishing today will have little effect on the fish population and therefore on future catches. If we don't prevent the fish population from growing by catching some of it, it will be prevented from growing by starvation.

These two cases, and the many other possibilities, are illustrated in Figure 29-2. This diagram shows how the *growth* in a fish population on the vertical axis depends on the *size* of the population on the horizontal axis. Point *D* indicates that the maximum size of the population is 10 million fish. This is the point at which there are so many fish that their population cannot increase further: For each new fish, an existing one will die. If there is no fishing, the fish population will grow toward this number, but not beyond. To confirm this, note that at any point to the left of *D*, such as *K*, the fish population will grow (by the height of *K*). As a result, the population will be greater in the next period, causing a movement to the right, which will continue as long as the yield curve lies above the axis. But once *D* is reached, there is no further growth in the number of fish.

There is no reason why a hungry human race should be particularly interested in this "no fishing" solution. There is little satisfaction in knowing that the sea is as full of fish as it can possibly get. Instead, let us consider a point like *C* that does involve fishing. Here the fish population is $X_c = 2$ million, and is increasing by $Y_c = 1\frac{1}{3}$ million fish per year. At this point,

we can take out the natural increase of $1\frac{1}{3}$ million fish year after year without reducing the 2 million population. Hence, this curve is known as the ***sustainable yield curve,*** where sustainable yield is the amount of a renewable resource (such as fish) that can be harvested while still leaving the population constant.

The highest point *M* on this sustainable yield curve represents the *maximum sustainable yield.* This is a point of particular interest because it shows the maximum number of fish (in this case, 2 million) that can be caught on a continuing basis without depleting the parent stock. To harvest fish at this maximum rate requires a parent population of 5 million, measured along the horizontal axis. A reasonable objective is to prevent the resource from falling below this 5-million quantity.

Now consider the situation long ago, before large-scale commercial fishing. This is illustrated by a point like *K*, with the ocean almost as full of fish as it could get. As human population and our demands on the seas increased, the fish population was reduced by heavy commercial fishing; there was a move to the left in this diagram. However, so long as the fish population still remained above 5 million (that is, to the right of the maximum sustainable yield at *M*), there was no conservation problem. As we harvested more, the fish population fell, but it became more able to regenerate itself. That is, the natural increase—as shown by the height of the curve—became greater as we moved from *K* toward *M*. It is only at point *M*, where the fish population is only 5 million, that we encounter the conservation problem. If at this point we continue to harvest more than the natural increase, we will continue to reduce the fish population. But now, with each such decline, the fish population becomes less able to regenerate itself; that is, each movement to the left leads to a lower point on the yield curve, closer to the point where the fish population can barely survive. If we do not limit catches, we may risk extinguishing a whole species, just as we nearly extinguished the buffalo.

Fishing out an ocean is not just a theoretical possibility. This almost happened with herring in 1969 as a result of the development of larger, more efficient fishing boats. Moreover, the introduction of sonar for chasing down whales has meant that some types of whale would face extinction if there were no controls over whaling.

To understand fully the dangers of overfishing, suppose the yield curve is the dashed curve on the left in Figure 29-2. In this case, heavy fishing may do irreversible damage to the species. This will occur, for example, if we have fished the population down to a quarter-million fish and are consequently at point *F*. There are still some fish, but they cannot find other fish to spawn. There is no longer a natural increase. Instead, there is a natural decrease in population: *F* lies below the horizontal axis. If we reach a point like *F*, the population will eventually die out on its own *even if we stop fishing altogether.* The first rule of conservation should be to prevent such irreversible disasters.

To sum up: Conservation measures should be taken to prevent the population from falling below the one which provides the maximum sustainable yield *M*.[†] For plentiful species where unrestricted catches occur far to the right at a point such as *K*, there is no need to limit catches.

[†] There are other complications that may move the desired target somewhat to the right or left of *M*. For example, an influence that tends to pull this target to the right is the fact that, as the fish population gets larger, the fish become easier and cheaper to find. However, because there are other influences that pull in the opposite direction, a target of *M* is a reasonable first approximation.

FIGURE 29-2
Sustainable yield curve
Point *C* indicates that if the population of fish on the horizontal axis is 2 million, this will increase by 1⅓ million per year, measured up the vertical axis. Therefore 1⅓ million fish can be caught each year and still leave the population constant at 2 million. As we move to the right along this curve it rises at first: The larger the fish population, the greater its natural increase. However, this increase reaches a maximum at *M*, where a fish population of 5 million generates an annual increase of 2 million. This 2 million is the maximum sustainable yield, the largest number that can be caught per year and still leave the fish population intact. To the right of *M*, the yield curve falls as the ocean becomes increasingly crowded with fish. When the population of fish reaches 10 million at point *D*, the ocean can support no further increase.

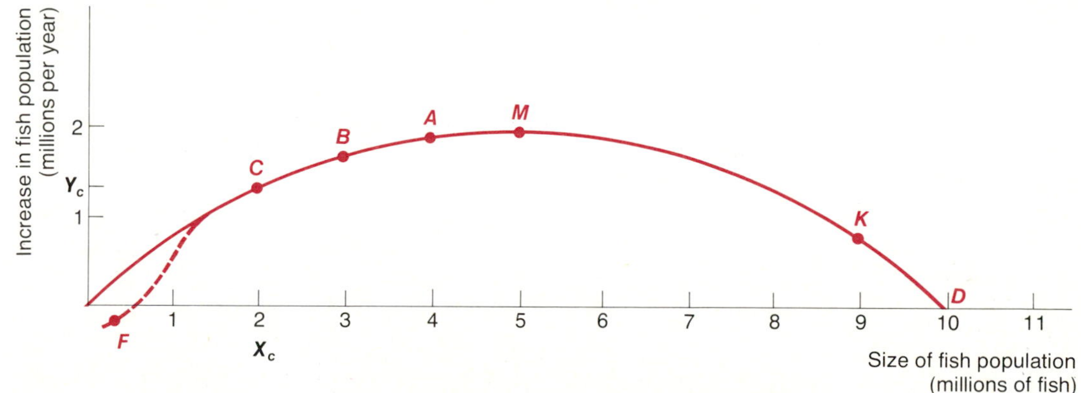

cient quantity Q^* and thus eliminate the triangular efficiency loss.

We will illustrate these three approaches by considering the problem of conserving fish in our inland lakes and rivers; thus we defer the more important and difficult problem of how fish off an ocean coastline should be conserved to a more advanced course. However, a few observations about ocean fishing are in order: If the government provides foreign fishing boats with free and unrestricted access to the waters off its coast, this may render useless any conservation by its own people. Therefore, recent attempts by a number of countries to extend their territorial limits—and thus control foreign fishing—should be judged not only in terms of the obvious issue of whether domestic or foreign fishing boats will get this year's catch, but also in terms of the more subtle issue of whether this policy is designed to conserve the resource. (The difficult task of conservation is complicated by the fact that fish swim. No matter how carefully a nation may protect them, they may be caught outside its territorial waters.)

Now let's turn to the simpler question: How can fish in our inland lakes and rivers be conserved?

1. Place Limits on the Catch

The government may limit the catch directly by restricting the number of fish each person can keep. Or, it may limit the fishing season, prohibiting any fishing whatsoever at certain times. (The off season is typically timed to minimize the disturbance to spawning.) In other cases, more peculiar nonprice restraints have been imposed; for example, the maximum number of nets each person can use has sometimes been carefully specified.

While this sort of limitation on nets may indirectly reduce the size of the catch, it is far from clear by how much. To rephrase this point in terms of Figure 29-1, there is no way of pinpointing whether the catch is reduced from Q to more or less than the desired target Q^*. This is important because—just as in the case of pollution—a restriction that is too severe may be worse than no restriction at all. Moreover, even if the government restriction on nets *were* to reduce the catch to exactly the desired target Q^*, it would be an expensive way of doing it. The reason is that labor would be wasted because each person would be able to use only a restricted number of nets; therefore, more people would be engaged in fishing. The same problem arises if each individual or fishing boat is limited in the number of fish it can keep: Too much labor or too many boats are expended in the effort. (Of course, this is more of a problem with commercial fishing than with sports fishing, where the whole point is to expend labor in a pleasant way.)

The problem with this first approach to conservation is that it does not use the market mechanism. We now turn to two alternative approaches that do.

2. Impose a Tax or a Fishing Fee

The government could deal with the externality by using a tax policy similar to the one suggested for controlling pollution in the previous chapter: Impose a tax equal to the external cost. Tax those who catch fish today according to the damage they do to future catches. In other words, tax them or charge them a fishing fee equal to the marginal external cost shown by the dark red arrow in Figure 29-1. This will raise their supply curve from S to S', thereby internalizing the externality. That is, this tax will force decision-makers to take into account the external as well as the internal costs of their actions. Accordingly, it will result in an efficient catch Q^*, where D intersects the new supply curve S'.

3. Create Property Rights

There may be an even simpler way of achieving efficiency. In certain cirumstances, a common property resource may be transformed into private property. For example, a large common pasture may be divided into 50 smaller fields, with one given to each of the families which previously used the commons. Once these fields have been fenced, each family will have an incentive not to overgraze its particular field.

It is not so easy to create property rights in the case of fish. However, in some cases it may be possible. For example, where fish are drawn from a number of small lakes, the fishing rights to each separate lake might be granted or sold to an individual, who would then have an incentive to limit the fishing in that lake.

To see how property rights result in desirable conservation, we will now consider the case of timber, much of which is already held by private owners.

A PRIVATELY OWNED RESOURCE: TIMBER

The market for timber is illustrated in Figure 29-3, with curve *S* representing the supply curve. Consider a single unit of output, *b*. The height of the supply curve *S* shows the price required to induce the owner to cut and sell that unit today. This price, sometimes known as the ***reservation price,*** covers two costs:

1. The direct cost of harvesting the timber—the wages of lumberjacks, the cost of hauling, etc.; plus
2. The cost to the owner because less timber will be left to cut in the future.

The *reservation price* of a privately owned resource includes both the cost of harvesting or extracting the resource today *and* the amount necessary to compensate the owner for the reduction in the resource available in the future. In other words, it is the height of supply curve *S* in Figure 29-3.

For more details on reservation price, see Box 29-2.

Observe that Figure 29-3 is very similar to Figure 29-1. In each diagram, there are two upward-sloping curves. The lower curve represents the direct cost of production—what it costs to cut the trees or catch the fish. The vertical distance between the two curves is a reflection of the conservation problem. It measures the cost of having fewer trees or fish available in the future.

However, there is one big difference between the two diagrams. In the case of a common property resource such as fish in Figure 29-1, the direct costs of production are all that the producers take into account.

FIGURE 29-3

Market for a privately owned natural resource: Timber

This is the same as the earlier example in Figure 29-1 except that the resource is now privately owned. In assessing what their harvesting today costs them, the private owners *do* include the dark red arrow of future cost. Thus their supply is *S*, and equilibrium is at *E*, with an efficient catch *Q*.

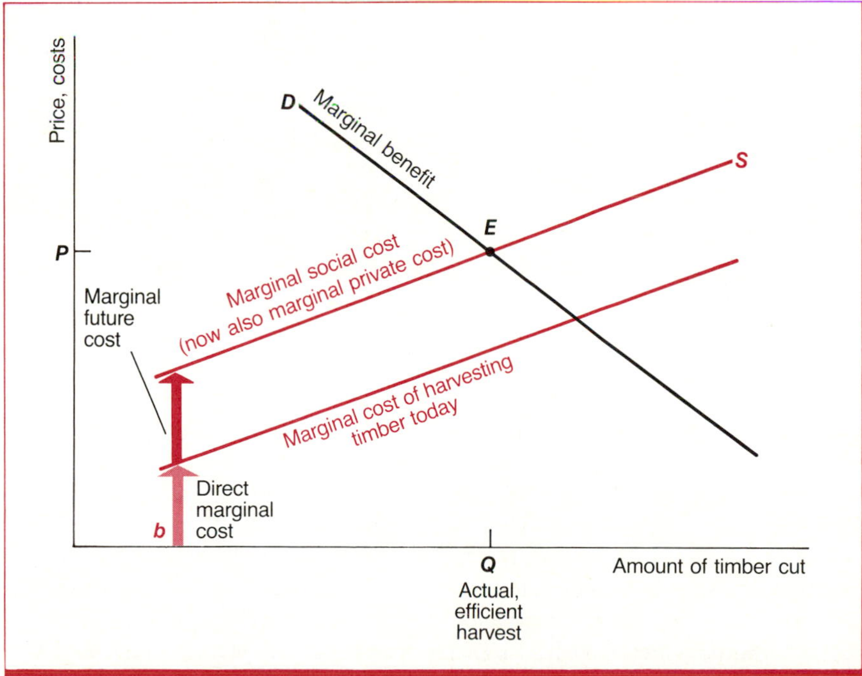

BOX 29-2

WHAT INFLUENCES THE RESERVATION PRICE OF A PRIVATELY-OWNED RESOURCE?

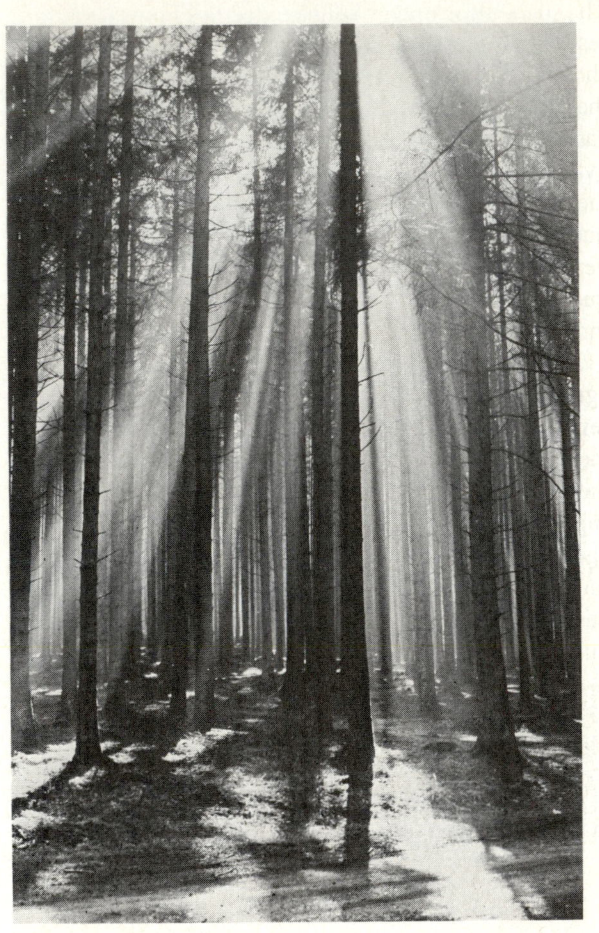

Some of the major influences on reservation price are:

1. The ***expected future price*** of the natural resource. The greater the expected price of timber next year, the greater the incentive to leave timber standing "in the bank," so to speak. Therefore, the higher will be the reservation price that owners will require before allowing their timber to be cut today.
2. The ***expected future cost of harvesting*** the resource. The higher the expected cost of cutting the timber next year, the less incentive the owners will have to leave the timber standing, and the lower will be the reservation price.
3. The ***rate of growth of the forest.*** If the forest has become fully mature, the owners will acquire no more timber by letting it stand for another year. Some trees may be harvested without substantial adverse effects on future harvests. Therefore the reservation price will be low.

For simplicity, we have assumed that the owner's decision is only whether to cut the timber this year or next year. But, of course, the issue is not so clear. Instead, the problem is to find the efficient pattern of harvesting over the next *n* years. If the owner is engaged in replanting the forest—rather than simply letting it grow up itself—this is another important cost to be taken into account.

Therefore, their supply curve is the lower curve, and the result is a socially inefficient output. Future costs are ignored and there is inadequate conservation. In contrast, timber owners in Figure 29-3 do conserve. They *do* take into account the dark red arrow that measures the cost in terms of fewer trees in the future. Therefore, their supply curve is the upper curve. Thus, for a privately owned resource such as timber, output is the socially efficient quantity.

Of course, private ownership may result in other inefficiencies. For example, if a single firm were to buy up all the timber land, it would be able to exercise monopoly power; that is, it would be able to raise price above P by reducing the quantity harvested to even less than Q. While this diagram therefore doesn't cover all cases, it does show how a privately owned resource in a *perfectly competitive* industry can lead to the efficient rate of production.

THE PROBLEM OF THE MYOPIC OWNER

Thus far it has been assumed that private owners of a resource take into account its future value. They do not shortsightedly consider only the present. However, if they do suffer from myopia and fail to see the full implications of their present harvests on the amount of timber available in the future, they will ignore or underestimate the dark red arrow of future costs in Figure 29-3. Consequently their supply curve will lie below S, and the harvesting of the resource will be more than the efficient quantity Q. In this case, private ownership does not provide adequate conservation.

An extreme example of this problem of myopia is aging owners who don't look into the future beyond a few years simply because they don't expect to be alive then. If their philosophy is "Cut the trees now and enjoy the income; who cares about ten years hence?" it's no suprise that they fail to adequately conserve. However, aged owners do not necessarily cause excessive harvesting. They do not, for example, if their objective is to pass on an asset of high value to their heirs. Even if their only concern is to live for the moment, a better option than excessive harvesting is to to sell the forest outright to someone who is younger and can take the long-term view. The sum received will provide the older person with even more money than clear-cutting the land.

THE CONSERVATION OF NONRENEWABLE RESOURCES

Timber and fish are examples of ***renewable*** resources. They reproduce and grow. A moderate rate of harvesting creates no danger that the forests or fish will disappear.

Other resources, such as oil and copper, are ***nonrenewable.*** There is a finite quantity of oil and copper in the ground, and if we use a constant amount each year, we will ultimately exhaust the available supply. Moreover, rising population creates pressures to increase the rate of extraction. We may therefore wonder if we are facing a day of reckoning in the not-too-distant future when we will face the exhaustion of our nonrenewable resources.

Simple Projections Spell Disaster

Anyone who projects the present rate of world population growth into the future finds that our requirement for nonrenewable resources is on a collision course with their available supply. Within the next hundred years or so, something must change. A number of models have been developed to show that, on our finite planet, today's trends in population growth and resource use cannot continue long into the future. A decade ago, a group of scholars at the Massachusetts Institute of Technology (MIT) concluded on the basis of a computer-based study that:

> If the present growth trends in world population, industrialization, pollution, food production, and resource depletion continue unchanged, the limits to growth on this planet will be reached sometime within the next one hundred years. The most probable result will be a rather sudden and uncontrollable decline in both population and industrial capacity.[1]

If present trends continue, by the middle of the twenty-first century disaster will be upon us—or, more precisely, upon our grandchildren.

But does it make any sense to assume that present trends *will* continue for a century? The assumption that they will has been questioned by Robert Solow, also of MIT:

> The characteristic conclusion of the Doomsday Models is very near the surface. It is, in fact, more nearly an assumption than a conclusion, in the sense that the chain of logic from the assumptions to the conclusion is very short and rather obvious. . . . The imminent end of the world is an immediate deduction from certain assumptions, and one must really ask if the assumptions are any good.

After all, if we are prepared to project present trends, we can bring our world to an end very easily, and we don't need a computer to show it. Any simple illustration will do. For example, if we project from a period in which the fruit fly population is growing, we can in a matter of a relatively few years bury the earth 2 miles deep in fruit flies. Any such projection provides an illustration, not of good economics or biology but of the

[1]Donella H. Meadows and others, *The Limits to Growth* (New York: Universe Books, 1972), p. 29.

mathematical magic of mechanically compounding a rate of growth.[2] A far more challenging and rewarding intellectual exercise is to ask: Why will the population of fruit flies eventually stop growing at a constant rate? Why will major changes in our present economic and social system occur?

Adjustments as Resources Become Scarcer

What changes can we expect in our present pattern of life as a growing population presses on a shrinking resource supply?

1. *Substitution in production.* As demand presses on available supply, the prices of resources rise and producers substitute other inputs. For example, as copper has become more scarce and expensive, construction firms have replaced copper pipe with plastic pipe.
2. *Induced innovation.* While plastics have been known substitutes for copper for many years, copper may also be displaced by products not yet developed. For example, copper wires are now being displaced in communications systems by far less expensive optical fibers made of glass. We couldn't have predicted this displacement of copper 20 years ago, since we knew almost nothing of fiber-optics then. Even though we can't precisely predict future technology, we can expect that copper will be further displaced in the future by more innovations.
3. *Substitution in consumption.* As forests have been cut down and quality wood has become scarcer, most consumers have found that solid wood furniture has become too expensive. Therefore they have turned to furniture made with veneers.
4. *Changes in population growth.* Population growth cannot be projected far into the future because the rate of population increase will be modified by the economic pressures that build up. As our planet becomes more crowded, bringing up children becomes more expensive—and this may influence the typical couple's decision on family size. Moreover, the population growth rate may fall for other reasons that have little to do with economics. In the highly industrialized countries, birthrates have recently been dropping because of changing social attitudes toward the family and children, and because of the development of birth control methods. True, much of the world's population is still in the less developed countries, where the rate of increase is still high. Reasons for this continued high rate include a decline in death rates because of better medical treatment, religious or social objections to birth control, and poverty. (Parents who are so poor that they can't afford insurance view children as a way of providing for their old age.) However, these influences are likely to weaken. Living standards are rising and death rates cannot be expected to fall as rapidly in the future as in the past.

With the increasing scarcity of resources, there is a major problem. But it is not the problem of some future doomsday; there are far more plausible reasons than a scarcity of resources for the human race to face Doomsday before the year 2100, particularly if we are unable to control nuclear weapons.

What, then, is the nature of the resource problem? Basically, it is one of *cost* and *technology*. To illustrate, consider one of our most essential resources, but one that we frequently take for granted: fresh, clean water. Suppose that some day we run so seriously short of it that certain areas are forced to tap a new, extremely expensive source of supply: the ocean, where the supply is unlimited. The use of seawater would involve the enormous cost of purifying and transporting it. Our problem is to keep these potential future costs in mind when we make decisions today, to ensure that we do not use our resources carelessly and wastefully. The more intelligently we conserve resources, the less the future cost of resource scarcity will be.

The central question, either in the case of resources or fruit flies, is therefore not: What would happen if current trends were to continue for 100 years? but rather: What is the likely process of adjustment? Even more to the point: What is the best path of adjustment? What can we do to make the process of adjustment work smoothly in terms of encouraging the discovery and development of substitutes? Finally, are resources being priced high enough today to protect our interests tomorrow? For a detailed analysis of this question, see Box 29-3.

*[2]To confirm the magic of compound growth, consider this: We will give you a million dollars, if you will give us just 1 cent today, 2 cents tomorrow, 4 cents the next day, and so on for just 1 month.

RESOURCES, THE ENVIRONMENT, AND ECONOMIC GROWTH

In earlier chapters, several arguments for growth were considered:

1. Unemployment is likely to be less severe in a rapidly growing economy.
2. Growth makes it easier to solve the poverty problem. Growth brings an across-the-board increase in income that lifts many families out of poverty; it is a "rising tide that lifts all boats." Moreover, growth makes it easier to change the *relative* position of the boats—to increase the percentage of the nation's income that goes to the poor. It is far easier to provide for the poor if the total income pie is growing. If it is not growing, any gains to the poor will require that someone else's income actually declines.
3. Growth increases not only our own future income but also the income of our children.

However, as already noted, this third point should not be overstated. If history is any guide, technological improvements will make our children wealthier than we are, no matter what growth policy we follow. As Robert Solow points out: "Why should we poor folk make sacrifices for those who will in any case live in luxury in the future?"

Growth has recently been questioned on other grounds as well: It depletes our resources and increases the pollution in our environment. Do these arguments justify slowing growth—or, as some suggest, setting a target growth rate of zero? Earlier we argued that a no-growth policy would be an extremely costly way to attack the pollution problem. Moreover, it would be relatively ineffective since it would not deal directly with the problem; it would only prevent pollution from growing, but it would not cut it back. There are similar reasons for being skeptical of a no-growth policy to conserve our resources. It would involve great cost, and it would not directly attack the problem of resource scarcity. Even if we were to end growth completely, we would still need to use resources, and we might still use them in a wasteful way. Better to deal specifically with the resource problem by encouraging the discovery and development of substitutes, and by ensuring that resources are priced high enough to induce us to cut back adequately on their use. In short, a policy of slowing growth is not specific enough to cure any single problem like resource depletion, pollution, or congestion.

Finally, in assessing the growth-versus-antigrowth debate, a helpful question to ask is this: Would the arguments now used against growth have applied equally well a hundred years ago? If so, has our growth over the past century been a mistake? Some people argue that, if we could, we should turn back the clock; but most would disagree. This is a judgment that you will have to make for yourself. However, in comparing the past with the present, don't forget the simple things we take for granted today. Before deciding in favor of the idyllic pastoral life of a few centuries ago, ask yourself this: What would you think of a world with less medical care, food, and the other things that we now view as essential?

OIL: A RESOURCE WITH VERY SPECIAL PROBLEMS

Any discussion of scarce natural resources would be incomplete without some reference to the resource problem that has been an important issue in public policy over the last two decades: oil. Recall that the world price of oil rose from less than $3 a barrel in 1973 to more than $30 in 1982. Although the $3 price in 1973 may have been insufficient to induce adequate world conservation, by the 1980s such a case could no longer be made. The problem was no longer the classic one of ensuring a high enough price to encourage conservation. That problem had already been more than solved by OPEC's huge price increases. Instead, the problem was an entirely different one. It was the problem of the dependence of the United States—and other oil importing countries—on foreign oil supplies that (1) were very expensive and (2) could be disrupted at any time. Indeed, in 1984 we became painfully aware of the risk of a supply disruption when warring Iran and Iraq began to sink oil tankers in the Persian Gulf. This risk gave us a strong incentive to reduce our dependence on OPEC oil.

When the international price of oil skyrocketed in 1973–1974 and 1979–1980, one of the most important policy decisions the U.S. government had to face was whether or not to intervene to control the domestic price

BOX 29-3

DYNAMIC EFFICIENCY IN PRICING A NONRENEWABLE RESOURCE[†]

How high should a nonrenewable resource be priced in order to ensure that our future requirements can be met? Although this is a difficult question, we can isolate some of the issues by considering the following simplified example. Suppose we have a limited quantity of a metal that will be completely replaced in 2 years by a cheaper plastic substitute of equal quality. The objective, then, is to completely use up the available supply of the metal in the next 2 years in the most efficient way. (Because cheaper plastic will then become available, there is no need to save any metal beyond this date.) How should it be priced this year and next year to achieve this objective?

The answer is shown in Figure 29-4. Select resource prices P_1 and P_2 in the 2 years so that the following two conditions are met:

1. The quantities used in the 2 years should exactly add up to the total available quantity Q. In other words, $Q_1 + Q_2 = Q$.

FIGURE 29-4
Efficient pricing pattern for a nonrenewable resource over 2 years
Efficient pricing requires that the gap AB between prices in the 2 years be equal to the interest rate. Efficiency also requires that the amount of the resource used up ($Q_1 + Q_2$) be equal to the total quantity available. Note that there is no reason for D_1 and D_2 to be the same; in fact, they are quite different in Figure 29-5.

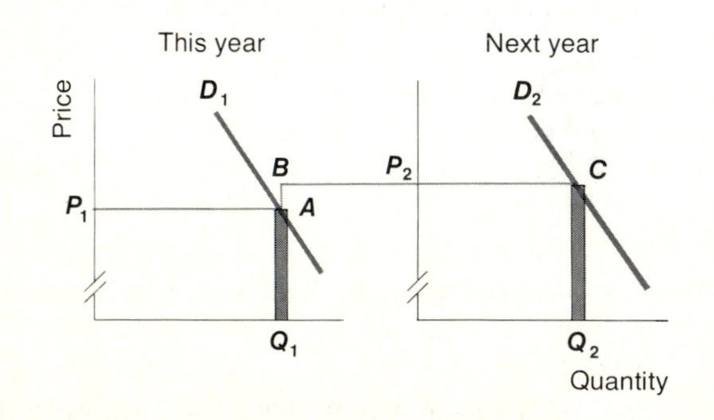

2. Price P_2 should be higher than P_1 by a gap AB equal to the interest rate. Thus, if the interest rate is 5%, P_2 should be 5% higher than P_1.

Why does this price pattern result in the efficient allocation of this resource over time? Why, in particular, should price be lower this year and higher next year? The answer is that there is an advantage in having goods or productive resources this year rather than next. If we have productive resources this year, we can use them to make capital, and this capital will allow us to produce more next year. For example, we have an option of (1) using 100 tons of steel to produce cars, refrigerators, or other consumer goods this year, or (2) using the 100 tons of steel to produce machinery that will allow us to have 105 tons next year. We can choose between 100 tons now or 105 tons next year. The rate of interest is a measure of the additional amount of goods we can have by waiting. Put another way, it is a measure of the advantage of having goods currently, rather than in the future. (This point will be explained in detail in Chapter 35.)

The most efficient pattern of pricing will reflect this advantage of goods now over goods in the future. In the special case shown in Figure 29-4, where the demand curves are the same this year and next, it is efficient to use more this year (Q_1) than next year (Q_2). In the general case, where the demand curves may or may not differ from year to year, the price should rise by the amount of the interest rate in order for there to be an efficient allocation over time.

To sum up the message of Figure 29-4: The fixed quantity of this resource is efficiently allocated if we use Q_1 this year and Q_2 next. This is what will occur in a competitive market if prices are P_1 and P_2 in the 2 years. We make no claim that this is the price pattern that will necessarily prevail; in fact, it may not. For example, if the supply of this resource is controlled by a small number of producers they may, like any other oligopolists, use their market power to set prices above P_1 and P_2. True, higher prices will mean that some of this resource will not be used up by the end of year 2, when it will be displaced by substitutes. However, the oligopolists may still have maximized profits because of the increased price on the amount that they actually *do* sell. This is just an extension of our conclusion in Chapter 26 that it may be profitable for colluding oligopolists to raise price, even though they sell less as a consequence.

In Figure 29-4, it has been assumed that the resource will be completely replaced by a substitute in 2 years. Figure 29-5 extends this analysis to the case where the resource is replaced after a longer period.

The resource in Figure 29-5 is replaced by a substitute after year 4. This does not necessarily mean that a substitute eliminates all demand in succeeding years. In fact, there is still demand for the metal in year 5, namely, D_5. However, this demand lies below P_5; the inexpensive substitute has "stunted" the demand for this metal. Of course, another reason that demand may be stunted may be that public taste turns against this resource; thus our use of it could end for this reason as well. An example is coal. Home furnaces were quickly converted away from coal about half a century ago, not only because oil and gas substitutes were developed, but also because no one wanted to shovel coal.

There are three crucial but highly unpredictable influences that will affect the efficient pricing pattern:

1. If existing deposits of the resource turn out to be less plentiful than expected, there will be less Q to distribute over time and the whole price "staircase" PP' will shift upward. (As this happens, note how the quantity used each year is reduced into line with the reduced total quantity Q.) On the other hand, if new deposits are discovered, there will be more Q available and the price staircase will shift down.
2. Price staircase PP' will shift if there is an unexpected change in demand. For example, if future demand is greater than expected, the price staircase will shift up.
3. The price staircase will fall (or rise) if substitutes are developed more (or less) rapidly than expected. It is very difficult to predict just when the development of substitutes will, in fact, occur.

In practice, therefore, it is very difficult to pin down specifically the efficient pricing and allocation pattern for any resource. But this box has highlighted some of the important considerations that should be taken into account.

†This box is based on Harold Hotelling's classic article that triggered the study of natural resource economics a half century ago: "Economics of Exhaustible Resources," *Journal of Political Economy,* April 1931, pp. 137–175. For a summary of some of the research that this article has stimulated, see S. Devarajan and A. C. Fisher "Hotelling's 'Economics of Exhaustible Resources': Fifty Years Later," *Journal of Economic Literature,* March 1981, pp. 65–73.

FIGURE 29-5

Efficient pricing pattern for a nonrenewable resource over a longer period

This figure extends Figure 29-4. Determining the efficient pattern of price and resource use over time may be viewed as fitting a price "staircase" PP' to the demand curves, with the restriction that $Q_1 + Q_2 + Q_3 \ldots$ be equal to the total fixed available quantity of the resource. As before, the height of each step in this staircase is the interest rate.

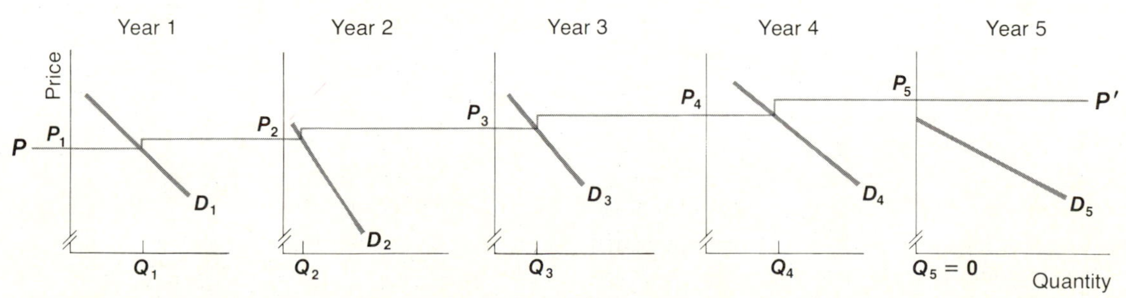

of oil. Specifically, the U.S. government considered two options:

1. Hands off—let the price of domestic oil within the United States rise as fast as the world price.
2. Control the domestic price of oil to keep it *below* the world price.

Initially, the government chose option 2, keeping the domestic price from rising as fast as the world price. However, in mid-1979, the Carter administration began to shift to option 1; it began a program of decontrol which was scheduled to be completed by October 1981. When President Reagan entered office, he moved the timetable forward; price controls on oil were abolished in early 1981. Thus both presidents ultimately judged that keeping the domestic oil price below the world price was a mistake.

This was not the first—nor is it likely to be the last—occasion for the government to be tempted to keep a domestic price below a rapidly rising world price. Accordingly, it is instructive to see in Figure 29-6 why this policy was a mistake.

Implications of Keeping the Domestic U.S. Price of Oil Below the World Price

Without government intervention, the U.S. price would be the same as world price P_W. (As long as the government doesn't interfere and oil can be freely bought and sold on the world market for P_W, U.S. buyers won't pay more for it than this, and U.S. producers won't sell it for less.) At this price, the quantity demanded in the United States would be P_WC, of which P_WB would be produced in the United States. The balance *BC* would be imported. Now consider the effect of government controls that kept the U.S. price below P_W, at P_1. As we shall see later, the actual system the government used for reducing price was *far more complicated* than the one we now describe; however, it is necessary to begin with a simplified case that will illustrate some of the basic issues.

Consumers responded to the lower price P_1 by picking point *F* rather than *C*. Thus the price control resulted in more consumption, as illustrated by arrow 1. In addition, the lower price induced domestic producers to pick point *A* rather than *B*. Price control thus resulted in less

FIGURE 29-6

The effects of keeping the domestic U.S. price of oil (P_1) below the world price P_W

The first effect was increased domestic consumption equal to arrow 1 that had to be satisfied by increased imports. The result was an efficiency loss because each of these barrels, such as *b*, cost more to import (the height of the empty bar plus the red bar) than the benefit it provided to consumers (the empty bar). Therefore, there was a loss on this barrel equal to the red bar. Adding up the similar losses on all the other barrels over the revelant range *CJ* of increased consumption, yielded the triangular efficiency loss *CJF*. At the same time, keeping the domestic price below P_W at P_1 also resulted in arrow 2 of reduced domestic oil production; this also had to be covered by increased imports. The result was an efficiency loss because each of these barrels, such as *a*, cost more to import (the height of the empty bar plus the red bar) than it would have cost if it had been produced domestically instead (the height of the empty bar). The result was a loss on this barrel equal to the red bar. Adding up the similar losses on all the other barrels over the relevant range *HB* of decreased U.S. production yielded the triangular efficiency loss *HBA*.

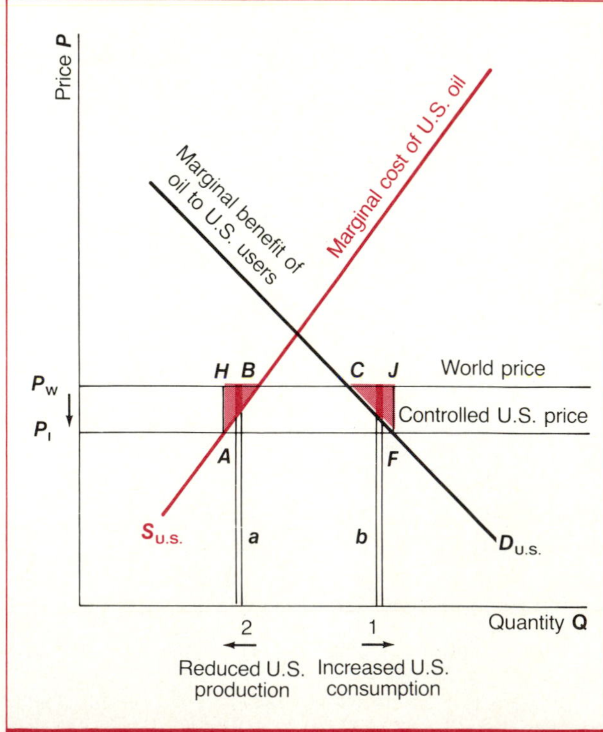

production, as shown by arrow 2. With greater consumption and less production, the difference between the two—that is, imports—increased from *BC* to *AF*.

In more detail, there were five effects of this policy.

1. Because the U.S. price was kept below the world price, U.S. oil consumers benefitted. (The "oil price shock" was not as severe for them as it would otherwise have been.) At the same time, U.S. producers were hurt because the price they received (P_1) was not as high as it would have otherwise been. Thus this policy benefitted consumers at the expense of producers. In other words, it transferred income from producers to consumers. But this was only a small proportion of the transfer *in the opposite direction*—from consumers to producers—that was taking place during the 1970s because the price of oil was skyrocketing. Thus this policy of keeping the domestic price from rising as rapidly as the world price was judged to be a "fair" or equitable one because it reduced the severe price shock to consumers by reducing the rapid increase in the price received by producers. (While the transfer described here was *domestic*—from one group to another within the United States—there was also an *international* transfer taking place, as described in Box 29-4).

2. Because the U.S. price control increased our imports from OPEC from *BC* to *AF*, it did exactly what we didn't want it to do. It increased our high-risk dependence on OPEC oil. Moreover, because we were buying more from OPEC, it made it easier for OPEC to increase the price it charged for its oil. Thus, paradoxically, the more we tried to keep the U.S. domestic price below the world price, the more OPEC was able to raise the world price.

3. U.S. oil consumers were not encouraged to conserve as much as they would have, if they had faced the full world price increase. Because their consumption was higher—as shown by arrow 1—there was an efficiency loss of red triangle *CJF*, as detailed in the caption to Figure 29-6. This loss reflected the fact that imported oil was costing more (the world price P_W) than the benefit consumers were getting from it (the height of the demand curve *CF*).

4. The reduction in U.S. oil production shown by arrow 2 resulted in another efficiency loss—red triangle *HBA*, also described in detail in the caption to this diagram. The reason for this efficiency loss is that we were importing oil at high cost P_W rather than producing it domestically at the lower cost shown by the height of the supply curve *AB*.

5. It was very expensive for the government to make such a simple price control system work. Importers had to pay P_W to buy oil on the world market. In forcing them to sell it at the lower price P_1, the government had to pay them the difference—that is, a subsidy of $P_W P_1 = HA$ per barrel. Thus the total subsidy that the government had to pay on the *AF* imported barrels was $HA \times AF$ = area *HAFJ*.

It was the hope of reducing problems 4 and 5 that led the government to use a more complex system than the one described so far.

The blended price system In the blended price system actually used, there were many prices, which fell into three basic categories:

1. The world price P_W for imports and "new oil"—that is, oil from newly drilled U.S. wells.

2. A lower price P_1 applicable to "old oil,"—that is, oil from U.S. wells already in production.

3. A blended price in between. To simplify a complicated story, this was found by pooling the oil in the first two categories and taking its average price. This was the price domestic U.S. buyers had to pay.

By allowing new oil to be sold at the world price P_W, the government hoped to avoid problem 4; with producers responding to this high price by operating at point *B* in Figure 29-6, the efficiency loss *AHB* would be eliminated. Because old oil was already in production and would be produced anyhow—or so it was hoped—keeping its price at the lower level P_1 would not significantly affect production. In addition, problem 5 was apparently solved. Oil buyers paid a blended price that was enough to cover the average price received by oil sellers (producers and importers). Therefore the government didn't have to pay any subsidy.

In theory, it was an ingenious solution. However, in practice it created a number of problems. To illustrate, consider just two: First, because there was no way of

BOX 29-4

THE INTERNATIONAL INCOME TRANSFER AS THE WORLD PRICE OF OIL INCREASED: OPEC AS A "CONSERVING MONOPOLIST"?

What we are witnessing in . . . oil and raw material prices is virtually the same as what is going on between trade unions and employers associations on the national level. It is a struggle for the distribution and use of the national product, a struggle for the world product.

HELMUT SCHMIDT,
then Minister of Finance and later Chancellor of the Federal German Republic

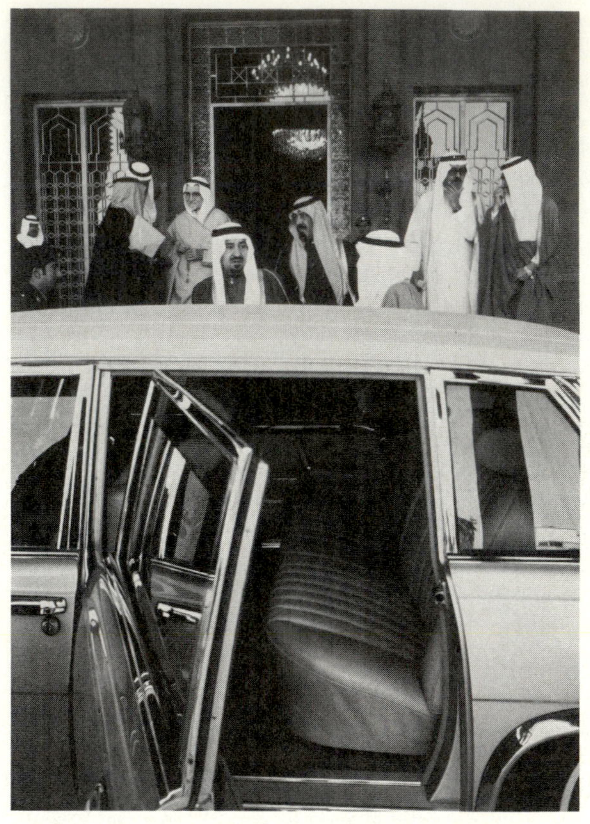

So far in this book we have analyzed a number of domestic transfers *within the United States*—like the transfer from American consumers to American producers that has occurred whenever an industry has been monopolized. Another example was the transfer from American oil consumers to American producers that occurred when the price of oil rose in the United States. However, one important thing to remember about such a domestic transfer is that it represented gains to one group of Americans and losses to another group that to some degree offset one another. However, with rising oil price an *international transfer* also took place. This was quite different because it involved a loss to one group of Americans (buyers of higher priced imported oil) which was *not* a gain to another group of Americans, but was instead a gain to OPEC. From the U.S. point of view, this transfer was a dead loss.

The OPEC countries argued that the large price increase was necessary to force the world to conserve; that is, the price of oil should be high enough to ensure that this important resource won't be used wastefully today, and consequently not be available for more important uses in the future. (It's important not to waste oil, since the demand for oil will be growing as the world increasingly industrializes.) Since countries such as the United States were not conserving, it was desirable for the price to be raised to a level at which they would conserve. So the OPEC nations claimed.

The oil-importing countries replied: "True, conservation did require some increase in the low 1973 price of less than $3—but not the more than ten times increase that occurred. The world is not rapidly running out of oil. Indeed, between 1950 and 1980, the world's oil reserves *increased by more than six fold.* Oil is not in the future crisis-supply situation that OPEC's high price implies. In raising price this much, the OPEC countries have not been primarily interested in the conservation of this resource. Instead, their real motive has been the same as that of any old-fashioned monopolist: They have raised price in order to *transfer income from us to them.*"

By the mid-1980s, OPEC's ability to transfer income in this way was being seriously eroded by its inability to control the world price.

physically distinguishing between old and new oil, illegal operators were given an incentive to use complex transactions to disguise the source of old oil. This then allowed them to sell it as new oil at a higher price. Second, the price controls were accompanied by a system of allocating gasoline during periods of scarcity. Unfortunately, the government miscalculated in making some of these allocations. The result was inadequate supplies of gasoline to many service stations, and long waiting lines of motorists in Florida and California.

These were only two of the reasons why the price controls were phased out.

Should the Domestic U.S. Price of Oil Be Pushed Above the World Price?

Thus far we have only considered the reasons for allowing the domestic U.S. oil price to rise to the world price. This world price is the marginal cost of oil to the United States because it is the amount that must be paid for imports. However, some economists—including James Tobin of Yale—have argued that the true cost to Americans of imported oil *exceeds the price paid for it*. Two of the points they make are those already noted in our introduction, where we recognized that oil involves special problems:

1. High risk is involved in large U.S. imports of oil from OPEC, since these imports could be cut off by war or revolution in the Middle East. A sudden reduction could involve a high cost; for example, it could cause a recession.
2. The more dependent we and our allies are on Middle East oil, the greater is the danger that we will become militarily involved, at great cost, in that volatile part of the globe.

These two risks can be viewed as costs we have to bear because we import oil from the Middle East. Such risk-related costs should be added to the world price P_W that we have to pay for oil in order to arrive at its true cost. According to this argument, efficiency requires that domestic U.S. price should fully reflect this cost and therefore also be above P_W. (Efficiency requires that the domestic price faced by consumers and producers provide a clear message to them of *all* the costs of a good.) Therefore, oil should be taxed to raise its price above P_W. However, these risk-related costs are controversial and hard to quantify, and proposals for higher taxes have been defeated (although there are some taxes that raise the U.S. price of gasoline and other oil products).

While raising the price of oil—or its products—is one way to reduce consumption and therefore our dependence on foreign oil, another approach is to develop other forms of energy.

CONSERVING OIL BY DEVELOPING SUBSTITUTE FORMS OF ENERGY

Our dependence on foreign oil may be reduced by the use of substitute forms of energy such as hydroelectricity, solar heating, or gasahol (a liquid fuel produced from vegetation). While there is a wide variety of such alternative forms of energy, we will now consider three of the most prominent substitutes—coal, natural gas, and nuclear power. Each of these—in particular coal and nuclear power—results in external costs to the environment. The important question is: What are the cheapest sources of energy when *both* costs of production *and* externalities are taken into account?

Natural Gas

Next to oil, natural gas is the largest American source of energy, accounting for about a quarter of U.S. consumption. Compared with nuclear power, it involves no waste disposal problem and less safety risk. Compared with coal, its extraction from the ground does little damage to the environment. Moreover, it burns much more cleanly than either coal or oil.

The problem has been that until recently, producers have been discouraged from finding and extracting natural gas by price controls. The resulting shortage of gas during the winters of 1976–1977 and 1977–1978 resulted in inconvience, hardship, and millions of dollars worth of lost industrial production. This spurred Congress to begin a gradual decontrol of gas prices.

The higher price for gas that came with decontrol has stimulated production; for the first time in years, new gas finds in 1980 were as great as the amount of gas used. Moreover, most geologists believe that the natural gas fields under the United States or its continental shelf are substantial enough to satisfy U.S. requirements into the next century—some say almost to the end of that century.

Coal: The Conflict between Energy and the Environment

The United States is the Saudi Arabia of coal, holding about 28% of the world's coal reserves; compare this with the U.S. holding of less than 10% of the world's natural gas and less than 5% of the world's oil reserves. At present rates of consumption, there is enough coal in the United States to last about 600 years. Yet the role of coal in satisfying U.S. energy requirements has been declining, from 75% in 1920 to less than 20% by the early 1980s. Coal has even failed to make a dramatic comeback in the last decade when oil prices have been so high.

An important reason has been the environmental cost of coal. Strip-mining leaves land scarred and mining companies facing the high cost of repairing the landscape. On the other hand, mining coal deep underground raises the problem of acid drainage and the risk of black lung disease. When coal is burned, the result is air pollution. The development of coal has been further complicated by inconsistent government policy, which has flipped-flopped between stimilating coal production and discouraging it.

The conflict between energy and the environment has been serious enough for coal, but it has been even more serious for nuclear power.

Nuclear Power

In the search for substitutes for oil, the last 15 years has been an era of disappointed expectations, but nowhere more so than in ***nuclear power***. In 1974, nuclear power was hailed as the key to reducing U.S. dependence on foreign oil. Yet, we now realize, that was the year in which growth of the industry virtually ceased: Orders for new nuclear plants almost completely collapsed in the face of unexpectedly high plant costs, tough regulations, and public opposition, which became even stronger after the Three Mile Island (3MI) accident in 1979.

In spite of the 3MI experience, the industry feels that it has a good safety record. Nuclear power has exposed the public to much less radiation than an equivalent use of coal, since coal contains traces of radioactive materials which are released into the atmosphere when it is burned. Moreover, while lives have been lost in accidents in coal mines, there have been no fatal accidents in commerical power plants. Consequently, the debate on safety has been less concentrated on the past than on three questions for the future: What is the chance of a much more serious accident than 3MI? Will a worldwide use of nuclear power contribute to the proliferation of nuclear weapons? And what will we do with nuclear wastes?

By the mid-1970s, the industry was battle-weary from fighting critics and vocal ''not-in-my-backyard'' groups opposed to nuclear plants or waste disposal units planned anywhere near their own communities. The debate over such issues was so heated and time-consuming that it was taking from 12 to 14 years to get nuclear power plants into operation; and this wasted time meant escalating costs. Time is money—big money: At a 14% interest rate, a $1 million cost incurred in day 1 grows over the next 10 years to $4 million—and this investment still hasn't earned a nickel of income. Moreover, with nuclear power, it's far from guaranteed that an investment will ever earn income. By the mid-1980s, failed nuclear projects had driven several large U.S. utilities nearly bankrupt.

KEY POINTS

1. In extracting common-property resources such as fish that are publicly owned, fishermen take no account of how this year's harvest will affect future harvests. The result is an efficiency loss: Too much is harvested today.

2. In an attempt to solve this problem by reducing the current catch of fish, the government may impose various restrictions, such as fishing licenses or off-season limits on fishing. In the case of ocean fishing, some governments have extended their territorial waters to limit the catch of foreign vessels. However, it is difficult to sort out how much of this territorial extension is a desire to conserve and how much is a desire to protect domestic vessels from foreign competition.

3. Another way to reduce the harvest to an efficient level is to establish property rights. This is a possibility if the fish are located in inland lakes. Once the resource becomes privately owned, its supply will reflect not only the current cost of harvesting it, but also the amount necessary to compensate the owner for the adverse effect of present harvests on future supplies.

4. Special problems arise when a resource is nonrenewable. If current rates of consumption continue, such a resource must someday be exhausted. This simple observation has led to a number of "Doomsday studies" that predict the collapse of our economic system. However, a problem with many of these studies is that they take inadequate account of price adjustments: As such resources become scarcer, their prices rise; this encourages conservation and stimulates the search for substitutes. An important question is: Are today's prices of nonrenewable resources high enough to ensure that existing supplies will not be used up too quickly and that the development of new substitutes will be encouraged?

5. The policy of keeping the domestic U.S. oil price below the world price has led to two kinds of efficiency loss: (1) It reduced conservation efforts by oil users and (2) discouraged production by domestic producers.

6. A case can be made for raising the U.S. domestic price not only to the world price but even above it. This would futher discourage oil imports and thus reduce the risks of trading with Middle Eastern OPEC countries.

7. Important current substitutes for oil include coal, natural gas, and nuclear power.

KEY CONCEPTS

common property resource
privately owned resource
reservation price
territorial limits
creation of property rights
renewable resource
nonrenewable resource
induced innovation
producer myopia
blended price system

PROBLEMS

29-1. Suppose 50 boats are fishing in an ocean area. Would there be any reason for the government to allow the boat owners to sign an agreement restricting the amount each catches? Is it possible that restricting the catch, which began as a conservation measure, may become a means of exercising market power? Explain. Can you think of any other examples of people who become conservationists because it is a way of providing themselves with more market power? When those who already have their ski chalets in Colorado become conservationists and prevent new ski runs and chalets from being built, what does this do to the value of their chalets?

29-2. Explain why a "myopic monopolist" might sell an inefficiently large or inefficiently small amount of a resource.

29-3. The problem of efficient timing in harvesting timber is illustrated in the diagram below. For example, point *A* indicates that if we wait 15 years before harvesting again, an acre will yield 10 units of timber. Which point represents a forest in which there is no longer any timber growth? Would you cut timber every 15, 30, or 66 years? Explain. (Assume that cutting and replanting costs are negligible.)

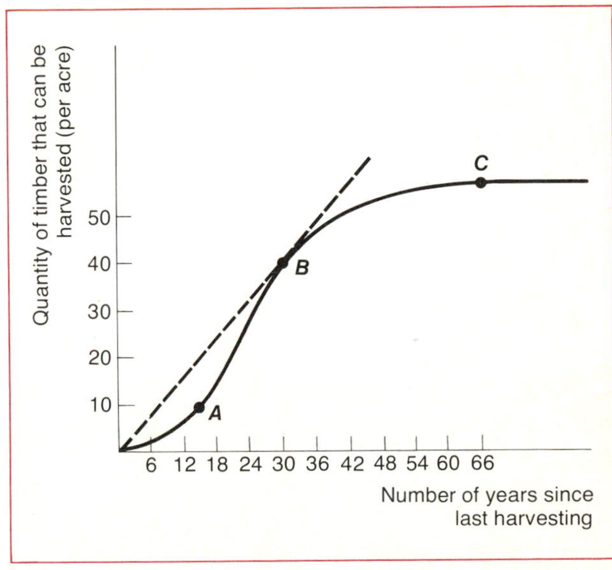

29-4. Doomsday models typically project a constant rate of growth of population and resource usage and, hence, forecast disaster. What economic forces tend to cause a change in the use of raw material resources? What forces affect the rate of population growth?

29-5. Equity among generations seems to suggest that we should not sacrifice much for our children, since they are likely to be wealthier than we are, regardless of what we do. How would you evaluate the following counterargument? Historically, each generation has sacrificed for the next. Is it fair for any generation to opt out of this process and thus become a "free rider," receiving benefits from the previous generation but making no attempt to pass on benefits to the next?

29-6. Using Figure 29-5, explain how conservation measures may be taken too far. Specifically, explain why it would be a mistake to cut back consumption one unit below Q_1 in year 1 in order to conserve that unit for use in year 5. Also, show why it would be a mistake to ignore conservation concerns and use one unit more than Q_1 in year 1.

29-7. Karl Marx recommended that the forests should no longer be privately owned; they should be made public property. In terms of conserving this resource, what would be the effect? Would this change the distribution of income? Explain both answers.

29-8. During the 1970s, there was a transfer from U.S. oil consumers to U.S. producers because OPEC increased its price. How was this transfer affected by the domestic U.S. price controls on oil?

CHAPTER 30

PUBLIC GOODS:

WHAT SHOULD THE GOVERNMENT PROVIDE?

Government is a contrivance of human wisdom to provide for human wants. EDMUND BURKE

Throughout this text, we have studied government intervention in the economy. For example, the government imposes regulations that prevent collusion between business firms (Chapter 27) and that limit pollution (Chapter 28). In these cases, government intervention is designed to influence the behavior of private firms and individuals. However, the economic decisions on what will be produced and how it will be produced are still made by private firms and individuals, subject to whatever constraints or incentives the government imposes. Although the market is *influenced* by government policies, it still delivers the goods.

In this chapter we consider instances where the free market does not adequately deliver the goods—or fails altogether—and there is a case for government intervention. As we study these goods, we will see once again that externalities are the key. However, the kind of externalities that are important now are not external costs such as pollution, but rather external *benefits* such as the two cited earlier: the benefits neighbors get when a homeowner hires a gardener, or the protection from disease that others receive when an individual gets a vaccination. To begin, consider the simplest possible analysis of such cases.

EXTERNAL BENEFITS AND RESOURCE MISALLOCATION

If there are any external or spillover effects, whether they be harmful or beneficial, the free market will not allocate economic resources efficiently. For example, because the good in Figure 28-2 had an external cost, a free, perfectly competitive market resulted in too much output. Accordingly, we might guess that, if a good has an external *benefit,* a free competitive market will result in *too little* output.

Figure 30-1 confirms that this guess is correct. The supporting argument can be stated briefly because it runs parallel to the argument used earlier in analyzing external costs. The key is to recognize that, instead of the external costs that were added to the *supply* curve in Figure 28-2, there are now external benefits to be added to the *demand* curve. Specifically, in Figure 30-1 the marginal external benefit shown by the arrow is added to the marginal private benefit MB to yield the marginal social benefit MB_S. An example might be flu shots. These provide both a private benefit MB to those who acquire them and an external benefit to others who become less likely to pick up the disease. Both these must be added to calculate the social benefit (MB_S) of the shots.

If this marginal social benefit MB_S is equated to the marginal cost MC, the result is an efficient outcome at E_2. However, in the absence of government interference, a free competitive market will reach equilibrium at E_1 instead, where marginal cost is equal to marginal *private* benefit. (This is the the only benefit taken into account by those buying the flu shots; thus it is their demand curve and is marked D_1.) With equilibrium at E_1 rather than E_2, the free market generates too little output—specifically, Q_1 rather than Q_2.

One Solution: A Subsidy

One way of getting to the efficient equilibrium E_2 is to provide buyers with a per unit subsidy equal to the external benefit arrow, thus shifting the demand curve up

FIGURE 30-1

Efficiency loss for a product with an external benefit, such as vaccinations

The height of the market demand D_1 shows the marginal benefit of vaccinations to the people vaccinated—that is, their own internal benefit because they don't get the disease. The black arrow shows the external benefit enjoyed by others because the disease isn't passed on to them. When these two benefits are taken into account, the result is the marginal social benefit MB_S. In a free market, equilibrium is at E_1, where marginal cost is equal to marginal *private* benefit. (This private benefit is the demand curve D_1 because it is the only benefit taken into account by those who make the decision to get vaccinations.) The result is an efficiency loss shown by the red triangle. To confirm, note that all units of output between Q_1 and Q_2 have a benefit—the height of MB_S—that exceeds their cost shown by the height of MC. Thus, producing them would result in a net benefit. In other words, because they are not produced, there is a net loss—as shown by the red triangle. This efficiency loss from "producing too little" is the same as the triangle in Figure 24-3*b*.

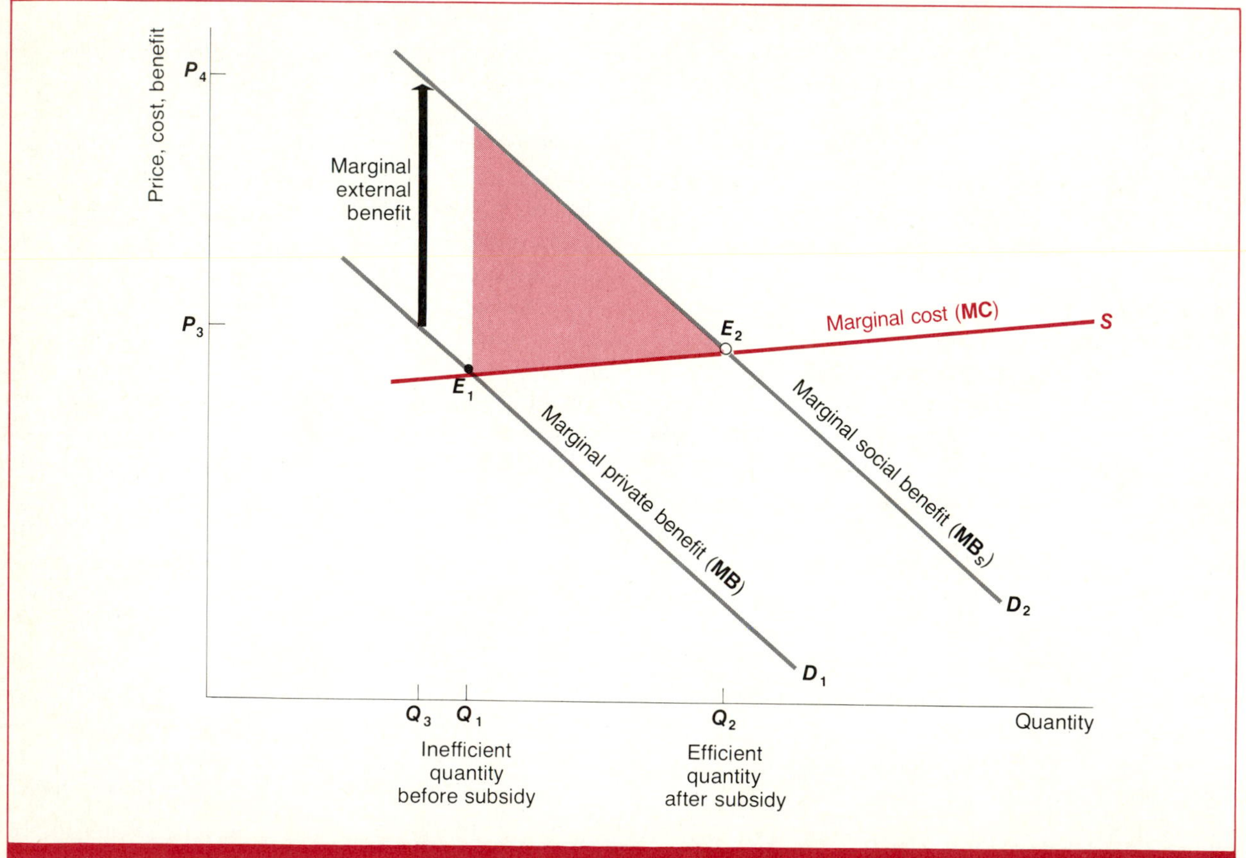

from D_1 to D_2. (Demand shifts in this way because, for example, the individual initially prepared to pay only P_3 for unit Q_3 is now prepared to pay P_4—that is, the original P_3 plus the subsidy received from the government shown by the black arrow.) With this shift in demand, a competitive market does the rest. Its new equilibrium is at E_2, where supply and new demand D_2 intersect. Thus efficient output Q_2 is achieved.

However, such an increase in efficiency alone does not necessarily justify a subsidy or any other form of government intervention. One must also examine the administrative costs of that intervention. Thus, for example, the government does not subsidize each homeowner for planting a garden, because the efficiency gains aren't sufficient to cover the costs of administering such a widespread subsidy program. On the other hand, in the case of many vaccinations, the efficiency gains *do* outweigh the costs of administration and a subsidy is justified.[1]

Notice in Figure 30-1 that efficiency is achieved by subsidizing a product with an external benefit, just as a product with an external cost was taxed in Figure 28-2. In either case, the government ''internalizes an externality.'' In Figure 28-2, polluting firms that paid the tax were made to ''feel internally'' the external damage they were causing, so they did less. On the other hand, purchasers of the sort of product we are now considering receive a subsidy that allows them to ''enjoy internally'' the external benefits it provides; thus this product is encouraged. In either the tax or subsidy case, *private firms or individuals act only after taking external effects into account*. This is as it should be.

Externalities may sometimes be internalized even without government action, but simply as a result of private market forces.

Private Market Transactions That Internalize an Externality

One example of this type of transaction is provided by the private real estate firm that purchases a whole block of houses in a run-down neighborhood. Its renovation expenditure on each house raises the value of that house and also provides a spillover benefit by raising the value of the other houses in the block as well. Once the firm has renovated all the houses in the block, it can capture both the internal and external benefits. Specifically, when it sells each house, it will enjoy *two* types of price increase: (1) the price increase because that particular house has been renovated and (2) the additional price increase because the neighborhood has improved as a result of the renovations to the other houses. Thus, while the firm may not be able to make a profit by purchasing and renovating a single house, it may be able to do so if it purchases and renovates the whole block, simply because it is able to capture the spillover effects.

As another example, if a firm constructs a ski lift on a mountain, it will be able to sell tow tickets. These receipts will be an internal benefit to the firm. At the same time, the ski lift will also generate an external benefit in the form of greater pleasure for those eating at a nearby restaurant who enjoy watching people ski. The internal benefit to the ski lift company from ticket sales may be insufficient to justify constructing the lift. But suppose the firm can buy the restaurant and, once the ski lift is built, start charging customers more. It thereby captures (internalizes) the external benefit it has created. It now becomes profitable to build the lift. The nation's output of ski lift services is no longer too low. It has now been increased to an efficient quantity because external benefits have been internalized. They are now being realized by the firm.

This suggests an alternative approach to externalities: Allow firms to merge into large enough units so that decision-makers will take such spillovers into account. However, this raises a conflict for policymakers. Mergers to internalize externalitites should be allowed. But mergers to accumulate market power should not. The problem is that mergers often do both.

Now let's pursue the issue of positive externalities further by considering a flood-control dam in a river valley. If a single farmer were to build such a dam, he would enjoy an internal benefit since his own crops and buildings would be protected from floods. However, such a benefit would be trivial compared with the enormous cost of constructing the dam. As a result, no indi-

[1] In the interests of simplicity, the government subsidy for vaccinations is typically in the form of a reduction in their cost (often to zero) rather than a grant paid to those who acquire them. However, either form of subsidy has a similar effect in encouraging people to acquire more.

vidual farmer builds it—even though its construction might be easily justified by the large external flood-control benefits it would provide for the thousands of other farmers in the valley. If the dam is to be built at all, it will have to be built *collectively*—by a large group of farmers acting together or by the government. Thus we come to the idea of a ***public good.***

PUBLIC GOODS

The simplest definition of a public good is ''anything the government provides.'' But this is too broad a definition for our purposes, for two reasons: (1) It includes all sorts of welfare payments such as free food or cash that are designed to achieve an equity objective by transfering income from one group to another. Such policies to achieve equity will be discussed in Chapter 37. For now, we continue to concentrate on efficiency. (2) ''Anything the government provides'' includes all sorts of activities that *could* be undertaken by private firms but are provided by the government instead; public transport systems and the U.S. Postal Service are examples. Since we are not interested in so broad a definition, we begin with the more narrow idea of goods—such as dams—that cannot be provided by private firms.

Since the idea of external benefits is important to our definition of a public good, we return to a detailed comparison of two of our previous examples. The first is hiring a gardener. Most of the benefits are internal; that is, they go to the family that hires the gardener to work on its own property. Therefore the private market works, at least to some degree: Individuals *do* have gardening done (although the amount is less than socially optimal).

Compare this with our example of a flood-control dam in a river valley. There are two important differences in this case. First, a free market will not work at all. No dam will be built because there is no individual farmer who will do it. The reason is that the internal benefits of flood control to that individual would be relatively small. Most of the benefits would be external—the protection from floods provided to other farmers in the river valley. Since no individual farmer will do it,

FIGURE 30-2
A private good
Individual demands in panels *a* and *b* are horizontally summed to get market demand in panel *c*. (At a price of $9, A buys one unit. If the price falls to $8, B also buys a unit. If the price falls to $7, A buys a second unit; and so on.) For such a private good with no external benefits, the market demand curve in part *c* represents marginal social benefit.

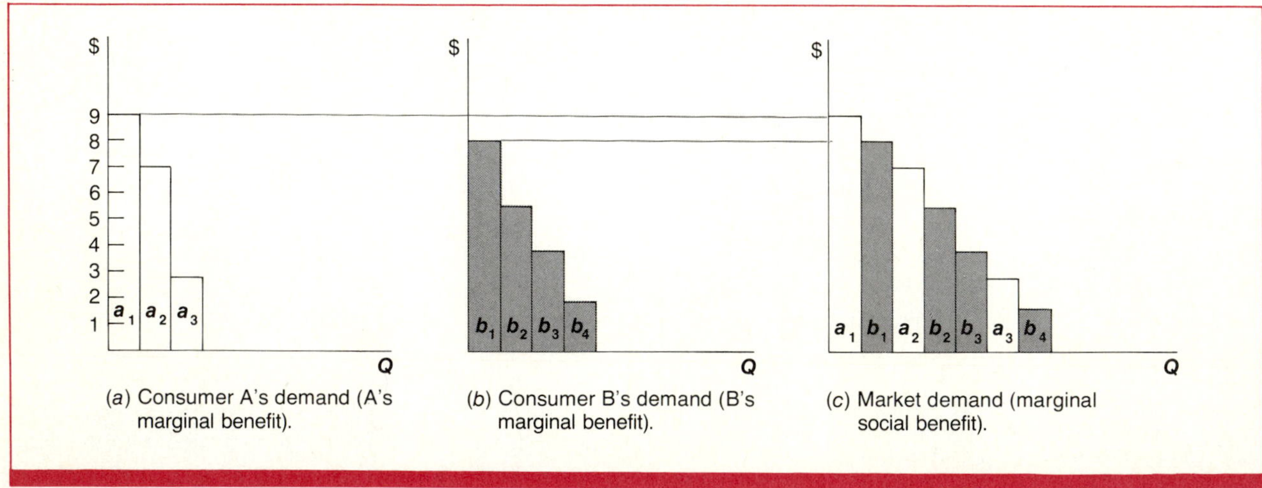

(*a*) Consumer A's demand (A's marginal benefit).

(*b*) Consumer B's demand (B's marginal benefit).

(*c*) Market demand (marginal social benefit).

any dam that is built will have to be constructed by the government. The second difference is more subtle: Once the government has built the dam, an individual farmer's benefit from it is the same as if he had built it himself.[2] Indeed, many economists use this as their definition of a public good: *It provides an individual with a benefit that does not depend on whether or not that person is the actual purchaser*. Another illustration is a lighthouse. Once it is built, no sailor can be excluded from using its services. All sailors are protected from the rocks whether or not they helped to pay for it.

A *public good* provides benefits that are available to everyone. No one can be excluded from enjoying this good, regardless of who pays for it.

The distinction between a public good and an ordinary private good is shown in Figures 30-2 and 30-3. A private good is illustrated in Figure 30-2. The first two panels show the marginal benefit (demand) of two individual consumers. Each consumer would actually have

[2]Notice that this is not true of gardening, where the benefit to a family does depend on who has the gardening done—the family itself, a neighbor, or someone far down the street.

FIGURE 30-3

A public good

For a public good, we *vertically* add the individual marginal benefits in panels *a* and *b* to get the marginal social benefit in panel *c*. For example, in panel *c*, b_1 is stacked on top of a_1 to show that *both* consumers get a benefit from this first unit. (There may be some individuals who get zero, or even negative benefit from a public good such as the army. While most people place a positive value on the defense service it provides, some place a negative value on it. Any such negative valuations should be taken into account, thus reducing MB_S in panel *c*.)

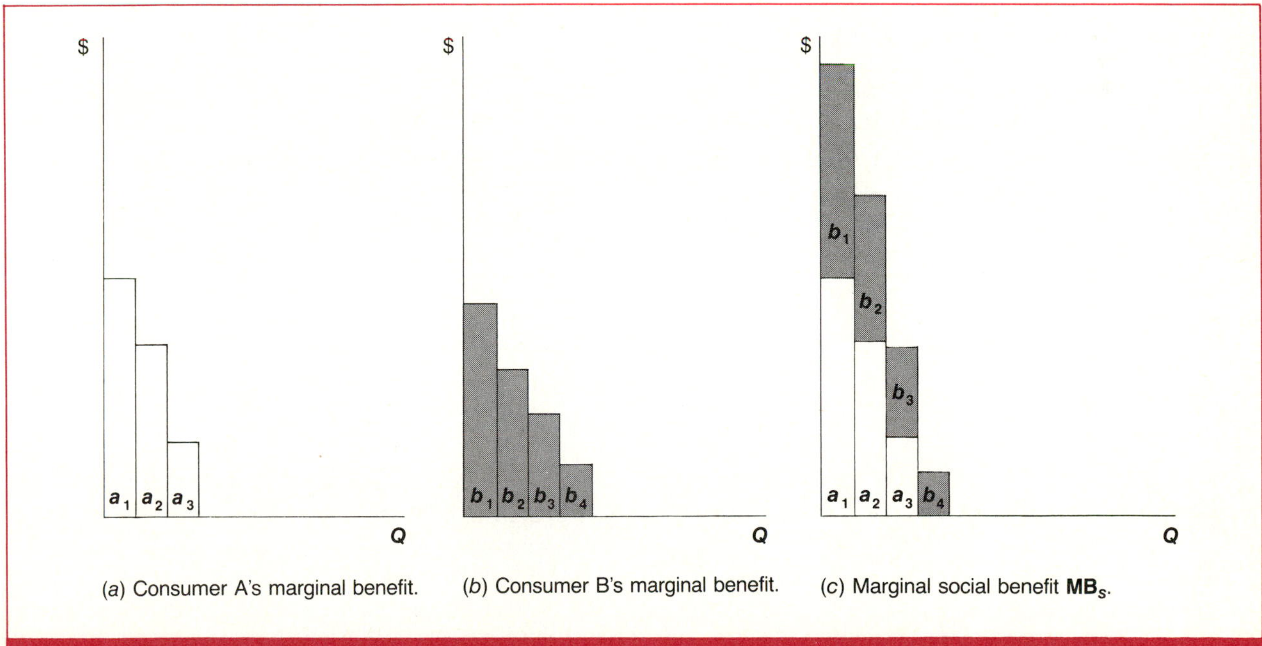

(*a*) Consumer A's marginal benefit. (*b*) Consumer B's marginal benefit. (*c*) Marginal social benefit $\mathbf{MB_S}$.

to purchase and acquire the good in order to realize this benefit from it. As we saw in Figure 21-1, a horizontal summation of the individual demands (marginal benefits) in panels *a* and *b* provides the total market demand in panel *c* (the marginal social benefit).

Figure 30-3 shows the alternative case of a public good, where all individuals can benefit from each unit produced. For example, consumer A gets benefit a_1 from the first unit. But this same unit also provides consumer B with benefit b_1. Since both individuals benefit from this first unit—both can, for example, see the warning beam from the same lighthouse—the benefit provided by this first unit is a_1 *plus* b_1, as shown in panel *c*. Thus, for such a public good, marginal social benefit (MB_S) is found by *vertically* adding the individual benefits—in contrast to the horizontal addition for a private good.[3]

It is important to recognize that the resulting marginal social benefit (MB_S) is not a demand curve. Nobody would buy the first unit if its price were $a_1 + b_1$. However, if it can be produced at this cost or less, the first unit should be produced. Moreover, if the second unit can be produced for $a_2 + b_2$ or less, it should be produced too, and so on.

PROBLEMS IN EVALUATING THE BENEFITS OF A PUBLIC GOOD

Suppose that panel *c* of Figure 30-3 shows the benefits of building a system of flood-control dams on a river. Further suppose that the first dam would indeed cost less than $a_1 + b_1$, so that it should be built. Let us now examine in more detail our earlier claim that this public good can be provided only by the government. Why can't it be provided by private enterprise instead? After all, since the two farmers value it at $a_1 + b_1$, why doesn't some entrepreneur collect this amount from them and build the dam? (The entrepreneur would be collecting more than the cost of the dam and therefore could pocket a profit.)

To answer this question, note that our two farmers A and B represent thousands of farmers in the valley. (For other public goods as well, there are very large numbers of consumers.) Thus you can visualize MB_S as the vertical sum, not of two individual marginal benefit curves but instead of thousands of them—with each individual curve being relatively insignificant. Now suppose that you are one of these individuals and the private entrepreneur who is promoting this project asks you for your valuation of the dam. Specifically, he asks how much you would be willing to contribute to its construction.

What would you reply? Clearly, you would have a strong incentive to understate your benefit, because you realize that it is very unlikely that your answer will influence the decision on whether the dam is built. You will either get a dam or not, depending on how the thousands of other farmers in the valley respond. All your reply will do is determine the amount that you will be contributing—and it's in your interest to minimize this. So you reply that you believe a flood-control system is exactly what this valley needs, and you believe your neighbors will value it very highly. However, it will provide little value for you; you personally are willing to pay very little for it.

Now, if the dam is built—as you secretly hope—it will cost you very little. Yet you cannot be excluded from enjoying its services: If the dam prevents a flood, your buildings and land will be protected. You get to be a ***free rider,*** enjoying the benefits while paying little of the costs. The problem, of course, is that you will not be the only one with an incentive to ride free. Every other individual in the valley also has exactly the same incentive, so that the entrepreneur gets a seriously biased response from everyone.

A *free rider* is someone who cannot be excluded from enjoying the benefits of a project, but who pays nothing (or pays a disproportionately small amount) to cover its costs.

[3]In Figures 30-2 and 30-3, we have dealt with only the two extreme cases: a "pure" private good, which provides benefit *only* to the purchaser, and a "pure" public good, which provides each individual with a level of benefit that does not depend *at all* on who purchases the good. There are, of course, many intermediate cases where a good provides benefit to the purchaser and to others as well, but where the level of benefit for each individual *does* depend on who purchases the good. (If I purchase it, I'll get more benefit from it than if you purchase it.) Such intermediate cases were illustrated earlier in the examples of gardening and vaccinations.

Accordingly, the dam does not get built by the private entrepreneur. It is natural therefore to turn to the government, which can solve the free rider problem by forcing everyone to pay taxes to build the dam.

Although it can collect enough taxes to build the dam, the government still faces the problem of evaluating the benefits of the dam in order to decide whether or not it should be built in the first place. In evaluating the benefits, the government, just like the private entrepreneur, encounters problems: It cannot simply ask people how highly they value the dam. If it were to ask you, and you believe that the government will build the dam without noticeably increasing your taxes, it will be in your interest to overstate your valuation in order to increase the chance that the dam will be built. Therefore, even though you previously told the private entrepreneur that the dam is worth almost nothing to you, you now turn around and tell the government it is worth $1 million to you since you know you won't actually have to pay the $1 million. In short, estimates by individuals of what the dam is worth are unreliable, regardless of who is collecting them.[4]

Another approach is to forget about canvassing people for their views, and instead estimate benefits of the dam in some other way. For example, by examining past records, the government can estimate the value of the crops that are likely to be saved from floods. Such benefits can then be compared with the estimated cost of the dam.

There are, however, two potential problems with such a ***benefit-cost analysis.*** First, unless it is treated with care, it may be used simply as an economic justification for projects which the government has already decided to build for political reasons. For example, a dam may have been promised to a key group of voters in the last election campaign. A politically motivated official with the task of evaluating this dam may estimate its construction costs on the low side, and add more and more benefits until the project is justified. Such benefits might include the recreational services of the new lake and the human lives saved by flood control. While these may be important benefits, a wide range of values can be placed on them, as we have already seen in our discussion of the evaluation of a human life (Box 27-4).

Another reason why it may be difficult to get an accurate estimate is that the engineers who expect to construct the dam may also be the ones who evaluate its benefits. There may be a real temptation for them to estimate the benefits on the high side in order to justify the dam and thus create future income and employment for themselves.

OTHER PROBLEMS WITH GOVERNMENT EXPENDITURE DECISIONS

Decision making by a government raises five problems that do not arise—or are less serious—when decisions are made by private firms.

1. The Difficulty in Reversing a Public Expenditure

If Coca-Cola announces a new formula, only to see its sales slip, it will reconsider its decision and bring back Coca-Cola "Classic." The reason is that a private company like Coca-Cola would sooner admit its mistake than lose market share; business executives will admit their mistakes to save their jobs. Not so in the public sector, where admitting mistakes may *cost* politicians their jobs: If a government expenditure program is dropped, the opposition party may be able to use this "admission of error" to defeat the government in the next election. Furthermore, politicians do not personally suffer out of pocket when they continue questionable expenditures. This also makes them less likely to admit a mistake and reverse an expenditure decision.

[4]Devising ways to get a better evaluation of public goods has become an important area of inquiry. One imaginative suggestion: Inform people that they will be taxed, but only if their individual valuation tips the scale in favor of building the dam; for such an individual, the tax would be the cost of the dam minus the sum of everyone else's valuation. Putting the question this way makes it less likely that people will provide a wildly inaccurate evaluation. In particular, it would prevent you from making your wild overestimate of a million dollars. Think about it: The more you exaggerate, the more likely it is that your answer will tip the scales in favor of the dam and you will be taxed. In addition, the more you exaggerate, the higher your tax bill could be.

For more detail on this sort of tax—and in particular on the proposal of Edward H. Clarke, see T. Nicolas Tideman and Gordon Tullock, "A New and Superior Process for Making Social Choices," *Journal of Political Economy,* December 1976, pp. 1145–1159.

2. Voting Politically for Products Is not Specific Enough

The Coca-Cola example suggests another important difference in public vs private decision making. When you buy a particular item, you register a clear vote for its production. However, in the public sector, you vote for a dam—at least in theory—by voting for a candidate committed to building it. Unfortunately, in practice it is not this simple; in fact, you may not get to vote on this issue at all. The reason is that in an election, you vote for a candidate who advocates a whole set of policies. Like most other voters, you may vote for this candidate because of some other completely unrelated issue, such as foreign policy, or even the personality of the candidate. It is therefore quite possible that the voters who have elected a candidate promising a dam don't really want the dam at all. While the issue is not quite this simple—the public can also express its preferences via campaign contributions, lobbying, and so on—it is nonetheless true that the political process is a relatively poor method for the public to express its preferences. The public does not vote often enough and specifically enough to provide a clear message to the government of who wants what. Compare this with the private market, where communication is much more effective: Each day millions of messages on millions of products are communicated to producers by consumers when they buy—or do not buy—those products.

3. The Incentive for Politicians to Support "Special-Interest" Groups

The diffuse and inchoate consumer interest has been no match for the sharply focussed, articulate and well-financed efforts of producer groups.

Walter W. Heller

In making decisions, our elected representatives have a number of motives. For example, they may honestly be trying to promote the public interest, or at least what they believe to be the public interest. (Unfortunately, it is often not clear what the public interest may be; see Box 30-1.) Frequently their desire to serve the public is their reason for entering politics in the first place. However, once they enter politics, they can't accomplish anything without being elected. Thus, of necessity, all politicians—no matter how noble—must be concerned with getting elected or reelected. One of the best ways to get reelected is to gain the backing of organized constituencies—or "special-interest" groups—who are able to deliver votes and/or financial support. In turn, the best way to get such backing is to support programs that are of intense interest to such groups, but of far less concern to the public that has to pay. The special interest of most people is their job—the goods or services they are producing; the source of our income is of intense interest to each of us. Politicians seeking special interest support therefore pay particular attention to people as producers rather than as consumers.

4. Short-Run, Crisis-Oriented Decision Making

The desire to be reelected also leads politicians to favor policies with costs that are hidden, and benefits that are obvious and will be realized quickly, before the next election. Why should politicians promote policies that the public won't understand, or policies that will provide benefits after the next election—and thus may help to reelect their successors? One of the reasons that politicians take this limited short-run view is that a busy public cannot be adequately informed about the hundreds of issues on which politicians must decide. Thus politicians tend to put off tough, long-run decisions, and when they finally do take action, it is often in response to a crisis.

5. Government Bureaucracy

Even if Congress has, with great foresight, made a decision that should benefit the nation overall, this policy must be introduced and enforced by the appropriate government department—for example, the Department of the Interior or the Department of Health and Human Resources. Each of these departments is a "bureau"; that is, it receives its income from a granting agency (Congress) rather than as a private firm does—from the sale of a product in the marketplace.[5]

[5]Departments of large private firms may develop many of the characteristics of a bureaucreacy, and to the extent they do, the difference between the operation of a government department and a business is diminished.

Difficulties in controlling a bureau's performance and cost The government bureau typically is a monopolist in the provision of its service to the public; indeed, the reason the government may have taken over this activity may be that it is a natural monopoly. For precisely this reason it is difficult for Congress to judge its performance: There is no equivalent private agency providing the same service with which the government bureau might be compared. Another difficulty is that a bureau's output can't be measured. Thus, for example, the Department of Agriculture can't be judged, like a private firm, on the number of bushels of wheat it produces, because it doesn't produce any. (This problem reaches right down through the ranks of a bureau. Difficulties in measuring output make it difficult for senior members in a bureau to evaluate the productivity of their juniors.)

This difficulty in evaluating performance is only one of the reasons why a bureau's costs are hard to control. Another reason is that a bureau's officials sometimes feel under pressure at the end of the year to inflate costs by spending any remaining funds in their budget: If they don't, their budget may be cut for the next year. Then there are the problems of bureaucratic waste that apply year round and that arise because a bureau is in a different situation than a private firm under pressure to sell its product in the marketplace. The private firm has great incentives to cut costs. These incentives come in the form of both a carrot (the desire to make profits) and a stick (the fear of bankruptcy if costs aren't kept in line). On the other hand, a bureau need not fear going broke. It is therefore under far less pressure to keep its costs down. Moreover, because officials in a bureau are not spending their own money, they may lose track of what it is worth. They simply don't "pay attention" in the same way that entrepreneurs do when they have their own money on the line. The result is enormous waste in, for example, the world's largest bureau: the Pentagon, which at one time paid $91 for screws available in any hardware store for 3 cents.

Unfortunately there has been evidence of waste not only in the Pentagon's purchases but also in its sales. For example, in 1983, the Pentagon sold $1.6 billion worth of surplus items for $89 million—less than 6 cents on the dollar. Moreover, many of these items were, at the same time, being *purchased at full price* by Pentagon officials unaware that the Pentagon already had them and was selling them off at a huge discount. There are few more telling examples of how the lack of cost controls in a bureau may lead to unnecessarily high costs.

In the absence of a profit motive, what incentives are there in a bureau? Government officials tend to substitute two other objectives: (1) the public interest (at least as they perceive it) and (2) their own interest, including establishing a public reputation, accumulating the power and perquisites of office, and—often most important—increasing the size of the bureau.[6]

The tendency for the government bureau and its budget to expand There are several reasons why the head of a bureau might try to increase its size. By increasing the number of employees, the official will seem to have more responsibility and thus may gain prestige. More employees may also mean more echelons of management—just as in a private firm—and therefore more jobs at the top; this in turn means improved prospects for promotion. Government officials may also seek more funds in order to serve the public or their constituents better; for example, the more funds going to the Department of Agriculture, the more benefits it can provide to the nation's farmers. And the more its constituents are thereby satisfied, the more they will put pressure on Congress if any attempts are made to cut the bureau's budget.

Monopoly inefficiency: Public vs. private Both a private monopoly and a monopolized public activity may operate in a technically inefficient way—that is, with unnecessarily high cost. One reason is that both have less incentive than a competitive firm to keep costs down. Both monopolies also result in allocative inefficiency—that is, the wrong amount of output. However, this kind of inefficiency appears in two different forms. On the one hand, a private monopoly produces too little output and therefore employs too few resources. On the other hand, a public monopoly—a bureau—has natural tend-

[6]The objectives of officials in a bureau are discussed in detail by Anthony Downs, *Inside Bureaucracy* (Boston: Little Brown, 1967), pp. 81–111.

BOX 30-1

PUBLIC CHOICE: WHAT'S "IN THE PUBLIC INTEREST"?

Majority rule is a basic principle of democracy. Surely we may take this simple and well-accepted principle as a straightforward way of determining what is in the public interest, right? Not necessarily—for several reasons.

1. The Problem of the Oppressive Majority

Under majority rule, if 51% of the public want a certain policy they can get it. It doesn't matter how small they value the benefit—as long as they get *some* benefit. Nor does it matter how heavy the cost of this policy may be to the minority. Thus it is possible for majority rule to leave society as a whole worse off, with the benefits to the majority falling short of the costs imposed on the minority.

To illustrate, consider the following modified version of an example suggested by Gordon Tullock of George Mason University. There are 100 farmers in a community. Each requires a small connecting road to get access to a main highway. It is in the interests of 51 of these farmers to vote to have access roads put into their own farms only, using taxes collected from all 100 farmers. However, this will involve a loss to society if the 49 losers who don't get roads suffer a great deal from the tax they have to pay, while the 51 winners who do get roads get a benefit that barely exceeds the tax they pay. Therefore, majority rule may be defective. Like private decision making, it may result in inefficiency—an overall loss to society.[†]

Is there a better voting procedure than majority rule? The answer is that there are a lot of alternatives, but each involves some weakness or other.[‡] For example, one could avoid the problem of the oppressive majority by requiring unanimous consent; then no policy could hurt anyone. But this rule is hopeless. By providing a veto to each individual, it paralyzes the government. Any policy that damaged even one voter would be vetoed. Rather than searching for a voting system which might conceivably be better than majority rule, a more common and reasonable approach is to protect minorities from an oppressive majority with a consititution, either written or unwritten.

Our example of the oppressive majority illustrates

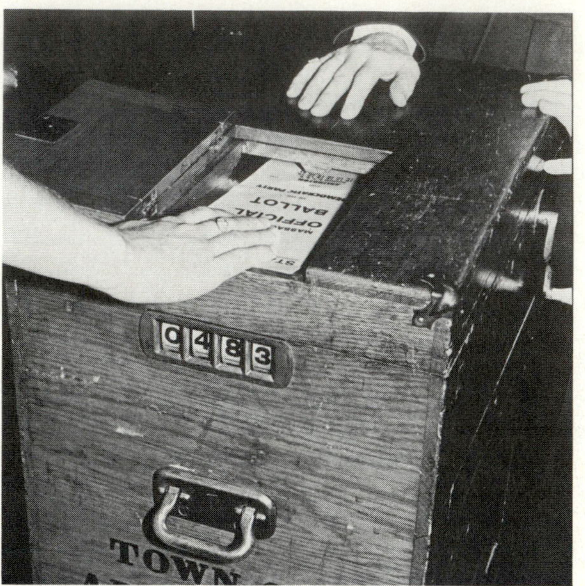

two additional points: (1) The government can redistribute income without transferring any cash. Suppose the 51 farmers who get roads receive more benefits than we have so far assumed. Specifically, suppose their net benefits are roughly equal to the loss borne by the minority. In this case, the majority receives a large transfer from the minority—even though no cash transfer takes place between the two. (2) Members of a minority have a strong incentive to try to break down the existing majority coalition in order to form a new ruling coalition including themselves. For example, the 49 excluded farmers are likely to try to get 2 farmers to leave the present majority and join them. Then the newly formed coalition can turn the tables on the 49 who were in a majority but now find themselves out of power. Of course, the new coalition may then come under the same pressure from outsiders as the old; there may be a cycle of changing coalition patterns.

2. The Voting Paradox: Why Majority Rule May Lead to No Clear Winner

Consider a population of only three individuals faced with a choice among three options, A, B, and C. Table 30-1 shows how each individual ranks each of these options. For example, the first column tells

TABLE 30-1
The Voting Paradox: Preferences of Three Individuals for Alternative Policies A, B, and C

Choice	Individual I	II	III
First choice	A	B	C
Second choice	B	C	A
Last choice	C	A	B

us that individual I prefers option A to option B, and B to C. Which of these options is the will of the majority?

If these individuals choose first between options A and B, a majority (individuals I and III) will vote for A. With A the choice so far, the only remaining question is how it compares with C. In voting between these two, the majority (individuals II and III) prefer C. So C is the final choice, reflecting the apparent will of the majority.

However, suppose instead that these individuals vote first between B and C. In this case, C is immediately rejected because individuals I and II prefer B. Thus the preference of the majority isn't clear at all; C may be the final choice or immediately rejected, depending on how the voting is set up.

We conclude that in a world in which individual preferences differ, an important determinant of the final choice may be the political process itself (in this example, the political decision on which options will be voted on first). Thus the individual who sets a committee's agenda or controls its voting procedure may be able to control the result.[§]

3. Logrolling

Logrolling occurs when several members of Congress agree: "You vote for my policy, and I'll vote for yours." Table 30-2 shows how it works in a simple case with three voters.

The first row in this table indicates that policy A provides a benefit of 3 to individual I, and a cost of 2 to each of the other two voters.

In a simple majority vote, both policies are defeated; individuals II and III vote against policy A, and I and III vote against B. However, I and II have an incentive to get together first: II agrees to vote for I's pet policy A, if I will vote for II's pet policy B. Because of this logrolling agreement, both policies pass. As

TABLE 30-2
Logrolling: Benefits (+) or Costs (−) of Each Policy to Each Individual

	Individual I	II	III
Policy A	+3	−2	−2
Policy B	−2	+3	−2
Net effect on each individual if *both* policies are passed because of logrolling:	+1	+1	−4

shown in the bottom row of this table, individuals I and II both benefit; indeed, that was the reason that they engaged in logrolling in the first place. However, III loses—and by even more than the combined gains of I and II. Thus logrolling hurts the community overall, even though it benefits the special interest groups who engage in it—in our example, individuals I and II.

This is the classical example of logrolling; but there is another possibility. Change the two entries of +3 in Table 30-2 to +5. As before, in the absence of logrolling, neither policy will pass. Logrolling occurs again for exactly the same reason as before, and once again I and II benefit while III loses. The difference this time is that the combined gain of I and II exceeds III's loss; thus logrolling results in a net overall benefit for this community. Therefore, logrolling isn't necessarily bad. In some cases, it may be the only way of achieving a socially desirable result.

[†]Majority rule can be inefficient not only because such undesirable policies *are* introduced but also because *desirable* policies are *not* introduced. For example, a desirable policy that benefits the minority a great deal may be rejected if it hurts the majority even slightly. Fortunately, majority rule may not be as inefficient in practice as these arguments might lead us to expect. The best evidence comes from Switzerland, where many issues are decided by a referendum in which the public votes yes or no on a single issue. In a study of 100 such votes, Columbia's Eli Noam concluded that there were only a few instances in which the result was inefficient; that is, the minority lost more than the majority gained. See "The Efficiency of Direct Democracy" *Journal of Political Economy,* August 1980, pp. 803–810.

[‡]For a discussion of some alternatives, see Dennis C. Mueller, *Public Choice,* (Cambridge: Cambridge University Press, 1979), especially pp. 49–58.

[§]This voting paradox, first described over a century ago, was extended by Kenneth Arrow in *Social Choice and Individual Values* (New York: John Wiley, 1951).

encies to expand; thus it often tends to employ too *many* resources.[7]

IS THE ENVIRONMENT A PUBLIC GOOD?

In Chapter 28 we concluded that, in a private market without government intervention, decisions by private firms may seriously damage the environment; and we have considered ways that the government may prevent such damage.

However, suppose that the environment is deteriorating of its own accord; no firm or individual is at fault in any way. For example, suppose that a species of wildlife is dying off in the wilderness. In this case, the proper approach is to recognize that the preservation of this species is a public good, just like the construction of a dam in our example earlier in this chapter. Since no individual values the species highly enough to incur the cost of personally preserving it, the private market generally won't deliver. Although private conservation organizations may act, the ultimate decision on whether to save the species—and how much to spend in the effort—is likely to rest with the government. If the government does act, everyone can enjoy the resulting benefits.

How large would these benefits be? This question is not easy to answer. While most people would put some value on the preservation of a wildlife species, it is very difficult to say how much. As Harvard's Richard Caves has put it: "How highly should we value wombats, if they are so far from civilization that no one will ever see them, let alone eat them?" One answer is that we may place some value on them, even though we don't ever see them, just as we may place a value on an air-conditioning system even though we may not actually turn it on this year. This phenomenon is described as *option demand*—the desire to have an option, whether or not we exercise it. Thus we may want to keep open the option of seeing a species, or drawing on it for medical research, even though we may never in fact exercise this option. Similarly, we may have an option demand for public parks which we may or may not actually visit. Option demand should be taken into account in the evaluation of environmental benefits.

Yet Caves' point is well taken: In discussing environmental protection, it is important to take a hard-headed view of the benefits and costs involved. For example, consider a caribou population that would be disturbed by the construction of an oil pipeline. A major cost would be involved in the extreme event that the pipeline were to cause the caribou to become extinct, since this could not be reversed by future generations. But if there is no such risk of extinction, what is the difference between reducing the population of caribou by 5% and reducing the population of cattle by 5% by slaughtering them for meat? Both policies provide obvious benefits: killing cattle provides food, while laying pipelines is essential to provide heat and power.

Again we conclude, as in Chapter 28, that keeping environmental damage down to an appropriately low level makes more sense than trying to avoid any damage whatever.

PUBLIC GOODS VS. PRIVATE GOODS: A REVIEW OF MICROECONOMIC MARKETS

In this section we compare the market for a public good described in this chapter with the other markets described in earlier chapters. Although a complete comparison would take us beyond the scope of this book, we can get a better understanding of how these markets compare by asking the following important question: In each market, how does the cost curve of a single producer compare with the total market demand curve?

In panel *a* of Figure 30-4, we answer this question for a perfectly competitive market; in the next three panels, the same question is answered for three other markets. (We defer discussion of the fifth panel until later.) In each of the first four cases, we see that the market that develops depends heavily on *how far the firm's average costs continue to fall*. To highlight this point, we have

[7]In *The Affluent Society* (Boston: Houghton-Mifflin, 1958) John Kenneth Galbraith argues that the government is *not* too large a part of the economy. Indeed, he argues that in some respects the government is too small; compared with a private business, it provides too few goods and services. One reason: Goods such as autos that are provided by private firms have their sales increased by advertising. However, goods such as roads that are provided by the government are not advertised. Therefore, we overspend on autos but underspend on roads.

assumed that the four products shown are similiar in other respects. For example, total market demand is exactly the same for each, and the average cost AC of each reaches a minimum at the same height, C. The only difference in these four products is that, as we move from left to right from panel to panel, AC reaches a minimum at an increasingly large output. Thus, in panel *a,* AC reaches a minimum at a very small output Q_1, while in panel *d,* AC reaches the same minimum height C at such a large level of output—that is, so far to the right—that it cannot even be shown in the diagram.

In the case of perfect competition in panel *a,* market demand can be satisfied at minimum cost by a large number of producers. There is little role to be played by the government, since this market is generally efficient when left to its own devices. (We assume here that there are no complications, such as serious price fluctuations over time, or important externalities.)

Panel *b* illustrates the case of natural oligopoly, where market demand can be satisfied at minimum cost by just a few firms. In such a market, a strong case can be made for the vigorous enforcement of antitrust laws to prevent collusion or the merger of these firms into a monopoly.

In the case of natural monopoly in panel *c,* market demand can be satisfied at lower cost by one firm than by more than one. Here, the application of antitrust legislation to split up a single firm makes little sense, since the split would raise costs. A preferred approach is price regulation, which prevents the firm from charging a high monopoly price, while allowing it to gain the cost advantages of large scale production.

In panel *d* costs have finally outrun demand. At no point do D and AC overlap, so there is no single price a firm can charge and still cover its costs. The product will not even appear on the market; there is no economic

FIGURE 30-4
The relationship of the costs of a single producer and total market demand

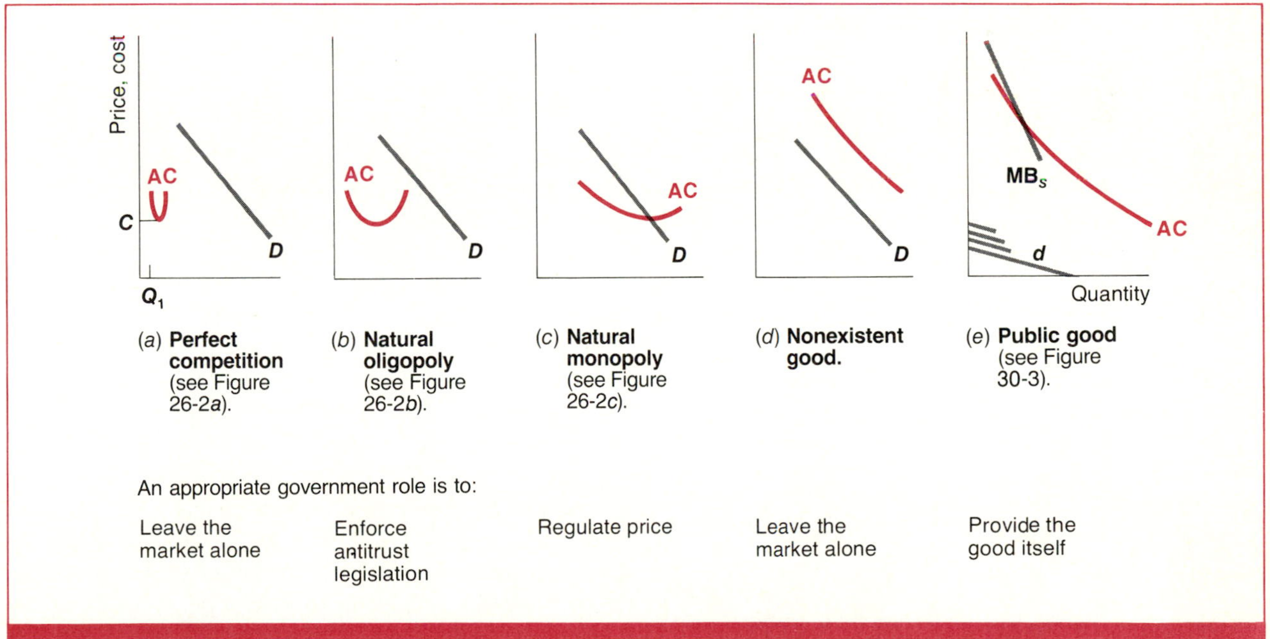

justification for its production.[8] The appropriate government policy is "hands off."

Finally, consider panel *e,* which shows a public good. In this case, the good is not produced by private firms; there is no standard market demand *D* (as the horizontal sum of individual demands *d*). However, the marginal social benefit MB_S of this good *does* exist. It is the *vertical* sum of the individual demand curves. If the MB_S curve overlaps the AC curve, it is in the public interest for the government to provide this good.

We conclude by noting that, in some cases, government intervention in the marketplace is not justified. But in other circumstances, when there is private market failure, a case can be made for such intervention. However, a word of warning is in order. Even in cases of private market failure, it should not be assumed that government intervention is a simple, fool-proof solution; it may also fail. Recall, for example, our earlier discussion in this chapter of the difficulties that arise in bureaucratic decision making, and the problems the government encounters in reversing a bad decision or in controlling its costs. Just because government intervention *could* increase efficiency, doesn't mean that it necessarily *will*; the government may improve things, or it may make them worse.

Now that we have completed our discussion of public goods, where the strongest case can be made for government intervention, we will turn in the next chapter to international trade, in which the case for government intervention is far weaker. In fact, economists have historically been extremely critical of government interference in this area.

KEY POINTS

1. If a good provides an external benefit, a perfectly competitive market will provide less than the efficient quantity of output. The government can induce the expansion of output to the efficient quantity by subsidizing buyers of this good by the amount of the external benefit. This "internalizes the externality" because buyers then personally enjoy not only the benefit the good provides to themselves, but also an amount equal to the benefit it provides to others.
2. No individual farmer would consider building a flood-control dam, because of its high cost and because the benefits he himself would receive would be trivial compared with the benefits that would go to thousands of neighboring farmers. This, then, is the general idea of a public good: It is a good that will not be produced by the private market; if it is to exist at all, it must be produced by the government.
3. A more precise and narrow definition is that a public good is one that can be enjoyed by everyone, regardless of who pays for it. For example, once a flood-control dam has been built, no one can be excluded from enjoying its flood-control services.
4. Building such a dam will be justified if its cost is less than the sum of its benefits to all the public.
5. In practice, there may be major problems in evaluating these benefits. Even if people have a clear idea in their own minds of what the benefits would be, they are unlikely to tell any government official (or, for that matter, any private entrepreneur). Therefore the alternative approach of benefit-cost analysis is often used. For example, the benefit of flood control is estimated by looking at past records of how often floods have occurred and the damage they have done to crops. But it still remains extraordinarily difficult to estimate some of the benefits, such as saving human lives.
6. When the government provides goods and services to the economy, a number of problems arise that are typically not encountered by private firms. For example, it is more difficult for the government to reverse an error; politicians fear losing votes if they admit mistakes.
7. When the public buys privately produced goods, producers have a clearcut indication that this is what the public wants. But when the public votes for a candidate who has promised to, say, build a dam, it's not clear whether the public wants the dam or not. It may have voted for the candidate for foreign policy or other reasons.
8. Politicians often make economic decisions not so

[8]An exception occurs in the case of the discriminating monopolist. If the gap between *D* and AC is small enough, a discriminating monopolist such as the doctor in Figure 25-8 may be able to cover her costs if she is able to charge different prices to different buyers. In this special case, the product does appear on the market, and its production can be justified by the benefits it provides to the public that would otherwise have to do without.

much in the interests of the general public as in the interests of their specific constituency (or some special interest group within that constituency). Moreover, they tend to favor policies with a payoff that is obvious and will be realized quickly—in particular, before the next election.

9. There is a natural tendency for a bureau and its budget to expand. One reason is that a bureau is typically not under the same cost-cutting pressures as a private firm which must sell its output on a competitive market.

10. There are two important ways to protect the environment. When it is being damaged by, say, polluting firms, the proper approach is to impose a tax or issue marketable emission permits (as described in Chapter 28). But when the environment is deteriorating of its own accord—for example, if a wildlife species is becoming extinct—the preservation of the environment may be viewed as a public good. Thus, government protection of the environment is justified if the costs of this protection are less than the benefits it provides to all individuals in society.

KEY CONCEPTS

external benefit
how a subsidy affects efficiency
internalizing an external benefit
public good
marginal social benefit for a private good and for a public good
free rider problem
benefit-cost analysis
private versus public decisions
difficulty in reversing public expenditures
special interest group
why government bureaucracies tend to expand
the environment as a public good
option demand

PROBLEMS

30-1. (*a*) In panel *c* of Figure 30-3, draw a horizontal marginal cost curve at a height just above the top of bar a_2. Now show the number of units of this public good that the government should provide. For example, how many dams should the government build in a flood-control network?

(*b*) In panel *e* of Figure 30-4, extend MB_S downward and to the right. Also extend curve AC to the right until it reaches a minimum, and then draw in the corresponding MC curve. How many units of this good should the government provide?

30-2. If a freeway is to be built into a city, discuss the benefits and costs that you think should be estimated. Explain why preparing such an estimate might be a difficult task.

30-3. Do you think national defense is a public good? Why? Would estimating its benefits be difficult? Why?

30-4. Suppose you are working for a government in the tropics and a proposal is being considered to spray a wide area of territory for malarial mosquitoes. A critic states that, if such an expenditure were justified, a private entrepreneur would already have seized this opportunity. What position would you take?

30-5. Equilibrium E_1 in Figure 30-1 is inefficient. Which, if any, of the efficiency conditions in Box 24-1 is violated?

30-6. Suppose the only three individuals who would benefit from a public good have the demand (marginal benefit) schedules shown on the next page. Assume also that each unit of this good involves a production cost of C and an external cost of K. Should this good be produced? If so, at what quantity of output? (Note: This problem is based on both Chapters 28 and 30.)

30-7. Suppose that, instead of the per-unit subsidy to the *buyer* equal to the arrow in Figure 30-1, the government provides exactly the same subsidy to the *seller*. Show the effect. Does this subsidy increase output to the efficient quantity? How does this policy compare with the policy of subsidizing the buyer?

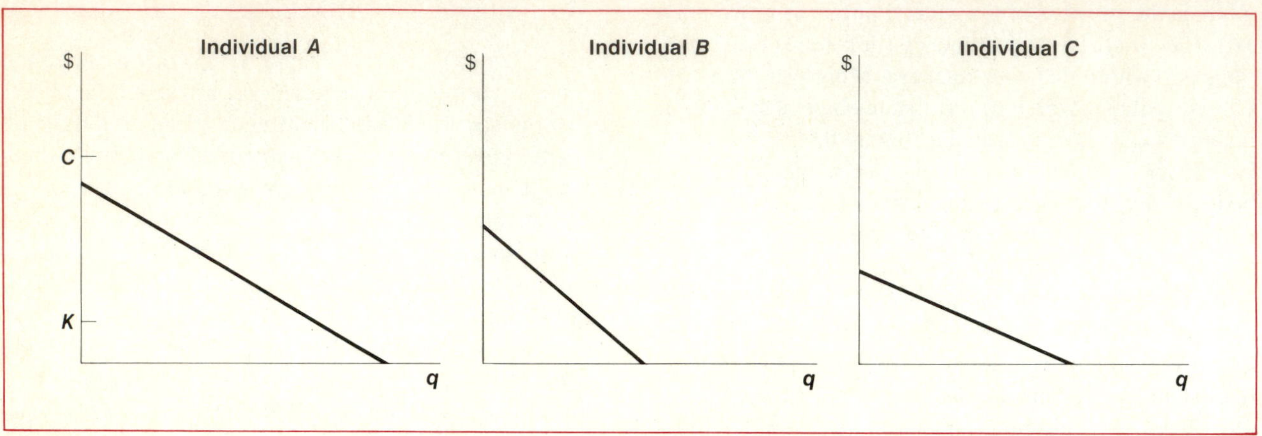
Individual A
Individual B
Individual C
$
C
K
q

CHAPTER 31

WHAT ARE THE GAINS FROM INTERNATIONAL TRADE?

Instructed ships shall sail to quick commerce
By which remotest regions are allied
Which makes one city of the universe
Where some may gain and all may be supplied.

JOHN DRYDEN (1631–1700)

Economic gains come from specialization. One of the reasons for the high material standard of living in the United States is our high degree of specialization. Steel is produced near the coal fields of Pennsylvania, wheat is produced in the western states, and citrus fruits are grown in California and Florida. By such specialization, we are able to increase our total output of goods.

Just as specialization within the United States increases output and efficiency, so too does specialization among the United States and other countries. Specifically, international trade and specialization between the United States and other countries bring the same benefits as domestic specialization, first noted in Chapter 3: namely, the gains from comparative advantage and economies of scale. International trade also exposes domestic producers to increased competition and thus reduces their market power. Because of international trade, we are not only able to buy inexpensive foreign goods. We also can get goods more cheaply from domestic producers who must keep their prices down in order to meet foreign competition.

The major objective of this chapter will be to consider in detail each of these benefits from trade. But before doing so, we ask two questions:

WITH WHOM DO WE TRADE? WHAT DO WE TRADE?

The first column of Table 31-1 shows that Canada and Japan are the two most important U.S. trading partners, by a wide margin. One reason Canada ranks first is that distance and transport costs—natural deterrents to trade—are at a minimum in U.S. trade with Canada.[1] Canada and Japan are followed by Mexico and the three largest countries in the European Economic Community.

The right-hand side of the table indicates that we trade a wide variety of goods. Our exports include such diverse items as grain from Iowa and aircraft from Seattle. Our imports include both primary materials essential to American industry and highly manufactured goods. For a nation on wheels, autos and oil account for an

[1]Many Americans don't realize the importance of trade with Canada. The reason is that U.S. purchases from Canada include raw materials (base metals) and manufactured goods (telecommunications equipment) that are less familiar to the U.S. public than the consumer goods (watches, cars, and radios) that Americans buy from Japan. (Also, the cars that are bought from Canada are built by GM, Ford, and Chrysler, and are virtually indistinguishable from similar U.S.-built cars.)

important part of our trade, although oil no longer plays such a dominant role in U.S. imports; between 1980 and 1984, oil and its products fell from 32% to 17% of U.S. imports.

This, then, describes *what* and *with whom* we trade. Now let us return to the advantages we reap from trade. We consider three basic sources of gain: (1) increased competition, (2) economies of scale, and (3) comparative advantage.

MARKETS BECOME MORE COMPETITIVE, AND HENCE MORE EFFICIENT

Consider the monopoly firm illustrated in Figure 31-1. Initially, without international trade, this firm has the U.S. market all to itself in panel *a*. If it is not subject to government regulation, it will be able to set a monopoly price. In panel *b*, we see what happens when trade is opened up. The potential demand facing the American producer is much larger, as shown by the total world demand curve. Therefore, the American firm is now able to go after foreign markets as well as the domestic market. However, it is no longer able to take the U.S. market for granted, since it faces stiff competition here from foreign producers. Thus, foreign trade can transform a natural monopoly in the domestic market in panel *a* into a natural oligopoly in the world market in panel *b*. In the process, this firm's monopoly control of the U.S. market is broken, and its ability to exercise market power (charge a high price) is reduced. As shown earlier, a lower more competitive price results in an improved allocation of resources, with a corresponding efficiency gain.

On the other hand, if the industry is originally a natural oligopoly, international trade can make it substantially more competitive. To illustrate, consider the U.S. firm in Figure 31-2 that, before trade, has about one-third of the domestic U.S. market. After trade is opened up in panel *b*, this firm will have a much smaller fraction of the market because the market is now the

TABLE 31-1
U.S. Merchandise Trade in 1980
(billions of dollars)

With whom do we trade?		What do we trade?	
Exports: U.S. sales to:		Exports	
Canada	$ 46.5	Food and live animals	$ 24.5
Japan	23.6	Crude materials, inedible (except fuels)	20.2
U.K.	12.2	Mineral fuels (including petroleum)	9.3
Mexico	12.0	Chemicals	22.3
West Germany	9.1	Machinery	60.3
France	6.0	Motor vehicles and parts	17.5
Asia (except Japan)	40.9	Other transport equipment	12.1
Latin America (except Mexico)	14.3	All other	45.9
Other countries	47.5	Total	$212.1
Total	$212.1		
Imports: U.S. purchases from:		Imports	
Canada	$ 66.5	Food and live animals	$ 18.0
Japan	57.1	Crude materials, inedible (except fuels)	11.1
Mexico	18.0	Mineral fuels (including petroleum and products)	61.0
West Germany	17.0	Chemicals	13.7
U.K.	14.5	Machinery	68.4
France	8.1	Motor vehicles and parts	45.4
Asia (except Japan)	63.0	Other transport equipment	5.4
Latin America (except Mexico)	24.3	All other	102.7
Other countries	57.2	Total	$325.7
Total	$325.7		

Source: U.S. Department of Commerce, *Survey of Current Business,* March 1985, pp. 16, 17.

whole world. Again, increased competition will tend to keep price down, with U.S. consumers benefitting. Furthermore, they gain in other ways as well if the domestic producer is forced to compete in nonprice aspects, such as quality or design. Thus, the U.S. automobile industry has been pressured into producing smaller cars as a result of foreign competition.

ECONOMIES OF SCALE

In the face of economies of scale and falling average costs, there are two additional gains from trade:

New Products Become Available

Specifically, international trade may make it profitable to produce goods which otherwise would not be produced at all. Panel *a* in Figure 31-3 illustrates such a product. Demand is too low in the domestic economy for this good to be profitably produced. But when the foreign market becomes available, demand becomes large enough to cover average costs (the rightward shift in *D* makes it now overlap AC) and the item is introduced. An example is Boeing, which in 1980 exported about half its output. Without exports, Boeing would have had difficulty in covering the enormous design and tooling costs of its 747 jumbo jet; at the very least, the jet's introduction would have been delayed. Perhaps it would not have been produced at all.

Existing Goods Can Be Produced More Efficiently

Where there are economies of scale, trade results not only in the introduction of new products but also in the more efficient production of old products. For example, European producers have been able to manufacture automobiles at larger volume and lower cost since the establishment of the European Economic Community. Because tariff barriers have been eliminated within the EEC, a manufacturer in any member country can sell freely to buyers in all member countries.

FIGURE 31-1
How international trade breaks down monopoly power

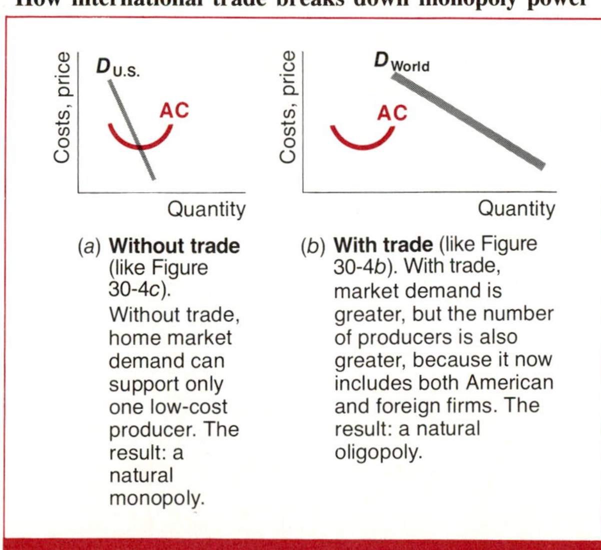

(*a*) **Without trade** (like Figure 30-4*c*). Without trade, home market demand can support only one low-cost producer. The result: a natural monopoly.

(*b*) **With trade** (like Figure 30-4*b*). With trade, market demand is greater, but the number of producers is also greater, because it now includes both American and foreign firms. The result: a natural oligopoly.

FIGURE 31-2
How international trade makes an oligopoly more competitive

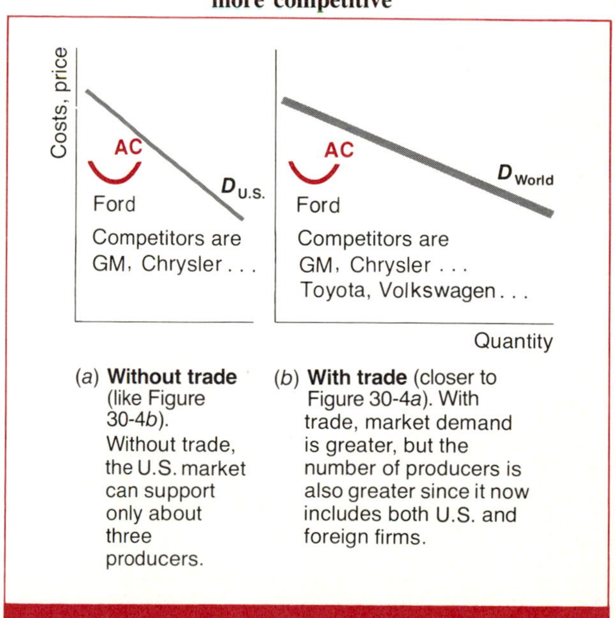

(*a*) **Without trade** (like Figure 30-4*b*). Without trade, the U.S. market can support only about three producers.

(*b*) **With trade** (closer to Figure 30-4*a*). With trade, market demand is greater, but the number of producers is also greater since it now includes both U.S. and foreign firms.

COMPARATIVE ADVANTAGE

Now suppose that there are no economies of scale; instead, suppose costs are constant. (The average cost curve is horizontal.) The theory of comparative advantage tells us that even in these circumstances, gains can be realized from international trade.

The basic idea of comparative advantage has already been introduced in Chapter 3. Even though the lawyer cited there may be more skillful (that is, may have an absolute advantage) in both law and gardening, she does not do her own gardening. Instead, she concentrates on law, the activity in which she has a comparative advantage. By specializing in this way, she can acquire more gardening service than if she were to take the time to do it herself.

Internationally, the idea is exactly the same: Even though the United States may be better—that is, have an absolute advantage—in producing both aircraft and radios, it may be in our interest to concentrate on aircraft and other products in which we have a comparative advantage, and leave radios to other countries. By specializing in aircraft, we may be able to acquire more radios through trade than we could produce ourselves.

The idea of comparative advantage was developed in the early nineteenth century by David Ricardo, an English economist, financier, and member of Parliament. In his simplified illustration of this idea, Ricardo assumed that markets were perfectly competitive, that there were no transport costs, that all production costs were constant, and that the only input was labor. He also assumed that there were only two countries (we shall call them America and Europe) producing two goods (we shall call them food and clothing).

Absolute Advantage

As a preliminary, Table 31-2 shows the case where each country has an *absolute advantage* in the production of one good. In the first column, we see that a clothing worker in Europe can outproduce a worker in America (4 to 3), so Europe has an absolute advantage in clothing. Similarly, in the second column we see that America has an absolute advantage in food, since an American worker can outproduce a European worker (2 to 1). The most efficient allocation of resources is to have America specialize in food and Europe in clothing, as the calculations at the bottom of Table 31-2 confirm.

So far, it seems that each country specializes in the good in which it has an absolute advantage. But this is

FIGURE 31-3

How international trade may create new products

The AC curves in these two figures are identical. But because of trade, the demand curve in part *b* is much farther to the right.

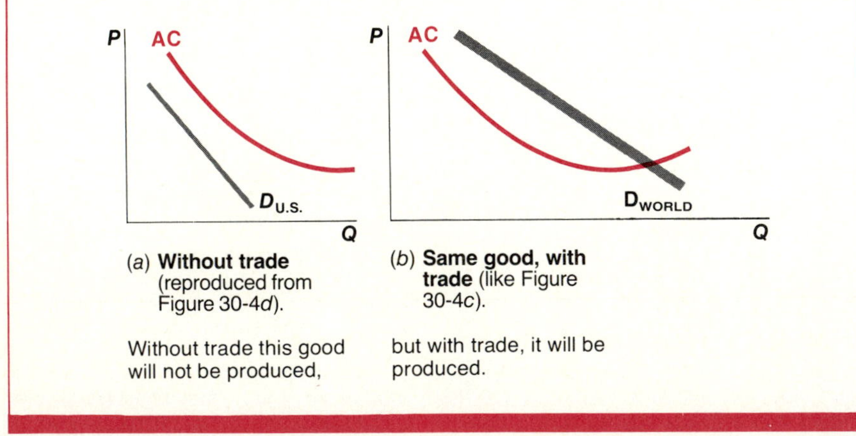
P
AC
$D_{U.S.}$
Q
P
AC
D_{WORLD}
Q
(*a*) **Without trade** (reproduced from Figure 30-4*d*).
Without trade this good will not be produced,
(*b*) **Same good, with trade** (like Figure 30-4*c*).
but with trade, it will be produced.

not always so. We shall now show that the key to specialization is *comparative advantage* rather than absolute advantage.

Comparative Advantage

Table 31-3 illustrates the more difficult case where one country, America (like the lawyer in Chapter 3), has an absolute advantage in the production of both goods: An American worker outproduces a European worker in both clothing (6 to 4) and food (3 to 1). Nonetheless, America—like the lawyer of Chapter 3—will not try to satisfy its requirements by producing both goods itself. Instead, it will specialize in one and buy the other from Europe, as we shall now explain.

Our first step is to calculate the opportunity cost of food in each country. First, in Europe: The second row of Table 31-3 tells us that a European worker who is now producing one unit of food could, instead, be producing four units of clothing. In other words, in Europe *the opportunity cost of one unit of food is four units of clothing*. Since prices reflect costs in a perfectly competitive economy, we would expect these two goods to exchange in Europe for the same 1:4 ratio; that is, in the absence of international trade, one unit of food will exchange in Europe for four units of clothing.

On the other hand, what is the opportunity cost of food in America? The first row of Table 31-3 tells us that an American worker who is producing three units of food could instead be producing six units of clothing. In other words, in America the opportunity cost of a unit of food is 6/3 = 2 units of clothing. Consequently, the two goods would exchange in America at this 1:2 ratio; that is, before trade, one unit of food will exchange in America for two units of clothing.

Since the opportunity cost of food in America is less (two units of clothing versus four in Europe), we say that America has a ***comparative advantage*** in food. By definition:

A country has a *comparative advantage* in the good that it can produce relatively cheaply, that is, at lower opportunity cost than its trading partner.

A similar set of calculations, again using the figures in Table 31-3, shows that in clothing, Europe has a lower opportunity cost and hence a comparative advantage.[2]

With this concept of comparative advantage in hand, we shall now see how both countries will benefit if they specialize in their product of comparative advantage and trade for the other—at any price ratio between the 1:2 price ratio which would prevail in an isolated America and the 1:4 in Europe. Suppose this price ratio—often called the "terms of trade"—is 1:3; that is, one unit of food exchanges internationally for three units of clothing. The determination of this price ratio depends not only on the cost conditions that we have been describing, but also on demand in these two countries. For example, the more strongly Europeans demand food—the U.S. export good—the higher the price of food will be.

Faced with an international price ratio of 1:3 (one unit of food exchanging for three units of clothing), let's first show how America can benefit by specializing in its product of comparative advantage, food, and trading to satisfy its clothing needs. Specifically, for each American worker taken out of clothing production, America loses six units of clothing. However, that worker instead now produces three units of food, which can then be traded (at the 1:3 international price ratio) for nine units of clothing—for a clear gain of three units of clothing.

Similarly, Europe also gains by specializing in its product of comparative advantage—clothing—and trading it for food. In switching a worker from food to clothing production, Europe loses one unit of food. But that worker produces four units of clothing instead; and this output can be traded (at the 1:3 international price ratio) for 4/3 = 1⅓ units of food—for a gain of 1/3 units of food.

To sum up this example, both countries gain from trade. America benefits by specializing in food (its comparative advantage) and trading for clothing. At the same time Europe benefits by specializing in clothing (its comparative advantage) and trading for food. The reason that

[2]In Europe the opportunity cost of clothing is 1/4 of a unit of food; that is, 1/4 of a unit of food must be given up to acquire 1 unit of clothing. Similarly, in America the opportunity cost of clothing is 3/6 = 1/2 unit of food. With its lower opportunity cost of clothing, Europe has a comparative advantage in clothing. Notice in this simple two-country, two-good example, that if America has a comparative advantage in one good (food), Europe *must* have a comparative advantage in the other (clothing).

there are gains from trade is that the cost ratios in the two rows of Table 31-3 (namely, 6/3 and 4/1) are different. If these ratios (that is, opportunity costs) were the same, there would be no comparative advantage and no gain from trade.

The gain to the United States from trade may be illustrated in another way. Figure 31-4 shows the American production possibilities curve (PPC), derived from the U.S. figures in the first row of Table 31-3, assuming that there are 200 million workers in America. For example, if they all work at producing clothing, each of the 200 million workers will produce six units, for a total of 1,200 million units of clothing, as shown at point *A*. Or, if they all work at producing food (three units each) they will produce 600 million units of food and no clothing at point *C*. Finally, if half the workers produce food and half clothing, the 100 million workers in clothing will produce 600 million units (six units each) while the other 100 million workers in food will produce 300 million units at point *B*. In this simple Ricardian example, the constant figures in the first row of Table 31-3 ensure that the production possibilities curve *AC* is a straight line: The opportunity cost of food in America remains constant as we move down this curve: No matter how much food we may be producing, we must give up two units of clothing in order to produce one more unit of food.

Before trade, America will produce and consume at a point on the production possibilities curve, such as *B*. With trade, America can benefit by the following two steps:

1. *Specialize*. Shift production from *B* to *C*, as shown by the red arrow in Figure 31-4; that is, produce 300 million more units of food by giving up 600 million units of clothing. Thus America concentrates on food, the good in which it has a comparative advantage.

TABLE 31-2
Illustration of Absolute Advantage
Hypothetical Output per Worker in Europe and America

	Clothing	Food
America	3 units	2 units
Europe	4 units	1 unit

In the first column, Europe has an absolute advantage in clothing production because a worker can produce 4 units compared with only 3 in America. In the second column, America has an absolute advantage in food, because a worker here can produce 2 units, compared with only 1 in Europe. Both countries together can produce more total output when America specializes in food and Europe specializes in clothing.

To confirm, suppose specialization has not occurred; in other words, suppose that each country is initially producing both goods. Now suppose that they begin to specialize—America in food, Europe in clothing. Therefore, a worker in America is switched out of clothing and into food production. At the same time, a worker in Europe is switched in the opposite direction (out of food and into clothing). As a result of these two switches:

	Clothing output changes by	Food output changes by
In America	−3	+2
In Europe	+4	−1
Therefore, net world output changes by	+1	+1

TABLE 31-3
Illustration of Comparative Advantage
Hypothetical Output per Worker in Europe and America

	Clothing	Food
America	6 units	3 units
Europe	4 units	1 unit

In the bottom row, one European worker can produce either 4 units of clothing or 1 unit of food. Thus, the opportunity cost of 1 unit of food in Europe is 4 units of clothing. In the row above, an American worker can produce either 6 units of clothing or 3 of food. The opportunity cost of food in America is therefore 6/3 = 2 units of clothing. [Notice how we calculate this opportunity cost by taking the ratio of the figures in the American row, just as we calculated the European cost (4/1) from the figures in the European row.] Since the opportunity cost of food in America is less than in Europe, America has a comparative advantage in food and specializes in this good.

To confirm that this specialization will increase total world output, again suppose that each country is initially producing both goods. Now suppose they begin to specialize: America switches one worker out of clothing and into food, and Europe switches two workers out of food and into clothing. Then:

	Clothing output changes by	Food output changes by
In America	−6	+3
In Europe	+8	−2
Therefore, net world output changes by	+2	+1

BOX 31-1

WAGES AND TRADE

In the example we have been describing on the preceding page, an important question arises: Will wages be higher in America or Europe? The answer is: In America, because labor is more productive here. (Remember, in Table 31-3 America has an absolute advantage in the production of both goods.) Because they can *produce* more goods, American workers can be *paid* "more goods," that is, a higher real wage. Moreover, Americans will have a higher real income whether or not the two countries trade. What trade and specialization make possible is an increase in real income in both countries.

FIGURE 31-4

Gains from trade

America's production possibilities curve *AC* is derived from the first row in Table 31-3 on the assumption that there are 200 million workers in America. Suppose that, without trade, America produces and consumes at point *B*. When trade is opened, America can (1) *specialize* in food by shifting production from *B* to *C* and (2) *trade* 300 million units of food for 900 million units of clothing at the prevailing 1:3 international price ratio. Thus America can move from *C* to *D*. The American gain from trade is the increase in clothing consumption from the original 600 million units at point *B* to the 900 million units at point *D*.

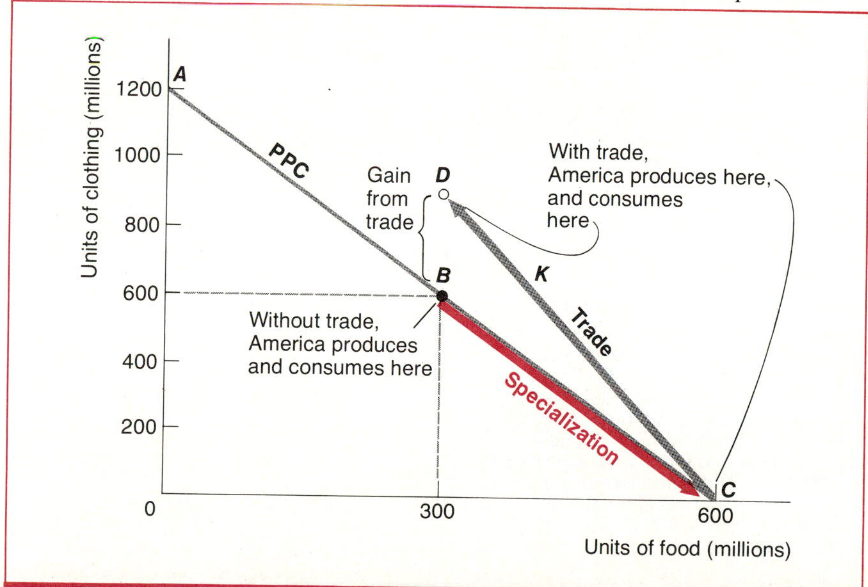

2. *Trade*. Trade these 300 million additional units of food at the 1:3 international price ratio for 900 million units of clothing. This second step is shown by the gray arrow.

As a result of this specialization and trade, America's consumption can rise from point *B* to point *D*. In other words, there are 300 million more units of clothing available for consumption. This is America's *real income gain*—or efficiency gain—from trade.

In panel *a* of Figure 31-5, we show that such a gain from trade exists even when opportunity costs are not constant, that is, in the more usual case when the production possibilities curve is not a straight line. This diagram also shows that, although trade induces a country to specialize, it will often not specialize completely. America moves from *B* to *C*, but not all the way to complete specialization at *F*. One frequently observes this pattern: A country not only specializes in and exports its product of comparative advantage—in this case, food. It also produces other goods as well—in this example, it produces *some* clothing at point *C*. (For details on why

FIGURE 31-5
Both trade and technological change allow us to increase consumption

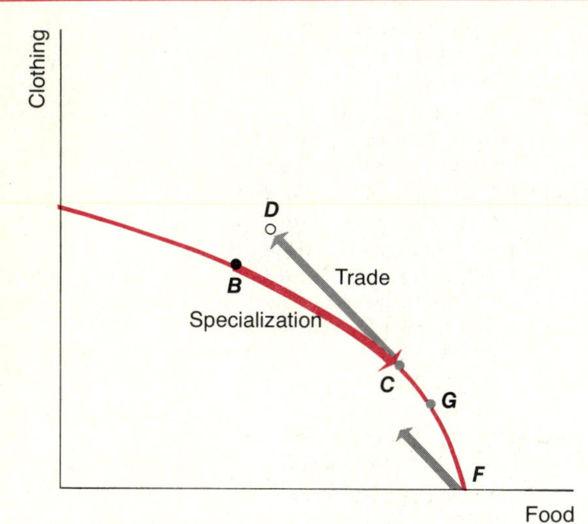

(*a*) **International trade.** Specialization and trade allow us to increase our consumption from ***B*** to ***D***. Note that the production possibilities curve does not shift. We just move to a different point ***C*** on this curve as we specialize in the production of food. Then, by exporting food and importing clothing, we reach consumption point ***D*** beyond the production possibilities curve. (Why don't we specialize completely, by moving from ***B*** not just to ***C***, but all the way to ***F***? The answer is that we would then be trading along the arrow at ***F***, and this doesn't allow us to reach the high consumption point ***D*** that is achievable by specializing to ***C*** and trading along the higher arrow. For exactly the same reason that ***F*** is inferior to ***C***, *any* other point on the production possibilities curve is also inferior to ***C***. Therefore tangency point ***C*** is best.)

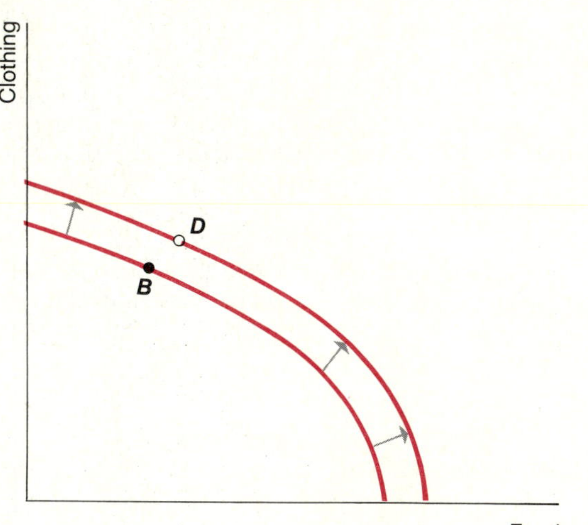

(*b*) **Technological change.** Technological change shifts the production possibilities curve outward, so that production and consumption may be increased from ***B*** to ***D***. (Similar to Figure 2-3.)

such a country will not specialize completely, see the caption to this diagram.)[3]

Comparative advantage thus leads to gains from trade. But why does comparative advantage exist? Why does America have a comparative advantage in wheat? One important reason is our large endowment of highly productive land, especially in the midwest. Similarly, the reason that Saudi Arabia specializes in oil is its huge endowment of this resource. On the other hand, a country like India, with its huge pool of unskilled labor, tends to have a comparative advantage in activities that require a great deal of labor. Comparative advantage depends not only on such resource endowments but also on skills and technology. For example, our highly developed technology gives us a comparative advantage in producing items such as computers and large airliners.

TRADE AND TECHNOLOGICAL CHANGE: THEIR SIMILARITIES

Panel *a* of Figure 31-5 shows how trade allows a country to consume at a point, such as *D*, that is beyond its production possibilities curve (PPC). True, *production* is always limited by a country's PPC, but consumption can be greater because of the gain from trade. In other words, international trade is the way for countries to break out of their production limitation and reach a point of consumption beyond it.

In panel *b* we see that technological change has the same effect of allowing us to move from point *B* to a higher point of consumption *D*. But it does so by shifting the production possibilities curve outward.

Trade and technological change are also alike in another significant respect: Though they generally provide a benefit to the nation as a whole, they do not necessarily benefit *every* group within the nation. Thus, there are often groups that object vehemently to trade or to technological change. For example, during the first period of rapid technological change in the textile industry about two centuries ago, workers feared that the new machinery being introduced would eliminate their jobs. (Some workers did indeed lose their jobs, even though machinery has ultimately made possible jobs with much higher productivity and pay.) This fear of job loss led some workers at that time to throw their wooden shoes—in French, *sabots*—into the machinery; hence, the word *sabotage* was coined. Similarly, international trade may displace textile workers if production is shifted from textiles—where some markets have been lost to imports—to computers or large aircraft, where we have a comparative advantage and export. Once again, those who are harmed may strongly object. In this case, they need not throw their shoes into the machinery; restrictions on imports are the way to seek protection. Note that trade restrictions and sabotage are similar in one respect: Both prevent a general improvement in the standard of living in order to protect a specific group.

The temporary unemployment that follows either trade or technological change is a problem but one that is frequently exaggerated. Workers displaced by technological change tend to be fairly quickly absorbed elsewhere, as are workers displaced by imports. For example, this was true in Europe, when the Common Market (the European Economic Community) opened up trade among countries on a very large scale and temporary unemployment was less than expected. It has also been historically true in the United States, although an exception occurred in the period 1981–1985, when imports increased dramatically because they were such a bargain. (Foreign goods were inexpensive because foreign currencies were so cheap.)

While there are striking similarities between trade and technological change, there is an important difference. Technological change is permanent: Once the production possibilities curve shifts outward in panel *b* of

*[3]Figure 31-5*a* can also be used to show how demand too influences specialization and trade. (In this elementary treatment we have emphasized the other side of the coin: the importance of costs, as reflected in the production possibilities curve. But demand is important too.) Suppose there is an increase in both countries in the demand for food; as a consequence its price rises. Therefore, less food is needed to buy a given quantity of clothing. In other words, the trade arrow becomes steeper. Consequently it is no longer tangent to the production possibilities curve at point *C*, but is instead tangent at a point to the right, say *G*. *G* is therefore the best production point for this country. (The reason the point of tangency is best is given in the caption to Figure 31-5*a*.) Thus this country specializes even more, by moving from *B* not just to *C* but to *G*. (And, of course, from point *G*, it trades up to the northwest along its new, steeper trade arrow.) To sum up: In response to increased demand, this country's production pattern changes; by producing even more food, it specializes to an even greater degree than before.

Figure 31-5, it doesn't shift back. In contrast, a trade gain is not necessarily permanent. If trade is sharply reduced—for example, because of the imposition of high tariffs—most of the gains from trade are lost; that is, the country in panel *a* moves from *D* back toward point *B*.

THE VARIOUS EFFECTS OF INTERNATIONAL TRADE ON EFFICIENCY

While this analysis illustrates the general case for trade, it is somewhat abstract since it lumps all American exports into a single food category and all imports into a single clothing category. Moreover, the only prices that exist are relative barterlike prices; for example, the price of one unit of food is three units of clothing. Now, let us return to the more familiar world of supply and demand, where goods are sold for dollars. For example, the price of a bushel of wheat may be $4.20. Here, we shall no longer think in abstract terms of only two goods—a collective export (food) and a collective import (clothing). Instead, we examine one specific American export item (wheat) and one specific U.S. import item (woolens). In this more familiar frame of reference, we shall illustrate how trade increases efficiency.

Efficiency Gain on a Typical Export: Wheat

Figure 31-6 shows the U.S. demand and supply curves for wheat. Without trade, equilibrium in the domestic market is at point *A*, where the nation's supply and demand intersect. Thus Q_A is produced at price P_A. At the same time, the price in the rest of the world is at the higher level *P*, reflecting the higher costs of producing wheat in foreign countries.

When trade is opened, U.S. producers discover that they can sell abroad at this higher price *P*, and they begin to do so. Moreover, since they can sell at *P* abroad, they are unwilling to sell at any lower price in the home market. Thus the domestic price rises to the world level *P*.[4]

American producers, earning this more attractive price, expand their output. Specifically, they move up their supply curve from *A* to *C*, increasing their output from Q_A to Q_2. But, of course, consumers view this higher price quite differently. They move up their demand curve from *A* to *B*, thus reducing their consumption from Q_A to Q_1. In short, Q_2 is now produced and Q_1 is consumed, with the difference (Q_1Q_2) being exported. Thus, these U.S. exports come partly from increased production and partly from reduced domestic consumption. We now examine each of these effects in turn.

First consider one of the units of reduced consumption Q_1Q_A, say unit *e*. The consumer's benefit from this lost unit of consumption is shown as the hollow bar under the demand curve. (Recall that demand reflects marginal benefit.) But the gain from exporting this unit is the export price *P* that is received for it, as shown by the hollow bar plus the solid bar above. Hence, the net gain from exporting it, rather than consuming it, is the solid bar. The sum of all such solid bars throughout the relevant range Q_1Q_A is the gray triangle 3. This is the gain from switching goods from consumption to a more highly valued use, namely, export.

Next consider one of the units of increased production for export Q_AQ_2, say unit *f*. The cost of producing it is the hollow bar under the supply curve. (Recall that supply reflects marginal cost.) But the benefit from producing it is the export price *P* received for it, which is the hollow bar plus the solid bar. Therefore the net gain from producing it for export is the solid bar. The sum of all such solid bars through the relevant range Q_AQ_2 is represented by the gray triangle 4. This is the efficiency gain from expanding production for export.

The total gain from exporting is shown as the sum of both these effects; in other words, the total gray area in Figure 31-6. In simple terms, this gain indicates that wheat can be sold to foreigners for more than it costs to produce it, or more than is lost by switching it away from domestic consumption.

Of course, this gray area will represent an efficiency *loss* if producers are *not* allowed to export. It demonstrates that interference in a competitive world market may be damaging, in the same way that we have seen that interference in a competitive home market may be damaging.

---

[4]More realistically, the American price rises to the foreign price, less transportation costs. However, to keep this illustration simple, we assume that transport costs and other similar complications do not exist.

Efficiency Gain on a Typical Import: Woolens

A parallel analysis illustrates the gain from importing a specific item. Figure 31-7 shows the U.S. supply and demand curves for an import-competing product like woolens. Without trade, equilibrium in the domestic market is at point *A*, with price P_A and quantity Q_A produced and consumed. At the same time, the price in the rest of the world is at the lower level *P*, reflecting the lower costs of production there.

When trade is opened, U.S. consumers can buy imported woolens at this lower price *P*. Since they are unwilling to buy from American producers at higher price P_A, the domestic price falls to the world level *P*. At this lower price, U.S. consumers increase their purchases; they move down their demand curve from *A* to *J*, increasing their consumption from Q_A to Q_6. At the same time, domestic producers respond to lower price *P* by moving down their supply curve from *A* to *H*, thus reducing their output from Q_A to Q_5. In short, Q_5 is now produced in the United States, while Q_6 is consumed; the difference (Q_5Q_6) is the amount imported. Thus, U.S. imports result both in decreased production and increased consumption.

FIGURE 31-6

Detailed effects of the export of an individual good: Wheat

With trade, price increases from P_A to *P* with Q_1Q_2 exported. In part, these exports come from reduced consumption (Q_1Q_A); the net gain on these units is area 3. The other part of these exports comes from increased production (Q_AQ_2); the net gain on these units is area 4. Thus, the total efficiency gain from exporting is the entire gray area. There is a transfer effect as well, shown by the arrow at the left: Because price has risen, producers gain at consumers' expense.

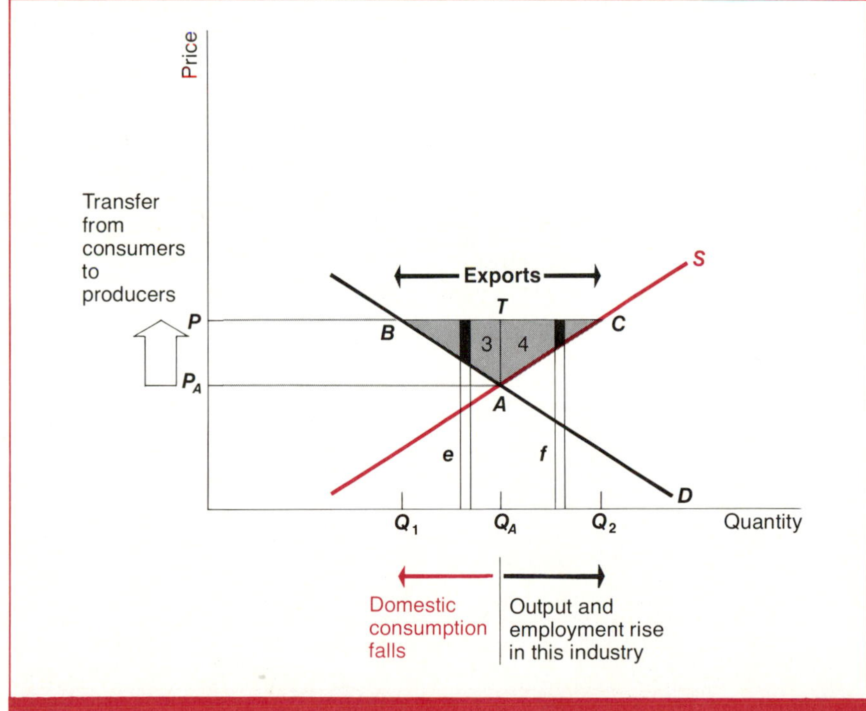

First, consider one of the units of decreased production Q_AQ_5, say unit *j*. The cost of importing it is the price *P* that must be paid for it, shown as the hollow bar. But because it is being imported, we save the cost of producing it ourselves, which is the hollow bar plus the solid bar—that is, its marginal cost as defined under the supply curve. Thus, the net gain from importing it, rather than producing it more expensively at home, is the solid bar. The sum of all such solid bars over the relevant range Q_5Q_A is gray triangle 1. This is the gain from allowing imports to displace relatively inefficient, high-cost domestic production.

Now consider one of the units of increased consumption Q_AQ_6, say unit *k*. Its cost is the import price *P* shown by the hollow bar. However, the consumer values it as the hollow bar plus the solid bar—that is, its marginal benefit defined under the demand curve. Therefore, the net benefit from this unit of increased consumption is the solid bar, and the sum of all such benefits is the gray triangle 2. This is the efficiency gain from allowing consumption to expand in response to a bargain international price.

The total efficiency gain on both accounts is the whole gray area in Figure 31-7. In simplest terms, this

FIGURE 31-7

Detailed effects of the import of an individual good: woolens

With trade, price decreases from P_A to P, with *HJ* imported. This reduces home production by Q_AQ_5; the net gain on these units is area 1. Imports also result in increased consumption of Q_AQ_6; the net gain on these units is area 2. Thus the total efficiency gain from importing this good is the entire gray area. There is also a transfer effect, shown by the arrow at the left: Because price has fallen, consumers gain at producers' expense.

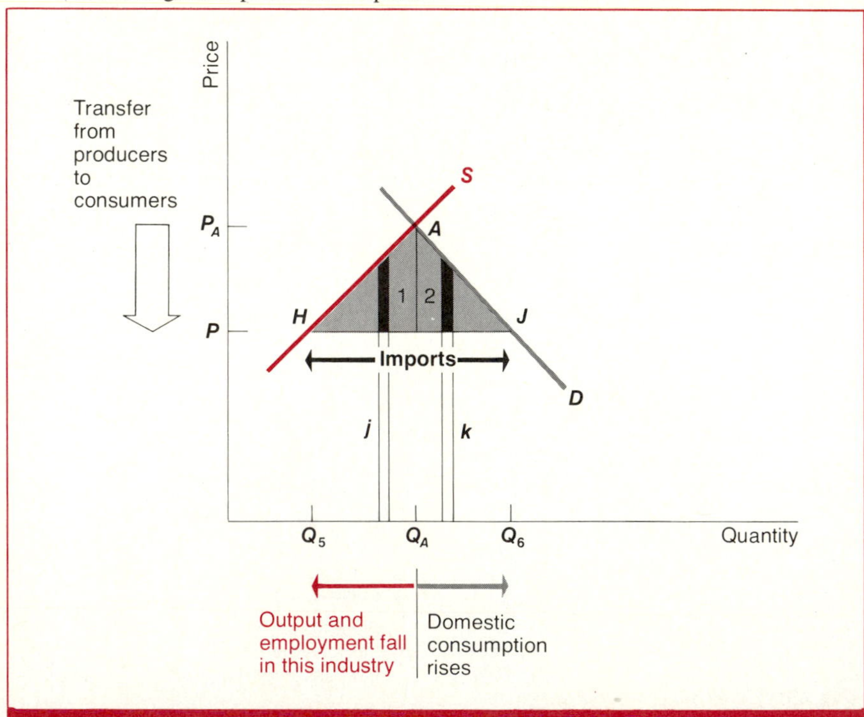

area shows that we can benefit by buying a low-cost import because it allows us to cut back our own inefficient high-cost production and also allows us to increase our consumption of a bargain-priced good.

WINNERS AND LOSERS FROM INTERNATIONAL TRADE

While trade leads to an overall gain in efficiency, it is important to emphasize again that not all groups benefit. For example, in Figure 31-6, trade brings an increase in the price of wheat. As a result, wheat farmers gain while consumers lose. This transfer is shown by the arrow to the left of the diagram. (Note: This is an important graphic device that will be used to show transfers throughout the rest of this book.) On the other hand, the import in Figure 31-7 results in the opposite sort of transfer. Because it lowers price, consumers benefit while producers lose.

These benefits and losses to each group as a result of imports are shown more precisely in the alternative analysis set out in Figure 31-8.[5] Each panel in this diagram reproduces the U.S. supply and demand curves for woolens from Figure 31-7. The gain to the nation's consumers from a lower price is shown by the gray area in panel *a* enclosed to the left of the demand curve. At the same time, producers receive a lower price and lose sales to imports. As a result, producers lose the red area in panel *b* enclosed to the left of the supply curve.[6] Because this area 5 also appears as a gray gain in panel *a*, it is a

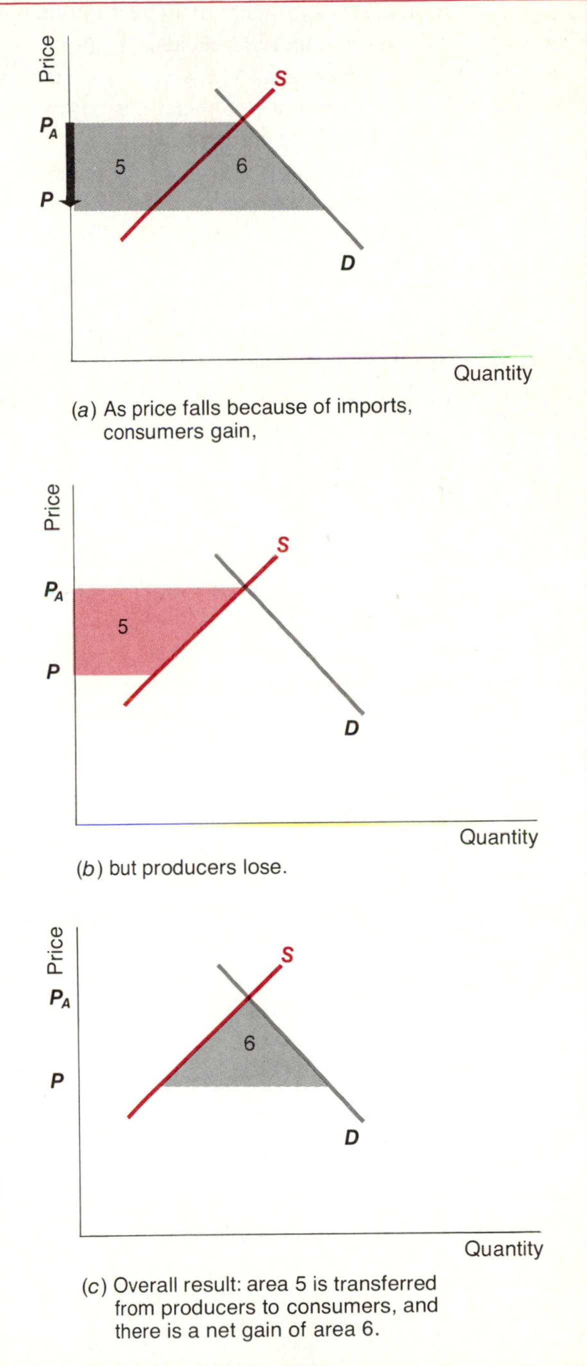

FIGURE 31-8
Detailed effects of an import of woolens (an alternative to Figure 31-7)

[5]*Note to instructors:* To a substantial degree, our analysis of transfer and efficiency effects in the balance of this book will be based on diagrams similar to Figure 31-7. Those who wish to supplement this with diagrams similar to Figure 31-8 will find examples in the Instructor's Resource Guide.

[6]For a review of how consumers are affected by a price change, see Figure 21-5. For a review of how producers are affected, see Figure 23-8.

transfer from the producers who lose it in panel *b* to the consumers who receive it in panel *a*. (This technique of identifying a transfer is important because it can be used on a wide variety of problems; for example, see problem 31-8.) At the same time, area 6 in panel *a* is a gray gain *not* offset by a red loss. This net gain of area 6 is reproduced in panel *c*. This is, of course, exactly the same gray efficiency gain that appeared in the preceding diagram.[7] Finally, in any such analysis, it's important to repeat an earlier warning: In concluding that there will be a net gain, we have assumed that the consumers' valuation of a $1 increase in income is roughly the same as the producers' valuation of a $1 reduction in income—or at least that they are sufficiently similar so that our conclusions are not upset.

As a current example of how imports affect various groups in the United States, consider our imports of textiles from the Far East. The effect on American textile producers is clear. They are damaged because these imports depress the domestic price of textiles and reduce their sales. At the same time, it is clear to American consumers that they benefit from a lower textile price. What is not always clear, however, is the net effect on the nation as a whole. This analysis suggests that the overall effect is favorable, since consumers gain more than producers lose.

Finally, note that while output and employment fall in import-competing industries (Figure 31-7), they rise in export industries (Figure 31-6). When both these effects are taken into account, there is no reason to expect either a large increase or decrease in employment as a result of trade—although unemployment may rise during the adjustment period. We emphasize: The principal point of international trade—like technological change—is *not* to increase employment; it is to increase real income.

KEY POINTS

1. In this chapter, a strong case has been made for international trade; the next chapter will deal with the case for tariffs and other restraints on trade.
2. There are three major sources of benefit from trade: (*a*) greater competition, (*b*) economies of scale, and (*c*) comparative advantage.
3. When trade is opened, countries specialize in certain products, increasing their output of these goods. If there are economies of scale, costs fall as a result of this increase in output.
4. Even if costs do not fall with rising output, trade will be beneficial if countries specialize in the goods in which they have a comparative advantage, that is, in those products in which they are relatively most efficient. We saw this not only in the Ricardian case where cost is constant, but also even in cases such as the one shown in Figure 31-6 where cost (supply) rises as output increases.
5. Because trade lowers the prices of goods we import and raises the prices of goods we export, it hurts some while benefitting others. Consumers of imports benefit, while consumers of exported goods are harmed. To some degree, but not completely, these are the same people, so that this transfer partly cancels out. In addition, producers of exports benefit, while producers of import-competing goods are hurt.
6. International trade is similar in many respects to technological change. Both increase real income by allowing a nation to consume more. Trade allows a country to consume beyond its production possibilities curve, while technological change shifts the production possibilities curve out. Trade and technological change can cause the same sort of short-run unemployment until workers who have lost their jobs shift to new, more productive employment.

KEY CONCEPTS

specialization
increased competition
economies of scale
greater availability of products
absolute advantage
comparative advantage
opportunity cost

[7]The method of Figure 31-8 can also be used to explain Figure 31-6 more fully. Specifically, as price rises in Figure 31-6: (*a*) consumers lose area $PBAP_A$, (*b*) producers gain $PCAP_A$, and thus (*c*) the net effects are a transfer of $PBAP_A$ from consumers to producers and an efficiency gain of *ABC*.

gain from trade
trade compared to technological change
exports: efficiency and transfer effects
imports: efficiency and transfer effects

PROBLEMS

31-1. "Foreign competition makes an industry more competitive." Should this result be viewed as an advantage or a disadvantage by (*a*) consumers of this good? (*b*) producers of the good? (*c*) the nation as a whole?

31-2. Suppose that there are economies of scale in the production of both X and Y. If Europe specializes in one and America in the other, is it possible for both countries to benefit? Explain your answer. Does this answer still hold if the cost curves for each good are identical in the two countries? Hint: Review the discussion of economies of scale in Chapter 3.

31-3. Return to Table 31-2, where costs are constant. (*a*) Change the "northwest" number 3 to 5. Does Europe now have an absolute advantage in either good? A comparative advantage in either? Draw a diagram like Figure 31-4 to show the potential American gain from trade, again assuming that there are 200 million workers in the United States and the international price ratio is 3:1. (*b*) Now change that same northwest number to 8. Which country now has a comparative advantage in food? In clothing? Are there potential gains from trade? Why or why not?

31-4. In moving from *B* to *D*, the country in Figure 31-4 consumes more clothing but not more food. Therefore, it takes all its gains from specialization and trade in increased clothing. Now suppose that it decides to consume less clothing; that is, it stops trading at point *K*, with its trade arrow now being only *CK* rather than *CD*. Will all the gains from specialization and trade be in clothing? In food? Or in some combination of the two? Graphically show exactly what the gains will be.

31-5. The following diagram shows the situation of Europe corresponding to the American situation in Figure 31-5*a*.

(*a*) How does Europe specialize when trade is opened?

(*b*) How does Europe trade? Fill in details of how much of each good Europe exports or imports.

(*c*) Are there any lines or curves in this diagram that must be similar to those that appear in Figure 31-5*a*?

(*d*) Does Europe gain from trade? If so, how much?

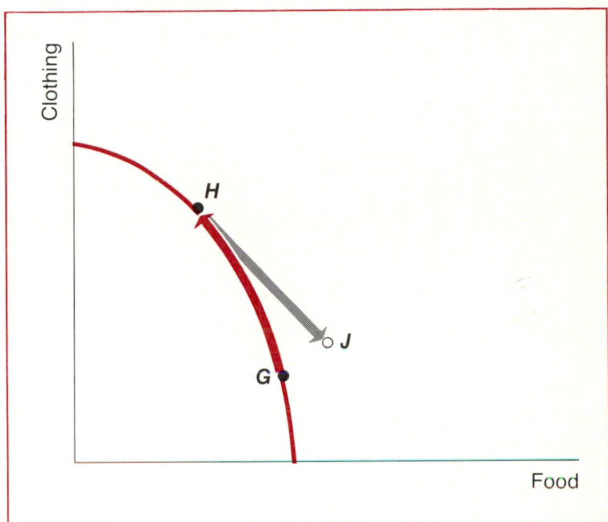

31-6. "Economists say that international trade and technological change are similar—but they are wrong. Technological change increases our real income by making us more productive. Trade does not." Evaluate this statement.

31-7. This problem looks ahead to Chapter 32. Suppose that the United States and Europe become involved in a trade war, with each imposing such heavy restrictions on imports that trade between the two is eventually cut off altogether.

(*a*) Use the diagram above and panel *a* of Figure 31-5 to show the gains or losses each would suffer. Is a trade war a "zero-sum game" (what one country wins, the other loses)? Or is it like any other kind of war, with losses on both sides?

(*b*) Use two diagrams like Figures 31-6 and 31-7 to show in more detail how the United States would be affected by such a trade war.

***31-8.** To see how the analysis of Figure 31-8 can be applied to an entirely different problem, consider the government price support policy for agriculture set out in Figure 24-11*b*.

(*a*) Use a series of colored diagrams like the panels in Figure 31-8 to show how each of the following three groups benefits or loses: consumers, producers, and U.S. taxpayers. (How much of the taxpayers' money does the Treasury pay out on the program?) By comparing these effects, indicate the transfers that take place, and in a final diagram show the net, overall efficiency effect of this policy.

(*b*) Confirm this efficiency effect by noting how this policy affects output and then applying the analysis of Figure 24-3.

CHAPTER 32

INTERNATIONAL TRADE:

POLICY DEBATES

Park your Japanese car in Tokyo

Detroit bumper sticker

Our interest will be to throw open the doors of commerce, and to knock off its shackles, giving freedom to all persons for the vent of whatever they may choose to bring into our ports, and asking the same in theirs.

THOMAS JEFFERSON

Despite the gains from trade discussed in Chapter 31, no country follows a policy of completely free trade; every nation erects barriers to restrict imports. These barriers include tariffs (taxes imposed on imported goods as they enter a country) or quotas (limits on the number of units that can be imported).

It is true that, since the 1930s, we have made great progress in reducing such trade restrictions. Much of the progress has come as a result of multilateral negotiations, by which countries reach agreement on tariff reductions and other trade matters. In the ''Kennedy round'' of trade negotiations in the 1960s, the United States and many other countries agreed to cut their tariffs by about one-third. In the Tokyo round agreement of 1979, these nations undertook to lower remaining tariffs by another third.

However, negotiating tariff reductions has been a long and arduous process. Moreover, as tariffs have been reduced, ''nontariff'' barriers such as quotas have become more important. Therefore, countries still retain substantial trade restrictions to protect their domestic industries from competition from imports. There are two basic reasons: (1) Trade barriers may be introduced for noneconomic motives. For example, a tariff may be imposed to protect an industry which might be essential to national defense in case of an emergency. (2) A country may restrict imports for special economic reasons, some of which are fallacious, but some of which may contain a kernel of truth.

NONECONOMIC EXPLANATIONS OF TRADE BARRIERS

The government may protect an industry for military or political reasons. Consider each objective in turn:

1. An Industry May Be Essential for National Defense

Two centuries ago, Adam Smith argued that national defense is an important goal. He maintained that, in pursuing this objective, we should be willing to protect our defense industries even if such protection involves an economic cost—that is, even if foreign countries have a comparative advantage in producing military supplies. This argument remains powerful more than 200 years later. Consider an extreme example: Even in the unlikely event that the Soviet Union agreed to sell us tanks more cheaply than we could produce them ourselves, we would not buy. Obviously, we don't want to ever find ourselves, in a time of crisis, dependent on the Soviet Union for our supply of tanks or spare parts. Therefore we buy from American manufacturers instead. We provide them with this protection because a defense industry is considered essential. Nor would we sell such equipment to the Soviet Union; in military goods we restrict our exports as well as our imports.

An important distinction can be made between consumer goods and weapons. Trade in consumer goods is mutually beneficial; both trading partners obtain more goods and therefore enjoy a higher standard of living. In the military area, however, we cannot say, "the more weapons the better." Defense depends on a country's military strength *relative to* other countries. Indeed, if all countries have more weapons, we all may be worse off, not better off. Therefore, in the case of military equipment, no general case can be made that trade is beneficial.

In protecting our defense industries, we face an important problem: Where do we draw the line? Do we protect just our military aircraft industry, or do we go one step beyond and protect our aluminium industry because it provides an input essential for military aircraft? Or do we take yet another step and protect the textile industry, which produces military uniforms? Although the defense argument makes sense in some cases, it can be taken too far, since almost every industry makes *some* indirect contribution to national defense. Furthermore, while we don't want trade in weapons with the Soviet Union, it does make sense to engage in some trade in weapons with our allies. This allows us all to gain economies of scale, which are generally very important in weapons production.

2. People Vote for Their Present Jobs

Increased international trade can mean that some jobs are lost in industries whose sales fall because of competition from imports. However, new jobs are created in export industries. The problem is that people are more concerned about the present jobs they may lose than the possibility of new jobs in an export industry. (After all, who knows for sure who will actually get these new export-based jobs?) Therefore, workers who don't want to take risks vote against increased trade; that is, they vote for the tariffs and other trade restrictions that protect their current jobs. As a consequence, too much attention may be paid to the employment that is lost from increased imports, and not enough to the employment that is gained from increased exports.

However, even if we look only at imports, we remember from Chapter 31 that the losses to producers from increased imports are more than offset by gains to consumers. By pointing this out, why can't a politician sell the idea of allowing imports in more freely?

The answer is that individuals tend to think and vote as producers, not consumers. To illustrate why, suppose that the import is shirts. There may be large benefits to consumers as a group from lower-priced shirts. But this gain is distributed widely among millions of purchasers, with each benefiting by such a small amount that nobody is likely to switch votes on this account. On the producers' side, however, things are different. Here, fewer individuals are affected by increased shirt imports, but the effect on each individual—whether in management or labor—is much greater. For people in this industry, the possible loss of jobs and profits will be important enough to determine how they vote; they become "one issue" voters. In brief, producers vote for politicians who will protect their jobs with a tariff, while consumers scatter their votes around on a whole variety of issues, with only a few voting against the tariff. Therefore, the interest of consumers in freer trade may be inadequately represented. (For a criticism of a policy that ignores the interests of consumers, see Box 32-1.)

A further, related reason that shirt producers may be able to exert strong political pressure is that they are not spread out all over the United States, as consumers are. Instead, they are concentrated in a few states or congressional districts. For members of Congress representing such districts, one very good way of getting political support may be to push for import restrictions on shirts. If they do, they will gain many votes from shirt producers, while losing very few from consumers. Moreover, this is not just a political sleight of hand. From the narrow point of view of just the shirt-producing districts, tariff-free imports of shirts may in fact be undesirable. The reason is that such districts would bear much of the loss from such duty-free imports (the red area in Figure 31-8). At the same time, these districts would receive little of the benefit (the gray area in panel *a* of that same diagram) because most consumers live elsewhere. For these districts, losses from increased shirt imports would exceed gains.

Therefore, it is no great surprise if the members of Congress from shirt-producing districts go to Washington committed to restricting imports of shirts. When they get there, they meet other members with similar problems: They too may be seeking protection for the goods produced in their own districts. The result is logrolling. The members from shirt-producing districts agree to vote to protect the products of other districts, in return for the promise of other members to vote for restrictions on shirt imports.

The result is continuous pressure in Congress for protection for industries that compete with imports. When imports on a wide variety of goods are restricted, the shirt-producing district may well be damaged after all because of the higher prices of a wide range of imported goods. However, the members from these districts may still be popular locally because they are remembered for their conspicuous support for the protection of the shirt industry, rather than for their less obvious support for the protection of other goods.

Thus, it is no surprise that some 200 years after the case for free trade was clearly stated by Adam Smith and David Ricardo, protection still lives on. In fact, we would have even more severe trade restrictions except for two things: (1) Producers in export industries have a strong interest in international trade, and recognize that foreigners won't buy our exports unless we buy imports from them. Thus, a concerted, producer-led lobby for freer trade may partially offset the protectionist lobbies. (2) The president is elected by all the people and carries a brief for the country as a whole. Most presidents have supported international initiatives to reduce trade barriers.

ECONOMIC ARGUMENTS FOR PROTECTION

In an attempt to counter the strong case for international trade, advocates of protection have put forward a number

BOX 32-1

WHAT HAPPENS IF THE CONSUMER IS FORGOTTEN: BASTIAT'S NEGATIVE RAILWAY

The absurdity of ignoring the interests of the consumer has never been more eloquently stated than by the French economist Frederic Bastiat (1801–1850):†

> It has been proposed that the railway from Paris to Madrid should have a break at Bordeaux, for if goods and passengers are forced to stop at that town, profits will accrue to bargemen, pedlars, commissionaires, hotel-keepers, etc. But if Bordeaux has a right to profit by a gap in the line of railway, and if such profit is considered in the public interest, then Angouleme, Poitiers, Tours, Orleans, nay, more, all the intermediate places, Ruffec, Chatellerault, etc., should also demand gaps, as being for the general interest. For the more these breaks in the line are multiplied, the greater will be the increase of consignments, commissions, transshipments, etc., along the whole extent of the railway. In this way, we shall succeed in having a line of railway composed of successive gaps, which we may call a Negative Railway.

†Abridged from Frederic Bastiat, *Economic Sophisms* (Edinburgh: Oliver and Boyd, Ltd., 1873), pp. 80–81.

of economic arguments. Some are fallacious, amounting to little more than weak rationalizations for protection, while others are stronger. The weakest arguments are considered first.

1. "Buy American Because It Keeps Our Money at Home."

This argument is sometimes expanded to: "If I buy a radio from Taiwan, I get the radio, and Taiwan gets the dollars. But if I buy a radio made in the United States instead, I get the radio and the dollars stay here." The problem with this argument is that it fails to recognize *why* the Taiwanese export to us. They do not work hard to produce radios for export merely for the joy of holding dollars. Like you or me, they want to earn dollars to buy things. To a large extent, they use dollars to buy such things as machinery and food from us. In other words, when we import radios it is machinery and food that we ultimately give up, not dollars. Similarly, if we buy radios at home, we will *also* be giving up machinery and food. (Some of our own resources will have to be diverted from producing machinery and food to producing radios.) Which way of acquiring radios—from the Taiwanese or ourselves—will cost us less machinery and food? The answer was given in Chapter 31: Radios will cost us less—in terms of foregone machinery and food—if we buy them from the Taiwanese, provided, of course, that the Taiwanese have a comparative advantage in radios.[1]

2. "We Can't Compete with Cheap Foreign Labor."

To clarify this issue, it is important first to ask: Why is labor more expensive in the United States? The answer is that wages are higher in America than in most foreign countries because labor here is more productive; it can produce more goods. Thus it can be "paid more goods"; that is, its real wage is higher than elsewhere—a point explained in Box 31-1, page 639. When we take into account both our higher wages *and* our higher productivity, we find that we can compete internationally in some goods but not others. While we cannot compete with cheap labor in other countries in products in which they have a comparative advantage, we can compete in products of our comparative advantage, where our higher labor productivity more than offsets our higher wage. These are the products on which we should be concentrating. (For more on the argument that we will be unable to compete with foreign producers, see Box 32-2.)

Foreign industries seeking protection from American goods sometimes turn this argument around as follows: "We can't compete with American labor, because it is more productive." Of course, the reply in this case is that, although U.S. labor productivity is higher than in most other countries, our wages are also higher. True, other countries will not be able to compete in activities where our productivity is particularly great and where we consequently have a comparative advantage—that is, in products such as large computers. On the other hand, foreign countries *can* compete successfully in those other activities where their wage advantage exceeds our productivity advantage and they consequently have a comparative advantage—for example, in products such as inexpensive shoes and clothing.

3. "Tariffs Should Be Tailored to Equalize Costs at Home and Abroad."

This recommendation may sound plausible, but it misses the whole point of international trade: *Gains from trade are based on cost differences between countries*; we import bananas or radios precisely because they can be produced more cheaply abroad than at home. Eliminate cost differences and you eliminate the incentive to trade; and when you eliminate this, trade disappears. Thus if we were to follow this recommendation, we would no longer be importing cheap bananas; instead we'd be producing them very expensively at home in greenhouses, with the costs of cheap imports from Central America being equalized by an extremely high tariff. In other words, to the degree that we were successful in the well-nigh impossible task of tailoring tariffs to make costs precisely equal at home and abroad, we would lose the

---

[1]Chapter 19 dealt with the situation in which American imports from foreign countries are substantially greater than foreign purchases from the United States. In this case, the argument in this section is no longer so clearcut; there may be a lag of months or years between our imports and foreign purchases of our goods. Nevertheless, our main point is still valid: The ultimate purpose of countries such as Taiwan in selling goods to the United States is to acquire the dollars to buy goods from us.

gains from trade we now enjoy. In a word: All that tailored tariffs would do is strangle trade.

While these three arguments for protection are false, the following arguments do contain at least some element of truth.

4. "If We Buy Steel from Pittsburgh rather than from Japan, Employment Will Rise in Pittsburgh rather than in Japan."

This statement may be true, particularly if there is large-scale unemployment in Pittsburgh. Why, then, does it not provide a very strong case for restricting trade, ranking in importance with the efficiency argument for free trade in the previous chapter? Why don't we use import restrictions to raise and maintain U.S. employment? There are two problems with this suggestion.

If we protect an industry's employment by import restrictions, how can its price be kept from rising rapidly? If the government becomes committed to pro-

BOX 32-2

THE PETITION OF THE CANDLEMAKERS

Sometimes the argument that we can't compete with cheap foreign labor appears in the slightly different form: "We can't compete with cheap foreign goods." This idea has never been more effectively criticized than by Frederic Bastiat over a hundred years ago. Here is his satirical description of an appeal by French candlemakers to the government to protect them from the free sunlight supposedly ruining their business:[†]

> We are subjected to the intolerable competition of a foreign rival, who enjoys, it would seem, such superior facilities for the production of light, that he is enabled to inundate our national market at so exceedingly reduced a price, that, the moment he makes his appearance, he draws off all custom from us; branch of French industry, with all its innumerable ramifications, is suddenly reduced to a state of complete stagnation. This rival is no other than the sun.
>
> Our petition is, that it would please your honorable body to pass a law whereby shall be directed the shutting up of all windows, dormers, skylights, shutters, curtains, in a word, all openings, holes, chinks, and fissures through which the light of the sun is used to penetrate into our dwellings, to the prejudice of the profitable manufactures which we flatter ourselves we have been enabled to bestow upon the country; which country cannot, therefore, without ingratitude, leave us now to struggle unprotected through so unequal a contest.

> Does it not argue the greatest inconsistency to check as you do the importation of coal, iron, cheese, and goods of foreign manufacture, merely because . . . their price *approaches zero,* while at the same time you freely admit, and without limitation, the light of the sun, whose price is during the whole day *at zero*?

[†]Abridged from Frederic Bastiat, *Economic Sophisms*, pp. 56–60.

viding an industry with whatever trade barrier it needs to protect it from losing sales and employment to foreign firms, this removes a very important restraint on the industry. If it can raise its price without fear of losing sales, it may well decide to do so.

The U.S. auto industry provides an instructive example. By 1979, it was already losing sales to imports. Nevertheless, labor contracts negotiated that year provided for large wage increases—even though auto wages were already well above the average for U.S. manufacturing. The resulting high cost of producing cars was one of the reasons that the U.S. companies lost even more sales to imports. Facing large-scale unemployment, U.S. autoworkers moderated their wage demands, in some instances accepting wage cuts. At the same time, they exerted great pressure on the government to protect the industry.

In 1981, the U.S. government pressured the Japanese into imposing ''voluntary'' limits on their auto exports to the United States. The resulting reduction in foreign competition led to higher auto prices in the United States and thereby imposed a high cost on the U.S. auto buyer. According to Wharton Econometric Forecasting Associates, restrictions on Japanese cars raised their price in the United States by $920 to $960 in 1981–1982 alone, and that price effect almost certainly increased in the years immediately following. The reduced competition from the Japanese also led to increased sales and profits to the American auto companies. This profit in turn allowed these companies to pay their executives large bonuses and their labor force increased wages. (However, wage increases were substantially smaller than they had been in earlier years, when competition from foreign cars was still weak). This raised the question: Why should other U.S. workers earning far lower wages be asked to subsidize U.S. autoworkers and auto executives by paying higher prices for cars? In 1985, the U.S. administration dropped its pressure on the Japanese to continue their strict limits on auto exports to the United States.

If employment is protected by import restraints, won't our trading partners retaliate by reducing their imports from us? To see why this might indeed happen, suppose we restrict specialty steel imports so that American purchases are switched from Europe to Pittsburgh. This is often called a ''beggar-my-neighbor'' policy because we would be trying to solve our unemployment problem by shifting it to the Europeans. The problem with this policy is that the Europeans may respond by restricting their imports of *our* goods, and thus shift the unemployment problem back onto us.

In periods of worldwide recession, all countries are tempted to initiate a beggar-my-neighbor policy of increased protection; it is tempting for each of them for exactly the same reason that it is tempting for us. If all countries attempt to solve unemployment this way, the result will be a general disruption of trade. Unemployment may consequently rise, not fall. For example, the increased U.S. protection that resulted from the Smoot-Hawley Tariff of 1930, combined with foreign retaliation, contributed to the severity of the worldwide depression of the 1930s. The Roosevelt administration undertook to reverse this destructive trend by pushing for the Reciprocal Trade Agreements Act and by negotiating lower tariffs.

If there is large-scale domestic unemployment, the cure should be sought in the domestic monetary and fiscal policies discussed in Parts 3 and 4 of this text, not in mutually destructive beggar-my-neighbor trade restrictions.

5. ''Restricting Trade Will Diversify a Nation's Economy.''

This is true. Just as trade leads a country to specialize, restricting trade leads to the opposite: diversification. Isn't it a good thing for a country to diversify—to avoid putting all its eggs in one basket?

The answer is, perhaps. But for countries, like individuals, the risks from specialization are often more than offset by the gains. (The risk of a future oversupply of lawyers or doctors does not prevent individuals from taking up these specialized careers. Their expected gains outweigh the risks they run.)

At the national level, an example of a high degree of specialization is Ghana's dependence on exports of cocoa, a product with a fluctuating price. It is true that Ghana's risks can be reduced by diversification. In turn, diversification may be encouraged by protecting new industries. However, even for a country like Ghana, the argument must be balanced against the advantages of specialization—the gains from trade. Moreover, fluctuations in cocoa price work both ways. There is the risk that price may fall, but there is also the possibility that price may rise. In this case, the greater the degree of specialization, the greater the benefit.

Finally, for an advanced industrial country such as the United States, policies to diversify the economy are hard to justify. No matter how freely we may trade and specialize, our activities are still likely to remain remarkably diversified. The evidence is that we would not give up the production of a whole category of goods (such as industrial products) to concentrate on another (such as agricultural products). Indeed, it would be unlikely that we would completely give up even one industry (say, sporting goods) in order to specialize in another (electrical machinery). Instead, the evidence suggests that trade leads to specialization in *certain kinds* of sporting goods and *certain kinds* of electrical machinery. For large industrial countries, trade has generally not resulted in a narrow range of products.

6. "We Need to Protect Our Infant Industries."

The basic idea here is this: A country may not be able to compete with other nations in an industry with economies of scale until this industry is well established and operating at high volume and low cost. This may be true even in an industry where the country will eventually have a comparative advantage and be able to produce very cheaply. This raises a question: Shouldn't such an industry be protected from being wiped out by tough foreign competition during the delicate period of its infancy?

Although this is an important question, it raises two problems: (1) How do you know that the only advantage of the foreign countries is that their industry is already established? For example, if a country is thinking of protecting an infant watch industry, how does it know that the only advantage of the Swiss and Japanese is that their industry is already established? Maybe they enjoy some basic advantage in watchmaking. If so, a watchmaking industry established elsewhere may never be able to compete. (2) When does an infant subsidy become an old-age pension? Industries that receive protection as infants never seem to grow up, but instead become forever dependent on their tariffs. Such industries can become a real problem. Once established, they employ many people who vote; thus protection continues to go to them, rather than to the real infants who have not yet hired a large enough labor force to give them voting clout.[2]

7. "Restricting Imports May Reduce the Price We Have to Pay for Them."

This argument applies to goods in which the United States purchases a large amount of the world's supply. The idea is this: If the United States imposes a tariff or some other trade restriction on such a good, say coffee, the U.S. buys less on the international market. As a result, the world demand for coffee decreases—that is, shifts to the left—and the price of coffee falls. Thus by restricting this import, the United States is able to acquire coffee at a more favorable price.[3] This is sometimes referred to as improving our *terms of trade,* that is, reducing the price of what we buy compared with the price of what we sell.

While the United States is a large enough purchaser to affect world price by such a restriction on its imports, this policy has limited applicability. While it would succeed if applied to our import purchases of coffee from Brazil or oil from OPEC, it would not succeed if applied to many of our other trading partners. The reason is that they, like the United States, are large enough buyers in world markets that they too can play the same game. For example, if we restrict our imports from Europe to reduce their price, the natural reaction of the Europeans would be to restrict their purchases from us, thus driving down the price of *our* exports. With the price of both our imports *and* exports depressed, it is far from clear that on balance we would benefit. The only certainty is that the

---

[2]A third question is this: If such an industry will eventually be a profitable one, why shouldn't its owners cover any initial losses out of their future profits? One possible answer is that the capital markets may not work very well. As a result, firms may be unable to raise the capital necessary to get them through the initial period of losses.

[3]Although the United States as a nation pays a lower price to, say, Brazil, the price paid by individual U.S. coffee buyers rises—because they must not only pay for the coffee but also the tariff that goes to the U.S. government. (It is in response to this higher price they are paying that individual U.S. buyers reduce their coffee purchases.)

volume of both European and U.S. exports would be reduced. Both sides are likely to lose.

8. "Restricting Imports Reduces Our Vulnerability to a Cutoff in Foreign Supplies."

Oil provides a good example of how dislocations may occur if we become highly dependent on an import whose supply is suddenly reduced or cut off. With a cutoff or serious reduction in imported oil, U.S. industry and American auto owners could face severe adjustment problems. One way of reducing this risk is to restrict oil imports so that we become less dependent on them.

This argument may possibly make sense for oil. However, even in this case, the argument for import restrictions is not conclusive. During the 1950s and 1960s we limited oil imports when the world price was only $2 per barrel, in order to reduce our dependence on foreign supplies. What was the result? Because of the import restrictions, the domestic U.S. oil price rose. In response, oil producers in the United States pumped more domestic oil, leaving less in the ground. Thus we became *more* dependent on foreign oil, thereby increasing our problem when the price rose later to over $30 a barrel. In other words, our attempt to reduce our vulnerability in earlier decades has increased our long-run vulnerability. Furthermore, it is difficult to think of another product to which the vulnerability argument might be applied. For almost any other good, a supply disruption would be less likely than for oil, since oil has a special problem: A sizable share of the world-traded supply comes from the politically unstable Middle East. For example, in the extremely unlikely event that our textile imports from Asia were to be cut off, we could continue to get supplies from Europe or produce more textiles at home. Or we could easily cut back on our purchases, using our existing clothing longer. In contrast, it is very difficult to reduce our consumption of oil quickly.

Free Trade vs. Protection: A Summary

This discussion shows that we should never judge an issue by adding up the number of arguments for and against it. There are only a few arguments for free trade, but they are very impressive. A reduction in trade barriers:

- Increases competition in our domestic market
- Provides consumers with a wider selection of goods
- Generates gains because of comparative advantage and economies of scale

Thus, free trade raises our standard of living.

On the other hand, there is a whole battery of arguments for protection. However, in summing them up, we first note that some are downright illogical. Moreover, even those that do have some element of truth (arguments 4 to 8 on the previous pages) don't provide a very strong case for U.S. protection—except perhaps in the special case of oil. The principal explanation for tariffs is not economic but political: In the political process, producers' interests are generally given greater weight than consumers' interests.

THE DEVELOPMENT OF TRADE POLICY

Figure 32-1 illustrates how U.S. tariff policy has changed. Historically, the liberalization of our trade has been a story of "two steps forward and one back." However, more or less steady progress has been made since the Smoot-Hawley Tariff raised U.S. protection to a peak during the depression. In 1934, the Reciprocal Trade Agreements Act provided for ***bilateral*** (two-way) negotiations in which the United States and one other country would bargain down their tariffs against each other. Then, in 1947, the United States and 22 other nations signed the General Agreement on Tariffs and Trade (GATT). This was based on the idea of ***multilateral*** negotiations in which all participating countries would lower their tariffs. Since 1947, U.S. policy, by and large, has been to concentrate on this multilateral approach and to bargain down tariffs in the GATT. An important exception was the bilateral 1965 Auto Pact, in which the United States and Canada agreed to eliminate auto tariffs against each other.

The European Economic Community (EEC)

In the late 1950s, the European Economic Community (EEC) was formed. West Germany, France, Italy, Holland, Belgium, and Luxembourg (later joined by Britain and several other countries) agreed to form a ***common market.*** Its provisions included tariff-free trade among all participating nations; a common tariff against goods coming into the EEC from other countries; and other measures of economic coordination, such as a common policy of agricultural price supports.

One of the reasons for the formation of the EEC was that the member countries eventually wanted to move some distance toward political union. But they also had a strong economic motive: to gain the benefits of freer trade among themselves. Since its formation, the EEC countries have made substantial economic progress, although it is difficult to assess how much has been due to the formation of the EEC, and how much has been due to other causes.

It is also difficult to assess how the EEC has affected outside countries like the United States. On the one hand, by inducing more rapid European growth, it has made Europe a better potential customer for U.S. exports. However, the formation of the EEC has raised two problems for the United States:

1. Because the United States is not an EEC member, American firms now face the special problem of being outsiders in competing in the European market. For example, before the EEC, American and German firms producing machinery faced the same tariff barriers in selling in the French market. But since the EEC has been formed, U.S. firms still face a tariff when going into the French market, while competing German firms do not.

2. The farm subsidies paid under the EEC's Common Agricultural Program (CAP) have generated European overproduction which has been sold at distress prices in traditional U.S. export markets in third countries. Thus

FIGURE 32-1
Average U.S. tariff rates
The United States has had high tariffs during some periods and low tariffs during others. Since the mid-1930s, the trend has been down, so that U.S. tariffs now average less than 5%. Nontariff barriers have become the most important impediments to trade.
Source: Statistical Abstract of the United States.

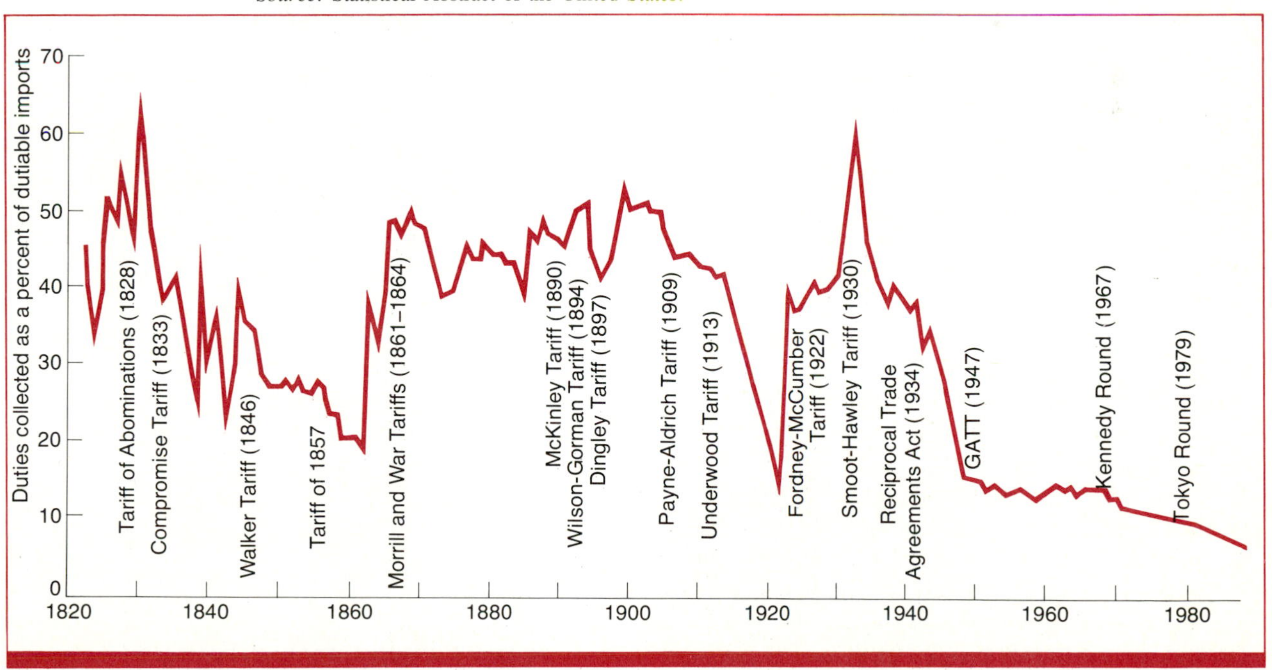

both the quantity and price of U.S. agricultural exports have been reduced. CAP has also been very expensive and divisive for the EEC. Recently, almost two thirds of the EEC budget has gone into subsidies to agricultural products. On balance, these subsidies benefit France (with its large farm population) at the expense of more urban countries like the United Kingdom. This has created severe conflicts among member countries of the EEC.

The Kennedy and Tokyo Rounds of Trade Negotiations

By the early 1960s, there were several good reasons for the United States to promote the idea of reducing tariffs through a new ''round'' of multilateral negotiations. By reducing all tariffs—and in particular, the U.S. tariff and the new common European tariff—such a move would (1) reduce the U.S. problem of being an outsider in its trade with Europe; (2) promote closer political ties with Europe; and (3) provide the familiar gains from freer trade to all participants. The result of this initiative was the Kennedy round of negotiations, which resulted in the 1967 agreement to cut existing tariffs on average by about one-third.

Following up this major success, there was a new set of negotiations during the 1970s to liberalize trade further—the Tokyo round. This led to the 1979 agreement to cut tariffs, on average, by another third in a series of steps during the 1980s. This agreement also provides for tariff-free trade in civilian aircraft.

By 1984, a remarkably high value for the U.S. dollar had made U.S. goods very expensive on world markets. This made it difficult for U.S. industries to compete, both in export markets and against relatively inexpensive imports coming into the United States. The result was a U.S. merchandise trade deficit of $113.5 billion—that is, U.S. merchandise imports exceeded exports by this amount—and pressures built up in the United States for protection. Since other countries were also considering protective measures at this time, President Reagan, in his state-of-the-union message in January 1985, called for a further round to negotiate down trade barriers. The objective of this round would be not only to make further cuts in tariffs but also to extend the ''codes of conduct'' introduced in the Tokyo round to limit nontariff barriers to trade.

Nontariff Barriers (NTBs)

We have already described one type of nontariff barrier (NTB)—a quota that limits the quantity of a good that can be imported. (The appendix at the end of this chapter shows why a quota may have many of the same effects as a tariff.) There are also many other, more subtle NTBs. A country may impose complex and costly customs procedures to discourage or delay imports. For example, in 1982 the French were determined to discourage imports of Japanese video cassette recorders (VCRs). They therefore required all imported VCRs to be cleared through the tiny customs office at Poitiers, an inland town far from any main port—ironically, the same small town referred to by Bastiat almost 150 years ago in his illustration of how ridiculous protection could become (Box 32-1).

Alternatively, countries may impose NTBs in the form of stiff quality or health standards that may be difficult for imports to satisfy. If such standards lead to an improvement in the nation's health, they may be justified even though they have the unfortunate side effect of restricting trade. On the other hand, they may have little effect on the nation's health; in this case the health issue may just be an excuse for introducing measures to reduce imports. For example, at one time, the Japanese effectively barred the import of Perrier (a natural sparkling water from France) by the requirement that it be boiled. The key question: ''Is a health standard imposed to protect health or to protect domestic industries?'' is often difficult to answer. For example, an outbreak of hoof-and-mouth disease in Argentina led to a U.S. ban on all imports of Argentine meat. This measure seemed clearly designed to protect health. However, the Argentines argued that the extension of this U.S. ban to mutton was designed to keep out imports, because the sheep-raising areas of Argentina were completely free of the disease. In cases like this, it is not easy to sort out how much of the health concern is valid and how much is an excuse for protection.

THE SPECIAL PROBLEM OF U.S.–JAPANESE TRADE RELATIONS

For many years, Japan has been viewed as a country that has imposed a wide variety of NTBs to reduce its imports; for example, it imposed quality standards on telecommunications equipment that, according to U.S. firms, made it almost impossible to export to Japan. By early 1985, Congress was in an ugly mood: The U.S. trade deficit with Japan was running almost $40 billion per annum; and in response to President Reagan's decision to allow the quotas on Japanese auto exports to lapse, the Japanese announced that these exports to the United States would increase. While that was no surprise, it added to the general frustration in Congress with the apparent unwillingness of the Japanese to take effective measures to open up their market. This led to a unanimous Senate vote of 92 to 0 asking the President to take action against the Japanese. Concerned that this could lead to a U.S.-Japan trade war, the Japanese Prime Minister made a remarkable national TV appearance asking all Japanese citizens to buy more foreign goods. It was not clear how effective this type of moral suasion would be. The question remained: ''How much concrete progress would Japan make in reducing its specific NTBs? This question applied to other countries as well, and had become a key issue in a world in which tariffs had been successfully reduced and NTBs had become a far more serious set of barriers to trade.

THE MULTINATIONAL CORPORATION (MNC)

No discussion of trade would be complete without a description of two important developments: (1) the growth of the multinational corporation and (2) recent rapid changes in technology. (For more on this issue, see Box 32-3.)

Multinational corporations (MNCs, pronounced ''monks'') are firms with their head office in one country and subsidiaries in other countries. For example, Ford produces cars not only in the United States, but also in subsidiary companies in Britain, Canada, West Germany, and elsewhere. Other countries have their multinationals too, such as Royal Dutch Shell, which is controlled by the Dutch and British.

Why does a company become a multinational? The traditional answer is that some firms go abroad to acquire raw materials. A good example is an oil company that has gone to the Middle East to find oil. But there are other important reasons as well. Once an American firm has developed a new product for the domestic market at great research and development costs, it will want to sell the product worldwide. Moreover, an American company that has decided to sell its product in, say, Europe may also decide to produce it there, if this is cheaper than producing it in the United States and exporting it over the European tariff wall.

A U.S. firm may go abroad in search of lower wages. For example, it may go to Korea or Taiwan to produce goods requiring a great deal of labor. This has led American labor unions to complain that the multinationals are ''exporting American jobs.'' In particular, labor has asked: Why should U.S. MNCs be allowed to transfer their technological know-how abroad, especially when some of it has been developed with the assistance of government funds provided by U.S. taxpayers? Moreover, when U.S. firms set up manufacturing operations abroad, doesn't this make it easier for foreign firms to copy their technology?

Multinational companies reply that you can't stop foreign competitors from copying your products. You can't prevent the spread of new technology. The most you can hope for, by keeping your technology ''at home,'' is to prolong the normal ''copying time''—but not by much. You can't prevent these goods from eventually being copied and produced in low-wage countries. If U.S. firms don't have subsidiaries there that do it, they will lose out to foreign firms. Furthermore, the technology which foreign countries gain from U.S. subsidiaries may be the best way to help these countries—better, say, than official assistance. Finally, foreign subsidiaries of U.S. firms create jobs in the United States. For example, auto engines, transmissions, and other parts are produced in the United States for export to a General Motor's subsidiary that assembles cars in Canada. (About one-fourth of U.S. exports are such shipments by American firms to their foreign subsidiaries.)

Because of the resources which MNCs have at their disposal to set up new factories, they may make it easier for countries to get established quickly in their activities of comparative advantage. By making specialization easier, MNCs help increase world income.

However, the growth of multinational corporations has raised problems, mostly for the host countries in which the MNCs have established subsidiaries. For ex-

BOX 32-3

CHANGING TECHNOLOGY IN THE INTERNATIONAL ECONOMY

Rapid technological change has complicated the traditional free-trade versus protection argument in the following way: In a stable, static world the most profitable course for a country is to concentrate on its comparative advantage. But in a world of rapid technological change, comparative advantage keeps changing. As a country switches from industry to industry in pursuit of its comparative advantage, the benefits of specialization may be eaten up by recurring turnaround costs, in the form of installing equipment and retraining labor in new industries.

After the Second World War, this argument was used to explain why some countries doubted their ability to benefit from growing trade with the technological leader, the United States. A simple analogy will illustrate: A rich and innovative man hires someone to fix his car and pays well for the job. But as soon as the employee has bought the necessary tools and mastered the job, the rich man announces he has discovered a brilliant way to do it himself. Now he wants the employee to look after the electrical system in his house. As soon as the employee masters this, the rich man announces that he has invented a completely automatic, trouble-free electrical system so he can shift the employee into some other activity.

Throughout this process, the employee's wage may rise rapidly, since it is very profitable to be associated with a man of such wealth and genius. But the employee still faces problems. First, he is spending a lot of money in tooling up for new jobs and is exhausting himself in learning how to handle them. Second, he may begin to wonder: "Given my employer's genius at replacing me, where will this all end? Will I eventually be shining his shoes for $50,000 a year?" So the employee begins to ask whether it would not be better to opt out of this game, even though quitting would mean a loss of income.

This sort of example was used to illustrate a problem faced by our trading partners. They agreed that free trade with us might maximize their income. But our rapid technological progress meant that their activities of comparative advantage were constantly changing and made some of their economists wonder: "Is the real income gain from trade worth the turnaround costs? And who wants to be a fifth wheel anyway?"

This argument has recently become far less compelling because our trading partners (especially Germany and Japan) have reduced the technological gap and, in some activities, have taken the lead. Instead, the argument now appears in somewhat different form, as follows: With the development of the international economy, any technological change that occurs in one country can be copied, within a brief period, by producers in another country. An American innovation may give us a comparative advantage in a certain good, but it will last only until the production of this good is copied in some other country with lower labor costs. At this point, the United States moves on to producing and exporting another good in which it has made an even more recent technological breakthrough. Thus the comparative advantage of the United States is in technologically advanced activities, and these keep changing. Notice that this new interpretation focuses on the heavy turnaround costs incurred by the technologically advanced country. To return to our earlier analogy: The Europeans and Japanese have not, as they might have feared, ended up shining our shoes. Instead, they began by producing clothing and radios. But now they have moved up into producing cars and TVs, leaving clothing and radios for the newly industrialized countries like Taiwan and Hong Kong.

ample, there is some concern that a large multinational may be able to acquire monopoly power in the host country's market. (On the other hand, the entry of a multinational may *reduce* the market power of an existing *domestic* monopolist.) Host countries are also concerned that they may become too dependent on foreign technology. They have also become concerned that their political independence may be eroded because decisions important for a host country may not be made there at all, but may instead be made elsewhere in the head offices of the parents. Worse yet, decisions may be made by the parent company's government. An example almost occurred when the U.S. government threatened legal action against U.S. parent companies unless they banned their subsidiaries in Western Europe from selling sensitive items to the Soviet Union. European countries viewed this as unwarranted U.S. interference in their sovereign decision over what and with whom they would trade, and the U.S. policy was dropped.

On other issues as well, governments in host countries find it difficult to deal with MNCs—in fact, more difficult than to deal with domestic firms, because a MNC can more easily exercise the option of simply leaving the country to produce somewhere else. Moreover, the reputation of multinationals has not been improved by the behavior of companies like Lockheed. In an attempt to secure foreign contracts, Lockheed at one time made payments to a number of politically influential foreigners. The resulting scandal touched a former Japanese prime minister and a member of the Dutch royal family. Finally, the image of multinationals was severely damaged by the Bhopal accident in India, where poisonous fumes from a subsidiary of Union Carbide killed over 2,500 local residents in the worst industrial disaster in history.

Although multinationals make a substantial contribution to world economic growth, they do, like domestic firms, often raise serious problems—problems that are sometimes particularly difficult because they extend across national borders.

KEY POINTS

1. Trade restrictions, such as tariffs or quotas, result in an efficiency loss: The gains from trade described in Chapter 31 are eroded as trade is reduced.

2. Trade restrictions on a good also transfer income from consumers to producers. One reason why countries have trade restrictions is that producers generally have more political power than consumers.

3. While many statements on the long list of economic arguments for protection are fallacious, some have a degree of validity. A less developed country, now exporting only a natural resource, may protect a domestic industry in order to diversify its economy, thus reducing its economic risks. An even stronger case can be made if that industry is a "promising infant," that is, an industry of comparative advantage if only it can be firmly established. The problem is, however, that assistance to infants can evolve into an old-age pension.

4. The United States, as a large buyer, might impose a tariff on an imported good to reduce the demand and hence the world price that we have to pay for it. This is the "terms-of-trade" argument. However, because other countries are likely to retaliate by imposing their tariffs on *our* goods, this is not a very strong argument for protection except, perhaps, in the special case of oil.

5. The same risk of foreign retaliation arises if we impose a tariff to try to ease our unemployment problem. Since this tariff would shift our unemployment problem to our trading partners, their likely reaction would be to impose their own tariffs, thus shifting the unemployment problem back to us—in particular to our export industries.

6. Multinational corporations transmit technology across national borders. Because of their ability to set up new plants quickly, they may make it easier for countries to develop their activities of comparative advantage. For example, multinationals often allocate labor-intensive activities to low-wage countries.

7. This in turn has led multinational corporations into conflict with U.S. unions that have accused them of exporting jobs. MNCs have also been criticized by host countries in which their subsidiaries are located. These countries may resent the fact that important economic decisions are made elsewhere, at some head office in a foreign country.

KEY CONCEPTS

tariff
quota
military argument for protection
political power of producers
a tariff tailored to equalize costs
beggar-my-neighbor policy
diversification versus specialization

infant industry protection
protection to improve terms of trade
retaliation
bilateral and multilateral negotiations
General Agreement on Tariffs and Trade (GATT)
European Economic Community (EEC)
Kennedy round
Tokyo round
nontariff barriers (NTBs)
multinational corporations (MNCs)
subsidiaries in host countries

PROBLEMS

32-1. If you don't know the answer to this question, you should be able to guess it. When the Japanese auto companies faced a limit on the number of cars they could ship into the U.S. market, did those companies concentrate on sending stripped down, inexpensive models or higher-priced models loaded with extras? Why?

32-2. In 1984, merchandise exports were equal to about 6% of U.S. GNP. They are more important for a number of other countries, where they account for even higher proportions of GNP—for example, more than 20% in Britain, Sweden, and Canada.

(*a*) Do you think the relatively low American percentage makes trade unimportant for the United States?

(*b*) Which of the four countries trades most in *absolute* terms, that is, which country has the largest number of dollars of trade?

(*c*) If the United States were, like Europe, split up into several countries, what would happen to the export/GNP ratio of each of these new countries?

32-3. The following statement was made earlier in this chapter: ". . . in activities of our comparative advantage, . . . our higher productivity more than offsets our higher wage." Along these same lines, what statement would you make about activities in which a low-wage foreign country has a comparative advantage?

32-4. "The higher the tariff on an import, the more revenue the government collects." Is this statement necessarily true or not? Explain.

32-5. (*a*) Following Figure 31-8, show the effect of a "prohibitive" U.S. tariff that completely eliminates our import of a good.

(*b*) Using a similar diagram, explain the effects of a foreign tariff that prevents us from exporting a good.

32-6. "Transport costs are like tariffs. Both deter trade. If either were reduced, countries would reap increased benefits from trade. Raising tariffs is much the same as going back to shipping goods in old, expensive clipper ships." Do you agree? Why or why not? (Hint: Don't forget that the government collects revenues from tariffs.)

32-7. Do you think it would pay Australian cement manufacturers to spend a lot of money to promote a tariff on cement? Why?

32-8. Explain why you agree or disagree with the following statement: "Because trade between countries provides benefits, a nation will benefit from an open border in goods. The same principle applies to fishing. Each nation should have an open border here as well. It should not have territorial rights, since they are just a way of protecting its domestic fishing industry."

APPENDIX

THE EFFECTS OF A TARIFF OR QUOTA THAT REDUCES IMPORTS

EFFECTS OF A TARIFF

Typically, a U.S. tariff will not end our import of a good but will only reduce it. In Figure 32-2, we consider this case, looking at a situation where the world price P_w remains unchanged in the face of a tariff; that is, we assume that there are no terms-of-trade effects.

First consider what happens if there is an extremely high tariff that eliminates trade altogether. Equilibrium occurs at point *A*, where the domestic demand *D* and supply *S* intersect. Next, consider what happens with free trade. At the world price P_w consumers buy at point *J*, while domestic producers supply at point *H*. Imports are *HJ*, the difference between domestic consumption and production.

Finally, consider the intermediate case of a tariff that reduces, but does not eliminate, trade in this product. The tariff *t* is added to the world price P_w, giving a new domestic price of P_t. Consumers respond to this price by moving to point *K*, which, as you would expect, is between free-trade point *J* and no-trade point *A*. At the same time, domestic producers pick point *R* on their supply curve. Imports are *RK*, the difference between domestic consumption and domestic production.

The effects of tariff *t* on all parties are shown in figure panels *b*, *c*, and *d*. As the U.S. price rises from P_w to P_t, consumers lose the red area enclosed to the left of the demand curve in panel *b*, while producers benefit by the gray area 3 enclosed to the left of the supply curve in panel *c*. However, there is now another effect, not encountered before, that is shown as area 4. This is the benefit to U.S. taxpayers because the U.S. Treasury is now collecting tariff revenue. A tariff *t*, equal to *RF*, is collected on each of the *RK* units imported—for a total revenue of area 4.

Since the two gray benefits in panel *c* also cover parts of the red loss in panel *b*, they are transfers. Specifically, area 4 is a transfer from consumers who pay more to the Treasury that collects the duty, while area 3 is a transfer from consumers to producers. However, some of the red loss in panel *b* is not cancelled out by gray gains in panel *c*. This balance is the net efficiency loss to society, shown as the two red triangles in panel *d*.[4] We conclude that a tariff results in these efficency losses and a transfer from consumers to producers. Moreover, when a tariff only reduces rather than eliminates an import, there is another transfer as well—from consumers to taxpayers.

EFFECTS OF A QUOTA

Trade may be restricted by a tariff or by a nontariff barrier (NTB) like a quota. Such a restriction limits the number of units of a good that can be imported, and has many effects similar to a tariff. For example, panel *a* of Figure 32-2 shows that a tariff *t* raises price in the U.S. market from P_w to P_t and thus reduces imports from *HJ* to *RK*. An equivalent, even more direct way of reducing imports by the same amount would be simply to prohibit any imports in excess of *RK*; in other words, impose a quota of *RK*. If the government does this, the new equilibrium will again be at point *K*, just as it was with the tariff.

Therefore a quota of *RK* is sometimes referred to as

[4] These two efficiency effects are marked 1 and 2 because they correspond to the two triangular efficiency effects first encountered in Figure 31-7. (We use red here to show the efficiency losses when trade is restricted, whereas in earlier Figure 31-7 trade was being opened up, and the resulting gains were shown in gray.) As an exercise, you should be able to confirm that triangle 1 in Figure 32-2*d* is the efficiency loss that results because inexpensive imports have been replaced by higher-cost domestic production, and that triangle 2 is the efficiency loss that results because consumers have been prevented from purchasing this good at the lowest possible price.

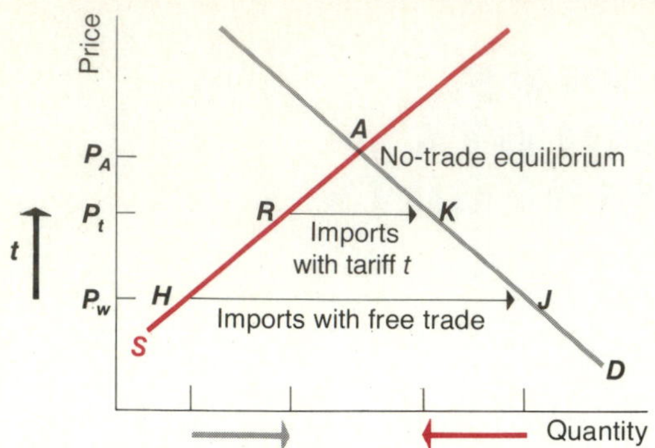

(*a*) Under free trade, the U.S. domestic price is the same as the world price $\boldsymbol{P_w}$; equilibrium is at ***J,*** with imports of ***HJ.*** With tariff ***t,*** the U.S. domestic price rises from $\boldsymbol{P_w}$ to $\boldsymbol{P_t}$; equilibrium is at ***K,*** with imports of ***RK.***

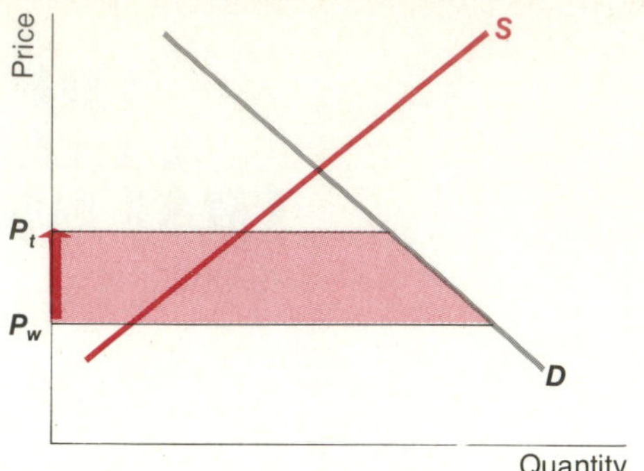

(*b*) Because price rises, consumers lose.

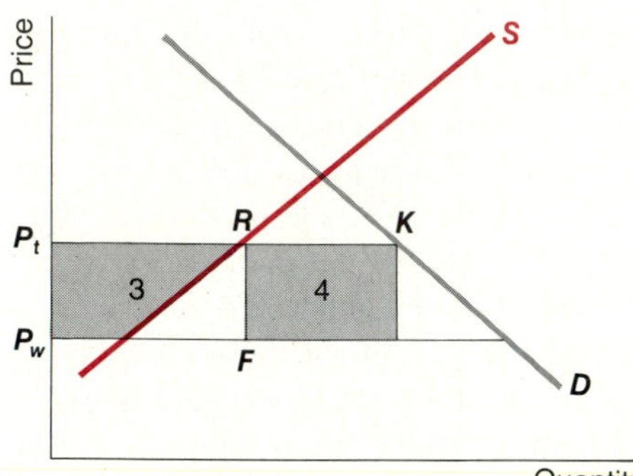

(*c*) But producers gain 3 and the treasury gains 4. As a result there is a transfer 3 from consumers to producers, and a transfer 4 from consumers to the treasury.

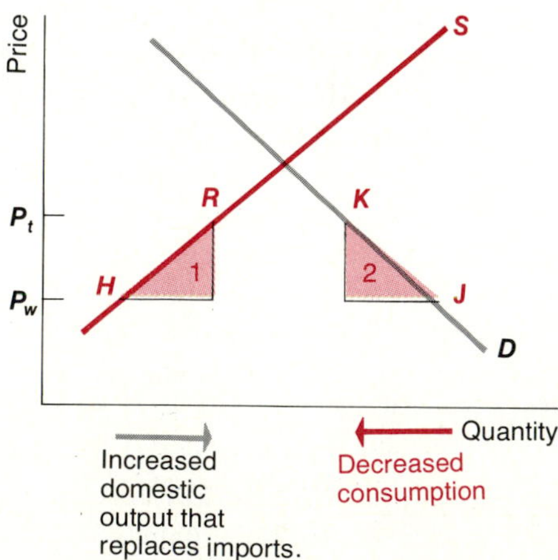

(*d*) There are also efficiency losses 1 + 2.

FIGURE 32-2
Effects of a tariff
The domestic American supply is S. Under free trade, there is assumed to be a completely elastic world supply at price P_w. Therefore, the total supply on the American market—from both domestic and foreign sources—is SHJ. This intersects American demand D at point J, the free-trade equilibrium where there are imports of HJ. However, when tariff t is imposed, the world supply shifts up by this same amount t. (Foreign suppliers now require their original P_w, plus an amount t to compensate them for the tariff they must pay at the U.S. border.) With this upward shift in foreign supply, the total supply on the American market—from both domestic and foreign sources—becomes SRK. This intersects American demand D at point K, which is the new equilibrium under the tariff. Note that price has increased from P_w to P_t by the amount of the tariff. Imports have decreased from HJ to RK, and American consumption has decreased by the red arrow below the baseline. At the same time, American output has increased by the gray arrow, hence employment in this industry has increased.

the "quota equivalent of tariff t."[5] It leads to the same inefficiency in resource allocation as tariff t. Specifically, it raises price in the U.S. market and so induces high-cost domestic production and decreased consumption. But there is one big difference. With a tariff, the higher price the consumer pays for imports goes to the U.S. Treasury in the form of the duty it collects (area 4 in panel c of Figure 32-2). But *with a quota, no such revenues are collected*. Therefore this amount goes not to the Treasury but instead to whoever is lucky enough to acquire the import quota rights—that is, to whoever is able to (1) acquire the good on the world market at cost P_w, (2) ship it into the United States, and (3) sell it there at price P_t. If the quota rights, or import licenses, are granted by the U. S. government to American importers, this windfall income 4 goes to these U.S. importers rather than to the Treasury. However, if the quota rights end up in the hands of the foreign firms that sell this good in the U.S. market, *this income goes to them rather than to the U.S. Treasury*. Consequently this is a loss to the United States, and this sort of quota becomes a much more costly protectionist device for America than a tariff. Isn't there some way to ensure against this loss to the United States? One answer would be for the U.S. government to auction off the import licenses. Since the total revenue raised by the U.S. Treasury from this sale would be roughly area 4, such a quota would have effects similar to those of the tariff shown in Figure 32-2.

A 1984 proposal for U.S. steel quotas provided a concrete example of how costly such a trade restriction may be on the country imposing it. According to estimates by the Congressional Budget Office,[6] efficiency losses similar to areas 1 and 2 in panel d of Figure 32-2 would have run as high as $1.1 billion by 1989. However this would not have been nearly as large as the $2.2 billion loss to the United States—roughly indicated by area 4 in panel b—which would have represented a transfer to foreign producers from U.S. buyers who would have paid a higher price for steel.

This raises serious questions about the U.S. policy of pressing hard to get certain countries to agree to impose so-called "voluntary" quotas on their exports to the United States. As a result of these quotas, we have lost income 4 to the foreign firms exporting to us, as well as efficiency losses 1 and 2 that follow from any form of protection. Why then do we pressure foreign countries to impose these quotas? Why don't we impose our own import restrictions instead, and thus avoid losing area 4? The reason is that, if we were to impose trade restrictions

[5]Figure 32-2, with its demand and supply curves, assumes perfect competition. Tariffs and quotas are not so easily compared when competition is imperfect.

[6]*The Effects of Import Quotas on the Steel Industry*, July 1984, p. 45.

ourselves, we would likely be judged in violation of the GATT (the General Agreement on Tariffs and Trade) and foreign countries would be entitled to retaliate against our exports.

Another question is: Why do *foreign countries* agree to restrict their exports to us? The answer is that they fear that, if they do not, the United States might go ahead and, disregarding its commitments to the GATT, impose its own tariff or quota instead. This would be damaging to these countries because it might restrict their exports even more. But whether it did or not, it would eliminate the benefit (area 4 in Figure 32-2) that these countries get so long as there are valuable quota rights held by their exporters.

The bonanza to foreign producers provided by area 4 has been illustrated in Hong Kong, where there is a thriving market for the quota rights to export clothing to the United States. At times, these rights have sold for about 10% of the value of the clothing. Some Hong Kong exporters with large quotas found that it was more profitable to sell the quota rights than to produce the goods. They closed down their factories and lived off the proceeds from the sale of their quotas.

PART SEVEN

MICROECONOMICS: HOW INCOME IS DISTRIBUTED

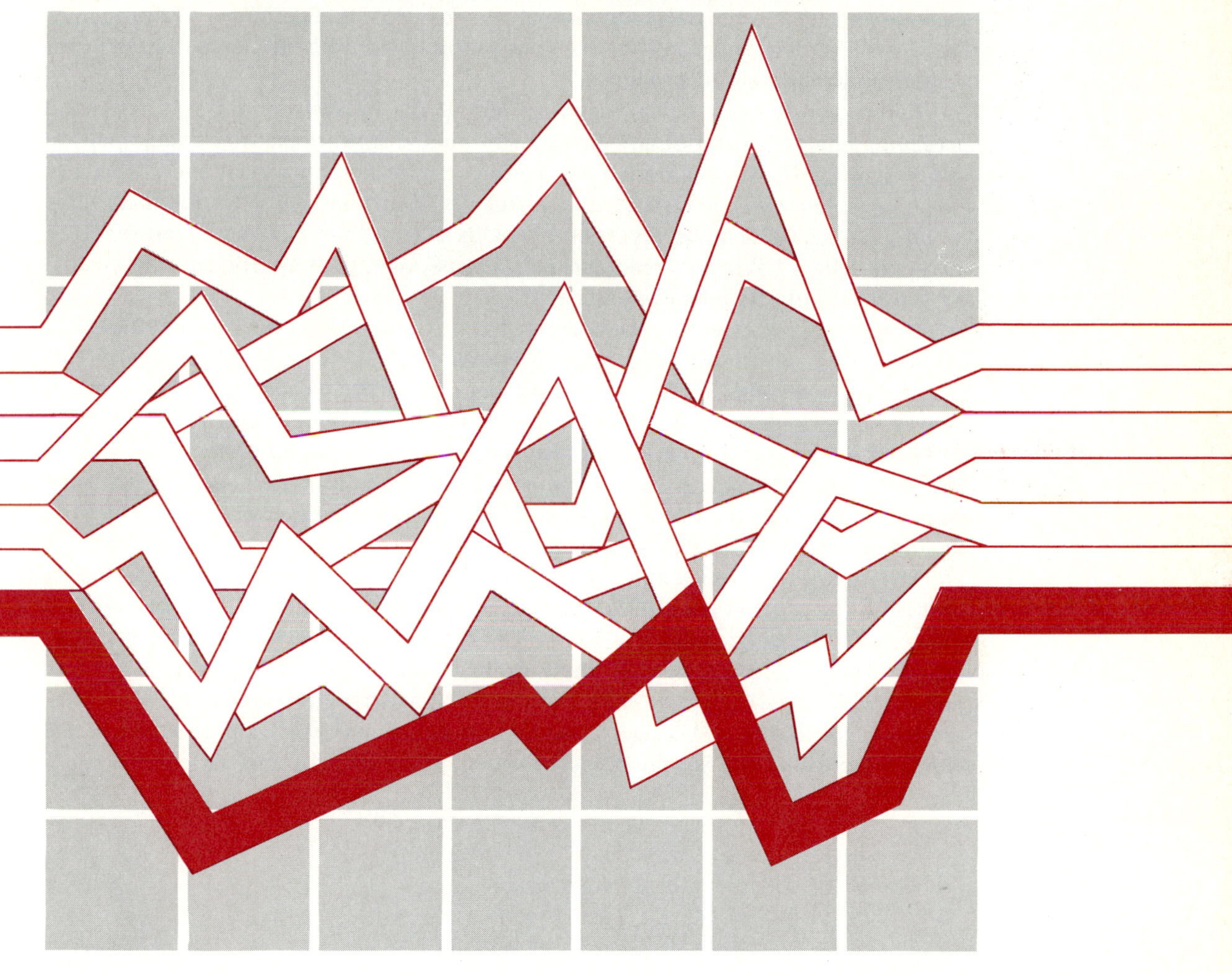

In Part 7, the central topic will be income distribution: *For whom* is the nation's output produced? We shall be asking questions such as: What determines the income that labor receives in the form of wages? What determines the interest and profit of owners of capital, and the rental income of landowners? Why does the heavyweight champion earn millions of dollars for every fight, while the nurse who looks after him in the hospital earns only a few thousand a year? And what policies can the government introduce if it wishes to change the nation's distribution of income?

To answer such questions, we shall be turning our attention from the markets for goods and services to the markets for labor, capital, and other factors of production. Fortunately, many of the principles developed in analyzing the markets for goods in Part 5 can now be applied with appropriate modifications to factor markets. It will be no great surprise to find that factor markets are like product markets. Sometimes they operate efficiently; sometimes they do not. Therefore, while much of Part 7 will be new, much will be the application of the tools developed in Part 5 to a challenging new set of problems.

Before proceeding, we reemphasize one of the important messages from the preceding chapters. Almost any government policy, from regulating a monopoly to imposing a tariff, will change a market price. And when a price changes, there are two effects: an *efficiency* effect and a *transfer* from one group to another. (For example, a price rise hurts buyers and benefits sellers; thus it causes a transfer from buyers to sellers.) When an economic policy is assessed, both its efficiency and transfer effects should be taken into account.

In the analysis of product markets in Parts 5 and 6, the focus was on efficiency. But we have seen that a policy that increases efficiency cannot be judged on this ground alone; its transfer effect must also be recognized. When we shift our major focus to income distribution in Part 7, a similar conclusion is reached: Any policy designed to transfer income cannot be judged on this ground alone; its effect on efficiency must also be carefully examined. In the box that follows on the next four pages, we illustrate the two concepts of efficiency and income transfer by reviewing several diagrams from Parts 5 and 6.

Whether or not you embark on this detailed optional review, you should look at Figures 1 and 2 to get the general idea of their message. Figure 1 shows two policies with exactly the same transfer effects (wide arrows on the left) but completely different efficiency effects (shaded triangles). On the other hand, Figure 2 shows two policies with exactly the same efficiency effects (gray triangles) but completely different transfers (arrows). Clearly, if we look at either only the transfer effect *or* the efficiency effect—but not the other—we may get a very incomplete picture.

WHY BOTH EFFICIENCY AND TRANSFER EFFECTS MUST BE CONSIDERED

An Important Message from Part 5

To see how similar transfer effects can be accompanied by different efficiency effects, we reconsider the commodity tax in Figure 1. Then, to show how similar efficiency effects can be accompanied by different transfer effects, we reconsider monopoly in Figure 2.

Reprise: The Commodity Tax on a Good that Pollutes and on One that Does Not

Panel *a* of Figure 1 shows the effect of a commodity tax on a good that creates no pollution nor any other externality. Panel *b* shows this same tax applied to a good that does involve pollution. Otherwise, these two panels are identical. In both panels, the commodity tax will involve exactly the same set of transfers, shown by the broad white arrows. The reason that the transfers are identical is that, in both cases, the tax shifts supply from S_1 to S_2, and equilibrium from E_1 to E_2. As a consequence, in each case consumers lose because the price they pay rises from P_1 to P_2, and producers lose because the price they receive (after paying the tax) falls from P_1 to P_3. But while consumers and producers lose, the treasury gains in the form of increased tax receipts. Thus, in each panel, the broad upward arrow shows the transfer from consumers to the treasury, and the arrow pointing down shows the transfer from producers to the treasury.

While transfers are the same in these two panels, the efficiency effects are quite different. Without pollution (panel *a*), the tax causes a red triangular loss of efficiency. But in the face of pollution (panel *b*), this same tax causes a gray triangular efficiency gain. (We assume the tax is equal to the marginal cost of pollution.) The reasons are detailed in the caption to Figure 1—but the basic idea is simple: In either case, the tax reduces output from Q_1 to Q_2. If there is no pollution (panel *a*), this output reduction moves the economy *away from* the efficient output at Q_1, and this results in an efficiency loss. But when pollution exists (panel *b*) the efficient output is not Q_1 but rather Q_2. The output reduction caused by the tax moves the economy *toward* this point, thus generating an efficiency gain.

Here is another way of seeing why this policy improves efficiency in panel *b* but not in panel *a:* When pollution exists (panel *b*) the tax provides a benefit that does not exist in panel *a*—the benefit to the public of having a polluting activity curtailed.

These two panels contain an important message. In two sets of circumstances, a policy can have identical transfer effects but completely different efficiency effects.

Reprise: The Problem of Monopoly

Figure 2 illustrates two ways in which monopoly output may be increased, thus increasing efficiency. In panel *a,* the traditional policy of price regulation is reproduced from Figure 25-7. The monopoly's initial equilibrium is at E_1. A policy of marginal cost pricing (that is, setting maximum price at P_2) will force the monopoly down its demand curve from E_1 to E_2, with the resulting transfer from the monopoly to consumers, as shown by the broad arrow on the left. In the process, monopoly output is increased from Q_1 to the efficient quantity Q_2, with the gray efficiency gain being the result.

Whereas in panel *a* the efficiency gain results from controlling the monopoly price, in panel *b* exactly the same efficiency gain is achieved by allowing the monopoly complete pricing freedom—including the freedom to charge different prices on different units. Suppose the monopoly is able to divide up its market and thus engage in price discrimination, just like the monopolist in Figure 25-8. However, where that earlier doctor-monopolist could divide the market into just two segments and thus quote only two prices, suppose that this present monopoly is in a strong enough position to quote a different price on each transaction. In other words, in dealing with the very first buyer, this monopoly refuses to sell even one unit unless it receives the maximum price that the buyer is prepared to pay, namely, the thin price arrow *a.* The monopoly then turns to the next buyer and similarly extracts *b,* the maximum price that the second purchaser is willing to pay. Thus the monopoly continues to work its way down its demand curve, exercising the ultimate degree of market power by squeezing every last nickel from every buyer along the way.† Because it can thus price each unit all the way up to its demand curve, it is able to convert its demand curve into a marginal revenue curve. For example, price *b* on the monopoly's demand curve is also a point on its marginal revenue curve because its additional revenue from selling the second unit is *b*.

FIGURE 1
Transfers the same, efficiency effects different: The effects of a commodity tax . . .

(*a*) . . . if there is no pollution (based on Figure 20-6)

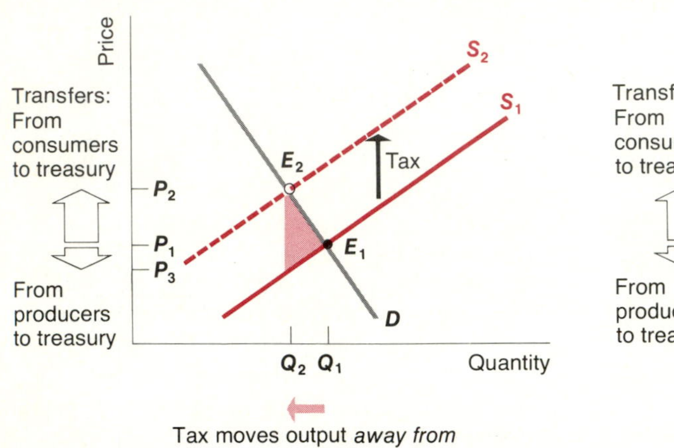

(*b*) . . . if pollution does exist (based on Figure 28-2)

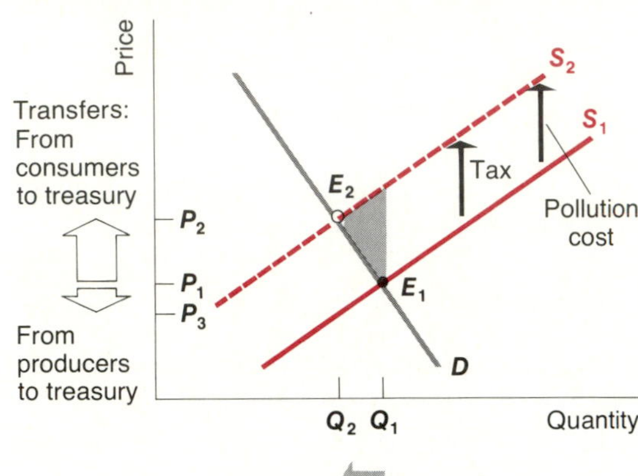

In both panels: Before the tax, equilibrium occurs at E_1, with price P_1 and output Q_1. The tax shifts supply up to S_2, thus shifting equilibrium to E_2. Consequently, output is reduced to Q_2 and price is increased to P_2.

Panel (*a*)

Transfer effects
The burden of the tax is divided between consumers and producers. Consumers lose because the price they pay rises from P_1 to P_2. Producers lose because the price they receive (after tax) falls from P_1 to P_3. (Producers actually receive P_2, but out of this, they must pay the tax of P_2P_3). Thus, there are two transfers: (1) the transfer from consumers to the treasury of P_1P_2 per unit (the white arrow pointing up); and (2) the transfer from producers to the treasury of P_1P_3 (the white arrow pointing down).

Efficiency effect
In this case, there are no externalities, so that *D* represents marginal benefit to consumers *and* to society, while S_1 represents marginal cost to producers *and* to society. Since *D* and S_1 are equal at output Q_1, this is efficient. Since the tax reduces output to Q_2, it results in an efficiency loss.

Panel (*b*)

Transfer effects
Exactly the same as in panel *a*.

Efficiency effect
Because pollution costs exist, the marginal cost of this good to society is S_2 rather than S_1. Since S_2 intersects marginal benefit *D* at E_2, Q_2 is the efficient quantity of output. By reducing output from Q_1 to this efficient quantity Q_2, the tax generates an efficiency gain, shown by the gray triangle.

FIGURE 2
Efficiency effects the same, transfers different

(*a*) Regulating monopoly price (based on Figure 25-7)

(*b*) Allowing the monopolist to discriminate completely (based on Figure 25-8)

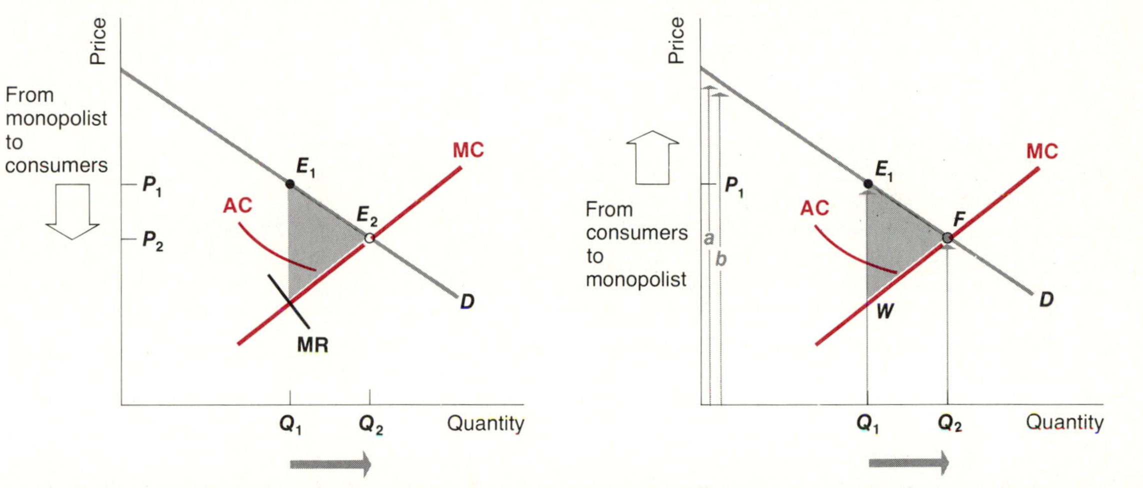

Original equilibrium is at E_1, with the monopoly selling output Q_1 at price P_1.

Panel (*a*)

A price ceiling set at P_2 drives the monopoly down its demand curve from E_1 to E_2.

Transfer effect
Since the price consumers pay is lowered from P_1 to P_2, there is a transfer from the monopolist to consumers shown by the broad white arrow.

Efficiency effect
Output is increased from Q_1 to the efficient quantity Q_2, where marginal cost equals marginal benefit *D*. The resulting efficiency gain is shown in gray.

Panel (*b*)

This discriminating monopoly prices "right up to its demand curve," charging the first buyer *a*, the second *b*, and so on. This allows it to convert its demand *D* into a marginal revenue curve. Hence, when it works its way down to E_1 it does not stop, since its marginal revenue (Q_1E_1) is still higher than its marginal cost (Q_1W). Instead it continues to produce to *F*, where these two are equal.

Transfer effect
Since the monopoly is able to squeeze a higher price (*a*, *b*, etc.) out of its original consumers, there is a transfer from consumers to the monopoly. (In fact, all the original consumer surplus is transferred to the monopoly.)

Efficiency effect
Exactly the same as in panel *a*.

Such a monopoly will not stop at E_1 but instead will continue to F, where its marginal cost MC now equals its new marginal revenue D. (To confirm this, observe that the monopoly selling at point E_1 will receive a marginal revenue equal to Q_1E_1. Since its marginal cost is only Q_1W, it will continue to expand production.) Therefore, in panel *b* the monopoly increases its output from Q_1 to Q_2, the efficient level, just as in panel *a*. Hence, there is exactly the same gray efficiency gain.

By now, you may be very uneasy about the way the monopoly in panel *b* is able to benefit from discriminatory pricing. The large transfer from consumers to this monopoly is shown by the broad arrow pointing up. (The height of this arrow is the average of the price increases the monopoly is now charging its original customers.) Note how this contrasts with the transfer in panel *a*, which was in exactly the opposite direction because the monopoly was forced to lower its price. [Note that there is one big difference between the discriminating monopolist discussed here and the discriminating monopolist in Figure 25-8. In that earlier diagram, the doctor-monopolist was not able to produce at all unless she could discriminate. (Her *D* was always below AC.) And it was better for consumers to be able to buy her services at a high price than not to be able to buy them at all. But there is no such justification for discrimination here, since the monopolist in Figure 2*b* is initially able to produce profitably at E_1 without discriminating.]

Panel *b* also illustrates why *monopoly profits may provide a poor indication of how monopoly distorts resource allocation* (that is, how it reduces efficiency). When the monopoly in panel *b* increases its profit by price discrimination, this does not increase the monopoly distortion in resource allocation. Quite the contrary: It eliminates this distortion altogether.

The message of Figure 2 may be recapped. The outcomes of the two panels involve exactly the same gray efficiency gain. But the transfers are completely different. Whereas the forced reduction in price in panel *a* transfers monopoly profit back to consumers, the unfettered exercise of monopoly power in panel *b* allows the monopolist to profit even more at the expense of consumers.

Conclusions

Any economic policy can have two effects: a transfer and an efficiency effect. If we consider only one of these effects, we will miss an important part of the total picture. For example, if we were to look only at the transfer effects in Figure 1, we would conclude: There is no difference between these two cases. And we would miss the completely different effects on efficiency. Or, if we were to look only at the efficiency effects of the two policies in Figure 2, we would conclude that they are the same. And we would miss their completely different transfer effects.

† Since one individual may appear in several locations on the demand curve, the monopoly must be able not only to quote a different take-it-or-leave-it price to each individual but also, in dealing with one individual, must be able to quote a different price for each purchase. Obviously, no firm does discriminate so completely. But the basic idea in this analysis still holds for firms that price-discriminate to a less complete degree. (For example, surgeons may have a widely varying set of rates.)

CHAPTER 33

WAGES IN A PERFECTLY COMPETITIVE ECONOMY

Let men . . . rate themselves at the highest value they can; yet their true value is no more than it is esteemed by others.

THOMAS HOBBES
Leviathan

The wage rate is the price of labor, and the market for labor is somewhat similar to the market for a good, such as wheat. Of course, these two markets are far from being completely the same. Labor is not just a commodity; labor involves people. Thus, there are major policy issues in labor markets which do not arise in the markets for other inputs or for final products. For example, if manufacturers wish to abuse their machines, that is pretty much their own business; the cost will come when the machines wear out quickly, and no major issue of public policy arises. Not so for labor. If a mine owner abuses workers by sending them to hazardous, dust-filled mines, the health of human beings is affected; the government has the right—and the responsibility—to intervene to set health standards. Or consider another example. Some business executives have peculiar quirks with respect to their products. In the early days of the automobile, Henry Ford's attitude was, "You can have any color of car you want—so long as it is black." No question of public policy arose; Ford paid for his views with lost sales when competitors were willing to give consumers their choice of colors. In contrast, personal quirks in the market for labor can be pernicious. If an employer just doesn't like some racial groups, the government may reasonably intervene to enforce nondiscrimination. Machines have no rights, but workers do.

Although the labor market is different in these respects from other markets, it may still be analyzed with some of the familiar tools we have already developed. What affects labor demand? What affects supply? In what circumstances does a free labor market result in an efficient wage rate and amount of employment and in what circumstances does it not? (An economy cannot be efficient overall, unless it has both efficient product markets—as explained in Chapter 24—*and* efficient factor markets, including the labor markets described in this chapter.) Other issues dealt with in this chapter include the policy question: Can the government intervene in the labor market to transfer income to labor, just as it sometimes intervenes in a product market to transfer income from one group to another? When it does, what effect does its intervention have on efficiency?

A PERFECTLY COMPETITIVE LABOR MARKET

In this chapter, we will study a perfectly competitive market for labor in a specific industry. Such a labor market has characteristics similar to a perfectly competitive product market:

1. Workers are mobile. They are not prevented from moving from one job to another.
2. There are so many buyers of labor service (employers) and sellers (workers) that none has any market power to influence the wage rate.
3. Labor is standardized. All workers are equally skillful and equally productive in the industry being studied.

Since the labor markets we observe in the United States are typically more complicated than this, we will eventually relax each of these simplifying assumptions. For example, later in this chapter we will relax the first assumption, that workers are mobile. Specifically, we will examine the economic effects of a rigid type of racial discrimination, where blacks are not mobile because they are not allowed into jobs traditionally held by whites. In the next chapter we will turn our attention to the second assumption and examine what happens when this condition is not met. What is the result when workers form a labor union in order to bargain for higher wages? Or when employers with market power are able to keep wages down? Finally, in Chapter 35 we will relax the third and most unrealistic assumption—that all workers are equally productive.

Our initial task, however, is to describe a perfectly competitive market, in which all three assumptions *do* hold. To do so, we first address the question: What determines the demand for labor? Although our main focus in this chapter is in the labor market in a specific *industry* (such as bicycles), we first set the stage by examining the labor demand by a single *firm* (the individual bicycle producer).

THE DEMAND FOR LABOR

In the United States, real hourly wage rates are now more than five times as high as they were in 1900. They have increased because of rising labor productivity.

The *real* wage is the nominal (or dollar) wage rate adjusted for inflation. The statement that the real wage is five times as high now as in 1900 means that the hourly wage will now buy five times as many goods and services as in 1900.

To describe the concept of labor productivity more precisely and examine its central role in determining the demand for labor, consider the firm in Table 33-1 with a given stock of plant and machinery.

In the first two columns, we see how this firm can increase its physical output in column 2 by hiring more labor in column 1.[1] In column 3, the ***marginal physical product*** of labor is the increase in total product in column 2 as each additional worker is hired. For example, hiring the second worker increases output from 5 to 12 units in column 2. Thus, the marginal physical product of that second worker is 7 units, shown in column 3.

However, the firm is even more interested in how its

[1]These figures are taken from the last row of the firm's production function in Table 23-1.

TABLE 33-1
Marginal Physical Product and Marginal Revenue Product of Labor†

(1) Number of workers	(2) Total physical product	(3) Marginal physical product, MPP (change in column 2 because one more worker is hired)	(4) Price per unit of product	(5) Marginal revenue product, MRP (5) = (3) × (4)
0	0			
		5	$20	$100
1	5			
		7	$20	$140
2	12			
		6	$20	$120
3	18			
		3	$20	$ 60
4	21			
		2	$20	$ 40
5	23			

In this hypothetical example, marginal physical product falls, provided that more than two workers are hired (column 3). Thus, beyond the second worker there are diminishing returns to labor.

†Shown for a hypothetical firm with a given capital stock and selling in a competitive market at a constant price.

revenue increases as it hires each additional worker. This is called its ***marginal revenue product.***

The *marginal physical product* (MPP) of labor is the additional number of units of output a firm can produce because it has hired one more unit of labor.

The *marginal revenue product* (MRP) of labor is the amount the firm's revenue increases because it has hired one more unit of labor.

The marginal revenue product for the firm in Table 33-1 is calculated in the last column on the assumption that this firm is selling its output in a perfectly competitive market in which it cannot influence price. Specifically, the price of its output remains $20 a unit in column 4 no matter how many units it sells. In this case, we calculate the additional revenue from hiring the second worker to be $140—that is, the seven additional units that the second worker produces times the $20 price of each unit. Observe that in this example, each marginal revenue product item in the last column is just the marginal physical product in column 3 times the $20 price; that is, it is just the ***value of the marginal product.***

***Value of the marginal product* (VMP) = marginal physical product × product price. If the firm's output is sold in a perfectly competitive market, VMP = marginal revenue product.**

We reemphasize that, as long as there is perfect competition in the product market, with product price being constant—as we assume hereafter—the firm's marginal revenue product will be the same as the value of its marginal product. However, when the product is sold in an imperfect market, with the prices in column 4 consequently changing rather than being constant, then MRP and VMP are *not* the same. (An example is given in problem 33-3.)

How many units of labor will the firm hire? To answer this question, we first take the marginal revenue product figures in the last column of Table 33-1 and graph them as the black line in Figure 33-1. If the daily wage paid to each worker is the $60 shown by the red line in Figure 33-1, this firm will stop hiring when it has employed four workers. (The fifth won't be hired because that worker would provide only $40 of additional revenue but would cost $60 to hire.) Note in Figure 33-1 that, in deciding on how much labor to hire, the firm is using a familiar guideline. It is hiring labor up to the point where the marginal benefit it provides (the marginal revenue product of labor) is equal to its marginal cost (the wage rate).

> **In a perfectly competitive labor market, the profit-maximizing firm hires labor to the point where the marginal revenue product (MRP) of labor equals the wage rate (W). (33-1)**

As we have seen, MRP = VMP when the firm sells its output in a perfectly competitive labor market. Therefore conclusion 33-1 can be restated:

> **If output is sold in a perfectly competitive market, the profit-maximizing firm will hire labor to the point where the value of the marginal product (VMP) equals the wage rate (W). (33-2)**

What is true of labor is also true of any other factor.

> **If factor markets are perfectly competitive, the profit-maximizing firm hires *each* factor of production to the point where its marginal revenue product equals the payment that must be made for it.[2] (33-3)**

The next question is: What is the firm's demand curve for labor? The answer is: Its marginal revenue product curve. To see why, note that point T on the firm's MRP curve is also a point on its demand curve (since, at a $60 wage, the firm hires four workers). Similarly, any other point on this MRP curve, say R, is also a point on the firm's demand curve. (At a $40 wage, the firm would hire five workers.) With each point on the MRP curve representing a point on the labor demand curve, the two curves coincide. Accordingly, the MRP curve in Figure 33-1 is labeled the demand curve for labor.

[2]A further example of this general principle will appear—in somewhat disguised form—in Figure 35-1.

***Essential idea for future chapters:* Whenever you see a demand curve for labor, you should visualize the bars enclosed beneath it, such as the bars shown in Figure 33-1. Each bar shows the marginal benefit of hiring another worker—that is, the marginal revenue product. (When output markets are perfectly competitive, this equals the value of the marginal product.)**

Finally, you should now work through problem 33-1 to see how the firm's income is divided between the wages it pays to labor and the amount it has left over to pay interest, profit, and rent to other factors of production. This will be a useful introduction to our discussion later in this chapter of how income is divided.

What Causes a Shift in the Demand for Labor?

Another way of asking this question is: What causes a shift in the marginal revenue product schedule in column 5 of Table 33-1? There are two reasons. First, there may be a change in the price of the firm's output in column 4. For example, if this price rises from \$20 to \$30, all the marginal revenue product figures in column 5 will correspondingly rise, causing the demand for labor to shift upward to d_2 in Figure 33-2. Examples of such a shift in demand include the increased demand for carpenters re-

FIGURE 33-1

A firm's demand for labor is the marginal revenue product of labor (column 5 of Table 33-1)

The points on the MRP curve represent points on the firm's demand curve. For example, point *T* on the MRP curve is also on the demand curve, because at a wage rate of \$60 the firm hires four workers.

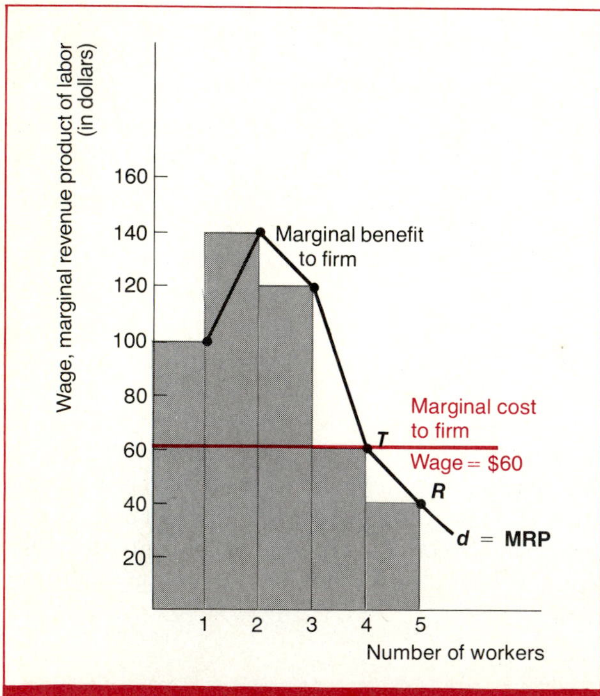

FIGURE 33-2

The firm's derived demand for labor

d_1 is the marginal revenue product of labor when product price is \$20. (It is calculated in column 5 of Table 33-1 and has already appeared as *d* in Figure 33-1.) d_2 is the marginal revenue product of labor if product price rises to \$30. (This is a recalculation of column 5 in Table 33-1, with \$30 replacing \$20 in column 4.)

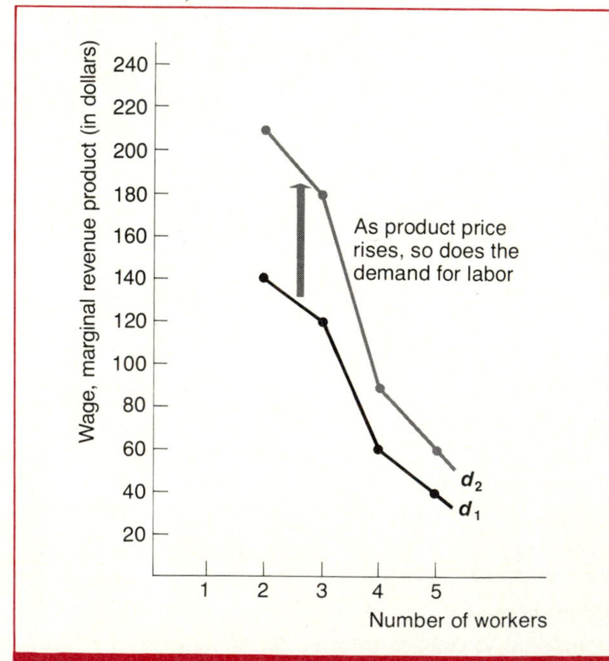

sulting from an increase in the price of houses, and the increased demand for farm labor following an increase in the price of wheat. Both these examples illustrate the *derived demand* for labor. Labor is demanded, not for its own sake directly, but for the goods and services it produces.

***Derived demand* exists when a good or service is demanded because of its usefulness in producing some other good or service. Thus, there is a derived demand for labor to produce cars and for land to grow wheat.**

The second reason that the demand for labor may shift up—that is, the MRP values in the last column of Table 33-1 may increase—is that the marginal physical product of labor in column 3 may increase. Such an increase can result from an increase in the education or training of the work force, an expanded use of *capital,* or an improvement in *technology*. For example, if more capital equipment is installed in a factory, the existing work force may be able to produce more.[3]

If a new type of machine is designed or a better layout for the factory is discovered, technology is improved and workers consequently may be able to produce more. Often changes in the quantity of capital come hand in hand with improvements in technology. For example, when computers improve, firms may increase the number of computers they use.

It should be recognized that, in some cases, improvements in technology may result in a short-run *reduction* in the demand for labor. For example, when new weaving machinery was introduced during the industrial revolution, some textile workers lost their jobs. However, in the long run, even such "labor-saving" improvements bring increased demand for labor and higher wages in the economy as a whole (as we shall see in Box 34-1).

The Labor Market for an Industry

Now let us turn from the demand for labor by a firm to the demand for labor by an industry. In a perfectly competitive economy, the industry's demand for labor is the horizontal sum of the demands by the individual firms in somewhat the same way that the market demand for a good (Figure 21-1) is the sum of the demands of individual consumers.[4] Such an industry demand curve for labor *D* is shown in Figure 33-3, along with the industry supply curve *S,* which will be described later. Together, industry *S* and *D* determine the industry wage rate *W*.

THE DEMAND FOR LABOR AND THE DIVISION OF INCOME

One of our major interests in the rest of this book is to examine how the nation's income is divided or "distributed." The marginal revenue product of labor curve (the demand for labor) can throw light on this issue. Specifically, in this section we shall show how the income going to labor and the income going to other factors of production in an industry can be read off the MRP curve shown in Figure 33-4.

Suppose equilibrium in this labor market is at *E,* with wage *W* (reproduced from Figure 33-3). What is the industry's total revenue?[5] The employment of the first worker produces output worth *a,* the bar on the left in

---

[3]For readers who have studied Appendix 23-A, suppose the amount of capital employed in Table 23-1 is increased from one unit to two. We now read along the second to last row rather than the last row. Regardless of how much labor is employed, more output is produced; that is, each output figure in the second to last row is larger than the corresponding figure in the last row.

What happens if there is a technological improvement? The answer: All numbers in the table increase.

[4]In fact, the industry's demand for labor is not exactly the horizontal sum of the demands by the individual firms. To see why, note that if the wage rate falls, each firm hires more workers, as shown by the individual labor demand curves. But this increased hiring results in increased industry output, which depresses the price of that output. This in turn shifts the labor demand curve of each individual firm. (Remember, each of these curves is drawn on the assumption that output price does *not* change.)

In short, the individual demand curves we are trying to sum do not remain fixed. In ignoring this problem, we recognize that the statements we make from now on will be only approximations. (As one might expect, there are many other such complications in economics.)

[5]More precisely, instead of an industry's total revenue, we mean the industry's value added—that is, the value of the industry's output after deducting the costs of all its inputs purchased from other industries (like the cost of steel to the auto industry). Throughout this analysis we define value of output in this value-added sense.

Figure 33-4; that is, the marginal revenue product of the first worker is a. The second worker adds b, and so on to the last worker, who adds j. The total revenue of the industry is the sum of all these bars—that is, shaded areas 1 + 2.

What part of this total revenue goes to labor? The answer is area 2, since wage W is paid to the N workers employed. Thus, if the labor market is competitive, we can summarize how the industry's revenue is distributed in the following two statements:

***Essential idea for future chapters:* Labor receives income equal to the wage rate times the number of workers employed. This labor income is the rectangle to the southwest of the equilibrium point on the labor demand curve.**

After labor is paid area 2, area 1 remains. This is what remains for other factors of production: interest and profit to capital, rent to land, and so on. Thus:

***Essential idea for future chapters:* After labor is paid, all other factors of production together receive the triangular area enclosed to the northwest of the equilibrium point on the labor demand curve.**

AN INDUSTRY'S SUPPLY OF LABOR IN A PERFECTLY COMPETITIVE ECONOMY

The labor supply for an industry, first shown in Figure 33-3, is now reproduced for more detailed examination in Figure 33-5. As the wage rate rises from W_1 to W_2, the labor supplied to this industry increases from N_1 to N_2; workers are drawn in from other industries by this increasingly attractive wage rate. As a specific example, the labor supply curve for this industry—say the furniture industry—tells us that when the wage rate rises to W_3, worker a is drawn into this industry.

FIGURE 33-3

Determination of an industry's wage rate

In a perfectly competitive labor market, the wage rate W is determined by the intersection of the demand and supply curves for labor.

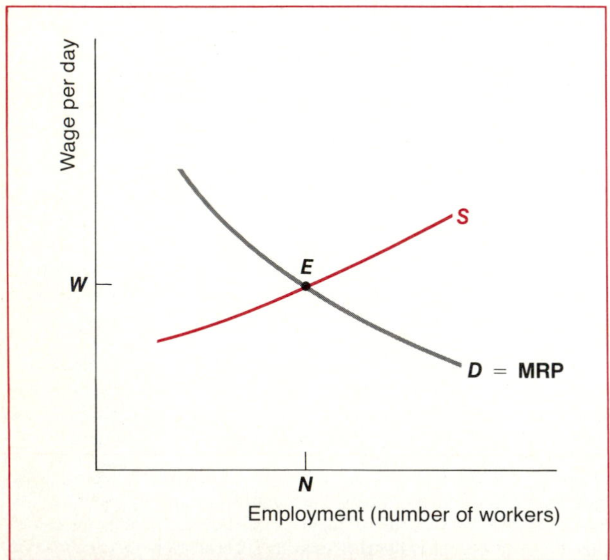

FIGURE 33-4

An industry's marginal revenue product of labor curve and the distribution of income

Total income earned by all factors of production is area 1 + 2. Of this, area 2 is paid to labor and area 1 goes to other factors of production.

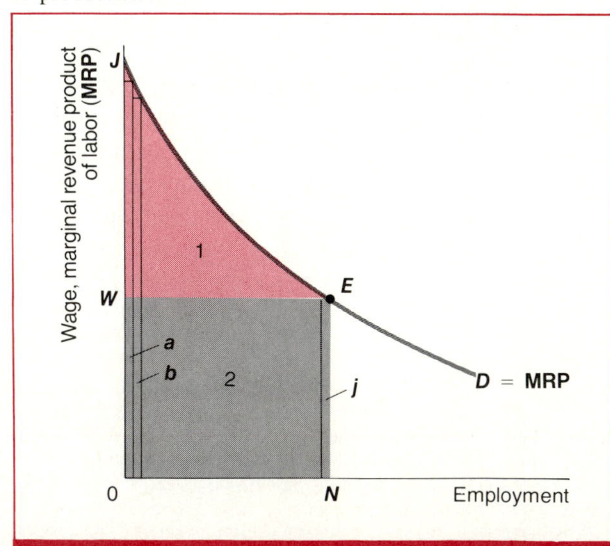

In order to persuade this worker to move, the wage rate W_3 must be high enough to cover the individual's *transfer price*. Specifically, the wage must be high enough to compensate the worker for:

1. The wage paid in the industry from which the worker is moving, say, the textile industry
2. Moving costs, both financial and psychological
3. Differences in the attractiveness of working in the furniture industry, compared with the textile industry

Item 2 need not be very great. It may be zero—if the worker is moving from a textile factory to a furniture factory next door, and needs to make no change in residence or commuting arrangements. Item 3 may be either positive or negative: If the new job in furniture is less attractive than the old job in textiles, a higher wage will be needed to induce the worker to move. If, on the other hand, the new job in furniture is more attractive, the worker may be willing to come for a *lower* wage than in the old textile job. (More detail on items 2 and 3 will be provided later.)

For the moment, we focus on the first item, which is usually the most important. The wage in the textile industry the worker is leaving was also the value of the worker's marginal product there. (Remember from conclusion 33-2 that, in the perfectly competitive economy we are studying, the wage in *any* industry is equal to the value of the worker's marginal product there.) Thus, the height of the bar *FC* represents the value of worker *a*'s output in the alternative activity of producing textiles. This is the opportunity cost of having this worker in the furniture industry. We conclude that:

In a perfectly competitive economy, the height of a single industry's labor supply curve measures the opportunity cost to society of having another worker hired in this industry.

This leads us to the appropriate way to view a labor supply curve:

Essential idea for future chapters: **Whenever you see a labor supply curve for an industry, you should visualize a whole set of bars beneath it, with each representing the value of the marginal product—or the wage—of that worker in another industry.**

In most of this chapter and the next, we will concentrate on the supply of labor facing an individual industry, leaving to the appendix our description of the supply of labor for the *economy as a whole*. However, note in passing that when we examine the economywide labor supply the question is no longer "As the wage rate rises, how many workers will be attracted in from other industries?" since there are no "other industries." Instead other questions come to the fore, such as "If the wage rate rises, will workers sacrifice some leisure to work more? Will a higher wage induce more people to immigrate?"

FIGURE 33-5
Supply of labor for the furniture industry
The rising supply curve for labor shows how an increase in the wage paid by the furniture industry increases the number of workers seeking jobs there. Moreover, in a perfectly competitive economy, the height of the supply curve at any point like *C* reflects the opportunity cost of hiring another worker *a* in the furniture industry—that is, the value of the worker's marginal product in the previous job in the textile industry. Thus, the supply curve for labor reflects the opportunity cost of hiring one more worker, just as the supply curve for a product reflects the cost of producing one more unit of output.

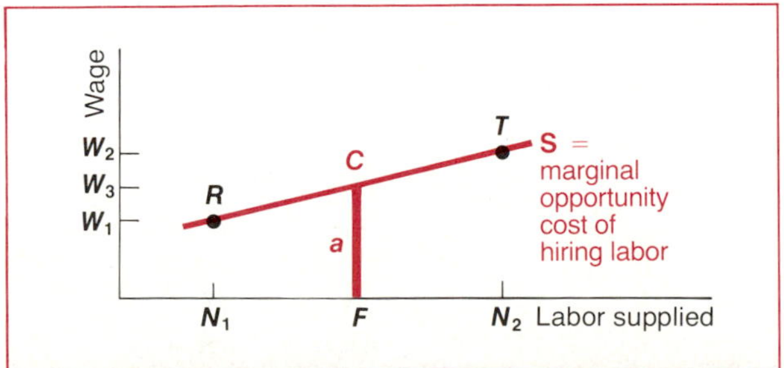

THE "INVISIBLE HAND" IN A PERFECTLY COMPETITIVE ECONOMY

Does Adam Smith's "invisible hand" work in factor markets as it did in product markets? In a perfectly competitive economy, will market prices result in an efficient allocation of labor?

Panel *a* in Figure 33-6 illustrates a labor market in a perfectly competitive economy. The quantity of employment is N_1 and the wage is W_1. This is efficient because it satisfies our criterion: The marginal benefit to society of any activity (in this case, hiring labor) must be equal to its marginal cost to society. The two are equal in panel *a* because demand reflects the marginal benefit of labor (that is, the value of the marginal product) while supply reflects its marginal cost. The efficiency of this result is perhaps most clearly seen by showing in panels *b* and *c* that any other solution is inefficient.

For example, consider panel *b*, where, for some reason, employment is greater than N_1. Specifically, suppose it is N_2. Let *f* represent one of the units of "excess employment." The benefit from employing this worker in this industry is the value of this worker's marginal product (which hereafter will be abbreviated to "marginal product"). This is shown graphically as the hollow bar under the labor demand curve. However, the cost of employing this worker in this industry is this worker's marginal product in an alternative activity, shown by the hollow bar plus the solid bar under the supply curve. The difference is the solid bar, which is the efficiency loss to society because this worker is in this industry rather than a higher-productivity job elsewhere. The total efficiency loss to society for all such excess workers in the range N_1N_2 is the red triangle.

On the other hand, at employment N_3 in panel *c*, there are *too few* workers in this industry. To confirm, consider one worker *g* who might be employed in this industry, but is not. The cost of employing this worker here is the value of this worker's marginal product in an alternative activity, shown by the hollow bar under the supply curve. However, the benefit from employing this worker here is this individual's marginal product in this industry, shown by the hollow bar plus the solid bar under the demand curve. The difference is the solid bar, which represents this worker's greater marginal product here than elsewhere; this is lost because this individual is not employed here. Finally, the sum of all such losses over the range N_3N_1 is the red triangle which shows the total efficiency loss to society. In brief this loss occurs because workers are not hired in this industry even though they would be more productive here than elsewhere.

To sum up: There is an efficiency loss if employment in this industry is greater or less than the perfectly competitive quantity N_1 in panel *a*. (Further detail on this point is provided in Box 33-1.) Thus, this analysis confirms the clear analogy between the labor market, where perfect competition generates an efficient level of employment in each industry, and the product market in Chapter 24, where perfect competition generates efficient output.

SOME COMPLICATIONS

As always, we can make no claim that perfect competition necessarily results in the "best of all possible worlds." It satisfies only one of our important objectives: the *elimination of deadweight inefficiency*. However, it does not address the question: How fair is the resulting distribution of income between labor and other factors of production? We will defer this important and difficult question to Chapter 36.

Moreover, in practice there may be a number of departures from the very simple perfectly competitive model we have described here. For example, there may be external spillover costs or benefits. Externalities can arise in a labor market just as in a product market. To illustrate, the public in a large city may judge that it receives an external benefit when musicians are hired for the local symphony orchestra. This external benefit arises because musicians are thought to make an important indirect contribution to the cultural life of the community merely by living there—in addition, of course, to the direct benefit they provide whenever they play in a concert. This external benefit will mean that a free, perfectly competitive market will result in "too little hiring of musicians"—just as external benefits lead to "too little production" of a good. (Recall that, because of the external benefits in Figure 30-1, equilibrium output Q_1 was "too little"; it was less than the efficient output Q_2.)

Now we consider two other departures from the very simple competitive outcome in Figure 33-6: (1) govern-

FIGURE 33-6 →
Why the labor market is efficient in a perfectly competitive economy

(*a*) At the perfectly competitive amount of employment N_1, there is an efficient number of workers in this industry—because ***D*** (the marginal benefit of hiring another worker) is just equal to ***S*** (the marginal cost of hiring another worker).

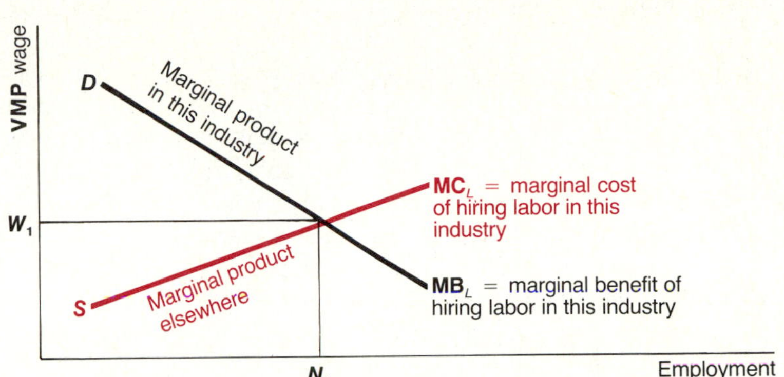

(*b*) N_2 is inefficient. There are too many workers in this industry—individuals like ***f*** who produce less here (the hollow bar) than they could elsewhere (hollow bar plus solid bar).

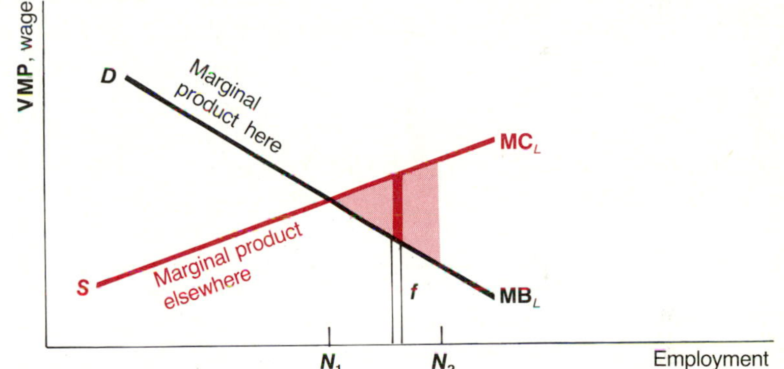

(*c*) N_3 is also inefficient. There are too few workers in this industry. Employment should be increased by hiring workers like ***g***, who would produce more here (the hollow bar plus the solid bar) than they do elsewhere (the hollow bar).

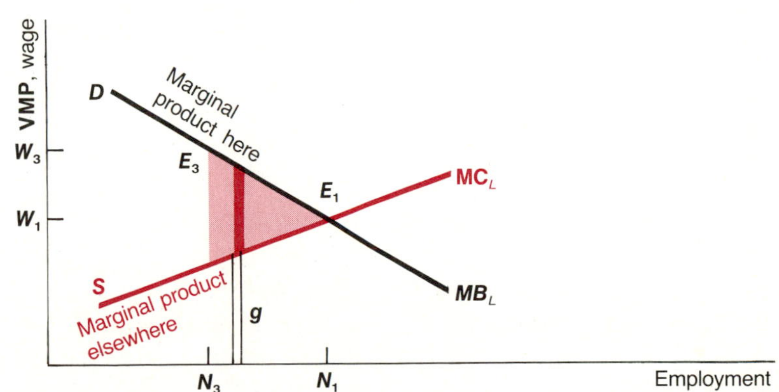

ment imposition of a minimum wage and (2) racial or sexual discrimination by employers hiring labor.

THE EFFECT OF A MINIMUM WAGE

The Fair Labor Standards Act of 1938 set a minimum wage of 25 cents an hour, covering 43% of the nonagricultural labor force. Since then the minimum wage has been increased over 10 times, and its coverage has more than doubled. However, not all workers in the industries covered by this legislation receive the minimum wage because some firms do not comply with the law, particularly when hiring illegal immigrants. One reason: The penalty for breaking the law is sometimes less than the cost of complying with the law by paying the minimum wage.

To analyze the minimum wage, consider two cases: (1) the effects on an industry, if it is the only one covered by the minimum wage; and (2) the effects if the *entire* economy is covered by the minimum wage. The U.S. economy is now somewhere between these two polar cases but moving closer over time toward case 2.

Case 1: Only One Industry Is Covered by the Minimum Wage

This case is described by panel *c* of Figure 33-6. Suppose that there is initially a perfectly competitive, free market wage of W_1 where supply equals demand for labor, and the government imposes a higher minimum wage W_3. Employers respond by moving up their demand curve from E_1 to E_3, thus reducing the number of workers they employ from N_1 to N_3. As a result, there is the triangular efficiency loss that follows because there are now too few workers in this industry.

Why then does the government introduce this policy? The answer is: to raise labor income and thus help to solve the poverty problem. In fact, this policy does lead to a redistribution of income. The winners are the N_3 workers who still have a job in this industry and who enjoy a wage increase from W_1 to W_3. The losers are the N_3N_1 workers who lose their jobs in this industry, or are not hired in the first place. They are left in lower-productivity jobs that pay lower wages.

Case 2: All Industries Are Covered by the Minimum Wage

The result in this case is the same in many respects. The winners are those who retain their jobs, while the losers are those who do not. However, there is one important difference. Now, those who lose their jobs do not get jobs elsewhere. Since the whole economy is covered, there are no other jobs for them to get. Because they become unemployed, they lose far more than in case 1. Moreover, the overall efficiency loss to the economy is greater because their lost output is no longer partially offset by their output in another job. They don't get another job.

Since most, but not all of our employment is covered by the minimum wage, the world in which we live lies somewhere between case 1 and case 2: It is likely that some workers who lose their jobs because of a minimum wage will get jobs elsewhere, but some will not.

BOX 33-1

ADAM SMITH'S "INVISIBLE HAND" IN THE LABOR MARKET

Our earlier analysis of Smith's "invisible hand" in the product market in Figure 24-2 is now extended to a factor market in Figure 33-7. If all individual employers and employees make decisions that are in their own self-interest, the result will be efficient, if perfect competition prevails throughout the economy. In panel *a*, employers hire labor up to the point where they maximize their profit—that is, up to the point where *their* marginal benefit is equal to their marginal cost. In panel *b*, workers pursue *their* self-interest by offering their labor services up to the point where *their* marginal benefit (the wage they can earn here) is equal to their marginal cost—that is, the wage they could earn elsewhere. The result in panel *c* is an efficient one for society, made possible because of the key role played by a competitive wage rate. It is the employers' reaction to a given market wage in panel *a* and the worker's reaction to that same wage in panel *b* that ensure in panel *c* that the value of the marginal product of labor will be the same in this industry and elsewhere. Therefore, the nation's output cannot be increased by shifting labor into this industry or out of it. In short, so long as no single individual on either side of the market can influence *W*, it is the key in orchestrating the actions of employers and employees in an efficient way.

In Figure 33-7, we have assumed that the height of the supply curve for labor measures the value of the marginal product in other industries from which labor is being drawn; that is, we have been focusing on item 1 on page 679. But what about items 2 and 3 which also determine the height of the supply curve; namely, the costs of moving and the pleasantness of the jobs? Do they upset the conclusion that a competitive market is efficient? The answer is no.

Here's why. Costs of moving can be important—for example, if a worker has to relocate in another city in order to get a new job. Resources are used in moving the worker's furniture and other possessions. From the point of view of society, it is not efficient for the worker to move unless that individual's marginal product (and wage) in the new industry is sufficiently higher to compensate for the move. But it must be—otherwise the worker won't move. Accordingly, the operation of the market leads to an efficient result.

Likewise, complication 3 does not cause inefficiency. Suppose that the new job is more attractive, and therefore the worker moves even though this individual's wage and marginal product are somewhat less here than elsewhere. Since this worker is producing less output, this seems to be an undesirable move. But that is not so. For economic welfare, we should count more than the goods and services produced. It is also important for people to enjoy their jobs. If the pleasantness of the new job at least compensates for the worker's lower wage, no loss of efficiency occurs. And this will be the case: The pleasantness of the new job must compensate for the lower wage—otherwise the worker won't move. Once again, we confirm the efficiency of the competitive market.

FIGURE 33-7
How the pursuit of private benefit in a perfectly competitive economy results in the efficient employment of labor (compare with Figure 24-2)

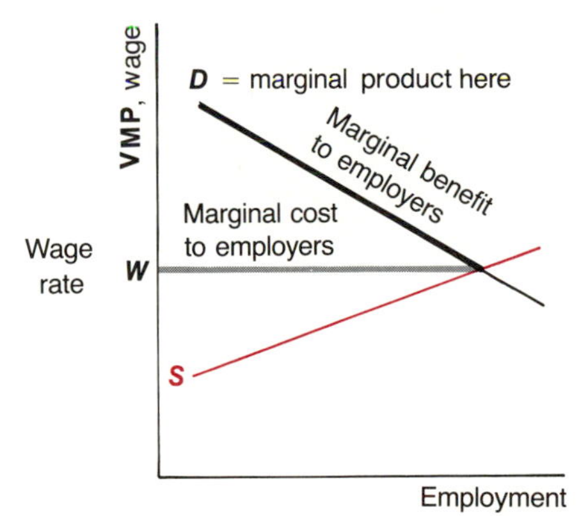

(*a*) If employers hire labor until *their* marginal benefit equals their marginal cost, . . .

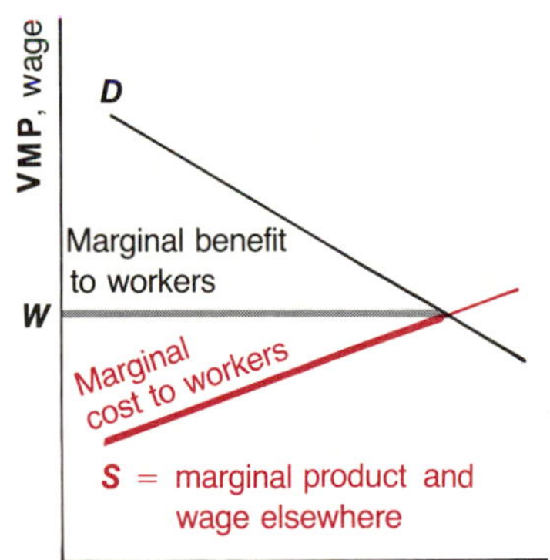

(*b*) and workers offer their labor until *their* marginal benefit equals their marginal cost, . . .

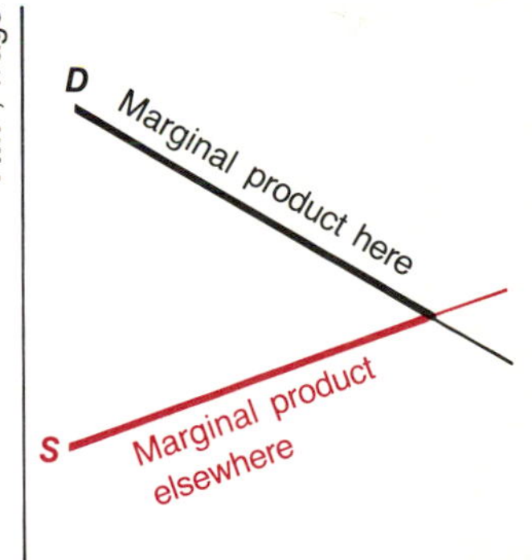

(*c*) then the marginal benefit to society (marginal product here) will be equated to the marginal cost to society (marginal product elsewhere) and the resulting outcome will be efficient.

For those who get a job elsewhere, there is an efficiency loss because they produce less. For those who remain unemployed, there is an even greater efficiency loss because they produce nothing.

Some Remaining Issues

Who are the workers who lose their jobs? The answer is often: minority groups who tend to be "last hired, first fired," and teenagers who lack work experience and skills. Minority teenagers get the worst of both worlds. Because the teenage unemployment rate is more than double the rate for adults, a number of economists have suggested a "two-tiered system," with a lower minimum wage for teenagers than for adults. In 1983, 1984, and 1985, the Reagan administration sent bills to Congress calling for a lower minimum wage for workers 16 to 19 years of age.

Such special treatment for teenagers was opposed by labor unions on the ground that employers might lay off adults with families to support, in order to hire teenagers at a lower wage. Moreover, if teenagers are given special treatment because of their lack of experience, why shouldn't groups facing other disadvantages also be given special treatment to encourage *their* employment? For example, why not also give special treatment—a lower minimum wage—to workers who are near retirement, who may have lost some of their mental or physical sharpness? With a two-tier system giving special treatment only to teenagers, people near retirement face a double problem. They have to convince employers not only that they are worth the standard minimum wage but also that they should be hired instead of low-wage teenagers.

Another problem with a minimum wage is that the increased income going to workers who keep their jobs may partly be an illusion. This will occur if employers who have to pay the higher wage cover this additional cost by cutting back on some of the other benefits they provide to their labor force—in particular, on-the-job training. Again this has important implications for teenagers. Because of their lack of experience, they have the most to lose if on-the-job training programs are cut back.

On the other hand, there is a good reason why a minimum wage may turn out *better* than we have suggested so far. In panel *c* of Figure 33-6, our conclusion that the minimum wage is inefficient depends critically on the assumption that before the minimum wage is introduced there is a perfectly competitive labor market. In particular, employers have no market power. However, if employers do have such market power, and have used it to depress wages below W_1, our conclusion may be reversed: *A minimum wage that raises wages may lead to greater employment and greater efficiency,* as we shall see in the next chapter.

DISCRIMINATION IN THE LABOR MARKET: AN INTRODUCTION

In our discussion of the minimum wage, we noted that minorities often bear a relatively heavy burden of any unemployment because they are among the first to be laid off. Worse yet: They may have trouble just getting a job in the first place. We shall now show how they may be the victims of discriminatory hiring by employers. In this analysis we will use labor demand and supply curves to identify some of the economic effects. However, it must be recognized that discrimination also has social, moral, and political effects which cannot be dealt with in such a simple framework.

What happens if employers favor one group for the better positions, and offer only inferior jobs to blacks or other minorities with equal skill and training?

To set the stage, the left panel in part *a* of Figure 33-8 shows the situation in an economy in which there is no discrimination. Notice that we are now describing the labor market for the economy *as a whole,* rather than for a single industry; discrimination is an economywide problem. Thus the demand curve *D* includes the demands of *all* hiring firms in the economy. As a first approximation, we assume that the number of workers in the economy as a whole is given, with the supply curve of labor consequently being vertical.

In the labor market shown in the first panel of part *a*

FIGURE 33-8 →
An introduction to the economics of labor-market discrimination

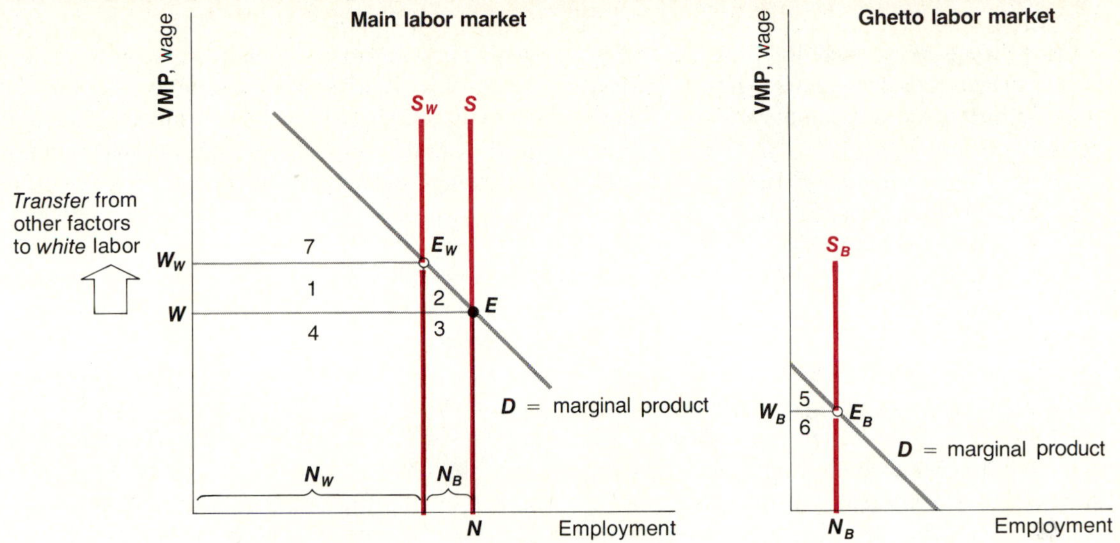

(*a*) **How discrimination affects wages and incomes.**
In a color-blind market *without discrimination,* equilibrium is at E in the left panel. The wage received by all workers is W, with N_W whites and N_B blacks employed. *With discrimination,* blacks are forced into the ghetto market on the right, where equilibrium is E_B. Thus black wages fall from W to W_B and the wage income of black workers falls from area 3 to area 6. Meanwhile, the forced departure of blacks from the main labor market on the left reduces labor supply there from N to N_W, thus raising wages of whites from W to W_W, and raising the wage income of white workers by area 1 (that is, from area 4 to area 4 + 1).

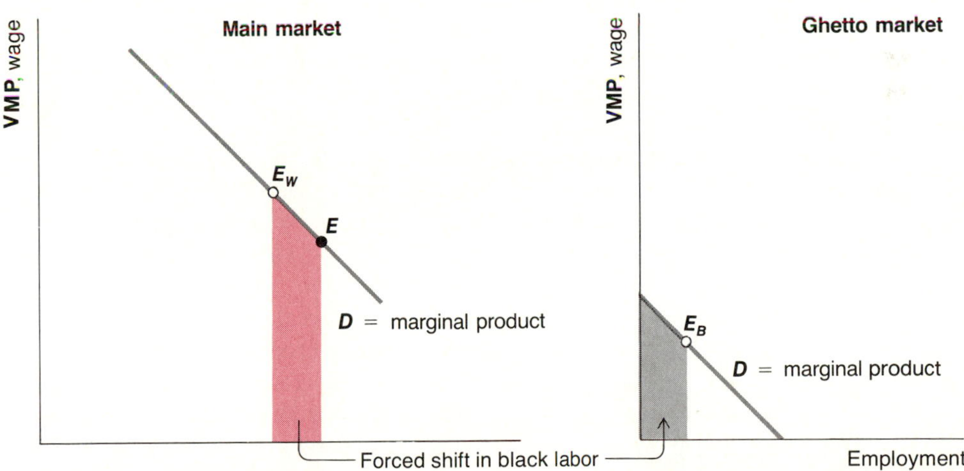

(*b*) **The efficiency effects of discrimination**
As a result of the forced departure of black labor from this main labor market, there is lost output of the red area under the demand curve. This is more than . . . the output (gray area) produced by black labor when it is hired in this low-productivity ghetto market. The efficiency loss is the difference in these two areas—the reduced output of black labor because it is shifted from high- to low-productivity jobs.

of Figure 33-8, wage W is paid to N workers—N_W whites and N_B blacks. No distinction is made between them; that is, in hiring workers, employers are "colorblind."

What happens if discrimination is introduced into this market? Specifically, consider the extreme case where employers no longer hire blacks to do the same jobs as whites in the main labor market, but hire them instead only for dead-end jobs where their marginal product is low.

In this extreme case, there is a ***dual labor market.*** The two quite separate labor markets are shown in the top two panels of Fig 33-8. In the left panel, showing the main labor market for whites only, supply shifts from S to S_W. The wage rate consequently rises from W to W_W. In the black labor market on the right, demand for labor D is low, reflecting the fact that the only jobs available are low-productivity tasks. Supply in this market is S_B. The wage rate is W_B, substantially less than the wage W that blacks received before discrimination.

The effects of such discrimination on each group and on the overall efficiency of the economy may be summarized:

1. *Black workers lose.* Because their wage rate is depressed from W to W_B, their total wage income falls from area 3 to area 6. (They may also suffer higher unemployment, which does not show up in this diagram.)
2. *White workers gain.* Because their wage rate rises from W to W_W, their total wage income rises by area 1—that is, it increases from area 4 to area 4 + 1.
3. *Owners of other factors of production lose.* Specifically, the income earned by capital and other nonlabor factors of production in the main labor market decreases by areas 1 + 2. (According to Figure 33-4, their income before discrimination was area 7 + 1 + 2; but afterward it is only area 7.) Of this, area 1 is a transfer from other factors to the white workers who receive this wage increase. This suggests that discrimination is not in the interest of employers because it depresses their profits (included in area 7). In other words, employers have an economic incentive *not* to discriminate; this incentive acts as a market pressure that tends to reduce discrimination. Another way to view this point is to note that there is a profit opportunity for employers who do not discriminate: They can increase their profit by hiring blacks at their low prevailing wage and putting them in high-productivity jobs in the main labor market. The more employers do this, the more the ghetto market shrinks and the greater the upward pressure on black wages; in other words, the more discrimination is reduced by market pressure.

Yet despite this market pressure, discrimination continues. One reason is given later in Box 34-3. Another is that economics is not a controlling influence over longstanding prejudices of employers. A third explanation is that employers may simply be responding to discriminatory pressure from their customers. A firm may not hire a black sales representative if its customers are prejudiced against buying from blacks. The problem is still prejudice, but it may be prejudice in society beyond the hiring firm.
4. *There may be little effect on whites overall.* Because nonlabor factors of production (like capital) are owned mostly by whites, there may be little effect on all whites taken together. True, white wage earners gain area 1; but this is just a transfer from other white-owned factors. The loss 2 incurred by other factors may be roughly offset by new income 5 earned in the ghetto market.
5. *There is an efficiency loss.* When we turn from the transfer effects to the efficiency effects show in part *b* of this diagram, we see that the total product of the economy falls. Because black workers are forced out of the main labor market, the value of output falls by the red area.[6] This is only partially offset by the new gray output produced in the segregated market. The difference is the reduced total output of the economy, that is, the efficiency loss that results from discrimination.
6. *This efficiency loss is borne primarily by blacks.* Because there is little net effect on whites, blacks suffer most—perhaps all—of the efficiency loss from discrimination. To confirm this, notice that the reduction in black income from area 3 to 6 in the two panels in part *a* is essentially the same as the efficiency loss (the difference between the red area and the gray area in the panels in part *b*).

[6]You can visualize this area as being made up of a whole set of vertical bars, each representing the marginal product that is lost when a black is forced out of this market and there is one less worker employed here.

Measuring the Effects of Racial Discrimination

Using a more complicated model, Barbara Bergmann of the University of Maryland has estimated how discrimination against blacks has raised the income of white labor by area 1 in Figure 33-8. In an article in the *Journal of Political Economy* (March 1971, pp. 294–313), she estimated that racial discrimination raised the income of white males with less than an elementary school education by 7% to 10%. Moreover, the income of poorly educated white females was raised by an even greater amount—between 10% and 15%.

In examining how blacks were affected, Bergmann estimated that discrimination reduced black labor income by about 25% to 40%. In other words, area 6 in Figure 33-8 was about 25% to 40% smaller than area 3. Finally, in evaluating the overall efficiency loss—that is, the difference between the red and gray areas in the lower panels—she estimated that over the economy as a whole, discrimination was unlikely to reduce total national income by more than 1½%.

What has happened since the period in the 1960s on which Bergmann's estimates were based? In the 12 years following the 1964 Civil Rights Act outlawing discrimination in employment, the income difference between black and white males entering the labor force was reduced. However by 1983, because of increased black unemployment, the average income of black families was still almost 40% below the income of white families.[7]

[7]Richard B. Freeman, *Labor Economics*, 2d ed. (Englewood Cliffs, N.J.: Prentice-Hall, 2d ed., 1979, p. 100) cites evidence that the income difference between black and white males was being reduced.

However, some of this progress may have been illusory because of the sort of on-the-job effects already noted in our discussion of the minimum wage. In an article in the *American Economic Review*, (September 1979, p. 553), Edward Lazear provided evidence that some employers who were legally forced to raise black wages compensated by reducing on-the-job black training. Thus blacks got higher current wages, but in exchange sacrificed future wages. (Notice that some employers seemed to be using reduced on-the-job training as a way to ''partially escape'' from antidiscrimination laws, just—as suggested earlier—as they might use this policy to try to escape from minimum wage laws.)

For the 1983 comparison of black and white family income, see Bureau of the Census, Department of Commerce, *Money Income and Poverty Status of Families and Persons in the United States: 1983* (Series P-60, No. 145, 1984).

Related Problems

Discrimation appears in other forms, and raises other thorny issues:

1. Housing Blacks are discriminated against in the market for housing. This is important, because restricting the entry of blacks into certain neighborhoods also restricts the access of their children to the educational facilities provided there. This in turn may affect their qualifications when they come to seek jobs. In short, blacks may get stuck in low-productivity low-wage jobs either because they are discriminated against by employers (as in Figure 33-8) or because they have lower qualifications as a result of other forms of discrimination, such as discrimination in the housing market, which may leave them with less access to a good education. Housing discrimination is examined in more detail in Box 33-2.

2. Discrimination against women ''Equal pay for equal work''—for example, paying a female and male teacher the same salary—is guaranteed under the 1963 Equal Pay Act. But special problems arise in any government program to ensure against sex discrimination when men and women have different jobs. To illustrate, suppose the government succeeds in getting men and women paid exactly the same salary of, say, $16,000 a year in nursing. Further suppose that the government also succeeds in getting both men and women paid exactly the same salary of, say, $24,000 a year as electricians. Isn't there still a problem? After all, most nurses are women, while most electricians are men. Aren't women being underpaid because their whole profession is underpaid? Isn't there discrimination unless you ensure that people get the same pay not only for the same job, but *also* for different jobs of ''comparable worth,'' like being nurses and electricians?

In recent years, the idea of equal pay for jobs of comparable worth has been a subject of controversy. To determine whether these two jobs do have equal worth—or that one has more worth than the other—one must address questions like: Which job is more demanding physically and mentally? Which job requires greater qualifications, knowledge, skill, and responsibility? Which involves more hazard or unpleasantness? And so on. When all jobs are rated in this way and a ''female'' job like nursing and a ''male'' job like being an electri-

BOX 33-2

DISCRIMINATION AGAINST BLACKS IN THE HOUSING MARKET†

Blacks have a lower standard of living not only because labor market discrimination lowers their wage, but also because discrimination in the housing market can increase the price they have to pay for a place to live, as illustrated in Figure 33-9.

Suppose the races are segregated, with blacks in the central core area and whites in the suburbs. Any increase in the white population can be accommodated by an expansion of new housing into the surrounding countryside. But an expansion of black population encounters resistance at the white boundary—in particular, the reluctance of whites there to rent or sell to blacks. (Moreover, population pressure in the black area may build up as blacks move into the city from depressed rural areas.) This pressure raises the price blacks have to pay to the point where whites near the border are finally willing to rent or sell to blacks. Thus, blacks pay more than whites—with the difference in price being the amount that whites require to overcome their reluctance to deal with blacks. (How can a houseowner sell to blacks at a higher price than whites? The answer is that the owner quotes a price above the market value, and accepts a lower bid if it is made by a white but not if it is made by a black.)

Exceptions to this pattern may occur. For example, prices in the white area next to the black core may even temporarily fall, if real estate agents stampede whites into selling quickly. In the past, agents have tried to do this by the now illegal practice of "blockbusting." This involved selling one or two houses in an all white block to blacks, and then using high-pressure tactics on the remaining whites to try to frighten them into quick sales "while there is still time." The incentive for real estate agents to engage in this practice was the commission they made from the rapid turnover of homes.

†This discussion of housing draws on Edwin Mills and Bruce Hamilton, *Urban Economics*, 3d ed. (Glenview, Ill.: Scott Foresman, 1984).

FIGURE 33-9
Housing discrimination
The white residential area can expand, but the black area is surrounded by white neighborhoods.

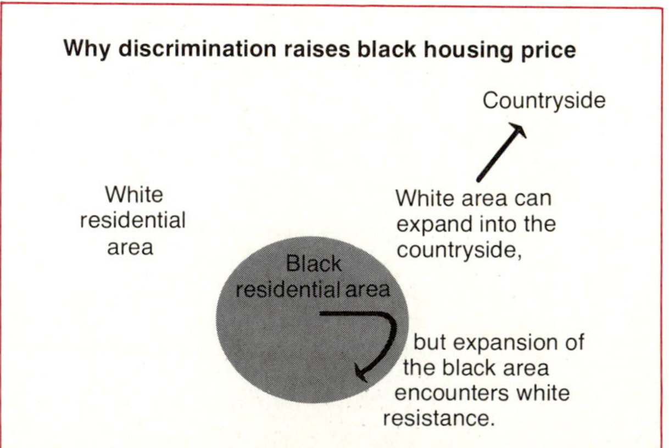
Why discrimination raises black housing price
Countryside
White residential area
White area can expand into the countryside,
Black residential area
but expansion of the black area encounters white resistance.

cian get the same rating—that is, are judged to have comparable worth—then the lower pay in nursing indicates sex discrimination. Salaries in this job should be raised. So say the proponents of comparable worth.

Its opponents see difficulties in putting the concept of comparable worth into practice. Here are the questions they ask: How can one possibly evaluate or trade off the greater risks required in washing windows in a skyscraper with the greater academic qualifications required in nursing? A job that 10% of the population views as pleasant may be viewed by others as downright unpleasant. In this case, do you put rating points on or take them off? Isn't the best way to answer this to look at workers' willingness to take such jobs, which will be reflected in supply conditions and therefore the wage rate? Do we really want the government overriding labor markets? In particular, if the government is involved in determining wages on the basis of comparable worth rather than market forces, how will the economy adjust when there is a shortage of one kind of labor and an oversupply of another—a problem normally solved by a change in the market wage rate?

In short, opponents of comparable worth argue that it would lead to a great deal of government interference based on the arbitrary and subjective judgment of those who rank jobs. On the other hand, proponents argue that continuing to rely on the market would allow discrimination to continue, and that's unacceptable.

The idea of comparable worth was given a substantial boost in 1983, when a court ordered the state of Washington to pay raises and back pay to 15,000 female employees in order to bring them into line with comparable men. Although that ruling is being appealed, the state has passed a law to eliminate pay differences by 1994. Other states, such as Minnesota and Iowa, have also launched comparable worth programs.

KEY POINTS

1. In a competitive labor market, a firm will hire workers until the marginal revenue product (MRP) of labor equals the wage rate. If output markets are perfectly competitive, MRP equals the value of the marginal product (VMP), and therefore the demand for labor reflects VMP.
2. Demand for labor in an industry, say textiles, may shift because of an increase in the price of textiles. Thus, the demand for labor is ''derived'' from the demand for textiles. Labor demand may also shift as a result of increased use of capital or the discovery of a new technique.
3. The supply of labor for an industry reflects the opportunity cost of labor, that is, the value of the marginal product that workers could have produced in other industries. (It also depends on other factors, such as the pleasantness of the job and costs of moving.)
4. Adam Smith's ''invisible hand'' works to allocate labor in the most efficient way in a perfectly competitive economy. If all market participants (employers and employees) pursue their individual economic gain, the result is an efficient solution for society as a whole.
5. If labor markets are competitive, the introduction of a minimum wage above the existing wage level will result in an efficiency loss. It will benefit workers who retain their jobs but hurt workers who become unemployed.
6. Racial discrimination by employers in hiring labor will result in an efficiency loss that is borne primarily by blacks who get segregated into low-wage and low-productivity jobs. Although white workers benefit, it may be largely at the expense of white owners of other factors of production.
7. To reduce sex discrimination by employers, women are guaranteed equal pay for equal work by the Equal Pay Act. It is more difficult to identify and deal with discrimination when men and women hold different jobs. One suggested solution is to pay women the same as men in jobs of comparable worth. Implementing such a policy involves a number of practical problems; however, it has been introduced in some recent contracts between state and local governments and their employees.

KEY CONCEPTS

real wage
marginal physical product of labor
marginal revenue product of labor
value of marginal product of labor
derived demand

share of income paid to labor
share of income paid to other factors
opportunity cost of labor
transfer price of labor
why labor supply reflects opportunity cost in a perfectly competitive economy
labor market efficiency
minimum wage
discrimination in layoffs
discrimination in hiring
discrimination in housing
dual labor market
comparable worth

PROBLEMS

33-1. In Figure 33-1 we concluded that, at a $60 wage, the firm hires four workers.

(*a*) What, then, is its total revenue? (Use the data in Table 33-1.) What is its total wage bill? How much of its total revenue remains after its wages have been paid; that is, how much does the firm have left over for interest, rent, and profit for its other factors of production?

(*b*) In that diagram, show the areas that represent: (*i*) the firm's total revenue; (*ii*) the part of this revenue that it pays to labor; and (*iii*) the part that is left for other factors of production.

33-2. The curve in Figure 33-1 showing the firm's marginal revenue product is drawn on the assumption of a given $20 price for the firm's output. But now suppose that because of decreased consumer demand for this output, its price falls to $10. Show graphically what happens to the firm's MRP curve. Does the firm change its employment? If so, by how much? Is this a further illustration of how "producers dance to the consumers' tune"?

33-3. In this chapter, perfectly competitive labor *and product* markets have been assumed. To see why imperfect competition in product markets is important, return to Table 33-1, but now make the assumption that the firm has influence over its price. Specifically assume that the figures reading down column 4 are $24, $23, $22, $21, and $20. Now, MRP in column 5 does *not* equal the value of the marginal product. Confirm this by calculating (*a*) MRP and (*b*) value of marginal product, VMP.

33-4. Because of a special commonwealth association, Puerto Rico has many close economic ties with the United States. What do you think of the idea of Puerto Ricans introducing the U.S. minimum wage on their island? In answering this question keep this in mind: Because of low labor productivity and a rapidly growing labor supply, Puerto Ricans have historically had a wage rate substantially lower than in the continental United States.

Would such a common minimum wage result in a more severe unemployment problem in Puerto Rico or the continental United States? In your view, should the Puerto Ricans have a minimum wage below the U.S. level? What do you think of the idea of setting a minimum wage in Puerto Rico low enough so that it would not cause any unemployment there? If it were set at this level, would it achieve the objective of reducing poverty by raising wages?

33-5. Would a minimum wage be more likely to raise the total income of labor if the elasticity of demand for labor is low rather than high? Explain why or why not.

33-6. "The wage rate acts as a screening device that determines where scarce labor will be employed and where it will be not." Illustrate this idea, using an argument parallel to the one used in Figure 24-5. Use the example of labor that is hired to build apartment buildings but is no longer hired to hoe field corn.

33-7. Suppose the New Jersey team in the U.S. Football League is considering spending a great deal of money to sign several college stars before they sign with the rival National Football League. The New Jersey owners request a subsidy from the owners of the other teams in their league, because they are otherwise unable to afford such a large outlay. How would you advise these other owners to respond? (Key: Would there be any externalities for the other owners?)

33-8. The efficiency loss illustrated in Figure 33-8 can be viewed as the result of splitting the labor market into black and white segments with different productivity in each. Explain why a similar efficiency loss occurs, at least to some degree, in the U.S. labor market because of its geographical divisions. (Because workers find it difficult and costly to move, they often stay in low-wage and low-productivity areas rather than move into higher-productivity areas.) Is it therefore true that barriers to labor mobility impose a cost on the economy? Do you see why a policy of increasing labor mobility raises the efficiency of the economy even when it doesn't reduce unemployment? (In fact, it may also provide another big benefit: It may indeed reduce unemployment.)

APPENDIX

THE ECONOMYWIDE SUPPLY OF LABOR

As a first approximation, the economywide labor supply might be viewed as a vertical line, reflecting a given labor force for the economy as a whole. This is the quantity of labor that will be supplied, if willingness to work is independent of the wage rate. However, there are two reasons why the supply curve may not be completely vertical after all—why the total amount of labor supplied may change if the wage changes:

1. The *labor participation rate* may change; that is, there may be a change in the proportion of the population in the labor market.
2. There may be a change in the average *number of hours worked* by the existing labor force.

However, it is not certain whether a higher wage will lead to an increase or decrease in the quantity of labor supplied. This is because a wage increase exerts two conflicting pressures:

1. The ***substitution effect.*** Since the reward for work (the wage rate) has increased relative to the reward from leisure, people have an incentive to substitute, working more and taking less leisure.
2. The ***income effect.*** This effect works in the opposite direction. A higher wage means higher income and thus allows workers to acquire more of everything they want: not only more goods, but also more leisure. In acquiring more leisure, they work less.

Which of these two conflicting effects dominates? We cannot be sure. As Figure 33-10 is drawn, the two are exactly balanced at wage W_3, where the quantity of labor supplied is at a maximum. However, if the initial wage is lower than this, the substitution effect dominates. As the wage rate rises from, say, W_1 to W_2, people increase the amount they work from Q_1 to Q_2. On the other hand, at a wage above W_3, the income effect dominates. Workers now have reached a high enough wage that they can say: "Let's use any further increase not only to buy more goods, but also to buy more leisure." In other words, an increase in the wage rate induces them to work less. Specifically, if the wage rate rises from W_3 to W_4, they *reduce* the quantity of labor they supply. In this range, the labor supply curve is described as "backward bending."

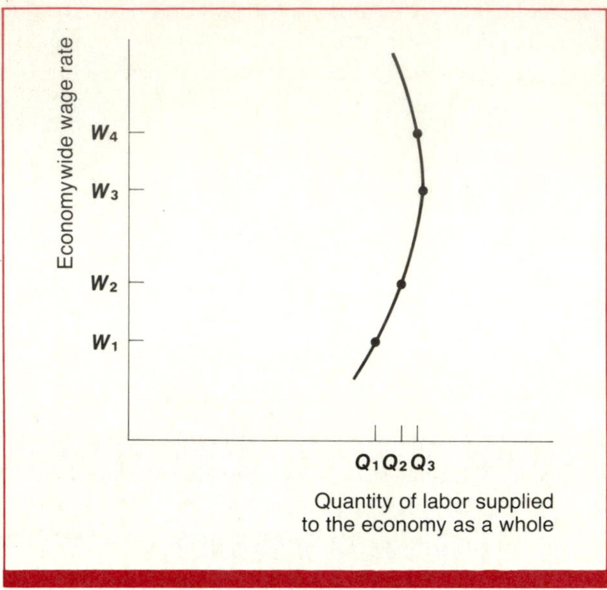

FIGURE 33-10
The supply of labor in the economy as a whole, rather than just in a single industry
At low wage W_1, an increase in the wage to W_2 results in an increase in the quantity of labor supplied from Q_1 to Q_2. However, at some higher wage rate (W_3) workers achieve a high enough income level that they can afford to take part of any further increase in income in the form of leisure. Accordingly, they work less; the labor supply curve is backward-bending.

CHAPTER 34

WAGES IN IMPERFECTLY COMPETITIVE LABOR MARKETS

Trade unionism is not socialism. It is the capitalism of the proletariat.

GEORGE BERNARD SHAW

In this chapter we study how the labor market departs from perfect competition. On the supply side, workers in many industries have formed unions in order to influence wage rates and working conditions. On the demand side, employers frequently have some control over the wage rate. An extreme example is a firm that is the only employer of industrial labor in a small town.

When market power exists on both sides of the market, the result is *bilateral (two-way) monopoly*. This is the situation that we wish eventually to study in this chapter. However, in order to work up to this complicated subject, we first address two preliminary questions: What happens if there is market power only on the supply side of the labor market? And what happens if there is market power only on the demand side?

First, we will examine unions. Although one of their major functions is to exercise market power to increase wages, they have other significant roles as well.

LABOR UNIONS: THE BENEFITS OF COLLECTIVE ACTION

It is sometimes said that a perfectly competitive labor market "has no memory, and no future." In such a market, people are hired or fired simply on the basis of what they can do *today*. However, in the real world, people work not only for the wage they receive today, but also in order to ensure a secure job for the future. In other words, people have a *stake* in their jobs. An important role of the union is to protect the stake of the workers, to give them a collective voice not only in the setting of wages but also, more generally, in the conditions of employment.[1] With the backing of unions, workers are protected from arbitrary dismissal or changes in the "rules of the game" by management. Because of these assurances, workers are able to commit themselves to an occupation more completely than they could in a timeless, impersonal, perfectly competitive market.

Collective Bargaining

When workers express their voice by getting together in a union, they overcome three disadvantages of "standing alone": (1) A single worker may have difficulty even getting management to listen, let alone negotiate to remove a grievance. (2) Management may retaliate personally against an individual who is complaining. The courts' interpretation of U.S. labor law is that workers acting collectively are protected from management retaliation, but as individuals they generally are not. (3) Even if an individual were to succeed in negotiating a change, it is unlikely to be worth the effort. Most of the benefits would go to other workers. In this sense, the resolution of a labor grievance is a public good; *all workers benefit, regardless of who negotiates it*. Negotiations are therefore undertaken collectively—by a union.

Collective bargaining **is any negotiation between a union and management over wages, fringe benefits, hiring policies, job security, or working conditions.**

[1]This chapter, in particular the discussion of labor's voice, draws heavily on Richard B. Freeman and James L. Medoff, *What Do Unions Do?* (New York: Basic Books, 1984).

In addition to raising wages by negotiating higher pay rates, unions may attempt to raise wages indirectly by negotiating other terms of employment. For example, unions may:

1. Negotiate a shorter work week and early retirement. Such changes reduce the supply of labor and thus put upward pressure on wages.
2. Negotiate with employers to hire only union members, and then limit union membership by imposing barriers to entry such as high initiation fees or long periods of apprenticeship. This approach also restricts the supply of labor, and thus raises wage rates.

In such negotiations, a union may, of course, have other objectives than just raising wages. For example, a shorter workweek may be desired for its own sake, and apprenticeship may be a way of screening bumbling amateurs out of dangerous occupations. Not surprisingly, motives are sometimes mixed. The charge has been made that the American Medical Association—the association of U.S. doctors—has acted like a union. For many years prior to a change in its policy about two decades ago, the association used its power to limit the number of medical schools and the number of students admitted to these schools. While the stated reason for this tough policy was to improve the quality of medical service, it also restricted the supply of graduating doctors and thus increased the incomes of the members of the association.

Another negotiating objective of unions is to establish clear rules on the conditions under which workers can be laid off or discharged. This is particularly important for older workers who would have difficulty finding other jobs. Accordingly, unions work hard to establish ***seniority rules*** to protect those who have been on the job longest, and who have the most to lose if they are discharged.

Seniority rules **give preference to those who have been longest on the job. Individuals with seniority are typically the last to be discharged or laid off and the first to be rehired.**

Without seniority rules, older workers might be in a vulnerable situation. Over the years, their productivity may have declined. In the absence of seniority rules they might be the *first* to be laid off. Thus union-negotiated rules can be viewed as a way of reducing older workers' vulnerability.

In addition to senority rules, unions attempt to provide job security in a number of other ways. For example, job security was a major concern of the United Auto Workers (UAW) during the labor negotiations of 1984. In response to union demands, GM agreed to spend up to $1 billion by 1990 to keep displaced workers on its payroll. GM also agreed to build a new subcompact car in the United States, thus reducing UAW fears that GM would go abroad for its small cars. The UAW and a number of unions in other industries have also pressed for restrictions on imports in order to protect U.S. jobs.

While unions in the past have focused their attention on wages, job security, and conditions on the shop floor, an important question is whether unions in the future will seek broader areas of influence, such as a voice in the nation's boardrooms. Germany is experimenting with ***codetermination:*** Labor and management have an equal number of seats on the board of directors, with the owners making the decision in the event of a tie. This experiment has had mixed success. It has improved communication. But both sides have reservations: Management feels that labor representatives sometimes waste time by raising "shop-floor" issues such as plant ventilation and sometimes leak secrets such as proposed plant layoffs. On the other hand, labor members of the board complain that the owners are in control because of the extra vote they get in the event of a tie. Moreover, some rank-and-file workers fear that their board members may begin to think like managers and soften their demands for higher wages and better working conditions.

In the United States, Douglas Fraser, president of the United Auto Workers, was on Chrysler's board of directors between 1980 and 1984. This marked the first time a union leader had a seat on the board of a major U.S. corporation. This was not so much the result of a change in any underlying philosophy of management-labor relations as an act of desperation to save a near-bankrupt company: Chrysler gave the union president a seat on the board when the UAW agreed to defer several hundred million dollars in wages and benefits. This innovation has been followed by Pan American, Eastern Airlines, and a number of smaller companies.

Before examining the detailed economic effects of unions, we first briefly review the long struggle to establish unions in the United States.

LABOR UNIONS: THEIR HISTORICAL DEVELOPMENT

You must offer the American working man bread and butter in the here and now, instead of pie in the sky in the sweet bye and bye.

The philosophy of early labor leader Samuel Gompers (as described by Charles Killingworth)

The beginning of the American union movement dates back to an era in which a relatively powerless labor force lived in poverty, or near it. In the last third of the nineteenth century, the Knights of Labor emerged, hoping to become the one great organization that might speak for all labor. Like the labor movement in England and a number of other European countries, the organization sought to make labor a unified force for radical political change.

However, American workers have never been sympathetic to such an overt political objective. The Knights disappeared, to be replaced in the 1880s by the American Federation of Labor (AFL), led by Samuel Gompers and devoted to the bread-and-butter issues of improving wages and working conditions, rather than the pursuit of a political class struggle. When asked what labor wanted, Gompers had a simple answer: "More."

The bread-and-butter approach remains an important characteristic of American labor. While unions sometimes support Democratic candidates, they often remain uncommitted, and on occasion support Republicans. Thus American labor has not followed the common pattern in England and some other European countries of formal, close association with one political party.

There are two kinds of unions in the United States:

1. *Industrial unions,* such as the United Auto Workers, draw on all workers in a specific industry or group of industries, regardless of the workers' skills.
2. *Craft unions,* such as the plumbers' or carpenters' unions, draw their members from *any* industry, provided the workers have a common skill.

Since its early beginnings, the history of American unions can be divided into the three periods sketched in Figure 34-1: (1) an initial low-membership period until the mid-1930s, (2) rapid growth for the next decade, and (3) the period since World War II.

The Period before the Great Depression

Until the early 1930s, unions developed in a hostile climate. On the one hand, business executives strongly resisted any attempts to unionize their firms, and would frequently retaliate against prounion workers by firing them and then blacklisting them with other potential employers. They would also sometimes use so-called ***yellow-dog contracts***: In order to get a job, a worker had to sign a commitment not to join a union.

An important question was how the courts would treat labor-management disputes. In particular, in light of the Sherman and Clayton antitrust acts, would the courts view unions as restraints on trade? Judgments either for or against unions seemed possible. On the one hand, a union could be viewed as a restraint on trade, since it is a combination of workers seeking to raise wages, just as a collusive oligopoly is a combination of sellers seeking to raise price. On the other hand, the Clayton Act seemed to exclude unions by stating that "labor is not an article of commerce." By and large, the courts' judgments during this early period did not favor labor.

For several reasons, union growth was thwarted during the 1920s and early 1930s. The AFL lost ground because it remained firmly committed to the idea of craft unionism on which it was founded. Therefore, it did not adequately appeal to the increasing number of unskilled workers in mass-production industries, such as steel and autos. Moreover, there was growth in employer resistance to unionism. Employers introduced paternalistic schemes providing labor with relatively generous benefits in an attempt to demonstrate that workers would do better without a union. Moreover, as a result of growing court hostility toward unions, employers were allowed to use injunctions (court orders) to prevent unions from picketing, striking, or pursuing almost any other activity judged threatening to business. Sometimes the courts issued injunctions without even hearing the union case.

The Period of Rapid Union Growth before and during the Second World War

In the depths of the depression in the 1930s, Congress passed several laws that improved the climate for unions. The first was the ***Norris-LaGuardia Act*** of 1932 that limited employers' use of what had become a prime weapon in the struggle against unions: the injunction. Court intervention in a labor dispute was to be limited to protecting property and preventing the use of violence.

In 1935, the ***Wagner Act*** (National Labor Relations Act) moved the government from a position of neutrality to one that favored labor. This act had three key provisions:

1. It declared the legal right of workers to form unions.
2. It prohibited employers from a number of unfair labor practices, such as firing or blacklisting prounion workers.
3. It established the National Labor Relations Board

FIGURE 34-1
Major trends in U.S. union membership, 1900–1984
American union membership remained low until the mid-1930s, then rose rapidly until the end of World War II. Since then, union membership has fallen as a proportion of the labor force.
Source: Department of Labor, *Handbook of Labor Statistics*.

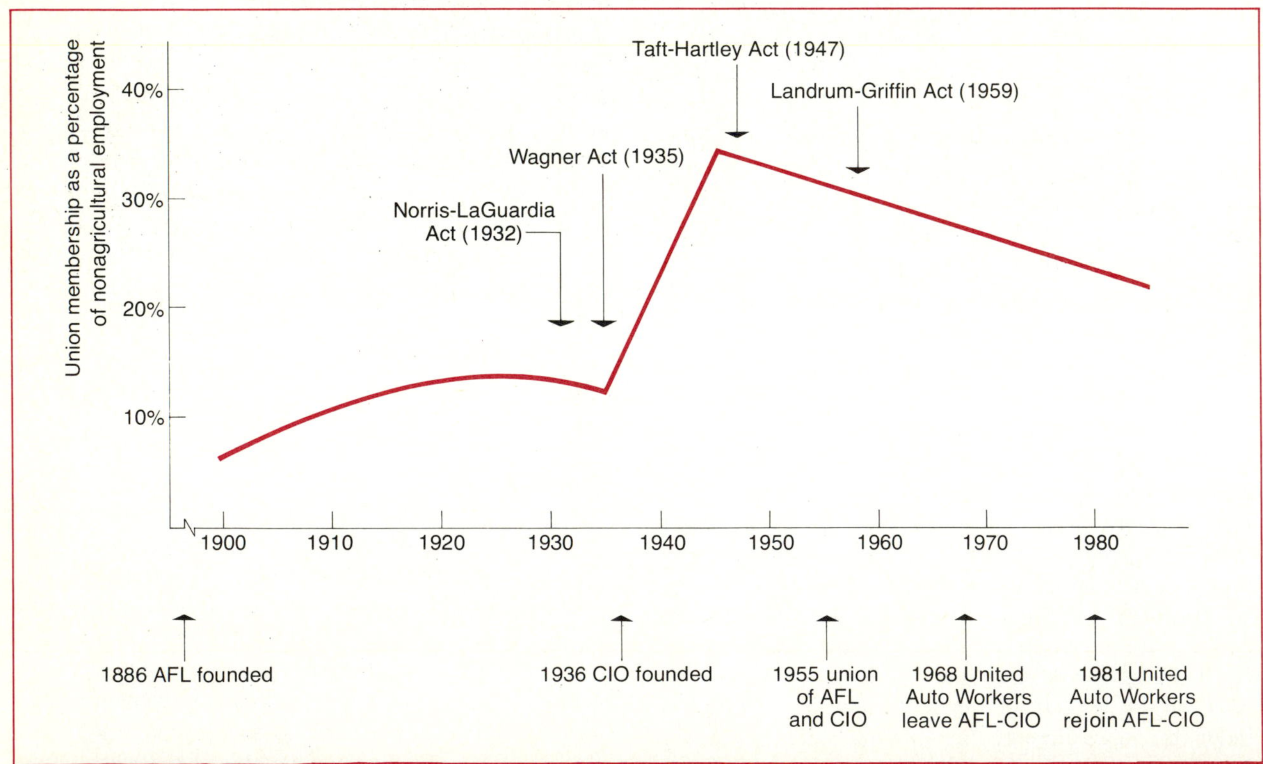

(NLRB) to control unfair labor practices by employers and to resolve disputes among unions. For example, the NLRB is empowered to hold elections in which workers decide which of two or more competing unions will represent them.

There is no question that the Wagner Act achieved its objective of removing the barriers to union growth. During the decade that followed, the proportion of the labor force that belonged to unions almost tripled. There was another important reason for this growth. In 1936, several union leaders, led by John L. Lewis, split away from the AFL because of its concentration on craft unions. They formed the Congress of Industrial Organizations (CIO), a collection of *industrial* unions. Between 1936 and 1945, the CIO had great success in unionizing the auto, steel, and other mass-production industries. (In 1955, the two unions resolved their differences and rejoined forces in the new AFL-CIO.)

The Postwar Period

Since World War II, unions have ceased to grow at the rapid rate of the preceding period. In fact, the percentage of workers in unions has actually declined. One reason has been that heavy industry—where union membership is most solidly concentrated—has had declining employment relative to other sectors of the economy. A second reason has been the shift in industrial jobs to the south, where unionism is weaker than in the north.

The popularity of unions began to decline during World War II, when the unions may have overplayed their hand. During the early years of the war, unions had added muscle in the form of a rapidly increasing membership. By 1944 they were flexing that muscle in a series of strikes that were viewed by many in the public as damaging to the war effort. The feeling that unions were becoming too powerful contributed to the passage of the Taft-Hartley Act in the face of stiff union opposition.

The Taft-Hartley Act (1947) Just as the Wagner Act 12 years earlier had dealt with "unfair" employer practices, the Taft-Hartley Act now attempted to outlaw "unfair" union practices. For example, it prohibited *closed shops* in industries engaged in interstate commerce. (Since only union members could be hired in a closed shop, it provided a union with veto power over who could be hired.) The Taft-Hartley Act also prohibited jurisdictional strikes—strikes arising from conflicts between unions over whose members will do specific jobs. It also forbade the "checkoff" of union dues unless workers agree to it in writing. (With a checkoff, employers collect dues for the union by deducting them from workers' paychecks.) In addition, the Taft-Hartley Act included provisions to increase the financial responsibility of union leaders. For example, it required pension funds to be kept separate from other union funds, and required union leaders to provide both their own membership and the National Labor Relations Board with detailed information on how union funds are spent. The act also contained a provision to delay strikes which "imperil the national health or safety." Specifically, the U.S. president was empowered to seek a court injunction in such circumstances to require strikers to return to work for an 80-day ***cooling-off period.***

However, the most controversial provision of the Taft-Hartley Act was contained in its famous section 14(b). This recognizes the right of states to enact ***right-to-work laws*** which give all workers the freedom to work, whether or not they belong to a union. Such laws make the ***closed shop*** and the ***union shop*** illegal. About 20 states—mostly in the south—have passed such laws. Union leaders consider section 14(b) to be overtly anti-union. They argue that, if membership in a union is not compulsory, workers can be free riders, participating in the benefits provided by a union without being members. Moreover, if many workers choose not to be members, it weakens the union's bargaining position. Consequently, unions have worked hard for the repeal of section 14(b). Indeed, opposition to 14(b) is considered an acid test of whether a politician is prounion or not.

A *closed shop* means that a firm can hire only workers who are already union members.

A *union shop* permits the hiring of nonunion members, but requires workers who are not yet members to join the union within a specified period, such as 30 days.

A *right-to-work law* outlaws the closed shop and the union shop in favor of the *open shop,* in which there is no requirement to join a union.

The Landrum-Griffin Act (1959) This act was passed by a Congress that was concerned over union corruption and wished to increase the restraints on union leaders. Among other stipulations, union officials were prohibited from borrowing more than $2,000 of union funds, the embezzlement of union funds became a federal offense, and restrictions were placed on ex-convicts seeking union offices. This act also sought to make union decisions more democratic by strengthening the power of members to challenge their leaders through the ballot box. It required regularly scheduled elections of union officers by secret ballot, with every member being eligible to vote. Moreover, a member's right to participate in union meetings was guaranteed, and any member was given the right to sue a union that tried to withhold any of these privileges.

While it is difficult to judge how effective this legislation has been in limiting union corruption, one conclusion is clear: It has still not completely solved the problem. In the last two decades, workers have found that it is not only their boss who may end up in jail; it may be their union leader as well. In recent decades, several Teamster presidents have gone to jail. Perhaps the most extreme example of crime occurred in the late 1960s, when Joseph Yablonski challenged Tony Boyle for the leadership of the United Mine Workers. After losing the election, Yablonski threatened to expose irregularities within the union. On December 31, 1969, an intruder murdered him, his wife, and his daughter in their sleep. In 1974, Boyle was convicted of arranging these murders and was sentenced to three life terms in jail.

The 1980s: Unions under Pressure

A combination of factors increased pressure on the unions during the 1980s. First, in August 1981, in response to an illegal strike by air-traffic controllers, President Reagan took an extremely strong action. He fired the striking workers and subsequently had their union decertified. Second, some unions—particularly in the airline industry—were adversely affected by deregulation. In order to survive in a much more competitive environment, the airline companies put pressure on employees to accept lower wages. Third, many unions were forced to make wage concessions because of the severity of the 1981–1982 recession and the threat by firms to move their plants to the less unionized sunbelt or abroad. For example, in wage settlements covering 1,000 workers or more in the first half of 1982, 58% of the workers got no wage increase at all. Two of the strongest unions—the United Auto Workers and the United Steel Workers—were under particular pressure because they had succeeded in the past in raising the wages of their members well above the U.S. manufacturing average, and both industries were suffering from intense foreign competition. Under threat of plant closures, both unions made wage concessions. (In the case of steel, some of the plants were closed anyway, in what the union viewed as a breach of faith; management argued that conditions had worsened since the agreement and there was no choice.)

The fourth reason that unions were under pressure was that management opposition had become stronger. In 1980, 15,000 workers were judged by the National Labor Relations Board to have been illegally fired for union activities; the reason for such widespread illegal practice by management was that the penalty for those who were caught was not high enough to discourage the practice. In order to escape from existing labor contracts, some firms were not only *threatening* bankruptcy but were actually entering bankruptcy voluntarily. As an example of how embattled and defensive the unions had become, the members of the United Food and Commercial Workers International Union had taken a cut in hourly wages from $10.69 to around $8 by 1983. Some members had lost their jobs altogether and had been replaced by nonunion workers earning $5.50 an hour. Furthermore, economic pressures forced a number of unions to accept a two-tiered wage structure. While existing workers continued to receive the old wage schedule, new workers could be hired at substantially lower rates. Boeing and American Airlines were among the firms that reduced labor costs with such contracts.

LABOR UNIONS: THE EXERCISE OF MARKET POWER

While union fortunes have ebbed and flowed, the evidence is that unions have succeeded in their major task of raising wages of their members. Statistical studies indicate that U.S. union members earn an average of 10% to

25% more than nonunion workers in comparable activities, with 20% being a figure that is frequently cited. However, it has been estimated that roughly half of this higher wage can be explained by the fact that unionized firms are able to hire more productive workers who could be earning a higher wage, whether they were in a union or not. This means that, for workers of *equal productivity,* a union is able to raise wages by only about 10%.[2]

In this section we consider the effects of a union that exercises its market power to raise the wage rate of its members. We also examine what happens when a union bargains to ensure employment for its members.

The Economic Effects When a Union Negotiates Higher Wages: A First Approximation

We begin by assuming a perfectly competitive labor market, with equilibrium at E_1 in Figure 34-2. Employers have no market power and take the wage rate as given. Workers have no market power and also take the wage rate as given.

Now suppose that this industry is unionized—that is, the workers who supply labor form a monopoly (a union) that raises the wage rate from W_1 to W_2. The enforcement of this higher wage requires "union discipline"; members must not be allowed to offer their labor services for less than W_2. Faced with this wage, employers react by moving up their demand curve from E_1 to E_2. Because the union has raised wages, employment is reduced from N_1 to N_2.

Efficiency effect There is the standard deadweight efficiency loss shown by the red triangle. This loss occurs because employment has been reduced from its perfectly competitive, efficient amount at N_1 to N_2, and displaced workers have had to move to industries where their productivity is lower. (This is the efficiency loss from too little employment described in detail in Figure 33-6*c*.)

Transfer effects Capital and other nonlabor factors of production lose area 3 + 4. (As explained in Figure 33-4, they earned 6 + 3 + 4 at initial equilibrium E_1. After the union is formed and equilibrium moves to E_2, they earn only area 6, for a net loss of 3 + 4.) Of this loss, 3 is a transfer to the N_2 workers who retain their jobs in this industry and enjoy a wage increase of W_1W_2. This is the reason they formed a union: to acquire area 3 of income that the owners of capital and other factors of production would otherwise receive. However, while these N_2 workers in the industry gain, there is a loss to the N_2N_1 workers who would like to work in this industry but who must instead take lower-productivity, lower-wage jobs elsewhere.

In conclusion, we emphasize two important points:

1. In judging that inefficiency results from the unionization of an industry—and from the other labor market changes we examine—we must make assumptions similar to those we made in analyzing product markets. For example, we assume that perfectly competitive conditions exist elsewhere in the economy. Moreover, we also keep in mind that, although we can make the statement that the move from E_1 to E_2 in Figure 34-2 is inefficient, we cannot make the stronger statement that this move has an adverse overall effect, without making some assumption about how the winners and losers compare in their evaluation of income. Remember: Efficiency is desirable, but it's not the whole story.
2. Figure 34-2 illustrates once again the similarity of the markets for labor and goods. Specifically note how the monopolization of a labor market in Figure 34-2 is similar to the monopolization of a product market in Figure 25-5 except, of course, that we are now talking about the wage and employment of labor rather than the price and quantity of a product.[3]

[2]See George Jakubson, "Effect of Unions on Wages: Estimation from Panel Data," Working paper, Department of Economics, NYSSILR, Cornell University, 1985. Also see C. J. Parsley, "Labor Union Effects on Wage Gains: A Survey of Recent Literature," *Journal of Economic Literature,* March 1980, p. 20.

*[3]There is an important reason why we cannot analyze monopoly in a labor market in exactly the same way as we analyze monopoly in a product market. In a product market, a monopoly firm will take into account any loss of sales (reduction in output) that results from its high price. However, in a labor market, it is not clear how fully a union will take into account any reduced employment that results from its high wage. This may be particularly true if the industry is growing and if the high wage does not displace any of the *current* union members, but instead reduces only the number of *new* workers coming into the industry. This difficulty prevents us from applying the standard analysis of monopoly to determine precisely how high the union will raise the wage rate.

Job Security

Job security may become the prime objective of a union if employment is shrinking—for example, because of reduced demand for the product, the introduction of labor-saving machines, or the growth of imports. There are three principal ways that a union may try to prevent the loss of jobs. First, it may seek protection from the government in the form of tariffs or quotas on imports. Second, it may negotiate a reduction in the number of hours in a standard workweek; if all workers work fewer hours, no worker need be laid off. (Moreover, if the union is able to negotiate a sufficient increase in the per-hour wage rate, its members may not suffer any income reduction; they may work less for the same pay.) The third way that a strong union may deal with falling employment is to use its bargaining strength to negotiate a ***featherbedding*** agreement. One example was the railroad firemen who had their jobs guaranteed even after coal-burning locomotives were replaced by diesels which had no fire.

FIGURE 34-2

The effects of unionizing an industry in a previously competitive labor market

When a union is formed and raises the wage rate from W_1 to W_2, equilibrium moves from the perfectly competitive point E_1 to E_2; that is, employers respond by reducing employment from N_1 to N_2. The result is the efficiency loss shown by areas 4 + 1. This reflects the fact that N_2N_1 workers don't have jobs in this industry where their productivity would be high, as shown by the height of the demand curve D; instead they have to take jobs elsewhere with lower productivity given by the height of the marginal cost for labor curve. The red triangular wedge between these two curves is the nation's lost productivity—its efficiency loss.

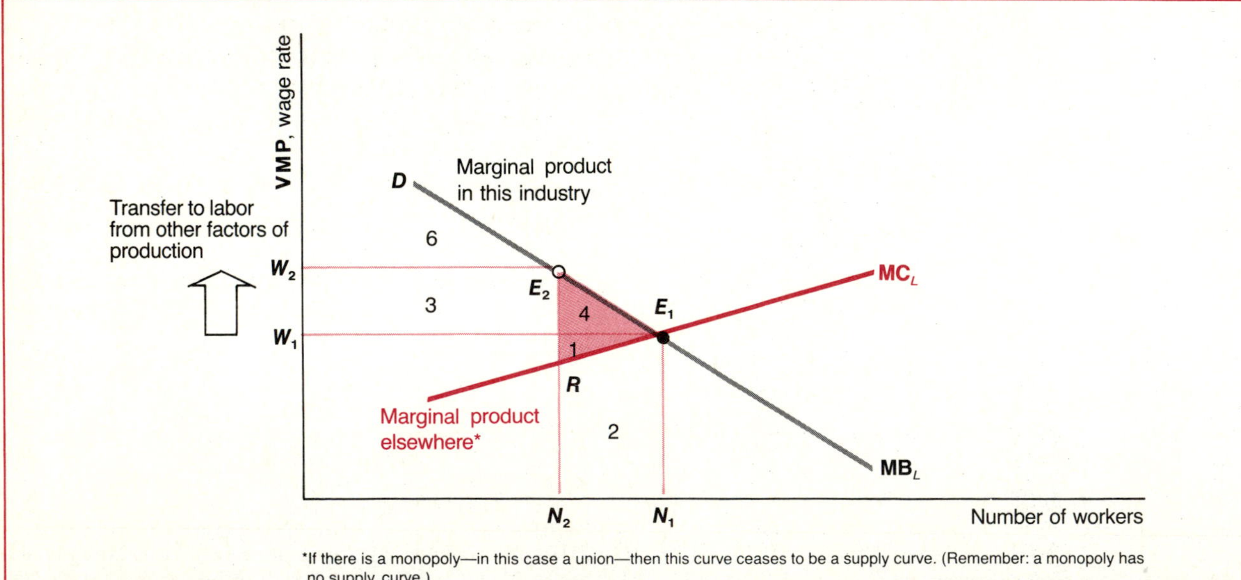

*If there is a monopoly—in this case a union—then this curve ceases to be a supply curve. (Remember: a monopoly has no supply curve.)

***Featherbedding* is the employment of labor in superfluous jobs.**[4]

What is the effect of such superfluous work? The answer is that it generally keeps employment in that industry higher than in a perfectly competitive labor market.[5] Specifically, it keeps the number of jobs at N_2 in Figure 33-6*b* rather than allowing it to decrease to the competitive number N_1. Moreover, it leads to an efficiency loss which often exceeds the red triangle shown in that earlier diagram. The reason is that this triangular efficiency loss is based on the assumption that employers use the extra workers they hire as productively as possible. However, many featherbedding contracts require employers not only to hire more workers, but also to assign them to tasks with low or even zero productivity. This makes the efficiency loss greater.

Is this criticism of featherbedding too severe? Because it protects workers who might otherwise have difficulty in getting another job, isn't it a way of introducing compassion into the economic system? The answer is yes, but it is a bad way to do it. Far better to ease labor's shift into other jobs than to have society carry an overhead of unproductive employment into the future. One compromise way of negotiating the end to a featherbedding contract is for the company to guarantee that all those individuals now holding jobs will continue to be employed, but they will not be replaced. Although this may be a costly solution, it at least guarantees that the problem will disappear as the present work force reaches retirement age. This is far superior to a featherbedding contract, where the inefficiency doesn't disappear when people in nonproductive jobs retire because they keep getting replaced. (More on the relation between efficiency and compassion is provided in Box 34-1.)

HOW UNIONS INCREASE EFFICIENCY: THE OTHER SIDE OF THE COIN

In our analysis so far, we have seen how a union may reduce efficiency by negotiating an increase in wages that reduces employment. But this is only part of the story. A union may also have *favorable* effects on efficiency.

1. Unions can improve the morale of the work force, and improve communication between workers and management. This may lead to better decision making.
2. By providing workers with a collective voice, a union makes it possible for them to improve their working conditions rather than quitting.[6] Because unions reduce ''quit-rates'' and labor turnover, there is less disruption in the workplace.
3. Even if there are none of these positive ''voice'' effects, there is another reason why a union that increases wages may still increase efficiency rather than reduce it. This will occur if the labor market is not initially perfectly competitive because market power is held by *employers* on the other side of the market. It will now be shown that in this case the formation of a union may be a counterbalance that increases efficiency.

MONOPSONY: MARKET POWER ON THE EMPLOYERS' SIDE OF THE LABOR MARKET

Employers typically quote the wage rate they will pay. In

[4]Featherbedding as defined by the Taft-Hartley Act (payment for work not actually performed) is illegal. Here we are concerned with a broader definition that includes cases where workers are on the job but the work is contrived; that is, the job would not exist were it not guaranteed by the union-management contract.

[5]This is not always the case, however. Featherbedding was a contributing factor in the death of some newspapers. In particular, some union contracts required that newpapers receiving typeset copy from advertisers had to reset this copy in ''bogus'' type which was not actually used. Featherbedding therefore may have resulted in fewer newspaper jobs even though it may have kept up the number of typesetting jobs.

[6]The fact that unions exist may even lead to an improvement in working conditions in firms that are *not* unionized. These firms may fear that, if they don't improve their working conditions, their workers may form a union. The existence of a union may also benefit nonunion workers *in the same firm*. In a number of instances, firms that have signed contracts with unions for higher wages have passed on the same increase to their nonunion labor force. However, the conclusion that unions raise nonunion wages is still a subject of debate, because in another respect unions exert downward pressure on nonunion jobs: The higher union wage reduces employment in union jobs; this in turn increases the number of workers looking for nonunion jobs, and consequently tends to lower wages there.

BOX 34-1

THE CONFLICTING OBJECTIVES OF COMPASSION AND EFFICIENCY

Two centuries ago, at the beginning of the industrial revolution in Britain, labor-saving machinery was introduced into the textile industry. Displaced workers in those days had much bleaker prospects than today: It was harder to find another job. Without a job, a worker's family faced severe malnutrition, or worse. Consequently, there were riots in which workers (the Luddites) broke into the factories and destroyed the new labor-saving machines. While recognizing their plight, we might ask: Suppose they had succeeded? Suppose labor-saving machinery had been banned and primitive handcrafting jobs guaranteed? If the Luddites and their heirs had been successful in thwarting technological change, wouldn't our situation today be very much like theirs two centuries ago? And if so, what progress would we have made against the problem that concerned them most: poverty?

Although labor-saving machinery may create transitional unemployment, it creates far better jobs in the long run. When bulldozers are introduced, whole armies of workers with shovels lose their jobs. But in the long run, this is highly beneficial both for society and also, in most cases, *for the workers who initially lose their jobs.* This is not only true of the ditchdiggers who get high-productivity and high-pay jobs driving the bulldozers. It is also true of other ditchdiggers who get high-productivity jobs in new, growing industries such as electronics, aircraft, and so on. These jobs exist because the introduction of bulldozers and other machines increases our ability to produce and therefore raises our income and purchasing power. This in turn means that we can afford to buy products that did not exist before.

In brief, society benefits because the labor force is engaged in more productive activities than ditchdigging. Because machines now perform menial jobs, we produce more. The resulting increase in our income allows us to afford more compassion—that is, we are able to ensure people against the extremes of poverty that had to be faced in earlier, less productive eras. The point is a simple one: In protecting people against severe economic adversity, it is important not to use methods that thwart progress by locking in inefficiency.

doing so, they frequently do not act like perfect competitors who take a market wage as given. Instead, they exercise a degree of market power. In particular, any firm that employs a large fraction of a local labor force will have an influence over the wage rate.

To analyze this situation, we initially assume exactly the same perfectly competitive market that we began with in the previous diagram, with equilibrium at E_1 reproduced in Figure 34-3. This time, instead of introducing monopoly (a single seller, in the form of a union) we introduce ***monopsony***—a single buyer, in the form of a single employer of labor. What happens if this single employer quotes a lower wage rate, while workers on the other side of the market act as perfect competitors, taking this wage rate as given? Specifically, suppose that the employer quotes a wage W_2 below the perfectly competitive wage W_1. In response to wage W_2, some workers leave this now unattractive industry for other jobs. In other words, the workers in this industry move down their supply curve from E_1 to a new equilibrium at E_2. The result is the red triangular efficiency loss because employment at N_2 is less than the perfectly competitive amount at N_1. (Details on this move from equilibrium E_1 to E_2 are given in Box 34-2.)

At the same time, the reduction in the wage paid by the employer results in the transfer shown by the arrow to the left of this diagram. This transfer is from workers who receive the lower wage, to other factors of production who benefit because there is more of the firm's income left for them. (An example of an even stronger exercise of market power by a monopsonist, and therefore an even greater transfer of income, is given in Box 34-3.)

Here we see another example of Adam Smith's "invisible hand" gone astray. The monopsonistic employer's pursuit of private benefit does *not* lead to public benefit. Quite the contrary. It leads to the deadweight efficiency loss shown by the red triangle in Figure 34-3.

In reality, there are few cases in which monopsony occurs in its pure form with only *one* buyer. There is more likely to be a small group of employers, that is, an *oligopsony* with a few buyers. In quoting a wage rate, each firm has some latitude; but to a greater or lesser degree it is influenced by the wages quoted by competing firms. On the one hand, competition among these firms may leave each with very little influence over the wage it

FIGURE 34-3

Effects when a perfectly competitive labor market is monopsonized

When a monopsony is formed, equilibrium moves from the perfectly competitive point E_1 to E_2. (Because the monopsonist quotes lower wage W_2, fewer workers offer their labor services and employment falls from N_1 to N_2.) As first explained in Figure 33-6*c*, there is the efficiency loss shown by the red triangle because too few workers are employed in this industry. The lower wage also results in a transfer from labor to other factors of production, as indicated by the arrow to the left of this diagram.

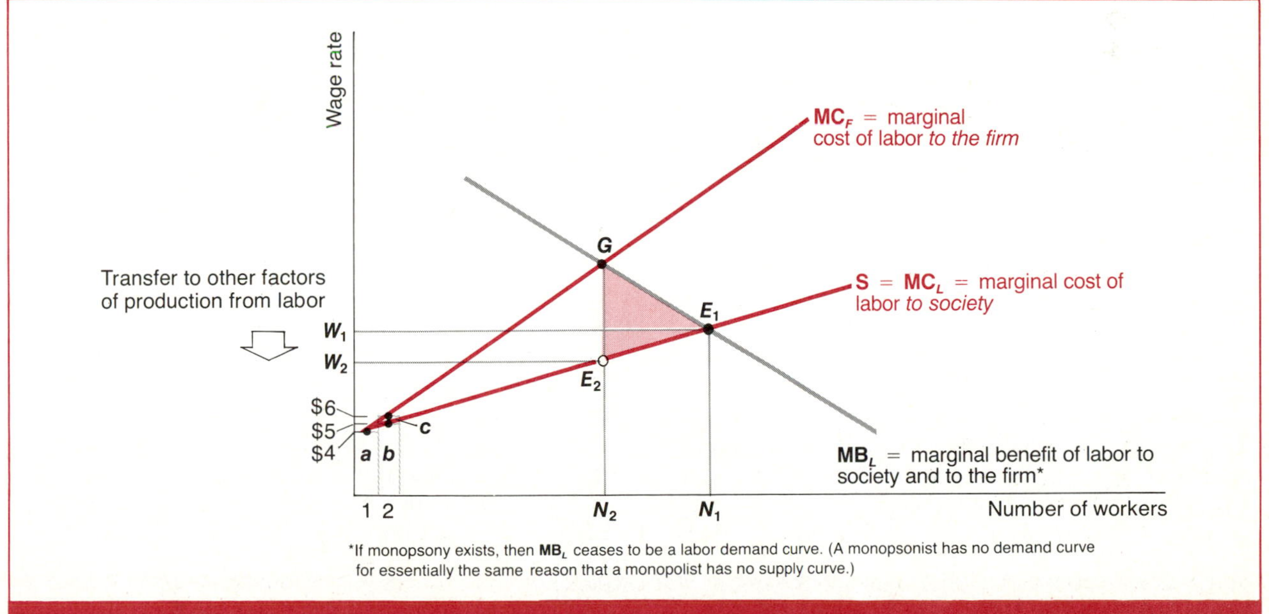

*If monopsony exists, then MB_L ceases to be a labor demand curve. (A monopsonist has no demand curve for essentially the same reason that a monopolist has no supply curve.)

BOX 34-2

HOW FAR DOES A MONOPSONIST TRY TO REDUCE THE WAGE RATE?

To choose the wage rate that will maximize its profits, the monopsony firm first calculates its marginal cost of hiring labor MC_F from the supply of labor *S*. This calculation is illustrated in the lower left hand corner of Figure 34-3: From the *S* curve we see that the firm must pay \$4 an hour at point *a* to hire one worker and \$5 an hour at point *b* to hire two. However, the firm's marginal cost MC_F of hiring the second worker is not \$5 but \$6—the \$5 × 2 = \$10 it costs to hire the two workers less the \$4 it cost to hire one. Thus MC_F, the marginal cost of labor to the monopsony firm, lies above the supply curve of labor *S*.

To maximize profit, this firm hires labor to point *G*, where its marginal cost of hiring labor MC_F is equal to the marginal benefit it receives from hiring labor. With its desired employment thus being N_2, what's the lowest wage it can quote? The answer is W_2, which is the point on the *S* curve above N_2. At this wage rate, the supply curve *S* indicates that just exactly the desired number of workers N_2 will offer their services to this firm.

Finally, Figure 34-3 provides another view of why a red efficiency loss arises from an employment level of N_2: The private firm equates the marginal benefit of labor MB_L not to *society's* marginal cost MC_L, but instead to its *own* marginal cost MC_F. Since the marginal benefit and cost of labor to *society* are not equated, the solution is not an efficient one.

can quote. In this case, the wage may be close to the competitive level W_1. On the other hand, if the few oligoposonists collude, perhaps in some covert way, they may together lower the wage rate well below W_1 toward the level W_2 that a monopsonist would choose.

Although monopsony rarely occurs in its pure form, with only one buyer, there has been one notable example: the monopsony power that the owners of baseball clubs used to have in buying the services of their players.

Monopsony and Baseball Salaries

I don't understand why grown men play this game anyhow. They ought to be lawyers or doctors or garbage men. Games should be left for kids.

Ted Turner,
owner of the Atlanta Braves

One reason grown men play baseball is because of the high income it offers, especially since the monopsony

BOX 34-3

MONOPSONY AND DISCRIMINATION IN THE LABOR MARKET

Monopsonists who use their market power to depress the wage rate of their entire labor force may go one step further and reduce even more the wage paid to a specific subset of their workers, such as a minority group. To illustrate, consider the monopsonistic firm that has used its market power to depress the wage rate in Figure 34-3 from the perfectly competitive level W_1 to W_2. It may then go one step further and offer the minority group an even lower wage. The firm may discriminate in this way for the same reason that the doctor who was a monopolist in a small town discriminated by charging different fees. In either case, discrimination is a way of increasing profit.

power of club owners like Ted Turner was broken in 1976. Before this, the "reserve clause" had made each major league owner a monopsonist, since a player could not sign a contract with any other major league team. However, beginning in 1976, a player in certain circumstances could become a free agent and negotiate with other clubs.

Figure 34-4 shows what happened to a few of the players who became free agents. A comparison of their before-and-after salaries indicates the remarkable way that the monopsony power of the reserve clause had depressed players' salaries. Moreover, since 1976 confirming evidence has continued to accumulate. In 1980, the baseball world was astonished when the New York Yankees signed outfielder and free agent Dave Winfield to a contract worth an estimated $1.5 million to $2 million *per year for 10 years*. Compare this with his $350,000 salary in San Diego the previous year before his escape, as a free agent, from the monopsony power of the reserve clause. To get some idea of Winfield's "before-and-after" situation, just increase the height of both bars for Baylor in Figure 34-4 by *ten times*. Further evidence that Winfield's high salary was due to his free agent status was to be found in the much lower salaries of equally good, or arguably better, players still held in the grip of the reserve clause.

The Effects of Unions Reconsidered

We are now in a position to show why our criticism of unions, which was valid if markets were initially competitive, is not necessarily justified if there is monopsony power on the other side of the market.

FIGURE 34-4
How monopsony (the reserve clause) depressed baseball salaries. (figures in $000s, rounded)

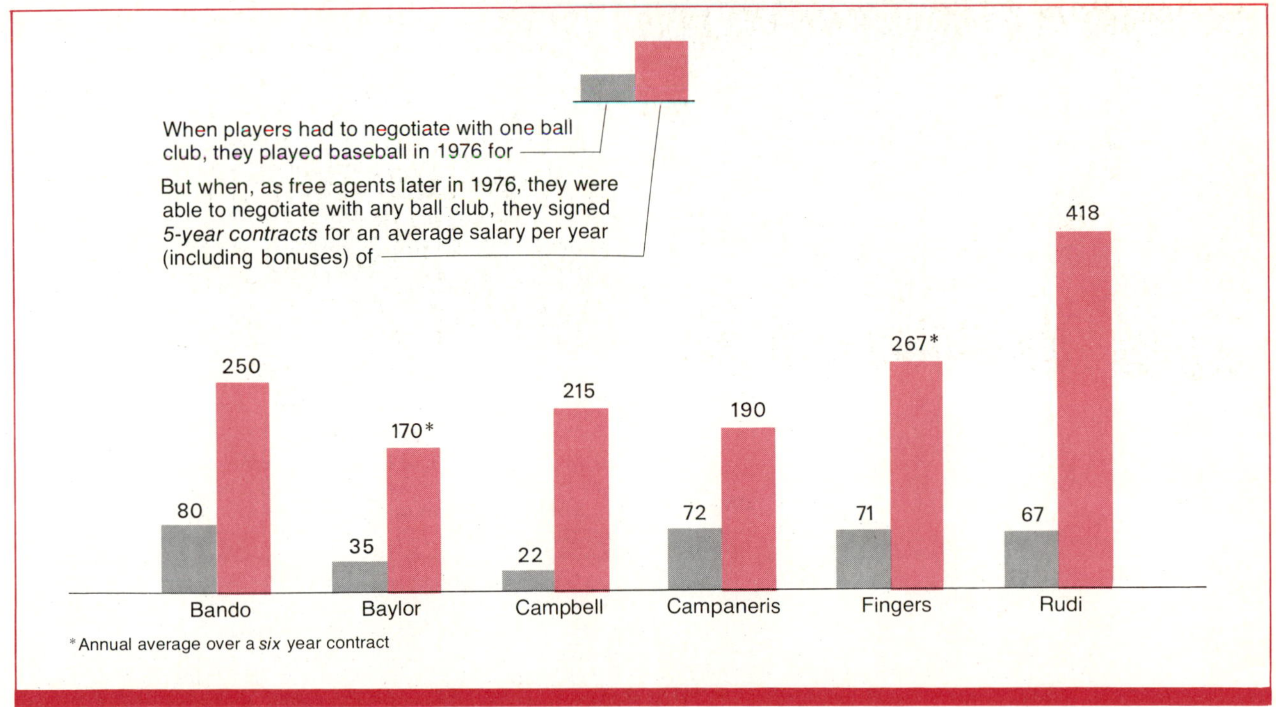
When players had to negotiate with one ball club, they played baseball in 1976 for
But when, as free agents later in 1976, they were able to negotiate with any ball club, they signed *5-year contracts* for an average salary per year (including bonuses) of
80
250
35
170*
22
215
72
190
71
267*
67
418
Bando
Baylor
Campbell
Campaneris
Fingers
Rudi
*Annual average over a *six* year contract

Figure 34-5 shows how a union that pushes up wages can actually raise, rather than lower, economic efficiency. This will occur, for example, if there has been a monopsony firm hiring labor, and this firm has lowered the wage rate from the competitive level W to W_1. At this lower wage, fewer workers have been offering their labor services to this industry. Therefore, because of monopsony in this labor market, employment has been reduced from N to N_1—that is, equilibrium has moved from E to E_1—with a consequent efficiency loss of areas 1 + 2. If a union is now formed and raises the wage rate from W_1 to W_2—moving the equilibrium from E_1 to E_2—the efficiency loss is reduced from areas 1 + 2 to just area 2. In other words, the formation of this union results in an efficiency gain of area 1. Of course, the union also benefits union members by recapturing some of the income previously lost to the monopsonist.

FIGURE 34-5

How inefficiency may be reduced if a union raises wages in a monopsonized labor market

Before the union, the monopsonist set the wage rate at W_1; with equilibrium at E_1, there was an efficiency loss of 1 + 2. When the union is formed it raises the wage to W_2. Equilibrium moves from E_1 to E_2, some employment is restored, and the efficiency loss is reduced to area 2. Consequently, the increased wage improves efficiency by area 1. It also transfers income from the monopsonist to labor. But if the union pushes the wage up past the competitive wage W—for example, toward W_3—equilibrium will be shifted away from E towards E_3 and efficiency will be reduced once again.

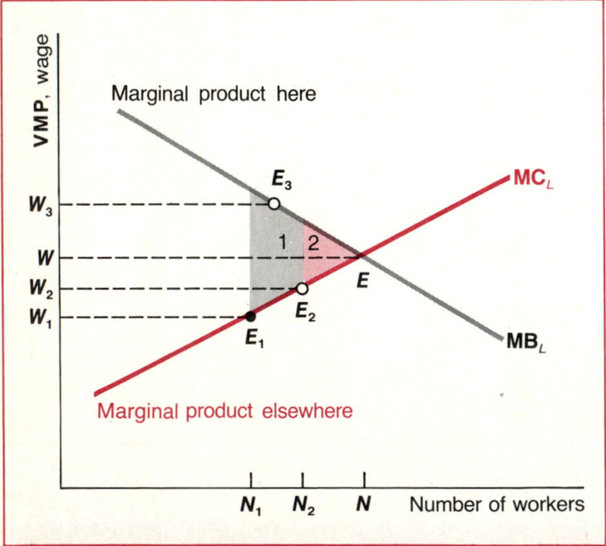

Thus, the following case can be made for unions. When workers form a union in a labor market dominated by a monopsonistic employer quoting a take-it-or-leave-it wage like W_1, they send a representative to the bargaining table who can counter by presenting the same sort of take-it-or-leave-it offer to management: "If you do not accept our wage claim, we will strike your firm, withdrawing all workers from the job and closing down your operations." Thus the union allows workers to speak from a position of strength, and the wage will then be negotiated between union and management. Typically, it will lie somewhere between the initial "take-it-or-leave-it" offers of the two parties, that is, somewhere between management's take-it-or-leave-it offer of W_1 in Figure 34-5, and labor's take-it-or-leave-it demand of, say, W_3. Only in this way can labor exercise what Kenneth Galbraith calls ***countervailing power*** to prevent the wage from being lowered all the way to management's target level of W_1. Moreover, if labor is able, through such bargaining, to raise its wage from W_1 to, say, W_2, it will not only be promoting its own interest. It will also be increasing overall economic efficiency.[7] Furthermore, union practices like picketing are a means of increasing the union's countervailing power by making it more difficult for the employer to hire strike breakers.

A Complication

Such is the case for unions. However, it does not justify

[7]This is another example of the *theory of the second best,* first encountered in Box 25-1. If there is only a single firm in a small town, it will be able to exercise monopsony influence over the wage rate. The economist's "first best" efficient solution—with perfect competition on both sides of the market—is simply not possible, no matter how desirable it might be. Instead, we must look for a second best solution. This may involve workers forming a union in order to influence price and thus counterbalance the power that the monopsonist already enjoys on the other side of the market. In his *American Capitalism: The Concept of Countervailing Power* (Boston: Houghton Mifflin Company, 1952) John Kenneth Galbraith favored strong unions as a way of balancing employers' power.

every exercise of market power. If a union gets very strong and pushes the wage up beyond W toward W_3, equilibrium will shift away from E toward E_3, and efficiency will once again be reduced.

Thus, the typical policy problem in the labor market is not that one side has market power and the other does not, but rather, that the relative power of the two may be unbalanced. If the government is pursuing the objective of making labor markets more efficient, it should be careful if it is reducing the bargaining power of one group and not the other. Such government action may sometimes make the situation better; but sometimes it may make it worse. If the government is reducing the market power of the group that is already in the weaker position, this government action will be making the problem of imbalance worse. On the other hand, if the government is increasing the market power of that group, it will be making the situation better.

This discussion also allows us to sharpen up our earlier conclusion about a minimum wage. If a minimum wage raises the wage rate in Figure 34-5 from an existing very low level like W_1 toward the competitive level W, employment and efficiency in this labor market are increased rather than decreased. On the other hand, if the minimum wage is set at a higher level and therefore raises the wage rate *away from* W and toward W_3, employment and efficiency are reduced. Therefore, a guideline for a minimum wage might be to set it near the competitive wage level in most industries. Unfortunately, this guideline is difficult to put into practice, because competitive wage rates are difficult to estimate and differ among industries. Furthermore, the government may be paying little attention to the objective of efficiency, concentrating on the redistribution of income instead.

BILATERAL MONOPOLY: RELATIVE BARGAINING POWER

When both sides have market power as in Figure 34-5, they push in opposite directions. While the employer tries to keep the wage rate down close to W_1, the union tries to push it up close to W_3. The outcome depends on the bargaining power of the two sides. We cannot tell by looking at the two curves in this diagram precisely where the final solution will be.

Which Side Has the Stronger Bargaining Position?

To see the importance of bargaining power, suppose that there is only one company in a mining town and that it faces an ineffective union representing only a minority of the workers. In this case, the company will be in a good position to keep the wage low. On the other hand, if there is one union facing a number of employers, the union may have the stronger bargaining position. It has sometimes been suggested that this used to be the situation in the auto industry—although Ford and GM could scarcely be considered weak bargaining adversaries.

If the United Auto Workers judges that its negotiations with the industry are not proceeding in a satisfactory way, it typically threatens to pull its workers out on strike in one of the auto companies, say Ford. If it does so, Ford workers on strike will get income support from a union strike fund drawn from workers from all the auto companies. But the company being struck (Ford) does not get the same sort of support from the other companies in the industry. True, Ford may get moral support from the other firms, but they still go on selling cars and cutting into Ford's market. And therein lies Ford's problem. If it is shut down by a strike and unable to produce cars, it will find that its share of the market is being eroded and that its profits are falling. In fact, a strong union may have the power to drive a company bankrupt—and sometimes this does happen, although not by design.

Workers rightly regard driving a firm out of business as "overkill," since this would destroy their jobs. Consequently, a union is unlikely to pick as its target one of the financially weak companies in an industry. If a firm is already close to bankruptcy, a strike threat may be very ineffective. It may be met only by the resigned observation: "If we agree to your wage demand, we go bankrupt. If we don't and you strike, we go bankrupt. There is nothing we can do." The negotiations may end there. Consequently, the union will select as its target a company that is reasonably sound financially—one that is both able to afford a sizable wage increase and can be hurt a great deal by a strike without being driven bankrupt.

STRIKES

The bargaining position of either side can also depend on its ability to outlast the other in a long strike. For example, the credibility of a strike threat by a union depends in part on the size of its strike fund. If this has been depleted by earlier strikes, the union is in a weak position. The company can play a strong hand, making a low offer near W_1 and sticking close to it, with the knowledge that the union cannot afford to strike. On the other hand, a company will be in a weak bargaining position if *it* cannot afford a strike. This may be the case for several reasons:

1. A construction company that has to pay heavy penalties for delay in completing a project may be forced to capitulate to a strike threat by the union.
2. A firm producing a perishable good or service may be in a weak bargaining position because sales and profits lost during a strike may be lost forever. ("Perishable" is used broadly, applying not only to physically perishable goods such as fruit but also to a good that goes out of date. For example, if a newspaper cannot deliver today's edition, the papers become worthless.)

Of course, firms producing goods that are not perishable are in a much stronger position—especially if these firms have accumulated large inventories and can consequently keep selling right through a strike. It is no accident that before critical wage negotiations, companies try to build up inventories, just as unions try to build up strike funds.

The Cost of a Strike

Strikes are costly to both sides: to labor in the form of lost wages, to management in the form of lost sales and profits. To illustrate this, suppose that, in the absence of a strike, the wage is W in Figure 34-6, with employment N. Then a strike that reduces employment to zero involves a temporary cost in terms of lost output valued at areas 1 + 2. Labor loses income 1—that is, its wage W times employment N—while the income lost by other factors is the remaining area 2.

Since both parties face a substantial loss in the event of a strike, it is often assumed that when a strike does occur, it is the result of an error in judgment by at least one of the conflicting parties. However, this need not be the case, as we will now show.

Labor-Management Negotiations to Avoid Strikes

Case *a* in Figure 34-7 illustrates the overwhelming majority of situations: Labor and management should be able to find a wage to agree on, and thus avoid a strike. The range of wages management is willing to pay (arrow *M*) and the range of wages labor is willing to take (arrow *L*) overlap through the shaded range W_1W_2. Any wage rate in this positive, shaded "contract zone" is acceptable to both parties. (Remember: The term "wage rate"

FIGURE 34-6

Short-run cost of a strike to labor and other factors of production

Without a strike, the value of total output in this industry is area 1 + 2, as first noted in Figure 33-4. Labor earns area 1, and other factors of production earn 2. But *if a strike does occur,* both these income areas are lost. (The cost may be less if some of the production lost during a strike can be made up after the strike is settled or if, in anticipation of the strike, the firm is able to increase its output and inventories.)

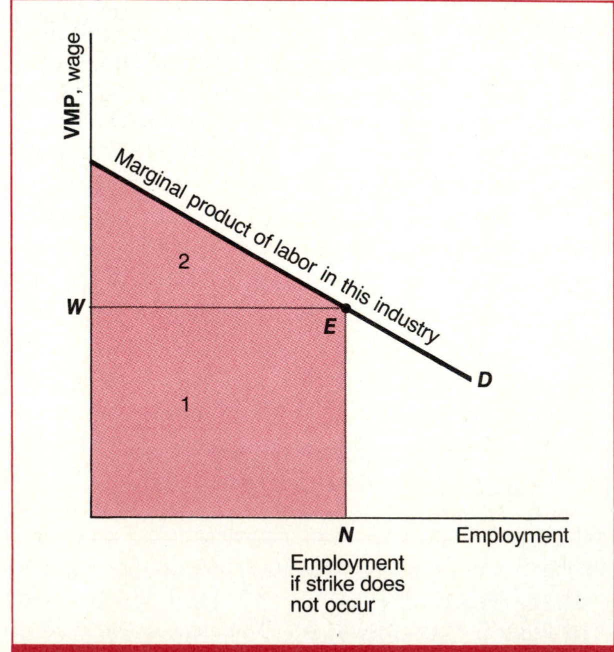

means total compensation to labor, including fringe benefits and improvements in working conditions.)

The actual negotiations may begin with labor demanding W_4 and management offering W_3. To the public, it appears that they are far apart and there is little hope of an agreement. However, as the negotiations proceed, both sides compromise, trading off one claim against another. Often neither party will officially concede anything; this may be viewed as a sign of weakness. Instead, each simply remains silent on a claim made by the other, and this "trade" is thereafter mutually recognized. Thus management moves up its arrow *M* and labor moves down its arrow *L*, until they reach a point of agreement at, say, W_5. In settling on this, management's negotiating team claims success; labor has been negotiated all the way down from its original demand of W_4. The union is also able to claim success; it has negotiated management all the way up from its original offer of W_3.

Most labor negotiations follow this sort of pattern and result in an agreement; a strike is avoided, and there are no stories in the newspapers. The highly publicized cases are those where a strike *does* occur. How does this happen? One answer is shown in panel *b*, where *L* and *M* do not overlap. There is *no* wage acceptable to both parties, regardless of the negotiating skill they may display. This case will be considered in a moment, but first it is important to explain why a strike may occur even in panel *a* where there *is* a mutually acceptable range of wage rates. Two reasons have been cited:

1. One of the parties may have some extraneous objective. For example, a company may want a strike as a means of weakening or destroying workers' support for their union. Alternatively, the union may want a strike in the belief that it will improve labor solidarity and morale. Or, either side may want a strike as a way to increase its long-run credibility—as a means of establishing that when it threatens a strike in future negotiations, it is not bluffing. Credibility is very important for each side because it makes it possible in the future to get a satisfactory settlement simply by *threatening* to strike, rather than having to rely on the far more costly method of *actually* striking.

2. One or both of the parties may engage in poor bargaining strategy. For example, suppose that management's initial offer is far below W_3—in fact, so low that it is viewed by labor as an insult. The anger that results may sour the negotiations enough to cause an unnecessary strike. An alternative bargaining error by management may be to make an initial offer that is too *generous*. Specifically, suppose management initially offers W_1, and states that this is its final, best possible offer (which it is; note that W_1 is right at the top of arrow *M*). The problem is that the union leaders may not believe it. They may view it as a standard opening offer and attempt to negotiate it up. When this attempt fails, a strike occurs because wage W_1 cannot be accepted by the union. It will look foolish to its membership if it has gone through weeks or months of trying to negotiate the company up, and has been unable to budge it an inch. It will seem that management has dictated the wage from the beginning, and all that the union has done is to make concessions. Why do the workers need such a union? Thus, although management has been very generous in offering W_1, it has inadvertently caused a strike because it has not "played the negotiating game." It has not followed the cardinal rule of "giving the other side a ladder to climb down."

Thus, even when there is a positive contract zone of acceptable wage rates (W_1W_2), an agreement may not be achieved because of inept negotiating. In the words of Lloyd Reynolds of Yale University:[8]

> Negotiators may stake out firm positions from which it is later difficult to retreat, may misread the signals from the other side, [or] may be unable to surmount the tactical difficulties of graceful concession.

While economic forces set the background and help to define the limits W_1W_2 within which the negotiated wage will fall, collective bargaining has some of the characteristics of a poker game: The wage negotiated is very much the product of the bargaining skills of the participants. Without minimal skills, there may be no bargain at all.

As already noted, the final reason that a strike may occur is that a positive contract zone does not exist—as

[8] *Labor Economics and Labor Relations*, 8th ed. (Englewood Cliffs, N.J.: Prentice-Hall, 1982), p. 447.

in case *b* in Figure 34-7. In this situation a strike cannot be avoided, because the positions (arrows) of the two parties do not overlap. On the eve of the strike, there is no wage that is acceptable to both. Each party would rather have a strike than agree to the other side's last offer.

However, the longer the strike goes on, the farther the two parties move to the right in this diagram, and the more likely it is that each side will modify its previous strong position—that is, the more likely it is that the two arrows L' and M' will approach each other. Workers on the picket lines increasingly feel the financial pinch of lost wages. Similarly, management sees its losses mount. Both recognize that the other *does,* in fact, mean business. Thus L' and M' eventually meet and the strike is settled, at a compromise wage such as W_8. But precisely because W_8 *is* a compromise wage, it is more attractive for each side than its opponent's last offer before the strike, as the short arrows on the far right indicate. Thus, achieving a more attractive wage is an incentive for each side to accept a strike rather than to capitulate to the other on the eve of the strike. (Sometimes, one side "loses a strike" and is forced to settle at or very near the prestrike offer of the other. In this case, it has made a mistake by not settling earlier.)

The Frequency of Strikes

Although strikes do occur, we have already noted that they are not very frequent. On average, just less than 1% of the working time of unionized labor was lost in strikes between 1971 and 1980. In the early 1980s, about 11% of unionized workers went on strike in an average year. (When we also include nonunionized labor, which is less frequently on strike, these figures become much smaller.[9])

However, strikes may be more costly than these figures suggest. They may result not only in lost output in the industries where the strikes occur; they may also inflict spillover costs on other industries.

Spillover Costs of a Strike

To illustrate, suppose that when the tire industry is on strike the value of the lost output and income *in that industry* is shown as area 3 in panel *a* of Figure 34-8; this is exactly the same as areas 1 + 2 in Figure 34-6. The loss may not end here: As tire supplies are depleted, auto production may be delayed or dislocated. This disruption involves a cost to the auto industry and inconvenience to

FIGURE 34-7
Some of the reasons why strikes occur

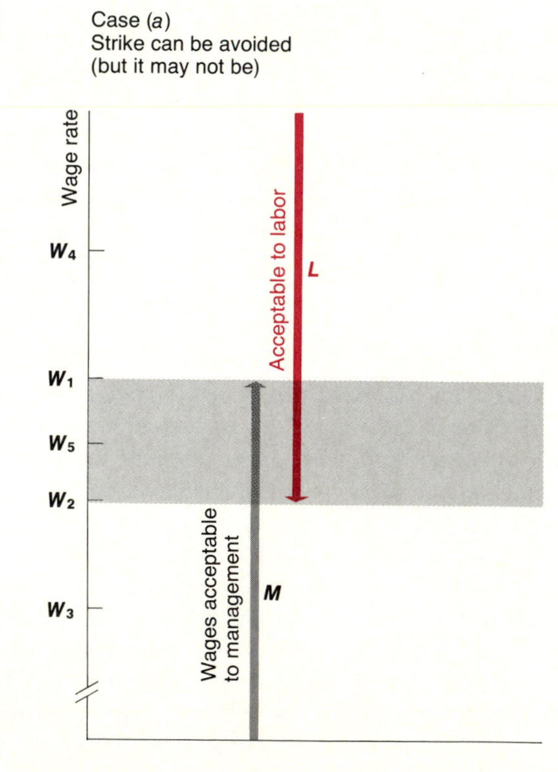

[9]These and some of the other figures cited in this chapter are drawn from Richard B. Freeman and James L. Medoff, *What Do Unions Do?* (New York: Basic Books, 1984).

Wildcat strikes—sudden walkouts by small groups of workers—are uncommon in the United States. However, they are more frequent in some other countries like Britain, where they have contributed to the decline of several important industries. Such strikes can be more disruptive than a full-scale strike that follows a breakdown in union-management contract negotiations. Wildcat strikes may be the result of unions that are *too weak* to prevent their members from taking actions that harm the workers in the industry as a whole.

the car-buying public. Since these are costs that are not incurred by any firm or individual in the tire industry, they are external spillover costs of the strike and are shown as area 4. In short, if a strike occurs in the industry, it will involve both internal cost 3 to the industry plus external cost 4 elsewhere in the economy.

In panel *b* we see that the situation could be worse. If one or more auto companies are eventually forced to shut down, the value of the lost output in the auto industry and the inconvenience to the public—shown as area 4—may exceed the value of the lost output in the tire industry, shown as area 3. An example of a strike with a substantial external cost occurred in Californian canneries. Lost income in these factories represented only a small part of the total cost. Far more important was the loss to the state's farmers: $10 million worth of tomatoes and $15 million worth of peaches and apricots had to be left to rot because the canning factories were closed down. Moreover, because so much of the nation's supply of canned fruit and vegetables comes from California, the American consumer also had to bear a cost in the form of higher prices.

Thus, the general public often has a stake in a strike decision in a specific industry. But the public *is not represented in the negotiations* that lead to a strike. Its attitude is often: "While labor and management in this in-

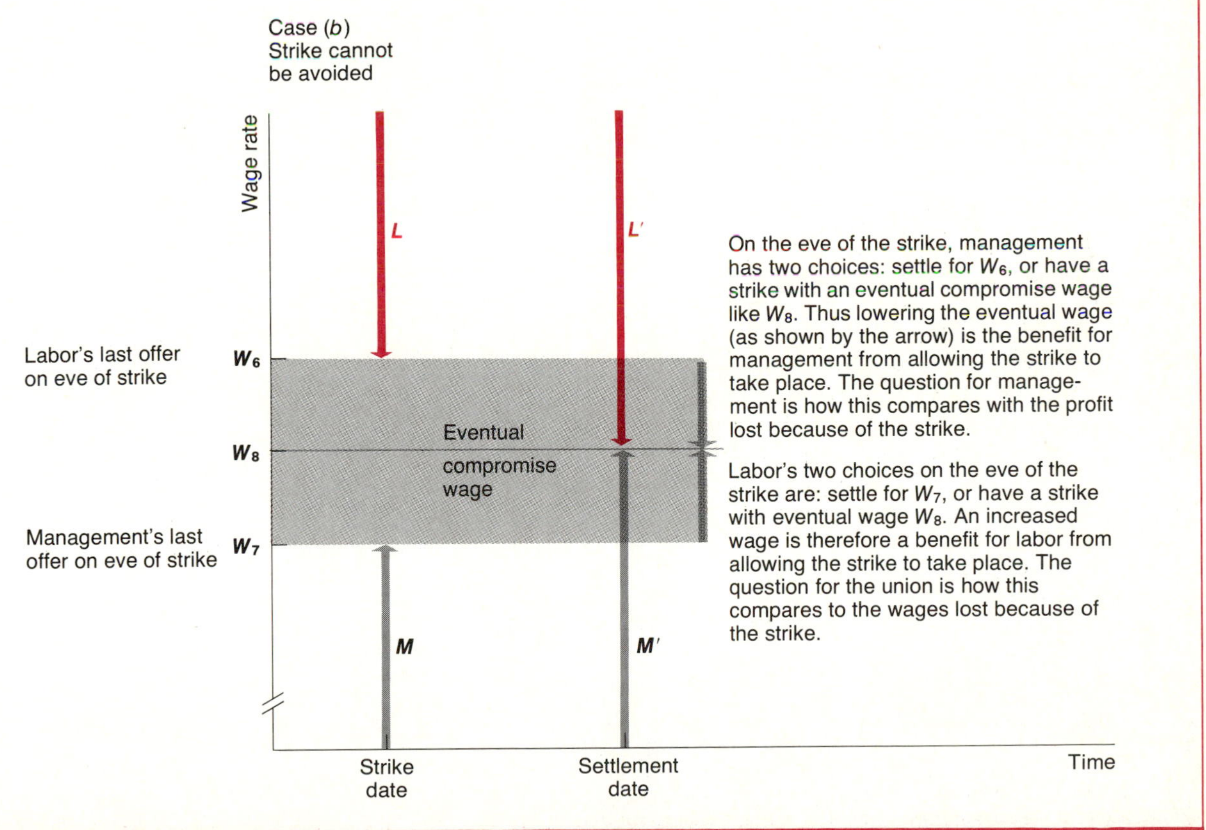
Case (b)
Strike cannot be avoided
Wage rate
L
L′
Labor's last offer on eve of strike
W6
W8
Management's last offer on eve of strike
W7
Eventual compromise wage
M
M′
Strike date
Settlement date
Time
On the eve of the strike, management has two choices: settle for W6, or have a strike with an eventual compromise wage like W8. Thus lowering the eventual wage (as shown by the arrow) is the benefit for management from allowing the strike to take place. The question for management is how this compares with the profit lost because of the strike.
Labor's two choices on the eve of the strike are: settle for W7, or have a strike with eventual wage W8. An increased wage is therefore a benefit for labor from allowing the strike to take place. The question for the union is how this compares to the wages lost because of the strike.

dustry are fighting over how area 3 is to be divided, we are losing area 4. Something is very wrong.''

Therefore, a number of ways have been sought to prevent strikes when negotiations between labor and management break down.

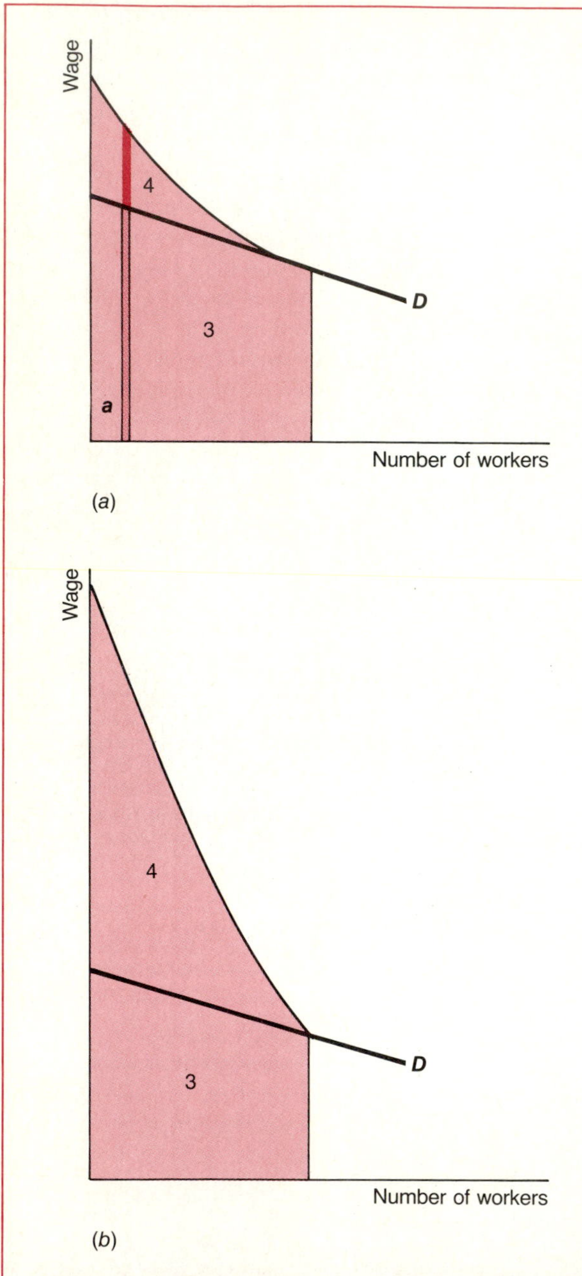

Last Resort Procedures to Prevent Strikes

As noted earlier, the Taft-Hartley Act empowered the president to seek a court injunction imposing an 80-day ''cooling-off period'' to delay a strike which threatens the national health or safety. Although this provides time for labor and management to negotiate a settlement, a strike may still occur after the 80-day period.

To assist deadlocked negotiations, the Federal Mediation Service has been established. ***Mediation***—or ***conciliation***—involves the appointment of an impartial third party to study the situation and suggest a compromise settlement. Although mediators cannot make binding recommendations on how the conflicts will be settled, they may be very helpful in resolving disputes for several reasons: A mediator may be able to (1) discover a solution that the two contending parties have overlooked; (2) find out who is bluffing and who is not, thus reducing the risk of a strike because one side has miscalculated the true position of the other; (3) provide a means of saving face for parties that are otherwise locked into highly publicized positions from which there is no graceful retreat. For example, a union can go back to its members and say: ''We didn't capitulate to the bosses. We accepted the recommendation of an impartial third party.'' Thus

FIGURE 34-8
Spillover cost of a strike
(*a*) When a strike occurs in tire production, area 3 shows the internal cost to the industry—the value of the lost output of tires. Area 4 shows the additional external cost to the public, in particular to the auto industry, where production is dislocated because tire supplies have dried up. More specifically, the fact that worker *a* becomes unemployed means that there is a loss of this individual's output of tires, as shown by the light red bar. However, there is a further cost, shown by the dark red bar, because of the dislocation in the auto industry, where car production is delayed because of the shortage of tires. (*b*) If the shortage of tires becomes so severe that auto companies have to lay off workers, area 4 of spillover cost from the strike may be more severe than area 3 of internal cost to the tire industry.

the two sides may be able to achieve a settlement because they are able to shift the responsibility (blame) onto the mediator.

If mediation fails, a second, more forceful technique is ***voluntary arbitration:*** Labor and management submit their conflict to an impartial third party, and *commit themselves in advance* to accept the arbitrator's decision. Provisions for voluntary arbitration are included in many collective bargaining agreements, as a way of settling disputes over the interpretation of the terms of the agreement.

A third, and much more drastic, approach is sometimes suggested: ***compulsory arbitration,*** whereby the government *forces* both parties to submit their dispute to an arbitrator, who then decides on a binding settlement. Although this seems like a simple solution, it has caused bitterness in countries which have relied on it. In particular, workers have sometimes felt that the government has favored management, and has therefore forced labor to work for unjustly low wages.

DISPUTES INVOLVING PUBLIC SERVICE EMPLOYEES

The most damaging strikes are usually those with large external spillover costs. These costs—illustrated in panel *b* of Figure 34-8—tend to be particularly large in the public sector. When subway workers go on strike, area 3 of lost income of these workers and the transit authority is typically far less than area 4—the spillover cost of tying up the city's economic activity. Serious spillover costs similiarly result from a strike of garbage collectors, firefighters, or air-traffic controllers.

Public service employees sometimes argue that, if they don't have a union, the government, as a monopsony employer, can exercise too much market power in setting their wage rate. They must accept whatever take-it-or-leave-it contract the government offers. Accordingly, public service employees have recently been organizing at a rapid rate. Membership in public service unions increased by roughly six times during the 1960s and 1970s. By the early 1980s, the American Federation of State, County and Municipal Employees (AFSCME) had become the largest of the unions affiliated with the AFL-CIO.

This growth in size is one source of strength for public employees' unions. But there are other sources as well:

1. Because public servants—such as the police or transit workers—provide essential services, their threat of a strike becomes a very potent weapon. Whereas a strike in the private sector puts pressure on employers to settle because of the income they will lose, a strike in the public sector puts pressure on the employers (the government) because of the votes it may lose from an irate public suffering from the suspension of some essential service.

2. A government may find it easier than a private employer to raise the funds necessary to pay a higher wage. For example, the government may increase taxes, or borrow. Another way to avoid a strike may be to provide a generous increase in pensions, a relatively painless measure because it commits a future—rather than the present—government to pay employees when they retire. Thus, it has appeal to politicians whose major concern is to win the next election. New York City proved how painful the long-run consequences of such a policy may be. By 1975, "the chickens had finally come home to roost." Wage and pension commitments—combined with other major problems, such as large welfare expenditures—drove the city to the brink of bankruptcy, where it was saved only by a period of austerity.

3. In private industry a strike may drive a firm out of business. Thus, strikers run the risk that their jobs may disappear, and this prospect acts as a restraint on labor demands. But there is far less restraint of this kind in the public service. True, a strike may cost the government an election. But this is a serious problem only for the government officials who are voted out of their jobs. It is far less of a threat to public service workers whose jobs are likely to exist no matter who wins the next election. This puts a public service union in a strong bargaining position.

4. Public employees and their dependents may become a significant percentage of the voting population. This weakens the resistance of elected officials to their demands.

At every level of government—federal, state, and local—strikes of public service workers are generally illegal. Nonetheless, some civil servants, particularly at the local level, do walk off the job or withdraw their services in more subtle ways, such as reporting in sick. Should they be allowed to strike? In passing antistrike laws, many legislators believe that they should not. If trash collectors go on strike, pollution may threaten public health. If firefighters or the police go on strike, people may die in fires or be victimized by criminals. In the face of such strike threats, a government may feel almost forced to meet labor demands. Surely no group of individuals should hold this sort of power over the public. This line of argument led President Reagan to take a strong stand when the air-traffic controllers struck. The strike was illegal. Therefore, he fired the strikers.

Many government workers argue that, if they are not allowed to strike, they may reasonably demand some other mechanism for achieving a fair wage. One approach adopted by the federal government is to provide civil servants with salaries equal to those in comparable private sector jobs. However, this provides neither a simple nor a complete solution. One difficulty is in defining what is meant by a "comparable" private sector job. Another problem is in determining what downward adjustment, if any, should be made to government salaries because of attractive pensions and greater job security.

WAGE DIFFERENCES: WHY DO THEY EXIST?

In answering this question, we shall draw together and expand on some of the points made in the last two chapters.

1. First, there may be ***dynamic differentials*** in wage rates. For example, if there is a large increase in the demand for construction workers in Alaska, their wages will rise above wages earned elsewhere; a dynamic differential is created. Eventually, this higher Alaskan wage will attract workers from other parts of the country, and this wage will settle back toward the wage level elsewhere; the dynamic differential declines. Such differentials are only temporary; the speed with which they disappear depends on the mobility of the labor force.

A *dynamic wage differential* arises because of changing demand or supply conditions in the labor market. It declines over time as labor moves out of jobs with relatively low wages and into those that pay a relatively high wage.

2. Some of the Alaskan wage differential may not disappear over time. To some degree wages may remain higher in Alaska to compensate for some disadvantage of working there, such as the colder climate. Similar ***compensating wage differentials*** may arise in jobs offering less security or less pleasant working conditions.

***Compensating wage differentials* result if labor views some jobs as less attractive than others. Employers have to pay a higher wage to fill the unattractive jobs.**

For example, jobs with high stress generally pay about 10% higher wages, and repetitive, boring jobs may also pay higher wages. On the other hand, some unpleasant jobs do not carry the higher wage one would expect. Instead, they have a higher turnover rate. This suggests that there may be a pool of available workers who take jobs without realizing they are unpleasant. When they do realize, they quit.

3. Some wage differences reflect ***monopsony or monopoly power.*** Thus workers in a small town facing a monoposony employer may receive a low wage. On the other hand, workers who are exercising market power through a union tend to get higher wages. A particularly high wage may be received by workers who are not only able to exercise market power in their own labor market through a strong union, but who are also employed by a firm with monopoly influence over *its* product market. For example, workers at General Motors have been able to earn a high wage, not only because of the strength of the UAW, but also because they work for a company that has been able to earn oligopoly profits in the car market. In short, this union has been able to negotiate wage increases out of GM's oligopoly profits in the car market. This was confirmed between 1980 and 1982, when the auto companies' oligopoly power was reduced by competition from imported cars. When combined with the effects of recession, this resulted not only in losses for the car companies but also pressure on the UAW to give up some wage increases won in earlier negotiations. The companies no longer were earning oligopoly profits that could be shared with labor.

4. *Other departures from perfect competition* may result in wage differentials. For example, ***barriers to entry*** in the form of long apprenticeship requirements may keep wages up in some crafts. ***Discrimination*** can depress the wages and salaries of minorities and women.

5. Finally, wage differences exist because people have different ***talents, education, and training.*** This is a major topic in the next chapter.

KEY POINTS

1. Labor markets are often imperfect. Workers form unions to exercise monopoly power on the supply side of the market. On the other side of the market, employers may exercise monopsony power. Examples include a government that hires public service employees, and a private firm that is the only major employer in a small town.

2. Unions provide labor with a collective voice. In collective bargaining, unions promote the interests of their workers by pressing for such improvements as (*a*) better working conditions, (*b*) seniority rules to protect long-time workers, and (*c*) higher wages.

3. If a union is formed in a perfectly competitive labor market without externalities and uses its market power to raise the wage rate, there is an overall efficiency loss. The reason is that some workers are not hired in this industry even though they would be more productive here than elsewhere. Moreover, by raising the wage rate, the union transfers income to labor from other factors of production.

   On the other side of the market, if employers acquire monopsony power and lower the wage below its perfectly competitive level, there will be the same sort of efficiency loss. But while the efficiency effects of monopoly and monopsony will be similar, their transfer effects will be in opposite directions. When a monopsonist lowers wages, the transfer is *from* labor *to* other factors of production.

4. If a labor market is already monopsonized by a single employer, it no longer necessarily follows that efficiency will be reduced if a union is formed to raise the wage rate. In fact, if the union's market power is used only to offset the market power of the employer, efficiency can be *increased.*

5. A union may increase efficiency in other ways, too. By providing workers with a collective voice, it may improve their performance and reduce costly turnover of the labor force. A union may increase productivity by improving morale and communication between labor and management. On the other hand, a union may negotiate featherbedding rules which reduce efficiency.

6. Bilateral monopoly occurs when market power exists on both sides of the labor market: Unions with monopoly power bargain with employers with monopsony power. The wage that results will fall between the high wage an unopposed union would seek and the low wage an unopposed monopsonist would offer. But, within these limits, it is impossible to predict precisely where the wage rate will be set. However, it will be heavily influenced by the bargaining power of each side. For example, a large union strike fund will increase the union's bargaining power, while a large inventory of finished goods will increase the bargaining power of management. Bargaining is also affected by the negotiating expertise of labor and management. An incompetent negotiator who won't provide the other side with a face-saving compromise may prevent an agreement from being reached.

7. Membership in public service unions has grown rapidly in recent years. Such a union may have a strong bargaining position, particularly if it provides an essential service. To avoid a strike, a government employer may be willing to tax or borrow to meet a wage claim that would drive a private employer out of business. An important policy issue is whether public employees should have the right to strike.

KEY CONCEPTS

industrial union

craft union
collective bargaining
seniority rules
codetermination
closed shop
union shop
yellow-dog contract
right-to-work law
open shop
Taft-Hartley injunction
transfer and efficiency effects of a union
featherbedding
transfer and efficiency effects of labor monopsony
bilateral monopoly
countervailing power
why a union may decrease or increase efficiency
relative bargaining power of union and management
why strikes occur
spillover costs of a strike
mediation
voluntary arbitration
compulsory arbitration
public service union
dynamic wage differential
compensating wage differential

PROBLEMS

34-1. Before deregulation, the Civil Aeronautics Board allowed the airlines to charge high fares, with some of the resulting profit being absorbed by high wage and salary payments. In such circumstances, would you expect that the deregulation that has made the airlines more competitive in setting their fares has affected their labor contracts as well? If so, how? What, in fact, did happen to the wages and salaries of employees when the airlines were deregulated?

34-2. "Monopsony in the labor market may have exactly the same effect on efficiency as a union." Is this possible? Explain. Would the transfer effects be the same in the two cases? (If you have studied Figure 2 on page 671, show how the two cases in the present example can involve identical efficiency effects but entirely different transfer effects.)

34-3. In the case of monopsony, which efficiency condition in Figure 33-7 has been violated? Explain.

34-4. In Figure 34-5, suppose that the initial wage rate in a unionized labor market is at W_3. If employers form a bargaining association and successfully negotiate a lower wage rate, show how efficiency is affected. Consider two cases: What happens if the association negotiates the wage down to W_2? Down to W_1?

34-5. Do you think that, as capital accumulates, the bargaining power of workers vis-à-vis management increases or decreases? Which workers can more effectively threaten to strike: Workers who would be leaving bulldozers idle? Workers who would be laying down their shovels?

34-6. Which union in each of the following pairs has the greater bargaining power? In each case, explain why. (*a*) A union of workers on the New York subway or a union of workers who build the trains. (*b*) A firefighters' union or a public school teachers' union. (*c*) A public school teachers' union or a university professors' union.

34-7. "Tying wage increases in the public sector to wage increases in private industry will not necessarily equalize wages. All it will do is keep them the same if they start out equal. If public sector wages are initially less than private sector wages, tying wages in this way only guarantees that inequities will be preserved." Do you agree? Do you think it is fair to pay both public and private employees the same wage if public employees have greater job security? If not, explain why, and give an estimate of the differential you consider desirable.

***34-8.** Use a diagram to show how the theory of the second best applies to labor forming a union in a market that is already monopsonized.

34-9. (*a*) Why might a union agree to a two-tiered contract, with a lower wage for new workers, provided the old higher wage continues for existing workers?

(*b*) If the lower wage for new workers is equal to the perfectly competitive wage, what will be the effect on efficiency? Why?

(*c*) Explain how a two-tiered wage may affect the job security of present high-wage workers.

CHAPTER 35

OTHER INCOMES

Buy land. They ain't making any more of the stuff.

WILL ROGERS

The last two chapters were devoted to the income of labor. The incomes of other factors of production such as capital and land will now be dealt with in this single chapter. The reason for such heavy emphasis on labor income is that wage and salary payments to labor constitute about three quarters of the total national income, with the incomes of other factors representing only the remaining one quarter. Nonetheless these other incomes still play an important role.

Consider first the income to capital, which comes in several forms. First, interest income is received by those who provide ***debt capital***; that is, those who lend money to businesses—or to others—to finance the purchase of machinery or the construction of new buildings. (One way to lend a firm money is to buy its bonds. Another way is to lend money to a bank or other financial intermediary which in turn lends it out to the firm.) Second, profits are earned by those who own ***equity capital***; that is, those who own small businesses outright or who own shares of a corporation's stock. Although the individual who buys stocks and bonds may view them quite differently, in this chapter we emphasize their similarity. Both represent a way in which people can contribute to the expansion of the nation's real capital and receive income in return.

Income is earned not only on physical capital, such as machinery and buildings, but also on ***human capital.*** An example is the human capital you are now accumulating in the form of an education. Your expenditure of time and money today will increase your productivity in the future and hence increase your income. Thus, an investment in human capital is like an investment in a machine or some other form of physical capital: It is an expenditure today that is expected to pay off in the future.

INTEREST: THE RETURN TO DEBT CAPITAL

To begin, let's suppose that firms finance investment only by borrowing. Borrowing takes place in the *market for loanable funds,* where lenders who supply funds come together with borrowers who demand funds. Like a competitive commodity market, a perfectly competitive market for loans can be studied with supply and demand curves.

How the Demand and Supply of Loans Determines the Interest Rate

Figure 35-1 shows the demand curve for loans by firms seeking the funds to finance investment projects—for example, funds to acquire new machinery. (People who need loans to buy houses or cars also participate in this market, but in this simple introduction we avoid such complications.) Just as the demand for labor depends on the productivity of labor, so too the demand for loans to buy machinery depends on how productive that machinery will be—that is, on the ***marginal efficiency of investment*** (MEI) shown in this diagram. Suppose bar *a* on the far left of Figure 35-1 represents the investment in machinery with the highest return (MEI) of 15%. For example, consider a machine that costs $100,000 and lasts only 1 year. If this machine generates enough sales to cover labor, materials, etc., and leave $115,000 in addition, it provides a rate of return of 15%. Specifically, this $115,000 repays the firm for its initial $100,000 investment and provides a $15,000 return—that is, a 15% return—on this investment.

The next most attractive investment is *b,* which yields a 14½% return; and so on. The result is the marginal efficiency of investment curve (MEI). This curve also represents the demand for investment loans. For example, if the interest rate is 10%, Q_1 of loans will be demanded. Firms will wish to invest in all the high-return opportunities to the left of *V*, but none to the right where the return has fallen below the 10% cost of borrowing money. (Further detail on the MEI was given in Chapter 14, in the section entitled "The Effects of Monetary Policy.")

Recall from Chapter 33 that firms hire labor to the point where its price (the wage rate) is equal to the marginal revenue product. Similarly, Figure 35-1 shows how firms acquire capital to the point where its price (the interest rate) equals the marginal efficiency of investment.

In Figure 35-2, the demand for investment loans (MEI) is reproduced from Figure 35-1, together with the supply of funds by lenders. This supply indicates how much businesses and households are willing to provide at various interest rates.[1] For example, the 4% interest rate that would just barely induce individual *f* to save and lend reflects how highly he or she values this money in its alternative use—current consumption. Individuals who value current consumption more highly won't be induced to save and lend until the interest rate rises above 4%. Therefore, they appear further to the right in this supply schedule. They are often described as having a stronger ***time preference***; that is, they have a stronger preference for consuming now rather than in the future.

In a perfectly competitive capital market, equilibrium is at *E*, where demand and supply intersect. In this example, the equilibrium rate of interest is 6%.

It is important to emphasize that this 6% interest rate reflects the height of the demand curve at *E*. In other words, *the marginal efficiency of investment is 6%.* We can take $1 worth of goods today and invest it to produce $1.06 of goods next year. In short, by investing we can convert present goods into a larger amount of future goods.

Through investment, present goods can be *exchanged for* a larger amount of future goods. Thus present goods are *worth more* than future goods, with the interest rate telling us how much more.

FIGURE 35-1
The marginal efficiency of investment and the demand for loans
Investment opportunities are ranked in order, starting with those yielding the highest return on the left. The resulting MEI schedule is also the demand for loans. For example, if the interest rate is 10%, firms will demand Q_1 of loans. They keep borrowing to point *V*, where the marginal benefit of borrowing (the MEI schedule) is equal to the marginal cost of borrowing (the interest rate).

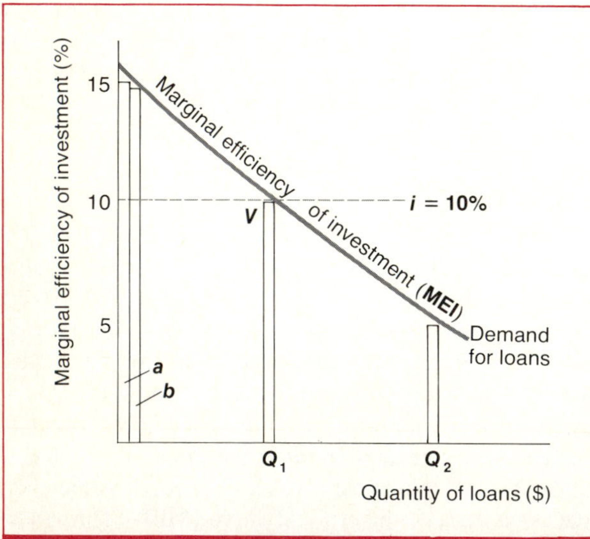

Roundabout Production, with Interest as the Reward for Waiting

Investment is often described as ***roundabout*** or ***indirect production.*** Rather than using resources today to produce consumer goods directly, society produces an even greater amount of consumer goods *indirectly* by a roundabout method: First, resources are used to produce capital goods, and then this capital is used—together with labor and land—to produce consumer goods.

The greater quantity of consumer goods that is eventually produced in this way is the incentive for undertaking roundabout production. However, roundabout production is not possible unless some people are prepared

[1]Here, we ignore a number of macroeconomic complications, including the effects of the banking system on the supply of loans. These complications were studied in Chapters 12 to 14.

to defer their consumption today; that is, people must be willing to save. This is necessary in order to release the resources that would otherwise go into producing consumer goods, and allow these resources to produce capital goods instead. For their decision to defer consumption—to wait before enjoying their income—savers receive an interest return. Thus the interest rate can be viewed as a *reward to savers for waiting,* just as the wage rate is a reward to labor for its time and effort.

Risk and Other influences on the Interest Rate

Although there is only one interest rate shown in Figure 35-2, in fact there are many rates of interest. A very large and financially sound corporation will be able to borrow funds at a low interest rate, since lenders view this loan as relatively risk-free. But a company in shaky financial condition will have to pay a higher interest rate to compensate lenders for the greater risk that the loan will not be repaid. Thus the interest rate shown in Figure 35-2 may be viewed as the "base rate of interest" that applies to a risk-free loan; as such, it is the best simple measure of the marginal efficiency of investment. Even though we continue to concentrate on this base rate, we should keep in mind that there is a whole array of interest rates on loans of varying risk.

Interest rates also reflect the *expectation of inflation*. (This macroeconomic issue was dealt with in Chapter 17. For simplicity, in this microeconomic analysis we describe a noninflationary world.) In addition, interest rates today depend on the *length of term of the loans* and the *expectation of future changes in interest rates*. For example, suppose interest rates today are expected to rise next year because of an increase in the demand for loans by business. In this case, lenders will now be reluctant to lend money for a long period of, say, 5 or 10 years. They will prefer instead to lend their money for a short period of, say, a year, at which time they can then lend it out again at the expected higher interest rate. Thus lenders now increase their supply of short-term loans, and this lowers the price (the interest rate) on these loans. At the same time, lenders now decrease their supply of long-term loans, raising the interest rate on these loans. Therefore, the expectation of a *future* change in interest rates will change the relationship between short-term and long-term interest rates *today*.

As we have seen in earlier chapters, an important question in product or labor markets is: What happens if the government intervenes to impose some restriction? This is also an important question in the capital market—that is, in the market for loans.

FIGURE 35-2

The market for loans

The demand for loans is reproduced from Figure 35-1. It reflects the marginal efficiency of investment. The supply of loans depends on how highly lenders value money in its alternative use—consumption. The equilibrium is at *E* with a 6% interest rate.

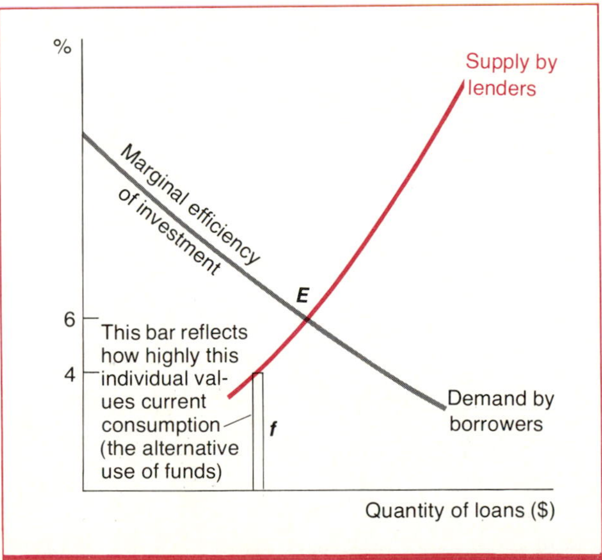

Effects of an Interest Rate Ceiling

Figure 35-3 shows what happens in a perfectly competitive capital market when the government imposes a ceiling on the interest rate that can be charged by banks. Original equilibrium before the ceiling is shown at *E*, with the interest rate at i_1. When the government sets a ceiling below this rate, say at i_2, the market no longer clears. There is a shortage of funds of *GF*. Unsatisfied borrowers cannot find loans.

One of the arguments in favor of an interest rate ceiling is that it will reduce the burden of interest payments that must be paid by relatively poor individuals and small firms. The lower interest rate does result in a transfer from lenders to borrowers—*but only to those borrowers lucky enough to get loans*. (This transfer is shown by the wide arrow on the left.) However, there is no guarantee that this redistribution will "help the poor." Some of the largest borrowers who get the bargain loans may be the rich who borrow to finance their big homes and business ventures. At the same time, some of the borrowers who are left unsatisfied may be the poor, who suffer as a consequence. Indeed, when funds are in short supply, poor borrowers are less likely to get them than are wealthy borrowers. If you had $100,000 to lend out and there were many groups who wanted to borrow it from you, would you lend it to the wealthy or to the poor?

Moreover, the interest rate ceiling has two unfavorable effects on efficiency. First, it reduces the quantity of loanable funds available for investment from Q_1 to Q_2. This shift in the market away from its initial, perfectly competitive equilibrium results in the efficiency loss shown by the familar red triangle in Box 35-1. However, this problem—that there are now too few investment funds available—is not the only reason for an efficiency loss. A second reason is that the wrong borrowers may get the limited funds.

While this second source of inefficiency is also described in detail in Box 35-1, the basic problem can be understood in a fairly simple way. Because the interest rate ceiling makes the demand for loans Q_3 greater than the supply Q_2, the limited supply of funds must be ra-

FIGURE 35-3

Effects of an interest rate ceiling

Before the interest rate ceiling, equilibrium in this competitive capital market is at E, with Q_1 of investment funds loaned out at interest rate i_1. When a ceiling of i_2 is imposed, borrowers are attracted by the lower rate and seek Q_3 loans; that is, borrowers try to move down their demand curve from E to F. However, only Q_2 of loans are available because lenders, discouraged by the reduced interest return, move down their supply curve from E to G. Thus, equilibrium shifts from E to G, loans are reduced from Q_1 to Q_2, and there is Q_2Q_3 unsatisfied demand for loans. Moreover, by lowering the interest rate that lenders receive and borrowers pay, the interest rate ceiling results in the wide-arrow transfer from lenders to those borrowers who get funds.

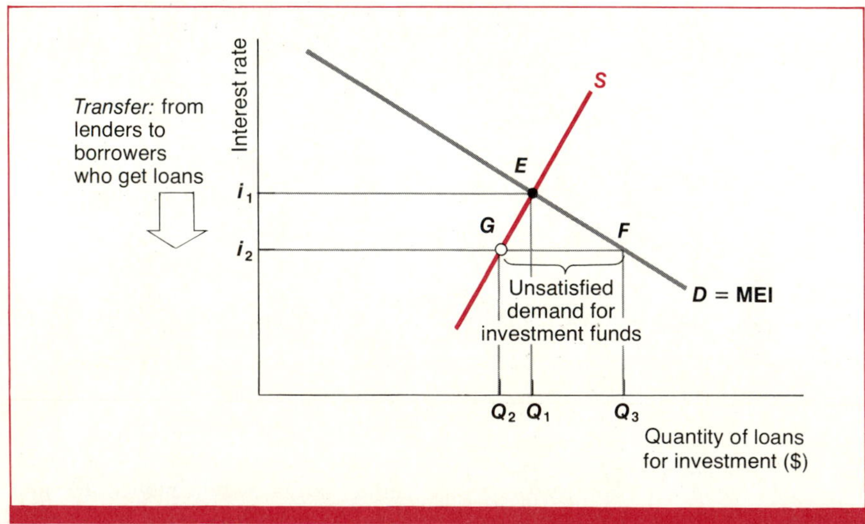

BOX 35-1

THE INEFFICIENCY OF AN INTEREST RATE CEILING

Figure 35-4 reproduces the market for loanable funds from Figure 35-3, along with the ceiling that reduces the interest rate from i_1 to i_2. The first efficiency loss from this policy is shown by the red triangle. This loss occurs because suppliers of funds (savers) are discouraged by the lower interest rate and provide fewer funds, as shown by arrow *a* at the bottom of the diagram. Consequently, economically justified investment projects like *g* are "knocked out"—they cannot be undertaken. This results in a loss because the cost of this project would have been only the hollow bar under the supply curve (the cost to the lender of having to reduce consumption), while its benefit would have been the hollow bar *plus* the solid bar under the demand curve (the return on this investment). Thus the net loss because this particular project is cancelled is the solid bar. The efficiency loss from all such cancellations in the relevant range shown by arrow *a* is the red triangle. Thus the principle previously established in the market for goods and for labor—that a shift away from a perfectly competitive equilibrium such as *E* will result in an efficiency loss—is now shown to hold in a perfectly competitive market for investment funds as well.

The efficiency loss will be limited to this red triangle *only if* the investment projects knocked out by a lack of funds are those (like *g*) in the range *a*. If this is not the case, there will be a second efficiency loss. To illustrate, suppose, for example, that project *j* on the left is the one that is knocked out, not *g*. (The promoter of *g* may have been able to borrow by being more persuasive to a banker who is rationing loans.) An even greater efficiency loss is now involved because an even more productive investment (*j* rather than *g*) is knocked out.

Moreover, this inefficiency may be even more serious. It is quite possible for *j* to lose out, not to *g*, but instead to an even lower-productivity project like *h*. In fact, *h*'s productivity is so low that it would not even be considered at the original interest rate i_1; nobody would try to borrow to undertake it. The only reason someone is now applying for funds for *h* is the attraction of the artificially low interest rate. If the funds go to *h* rather than *j*, the efficiency loss from this rationing error—the reduction in the nation's output—will be even more severe. In this case, the loss will be the difference in *j*'s high productivity and *h*'s low productivity.

FIGURE 35-4

The inefficiencies created by an interest rate ceiling

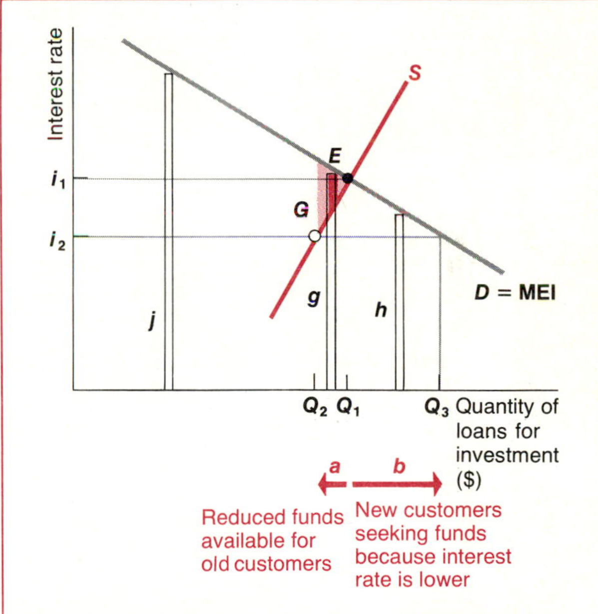

tioned in some way. Bankers may do this by a first come, first served procedure or some more complex method. But whatever the method, there will be a second efficiency loss unless the funds are rationed out to exactly the right set of borrowers—that is, those borrowers to the left of Q_2 in Figure 35-3, who have the investment projects with the highest productivity (MEI). It is unlikely that this will happen. Because the interest rate is so low, borrowers in the range Q_2Q_3, with lower-productivity investments, will also be trying to obtain funds, and some may succeed. If such a ''rationing error'' does occur, the second efficiency loss results: In the market for investment funds, high-productivity investments lose out to low-productivity ones.

This second source of inefficiency—above and beyond the red triangle in Figure 35-4—may be summarized as follows. In an unrestricted, perfectly competitive capital market, the interest rate is a price that allocates funds to the most productive investment projects. When the government intervenes to set an interest rate ceiling, some other allocating device must be used, and there is then a risk that the wrong set of projects will get the funds.

We emphasize that this is just another illustration of the general problem that applies to *any* form of price fixing, such as our earlier example of rent control. Not only does rent control result in fewer apartments for rent. In addition, the ''wrong'' people may get the apartments. For example, a retired couple may continue to hang on to a choice New York apartment even though they now spend 9 months a year in Florida and would give up the apartment if they had to pay the higher free-market rent.

Returning to the interest rate ceiling, we once again conclude: If we wish to transfer income from the rich to the poor, changing a market price like the interest rate may be an unwise way to do it. In the first place, an interest ceiling may be an ineffective form of transfer because it may not move income from the rich to the poor at all. The statement that ''borrowers benefit, therefore the poor benefit'' involves two possible errors. First, borrowers as a group may not benefit, since some no longer get funds. Second, the borrowers who get cut off from funds tend to be the poor. Therefore, they bear the cost of this policy, whereas the rich who are still able to borrow are the ones who benefit from the lower interest rate. Moreover, an interest ceiling may have damaging effects on efficiency. Isn't it better for the government to do any transferring directly, by taxing the rich and subsidizing the poor? The answer is yes, *provided* the government can do so without incurring large efficiency losses of a different sort—an issue to be discussed in Chapter 37.

NORMAL PROFIT: A RETURN TO EQUITY CAPITAL

Thus far, we have assumed that all investment projects are financed by borrowing. Now let's broaden our analysis to include ''equity finance''—that is, funds a firm raises by selling its stock (or by retaining some of its earnings). When a firm sells its stock, those who buy it obtain a share of the ownership and future profits of the firm.

In Chapter 22, we drew a distinction between two kinds of profit. First, ***normal profit*** reflects opportunity cost—the return necessary to induce and hold funds in one activity rather than another. Second, ***above-normal profit*** is any additional return beyond this. We defer discussion of above-normal profit to a later section and concentrate here on normal profit.

For those who provide equity funds, what is their normal profit; that is, what is the opportunity cost of these funds? The answer is the return the funds could earn in their best alternative use. An alternative to buying stock is to buy interest-bearing securities. Thus normal profit can be viewed as the base rate of interest plus an appropriate premium for risk—a risk which may be substantial because the entire amount that is put into the ownership of a firm may be wiped out. (Profit is sometimes described as a reward for risk taking. However, it is more than this, since it must also include a base rate of return needed to attract funds away from interest-bearing alternatives.)

Figure 35-2 can now be recast in the more general form shown in Figure 35-5, which represents the total market for investment funds. Now D includes the total demand by business for investment funds, whether these funds are raised by borrowing or by the sale of stock; and S is the corresponding supply. The resulting equilibrium

Q is the quantity of both debt and equity funds provided by savers to those who invest.

THE ROLE OF FACTOR PRICES

We have examined the pricing of two factors of production—labor and capital. We now pause to consider how factor prices influence both the individual firm's decisions on using these factors and the allocation of these factors across the economy as a whole.

How Factor Prices Influence Decisions by Individual Firms

In its decision making, a firm must address several issues. On the one hand, it must decide on how much labor and how much capital equipment it will use. At the same time, it must also decide which goods to produce and how much of each. To illustrate, suppose the wage rate rises. The firm responds by using less labor and more capital; that is, it substitutes capital for labor because labor has become more expensive. Moreover, because of the higher wage, the firm may also reduce the output of its final products, especially those requiring a great deal of labor.

As a further example of how factor and product decisions are interrelated, suppose there is an increase in the price of one of the firm's products. In response, the firm will increase its output of this good by hiring more factors of production and/or by shifting production away from one of its other outputs. In short, the firm's decisions on what to produce and the amount of factors to employ are not separate decisions. Instead, they are all *elements of one overall decision.*

FIGURE 35-5

The market for investment funds (a generalization of Figure 35-2)

Whereas Figure 35-2 showed only borrowing, this diagram shows two ways that business may raise funds: by borrowing or by equity finance (the sale of stock). D is the demand for funds—in either debt or equity form—to finance new investment, while S is the corresponding supply of funds. In equilibrium, the base rate of return, in the absence of risk, would be r. However, in a risky world, the return any specific business must actually pay for the funds it raises will be r plus an appropriate amount to compensate the lender for risk.

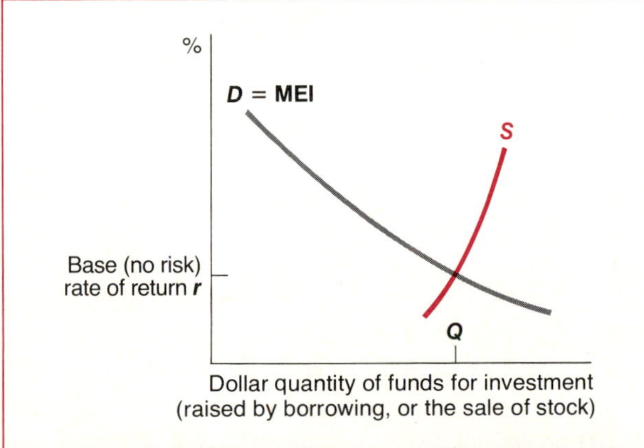

How Factor Prices Influence the Allocation of Scarce Resources throughout the Economy

Just as price acts as the screening mechanism for deciding who will consume a good and who will not (Figure 24-5), so a factor price acts as a screening device to determine how a scarce resource will be used. For example, the wage rate acts as a screen to determine the particular activities in which society's scarce labor will be employed. In a competitive, fully employed economy, the wage rate rises as productivity increases. This conveys a clear message to those producers who can no longer afford the higher wage. The message is: Society can no longer afford to have its scarce labor employed in your activity. There are now too many other, more productive pursuits. This may seem harsh, but it is the sign of economic progress. Think back, for a moment, to all the things that labor used to do, but no longer does. At our current high wage rates, it doesn't pay to hire workers to hoe field corn anymore, as in the "good old days." Household servants have almost vanished.

Similarly, we have seen how the interest rate is a market price that acts as a screen to determine in which particular projects investment will take place. When that screening device is replaced by another—such as the rationing that occurs when an interest rate ceiling is imposed—investment funds are unlikely to go to the most productive projects.

THE RETURN TO HUMAN CAPITAL

Income is earned not only by investment in machinery and other physical capital, but also by investment in *human capital*—the acquisition of skills, training, and education.[2] In many essential respects, an investment in human capital is similar to an investment in physical capital: Current consumption is reduced in the expectation of higher future income and consumption. For example, students give up the income they could make if they were not busy studying; they live frugally in the hope that the education will pay off in higher income after graduation. Similarly, apprentices may be willing to work for abnormally low wages if they are receiving training that is likely to lead to a better job.

By recognizing the importance of human capital, we recognize that everyone in the labor force is not equally productive; we are relaxing our earlier assumption that all workers are similar. In fact, the quality of labor depends on the amount of education, skill, and experience that various individuals have acquired. Some have a lot of human capital, others very little. Frequently their incomes reflect this. This means that when we say that three quarters of the national income is paid in the form of wages and salaries, we recognize that this includes not only a basic payment for the time and effort of unskilled labor, but also a return on the human capital that skilled workers have acquired.

Who pays for the investment in human capital? In the case of education, much of the investment is undertaken by the individuals who spend their time studying instead of earning an income. However, governments also invest: Federal, state, and local governments all help to finance education. One justification for these expenditures is that it is only fair to provide educational opportunity for all. Another is that education provides not only a benefit to those who acquire it, but also spillover benefits to others in society as well. For example, if a highly educated doctor discovers a new vaccine, it may not only increase the discoverer's own income, but will also benefit the public, which now has protection from a disease. In the face of such spillover benefits, the unaided free market may not provide enough investment in human capital, so the government also contributes.

On-the-job apprenticeship or training in industry also represents an investment in human capital. There are several ways the initial cost of this investment may be covered. For example, workers may accept a low wage during the apprenticeship period when their productivity is still low. However, as noted earlier, the possibility of using this arrangement is limited by the minimum wage laws. Alternatively, employers may pay apprentices a standard wage and thereby bear the initial costs of this investment. But this option raises a serious problem for employers, since they are investing in an asset—in the form of skill or training—which they do not own. Workers are not slaves, and they can always quit and go to work elsewhere, taking the training with them. (Of course, the ease with which they can do so depends on how specific their expertise is to the company that trained them.) This is another reason why there may be underinvestment in human capital: Employers may not invest as heavily in training programs as they would if workers would guarantee to stay on the job and thus allow employers to "get their money back." More detail on this issue is provided in Box 35-2.

Human Capital and Discrimination

The problem of low income for a minority may reflect more than present discrimination by employers. It may also be the result of the past inability of the minority to acquire human capital. The members of such a group may be caught in the following vicious circle. Past discrimination has meant that they have been receiving lower wages. Consequently, they have been unable to provide their children with an adequate education. As a result, their children are now paid lower wages—*even if employers today don't discriminate*. For example, blacks remain at a disadvantage even if those now making important economic decisions are color-blind.

One way of breaking this vicious circle is to ensure

---

[2]For a sample of early work in this field, see G. S. Becker, *Human Capital: A Theoretical and Empirical Analysis, with Special Reference to Education,* 2d ed. (New York: National Bureau of Economic Research, 1975) and Jacob Mincer, *Schooling Experience and Earning* (New York: National Bureau of Economic Research, 1974). For a survey of more recent research on the value of an education, see R. J. Willis, "Wage Determinants: A Survey and Reinterpretation of Human Capital Earnings Functions," in O. C. Ashenfelter and R. Layard (eds.), *Handbook of Labor Economics* (Amsterdam: North Holland Press, 1985). This article is drawn on for many of the estimates in this section.

equal educational opportunity for minorities. To make up for past discrimination, special efforts have been made under affirmative action programs to get blacks, other minorities, and women into training programs and positions where they can accumulate human capital. How far affirmative action should be extended to ''reverse discrimination''—whereby minorities and women are given preferential treatment—is a very controversial legal, moral, and social question, on which even Supreme Court justices have difficulty passing judgment. In one of the most important early cases in 1978, a California medical school was sued by a rejected white applicant named Bakke, who claimed to have better qualifications than some nonwhites who had been admitted. While upholding affirmative action in principle, the Supreme Court seemed to back down in this specific case; it ordered Bakke admitted.

Measuring the Return on Human Capital: What Is a College Education Worth?

Acquiring a college education involves substantial costs. Two of the most important are illustrated in Figure 35-8, which shows the income pattern of those with a college degree and those without.

The first cost is the income foregone during the actual period of study. This cost can be visualized as a set of arrows like *a*, one for each year spent in college. But that's not the only sacrifice college students make. Even after their education is complete, their average incomes at first are below the incomes of people without a degree who have 4 years of experience and seniority instead. This cost to college students is the set of postcollege arrows like *b*. However, this income disadvantage of college graduates disappears fairly quickly. By point *F* in their late twenties they have caught up. Arrow *c* shows that by their late thirties they have gone well ahead—and they stay ahead.

Thus the costs and benefits of a college education can be summed up as follows:

1. The *costs* include both (*a*) the income foregone during college and the later ''catch-up period,'' shown as the red area in this diagram, and (*b*) a set of costs not shown in this diagram, including tuition and any higher costs of living in college residence than elsewhere.

2. The *benefits* are in the form of a higher income later, as shown by the gray area.

By comparing these initial costs and eventual benefits, we can calculate a percentage return on a college education (an investment in human capital) in much the same way as we earlier estimated the percentage return on physical capital such as machinery.

However, such calculations raise problems. For example, is it reasonable to claim that the higher income of college graduates—shown by the gray area in Figure 35-8—is all due to their college education? The answer is no. One reason for their higher earnings is that they are, on average, more talented and hardworking; they aren't dropouts. Thus, even without a college education, they would still earn more, on average. Accordingly, one task is to sort out how much of their higher income should be attributed to their college education, and how much to their greater talent and perseverance. A second difficulty is that the *private* rate of return to the individual acquiring an education is not the same as the *social* rate of return to the nation as a whole. (For adjustments in the private rate necessary to derive the social rate, see Box 35-3.)

Studies that have attempted to take some of these complications into account provide the following picture. The return to a college education tended to decrease between 1900 and 1940. However, at that time it stopped falling and remained at the relatively stable rate of 10% to 12% until 1970. During the next decade it began to decrease again, and by the early 1980s it had fallen to 5% to 9%. For students who incurred the much heavier cost of continuing on to a Ph.D., the return to this extra effort was only about 2%.

Why did the rate of return to a college education fall during the 1970s? One reason seems to have been a decrease in its benefits—in terms of the additional future income it yielded. Another reason was the increase in its costs such as tuition.

However, by 1985 some experts were speculating that the return on higher education might be increasing again, for two reasons: (1) the two recessions in the early 1980s hurt those with a college degree less than those without a degree, and (2) there was a reduction in the population bulge of college graduates looking for jobs.

Thus we see that education is indeed an investment; costs incurred in acquiring an education today do yield a return in terms of higher income in the future. This is particularly true of a high school education, which has traditionally had a higher return than a college education. Moreover, a high school education is a relatively good investment in another sense: it yields returns that are favorable relative to returns to physical capital. Thus if you wish, you could view your high school education purely and simply as an investment; it needs no further justification.

While a college education may also be viewed as an investment, it has had a return—especially during the 1970s—that has not compared favorably with the return on physical capital. Therefore, it can only partly be justified as an investment. Unless its return rises dramatically

BOX 35-2

WHO SHOULD INVEST IN APPRENTICESHIP TRAINING?

As one form of investment in human capital, on-the-job training of apprentices involves an initial cost that is expected to pay off with increased productivity in the future. In this box we consider the question: Who should pay this initial cost, the employees who receive the training or the employers?

The Employees

In Figure 35-6, the employees' wage (the red line) is always kept the same as their productivity (the black line). Therefore the investment in the initial apprenticeship period (area 1) is paid by the employees who accept a wage during this period that is lower than the wage W_o they could earn in alternative jobs. They also get all the later payoff from the investment (area 2), since the wage W_n that they earn then is higher than the W_o they could earn without the training.

The Employers

In Figure 35-7, the employees bear none of the cost of the investment, nor do they capture any of the payoff from it. Throughout, their wage remains the same W_o

FIGURE 35-6
The employees invest in apprenticeship

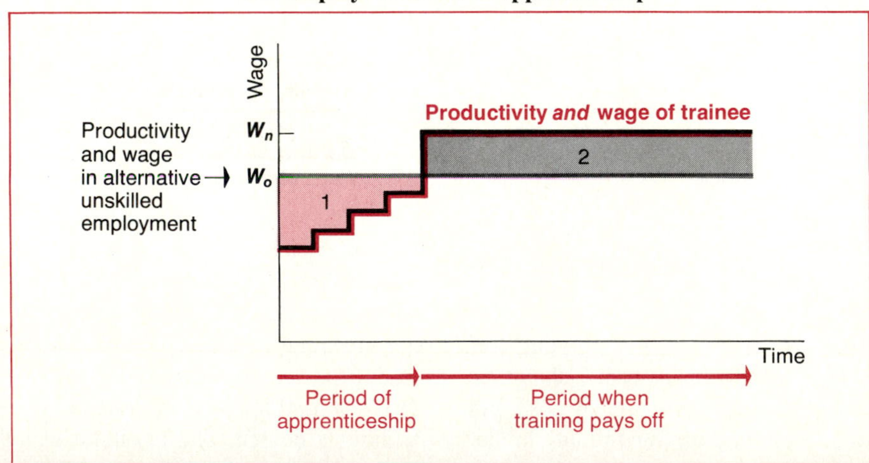

in the future, part of its justification depends on its other benefits in the form of "consumption" gains. For example, a college education provides many individuals with a greater appreciation of history and literature. One might also consider the psychological benefits that well-educated people receive because they have more interesting and challenging jobs. To illustrate: Even if the income were the same, it would be more interesting and pleasant to design a bridge than to pour the cement. Then, too, jobs may come with what the British call "perks" (perquisites). For example, expense-paid business trips are often fun. On the other hand, those at the top often work very hard, under great pressure.

The Complex Nature of Wages and Salaries

In the preceding section, we have seen some of the rea-

that they could have earned in other jobs. It is now the employers who pay the total cost of the investment (area 1). The reason is that during the apprenticeship period they get less productivity from the employees (black line) than the wage they pay them (red line). In theory, employers also get the later payoff from this investment (area 2) when the productivity of the employees exceeds their wage W_o.

However, the problem for employers is that they may not get this later payoff, since workers may leave once their training is completed. Specifically, workers may be attracted away by another employer offering higher wage W_n; there is now a very good chance of such an offer, since this is now what the workers' services are worth. This risk that employees will leave once their training is complete reduces the incentive for employers to undertake investment in human capital, even though it might yield high returns to society in terms of greater labor productivity.

These two panels represent the two sharpest alternatives. In practice, other more complicated arrangements are often introduced. For example, even employers in panel *b* who pay the whole training cost almost always give the trainees some of the eventual payoff 2, in order to keep them from leaving.

FIGURE 35-7
The employers invest in apprenticeship

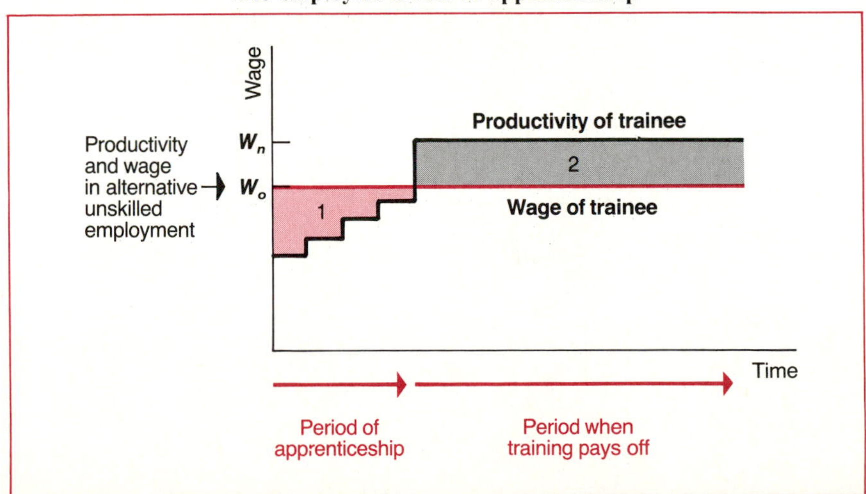

sons why an individual's wage or salary may reflect far more than just a basic wage rate. For example, an individual's income may be higher because of education. Or, it may be higher because of some specific talent or ability: Tom Watson was born with a great natural ability to hit a golf ball; others are born with a special talent for solving mathematical problems.

Figure 35-9 illustrates this idea. An initial point of reference is provided on the left by the base income of $15,000 earned by an unskilled laborer with no special talent or training. The remaining three individuals work for a large firm. Individual A is educated up to an MBA and has 5 years experience. He earns $33,000 income; this is also what he could earn in an alternative occupation. (This includes the $15,000 base wage plus a $18,000 return on his education and experience.) In other words, $33,000 is his income and also his opportunity cost. Individual B has exactly the same education and experience as A, and the same $33,000 opportunity cost. However, her income is another $14,000 higher because she has a special flair for solving the problems encountered by this firm. Finally, individual C has exactly the same education, experience, and opportunity cost as A and B. But he has an even more incisive mind in dealing with this firm's problems. His income consequently is a hefty $75,000.

FIGURE 35-8
Lifetime profile of people's incomes, with and without a college education
White male earnings for high school graduates and for college graduates in 1973.
Source: Richard B. Freeman, *Labor Economics* (Englewood Cliffs, N.J.: Prentice-Hall, 1979), p. 39.

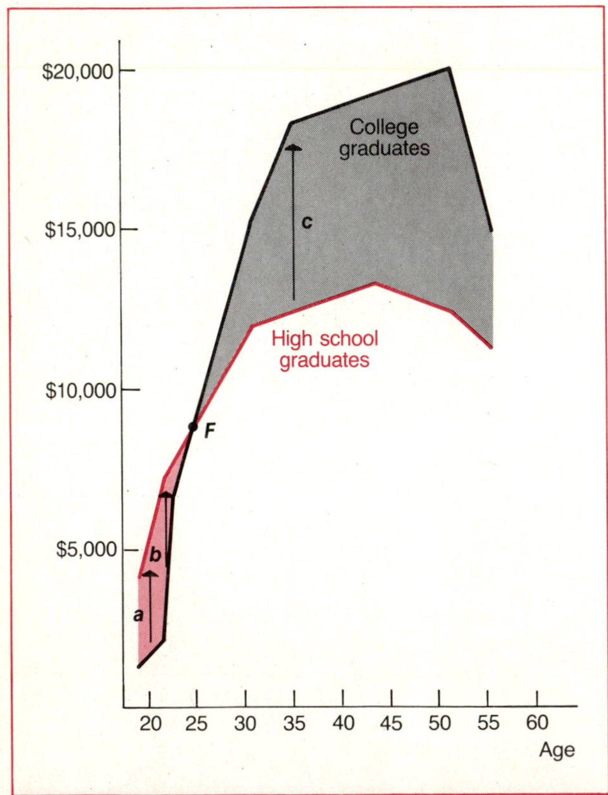

Three components of income can be distinguished:

1. The $15,000 base income for unskilled work.
2. The additional $18,000 of income that these consultants could earn in other jobs because of their education and experience.

The first two components represent opportunity cost. The last one does not:

3. Additional returns to those with special talents. This third item falls under the economists' broad definition of ***rent***.

Economists use the term *rent* in a broad sense, to identify the return to any factor of production in excess of its opportunity cost.

Thus, rent is the gap between what a factor *is* earning and what it *could* earn elsewhere. Expressed this way, we see that there are two reasons why an individual's income might include a very large rent component: (1) The income he or she *is* earning may be very high, and (2) what he or she *could* earn elsewhere is low. We continue to focus on the first reason here, while the second is considered in Box 35-4.

RENT

What do Martina Navratilova, Placido Domingo, and an

acre of Iowa farmland have in common? The answer to this question is: They all are like business executive C in Figure 35-9; they all earn an economic *rent* because of their superior quality. Domingo has an exceptional voice. Navratilova plays outstanding tennis. An acre of Iowa land yields unusual quantities of grain.

Rent on Agricultural Land, Based on Differences in Quality

All economic analyses begin with the cultivation of the earth. . . . To the economist, . . . the green plain is a sort of burial place of hidden treasure, where all the forethought and industry of man are set at naught by the caprice of the power which hid the treasure. . . . Thus is Man mocked by earth his stepmother, and never knows as he tugs at her closed hand whether it contains diamonds or flints, good red wheat or a few clayey and blighted cabbages.

George Bernard Shaw

Figure 35-12 shows three plots of land with no alternative use but to grow a crop. In other words, their opportunity cost is zero. It therefore follows from the preceding definition that any income they earn is rent. In this special case, economists' and the public's definition of rent coincide: It is the income earned by land.

Relatively poor land *C* has such low productivity that with a $3 price of wheat, it has just been brought into cultivation. The value of the wheat it produces is barely sufficient to cover the costs of fertilizer, machin-

BOX 35-3

WHY PRIVATE AND SOCIAL RETURNS TO EDUCATION DIFFER

To estimate the social return to investment in higher education, the estimated private rate of return should ideally be adjusted as follows:

1. Adjust it *upward* to take account of any external benefits, such as the spillover benefit from the education of the doctor who discovers a new vaccine.
2. Adjust it *downward* to take account of government subsidies to higher education. These are costs of the investment to society but not to the private individuals being educated. Because private individuals do not take these costs into account, they are not included in the calculation of private rates of return.

There are other reasons why private and social rates of return may differ. Employers pay college graduates more, not only because education has made them more productive but also because it has given them a "credential." In other words, education acts as a screening device that tells employers which individuals have the capacity and diligence to learn. Because it gives college graduates the best jobs, it provides them with a private return in the form of a

higher income. But what benefit to society overall is provided by such a mechanism that gives the best jobs to one group rather than another? The traditional answer has been: Very little. However, it may be argued that there is some social benefit to screening because it tends to match up the more talented people with the best jobs. If there were no college screening mechanism, it would take longer for these jobs and people to "find" each other, with some national output and income being lost during this period.

ery, the farmer's time, and other inputs. Therefore, it earns no rent. Land *B* is more fertile soil that grows enough wheat per acre to pay for other inputs and leave $60 per acre; that is, its rent is $60 per acre. Land *A* is even more productive and earns a rent of $150.

Of course, the rent on these plots of land depends on the price of wheat. Suppose that, because of crop failures elsewhere in the world, the price of wheat rises from the initial $3 a bushel (in Figure 35-12) to $4. The result is shown in Figure 35-13. Land *C*, which previously earned no rent, now does. And the rents earned by plots *A* and *B* increase. Land *D* is now the marginal land, just brought into cultivation and earning zero rent.

Another Example of Rent: The Income from Mineral Deposits

A mineral deposit may also earn an economic rent. To confirm this statement, reinterpret Figures 35-12 and 35-13 as follows. Mineral deposit *A* is a rich vein of ore, easy to reach. Mineral deposit *B* is also a rich vein of

FIGURE 35-9

Dividing income into its components

Individuals A, B, and C have the same qualifications—an MBA plus 5 years experience—and the same $33,000 opportunity cost, shown by the red dashed line. Any surplus income above this is rent. Thus A earns no rent, B earns $14,000 rent, and C—with the greatest natural talent for the job—earns $42,000 rent.

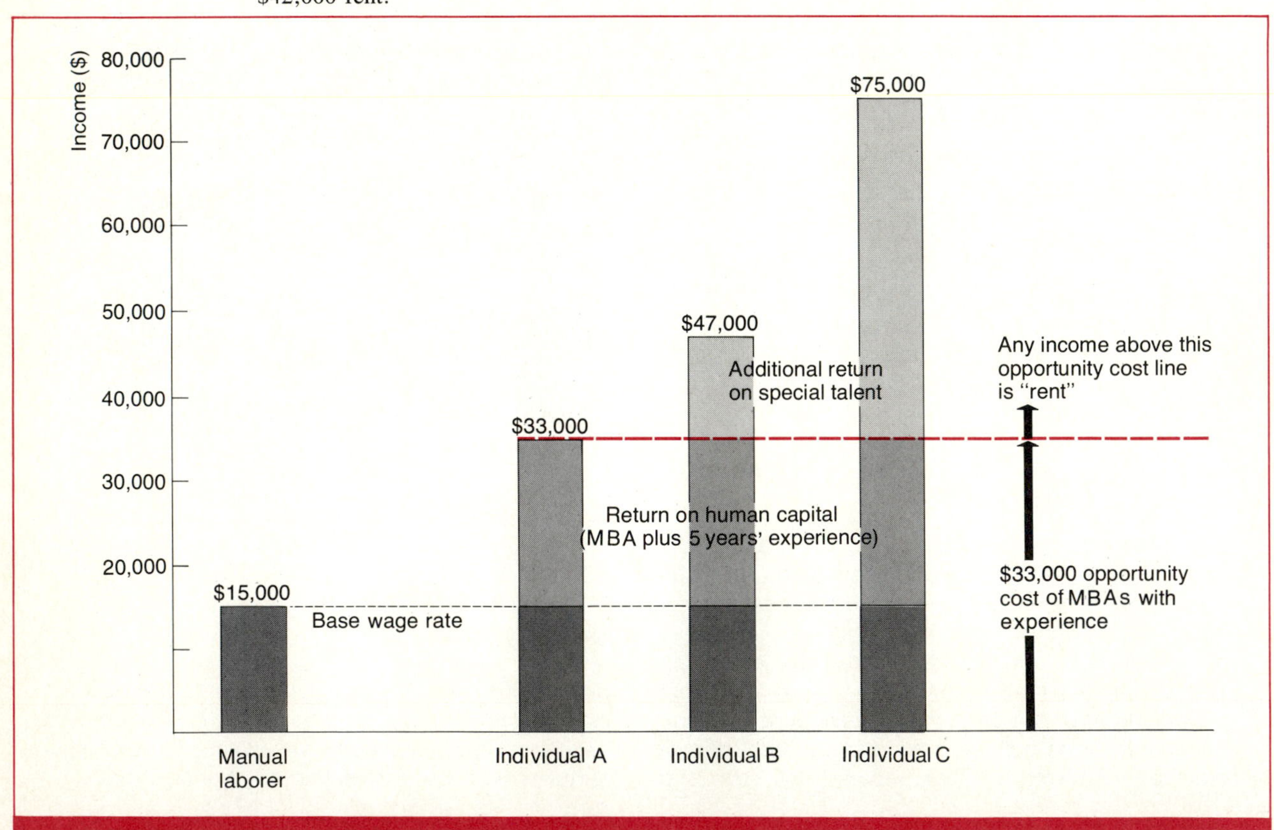

BOX 35-4

RENT AND OPPORTUNITY COST

Recall that rent is defined as the difference between what a factor *is* earning and what it *could* earn elsewhere (its opportunity cost). The three business executives in Figure 35-9 had the same $33,000 opportunity cost but different incomes, so they had different rents. Here, we consider individuals who have the same *income* but different *opportunity costs.* Differences in rent occur in this case as well, as we shall now show.

In Figure 35-10 we show a labor market in which all individuals have the same salary *Y.* But their opportunity costs vary. Thus individuals *a* and *b* have the two different opportunity costs shown by the two hollow bars. Therefore their rents will vary.

To show this in detail, first consider individual *a.* She has barely been attracted into this industry by income *Y,* since this is what she can earn elsewhere (her opportunity cost). Because there is no difference between her income and her opportunity cost, she earns no rent.

The situation for individual *b* is different. His opportunity cost (potential income elsewhere) is shown by the lower hollow bar. The difference between this and his *actual* income *Y* is the red bar; this is his rent. Visualizing similar red bars representing the rents of other workers, we conclude that the rent earned by all *N* workers in this industry is the shaded triangle 2.

To sum up this example: The *N* workers, all earning salary *Y,* have a total salary income of areas 1 + 2.

FIGURE 35-10
Rent of a factor of production that (*a*) has an alternative use (such as labor) and (*b*) one that does not (such as some types of land)

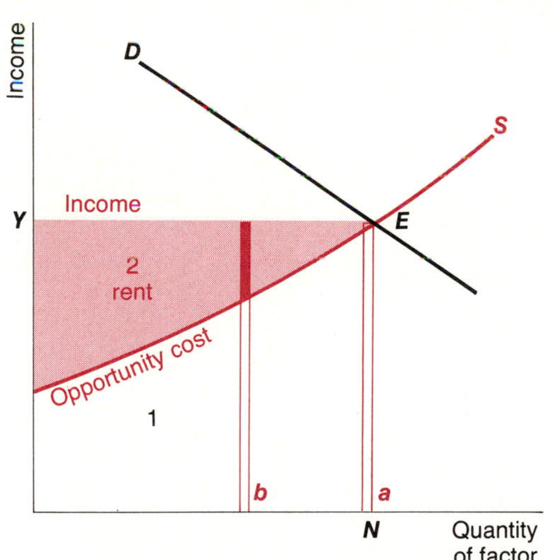

(*a*) All individuals in this panel earn the same income **Y**, but they have different opportunity costs, as given by the height of the curve **S**. The difference between their income and opportunity cost is rent. For individual ***b***, this is the dark bar, while for individual ***a***, it is zero. For all individuals, it is the shaded area.

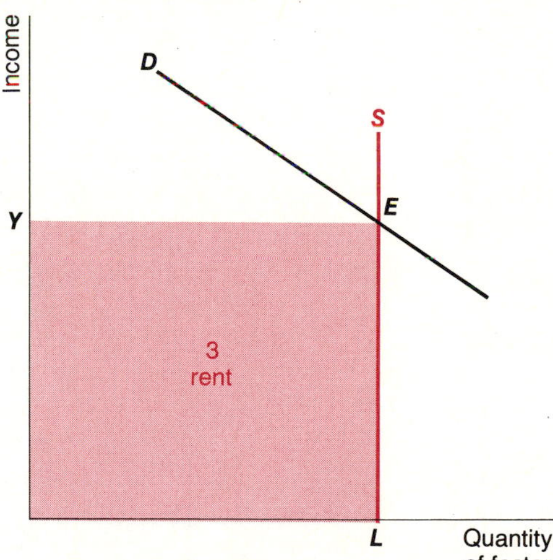

(*b*) None of the plots of land in this panel has any other use. All plots have zero opportunity cost, and their supply is completely inelastic. Therefore, their entire income 3 is rent.

Of this, area 1 is their opportunity cost, while area 2 is their rent.

The income of any other factor of production can similarly be divided into opportunity cost and rent components. In particular, we are interested in the land shown in panel *b* which has a completely inelastic supply because it can't be used for anything but agriculture. In other words, quantity *L* will be supplied no matter what its price may be. Because this land can't earn anything in any other use (its opportunty cost is zero) *all* its income 3 is rent.

Finally, we can recap our discussion of rent with the simple example shown in Figure 35-11, which illustrates how an individual can earn rent because (1) he's very good at what he's doing (the issue addressed in the main text) or (2) he's very bad at anything else (the issue addressed in this box). Washington is a better basketball player than teammate McTavish, and his higher income reflects this. If they had the same opportunity costs—that is, the same ability to earn income elsewhere—Washington would have a higher rent. But they don't have the same opportunity costs. Whereas Washington could play pro football instead for $100,000 a year, McTavish has no other talent than basketball. His opportunity cost is the bare $15,000 that he could earn in unskilled manual labor. Because his opportunity cost is so low, almost all his income is rent; indeed, for this reason there's a higher rent component in his income than in Washington's.

FIGURE 35-11

Why rent depends both on (1) how productive a factor is in its present use and (2) how unproductive it is in any other use

Washington has more basketball talent and earns a higher salary. If the opportunity costs of the players were the same, Washington would earn the higher rent. But their opportunity costs are not the same. In fact, McTavish's is so much lower that rent makes up a larger part of his income than Washington's.

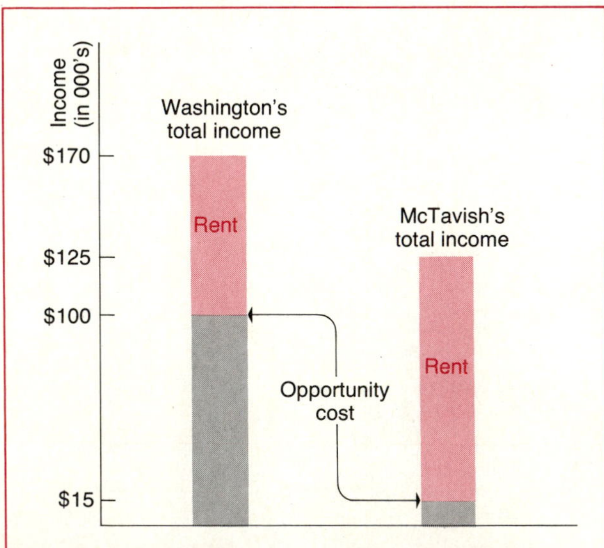

ore, but difficult to reach and extract. Deposit *C* is of poorer quality and so difficult to reach that initially in Figure 35-12 it is barely being mined. In Figure 35-13 we see how an increase in the price of ore increases the rent earned on each of these deposits and induces the mining of low-yield deposit *D* for the first time.

Rent on Land Because of Its Location

Land may yield economic rent not only because of its fertility but also because of its location. To illustrate, land *A* in Figure 35-14 is in the prime business district of a city and can be used in a highly productive way. A business might wish to locate there for a variety of reasons: It might want to be close to suppliers and competitors so that it can easily keep up with new developments and innovations in the industry. Or, it might wish to have access to the large labor pool that exists in this area of high-density population. Or, it might wish to be close to the population center in order to reduce the cost of transporting its product to market.

For all these reasons, location *A* earns a rent. Land *B* is less attractive since it is not in this prime district, and it earns a smaller rent. Finally, land *C* earns no rent because it is even farther away and therefore involves even higher costs of inconvenience and transportation.

These blocks in Figure 35-14, just like the bars in the previous diagram, give us a picture of how rents compare. Because the selling price of land depends on the rent it can earn—as we shall soon see in more detail—these blocks also give us a picture of how land prices over an urban area will compare.

Finally, note that although the heights of the blocks have been drawn to reflect rents and land values, they may also provide some rough indication of where the tallest buildings will be constructed. Office space be-

FIGURE 35-12

Rent based on differences in quality of land (based on wheat price of $3 per bushel)

Marginal land *C*, which is just barely fertile enough to cultivate, earns no rent. High-productivity land *A* earns the highest rent.

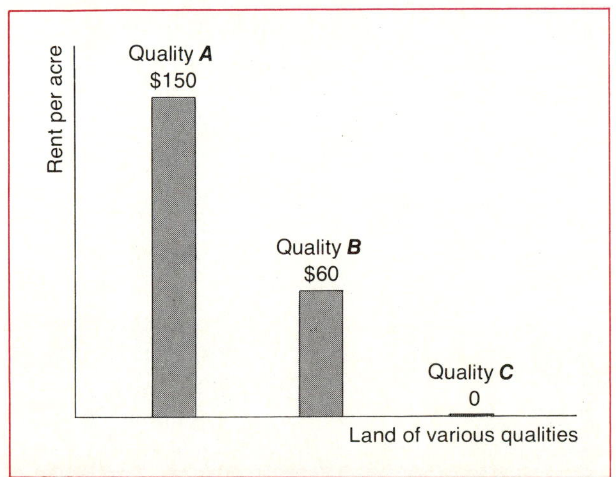

FIGURE 35-13

How rents increase when the price of wheat increases

This figure is the same as Figure 35-12 except that the price of wheat has risen from $3 to $4 per bushel. Because of this increased price, all existing plots of land earn greater income—that is, greater rent. Moreover, less productive plot *D* is brought into cultivation for the first time.

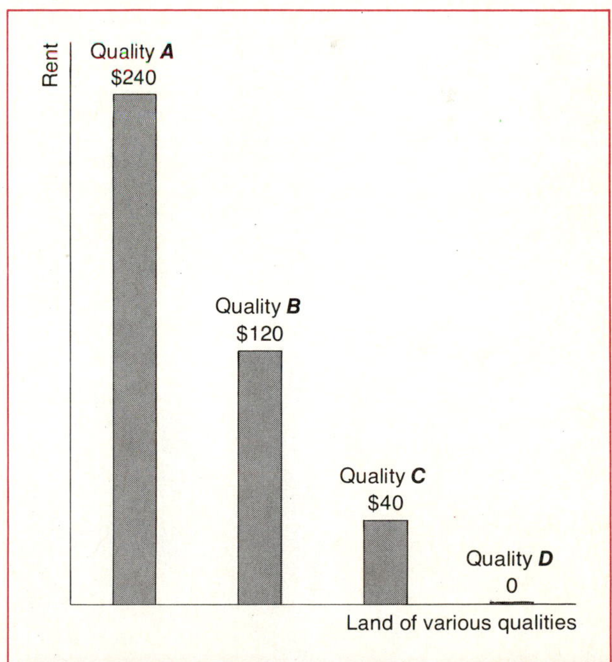

comes more and more expensive to construct as a building gets higher and higher. Consequently, if land is cheap, you buy more land and build sideways. But if land is expensive enough, you conserve it by building up. Thus, buildings tend to be tallest in the prime, most expensive locations.

Above-Normal Profit as a Rent

Since above-normal profit is defined as a return above opportunity cost, it is, by definition, a rent. The most obvious illustration occurs in the case of monopoly. Specifically, the shaded area of above-normal profit in Figure 25-4 is a ***monopoly rent.*** It exists because entry by new firms into the industry is restricted. Therefore, it is a rent on whatever restricts entry. For example, it may be rent on a government license that is granted to one firm (or a few) that blocks out other potential competitors. Or, it may be rent on a patented product that other firms cannot copy. Or, if there are economies of scale, the existing firm may earn a rent since no other firm can afford to enter.

FIGURE 35-14

Rent based on differences in the location of land

Compare with Figure 35-12. Because of its greater convenience and lower transport costs, land *A* earns a higher rent than land *B*. Land *C*, in a relatively poor location, earns no rent.

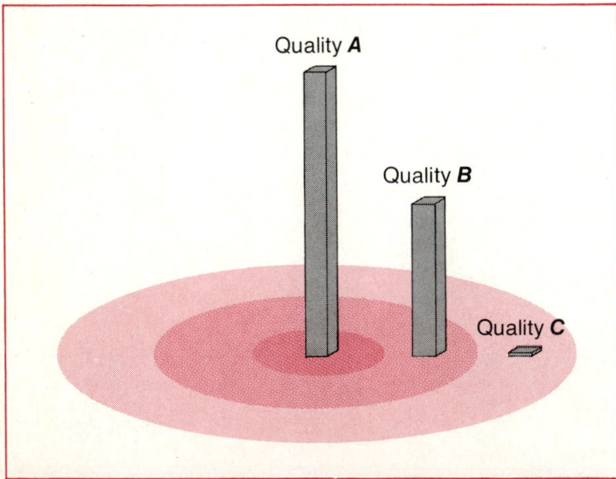

HOW RENTS ARE CAPITALIZED

If land plots *A* and *B* in Figure 35-14 are put up for sale, we would expect *A* to sell for a higher price; it will be more valuable because of the higher rent it can earn. This is generally true: Higher rents result in higher land values. But can't we be more precise about how the value of land is determined?

If you had the money and you were interested in buying land *B* in Figure 35-12, how much would you be willing to pay for it? Bear in mind that, as an alternative, you can always purchase bonds (or stocks) instead and earn a rate of return of, say, 6%. Because the rent of land *B* is $60 per year, you should be willing to pay about $1,000 for it. This gives you the same 6% rate of return on your land (a $60 return on $1,000) as on the alternative of buying bonds. Moreover, the competition of other potential buyers who feel the same way will ensure that the price of land *B* will settle at about $1,000—so long as the rent on *B* is expected to remain at $60 per year.

However, when the rent on land *B* doubles in Figure 35-13 to $120, potential buyers will be attracted by this higher income it can earn, and will begin to bid up the price of this land. This process will continue until the price of this land roughly doubles to $2,000, where its rate of return will again be the same 6% as before—that is, a $120 return on $2,000. To describe this process, we say that an increase in rent is ***capitalized*** in the value of the land.

In practice, there are many complications. In particular, the price of land will be affected not only by present rents but by expected *future* rents too. If a single year's rent increases by 20%, the price of land may increase by more than 20% if people expect rents to continue rising.[3]

The fact that land prices reflect rents leads us to be skeptical of any government program to raise farm income by raising the price of commodities, such as wheat. The major effect of such a program may be to cause higher rents (a shift from Figure 35-12 to 35-13) and consequently a higher value for farmland. Thus its benefit tends to go to the owners of farmland when the price supports are introduced. By and large, it does not

[3]Further detail on how an income flow (such as rent or interest) is capitalized in the value of an asset (such as land or a bond) was given in Box 13-1. The "capitalization of an income flow" is just another way of saying "the calculation of the present value of an income flow."

go to those who want to farm by renting land. And, if new farmers purchase the land, they will be passing their eventual increase in income from farming over to those who have sold them the land at a high price. Paradoxically, the higher wheat price may make farming *less* attractive for newcomers. They now have a greater problem of raising the funds necessary to purchase the higher-priced farm land. Thus government price supports designed to "help out the small farmer" may, in fact, keep those of limited means out of farming altogether.

Moreover, serious problems arise even for those who do raise the necessary funds to get into farming by borrowing heavily on a big mortgage. They will be able to earn a living—and make those big mortgage payments—only if the government price-support program continues. So these farmers *of necessity* become strong supporters of the government program; without it, agricultural prices would fall and they would no longer be able to make their mortgage payments. In short, when government support programs are introduced, they tend to benefit one group—those who initially own the land. But if these initial owners sell it, they are "out-of-reach." For example, if they have retired to Florida on the proceeds of their land sale, they cannot be damaged if the farm support program is then ended. Instead, the damage falls on the *new* owners.

By 1985, this had become a serious problem, because many U.S. farmers had bought land at the high price prevailing in the late 1970s. During the early 1980s there was downward pressure on agricultural prices, and price support programs by the government had become so costly that President Reagan proposed dramatic reductions in these subsidies. Because this policy would lower farm income, the President found himself in direct conflict with U.S. farmers. Although they were among the world's most efficient food producers, many had made the mistake of borrowing to buy land earlier at an inflated price. Any fall in the price of food would leave them unable to make their mortgage payments and facing bankruptcy.

Other economic rents—as well as those on land—may also be capitalized. The number of taxis in New York is limited, since each must have a "medallion." Because this requirement makes taxis scarce, the fares collected by each taxi are greater. This higher income (rent) becomes capitalized in the value of a medallion. By 1985 the price of a medallion had risen to $86,000, many times the cost of even the most expensive cab. Thus, someone who wants to own and operate a cab in New York may be able to do reasonably well once he gets into the business. But how does he raise the money to get started in the first place?

Finally, taxi medallions raise one more question. Rather than let the medallion owners benefit from the policy of restricting the number of cabs, would it not have been better for New York to auction off the rights to operate cabs only for 1 or 2 years at a time? Then the city would have been able to collect the rents. Moreover, individual drivers could now enter the industry far more easily. They would have to buy only the right to operate a cab for 1 or 2 years rather than the far more expensive medallion, which represents the right to operate a cab permanently. (Once a permanent medallion system has been introduced, the government cannot switch to an auctioning of annual permits without inflicting a loss on present owners of medallions. This is similar to the problem with agricultural price supports. They cannot be lowered without inflicting a loss on present owners of land.)

Taxing Rent

Rent has always been a natural target for taxation. About a century ago, Henry George built a powerful single-tax movement on the idea that nothing should be taxed but land rents. (His book *Progress and Poverty* sold millions of copies, and he almost won an election as mayor of New York.) Why, asked George, shouldn't we tax land rents, since they represent a pure windfall? Owners obviously don't produce the land, nor do they work for their rental incomes. Instead, they just hold the land and become wealthy from "unearned increments" as the population increases and rents rise. George argued that the land rents belong to the public as a whole, and should be taxed away from the owners and used for public purposes.

George's case was based not only on equity but also on efficiency. A levy on land rents is one of the few taxes that need not distort resource allocation. Even if half the rent on land is taxed away, it will still remain in cultivation. What else can the owner do with it? And because the quantity of land in use is not affected, there is no reason to expect an efficiency loss. (Compare this with a tax on any other factor of production. For example, a tax on wages can affect the incentive to work and might thus affect the amount of work done.)

However, George's proposal to tax land rent raises two serious difficulties—in addition to the obvious problem that, as a single tax, it would not raise nearly enough money to cover today's large government expenditures. First, if present owners paid the current high price when they bought their land, rents are not a windfall to them at all but just a reasonable return on their large initial expenditure. (Why tax those who bought land and not those who bought stocks or bonds instead?) The only windfall is to the previous owners who sold the land for a high price. But they may now be living in Bermuda, beyond the reach of the taxing authority. Second, in practice it may be impossible to separate the rent on land from the return to buildings. If you tax a landlord's income, you will be taxing *both*. But the return to buildings—or to any other improvements on the land—is not a return to the land itself. Instead, it is a return to *capital,* and it cannot be taxed without causing distortion and inefficiency. For example, a tax on the returns from apartments will discourage the construction and maintenance of buildings.

KEY POINTS

1. Those who provide the nation's capital receive income in several forms. For example, those who own businesses receive profits. Those who lend money to businesses to purchase plant or equipment receive interest.
2. In a perfectly competitive capital market, the interest rate is determined by the demand and supply of loanable funds. Demand reflects how productive these funds will be when they are invested (the marginal efficiency of investment). Supply reflects how highly savers value money in its alternative use—consumption.
3. Because capital is productive, present goods can be exchanged for even more future goods. Therefore, present goods are worth more than future goods. The interest rate indicates how much more.
4. The interest rate also acts as a screening device that allocates funds to investment projects with the highest productivity. A government ceiling that lowers the interest rate below its perfectly competitive level results in two kinds of efficiency loss: (1) It reduces the total funds available for investment, and (2) it may result in funds being allocated to the wrong set of projects. It also results in a transfer from lenders to those borrowers who are able to get loans. This doesn't necessarily benefit poor individuals or small businesses, because they may be the potential borrowers who do *not* get loans; banks prefer to lend to wealthy individuals and large businesses.
5. Income is earned not only on machinery and other forms of physical capital, but also on human capital—that is, on skills, training, and education. The individuals who own the human capital are not the only ones who bear the initial cost of the investment. Governments also invest by subsidizing education, and businesses invest by subsidizing training programs. An inadequate past opportunity to accumulate human capital is one significant reason why the income of minority groups is depressed.
6. The return to an individual from an investment in a college education has been estimated as about 5% to 10%. Although this return had fallen during the 1970s, there was some evidence in the early 1980s that it was rising again.
7. Economists define rent as the return to any factor of production above its opportunity cost. Those with superior talents in any occupation, whether it be business or basketball, earn a rent.
8. Land also earns a rent—except for plots that are not cultivated or have just barely been brought into cultivation. The most fertile plots earn the largest rent. If the price of farm products increases, rents on all cultivated plots of land rise and new plots are brought into cultivation.
9. Rent is also earned on land because of its location. Mineral deposits similarly earn rent, with the richest, most accessible deposits earning the highest rents. Above-normal profits earned by a firm are also a form of rent. In the case of monopoly, these rents are typically due to something—such as a patent or a government license—that blocks entry by potential competitors.
10. The higher the rent earned by an asset such as a

plot of land, the higher its value; thus, rents are ''capitalized.'' This in turn has important implications for any agricultural price support policy that raises rents and therefore the price of farms. Although such a policy obviously benefits those who own farms, it won't necessarily increase the income of those who want to buy farms and work them. Quite the contrary: It tends to discourage new entrants by increasing the initial cost of buying a farm.

KEY CONCEPTS

debt and equity capital
physical and human capital
marginal efficiency of investment (MEI)
roundabout production
time preference
why present goods are worth more than future goods
base (risk-free) rate of interest
transfer and efficiency effects of an interest rate ceiling
misallocation due to rationing of funds
normal and above-normal profit
substitution between factors of production
interest rate as an allocator of investment funds
human capital and discrimination
affirmative action programs
private and social returns to education
economists' broad definition of rent
rent on land due to fertility
rent on land due to location
monopoly rent
capitalization of rent

PROBLEMS

35-1. This is a review of Chapters 33, 34, and 35. Why are wages and salaries higher in the United States than in most other countries? Why are our other forms of income also higher? The highest per capita incomes are not in the United States or Western Europe, but in some of the smaller states along the Persian Gulf. Why?

35-2. Using a three-panel diagram like Figure 24-5, show how the interest rate acts as a monitoring device to determine which investments will be undertaken and which will not.

35-3. If expectations change, with borrowers and lenders expecting that interest rates will fall in the future, what is likely to happen to the interest rate that a firm has to pay in order to sell long-term bonds today?

35-4. When economists speak of labor, capital, and land as factors of production, resources such as oil are included in the broad ''land'' category. Explain how the rapidly rising price of oil in the 1970s affected (1) decisions by individual firms on the combination of factors they would use, and (2) the mix of final goods that was produced. (Use plastics and fertilizer—which both require a large quantity of oil to produce—in your answer.)

35-5. ''In a world in which labor is free to switch jobs, there will be inadequate investment in human capital in the form of job training.'' Do you agree? Explain why or why not. How might our minimum wage laws be changed to reduce this problem? Would such changes raise other problems? (Read Box 35-2 before answering this question.)

35-6. Explain why the armed services have subsidized the college education of students who sign up to serve for several years after graduation. Explain why your answer is similar to one of the cases in Box 35-2.

35-7. Why might a firm pay a very high salary to attract an executive from a competing firm?

35-8. In Figure 35-9, does individual A receive more income than a manual laborer because of rent? Does B receive more than A because of rent? Explain your answer.

35-9. The public's idea of rent does not coincide with the economist's definition. How are the two concepts different? Give an example of (*a*) a return which an economist considers rent, but the public does not; (*b*) a return which the public considers rent, but the economist does not; and (*c*) a return which both consider rent.

35-10. Do you think that rent is an important or an insignificant part of the income of: (*a*) Robert Redford, (*b*) an elevator operator, (*c*) a textile worker?

35-11. Are these statements true or false? ''An increase in the price of oil not only stimulates the search for oil. It also brings previously uneconomic sources of oil into production. But it does not affect rent on existing oil fields.'' If any of these statements is false, correct it.

35-12. Suppose that all the agricultural land within 100 miles of Kansas City is equally fertile. Suppose, also, that all corn must be sold in Kansas City and that the cost of transporting it there depends only on distance. What pattern of land rent would you expect over this area?

35-13. Suppose New York City imposed its taxi restriction by allowing only a restricted set of *individuals* to drive cabs. Would rents be generated in this case? If so, who would earn these rents?

35-14. The number of doctors is limited because anyone practicing medicine must have a license. Are rents generated in this case? To whom do they go? Is the objective of licensing to affect doctors' income, or is there some other reason?

35-15. When Dave Winfield decided to play baseball he turned down offers to play pro football (where, let's suppose, he might be now working for $100,000 a year) and basketball (for $500,000 a year). Divide his current income of about $2 million a year into rent and opportunity cost.

CHAPTER 36

INCOME INEQUALITY

The most difficult issues of political economy are those where goals of efficiency . . . and equality conflict.

JAMES TOBIN

By 1984, New York Yankee outfielder Dave Winfield—with his $2 million a year contract for 10 years—was not the only rich athlete. The top salaries of superstars in other sports were $1 million a year or more, with the only question being, "For how many years?" Wayne Gretsky's hockey contract covered 21 years, while Magic Johnson's basketball contract was for 25 years. Steve Young, a college quarterback who didn't even own a credit card, signed a contract for almost $1 million each year until his retirement at age 65—43 years in the future.

This raises a question: Should an athlete earn that much more than the President of the United States? Should a disc jockey earn five times as much as a violinist with a symphony orchestra? Should anchorman Tom Brokaw earn almost three times as much as his boss, the Chairman of the Board of RCA?

The distribution of income in the United States is riddled with such glaring differences. In this chapter we will look at the income of Americans to see whether such examples are the exception or the rule. How unequal are American incomes, overall? Is inequality increasing or decreasing?

Our second task will be to address the question: What is a *fair* distribution of income? Is it the income distribution that results from the free play of market forces? Or, is it an equal income for all? Or, is it some compromise between the two?

To begin, we review why income differences arise in the first place. Why do some people earn so much more than others?

REVIEW: WHY DO INCOMES DIFFER?

When Babe Ruth was told that he earned more than the President, he replied: "I had a better year than he did."

In earlier chapters, we saw how market forces result in quite different incomes for different people. For example, the high income of a surgeon is in part a return to *human capital*; it provides compensation for the years of foregone income and hard study in medical school. It may also be partly a *rent* on greater-than-average *innate talent*. Of course, other individuals have gifts of quite a different sort; star athletes and entertainers also earn very large rents.

Income differences also arise because of *wealth*. Those who own stocks, bonds, and other forms of property receive income from them. There are even greater differences in wealth than in income. The richest 1% of the population holds about 20% of the nation's wealth. The richest half holds about 94%, leaving only about 6% to the poorest half. The poorest quarter holds almost no wealth at all.

Family background explains some income differences. America may be the land of opportunity where someone from a poor, low-status family can achieve prominence and success. However, coming from the "right family" does help, especially if parents provide not only a silver spoon but also practical advice and inspiration. And an individual in a minority group may have a lower income because of *discrimination*.

In addition, income differences may arise because of the exercise of *market power*. People who find themselves in a monopoly position may be able to profit handsomely in terms of increased income.

There are also income differences because some people work at more dangerous or unpleasant jobs. Thus the construction worker in a dangerous job may receive a *compensating wage differential,* that is, a higher wage to compensate for the risks faced. At the other extreme, artists may accept a lower income in order to pursue a career that they find particularly pleasant.

Income differences may also arise because some people *work harder* than others. For example, a specific doctor's income may be lower because of a personal decision to sacrifice income for leisure; an example is the doctor with a clinic at the base of Mount Tremblant who skis in the morning and sets broken bones in the afternoon. On the other hand, many doctors work very long hours, and this helps to explain their high incomes.

Some income differences may be the result of differences in *health,* or just plain *luck*. An example is the star quarterback who is injured by a vicious tackle and must give up football and the large income that goes with it.

Just as bad luck can lower income, good luck can raise it. One form of good luck is "being the right person at the right time." An example is the second-string quarterback who is headed nowhere, but suddenly gets a chance to step into the injured star's shoes. If this leads to a high-income career, some—but not all—of this success is attributable to luck.

Of all the causes of income differences, can we say which is most important? In a surprising study, Jacob Mincer of Columbia University concluded that the answer was: human capital. He found that *differences in human capital explained roughly 60% of the differences in American incomes.*[1]

HOW MUCH INCOME INEQUALITY IS THERE?

It's the rich whot gets the gryvy,
It's the poor whot gets the blime.

English ballad, World War II

Are wide differences in individual incomes the exception or the rule? When we look at the income of all Americans, how much inequality is there?

Panel *a* in Table 36-1 shows the distribution of U.S. incomes. However, these figures were calculated before taking into account government policies that tend to raise the relative income of the poor, such as unemployment insurance, social security, and taxes. Excluding these policies, the poor are very poor indeed: The lowest-income fifth of the population receive less than 1% of the nation's income. At the other extreme, the highest-income fifth of the population receive over half the nation's income.

This unequal distribution is illustrated with a ***Lorenz curve.*** The first step in drawing such a curve is to rearrange the data in panel *a* of Table 36-1 into *cumulative* form in panel *b*. For example, in the second row, the poorest 40% of the population earn 7.3% of the nation's income. (To get this figure, we add the first two numbers in panel *a*.) This point, labeled *J,* is then plotted in Figure 36-1, along with other points that are similarly calculated. The result is the Lorenz curve of U.S. income.

To get some feel for how much inequality this curve represents, we ask: What would this Lorenz curve look like if all families received exactly the same income? In that case, we would observe point *F* instead of point *J:* The "lowest" 40% of the population would receive 40% of the income. And instead of point *K* we would observe point *G*; 60% of the population would receive 60% of the income. When we join all points like *F* and *G,* the result is the "complete equality" line *OFGM,* which is the 45° straight line from the origin. Thus income inequality is shown by the amount of bow in the Lorenz curve; that is, by the size of the red slice between the curve and the 45° line.

In fact, *inequality is not as serious a problem as this diagram suggests*. One reason: Even if each family were earning exactly the same *lifetime* income, the Lorenz curve would still not coincide with that 45° line. We would still observe some "inequality slice." The reason is that, during any single year, we would observe some young families starting out with low incomes, and some middle-aged families in their earning prime with high incomes. Inequality exists in that year for these families, even though they have exactly the same lifetime income pattern.

Nonetheless, even when such influences are fully taken into account, a substantial degree of inequality

[1]His study covered white urban males. See Jacob Mincer, "Education, Experience, Earnings and Employment," in F. Thomas Juster (ed.), *Education, Income and Human Behavior* (New York: McGraw-Hill, 1975), p. 73.

TABLE 36-1
Estimated Income Distribution of U.S. Families, before Taxes and Transfers

(a) Income distribution		(b) Cumulative income distribution		
Population	Share of total income	Population	Share of total income	Point in Figure 36-1
Lowest 20%	gets less than 0.3%	First 20%	gets less than 0.3%	*H*
Second 20	gets 7.0	First 40	gets 0.3 + 7.0 = 7.3	*J*
Third 20	gets 16.1	First 60	gets 7.3 + 16.1 = 23.4	*K*
Fourth 20	gets 26.0	First 80	gets 23.4 + 26.0 = 49.4	*L*
Highest 20	gets 50.6	Total	gets 49.4 + 50.6 = 100.0	*M*

Source: Congressional Budget Office, *Poverty Status of Families under Alternative Definitions of Income,* Background Paper no. 17, rev. (Washington: Congress of the United States, June 1977), p. 24, updated to 1984 by authors.

FIGURE 36-1
Lorenz curve showing before-tax-and-transfer income distribution of U.S. families

If every family had exactly the same income, the American income distribution would follow the 45° "complete equality" line. The actual income distribution is shown by the curve that lies below this—with the red slice between the two showing the amount of income inequality.

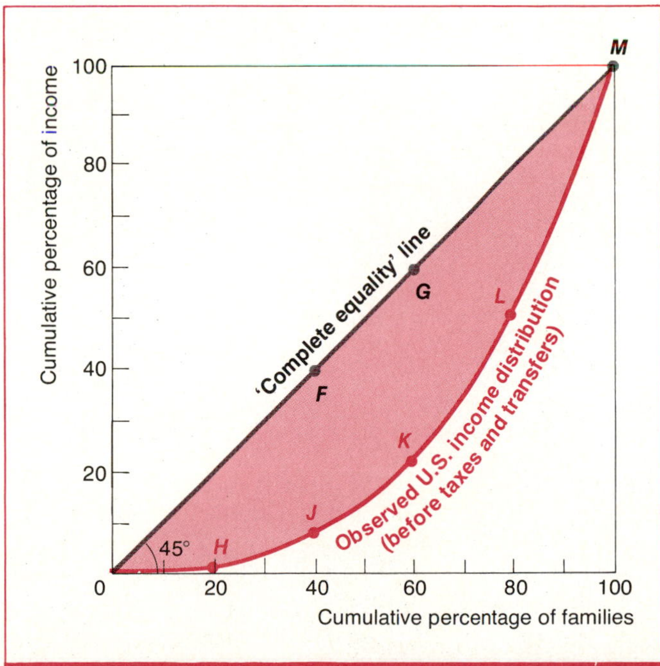

exists. Society's response is to reduce this inequality by government taxation that concentrates more heavily on the rich, and government expenditure programs such as social security, unemployment insurance, and food stamps that raise the relative income of those who are poor.

HOW MUCH INEQUALITY DOES THE GOVERNMENT NOW ELIMINATE?

The degree to which government taxes and transfer payments reduce inequality in the nation's income distribution is shown in Figure 36-2. The colored area is exactly

FIGURE 36-2

How government taxes and transfers reduce U.S. income inequality

Taxes and transfers by all levels of government reduce income inequality by about one third. Taxes, which shift the curve from *d* to *e,* are a relatively unimportant form of equalization compared with government transfer programs—especially social insurance, which reduces inequality from curve *a* to curve *b*.

Sources: Curve *a* is a reproduction of Figure 36-1. Curve *e* is derived from the figures in the 1984 column of Table 36-2 in exactly the same way that curve *a* was derived from Table 36-1(*a*). The breakdown of the slicing between *a* and *e* is based on an updating of Congressional Budget Office, *Poverty Status of Families under Alternative Definitions of Income,* Background Paper No. 17 rev. (Washington, June 1977), p. 24.

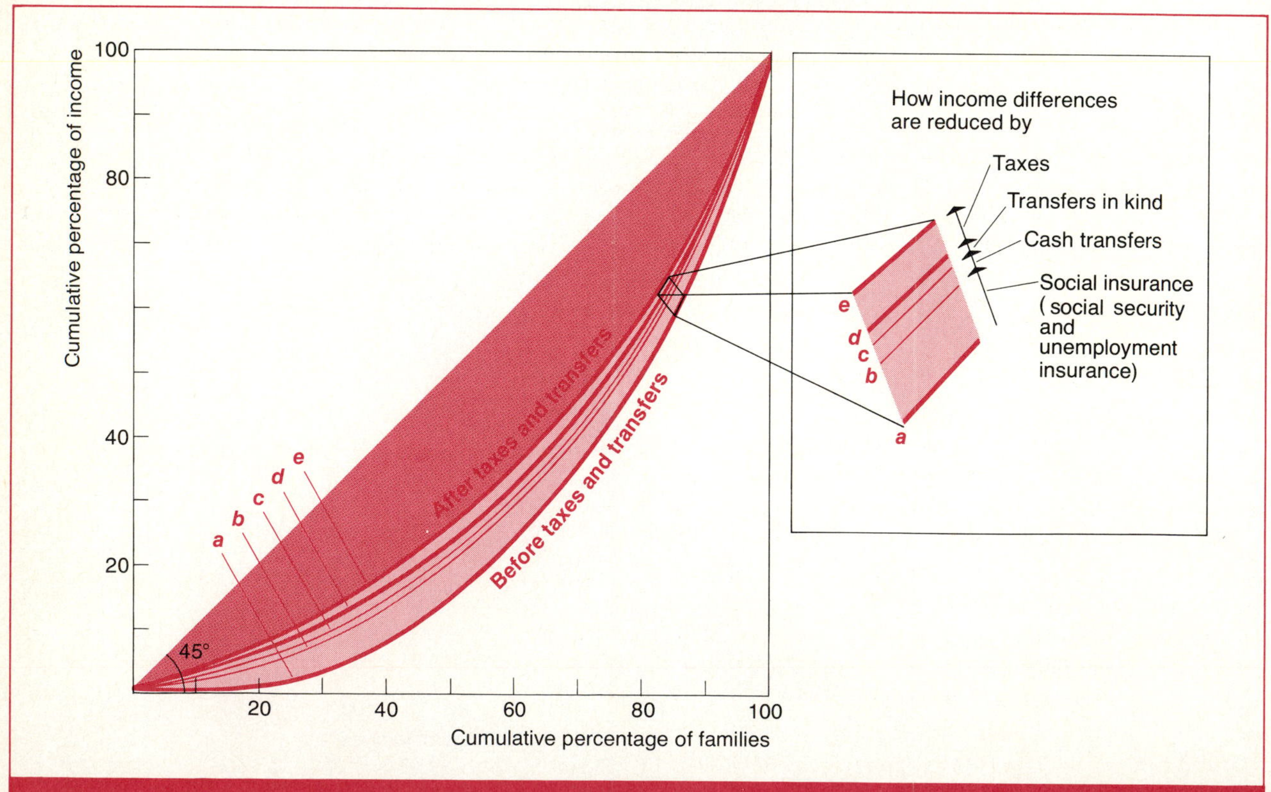

the same as in Figure 36-1. However, here it is broken down into a light area that shows how much the government reduces inequality, and a darker area that shows how much still remains.

Whereas curve *a* is a reproduction of the before-taxes-and-transfers curve graphed in Figure 36-1, curve *b* shows the major shift toward equality that occurs as a result of social insurance, including social security and unemployment insurance. (Social security and other government programs that shift this curve are discussed in more detail in the next chapter.) Curve *c* shows the further shift that results from cash transfers such as Aid to Families with Dependent Children. Curve *d* shows the shift as a result of transfers-in-kind, where the government provides goods such as food, or services such as medical assistance, instead of cash. The final shift to curve *e* shows the effect of taxation. When all programs are considered, the overall picture is one of a government that is making substantial transfers of income to the poor, in the process eliminating roughly a third of the nation's income inequality. Claims that the government is not very effective in changing the nation's income distribution have frequently been based on calculations that do not take into account all of these programs, in particular, in-kind transfers.

One surprise in this diagram is that taxation, often supposed to be a great income redistributor, is relatively ineffective in reducing income inequality. Certainly taxes are a large enough item in our income to make a big difference. But they do not change the nation's income distribution as much as one might expect because, on balance, they are not highly progressive. While it is true, as noted in Chapter 5, that *income* taxes are progressive—that is, the rates rise as incomes rise—other taxes are regressive. Moreover, loopholes ease the burden of income taxes on the wealthy.

On the other hand, the more explicit transfer programs such as unemployment insurance, social security, and other forms of cash transfer seem, when taken together, to be more effective. However, we must be cautious about this conclusion. It is quite true that the payments they provide to the poor *directly* reduce inequality—that is, shift the Lorenz curve up from *a* to *d*. But *indirectly* they *increase* inequality (make the Lorenz curve *a* lower than it would otherwise be) because of their side effects. For example, the income guarantee provided by programs such as unemployment insurance makes unemployed people less desperate to get a job quickly, because they can at least survive without one. Moreover, for some couples the incentive to stay together may be reduced by an income guarantee that ensures that they can get welfare if they separate. When a couple breaks up, one medium-income family may become two poor families.

These effects reduce the per-family earned income at the low end of the scale, and give Lorenz curve *a* a bigger bow than it would otherwise have. In short, income-support programs have two conflicting effects on income inequality. Indirectly they make it worse by giving the "before transfers" curve *a* a bigger bow. But directly they make it better by shifting the Lorenz curve up from *a* to the "after transfers" curve *d*.

Has the Lorenz curve *e* been changing over time? During the 1980–1984 period, there was some increase in inequality, as shown in Table 36-2. A comparison of the 1980 and 1984 columns indicates that there was a shift of 1.9% of the nation's income to the highest 20% of the population. Most of this came from the lowest 40% of the population. While part of this shift was due to some of President Reagan's policies, such as changes that made it more difficult for the poor to qualify for welfare, there were also other influences at work, such as the recessions of 1980 and 1981–1982 that resulted in

TABLE 36-2
Income Distribution of U.S. Families, after Taxes and Transfers, 1980 and 1984

Population	Share of income 1980	1984
Lowest 20%	6.8%	6.1%
Second 20	13.2	12.5
Third 20	18.5	18.1
Fourth 20	24.5	24.5
Highest 20	37.0	38.9
	100%	100%

Source: John L. Palmer and Isabel V. Sawhill, *The Reagan Record* (Cambridge, Mass.: Ballinger, 1984), p. 322.

a more severe job and income loss by the relatively poor. These pressures that shifted the Lorenz curve toward greater inequality also made another problem worse: The percentage of the population below the poverty level increased, as we shall see in the next chapter.

Barry Bluestone of Boston College and Bennett Harrison of MIT have recently argued that a fundamental change is taking place in the pattern of the nation's income.[2] Middle-income jobs are disappearing, while the number of low-income jobs is expanding. The reasons they cite include the contraction of heavy industry, such as autos and steel, which has meant the loss of highly paid union jobs. At the same time there has been, according to these authors, a rapid growth in the low-wage, generally nonunion service industries. They argue that even the expansion of the high-tech, computer-related sector has not helped, because its employment is divided between managers and engineers with high incomes and workers on the production line with low incomes. Critics of this theory contend that the sharp division between high- and low-paying jobs in the computer industry is exaggerated, and that much of the pressure on heavy industry is temporary—caused by an unusually high value of the U.S. dollar that has made it difficult to compete with foreign firms.

Now let's turn from the question "What *is* the income distribution?" to "What *should* the income distribution be?"

In deriving policies which affect the distribution of income, what should we set as a target? Is there such a thing as a "fair" or "equitable" distribution?

WHAT IS AN EQUITABLE INCOME DISTRIBUTION?

See how the fates their gifts allot,
For A is happy—B is not.
Yet B is worthy, I dare say,
Of more prosperity than A!

If I were fortune—which I'm not—
B should enjoy A's happy lot,
And A should die in miserie—
That is, assuming I am B.

Gilbert and Sullivan
The Mikado

A search for an equitable or just distribution of income for society will lead us into treacherous intellectual terrain, from which some of the world's noted philosophers have been unable to escape with reputations intact. Although we cannot expect to arrive at any definitive answer in this elementary treatment, we can at least identify some of the important issues.

To begin, we reemphasize two important points made in Chapter 1:

1. *Equity and equality are two different concepts.* In our Lorenz curve description of income distribution, we have addressed only the question of equality: How equal *are* incomes? This is an empirical question. We can answer it by looking at the facts—by examining how much each American family earns. On the other hand, the question of equity is not what incomes are, but rather what they *should be*. What income distribution is fair and just? This is an ethical issue on which people are not unanimous. Some believe that equity is equality—that it is fair for everyone to receive the same income. On the other hand, many believe that equity is not equality—for example, the individual who works harder or more effectively should be paid more.

***Equal* means "of the same size." *Equitable* means "fair." The two are not necessarily the same.**

2. We reemphasize that government policy cannot be designed just to achieve equity—that is, a fair division of the nation's income pie. Instead it must also take into account other, often conflicting goals such as efficiency—increasing the size of that pie. However, to sharpen our idea of equity, suppose for now that this is our only concern. *On grounds of equity alone,* what is the best distribution of income?

Of the many possible answers, consider three: first, the distribution that results from the free play of the economic marketplace; second, a completely equal distribution of income; and third, some compromise between the two.

[2] Barry Bluestone and Bennett Harrison, *The Deindustrialization of America: Plant Closings, Community Abandonment, and the Dismantling of Basic Industries* (New York: Basic Books, 1982).

Is the Free Market's Distribution of Income Equitable?

> **Whatever is, is right.**
> Alexander Pope
> *Essay on Man*

In economics, few would agree that whatever is, is necessarily right. *The free market does not do an entirely satisfactory job of distributing income.* Consider a monopolist who makes a fortune by successfully cornering the supply of a good, selling some at a very high price and letting the unsold balance rot. In such cases it is very difficult to argue that the free market distributes income in a fair, equitable way.

However, our reservations about the free-market distribution are far more fundamental than this and apply even when markets are perfectly competitive. Such markets will, under certain conditions (no externalities, etc.) allocate factors of production in an *efficient* way that will maximize the nation's total income. In the process, they determine a set of prices of both goods and factors of production—the wages of labor, rents on land, etc. Thus they both maximize the nation's income pie and determine how it will be divided. But we can make no claim that they necessarily divide the pie up in a fair, equitable way. Remember: The size of the pie is maximized for *those who have the income to pay for it.* Output in a competitive market economy may include luxuries for the rich and too few necessities for the poor. Moreover, in many cases the poor—in particular the disabled—may be destitute for no fault of their own.

Even the strongest supporters of the free market, while championing its efficiencies, will still vote for aid for those who are destitute. This point is important enough to repeat: The demonstrable virtues of a free, perfectly competitive market have to do with its efficiency, not its equity.

Perhaps the best illustration is this. In a perfectly competitive economy, rents on land efficiently direct the nation's scarce land into its most productive uses; if rents are forced below the competitive level, land may be used in wasteful ways. However, the payment of these rents to those who own the land does not necessarily give us a fair distribution of income. We can see this point by considering an extreme example of land that has been inherited by the idle rich. Why should they earn an income many times that of the able and hardworking people whom they hire to manage and work this land?

Equality as a Target

The idea that we should aim for complete equality has an immediate appeal (see Box 36-1). Since everyone has certain other rights, such as the right to vote and equality before the law, why should each of us not have equality in our access to the marketplace—the right of equal economic reward? In other words, since everyone has an equal vote to cast in elections, why shouldn't everyone have equal dollar "votes" to spend in the marketplace? In practice, it would be prohibitively costly to give everyone this right: An equal division of the pie would greatly shrink its size.

However, even if this cost did not exist, there would still be fundamental philosophical problems. For example, the right to an equal economic reward would come into conflict with the right of equality before the law—in particular, the principle that those who break the law should be punished for their crimes. Those who have to pay fines should *not* be left with an equal number of economic votes.

Moreover, there are practical problems. For example, how is equality to be defined? One way is to define it, most simply, as "equal money incomes." But this answer is not satisfactory, because not everyone works the same number of hours. Those who decide on shorter working hours are taking some of their potential income in the form of leisure, rather than cash. Therefore, income should be defined more broadly to include both income taken in the form of cash and "income" taken in the form of leisure. Fairness requires that an individual who takes a lot of income in one form—leisure—should get less in the other form—cash. Similarly, those whose work is dangerous should be paid higher money wages to compensate them for the risk. According to this approach, the *overall* economic position (rather than just money income) should be equalized.

Unfortunately, this broader approach raises as many problems as it solves. If the overall position of individuals is to be equalized, those who have unpleasant jobs should be paid high enough wages to compensate them, and those whose jobs are fun should accordingly be paid

BOX 36-1

RAWLS ON EQUALITY

Harvard philosophy professor John Rawls has argued that income equality is a desirable goal—except in special circumstances. His analysis starts in a promising way. A consensus on the fair distribution of income is difficult to achieve because everyone has a special ax to grind. Those with high incomes favor a system in which inequality is allowed because it lets them keep their higher income. Those with low incomes are likely to advocate equality because it will improve their position. Rawls therefore suggests that, to get an objective view, people must be *removed from their present situation* and placed in an ***original position*** where they decide what the distribution of income should be, without knowing the specific place they themselves will eventually take in this distribution. What income distribution will they choose?

Here are the essentials of Rawls' argument. The typical person in the original position will think something like this: "Whatever income distribution is chosen, with my luck, chances are that I'll end up at the bottom. So I'll vote for the income distribution that will leave me, the lowest one on the totem pole, as well off as possible." Since everyone is similarly situated in the original position, Rawls argues that all will reason in the same way. He concludes that a consensus will develop in favor of an equal distribution of income—unless there is an unequal distribution that leaves *everyone* better off. This is what Rawls calls the ***difference principle.***†

While Rawls' approach will generally lead to equality, there are circumstances in which it will not. To illustrate, we use two extreme examples, but the argument applies in less extreme cases as well. For the first example, suppose people in the original position choose between the two income distributions shown in Table 36-3. Option A represents complete equality, with everyone's annual income at $5,000. Now suppose it is possible to move to option B, where everyone's income is $10,000 except for the last individual, whose income is $5,100. (Suppose that this move is possible because there was previously a very high tax aimed at equalizing income. When the tax is removed, people respond by working more.) Because everyone benefits, Rawlsian logic leads to a move from A to B—a move *away from equality.*‡ Most people would agree with such a move. So far, Rawl's theory is not controversial. In the circumstances shown in Table 36-3, Rawls, like almost everyone else, would allow inequality.

Table 36-4 illustrates the second, more likely situation, with options A and C. As before, the move away from equality (in this case, from A to C) benefits almost everyone by $5,000. But now we recognize that any such substantial change is likely to leave at least one person worse off. (Note in the last column how the income of the last individual is reduced by $100.) In this case, Rawls argues that people in an original position would choose option A. With their concern about ending up at the bottom of the totem pole, they would focus on the figures in the last column and prefer A with its $5,000 income to C with its $4,900 income. Thus, according to Rawls, people would choose equality.

TABLE 36-3
When Rawls' Theory Leads to Inequality: An Example

	Income of all individuals but one	Income of last individual
Option A (equality)	$ 5,000	$5,000
Option B (inequality)	$10,000	$5,100†

†Option B chosen because everyone is better off

TABLE 36-4
When Rawls' Theory Leads to Equality: An Example

	Income of all individuals but one	Income of last individual
Option A (equality)	$ 5,000	$5,000†
Option C (inequality)	$10,000	$4,900

†Option A chosen because a move to C would damage the last individual

It is here, when he puts forward a strong argument in favor of equality, that Rawls' theory is open to criticism. Ask yourself: If you were in Rawls' original position, without knowledge of where you would eventually end up, which option would you choose? Would you join the consensus Rawls expects in favor of option A? Most people would find C difficult to resist. The miniscule risk of being $100 worse off seems trivial in comparison with the near certainty of being $5,000 better off. This seems to be a risk well worth taking. Indeed, those who would select Rawls' option A are those who would *avoid risk at almost any cost.* How in the world would you find anyone so risk-averse? Observe that the risk you would be taking in choosing income distribution C rather than A would be the same as your risk at the race track or the stock exchange if you were to bet $100 for a chance to win $5,000, with odds *in your favor* of 240 million to 1. Why those odds? There are 240 million people in the United States. In moving from option A to C, they would all "win" $5,000—except for the one who would lose $100. With such odds, who in the world would turn down such a bet?

Try an experiment to see the difficulty with Rawls' argument. Change the number in the southwest corner of Table 36-4 to $100,000. Rawls' argument still leads to the choice of equality (option A). Would this be your choice? If so, would you choose option A or C if the number were even higher, say $1 million? Or $1 billion? Won't you eventually come around to option C and give up voting in a Rawlsian way?

Because people in an original position would not necessarily vote for equality option A over C, Rawls does not make a convincing case for equality. The difficulty is that his argument is based on the assumption that people's only concern is with what is happening in the last column in those two tables—that is, with that last, poorest individual. Specifically, the choice is based on *maximizing* the *minimum* income; hence, this is often referred to as the *maximin* criterion. But why should we completely ignore the vast majority and be totally preoccupied with that last individual?

In a later reconsideration of the maximin criterion,[§] Rawls concluded that although he still viewed it as attractive, "a deeper investigation . . . may show that some other conception of justice is more reasonable. In any case, the idea that economists may find most useful . . . is that of the original position. This perspective . . . may prove illuminating for economic theory."

[†] In his *Theory of Justice* (Cambridge, Mass.: Harvard University Press, 1971), p. 63, Rawls was concerned with more than income: "All social values—liberty and opportunity, income and wealth, and the bases of self-respect—are to be distributed equally unless an unequal distribution of any, or all, of these values is to everyone's advantage."

While we consider the lowest-income individual in our examples, Rawls' focus is on a typical individual in the lowest-income group. But this does not seriously affect his conclusion or our evaluation of it.

[‡] Envy is not taken into account: It is assumed that nobody's happiness is reduced by the knowledge that someone else has become richer.

[§] See John Rawls, "Some Reasons for the Maximin Criterion," *American Economic Review,* May 1974, pp. 141–146.

Advocates of income equality were immediately attracted to Rawl's theory because it seemed to provide a firmer foundation for equality than the traditional argument. According to the earlier argument, equality is a desirable goal because it would maximize the total utility of all individuals in society. However, this conclusion follows only if it can be assumed that all individuals have the same capacity to enjoy income. (If this assumption does not hold, we can improve the outcome by moving away from complete equality, by transferring some income away from those who are less able to enjoy it, to those who are more able to enjoy it.) Unfortunately, there is no way we can confirm or deny the assumption that people enjoy income equally. Remember, there is no way to meter people's heads to compare the satisfaction they get from $1 of income.

Therefore this traditional argument does not provide convincing support for income equality. Nor, as we have seen in this box, does Rawls' theory. Like the older theory, it has a weak link—in this case the assumption that the only concern is for the lowest person on the totem pole. Moreover, many of those who believe in equality became less enthusiastic about Rawls' theory when they discovered that it allows for a very substantial degree of inequality—as we have seen in Table 36-3 and as Rawls himself has reemphasized. (Rawls, "Some Reasons for the Maximin Criterion," p. 145.)

less. But how do we handle the following problem. Some people find a particular job—like teaching—extremely rewarding, while others find it a bore. Should the first group be paid less than the second, in order to make them equal? Quite apart from the practical problem of determining how much each teacher likes the job—in a situation in which they would all have an incentive to lie—this broad approach would lead to an unsatisfactory result: People would be paid for hating their jobs. Since those who love teaching generally make the best teachers, this would mean that the best teachers would be paid the least. Surely this would not be fair.

Worse yet, bored, dissatisfied teachers often don't work so hard; they take "leisure on the job." Would it be fair to pay them a premium salary, when those taking a lot of leisure at home would receive low pay?

Therefore we conclude that considerations of *equity alone* have not led us to complete equality as a meaningful objective. We are skeptical of this objective, just as we were skeptical earlier of the free-market determination of income. How about some compromise between the two?

A Compromise between the Free Market and Complete Equality

It is easy to conclude that both the free-market and complete equality approaches involve serious problems. What is far more difficult is to say where in the broad range in between we should aim. We will not be able to answer that question. But here are some suggestive ideas for you to consider as you grapple with it (and you must, as a voter).

Make it a fair race, . . . Suppose we think of participating in the economy as being in a race in which each runner's income is determined by his or her finish. The egalitarian view that "justice is income equality" implies that the government should equalize all rewards at the end of the race: Give everyone a bronze medal—no golds, and no booby prizes. As the Dodo in *Alice in Wonderland* put it, "Everybody has won, and all must have prizes."

An alternative view is that the responsibility of the government is only to ensure that the race is fair. Disadvantages should be eliminated: No one should start with a 50-yard handicap because of being a woman, or a black, or the child of parents who are not influential. In this race, everyone has a right, but it is the right of equality of *opportunity,* not equality of *reward*. In brief, everyone should have the right to an equal *start*—but not to an equal *finish*.

While the idea of equal opportunity is appealing, it too is difficult to define. Buried in any definition of a fair race is a judgment on *which advantages are unfair and should be removed, and which advantages should not*. Advantages of race, color, and ethnic background clearly should be removed. But what should we do about advantages arising from differences in natural ability? Should an individual in the economic race be penalized for natural business talent so that all may start equal? Does it make any more sense to do this than to penalize a marathon runner for strong legs? If we were to embark on such a penalty or handicap system, we would end up in the world of Box 36-2, where Kurt Vonnegut's Handicapper General weighs down naturally talented ballerinas with bags of birdshot. In such a world, nobody would come close to breaking the 4-minute mile; the economy would fall far short of its potential.

. . . but modify the rewards It is quite possible to have a fair race, yet still have a bad system of rewards. For example, suppose the winner were to be given a million dollars and the loser were to be thrown, Roman style, to the lions? Believing in a fair economic race does not prevent us from modifying its rewards—in other words, using taxes and transfer payments to reduce the income differences that result.

To the authors, this idea of a fair race and a modified system of rewards that reduces but does not eliminate income inequality seems to be an appealing principle. But again, the idea is not as simple as it sounds. Is not an individual's economic life less like a standard race than like a relay race? Moreover, a relay race with no beginning or end? The race you run depends on the start you get, in terms of your whole background, including your family wealth. A first reaction is that it should not be like this. To keep the race fair, everyone should be started off equally, without any advantage of inherited wealth. Should we therefore tax away all inheritances and, for the same reason, gifts?

This is a difficult proposal to defend, even on equity grounds. Consider two men with equal incomes. One spends it all. The other wishes to save in order to pass wealth on to his children. Is it fair to impose a tax that prohibits him from doing so? Is not charity a virtue? What can one say of a society that prevents gifts to family or friends?

BOX 36-2

KURT VONNEGUT ON WHY ONLY HORSES AND GOLFERS SHOULD BE HANDICAPPED[†]

The year was 2081, and everybody was finally equal. They weren't only equal before God and the law. They were equal every which way. Nobody was smarter than anybody else. Nobody was better looking than anybody else. Nobody was stronger or quicker than anybody else. All this equality was due to the 211th, 212th, and 213th Amendments to the Constitution, and to the unceasing vigilance of agents of the United States Handicapper General. . . .

George [Bergeron, whose] intelligence was way above normal, had a little mental handicap radio in his ear. He was required by law to wear it at all times. It was tuned to a government transmitter. Every twenty seconds or so, the transmitter would send out some sharp noise to keep people like George from taking unfair advantage of their brains. . . .

On the television screen were ballerinas. . . . They weren't really very good—no better than anybody else would have been anyway. They were burdened with sashweights and bags of birdshot and their faces were masked, so that no one, seeing a free and graceful gesture or a pretty face, would feel like something the cat drug in. George was toying with the vague notion that maybe dancers shouldn't be handicapped. But he didn't get very far with it before another noise in his ear radio scattered his thoughts. . . .

George began to think glimmeringly about his abnormal son who was now in jail, about Harrison, but a twenty-one-gun salute in his head stopped that. "Boy!" said Hazel, "that was a doozy, wasn't it?" It was such a doozy that George was white and trembling, and tears stood on the rims of his red eyes. Two of the eight ballerinas had collapsed to the studio floor, were holding their temples. . . .

The television program was suddenly interrupted for a news bulletin. It wasn't clear at first as to what the bulletin was about, since the announcer, like all announcers, had a serious speech impediment. For about half a minute, and in a state of high excitement, the announcer tried to say, "Ladies and gentlemen—"

He finally gave up, handed the bulletin to a ballerina to read. . . . "That's all right—" Hazel said of the announcer, "he tried. That's the big thing. He tried to do the best he could with what God gave him. He should get a nice raise for trying so hard."

"Ladies and gentlemen—" said the ballerina, . . . "Harrison Bergeron, age fourteen . . . has just escaped from jail, where he was held on suspicion of plotting to overthrow the government. He is a genius and an athlete, is under-handicapped, and should be regarded as extremely dangerous."

A police photograph of Harrison Bergeron was flashed on the screen. . . . Harrison's appearance was Halloween and hardware. Nobody had ever born heavier handicaps. . . . Instead of a little ear radio for a mental handicap, he wore a tremendous pair of earphones, and spectacles with thick wavy lenses. The spectacles were intended to make him not only half blind, but to give him whanging headaches besides.

Scrap metal was hung all over him. Ordinarily, there was a certain symmetry, a military neatness to the handicaps issued to strong people, but Harrison looked like a walking junkyard.

[†]Abridgment of "Harrison Bergeron" from *Welcome to the Monkey House* by Kurt Vonnegut Jr. Copyright © 1961 by Kurt Vonnegut Jr. Originally published in *Fantasy and Science Fiction.* Reprinted by permission of Delacorte Press/Seymour Lawrence.

Conclusions: Can We Pin Down the Idea of Equity?

Unfortunately, the answer is no. The only conclusions we have been able to reach are both negative. Equity is not complete equality of income, nor is it the income distribution that the free market generates. We are left somewhere between. We conclude that, in terms of equity considerations alone, we should move from a free-market distribution some distance, but not the whole way, toward equalizing incomes.

To further complicate matters, any such move tends to involve an efficiency cost in terms of a shrinking national pie. The reason—to be examined in detail in the next chapter—is that guaranteeing people an income tends to reduce their incentive to work, and they produce less. Because of this efficiency cost, it is desirable to stop short of the degree of equality which would be chosen if equity were the sole objective.

In practice, we have already introduced tax and expenditure policies that have moved us some distance toward equalizing incomes, as Figure 36-2 has illustrated. It is possible that we have not yet moved far enough; it is also possible that we have moved too far. The question of how the nation's income should be distributed is likely to remain an issue of continuing debate. However, it is important that the dispute about how the national income pie should be divided does not become so heated and exhausting that the total size of that pie is substantially reduced. To return to our earlier analogy: If all participants had spent their energies in a squabble about how the race should be run and how the rewards should be divided, no one would have broken the 4-minute mile.

KEY POINTS

1. Large differences exist in the incomes of individual Americans. Some have high incomes because of their human capital, wealth, native talent, family background, market power, or just plain luck. Others have low incomes because they enjoy none of these advantages or for some other reason. For example, they may suffer from discrimination.
2. If we examine the U. S. income distribution *before government taxes and transfers* are taken into account, we observe a great deal of inequality. The poorest 20% receive only 0.3% of the nation's income, while the highest 20% get over half.
3. About a third of this inequality is eliminated by government transfer expenditures that are concentrated heavily on the poor, and by progressive taxes that draw heavily from the rich. However, our tax system overall is not as progressive as the income tax alone, and taxes do much less equalizing than government transfer payments.
4. The most effective government expenditure in equalizing income is social insurance such as social security and unemployment insurance. But other government expenditures, both in cash and in kind, also play a role.
5. Equality is a question of fact: How equal *are* incomes? On the other hand, equity is a matter of judgment: What pattern of incomes is fair? A strong case can be made that neither a completely equal distribution of incomes nor the unequal free-market distribution is equitable. A desirable target seems to lie somewhere between.
6. While it is very difficult to be more precise than this, some rough guidelines have been suggested. For example, the ''economic race'' should be kept as fair as possible. In other words, everyone should have an equal opportunity. The government should ensure that no one starts at a disadvantage because of race or sex. However, the appealing principle of equality of opportunity conflicts with the equally appealing principle that parents should be able to help their children.
7. Equal opportunity need not result in equal reward. Even if everyone could be given an equal start, there is no reason to expect that all will finish in a tie. Some will get greater rewards than others. The second responsibility of the government is to modify rewards—that is, to reduce income inequality by taxes and transfer payments.
8. Finally, even if we could determine an equitable income distribution, it does not follow that the government should continue to redistribute income up to this point. The reason is that the act of redistributing income—changing the division of the national pie—affects the incentive to work and hence the level of efficiency (the size of that pie). Therefore, a compromise should be selected between the conflicting objectives of equity and efficiency.

KEY CONCEPTS

cumulative income distribution (Lorenz curve)
social insurance
cash transfers
transfers in kind
difference between equity and equality
limitations of the free market as a distributor of income
difference between equalizing opportunity and equalizing reward

PROBLEMS

36-1. Explain to your very bright roommate (who is not studying economics) why some Americans have much higher incomes than others.

36-2. Mark McCormack is, in his own words, an ''engineer of careers.'' In one year, his company is reported to have grossed \$35 million by charging a 15% to 40% agent's fee for managing 250 tennis stars and golfers. Do you think McCormack's large income is the result of (*a*) only luck, (*b*) luck and other reasons, or (*c*) just other reasons? If you answer (*b*) or (*c*), explain what the other reasons might be.

36-3. Explain how the marketplace generates a rental income for those with high reputation, just as for those with great skill.

36-4. Explain why you agree or disagree with the following statement: ''Free-market prices of factors of production help to maximize the total national income pie and also divide it in an equitable way.''

***36-5.** This question is based on Box 36-1. Is the following statement true or false? If true, explain it. If false, correct it:

Rawls' maximin principle is to *maximize* the *minimum* possible income. However, this is the preference only of people who are unwilling to risk any of their income in the hope of acquiring more. Many people are not like this, including all those individuals who bet a small part of their income at the races or Monte Carlo in the hope of winning more.

***36-6.** In 1899, John Bates Clark wrote in the *Distribution of Wealth* that ''free competition tends to give to labor what labor creates (that is, the value of the marginal product of labor), to capitalists what capital creates (that is, the marginal product of capital), and to entrepreneurs what the coordinating function creates.'' This sounds as though everyone gets what he or she deserves; that is, free competition distributes income in an equitable way. Do you agree? In your view, what does a free competitive market do well and what does it do not so well?

CHAPTER 37

GOVERNMENT POLICIES TO REDUCE INEQUALITY:

CAN WE SOLVE THE POVERTY PROBLEM?

If a free society cannot help the many who are poor, it cannot save the few who are rich.

JOHN F. KENNEDY

Although Americans may differ on the question of how far we should go in reducing income inequality in general, there is one specific issue on which the overwhelming majority agree: Nobody should starve, nor should children grow up in abject poverty. Yet, in 1983, poverty was still a fact of life for more than 1 in 8 American families. You can confirm the grinding effect of poverty by driving from a wealthy suburb of any large American city into a depressed core area. In the United States, overall wealth stands in stark contrast to the poverty faced by those who are insufficiently fed, housed, and clothed. In the mid-1960s this problem was recognized to be so important that the federal government declared a ''war on poverty'' and introduced a number of new measures to improve the lot of the poor. Although these efforts initially did reduce the problem, progress has been disappointing; since 1979, the incidence of poverty has increased.

This chapter is a study of the poor—the individuals who appeared in the bottom left-hand corner of the Lorenz income curve in the last chapter. Who are the poor? Why are they poor? What programs has the government introduced to fight the war on poverty? Should these programs be viewed as a way of cleaning up an economic mess created by the system, or do they create the mess? And finally, can the faults in these programs be cured—and, if so, how?

POVERTY

The economic definition of poverty is ''inadequate income.'' But this does not mean that poverty is strictly an economic condition. It is often also a state of mind, a condition in which the individual feels helpless. Therefore, poverty is a subject for sociologists and political scientists as well as economists. One of the difficulties encountered in studying poverty is the chicken-or-egg problem. Are people unable to cope with their economic problems because they are poor? Or are they poor because they are unable to cope? Undoubtedly the answer is, partly both.

Poverty exists when people have inadequate income to buy the necessities of life. In 1984, a family of four fell below the poverty line if it had an income of less than $10,610.

How the Poverty Line Is Defined

In defining the poverty line—officially known as the ''low-income line''—the government starts with the idea that food is the first essential. Accordingly, the Department of Agriculture calculates the cost of a diet that satisfies the requirements of minimum nutrition. As in any such definition of subsistence or bare necessity, judgment is important. To illustrate: $200 or $300, spent on just the right combination of things like soybeans, orange juice, and liver, will provide a medically balanced diet for one person for a year. Moreover, this menu will be healthier than the present diet of some well-to-do Americans. But who would you get to eat it? Consequently, the Department of Agriculture does not use this, but instead calculates the cost of a barely adequate and acceptable, but certainly not luxurious, diet.

Since low-income families typically spend about one-third of their income on food, the cost of this diet is multiplied by 3 to arrive at the official low-income line. This figure is then adjusted to take account of the size of the family. Whereas the 1984 poverty line for a family of four was $10,610, for a family of six it was $14,210. (For more detail, see Table 1-1.)

To take account of inflation, the poverty line periodically has to be adjusted upward. Furthermore, it rises over the long term because our concept of poverty keeps changing. The poverty income of $10,610 in 1984 would have been regarded in colonial times as a very handsome income indeed—even after full adjustment is made for inflation. In fact, it would still have been considered a good income as late as the 1930s. When President Roosevelt spoke at that time of one-third of the nation living in poverty, he implied a poverty-line income that was far lower, and that would buy far less, than the poverty income of 1984. Thus, upward adjustments in the definition of poverty do occur. But beware: If the definition of poverty is made too flexible, the concept becomes meaningless. If, for example, poverty were defined as the income of the bottom one-tenth of the population, there would be no hope of curing it. By definition, 1 in 10 Americans would *always* be poor, no matter how much we raised everyone's income. And the statement that 1 American family in 10 was living in poverty would tell us absolutely nothing about the seriousness of the problem or about our success in curing it.

Who Are the Poor?

Poverty is more likely to occur in some groups than in others. For example, a person living in the south is more likely to be poor than a person living in the north. Someone with less than 8 years of education is more likely to be poor than someone who has finished high school; and completion of a college education almost—but not quite—guarantees one against poverty. People living in the core area of a big city are more likely to be poor than those living in its suburbs. Part of the reason is that many of those who have been able to afford to move from the core to the suburbs have already done so. However, poverty is not limited to centers of big cities. Many of the poor live on farms or in small towns or cities.

Figure 37-1 shows some of the other faces of poverty. A black is almost three times as likely to be living in poverty as a white,[1] and people of Spanish origin fare little better. Persons in fatherless families are far more likely to be poor than those living in a home with both parents. One out of five children is now living apart from one parent, and it is estimated that nearly half the children born today will spend part of their first 18 years in a family headed by a single parent. Being both black and in a single-parent family is a particularly unfortunate combination: Over half of those in this category are below the poverty line. This is an increasing problem because the number of these families has been growing; between 1969 and 1982 it doubled.

A comparison of the two left-hand bars in Figure 37-1 shows how the overall incidence of poverty increased between 1979 and 1983 from 9% to 13%. Moreover, except for the elderly, the poverty problem for each of the detailed categories shown in the rest of this diagram also increased. One of the questions addressed in this chapter will be ''Why?''

THE WAR ON POVERTY

Following the declaration of the war on poverty, government transfer programs such as unemployment insurance and food stamps grew by about ten times between 1965 and 1981 in dollar terms and about four times when adjusted for inflation. When the public thinks of antipoverty programs, these are two that often come to mind. However, these outlays relieve only the *symptoms* of poverty. They make it more bearable without providing much hope that the problem will be cured—that is, that the poor will be able to increase their earnings. A more promising long-run approach to poverty is to attack its *causes*. For example, expenditures on education or training are designed to cure one of the causes of poverty: inadequate human capital. The objective is to allow people to accumulate this capital in order to provide for their

[1]However, there are more poor whites than poor blacks. Without reading further, can you see why? The answer is: There are more poor whites because most of the population is white.

own support in the future. (Although it is usually more promising to attack the causes of a problem than its symptoms, this is not always the case. In extreme cases of "clinical" poverty, where individuals have such a low innate capacity or skill that no amount of training will allow them to earn a living, straight support programs may be the more effective form of assistance.)

POLICIES TO REDUCE THE CAUSES OF POVERTY

Before turning to policies dealing with the symptoms of poverty, we consider those that attack its causes.

Subsidizing Investment in Human Capital

Federal, state, and local governments subsidize education in various ways. The provision of free elementary and secondary schooling is the most important, but there are also other programs that provide job training. For example, under President Carter the Comprehensive Employment and Training Act (CETA) provided federal subsidies for training unemployed workers. This was superseded during the Reagan administration by a smaller-scale program under the Jobs Training Partnership Act (JTPA). While this program also provides retraining and relocation assistance, it has put greater emphasis on subsidizing employment in the private rather than the public sector.

Antidiscrimination Policies

Another cause of poverty is job discrimination, which reduces the income of minorities and women. As noted earlier, the Equal Pay Act (1963) requires that women be paid the same as men for equal work, and the Civil Rights Act (1964) outlaws discrimination in hiring, firing, and other employment practices.

Dealing with Unemployment and Disability

In the case of unemployment, the most promising government policies are those designed to keep the economy operating at a high level of output. Permanent disability is quite a different problem because it cannot be cured once it has happened. It is then too late to deal with the cause. However, when we consider *future* disabling accidents, it is *not* too late to deal with the cause; some of these accidents can be prevented. This is the task of the Occupational Safety and Health Administration.

Other Policies

The Work Incentive Program (WIN) subsidizes the training and employment of people on welfare. It also enables parents to take jobs by providing day-care facilities for children. This provision is particularly important in reducing the incidence of poverty in the increasingly important group of families with only one parent in the home. Although the Reagan administration did not succeed in its proposal to eliminate WIN, this program has been substantially cut back.

POLICIES TO REDUCE THE SYMPTOMS OF POVERTY: GOVERNMENT PROGRAMS TO MAINTAIN INCOMES

Even if it is not possible to cure a disease, it is very important to provide the patient with relief from the symptoms. While we are in the process of developing long-run cures for poverty—such as upgrading human capital and ending discrimination—we also provide the public assistance programs in Table 37-1 that reduce the symptoms of poverty by keeping many families from falling below the poverty line.

Social Insurance Programs

Social insurance programs to protect the elderly and the unemployed were not designed specifically to deal with the poverty problem; people need not be poor to receive benefits. Nonetheless, such programs play a key role in keeping many of the population from living in poverty.

1. *Unemployment insurance* provides temporary assistance to people who have lost their jobs.
2. *Social security* is by far the most important income maintenance program. The government collects contributions from both employees and employers and from self-employed individuals. In turn, these contributions are paid out in retirement, disability, and other benefits.
3. *Medicare,* a health insurance program, provides medical services for the elderly.

Between 1970 and 1979, these last two programs helped to reduce the incidence of poverty among the elderly from over 25% to less than 10%. Moreover, this rate continued to fall during the difficult period 1979–1983 when the rate of poverty over the economy as a whole was increasing substantially. Table 37-1 confirms that the reason for this favorable performance was the large increase between 1979 and 1985 in government payments for social security and medicare. (Part of this increase occurred because a larger proportion of the population was reaching retirement age.)

Welfare Programs

Welfare programs *have* been designed specifically to combat poverty. Unlike social insurance programs, for which people qualify whether or not they are poor, benefits from welfare programs are intended exclusively for the poor. They have traditionally been far smaller than the social security and medicare programs for the elderly. Moreover, these were among the programs targeted by the Reagan administration in its attempts to re-

FIGURE 37-1

Incidence of poverty, 1979 and 1983

Sources: U.S. Department of Commerce, Bureau of the Census, "*Estimates of Poverty, Including the Value of Non-Cash Benefits,*" Technical Paper 51, p. xviii; and Technical Paper 52, pp. xi, xiv, 20.

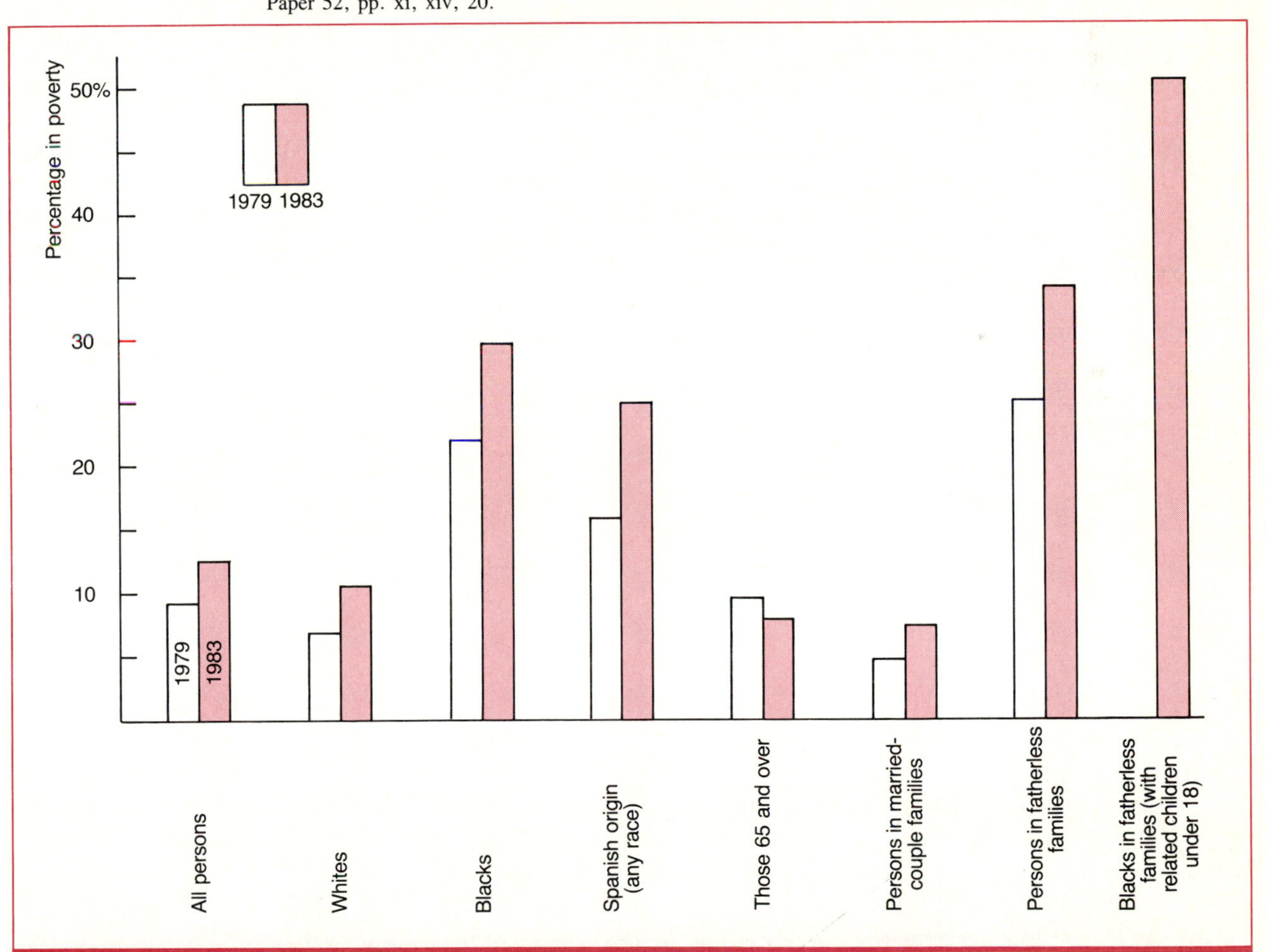

duce government spending. The first program we now consider is one that was subject to a large cutback.

1. *Aid to Families with Dependent Children (AFDC).* This program is administered by the states but is financed in part by grants from Washington. Under this program, cash benefits are provided for poor families with dependent children. Generally, this aid goes to families headed by a single parent. In fact, in some states a family cannot qualify for AFDC if an able-bodied man is in the home. While this provision has the desirable objective of encouraging able-bodied fathers to go to work, it sometimes drives them out of the home instead; they may feel that the simplest way for them to support their dependents is to leave, and thus allow their families to qualify for welfare.

2. *Supplementary Security Income (SSI).* This program provides cash assistance to aged, blind, and otherwise disabled persons who are poor.

3. *Medicaid.* This health insurance program is similar to medicare except that it provides medical services for those with low incomes. A discussion of some of the problems the government faces in providing medical care is provided in Box 37-1.

TABLE 37-1
Income Transfer Programs

	Date enacted	Public expenditures (billions of current dollars) 1965	1979	1981	1985 (preliminary estimates)
(*a*) Social insurance					
Cash benefits:					
Social security	1935	$16.5	$102.6	$137.0	$191.4
Unemployment insurance	1935	2.5	11.2	18.7	24.6
Workers' compensation	1908	1.8	9.9	14.8	
Veterans' disability compensation	1917	2.2	6.8	7.5	10.6
Railroad retirement	1937	1.1	4.3	5.2	
Black lung	1969	†	0.6	0.9	
In-kind benefits:					
Medicare	1965	†	29.1	38.4	74.9
(*b*) Welfare (public assistance)					
Cash benefits:					
Aid to families with dependent children (AFDC)	1935	1.7	10.8	12.8	8.4
Supplement security income (SSI)§	1972	2.7	6.8	8.5	8.8
Veterans' pensions	1933	1.9	3.6	4.1	3.7
General assistance	‡	0.4	1.2	1.5	
In-kind benefits:					
Medicaid	1965	0.5	21.8	27.6	24.2
Food stamps	1964	0.04	6.8	9.7	12.5
Housing assistance	1937	0.3	4.4	6.6	10.9
Total expenditures		31.5	219.9	293.2	
Total expenditures as a percentage of GNP		4.6%	9.1%	10.0%	

†Nonexistent.
‡Varied by states.
§Prior to 1972, Aid to the Blind, Aid to the Permanently and Totally Disabled, and Old Age Assistance.
Source: Sheldon Danziger, Robert Haveman, and Robert Plotnick, "How Income Transfer Programs Affect Work, Savings and the Income Distribution: A Critical Review," *Journal of Economic Literature*, September 1981, table 1. The incomplete set of estimates for fiscal year 1985 are taken from John L. Palmer and Elizabeth Sawhill, *The Reagan Record* (Cambridge, Mass.: Ballinger, 1984), p. 185.

4. *Food stamps*. The federal government provides the poor with food stamps, which they can exchange for food.

5. *Public housing*. This form of assistance, first offered in 1937, has been modified on numerous occasions. The basic idea is this: A local government is subsidized by the federal government to acquire housing and rent it out to low-income tenants, who pay 25% of their income in rent, with the federal government paying the rest. (For more on housing subsidies, see Box 37-2.)

It is worth reemphasizing that while AFDC and SSI provide *cash benefits,* the other three programs—medicaid, food stamps, and public housing—provide benefits ***in kind.*** For the 16 years between 1965 and 1981, these in-kind transfers were by far the most rapidly growing welfare programs, with each increasing by more than 20 times in dollar terms, or more than 8 times when adjusted for inflation.

***Benefits in kind* are payments, not of cash, but of some good such as food, or service such as medical care.**

Because these in-kind transfers lift many families above the poverty level, they should be taken into account in any assessment of the incidence of poverty. Recognition of these benefits reduced the 1983 percentage of the population in poverty from the "official level" of 15.2% to 13%. Moreover, for the elderly this percentage reduction was even greater—from 14% to less than 9%. One reason is that the medical benefits on which the elderly depend so heavily are paid in kind, not in cash.

ASSESSING THE PRESENT WELFARE PACKAGE

In spending large sums, are we making headway against the poverty problem? Figure 37-2 suggests that until the 1970s, the answer was a resounding yes. By recent poverty standards, one in two Americans was poor in 1929; by 1947, the figure was one in three; and by 1970, it was one in eight. In particular, the 1960s brought a rapid reduction in poverty because of declining unemployment plus a big expansion in transfer programs. However, by the early 1970s, the poverty rate stopped falling, and the

BOX 37-1

THE RISING COST OF HEALTH CARE

It is widely recognized that the quality of medical services in the United States is as good as anywhere in the world—at least for those who can afford it. However, it has become *very* costly. In 1984–1985, Americans spent 10.8% of GNP on health care. While the government provides medical services to the elderly (medicare) and the poor (medicaid), it does not provide such services for the rest of the population. Broader government medical programs have been suggested by Senator Kennedy and others. However, such proposals have met a cool reception in Congress, largely because they would add to the bill the goverment would have to pay for medical services—a bill which has been rising rapidly.

One reason that such a large proportion of the nation's GNP is devoted to health care is that medical research has now made it possible to save lives in a variety of new ways. But most methods, such as heart transplants, are very expensive. All available lifesaving opportunities cannot be seized unless a larger and

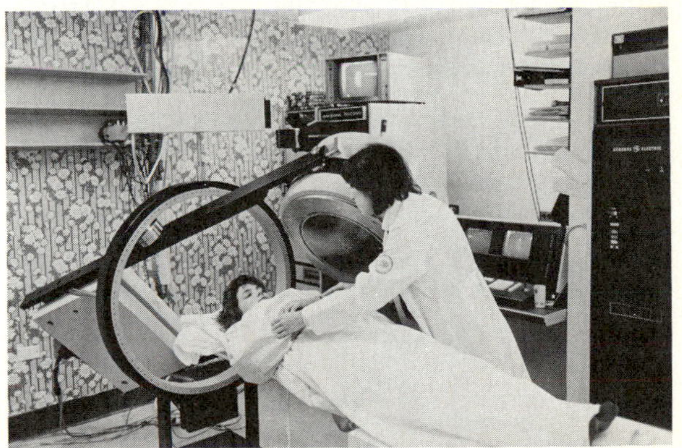

larger percentage of the nation's GNP is directed into this effort. One can argue that, with the opening up of new lifesaving opportunities, more of our GNP *should* be spent in this way. However, if we try to capture *all* of these opportunities, the cost would become extremely high.

Therefore, society must have some way of deciding at what point its lifesaving efforts will be limited—that is, at what point funds that could save lives will be cut off. Which patients will be the lucky ones who will live because they get access to the limited number of lifesaving machines and treatments that society can afford?

No one likes to make this life-and-death decision on "who will get a seat in the lifeboat" and who will not. For this reason, there are a number of alternative ways of making this decision.

1. *Delay.* In 1984, the British National Health Service provided about 110 free heart transplants. However, there was a waiting list of up to a year, during which most of those in line simply died.
2. *Set an age limit.* Unofficially, heart transplants are given only to those less than 50 years of age. This was one reason why Barney Clark and William Schroeder, both over 50, tried artificial hearts instead.
3. *Use chance.* Decide on who will live and die in some sort of a doomsday lottery. However, this makes no sense at all, because an Einstein may lose out in such a lottery to a suicidal derelict who places no value on his own life. [For more on this life-or-death choice, see Victor R. Fuchs, *Who Shall Live?* (New York: Basic Books, 1983).]

Because these methods are unsatisfactory or inadequate, the life-or-death decision frequently has to be made by doctors on the spot—or administrators or committees allocating funds. It's an exceedingly difficult decision. We've seen earlier how difficult it is to put a value on a life. But the task of saying that one *particular* life is worth more than another—and therefore is the one that should be saved—is even more difficult. Therefore, whenever possible, those making such decisions understandably argue: Instead of choosing between two lives, let's save them both—if there is any *conceivable* way we can get the cost covered. This, then, is one reason there is persistent upward pressure on costs.

Another reason is that, with such a substantial share of medical bills paid for by medicare, medicaid, or private insurance schemes, there is inadequate pressure to cut costs. Patients have little incentive to seek out low-cost treatment; when your health is at stake you don't go bargain hunting, especially when an insurance company is paying the tab.

In the eyes of the critics, a more efficient and less costly system of health care would require that individuals pay more of the money cost of this service. We may not want to allow money to make the life-or-death decision on who will get lifesaving care and who will not; that is, we may not want to put "seats on the lifeboat" up for sale. Nonetheless, we may still want to use money in a far more limited way to provide an incentive for people to seek out low-cost care. One way is to have insurance schemes with larger "deductible" clauses that leave part of the cost of treatment for patients to bear. With patients becoming more cost-conscious, competition would be stimulated among doctors and hospitals.

Finally, there is evidence that medical costs are rising for a third reason: Some doctors and hospitals are defrauding the plans. A U.S. Senate committee investigating the cost of medicaid found that some doctors would carry out complete physical examinations—with the whole battery of laboratory tests—on essentially healthy people who came to their offices with a minor complaint. Through referrals, a group of specialist doctors may "ping-pong" patients back and forth among themselves. Medicaid patients getting a doctor's appointment have sometimes been told to bring their children, too. The doctor can then take a brief look at the children and charge medicaid the fee for an office visit for each. The vast majority of physicians, of course, do not waste time and money in this fraudulent way. However, according to the Department of Health and Human Resources, there are enough doctors who do engage in these practices that the costs of medicare and medicaid have been raised by a substantial amount. In turn, attempts to fight this problem of "medifraud" have entailed the creation of costly administrative machinery to supervise the payments made under the plans.

While some critics concede that an extension of medicare to the whole population may be desirable on equity grounds, they are concerned that it could mean an economywide extension of these problems. It could become extremely costly.

BOX 37-2

HOUSING SUBSIDIES: WHO BENEFITS?

Many voters believe that better housing is an important social goal—better housing for the poor and better housing for the average citizen, too. Of the numerous incentives for housing, the most notable is a provision which allows homeowners to reduce the income tax they have to pay. (In calculating their taxable income, they are permitted to deduct the property taxes and interest payments on their mortgages.) The idea is to encourage people to own their own homes. As a consequence, the United States now has the highest rate of owner-occupied housing in the world. Far from being an antipoverty program, this policy benefits the average homeowner more than the poor who own small homes or none at all.

Another government housing policy is urban renewal, which is designed to improve slum housing, revitalize downtown business areas, and attract middle-class residents from the suburbs back into the big cities. This program involves federal subsidies to local governments to tear down central city slums and rebuild these core areas. This policy has generated heated controversy: Its supporters view it as the last hope of saving the big cities, while its critics point out that, initially at least, it resulted in many more dwellings being torn down than constructed. As a consequence, the central city poor found that their housing supply was shrinking. Another reason for the shrinkage was the success of this program in its important objective of attracting the middle class back from the suburbs. Thus, more of the new available space was occupied by the nonpoor. To ensure that the poor will be better accommodated, attempts have been made to guarantee that any renewal program includes specified amounts of low-income housing.

rest of that decade brought no further reduction. During that period, the continued expansion of transfer programs was just sufficient to offset the negative effects of increased unemployment.[2]

In the early 1980s, the poverty rate increased because of high unemployment and the tightening of transfer programs. It was also due to long-term trends, such as the growth in the number of single-parent households. This increase in poverty continued until 1984, when the official rate dropped from 15.2% to 14.4% (not shown in Figure 37-2). This reduction in poverty during 1984, when unemployment was decreasing, confirms that some of the poverty problem in the previous years was due to relatively high levels of unemployment.

[2]Transfer programs may be less successful than expected in reducing poverty. True, transfers do have a positive effect; many families that would otherwise be below the poverty line are raised above that line by transfers. However, while this direct effect is positive, there is also a negative indirect effect noted in the previous chapter: If transfer payments did not exist—that is, if there were no welfare to fall back on, people would have a greater incentive to work; and with more people working, fewer would be initially below the poverty line. In other words, because transfers have the indirect effect of reducing incentives to work, they are less effective in reducing poverty than they initially appear.

Problems with the Present Welfare System

Perverse incentives It is difficult to design a welfare system without creating perverse incentives. Indeed, it is so difficult that the problem of incentives will be one of the main themes in this chapter. We have already noted that Aid to Families with Dependent Children (AFDC) may, in certain circumstances, encourage a parent to desert the family. Unfortunately, the problem of incentives is broader than this.

Consider the public housing program. As we have seen, families pay 25% of their income in rent under this program. This means that, for every $1 more they earn in income, they must pay 25 cents more in rent because the government reduces their subsidy by this amount. By itself, this effect on the incentive to work may not be very important. However, some of the other subsidies in Table 37-1 are also reduced as a family's income rises. When the effect of all these subsidy reductions is taken into account, the accumulated impact on the incentive to work may be very substantial. The poor may well wonder: "Why go to work to earn an additional $1,000 of income, if it means that we will have our housing subsidy reduced by $250, and our AFDC by $450—for a total reduction of $700? It's as though we had to pay a $700 tax on this $1,000 of additional income." Such a family is paying an ***implicit tax*** of 70% on its additional income. Worse yet, the implicit tax may be even higher than this. If this family were to lose even more subsidies, its implicit tax could approach 100%. In some cases it is even higher; for such families, going to work *lowers* their income.

The *implicit tax* built into a welfare program is calculated by examining the *benefits lost* when a family

FIGURE 37-2

How the U.S. poverty rate has been changing over time

By recent poverty standards, the percentage of the population in poverty followed a downward long term trend until the early 1970s. However, in the early 1980s there was an increase in the incidence of poverty.

Sources: Trend line only from 1929 to 1960. The 1929 figure is a rough approximation that follows from the fact that the average real income in 1929 was about the same as the poverty level as defined in the mid 1970s. The 1947 figure is from the Council of Economic Advisers, *Annual Report, 1964*. The before-transfer series from 1979–1983 is taken from John L. Palmer and Elizabeth V. Sawhill, *The Reagan Record* (Cambridge, Mass.: Ballinger, 1984) p. 197. The official poverty series since 1960 is from Council of Economic Advisers, *Annual Report,* 1984, p. 252, and 1985, p. 264.

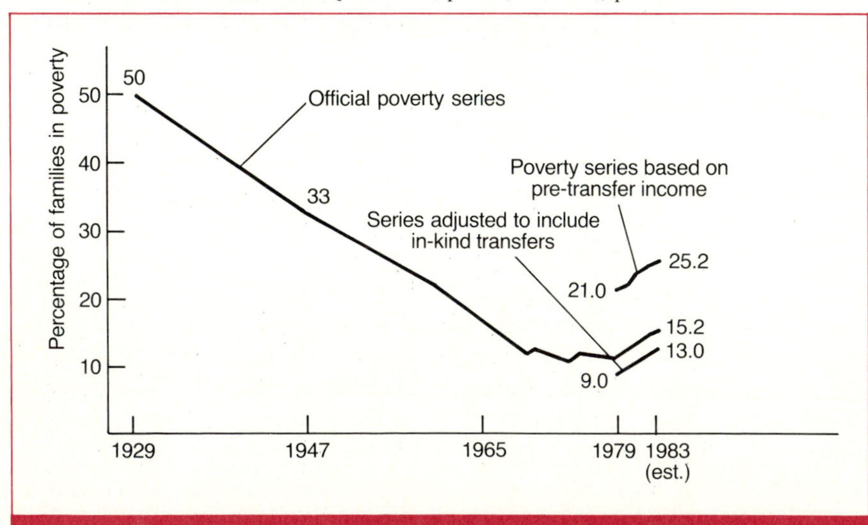

earns another $1 of income. (If its benefits are reduced by 46 cents, the implicit tax is 46%.)

Complexity

Two messages stand out clearly in Table 37-1. First, a great deal of money is being spent on transfer expenditures. Second, there is a whole set of programs. Inequity arises because some families qualify for more of these programs than other equally poor families. By drawing on several of these programs, some poor families are lifted not only to the cutoff poverty level but somewhat above it, while other families are left substantially below it. In some cases, welfare recipients end up with a higher income than some of the workers who pay taxes to support them. (Little wonder that these workers become vocal critics of welfare.) To top it all off, the poor sometimes feel that the welfare workers who administer these programs hold far too much arbitrary power over them; those on welfare are subjected to hassles and humiliation. In turn, some welfare workers view the programs as a nearly hopeless administrative tangle. On receiving the *Public Assistance Handbook,* former Senator Clifford P. Case declared: "I was appalled to receive a package of regulations weighing almost six pounds, as thick as the Washington, D.C. telephone directory. Leaving the human element aside, this handbook is the best possible evidence that the present welfare program is a bureaucratic nightmare." In view of these problems, why not replace the whole checkered pattern of policies with a single program that guarantees each family the same minimum income—adjusted, of course, for differences in family size?

A GUARANTEED MINIMUM INCOME: A CURE FOR THE POVERTY PROBLEM?

Why not eliminate poverty in one stroke by setting a minimum income at the poverty level? If any family's income were to fall below that level, the government could cover that shortfall with a direct grant. What would this cost? If we add up the shortfall in income of all families below the poverty line, the sum would be only 1% or 2% of U.S. GNP. Considering what we are already spending, why shouldn't we just commit ourselves to this sort of relatively modest increase in expenditure, and end poverty?

Unfortunately, it is not that easy.

Inefficiencies in a Subsidy Program

The problem is this. A program that raises the income of the poor by $10 billion costs far more than $10 billion. Waste occurs because such a program has several adverse effects on incentives.

Disincentives for those paying for the subsidy The first adverse incentive applies to those who pay the higher taxes necessary to finance this scheme. The heavier the tax rate, the more likely it is that an individual will ask, "Why am I working so hard when the government gets such a large slice of what I earn?" Thus, by reducing the reward for working, a high tax has a negative effect on the incentive to work. However, this is partly offset by a positive effect: A high tax makes working more necessary for those trying to maintain previous levels of spending. Nevertheless, on balance, high taxes tend to have a negative effect on work effort. They also encourage the search for tax loopholes. As higher-income individuals engage in socially unproductive efforts to reduce their tax payments—or hire accountants or lawyers to help them—there is a consequent waste imposed on society. As Arthur Okun described it: "High tax rates are followed by attempts of ingenious men to beat them, as surely as snow is followed by little boys on sleds."[3]

Disincentives for those receiving the subsidy Now let's turn to those at the bottom of the income scale who will receive this subsidy. Here one would expect more substantial incentive effects, for the reasons shown in Figure 37-3. (In this diagram we concentrate on what happens to people at the bottom of the income scale. For simplicity, we disregard any taxes paid now by these people. To simplify further, we use a "round figure" poverty line of $10,000.) Families are plotted along the horizontal axis according to how much income they originally earn. Thus, family *h* with a $8,000 earned income

[3]Arthur Okun, *Equality and Efficiency: The Big Trade Off* (Washington: Brookings Institution, 1975), p. 97.

is plotted at point Q along the horizontal axis. Income after the implementation of this policy is measured up the vertical axis. If no subsidy were paid to family *h*, its "income after" would also be $8,000, as shown by the red bar. In other words, family *h* would be shown by *F* on the 45° line, where its before and after incomes are equal. Hence this 45° line may be called the "same-before-and-after" line, or just the "no-subsidy" line.

However, our minimum income program does pay family *h* a subsidy—specifically, the $2,000 solid bar *FG* that is necessary to raise its income to the poverty line of $10,000. Since the income of any other family below the poverty line is similarly subsidized up to this $10,000 level, the "income after subsidy" line is the heavy line *CAB*. Shaded triangle 1 represents the shortfall that the government must fill at a cost of 1% or 2% of GNP—*provided people continue to work and earn as much after the subsidy as before.*

The problem is that, because they are being subsidized, some people will *not* work as hard as before. For example, the father of family *h* may realize: "If I don't work at all, the government will still guarantee us the same $10,000; so why should I work?" If he stops working, that $8,000 of income he earned disappears. The position of that family on the horizontal axis therefore shifts all the way to the left, from situation *h* to situation

FIGURE 37-3

Possible disincentive effects of a guaranteed $10,000 minimum income

The 45° line *OAB* is the no-subsidy line. For example, at point *F* on this line, family *h* that earns $8,000 (measured left to right) would end up with $8,000 (measured up). On the other hand, heavy line *CAB* shows income after the subsidy. Family *h* is paid the $2,000 (gray bar) subsidy necessary to raise it to the guaranteed $10,000 level, while family *g* which earns no income must be paid a full $10,000 subsidy. This program erodes the incentive to work: Because *h*'s income will remain at the same $10,000 level, this individual may stop working and thus join *g*.

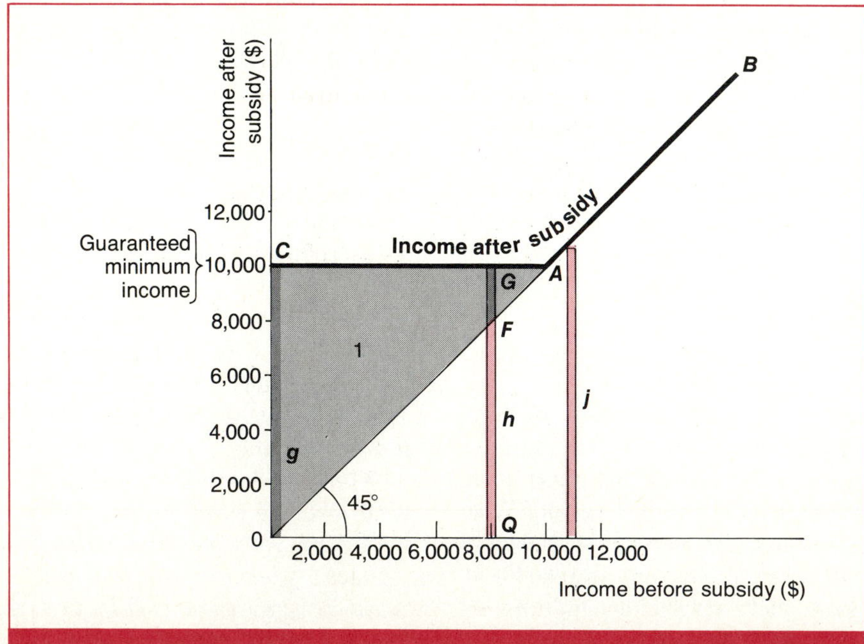

g. At this point, nothing is being earned, that family has become totally unproductive, and it must be subsidized by the full \$10,000. Therefore, in order to raise this family's income by the original \$2,000 shortfall, the government ends up paying \$10,000. This example illustrates what Arthur Okun referred to as transferring income "with a leaky bucket." Although \$10,000 has been spent to increase the income of a poor family, it has increased their income by only \$2,000. The other \$8,000 has "leaked away" because the family has stopped working. In other words, the "transfer bucket" in this hypothetical example has an 80% leak. This leakage of the red bar at *h* also represents the efficiency loss from this policy. The original income this family produced was the \$8,000 red bar at *h*, but this is now lost to society because no one in the family any longer works.

Disincentives that apply to the nonpoor Disincentive effects may apply not only to poor families like *h* with initial incomes below the \$10,000 support level; they may also apply to nonpoor families like *j* with incomes above \$10,000. Suppose the breadwinner in family *j* has been earning \$11,000 in a boring and unpleasant job. The subsidy program will now offer a tempting option: Go fishing and receive a \$10,000 income from the government. If this happens, family *j* also shifts to the far left into position *g*, where it too qualifies for the full \$10,000 subsidy. Thus the government has to subsidize not only those with initial incomes below the \$10,000 poverty level but *also* some with incomes above the poverty line for whom this program was never intended.

In short, when the government attempts to fill an income gap by such a simple subsidy, its cost may far exceed the initial income shortfall that it set about to cure. The reason is that the subsidy disturbs incentives; some people may work less or stop working altogether. From the viewpoint of the government paying the subsidy, the problem appears in two forms. On the one hand, some poor families like *h* may absorb more subsidy than expected. On the other hand, a whole new and unexpected group of families like *j* may appear on the scene, hat in hand. Moreover, when a family like *j* goes on the subsidy program, the overall efficiency loss to society is particularly severe. It is the red bar at *j*—the \$11,000 of income that is no longer produced because someone who used to work is now off fishing.

The reason that this policy is so inefficient is that the portion *CA* of the "income after subsidy" line is completely horizontal, leaving the poor *no* incentive to work; that is, they face an implicit tax of 100%. They have nothing to show for any additional \$1 they earn, because their subsidy is reduced by the same \$1.

Critics charge that, in terms of its antiwork incentives, the present U.S. welfare system is quite close to this simple subsidy scheme. In some cases, the present system involves an implicit tax of less than 100%, but in some special cases it is more. (See Box 37-3.) Thus the guaranteed annual income scheme described in Figure 37-3 can be used as a very rough-and-ready approximation, to illustrate some of the problems of the current system. However, we emphasize: The present system—with its wide variety of programs—cannot be *fully* described by *any* simple diagram.

CONFLICTING VIEWS ON WELFARE

Figure 37-3 illustrates why some observers view welfare as the *cure* for society's failure while others view it as the *cause* of this failure.

Economic Failure: Is It Cured or Caused by Welfare?

Proponents of welfare programs point to individuals who are disabled or just cannot cope. Because they are unable to succeed economically, they are initially left at *g* in Figure 37-3. The (gray bar) welfare benefits raise them above the poverty line, solving a serious social problem.

On the other hand, welfare critics point to the individuals we've described who start out at *h* or *j* and respond to welfare by shifting to *g*. According to this view, welfare payments provide potentially productive people with an incentive to stop producing—to stop earning the red bar of income at *h* or *j* and instead go on the dole at *g*. In such cases, welfare *creates* a social problem.

In practice, a welfare system has *both* effects: It solves the poverty problem for people who start at *g*, and it creates a problem by inducing some of the people who start at *h* or *j* to move to *g*. In the U.S. system, what is the relative importance of these two effects? In particular, how much does welfare erode the incentive to work? The answer is apparently not as much as the discussion of Figure 37-3 might suggest. Many families at *h* or *j* *don't* stop working; they don't move to the left. Their (red bar) productivity is not lost. Moreover, many people start at *g*. In their case, there is no leak in the bucket at all. Welfare can't reduce their productivity because they don't produce anything in the first place. Thus, the Okun transfer bucket is not completely shot through with holes.

Nonetheless, available evidence suggests that a substantial leak does exist. For $1 of welfare expenditure, an estimated 25 cents leaks away because welfare recipients work less. In addition, there are other leakages in the transfer bucket. In particular, there are losses from collecting the taxes necessary to finance the welfare expenditure, because taxation encourages the search for loopholes and reduces the incentive to work of those who are taxed. Estimates of this "excess cost of taxation" vary widely but suggest that 25% to 35% is the best range for estimating this second leak, with 30% being perhaps the best single round number. This means that there is a leak on both the taxation and expenditure ends of roughly 50%. When account is taken of the other costs—such as the administrative costs of running a welfare program—the picture is one of a bucket with somewhat more than a 50% leak.[4]

[4]Estimating this leak is difficult because it depends on how the government is raising taxes and how it is spending the funds. Nonetheless, a fairly clear, though not precise, picture still emerges. In simulations 1 and 6 in Table 2 of "Welfare Costs per Dollar of Additional Tax Revenue in the United States," *American Economic Review*, June 1984, Charles Stuart estimates that the excess cost of taxation ranges from 7% to 53%. In his judgment, 30% to 40% is the most likely range. In Table 3 of "General Equilibrium Computations of the Marginal Welfare Costs of Taxes in the United States," *American Economic Review*, March 1985, C. L. Ballard, J. B. Shoven, and John Whalley provide estimates of the marginal excess burden of taxation that range between 17% and 56%, with their best estimate being roughly 33%. In the NBER Reporter, Spring 1983, Jerry Housman estimates this leak to be 28%. Thus we conclude that the leak on the taxation end is 25% to 35%. How about the second leak when the funds are spent because welfare recipients work less? The 25% estimate that we quote is from Danziger et al., "How Income Transfer Programs Affect Work, Savings and the Income Distribution: A Critical Review," *Journal of Economic Literature*, September 1981, pp. 975–1028. (The calculations of Edgar Browning and William R. Johnson in "The Trade-Off between Equality and Efficiency," *Journal of Political Economy*, April 1984, pp. 175–203, imply that, for some taxation/expenditure programs, these two leaks may be much greater.)

To recap this discussion, it is worth considering what we mean by a leak in the transfer bucket of about 50%. It does *not* mean that the government raises $100 in taxes but only delivers $50 to the poor. Instead, the hypothetical example in Figure 37-4 shows what happens. We begin at line 2 with the $100 the government collects in taxes. Most, but not all, of this is delivered to the poor. In our example, we suppose that the government has $10 of administrative costs, so that only $90 can be delivered to the poor. The problem is that about 25% of this—let's say $25—leaks away. It does not raise the income of the poor at all; it just replaces the income they lose because they work less. (An extreme example was family *h* in Figure 37-3.) Thus the income of the poor is increased by only $90 − $25 = $65. Finally we return to the top of this diagram and see that when the government raises the original $100 in taxes, this imposes a $30 excess cost on the economy because, for example, those who are taxed work less. When this $30 of excess cost is added to the $100 of taxes, it is costing the American public $130 to provide a net benefit of $65 to the poor. It is in this sense that there is a 50% leak.

Such a large leak does not mean that welfare expenditures should necessarily be cut back because of the waste in the transfer process. However, it does illustrate that solving the poverty problem is a more expensive task than was once assumed.

Noneconomic Benefits and Costs

It is no suprise that economists focus on the economic effects of welfare programs; for example, how much does the "bucket" leak? But such programs have effects that go beyond economics.

On the positive side, welfare programs are society's way of stating its commitment to the less fortunate. We would not want to live in a callous nation which paid no heed to the sick and helpless. By contributing to a humane society, a welfare program can have social gains which go beyond the benefits to the welfare recipients themselves.

Because of the way in which welfare programs are a symbol of society's values, flaws in these programs can be demoralizing. Critics suggest that our welfare system has unintended social costs:

1. One of the many reasons that fathers remain in the

BOX 37-3

HOW A HIGH IMPLICIT TAX ERODES WORK INCENTIVES IN OUR EXISTING WELFARE SYSTEM

Failure to understand the concept of the implicit tax in a welfare program can lead to costly policy errors. For example, in 1981 the Reagan administration, which was committed to reducing welfare dependency by encouraging work, introduced a policy change to AFDC (Aid to Families with Dependent Children) that had the opposite effect. To understand why, we turn the clock back to the 1960s, when recipients of AFDC who took a job lost $1 of benefits for every $1 they earned. Their implicit tax rate was 100%; there was no monetary incentive to go to work. In the late 1960s, Congress reduced this problem by lowering the implicit tax to approximately 66%. In other words, for every $3 they earned, their AFDC subsidy was reduced by $2; they still had a $1 incentive to get a job. However, in 1981, the administration removed or reduced that $1 incentive for anyone employed for 4 months. Consequently, many of those earning $3 lost $3 of AFDC subsidy. Because the implicit tax for them was 100%, they no longer had any financial incentive to get or hold a job.

In some cases, it was even possible for someone earning $3 to lose not only $3 of AFDC benefit, but some other benefit like medicaid as well. In this case, the implicit tax was *more* than 100%; there was an incentive *not* to work.

Critics of this change charged that it left the poor with little or no encouragement to work. In response, the administration cited evidence that most AFDC recipients with jobs continued to work despite the change.[†] However, there was still another question: Would AFDC recipients *without* jobs still try as hard to find work?

Of course, there were many people on welfare who benefitted from programs *other* than AFDC and who therefore did not face AFDC's implicit tax of 100%. However, that also raised a problem. The wide variation in implicit taxes faced by those who were at essentially the same poverty level made the welfare system inconsistent and inequitable.

[†]The administration also pointed out that the tightening of the requirements to qualify for AFDC meant that 10% to 15% of previously covered families were no longer eligible. For this group, the marginal tax rate due to AFDC *fell* from 66% to zero. (Since they were no longer getting any AFDC benefits, they had none to lose if they earned more income.) Thus those families that were dropped from the program *did* have a strong incentive to get a job.

home and support their families is the fear of what might happen if they were to leave. If a government welfare program removes this fear by guaranteeing child support, won't some fathers feel freer to leave? Thus, welfare programs may affect our social structure and, in particular, the family unit.

2. Does welfare encourage a problem it is designed to cure: the "culture of poverty"? Does it encourage dependence and destroy pride and self-respect? Being the breadwinner may be one of the few sources of pride and self-respect for those with low-paying, no-promise jobs. If welfare provides as adequately for their families as they can, does it make them feel like so much excess baggage and destroy their self-respect?[5]

THE KEY TRADE-OFF: EQUITY VS. EFFICIENCY

It all seemed so simple. As we look back over the microeconomic half of this book, the following message

[5]Many have held the view that there is a "welfare trap": Welfare tends to be addictive, inducing those who are on it to stay on. Moreover, children in a family receiving welfare may in turn grow up to depend on welfare rather than work as the source of their support. Thus welfare creates a welfare-dependent society. This view has recently been challenged by Mark W. Plant in "An Empirical Analysis of Welfare Dependence," *American Economic Review,* September 1984.

For the view that government programs destroy the dignity of those who keep low-paying jobs, see Charles Murray, *Losing Ground: American Social Policy, 1950–1980* (New York: Basic Books, 1984).

seemed to be emerging: Where product or factor markets are inefficient, the government should intervene to increase efficiency. For example, it should intervene to tax polluters or to regulate monopoly price. This intervention is particularly desirable if it also has favorable equity effects—for example, if it benefits a low-income, disadvantaged group. Then there are no conflicts, and the appropriate policy choice is a simple one. An illustration is eliminating discrimination in the labor market. This policy increases efficiency and also transfers income to those who have faced disadvantages because of their race or sex. However, such cases are the exception rather than the rule; most policies do involve a conflict between equity and efficiency. Thus the attempt to achieve equity by intervening in product or factor markets often leads to inefficiency. To achieve equity, we should therefore rely on direct government transfers rather than inefficient interventions into factor or product markets—like the imposition of an interest rate ceiling.

Unfortunately, it's not so easy after all, because of one weak link in this argument. Direct government transfers may not be very efficient either. In particular, government spending on the poor erodes the incentive to work and reduces national output. Thus, we are still left with the trade-off between the objectives of equity and efficiency. The size of the national pie is typically reduced if we try to carve it up in a more equitable way.

This is not a recommendation that we go back to transferring income by the inefficient market interventions we have criticized in earlier chapters. Not only are they inefficient. Worse yet, as a means of raising the income of the poor, they are often ineffective. An interest rate ceiling is again a good example because it benefits rich borrowers as well as poor. In fact, it may leave many relatively poor borrowers in deep trouble because they are completely cut off from funds. As another example, price supports benefit the affluent farmer without lifting many poor farmers out of poverty.

The message remains: The way to reduce poverty is by direct government policies to aid the poor. However, we should be searching for a better way of making these transfers than the simple subsidy programs we have been

FIGURE 37-4
Leaks in the transfer bucket

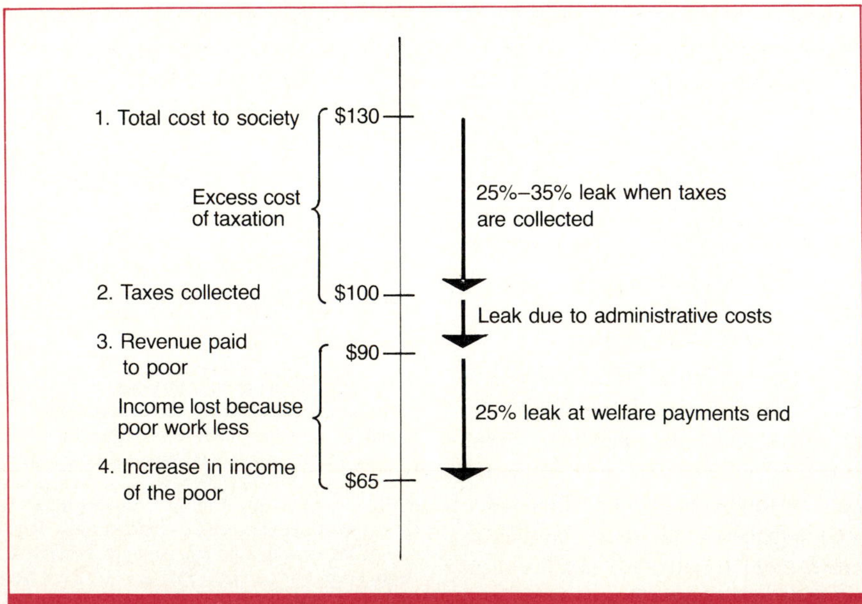

discussing so far. In particular, we should be seeking a way that is not only *equitable* but is also *efficient*—that is, a way that does not destroy the incentive to work.

THE NEGATIVE INCOME TAX: CAN WE COMBINE EQUITY AND EFFICIENCY?

How can we guarantee families a minimum income (for example, $10,000) without destroying their incentive to work? This is an essential question, and it is not an easy one to answer. One proposal is the ***negative income tax,*** which has been advocated by many of those on both the "left" and "right" of the political spectrum who are critical of the present welfare system. To explain this proposal, let's put the guaranteed minimum income in Figure 37-3 back on the drawing board in Figure 37-5. This new diagram has the same frame of reference as the earlier one, except that it is extended to the right to allow us to take account, not only of families that receive a subsidy, but also of higher-income families that pay the government a tax. The 45° "same-before-and-after" line *OQB* now represents the "no-subsidy, no-tax" line where families would be if the government neither subsidized nor taxed them.

Design of a Negative Income Tax

To see how a negative income tax would work, begin by assuming, as before, that the minimum income level is set at $10,000. Now, rather than subsidizing incomes just up to the line *CA* by filling gap 1 as we did in Figure 37-3, the government instead pays subsidies—that is, "negative taxes"—equal to areas 1 + 2 + 3, thereby bringing incomes up to the heavy line *CQ*. (Beyond an income of $20,000, a family pays "positive" taxes to the government, as shown by the red area 4.) Because the "income-after-tax" line *CQH* slopes upward, people have an incentive to work. The more income they earn (the more they move to the right in this diagram) the more income they get to keep (the higher they rise on line *CQ*). By providing this incentive to earn income, we attempt to reduce the leak in the bucket that occurs because people prefer to go on welfare rather than to work. Proponents of the negative income tax emphasize that it must replace *all* existing welfare programs, such as food stamps. If some of these subsidies remain, the poor may get a higher income from these subsidies and the negative income tax than from working. They may therefore quit work to draw government benefits.

The negative income tax should not only improve efficiency. It should also move us toward a greater degree of equity in several ways: (1) It would guarantee a minimum income for all, (2) it would replace the wide variety of existing welfare programs with one consistent policy that would treat all families at the same income level in the same way, and (3) it would also satisfy another equity objective of most Americans—it would leave those who work with a higher income than those who do not.

However, this would apparently be a very expensive program, since the subsidy is now area 1 plus areas 2 and 3. Specifically, the government now provides an even greater subsidy (areas 1 + 2) to poor families earning less than $10,000, *plus* a subsidy 3 to *nonpoor* families with incomes all the way up to $20,000. Of course, families earning even higher incomes pay a tax. For example, a family earning $24,000 pays the $2,000 tax shown as the dark red bar *t*. Thus, heavy line *CQH* shows how the government pays gray subsidies all the way up to point *Q*, and levies the red tax on incomes above this. (Although this line need not have a constant slope, it does in this simple example. Any family keeps half of any additional income it earns. For example, those with earned incomes of less than $20,000 get to keep half of any additional income they earn; in other words, they lose half of it, which means they face a 50% implicit tax. At the same time, those at the higher end of the income scale face a 50% regular tax on all their income over $20,000.)

Another problem with the negative income tax is that its apparent high cost is not limited to filling new gaps 2 + 3. In addition, the treasury loses the taxes previously collected from many nonpoor families with incomes between $10,000 and $20,000. This leads to some extraordinary results. In 1982, more than half of U.S. families had an income of less than $20,000. (The proportion is lower now, but it is still very large). Under this program they would pay no tax; instead they would receive a subsidy. Moreover, this program would also reduce the taxes paid by some families with incomes

FIGURE 37-5

A negative income tax (compare with Figure 37-3)

Family *g* with a zero earned income is paid the gray bar grant of $10,000. But what do we do with family *d* with $2,000 of earned income? If we make the same mistake we made in Figure 37-3 and raise this income up only to that same $10,000 (by a $8,000 grant), this will leave that family with no incentive to keep working to earn that $2,000. So to provide an incentive to work, we grant this family $9,000 instead (as shown by the gray bar), thus bringing its total up to $11,000 at point *D*. If we continue in this way, always providing a $1,000 incentive for families to earn an additional $2,000 of income, we move up heavy line *CQ* to cutoff point *Q*, where no subsidy is paid. Moreover, if we continue to allow families to keep half of any additional income they earn, we will tax incomes above this level down from *QB* to *QH*. Thus, red area 4 shows us how any income above $20,000 is subject to a tax; for example, family *f* with a $24,000 income pays the $2,000 tax *t*. At the same time, gray area 1 + 2 + 3 shows us how any income below $20,000 is subsidized—that is, ''taxed in reverse.'' Hence the name: negative income tax.

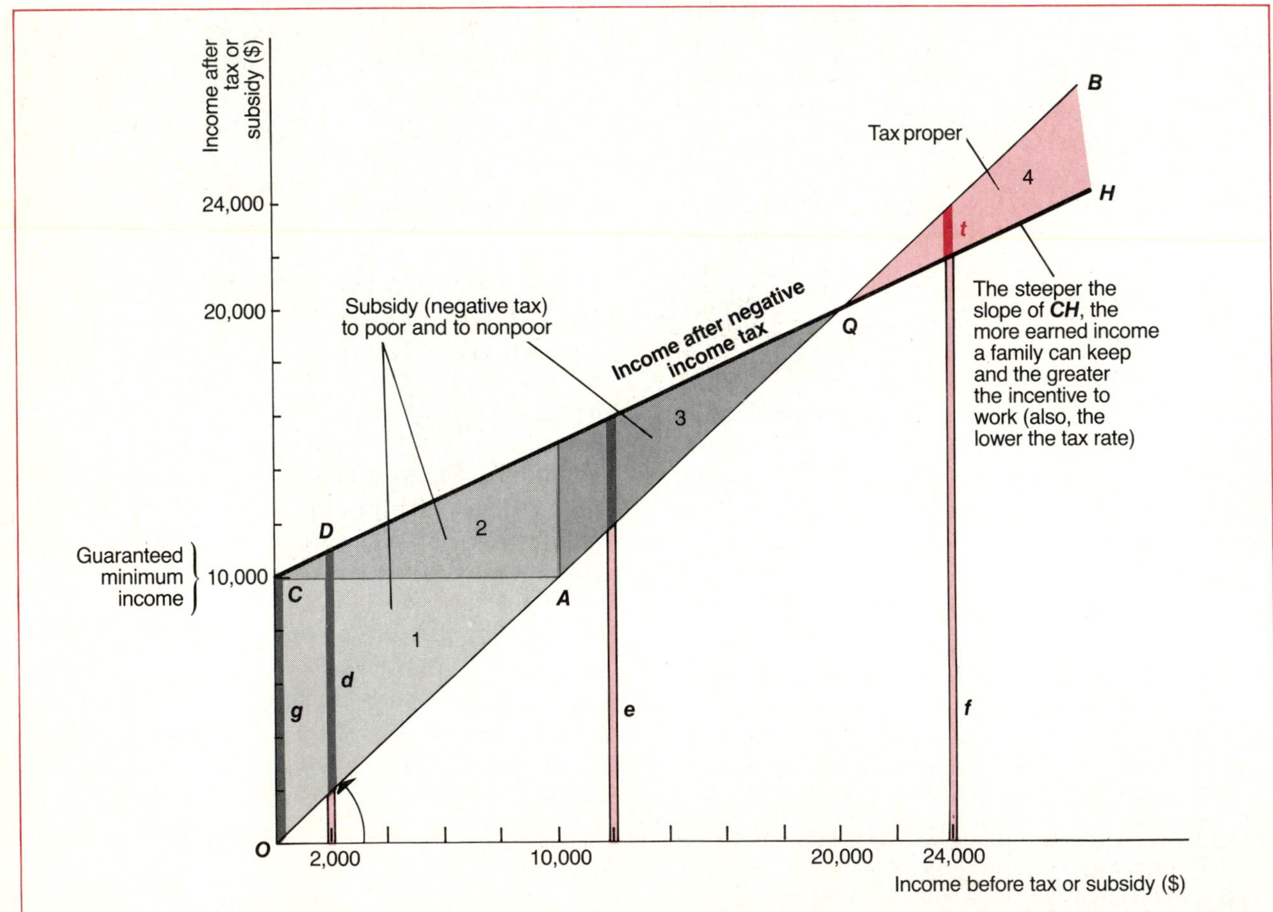

above \$20,000.[6] Benefitting such families was scarcely the objective when we set out to raise families to the poverty level of \$10,000!

When one takes into account all these considerations, doesn't the negative income tax come out badly in comparison with the simply subsidy scheme in Figure 37-3? Why would anyone recommend it? The answer is that it should have a favorable effect on incentives. The negative income tax should be a far less leaky bucket than a simple subsidy scheme or our present welfare system. This point is worth considering in detail.

Why the Negative Income Tax Should Reduce the Leaks in the "Welfare Bucket"

By allowing families to keep half of any additional income they earn, the negative income tax should induce them to get out and earn more, and thus "move to the right" in Figure 37-5. Since this would reduce—and in some cases, perhaps even eliminate—the subsidy some families receive, the cost of this scheme should be less than the gray subsidy area in Figure 37-5 suggests.

Moreover, the cost of this scheme may be reduced even further by modifications. For example, the "after-tax" line CQH might be lowered by, say, \$2,000. This would maintain the same incentive to work (the same slope of CQH) but would substantially reduce the cost (the subsidy areas 1 + 2 + 3). Moreover, by shifting critical point Q to the left, it would mean that families with an income in the \$16,000 to \$20,000 range would no longer receive a subsidy; instead they would pay a tax. Thus this program would no longer allow so many U.S. families to escape taxes. However, one problem would remain: Those at C doing no work would now receive less than the \$10,000 poverty minimum.

This problem might be reduced by providing a guaranteed \$10,000 income to those who are aged, infirm, or disabled and *cannot* work. If these people can be clearly identified, guaranteeing them a minimum income would result in no inefficiency; it would not affect the amount they work, because they can't work. Such a program would also score high in terms of equity, by providing an adequate safety net for those who cannot do without it. Such a policy—of identifying specific groups with special needs—is called *categorization* or *tagging*. The big problem is that, in practice, it is difficult to identify exactly who should be tagged as unable to work; it is often difficult to determine who is disabled. While people don't blind themselves to get welfare, some may falsely argue that they have been disabled because, say, of minor backaches that they exaggerate.

The Negative Income Tax Does Not Resolve All Conflicts

We can now extend this theoretical discussion of the negative income tax by noting how it gives rise to tension among the following three objectives:

1. Set the minimum income level C high enough so no one will be left destitute.
2. Give CQH enough slope to provide people with a strong incentive to work. (Many would view the slope of CQH in Figure 37-5 as being too low and therefore providing inadequate incentive to work. Since people can keep only half of any additional income they earn, they all "spend half their time working for the government.")
3. Keep the subsidy areas 1 + 2 + 3 small, in order to keep the cost of the program down and avoid heavily subsidizing the nonpoor.

It is impossible to achieve all these objectives at once because they are in conflict. For example, the way to achieve the second objective is to make line CQH steeper. But a greater slope means that either C must be lower or subsidy areas 1 + 2 + 3 must be larger. Thus objective 2 conflicts with objectives 1 and 3.

While the negative income tax does not resolve all conflicts, it nonetheless does look like a promising approach—at least in theory. Unfortunately, in cases where it has been tested, it has been disappointing in two respects.

The Negative Income Tax in Practice: Results of Recent Experiments

In several experiments, a number of families have been

[6]To confirm this statement, consider a family with income just barely over \$20,000. In Figure 37-5, it pays a minuscule tax that is less than the tax it used to pay.

For evidence that more than half of U.S. families in 1982 had an income of less than \$20,000, see the *Federal Reserve Bulletin*, September 1984, p. 680. The median U.S. family income in 1982 was \$19,446.

put on a negative income tax. How have they behaved, compared with families under the present welfare system?

The economic effects In experiments in Seattle and Denver, a negative income tax specifically designed to encourage people to work more led to paradoxical results: People actually worked less. As a result, the negative income tax seemed to add as much to their leisure as to their income. The explanation for this surprising result seems to be that the expected positive work incentive is more than offset by three influences that encourage them to work less:

1. Being on a negative income tax eliminates the ***hassle*** people often encounter when they quit work and go on welfare. Under a negative income tax people feel freer to quit work and don't search as hard for a new job.
2. Under a negative income tax, people can quit their jobs without feeling the ***social stigma*** faced by those on traditional welfare.
3. When people have participated in the negative income tax experiment, its characteristics have been ***clearly explained.*** Participants are told of their rights—in particular, their right to stop working and still continue to receive an income. Consequently, they are more likely to exercise this no-work option simply because they know about it. In contrast, some of those who might draw ordinary welfare stay on the job because they are not so well informed about their options. (Because of the hassle, it may not be clear exactly what their options are.)

Noneconomic effects of the negative income tax Some noneconomic effects are favorable. For example, there is evidence that a negative income tax may increase the number of adults finishing high school. On the other hand, the 5-year experiments in Seattle and Denver indicated that a negative income tax may increase the incidence of marriage breakups by as much as 50%. This was another puzzling result because the negative income tax was expected to help keep families together—for example, by taking them off AFDC with its incentive for fathers to leave home. It isn't entirely clear *why* the negative income tax had this perverse effect. Perhaps, once again, it was because participants were fully informed about their options. (Specifically, they were informed about the financial support their families would continue to receive if they were to leave home.) If strengthening marriages is viewed as a public policy objective, the negative income tax has been a major disappointment. Moreover, this effect on families may indirectly have important economic implications. When a middle-income family breaks up, the result is often two new families, with one or both living below the poverty line.

WHERE DO WE GO FROM HERE?

Because of unfavorable experimental results, it has now become difficult to argue that the negative income tax—so promising on the drawing board—is the hoped-for "solution" to the welfare problem. Paradoxically, if it is to be introduced, it should probably not be in the hassle-free, stigma-free way that was once viewed as one of its great advantages. Unfortunately, it seems necessary to have some hassle and stigma attached to any income-support program to give people an incentive to go to work instead.

In the light of these results, many are looking less to a single solution to the poverty problem, and are instead recommending a variety of different programs for different groups. For example, there is now strong bipartisan support for stronger enforcement of child support laws to raise the income of families headed by women, thus reducing poverty in this most seriously afflicted group. Another suggestion is to raise the take-home pay of low-income workers by paying them a ***wage subsidy*** that would increase as the number of their dependents increased. Because such a government subsidy would come to the family via the worker's paycheck, it would increase the worker's pride in having a job and supporting a family. Moreover, to the degree that a wage subsidy were to replace existing welfare programs, it would also increase the fear of severe financial distress at home if that individual were to walk out; this should increase the incentive for wage earners to stay with their families. Finally, by increasing the take-home wage, a wage subsidy would increase the incentive to work.[7]

[7]For further specific suggestions to reduce poverty, see Alice Rivlin (ed.), *Economic Choices 1984* (Washington: Brookings, 1984), chap. 7.

Unfortunately this wage subsidy proposal is far from being problem-free. In particular, it's essential to remember that small but important group who, because of disability or low innate capacity, are unable to earn a living. A wage subsidy would do nothing to solve their problem. They would have to be tagged as valid recipients of straight welfare subsidies. But this in turn means facing one of the most difficult issues in dealing with poverty: How do you decide who's in the tagged group that doesn't have to work, and how do you keep out others who want to get in?

KEY POINTS

1. Poverty is defined as inadequate income to buy the necessities of life. A specific poverty-line figure is determined by calculating the minimum cost of a nutritious and barely appealing diet and multiplying that figure by 3. In 1985 the poverty line for a family of four was about $10,610.
2. Since 1979, the incidence of poverty has risen. The increase was a result of a number of factors: the double recessions of 1980 and 1981–1982, a tightening of welfare programs, and long-term influences, such as growing divorce and separation rates. By 1983, 13% of American families were living in poverty.
3. Blacks and those of Hispanic origin are more likely to be poor than whites, and southerners are more likely to be poor than northerners. The less an individual is educated, the greater the risk of poverty. The problem exists in cities, towns, and farms, with the areas least affected being the suburbs of big cities. Poverty is a particularly serious problem in fatherless families, especially those that are black.
4. In the long run, the most promising government antipoverty policies are those that deal with the causes rather than the symptoms of poverty. These policies include eliminating employment discrimination against minorities and women, and subsidizing investment in human capital, including both education and on-the-job training.
5. Government income maintenance programs include social security and unemployment insurance, which are paid to poor and nonpoor alike. But there are also many programs, like Aid to Families with Dependent Children, food stamps, and housing assistance, that are designed specifically for the poor. The problem with these programs is that when the poor earn more income, they face an implicit tax, in the form of a reduction in the subsidies they receive. This implicit tax reduces their incentive to work, thus lowering the nation's output.
6. The package of present programs is also inequitable. Some of the poor are not lifted up to the poverty line, while others who qualify under several of these programs are lifted above it—indeed, in some cases, even above the income earned by some of the people who pay taxes to support the antipoverty program.
7. Why not, then, replace this present system with a single policy that would lift all the poor up to the same minimum income level? One answer is that the poor, with their incomes thus guaranteed, would have little or no economic incentive to work, and the nation's output would be reduced. Thus, the conflict between greater equality and efficiency persists: As we try to carve up the national pie more equally by raising the income of the poor, the total size of that pie is reduced.
8. In theory, a negative income tax is a good method of reducing, but not entirely eliminating, this conflict. Under this policy, families would be allowed to keep part of any additional income they earn. This would leave them with an incentive to work. The program would also guarantee every family a minimum income. Unfortunately, in experiments so far, the negative income tax has been a disappointment. People tend to work less rather than more.

KEY CONCEPTS

poverty line
causes of poverty
symptoms of poverty
policies to increase human capital
policies to eliminate discrimination
Work Incentive Program
social security
unemployment insurance
medicare
medicaid

Aid to Families with Dependent Children
food stamps
public housing
benefits in kind versus in cash
implicit tax in a welfare system
leak in the transfer bucket
guaranteed minimum income
tagging
negative income tax
hassle and stigma
wage subsidy

PROBLEMS

37-1. What is meant by an implicit tax rate of 90%? Of 105%? What is the effect of each of these tax rates?

37-2. Review the efficiency losses from the income redistribution policy in Figure 37-3. What is the efficiency loss if this subsidy induces the income earner(s) of family *h* to go fishing? The income earner of family *j*? What is the efficiency loss if the income earner of family *j* takes one day off each week to go fishing? What is the efficiency loss from subsidizing a family like *g* that originally earned no income?

If the minimum income level were set at $12,000, rather than $10,000, would the efficiency loss be greater or smaller?

37-3. Explain to your bright roommate (who is taking economics but hasn't yet reached this chapter) exactly what is meant by a ''leaky bucket.''

37-4. In Figure 37-5, the incentive to work is the $1,000 a family can keep out of each additional $2,000 it earns. Now suppose that the amount it can keep is reduced from $1,000 to $600.

(*a*) Redraw Figure 37-5 to take this into account.

(*b*) What has happened to the incentive to work?

(*c*) What has happened to the implicit tax in this welfare proposal?

(*d*) Are your answers to (*b*) and (*c*) related in any way? If so, how?

(*e*) What has happened to the total amount of subsidy the government must pay? (Be careful.)

(*f*) Has this transfer bucket become more or less leaky?

(*g*) Now regraph this policy making one further change: Set the poverty level at $8,000, rather than $10,000. Again answer questions (*b*), (*c*), and (*e*). What are the pros and cons of the two policies you have graphed?

37-5. Suppose you are designing a negative income tax. Graph your answers to each of the following questions:

(*a*) What do you consider a reasonable minimum family income (*OC* in Figure 37-5)?

(*b*) What do you consider to be the maximum reasonable implicit tax rate? How does the slope of *CQ* in your diagram therefore compare with *CQ* in Figure 37-5?

(*c*) From your answers to (*a*) and (*b*), calculate the break-even level of income (like the $20,000 at *Q* in Figure 37-5).

(*d*) Do you think the tax on families to the right of the break-even point *Q* should be greater or smaller than the implicit tax on families to the left of *Q*?

(*e*) Explain the possible ''public finance problem'' in your scheme. In other words, do you think your scheme would make it difficult for the government to collect enough taxes from those to the right of *Q* to cover the costs of subsidizing those to the left of *Q*—and cover other government costs as well? As real incomes rise, would this public finance problem become more serious, or less? Would you agree with the view that we should institute a negative income tax some day, but there is a serious question of how soon we can afford it?

CHAPTER 38

MARXISM AND MARXIST ECONOMIES

The capitalist gets rich . . . at the same rate as he squeezes out the labor power of others, and then forces on the laborer abstinence from all life's enjoyments.

KARL MARX
Das Kapital

Historically, one of the major criticisms of the free enterprise system has been that it does not distribute income in an equitable way—largely because of the income payments that go to private owners of factories and other forms of physical capital (''capitalists''). Moreover, many critics believe that the economic and political power held by capitalists limits the government in its attempts to achieve a more equal and just society. The solution, according to some of these critics, is to replace our system with one that is fundamentally different—specifically, a system in which capital is owned by the state and used on behalf of all the people.

This chapter begins with a discussion of the ideas of Karl Marx, whose writings over a century ago have proved to be the most influential and durable criticisms ever leveled against the free enterprise system. This is followed by an examination of the socialist systems of the Soviet Union and Yugoslavia, two illustrations of the many alternative ways in which the philosophy of Karl Marx can be put into practice. Finally, we have a few brief observations about the Peoples' Republic of China.

KARL MARX

In proportion as capital accumulates, the lot of the laborer, be his payment high or low, must grow worse.

Karl Marx
Das Kapital

Today about one-third of the world lives under some form of Marxist-communist economic system. In addition, there are many followers of Marx who do not support any of the existing communist states, but who believe his ideas should be implemented in a different way. Clearly, this means that whether or not Marx was right, he was certainly one of the most influential writers in history.

Marx's criticism of the free market was based on two theories. While both were controversial, even in Marx's day, they were nonetheless accepted by many orthodox economists. These two theories were: (1) the labor theory of value and (2) the theory that wages tended toward a socially defined subsistence level. According to the labor theory of value, the value of any good is determined by the amount of labor that goes into producing it. (But be careful: As Marx recognized, this value must include both the labor time directly required to produce the good and the labor time spent on, or ''congealed in,'' the machinery used to produce the good.) Marx then asked: With labor being the source of all value, does it receive the total value of the nation's output in return for its effort? His answer was no: All that labor receives is a low wage representing only a fraction of what is produced. The rest is ***surplus value*** that goes to the employer or capitalist (the owner of the capital equipment which labor uses). Marx's conclusion: This surplus value should go to labor. Because it does not, the working class is exploited.

Surplus Value and the Class Struggle

According to Marx, the exploitation of the proletariat

(workers) by the bourgeoisie (capitalists) results in a ***class struggle.*** He urged workers to organize themselves to fight this struggle. In his words, "Let the ruling classes tremble at a Communist revolution. The proletarians have nothing to lose but their chains. They have a world to win. Working men of all countries, unite!"[1] In his view, the capitalist class would continue to accumulate more and more capital and use it to exploit labor more and more. Thus there would be "an accumulation of misery, corresponding to the accumulation of capital." Marx's cure was a revolution—which he viewed as inevitable[2]—in which the workers would seize power and abolish the ownership of capital by individuals: "By despotic inroads on the rights of property [workers would] centralize all instruments of production in the hands of the State." Finally, after this new ***socialist*** system has been firmly established, the state would wither away, leaving Marx's ideal ***communist*** society.

Socialism **is an economic system in which the "means of production" (capital equipment, buildings, and land) are owned by the state.[3]**

In Marxist countries like the Soviet Union, *communism* means an ideal system in which all means of production and other forms of property are no longer owned by individuals or the state, but instead are owned by the community as a whole; and all members of the community share in its work and income. The Soviet Union makes no claim to having achieved communism. Rather, it claims to be working "through socialism towards communism."

In the West, communism has a quite different meaning. It refers to the present economic and political system of countries like the Soviet Union.

How the Critic Has Been Criticized

Marx's critics have pointed out that a number of his predictions have proven false. For example, there is little evidence that any existing governments, such as that of the Soviet Union, are withering away, even though the Soviet state has existed for about 70 years. The idea that the state would "wither away" ranks as one of the most curious in the history of economic and political thought. One need not be as cynical as Lord Acton ("Power corrupts; absolute power corrupts absolutely") to doubt that those who have struggled for power will be prepared to give it up voluntarily.

Indeed, the most significant single weakness of Marxism, in the view of a number of its sympathetic critics, is that it provides enormous political power to individuals without providing adequate ways to control them—such as free elections in which the public can throw them out.[4] (Voting yes or no to a single slate of candidates is obviously not enough.) Thus Marxism provides inadequate restraints against the ruthless exercise of power by a ruler like Joseph Stalin. The majority of Marxists now view Stalin as an abberation that no better reflects true Marxism than the Holy Wars reflected Christianity. While there may be some truth in this defense, we should be careful with it. Specifically, it is inappropriate to argue, as Marxists sometimes do, that every Marxist failure like Joseph Stalin is not true Marx-

[1]The source of quotes in this paragraph is Karl Marx and Friedrich Engels, *Manifesto of the Communist Party* (Peking: Foreign Languages Press, 1975), pp. 59 and 77. Note that Marx went far beyond an analysis of economic forces to suggest what should be done to change them. In taking such a normative approach, Marx and the Marxists strongly dispute the view of some economists that a positive, "value free" economic analysis is possible.

[2]If this revolution is the inevitable result of a historical process governed by unchangeable economic laws—as Marx believed—what's the point of exhorting workers to struggle hard to achieve it? One possible answer: Even an inevitable event may be speeded up.

[3]"Socialism" has become an emotion-laden word that is now used loosely in a wide variety of meanings. To the campus radical, it is a tool for attacking the shortcomings of American society. To the American millionaire, it is a plot to deprive the wealthy of their hard-earned fortunes. To the Swedish politician, it means a mixed economic system, combining substantially free markets and a large degree of private ownership with a highly developed social welfare system. To Nobel prizewinner Friedrich Hayek, it represents a loss of freedom by the individual to the state and thus is a step along "the road to serfdom." To the British Fabian Socialist, it means the gradual evolution of a more humane economy, with a more equal distribution of income. With such diversity on the meaning of socialism, it is little wonder people have difficulty in debating its virtues and vices.

[4]See Robert Heilbroner, *Marxism For and Against* (New York: Norton, 1980).

ism, while every capitalist failure proves that this system is corrupt and headed for collapse.

The principal point remains: There were in fact no controls in the Soviet system to prevent Stalin from rising to the top and, worse yet, from staying there. Nor are there safeguards against the accumulation of power by more recent Soviet leaders. Thus, Marxism is paradoxical. While it promises greater political freedom, it has delivered less wherever it has been tried. Although a Marxist society is initially revolutionary, it may become very conservative, with aging leaders clinging to power and maintaining the status quo.

Another criticism of Marxism is that, as capital has accumulated, there has not been the accumulation of misery that Marx predicted. Quite the contrary: Misery has been reduced. And for good reason. Over the long run, the accumulation of capital has raised the demand for labor and thus has raised, rather than lowered, the wage rate. To cite an earlier example: Workers driving bulldozers are paid more than workers with shovels. While many Marxists concede that workers' income has indeed risen in *absolute* terms, they reinterpret Marx's prediction to mean that workers would become poorer, not in any absolute sense, but *relative* to other classes in society. Even this weaker claim is difficult to support with historical data.

Another way in which Marxists have reinterpretted Marx is to argue that although capitalists may have been unable to exploit labor in Europe and North America to the degree that Marx predicted, they have succeeded in exploiting labor in the less developed countries (LDCs), which have become today's economically subjugated proletariat. Sometimes, this argument is put very simply: "We are rich. They are poor. Therefore, we must have become rich by making them poor." This conclusion does not follow, because it is based on the "zero-sum" assumption—that the LDCs lose what we gain and vice versa. Our foreign investment in the LDCs can provide both a profit to investors and benefit to the LDCs, when foreign investors bid up wages and pay out part of their profits in taxes to LDC governments. Our trade with the LDCs isn't a zero-sum game either. As we saw in our earlier discussion of comparative advantage, both parties typically gain from trade.

We conclude that, short of a major reinterpretation of what Marx said, his prediction that workers would become poorer has proven false. Nonetheless, it is true that workers are paid less than what the nation produces. We have referred to the gap between the two as payments to other factors of production. Marx called it surplus value. In particular, he focused his attack on the payments going to owners of capital. Was he justified in dismissing these payments as simply the exploitation of labor?

How Are Capital Costs to Be Covered?

Here we must be careful. Part of the cost of capital is the payment for the labor time spent on producing machinery. As Marx recognized, this is an appropriate payment to labor; therefore, it is not surplus value. However, Marx did regard as surplus value the interest and profit paid to those who provide the funds to finance investment.

The Marxist contention is that it is precisely these interest and profit payments that make our system inequitable. Moreover, Marxists maintain, it is possible to set up a system in which investment occurs even though there is no interest rate to act as an incentive to get the public to provide the necessary funds. The way to ensure that investment takes place is for the state to impose taxes high enough not only to cover current government expenditures, but also to provide the funds for investment. Under such a system, the ownership of capital is held by the state on behalf of the people, rather than by capitalists.

While communism may achieve Marx's objective of ending income payments to capitalists, it raises several new problems. First, raising investment funds by such a system of involuntary saving—that is, by taxes—may "hurt" more than our system of voluntary saving. Under our system, people can save when it is most convenient, and need not save when it is difficult to do so. Under a Marxist system, they are forced to save throughout their taxpaying lives. Taxes must be paid, no matter how much they hurt.

Second, can investment decisions made by government officials in a communist state be as flexible and innovative as decisions made by the owners of capital in a free enterprise system?

Investment Decisions

To invest wisely, two questions must be answered: (1) Should existing types of plant and equipment be expanded? (2) What *new* products and processes should be developed? There is less incentive for the second question to be asked in the Soviet Union than in a free enterprise economy. Whenever you compare the two systems in the future, ask yourself: Which innovations from free enterprise economies are the Soviets using? Which of their innovations are we using?

Consider the practical problems communist countries encounter in allocating investment funds across the economy, as they do when drawing up a 5-year plan. To illustrate, first consider what happens in our economy if there is a major new discovery of, say, oil in Alaska. To finance its development, the oil companies increase their borrowing (or issue new stock) and the interest rate rises slightly. In response to this, marginal investments elsewhere in the nation are cut back. Thus, funds for this development are raised from all over the country, as a result of a large number of individuals and firms reacting to a rise in the market interest rate. In comparison, what occurs in a communist country that, 6 months ago, set its 5-year investment targets for each sector? Do the planners sit down and go through the planning process all over again? For a big enough discovery, they might. However, for less significant events—such as a modest discovery of copper ore in Montana—they can't be continuously rewriting the plan. The plan tends to get "locked in." New opportunities are not incorporated into the plan until the next time it is recalculated. Thus adjustment to unexpected changes is much more difficult in a planned economy than in a free enterprise economy, in which markets are responding continuously to changes that occur.

Any society must have some mechanism to determine which investments are undertaken and which are not. In our economy, the interest rate and expected profits are the mechanism. They are used to direct funds toward the high-return investments, not to the low-return ones. While this system is far from perfect, it does provide a framework within which to make choices. Recognizing this, central planners now quietly make their interestlike calculations after all. (Nevertheless, major blunders are still made. A contributing factor in Poland's economic difficulties was the construction of a \$5 million steel mill in a location that was poor from an economic point of view, but was the home town of the Communist party secretary. True, politicians anywhere may thus "feather their own nest"; however, this problem is potentially more serious in a Marxist economy, where most capital is owned by the state and controlled by government officials.)

The Role of Profit

Recall that normal profit is a return to a firm's capital equal to the return that could be earned elsewhere. Above-normal profit is any additional return beyond this; in a free enterprise economy, it goes to those who take risks—in particular, to entrepreneurs. Is this justified? To throw light on this issue, consider two kinds of above-normal profit—monopoly profit and profit from a successful innovation.

Above-normal monopoly profit Many non-Marxist economists would agree that monopoly profit should be reduced or eliminated by "trustbusting" or regulation. However, Marxists charge that we are naive if we believe that we can effectively deal with monopoly in our present economic and political system. The reason, Marxists argue, is that in our system, monopolists can translate their economic power (money) into political power (votes) via campaign contributions. This power then allows them to thwart antimonopoly action. In short, our elected officials are too often committed to the interests of the rich and powerful rather than to the interests of the public. Thus, Marxists contend, the only effective way to deal with this problem is to change the system, and to prevent the accumulation of wealth that makes such political corruption possible.

There is, of course, an element of truth in this criticism—more, perhaps, than we like to admit.[5] But the question is one of alternatives. If a system is to be set up

[5]For a thoughtful, non-Marxist view of this problem, see the brief book by Elizabeth Drew, *Politics and Money: The New Road to Corruption* (New York: Macmillan, 1983).

based on the "public interest," how is that elusive concept to be defined? What better way is there to determine it than by elections? If there are no elections, and one party has the monopoly of power, what protection is there against the abuse of that power? It is scarcely satisfactory to say that elections between two or more contending parties are unnecessary in the Soviet Union because the Communist party represents the interests of the workers. (This belief is one reason why communist governments strongly resist the development of independent sources of power, such as the Solidarity union in Poland. An independent union implies that the Communist party does not invariably represent the interests of the working people.) In Western countries, the prevailing practice is to let voters decide between two or more competing political parties.

Above-normal profit from innovation In our system, there are various kinds of innovation that may allow a firm to earn an above-normal profit. For example, a firm may develop a new product that better satisfies consumers. True, in the long run, such above-normal profit may disappear as competing firms follow suit. Nonetheless, this profit still provides the incentive for businesses to innovate and respond to changing consumer tastes. In short, the opportunity for profit is what makes our system go; it determines what will be produced and how. We tax away part of profits, but not all; some incentive to innovate must be left. However, many Marxists take the view that although this profit system may have worked well enough in our early stages of development,[6] it is no longer satisfactory. The whole incentive system should be changed and the economy directed in some other way. Precisely how, of course, is the big question.

This question is not answered by Marx's recommendation: "From each according to his ability; to each according to his need." This sounds fine in theory, but in practice it is a totally impractical guideline. If individuals define their own needs, the sum will always outrun a nation's ability to produce. Alternatively, if needs are defined by someone else, two questions remain. Who is to decide? and How does that person decide who needs what? (For a socialist country in the transition stage to communism, this guideline has been modified to: "From each according to his ability; to each according to his *work*." This is the policy in the Soviet Union.)

THE COMMAND ECONOMY OF THE SOVIET UNION

The Soviet Union is a riddle wrapped up in a mystery inside an enigma.

Winston Churchill

The first country to attempt to put Marx's philosophy into practice was the Soviet Union, and for almost 30 years it was the only communist nation of any significance.

In 1917, the repressive and decaying czarist regime in Russia was overthrown by a moderate group led by Kerensky. In turn, Kerensky was overthrown by a small, militant group led by Lenin, a Marxist revolutionary. Lenin's control was consolidated when the Red Army defeated the White Russians in a bitter civil war and turned back an invasion by Western countries. It was only then that Lenin and the other communist leaders could turn their attention fully to the design of a new kind of economy.

As it has developed, that economy has differed from ours in two major respects: (1) Productive assets are predominantly owned by the state rather than by individuals, and (2) many production decisions are made on the command of a central authority. Our discussion of each of these is summarized for easy reference in Table 38-1.

Public vs. Private Ownership

In the United States, the basic pattern is private ownership—with some exceptions, such as school buildings and public works like the Tennessee Valley Authority. In the Soviet Union, in contrast, the basic pattern is public ownership, with some exceptions. For example, some retail and wholesale businesses are privately owned. In addition, over one-third of the houses in cities and virtually all houses on farms are privately owned. Moreover, private ownership in agriculture extends beyond housing. For example, each family working on a collective

[6]In the Communist Manifesto, Marx and Engels expressed great admiration for the growth generated by capitalism, which in the preceeding 100 years "created more massive and colossal productive forces than have all preceding generations together."

farm can use a small plot of land and the livestock and equipment to go with it. Finally, of course, personal assets like clothing and household tools are privately owned.

Otherwise, assets in the Soviet Union are predominantly owned by the state. These assets include the "means of production" that, in Marx's view, were used to exploit labor, such as factories, industrial machinery, transport and banking facilities, and natural resources.

Central Planning in the Soviet Economy

The second big difference in the two systems is that the important decisions on what will be produced in the Soviet Union are made "by command," by a central state planning agency—GOSPLAN. ("Gos" is the abbreviation for the Russian word for "state.") In comparison, in our economy most such decisions are made by individual producers responding to a profit incentive. (But not all: A number of our production decisions, such as the number of new schools or military aircraft, are made by federal, state, or local governments.)

In a complex planning process, the Soviet government decides on a 5-year plan which establishes the desired rate of growth, including the necessary investment for that growth. Within this broad framework, a more detailed plan is drawn up for each year, specifying output targets throughout the economy. The targets are not chosen in a completely arbitrary way by government planners. Instead, they are the result of an elaborate set of consultations, in which each firm and industry suggests amendments to its targets. Nonetheless, the targets are eventually set by the planners, and each plant manager is given a specific quota to fulfill. The manager faces an array of incentives (bonuses, promotions, etc.) to reach or exceed the quota. Profits do exist in the Soviet Union, and can be calculated just as in our economy. However, profits do not provide the same sort of incentive as in our system because most go to the state. Moreover, profits are calculated from output and input prices that are set by planners and are not very closely related to demand and supply conditions. *Since profits do not provide the same information, nor the same incentive to produce as in our system, they do not play the same key role in allocating resources.* To illustrate: The central planners may decide to contract an activity that is profitable in order to expand one that is unprofitable—a pattern exactly the opposite of what normally happens in our system. Thus the plant manager tends to be a hired official carrying out a directive of what to produce, rather than an entrepreneur making decisions about what output will be.

The surprising thing about such a highly complicated planning system is not that it sometimes works badly but that it works at all. Consider the problem that arises if the planners increase the target for steel to be used in building bridges. Because steel production requires machinery, the machinery target must also be increased. But machinery production requires steel, so the steel target must be increased again. In turn, this results in a second-round increase in the machinery target, and so on, and on. Because steel is an input for machinery production and machinery is an input for steel produc-

TABLE 38-1
How the Soviet System of Public Ownership and Central Planning Differs from Our System

Basic issues	Soviet system	Modified free enterprise
1. Is ownership of productive assets held by the state or by private individuals?	State ownership—with some exceptions; for example, in parts of agriculture and retail trade	Private ownership—with exceptions like the post office, some utilities, and some transport systems
2. How are prices and outputs determined?	Largely by central planning agency	Largely in individual markets, in response to profit motive
3. How much freedom of choice do consumers have?	In theory, free choice in spending income; but in practice, items of desired style, size, etc., may be difficult to obtain	Essentially free choice in spending income, with producers more responsive to a wide variety of tastes

tion, one target cannot be set without regard to the other. Moreover, this interdependency illustrates only the simplest possible "loop" in the economic system. In reality, a complex economy like that of the Soviet Union is characterized by a myriad set of much more complicated loops, with the output of one industry being used directly or indirectly as an input of almost all the others. Thus, a target cannot be set in isolation.

It is sometimes assumed that if there are economic problems, they can be solved by planning. Some may be solved, but others cannot. In particular, central planning tends to be inflexible, slowing the response of the economy to changing conditions (the weather, changes in the availability of raw materials, etc.). Moreover, the act of planning introduces a number of problems of its own. In theory, it should be possible to "get the plan right"—that is, to come up with a consistent set of outputs. However, there are millions of items produced in the Soviet Union. Such an economy is too complex and unpredictable to be adequately managed by any plan, and bottlenecks frequently occur. What happens if the production of steel is inadequate to meet the needs of the machinery industry and other steel-using industries? What can be done by a plant manager desperate to acquire steel? The answer often is: Dispatch a *tolkach* (fixer), cognac and rubles in hand, to acquire steel with the appropriate bribe. While bribery occurs in any economy, the difference is that this, and other similar forms of "fixing," are often quietly condoned in the Soviet Union because of the role they play in making the Soviet economy operate. Without such emergency measures, quotas would be even more difficult to achieve. Thus in the Soviet Union, a market economy has been replaced by a central-command quota system *and* a "second economy" that fills the inevitable cracks in the quota system. Black markets also exist in goods stolen from the state. In such a system, there is no clear line between what is silently tolerated and what is punished. An executive of GUM (a large department store in Moscow) was unable to make this distinction and was executed for "excessive" operations in the second economy.

A second way in which bottleneck problems are reduced—but not eliminated—is for Soviet planners, faced with a shortage, to simply let consumers do without. If steel is in short supply, use it to produce industrial machinery rather than home refrigerators. With this set of priorities, it is no surprise that Soviet performance in heavy industry is better than in consumer goods and housing.

Growth in the Soviet Economy

The example just given is but one reflection of the Soviet emphasis on industrial growth at the expense of the consumer. In addition, planners aim for a high growth rate by diverting a large proportion of production away from consumption and into investment. Since investment has typically accounted for about 30% of GNP in the Soviet Union—a percentage almost twice as high as in the United States—it is no surprise that, until recently, the Soviet growth rate often exceeded the U.S. rate. If the Soviets had been able to continue their 6% to 10% real growth rates of the 1960s, they would have eventually overtaken the United States. However, the higher Soviet growth rate in the past must be interpreted with care. It did not necessarily mean that the communist system was a relatively efficient way of generating growth. Instead it reflected the fact that a very large share of Soviet GNP was being directed toward investment. The Soviet experience might be compared with that of Japan, a noncommunist market economy that has been also investing about 30% of its GNP. Japanese growth has far exceeded that of the Soviet Union.

Despite the continued heavy diversion of Soviet income from consumption into investment, the growth rate in the Soviet Union has recently become very disappointing.[7] In spite of its substantial insulation from the world economy, the Soviet Union has followed a pattern similar to that of most other countries, growing much more slowly since 1973 than before; indeed, by the end of the 1970s, Soviet growth had fallen close to zero.

Soviet planners have two principal ways to divert production away from consumption. First is the planning process, which gives priority to investment rather than consumption, and often results in shortages of consumer goods. Second is a tax on consumer goods that accounts, on average, for about one-third of their price.

[7]For detail on this and some of the other issues discussed in this chapter, see E. A. Hewett "Economic Reform in the Soviet Union," *The Brookings Review*, Spring 1984.

This tax helps to finance investment and takes income out of the hands of consumers, thus reducing their purchasing power. Consequently, shortages of consumer goods are reduced, although not avoided.

The Position of the Soviet Consumer

Consumers tend to be the forgotten people in the Soviet system—although their lot has been gradually improving. We have already seen how they are forced—via heavy taxation—to sacrifice current consumption to finance the investment the government undertakes, and how they are also forced to shoulder a special burden when bottlenecks develop. In addition, there is another cost in the Soviet command economy that consumers have to bear. To understand it, consider again the Soviet plant manager whose major concern is to produce a given quota of, say, nails. If planners have set the quota in terms of kilograms, the manager can most easily satisfy it by producing a relatively small number of large nails. (Visitors often wonder why so many things seem "heavy" in the Soviet Union. The reason is than many quotas are expressed in kilograms. Thus an easy way to achieve a quota is to build weight into the product. It is no suprise that the Soviet Union is the world's largest producer of steel.)

On the other hand, suppose that the quota of nails is defined as a certain *number*. In this case, the manager will produce mostly small ones. Again, the resulting nail production will not satisfy the consumer, who wants a selection of various kinds. Of course, the consumer may be able to make a wrong-sized nail do in a pinch. But what does a person with big feet do if shoe producers meet their quota by concentrating on small sizes? The poor quality of goods and other problems facing the consumer (Box 38-1) remain one of the major weaknesses of the Soviet system. The problem can be stated very simply: The consumer is not king; the "customer" that producers are most concerned about is the central authority to which they must report.

Recently, Soviet leaders have, with mixed success, been trying to pay more attention to consumers. For example, auto production has been raised substantially in cooperation with the Italian automaker Fiat. The result is the rugged but technologically backward Lada, which is sold on world markets at bargain prices but is very expensive for Soviet purchasers.

How Much Can the Soviet Consumer Buy?

In 1982, feeding a family required more than twice as many hours of work in Moscow as in Paris or Washington. The purchase of a color TV required over 700 hours of labor time in Moscow compared with 106 in Paris or 65 in Washington; and for a small car, 53 months of work was required in Moscow versus 8 months in Paris or 5 in Washington.

However, the lot of Soviet citizens is not as bad as this sounds, because government subsidies provide Soviet citizens with bargain housing and free medical care. While this reduces the gap in living standards, it would be even more significant if Soviet citizens were able to acquire more of these services. Unfortunately, because of a housing scarcity, the average Soviet urban dweller doesn't get much housing—only about one-third the average for an American family or one-half the average in Western Europe.

The Interplay of Economic and Political Systems

The Soviet system of rule by a single party is quite consistent with Marx's prediction that the overthrow of the capitalist system would be followed by a "dictatorship of the proletariat." One of the interesting questions is whether a centrally planned economy like the Soviet system would work at all with the degree of political freedom that we enjoy. The more economic commands are issued by a central authority, the more dictatorial a system generally becomes.

This is an important issue, because a major Soviet criticism of our system—one that contains an element of truth—is that economic power corrupts political institutions. But if the Soviets' alternative economic system leads to an even worse form of government, what sort of cure is that?

Better Macroeconomic Balance?

The Soviets seem to be able to do a better job of curing unemployment than we do, since they can set their target outputs at a level to closely approximate full employment. However, while they face less overt unemployment, they have a greater problem with "disguised" unemployment—that is, workers on the job who seem to be producing something, but who are in fact contributing little or nothing to the national product. An example is the labor used to produce undersize shoes that never get worn. While this may appear to be productive employment, it is, in fact, wasted effort. An oft-cited failure of the U.S. economy was Ford's decision in the 1950s to introduce the Edsel, an automobile that sold very poorly. Its failure represented a loss not only to Ford but to the nation as a whole in terms of the resources wasted in the development of this car. In the Soviet Union, such a failure would not have occurred. Instead, the public would have bought the Edsel. It might not have been quite what people wanted, but they would not have had much choice. In the United States, an incorrect decision results in a loss to producers and short-run unemployment in an industry; both of these can be identified and evaluated. On the other hand, a similarly erroneous decision in the Soviet Union results in a loss to consumers that may not be so obvious and so easy to measure, but may be just as real. This suggests another question to keep in mind when comparing the Soviet and American systems: Do Edsel-type goods that the public does not like still exist in the Soviet Union, or are they disappearing?

Which is the worse problem—the Soviets' disguised unemployment or our overt unemployment? Our problem may be less damaging in the long run, because it is

BOX 38-1

A SHOPPER'S GUIDE TO THE SOVIET UNION[†]

Shopping in the Soviet Union is often a lottery. The stores seem well stocked, but typically with inferior or out-of-fashion items that nobody wants. When attractive goods arrive they are quickly snapped up. Long lines immediately form as passersby queue up, sometimes without even asking what's on sale. (They find that out later; sometimes nobody in the last 20 or 30 yards of a lineup will yet know.) When you get to the head of the line, chances are you may have to deal with rude salesclerks who know that you will buy anyway, and who may be getting even for the frustrations they face in doing their own shopping. But all this you disregard in order to buy for yourself, your friends, your parents, and your cousins.

Buying this way involves a lot of luck and a lot of good management. Shoppers know by heart the sizes and color preferences of relatives and friends; they carry a lot of cash, because credit cards and checks aren't used and one never knows where lightning will strike next. To be ready, women carry a bag called an *avoska,* which is derived from the Russia word for "maybe." Soviet citizens have lined up through a freezing December night just to get on an 18-month-

long waiting list to buy a car, and viewed themselves as lucky when they succeeded. Thus the efficiency loss in this centrally planned system includes not only the loss because consumers often get inferior products; it also includes the loss because consumers waste time in queues. The Soviet press estimates that the public spends 30 billion hours in line per year—a waste equal to having 15 million unemployed.

[†]This box draws heavily on Hedrick Smith, *The Russians,* chap. II (New York: Quadrangle-New York Times Book Co., 1976). The situation for shoppers remains much the same a decade later.

obvious to all. Therefore a government is brought under pressure to reduce it. (There may be no similarly strong pressure in the Soviet Union to reduce disguised unemployment, precisely because it *is* disguised and therefore may go unrecognized.) A second consideration is that a system with overt unemployment allows rapid growth following a recession as the unemployed are put back to work. When growth slows in the Soviet Union—as it has in recent years—there is no pool of unemployed labor to fuel a rapid recovery; everyone already has a job.

However in some respects, the Soviet problem of disguised unemployment may be less damaging than ours: The individuals involved are at least working and hence *feel* productive, even though they are not. Therefore, its psychological and social effects are less serious. One might also argue that disguised unemployment is more equitable than overt unemployment, because the winners are those who get a job who are able to earn an income to support their families; in other words, the winners are those who would otherwise be jobless and at the low end of the economic ladder. The losers are those at all levels on the ladder—the poor and rich alike who get inferior products.

In the Soviet Union, the balance between aggregate demand and aggregate supply has been substantially different from that in the United States and other market economies. In the United States, demand has at times fallen, resulting in recessions, high unemployment, and a low rate of capital utilization. At other times, aggregate demand has risen rapidly, putting pressure on productive capacity and causing inflation. In the Soviet Union, demand has consistently been high compared to productive capacity. This is one reason for the low Soviet rate of unemployment. Inflation has been suppressed—though not completely—with price controls, and the resulting shortages mean that many consumer goods are hard to find. Even though capital-goods industries have been favored in the planning process, shortages have also occurred there. The result has been a stretch-out of investment projects—projects planned for 3 or 4 years often take 10 years or longer. The resulting inefficiencies provide one reason for the disappointing payoff from the large volume of capital formation. In the smaller, more open economies of Eastern Europe, the macroeconomic imbalances have also been reflected in stretch-outs of investment projects and shortages of consumer goods. Since such shortages create pressures to buy abroad, these countries have often had rising imports that have led to balance-of-payments crises.

Is there Equality of Income in the Soviet Union?

The answer is no. The Soviets have allowed large differences in income to creep back into their system, as they have tried to increase production by providing incentives. Thus scientists receive a much higher income than clerks, and skilled workers earn much more than unskilled workers. As a result, human capital is becoming a significant source of income difference in the Soviet Union, as well as in the United States. (Recall Jacob Mincer's evidence, that about 60% of American income differences are due to human capital.) Because of this growing importance of *human capital,* a socialist policy that deals only with *physical capital* (by putting it in the hands of the state) can, at best, provide no more than a partial solution to the problem of serious income inequality. This raises the question: Will the appeal of socialism to those who believe in equalizing incomes become less strong than in Marx's day?

Concluding Observations on the Soviet System

The ability of Soviet leaders to impose high taxes has provided substantial resources for investment, and for many years there was rapid growth in Soviet heavy industry. However, this growth has become particularly disappointing in the last decade. Moreover, the Soviet system has performed poorly in the many areas where decentralized decision making is the key to success. Nowhere is this more true than in agriculture, into which the Soviets pour more than 25% of their investment—about five times as large a percentage as in the United States. Yet despite this, Soviet agricultural productivity remains low. The principal problem is the organization of labor into collective farms where individuals have little incentive to work or innovate. (As much as a quarter to a third of the nation's total agricultural output is produced on the miniscule 2% of the Soviet farmland that is privately owned, where individuals are rewarded for hard work and initiative.) Soviet leaders have often attributed poor harvests to the weather, but grain was exported from these same lands before the First World War, and the weather doesn't raise the same problems on adjacent privately owned plots of land. Some critics quip that, since 1917, the Soviet Union has announced a poor harvest due to bad weather 68 times.

The same sort of problems have dogged the Soviets' efforts over the last 50 years to close the technology gap. True, they have performed impressively in some ways. As early as 1957 they were graduating 80,000 engineers compared with 29,000 in the United States. Now they are world leaders in a number of fields, from theoretical mathematics to applied areas such as oceanography and polar research. Moreover, Soviet scientists developed the most promising line of research for the harnessing of power from nuclear fusion. However, they have not been successful in getting innovation across the board in a society that rewards caution and conformity rather than risk taking. An important area in which Soviet technology has lagged is computers. Despite the Soviets' theoretical contributions to computer development and their ability to produce the large scale computers necessary to put astronauts into space, they are concerned that they may have missed out on some of the early stages of the small computer revolution. One of the first policy changes of Soviet leader Mikhail Gorbachev in 1985 was to introduce a crash program to get high school students familiar with computers.

It is not only the political leaders, concerned with maintaining power, who become devoted to the status quo. Plant managers do also, and resist experimenting with promising but risky new techniques because this may make it difficult for them to meet their quotas. Indeed, they may even resist *proven* risk-free innovations or style changes because introducing them will temporarily reduce their production and make their quotas more difficult to achieve. Moreover, Soviet managers lack an incentive to reduce costs by economizing in the use of inputs. Consequently, for example, the Soviet Union uses 35% more energy per unit of output than does the United States, and 150% more than Western Europe. This profligate use is a cause—along with central planning—of the serious shortages of inputs.

One of the most critical problems in the Soviet economy is the limited incentive to work. The scarcity of consumer goods means that additional pay may not provide a strong incentive—as illustrated by the Soviet joke: "They pretend to pay us, and we pretend to work." Alcoholism and absenteeism are serious problems. A cartoon shows two workers embracing in a factory, with the caption "Old friends meet. They haven't seen each other for two months; one or the other has been absent every day." This lack of incentives seems strange, since the authorities have introduced a number of incentives for individual workers that appear to be similar to—and sometimes even seem to exceed—those available to American workers. Not only are Russian workers paid higher wages in some occupations than in others; in addition, high piecework rates (that is, payments according to the number of units produced) are more common as an incentive in the Soviet Union than in the United States. Often the most productive workers are granted tangible rewards, such as free government-financed holidays. Finally, there are other incentives which may seem odd to us but appear to have a certain appeal in the Soviet Union. For example, highly productive workers are decorated and cited as "Heroes of Socialist Labor."

Why then have Soviet workers not responded? Why has their productivity been disappointing? One possible reason is that wages are paid whether or not a factory meets its quota, and in the Soviet system there is no risk that a factory will go bankrupt. Another is that, after so many years of being told to reduce consumption today in order to enjoy a higher standard of living in the future, Soviet citizens have become cynical. While their paychecks are guaranteed, the goods they can buy continue to be disappointing.

In the Soviet system, problems of quality, preoccupation with quotas, and the heavy diversion of resources by the state from consumption into investment all mean that the consumer has been short-changed. This is one of the reasons why the Soviets have not, after all, achieved their objective of income equality. The elite not only receive a higher income; they also get to spend it on Black Sea resorts and in special stores which stock highly desirable items such as the French perfume and Yugoslavian toothpaste that are not available to the general public. The Soviets, like us, do not have complete equality. Their reply is that they are far closer to it than we are, because huge accumulations of wealth cannot be passed on from generation to generation. But there is an increasingly important kind of wealth that *can* be passed on: human capital. By arranging the best education and careers for their children, the Soviet elite pass on their privileged status.

However, as already noted, many Marxists in the West would argue that the Soviet Union is an example of communism gone wrong, not of any fundamental weaknesses in communism itself. The degree to which you accept this claim is a matter of judgment, on which you will have to decide for yourself. But before doing so, it is enlightening to consider the case of Yugoslavia, a communist country in which there is less accumulation of power by the central authority.

THE SOCIALIST MARKET ECONOMY OF YUGOSLAVIA

By the end of the Second World War, Soviet armies had swept the Germans out of the countries of Eastern Europe, imposing communist political and economic systems in their wake. Since that time, the history of these countries has been marked by a long and sometimes unrewarding struggle for political and economic reform. The story of Yugoslavia is somewhat different. That country was liberated from the Germans, not by the Soviet army, but instead by a Yugoslavian guerrilla movement. The civil war that followed was won by Marshall Tito, a communist who nonetheless was sufficiently independent to break politically with Moscow in 1948. He was then able to introduce his own kind of communism, which can best be described as ***market socialism.*** As in the Soviet Union or any other Marxist country, most capital is owned by the government. But Yugoslavia has a less centralized economy than the Soviet Union. The decision on what will be produced depends more heavily on market signals from consumers than on decisions by central planners.

Market socialism **is an economic system which is based on the socialist idea of government ownership of the "means of production" (capital equipment, buildings, and land). At the same time, most of the decisions on what will be produced are made by the market—that is, by the interaction of consumers and producers, rather than by central planners.**

Before we consider how the Yugoslavs have introduced a greater reliance on the market, it is important to keep their economy in perspective by noting the respects in which their government still does exercise a high degree of control. First, although many prices vary as a result of market pressures, they typically do so only within specified limits. Moreover, in some sectors, prices are controlled by the government. Second, the government follows a high-growth policy. As in the Soviet Union, about one-third of GNP is directed into investment. Third, the government determines which sectors will grow more rapidly than others by allocating investment funds to each. However, within each sector there is, typically, considerable competition among enterprises for available funds. Finally, the Yugoslavs, like the Soviets, draw up a 5-year plan. However, the Yugoslav plan is less in the Soviet style of setting target outputs in each sector than in the French style of simply indicating what output levels are likely to be. Thus, a steel firm can see the expected level of output in industries that use steel, such as machinery and home appliances. It can then use this information in making its own decision on how much steel to produce.

The Greater Degree of Market Freedom in Yugoslavia

In Yugoslavia, a firm may be owned by the state, but it is operated by its workers, who elect a manager to make day-to-day decisions. The manager acquires labor and other factors of production and sells the firm's output in more-or-less free markets, with the objective being to earn profits, which in turn are shared with the workers. The enterprise may succeed or it may not, depending on its ability to earn profits by responding to changes in consumer tastes and other market pressures. Moreover, within limits, the firm can change its prices.

Because production decisions are influenced by the profit motive and are sensitive to consumer wants, the Yugoslav system achieves some of the efficiencies of ours. But (no surprise) it consequently also encounters some of our problems. First, managers who are in a monopoly position soon discover that they can exploit this position. They can increase their workers' profits by restricting supply and raising price.[8] Thus the efficiency losses of monopoly may arise in such an economy, just as they do in ours.

Second, workers' income depends on earnings from the enterprise rather than on just a formal wage. Since some enterprises are more successful financially than others, some workers have higher incomes. Thus, workers' ownership introduces incentives for labor to work harder (thereby increasing efficiency), but it also results in an uneven distribution of income that many socialists view as inequitable. Even in this socialist state, *there is still a conflict between the objectives of efficiency and equity*.

Third, compared with the Soviets, the Yugoslavs face a greater problem of overt unemployment[9]—though a smaller problem of disguised unemployment. The reason is that, in Yugoslavia, profits determine whether an enterprise will prosper or not, and if it does, it may expand. Hence, regions that have profitable enterprises may have no problem in absorbing a growing labor force and thus maintaining full employment. However, regions with unprofitable firms that do not grow may face an unemployment problem. There is no Soviet-type command for production to expand in these areas.

[8]At first, socialist theoreticians were optimistic that the monopoly problem could be solved by setting up a system in which planners would announce prices. This would force producers into the role of price takers. As a consequence, they would produce to the point where their marginal cost would be equal to price. At the same time, consumers would also take market price as given, and would consume to the point where their marginal benefit would be equal to price.

How would a planner decide on the price to announce? If the price that had been previously announced did not equate producers' supply and consumers' demand, the planner would change it until it did. With producers and consumers all acting as price takers, wouldn't such a socialist system provide the efficiency of perfect competition—even better than our imperfectly competitive free enterprise system? The answer is: Not necessarily. The profit-seeking manager with monopoly power would still be able to exercise it. As the only producer, the manager could just reduce the quantity supplied. The planner would then observe that supply was falling short of demand, and would raise price to the monopoly level the producer was seeking. In other words, a monopolist who figures out how the system works may not take price as given, even if it is announced by a central planner.

[9]See A. Sapir, "Economic Growth and Factor Substitution: What Happened to the Yugoslav Miracle?" *Economic Journal*, June 1980, p. 305.

Special Problems

In Yugoslavia, there is still a relatively healthy, small-scale, privately owned sector where new firms are set up by individuals, just as in our system. However, if we concentrate on the rest of the economy where capital is publicly owned, an important question for this or any other socialist economy is: Who sets up new enterprises? In Yugoslavia, existing firms develop new product lines and open up new branches. But how are *new* firms established?

This is a major issue because the entry—or even just the threat of entry—of new firms into an industry may reduce or prevent monopoly abuse, thus increasing the efficiency of the economy. Moreover, new firms may mean an even greater variety of new products to satisfy consumer demand more effectively, as well as new jobs in regions of severe unemployment. New firms in our system are formed by entrepreneurs who know they will own them and expect to earn profits from them. But where private ownership is not allowed, what then? In Yugoslavia, new firms may be set up by a local community using government-supplied funds. But the problem is that the initiator loses control of the enterprise as soon as it is established and passes into the hands of its workers—so the incentive to exercise such an initiative is reduced.

CHINA: ANOTHER SOCIALIST EXPERIMENT

While the Soviet Union is the oldest of the communist governments, the Communist party of China rules by far the largest population. For the first three decades after the 1949 victory of the Communist party in the Civil War, China's economy was dominated by central planning, somewhat similar to that in the Soviet Union. Under Mao, China embarked on several nationwide campaigns—the "Great Leap Forward" of the late 1950s, aimed at spreading small-scale industrial production, and the "Cultural Revolution," aimed at ensuring ideological purity. Since Mao's death, there has been less emphasis on rigid ideological conformity. By 1984, the official People's Daily newspaper went so far as to suggest that Marxism might be out of date, and could not be relied upon to solve all of China's problems.

A major reason for this change in view was the favorable experience in agriculture, which was reformed in 1979. An incentive system was established that allowed peasants, once they had turned over a relatively modest quota of their crops to the government, to sell the rest on the open market. According to some estimates, Chinese grain output almost doubled between 1979 and 1985, and the Chinese were encouraged to reform other sectors of the economy. Private enterpreneurs are no longer considered enemies of the people. Private enterprise has been encouraged in some areas, and foreign investment welcomed, as China has taken major steps toward a market-oriented economy.

Moreover, the Chinese have been also moving away from the earlier Soviet-style emphasis on reduced consumption to finance investment and growth. By 1984, investment had fallen from a high of over one-third of national product to just over one-quarter.

The incentive systems that have been so successful in agriculture have been introduced in industry as well. State-owned enterprises have been encouraged to aim their efforts at increasing efficiency and better satisfying consumer wants. These enterprises have been made responsible for their profits or losses. Many of the enterprises incurring losses have been informed that their government subsidies will eventually be ended. Nowhere has reform gone further than in the area that borders Hong Kong.

By 1985, there was some indication that the Chinese authorities were becoming concerned that the market reforms were moving too fast and that they might lose control. There was a report that there had been a crackdown; for example, the President of the Bank of China was reported to have been fired because he had violated discipline by giving himself and other bank officials excessive pay increases. The question was: Would the apparently successful move by the Chinese toward a market economy be allowed to continue? And if so, what sort of pressure for reform would this put on the Soviet Union, with its highly centralized system that lacks innovation and initiative?

CONCLUSIONS

In previous chapters we saw how, in our system, redistributing income via government transfer payments reduces incentives—in particular, the incentive to work of those receiving the payments. In this chapter we have seen how incentives are also reduced in a socialist system where income is redistributed by the more drastic measure of giving the ownership of capital to the state. Most notably, a socialist system such as the Soviet Union reduces the incentives to initiate and innovate. Thus, there is no system that works ideally, solving all problems at once.

Judgment on which economic system is better depends not on what it promises but on what it delivers. *In practice,* which system does a better job of solving the basic economic problem of transforming resources into the satisfaction of human wants? As you evaluate this issue for yourself in the future, remember that the standard criticism of socialism is that it does not do a particularly good job of satisfying these wants. Also remember the basic criticism of free enterprise: It does a far better job of satisfying the wants of the rich than of the poor.

Another criticism of free enterprise is that large corporations often exercise too much economic and political power—power that should be exercised by the government on behalf of the people. However, if communism cures this problem by transferring a great deal of economic power (including the ownership of capital) to the government, does too much power then fall into the hands of the state? Lane Kirkland, president of the AFL-CIO, has expressed American labor's reservations about dealing with a powerful state:

> We on the whole prefer to negotiate with private companies that have roughly equivalent bargaining power than with [government] corporations that control the courts, the police, the army, the navy, and the hydrogen bomb.

The problem of dealing with a powerful communist state has been faced recently by Polish workers when they formed a union. They discovered that a state that had always paid lip-service to the interests of the workers could still strongly resist any attempt by workers to set up their own organization.

Finally, we must distinguish between the physical capital that a socialist state brings under government ownership and control, and the human capital that cannot be dealt with in this way: the skills, experience, and expertise we carry around in our heads. Labor is no longer as unskilled as when Marx wrote over 100 years ago; workers now have widely differing skills. Consequently, our nation's capital today is in the hands not only of those who own physical plant and machinery, but also of those who own human capital. These people range all the way from semiskilled workers to managers and professionals. As a result, it is now much more difficult to argue that our society is simply divided into two groups: those who exploit (the capitalists) and those who are exploited (the workers). Most workers are also ''capitalists''—some because they own physical capital, but most because they own significant quantities of human capital.

KEY POINTS

1. Most of the physical capital in our free enterprise system is owned by individuals; under socialism it is owned by the state on behalf of all the people. The theoretical appeal of socialism is that it eliminates one of the major causes of inequality in our system: the power and income enjoyed by those who own capital.
2. The two major economic characteristics of the system that exists in the Soviet Union today are (*a*) physical capital is owned publicly rather than privately and (*b*) investment and output levels are determined by a central planning authority.
3. One of the advantages of Soviet economywide central planning is that industry output targets can be set at a level that keeps unemployment low. But there are disadvantages. Central planning results in a great accumulation of power in the hands of the central political authorities. The more such power is centralized, the greater the risk that this power will be abused. A key question is: Could a Soviet-style command economy be run without political dictatorship?
4. A further problem with economywide planning is that it is extremely difficult to administer, and therefore often results in bottlenecks and other inefficiencies. Accordingly, central planning tends to result in higher levels of disguised unemployment, with workers engaged in unproductive activities such as producing goods that poorly satisfy consumer tastes.
5. In recognition of this problem, the Soviets have recently been attempting to make their system more sensitive to ''messages from the marketplace.'' This approach has brought them closer to Yugoslavia's economic system.
6. Yugoslavia is, like the Soviet Union, a socialist country in which productive capital is owned by the state. But it differs from the Soviet Union because much less economic decision making is done by a central authority, and much more is handled by individual enterprises responding to profits and subject to market pressures.
7. For this reason, the Yugoslavian economy is closer to our system; as a consequence, the government encounters some of the same problems that we face, such as unemployment. Moreover, the fact that the Yugoslavs' capital is publicly owned means that they face a problem common to the Soviet Union or any other socialist country: how to attain the high levels of innovation and initiative that exist in a free enterprise system, where the people who own capital take great risks in order to earn future profits.
8. The Chinese have recently been moving away from the central planning of the Soviet Union towards a market-oriented economy.

KEY CONCEPTS

capitalist
labor theory of value
subsistence level of wages
surplus value
proletariat
bourgeoisie

class struggle
socialism
communism
Gosplan
5-year plan
output target
overt vs disguised unemployment
market socialism
worker management of firms

PROBLEMS

38-1. What did Marx mean by ''surplus value''? Does it include some, all, or none of the costs of capital that must be paid by firms undertaking investment?

38-2. What are the two forms of unemployment? Which is worse in the Soviet system? Which is worse in our system? Explain.

38-3. In your view, what is the most important difference between the Soviet and the Yugoslav systems?

38-4. ''Because many workers are hostile to capital, they oppose a rapid accumulation of it—either by a firm or by the nation as a whole. Thus they fail to understand their own interest, which is to be working with more, rather than less, capital.'' Do you agree that it is in the workers' interest to be working with more capital? Or with less? Explain your answer.

38-5. Give your own concrete example to explain how a bottleneck may occur in a centrally planned economy. To what degree do you think socialism requires central planning?

38-6. Do we acquire more new technology from the Japanese, British, and Germans, or from the Russians and Czechs? Are there several reasons for your answer?

38-7. ''Under unrestricted free enterprise, a stupid, shiftless individual who has inherited a great deal of valuable land can charge a high rent, and through the diligent pursuit of idleness, become very wealthy—indeed, far wealthier than the intelligent, hardworking person who rents the land. Something is wrong.'' Explain why you agree or disagree.

Now consider three alternative solutions to this problem, carefully criticizing each:

(*a*) Put a ceiling on rent. This would transfer income from landlords to tenants.

(*b*) Charge the maximum rent, but have the land owned by the state, with all income going to the state.

(*c*) Let the shiftless owner continue to own the land and charge a maximum rent. But place a heavy percentage tax on his income.

Which solution is closest to the socialist blueprint? Which is closest to our modified free enterprise system?

38-8. ''Although socialism and communism promise less, they deliver more.'' Explain why you agree or disagree.

GLOSSARY

Not all these terms appear in the text; some are included here because they occur frequently in readings or lectures. Page numbers provide the primary references for the terms. For additional references, see the index.

ability-to-pay principle. The view that taxes should be levied according to the means of the various taxpayers, as measured by their incomes and/or wealth. Compare with *benefit principle*. (p. 93)

absolute advantage. A country (or region or individual) has an absolute advantage in the production of a good or service if it can produce that good or service with fewer resources than other countries (or regions or individuals). See also *comparative advantage. (p. 46)*

accelerationist. One who believes that an attempt to keep the unemployment rate low by expansive demand policies will cause more and more rapid inflation. (p. 330)

accelerator. The theory that investment depends on the change in sales. (p. 315)

accommodative monetary policy. (1) A monetary policy that allows the money stock to change in response to changes in the demand for loans. (p. 266) (2) A monetary policy that increases aggregate demand when wages and other costs increase, in order to prevent an increase in unemployment in the face of cost-push forces.

accounts payable. Debts to suppliers of goods or services. (p. 103)

accounts receivable. Amounts due from customers. (p. 102)

action lag. The time interval between the recognition that adjustments in aggregate demand policies are desirable and the time when policies are actually changed. (p. 298)

actual investment. Investment as it appears in the GNP accounts; investment including undesired inventory accumulation. (p. 180)

adjustable-rate mortgage. A mortgage whose interest rate is adjusted periodically in response to changes in a market rate of interest. (p. 359)

adjustable peg system. A system where countries peg (fix) exchange rates but retain the right to change them in the event of fundamental disequilibrium. (In the adjustable peg system of 1945–1973, countries generally fixed the prices of their currencies in terms of the U.S. dollar.) (p. 388)

ad valorem tax. A tax collected as a percentage of the price or value of a good.

aggregate demand. (1) Total quantity of goods and services that would be bought at various possible average price levels. (pp. 158–159) (2) Total expenditures on consumer goods and services, government goods and services, (desired) investment, and net exports. (p. 165)

aggregate supply. (1) Total quantity of goods and services that would be offered for sale at various possible average price levels. (p. 160) (2) Potential GNP.

allocative efficiency. Production of the best combination of goods with the best combination of inputs. (p. 12)

annually balanced budget principle. The view that government expenditures should be limited each year to no more than government receipts during that year. (p. 214)

antitrust laws. Laws designed to control monopoly power and practices. Examples: Sherman Act, 1890; Clayton Act, 1914. (p. 561)

appreciation of a currency. In a flexible exchange-rate system, a rise in the price of a currency in terms of another currency or currencies. (p. 395)

arbitrage. A set of transactions aimed at making a profit from inconsistent prices.

arbitration. Settlement of differences between a union and management by an impartial third party (the arbitrator) whose decisions are binding. (p. 713)

arc elasticity of demand. The elasticity of demand between two points on a demand curve, calculated by the equation

$$\frac{\Delta Q}{Q_1 + Q_2} \div \frac{\Delta P}{P_1 + P_2}$$

(p. 415)

asset. Something that is owned. (p. 102)

automatic stabilizer. A feature built into the economy that reduces the amplitude of fluctuations. For example, tax collections tend to fall during a recession and rise during a boom, slowing the change in disposable incomes and aggregate demand. Thus they are an automatic fiscal stabilizer. (p. 211) Interest rates tend to fall during a recession and rise during a boom because of changes in the demand for funds. These changes in interest rates tend to stabilize investment demand. Thus they are an automatic monetary stabilizer. (p. 265)

average-cost pricing. Setting the price where the average-cost curve (including normal profit) intersects the demand curve. (p. 524)

average fixed cost. Fixed cost divided by the number of units of output. (p. 462)

average product. Total product divided by the number of units of the variable input used. (p. 457)

average propensity to consume. Consumption divided by disposable income. (p. 177)

average propensity to save. Saving divided by disposable income.

average revenue. Total revenue divided by the number of units sold. Where there is a single price, this price equals average revenue. (p. 514)

average total cost. Total cost divided by the number of units of output. (p. 462)

average variable cost. Variable cost divided by the number of units produced. (p. 462)

balanced budget. (1) A budget with revenues equal to expenditures. (2) More loosely (but more commonly), a budget with revenues equal to or greater than expenditures. (p. 83)

balanced budget multiplier. The change in equilibrium national product divided by the change in government spending when this spending is financed by an equivalent change in taxes.

balance of payments. The summary figure calculated from balance-of-payments credits less balance-of-payments debits, with certain monetary transactions excluded from the calculation. (There are various ways of defining monetary transactions; thus, there are various balance-of-payments definitions. The most common excludes official reserve transactions.) (p. 404)

balance-of-payments accounts. A statement of a country's transactions with other countries. (p. 401)

balance-of-payments surplus (deficit). A positive (negative) balance of payments. (p. 404)

balance of trade (or balance on merchandise account). The value of exports of goods minus the value of imports of goods. (p. 404)

balance sheet. The statement of a firm's financial position at a particular time, showing its assets, liabilities, and net worth. (p. 102)

band. The range within which an exchange rate could move without the government's being committed to intervene in exchange markets to prevent further movement. Under the adjustable peg system, governments were obliged to keep exchange rates from moving outside a band (of 1% either side of parity). (p. 389)

bank reserve. Bank holding of currency and reserve deposits in the Federal Reserve. (p. 234)

bank run. A situation in which many owners of bank deposits attempt to make withdrawals because of their fear that the bank will be unable to meet its obligations. (p. 232)

bankruptcy. (1) A situation in which a firm (or individual) has legally been declared unable to pay its debts. (2) More loosely, a situation in which a firm (or individual) is unable to pay its debts.

barrier to entry. An impediment that makes it difficult or impossible for a new firm to enter an industry. Examples: patents, economies of scale, accepted brand names. (p. 551)

barter. The exchange of one good or service for another without the use of money. (p. 40)

base year. The reference year, given the value of 100 when constructing a price index or other time series. (p. 127)

beggar-thy-neighbor policy (or beggar-my-neighbor policy). A policy aimed at shifting an unemployment problem to another country. Example: an increase in tariffs. (p. 654)

benefit-cost analysis. The calculation and comparison of the benefits and costs of a program or project. (p. 573)

benefit principle. The view that taxes should be levied in proportion to the benefits that the various taxpayers receive from government expenditures. Compare with *ability-to-pay principle*. (p. 93)

benefits in kind. Payments, not of cash, but of some good (like food) or service (like medical care). (p. 757)

bilateral monopoly. A market structure involving a single seller (monopolist) and a single buyer (monopsonist). (p. 707)

bill. See *Treasury bill*.

blacklist. A list of workers who are not to be given jobs because of union activity or other behavior considered objectionable by employers. (p. 695)

black market. A market in which sales take place at a price above the legal maximum. (p. 68)

block grant. Grant that may be used in a broad area (such as education), and need not be spent on specific programs (such as reading programs for the handicapped). (p. 87)

bond. A written commitment to pay a scheduled series of interest payments plus the face value (principal) at a specified maturity date. (p. 100)

bourgeoisie. (1) In Marxist doctrine, capitalists as a social class. (2) The middle class. (3) More narrowly, shopkeepers. (p. 774)

book value. The book value of a stock is its net worth per share. (It is calculated by dividing the net worth of the firm by the number of its shares outstanding.) (p. 103)

boycott. A concerted refusal to buy (buyer's boycott) or sell (sellers' boycott). A campaign to discourage people from doing business with a particular firm.

break-even point. (1) The output at which costs just equal revenues and therefore profits are zero. (2) The level of disposable income at which consumption just equals disposable income and therefore saving is zero. (p. 176)

broker. One who acts on behalf of a buyer or seller. (p. 108)

budget deficit. The amount by which budgetary outlays exceed revenues. (p. 83)

budget line (or income line or price line). The line on a diagram that shows the various combinations of commodities that can be bought with a given income at a given set of prices. (p. 449)

budget surplus. The amount by which budgetary revenues exceed outlays. (p. 83)

built-in-stabilizer. See *automatic stabilizer*.

burden of tax. The amount of the tax ultimately paid by different individuals or groups. (For example, how much does a cigarette tax raise the price paid by buyers, and how much does it lower the net price received by sellers?) The incidence of the tax. (p. 93)

business cycle. The more or less regular upward and downward movement of economic activity over a period of years. A cycle has four phases: recession, trough, expansion, and peak. (p. 137)

capital. (1) Real capital: buildings, equipment, and other materials used in the production process that have themselves been produced in the past. (p. 28) (2) Financial capital: either funds available for acquiring real capital *or* financial assets such as bonds or common stock. (p. 28) (3) Human capital: the education, training, and experience that make human beings more productive. (p. 724)

capital consumption allowance. Depreciation, with adjustments for the effects of inflation on the measurement of capital. Loosely, depreciation. (p. 123n)

capital gain. The increase in the value of an asset over time.

capitalism. A system in which individuals are permitted to own large amounts of capital, and decisions are made primarily in private markets, with relatively little government interference. (p. 52)

capitalized value. The present value of the income stream that an asset is expected to produce. (pp. 252, 734)

capital market. A market in which financial instruments such as stocks and bonds are bought and sold.

capital-output ratio. The value of capital divided by the value of the annual output produced with this capital. (p. 317)

capital stock. The total quantity of capital.

cartel. A formal agreement among firms to set price and market shares. (p. 538)

categorical grant. A federal grant to a state or local government for a specific program. Such a grant generally requires the recipient government to pay part of the cost of the program. (p. 87)

cease-and-desist order. An order from a court or government agency to an individual or company to stop a specified action. (p. 563)

central bank. A banker's bank, whose major responsibility is the control of the money supply. A central bank also generally performs other functions, such as check clearing and the inspection of commercial banks. (p. 232)

central planning. Centralized direction of the resources of the economy, with the objective of fulfilling national goals. (p. 778)

certificate of deposit. (CD). A marketable time deposit.

ceteris paribus. "Other things unchanged." In demand-and-supply analysis, it is common to make the *ceteris paribus* assumption; that is, to assume that none of the determinants of the quantity demanded or supplied is allowed to change, with the sole exception of price. (p. 58)

check clearing. The transfer of checks from the bank in which they were deposited to the bank on which they were written, with the net amounts due to or from each bank being calculated. (p. 237)

checking deposit. A deposit against which an order to pay (that is, a check) may be written.

checking deposit multiplier. The increase in checking deposits divided by the the increase in bank reserves. (p. 239)

checkoff. The deduction of union dues from workers' pay by an employer, who then remits the dues to the union. (p. 697)

circular flow of payments. The flow of payments from businesses to households in exchange for labor and other productive services and the return flow of payments from households to businesses in exchange for goods and services. (p. 43)

classical economics. (1) In Keynesian economics, the accepted body of macroeconomic doctrine prior to the publication of Keynes' *General Theory*. According to classical economics, a market economy tends toward an equilibrium with full employment; a market economy tends to be stable if monetary conditions are stable; and changes in the quantity of money are the major cause of changes in aggregate demand. (p. 162) (2) The accepted view, prior to about 1870, that value depends on the cost of production. In the late nineteenth century, this was replaced with the ''neoclassical'' view that value depends on both costs of production (supply) and utility (demand).

class struggle. In Marxist economics, the struggle for control between the proletariat and the bourgeoisie. (p. 773)

clean float. A situation where exchange rates are determined by market forces, without intervention by central banks or governments. (p. 394)

closed economy. An economy with no international transactions.

closed shop. A business that hires only workers who are already union members. (p. 697)

cobweb cycle. A switching back and forth between a situation of high production and low price and one of low production and high price. A cobweb cycle can occur if there are long lags in production and if producers erroneously assume that price this year is a good indicator of price next year.

collective bargaining. Negotiations between a union and management over wages and working conditions. (p. 693)

collective goods. Goods that, by their very nature, provide benefits to a large group of people.

collusion. An agreement among sellers regarding prices and/or market shares. The agreement may be explicit or tacit. (p. 538)

commercial bank. A privately owned, profit-seeking institution that accepts demand and savings deposits, makes loans, and acquires other earning assets (particularly bonds and shorter-term debt instruments). (p. 233)

commons. Land that is open for use by all or by a large group; for example, commonly owned pasture land. (p. 598)

common stock. Each share of common stock represents part ownership in a corporation. (p. 98)

communism. (1) In Marxist theory, the ultimate stage of historical development in which (*a*) all are expected to work and no one lives by owning capital, (*b*) exploitation has been eliminated and there is a classless society, and (*c*) the state has withered away. (2) A common alternative usage: the economic and political systems of China, the Soviet Union, and other countries in which a Communist party is in power. (p. 774)

company union. A union dominated by the employer.

comparable. Of equal value, requiring equivalent effort, responsibility, training, and skills. The *comparable worth issue* is the question of whether employers should be required to pay women as much as men working in different but comparable jobs. Comparable worth—also sometimes known as *pay equity*—takes the anti-discrimination idea beyond the requirement that people be paid the same amount for doing the same job. (p. 687)

comparative advantage. If two nations (or cities or individuals) have different opportunity costs of producing a good or service, then the nation (or city or individual) with the lower opportunity cost has a comparative advantage in that good or service. (p. 48)

compensating wage differentials. Wage differences that may result if labor views some jobs as less attractive than others. (Employers have to pay a higher wage to fill the unattractive jobs.) (p. 714)

competition. See *perfect competition*.

competitive devaluations. A round of exchange-rate devaluations in which each of a number of countries tries to gain a competitive advantage by devaluing its currency. (Not all can be successful; each must fail to the extent that other countries also devalue.)

complementary goals. Goals such that the achievement of one helps in the achievement of the other. (Contrast with *conflicting goals*.) (p. 15)

complementary goods. Goods such that the rise in the price of one causes a leftward shift in the demand curve for the other. (Contrast with *substitute*.) (p. 59)

complements in production. Goods such that the rise in the price of one causes a rightward shift in the supply curve of the other. Joint products. (p. 61)

concentration ratio. Usually, the fraction of an industry's total output made by the four largest firms. (Sometimes a different number of firms—such as eight—is chosen in calculating concentration ratios, and sometimes a different measure of size—such as assets—is chosen.) (p. 534)

conflicting goals. Goals such that working toward one makes it more difficult to achieve the other. (p. 15)

conglomerate merger. See *merger*.

consent decree. An agreement whereby a defendant, without admitting guilt, undertakes to desist from certain actions and abide by other conditions laid down in the decree.

conspicuous consumption. Consumption whose purpose is to impress others. A term originated by Thorstein Veblen (1857–1929).

constant dollars. A series is measured in constant dollars if it is measured at the prices existing in a specified base year. Such a series has been adjusted to remove the effects of inflation or deflation. (p. 127) Contrast with *current dollars*.

constant returns (to scale). This occurs if an increase of x percent in all inputs causes output to increase by the same x percent.

consumer price index (CPI). A weighted average of the prices of goods and services commonly purchased by families in urban areas, as calculated by the U.S. Bureau of Labor Statistics. (p. 128)

consumer surplus. The net benefit that consumers get from being able to purchase a good at the prevailing price; the difference between the maximum amounts that consumers would be willing to pay and what they actually do pay. It is approximately the triangular area under the demand curve and above the market price. (p. 440)

consumption. (1) The purchase of consumer goods and services. (p. 119) (2) The act of using goods and services to satisfy wants. (3) The using up of goods (as in capital consumption allowances).

consumption function. (1) The relationship between consumer expenditures and disposable income. (p. 175) (2) More broadly, the relationship between consumer expenditures and the factors that determine these expenditures.

contestable market. A market with only one or a few producers, whose market power is nevertheless severely limited by the ease with which additional producers may enter. (p. 554)

convertible bond. A bond that can be exchanged for common stock under specified terms and prior to a specified date, at the option of the bondholder. (p. 100)

convergence hypothesis. The proposition that the differences between communistic and capitalistic societies is decreasing.

coincidence of wants. This exists when *A* is willing to offer what *B* wants, while *B* is willing to offer what *A* wants. (p. 41)

cornering a market. Buying and accumulating enough of the commodity to become the single (or at least dominant) seller, and thus acquire the power to resell at a higher price. (p. 498)

corporation. An association of stockholders with a government charter that grants certain legal powers, privileges, and liabilities separate from those of the individual stockholder-owners. The major advantages of the corporate form of business organization are limited liability for the owners, continuity, and relative ease of raising capital for expansion. (p. 98)

correlation. The tendency of two variables (like income and consumption) to move together.

cost-benefit analysis. See *benefit-cost analysis*.

cost-push inflation. Inflation caused principally by increasing costs—in the form of higher prices for labor, materials, and other inputs—rather than by rising demand. (p. 326) Contrast with *demand-pull inflation*.

countercyclical policy. (1) Policy that reduces fluctuations in economic activity. (2) Policy whose objective is to reduce fluctuations in economic activity.

countervailing power. Power in one group which has grown as a reaction to power in another group. For example, a big labor union may develop to balance the bargaining power of a big corporation. A term originated by Harvard's John Kenneth Galbraith. (p. 706)

Cournot-Nash equilibrium. Equilibrium that exists when each firm assumes that none of its competitors will react to any changes it makes. (p. 548)

craft union. A labor union whose members have a particular craft (skill or occupation). Examples: an electrician's union, or a plumbers' union. Contrast with *industrial union*. (p. 695)

crawling peg system. An international financial system in which par values would be changed frequently, by small amounts, in order to avoid large changes at a later date.

credit crunch. A situation of severe credit rationing. (p. 281)

credit instrument. A written promise to pay at some future date.

credit rationing. Allocation of available funds among borrowers when the demand for loans exceeds the supply at the prevailing interest rate. (p. 281)

creeping inflation. A slow but persistent upward movement of the average level of prices (not more than 2% or 3% per annum).

cross-section data. Observations taken at the same time. For example, the consumption of different income classes in the United States in 1986.

crowding out. A reduction in private investment demand caused when an expansive fiscal policy results in higher interest rates. (p. 285)

currency. (1) Coins and paper money (dollar bills). (p. 228) (2) In international economics, a national money, such as the dollar or the yen. (p. 387)

current account surplus. The amount by which a country's export of goods and services is greater than the combined sum of its imports of goods and services plus its net unilateral transfers to foreign countries. (p. 404)

current dollars. A series (like GNP) is measured in current dollars if each observation is measured at the prices that prevailed at the time. Such a series reflects both real changes in GNP *and* inflation (or deflation). Contrast with *constant dollars*. (p. 127)

current liabilities. Debts that are due for payment within a year.

customs union. An agreement among nations to eliminate trade barriers (tariffs, quotas, etc.) among themselves and to adopt common tariffs on imports from nonmember countries. Example: the European Economic Community.

cutthroat competition. Selling at a price below cost, with the objective of driving competitors out of the market (at which time prices may be raised and monopoly profits reaped). (p. 540)

cyclically balanced budget. A budget whose receipts over a whole business cycle are at least equal to its expenditures over the same cycle. Unlike an annually balanced budget, a cyclically balanced budget permits the use of countercyclical fiscal policies. Surpluses during prosperity may be used to cover deficits during recessions. (p. 215)

debasement of currency. (1) Reduction of the quantity of precious metal in coins. (p. 44) (2) More broadly, a substantial decrease in the purchasing power of money.

debt instrument. A written commitment to repay borrowed funds.

declining industry. An industry whose firms make less than normal profits. (Firms will therefore leave the industry.)

decreasing returns (to scale). Occurs if an x percent increase in all inputs results in an increase of output of less than x percent.

deficit. The amount by which expenditures exceed revenues. (p. 83)

deflation. (1) A decline in the average level of prices; the opposite of inflation. (p. 10) (2) The removal of the effects of inflation from a series of observations by dividing each observation with a price index. The derivation of a constant-dollar series from a current-dollar series. (p. 129)

deflationary bias. Such a bias exists in a system if, on average, monetary and fiscal authorities are constrained from allowing aggregate demand to increase as rapidly as productive capacity. (The classical gold standard was criticized on the ground that it created a deflationary bias.)

deflationary gap. See *recessionary gap*.

deindustrialization. A reduction in the size of the manufacturing sector, usually as a result of competition from imports. (p. 397)

demand. A schedule or curve showing how much of a good or service would be demanded at various possible prices, *ceteris paribus*. (p. 55)

demand deposit. A bank deposit withdrawable on demand and transferable by check.

demand-pull inflation. Inflation caused by excess aggregate demand. (p. 326)

demand management policy. A change in monetary and/or fiscal policy aimed at affecting aggregate demand. (p. 200)

demand-pull inflation. Inflation caused by excess aggregate demand. (p. 326) Contrast with *cost-push inflation*.

demand schedule. A table showing the quantities of a good or service that buyers would be willing and able to purchase at various market prices, *ceteris paribus*. (p. 55)

demand shift. A movement of the demand curve to the right or left as a result of a change in income or any other determinant of the quantity demand (with the sole exception of the price of the good). (p. 58)

demand shifter. Anything except its own price that affects the quantity of a good demanded. (p. 59)

depletion allowance. A deduction, equal to a percentage of sales, that certain extractive industries are permitted in calculating taxable profits.

depreciation. (1) The loss in the value of physical capital due to wear and obsolescence. (2) The estimate of such loss in business or economic accounts. (3) The amount that tax laws allow businesses to count as a cost of using plant or equipment. (p. 105)

depreciation of a currency. A decline in the value of a floating currency measured in terms of another currency or currencies. (p. 395)

depression. An extended period of very high unemployment and much excess capacity. (There is no generally accepted, precise numerical definition of a depression. This text suggests that a depression requires unemployment rates of 10% or more for 2 years or more.) (p. 139)

derived demand. The demand for an input that depends on the demand for the product or products it is used to make. For example, the demand for flour is derived from the demand for bread. (p. 677)

devaluation. In international economics, a reduction of the par value of a currency. (p. 390)

dictatorship of the proletariat. In Marxist economics, the state after a revolution has eliminated the capitalist class and power has fallen into the hands of the proletariat. (p. 780)

differentiated products. Similar products that retain some distinctive difference(s); close but not perfect substitutes. Examples: Ford and Chevrolet automobiles, different brands of toothpaste. (p. 551)

diminishing returns, law of eventually. If technology is unchanged, then the use of more and more units of a variable input, together with one or more fixed inputs, must eventually lead to a declining marginal product for the variable input. (p. 455)

dirty float. See *floating exchange rate*.

discounting. The process by which the present value of one or more future payments is calculated, using an interest rate. (See *present value*.) (p. 252) (2) In central banking, lending by the central bank to a commercial bank or other financial institution. (p. 253)

discount rate. (1) In central banking, the rate of interest charged by the central bank on loans to commercial banks. (p. 251) (2) The interest rate used to calculate present value. (p. 252)

discouraged worker. Someone who wants a job but is no longer looking because work is believed to be unavailable. A discouraged worker is not included in either the labor force or the number of unemployed. (p. 145)

discretionary policy. Policy that is periodically changed in the light of changing conditions. The term is usually applied to monetary or fiscal policies that are adjusted with the objectives of high employment and stable prices. Contrast with *monetary rule*. (p. 295)

disposable (personal) income. Income that households have left after the payment of taxes. It is divided among consumption expenditures, the payment of interest on consumer debt, and saving. (p. 126)

dissaving. Negative saving.

dividend. The part of a corporation's profits paid out to its shareholders. (p. 100)

division of labor. The breaking up of a productive process into different tasks, each done by a different worker (for example, on an automobile assembly line). (p. 48)

dollar standard. An international system in which many international transactions take place in dollars and many countries hold sizable factions of their reserves in dollars. Also, other currencies may be pegged to the dollar. (p. 392)

double-entry bookeeping. An accounting system in which each transaction results in equal entries on both sides. When double-entry bookkeeping is used, the two sides of the accounts must balance. (p. 401)

double taxation. The taxation of corporate profits first when they are earned and second when they are paid out in dividends. (p. 99)

dumping. The sale of a good at a lower price in a foreign market than in the home market—a form of price discrimination.

dual labor market. A double labor market, where workers in one market are excluded from taking jobs in the other market. (p. 686)

duopoly. A market in which there are only two sellers.

dynamic efficiency. Efficient change in an economy, particularly the most efficient use of resources, the best rate of technological change, and the most efficient rate of growth. (p. 493)

dynamic wage differential. A wage difference that arises because of changing demand or supply conditions in the labor market. It tends to disappear over time as labor moves out of relatively low wage jobs and into those that pay a relatively high wage. (p. 714)

econometrics. The application of statistical methods to economic problems.

economic efficiency. See *allocative efficiency, dynamic efficiency*, and *technological efficiency*.

economic integration. The elimination of tariffs and other barriers between nations. The partial or complete unification of the economies of different countries.

economic rent. The return to a factor of production in excess of its opportunity cost. (p. 730)

economics. (1) The study of how people acquire material necessities and comforts, the problems they encounter in doing so, and how these problems can be reduced. (p. 3) (2) Frequently, a narrower definition is used—the study of the allocation of scarce resources to satisfy human wants. (p. 39)

economies (diseconomies) of scale. Occur if an increase of x percent in all inputs results in an increase in output of more (less) than x percent. (p. 48)

economize. To make the most of limited resources; to be careful in spending.

efficiency. The goal of getting the most out of our productive efforts. See also: *allocative efficiency, dynamic efficiency*, and *technological efficiency*. (p. 12)

effluent charge. A tax or other levy on a polluting activity based on the quantity of pollution discharged. (p. 586)

elastic demand. Demand with an elasticity of more than one. A fall in price causes an increase in total expenditure on the product in question, because the percentage change in quantity demanded is greater than the percentage change in price. (p. 414)

elasticity of demand. The price elasticity of demand is

$$\frac{\text{Percentage change in quantity demanded}}{\text{Percentage change in price}}$$

Similarly, the income elasticity of demand is

$$\frac{\text{Percentage change in quantity demanded}}{\text{Percentage change in income}}$$

The unmodified term "elasticity" usually applies to price elasticity. (p. 414)

elasticity of supply. The (price) elasticity of supply is

$$\frac{\text{Percentage change in quantity supplied}}{\text{Percentage change in price}}$$

(p. 417)

elastic supply. Supply with an elasticity of more than one. A supply curve which, if extended in a straight line, would meet the vertical axis. (p. 417)

emission fee. See *effluent charge*.

employer of last resort. The government acts as the employer of last resort if it provides jobs for all those who are willing and able to work but cannot find jobs in the private sector. (p. 340)

employment rate. The percentage of the labor force employed.

endogenous variable. A variable explained within a theory.

Engel's laws. Regularities between income and consumer expenditures observed by nineteenth-century statistician Ernst Engel. Most important is the decrease in the percentage of income spent on food as income rises.

entrepreneur. One who organizes and manages production. One who innovates and bears risks. (p. 28)

envelope curve. A curve that encloses, by just touching, a series of other curves. For example, the long-run average-cost curve is the envelope of all the short-run average-cost curves (each of which shows costs, given a particular stock of fixed capital). (p. 471)

equation of exchange. MV = PQ. (p. 283)

equilibrium. A situation where there is no tendency for change. (p. 57)

equity. (1) Ownership, or amount owned. (p. 103) (2) Fairness. (p. 12)

escalator clause. A provision in a contract or law whereby a price, wage, or other monetary quantity is increased at the same rate as a specified price index (usually the consumer price index). (p. 361)

estate tax. A tax on property owned at the time of death.

Eurodollars. Deposits in European banks that are denominated in U.S. dollars.

excess burden of a tax. The decrease in efficiency that results when people change their behavior to reduce their tax payments. (p. 219)

excess demand. The amount by which the quantity demanded exceeds the quantity supplied at the existing price. A shortage. (p. 58)

excess reserves. Reserves held by a bank in excess of the legally required amount. (p. 236)

excess supply. The amount by which the quantity supplied exceeds the quantity demanded at the existing price. A surplus. (p. 58)

exchange rate. The price of one national currency in terms of another. (p. 384)

exchange-rate appreciation (depreciation). See *appreciation (depreciation) of a currency*.

excise tax. A tax on the sale of a particular good. An *ad valorem tax* is collected as a percentage of the price of the good. A *specific tax* is a fixed number of cents or dollars on each unit of the good.

exclusion principle. The basis for distinguishing between public and nonpublic goods. If those who do not pay for a good can be excluded from enjoying it, then it is not a public good. (p. 621)

exogenous variable. A variable not explained within a theory; its value is taken as given. Example: investment in the simple Keynesian theory.

expansion. The phase of the business cycle when output and employment are increasing. (p. 138)

export (E). Good or service sold to foreign nationals. (p. 122)

export of capital. Acquisition of foreign assets.

external cost. Cost borne by others. Pollution is an example of an external cost (sometimes called a cost spillover or a neighborhood cost). (p. 89)

externality. An adverse or beneficial side effect of production or consumption. Also known as a *spillover* or *third-party effect*. (p. 88)

externally held public debt. Government securities held by foreigners. (p. 219)

Fabian socialism. Form of socialism founded in Britain in the late nineteenth century, advocating gradual and evolutionary movement toward socialism within a democratic political system.

face value. The stated amount of a loan or bond. The amount that must be paid, in addition to interest, when the bond comes due. The principal. (p. 100)

factor mobility. Ease with which factors can be moved from one use to another.

factor of production. Resource used to produce a good or service. Land, labor, and capital are the three basic categories of factors. (p. 28)

fallacy of composition. The unwarranted conclusion that a proposition which is true of a single sector or market is necessarily true for the economy as a whole. (p. 198)

fair return. Return to which a regulated public utility should be entitled.

featherbedding. (1) Commonly: Make-work rules designed to increase the number of workers or the number of hours on a particular job. (2) As defined in the Taft-Hartley Act: Payment for work not actually performed. (p. 701)

federal funds rate. The interest rate on very short term (usually overnight) loans between banks.

fiat money. Paper money that is neither backed by nor convertible into precious metals but is nevertheless legal tender. Money that is money solely because the government says that it is. (p. 260)

final product. Product that has been acquired for final use and not for resale or for further processing. (p. 119)

financial instrument. A legal document representing claims or ownership. Examples: bonds, Treasury bills.

financial intermediary. An institution that issues financial obligations (such as checking deposits) in order to acquire funds from the public. The institution then pools these funds and provides them in larger amounts to businesses, governments, or individuals. Examples: commercial banks, savings and loan associations, insurance companies. (p. 105)

financial market. A market in which financial instruments (stocks, bonds, etc.) are bought and sold. (p. 105)

fine-tuning. An attempt to smooth out mild fluctuations in the economy by frequent adjustments in monetary and/or fiscal policies. (p. 296)

firm. A business organization that produces goods and/or services. A firm may own one or more plants. (p. 55)

fiscal dividend. A budget surplus, measured at the full-employment national product, that is generated by the growth of the productive capacity of the economy. (This term was most commonly used during the 1960s.)

fiscal drag. The tendency for rising tax collections to impede the healthy growth of aggregate demand that is needed for the achievement and maintenance of full employment. (This term was most commonly used during the 1960s.)

fiscal policy. The adjustment of tax rates or government spending in order to affect aggregate demand. (p. 203) *Pure fiscal policy* involves a change in government spending or tax rates, unaccompanied by any change in the rate of growth of the money stock. (p. 286)

fiscal year. A 12-month period selected as the year for accounting purposes.

Fisher equation. The equation of exchange: MV = PQ. (p. 283)

fixed asset. A durable good, expected to last at least a year.

fixed cost. A cost that does not vary with output. (p. 454)

fixed exchange rate. An exchange rate that is held within a narrow band by the monetary authorities. (p. 388)

fixed factor. A factor whose quantity cannot be changed in the short run. (p. 453)

flat tax. A tax with only one rate applying to all income. A proportional tax. (pp. 91–92)

floating (or flexible) exchange rate. An exchange rate that is not pegged by monetary authorities but is allowed to change in response to changing demand or supply conditions. If governments and central banks withdraw completely from the exchange markets, the float is *clean*. (That is, the exchange rate is *freely flexible*. A float is *dirty* when governments or central banks intervene in exchange markets by buying or selling foreign currencies in order to influence exchange rates. (p. 394)

focal-point pricing. This occurs when independent firms quote the same price even though they do not explicitly collude. They are led by convention, rules of thumb, or similar thinking to the same price. (For example, $39.95 for a pair of shoes.) (p. 548)

forced saving. A situation where households lose control of their income, which is directed into saving even though they would have preferred to consume it. This can occur if the monetary authorities provide financial resources for investment, creating inflation which reduces the purchasing power of households' incomes (and therefore reduces their consumption). Alternatively, forced saving occurs if taxes are used for investment projects (such as dams).

foreign exchange. The currency of another country. (p. 384)

foreign exchange market. A market in which one national currency is bought in exchange for another national currency. (p. 384)

foreign exchange reserves. Foreign currencies held by the government or central bank. (p. 387)

forward price. A price established in a contract to be executed at a specified time in the future (such as 3 months from now). See also *futures market*.

fractional-reserve banking. A banking system in which banks keep reserves (generally in the form of currency or deposits in the central bank) equal to only a fraction of their deposit liabilities. (p. 231)

freedom of entry. The absence of barriers that make it difficult or impossible for a new firm to enter an industry. (p. 473)

free enterprise economy. One in which individuals are permitted to own large amounts of capital, and decisions are made primarily in private markets, with relatively little government interference. (p. 53)

free good. A good or service whose price is zero, because at that price the quantity supplied is at least as great as the quantity demanded.

free-market economy. An economy in which the major questions "What?" "How?" and "For whom?" are answered by the actions of individuals and firms in the marketplace rather than by the government. (p. 51)

free rider. Someone who cannot be excluded from enjoying the benefits of a project, but who pays nothing (or pays a disproportionately small share) to cover its costs. (p. 622)

free trade. A situation where no tariffs or other barriers exist on trade between countries.

free-trade area (or free-trade association). A group of countries that agree to eliminate trade barriers (tariffs, quotas, etc.) among themselves, while each retains the right to set its own tariffs on imports from nonmember countries. Compare with *customs union*.

frictional unemployment. Temporary unemployment associated with adjustments in a changing, dynamic economy. It arises for a number of reasons. For example, some new entrants into the labor force take time to find jobs, some with jobs quit to look for better ones, and others are temporarily unemployed by such disturbances as bad weather. (p. 149)

front-loaded debt. A debt on which the payments, measured in constant dollars, are greater at the beginning than at the end of the repayment period. (p. 354)

full employment. (1) A situation in which there is no unemployment attributable to insufficient aggregate demand; that is, where all unemployment is due to frictional causes. (2) A situation where all who want to work can find jobs reasonably quickly. (p. 151)

full-employment budget (or high-employment budget). Full-employment government receipts (that is, the receipts that would be obtained with present tax rates if the economy were at full employment) minus full-employment government expenditures (that is, actual expenditures less expenditures directly associated with unemployment in excess of the full-employment level). (p. 211)

full-employment GNP. The GNP that would exist if full employment were consistently maintained. Potential GNP. (p. 151)

full-line forcing. See *tying contract*.

fundamental disequilibrium (in international economics). A term used but not defined in the articles of agreement of the International Monetary Fund. The general idea is that a fundamental disequilibrium exists when an international payments imbalance cannot be eliminated without increasing trade restrictions or imposing unduly restrictive aggregate demand policies. (p. 389)

futures market. A market in which contracts are undertaken today at prices specified today for fulfillment at some specified future time. For example, a futures sale of wheat involves the commitment to deliver wheat (say) 3 months from today at a price set now.

gain from trade. Increase in real income that results from specialization and trade. (p. 639)

game theory. Theory dealing with conflict, in which alternative strategies are formally analyzed. Sometimes used in the analysis of oligopoly.

general equilibrium. Situation where all markets are in equilibrium simultaneously.

general equilibrium analysis. Analysis taking into account interactions among markets.

general glut. This occurs when excess supply is a general phenomenon. The quantity of goods and services that producers are willing to supply greatly exceeds the quantity buyers are willing and able to purchase.

general inflation. An increase in all prices (including wages) by the same percent, leaving relative prices unchanged. (p. 160)

general price level. Price level as measured by a broad average, such as the consumer price index or the GNP deflator.

Giffen good. A good whose demand curve slopes upward to the right. (p. 451)

Gini coefficient. A measure of inequality derived from the Lorenz curve. It is the "bow" area (in Figure 36-1 on p. 741) between the curve and the diagonal line divided by the entire area beneath the diagonal line. It can range from zero (if there is no inequality and the Lorenz curve corresponds to the diagonal line) to one (if there is complete inequality and the Lorenz curve runs along the horizontal axis).

GNP (price) deflator. Current-dollar GNP divided by constant dollar GNP, times 100. Measure of the change in prices of the goods and services in GNP. (p. 128)

GNP gap. Amount by which actual GNP falls short of potential GNP. (p. 152)

gold certificate. Certificate issued by the U.S. Treasury to the Federal Reserve, backed 100% by Treasury holdings of gold.

gold exchange standard. International system in which most countries keep their currencies pegged to, and convertible into, another currency that in turn is pegged to and convertible into gold. (p. 391n)

gold point. Under the old gold standard, an exchange rate at which an arbitrager can barely cover the costs of shipping, handling, and insuring gold.

gold standard. System in which the monetary unit is defined in terms of gold, the monetary authorites buy and sell gold freely at that price, and gold may be freely exported or imported. If central banks follow the "rule of the gold standard game," they allow changes in gold to be reflected in changes in the money stock. (pp. 262, 387)

gold sterilization. A gold flow is sterilized when the central bank takes steps to cancel out the automatic effects of the gold flow on the country's money supply (that is, when the "rule of the gold standard game" is broken).

good. Tangible commodity, such as wheat, a shirt, or an automobile.

graduated-payment mortgage. A mortgage on which the money payments rise as time passes, in order to reduce front loading. If the money payments rise rapidly enough to keep real payments constant, then the mortgage is *fully* graduated. (p. 354)

Gresham's law. Crudely, ''Bad money drives out good.'' More precisely: If there are two types of money whose values in exchange are equal while their values in another use (like consumption) are different, the more valuable item will be retained for its other use while the less valuable item will continue to circulate as money. (p. 44)

gross national product (GNP). Personal consumption expenditures plus government purchases of goods and services plus gross private domestic investment plus net exports of goods and services. The total product of the nation, excluding double counting. (p. 125)

gross private domestic investment (I_g). Expenditures for new plant, equipment, and new resdential buildings, plus the change in inventories. (p. 123)

growth. An increase in the productive capacity of the economy. (p. 33)

Herfindahl index. A measure of concentration. Specifically, the sum of the squared market shares of all the firms. (p. 536)

high-employment GNP. The GNP that would exist if a high rate of employment were consistently maintained. Potential GNP. (p. 151)

holding company. A company that holds a controlling interest in the stock of one or more other companies.

horizontal merger. See *merger*.

human capital. Education and training that make human beings more productive. (p. 725)

hyperinflation. Very rapid inflation. (p. 10)

identification problem. The difficulty of determining the effect of variable *a* alone on variable *b* when *b* can also be affected by variables *c, d,* etc. (p. 431)

impact lag. The time interval between policy changes and the time when the major effects of the policy changes occur. (p. 298)

imperfect competition. A market in which some buyer(s) or seller(s) are large enough to have a noticeable effect on price. (p. 55)

implicit (or imputed) cost. The opportunity cost of using an input that is already owned by the producer. (p. 464)

implicit tax built into a welfare program. The benefits a family loses when it earns another $1 of income. For example, if its benefits are reduced by 46¢, the implicit tax is 46%. (p. 760)

import (M). Good or service acquired from foreign nationals. (p. 122)

import of capital. Sale of assets to foreign nationals.

import quota. A restriction on the quantity of a good that may be imported. (p. 649)

incidence of a tax. The amount of the tax ultimately paid by different individuals or groups. (For example, how much does a cigarette tax raise the price paid by buyers, and how much does it lower the net price received by sellers?) (p. 93)

income-consumption line. The line or curve traced out by the points of tangency between an indifference map and a series of parallel budget (income) lines. It shows how a consumer responds to a changing income when relative prices remain constant.

income effect. Change in the quantity of a good demanded as a result of a change in real income with no change in relative prices. (p. 451)

income elasticity of demand. See *elasticity of demand*.

income line. See *budget line*.

incomes policy. A government policy (such as wage-price guideposts or wage and price controls) aimed at restraining the rate of increase in money wages and other money incomes. The purpose is to reduce the rate of inflation. (p. 341)

income statement. An accounting statement that summarizes a firm's revenues, costs, and income taxes over a given period of time (usually a year). A profit-and-loss statement. (p. 104)

increasing returns to scale. This occurs if an increase of *x* percent in all inputs results in an increase in output of more than *x* percent. (p. 470)

incremental cost. The term that business executives frequently use instead of ''marginal cost.''

incremental revenue. The term that business executives frequently use instead of ''marginal revenue.''

index. A series of numbers, showing how an average (of prices, or wages, or some other economic measure) changes through time. Each of these numbers is called an index number. By convention, the index number for the base year is set at 100. (p. 127)

indexation. The inclusion of an escalator clause in a contract or law. An increase in the wage rate, tax brackets, or other dollar measure by the same proportion as the increase in the average level of prices. (pp. 356, 361)

indifference curve. A curve joining all points among which the consumer is indifferent. (p. 447)

indifference map. A series of indifference curves, each representing a different level of satisfaction or utility. (p. 448)

indirect tax. A tax that is thought to be passed on to others, and not borne by the one who originally pays it. Examples: sales taxes, excise taxes, import duties. (p. 125n)

induced investment. Additional investment demand that results from an increase in national product. (p. 197)

industrial union. A union open to all workers in an industry, regardless of their skill. (p. 695)

industry. The producers of a single good or service (or closely similar goods or services). (p. 55)

inelastic demand. Demand with an elasticity of less than one. See *elasticity of demand*. (p. 414)

infant-industry argument for protection. The proposition that new domestic industries with economies of scale or large requirements of human capital need protection from foreign producers until they can become established. (p. 655)

inferior good. A good for which the quantity demand decreases as income rises, ceteris paribus. (p. 59)

inflation. A rise in the average level of prices. (p. 10)

inflationary gap. The vertical distance by which the aggregate demand line is above the 45° line at the full-employment quantity of national product. (p. 206)

inheritance tax. Tax imposed on property received from a person who has died.

injection. Demand for a GNP component other than consumption. (p. 182)

injunction. Court order to refrain from certain practices or requiring certain action. (p. 695)

innovation. A change in products or in the techniques of production.

inputs. Materials and services used in the process of production.

interest. Payment for the use of money.

interest rate. Interest as a percentage per annum of the amount borrowed.

interlocking directorate. Situation where one or more directors of a company sit on the boards of directors of one or more other companies that are competitors, suppliers, or customers of the first company. (p. 561)

intermediate product. A product intended for resale or further processing. (p. 119)

internal cost. Costs incurred by those who actually produce (or consume) a good. (p. 582) Contrast with *external cost*.

internalization. A process that results in a firm or individual taking into account an external cost (or benefit) of its actions. (p. 583)

international adjustment mechanism. Any set of forces that tends to reduce surpluses or deficits in the balance of payments. (p. 388)

international liquidity. The total amount of international reserves (foreign exchange, SDRs, etc.) held by the various nations. (p. 392)

inventories. Stocks of raw materials, intermediate products, and finished goods held by producers or marketing organizations. (p. 121)

investment. Accumulation of capital. (p. 28)

investment bank. A firm that merchandises common stocks, bonds, and other securities. (p. 105)

investment demand. (Also known as *desired investment* or *planned investment*). This is the amount of new plant, equipment, and housing acquired during the year, plus additions to inventories that businesses wanted to acquire. Undesired inventory accumulation is excluded. (If undesired inventory accumulation is included, the result is *actual investment*.) (p. 180)

investment good. A capital good. Buildings, equipment, or inventory.

investment, private domestic (I). See *gross private domestic investment* and *net private domestic investment*.

investment tax credit. A provision in the tax code providing a reduction in taxes to those who acquire capital goods. (p. 93)

invisible. An intangible; a service (as contrasted with a good).

"invisible hand." Adam Smith's phrase expressing the idea that the pursuit of self-interest by individuals will lead a desirable outcome for society as a whole. (p. 6)

iron law of wages. The view (commonly held in the nineteenth century) that the high birth rate creates a tendency for the supply of labor to outrun the productive capacity of the economy and the demand for labor. As a consequence, it was an iron law of nature that wages would be driven down to the subsistence level. (Any excess population at that wage would die from starvation, pestilence, or war.) (p. 74)

jawbone. Persuade; attempt to persuade, perhaps using threats.

joint products. Goods such that the rise in the price of one causes a rightward shift in the supply curve of the other. Complements in production. Products produced together. Example: meat and hides. (p. 61)

joint profit maximization. Formal or informal cooperation by oligopolists to pick the price that yields the most profit for the group. (p. 538)

jurisdictional dispute. Dispute between unions over whose workers will be permitted to perform a certain task. (p. 697)

key currency. A national currency commonly used by foreigners in international transactions and by foreign monetary authorites when intervening in exchange markets. Examples: the U.S. dollar, and, historically, the British pound. (p. 392)

Keynesian economics. The major macroeconomic propositions put forward by John Maynard Keynes in *The General Theory of Employment, Interest and Money (1936)*: A market economy may reach an equilibrium with large-scale unemployment; steps to stimulate aggregate demand can cure a depression; and fiscal policies are the best way to control aggregate demand. (p. 163) Contrast with *classical economics*.

kinked demand curve. A demand curve that an oligopoly firm faces if its competitors follow any price cut it makes but do not follow any of its price increases. The kink in such a demand curve occurs at the existing price. (p. 546)

L. M3 + U.S. savings bonds + short-term Treasury securities + short-term marketable securities issued by corporations; liquid assets. (p. 230)

labor. The physical and mental contributions of people to production. (p. 28)

labor force. The number of people employed plus those actively seeking work. (pp. 144–145)

labor-intensive product. A good whose production uses a relatively large quantity of labor and relatively small quantity of other resources.

labor participation rate. See *particiption rate*.

labor productivity. See *productivity of labor*.

labor theory of value. Strictly, the proposition that the sole source of value is labor (including labor ''congealed'' in capital). Loosely, the proposition that labor is the principal source of value. (p. 773)

labor union. See *union*.

Laffer curve. A curve showing how tax revenues change as the tax rate changes. (p. 379)

laissez faire. Strictly translated, ''let do.'' More loosely, ''leave it alone.'' An expression used by the French physiocrats and later by Adam Smith, meaning the absence of government intervention in markets. (p. 6)

land. This term is used broadly by economists to include not only arable land but also the other gifts of nature (such as minerals) that come with the land. (p. 28)

law of diminishing marginal utility. As a consumer gets more and more of a good, the marginal utility of that good will (eventually) decrease. (p. 438)

law of diminishing returns. See *diminishing returns, law of eventually*.

leading indicator. A time series that reaches a turning point (peak or trough) before the economy as a whole. (p. 310)

legal tender. The item or items that creditors must accept in payment of debts. (p. 259)

leakage. (1) A withdrawal of potential spending from the circular flow of income and expenditures. (p. 181) (2) A withdrawal from the banking system that reduces the potential expansion of the money stock. (p. 242)

leakages-injections approach. The determination of equilibrium national product by finding the size of the product at which leakages are equal to injections. (p. 209)

legal tender. An item that creditors must, by law, accept in payment of a debt. (p. 259)

leverage. The ratio of debt to net worth. (p. 107)

liability. (1) What is owed. (p. 102) (2) The amount that can be lost by the owners of a business if that business goes bankrupt. (p. 98)

life-cycle hypothesis. The proposition that consumption depends on expected lifetime income (as contrasted with the early Keynesian view that consumption depends on current income).

limited liability. The amount an owner-shareholder of a corporation can lose in the event of bankruptcy. This is limited to the amount paid to purchase shares of the corporation. (p. 98)

line of credit. Commitment by a bank or other lender to stand ready to lend up to a specified amount to a customer on request. (p. 107)

liquid asset. An asset that can be sold on short notice, at a predictable price, with little cost or bother. (p. 230)

liquidity. Ease with which an asset can be sold on short notice, at a predictable price, with little cost. (p. 106)

liquidity preference. The demand for money—that is, the willingness to hold money as a function of the interest rate.

liquidity preference theory of the interest rate. The theory put forward by J. M. Keynes that the interest rate is determined by the willingness to hold money (liquidity preference) and the supply of money (that is, the stock of money in existence). (p. 275) Contrast with *loanable funds theory of interest*.

liquidity trap. In Keynesian theory, the situation where individuals and businesses are willing to hold all their additional financial assets in the form of money—rather than bonds or other debt instruments—at the existing interest rate. In such circumstances, the creation of additional money by the central bank cannot depress the interest rate further, and monetary policy cannot be effectively used to stimulate aggregate demand. (All additional money created is caught in the liquidity trap and is held as idle balances.) In geometric terms, the liquidity trap exists where the liquidity preference curve (the demand for money) is horizontal.

loanable funds theory of interest. The theory that the interest rate is determined by the demand for and the supply of funds in the market for bonds and other forms of debt. Contrast with *the liquidity preference theory of interest*.

lockout. Temporary closing of a factory or other place of business in order to deprive workers of their jobs. A bargaining tool sometimes used in labor disputes; the employer's equivalent of a strike.

logarithmic (or log or ratio) scale. A scale in which equal proportional changes are shown as equal distances. For example, the distance from 100 to 200 is equal to the distance from 200 to 400. (Each involves a doubling.) (p. 21)

long run. (1) A period long enough for prices to adjust to their equilibrium level. (p. 162) (2) A period long enough for equilibrium to be reached. (3) A period of time long enough for the quantity of capital to be adjusted to the desired level. (p. 453) (4) Any extended period.

long-run Phillips curve. The curve (or line) traced out by the possible points of long-run equilibrium; that is, the points where people have adjusted completely to the prevailing rate of inflation. (p. 330)

long-run production function. A table showing various combinations of inputs and the maximum output that can be produced with each combination. For a simple firm with only two inputs (labor and capital), the production function can be shown by a two-dimensional table. (p. 480)

Lorenz curve. A curve showing cumulative percentages of income or wealth. For example, a point on a Lorenz curve might show the percentage of income received by the poorest half of the families. (The cumulative percentage of income is shown on the vertical axis. The family with the lowest income is counted first, and then other families are successively added in the order of their incomes. The cumulative percentage of families is on the horizontal axis). Such a curve can be used to measure inequality; if all families have the same income, the Lorenz curve traces out a diagonal line. See also Gini coefficient. (p. 740)

lump-sum tax. A tax of a constant amount. The revenues from such a tax do not change when income changes. (p. 207)

M1. The narrowly defined money stock; currency (paper money plus coins) plus checking deposits held by the public (that is, excluding holdings by the federal government, the Federal Reserve, and commercial banks). (p. 228)

M2. The more broadly defined money stock; M1 plus noncheckable savings deposits and small time deposits. (p. 229)

M3. An even more broadly defined money stock; M2 plus large time deposits (p. 230)

macroeconomics. The study of the overall aggregates of the economy, such as total employment, the unemployment rate, national product, and the rate of inflation. (p. 116)

Malthusian problem. The tendency for population to outstrip productive capacity, particularly the capacity to produce food. This is the supposed consequence of a tendency for population to grow geometrically (1, 2, 4, 8, etc.) while the means of subsistence grows arithmetically (1, 2, 3, 4, etc.). The pressure of population will tend to depress the wage rate to the subsistence level and keep it there, with the excess population being eliminated by war, pestilence, or starvation. A problem described by Thomas Malthus in his *Essay on the Principle of Population* (1798). (p. 74)

managed float. A dirty float. See *floating exchange rate*.

marginal. The term commonly used by economists to mean "additional." For example: *marginal cost* is the additional cost when one more unit is produced; *marginal revenue* is the addition to revenue when one more unit is sold; *marginal utility* is the utility or satisfaction received from consuming one more unit of a good or service.

marginal cost pricing. Setting price at the level where MC intersects the demand curve. (p. 520)

marginal efficiency of investment. The schedule or curve relating desired investment to the rate of interest. The investment demand curve. (p. 277)

marginal physical product. The additional output when one more unit of an input is used (with all other inputs being held constant). For example, the *marginal physical product of labor* (often abbreviated to the *marginal product of labor*) is the additional output when one more unit of labor is used. (p. 457)

marginal product. (1) Strictly, the marginal physical product. (2) Sometimes, the value of the marginal physical product.

marginal propensity to consume (MPC). The change in consumption expenditures divided by the change in disposable income. (p. 176)

marginal propensity to import. The change in imports of goods and services divided by the change in GNP.

marginal propensity to save (MPS). The change in saving divided by the change in disposable income. 1 − MPC. (p. 177)

marginal rate of substitution. The slope of the indifference curve. The ratio of the marginal utility of one good to the marginal utility of another. (p. 447)

marginal revenue product. The additional revenue when the firm uses one additional unit of an input (with all other inputs being held constant). (p 675)

marginal tax rate. The fraction of additional income paid in taxes. (p. 82)

marginal utility. The satisfaction an individual receives from consuming one additional unit of good or service. (p. 438)

margin call. The requirement by a lender who holds stocks (or bonds) as security that more money be put up or the stocks (or bonds) will be sold. A margin call may be issued when the price of the stocks (or bonds) declines, making the stocks (or bonds) less adequate as security for the loan. (p. 256)

margin requirement. The minimum percentage that purchasers of stocks or bonds must put up in their own money. For example, if the margin requirement on stock is 60%, the buyer must put up at least 60% of the price in his or her own money and can borrow no more than 40% from a bank or stockbroker. (p. 256)

market. An institution in which purchases and sales are made. (p. 51)

market economy. See *free-market economy*.

market failure. The failure of market forces to bring about the best allocation of resources. For example, when production of a good generates pollution, too many resources tend to go into the production of that good and not enough into the production of alternative goods and services.

market mechanism. The system whereby prices and the interaction of demand and supply help to answer the major economic questions "What will be produced?" "How?" and "For whom?" (p. 53)

market power. The ability of a single firm or individual to influence the market price of a good or service. (p. 55)

market-power inflation. See cost-push inflation (p. 326)

market share. Percentage of an industry's sales accounted for by a single firm.

market structure. Characteristics that affect the behavior of firms in a market, such as the number of firms, the possibility of collusion, the degree of product differentiation, and the ease of entry.

Marxist economy. One in which most of the capital is owned by the government. (Individuals may of course own small capital goods, such as hoes or hammers, but the major forms of capital—factories and heavy machinery—are owned by the state.) Political power is in the hands of a party pledging allegiance to the doctrines of Karl Marx. (p. 53)

measure of economic welfare (MEW). A comprehensive measure of economic well-being. Per capital real national product is adjusted to take into account leisure, pollution, and other such influences on welfare. (p. 131)

median. The item in the middle (that is, half of all items are above the median and half are below).

medium of exchange. Money; any item that is generally acceptable in exchange for goods or services; any item that is commonly used in buying goods or services. (p. 43)

member bank. A bank that belongs to the Federal Reserve System.

mercantilism. The theory that national prosperity can be promoted by a positive balance of trade and the accumulation of precious metals.

merchandise account surplus. The excess of merchandise exports over merchandise imports.

merger. The bringing together of two or more firms under common control through purchase, exchange of common stock, or other means. A *horizontal merger* brings together competing firms. A *vertical merger* brings together firms that are each others' suppliers or customers. A *conglomerate merger* brings together firms that are not related in any of these ways. (p. 564)

merit good. A good or service that the government considers particularly desirable and that it therefore encourages by subsidy or regulation—such as the regulation that children must go to school to get the merit good of education. (p. 89)

microeconomics. The study of individual units within the economy—such as households, firms, and industries—and their interrelationships. The study of the allocation of resources and the distribution of income. (p. 116)

military-industrial complex. A loose term referring to the combined political power exerted by military officers and defense industries; those with a vested interest in military spending. (In his farewell address, President Eisenhower warned against the military-industrial complex.)

minimum wage. The lowest wage that an employer may legally pay for an hour's work. (p. 682)

mint parity. The exchange rate calculated from the official prices of gold in two countries under the gold standard.

mixed economy. An economy in which the private market and the government share the decisions as to what shall be produced, how, and for whom. (p. 52)

model. The essential features of an economy or economic problem, explained in terms of diagrams, equations, or words—or some combination of these.

monetarism. A body of thought that has its roots in classical economics and that rejects much of the teaching of Keynes' *General Theory*. According to monetarists, the most important determinant of aggregate demand is the quantity of money; the economy is basically stable if monetary growth is stable; and the authorities should follow a monetary rule, aiming for a steady growth of the money stock. Many monetarists also believe that the effects of fiscal policy on aggregate demand are weak (unless accompanied by changes in the quantity of money), that the government plays too active a role in the economy, and that the long-run Phillips curve is vertical. (The most famous monetarist is Milton Friedman, a retired University of Chicago professor.) (p. 168)

monetary base. Currency held by the general public and by commercial banks plus the deposits of commercial banks in the Federal Reserve.

monetary policy. Central bank policies aimed at changing the rate of growth of the money stock; for example, open market operations or changes in required reserve ratios. (p. 246)

monetary rule. The rule, proposed by monetarists, that the central bank should aim for a steady rate of growth of the money stock. (p. 168)

money. Any item commonly used in buying goods or services. Frequently, M1.

money illusion. Strictly defined, people have money illusion if their behavior changes in the event of a proportional change in prices, money incomes, and assets and liabilities measured in money terms. More loosely, people have money illusion if their behavior changes when there is a proportional change in prices and money incomes.

money income. Income measured in dollars (or, in another country, income measured in the currency of that country).

money market. The market for short-term debt instruments.

money multiplier. The number of dollars by which the money stock can increase as a result of a $1 increase in the reserves of commercial banks. (p. 239)

money stock (or supply). Narrowly, M1. More broadly and less commonly, M2 or M3. (p. 229)

monopolistic competition. A market structure with many firms selling a differentiated product, with low barriers to entry. (p. 552)

monopoly. (1) A market in which there is only a single seller. (p. 54) (2) The single seller in such a market. A *natural monopoly* occurs when the average total cost of a single firm falls over such an extended range that one firm can produce the total quantity sold at a lower average cost than could two or more firms. (p. 511)

monopoly rent. Above-normal profit of a monopoly. (p. 734)

monopsony. A market in which there is only one buyer. (p. 76)

moral suasion. Appeals or pressure by the Federal Reserve Board intended to influence the behavior of commercial banks. (p. 257)

most-favored-nation clause. A clause in a trade agreement that commits a country to impose no greater barriers (tariffs, etc.) on imports from a second country than it imposes on imports from any other country.

multinational corporation. A corporation that carries on business (either directly or through subsidiaries) in more than one country. (p. 659)

multiplier. The change in equilibrium real national product divided by the change in investment demand (or in government expenditures, tax collections, or exports). In the simplest economy (with a marginal tax rate of zero and no imports), the multiplier is 1 ÷ (the marginal propensity to save). (p. 184) See also *checking deposit multiplier*.

municipals. Bonds or shorter-term securities issued by municipal governments.

national bank. A commercial bank chartered by the national government.

national debt. (1) The outstanding debt of the federal government. (2) The outstanding federal government debt excluding that held by federal government trust funds. (3) The outstanding federal government debt excluding that held by federal government trust funds and the 12 Federal Reserve Banks.

national income. The return to all factors of production owned by the residents of a nation. (p. 119)

national product. See *gross national product* and *net national product*.

natural monopoly. See *monopoly*

natural oligopoly. See *oligopoly*

natural rate of unemployment. The equilibrium rate of unemployment that exists when people have adjusted completely to the existing rate of inflation. The rate of unemployment to which the economy tends when those making labor and other contracts correctly anticipate the rate of inflation. The rate of unemployment consistent with a stable rate of inflation. (p. 330)

near money. A highly liquid asset that can be quickly and easily converted into money. Examples: a savings deposit or a Treasury bill. (p. 230)

negative income tax. A reverse income tax, whereby the government makes payments to individuals and families with low incomes. (The lower the income, the greater the payment from the government.) (p. 767)

negotiable order of withdrawal (NOW). A check-like order to pay funds from an interest-bearing savings deposit.

neocolonialism. The domination of the economy of a nation by the business firms or government of another nation or nations.

net exports. Exports minus imports. (p. 122)

net national product. (NNP). Personal consumption expenditures plus government purchases of goods and services plus net private domestic investment plus net exports of goods and services. GNP minus capital consumption allowances. (p. 125)

net private domestic investment I_n. Gross (private domestic) investment minus capital consumption allowances. (p. 123)

net worth. Total assets less total liabilities. The value of ownership. (p. 102)

neutrality of money. Money is neutral if a change in the quantity of money affects only the price level without affecting relative prices or the distribution of income.

neutrality of taxes. (1) A situation where taxes do not affect relative prices. (2) The absence of an excess burden of taxes. (p. 90)

New Left. Radical economists; Marxists of the 1960s and 1970s.

nominal. Measured in money terms. Current dollar as contrasted to constant-dollar or real. (p. 127)

noncompeting groups. Groups of workers that do not complete with each other for jobs because their training or skills are different.

non-price competition. Competition by means other than price; for example, advertising or product differentiation. (p. 549)

non-tariff barrier. Impediment to trade other than tariffs. Example: an import quota. (p. 658)

normal good. A good for which the quantity demanded rises as income rises, *ceteris paribus*. Contrast with an *inferior good*. (p. 59)

normal profit. The opportunity cost of capital and/or entrepreneurship. (Normal profit is considered a cost by economists but not by business accountants.) (p. 466)

normative statement. A statement about what should be. (p. 37) Contrast with a positive statement.

NOW account. A savings account against which a negotiable order of withdrawal (a check) may be written.

official settlements surplus. The balance of payments surplus of a country acquiring net international reserves (that is, a country whose international reserves are increasing more rapidly than foreign countries' reserve claims on it). (p. 404)

Okun's law. The observation that a change of 2% to 3% in real GNP (compared with its long-run trend) has been associated with a 1% change in the opposite direction in the unemployment rate. (Named after Arthur M. Okun.) (p. 146)

old age, survivors, and disability insurance. Social security.

oligopoly. A market in which there are only a few sellers who sell either a standarized or differentiated product. (p. 54) A *natural oligopoly* occurs when the average total costs of individual firms fall over a large enough range that a few firms can produce the total quantity sold at the lowest average cost. (p. 536) (Compare with *natural monopoly*.)

oligopsony. A market in which there are only a few buyers.

open economy. An economy that has transactions with foreign nations.

open market operation. The purchase (or sale) of government (or other) securities by the central bank on the open market (that is, not directly from the issuer of the security). (p. 248)

open shop. A business that may hire workers who are not (and need not become) union members. Contrast with *closed shop* and *union shop*. (p. 697)

opportunity cost. (1) The alternative that must be foregone when something is produced. (pp. 31–32) (2) The amount that an input could earn in its best alternative use. (p. 466)

output gap. The amount by which output falls short of the potential or full-employment level. The GNP gap. (p. 204)

panic. A rush for safety, historically marked by a switch out of bank deposits into currency and out of paper currency into gold. A run on banks. (p. 232) A *stock-market panic* occurs when there is a rush to sell and stock prices collapse. (p. 108)

paradox of thrift. The paradoxical situation, pointed out by Keynes, where an increase in the desire to save can result in a decrease in the equilibrium quantity of saving. (p. 197)

paradox of value. The apparent contradiction, pointed out by Adam Smith, when an essential (such as water) has a low price while a nonessential (such as a diamond) has a high price. (p. 438)

Pareto improvement. Making one person better off without making anyone else worse off. (Named after Vilfredo Pareto, 1848–1923.) (p. 491)

Pareto optimum. A situation where it is impossible to make any Pareto improvement. That is, it is impossible to make any individual better off without making someone else worse off. (p. 491)

parity price. The price of a farm product (such as wheat) that would allow a farmer to exchange it for the same quantity of nonfarm goods as in the 1910–1914 base period. (A concept of fair price used in American agricultural policy since the Agricultural Adjustment Act of 1933.) (p. 428)

partial equilibrium analysis. Analysis of a particular market or set of markets, ignoring feedbacks from other markets.

participation rate. Number of people in the civilian labor force as a percentage of the civilian population of working age. (p. 145)

partnership. An unincorporated business owned by two or more people. (p. 98)

par value of a currency. Up to 1971, under the IMF adjustable peg system, the par value was the official price of a currency specified in terms of the U.S. dollar or gold. (p. 389)

patent. Exclusive right, granted by the government to an inventor, to use an invention for a specified time period. (Such a right can be licensed or sold by the patent holder.)

payroll tax. A tax levied on wages and salaries, or on wages and salaries up to a specified limit. Example: social security tax.

peak. The month of greatest economic activity prior to the onset of a recession; one of the four phases of the business cycle. (p. 138)

peak-load pricing. Setting the price for a good or service higher during periods of heavy demand than at other times. The purpose is to encourage buyers to choose nonpeak periods and/or to raise more revenue. Examples: electricity, weekend ski tow.

pegged. Fixed by the authorities, at least temporarily. Examples: pegged interest rates (1941–1951), pegged exchange rates (1945–1973).

penalty rate. A discount rate kept consistently above a short-term market rate of interest. (p. 255)

perfect competition. A market with many buyers and many sellers, with no single buyer or seller having any (noticeable) influence over price. That is, every buyer and every seller is a *price taker*. (p. 54)

permanent income. Normal income; income that is thought to be normal.

permanent-income hypothesis. The proposition that the principal determinant of consumption is permanent income (rather than current income).

perpetuity (or "perp"). A bond with no maturity date that pays interest forever. (p. 252)

personal consumption expenditures. See *consumption*.

personal income. Income received by households in return for productive services, and from transfers prior to the payment of personal taxes. (p. 126)

personal saving. (1) Loosely but commonly, disposable personal income less consumption expenditures. (p. 176) (2) More strictly, disposable personal income less consumption expenditures less payment of interest on consumer debt. (p. 124)

petrodollars. Liquid U.S. dollar assets held by oil exporting nations, representing revenues received from the export of oil.

Phillips curve. The curve tracing out the relationship between the unemployment rate (on the horizontal axis) and the inflation rate or the rate of change of money wages (on the vertical axis). (p. 322) The *long-run Phillips curve* is the curve (or line) tracing out the relationship between the unemployment rate and the inflation rate when the inflation rate is stable and correctly anticipated. (p. 330)

planned investment. Desired investment; investment demand; *ex ante* investment. (p. 180)

plant. A physical establishment where production takes place. (p. 55)

policy dilemma. This occurs when a policy that helps to solve one problem makes another worse. (p. 324)

political business cycle. A business cycle caused by actions of politicians designed to increase their chances of reelection. (p. 304)

positive statement. A statement about what is (or was) or about how something works. (p. 37) Contrast with a *normative statement*.

potential output (or potential GNP). The GNP that would exist if a high rate of employment were consistently maintained. (p. 151)

poverty. Exists when people have inadequate income to buy the necessitites of life. (p. 13)

poverty level (or poverty standard). An estimate of the income needed to avoid poverty. In 1984 it was $10,610 for a family of four. (p. 13)

precautionary demand for money. The amount of money that households and businesses want to hold to protect themselves against unforeseen events.

preferred stock. A stock that is given preference over common stock when dividends are paid. That is, specified dividends must be paid on preferred stock before any dividend is paid on common stock. (p. 101)

premature inflation. Inflation that occurs before the economy reaches full employment.

present value. The value now of a future receipt or receipts, calculated using the interest rate, i. The present value (PV) of $\$X$ to be received n years hence is $\$X \div (1 + i)^n$. (p. 252)

price ceiling. The legally established maximum price.

price discrimination. The sale of the same good or service at different prices to different customers or in different markets, provided the price differences are not justified by cost differences such as differences in transportation costs. (p. 521)

price-earnings ratio. The ratio of the price of a stock to the annual (after-tax) earnings per share of the stock.

price elasticity of demand (supply). See *elasticity of demand (supply)*.

price floor. (1) The price at which the government undertakes to buy all surpluses, thus preventing any further decline in price. (p. 421) (2) The legally established minimum price.

price index. A weighted average of prices, as a percentage of prices existing in a base year. (pp. 127–128)

price leadership. A method by which oligopolistic firms establish similar prices without overt collusion. One firm (the price leader) announces a new price, confident that the other firms will quickly follow. (p. 547)

price line. See *budget line*.

price maker. A monopolist (or monopsonist) who is able to set price because there are no competitors. (p. 513)

price mechanism. See *market mechanism*.

price parity. See *parity price*.

price searcher. A seller (or buyer) who is able to influence price, and who has competitors whose responses can affect the profit-maximizing price. An oligopolist (or oligopsonist). (p. 537)

price support. A commitment by the government to buy surpluses at a given price (the support price) in order to prevent the price from falling below that figure. (p. 421)

price system. See *market mechanism*.

price taker. A seller or buyer who is unable to affect the price and whose market decision is limited to the quantity to be sold or bought at the existing market price. A seller or buyer in a perfectly competitive market. (p. 513)

price-wage flexibility. The ease with which prices and wages rise or fall (especially fall) in the event of changing demand* and supply. (p. 161) Contrast with *price-wage stickiness.*

price-wage stickiness. The resistance of prices and wages to a movement, particularly in a downward direction. (p. 161)

primary burden of tax. The amount of tax collected. Compare with excess burden. (p. 219)

prime rate of interest. (1) a bank's publicly announced interest rate on short-term loans. (2) Historically, the interest rate charged by banks on loans to their most credit-worthy customers. (p. 251)

private domestic investment. The production of private (nongovernmental) capital during a time period, including (1) plant and equipment, (2) residential buildings, and (3) additions to inventories. (p. 120)

procyclical policy. A policy that increases the amplitude of business fluctuations. ("Procyclical" refers to results, not intentions.)

producer surplus. Net benefit that producers get from being able to sell a good at the existing price. Returns to capital and entrepreneurship in excess of their opportunity costs. Rents on capital and enterpreneurship. Measured by the area left of the supply curve between the breakeven price and the existing price.

product differentiation. See *differentiated products.*

production function. The relationship showing the maximum output that can be produced with various combinations of inputs.

production possibilities curve. A curve showing the alternative combinations of outputs that can be produced if all productive resources are used. The boundary of attainable combinations of outputs. (p. 29)

productivity. Output per unit of input.

productivity of labor. The *average* productivity of labor is total output divided by the units of labor input. (pp. 146, 367) The *marginal* productivity of labor is the additional output when one more unit of labor is added, while all other factors are held constant. (p. 457)

profit. In economics, return to capital and/or entrepreneurship over and above normal profit. (p. 466) In business accounting, revenues minus costs. (p. 104) Also sometimes used to mean profit after the payment of corporate income taxes. (p. 104)

profit-and-loss statement. An accounting statement summarizing a firm's revenues, costs, and income taxes over a given period (usually a year). An income statement. (p. 104)

progressive tax. A tax that takes a larger percentage of income as income rises. (p. 82)

proletariat. Karl Marx's term for the working class, especially the industrial working class.

proportional tax. A tax that takes the same percentage of income regardless of the level of income. (p. 82)

proprietors' income. The income of unincorporated firms. (p. 126)

prospectus. A statement of the financial condition and prospects of a corporation, presented when new securities are about to be issued. (p. 111)

protective tariff. A tariff that is intended to protect domestic producers from foreign competition (as contrasted with a revenue tariff, intended as a source of revenue for the government).

protectionism. The advocacy or use of high or higher tariffs to protect domestic producers from foreign competition.

proxy. A temporary written transfer of voting rights at a shareholders' meeting. (p. 101)

proxy fight. a struggle between competing groups in a corporation to obtain a majority vote (and therefore control of the corporation) by collecting proxies of shareholders. (p. 101)

public debt. See *national debt.*

public good. See *pure public good.*

public utility. A firm that is the sole supplier of an essential good or service in an area and is regulated by the government. (p. 532)

pump priming. Short-term increases in government expenditures aimed at generating an upward momentum of the economy toward full employment.

purchasing power of money. The value of money in buying goods and services. The change in the purchasing power of money is measured by the change in the fraction 1 ÷ the price index. (p. 159). ***general purchasing power.*** Something that can be used to buy any of the goods and services offered for sale; money. (p. 41)

purchasing power parity theory. The theory that changes in exchange rates reflect and compensate for differences in the rate of inflation in different countries.

pure public good. A good (or service) with benefits that people cannot be excluded from enjoying, regardless of who pays for the good. (p. 621)

qualitative controls. In monetary policy, controls that affect the supply of funds to specific markets, such as the stock market; selective controls. (p. 255) Contrast with *quantitative controls.*

quantitative controls. In monetary policy, controls that affect the total supply of funds and the total quantity of money in an economy. (p. 255)

quantity theory (of money). The proposition that velocity is reasonably stable and that a change in the quantity of money will therefore cause nominal national product to change by approximately the same percentage. (p. 283)

quota. A numerical limit. For example, a limit on the amount of a good that may be imported. (p. 649)

random sample. A sample chosen from a larger group in such a way that every member of the group has an equal chance of being chosen.

rate base. Allowable capital of a public utility, to which the regulatory agency applies the allowable rate of return.

rate of exchange. The price of one national currency in terms of another. (p. 384)

rate of interest. Interest as a percentage per annum of the amount borrowed.

rate of return. (1) Annual profit as a percent of net worth. (2) Additional annual revenue from the sale of goods or services produced by plant or equipment, less depreciation and operating costs such as labor and materials, expressed as a percent of the value of the plant or equipment. (p. 276)

rational expectations. Expectations based on available information, including information about the policies being pursued by the authorities. If expectations are rational, people do not consistently make the same mistake. (p. 335)

rationing. (1) A method for allocating a good (or service) when the quantity demanded exceeds the quantity supplied at the existing price. (2) More loosely, any method for allocating a scarce resource or good. In this sense, we may speak of the market *rationing by price*.

ratio (or logarithmic) scale. A scale in which equal proportional changes are shown as equal distances. For example, the distance from 100 to 200 is equal to the distance from 200 to 400. (Each involves a doubling.) (p. 21)

Reaganomics. The economic program of President Reagan, including: (1) tax cuts, (2) restraint in domestic spending, (3) increases in defense spending, and (4) less regulation. (p. 83)

real. Measured in quantity terms; adjusted to remove the effects of inflation. (p. 127)

real capital. Buildings, equipment, and other materials used in production, which have themselves been produced in the past. Buildings, equipment, and inventories.

real wage. The quantity of goods and services that a money wage will buy; the money wage adjusted for inflation.

recession. A decline in output, income, employment, and trade, usually lasting 6 months to a year, and marked by widespread contractions in many sectors of the economy. (pp. 10, 138)

recessionary gap. The vertical distance by which the aggregate demand line is below the 45° line at the full-employment quantity of national product. (p. 204)

recognition lag. The time interval between the beginning of a problem and the time when the problem is recognized. (p. 298)

regression analysis. A statistical calculation of the relationship between two or more variables.

regressive tax. A tax that takes a smaller percentage of income as income rises. (p. 82)

regulation Q (of the Federal Reserve). A limit on interest rates that commercial banks may pay on deposits.

rent. (1) In economics, any payment to a factor of production in excess of its opportunity cost. (p. 728) (2) A payment by the user of land to the owner. (3) Payments by users to the owners of land, buildings, or equipment.

replacement-cost depreciation. Depreciation based on the current replacement cost of buildings and equipment rather than their original acquisition cost. (p. 358)

required reserves. The reserves that a bank legally must keep. For members of the Federal Reserve System, these reserves are held in the form of currency or deposits with a Federal Reserve Bank. (p. 234)

required reserve ratio. The fraction of deposit liabilities that a bank must keep in reserves. (p. 234)

rescheduling of debt. The renegotiation of the terms of the debt, to give the debtor more time to repay, and sometimes including a reduction in the interest rate. (p. 397)

reservation price of a resource. The cost of harvesting the resource today plus the amount necessary to compensate for the reduction in the quantity of the resource available in the future. (p. 603)

resource. Basic inputs used in the production of goods and services, namely, labor, land, and capital. (pp. 27–28)

restrictive agreement. Agreement among companies to restrain competition through practices such as price fixing or market sharing.

retail price maintenance. Practice whereby a manufacturer sets the minimum retail price of a product, thereby eliminating price competition among retailers of that product. (p. 563)

return to capital. See rate of return.

revaluation of a currency. An increase in the par value of the currency. (p. 390)

revenue sharing. Grant by the federal government to a state or local government. *General revenue sharing* involves grants whose use is (practically) unrestricted. (p. 87)

revenue tariff. See protective tariff.

right-to-work law. State law making it illegal to require union membership as a condition of employment. State prohibition of closed shops and union shops. (p. 697)

risk premium. The difference between the yields on two grades of bonds (or other securities) because of differences in their risk. The additional interest or yield needed to compensate the holder of bonds (or other securities) for risk. (p. 107)

roundabout production. The production of capital goods and

the use of these capital goods in the production of consumer goods. The production of goods in more than one stage. (p. 718)

rule of the gold standard game. The understanding that each country would permit its money stock to change in the same direction as the change in its gold stock. That is, if a country's gold stock were to rise, it should allow its money supply to increase, and vice versa.

rule of 70. A rule that tells approximately how many years it will take for something to double in size if it is growing at a compound rate. For example, a deposit earning 2% interest approximately doubles in $70 \div 2 = 35$ years. In general, a deposit earning x percent interest will double in about $70 \div x$ years. (p. 355)

run. A rush to switch into safer assets; for example, a *run on banks*. (p. 232)

satisficing theory. The theory that firms do not try to maximize profits but rather aim for reasonable target levels of profits, sales, and other measures of performance.

saving. See *personal saving*.

saving function. (1) The relationship between personal saving and disposable income. (p. 176) (2) More broadly, the relationship between personal saving and the factors (like disposable income) that determine saving.

Say's law. The discredited view that supply in the aggregate creates its own demand (regardless of the general price level). (p. 195)

scarcity. (1) The inability to satisfy all wants because they exceed what we can produce with our available resources. (p. 27) (2) A shortage.

SDRs. See *special drawing rights*.

seasonal adjustment. The removal of regular seasonal movements from a time series. (p. 140)

secondary boycott. Boycott against a firm to discourage it from doing business with a second firm, in order to exert pressure on the second firm (which may be in a strong position to withstand other forms of pressure).

secondary reserves. Bank holdings of liquid assets (Treasury bills, etc.) that can readily be converted into primary reserves (currency or reserve deposits).

second best, theory of the. The theory of how to get the best results in remaining markets when one or more markets have defects about which nothing can be done. (p. 518)

secular stagnation. A situation of inadequate aggregate demand extending over many years. Consequently, large-scale unemployment persists, and it may even become increasingly severe.

secular trend. The trend in economic activity over an extended period of years.

selective controls. In monetary policy, controls that affect the supply of funds to specific markets, such as the stock market; qualitative controls. (p. 255)

sell short. See *short sale*.

seniority rules. Rules giving preference to those who have been longest on the job. Individuals with seniority are typically the last to be discharged or laid off, and the first to be rehired. (p. 694)

shortage. (1) The amount by which quantity supplied is less than quantity demanded at the existing price; the opposite of a surplus. (2) Any deficiency. (p. 58)

short run. (1) The period before the price level has adjusted to its equilibrium. (2) The period in which the quantity of plant and equipment cannot change. (3) The time period before equilibrium can be reestablished. (4) Any brief time period.

short-run production function. The table showing the relationship between the amount of variable factors used and the amount of output that can be produced, in a situation where the quantity of capital is constant. For the simple case of a firm with just two inputs—capital and one variable factor—the short run production function is one row in the long-run production function. (p. 457)

short sale. A contract to sell something at a later date for a price specified now.

single proprietorship. A business owned by an individual person. (p. 97.) Contrast with partnership and corporation.

single-tax proposal. The proposal of Henry George (1839–1897) that all taxes be eliminated except one on land. (George argued that all returns to land represent an unearned surplus.) (p. 735)

slope. The vertical rise in a function divided by the horizontal run. (p. 25)

snake. An agreement among some Western European countries to keep their currencies within a narrow band of fluctuation (the snake). Prior to 1973, they allowed their currencies to move jointly in a wider band with respect to the dollar. (This was called the *snake in the tunnel*.) (Since 1973, the snake has not been tied to the dollar.)

socialism. An economic system in which the means of production (capital equipment, buildings, and land) are owned by the state. (p. 774)

soil bank program. A government program under which the government pays farmers to take land out of production (in order to reduce crop surpluses).

special drawing rights (SDRs). Bookkeeping accounts created by the International Monetary Fund to increase the quantity of international reserves held by national governments. SDRs can be used to cover balance-of-payments deficits. (p. 393)

specific tax. A fixed number of cents or dollars of tax on each unit of the good. Contrast with *ad velorum tax*.

speculation. The purchase (or sale) of an asset in the hope of making a quick profit from a rise (fall) in its price. (p. 390)

speculative demand for money. The schedule or curve showing how the rate of interest affects the amount of assets that firms and households are willing to hold in the form of money, rather than in bonds or other interest-bearing securities.

speculator. Anyone who buys or sells a foreign currency (or any other asset) in the hope of profiting from a change in its price. (p. 390)

spillover. See *externality*.

stagflation. The coexistence of a high rate of unemployment (stagnation) and inflation. (p. 322)

standard of value. The item (money) in which the prices of goods and services are measured. (p. 228)

state bank. A commercial bank chartered by a state government.

sterilization of gold. See *gold sterilization*.

store of value. An asset that may be used to store wealth through time; an asset that may be used to finance future purchases. (p. 228)

structural unemployment. Unemployment due to a mismatch between the skills or location of the labor force and the skills or location required by employers. Unemployment due to a changing location or composition of jobs. (p. 150)

subsidy. A negative tax.

subsistence wage. Minimum living wage. A wage below which population will decline because of starvation or disease. (p. 74)

substitute. A good or service that satisfies similar needs. Two commodities are substitutes if a rise in the price of one causes a rightward shift in the demand curve for the other. (p. 59)

substitution effect. The change in the quantity of a good demanded because of a change in its price when the real income effect of the change in price has been eliminated. That is, a change in the quantity demanded as a result of a movement along a single indifference curve. See also *income effect*. (p. 451)

sunspot theory. The theory put forward in the late nineteenth century that cycles in sunspot activity cause cycles in agricultural production and hence cycles in business activity.

superior good. A good for which the quantity demanded rises as income rises, *ceteris paribus*. A *normal good*. Contrast with an *inferior good*. (p. 59)

supply. The schedule or curve showing how the price of a good or service influences the quantity supplied, *ceteris paribus*. (p. 57)

supply of money. See *money stock*.

supply schedule. A table showing the quantities of a good or service that sellers would offer at various market prices, *ceteris paribus*. (p. 57)

supply shift. A movement of the supply curve of a good (or service) to the right or left as a result of a change in the price of inputs or any other determinant of the quantity supplied (except the price of the good or service itself). (p. 61)

supply shifter. Anything that affects the quantity of a good or service supplied except its own price. (p. 61)

supply side. The view that it is supply factors—such as the quantity of capital and the willingness to work—that are the principal constraints to growth. According to this view, a lack of aggregate demand is not the main constraint.

surplus. (1) The amount by which quantity supplied exceeds quantity demanded at the existing price. (2) Any excess or amount left over. (p. 58) Contrast with *shortage*.

surplus value. In Marxist economics, the amount by which the value of a worker's output exceeds the wage; the share of output appropriated by capitalists. (p. 773)

sustainable yield. The amount of a renewable resource (like fish) that can be harvested while still leaving the population constant. (p. 600)

sympathy strike. A strike by a union that does not have a dispute with its own employer but rather is trying to strengthen the bargaining position of another striking union.

syndicate. An association of investment bankers to market a large block of securities. (p. 106)

tacit collusion. The adoption of a common policy by sellers without explicit agreement. (p. 547)

takeoff. The achievement of sustained growth, in which capital can be accumulated without depressing the standard of living below its existing level. (p. 36)

target price. Agricultural price guaranteed to farmers by the government. (If the market price falls short of the target price, the government pays farmers the difference.) (p. 421)

tariff. A tax on an imported good. (p. 649)

tax-based incomes policy (TIP). An incomes policy backed up with tax penalities on violators or tax incentives for those who cooperate. (p. 343)

tax credit. A subtraction from the tax payable. (For example, if a $1000 machine is bought, a 10% investment tax credit means that $100 can be subtracted from the taxes that must be paid to the government.) (p. 90)

tax deduction. A subtraction from taxable income. Suppose an individual pays $1000 in interest on a home mortgage. This $1,000 can be deducted from taxable income. For someone in the 36% tax bracket, this results in a $360 reduction in taxes. (Note that the tax saving depends on the tax bracket. Thus, a $1,000 deduction reduces taxes more for someone in the 36% tax bracket than for a person in a lower bracket. Note also that the \$1,000 deduction is worth only \$360 to this individual, while a \$1,000 tax credit is worth the full \$1,000 in tax savings.)

tax incidence. See *incidence of tax*.

tax neutrality. (1) A situation where taxes do not affect relative prices. (2) A situation where the excess burden of taxes is zero.

tax shifting. This occurs when the initial taxpayer transfers all or part of a tax to others. (For example, a firm that is taxed may charge a higher price.) (p. 420)

technological (or technical) efficiency. Providing the maximum output with the available resources and technology, while working at a reasonable pace. The avoidance of wasted motion and sloppy management. (p. 12)

terms of trade. The average price of goods sold divided by the average price of goods bought. (p. 655)

theory of games. See *game theory*.

theory of public choice. Theory of how government spending decisions are made and how they should be made.

third world. Countries that are neither in the ''first'' world (the high-income countries of Western Europe and North America, plus a few others such as Japan) nor in the ''second'' world (the countries of Eastern Europe). Low-and middle-income countries other than those run by Communist parties.

time preference. The desire to have goods now rather than in the future. The amount by which goods now are preferred over goods in the future. (p. 718)

time series. A set of observations taken in successive time periods. For example, GNP in 1974, in 1975, in 1976, etc. (p. 20)

TIP. *See tax-based incomes policy.*

total cost. The sum of fixed costs and variable costs. (p. 455)

total revenue. Total receipts from the sale of a product. Where there is a single price, total revenue is the price times the quantity sold.

transactions demand for money. The amount of money that firms and individuals want to cover the time between the receipt of income and the making of expenditures.

transfer payment. A payment, usually made by the government to private individuals, that does not result from current productive activity. (p. 80)

Treasury bill. A short-term (less than a year, often 3 months) debt of the U.S. Treasury. It carries no explicit interest payment; a purchaser gains by buying a bill for less than its face value. (p. 251)

trough. The month of lowest economic activity prior to the beginning of a recovery; one of the four phases of the business cycle. (p. 138)

turnover tax. A tax on goods or services (whether they are intermediate or final products) whenever they are sold.

turning point. The trough or peak of a business cycle. (p. 138)

tying contract. Contract that requires the purchaser to buy another item or items in a seller's line of products in order to get the one that is really wanted. (p. 561)

underemployed. (1) Workers who can find only part-time work when they want full-time work. (2) Workers who are being paid full time but are not kept busy because of low demand for output. (p. 146)

underground economy. Economic activity unobserved by tax collectors and government statisticians. (p. 132)

underwrite. Guarantee that a new issue of stock will all be sold. (An investment banker who underwrites stock but is unable to sell it all must buy the remainder.) (p. 105)

undesired inventory accumulation. Actual inventory accumulation less desired inventory accumulation. (p. 180)

undistributed corporate profits. After-tax corporate profits less dividends paid.

unemployment. The condition of people who are willing to work but cannot find jobs. More generally, the condition of any underutilized resource. (p. 144)

unemployment rate. The percentage of the labor force unemployed. (p. 145)

union. An association of workers, formed to negotiate over wages, fringe benefits, and working conditions. (p. 693)

union shop. A business where all nonunion workers must join the union within a brief period of their employment. Compare with *closed shop* and *right-to-work law*. (p. 697)

unit elasticity. Elasticity of one. If a demand curve has unit elasticity, total revenue remains unchanged as price changes. (The demand curve is a rectangular hyperbola.) If a supply curve has unit elasticity, it is a straight line that would, if extended, go through the origin. (pp. 416–417)

unlimited liability. Responsibility for debts without limit. (p. 98)

utility. The ability to satisfy wants. (p. 438)

value added. Value of the product sold less the cost of intermediate products bought from other firms. (p. 119)

variable costs. Any costs that increase as output increases. (p. 454)

velocity of money. The average number of times per year that the average dollar in the money stock is spent. There are two principal ways of calculating velocity. (1) *Income velocity* is the number of times the average dollar is spent on final products (that is, GNP ÷ M). (2) *Transaction velocity* is the number of times the average dollar is spent on *any* transaction (including those for intermediate goods and financial assets). That is, total spending ÷ M. (p. 283)

vertical merger. See *merger*.

workable competitition. A compromise that limits monopoly power while allowing firms to become big enough to reap the economies of scale. A practical alternative to the often unattainable goal of perfect competition. (p. 569)

yellow-dog contract. Contract in which an employee agrees not to become a member of a union. (p. 695)

yield. The annual rate of discount that would make the present value of a stream of future payments equal to the price or present value of an asset. (p. 276n) The *rate of return*.

zero-base budgeting. A budgeting technique that requires items to be justified anew ''from the ground up,'' without regard to how much has been spent on them in the past.

BIOGRAPHY

ADAM SMITH
ALFRED MARSHALL
KARL MARX
LORD JOHN MAYNARD KEYNES

Adam Smith (1723–1790)

Modern economics is often dated from 1776, the year that Adam Smith published his *Inquiry into the Nature and Causes of the Wealth of Nations.* In the same year, the Declaration of Independence was signed in Philadelphia. The timing was not entirely a coincidence. The Declaration of Independence proclaimed the freedom of the American colonies from British rule. The *Wealth of Nations* put forth the doctrine of economic freedom.

In his book, Smith argued for economic liberalism—that is, free enterprise within a country and free trade among countries. The government should interfere less in the market place; it should leave people alone to pursue their own self-interest. Smith believed that there is an "invisible hand" that causes the producer to promote the interests of society. Indeed, "by pursuing his own interest he frequently promotes that of society more effectually than when he really intends to promote it." [In advocating laissez faire (French for "leave it alone"), Smith did however recognize that government intervention might be desirable in some circumstances; for example, when the nation's defense is at stake.]

Smith was born in 1723, soon after his father died, in the small Scottish seaport of Kirkaldy, where some of the townsfolk still used nails as money. It is said that when he was 4, he was carried off by gypsies, who later abandoned him. One biographer comments: "He would have made, I fear, a poor gypsy."

He remained a bachelor throughout his life. "I am a beau in nothing but my books" was the way he described his lack of appeal for the opposite sex. He suffered from severe absent-mindedness. One biographer describes how Smith, the most illustrious citizen of Edinburgh, would stroll its streets "with his eyes fixed on infinity and his lips moving in silent discourse. Every pace or two he would hesitate as if to change his direction, or even reverse it." In his mannerisms he may have been awkward, but when he picked up a pen, he became a giant; he was one of the foremost philosophers of his age.

His writing caught the eye of Charles Townshend, an amateur economist of great wit but little common sense. (As British Chancellor of the Exchequer, he was responsible for the tea tax that brought on the American Revolution.) When Townshend offered Smith the lucrative job of tutoring his ward, Smith accepted and spent 4 years in Switzerland and France, where he met Voltaire and other leading French philosophers. When the brother of his ward was murdered on a French street, Smith returned to Britain. There, thanks to a pension provided by Townshend, he completed *The Wealth of Nations*.

This was his second and last book. He went into semiretirement, occasionally revising his books and beginning two new ones. But he wrote that "the indolence of old age, tho' I struggle violently against it, I feel coming fast upon me, and whether I shall ever be able to finish either is extremely uncertain." He lost the struggle, dying at the age of 67—but not before he had his two unfinished works burned.

Alfred Marshall (1842–1924)

By blending themes developed by other economists and by adding his own contributions, Alfred Marshall became the father of modern microeconomics (the detailed study of how individual goods are produced and priced).

Marshall was born in 1842 in Clapham, then a green suburb of London. His father, a cashier in the Bank of England, was a man of tyrannical disposition who wrote a book called *Man's Rights and Woman's Duties*. As a good Victorian, he exercised strong parental control: He overworked his son, insisted that he prepare himself for the Ministry, and even made him promise not to play chess—"a waste of time." This childhood repression may have left lasting scars: For the rest of his life, Marshall remained fearful of idleness, hypercritical of his own writing, and nervous about his health almost to the point of hypochondria.

Young Marshall did eventually rebel against the father, rejecting the Oxford scholarship he had won to study classics and theology and turning to mathematics instead. This was important to him later in economics: He used diagrams to illustrate economic theory (for which, it is said, some students have never forgiven him). Marshall eventually became a professor at Cambridge, where he reigned over the British economics profession for almost 25 years until his retirement in 1908. He was everyone's idea of a professor—white hair, white mustache, and bright eyes.

Although a man of overflowing ideas, Marshall—like Adam Smith—was in no hurry to rush into print. Just as Smith had burnt his unfinished writing, Marshall threw much of his into the wastebasket. He kept back printed proofs of one book for 15 years before allowing it to be published. Such long delays meant that many of the ideas he had developed and taught years before had become common knowledge by the time they reached the printed page. (Indeed, this makes it difficult for historians to sort out exactly what he discovered and what he did not.)

Marshall's masterpiece was his *Principles of Economics,* first published in 1890. One of his concerns was the problem of poverty: "The study of the causes of poverty is the study of the causes of the degradation of a large part of mankind."

The many dimensions of Marshall's genius are perhaps best summarized by this tribute:

> The master-economist must possess a rare combination of gifts. He must be mathematician, historian, statesman, philosopher. . . . He must be purposeful and disinterested . . . ; as aloof and incorruptible as an artist; yet sometimes as near the earth as a politician.

This tribute was written by Marshall's most illustrious student, John Maynard Keynes, who himself achieved such fame that he is described on page 815.

Karl Marx (1818–1883)

"Workers of the world unite; you have nothing to lose but your chains." This popular paraphrase of Marx's most famous quote illustrates his passionately held views. In his writings, passages of dry economics are punctuated by emotional outbursts against the existing economic system. Marx is most eloquent when he describes the misery of the working class in England over a century ago. On the other hand, he is least convincing when he predicts that this misery will increase.

Whereas Smith and Marshall believed in free enterprise—with the government intervening only in special circumstances—Karl Marx believed the free enterprise system should, and inevitably would, be replaced by a wholly different system: communism. Under communism the nation's wealth (capital) would be held, not individually, but instead by everyone collectively. *Das Kapital* (or *Capital,* in its English translation) was Marx's most important book; and the *Communist Manifesto* (written with Friederick Engels in 1848, the year when revolutionary fires swept across Europe) is still the most celebrated pamphlet in the history of communism.

Marx was born in 1818 in the city of Trier in the Prussian Rhineland, now part of West Germany. As an undergraduate of the University of Bonn and as a graduate student in Berlin, he became increasingly associated with radical groups; his best friend was jailed for radical activity. (Although Marx in later life had periodic difficulties with the authorities, the only day he ever spent in jail was when he was a student—on a charge of being drunk and disorderly.)

Marx was a man of great contradictions. He remained something of an intellectual recluse, avoiding other economists and sociologists, with whom he might have had much to discuss. Despite his broad intellectual attainments, he was the victim of strange obsessions. (He believed that Lord Palmerston, the British foreign minister, was an agent of the Russians.) He was determined not to let a capitalist society turn him into a "money-making" machine, yet he was willing to live off gifts from Engels, himself a capitalist. Marx was an affectionate father, yet he sacrificed the health of his children because he could seldom bring himself to seek paid employment. (His one steady source of earned income was writing articles for the *New York Herald Tribune*.) Before Engels was able to afford sizable gifts, Marx lived with his family in poverty; once they were evicted and their possessions seized. Several of his children died, "a sacrifice to [capitalist] misery." In one case his wife had to borrow to buy a coffin.

In 1883, broken by the death of his wife and eldest daughter, and having made the remarkable statement that has bewildered his disciples ever since ("I am not a Marxist"), Marx died. He could little realize the influence he would have on history. Today about one-third of the word lives in a communist system, where Marx is revered. In much of the other two-thirds of the world, he is viewed as the most controversial economist who ever lived.

John Maynard Keynes (1883–1946)

Just as Marshall fathered modern microeconomics, so Keynes became the father of modern macroeconomics (the broad-brush study of the economy "in the large," focusing on overall employment and production). Keynes' great contribution to economics is *The General Theory of Employment, Interest and Money,* published in 1936. This book was eagerly anticipated: Keynes was already famous for his views on a variety of topics, from the gold standard to the 1919 peace treaty imposed on Germany. Moreover, it was widely known that he was writing on the economic problem that concerned people most in the 30s: the worldwide depression, when there were 14 million unemployed in the United States alone.

The General Theory turned out to be a blistering attack on traditional (classical) economists who believed that, with time, unemployment would cure itself. Not so, said Keynes. Unemployment could persist. In such circumstances, the government should step in and increase its spending. Then more goods would be produced, and more people put to work.

In the 19th century, Karl Marx had prophesied the doom of the existing economic system. Keynes recognized that the system had serious flaws, but he believed that it could be reformed. Thus, his views lay somewhere between those of a laissez faire economist like Adam Smith and those of a revolutionary like Karl Marx.

Keynes was born in 1883, the year that Karl Marx died. Keynes' father was an eminent logician and political economist and his mother was a justice of the peace and mayor of Cambridge, England. The intellectual gifts of their son were almost immediately evident; by age 6, young Keynes was trying to figure out how his brain worked. On scholarship at Eton, Keynes blossomed. He grew a mustache, bought a lavender waistcoat, and developed his life-long taste for champagne. Then he went to undergraduate studies at Cambridge, where his brilliance was quickly evident to his teachers, including Alfred Marshall.

Keynes went from success to success. Biographers have speculated that, just as Marx's prophecy of economic doom reflected the privation that marked his personal life, so Keynes's optimistic promotion of solutions reflected a life of accomplishment. At only 28, he became editor of the most prestigious British economic journal, a post he held for most of the rest of his life. He became a teacher at King's College, Cambridge, and a shrewd investor. Under his financial guidance, a small £30,000 King's College fund was expanded by more than ten times. And by applying himself for only half an hour each morning—before he got out of bed—he was able to earn a personal fortune of more than $2 million through speculation on the foreign currency and commodity markets. (But his own personal success did not soften his harsh judgment of the costs to society when the public becomes caught up in a whirlpool of speculation: "When the capital development of a country becomes a by-product of the activities of a casino, the job is likely to be ill-done.")

PHOTO CREDITS

Endpapers: Adam Smith (Bettmann Archive); Thomas R. Malthus (Bettmann Archive); David Ricardo (Bettmann Archive); John Stuart Mill (Bettmann Archive); Karl Marx (Bettmann Archive); Alfred Marshall (Historical Pictures Service, Chicago); Knut Wicksell (Historical Pictures Service, Chicago); Irving Fisher (Culver Pictures); John Maynard Keynes (United Press International); Simon Kuznets (Wide World Photos); Paul Samuelson; Milton Friedman (American Economic Assn.); John R. Hicks (United Press International); Wassily Leontief (Wide World Photos); Frank Hyneman Knight (Wide World Photos); Jacob Viner (Wide World Photos); Gunnar Myrdal (Wide World Photos); James Tobin (Wide World Photos); Paul Wonnacott and Ronald Wonnacott (Tim Condon)

Biographies in backmatter:
(John Maynard Keynes) Bettmann Archive
(Karl Marx) Bettmann Archive
(Alfred Marshall) Historical Pictures Service

Boxes:

1-1 Bruce Roberts/Photo Researchers
2-2 (Jobs, Sculley, Wozniac) UPI/Bettmann Newsphotos
(Delorean) Wide World
6-1 *The Solid Gold Cadillac*. Copyright © 1956 Columbia Pictures Corp. All rights reserved. Courtesy of the Museum of Modern Art Film Stills Archive.
8-2 Peter Menzel/Stock, Boston
20-2 Wide World
20-3 (old gas station) UPI/Bettmann Newsphotos
(old car) Bettmann Archive
(new gas pump) Arthur Glauberman/Photo Researchers
(new car) Courtesy of Ford Motors
20-4 (Eniac) UPI/Bettmann Newsphotos
(memory chip) Courtesy of IBM
22-1 Steven Lewis/The Picture Cube
22-3 Wide World
23-1 Wide World
26-1 Kenneth Karp
26-3 Kenneth Karp
27-1 Don Rutledge/Black Star
27-3 Wide World
27-4 Robert Houser/Photo Researchers
28-1 Ellis Herwig/Stock, Boston
28-2 Fred Ward/Black Star
29-1 Russ Kinne/Photo Researchers
29-2 Werner H. Müller/Peter Arnold, Inc.
29-4 Robert Azzi/Woodfin Camp & Assoc.
30-1 Dan Walsh/The Picture Cube
32-1 Culver Pictures
32-2 Gordon S. Smith/Photo Researchers
34-1 Tom McHugh/Photo Researchers
35-3 Richard Frear/Photo Researchers
37-1 Michael Kagan/Monkmeyer
37-2 Michael Uffer/Photo Researchers
38-1 Marcel Minée/International Stock Photo

INDEX